REVELATIONS FROM THE RUSSIAN ARCHIVES

REVELATIONS FROM THE RUSSIAN ARCHIVES

Documents in English Translation

edited by Diane P. Koenker and Ronald D. Bachman

Library of Congress • Washington, 1997

Opposite the title page is a photograph of Stalin's daughter Svetlana seated on Beria's lap, taken in 1930, when Beria enjoyed Stalin's patronage. From the Central Archive of Cinema and Photographic Documents. See p. 346. (Cropped.)

Library of Congress Cataloging-in-Publication Data
Revelations from the Russian archives : documents in English
  translation / edited by Diane P. Koenker and Ronald D. Bachman.
      p.   cm.
  Includes bibliographical references and index.
  ISBN 0-8444-0891-3 (alk. paper)
  ———— Copy 3 Z663.17 .R488   1996
      1. Archives—Soviet Union—Exhibitions. 2. Soviet Union—
History—Sources—Exhibitions. I. Koenker, Diane, 1947– .
II. Bachman, Ronald D., 1947– . III. Library of Congress.
CD1711.R488 1996
947.084—dc20
                                            96-24752
                                              CIP

♾ The paper used in this publication meets the minimum
requirements of the American National Standard for Information
Sciences—Permanence of Paper for Printed Library Materials, ANSI
Z39.48-1984.

For sale by the U.S. Government Printing Office
Superintendent of Documents
Washington, D.C. 20402-9328
ISBN 0-8444-0891-3

CONTENTS

ARCHIVAL ABBREVIATIONS

APRF	Arkhiv Prezidenta Rossiiskoi Federatsii (Archive of the President of the Russian Federation)
AVP RF	Arkhiv vneshnei politiki Rossiiskoi Federatsii (Archive of Foreign Relations of the Russian Federation)
KGB	Archives of the USSR Committee on State Security
RTSKhIDNI	Rossiiskii tsentr khraneniia i izucheniia dokumentov noveishei istorii (Russian Center for the Storage and Study of Documents of Recent History [former Central Party Archive])
TSGAKFD	TSentral'nyi gosudarstvennyi arkhiv kino-foto dokumentov (Central State Archive of Cinema and Photographic Documents)
TSGALI	TSentral'nyi gosudarstvennyi arkhiv literatury i iskusstva (Central State Archive of Literature and Art)
TSGANKh	TSentral'nyi gosudarstvennyi arkhiv narodnogo khoziaistva (Central State Economic Archive)
TSGAOR	TSentral'nyi gosudarstvennyi arkhiv Oktiabr'skoi revoliutsii (Central State Archive of the October Revolution) [renamed Gosudarstvennyi arkhiv Rossiiskoi Federatsii (State Archive of the Russian Federation)]
TSGASA	TSentral'nyi gosudarstvennyi arkhiv Sovetskoi Armii (Central State Archive of the Soviet Army)
TSGOA	TSentral'nyi gosudarstvennyi osobyi arkhiv (Central State Special Archive)
TSKhSD	TSentr khraneniia sovremennoi dokumentatsii (Center for the Storage of Contemporary Documentation [former Central Committee Archive])

PREFACE

Some four years have passed since the Library of Congress staged "Revelations from the Russian Archives," one of the most important exhibits in the history of this institution. Since the closing of the exhibit, researchers have continued to enjoy electronic access via the Internet to many of the documents that so interested scholars and the general public in July 1992. The present volume provides, for the first time, English translations of all the documents in the exhibit along with several dozen additional papers selected by our curatorial team in Moscow. Some of these materials were hand-carried to the Library—literally on the eve of the exhibit's opening—by the then head of the Russian State Archives, Rudol'f Pikhoia, and by the late Dmitrii Volkogonov, President Yeltsin's close adviser on defense issues. These brave men shared the conviction that the Russian people had a right to know their own history. And they understood the Jeffersonian principle that democracy cannot flourish where freedom of information is denied. Their efforts to preserve the historical record and open to public view the darkest secrets of the Soviet archives were nothing short of heroic. Thanks to their initiative, imagination, and determination and to the hard work of our staff at the Library of Congress, the exhibit "Revelations from the Russian Archives"—and, hence, this volume—became reality.

Like the several documents that received considerable publicity during the 1992 exhibit—for example, letters revealing Lenin's ruthless treatment of his political enemies, Bukharin's pathetic plea for his life, and the early report of construction flaws in the Chernobyl Nuclear Power Plant—the primary contribution of the present publication is the opportunity it provides to glimpse the inner workings of the world's first and longest-lived totalitarian state. The Soviet system was a ruthlessly effective, self-perpetuating political machine, operated by apparatchiks taught not to think for themselves. Perusing the reports of politburo meetings, NKVD orders, and sundry governmental decrees, one almost grows numb to the horrible realities they describe because of the detached, banal tone in which the documents were written. Document 30, for example, giving detailed instructions on how to conduct a purge of the Russian Communist Party rank and file, employs a pseudoscientific matrix by which each party member is to be evaluated. Were the consequences not so tragic, one might even find the rating elements laughable. Similarly, one is struck by the cold statistics of Documents 106 and 107, which inform Stalin that there were "no incidents" during the forced resettlement of a quarter million Tatars, Bulgarians, Greeks, and Armenians from Crimea.

The years since the exhibit at the Library have been a tumultuous period in Russian history. The creation of democratic institutions, a market-based economy, and a civil society may require more time than most Russians believed, and progress toward making Russia "a normal country" has been painfully slow. Indeed, as I write, the strident voices of Russian authoritarian nationalism on both the left and the right extremes of the political spectrum are heard. Researchers report that access to the vast archives of the Communist Party, the KGB, the Foreign Ministry, and other repositories has become more restricted in recent months, and the outlook for archival research at this writing is not encouraging. I hope that this volume may remind readers how far Russia has come and how much the world stands to lose should Russia's experiment in democracy fail.

JAMES H. BILLINGTON
Washington
March 18, 1996

ACKNOWLEDGMENTS

The editors wish to thank the many Library of Congress staff members, outside specialists, and volunteers who transformed an amorphous mass of often barely legible Russian-language manuscript material into the present handsome volume. Michael H. Haltzel, chief of the European Division, guided the project in its early stages. When in mid-1994 Dr. Haltzel left his position as chief of the division, Assistant Chief David H. Kraus took up the project. Dr. Haltzel—in consultation with Mr. Kraus, area specialists Harold M. Leich and myself, and John Y. Cole and Evelyn E. Sinclair of the Publishing Office—named Professor Diane P. Koenker of the University of Illinois substantive editor of the volume, myself translation editor, and Lawrence D. Orton line editor. Professor Koenker thus selected the documents and illustrations for inclusion in the volume, arranged them thematically, reviewed the translated documents, wrote all the introductory and analytical material, and produced the glossaries. Dr. Orton reviewed the manuscript, ensuring stylistic consistency within the constraints presented by the formal and stylistic diversity of the original documents. As an East European historian, he also was sensitive to errors, omissions, ambiguities, and other substantive problems. In my role as translation coordinator and editor, I took responsibility for maintaining document control, translated much of the handwritten material, and edited the translations. As the project progressed, I became the liaison with Professor Koenker and Dr. Orton, ensuring that editorial revisions were coordinated and executed, incorporating improvements made by European Division staff members, and delivering final manuscript to the Publishing Office. Special thanks go to W. Ralph Eubanks, Evelyn Sinclair, and Gloria Baskerville-Holmes of the Publishing Office for overseeing the final stages of the undertaking and bringing the volume to publication.

RONALD D. BACHMAN
European Division

A NOTE ON THE TRANSLATIONS

Most of the documents included in this volume have been translated in their entirety. In some instances, however, it was necessary to omit lengthy passages judged to be of marginal research value. Omitted sections are marked by the ellipsis symbol within brackets, e.g., [. . .]. Ellipsis markings that occurred in the original text are preserved. The phrase "break in the text" identifies gaps and missing pages in the original documents themselves.

The Library of Congress system of Cyrillic transliteration—without ligatures, however, on the digraphs ts, iu, and ia—is used throughout the volume. Although the editorial team rendered some of the most commonly known names and terms in their conventional English spellings, the list of exceptions to Library of Congress transliteration is relatively short. While specialists may find adherence to this system occasionally disconcerting, it is also true that specialists themselves disagree on both the composition of exceptions lists and the transliteration of such "household names" as Lavrentii (Lavrenty, Lavrenti) Beria (Beriia). Abbreviations and acronyms are not recast according to their English expansions, e.g., *TSK KPSS* rather than CC CPSU (Central Committee of the Communist Party of the Soviet Union). All Russian terms, abbreviations, and acronyms are italicized regardless of their frequency of occurrence in the scholarly and popular literature, e.g., *perestroika*. Russian loanwords whose standard English spelling is not consistent with the Library of Congress transliteration system, however, are not italicized, e.g., politburo instead of *politbiuro*.

An attempt has been made to preserve the general appearance of the original documents in the arrangement of headers, signature blocks, and text and in the use of underscoring, capitalization, and through-striking. In addition, stamps, annotations, and instructions appearing on the original documents are translated and preceded by brief bracketed descriptors, e.g., [Stamp in upper left corner:] Archive of F. Z. Dzerzhinsky. Finally, the translations attempt—to the degree this is possible—to preserve the style and tone of the original documents.

INTRODUCTION

Shortly after the defeat of the attempted coup by Kremlin hard-liners in August 1991, a group of democrats led by the chief archivist of Russia, Rudol'f Pikhoia, took over the secret archives of the Central Committee of the Communist Party and began the process of gaining control over all of Russia's archives, attempting to organize them for study by independent researchers. Dr. Pikhoia asked for the cooperation of the Librarian of Congress, James H. Billington, a historian of Russian culture, in this endeavor, and their collaboration led to an exhibit at the Library of Congress from June 17 to July 16, 1992, displaying in Russian and English over three hundred previously secret Soviet documents. Tens of thousands of visitors passed through the exhibit during the four weeks the documents were on display; another forty thousand Americans accessed selections of the exhibit "on-line" via electronic networks across the country. In addition to the documents, the library displayed a large number of photographs and selected films from the party archives: the film excerpts came from newsreels and propaganda films never before seen outside the USSR, including rare footage of the Winter Palace and the Kremlin weeks after the October 1917 coup; extended coverage of the Thirteenth Party Congress, convened four months after Lenin's death; churches and synagogues razed by Soviet officials; forced collectivization; the building of the White Sea Canal; and extraordinary sound footage from one of the very first public show trials, held in 1930 to prosecute the so-called Industrial Party.

This publication constitutes the compendium of English translations of all the documents used in the exhibit, plus photographs and other documents that had to be excluded from the exhibit for reasons of space. These additional documents were selected from the seventy million that were available from the newly opened archives of the Communist Party, supplemented by formerly secret materials from other state archives. Knowing that it would be impossible to select materials comprehensively, the library's curatorial team instead decided to choose core samples of the types of documents that are now accessible to researchers. The Library of Congress staff and Soviet archivists worked together to compile a list of topics that would be most likely to yield interesting new information and illustrations of some of the most critical periods of Soviet history. Hence, scholars looked for items that might shed light on the origins of the Soviet system, in particular the system of state terror and concentration camps and early trade relations between the U.S. and the USSR. The curatorial team also looked for documents that would illustrate specific U.S.-USSR relations, including those on the wartime alliance, prisoners of war, the Cold War, and the Communist Party of the U.S.A. The team did not always find significant new documents on all subjects: nothing turned up on Marshal Zhukov or on the fall of Stalin's secret police chief, Lavrentii Beria, for example, and the August 1991 coup also yielded little new in the way of documentation.

These documents were delivered to the Library of Congress, some in their original and some in photocopy, where they were evaluated by the professional staff in the Library's European Division. Those selected for the exhibit were translated into English by a team of translators at the library. In many cases, given the constraints of space and the time required to complete the translations, only portions of the original documents were displayed. All of the documents and photographs on view in the library exhibit have been included in this volume, and many of them appear here for the first time in their complete, unabridged form. From the additional documents that were not included in the exhibit or arrived too late to be put on display, the editor chose to add to this volume all of those that have not already been published or do not duplicate sources or information available elsewhere. Photocopies of all of the original documents, in their original language, can be examined by scholars at the European Reference Desk in the Library of Congress Jefferson Building.

The exhibit, which received extensive press coverage in the United States and abroad, marked the culmination of a remarkable period of growing Soviet candor about its secrets, a period that had begun with the selection of Mikhail S. Gorbachev as general secretary of the Communist Party in 1985. Gorbachev's reform plans for the Soviet Union included *glasnost'*, or openness, as the essential ingredient for improving the way the system worked by giving individuals more incentives to help reform the system. "Broad, up-to-date, and honest information is a sign of trust in people, respect for their intelligence and feelings, and their ability to make sense of developments," said Gorbachev in 1984. Later he added, "The better people are informed, the more consciously they act, the more actively they support the party, its plans and programmatic objectives."[1] Intellectuals jumped aboard the *glasnost'* bandwagon, starting with novelists and dramatists who dared to explore themes that had once been forbidden, such as conflicts within the Communist Party in the early days of the revolution or the treachery and personal duplicity of individuals during Stalin's purges. Soviet historians, ever sensitive to state policies and state secrets, moved more cautiously into the new era of *glasnost'* but began tentatively to extend the range of what was permissible to research and write.[2] They were encouraged by Gorbachev's pronouncement in March 1987, "There should be no blank pages in history and literature. Otherwise, it is not history or literature, but artificial constructions."[3] Journalists and historians alike began to probe these "blank pages," still wondering whether and where limits would be drawn. Later that year Gorbachev announced that he planned to give a major address on the "blank spots" of Soviet history, and intellectuals rejoiced. "Gorbachev's speech will give us back our past, both the good and the bad, so we may create our future."[4] The dynamic new rector of the Moscow Historical Archival Institute (which has since become the Russian State University for the Humanities), IUrii N. Afanas'ev, also called for more investigation of "veiled periods" of Soviet history. Others who had built their careers around packaging history for the regime's consumption disagreed. The ninety-year-old dean of Soviet historians of the 1917 revolution, I. I. Mints, declared at a roundtable discussion, "Names ought to be mentioned, but we have to acquit only those who deserve it. We can't forget Trotsky's damage to our country."[5] And Gorbachev's speech, nationally televised and lasting for two hours and forty-one minutes, disappointed many hopeful citizens. The Soviet leader called for the rehabilitation of Nikolai Bukharin, long the darling of Soviet reformers, but also warned against succumbing "to the pressure of the overly zealous and impatient." In other words, Leon Trotsky remained a non-person; the "crime of collectivization" was not the policy to dispossess rich peasants, or *kulak*s, but rather the incorrect labeling of too many middling peasants as *kulak*s. Likewise, there was no mention of the millions of victims of Stalin's purges or of Stalin's record in World War II.[6]

Historians, however, were encouraged by the signals Gorbachev sent in his November 2 speech and became emboldened to call for even more openness. Leading Soviet historians just after the speech admitted at a news conference that they had indeed been more conservative than novelists but that it was time to respond to the calls for new approaches to the past. The representative

1. Quoted in Stephen White, *Gorbachev in Power* (Cambridge, 1990), p. 58.
2. Robert W. Davies, *Soviet History in the Gorbachev Revolution* (Bloomington, Ind., 1989), pp. 167–79.
3. *New York Times*, March 15, 1987.
4. *New York Times*, October 26, 1987.
5. *New York Times*, October 26, 1987.
6. *New York Times*, November 3, 1987.

of the Institute of Marxism-Leninism, the repository of Communist Party history and the legacy of Lenin, openly expressed his frustration with the continuing policy of closed archives: party archives that had been opened in the 1950s and early 1960s, during the "thaw" of Soviet cultural life under Khrushchev, had later been resealed. It was time to reverse this decision.[7]

Gorbachev himself did not insist that his November 2 speech had drawn a line in the sand of historical revelation and soon signaled an even greater permissibility in the realm of historical writing.[8] In libraries forbidden books and materials began to make their way out of the closed "special collections" and into regular circulation. Closer cooperation between the U.S. and the USSR had already been heralded earlier in 1987, when the American Council of Learned Societies and the USSR Main Archival Administration agreed to co-ordinate exchanges of official records between the Soviet state archives and the U.S. National Archives.[9]

The central state began to lose its monopoly on the historical record. Individuals working in closed archives now began to write about their findings in the public press. A journalist, Vasilii Seliunin, published an article in the leading literary-political monthly *Novyi Mir* that publicly criticized Lenin for the first time. Relying on early Soviet decrees and some of the writings of Lenin that had never been published (some of which are included in this volume), Seliunin detailed Lenin's call for the use of coercion and terror against *kulak*s and other "enemies of the people." The military historian Dmitrii A. Volkogonov, who was a leading member of the Russian team that assembled the documents in this volume, was amassing a large collection of formerly secret documents for new biographies of Stalin and Trotsky. An independent organization, "Memorial," began to collect individual archives and materials on victims of Stalin's repressions. Soliciting funds from the broad public, they sponsored exhibits across Russia devoted to restoring to memory the victims of the purges and to detailing their suffering. An exhibit in November 1988, held at the House of Culture in a Moscow factory, drew thirty-five thousand visitors in nine days.[10] Local "Memorial" affiliates in libraries and universities began to mount their own exhibits—tributes to members of their professions who had fallen victim to the purges. On January 10, 1989, the Central State Archive announced that it was opening five hundred thousand secret files on such subjects as the White opposition to Bolshevik rule, the Russian Orthodox Church, and numerous public organizations that existed in the 1920s and 1930s.[11] Not only the documents themselves, but the all-important inventories and other finding aids were made available to the international scholarly public. Finally, after the failure of the August 1991 coup to restore centralized authoritarian rule in the USSR, the Communist Party was dissolved as a criminal organization, and its assets, including the vast treasures of the party archives, fell under the control of the Russian Federation.

7. *New York Times*, November 5, 1987.
8. Davies, *Soviet History*, pp. 136–37.
9. *New York Times*, February 16, 1987.
10. *New York Times*, November 28, 1988.
11. *New York Times*, January 10, 1989.

The opening up of these riches to scholars to whom they had long been denied, both inside and outside the USSR, also brought sober new realities. The archives, like many other facets of Soviet cultural life, had been woefully underfunded. The cooperative effort that led to this exhibit was one of a number of ventures intended to provide greater access to the materials and material support for the preservation and cataloging of those materials. In early 1992 the British firm Chadwyck-Healey reached an agreement with the Russian government to microfilm the entire party archive, estimated at 70 to 100 million documents. The first batch of materials was made available to scholars—at gold-plated prices—in 1993. The Hoover Institution at Stanford University announced in March 1992 that it had agreed to finance a $3 million preservation project in the party archives, which would include making microfilm copies available worldwide.[12] Collaborative projects between Western and Russian institutions and individuals, designed both to make new materials available to the scholarly public and to subsidize the continuing operation of the archival repositories, have been initiated in a number of areas. In December 1992 the Council of the American Historical Association, representing fifteen thousand professional historians in the United States, supported these efforts in a resolution that called for the promotion of international cooperative endeavors to defray the costs of preservation and maintenance, for the generation of finding aids and printed guides, and for open access to the archives for scholars of all countries.[13]

Problems remain regarding access to these remarkable records of twentieth-century world history. Scholars in many countries worry about the growing commercialization of the Russian archives and about the fact that large-scale microfilming projects may require the withholding of materials from general circulation for unacceptably long periods of time. Individual archives establish independent and arbitrary fees for the use of their materials and for photocopying. The appropriate rules for release of personal materials and for more generalized access have yet to be developed in Russia: should there be a ten-year limit on the opening of files? a forty-year limit? What other restrictions ought to be placed on materials that pertain to people still living? Meanwhile, as IUrii Afanas'ev pointed out in a recent interview, "While there is not universal access, a significant number of historians are granted access to documents still labeled secret. They photocopy them, collect data, prepare future publications. . . . Why shouldn't they deny access to those documents for seventy years, when they have already worked with them and have photocopies of them?"[14] He goes on, "The archival resources constitute our national treasure, our society's memory. Who has the right to arbitrarily manage a national treasure? This should be decided openly and on the basis of legal norms."

Such controversy and debate over the disposition of "Russia's memory"—

12. *New York Times,* March 11, 1992.
13. Reprinted in *Slavic Review,* 52, no. 1 (spring 1993): 105–6.
14. *Slavic Review,* 52, no. 2 (summer 1993): 339–41, interview with IU. N. Afanas'ev.

its archives—are a natural corollary to the colossal upheavals in structures and mentalities that have accompanied the new Russian revolution since 1991. Against the background of these disputes and legitimate arguments about the future of Russian archival policy, the June 1992 exhibit of newly released documents provided an important opportunity for taking stock of the impact of the new archival revelations and their meaning for the writing of Russian history. On June 18, 1992, a symposium of leading scholars and archivists connected with the exhibit met to discuss the implications of the documents on display. Representing the Russian archival commission were Rudol'f Pikhoia, chairman of the Russian Federation Committee of Archival Affairs, and Dmitrii Volkogonov, director of the Institute of Military History. Moderated by James H. Billington, Librarian of Congress, the panel included Robert Tucker, professor emeritus of politics at Princeton University; Paul Nitze, former director of the U.S. State Department Policy Planning Staff and a participant in some of the decisions reflected in the documents; and Adam Ulam, professor of political science and director of the Russian Research Center at Harvard University.

Pikhoia and Volkogonov discussed some of the levels of secrecy that the exhibit now revealed. Volkogonov explained that all archives were placed under the control of the secret police in 1924, and "Lenin himself established a whole classification scheme, under which there were 15 degrees of secrecy—ultra secret, top secret, secret, confidential, single copy for eyes only, to be returned to sender, etc."[15] The panelists also discussed the significance of this particular set of documents for understanding the Soviet period of Russian history. Tucker warned against expecting too much from these new materials or relying on them to the exclusion of other types of sources that have long provided valuable documentary evidence themselves, such as the daily press. Such documents as the press "are of incalculable importance because they did not necessarily tell the truth at any one given point but, what they did tell was the truth about what the regime, the dictatorial regime of Stalin, wanted people and the world to think, and that in itself was a self-revelation of that regime."[16] Nonetheless, he agreed that the new materials would be of enormous benefit in clearing up certain matters of interpretation, for example the extent of the famine in the early 1930s or the numbers of *Gulag* victims. The archival revelations, he felt, were especially helpful in understanding how decisions were reached at the highest echelons of Soviet power. He himself was able to consult Stalin's personal library, and seeing the marginal comments and underlining that Stalin made has helped him to refine his interpretation of Stalin's thinking at the time. Other documents, such as the decisions made in the Politburo about military intervention in Afghanistan, help to explain specific decisions and specific events, but, as Tucker argued, the long-term

15. *Revelations from the Russian Archives: A Report from the Library of Congress* (Washington, 1993), pp. 39–42.
16. *Revelations*, p.46.

value of these revelations will "not turn on the specific bits of information, or even the collective upshot of all those specific bits of information," but on the ways of thinking, the interpretations, that historians and scholars bring to the information.

The symposium that marked the opening of the exhibit of Russian archives at the Library of Congress, the exhibit itself, and this compendium of the documents provided for the exhibit should all be taken as a single moment in the continuing unfolding of Russian history. The exhibit and this volume provide an occasion for reflecting on the terrible damage done to our collective memories by the secrecy practiced by the Soviet regime, as well as a reminder of certain key moments in the history of the Soviet Union in the twentieth century. Neither the exhibit nor the volume claims to offer a complete "documentary history of the USSR." In fact, as Tucker suggested at the exhibit symposium, scholars of the USSR have not been bereft of sources for the study of that system. Even more to the point, much of the information confirmed in these documents has long been assumed on the basis of other types of sources, including publications based on Western sources, memoirs, and dissident literature published by courageous intellectuals who had access to some of this very material. The significance of this exhibit and volume lie in the fact that these documents, once secret, strictly secret, and top secret, have now been disclosed.

The curatorial team chose the documentary material to illustrate two broad areas in Soviet history and current affairs: Soviet domestic affairs and the relations between the United States and the Soviet Union. Within the two sections, documents have been further grouped into subject categories. Each category is introduced with a short essay setting the context of the material and discussing some of the specific background to particular documents. Some especially significant documents have been provided with their own specific introductions.

The largest number of documents in the exhibit and the collection relate to an area whose secrets had been the most closely guarded in the history of the USSR: the nature and operation of the coercive apparatus of repression and terror. More than one hundred documents in this section have been further grouped into topical sections. Documents on the origins and operations of the secret police relate to the creation of the *Cheka,* the first secret police agency, and to comments on and criticisms of its operations. Included here are a few of the four thousand letters written by Vladimir Lenin that had remained unpublished in his collected works. A second section groups political reports and sources of public opinion available to the regime. The secret police generated regular political summaries of activism and popular attitudes that were forwarded to leading party, economic, and trade union organizations; such reports should provide scholars with a valuable new source for assessing relationships between leaders and led. Also included in this category are samples of letters written to Soviet leaders by ordinary citizens, many but not all of them critical of the regime's policies and showing substantial political engagement in the affairs of the day. The largest number of documents in this group of materials on the repressive apparatus deal with the period in Soviet history known as the "Great Terror," or the "Great Purge." Beginning with the assassination of the second most important party leader, Sergei Kirov, this wave of repression spread to the highest echelons of party, government, and military organizations. Documents here include materials on the Seventeenth Party Congress of 1934, which perhaps set the stage for the murder of Kirov; a collation of several investigations of the Kirov murder, none of which implicate Stalin in the crime; materials from the trials and sentencing of Communist leaders Lev Kamenev, Grigorii Zinoviev, Nikolai Bukharin, and Aleksei Rykov; and a set of materials on the "Doctors' Plot," which raised new fears of a wholesale purge on the eve of Stalin's death.

A set of documents illuminates the labor camp and concentration camp system that the writer Alexander Solzhenitsyn described as the Gulag Archipelago. The materials document the beginnings of this system, include complaints from some of its inmates, and extend to the treatment of Polish prisoners in Soviet captivity, including the order for the execution of Polish army officers at the prison camp in Katyn forest in 1940. Documents on censorship, particularly relating to published works, constitute a separate section, and include lists of banned books, some with explanations of how their authors fell afoul of Soviet norms. This section concludes with the first of the orders to restore some of these works to public circulation. Finally, the state's repressive practices directed against specific national groups are documented, with particular emphasis on the wholesale resettlement of Crimean Tatars, Germans, Greeks, and other groups during World War II. The government persecution of Jews and Jewish culture after the war is also documented here.

The second major group of documents on the internal workings of the Soviet system relates to the very important relationship between the state and intellectuals. Early hostility of the regime to politically hostile or even neutral intellectuals included arrests and deportations. The collection contains a particularly spiteful letter from Lenin to the writer Gorky on the worthlessness of intellectuals. A small group of documents relates to the period at the start of the first five-year plan and the beginning of the cultural revolution, symbolized by attacks on engineers, economists, and other specialists accused of forming a hypothetical Industrial Party with links to Western espionage agencies. The Communist Party returned to a policy of strict control over the content and ideology of creative writings after World War II, led by Stalin's chief lieutenant, Andrei Zhdanov. Some of the most important decrees of this period, with the originals in Zhdanov's own handwriting, are included. Finally, this section presents a number of documents relating to the emergence and persecution of dissident writers and activists during the Brezhnev era from 1964 until 1982, and after. These materials include petitions on behalf of persecuted writers, internal Communist Party policy statements on counterpropaganda, and materials on the writers Boris Pasternak, Alexander Solzhenitsyn, and the physicist Andrei Sakharov, among others.

The inner workings of the Communist Party gave rise to a third group of documents. In the culture of the Communist Party, personnel matters were always considered to be confidential and highly secret: the very publication of the party membership records of Soviet leaders from Dzerzhinsky to Gorbachev constituted an enormous break with tradition. Documents in this section also illustrate the development of the Soviet *nomenclatura* system, by which key appointments in every sphere of administration were monitored and controlled according to the interests of the Communist Party apparatus.

Documents on the Soviet Union's economic development relate primarily to the agricultural sphere: materials include government reports and citizens' complaints about the collectivization process that accompanied the first five-year plan in 1929–30. Another set of documents reveals the extent of the terrible famine that gripped Ukraine and other grain-growing areas in 1932 and 1933. Such documents represent only the tip of the iceberg of materials on this episode in Soviet history, which was long denied outright by Soviet scholars and whose historical interpretation invites further research into these and many additional documents.

The relationship between the state and religion was another area in which information was kept tightly controlled and highly restricted. One group of documents here relates to the history of the state's treatment of religion from the violent seizure of church valuables in 1922 to the more cautious coexistence and state control of the 1950s and 1960s. Materials on the persecution of the Orthodox Church Patriarch Tikhon, political reports on religious attitudes of the peasantry, and attempts to expropriate the Church's cultural symbols are among the many documents that trace the church-state relationship in the USSR from 1918 to 1990. A second, smaller category of materials relates more specifically to the antireligious activities of the state, most of them dealing with the period of cultural revolution of 1929–32, which coincided with the first five-year plan in the economy and the mass drive for collectivization.

Another set of documents constitutes a category by itself: papers concerning the accident at the Chernobyl nuclear electricity-generating plant in Ukraine. These documents include an early 1979 warning about defects in the plant, as well as papers on the regime's immediate response to the tragedy in 1986. The final group of documents on the internal workings of the Soviet system relates to the reforms begun by Gorbachev in 1985 and some of the setbacks to those reforms. This was a period in which the lid was off much of the secrecy of the Soviet system, and an increasingly open press provided masses of information of the type that was formerly highly secret. Documents include the Central Committee's response to the violent repression of nationalist demonstrators in Tbilisi, Georgia, in 1989 and Vilnius, Lithuania, in 1991. Only two documents relating to the August 1991 coup attempt were provided for the exhibit, in some measure because the prosecution of the instigators of the coup was still in process.

The second major group of documents—roughly one-third of the total—concerns areas of conflict and cooperation between the Soviet Union and the United States. The relationship between the U.S. and the USSR has always been a special one, with shared experiences as frontier societies and as new republics in their own time. Both countries became major world powers after World War II, and their mutual antagonism and search for modes of coexistence have driven much of the international history of the second half of the twentieth century. Both rivalry and détente, in other words, have always been on the agenda of U.S.-USSR relations.

The first group of documents in this second part of the volume relates to economic cooperation and contacts between the two countries, a topic that has once again become timely. A set of materials describes the involvement of U.S. agencies, both governmental and voluntary, in assisting victims of the Volga region famine in 1921. A second set of materials concerns efforts of U.S. capitalists to find markets and establish joint ventures with the Soviet economy. One of the earliest of the Americans to do business was Dr. Armand Hammer, who first journeyed to Soviet Russia with supplies to aid famine victims, developed a number of enterprises during the 1920s, and remained active in U.S.-Soviet economic relations his entire life. Finally, joint ventures initiated by American sympathizers with the Soviet regime are chronicled in a brief set of documents.

Relations between the Communist Party of the Soviet Union and the Communist Party of the U.S.A. are illustrated in a set of materials taken from the subset of the party archive devoted to the Communist International (Comintern). The documents indicate sources of financial aid for early supporters of the Comintern, and indicate some of the points of conflict and controversy in the history of the U.S. party. Materials include both Soviet commentaries on events and problems and documents generated by American participants in the communist movement.

The next two groups of documents primarily concern U.S.-USSR interactions during World War II, but also included are two very important documents on Soviet foreign policy. One is a 1934 discussion of plans for the development of bacterial warfare; the other is the secret protocol of the Nazi-Soviet Nonaggression Pact of 1939, of which Soviet authorities had either denied the existence or which they claimed to be unable to find in their own archives until shortly before the Library exhibit of 1992. Materials here also include military documents on the disposition of troop strength just before the Nazi invasion of the USSR in 1941, correspondence between Stalin and U.S. leaders, and documents on treatment and repatriation of U.S. prisoners of war liberated from German prison camps by the Soviet Army.

These documents are followed by two groups of materials that chronicle the Cold War, the period of hostility between the two nations that began in

1947 and ended with the new foreign policy initiated under Mikhail Gorbachev and his successor, Boris Yeltsin. The documents here focus on disagreements over control of Germany and Berlin after the war and on propaganda initiatives adopted to counter American hostility in the 1970s and 1980s. No materials were provided about the Korean War or the Vietnam War. A special set of documents discusses what many consider the defining moment of the Cold War, the crisis over the Soviet deployment in Cuba of ballistic missiles in 1962.

Materials relating to the post-Stalin policy of peaceful coexistence, enunciated in a 1955 letter from the Soviet leader Bulganin, also include Soviet intelligence reports about U.S. leaders from Wendell Wilkie to John Foster Dulles to William O. Douglas and conclude with a 1986 agreement on cooperation in space exploration. The final section of documents deals with the Soviet involvement in Afghanistan. The materials include minutes of a Central Committee decision to intervene in Afghan internal politics in 1979 and high-level considerations of propaganda strategies to employ with respect to the Soviet involvement in Afghanistan.

Illustrative material for the exhibit and this volume came both from the Soviet archives and from the collections of the Library of Congress. Photographs include images of the campaign to collectivize agriculture, the assault on the Orthodox Church, and the prison camp system, including a photo dating from as early as 1919. Other photographs depict Soviet leaders or memorialize key congresses and meetings. Posters from the Library of Congress depict many of the key campaigns in Soviet history directed against religion, against fascism, or promoting industrialization and good work habits.

The documents are identified by number, consecutively. The archival location of documents was provided by the Russian curators, and it is hoped that this core sample of documents will indicate to serious researchers the nature of available materials and their location, so that they can plan research efforts accordingly. A number of documents arrived at the exhibit late and by different channels, and it was not always possible to verify their location, although little doubt exists about their authenticity. The Molotov-Ribbentrop secret protocols, for example, were released from the Central Committee archive, and it is assumed that most of the other unattributed documents can also be found in that sprawling inner sanctum of the best kept secrets of the Soviet regime. Finally, to help guide the reader through the complicated forest of personalities and institutions represented in this volume, the editors have appended a brief biographical appendix of some of the most significant individuals mentioned in the documents and a glossary of abbreviations and terms.

PART I. INTERNAL WORKINGS OF THE SOVIET SYSTEM

chapter 1

THE APPARATUS OF REPRESSION AND TERROR

Two of the most interesting "blank spots" in Soviet history have been documentary evidence on the apparatus of repression used to support Soviet rule and a unified theory to explain the regime's (or Stalin's) repression and terror. Western readers have long had evidence of the police apparatus, instruments of repression, labor camp system, censorship, and hostility toward national minorities, but documentation on the internal workings of this system was rigidly suppressed by the Communist regime. Some of the documents presented here illustrate and corroborate facts and conclusions drawn long ago by skilled scholars using other kinds of sources such as the press and memoirs by eyewitnesses. The Smolensk regional Communist Party archive captured by Germans in World War II and acquired by the United States has also indicated the extent of this system and allowed scholars to extrapolate conclusions about the system more generally.

These documents offer a variety of glimpses of this system. They include the minutes of high-level meetings in which basic institutions such as the labor camp system were created; procedural instructions for the verification of party documents, the instrument that accompanied the Great Purge of the 1930s; lists of dangerous books and internal debates on the nature of these dangers in particular books; and orders and reports documenting in matter-of-fact tones the expulsion of national minorities. Such documents provide important insight into the process and procedure of state control and state policies. Other documents chillingly illustrate moments that are well known to students of Soviet history. The pleas for clemency by the purged party leaders Zinoviev, Rykov, and Bukharin are particularly poignant.

Some issues cannot be so readily resolved by the evidence from these documents, and unanswered questions remain. Chief among these is a comprehensive explanation of the Great Purge, the sweeping assault on party cadres and intellectuals that began with the murder of Sergei Kirov in December 1934 and reached its climax with the show trials of 1937. Millions of people were victims of this wave of repression, but the exact magnitude of the human costs of this repression is still unknown. Much more extensive work in these opened archives will be required to determine with greater certainty the final toll.

Nor do the documents offered by the Russian state archives yield sufficient evidence on motivation and cause. In particular, one of the key episodes in the Great Terror, the murder of Kirov, remains unexplained. Many people saw the hand of Stalin in this murder, and it has been widely believed that the investigations and evidence were tampered with in order to protect this secret. An extensive review of the evidence carried out in 1990 at the behest of Gorbachev's advisor Alexander Yakovlev does not implicate Stalin (Document 35); but Yakovlev remains unconvinced. Another explanation for Stalin's assault on party cadres was the rumor that the party faithful at the Seventeenth Party Congress in 1934 had not voted overwhelmingly to elect Stalin to the party's central committee. The documents provided here show this not to be the case, but these may be part of the cover-up. There are no smoking guns in these documents, and there is no guarantee that the ultimate truth lies yet undiscovered in Moscow. Historians must continue to search for answers to these ambiguous questions by gathering multiple sources of evidence, examining context, and using their interpretive skills to devise plausible, if not definitive, explanations.

On the other hand, the political context of this repressive state can now be more clearly understood. The documents grouped here as political intelligence reports indicate a government deeply suspicious of its citizens, and a citizenry far more willing to criticize that government than has been previously understood. The letters from Lenin printed here and in the next section help to dispel the theory that Stalin's repressive policies were an aberration of "Leninism." Lenin's order, dated August 1918 (Document 4), to set an example by punishing rich peasants presages the class militance and the punitive tone later used by Stalin.

Secret Police: Origins and Operations

The end of the tsarist regime in February 1917 also brought an end to the tsarist secret police organization, the *Okhrana*, whose task was to monitor political opposition and to enforce obedience to the regime. Less than two months after taking power—amid threats of counterrevolution, conspiracies, political opposition from all points of the spectrum, armed bands of demobilized soldiers and sailors roaming the towns, and a general lawlessness stemming from weak political authority in the center—the Council of People's Commissars voted to create an emergency commission to combat "sabotage" and all counterrevolutionary politics. The *Cheka,* as the agency came to be known, took its nickname from the first letters of the first two Russian words of its long title, the Extraordinary Commission for Combatting Counterrevolution and Sabotage. Later, the commission added "the struggle with speculation" to its title and to its mandate. The founding chief of the *Cheka* was a Polish revolutionary of aristocratic background, Felix Dzerzhinsky, a veteran of tsarist prisons and the underground movement. Although the absolute power invested in the *Cheka* would lead to corruption and abuses of power, as pointed out, for example, in Lenin's letter to Latsis of June 4, 1919 (Document 7), Dzerzhinsky himself was a revolutionary ascetic, known to be morally incorruptible and dedicated absolutely to the revolutionary cause.

The *Cheka* was created at a moment of extreme political danger for the regime, and it developed its apparatus and methods of operation during the Russian Civil War, a period when the principle of the survival of the revolutionary state dominated all other considerations of justice and equity. But the military victory of the Red Army over the Whites by 1920 did not end political opposition even within the Bolshevik Party (renamed the Communist Party in 1918), and the *Cheka* would continue to play the leading role in reporting on and enforcing conformity to the rules of the regime. The *Cheka* was dissolved on February 6, 1922, and its functions were transferred to a new State Political Administration (*GPU*) under the People's Commissariat of Internal Affairs (*NKVD*). Dzerzhinsky remained the chairman of the *GPU*. The following year, the *GPU* was removed from the *NKVD* and given the status of an independent agency, named the Unified State Political Directorate (*OGPU*). Upon Dzerzhinsky's death in 1926, V.R. Menzhinskii, his former deputy, assumed the leadership of the agency. In July 1934 the *OGPU* lost its independent status and once again became a part of the *NKVD*. Under this title, the agency would become responsible for executing the arrests and investigations of the period of the Great Purges. Several documents in this chapter describe *NKVD* procedures, and extensive documentation on the purges themselves will be found here as well. After World War II, the *NKVD* was divided into two agencies, the Ministry for Internal Affairs (*MVD*), responsible for ordinary police and the labor camps, and the Ministry for State Security (*MGB*), the security police. In 1954, after Stalin's death, the *MGB* was demoted in status to a Committee on State Security, the *KGB*, and continued under this title until the breakup of the Soviet Union in 1991.

DOCUMENT 1   *Agenda of the December 20, 1917, meeting of the Council of People's Commissars, including Dzerzhinsky's report on the creation of the Cheka, the secret police organization*

Meeting of the Council of People's Commissars, December 7, 1917

Chairman: Vl. Il'ich Lenin
Present: Trotsky, Kollontai, Stuchka, Dybenko, Petrovskii,
             Menzhinskii, Raskol'nikov, Stalin, Glebov, Bogolepov,
             Uritskii, Aksel'rod, Shotman, Elizarov, Shliapnikov,
             Essen, Sverdlov, Bonch-Bruevich

	Discussed:		Resolved:
1.	Exchange of views on hiring Socialist Revolutionaries [*SRs*] in government ministries.	1.	After a general discussion it was decided that it was acceptable to hire *SRs* in government ministries by adjusting certain conditions requested by them. Comrades TROTSKY and STALIN are instructed to meet tomorrow at 10:30 A.M. with representatives of the *SRs* to inform them of the viewpoint on this matter of the Council of People's Commissars.
2.	The extra-agenda announcement of Comrade STALIN about the visit of a delegation from the Ukrainian Revolutionary Staff of the Petrograd Regional Military Command, representing the Central Ukrainian Rada, to conduct talks with the Council of People's Commissars.	2.	Comrades TROTSKY and STALIN are assigned to receive the delegation.
3.	The petition from four People's Commissars about the new railroad wage scale adopted by the Executive Committee [*TSIK*].	3.	In view of the petition of the four People's Commissars on the new wage scale for railroad employees authorized by the *TSIK*, the *TSIK* is requested to review its decision if possible. The People's Commissars who introduced the corresponding petition are charged with this.
4.	The demands of the Central Committee of the Trade Union of Postal and Telegraph Employees about the possibility of a Russia-wide postal and telegraph strike and about the possibility of a Russia-wide general strike of all government agency employees.	4.	In view of the fact that the commission that was appointed yesterday by the Council of People's Commissars to deal with this matter is still deliberating, do not adjourn until the commission delivers its decision to the Council of People's Commissars.
5.	Sending a delegation abroad.	5.	In principle, sending a delegation abroad is seen as desirable; matter referred to *TSIK*.
6.	Coordinating military and revolutionary activities.	6.	A commission is to be established, consisting of representatives of the Ministries of Military, Naval, and Internal Affairs.
7.	Immediate confirmation by telegram of signatures of Samara Revolutionary Committee presidium members—Comrades Kuibyshev, Gerasimov, and Mitrofanov—to obtain allocations from local State Bank branch.	7.	Matter assigned to Comrade Petrovskii.

8.	The necessity of immediate aid to the revolutionary committee of the city of Samara.	8.	PETROVSKII is instructed to ascertain whether the 200,000 [rubles] that were sent to them by the Main Treasury were received.

Present: Dzerzhinsky, Stalin, Petrovskii, Glebov, Menzhinskii, Aksel'rod, Shotman

9.	Dzerzhinsky's report on the organization and staff of a commission to combat sabotage. Staff (incomplete): 1. Ksenofontov 2. Zhedilev 3. Averin 4. Petersen 5. Peters 6. Evseev 7. V. Trifonov 8. Dzerzhinsky 9. Sergo? 10. Vasil'evskii? Purpose of the commission: 1. Search for and liquidate all counterrevolutionary and sabotage politics and activities throughout Russia, attempting to see that none succeed. 2. Bring to trial before the Revolutionary Tribunal all saboteurs and counterrevolutionaries and develop means to combat them. 3. The commission carries out preparatory investigations insofar as they are necessary for the search. 4. The commission is divided into departments—information, organizational department (for organizing the struggle against counterrevolution in all of Russia), and a sub-department, a department for struggle. The commission structure will be finalized tomorrow [illegible]. The commission should pay chief attention to the press, sabotage, and other rightist *SR* sabotage. [remainder illegible]	9.	Name the commission the All-Russian Extraordinary Commission under the Council of People's Commissars to Combat Counterrevolution and Sabotage. The commission is approved.

RTSKhIDNI, fond 19, opis 1, delo 21, listy 2, 2 ob.

Cheka director F. E. Dzerzhinsky (center) with board members (left to right) S. G. Uralov, K. M. Volobuev, I. D. Chugurin, I. K. Ksenofontov, G. S. Moroz, and V. V. Fomin, 1918–19. TSGAKFD. N 4-16290

DOCUMENT 2 *Warrant issued by Dzerzhinsky, head of the* Cheka, *May 23, 1918, to detain Ernest Kal'nin and to seize his personal possessions*

All-Russian Extraordinary Commission
under the Council of People's Commissars
in the Struggle against Counterrevolution and
Official Crimes

Dept. No. 1524. Good for one day
Warrant

Comrade Ovchinnikov is commissioned to carry out a search, inspection, seizure of documents and books, imposition of an arrest of the goods of Ernest Kal'nin.
Depending on the results of the search, detain this citizen at your discretion and requisition or confiscate his goods and weapons.

Commission Chairman: F. Dzerzhinsky
Secretary: Il'in
May 23, 1918

RTSKhIDNI, fond 17, opis 4, delo 187, list 56

Execution of Nicholas II

The 300-year-old Romanov dynasty came to an end on March 2, 1917 (old style), when Nicholas II abdicated his office in favor of his brother Michael, and Michael declined to ascend to the throne. The Provisional Government was unable to decide what should be done with the former tsar and his family, who lived under house arrest in their country palace after the February Revolution. Monarchists hoped to restore him to power, while others negotiated on the Romanovs' behalf for asylum in England. When these discussions came to naught, and with the increasingly unstable political situation in Petrograd, the prime minister, Alexander Kerensky, decided in August 1917 to move the royal family secretly to a safer location in Tobol'sk, in Siberia. They remained quietly there until April 1918, when Bolshevik authorities decided that Tobol'sk was too vulnerable to monarchist forces, and they ordered the Romanovs transferred to the more solidly revolutionary city of Ekaterinburg, in the Urals.

In mid-May Nicholas, Alexandra, their five children, and some servants were installed in a house that had belonged to the merchant family Ipatiev. By July 1918, even Ekaterinburg was not safe, and there were fears that White forces might liberate the Romanovs and use them to rally the anti-Bolshevik forces. The *Cheka* increased its security around the Ipatiev home in the beginning of July. Meanwhile, the Regional Soviet of the Urals had voted for the Romanovs' execution, but first they sent a representative to secure Moscow's approval. The Bolshevik leadership decided to use the occasion for a public trial of the Romanovs. But with the Whites advancing rapidly on Ekaterinburg, the Bolsheviks feared they had only two or three days in which to act, or Nicholas would fall into the hands of the enemy. The Regional Soviet ordered the execution to be carried out immediately. The family was shot in the basement of the Ipatiev house early in the morning of July 17, and their bodies were burned and buried in deserted mine shafts outside of the city.

Many of the facts of the execution were uncovered by investigators for Admiral Kolchak when his White forces captured the city. In 1993 scientists confirmed, using DNA matching, that the bones discovered in the mine shaft were indeed the remains of the Romanovs. But there has always been controversy about whether the execution was a decision taken at local initiative in the heat and chaos of the Civil War, or whether the order to eliminate the tsar and his family came from Moscow, from Lenin. Trotsky reported in 1935, for example, that he was told Lenin had approved the execution. If indeed the Council of People's Commissars decided to authorize the execution on July 2, as circumstantial evidence suggests, then Lenin's July 16 telegram reassuring the Danish press, "czar safe," is utterly and deliberately misleading and false.

DOCUMENT 3   *Telegram from* National Tidende *(Copenhagen), July 16, 1918, inquiring about the Tsar, and Lenin's reply*

MOSCOW TELEGRAPH   TELEGRAM
[illegible]   LENIN: MEMBER OF TEM[?]
Form no. 99   GOVERNMENT: MSRT[?]
Received by [illegible]

FROM COPENHAGEN 354/4/26 T9 6 30

   RUMOUR HERE GOING THAT THE OXSZAR HAS BEEN MURDERED KINDLY WIRE   FACTS I=NATIONALTIDENDE

       [handwritten:] *National Tidende Kjobenhavn*
                    Rumour not true   czar safe   all rumours are only lie of capitalist press   Lenin

                 [stamped:] NOT FOR PUBLICATION

RTSKhIDNI, ll. 333.

Bolshevik Terror

The use of terror had been an integral part of the revolutionary movement in Russia well before the Bolsheviks came on the scene. Inspired by the systematic terror of the French Revolution, nineteenth-century Russian Socialist Revolutionaries had directed their terrorist actions against members of the tsarist regime as a class, assassinating officials of high and low rank. Bolshevik terror also had a class component as its base. Class conflict was the essence of the revolution, and this justified the policy described by a *Cheka* leader: "We are eliminating the bourgeoisie as a class." In the face of resistance by this class enemy, any and all repressive measures could be justified, as long as they were used against those who belonged to the enemy class. In January 1918 Lenin had said, "Until we use terror against speculators—shooting them on the spot—nothing will happen." With the intensification of the Civil War on the borderlands and increasing opposition in the center, the Central Executive Committee of Soviets declared "the Socialist Fatherland in Danger" and called for mass terror against the bourgeoisie.

Strong-arm Bolshevik attempts to requisition grain from the peasantry combined with this rhetoric of terror produced violent opposition. In early August 1918 peasants in Penza province rose up against the regime. The Bolsheviks claimed the "mutiny" was led by *kulak*s, the richest stratum of the peasantry, who, they asserted, duped average and poor peasants into joining the revolt. Besides the note included here (Document 4), Lenin sent several other telegrams to Penza Communist leaders. The same day he gave this order to Penza, Lenin also wrote to officials in Nizhnii Novgorod to "organize immediately mass terror, shoot and deport the hundreds of prostitutes who are making drunkards of the soldiers, as well as former officers, etc. . . ."

The terror escalated in the beginning of September 1918. On August 30, as Lenin was leaving a factory meeting where he had spoken, a Socialist Revolutionary named Fania Kaplan shot and seriously wounded him. Kaplan's assault became the signal for the inauguration of an official policy of "Red Terror," of revenge for the attack on the revolution's leader. The leading Bolshevik newspaper in Petrograd proclaimed, "For the blood of Lenin . . . let there be floods of blood of the bourgeoisie—more blood, as much as possible." Document 5 from the *Cheka*'s weekly bulletin (a complete run of which is held at the Hoover Institution at Stanford University) indicates the local *Cheka* responses to the call for terror: arrests of hostages and escalating apocalyptic rhetoric.

Letter from Lenin to Communist leaders in Penza, August 11, 1918, on dealing with peasant revolts in the province

11-8-18

Send to Penza
To Comrades Kuraev,
Bosh, Minkin, and
other Penza
Communists

Comrades! The revolt by the five *kulak volost*'s must be suppressed without mercy. The interest of the entire revolution demands this, because we have now before us our final decisive battle "with the *kulak*s." We need to set an example.

1) You need to hang (hang without fail, so that the public sees) at least 100 notorious *kulak*s, the rich, and the bloodsuckers.

2) Publish their names.

3) Take away all of their grain.

4) Execute the hostages—in accordance with yesterday's telegram.

This needs to be accomplished in such a way that people for hundreds of miles around will see, tremble, know, and scream out: let's choke and strangle those blood-sucking *kulak*s.

Telegraph us acknowledging receipt and execution of this.

Yours, Lenin

P.S. Use your toughest people for this.

[not numbered]

RTSKhIDNI, fond 2, op. 1, d. 6898, l. 1-1ob.

DOCUMENT 5 *Excerpts from the* Cheka *Weekly of 1918 concerning the response of the* Cheka *to an attempt on Lenin's life and the murder of Uritskii*

RED TERROR

In response to the attempt on Comrade Lenin's life and the murder of Comrade Uritskii, the Extraordinary Commissions [*Cheka*s] in many cities have issued warnings that if anyone makes the slightest attempt to encroach on the rule of workers and peasants, the iron dictatorship of the proletariat will discard its generosity to its enemies. Below we print one of these warnings, issued by the Torzhok *Cheka*.

DECLARATION

To all citizens of the city and *uezd* of Torzhok.

Hirelings of capitalism have targeted the leaders of the Russian proletariat. In Moscow, the chairman of the Council of People's Commissars, Vladimir Lenin, has been wounded, and in Petrograd, Comrade Uritskii has been killed. The proletariat must not allow its leaders to die at the vile, filthy hands of counterrevolutionary mercenaries and must answer terror with terror. For the head and life of one of our leaders, hundreds of heads must roll from the bourgeoisie and all its accomplices. Putting the general citizenry of the city and *uezd* on notice, the Novotorzhsk *Cheka* announces that it has arrested and imprisoned as hostages the following representatives of

Surrender of grain by peasants in Kurgan *oblast'*, demanded by the surplus appropriation system, 1918. TSGAKFD. N 1544

the bourgeoisie and their accomplices, the rightist *SR*s [Socialist Revolutionaries] and Mensheviks. These individuals will be shot immediately by the *Cheka* if there is the slightest counterrevolutionary action directed against the Soviets, or any attempt to assassinate the leaders of the working class.

List of hostages.

Grabinskii, Konstantin Vasil'evich—director of the "Koz'miny" factory. Golovnin, Vasilii Petrovich—director of the Golovnin factory. Raevskii, Sergei Petrovich—priest of the Ascension church. Gorbylev, Ivan Ivanovich—merchant. Arkhimandrit, Simon—prior of the men's monastery. Golovnin, Aleksandr Ivanovich—owner of the Tannery. Novoselov, Vasilii Efremovich—plant owner-engineer. Ganskii, Bruno Adol'fovich—officer, rightist *SR*. Petrov, Semen Filippovich—officer, rightist *SR*. TSvylev, Mikhail Stepanovich—engineer, merchant. Shchukin, Ivan Petrovich—retired artilleryman, captain, rightist. Pannichkin, Sergei Ivanovich—former agent of the Tsarist secret police. Mel'nikov, Efrem Aleksandrovich—broker, rightist. Anitov, Nikolai Dmitrievich—rightist *SR*. Anan'in, Andrei Trofimovich—rightist *SR*. Leshchov, Mikhail Stepanovich—rightist *SR*. Poliakov, Nikolai Ivanovich—merchant, Black Hundreder. Grabinskii, Nikolai Vasil'evich—merchant, speculator. Garmonov, Il'ia Aleksandrovich—rightist *SR*. Prokhorov, IAkov Egorovich—merchant.

Chairman, Novotorzhsk Extraordinary Commission

M. Kliuev.

Members of the Commission: I. Shibaev.
TSvetkov.

Urgent Bulletin from the Extraordinary Commission on Combating Counterrevolution in the City and *Uezd* of Morshansk

Comrades . . . He who would fight for a better future must be merciless to his enemies. He who would strive to defend the poor must temper his compassion and become cruel. Revolution is not a game and one must not toy with it. If they strike us on one cheek, we will repay it a hundred times over to their entire body. You who are oppressed, value yourselves . . . .

Do not believe the agents provocateurs . . . .

You know that a few days ago an attempt was made on the life of Comrade Lenin and Comrade Uritskii was killed; this was organized by rightist parties and the bourgeoisie; i.e., they are inflicting wounds to our head. It is obvious they are systematically eliminating the leaders of the revolution. Measures have been taken to forestall this vile enterprise, and antidotes have been devised to stop the contagion, i.e., RED TERROR, massed against the bourgeoisie, the former gendarmerie, the constables, sheriffs, and other police and officers guiding the counterrevolutionary element. All of Russia has been vaccinated, especially in the city of Morshansk, where in retaliation for the murder of Comrade Uritskii and the wounding of Comrade Lenin, we have shot the former sheriff of Morshansk *uezd,* Vasilii Zasukhin; the former Morshansk city police chief, Pavel Arkhipov; the former constable of section 3, Morshansk *uezd,* Mikhail Kurgaev; the former constable of sections 5 and 6, Viacheslav Lazov. If there is another attempt to assassinate the leaders of our revolution or in general communists holding responsible posts, the cruelty of the workers and the poor people of the countryside will be revealed in even harsher form for the bourgeoisie, because they need to react against such vile actions as the implementation of "white terror."

You, comrade workers and rural poor, do not be afraid. View the red terror as a necessity to force the bourgeoisie and its lackeys to be quiet. Furthermore, be aware that the capitalist rulers in Ukraine, on the Don, are shooting workers and peasants, the number of victims reaching 20,000. They are not standing on ceremony in Finland either, and the jails are full; they are packing our brothers in where there are already as many as 80,000 incarcerated. Remember that we will not move them with our softness and good will toward them, because they are acting with a purpose, striving to extinguish and deny the rights of the workers and peasants. Thus we answer and we must answer a blow with a blow ten times stronger.

Comrade poor people . . . . Calm confidence and organization . . . .

6-IX. Mozhaisk. At the direction of the *Cheka,* 6 persons have been shot, including the doctor Sazykin for hiding a wagon of weapons; the priest Tikhomirov for inciting the peasants to riot against the Soviets; Plokhovo, the former police inspector of Mozhaisk *uezd;* Rusanov, the former constable and large landowner; and Tikhomirov and Nikulin, agents provocateurs of the tsarist secret police, former civil servants.

Published, in a bound volume, no. 1, pp. a,b, *KGB* Archive

DOCUMENT 6   *Council of People's Commissars' certificate, signed by Lenin, March 29, 1919,*
confirming M. IA. Latsis as a member of the **Cheka** *collegium*

RUSSIAN
SOCIALIST
FEDERATED
 SOVIET REPUBLIC
 - - - - - - -
COUNCIL
OF PEOPLE'S COMMISSARS

- - - - * - - - -   CERTIFICATION.

Moscow, the Kremlin.

 March 29, 1919

  No. A 2354.

        The bearer of this, Comrade MARTYN IANOVICh L A T S I S /SUDRABS/ is confirmed by the Council of People's Commissars on the 27th of March of this year as a Member of the Collegium of the All-Russian Extraordinary Commission for Combatting Counterrevolution, Speculation and Official Crimes.

Chairman of the Council
of People's Commissars   [signed] V. I. Ul'ianov (Lenin)

        Secretary of the Council
        of the People's Commissars   [signed] L. Fotieva

RTSKhIDNI, fond 2, opis 1, delo 9037, list 1

DOCUMENT 7   *Letter from Lenin to Latsis, June 4, 1919, concerning excesses committed in the*
name of the **Cheka**

RUSSIAN
 Federated
Soviet Republic
 - - - - - - - - -
CHAIRMAN OF THE COUNCIL
OF WORKERS' AND PEASANTS'
 DEFENSE
    - - - -o- - - -   To Comrade LATSIS.

 Moscow, Kremlin
 June 4, 1919

        Dear comrade! I received your letter and the enclosure.

        Kamenev says—and declares that some very prominent Extraordinary Commission for Combatting Sabotage and Counterrevolution [*Cheka*] operatives confirm it—that the *Cheka* has brought about a multitude of evils in Ukraine, having been established there too early and having admitted into their ranks a mass of hangers-on.

The personnel [of *Cheka*] must be checked out very strictly. Dzerzhinsky, I hope, will assist you in this matter from here. At all costs, the *Cheka* operatives must be taken firmly in hand and the hangers-on expelled. At your convenience, report to me in more detail about the purge of *Cheka* personnel in Ukraine and about the results of this action.

Regards!

Yours, Lenin

Source:?

DOCUMENT 8   *Undated letter from Latsis to Lenin, on excesses in the Ukrainian* **Cheka**

Dear VLADIMIR IL'ICh!

In your letter, you press for a purge of the Ukrainian Extraordinary Commissions for Combatting Sabotage and Counterrevolution [*ChKs*].

I have set myself to this work from the first first day of my work, since April 10.

All our misfortune comes from the fact that [we have] nothing with which to build.

Those officials whom we got rid of in Moscow as both of meager talents and poor reliability have gathered in Ukraine.

The party committees can give us nobody. Compared to other agencies, we nevertheless have proportionally three times more Communists than they.

Now, we have decided to accept only Communists (Bolsheviks) and Socialist Revolutionaries [*SRs*].

I have made very great concessions to upgrade the composition of the *ChK*, and, to rid myself of the constant censures and pogroms, I have abolished the *uezd ChK* and I have gotten rid of petty speculation.

Since the very first day I have forbidden the seizure of anything except material evidence during arrests.

But our Russian figures: "Don't I really deserve those pants and boots that the bourgeoisie have been wearing until now? That's a reward for my work, right? So, I'll take what's mine. And there's no sin in that."

This is where the constant petty attempts come from.

Even executions of officials don't help. Death has already become an all-too-common occurrence.

Now, an inspection commission of six specialists in all branches has been sent throughout all the *guberniia*s.

As you see, we are doing what we can.

It must be said that the situation is improving, but not so much as to be insured against the attack of Red troops.

With comradely greetings.

[signed] Latsis

Stamp (at bottom center): Archive of the Marx-Engels-Lenin-Stalin Institute, No. 4226, kl. 2, l. 2

Source:?

DOCUMENT 9   *Letter from Deputy People's Commissar of Foreign Affairs L. M. Karakhan to Stalin and all members of the Politburo, May 6, 1922, regarding tendentious reports by United Press representative Gullinger*

<u>TO THE POLITBURO</u>

1. To Comrade Stalin.

----

2. Copies to all members of the Politburo.

For some time now, particularly during the period of the Genoa Conference, the Moscow representative of the American Telegraph Agency "United Press," Citizen Gullinger, has started sending abroad telegrams tendentiously reflecting events in Russia. This has been particularly so in his telegrams on the removal of church properties and in telegrams that have anticipated the "united front" of Germany and Russia at the Genoa Conference. We have repeatedly brought to his attention the distortion of the facts permitted by him in his telegrams. We have not let pass several of his telegrams, while in others we have expunged the particularly tendentious passages that might serve as the basis for propagating false rumors about Russia abroad. In response to this, Citizen Gullinger has begun to slip into his telegrams phrases about the tightening of censorship in Moscow. On April 26, he brought for transmission a telegram, a copy of which is enclosed with this letter. This telegram was not let through; nevertheless, Gullinger sent it, apparently through some mission, as we learned from the response he received to his suggestion.

I feel that it is intolerable to permit such crooks to live in Moscow and to continue to do such dirty tricks. I suggest that he be deported immediately.

I have asked Genoa about this matter and received the response that they have no objection to deporting Gullinger.

Since it is necessary to deport him immediately, I would request that the question be resolved by Thursday by an arrangement over the telephone. (A copy of this letter has been circulated to all members of the Politburo).

       With Communist Greetings

....

[Stamp bottom right:] Secret Archive of the Central Committee
           of the All-Union Communist Party (of Bolsheviks)

                   Inventory No 290; Convocation; F-GR;
          Archive No.—

RTSKhIDNI, fond 17, opis 86, delo 146, listy 2,3

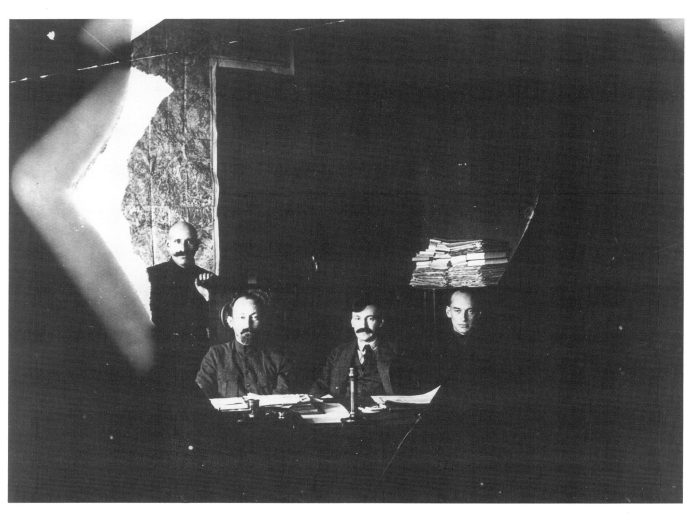

Meeting of the board of the *Cheka*, Moscow, 1923, (left to right) A. IA. Belen'kii, chief of protection for Lenin; F E. Dzerzhinsky, director; V. R. Menzhinskii, assistant director; and G. I. Bokii. TSGAKFD. N2-100916

DOCUMENT 10   *Letter from Nikolai Bukharin, editor of* Pravda, *to Felix Dzerzhinsky, December 1924, on the necessity for more liberal policies*

Dear Feliks Edmundovich,

I was not at the last meeting of the executive group. I heard that you, by the way, said there that I and Sokol'nikov are "against the *GPU*" etc. I was informed about the argument that took place the day before yesterday. And so, dear Feliks Edmundovich, lest you have any doubt, I ask you to understand <u>what</u> I do think.

I believe that we should move <u>more rapidly</u> toward a more liberal form of rule: fewer acts of repression, more rule by law, more discussion, self-government (under the direction of the party, naturally) and so on. In my article in *Bolshevik*, which you <u>approved,</u> I laid out the theoretical underpinnings of this course. <u>Therefore,</u> I occasionally come out against proposals that expand the powers of the *GPU* and so on. Understand, dear Feliks Edmundovich (you know how fond I am of you) that you do not have <u>the slightest</u> reason to suspect me of any sort of ill will, either toward you personally or toward the *GPU* as an institution. It's a question of <u>principle</u>—that is what is at issue.

Because you are a man deeply passionate about politics but at the same time [one who] can be impartial, you will understand me.

I warmly embrace you, warmly press your hand, and wish you a speedy recovery.

Yours,
N. Bukharin

RTSKhIDNI, fond 76, opis 3, delo 345, listy 2, 2ob

DOCUMENT 11   *Letter from Dzerzhinsky, head of the* GPU, *to his deputy chief, V. R. Menzhinskii, December 24, 1924, on how to counteract the liberal attitudes expressed in Bukharin's letter calling for more open policies*

To Comrade Menzhinskii   For your eyes only
                                         [copying forbidden]

Here attached is Bukharin's letter to me which I would like you to return to me after reading.

We have to take into consideration that such attitudes exist among the Central Committee members, and [we have] to think it over. It would be the greatest political blunder if the party yielded on the fundamental question of the *GPU* and gave "new life" to the Philistines—as a line, as a policy, and as a declaration. It would mean a concession to Nepmanism, Philistinism, and tending toward a rejection of bolshevism; it would mean a victory for Trotskyism and a surrender of our positions. To counteract these attitudes we need to review our practices, our methods and eliminate everything that can feed such attitudes. That means that we (the *GPU*) must become quieter, more modest. We should use searches and arrests more carefully, with better incriminating evidence; some categories of arrests (Nepmanism, official misconduct) should be limited, and carried out under pressure, or by mobilizing popular party support for us; we must better inform the Moscow committee about all matters, more closely involving the party organization in these affairs. We need to review our policy on granting permission to go abroad and on visas. We must pay attention to the struggle for popularity among peasants, organizing help for them in the struggle against hooliganism and other crimes. And in general, we need to plan measures to gain support among workers and peasants and mass party organizations.

In addition, once again, we need to pay attention to our information summaries so that they provide the members of the Central Committee an accurate picture of our work in brief, very specific terms. Our information summaries are presenting a one-sided picture, completely black, without the proper perspective and without describing our real role. We must compile accounts of our work.

December 24, 1924 F. Dzerzhinsky

[Stamp, upper left corner:] Archive of F. Z. Dzerzhinsky

RTSKhIDNI, fond 76, opis 3, delo 345, listy 1, 1 ob.

DOCUMENT 12   *Verdict of the Supreme Court of the RSFSR, November 5, 1935, concerning the formation by several "agitators" of an anti-Soviet group at the October Revolution dockyard in the city of Ufa [supplement to a report to Stalin and Molotov on review of the activities of the Supreme Court]*

[stamp] Commission of Soviet Control under the Council of People's Commissars of the
USSR [*KSK pri SNK SSSR*]
Secret
No. 1785c

COPY

Verdict of the
Russian Socialist Federated Soviet Republic [*sic*]

On March 25, 1935, the Water Transport Court of the Kama River Basin in the city of Ufa, composed of Chairman Kalinin, the People's Jurors Naumochin and Smykova, and secretary Volkov, reviewed, in closed session, the accusation against:

> 1) Esin, Anatolii Alekseevich: 39 years old; from a working-class family in Sormovo; a lathe operator by profession; married, supporting wife and daughter; has worked in water transport since 1924; literate; a member of the *VKP(b)* from 1917 through 1923; left the party under the influence of the *SR* organization; became a *VKP(b)* candidate member in 1932; expelled in 1935 for counterrevolutionary activities; resides at the October Revolution dockyard.

> 2) Beliankin, Efim Mikhailovich: 44 years old; from a poor peasant family in the Chistopol' region, Tatar Republic; severed ties with the peasantry in 1902; a lathe operator by profession, has worked in water transport since 1924; married, supporting wife and daughter; candidate member in the *VKP(b)* since 1932; expelled for counterrevolutionary activities; a red partisan; resides at the October Revolution dockyard.

> 3) TSinarev, Nikolai Andreevich: 37 years old; from a working-class family in Blagoveshchensk, Bashkir Republic; poorly educated; a metal worker since 1922; has worked in water transport since 1925; was a member of the *VKP(b)* after 1925; expelled for counterrevolutionary activities; married, supporting 3 dependents; a red partisan; resides at the October Revolution dockyard.

The crime is covered by article 58, paragraph 10 of the Criminal Code.

After hearing the testimony of the defendants and witnesses, the court in a preliminary inquest established the presence of an anti-Soviet group at the October Revolution dockyard consisting of Esin, Beliankin, and TSinarev.

The accused group of like-minded workers, being unhappy with the policies of the party and government and hiding behind their party membership cards, spread openly hostile views against the party and government among the workers of the dockyard, exploiting certain shortcomings in the operation of the dockyard organization for their purposes, interpreting everything in a counterrevolutionary spirit, and in this way stirring discontent among the workers. For example, Esin would say, "Wage rates are low, earnings are small, one must leave the water transport business, all the newspapers tell lies. They claim that there is a lot of bread available, and yet we ourselves are hungry."

Beliankin and TSinarev agreed fully with the above; i.e., they backed Esin at all times, and Beliankin would say, "The trade unions do not defend the workers and side with the bosses. A dog does not eat another dog."

When it became known at the dockyard that Sergei Mironovich Kirov, a member of the Presidium of the *TSIK* of the USSR and the Politburo of the *TSK VKP(b)*, had been murdered by the treacherous hand of an agent sent by a Trotskyite-Zinovievite counterrevolutionary organization, the working class bowed its heads and drew even more closely together around the Communist Party and its leader, Comrade Stalin. At a December 3 memorial meeting to honor Sergei Mironovich Kirov, Esin, Beliankin, and TSinarev were in attendance and openly expressed among the workers their solidarity with the traitors of the working class. At the same time, they conducted counterrevolutionary agitation, focusing their cynicism on Kirov and Stalin.

The court considers it a proven fact that Esin, the main instigator of counterrevolutionary opinions, at the December 3 meeting openly told the workers, "The dog Kirov has been killed; there remains one more dog, Stalin." Leaving the meeting, he looked at the portrait of Stalin at the club and said, "He should be hung along with Lenin from the antenna; let him swing." Earlier Esin also said, "Nowadays the unions do not protect the workers and wages are too low." These remarks in themselves were sufficient to stir up discontent among the workers and to subvert measures undertaken by the Soviet authorities and the party.

Beliankin agreed with all the counterrevolutionary views of Esin, and he remarked, on December 2 when Esin told him that Kirov had been murdered, "To a dog, a dog's death." Up to the moment of arrest Beliankin told the workers that it was hopeless to petition for increased salaries through the trade unions, that the unions work hand in hand with the bosses, and that "a dog will not eat another dog."

TSinarev also sympathized with and shared the counterrevolutionary views of Esin and Beliankin and, in connection with the villainous assassination of Kirov, said, "Kirov was killed because he was scum." He did not report the counterrevolutionary activities of Esin and Beliankin even though he was a member of the party.

Esin, Beliankin, and TSinarev admitted their partial guilt; however, as a result of TSinarev's complete testimony and admission, Esin's and Beliankin's counterrevolutionary activities were unmasked.

Governed by articles 319–320 of the Criminal Procedure Code and article 58, paragraph 10 of the Criminal Code of the Russian Republic, the following sentence is declared:

1) Esin, Anatolii Alekseevich, in accordance with article 58, paragraph 10, has been declared guilty and is sentenced to be deprived of his freedom for 7 years.
2) Beliankin, Efim Mikhailovich, in accordance with article 58, paragraph 10, has been declared guilty and is sentenced to be deprived of his freedom for 5 years.
3) TSinarev, Nikolai Andreevich, in accordance with article 58, paragraph 10, has been declared guilty and is sentenced to be deprived of his freedom for 3 years.

1) No material evidence relevant to the case.
2) Hold Beliankin, Esin, and TSinarev under armed guard at Bash. Central [illegible]
3) Verdict is final but can be contested in an appeal to the Supreme Court of the RSFSR within 72 hours from receipt of a copy of the verdict.

Original signed by: Chairman Kalinin, members Naumochkin, Smykova
True copy of the original: Court Secretary, Bel'sk section—signature
(M.P.)

RTSKhIDNI, fond 17, opis 120, delo 171, listy 38, 39, 46.

DOCUMENT 13   *Resolution by the USSR Council of People's Commissars and the Party's Central Committee, June 17, 1935, on the procedure for executing arrests*

SUPPLEMENT to point 157,
Politburo Minutes No.27.

ON THE PROCEDURE FOR EXECUTING ARRESTS.

Resolution of the Council of People's Commissars of the USSR and the Central Committee of the All-Union Communist Party (of Bolsheviks) [*VKP(b)*]

The Council of People's Commissars of the USSR and the Central Committee of the All-Union Communist Party (of Bolsheviks) resolve:

1. As a change to the instructions of May 8, 1933, *NKVD* arrests on all matters without exception henceforth can be executed only with the consent of the appropriate procurator.

2. If it is necessary to carry out an arrest at the scene of a crime, responsible *NKVD* personnel, legally so authorized, are obliged to report the arrest immediately to the appropriate procurator to obtain confirmation.

3. Permission for arrests of members of the USSR Central Executive Committee [*TSIK*] and the union republic *TSIK*s is granted only after organs of the Procuracy and *NKVD* have obtained the consent of the USSR *TSIK* chairperson or the union republic *TSIK* chairpersons as appropriate.

Permission for arrests of supervisory personnel of people's commissariats [*narkomat*] of the USSR and union republics and equivalent central institutions (chiefs of directorates and department heads, industrial association heads and their deputies, directors and deputy directors of industrial enterprises, *sovkhoze*s, etc.), as well as engineers, agronomists, professors, physicians, and directors of academic and scientific research institutions is granted with the consent of the appropriate People's Commissars.

4. Permission for arrests of *VKP(b)* members and candidates is granted with the consent of the secretaries of *raion, krai, oblast' VKP(b)* committees, the central committees of national communist parties, as appropriate. As regards communists holding administrative positions in the Union People's Commissariats [*narkomats*] and in equivalent central institutions, permission is granted after obtaining the concurrence of the Party Control Commission chairperson.

5. Permission for arrests of military personnel of the higher, senior, and intermediate command staff of the Workers' and Peasants' Red Army is granted with the consent of the People's Commissar of Defense.

6. Permission for arrests in a *raion* is granted by the *raion* procurator, in autonomous republics by the procurator of these republics, in the *krai*s (*oblast'*s) by the *krai* (*oblast'*) procurators.

On matters involving crimes in railroad and water transport, permission for arrests is granted by section procurators, route procurators, and navigation basin procurators as appropriate; on matters under the jurisdiction of military tribunals, permission is granted by the military district procurators.

Permission for arrests executed directly by the People's Commissariats of Internal Affairs of the Union Republics is granted by the procurators of these republics.

Permission for arrests executed directly by the People's Commissariat of Internal Affairs of the USSR is granted by the Union Procurator.

CHAIRMAN OF THE SOVIET OF   SECRETARY OF THE CENTRAL
PEOPLE'S COMMISSARS OF THE USSR   COMMITTEE OF *VKP(b)*
V. MOLOTOV.   J. STALIN.
June 17, 1935

RTSKhIDNI, fond 17, opis 3, delo 965, list 75

DOCUMENT 14   *Resolution by the USSR Council of People's Commissars and the Party's Central Committee, November 17, 1938, on improving NKVD arrest procedures*

To the People's Commissars of Internal Affairs in the union and autonomous republics, the *krai* and *oblast'* chiefs of the *NKVD* Administration, and the chiefs of *okrug*, municipal, and *raion* branches of the *NKVD*.

To procurators in the union and autonomous republics, *krai*s, and *oblast'*s, and procurators in the *okrug*s, cities, and *raion*s.

To central committee secretaries of the national communist parties and the *krai, oblast', okrug*, municipal, and *raion* committees of the All-Union Communist Party (of Bolsheviks) [*VKP(b)*].

ON ARRESTS, PUBLIC PROSECUTIONS, AND CONDUCT OF INVESTIGATIONS

Resolution of the USSR Council of People's Commissars [*SNK SSSR*] and the Central Committee [*TSK*] of the All-Union Communist Party (of Bolsheviks)

The Council of People's Commissars and the Central Committee of the Communist Party observe that during 1937–38, under the party's guidance, *NKVD* agencies accomplished a great deal in the effort to crush the enemies of the people and to purge the USSR of countless spies, terrorists, diversionary agents, and saboteurs, including Trotskyites, Bukharinists, Socialist Revolutionaries, Mensheviks, bourgeois nationalists, White Guards, fugitive *kulak*s and criminals that provided serious support to foreign intelligence services operating in the USSR, particularly those of Japan, Germany, Poland, England, and France.

At the same time, *NKVD* agencies also have accomplished a great deal toward crushing espionage and diversionary activities by agents from foreign intelligence services that have infiltrated the USSR in great numbers from beyond the cordon disguised as so-called political refugees and deserters, including Poles, Romanians, Finns, Germans, Latvians, Estonians, Harbin residents, and others. Purging the country of diversionary, insurgent, and espionage agents has played a positive role in ensuring the future successes of socialist construction.

But we must not think that the business of purging the USSR of spies, saboteurs, terrorists, and diversionary agents is over and done with.

Now the task at hand in continuing the merciless battle against all enemies of the USSR is to organize the battle using more effective and reliable methods.

This is all the more necessary as the mass operations to crush and root out hostile elements carried out by *NKVD* agencies in 1937–38 employing simplified investigation and prosecution could not but result in a number of gross inadequacies and distortions in the operations of the *NKVD* agencies and the Procuracy. More importantly, enemies of the people and spies from foreign intelligence services who have infiltrated *NKVD* agencies (both central and local), continuing to carry on their subversive activity, have tried in all conceivable ways to confound investigative and undercover activities, have knowingly violated Soviet laws, have carried out unfounded mass arrests, while protecting their collaborators, particularly those planted in *NKVD* agencies.

Below are described the most significant shortcomings recently uncovered in the operations of agencies of the *NKVD* and Procuracy.

First of all, *NKVD* employees have completely abandoned undercover work, preferring to work in an oversimplified manner using mass arrests, paying no attention to the thoroughness and quality of the investigation.

NKVD employees have grown so unaccustomed to painstaking, systematic undercover work and have taken such a liking to the oversimplified modus operandi that until very recently they have objected to placing limits on their execution of mass arrests.

This has resulted in further deterioration of already poor undercover work, and worst of all, many *NKVD* agents have lost their taste for undercover measures that play an exceptionally important role in *Cheka* operations.

Naturally, as a result of all this, the investigation as a rule has not succeeded in totally unmasking arrested spies and diversionary agents from foreign intelligence services and has not completely revealed all their criminal connections because the requisite undercover work has been absent.

This lack of appreciation of the importance of undercover work and the unacceptably lax attitude about arrests are all the more intolerable in view of the fact that the *SNK SSSR* and the *TSK VKP(b)* on May 8, 1933, June 17, 1935, and finally March 3, 1937, categorically pointed out the necessity of properly organizing undercover work, restricting arrests, and improving investigation.

Second, a very gross inadequacy in the operation of *NKVD* agencies is the deeply rooted, oversimplified procedure of investigation, whereby, as a rule, the examining magistrate limits himself to obtaining a confession of guilt from the accused and completely ignores substantiating this confession with the necessary documentary evidence (testimony of witnesses, expert depositions, statements, material evidence, etc.).

Frequently the arrested person is not interrogated for a month after arrest, sometimes for even a longer time. Standard interrogation procedures are not always observed. Frequently there are cases when the arrested person's testimony is written down in the form of rough notes, and after a prolonged interlude (ten days, a month, even longer) a complete transcript is compiled that totally violates the requirement of article 138 of the Code of Criminal Procedures on a verbatim (to the extent possible) rendering of the arrested person's testimony. Very often, the interrogation transcript is not compiled until the arrested person confesses the crimes he has committed. There are many instances when the transcript totally omits the defendant's testimony refuting this or that charge.

Investigative papers are executed sloppily and contain rough-draft, illegibly corrected and overwritten pencil notations of testimony, as well as testimony transcripts not signed by the interrogated person nor certified by the examining magistrate. Sometimes unsigned, unconfirmed indictments are included.

For its part, the Procuracy does not take the necessary steps to eliminate these deficiencies, generally limiting its role in the investigation to simple registration/stamping of investigative documents. Procuracy agencies not only do not eliminate violations of revolutionary legality, they actually legitimize these violations.

Enemies of the people, having infiltrated *NKVD* and Procuracy agencies (both central and local), often have skillfully exploited this irresponsible attitude toward investigative work and this gross violation of established legal procedures. They have knowingly twisted Soviet law, committed forgery, falsified investigative documents, indicted and arrested on trumped-up charges and even without any grounds whatever, brought charges (for provocation) against innocent persons, while doing everything possible to conceal and protect their collaborators in criminal anti-Soviet activity. These kinds of things went on in both the central and local bureaucracy of the *NKVD*.

All these intolerable failings in the work of *NKVD* and Procuracy agencies were possible only because the enemies of the people, having infiltrated the *NKVD* and Procuracy agencies, made every conceivable attempt to sever the work of *NKVD* and Procuracy agencies from party organs, to escape party control and supervision, and thus make it easier for themselves and their collaborators to continue their anti-Soviet, subversive activity.

In order to eliminate the above-described failings and properly organize the investigative work of *NKVD* and Procuracy agencies, the *SNK SSSR* and the *TSK VKP(b)* resolve:

1. To prohibit *NKVD* and Procuracy agencies from carrying out any kind of mass arrests or evictions.

In accordance with art. 127 of the Constitution of the USSR, arrests are to be conducted only with a court order or with a procurator's approval.

Eviction from the border region is to be permitted on a case-by-case basis with the approval of the *SNK SSSR* and *TSK VKP(b)* only with a special presentation from the appropriate *oblast'* or *krai* party committee or the Central Committee of a republic Communist Party coordinated with the *NKVD SSSR*.

2. To eliminate judicial troikas established by special decrees from the *NKVD SSSR* as well as troikas in the *oblast'*, *krai*, and republic Administrations of Workers' and Peasants' Militia.

Henceforth all cases are to be submitted for review by the courts or a Special Conference of the *NKVD SSSR* in strict accordance with existing jurisdictional laws.

3. In making arrests, *NKVD* and Procuracy agencies are to abide by the following requirements:

a) execute the arrests in strict adherence to the *SNK SSSR* and *TSK VKP(b)* resolution of June 17, 1935;

b) when a procurator's approval is required for an arrest, *NKVD* agencies are obliged to present a statement of justification and all materials substantiating the need for the arrest;

c) Procuracy agencies are obliged to carefully and substantively validate the arrest statements of the *NKVD* agencies and if necessary demand supplementary investigative actions or submission of supplementary investigative materials;

d) Procuracy agencies are obliged not to allow execution of arrests without adequate justification. The procurator approving an arrest is to bear responsibility for any improper arrest along with the *NKVD* personnel executing it.

4. Require *NKVD* agencies to observe all provisions of the Code of Criminal Procedures in conducting investigations, particularly:

a) to complete the investigation within the legally specified timeframe;

b) to interrogate the arrested persons within 24 hours of their arrest; to immediately compile a transcript after each interrogation in accordance with article 138 of the Code of Criminal Procedures, precisely indicating when the interrogation began and ended.

In reviewing their interrogation, the procurator is required to write on the transcript that he has reviewed it, indicating the time, day, month, and year;

c) Documents, correspondence, and other objects removed during a search are to be sealed immediately at the search site in accordance with article 184 of the Code of Criminal Procedures, and a detailed inventory of everything sealed is to be compiled.

5. Require Procuracy agencies to observe precisely the provisions of the Code of Criminal Procedures for executing procuratorial oversight of investigations conducted by *NKVD* agencies.

In accordance with this, require Procuracy agencies to systematically monitor the investigative agencies' observance of all legally established rules for conducting investigations and to promptly eliminate violations of these regulations; take measures to guarantee the accused person the procedural rights afforded him by the law, etc.

6. In connection with the growing role of procuratorial oversight and the increased responsibility placed on Procuracy agencies for arrests and investigations conducted by *NKVD* agencies, it must be viewed as essential to:

a) establish that all procurators overseeing an investigation conducted by *NKVD* agencies are confirmed by the *TSK VKP(b)* based on inputs from the appropriate *oblast'* and *krai* party committees, the republic communist parties' central committees, and the Procurator of the USSR;

b) require the *oblast'* and *krai* party committees and the central committee of the republic communist parties to validate and present for confirmation to the *TSK VKP(b)* all candidacies of all procurators overseeing investigations by *NKVD* agencies;

c) require the Procurator of the USSR, Comrade Vyshinsky, to identify politically trustworthy, qualified procurators in the central administration to oversee investigations conducted by the central *NKVD* bureaucracy and within twenty days present them for confirmation to the *TSK VKP(b)*.

7. Approve *NKVD* measures presented in the October 23, 1938, order to regulate the conduct of investigations by *NKVD* agencies. In particular, approve the *NKVD* decision concerning the organization of special investigation units in the operations divisions.

Stressing the importance of properly organized investigative work by *NKVD* agencies, require the *NKVD* to ensure that the best, most politically trustworthy and most qualified members of the party (based on performance) are designated to be investigators in the center and in the field.

Establish that all investigators in central and local *NKVD* agencies are designated solely by order of the *NKVD*.

8. Require the *NKVD* and Procurator of the USSR to give their local agencies instructions to fulfill the present resolution precisely.

The *SNK SSSR* and the *TSK VKP(b)* direct the attention of all *NKVD* and Procuracy staff to the necessity of resolutely eliminating the above-described failings in the operations of *NKVD* and Procuracy agencies and to the extreme importance of reorganizing all investigative and procuratorial work.

The *SNK SSSR* and the *TSK VKP(b)* warn all *NKVD* and Procuracy staff that for the slightest infraction of Soviet laws or party or government directives, each *NKVD* and Procuracy employee, whoever it may be, will be held strictly accountable before a court of law.

Chairman of the Council of People's   Secretary of the Central
Commissars of the USSR V. MOLOTOV.   Committee of the *VKP(b)*
                                             J. STALIN.

November 17, 1938
No. P 4387

Source?

DOCUMENT 15   *Letter from members of the Procuracy of the USSR, October 28, 1939, appealing to A. A. Zhdanov for changes in the Procuracy and calling for a halt to the criminal behavior of the* NKVD

Dear Comrade Zhdanov!

We, the employees of the Procuracy of the USSR ask that you attentively read this letter, which was written by us after long reflection and with a single purpose—to inform the Central Committee of the party about shocking occurrences in the operation of the Procuracy and the *NKVD*.

The party's Central Committee decision of November 17, 1938, identified the grossest distortions of Soviet laws by *NKVD* organs and obligated those organs and the Procuracy not only to stop these crimes but also to correct the gross violations of law that have resulted in mass sentencing of totally innocent, honest Soviet persons to various sorts of punishment, often even execution. These persons—not a few, but tens and hundreds of thousands—sit in camps and jails and wait for a just decision; they are perplexed about why and for what they were arrested and by what right the bastards from Ezhov's band persecuted them, using medieval torture.

It would seem that the party's Central Committee decision of November 17,1938, should have mobilized all attention on immediately rectifying the criminal policy of the bastard Ezhov and his criminal clique, which has literally terrorized Soviet persons, upright, dedicated citizens, old party members, and entire party organizations.

In reality, something else is happening.

Comrade Pankrat'ev, who has replaced Comrade Vyshinsky, cannot guarantee implementation of this critical decision of the party Central Committee because of his lack of authority in the Procuracy and particularly in the eyes of *NKVD* personnel.

It is strange to say, but it is a fact that Comrade Beria not only is not burning with desire to free totally innocent people, but to the contrary is conducting a definite policy to hinder this effort and is using his authority to maintain the "honor of the uniform."

Therefore, the decision to charge a special conference of the *NKVD* with reviewing its own decisions executed by Ezhov's band is a big mistake.

Here, at a special conference, the decisive role and final word belong not to the representative of supervision—the Procurator—but to Comrade Beria and his entourage, who, with all the means and resources at their disposal, are violating the requirements of the Procuracy to stop these actions.

Comrade Pankrat'ev, who attends these meetings, bows his head to Politburo candidate member Comrade Beria and silently goes along with obviously wrong decisions.

Thus, at these special conferences the absolutely correct and lawful protests of the Procuracy of the USSR are crushed with the direct connivance of the Procurator of the USSR, Comrade Pankrat'ev.

One only needs to review what took place at the last special conference sessions and speak with the procurators who directly prepared these matters and it becomes apparent that the line followed by Comrade Beria has nothing in common with party directives.

Such practices have disoriented the staff of the Procuracy of the USSR, those honest procurators who directly monitor these scandalous cases and spend sleepless nights and grieve for guiltless Soviet persons condemned by Ezhov's band.

We earnestly beseech you, Comrade Zhdanov, to take up this matter of utmost importance, and if there is no chance of changing the criminal practices pursued within the walls of the *NKVD*, to change the system, to entrust the Procuracy with reviewing matters incorrectly handled by Ezhov's band—excluding from these matters the authority of Comrade Beria, who intentionally or unintentionally is cultivating a defense of the "honor of the uniform" of *NKVD* personnel at all costs.

Just consider that hundreds of thousands of people guilty of nothing continue to sit in jails and camps, and nearly a year has passed since the party's Central Committee took its decision.

Can it really be this does not worry anyone?

Speak with the procurators of the special procuracies (railroad, navigation) and they will tell you facts that will make your hair stand on end, and they will show you these "cases," this disgrace to Soviet power.

At the same time, we ask you to correct the very grave error of Comrade Pankrat'ev's appointment. Give us a director with a high degree of authority who can take on even Beria.

We senior employees have always been puzzled by the relationship of the party leadership and government to the staff of the Procuracy, the sharpest tool of the dictatorship of the proletariat.

Can it really be so hard to understand that the procuracies, by virtue of the special obligations entrusted to them, must be properly compensated?

A procurator on the staff of the Procuracy of the USSR who has worked honestly for 10–15 years and who performs the most serious work earns 650–750 rubles, whereas a newly hired *NKVD* staff member, a semiliterate youth, earns more than 1200–1500 rubles, enjoys all the benefits, receives a bonus, a uniform allowance, etc.

Where is the logic? For what is this wrongheaded policy followed?

Procurators cannot be kept in a state of semistarvation for decades!

We ask you to think about this. We are completely convinced that all that has been described here is being concealed from the party's Central Committee—obviously it is more advantageous that way for someone.

The procurators of the Procuracy of the USSR.

October 28, 1939

RTSKhIDNI, fond 77, opis 1, delo 194a, listy 4, 4 ob, 5 ob

Political Intelligence Reports and Public Opinion

One of the important contributions of *glasnost'*, the new policy of openness introduced during the leadership of Mikhail Gorbachev, was to make "public opinion" available to the public, and since 1985 the publication of opinion polls has become an important part of Soviet and Russian life. Assessing public attitudes, moods, and reactions to policies and events was always much more difficult under the old system. These documents reveal, however, the extent to which the regime had access to detailed and regular reports on local opinions and local activism. Each province-level *Cheka* organization reported regularly on all kinds of cases of unrest, protest, illness, and crime, economic dislocations, and also the absence of protest. These reports were forwarded to central organs in the form of "Information summaries" (*Info-svodka*) and distributed to leading party, economic, and trade union organizations. In this way the *Cheka* carried on the tradition of political reporting developed by the tsarist *Okhrana*, and these reports, as they become available to scholars, will provide a rich new source of information on public life during the Soviet regime.

One must be careful in assessing the reliability of these documents: reports from the field were only as good as the agents who provided them. Moreover, as Dzerzhinsky noted in Document 11, "Our information summaries are presenting a one-sided picture, completely black . . . " Security agencies often exaggerate the dangers they report in order to enhance their own institutional importance.

A second valuable source of popular opinion are letters written to party officials, institutions, and newspapers. Letters such as the one to Trotsky (Document 19) and to Stalin (Document 20) indicate a surprising depth of public political consciousness and criticism of the regime. Letters could be positive as well, as with the postcard to Stalin from the grateful Armenian collective farm worker in 1937 (Document 27). Many documents reporting on political dissidence are included in the section of this volume on the dissident movement, but Document 29, a *KGB* report on sources of criticism of the Soviet government in 1988, continues the tradition of comprehensive reporting on opposition to the system.

Summary report on political groups, June 2, 1920, by the Information Section of the Secret Division of the Cheka

POLITICAL GROUPS
No. 75

Summary Report of the Information Section of the Secret Department of the All-Union Extraordinary Commission for Combating Counterrevolution and Sabotage [*VChK*].

TVER' *GUBERNIIA*. There are parties of left Socialist Revolutionaries [*SRs*] and anarchists in Bezhetskii *uezd*. The anarchists have their own federation and club. They do not hold meetings, only conferences concerning their program. (Report of the *Guberniia* Extraordinary Commission [*GubChK*], April 15–May 1, 1920)

IVANO-VOZNESENSK [*sic*] *GUBERNIIA*. Operating legally is a "committee of revolutionary communists" and an *SR* minority group, whose members are former right *SR*s. Their relationship to Soviet power is somewhat dubious. (Report of the *GubChK*, April 30, 1920)

UKRAINE. The majority of members of the Petliurist counterrevolutionary organization *TSupok* are *SR*s, chiefly Lozanovskii, Petrenko, Shadilo. (The Kiev organization Ukrainian Socialist Revolutionaries [*USR*] claims to represent the trend of the entire party. A few are involved in the Petliurist movement and the Ukrainian Social Democrats [*USD*], left *SR*s, and the Ukrainian Communist Party [*UKP*] (Borotbists). (From a report of the Plenipotentiary of the *SOOGChK*, April 19)

TSARITSYN *GUBERNIIA*. There are organizations of *SR*s and anarchists. These organizations have yet to show any signs of activity (Report of *GChK* for January 16–April 1)

TOMSK *GUBERNIIA*. Menshevik and *SR* sympathizers have been discovered among the white collar workers of the Omsk Railroad. (Report No. 4 of Omsk *Raion* Transportation *ChK* for Mar. 15–Apr. 1)

TOMSK *GUBERNIIA*. Counterrevolutionary attitudes among workers of the Tomsk Water Transportation Authority (5000 employees). Large numbers of *SR*s, Mensheviks, and monarchists. (Report No. 4 of Omsk *Raion* Transportation *ChK*, Mar. 15–Apr. 1 1920)

ANARCHISTS

VOLOGDA. Agitational activity by anarchists has taken on a more malicious, intensified character. (Report of *VGChK*, May 1–15)

VOLOGDA *GUBERNIIA*. Recently, anarchists have become more active not only in the city, but in the *uezd*s and at the military garrison (Sixth Regiment stationed in the suburbs of Vologda). Activists were arrested early in the morning on May 1 for the purpose of preventing any further propaganda. (From the report of the Secret Department of the *GChK* of May 4, 1920)

VLADIMIR. Anarchism has been developing in the Aleksandrov, Pereiaslavl', and IUrev *uezd*s. (Report of *VGChK* for Apr. 15–May 1)

EKATERINBURG. Anarchists have been gradually becoming more active. (Report of Ekaterinburg *KGChK* Apr. 15–30)

ASTRAKhAN *GUBERNIIA*. There was an incident where anarchist leaflets in opposition to Soviet power were distributed. (Report of *GubChK* of March 20, 1920)

UKRAINIAN COMMUNIST PARTY

UKRAINIAN COMMUNIST PARTY ABROAD. In Vienna a Ukrainian Communist Party has formed around Vinnichenko, Golubovich and others and has contacts with the Communist Party (Bolshevik) of Ukraine and the Soviet government. This foreign *UKP* has been formed by leftist groupings of the Ukrainian Social Democrats [*USD*] (Chekhovskii) and the Ukrainian Socialist Revolutionaries [*USR*] (A. Stapnenko) who oppose the government of the Ukrainian Revolutionary Party [*UPR*]. All adherents of this tendency sent to Ukraine were instructed to join the *UKP* of Borotbists. Together with the truly dissenting Petliurists, agents of Petliura went to Ukraine to conduct underground activity. (Report of the plenipotentiary of the *SOOKChK*, April 19, 1920)

MAXIMALISTS

VLADIMIR. The maximalists are inciting the population against Soviet power, especially in Suzdal' *uezd*. (Report of the Vladimir *GChK*, April 15–May 1)

VIATKA *GUBERNIIA*. At the Izhevsk Works 5 Maximalists [Social Revolutionary faction] were arrested after they had gone out to villages and called on the peasants to rise up. These individuals had been making preparations for an armed uprising in Izhevsk *raion* (*GChK* report of Apr. 16–Apr. 30, 1920)

REVOLUTIONARY COMMUNISTS

IAROSLAVSKAIA. A purge of undesirable elements is being conducted in the party of Revolutionary Communists. (Information Section of the Iaroslavl' *GChK*, April 20, 1920)

VOLGA GERMAN *OBLAST'*. There is a small but influential organization of Revolutionary Communists. (From report of Secret Department of *ObChK* for Feb. 1–Apr. 15, 1920)

SOCIALIST REVOLUTIONARY INTERNATIONALISTS

DONETSK. S. R. Internationalists work openly. There are committees of the party in Mariupol' and other cities. (Report of the Donetsk *GChK*, April 15–30)

LEFT SOCIAL REVOLUTIONARIES

VORONEZh. In Novokhopersk Left *SR*s have organized a "Russian allied terrorist fighting squad," whose aim is to terrorize officials of the Russian Communist Party [*RKP*]. (Report of the *GChK*, April 1–15, 1920)

KOSTROMA. In Kologrievsk *uezd* an organization of leftist *SR*s was discovered, the majority of whose members are former officers of the old army. (Report of the Kostroma *GChK*, April 15–30)

DONETSK. The Left *SR*s have an organization in the province which is engaged in underground agitation and has been active in Lugansk, IUzovka, Mariupol', and Grishin *uezd*s (Report of Donetsk *GChK* of Apr. 15–30)

KhERSON. Thanks to intense agitation, a Left *SR* organization has gained the sympathy of the peasants, especially in Elizavetgrad and Kherson *uezd*s (Report of Kherson *GChK*)

MINORITY GROUP OF THE SOCIALIST REVOLUTIONARY PARTY

DONETSK. There is a committee of *SR*s (minority) in Lugansk. It works mostly clandestinely and in institutions hopes to conduct business in its own way. (Report of the Donetsk *GChK*, April 15–30)

KhERSON. The Menshevik Party is stronger than the Right *SR* faction. It does not behave actively but tries to get elected to the Soviets (Report of Kherson *GChK*, Feb. 12–Apr. 15)

EKATERINBURG. The Mensheviks have emerged on the political scene, but they have not been operating out in the open. They have been holding discussions of political topics for agitation purposes, especially among the railroad workers (Report of *KGChK* of Apr. 15–30, 1920)

MONARCHISTS

KhERSON. A definite organization of monarchists has not been established, only agitation by individuals has been observed. (Report of the Kherson *GChK*, February 12–April 15)

[signed] Director of the Secret Division of the *VChK*: Latsis
[signed] Director of the Section: D. Kats
June 2, 1920

RTSKhIDNI, fond 5, op. 1, d. 2617, ll. 1,2,4

DOCUMENT 17   *Report on military action against bandits, March 31, 1921*

SECRET

Moscow, March 31, 1921

SITUATION REPORT FOR MARCH 30, 1921

Map Scale: 10 *verst*s per inch

Ukraine, Lozovaia Station area. A band of 120 men (whose gang's name is unknown and who were also spotted on March 28 attacking Zhemchuzhnoe Station) captured Raduevo Station on March 29 and, after destroying the telegraph apparatus, proceeded to Nadezhdino, where they were driven off and scattered by fire from our armored train.

Orel Military District, Tambov *guberniia*, Chakino Station area. On March 29 our cavalry units fought and drove off a band of up to 100 horsemen from Bakharevka (12 *verst*s northwest of Chakino Station). The band retreated to Ponzar (15 *verst*s west of Chakino), from which they were driven off again and scattered in different directions. Otkhozhaia Station area. On March 29 our units launched an attack on Semenovka (7 *verst*s northeast of Otkhozhaia Station), which had been occupied by a band of 1,000 men with 2 machine guns, in two columns from the south and the west. The band was unable to withstand our assault and retreated to Nikol'skoe-Rzhaksa (3 *verst*s east of Semenovka). Our cavalry detachment charged, slashing into Nikol'skoe on the heels of the bandits, and took the south side of the village but was forced back to its starting point by heavy enemy machine gun fire. Nothing particularly noteworthy happened elsewhere.

Trans-Volga Military District, Petrov *raion*. Popov's bands, who advanced on Sapolga on March 28 (25 *verst*s northwest of Petrovska) and from there to the village of Serdoba, took Serdoba and have been moving on Aleksandrovka (15 *verst*s north of Serdoba) since March 29. The bands are under pursuit by our units.

Caucasus Front, Delizhan *raion*. In the Karakli Sector our offensive is underway. We have occupied Pamb-arm, Mandzhukhli, Pamb-kurd, and Chaban-Karakmaz (all of these points are 10 to 12 *verst*s southwest and southeast of Amaml').

Siberia, Tobol'sk *raion*. Our units are engaged in fierce fighting with rebels on the line running from the village of Kularevskoe to the village of Bagaiskoe (50 *verst*s south of Tobol'sk). Ishim *raion*. Bordakov's band of 300 men, with two cannon and three machine guns, is in retreat and under pursuit by our units east of the village of Kokhanskoe towards the main line of the Ishim-Omsk Railroad. Petropavlovsk *raion*. 70 *verst*s north of Petukhova our men overtook and routed Bukhvalov's band. The chief of staff of the Siberian Front and the chief of staff of the People's Rebel Army were taken prisoner, while Bukhvalov shot himself. No. 1898/*op.*

Chief of Operations for the Republic   War Commissar
[illegible signature]   [illegible signature]

RTSKhIDNI, fond 17, op. 86, d. 144, ll.5

Digest of reports from the Information Section of the Cheka, January 9, 1922, concerning the political and economic situation in various provinces

Top Secret

Moscow, January 9, 1922
Lenin Archive
Entry no. 26
Item no.[illegible]

1820 hour
copy no. 1

To Comrade Lenin

G O S I N F S V O D K A [State Information Summary]
OF THE INFORMATION SECTION OF THE
All-Russian Extraordinary Commission for Combating
Counterrevolution, Sabotage, and Speculation [*VChK*]:

For January 6, 7, and 8, No. 6/244/.

CENTRAL *GUBERNIIA*S

MOSCOW *GUBERNIIA*/State information summary of the *MChK* [Moscow Extraordinary Commission] No. 4, 5, pages 5 and 6 (1.)

1. Veteran workers were dismissed at the 2nd Model Print Shop. Hiring of new workers is progressing slowly. The print shop has stopped. Not having received their pay for the month of December, the workers at the *Tekhnika i Meditsina* plant stopped work on January 5. The *Mars* uniforms factory has been stopped for two weeks. The textile factory of Petrov and Galakteev is not operating due to a shortage of fuel.
(Abstract sent to Comrade Bogdanov)

10. Workers of the Briansk Railroad Depot, as a result of the absence of wages for the month of December, began a slowdown on January 4.

BRIANSK *GUBERNIIA*/State information summary No. 2 5(1.)

2. The mood of the population is satisfactory. (Abstract sent to Comrade Zalutskii)

4. The work of the union cells within enterprises is weak.

8. Epidemics are developing especially virulently among the children. Medical supplies are lacking. (Abstract sent to Comrade Semashko)

VLADIMIR *GUBERNIIA*/State information summary No. 60696 5(1.)

1. As a result of a rise in market prices, the mood of the workers and employees is unsatisfactory. (Abstract sent to Comrade Zalutskii and Comrade Khinchuk)

3. Trade is developing poorly as a result of a shortage of goods and a lack of high quality. (A copy of this abstract sent to Comrade Khinchuk.)

IVANO-VOZNESENSK *GUBERNIIA* (Political information summary No. 2, January 1)

2. The mood of the peasants is satisfactory. One exception is IUr'evets *uezd,* where the peasants are dissatisfied with the levies for schools and hospitals. (Copies sent to Comrades Zalutskii and Khalatov)

KALUGA *GUBERNIIA* (Political information summary No. 2, January 5)

2. The two-week food procurement drive has been extended to January 20. Party organizations and trade unions have organized 447 individuals to procure foodstuffs. The food has been slow in coming. To this point only 58% of the quota has been met. (Copies sent to Comrades Khalatov and Zalutskii)

KURSK *GUBERNIIA* (Political information summary No. 5, January 5)

3. Market prices have risen. (Copy sent to Comrade Khinchuk)

NORTHERN *KRAI*

VOLOGDA *GUBERNIIA* (Political information summary No. 5, January 5)

1. The mood of the general public is satisfactory. As of December 31, 91% of the quota for the tax-in-kind on food had been collected. 80.2% of the quota for seed loans has been met. Peasants are heavily involved in the production of moonshine. (Copies sent to Comrades Khalatov, Zalutskii, and Doletskii)

6. The military units are in satisfactory condition. (Copy sent to Comrade Zalutskii)

8. The blue- and white-collar workers of Vologda have resolved to contribute 5% of their food rations to the famine victims and adopt 73 refugee children. The last *guberniia* famine relief drive collected 7,756,935 rubles and 523 poods of flour. (Copies to All-Union Famine Relief Central Executive Committee and Comrade Doletskii)

NORTHWEST *KRAI*

PSKOV *GUBERNIIA* (Political information summary No. 289, January 5)

6. The mobilization of the public for the Karelian Front was successful. (Copy to Comrade Zalutskii)

MURMANSK *GUBERNIIA* (Political information summary No. 50, January 4).

3. A Norwegian steamship carrying 2,257 tons of coal arrived in Murmansk from Great Britain. A Russian steamer carrying 1,600 tons of colonial goods arrived on January 4.

(Copy to Comrade Khinchuk)

PETROGRAD *GUBERNIIA* (Political information summary No. 6, January 5)

1. The workers of *Caravan* No. 2 went back to work after receiving their pay on January 4. (Copy sent to Comrade Bogdanov)

KARELIAN LABOR COMMUNE (Bandit report No. 7945, December 31 and January 5–6)

7. The rebels are getting skis at Finnish border villages. On the central sector of the front the bandits are recruiting new members from the local population.

FOREIGN INFORMATION (Bandit report No. 5, January 6)

1. Estonia. A Russian organization is headquartered in the city of Pechora and is recruiting volunteers for Karelia. They have succeeded in recruiting many unemployed individuals from the northwest. The volunteers are paid three months in advance. As of December 26, 145 veterans of the Kronstadt uprising had been sent from Vyborg to Karelia.

WESTERN *KRAI*

SMOLENSK *GUBERNIIA* (Political information summary No. 139, January 5)

2. The peasants are dissatisfied with the efforts to inventory secluded farmland. As of January 1, 96% of the quota for the tax-in-kind on food had been collected. In terms of rye, 3,830,967 poods have been collected. The procurement of firewood has been going well. From July 1 through December 1, 54,504 cords (51,206 cubic *sazhen*s) had been collected, amounting to 94% of the quota. 27,269 cubic *sazhen*s have been transported to the center. (Copies sent to Comrades Khalatov, Danishevskii, and Doletskii)

3. Market prices are rising. On the eve of the New Year a pood of grain cost 140,000 rubles. The rise in prices can be attributed to the influx of refugees from the Volga. (Copy sent to Comrade Khinchuk)

5. The Executive Committee of IArtsevo *Uezd* is in the process of disbandment. There is a shortage of paper currency in the *guberniia*. Government workers are disgruntled because they have not been paid. (Copies sent to Comrades Vladimirskii and Alskii)

9. The introduction of the new supply system has led rural schoolteachers to engage in counterrevolutionary agitation among the peasants. (Copies sent to Comrades Pokrovskii and Zalutskii)

UKRAINE AND CRIMEA

No reports received.

URAL *GUBERNIIA* (Bandit report No. 4, January 5)

7. According to a report dated December 31, Serov's band consisting of 800 cavalrymen with 3 machine guns occupied the village of Topolinskii on December 28. The local *kulak*s are joining bands in Gur'evo.

BUKEEVSKAIA *GUBERNIIA* (Bandit report No. 79, December 31)

7. According to a report dated December 29, negotiations to effect a voluntary surrender of Tugiz-Baev's band to the Soviet authorities are underway.

KIRGHIZ *KRAI*

No reports received.

URALS

BASHKIR REPUBLIC (Political information summary No. 56, January 5)

1. The workers are in a bad mood because of the famine. (Copy sent to Comrade Zalutskii)

2. The drive to collect the tax-in-kind on food is going well. The peasants in the Duvkush cantons are in a bad mood because of the famine. (Copies sent to Comrades Zalutskii and Khalatov)

4. Political agitation and propaganda efforts have been ineffectual. (Copy sent to Comrade Zalutskii)

7. Petty banditry has broken out in the republic. Efforts to suppress the bandits have been hindered by the indulgence of the local population.

9. The care of children is extremely poor at the orphanages. Staff members have been beating the children. (Copy sent to Comrade Pokrovskii)

SIBERIA

FOREIGN INFORMATION (Bandit report No. 5, January 6)

11. According to a report dated December 15, 2 regiments consisting of Tatars and Tunguses mutinied against Bakich in Urunichi *raion.*

TURKESTAN

No reports received.

HEAD OF THE INFORMATION DEPARTMENT OF THE *ChEKA*: BORTNOVSKII
HEAD OF THE STATE INFORMATION DEPARTMENT OF THE *ChEKA* KhUDIAKOV.

33 copies of this report were typed and distributed:

Copy No. 1	Comrades	Lenin
" No. 2		Stalin
" No. 3		Trotsky and Sklianskii
" No. 4		Meletov and Mikhailov
" No. 5		Dzerzhinsky and Emshanov
" No. 6		Unshlikht
" No. 7		Menzhinskii and IAgoda
" No. 8		Medved' and Avanesov

" No. 9	Samsonov and Blagonravov
" No. 10	Redens and Mogilevskii
" No. 11	Artuzov
" No. 12	Chicherin and Litvinov
" No. 13	Andreev and Shmidt
" No. 14	Steklov
" No. 15	Meshcheriakov and Sol'ts
" No. 16	Zelenskii
" No. 17	Radek
" No. 18	Khalatov
" No. 19	Mantsev (to be passed on and read to Central Committee of the Communist Party of Ukraine)
" No. 20	Pavlunovskii (to be passed on and read to Siberian Bureau of Russian Communist Party)
" No. 21	Trushin (to be passed on and read to Southern Information Bureau of Russian Communist Party)
" No. 22	Pankratov (to be passed on and read to Central Bureau of the Communist Party of Belorussia)
" No. 23	Peters (to be passed on and read to the Turkestan Bureau of the Russian Communist Party)
" No. 24	Moroz (to be passed on and read to the *Oblast'* Committee of the Russian Communist Party)
" No. 25	Voroshilov (to be passed on and read to the Rostov Committee of the North Caucasus Military District)
" No. 26	Ivanov (to be passed on and read to the Volga Region *Cheka*)
" No. 27	Messing (to be passed on to Comrade Zinoviev)
" No. 28	Katsnel'son
" No. 29	Gus'ev
" No. 30	El'tsin
" No. 31	Kratt
" No. 32	file (Information Department of *Cheka*)
" No. 33	" " "

(for monthly summary)

(True copy of original)

Secretary of Information Department of *Cheka*: [signed] Falakin [?]

RTSKhIDNI, fond 5, op. 1, d. 2627, ll. 31,32,35,35ob.

Declaration by three factory workers on behalf of Trotsky, December 29, 1924, expressing disagreement with state policies and the difficult material situation

[handwritten, upper left corner:] <u>Comrade Kalinin,</u> January 23, 1925

COPY

ALL-RUSSIAN CENTRAL COMMITTEE
SOVIET OF WORKERS', PEASANTS', AND RED ARMY SOLDIERS' DEPUTIES

Workers of the *Krasnyi Kashevar*
[Red Cook] and *Serp i molot*
[Hammer and Sickle] Factories

DECLARATION

The contrived "permanent revolution" split between the Bolshevik Communist Party and Trotsky, whom the entire Soviet and the press have so fiercely attacked without allowing him to respond and with no intention of allowing him to respond, is designed to get him out of the way and keep anyone from interfering with the shady characters as they do their dirty work in the country. You accuse Trotsky, calling him a Menshevik and an *SR,* but you defend Lenin. One man can't make a revolution, the revolution makes people. We are all well aware that Lenin was an emigre and never lived in Russia, but lived abroad and had absolutely no idea of the needs of the Russian people. On the other hand, who created the Red Army and who was its leader (Order No. 14; Trotsky)? Who wiped out the Dutov, Kaledin, Kornilov, Merkulov, Wrangel, Semenov, Kolchak, IUdenich, Petliura, Makhno, Bolo-Molokhovich, Marusia, Antonov, and Kozlovskii gangs? Who put down the Kronstadt uprising? Zinoviev fled from Petrograd to Moscow with his briefcase, while Trotsky and the officer-trainees went to Kronstadt, routed the gang, and restored order. Who nipped the priestly provocation in the bud? Trotsky. Who organized the Air Force and the Red Navy, and who created the Voluntary Association to Assist the Development of the Chemical Industry (*Dobrokhim*)? Trotsky did it all.

All we get from you is talk, but no action. You've been saying and are now writing that Russia is a free country, but in reality it's quite the opposite. In reality we have tyranny, repression, serfdom, tax after tax. Every day we have seizures and auctions of peasant property, arrests, imprisonment, eviction, and exile to distant *guberniia*s. Just think of all the taxes now, how high they are, and who has to pay them. 600 million rubles worth of agricultural taxes, 1,000 million rubles from the unemployed, and 1,000 million more rubles in the form of proceeds from their property sold at auction and fines. Every day in Moscow alone 1,000 million rubles worth of property confiscated from needy persons unable to pay their taxes is sold in the markets, while only 300 million rubles are collected from the "haves." And what about the proceeds from the sale of forests, meadows, coal, anthracite, and animals, and the income from factories, mills, and sales of wine, kerosene, gasoline, matches, tobacco products, railroads, streetcar lines, electricity, water, cooperatives, trusts, syndicates, and the Moscow Agricultural Commodity Processing Consortium? And what about the sale of territory, as Trotsky reminded us? Bessarabia has been sold, Wrangel Island has been sold, Turkestan has been sold, Moldavia has been sold, and Krasin has even begun to sell Georgia to France, which means that soon the Caucasus will be sold, and Karelia might already have been sold, in the same way that the fisheries and the Chinese Eastern Railroad were sold. And if we added it all up, not only are the peaceful Russian people being robbed, everyone will have to give up everything we've worked for in the last seven years for a few pennies. It would have been easier to get all the factories and plants working at full speed, and then we wouldn't have any unemployment. But of course, then there wouldn't be anyone to rob, the prisons would be completely useless, and the Yids would have to go to work instead of sitting around thinking up taxes and ways to rob us. We have seen all of this and have been waiting and hoping that someone who's a little smarter and doesn't have a heart of stone would come around to lead the Russian people to liberation. But we don't have anybody like this. The people in power are brutal careerists who want to turn Russia into a mass graveyard by systematic starvation. All of us go to bed worried and believing that the morrow will bring a new tax, higher rent, or a property or income tax from our wallets or who knows what kind of one-time government or property assessment. Once again we get confiscations and auctions, and more people get thrown out in the cold, more people get exiled, more people get thrown in prison, more wives and children are crying, and if people try to do anything about it they get shot. All these commissars, inspectors, agents, tax collector executioners, and cops are under orders from the *TSK*, but we don't have a *TSK*. We ought to elect a new one, but the people in the *TSK* now don't want to stand for reelection and don't want to look at the kind of tyranny, brutality, and robbery that's going on here. They should leave Moscow for a day and go for example to Zatsepskii market undercover and see how the mounted and foot police wave their sabres and pistols around and threaten everybody, how they trample women and children with their horses, how they haul innocent people to the committee, and how sometimes they beat them almost to death and don't hesitate one bit to rob them worse than the *Oprichniki,* just like the Roman Emperors Nero and Trajan used to do to the martyrs. All the workers are getting sick of this comedy. It's not right for a free country. The entire Russian people is waiting for the right time, and then a lot of people will be crying. We see who you're protecting and who you're ruining and how you're protecting the stall owners and the store owners and how you're robbing the unemployed poor people. We see how you've shut down the factories. We've seen all your taxes and your assessments, and we know all your ranks, categories, and grades. We've seen how many people you've driven to an early grave, but you can't kill everyone. Your time is coming, and you will pay with your blood for everything. Then the hour of liberation will come, and we'll make Trotsky our leader or king or maybe Kerensky because he liberated us from tsarist oppression. Down with tyranny, down with repression, and long live the freedom of the workers.

Afianskoi K., Gorbunov, IUshkin. December 29, 1924

True Copy: Correspondence Secretary of the
               Chairman of the All-Union
               Central Executive Committee

RTSKhIDNI, fond 78, op. 1, d. 142, ll. 10–11.

DOCUMENT 20   *Letter from a Urals peasant to Stalin, undated, on inequalities in the country-side*

COPY
Comrade STALIN

Having read *Krest'ianskaia gazeta* [Peasant Newspaper] published in Ural *oblast',* I have found an entire page of interesting articles under the heading: "Has the Party Lost Its Way?, an article was written by peasants and contains a bitter truth. It may be that you live far from peasants and will not believe this, but it is true. For the most part, bureaucrats, bribe-takers, and toadies sit in our district and regional administrative agencies, which deeply infuriates the peasants. I, myself, went to the *oblast'* center and saw how the city lives in luxury and satisfaction and never thinks of the poor circumstances of the villages, it lives care-free (like the old nobility), but in the villages it is the opposite, the needs of the peasants burn them from behind and from in front and he thinks about the city because it depends on him, but his own needs can't be met. I appeal to you as a high-standing person in the party. Let the villages breathe easier, give them satisfaction and privileges like the cities. Have we not spilt our blood together for the revolution, but it turns out that the revolution was only for the office workers and factory workers, we feel wronged somehow. Read the newspaper which I am sending you and reply in the newspaper of the Ural peasants, if necessary, I will write again. I await your reply.

Ural. Troitskii *okrug,* Step. P/o Streletskii pos. NEVEROV, ALEKS

True copy:

[Punctuation errors and poor style of original retained.]

Source: ?

Partial letter of a peasant from Riazan' guberniia to Stalin, September 3, 1926,
criticizing the Soviet leadership for the difficult conditions in the country

. . . from today, Sept. 3, 1926, you, generally speaking the leaders of Soviet society, bear the blame for all those comrades, i.e. members of society, who languish in jails, poverty, and back-breaking labor. You impede the march of life towards communism. You don't allow discussions of the concerns of the working masses with you by their representatives, who come to the capital to see the leaders.

If you have not yet totally forgotten the basic goal of the life of Mankind, send the address of where you are staying to me, who has come to the capital on the issue "Communist science." My address: House of Soviets Hostel, no. 3, room 15, Velichko, Petr Iv. Please, without delay. And if not, then know that you will have to answer for the obstacles which will be created as a result of your negligent attitude toward the cause of labor.

I am waiting.   September 3, 1926
       Velichko P. I.   1:15 p.m.

[The beginning of the letter is missing. The poor style of the original is retained.]

RTSKhIDNI, fond 17, op. 85, d. 494, l. 143 (in annot.), 142 (in checklist)

DOCUMENT 22   *Letter from a peasant, A. Shaburov, to M. I. Kalinin, June 20, 1926, protesting*
state tax policies

COPY
TO COMRADE <u>KALININ</u>

I would definitely appreciate an answer from you, however brief, to my main question and a number of other questions and contradictions which follow from it.

Is it true that the Central Executive Committee [*TSIK*] of the USSR has approved a law which would require peasant migrant workers to pay a tax of 15 to 25% on their gross annual wages at any factory?

You might say, Comrade Kalinin, what nonsense! And it's the kind of nonsense rarely seen in human history.

At a plenum of its Central Committee [*TSK*], the Communist Party, which is the leader of the Nation and has proven itself to be the benefactor and savior of the toiling masses from capitalist oppression and exploitation, approved the draft of an agricultural tax law, which was followed by approval of the law by the *TSIK*, which gives the republic's tax agencies unlimited power to tax hardworking peasant migrant workers 25% of their gross annual earnings at a time when these workers are unable to feed themselves on their tiny plots of land and have been forced to go earn a living by working somewhere else.

Everyone smiled and laughed when they first heard the news of this tax, thinking that it was just a joke and that the person who told them the news was joking. And in fact, could any worker in the Soviet republic possibly imagine that such a horrible tax, which would have been unimaginable in the capitalist era, would be collected from him, who is already being exploited by the state at the plant where he works (which has already been acknowledged, especially after the 14th Party Congress). Could even one worker imagine that after making 400 rubles from May 1, 1925, to May 1926 the state, a revolutionary state at that, would tell him, "You've made a ton of money, so give me 100 rubles, and 300 will be enough for you." It would be hard enough for a draft horse exploited two times over to imagine this, let alone a worker and a human being.

But in the Soviet Republic it has become a reality, as the IAroslavl' *Uezd* Executive Committee and the Gavrilo-IAmskii *Volost'* Executive Committee officially stated in their reports.

After obtaining and reading the agricultural tax law, I understood that nonagricultural wages would be taxed, but that the law set no definite limits for the taxes, leaving everything up to the discretion of the *volost'* executive committee, which is to say to the will of Allah. The law goes into detail on taxes for basic and specialized agricultural sectors, but is too vague when it comes to nonagricultural earnings, and I simply don't understand it. The example of 300 rubles earned in six months given in the comments for Article 22 says very little. First of all, it only covers the temporary (winter) earnings of peasants and says absolutely nothing about the earnings of migrants who work in town year round. Secondly, the example isn't very complete and reeks of arbitrariness. Between the lines of this example you can read the words "Do whatever you want, *volost'* Executive Committee." *Guberniia* Executive Committee Order No. 45, which was issued for the purpose of elaborating this law, provides satisfactory limits for the income of craftsmen, carpenters, and so forth, but doesn't say a word about peasants who are permanently employed at factories and other enterprises or how their earnings are supposed to be counted as part of their agricultural income.

So where can we find the standard? After all, theoretically, a law is a standard. So where is it? Has the Soviet Government passed it down to the lower echelons?

In order to untangle the confusion in my head after reading the law, I went to the *volost'* Executive Committee. They told me the following: my wages of 33 rubles 20 kopecks a month, or 396 rubles per year would be taxed in full with deductions for union dues (minus 8 rubles), for rent at the communal apartment rates of 50 kopecks per month (minus 6 rubles)—396 minus 8 minus 6 = 382; the farm: land 3.45 *desiatina*s x 35 rubles = 120 rubles; meadow: 1 *desiatina* = 20 rubles; one horse and two cows at 25 rubles each = 75 rubles; for a total of 600 rubles per year for six mouths = 100 rubles per mouth, for a total tax of 76 rubles and 20 kopecks.

While I only have to pay 6 rubles and 15 kopecks on the farm, I have to pay 70 rubles from my wages of 33 rubles per month, which means that I have to turn over 20% of my gross income to the state, or 20 kopecks out of every ruble I earn. This means that if I didn't eat or drink and slept under a bush, because there aren't any apartments at communal rates, I would have to work a little over two months just to pay the tax. But if I eat and drink and live in an apartment, I'd have to work five months, which is terrible! After all, I pay 3 rubles a month for a place to live, not 50 kopecks, which means I have to spend half my pay without giving it to the farm, but the *uezd* and *volost'* executive committees have ordered me to put all my pay into the farm.

I told the members of the *volost'* committee that this was robbery of a kind rarely seen in human history and asked them where was the justice our leaders spend so much time talking about. I told them that I thought they didn't understand the law and that probably the Central Executive Committee had absolutely no intention of taking 20% of the income away from workers in the form of a direct tax, but they told me they didn't make this up by themselves and were just doing what their superiors told them to do. And we continue to believe that the only thing that's holding back the imminent prosperity of the Russian people is the "lower levels," i.e. the lower-level government administrators and managers on the periphery, and that the top people in Russia who run the country are so smart, farsighted, and pure-hearted that they could never cause an economic crisis or their programs could not result in any excesses, and that all the problems are the fault of the lower levels and their incompetent execution of the programs, which is also the explanation the higher-ups prefer.

Now government officials are travelling around the countryside explaining the agricultural tax and finding out what the peasants think about it. Of course, the results aren't worth mentioning, because anyone could guess what they would be ahead of time. If an official goes up to Ivan Petrov and says: "Your tax would be 50 rubles, but Petr Ivanov will pay 45 rubles of it for you, and you'll only have to pay 5 rubles. So is the tax OK or what?" Ivan Petrov would say, "It's good, it's good," and "that's the only kind of tax that would be fair."

And after all, I did hear an official of the *Uezd* Executive Committee say that 14% of the taxpayers would pay 53% of the total tax.

Comrade KALININ, the law is basically good, and with respect to agriculture it is very good, but with respect to nonagricultural wages it is extremely bad and verges on robbery and is causing such nonsocialist and archcapitalist contradictions in the Soviet Republic, which is only dreaming of becoming the socialist country it now calls itself, that it's even shameful for me as a citizen of the Republic to talk about it.

Any citizen of Russia or any country in the world who sees the Soviet government committing such nonsocialist excesses with these kinds of programs is quite justified in saying that he is witnessing the historical collapse and bankruptcy of socialist ideas.

The contradictions are as follows: there is a law which says that a person who earns 75 rubles per month has to pay a tax of 9 rubles per year, or 1%, which is an income tax. At the same time there is another law which says that a person who earns 33 rubles per month has to pay 70 rubles, or 20%, which is an agricultural tax, and there is also a law which says that people who earn salaries of up to 75 rubles per month don't have to pay any taxes at all. And all of these laws have been passed in the name of the toilers, not the bourgeois exploiters, but the pure-hearted toilers and citizens of the same republic. These are gaping contradictions which not even a capitalist country could permit.

The new law has given rise to scenarios such as the following ones:

Let's say there are two looms, with one worker standing beside each of them. One of the workers comes from the workers' housing development, while the other is a peasant migrant worker. One of the workers can spend his pay as he sees fit, while the other, and it hurts me to say this, has to turn over one-fifth to the government!!! That's what you call complete and total equality! The dictatorship of the proletariat 1000%!

Under Soviet power we've started to get favorite sons and stepchildren.

And what sort of needs do the first and second weavers have? What sort of advantages does each of them have? And which one of them lives better?

The first weaver can hire a nanny—because his wife also works—for 5 to 8 rubles a month and pays about 10 rubles a month for rent (and if he is a homeowner, it will only make him money). This would amount to 15 rubles a month, while their combined wages are 60 to 100 rubles a month. They work 88 hours a month, and the rest of the time they can relax, recreate, and so forth.

The second weaver lives away from his family, sleeps wherever he can, either eats dry crusts of bread or spends 2/3 of his pay on food for himself, and has to forego any of the happiness he would get from being with his family. If he works 5 to 10 *verst*s away from home, in the summer he'll rush home almost every day to work on the farm with his wife. After 8 hours of work at the factory, he spends four hours a day working at home.

His wife has to stay in the country alone with the children, work in the house and in the field, and worry endlessly. She doesn't have a single bright or happy moment in her life. If something goes wrong her work in the field will go for naught. The family grows enough to last six months, her husband earns 45 rubles a month, and where can they go? Any problem with the farm is a nightmare: if the barn rots she has to fix it, if the plow breaks she has to fix it or buy a new one. The wife wears out the horse because she doesn't know how to handle it and has to buy another one, and so on and so forth. One need after another, nothing but need, need, need, at every step.

And the government says the petty bourgeoisie elements who are making 45 rubles a month have to pay 100 rubles in taxes.

Perhaps if the government says we have to choose between the machine or the wooden plow, maybe we could do so, but the most important point is that we should not be forced to do so by beating us over the head with a club or robbing us. We should be persuaded like human beings, in the language of socialist justice, something like "Comrades, etc.," but not like the way they did when they announce a law in June and say they will only consider land partition and transfer deeds that were signed before May 1. That kind of law isn't a socialist law, it's a bandit law.

Let's look at the following scenarios which the new law has created:

Until the new law was passed, the peasant migrant worker was practically the only MESSENGER between the city and the countryside, the only bringer of light, and the only supporter of Soviet power in the country and at peasant meetings and in discussions with peasants. Only the migrant worker put up any resistance to all the lame anti-Soviet arguments of the *kulak* elements by holding forth in endless debates and even fights. Now the *kulak* has triumphed. He is holding his sides and is laughing at the whole village, saying "Well, Petr Ivanov, what do you think about Soviet power now?" and "Look at how Soviet power has robbed its supporters, ha, ha, ha!!!" And the migrant worker walks away in silence with an aching heart and doesn't know what to say.

I won't spend a lot of time talking about how the tax will affect the farms of the migrant workers, because it wouldn't be hard to imagine. But as a typical example I can quote one migrant worker: "I only wanted to buy a winnower for the farm, but I got hit with a 100 ruble tax, and now I'm thinking about selling our last plow."

With respect to collecting the tax, the authorities will be able to collect all of the tax from the settled peasants (from the Ivan Petrovs), but all I've been hearing from the migrant workers is: "I won't pay the tax", "I'll quit work and won't leave anything for them to take from my house," "I'll go to prison if I have to," "I'll do whatever it takes, but I won't pay that much tax." And one migrant worker, who was awarded the Order of the Red Banner for his courage at Kronstadt, said, "I'll go and tell them to take my medal for the tax, but I just can't pay 100 rubles out of a salary of 35 rubles a month."

I would recommend the following amendments to the law (in order to add the necessary details it is now lacking). Granted, the principle behind the tax is good, and no one would deny it. It's true that our state is still in the building process and that construction requires money, and this might be a compelling reason for deviating from socialist principles, but any deviations should be moderate, not extreme. And every migrant worker realizes this and would be willing to pay more than his neighbor the peasant and more than the worker at the next machine. He is willing to pay twice or three times as much taxes as his neighbor, but you can't ask him to pay twenty times more than his neighbor. This is nothing more than robbery, and it can't stand the slightest scrutiny.

So let the government set a maximum tax for nonagricultural wages at 2% or, at most, 3% of gross earnings and tell the *volost'* executive committees they can't collect any more than that, or as an alternative, provide a minimum subsistence deduction of 18 to 25 rubles a month.

In 1918, when it took over the leadership of Russia, the Communist Party stopped standing on firm ground, became detached from reality, and has been floating in the clouds of communist daydreams so long that it has been unable to put its feet back on the ground long enough to build a state there. As everyone knows, all individual and social life is based on an economic foundation, but the pillars on which Russia rests are so shaky and so poorly built that they have to be replaced quite frequently with new ones. But the fact of the matter is that the process of changing pillars is expensive, and, moreover, every time the pillars are changed the entire edifice shakes a little more and crashes down on the heads of one, and then another, segment of the Russian population. Peasant heads are aching the worst of all from the economic crises and all the changes in the pillars. Now, the new law has shifted the brunt of the blow from the majority of peasants to a minority (14%), i.e., the hardest toiling semi-proletarian segment of the peasantry, whose meager farms have forced them to work for wages. The blow has bypassed the *kulak*s, who don't have to go to factories and mills to eat the dust and can earn just as much money (which is easy for them to hide from the tax collector) by speculation and other chicanery.

Some people might say that I am too deeply submerged in materialistic and egotistical concerns, that I am looking at life and judging everything from the standpoint of my own personal advantage, and that I have forgotten about ideological principles and socialist ideals. To this I can only respond with the following: what sort of principles have our Communist ideologues such as the STALINs and KALININs based their personal lives on with their huge salaries? What about the Russian progressive intelligentsia? Did Comrade KAMENEV, Comrade KALININ, or any of the educated cultured people say that they were sacrificing themselves for the construction of a socialist state and would be content with salaries of 50 rubles a month? None of them said this or did this. And what about Comrade KAMENEV, who gives us all his apostolic preaching about communism while his belly continues to grow? He's not exactly living a communist life, especially in the situation the republic finds itself in now.

So what's the point in asking unsophisticated country folk who barely get by from one crust of bread to another, from kopeck to kopeck, about the ideological principles of life? If you were Ivan Petrov, wouldn't you be happy if Petr Ivanov were paying your tax for you?

So, Comrade Kalinin, I am asking you, as the chairman of the *TSIK* and a member of the Political Bureau of the country's ruling party, to explain why the *TSIK* approved a law giving the authorities the right to take 20% of a worker's wages in the form of taxes.

I would definitely appreciate it if you would answer my question with a brief reply in the newspaper *Bednota* [For the Poor] and rid me of the oppressive and dreary thoughts which I've set forth in this letter and which the *volost'* and *uezd* executive committees planted in my head because, as I believe, of their misinterpretation of the new law.

Aleksei ShABUROV, a peasant from the village of Kurdumovo, Gavrilo-IAmskii *volost'*, IAroslavl' *uezd* and *guberniia*.

June 20, 1926

                True Copy:

(17-2)

Source: ?

DOCUMENT 23   *Letter from a peasant of Riazan' guberniia to Stalin, March 22, 1926, discussing the socialist state and suggesting needed changes in the system*

To: J. V. Stalin

From a nonparty peasant   [date stamp] Mar. 22, 1926

Respected Comrade!

No one, it seems, questions that the dictatorship of the proletariat is a distinguishing feature of the entire period of the revolution. This is an axiom well known to every young pioneer. According to this fine theory, the toiling classes are granted broad civic rights. But in fact it didn't happen that way at all: These classes, even if they did get citizenship, it was limited; and up to now they have not enjoyed freedom, in the full meaning of that word. This assertion is based upon universally recognized facts, which I don't need to expand upon, considering certain social conditions.

Of course one can object, pointing to our newspapers, magazines, unions, committees, etc.: Isn't all this proof of genuine, democratic freedom? Surely these institutions work freely and express everything they need to. This is true in part but there are also phenomena that appear quite definitely to be headed in a negative direction. Just as no army limits itself to only a certain type of force, e.g., infantry, no matter how advanced it may be, no state should hinder those social trends that fail to march in step with the country's predominant political views. The society that is based on only its own opinions, that does not permit opposing views, is a one-dimensional society.

How goes it at the present time in the first socialist country? Alas, not totally as might have been expected. One cannot question its progressive beginnings and all the other virtues of Soviet power, but major sources of regressive qualities stand out so starkly in our public life that it's impossible not to notice them. For example, who does not know that most of the publications from our periodical literature suffer from a lack of substance and boldness and are monotonously run. Who does not know that our newspapers and journals often get carried away with boasting; no matter what issue you pick up, you see embellishment and boasting everywhere: "our side has won," "we are accomplishing our goal," "we are victorious." All we need are fine-sounding patriotic slogans and any task becomes a piece of cake. But what are all the practicing and accomplished Demostheneses yammering about? The same thing as the belles lettres. The only difference is that the blabbermouths shamelessly copy their world views and phrases from the newspaper columns, then they release them into their gramophone's ear horn. But belles lettres possess a certain originality. Once again, I qualify this and say there are a few positive exceptions. As a result of this kind of activity, the view is being established that they want to put out something dubious as "authentic," that they want to be absolutely convincing.

Of course no one denies the successes and achievements of the socialist state, but our public figures make so much of them that I'm unconsciously reminded of the merchant who overpraises his goods in an effort to "con" a buyer. The one-sidedness of our social life also is reflected in the fact that the state enjoys a press monopoly. There is no disagreement that in the past this measure was necessitated by the struggle for power, but at this time, it seems, the need for this prop has passed.

The dictatorship of the proletariat is, according to socialist teaching, a transitional stage that must in time fade into the realm of legend; consequently, during its existence, it should, year by year as it were, lose its rough edges and take on more and more gentle forms, in conjunction with which corresponding changes should take place in the public life of the state. In our [Soviet] union, although these changes have taken place in part, much remains the same. In this regard, much is being done with great delay and with errors.

At this time, it seems to me that among the essential changes that the government must implement in our society in the near future undoubtedly are: abolishing the monopoly of the press; abolishing the monopoly of the party, i.e., legalizing democratic political parties; and other things in this vein. Why don't we bring this to reality?

Some people will say that it's too early to grant legal existence and publishing rights to all democratic political parties and that it will harm the dictatorship of the proletariat. On the contrary, it's time, and there's nothing dangerous in it. Of course, monarchist and bourgeois parties should not be included on the list of legal ones, but as for democratic ones, if they work toward a state revolution, they can be repressed with the help of the *GPU*.

Before, Soviet power couldn't do that; but now it wouldn't damage its interests, and this measure would be very beneficial. It's time at last to replace one phonograph record with another one that's more appropriate. To be sure, there are differences in records, and another one might give you a headache.

If the ruling circles of the USSR were to find it possible to make such changes in our public life, then that egregious, self-aggrandizing one-sidedness and some other things would tone down and take on a more attractive face. Most of the newspapers, magazines, and loudmouths would be pressured in their respective spheres of activity to behave more modestly, preach less vainly, be more businesslike. People with vigor and innovative ideas, ideas that are now impossible to conceive, will appear.

Answer me please, Comrade Stalin, what is the obstacle?

N. Zharikov

Village Neznanovo, Karab. *volost'*, Ryzhskogo *uezd*, Riazan' *guberniia*. Postal address: p.o. Chemodanovka, Riazan' *guberniia*, village Neznanovo

RTSKhIDNI, fond 17, op. 85, d. 495, ll. 284, 284ob, 285, 285ob

First tractor in the village, 1926. TSGAKFD. N 297146

Secret Archives of the
Central Committee of the
All-Russian Communist Party (Bolshevik)

INV. NO.

Session	Volume-Group [?]	Archive No.

Copy No. 120
TOP SECRET
Archive as Encrypted

USSR
UNIFIED STATE POLITICAL DIRECTORATE [*OGPU*]
Information Department
April 1927
Moscow

The attached report provides an overview of the political situation in the USSR in February 1927. This summary was written on the basis of classified information supplied by the Information Department of the *OGPU* supplemented with material from the Secret (Clergy) and Counterintelligence (Banditry) Departments of the *OGPU*.

In view of the top secret nature of this survey, it should be archived in the same manner as encrypted material. Copying or excerpting from this survey is absolutely prohibited.

The authorized representatives of the *OGPU* and the heads of the *guberniia* and *oblast'* branches of the *OGPU* may make this survey available to the secretaries of *oblast'* committees, *guberniia* committees, and *krai* committees and bureaus of the Central Committee of the All-Russian Communist Party (Bolshevik) for reading.

The survey includes 5 appendices and 1 table.

DEPUTY DIRECTOR OF THE *OGPU*   [signed] IAgoda

HEAD OF THE INFORMATION

DEPARTMENT OF THE *OGPU*   [signed] Alekseev

WORKERS

The political attitudes of the workers were revealed in the course of the election campaigns for the Soviets.

The workers were much more active than other segments of the urban population. Statements at workers' meetings have demonstrated both the political and cultural growth of the working masses.

We must point out the apathetic attitudes of the unemployed toward the election campaigns and a number of anti-Soviet comments at meetings of the unemployed.

Strikes became somewhat more frequent in February and primarily revealed the dissatisfaction of certain groups of workers with the new collective bargaining agreements. The dissatisfaction spread to certain categories of skilled metalworkers (wage cuts) and textile workers (dissatisfaction with wage leveling in the new agreements). Of the 67 strikes involving a total of 5,594 strikers (as opposed to 58 strikes with 4,263 strikers in February [sic!]), 41 (with 3,114 strikers) occurred in the metal and textile industries.

Metalworkers

(Strikes) There was an increase in the number of strikes among metalworkers in February (12 strikes with 1,514 strikers as opposed to 6 with 1,208 strikers in January). The strikes primarily occurred in response to wage cuts.

At the Lenin Shipyard 400 workers went on strike in response to pay cuts of 30 rubles per month (the pay cuts were attributed to the transfer of the shipyard to the machinery trust where piece rates are lower than in the shipbuilding trust) and the failure of the factory committee and party cell to give the necessary explanations for the forthcoming cuts. A few party members joined in the strike.

At the Kiev Arsenal 230 workers went on strike. It is typical that piece rates for several jobs at the arsenal are much lower than the prewar rates.

The smiths at the Petrovskii Locomotive Works (Kherson *okrug*) went on strike in response to a 50% cut in piece rates.

(Wage Cuts) Wage cuts (not only for certain categories of skilled workers but for entire departments) went into effect at 32 metal works in Leningrad, Ukraine, and Moscow (as opposed to 23 plants in January). The cuts brought about a number of fierce disputes and strikes at the plants. The dissatisfaction was especially high among the workers at the large Leningrad plants (15).

In most cases the managers of the plants implemented the wage cuts to circumvent the new rate agreements (at the same time, as the wage floor was raised, bonuses were cut, pay increments were cut 15% to 30% or at times by as much as 50%, and new formulas for calculating wages were introduced). This led the workers at several plants to threaten to "beat up the directors and wheel them out in a barrow." Labor-management relations became particularly bad at a number of shops at the Putilov Works. In the boiler department two groups of stokers (more than 100 individuals) conducted a sitdown strike in response to a 30% cut in bonuses and threatened to beat up the supervisor of the shop and wheel the labor protection supervisor out in a barrow.

At the electrical shop the shop supervisor decided that January's wages should not be higher than December's wages and cancelled the wage hike established by the new agreement. At the yard the workers got only one ruble instead of the 10 rubles they were promised, and after calling in the yard supervisor they declared: "Where's the justice in all this? Moscow raised our pay, and all we get is a few pennies. Only the parasite bosses will see any of the kopecks we've earned with our toiling blood." Disputes also broke out at a large number of shops (the brass foundry, the boiler works, the tractor works, and the new forge shop). A 30% cut in piece rates at the Kalinin Pipe Factory caused the workers to mutter that "they would have to stuff the rate-setter in a sack, paint him red, and wheel him to the river."

There were also blatant violations of collective bargaining agreements. One of the articles (22) of the new collective bargaining agreement for the Evdokimov Precision Instruments Factory contains a clause stipulating that the management cannot cut piece rates. But the director of the Optical Instruments Trust ordered a rate cut anyway. A general assembly of the workers resolved to ask the union to implement immediately Article 22 of the new collective bargaining agreement.

(Layoffs) In February large groups of workers (100 to 200) were laid off at a number of metal works in Ukraine and the Volga basin. Most of the layoffs were due to a shortage of raw materials and orders. Major layoffs occurred at the Izhevsk Works (more than 800 workers). The management and factory committee decided to "lay off the old and the infirm first." The individuals affected are being examined by a medical commission.

The dissatisfaction has been compounded by the fact that workers with absolutely no wherewithal are being laid off (workers recently discharged from the military and so forth).

Workers are also dissatisfied with the surreptitious layoffs underway at a number of plants in Ukraine (the transfer of skilled workers to outdoor work).

At the *Red Star* plant in Zinov'evsk *okrug*, the wages of skilled workers reassigned to unskilled labor have fallen from 200 to 40 rubles.

At most of the plants the workers, while protesting the layoffs, would not object to a shorter work week to prevent layoffs.

(Late Wage Payments) Cases of late wage payments in the metal industry were fewer in February than in January (16 as opposed to 30). There was also a 50% reduction in the number of lengthy delays (8 as opposed to 15 in January). Wage payment delays continue to be a problem at Urals plants (6). Workers at the Koliushchenko *Uralsel'mash* [Urals Agricultural Machinery] Plant have indicated that many workers "panhandle" on their way to work in the morning because their pay is late. At the Ust'-Katav Plant of the Southern Urals Trust, where wages for the second half of December were paid on January 17 (and then only 50%), the workers at the forge shop on their own initiative called a meeting at which there were caustic comments such as the following: "they dole out our wages in small pieces, they harass us like we're dogs, the party doesn't pay any attention to us, they just try to pacify us with all kinds of promises." The workers (1000) of the Bytoshevskii Plant in Briansk are still agitated because of long wage payment delays (they went on strike in November and December of 1926 and in January and February of this year). The strike in February lasted 5 days (I, 1–16).

Textile Workers

(Strikes) Strikes among the textile workers are still taking place with great frequency (29 strikes with 1600 strikers as opposed to 20 with 1497 strikers in January). The strikes are still encompassing mainly the workers in the main shops and have taken place in response to wage cuts due to rate-setting errors and the adverse impact of the wage levelling included in the new collective bargaining agreement on certain categories of workers. Strikes have been particularly common among the weaver apprentices (factories in the city of Ivanovo-Voznesensk).

(Dissatisfaction with Rate System) Rate-setters at most factories have failed to properly take into account the quality of the raw materials, changes in working conditions, and the condition of the machinery, which has resulted in wild swings in wages. At the First Republican Factory (Kostroma), at Bol'shaia Dmitrovskaia, and at Nizhne-Seredskaia (Ivanovo-Voznesensk *guberniia*), strikes broke out in response to a wage cut, in connection with the worsening quality of raw materials; the wages of warpers at the First Republican Factory fell by 30%. At the Glukhov Mill 2 shifts of weavers working on three machines went on strike in response to a 5–10 ruble wage cut caused by a switch to new yarn (zephyr). The poor quality of rate-setting is exemplified by an incident which took place at the cotton print department of the Proletarian Mill (Tver' *guberniia*), where rates were reset 3 times after the conclusion of a collective bargaining agreement, evoking extreme dissatisfaction among the workers. A decline in the quality of the raw material at the plant caused the weavers to demand higher wages and threaten a strike. They became even more dissatisfied when the rate-setter, whom they'd asked to explain why their wages were cut, replied that "payroll calculations are privileged information." The assistant director of the plant refused to carry out an order from a board of arbitration which directed that the weavers be paid the average wage, and this order was carried out only after a directive from the director of the Trust.

At the canvas department of the First Republican Factory 100 workers went on strike after the management of the plant set arbitrary piece rates (without notifying the rates and conflict commission [RKK]), reducing the workers' pay. The management stubbornly refused to pay the workers the average wage, even though a provision to this effect was included in the collective bargaining agreement.

(Strike movement among apprentices) In early February, in conjunction with the signing of new collective bargaining agreements, there was an organized demonstration by apprentices from 6 factories in the city of Ivanovo-Voznesensk (the *NIVM*, the *BIVM*, the *Rabkrai*, the *Zariad'e*, [italicized acronyms unclear] the Bol'shaia Dmitrovskaia, and the Staro-Dmitrovskaia Mills), who were primarily striking for much higher wages. Strike fever also spread to apprentices at a number of factories in different districts of Ivanovo-Voznesensk *guberniia*. A strike also broke out at the Vagzhanov Factory in Tver' *guberniia*. Individual members of the Communist Party took part in the strikes. The strike of the apprentices did not receive widespread support among most of the workers, and the apprentices went back to work on the old terms. [break in the text]

THE ELECTION CAMPAIGN

A Rise in Attendance at Election Meetings

The aforementioned factors resulted in a certain realignment of the forces contesting the elections. It included much greater activity by the poor peasants in these elections over the previous elections, which was at times offset by a decline in the activity of the middle-income peasants. The elections have also been accompanied by greater attendance at election meetings in most areas of the country over last year. For example, in Moscow *guberniia* attendance at election meetings has averaged 58% as opposed to 53.2% last year; in 5 *uezd*s of the Karelian Republic attendance ranged from 45 to 60%; in 5 *uezd*s of Cherepovets *guberniia* it ranged from 53 to 67%; in Novgorod *guberniia* (859 rural soviets) it ranged from 45 to 56%, in Smolensk *guberniia* (8 *uezd*s) it ranged from 44 to 72%, and so on. In Ukraine (659 rural soviets, 34 *okrug*s), average attendance at election meetings was 56.5% and in some cases, was as high as 70 to 90%. In the North Caucasus (400 rural soviets), attendance at election meetings was 45.4%. In Siberia (11 *okrug*s, 1361 rural soviets), attendance was 50.3%, while in certain *okrug*s it was much higher (53.8% in Kuznetsk *okrug*, 61.5% in Oirat *oblast'*, 60.4% in Khakass *okrug*, 53% in Novosibirsk *okrug*, and so on). Attendance was lowest in Minusinsk *okrug* (40%).

There was a decline in electoral participation from last year in Tver' *guberniia* (48.6% as opposed to 51.6%), in Vologda *guberniia* (in 11 *volost*'s in Kargopol *uezd*, attendance at election meetings varied from 14 to 32%, while in certain cases it was as low as 8%).

The attitudes of different segments of the rural population at the elections may be described as follows:

Poor Peasants and Elections

(Poor peasants more active) While the middle-income peasants played the leading role in the coalition of middle and poor peasants in the last campaign, in a number of regions (Ukraine, North Caucasus, Siberia) the leading role passed to the organized poor peasants. The greater activity of the poor peasants was primarily evident in their interest in the poor peasants' meetings, which were attended by 50 to 60% of the poor peasants, while in some places attendance was 80 to 90% or higher. The attendance of poor peasants at pre-election and election meetings was much higher than last year's, and in places the poor peasants attended in higher numbers than other groups of voters. For example, in Samara *guberniia*, in the Bogdanov *volost'*, practically none of the poor peasants used to attend the meetings, while now all of them go. In some *okrug*s in the Urals (Shadrino, Chelyabinsk) the poor peasants accounted for 50 to 60% of all attendance at the election meetings. In Biisk *okrug* of Siberia an average of 44% of the voters at each electoral district attended the elections to the Srostinskii Rural Soviet, while 100% of the poor peasants showed up. In Minusinsk *okrug* (200 rural soviets), 356 pre-election meetings were attended by a total of 38,560 voters, including 19,617 poor peasants, 15,440 middle peasants, and 1,475 wealthy peasants, 456 party members, 468 *komsomol* members, and 1,104 others (office workers, members of the intelligentsia).

In most cases, the activity of the poor peasants was quite healthy and was aimed at isolating the *kulak*s and their supporters in the elections. In certain cases, when attempts were made to convene separate poor peasant meetings, poor peasants spoke out against these meetings, fearing that they might result in a worsening of relations with the middle peasants and stating that "the organization of separate meetings for the poor peasants would stir up hostility between the poor peasants and the middle peasants" (Voronezh *guberniia*), "the middle peasants should be invited to our meeting, for otherwise the organization of separate meetings for poor peasants might lead to the same situation as during the revolution, when the poor and middle peasants were at odds" (Komi-Zyrian region) (III, 37–40).

(Attitudes of Committees of Poor Peasants [*Kombedy*]) At the same time, the greater activity of the poor peasants, especially in Ukraine, has resulted in a rebirth of "committee of the poor" attitudes, which were evidenced in a tendency to ignore the middle peasants in the elections. These were especially manifest in the tendency to elect exclusively "poor peasant" soviets. At the elections the poor peasants often said that "we don't need the middle peasants because they will defend their own interests," "we only need a soviet which will defend the interests of the poor," and so forth. In Glukhov *okrug,* in the village of Pogrebka, the poor peasants stated that "as long as poor peasants are on the rural soviet, then everything is OK, and for the sake of appearances we might include a couple of middle peasants. In the Moldavian Republic at the elections to the Vzdoturkovskii Rural Soviet, the poor peasants stated that "last year, when there was a majority of middle peasants on the rural soviet, the members of the Committee of Poor Peasants [*KNS*] had to meet in back alleys, and all the goodies were handed out by soviet power to the middle-income and wealthy peasants, and we poor peasants were kept down. This year we aren't going to be stupid and will prove that power in the countryside should belong to us." In Nikolaev *okrug* at the Kalinin Rural Soviet the poor peasants who worked hard in preparation for the elections said that "we've gotten another chance to take power into our own hands and we must take advantage of it." Similar attitudes prevailed in certain places, especially in Ukraine, and were supported by some low-level government workers. A typical comment came from a member of the Tomakovskii Executive Committee in Zaporozh'e *okrug* at a meeting of the peasants of the Ilyin Rural Soviet: "Last year the authorities gave us broad democracy, which resulted in the middle peasants and *kulak*s coming to power and the poor peasants losing power and moving to the end of the line. So this year we are faced with the task of bringing the poor peasants back into positions of power and letting the wealthy and middle peasants stay in the rear."

This tendency towards the removal of middle peasants was clearly evident in the nomination of candidates for rural soviets at poor peasant and pre-election meetings, when the majority of the nominees were poor peasants (Samara *guberniia,* Ukraine, Siberia). In Priluki *okrug* several rural party cells and *KNS*s appointed 75% poor peasants, 5% middle peasants, and 20% women to the new soviets. In Samara *guberniia,* in six villages of the Berevo-Luka *volost'* and in Pugachev *uezd,* poor peasants' meetings nominated 154 candidates to the rural soviets, 62% of whom were poor peasants and 38% of whom were middle peasants. In Novosibirsk *okrug* 65 to 70% of the candidates nominated to the rural soviets at poor peasants' meetings were poor peasants, while the rest were middle peasants (III, 41–47).

Apathy among the poor peasantry in the current campaign has been less frequent and can be mainly attributed to deficiencies in the work of rural party cells and public organizations in the villages or the financial dependence of the poor peasants on wealthy peasants and *kulak*s (which was observed to some extent in Briansk and Orenburg *guberniia*s, the Urals, and other places).

Quite often the apathy of the poor peasants is manifest in their unwillingness to work for the soviets due to the low salaries paid to soviet employees and their unwillingness to "neglect their farms" (III, 48–52).

The Attitudes of Middle Peasants at the Elections

(Middle peasant-poor peasant coalition) In most parts of the country the vast majority of the middle peasants entered into a coalition with the poor peasants in the elections, which was largely made possible by extensive organizational work by the poor peasants. At the same time, the greater activity of the poor peasants changed the role of the middle peasants from the last campaign. While the middle peasants played a dominant role in the last elections and led the poor peasants after them, this year the poor peasants largely took the lead and controlled the middle peasant-poor peasant coalition. This was clearly evident in the lists of candidates, which were nominated at poor peasants' meetings and in most cases received the organized support of the middle peasants, and in the vocal opposition to the candidates put forth by the *kulak*s and wealthy peasants. The realignment of forces was most pronounced in areas with the sharpest rural social divisions (Ukraine, North Caucasus, and Siberia, and several other areas), where the campaign unleashed the energy of the poor peasants in opposition to the rich peasant and *kulak* segments of the rural population. In a large number of other areas, especially the central region, the middle peasants were just as active and sometimes more active than the poor peasants (III, 53–56).

(Independent activities on the part of the middle-income peasants) Although they did not evoke sharp opposition among the middle peasants, in places the excessive steps of depriving some middle peasants of their voting rights in the period preceding the elections and the removal of middle peasants from the new soviets did result in a certain amount of alienation of the middle peasants from the poor peasants. At the election meetings expressions of opposition by middle peasants to the lists of candidates prepared jointly by the party cells and the poor peasants were especially sharp in places where only token numbers of middle peasants were nominated or no middle peasants at all were included. In Ukraine there were incidents where middle peasants, as a kind of protest against the pressure of the poor peasants, acted independently in the elections, either rejecting the poor peasants' lists or (which was much less common) . . . [narrative ends here]

TABLE
STRIKES IN JANUARY AND FEBRUARY OF 1927

Reason for strike	Dissatisfaction with wages		Dissatisfaction with piece rates and additional pay		Dissatisfaction with output norms		Late or incomplete pay and irregularities in payments	
	January	February	January	February	January	February	January	February
Metalworkers	3	1	——	8	——	——	1	2
Textile workers	6	17	3	7	——	——	1	2
Miners	5	——	——	——	——	2	——	1
Transportation workers	3	1	3	——	——	——	1	1
Local transportation workers	1	5	——	2	——	——	——	——
Chemical workers	——	1	——	——	——	——	——	——
Seasonal workers	1	3	——	——	——	——	1	2
Others	2	2	——	——	——	——	2	1
Total	21	30	6	17	——	2	6	9

TABLE (CONTINUED)
STRIKES IN JANUARY AND FEBRUARY OF 1927

Reason for strike	Dissatisfaction with management of plant and working conditions		Other reasons		Total strikes		Total strikers		Total worker-days lost	
	January	February	January	February	January	February	January	February	January	February
Metalworkers	——	——	2	1	6	12	1208	1514	1133	3612
Textile workers	1	2	9	1	20	29	1497	1600	1072	692
Miners	2	——	——	1	7	4	393	134	376	184
Transportation workers	——	——	3	——	10	2	509	45	641	72
Local transportation workers	——	——	——	——	1	7	125	702	25	886
Chemical workers	——	——	1	1	1	2	70	65	70	23
Seasonal workers	——	——	——	1	2	6	163	1348	152	1993
Others	——	——	7	2	11	5	298	186	278	128
Total	3	2	22	7	58	67	4263	5594	3747	7590

Secretary of the Information Department of the *OGPU*   [signed]   (Kucherov)

RTSKhIDNI, fond 17, op. 87, d. 201, ll. 44, 45, 45ob, 49, 84.

DOCUMENT 25   *Postcard to M.I. Kalinin from a worker at the Lenin plant in Voronezh, February 14, ca. 1930, describing the miserable life of the workers*

Voronezh February 14

[Back of postcard]

Dear comrade Mikhail Ivanovich!

The life of a worker is very hard Our wives cannot manage to feed us They leave at five o'clock in the morning to buy bread, meat, potatoes and return home around four o'clock [in the afternoon] and even at that they don't bring back enough There is nothing to eat I am always hungry and the children are barefoot and starving Every day things go from bad to worse The peasant-farmer does not bring anything to the marketplace, what are we to do You are our hope.

Respectfully yours

A worker of the Lenin Plant

[On the side] Help us

[Front of postcard, upper left corner] Coat of arms, over which is written "Inquiry to *Oblast'* Executive Political Committee."

[Front of postcard, upper right corner] Postmark of the city of Voronezh, date unclear except for 14th of a month.

Post Card
Posta Karto

Address: <u>Voronezh-local</u>

Addressee: <u>Mikhail Ivanovich Kalinin</u>

<u>Father of the Working People</u>

RTSKhIDNI, fond 78, op. 1, d. 378, ll. 46, 46ob

DOCUMENT 26   *Report on anti-regime political attitudes and low morale of working-class and professional employees in the transportation industry, June 1933*

[Handwritten:] To Comrade Andreeev
TOP SECRET

[Stamp illegible except for:]
JUNE 1933

REPORT

ON THE POLITICAL ATTITUDES AND MORALE OF
THE TRANSPORTATION WORKERS

Negative attitudes have become widespread among all categories of transportation workers.

These attitudes are primarily in response to inadequate supplies, the pressure which has been applied in the grain procurement drive and its resultant problems, and delays in wage payments.

Some typical negative attitudes are reflected in the quotes provided below.

WORKERS

"IT'S DISGUSTING. THEY AREN'T GIVING US OUR PAY. WE NEED ANOTHER REVOLUTION TO WIPE OUT EVERY LAST ONE OF THEM (THE COMMUNISTS)."
(MALAPURA, a machinist at the Artemovsk Depot)

"SOVIET POWER IS DRIVING THE WORKERS INTO THE GRAVE. NO MATTER WHAT WE DO, IT'S NOT ENOUGH, AND DON'T EVEN ASK ABOUT EATING. IN THE OLD DAYS THE GENTRY MADE US WORK, BUT AT LEAST THEY LET US EAT."
(BALABAS, a coppersmith at the Izium Steam Locomotive Repair Works)

"IN THE COUNTRY THEY'RE TAKING AWAY THE PEASANTS' LAST BIT OF GRAIN. IT'S OUTRIGHT ROBBERY."
(MATKOVSKII, a worker at the Komarovtsy Station in Gaivoron *raion*)

"DID WE REALLY FIGHT SO THAT THE WORKERS AND THE PEASANTS COULD LIVE THE WAY THEY'RE LIVING TODAY? THERE'S NOTHING BUT BUREAUCRACY AND RED TAPE. THE PEASANTS HAVE BEEN DRIVEN OFF AND ROBBED OF EVERYTHING. IF I GET MY CHANCE, I'LL PICK UP A RIFLE AGAIN AND KILL THE HIGH-RANKING BASTARDS WHO REDUCED THE COUNTRY TO THIS CONDITION."
(KALAShNIKOV, a metalworker at the Nizhne-Dneprovsk Rail Car Repair Works and a former Red partisan)

"LET'S STOP KIDDING AROUND. THE PEOPLE ARE STARVING. THE WORKING CLASS SEES EVERYTHING QUITE CLEARLY AND WON'T FOLLOW YOU ANY MORE."
(A comment by MARKIN, a metalworker at Krinichnaia Station in Debaltsevskii *raion*, at a workers' meeting).

"EVERYBODY TALKS ABOUT HOW THE WORKERS IN FOREIGN COUNTRIES ARE SUFFERING, BUT DOESN'T SAY ANYTHING ABOUT WHAT'S GOING ON OVER HERE. OVER THERE THEY'RE DESTROYING FOOD BECAUSE OF SURPLUSES, AND WE'RE TOLD THERE'S A CRISIS OVER THERE. WE NOT ONLY HAVE A CRISIS, WE HAVE NOTHING AT ALL."
(OVChARENKO, a smith at the Dnepropetrovsk Depot).

WHITE-COLLAR
WORKERS

"THIS ISN'T A GOVERNMENT, IT'S A GANG. THEY'VE REDUCED THE PEASANTS TO A CONDITION WHERE THEY HAVE NOTHING TO LIVE ON. THEY'VE TAKEN THEIR LAST BIT OF GRAIN, THEY'VE TAKEN ALL THE POTATOES, AND THEY'VE LEFT THE PEASANTS TO THE MERCY OF FATE."
(BUBYREV, an assistant station master at Zolotnitskaia Station, Belgorod *raion*)

"ALL OF US SHOULD STOP WORK IMMEDIATELY, AND THEN OUR SITUATION WOULD IMPROVE."
(GRIGORUK, a clerk at Krasilov Station, Gaivoron *raion*)

"THE PEOPLE IN POWER ARE A BUNCH OF SABOTEURS WHO DON'T KNOW HOW TO PLAN. THEY'RE EXPORTING EVERYTHING TO FOREIGN COUNTRIES, WHICH MEANS THINGS WON'T GET ANY BETTER OVER HERE."
(POGORELOV, a conductor in the Dnepropetrovsk Reserve)

"NOBODY FEELS LIKE DOING ANYTHING ON AN EMPTY STOMACH. IF WE GOT OUR SUPPLIES AND OUR FOOD QUICKER, THEN WE MIGHT BE ABLE TO FULFILL THE FIVE-YEAR

PLANS. IT'S FINE FOR STALIN WITH HIS FULL STOMACH TO SIT IN MOSCOW AND THINK UP THINGS. LET HIM TRY TO LIVE ON OUR RATIONS."
(TSVETKOVSKII, a telegraph operator at Ovruch Station)

PROFESSIONALS
AND TECHNICIANS

"THE SOVIETS HAVE MISMANAGED US TO THE BRINK OF DISASTER. THE INTELLIGENTSIA IS SUFFERING. AN ENGINEER OR A DOCTOR CAN'T LIVE WITHOUT WORKING TWO JOBS. PEOPLE ARE WALKING AROUND LIKE GHOSTS. OUR GOVERNMENT DOESN'T CARE IF WE GET ANY FOOD OR NOT. THE ONLY THING I CAN CALL IT IS SABOTAGE."
(ShAPOVALOV, a doctor at the Railroad Clinic in Dnepropetrovsk)

"WE CAN'T EXPECT ANYTHING GOOD FROM THE IDIOTS IN POWER NOW. THE ONLY THING WE HAVE TO LOOK FORWARD TO IS HORRORS WHICH MANKIND HAS NEVER SEEN BEFORE."
(GROShEV, an engineer at Ilovaisk Station)

"THE CLASSLESS SOCIETY MEANS THE PRIVILEGED CASTE OF COMMUNISTS, BECAUSE EVERYONE ELSE CAN'T EXPECT ANYTHING BUT A STEEL YOKE."
(TKAChENKO, an engineer in Ilovaisk *raion*).

"THE NEWSPAPERS SAY THAT THE CRISIS HASN'T REACHED US. BUT I SAY THAT THE CRISIS HAS HIT US HARDER THAN IT HAS THE CAPITALIST COUNTRIES. WE AREN'T GETTING ANY SUPPLIES OR ANY NEW CONSTRUCTION. ALL THE CONSTRUCTION PROJECTS, EVEN THE MILITARY ONES, ARE BEING MOTHBALLED. MAJOR LAYOFFS ARE ON THE HORIZON. AREN'T THESE THE SYMPTOMS OF A CRISIS?"
(SLOPOVRONSKII, a doctor at the Railroad Clinic in Dnepropetrovsk).

"I WOULD BE GLAD TO GO TO A FOREIGN COUNTRY WHERE THE NEWSPAPERS SAY THERE'S HUNGER AND CRISIS. ALL A WORKER HERE HAS TO DO TO BECOME COLD AND HUNGRY IS SKIP ONE DAY OF WORK."
(SIKIRSKII, an agronomist in Ilovaisk *raion*)

Source: ?

DOCUMENT 27   *Letter from Armenian collective farm worker A. N. Tolmosova to M. I. Kalinin, December 13, 1937, expressing gratitude to the Soviet government and to party leaders*

Moscow, The Kremlin
To Chairman of the Central Executive Committee of the USSR
Mikhail Ivanovich Kalinin.

From collective farm worker Agaf'ia
Nikolaevna Tolmosova. Armenian SSR
Dilizhan *raion*, Krasnoe village.

Dear Mikhail Ivanovich!

I am a woman collective farm worker at the Voroshilov Collective Farm in Krasnoe, Dilizhan *raion* of the Armenian SSR. [I], Tolmosova, A. N., in the name of my entire family, consisting of my fourteen children who live with me, would like to express my Great gratitude to Our Soviet Government and to our leader, the Communist Party . . .

[The document is incomplete. Handwritten across the right side is the number 140 and the underlined name T. Markov.]

RTSKhIDNI, fond 78, op. 1, d. 593, ll. 139–140

DOCUMENT 28   *Letter from party member Alekseev to Stalin, February 17, 1939, asking for a reduction in penalties for reinstated party members*

Proletarians of all Countries, Unite!
SECRET

All-Union Communist Party (Bolshevik) (*VKP(b)*)
CENTRAL COMMITTEE (*TSK*)

SPECIAL SECTOR

No. 5/125   February 17, 1939

to the *TSK VKP(b)* SECRETARY
to Comrade ZhDANOV

The letter of Comrade A. Alekseev is directed to your consideration.
HEAD OF THE SPECIAL SECTOR *TSK VKP(b)*

[signed] A. Poskrebyshev

Copy

Comrade Stalin!

Before the Congress, I beg to make one suggestion which only you can understand and authorize.

My suggestion is the following:

In 1936–1937 many, many people were expelled from the party who were undeserving of this, although some of whom were indeed guilty, but often out of necessity. The majority of them were cut off from their own party for not less than a year before the January *TSK* Plenum.

During the period of their expulsion these people suffered and endured much. After the wise decision of the January *TSK* Plenum they were all reinstated, having been given one penalty or another.

These penalties were accepted by these people, at the time even joyfully, because what is a penalty in comparison with being cut off from the party in which you have stayed for dozens of years and to which you have devoted all your energies.

The penalties received hang over these people right up to the present time. They weigh on them mentally, and they force them to feel themselves *VKP(b)* members without full rights, to whom this or that public work (reports, propaganda, etc.) cannot be entrusted.

However, the overwhelming majority of them have already redeemed their faults three-fold, both by their work and by these sufferings which they have gone through in the period of their expulsion. Indeed, by the very fact of their expulsion they have been punished severely and for their entire life. Therefore, the penalty hanging over them is already an unnecessary weight, which is not educational in its results.

Hence, it would be very good if the *TSK VKP(b)* passed a resolution or introduced a draft resolution at the Party Congress, approximately thus: "The Congress resolves to propose to all party organizations for a specific period (1–2 months) to remove the party penalties from all *VKP(b)* members who had been expelled during the period of 1936–1937 and who have shown their worth through public work after reinstatement."

Thousands and thousands of people would greet this resolution with such joy and enormous gratitude toward you—the wise party leader. It would be in keeping with the entire spirit of the approaching 18th Party Congress.

A. Alekseev.

VKP(b) member, party card no. [illegible]

February 7, 1939

Moscow, Leningrad Highway
Building 36, Apt. 24, instructor at an automotive school.
tel. D-2-35-61.

P.S. I urgently request that Secretariat workers bring my suggestion to the attention of Comrade Stalin.

True copy: [signed] Kriapkina

Received at the Special Sector *TSK VKP(b)* February 9, 1939

Source: ?

Top Secret
Special Folder

Committee of State Security [*KGB*] of the USSR
March 21, 1988 No. 458-Ch
Moscow   TO THE CENTRAL COMMITTEE of the *KPSS*

On results of the work of the *KGB* in
investigating authors of anonymous
materials of a hostile nature.

In 1987 the measures implemented in the country for economic *perestroika* and the broadening of democratization and *glasnost'* resulted in a 29.5% reduction in the distribution of anonymous materials of an anti-Soviet, nationalistic, and politically injurious content as compared with the previous year. However, the number of persons who took part in their preparation and distribution (1,663) increased by 9.4% because of some growth of cliquish, negative occurrences among the youth of the Kazakh SSR and Latvian SSR.

The number of instances of distributed materials criticizing internationalist assistance to Afghanistan by the USSR declined by 77%, and the number of profascist slogans and symbols fell by 24%.

During the year 44 instances of distribution of anonymous materials containing terrorist statements against leaders of the *KPSS* and the Soviet government, 108 threats of physical violence against representatives of the local party, soviet activists, and functionaries, 309 nationalist, basically anti-Russian fabrications, and 46 instances of disagreement with the measures for restructuring Soviet society were recorded.

A significant number of anonymous incidents occurred in Ukraine, Kazakhstan, Latvia, Lithuania, Moscow, and Leningrad.

In 1987, 1,312 authors of pamphlets, letters, and graffiti were identified. Of this number, 33 persons admitted to statements of a terrorist nature about the leaders of the party and the government, and 67 to threats of physical violence against local party and soviet activists and functionaries.

Of the total number of authors investigated, 37.2% are university students, high school students, and students in vocational schools, 18.6% are workers, 16.8% are office workers, 9.5% are retired persons, 17.9% are other categories of citizens, including persons serving time in correctional-labor facilities.

Among the authors who were identified are 59 members and candidate members of the Communist Party and 361 members of the Young Communist League.

Reasons for preparing and distributing anonymous materials are: nationalist sentiments (248 persons); dissatisfaction with measures taken to strengthen discipline and fight drunkenness and alcoholism (187 persons); inadequacies in the food supply to the population and also high prices for certain manufactured goods (43 persons); difficulties with housing and household needs (41 persons); hooliganism (238 persons); mercenary motives (86 persons); mental illness (86 persons); illegal actions by some local leaders manifested in coarse treatment of subordinates, officious treatment of citizens' petitions, violations of ethical behavior, etc. (23 persons).

The reasons for the preparation and distribution of anonymous materials by the remaining 276 authors are now being investigated.

After appropriate review, the majority of the authors under investigation (55.6%) were dealt with through measures of a preventive nature; 66 persons were tried pursuant to articles of the general Criminal Code of the RSFSR and the criminal codes of other union republics.

The *KGB* is implementing measures to prevent and suppress in a timely fashion negative incidents connected with the distribution of anonymous materials of hostile content and to increase the effectiveness of the effort to identify the authors and distributors of these materials.

For your information.

Committee Chairman   [signed] V. Chebrikov

Source?

Party Purges from Kirov to the Doctors' Plot

The party purge, or cleansing, emerged as an important ritual of Communist political culture in the critical months of the Civil War. Aware that party growth had been fueled not just by zealous activists but also by careerists and free-riders seeking merely to enjoy the perquisites of party membership, party organizations in 1919 launched a systematic review of their membership, weeding out or purging those individuals who did not measure up to the high standards expected of Communists. Such purges were repeated in 1921, 1924, 1925, 1928, and 1929: grounds for expulsion included being a member of the wrong class, corruption, passivity, religious belief, and immorality. In 1921, faced with severe political opposition within and outside its ranks, the party's Tenth Congress also adopted a policy that organized opposition to party policy be punished by expulsion from the party. This policy was used to expel dozens of important party figures, oppositionists who attempted to displace Stalin at the Fifteenth Party Congress in 1927. Trotsky, Bukharin, Zinoviev, Kamenev, and other future victims of the purges of the 1930s were formally expelled by the Fifteenth Congress. Most of them were subsequently readmitted to the party, after apologies and new professions of loyalty, only to become victims once again in the Great Purge that culminated in 1937–38.

The next, more bloody round of purges began with the mysterious murder of the Leningrad party leader, Sergei Kirov, in December 1934. The investigation implicated high party officials, and hundreds of party members were questioned, arrested, and forced to incriminate ever widening circles in society. "Enemies of the people" were found everywhere. A so-called conspiracy among military commanders was tried in secret and revealed only after their execution. The public prosecution of these enemies culminated in three grand show trials in Moscow. In August 1936 sixteen defendants went on trial as members of the "Trotskyite-Zinovievite Terrorist Center," including Zinoviev and Kamenev. (Trotsky, after his expulsion from the party in 1927, was subsequently exiled to Central Asia and then expelled from the country. The archvillain behind all of these accusations, he was assassinated in Mexico by a Soviet agent in 1940.) Seventeen members of the "Anti-Soviet Trotskyite Center," including Karl Radek and IUrii Piatakov, faced trial in January 1937.

The final trial, of the "Anti-Soviet Bloc of Rights and Trotskyites" in March 1938, included Nikolai Bukharin and Aleksei Rykov. Firsthand accounts of many survivors of this nightmarish period in Soviet history have provided many facts and details of the process; the documents included here offer poignant insights into the tragic personal side of this era.

Scholars disagree on how many victims perished as a result of these purges and of Stalin's other policies. The documents revealed here provide no quick resolution to this disagreement, nor is an answer likely to be easily or conclusively found. Likewise, the question of motive remains unresolved. Why did Stalin launch these purges? Some have argued that he faced opposition within the party after the collectivization travails and that the Seventeenth Party Congress in 1934 was prepared to replace him with Kirov. Others have suggested that the purges were an elaborate cover-up of Stalin's secret past as a tsarist police agent. Roy Medvedev argued that one factor was the contradiction between Stalin's limitless ambition and his limited abilities, causing him to believe that all his associates, past, present, or future, had to be seen as potential enemies. The linkage between Stalin and the purges was critical: just before Stalin died in 1953 a new round of purges was signaled with the arrest of a group of Kremlin doctors who were charged with assassinating high officials. Stalin's death in March 1953 and the arrest of his police chief Beria put an end to these accusations, and although arrest and repression continued as part of the repertoire of Soviet politics, nothing on the scale of Stalin's purges ever recurred.

DOCUMENT 30 *Instructions for carrying out verification of party documents and purging the party membership, June 15, 1921*

MINUTES OF A MEETING OF THE ORGANIZATIONAL
SUBCOMMISSION TO REVIEW AND PURGE
THE MEMBERSHIP OF THE
RUSSIAN COMMUNIST PARTY

June 15 of this year [1921]

Persons in attendance: Comrades Zalutskii, Krinitskii, Mikhailov, Unshlikht, Kuchmenko, and Laida

SUBJECT:
1) Draft of an investigative procedure and guidelines for reviewing and purging the membership of the Russian Communist Party submitted by Comrade Zalutskii.

DECISIONS:
1) Initiate a purge of the party from the top down regardless of position.
2) Eliminate the passive element from Soviet government agencies.
3) Rid the factories and plants of nonproletarian elements.
4) Purge the *kulak*s in the countryside.
Organize a subcommission consisting of Comrades

Zalutskii, Krinitskii, and Unshlikht to draft detailed guidelines for these processes.

Form a subcommission consisting of Comrades Gusev and Laida to develop proposals for purging military organizations.

The subcommissions have three days to complete their work.

GENERAL GUIDELINES FOR REVIEWING, VERIFYING, AND PURGING PARTY MEMBERS

The Elements That Should Be Eliminated from the Party

The primary objectives of the process of reviewing, verifying, and purging the party's membership are: 1) remove from the party non-Communist, antiproletarian elements who are indifferent to the interests of the working class; and 2) remove elements that are not amenable to Communist reeducation and reform, including members of the old bourgeoisie, officials of the old regime, and various specialists and petty-bourgeois intelligentsia who are almost completely alien to the proletariat and party but who joined the party in recent years.

The very fact that the party contains these elements, including elements that are alien to the party and the working class, can be attributed to a large number of factors and circumstances in the era of the dictatorship of the proletariat, an era in which the Communist Party is the ruling party and has been in power for several years as the ruler of a gigantic country; this is one of the main factors attracting undesirable non-Communist and even anti-proletarian elements into the party. We must thoroughly rid ourselves of these elements by checking each member individually and by interviewing his coworkers who know him with regard to his performance, actions, and day-to-day attitudes towards the proletarian revolution and Soviet power and who could provide an objective, impartial evaluation of the individual.

Even during the war, when the outcome of the fighting at the fronts was very uncertain and when it was difficult to tell which side would win, alien and hostile elements were able to infiltrate the party for different motives and reasons. Many philistine, petit bourgeois elements in Soviet government agencies were nominated for membership and joined the party for reasons quite different from their ideals and revolutionary motives and aspirations. They wanted to take advantage of their party membership to get promoted to more responsible positions and jobs and thus get better living conditions, better rations, and so forth. Hence in reviewing, verifying, and purging the membership, we must focus special attention on and thoroughly review, verify, and purge the membership in government office cells. But if hostile and at best apolitical philistine elements more concerned with their personal well-being than the interests of proletarian struggle and revolution were able to infiltrate the party, albeit in small numbers, even during the war, even when the outcome was unclear, one might expect an even greater influx of antiproletarian elements into the party once the victory of Soviet power was certain and once party membership did not entail even the slightest risk of retaliation for party membership, which was the fate hanging over every member during the war against Kolchak, Denikin, IUdenich, and the others if the wrong side had won. These dangers and risks obviously required a more sincere and conscientious attitude and willingness to sacrifice on the part of the individuals joining the party. The barriers and safeguards which protected the party from non-Communist elements were lowered as the fighting died down and the counterrevolutionary hopes of crushing Soviet Russia with military force were dashed. This period was marked by the admission of small groups and entire factions from other parties who had previously wavered or opposed the Communist Party and Soviet power. The truce with Poland and Wrangel's defeat were followed by a period in the history of Soviet Russia similar to the one we are experiencing today, in which there are no external fronts and a quasi-peaceful balance prevails. The international bourgeoisie and the Russian counterrevolutionaries were forced to change their tactics, abandon their hope of strangling Soviet Russia by force, and engage in a more prolonged conflict using different tactics. The same period has been characterized by a rather slow and gradual change in the economic policy of the capitalist countries towards Soviet Russia, i.e., the gradual abandonment of the embargo and the beginning of trade agreements between individual capitalist countries and major capitalist corporations with Soviet Russia.

It goes without saying that the lack of any clear and obvious risk of deprivation and persecution for party membership and, conversely, the possibility of taking advantage of party membership for personal goals and privileges has drawn alien and even hostile bourgeois and petit bourgeois elements into the party, because the party, through the government and its officials, is beginning to rebuild the country's economy on the basis of the money economy of the transitional era, is organizing wholesale and retail trade in the country, is concluding trade agreements and business deals with other countries, is taking steps to secure supplies and food for the country, and is the owner of the remnants of large-scale industry and transportation. All of these activities have tempted both unproletarian and anti-proletarian elements to join the party. Hence we should subject individuals who have joined the party recently, especially former members of other parties such as the Mensheviks, Socialist Revolutionaries, and so forth, to the same type of thorough, meticulous, and comprehensive investigation and review.

Because the RKP is the country's ruling party, outright enemies of the proletariat and hired agents and provocateurs of the Western European bourgeois countries and counterrevolutionary Russian organizations have made every conceivable effort to infiltrate our party, in the same way that our illegal party was infiltrated by agents and provocateurs of the tsarist secret police for provocation purposes and to destroy our party from within. Hence in reviewing and purging the membership of the party, we should concentrate on eliminating individuals who are undermining party discipline, spreading provocative rumors, and slandering the party, party institutions, and Soviet power. The same kind of alertness and thoroughness should be exercised in purging criminal, quasi-gangster, and shady and corrupt elements in various important positions. Finally, we must exercise extreme caution, alertness, and thoroughness in purging, reviewing, and investigating peasant cells in the countryside and villages, which in all probability might be infiltrated by *kulak* bourgeois elements, as well as peasants who do not exploit the labor of others, especially if we consider that proletarian power in Russia, with its current semibourgeois, transitional economic base, its very weak nationalized socialist industry, and its encirclement by capitalist countries, has had to do everything it can to assist the growth of proletarian revolution in the Western European and Transatlantic countries and, at the same time, take all possible steps to preserve its alliance with the millions and millions of peasants by protecting them from the gentry and the moneylenders and assisting them in improving their farming operations, which in turn has attracted the more sincere and conscientious elements of the working peasantry to the party, along with hostile *kulak* elements who are not amenable to party reform.

Last name. . . . .
First name and patronymic . . . .
City of assignment. . . . .   Agency/office. . . . .
Job title . . . .

Category	Item	5	4	3	2	1
1.	Stability, and steadfastness of party convictions, political training	Stable and steadfast party member	Stable party member	Maturing party member	Unpredictable party member	Vacillating and wavering party member
2.	Ulterior motives for joining movement (Communist Party)	Dedication to ideology and working class	Job satisfaction	Vanity	Minor personal benefits	Personal well-being
3.	Tact, flexibility of behavior, thinking, attitude towards others	Liked by everyone	Diplomatic and easy to get along with	Sometimes hostile	Troublemaker	Intriguer
4.	Interest in Marxism, Marxist training	Profound and comprehensive knowledge	Extensive knowledge of certain subjects	Superficial knowledge	Fragmentary knowledge based on hearsay	Not interested
5.	Discipline, attitude towards party and government directives	Eager	Conscientious	Procrastinator	Faker	Disobedient

Category	Item	5	4	3	2	1
6.	Character, courage of convictions	Persistent	Firm	Gives up easily	Weak character, unprincipled	Shameless compromiser
7.	Tact, temperament	Polite, restrained	Even-tempered	Hot-tempered	Easily upset	Irritable
8.	Mental agility	Quick and inventive	Resourceful	Somewhat clumsy	Slow	Dull and unresponsive
9.	Objectivity and self-criticism	Self-critical	Admits mistakes	Doesn't admit mistakes, but corrects them	Stubborn and argumentative	Combative and easily offended
10.	Receptivity to knowledge, sophistication, capacity for self-improvement	Doesn't know that he knows (modest)	Knows that he knows	Knows that he doesn't (wants to know)	Doesn't know that he doesn't know (ignorant)	Doesn't want to know that he doesn't know
11.	Lifestyle (financial status)	Satisfied with what he has	Reasonable needs	Desire for comfort	*Bon vivant*	Love of luxury
12.	Ability to handle work and people	A leader. People find it easy to follow him	Good leader	Poor leader	(Helpless) Easily influenced by others	Other people control him
13.	Initiative, originality of thinking, willingness to try new methods	Great initiative	Average initiative	Quite progressive-minded	Does what he's told.	Sticks to the same old routine
14.	Teamwork. Awareness and understanding of common goals.	Close contact (aware)	Works well with others	Narrow specialist (bureaucratic)	Finds it difficult to work with others	Obstructionist
15.	Ability to plan, organize, and systematize work	Aware of and in control of every detail	Good when everything is going well	Takes up the slack for his co-workers	Spins his wheels	Disorganized (dull)
16.	Ability to inspire interest and enthusiasm in his colleagues	Interesting and inspiring person	Impressive	Average	Boring and listless	Kills any enthusiasm
17.	Approach to the task, ability to separate the important from the unimportant, ability to set the tone and the pace	Breadth and vision	Gets a feel for the job and thinks	Absorbed in petty details, doesn't see the big picture	Can't see the forest for the trees	Just doesn't get the point

RTSKhIDNI, fond 17, op. 86, d. 8, ll. 2

The Seventeenth Party Congress, 1934

The Communist Party's Seventeenth Congress assembled in January 1934, the first party congress to be held since the breakneck days of rapid industrialization and collectivization in the period from 1929 to 1931. This was to be the "Congress of Victors" and of reconciliation. The worst travails of the collectivization process were over, opposition within the party had been defeated, and the themes of this congress were to be victory over economic backwardness, reconciliation between state and society, and a return to normalcy. This yearning was accompanied, in some party circles, by an anti-Stalin backlash. The cult of Stalin continued to be fostered by those around the General Secretary, but he had antagonized many comrades with his handling of opposition within the party in 1932 and 1933. Perhaps it was time for a new type of leader to take the reins of power. To this end, certain party oligarchs gathered conspiratorially on the eve of the Seventeenth Congress to plot a change in the leadership: many saw the dynamic leader of the Leningrad party organization, Sergei Kirov, as the natural and appropriate successor to Stalin, and, on the tenth anniversary of his death, to Lenin himself. Reports differ as to whether Kirov seriously considered joining the plot, or whether he reported its existence to Stalin as soon as he was approached. But there was no question that Kirov's speech to the Congress, though utterly loyal to Stalin, inspired spontaneous enthusiasm from the delegates and led naturally to talk about which of the two was more popular. According to a number of eyewitnesses, the challenge to Stalin became even more overt in the normally pro forma elections to the next Central Committee, which occurred at the end of the Congress. On the list of candidates for the Central Committee [listed in Document 34], delegates were to cross out the names of any they wished to vote against; an absolute majority of ballots was required for election. Kirov received only 3 or 4 negative votes, but Stalin received many more, 100 to 300 according to recollections. Kirov allegedly informed Stalin of these totals, and Stalin thereupon ordered that most of the negative ballots be destroyed. The official number of delegates voting became 1,059 instead of 1,225, Stalin received 1,056 votes, and Kirov 1 less. These accounts remain unconfirmed by the documents presented here, which reflect the cover-up rather than the true depth of anti-Stalin sentiment at the Seventeenth Congress of the Communist Party.

S. Kirov and M. Chudov at the 17th Congress of the *VKP(b)*, Moscow, January 1934. TSGAKFD

DOCUMENT 31   ***Delegate card of S. M. Kirov for the Seventeenth Party Congress, January 26, 1934***

Proletarians of all Countries, Unite!

ALL-UNION
COMMUNIST PARTY
(Bolshevik)

CREDENTIAL No. <u>9</u>

The bearer of this, Comrade <u>Kirov S.M.</u> has been selected as a delegate to the 17th Congress of the All-Union Communist party (of Bolsheviks) from the <u>Leningrad</u> organization, with full voting rights.

Secretary of the Central Committee
[signature illegible]

Member of the Credentials Commission   [signature illegible]

RTSKhIDNI, fond 80, op. 18, d. 151, l. 1

DOCUMENT 32   *Minutes of the Vote-Counting Commission of the Seventeenth Party Congress, February 9, 1934, on procedures and ballot box assignments*

MINUTES No. 1

OF THE JANUARY 9, 1934, SESSION OF THE VOTE-COUNTING COMMISSION
AT THE XVII CONGRESS OF THE ALL-UNION COMMUNIST PARTY (BOLSHEVIKS)

Chairman — Zatonskii
Secretary — Osvenskii

On the procedure for counting votes and assigning commission members to ballot boxes

Distribute commission members in the following manner:

Ballot box no. 1 (1–100) — Comrades Kontorin, Shakhgil'dian, Il'in, Voltsit, Kuznetsov.
Ballot box no. 2 (101–200) — Comrades Semin, Gorchaev, Grishin, Akbotin, Kekediia.
Ballot box no. 3 (201–300) — Comrades Viatkin, Kudriavtsev, Stakun, Popok, Vatsek.
Ballot box no. 4 (301–400) — Comrades Gorbunov, Slavin, Starukhin, Kelarev.
Ballot box no. 5 (401–500) — Comrades Viksnin, Kulagin, Druian, Vaichurin.
Ballot box no. 6 (501–600) — Comrades IAkobson, Vakhlamov, Amelin, Velen'kii.
Ballot box no. 7 (601–700) — Comrades Gurevich, Ivanov, Vainov, Levitin, Akopov.
Ballot box no. 8 (701–800) — Comrades Kolotilin, Shir-Mukhamedov, Markitan, Isanchurin, Ryskin.
Ballot box no. 9 (801–900) — Comrades Lapidus, Andreev, Murafer, Marchik, Shilkhin.
Ballot box no. 10 (901–1000) — Comrades Kalnin, IAstrebov, Smirnov, Fedorovich, Podarin.
Ballot box no. 11 (1001–1100) — Comrades Butkevich, Arkhipov, Pakov, Kogan, Tarasov.
Ballot box no. 12 (1101–1200) — Comrades Shestakov, Karklin, Karavaev, Andreasian, Margulis.
Ballot box no. 13 (1201–1300) — Comrades Esiak, I. Alekseev, Levitin (Crimea) Verkhovykh.

CHAIRMAN [signed] V. Zatonskii
SECRETARY [signed] M. Osvenskii

RTSKhIDNI, fond 59, op. 2, d. 46, l. 1

DOCUMENT 33   *Report on the voting at the Seventeenth Party Congress, February 10, 1934*

MINUTE NO 2
OF THE MEETING OF THE
COMMISSION TO COUNT VOTES
AT THE 17TH CONGRESS OF THE
ALL-UNION COMMUNIST PARTY (BOLSHEVIK) (*VKP(b)*)
ON FEBRUARY 10, 1934

The Commission has established that a total of 1,059 ballots were cast at the 17th Congress of the *VKP(b)*.

All of the individuals nominated by the conference of delegations for membership in the Central Committee [*TSK*] of the *VKP(b)*, candidate status for membership in the *TSK*, membership in the Inspection Commission, membership in the Party Control Commission, and membership in the Soviet Control Commission are hereby declared elected as having received an absolute majority of votes.

Tallies of the number of votes received by each comrade elected to a specific body are attached to this document.

CHAIRMAN OF THE VOTE COUNT COMMISSION [signed] (Zatonskii)

SECRETARY OF THE COMMISSION [signed] (Osvenskii)

RTSKhIDNI, fond 59, op. 2, d. 46, l. 2.

DOCUMENT 34   *List of members and candidates for the* TSK KPSS *and Soviet and Party Control Commissions, with vote totals of the "aye" votes, February 5–10, 1934*

17TH CONGRESS OF THE ALL-UNION COMMUNIST PARTY (BOLSHEVIK)
LIST OF MEMBERS AND CANDIDATES FOR MEMBERSHIP IN THE CENTRAL COMMITTEE [*TSK*] OF THE *VKP(b)* [BALLOT]

Proposed by a conference of representatives of all the delegations to the congress
NOMINEES FOR FULL MEMBERSHIP:

Name	Votes	Name	Votes
1. Alekseev P. A.	1057	30. Krzhizhanovskii G. M.	1058
2. Andreev A. A.	1044	31. Krinitskii A. I.	1026
3. Antipov N. K.	1039	32. Krupskaia N. K.	1057
4. Badaev A. E.	1054	33. Kuibyshev V. V.	1045
5. Balitskii V. A.	1046	34. Lavrent'ev L. I.	1045
6. Bauman K. IA.	1046	35. Lebed' D. Z.	1019
7. Beria L. P.	1028	36. Litvinov M. M.	1055
8. Bubnov A. S.	1054	37. Lobov S. S.	1042
9. Vareikis I. M.	1054	38. Liubimov I. E.	1038
10. Voroshilov K. E.	1057	39. Manuil'skii D. Z.	1058
11. Gamarnik IA. B.	1057	40. Mezhlauk V. I.	1050
12. Evdokimov E. G.	1053	41. Mikoyan A. I.	1056
13. Ezhov N. I.	1043	42. Mirzoian L. I.	1034
14. Enukidze A. S.	1057	43. Molotov V. M.	1054
15. Zhdanov A. A.	1052	44. Nikolaeva K. I.	1045
16. Zhukov I. P.	1034	45. Nosov I. P.	1034
17. Zelenskii I. A.	1039	46. Ordzhonikidze G. K.	1056
18. Ivanov V. I.	1056	47. Petrovskii G. I.	1044
19. Ikramov Akmal'	1054	48. Postyshev P. P.	1044
20. Kabakov I. D.	1055	49. Piatakov IU. L.	1044
21. Kaganovich L. M.	1045	50. Piatnitskii I. A.	1058
22. Kaganovich M. M.	1009	51. Razumov M. O.	1052
23. Kalinin M. I.	1059	52. Rudzutak IA. E.	1053
24. Kirov S. M.	1055	53. Rumiantsev I. P.	1057
25. Knorin V. G.	1056	54. Rukhimovich M. L.	1049
26. Kodatskii I. F.	1059	55. Ryndin K. V.	1026
27. Kosarev A. V.	1052	56. Stalin J. V.	1056
28. Kosior I. V.	1039	57. Stetskii A. I.	1046
29. Kosior S. V.	1028	58. Sulimov D. E.	1058

Name	Votes	Name	Votes
59. Ukhanov K. V.	1029	66. Shvernik N. M.	1050
60. Khataevich M. M.	1035	67. Sheboldaev B. P.	1047
61. Khrushchev N. S.	1037	68. Eikhe R. I.	1058
62. Chernov M. A.	1018	69. IAgoda G. G.	1039
63. Chubar' V. IA.	1050	70. IAkir I. E.	1049
64. Chuvyrin M. E.	1042	71. IAkovlev IA. A.	941
65. Chudov M. S.	1053		

NOMINEES FOR CANDIDATE MEMBERSHIP STATUS:

Name	Votes	Name	Votes
1. Bagirov M. D.	1045	35. Mikhailov V. M.	1003
2. Blagonravov G. I.	1035	36. Mikhailov M. E.	1044
3. Bliukher V. K.	1051	37. Musabekov G.	1054
4. Budennyi S. M.	1025	38. Osinskii V. V.	1042
5. Bulganin N. A.	1050	39. Pavlunovskii I. I.	1011
6. Bulin A. S.	1048	40. Pakhomov N. I.	1055
7. Bukharin N. I.	978	41. Pozern B. P.	1044
8. Broido G. I.	983	42. Polonskii V. I.	969
9. Bykin IA. B.	1050	43. Popov N. N.	1040
10. Veger E. I.	1039	44. Poskrebyshev A. N.	1022
11. Veinberg G. D.	959	45. Ptukha V. V.	1037
12. Gikalo N. F.	1038	46. Rozengol'ts A. P.	1034
13. Goloded N. M.	1042	47. Rykov A. I.	858
14. Grin'ko G. F.	858	48. Sarkisov S. A.	1036
15. Griadinskii F. N.	1056	49. Sedel'nikov A. I.	1033
16. Demchenko N. N.	1024	50. Semenov B. A.	1048
17. Deribas G. D.	1042	51. Serebrovskii A. P.	1029
18. Egorov A. I.	1030	52. Smorodin P. I.	1054
19. Eremin I. G.	1054	53. Sokol'nikov G. IA.	1003
20. Zaveniagin A. P.	1042	54. Strievskii K. K.	1041
21. Zatonskii V. P.	1019	55. Struppe P. I.	1053
22. Isaev U. D.	1054	56. Tovstukha I. P.	1053
23. Kalmanovich M. I.	1046	57. Tomskii M. P.	801
24. Kaminskii G. N.	1055	58. Tukhachevskii M. N.	1045
25. Kalygina A. S.	1047	59. Uborevich I. P.	965
26. Komarov N. P.	1011	60. Ugarov A. I.	1037
27. Kubiak N. A.	962	61. Unshlikht I. S.	1053
28. Kul'kov M. M.	1047	62. Filatov N. A.	1014
29. Kuritsyn V. I.	1051	63. Shvarts S.	1040
30. Lena A. K.	1046	64. Shteingardt A. M.	1015
31. Lozovskii S. A.	1046	65. Shubrikov V. P.	1057
32. Liubchenko P. P.	844	66. Eliava Sh. Z.	1044
33. Makarov I. G.	1044	67. IUrkin T. A.	1039
34. Mekhlis L. Z.	1038		

Comments: a) Voting is allowed only with these ballots, and any changes to the list must be made on this ballot.

b) If you want to replace any of the candidates listed on the ballot, cross his name out and write the last name of your candidate next to it.

c) Writing in any names in excess of the number indicated on the ballot is prohibited.

[Illegible note indicating person responsible for preliminary tally of the votes before the commission made its final count.]

[handwritten:] The number of votes received by the comrades listed have been verified. Chairman of the Vote Counting Commission

17TH CONGRESS OF THE *VKP(b)*

LIST OF MEMBERS OF THE PARTY CONTROL COMMISSION
[BALLOT]
Proposed by a conference of representatives of all the delegations to the congress

Name	Votes	Name	Votes
1. Kaganovich L. M.	1053	31. Lychev I. A.	1052
2. Ezhov N. I.	1052	32. Meerzon Zh. I.	986
3. Shkiriatov M. F.	1054	33. Moskatov P. G.	1051
4. IAroslavskii Em.	1049	34. Murugov I. V.	1053
5. Akulov I. A.	1052	35. Os'mov N. M.	1056
6. Peters IA. Kh.	1054	36. Pospelov P. N.	1052
7. Bulatov D. A.	1055	37. Paparde L. A.	1056
8. Akulinushkin P. D.	1044	38. Pshenitsyn K. F.	997
9. Bekker I. M.	1051	39. Petrovskii A. N.	1057
10. Berezin N. S.	1055	40. Rabichev N. N.	1016
11. Bogushevskii V. S.	890	41. Rubenov R. G.	1030
12. Brikke S. K.	1012	42. Rubinshtein M. I.	1059
13. Zalikin A. T.	1047	43. Sakharova P. F.	1041
14. Bukharin K. I.	1051	44. Sakh'ianova M. M.	1055
15. Vasil'ev S. V.	1057	45. Stavskii V. P.	1049
16. Volkov V. L.	1053	46. Stepanov M. T.	1058
17. Genkin E. B.	1036	47. Saltanov S. A.	1041
18. Granovskii M. L.	1049	48. Sorokin M. L.	1052
19. Grossman V. IA.	1030	49. Temkin M. M.	1019
20. Davidson R. E.	1051	50. Frenkel' A. A.	1032
21. Dvinskii B. A.	1053	51. Khavkin S. T.	1041
22. Zhukovskii S. B.	1057	52. Chubin IA. A.	1050
23. Zaitsev F. I.	1047	53. Shadunts S. K.	1041
24. Zashibaev A. S.	1059	54. Sharangovich V. F.	1049
25. Zimin N. N.	1010	55. Shaburova M. A.	1044
26. Karavaev P. N.	1056	56. Shestakov V. I.	1058
27. Kakhiani M. I.	1041	57. Shokhin A. P.	1055
28. Kubar' T. F.	1052	58. Shustin A. IA.	1046
29. Kuibyshev N. V.	1048	59. IUrevich E. I.	1055
30. Levin A. A.	1044	60. IAkovlev A. I.	1026

Comments: a) Voting is allowed only with these ballots, and any changes to the list must be made on this ballot.

b) If you want to replace any of the candidates listed on the ballot, cross his name out and write the last name of your candidate next to it.

c) Writing in any names in excess of the number indicated on the ballot is prohibited.

LIST OF MEMBERS OF THE SOVIET CONTROL COMMISSION
[BALLOT]

Proposed by a conference of representatives of all the delegations to the congress

Name	Votes	Name	Votes
1. Kuibyshev V. V.	1056	36. Kissis R. IA.	1043
2. Antipov N. K.	1048	37. Krivin M. G.	1055
3. Belen'kii Z. M.	1044	38. Kozlovskaia A. IA.	1054
4. Antselovich N. M.	1044	39. Kalashnikov V. S.	1029
5. Gaister A. I.	1044	40. Korostashevskii I.E.	1053
6. Prokof'ev G. E.	1052	41. Soms K. P.	1051
7. Lomov G. I.	1049	42. Mal'tsev K. A.	1054
8. TSikhon A. M.	1053	43. Manfred S. A.	1054
9. Zemliachka R. S.	1042	44. Miroshnikov I. I.	1056
10. Moskvin I. M.	1034	45. Melamed G.	1059
11. Roizenman B. A.	1046	46. Morgunov N. S.	1057
12. Bogdanov I. A.	1056	47. Mezhlauk I. I.	1050
13. Bazilevich G. D.	1048	48. Nazaretian A. M.	1039
14. Bauer IA. IA.	1054	49. Uralov S. G.	1054
15. Bukhanov A. A.	1059	50. Gusev A. N.	1055
16. Balakhnin S. M.	1055	51. Oshvintsev M. K.	1038
17. Bukatyi V. L.	1039	52. Perekatov I. G.	1043
18. Bogat A. P.	1056	53. Pylaev G. N.	1057
19. Voznesenskii N. A.	1050	54. Petrunichev I. A.	1054
20. Veinbaum E. I.	1058	55. Pronin I. S.	1049
21. Vengerova R. S.	1057	56. Paskutskii N. A.	1051
22. Gemmervert M. I.	1057	57. Remeiko A. G.	1033
23. Gindin IA. I.	1046	58. Rozit A. R.	1052
24. Gei K. V.	1049	59. Remizov M. P.	1059
25. Gladshtein IU. M.	1056	60. Romanovskii V. I.	1057
26. Gol'dich L. E.	1039	61. Sulkovskii F. V.	1045
27. Deich M. A.	1044	62. Strel'tsov G. M.	1037
28. Dogadov A. I.	1027	63. Sud'in S. K.	1058
29. Egorov IA. G.	1057	64. Trilisser M. A.	1050
30. Zhuchaev D. A.	1053	65. Terekhov R. IA.	974
31. Il'in N. I.	1057	66. Ulianova M. I.	1057
32. Ivanov N. G.	1057	67. Feigin V. G.	1026
33. Ivanov A. A.	1057	68. TSarev P. S.	1055
34. Karpov V. I.	1057	69. Shablievskii G. V.	1052
35. Karlik A. I.	1044	70. Khakhan'ian G. D.	1056

Comments: a) Voting is allowed only with these ballots, and any changes to the list must be made on this ballot.

b) If you want to replace any of the candidates listed on the ballot, cross his name out and write the last name of your candidate next to it.

c) Writing in any names in excess of the number indicated on the ballot is prohibited.

[Handwritten, upper left corner:] The number of votes received by the comrades listed has been verified. Chairman of the Vote Counting Commission

RTSKhIDNI, fond 58, op. 46, d. 2, ll. 3, 30b, 4–5 [or, per Russian final list, fond 59, op. 2, d. 46, ll. 3–5]

The Kirov Murder

Less than a year after the Seventeenth Party Congress had accorded Sergei Kirov a prominent place in the hearts of party delegates, the popular Leningrad party leader was assassinated in the corridor leading to his office by a young Communist, Leonid Nikolaev. The murder provoked immediate accusations of a widescale conspiracy against the Soviet Union itself: Nikolaev had acted as part of a plot involving a "Trotskyite-Zinovievite platform," a "Leningrad center" whose purpose was to overthrow the regime. The investigation of the murder led to new sensational revelations about "enemies" and launched the wholesale attack on the party, the Great Purge.

The question of who planned the murder of Kirov and why he was killed has remained one of the great mysteries of Soviet history. Stalin ordered an immediate investigation and traveled to Leningrad to direct the interrogations personally. One of the witnesses to the murder was killed mysteriously in an automobile crash en route to the interrogation. Gossip on the street in Leningrad linked Stalin with the killing, and most historical accounts conclude convincingly that Stalin arranged the murder, probably with a twofold purpose in mind. Killing Kirov would remove a powerful rival, and it would justify a new all-out assault on other waverers and dissidents, consolidating Stalin's control of the party, and the party's control of the country. Nonetheless, Stalin's guilt has never been proven, although the case has been revisited at the highest levels of the Soviet leadership several times since the death of Stalin. Khrushchev, in his secret speech to the Twentieth Party Congress in 1956, alleged that Stalin was responsible for Kirov's murder, and several commissions were appointed to sift the evidence in the following years. Their conclusion was that there was no conspiracy, that Nikolaev, a disgruntled and unstable party member, had acted alone. Another Central Committee commission was appointed under Gorbachev to investigate the affair; again, the direct hand of Stalin was not found, although the chairman of the commission, Yakovlev, concluded, "Questions have arisen for which there are still no convincing answers."

To Comrade B. K. Pugo

<u>TO MEMBERS OF THE COMMISSION OF THE POLITBURO OF THE CENTRAL COMMITTEE OF THE COMMUNIST PARTY OF THE SOVIET UNION CONCERNED WITH ADDITIONAL STUDY OF THE MATERIALS ON THE REPRESSIONS OF THE 30S, 40S, AND EARLY 50S.</u>

Return to *TSK KPSS*
(General Department, Section II)

NOT FOR PUBLICATION

No St-87(k)
March 26, 1990

<u>Some Thoughts on the Results of the
Inquiry Into the Circumstances
Surrounding the Murder of S. M. Kirov</u>

A memorandum examined by the commission provided a comprehensive analysis of facts and documents gathered by the Central Committee commissions appointed in the 1950s and 1960s to explore the circumstances surrounding S. M. Kirov's murder. The basic conclusions of the most recent investigation were that the available evidence indicates that the act of terrorism perpetrated against S. M. Kirov was planned and committed by Nikolaev alone. In 1933–34 there was no counterrevolutionary terrorist organization in Leningrad, nor any so-called Leningrad Center. There is no proof on which to base any accusations that G. IA. Biseneks, the former consul of bourgeois Latvia in Leningrad, was involved in arranging Kirov's murder. There is also no proof of a plot to murder Kirov involving his bodyguard, M. V. Borisov, who died in an automobile accident. And finally the memorandum states that there is no evidence confirming the involvement of J. V. Stalin and the People's Commissariat of Internal Affairs [*NKVD*] in organizing and carrying out Kirov's murder, either in the criminal case files on Nikolaev, Kotolynov, et al., or in the documents uncovered by the investigations conducted in 1956–1967 and 1988–1989.

In my personal opinion, these findings and the supporting evidence for them cannot be accepted unconditionally, because questions have arisen for which there are still no convincing answers. [break in the text]

Why did IAgoda take the blame for arranging Kirov's murder? At his trial in 1938, he publicly stated that agents from *NKVD* central headquarters and the Leningrad Directorate of the *NKVD* had arranged and committed this murder. So why did he make this public confession, fabricated by the investigators, of crimes that IAgoda and the persons he named did not commit? IAgoda was included in an imaginary "rightist Trotskyite bloc" that never existed. Not only did he not associate with any of the imaginary members of this faction in any way, he even had unfriendly and often hostile relations with them. We have no idea what was said at the closed sessions of the trial where IAgoda gave his testimony. Were any attempts ever made to determine which cases IAgoda asked the court to examine separately and in closed session? IAgoda had one and only one boss, and that was Stalin. Is that whom they were talking about at the closed sessions of the judicial panel?

So how did IAgoda behave in the latter part of November and on the morning of December 1, 1934? Where was he, what was he doing, whom did he see, what was he interested in, and did he go see Stalin?

The memorandum also ignored the trials at which top officials and agents of the Leningrad *NKVD* were convicted twice on the same charges. Did the persons who drafted the memorandum ever examine the investigation, the material evidence, or the indictments against the *NKVD* agents? If we assume that the murder was arranged by *NKVD* agents, then we must determine who was behind Nikolaev. By the time of the 20th Party Congress, only three of the 12 agents from the Leningrad Directorate of the *NKVD* convicted of dereliction of duty in guarding Kirov were still alive: F. T. Fomin, the deputy chief of the *oblast' NKVD* directorate, and P. M. Lobov, the chief. [break in the text]

. . . of the *oblast'* and city party committees at the time. There is evidence which indicates that even the employees of the department of the Leningrad City Soviet, which was located on the ground floor, had to get a special pass to go to the third floor, where the party *oblast'* committee's offices were located. As we know, not too long before the attempt on Kirov, his retinue of bodyguards had been enlarged from three to fifteen men. But there has been no careful study of how Kirov's personal security was organized or where these bodyguards were at the time of the murder. Obviously, all of these questions are in need of further investigation.

The main conclusion of the Procuracy and *KGB* examination of the circumstances surrounding Kirov's murder was that the act of terrorism was planned and carried out by Nikolaev alone. But the memorandum devotes very little attention to Nikolaev's character and his possible motives for the act and spends very little time analyzing the murder or explaining a number of circumstances which allowed the murder to occur, all of which are extremely important questions. The basic thrust of the memorandum is, first of all, to prove that Stalin was unaware of and had nothing to do with the planning and arrangement of the attempt on Kirov and, second, had absolutely nothing to do with the murder. The third point is that there was absolutely no connection between Nikolaev's actions and any former opposition members and that no such counterrevolutionary terrorist organization as the so-called Leningrad Center ever existed. And finally, the memorandum's fourth point is that Stalin took full advantage of Kirov's murder to organize mass repression in the country. [break in the text]

So what led to this attitude, and what consequences did it have? All of this is completely ignored.

In short, all of the above forces us once again to reopen the investigation of all the circumstances surrounding the murder of S. M. Kirov.

March 23, 1990   [signed] A. Yakovlev

CONCERNING THE RESULTS OF THE EXAMINATION OF MATERIALS OF THE COURT PROCEEDINGS IN THE CASE OF S. M. KIROV'S MURDER

[This is the *KGB* report completed in 1961.]

On December 1, 1934, at 1630 hours in the City of Leningrad, in the headquarters of the *oblast'* committee of the All-Union Communist Party (Bolshevik) [*VKP(b)*], in the third floor corridor, a shot from a revolver killed S. M. Kirov, a member of the Presidium of the Central Executive Committee of the USSR and the Secretary of the Central Committee and the Leningrad *Oblast'* Committee of the *VKP(b)*. The foul murder of S. M. Kirov was committed by one Nikolaev L. V., who was arrested at the scene of the crime.

The following persons were arrested in connection with this terrorist act in December 1934 and were bound over for trial as members of an underground counterrevolutionary terrorist group responsible for arranging S. M. Kirov's murder: Nikolaev L. V., Kotolynov I. I., Shatskii N. N., Rumiantsev V. V., Mandel'shtam S. O., Miasnikov N. P., Levin V. S., Sositskii L. I., Sokolov G. V., IUskin I. G., Zvezdov V. I., Antonov N. S., Khanik L. O., and Tolmazov A. I., a total of 14 individuals.

On December 28 and 29 the case against Nikolaev and the others was heard by the Leningrad Military Collegium of the Supreme Court of the USSR following a streamlined procedure, without calling any witnesses and without a prosecutor or defense attorney.

In its verdict the court stated that in 1933–1934 in Leningrad, an underground terrorist group consisting of former members of the Zinovievite opposition was organized and operated under the direction of a "Leningrad Center," consisting of Levin, Rumiantsev, Kotolynov, Mandel'shtam, Miasnikov, Sositskii, Shatskii, and Nikolaev. This center planned and organized the murder of S. M. Kirov. Under the direct supervision of Kotolynov and with the active cooperation of Shatskii, IUskin, Sokolov, Antonov, Zvezdov, Tolmazov, and Khanik, after lengthy preparations, Nikolaev, under the direct orders of the "Leningrad Center," murdered S. M. Kirov.

The court also determined that the leaders of this terrorist group were hoping for an armed intervention by foreign countries and that for this purpose Nikolaev, on Kotolynov's suggestion, had established criminal relations with Biseneks, the Latvian consul in Leningrad, in September 1934.

The Military Collegium of the Supreme Court of the USSR found all the defendants guilty of participating in the commission of a terrorist act (Article 58-8 of the Criminal Code of the Russian Soviet Federated Socialist Republic (RSFSR)) and being members of an anti-Soviet organization (Article 58-11 of the Criminal Code of the RSFSR) and sentenced them to death by shooting and confiscation of all their personal property. The sentence was not subject to appeal and was executed the very same day, December 29, 1934.

<u>Moral and Political Characteristics of Nikolaev.</u>
<u>His Planning and Execution of the Murder of S. M. Kirov.</u>

S. M. Kirov's murderer, Leonid Vasil'evich Nikolaev, was born in 1904 in the city of Leningrad into a working-class family, had a sixth-grade education, joined the *Komsomol* in 1920, joined the *VKP(b)* in April, 1924, and was expelled from the party by decision of the Party Control Commission of the *TSK VKP(b)* after his arrest as a counterrevolutionary.

Nikolaev's personal papers and official documents provided the following information on his employment history:

1919–20: secretary of a rural soviet in Saratov *guberniia*;
1920–21: orderly at a military hospital in Leningrad;
1921–22: city services employee, Vyborg District, Leningrad;
Sept. 1922–Aug. 1923: business manager of Vyborg District *Komsomol* Committee;
1923–25: metalworker, *Krasnaia Zaria* Plant, Leningrad;
1925–26: business manager, Luga District *Komsomol* Committee, City of Luga;
1926–31: cultural worker, institute construction site; metal worker at *Krasnyi arsenal* and *Karl Marx* plants;
May–Sept. 1931: instructor and consultant of Leningrad *Obkom VKP(b)*
1931–32: Head of Finance Department of the Leningrad *Oblast'* Council of the "Down with Illiteracy!" Society;
Aug. 1932–Oct. 1933: inspector, national price inspectorate of Leningrad *Oblast'* Control Commission and
        Workers' and Peasants' Inspectorate;
1933 to April 1, 1934: instructor at Leningrad Institute of the History of the *VKP(b)*.

In January 1929 Nikolaev was fined by a people's court for riding his bicycle in a reckless manner. The Vyborg District Control Commission of the *VKP(b)* subjected him to public censure on February 22, 1929, for the same offense. During a party purge, on October 16, 1929, a general meeting of his shop cell at the *Krasnyi arsenal* Plant (Plant No 7) reprimanded him "for "stirring up a squabble in the press."

The Primary Party Organization of the Institute of the History of the *VKP(b)* expelled Nikolaev from the party for refusing a mobilization summons to work on the railroads, and on April 1, 1934, he was fired from his job at the institute.

RECOMMENDATIONS

1. In light of the blatant fabrications and obvious flaws in the accusations that Kotolynov, Shatskii, Rumiantsev, Mandel'shtam, Miasnikov, Sositskii, Levin, Antonov, Khanik, Tolmazov, Sokolov, IUskin, and Zvezdov took part in organizing a so-called underground, terrorist, Zinovievite organization headed by the "Leningrad Center," which in reality never existed, and the total lack of involvement of these individuals in preparing and committing the terrorist act against S. M. Kirov, we deem it necessary to invalidate the verdicts against these individuals and close the case against them due to a lack of the elements of a crime in their actions.

The verdict against S. M. Kirov's actual murderer, L. V. Nikolaev, and the classification of his actions as a crime under Article 58-8 of the Criminal Code of the RSFSR (terrorist act) were proper and do not require review.

2. In light of the noninvolvement of G. IA. Biseneks, the former Latvian consul in Leningrad, in Niko-

laev's planning and commission of the murder of S. M. Kirov, and the untruth of the accusations of espionage on behalf of British intelligence against G. IA. Biseneks and his brother V. IA. Biseneks, we deem it necessary to invalidate the verdicts against these individuals and close the case against them due to a lack of the elements of a crime in their actions.

Executive Controller of the Party Control Commission of the Central Committee of the Communist Party of the USSR (*TSK KPSS*) [signed] (A. Kuznetsov)	Assistant Head of the Department of Administrative Agencies of the *TSK KPSS* [signed] (K. Nikitin)
Assistant Chief Military Prosecutor [signed] (A. Ivanov)	Senior Investigator for Sensitive Cases of the Investigative Department of the Committee for State Security [*KGB*] of the Council of Ministers of the USSR [signed] (K. Ushakov)

July 17, 1961

[Recollections of Poskrebyshev, written in 1961]

TO THE PARTY CONTROL COMMISSION
OF THE CENTRAL COMMITTEE
OF THE COMMUNIST PARTY OF THE USSR [*TSK KPSS*]

To Comrade N. M. ShVERNIK

Two officials of the Party Control Commission of the *TSK KPSS*, Comrades V. P. Ganin and A. I. Kuz'min, recently asked me for information on my recollections of events in the distant past related to the murder of S. M. Kirov, in particular: a) the routing and review by the Central Committee of the indictment in the case of Zinoviev, Kamenev, and other persons accused of S. M. Kirov's murder, a copy of which they showed me with additions and corrections in the text in Gertsenberg's handwriting and a few words in my handwriting; and b) the information that Chudov provided to Stalin on Kirov's murder. They asked me to put my answers in writing, which I am doing.

I will qualify my testimony by saying that these events took place 26 years ago, and my age (70) makes it difficult for me to reconstruct much of what took place.

1. The information that Chudov provided to Stalin on Kirov's murder

On December 1, 1934, in the daytime, Chudov, the Secretary of the Leningrad *Obkom* called from Leningrad and asked me to put him through to Stalin because of an emergency, which I did. But Stalin didn't answer the call. Then Chudov asked me to inform Stalin that on this day (December 1), as Kirov was walking down the corridor at Smolny to his office, he was seriously wounded by a shot in the back of the head, that the doctors' efforts to save him were futile, that he died, and that the murderer had been arrested. I asked the secret policemen assigned to guard Stalin to find him and, if he was asleep, to wake him and inform him of Chudov's call and Kirov's murder. A few minutes later Stalin called, and I informed him of Chudov's call and his report of Kirov's murder. He ordered me to put him through to Chudov immediately. After talking with Chudov, Stalin came quickly to the *TSK* and ordered me to call the members of the Politburo and the *TSK* Secretaries to his office.

After the meeting it became clear that Stalin, Voroshilov, and a number of other individuals would have to leave for Leningrad immediately to survey the situation and conduct an investigation of Kirov's murder. They left that very same night.

After returning from Leningrad, Stalin said that Kirov's murder was the work of Zinoviev, Kamenev, and other members of the Leningrad opposition. Subsequently, in 1935, criminal proceedings were initiated against Zinoviev, Kamenev, and other individuals in connection with Kirov's murder.

2. The Routing and Review of the Draft of the Indictment
Against Zinoviev, Kamenev, and Others Accused of Kirov's Murder

In 1935 the prosecutor's office forwarded a draft of an indictment "on the case of Zinoviev, Kamenev, and other individuals accused of Kirov's murder" to the Politburo. This draft was discussed at a special meeting of the Politburo and representatives of the prosecutor's office. Obviously, the decision made at the meeting was not recorded in any kind of official transcript. I don't remember how the draft was routed for additions and corrections. I would imagine that the handwritten corrections were either made by Vyshinsky from Stalin's copy or were dictated to Vyshinsky once the discussion of the draft had concluded.

In turn, Vyshinsky, either at our request or on his own initiative, gave us his copy so that the additions could be included in the other copy to be used as the *TSK* file copy. Gertsenberg, who worked in the same office as Dvinskii and I, made these additions (on a clean copy). With respect to the three words in my handwriting, Gertsenberg might have left them out when he was copying the corrections and the omissions might have been discovered when the two copies were collated, or Vyshinsky might have dictated them to me over the telephone.

Former Head of the
Special Section of the *TSK*
A. Poskrebyshev

July 28, 1961

True copy: [illegible signature]

The original is contained in the files of the commission assigned to review the case of the Zinovievite counterrevolutionary organization "The Moscow Center" (Volume No. 4).

1 of 1 copy
September 9, 1965

Comrade Kirov was wounded at 4:37 P.M. near the waiting room of Comrade Chudov's office. He was found lying face down. Another unknown individual was discovered sprawled in a prone position two or three paces away from him.

An initial examination by Vogin and Rosliakov revealed no signs of a pulse or breathing. Comrade Kirov lay face down, totally immobile, with his legs stretched out, his hands lying by his sides, and with blood flowing copiously from his mouth and nose and some blood on the floor. Seven or eight minutes later Kirov was moved to his office.

As the body was being moved, Doctor Gal'perina arrived and diagnosed facial cyanosis, detected no pulse or respiration, and found dilated pupils with no response to light. They put hot water bottles on Kirov's legs and gave him artificial respiration. At 5:10 P.M. Dr. Vabib [?], Dr. Fel'tstag [?], and Dr. TSatskin arrived, and then at 5:15 Professor Dobrotvorskii arrived and diagnosed a wound in the occipital area. The doctors diagnosed a large hematoma in the frontal portion, applied a tourniquet, and administered three doses of two cubic centimeters of camphor each and two cubic centimeters of caffeine and performed artificial respiration.

Doctor Cherniak arrived at 4:55 P.M.

Doctor Cherniak found Comrade Kirov on the table, with absolutely no pulse, facial cyanosis, cyanosis of the extremities, and dilated pupils with no response to light. He gave Kirov injections of camphor and caffeine and performed artificial respiration . . . [illegible handwritten text] Professor Dobrotvorskii arrived at 5:15 P.M. and diagnosed severe facial cyanosis, dilated pupils with no response to light, and detected no pulse and no heartbeat when he listened to the patient's heart. He performed artificial respiration, administered oxygen, and administered an intracardiac injection of adrenaline and also digalen. The professor observed that the cyanosis was disappearing. He continued to perform artificial respiration for twenty-five minutes.

Professor Dzhanalidze arrived at 5:40 P.M.

He arrived when the other doctors on the scene were performing artificial respiration. He detected no pulse, no breathing, and no heartbeat. He pronounced the situation completely hopeless. In spite of this, the doctors continued to perform artificial respiration for some time. Kirov's pupils were completely dilated and did not respond at all to light. He was pronounced dead.

On the back side of Kirov's cap, on the left, the doctors discovered a clean bullet hole. On Kirov's skull, five fingers from the left ear in the vicinity of the cerebellum, the doctors discovered an entrance wound with slight ecchymosis. One of the doctors used his fingers to probe the entrance wound in the squama occipitalis. The doctors discovered swelling from subcutaneous hemorrhaging above the left arcus superciliaris.

Conclusion: Death occurred instantly as a result of damage to vital nerve centers.

December 1, 1934
7:55 P.M.

Signatures of: Bogen (Director of City Health Department)
Professor Dobrotvorskii
Professor Dzhanalidze
Professor Gesse
Citizen Fridman
Doctor Gal'perina
Doctor Cherniak
Doctor Feierman
Doctor TSatskin [?] (Deputy Director of City Health Department)
Doctor S. Mamushin [?]

True copy of original

[Seal of Leningrad *Oblast'* Committee of Communist Party]

[signed]

Secret
Copy No. 1

MEMORANDUM

According to the records of the Records Department of the Committee for State Security [*KGB*] of the Council of Ministers of the USSR, Leonid Vasil'evich Nikolaev, born in 1904, is not listed as an agent. L. V. Nikolaev also does not appear in lists of candidates nor in documents pertaining to the destruction of personal archival records of the *KGB* central apparatus.

Senior Operations Representative of the
Records Department of the *KGB* of the USSR
Council of Ministers
[signed] (Astashov)

July 23, 1966

MEMORANDUM

The records of the Office of the *KGB* of the Council of Ministers of the USSR for Leningrad *oblast'* contain no reference to NIKOLAEV Leonid Vasil'evich as an agent or informant.

DEPARTMENT HEAD
OFFICE OF THE *KGB*
FOR LENINGRAD *OBLAST'*

[signed] (LOBANOV)

February 16, 1967

Copy

MEMORANDUM

On December 1, 1934 the following personnel were on security duty at Building No 26/28 on Krasnye Zori Street and Smolny:

1. SMIRNOV A. V. n/n agent [acronym unclear] dressed as doorman.

2. TRUSOV N. M. n/n agent near Building No. 26/28.

3. PAUKER K. M. Operations Commissar (inspection of shift in vehicle).

4. LAZIUKOV P. P. n/n agent (inspection of shift in vehicle).

5. AUZIN A. B. n/n agent (guard duty and reception at Smolny).

6. BALYKOVSKII N. L. n/n agent (guard duty and reception at Smolny).

7. ALEKSANDROV I. A. n/n agent (guard duty and reception at Smolny).

8. BORISOV M. V. Operations Commissar (on permanent guard at Smolny Building).

9. DUREIKO N. N. n/n agent (walking patrol on third floor).

HEAD OF FOURTH OPERATIONS UNIT:
(Kotomin)

December 2, 1934

Original in Archives Case File No. OS-100807 for Nikolaev et al.

(Volume 24, *l.d.* 335)

True Copy: [signed]

1 of 1 (copies)

June 28, 1966

[handwritten:] The document from which the copy was made was unsigned but was certified by an unknown individual whose signature is illegible.

<u>AFFIDAVIT</u>

On February 17, 1965, we the undersigned interviewed Comrade Nikolai Sidorovich VLASIK, the former chief of Stalin's personal bodyguard. During the interview Comrade Vlasik was very reticent and hesitant to talk. For the most part, his answers to our questions were very brief. He reacted irritably to some of our questions and refused to say anything. In consideration of Comrade Vlasik's age and complaints of poor health, we offered to interview him in the presence of a stenographer, but he rejected our offer. He also refused to write out a statement in his own hand or dictate it to a stenographer. Comrade Vlasik would only agree to sign a handwritten statement taken by another person from his testimony and in his presence immediately after the conclusion of the interview.

Because of Comrade Vlasik's behavior, several topics of interest discussed in the interview are not mentioned in his statement. These topics can basically be summarized as follows.

According to Comrade Vlasik's testimony, prior to December 1, 1934, personal security for Stalin was provided by an operations group of nine men (a "nine"). After Kirov's murder, Stalin's security was strengthened considerably. While prior to Kirov's murder Stalin's guards had only kept a visitors' log for his office (at the Kremlin), after December 1, 1934, a visitors' log was also kept at his residence.

As Comrade Vlasik described it, Stalin and Kirov had a friendly relationship. When Kirov came to Moscow, he would always go to Stalin's home and would often send him fresh fish and game from Leningrad. Vlasik also informed us that he personally never knew of anything and hadn't heard anything from anyone else which would suggest that relations between Stalin and Kirov were anything but friendly. The only member of Kirov's personal bodyguard that he knew was Bukovskii, the operations commissar, who accompanied Kirov when the latter came to visit Stalin.

Comrade Vlasik refused to answer when we asked him whether he knew anything about the circumstances of Kirov's murder. He was deeply upset by the talk that Kirov's murder had been arranged by Stalin. As Comrade Vlasik put it, such rumors were completely groundless. Although he considers himself one of Stalin's victims, having been twice fired from his job and placed under arrest in 1952, he, as a person who was in close contact with Stalin and knew him personally for many years, refuses to entertain the notion that Stalin had anything to do with this crime.

Vlasik knew well Medved', the former director of the *NKVD* Directorate for Leningrad *Oblast',* from the time they both worked in the Moscow *Cheka.* He also knew Medved''s deputy, Zaporozhets. Vlasik claims that he has no memory of Stalin ever summoning Medved' or Zaporozhets prior to Kirov's murder and has absolutely no knowledge of any personal contact between Stalin and these individuals.

In Vlasik's words, Stalin treated IAgoda rather coolly and only met with him for official business.

In his recollections of Stalin, Molotov, and Voroshilov's trip to Leningrad after December 1, 1934, he said that after Stalin received the news about the auto accident and the death of Operations Commissar Borisov, Stalin became visibly upset in Molotov's presence and expressed extreme dissatisfaction with the secret policemen who were unable to get Borisov to Smolny safely.

When the subject of the circumstances of Allilueva's death came up during the interview, Comrade Vlasik stated that he didn't consider it possible to discuss the subject and advised us to talk to Molotov, who was well informed on the details of Allilueva's demise.

Signatures of:
    Klimov
    Baturin
    Zanaraev
    Kuz'min

TO THE PARTY COMMISSION OF THE *TSK KPSS*

Statement

With respect to the questions posed to me, I can provide the following information:

Pauker, the *NKVD* Operations Commissar, informed me of Kirov's murder and the need to go to Leningrad. No one ever discussed the circumstances of Kirov's murder in my presence. Stalin, Molotov, and Voroshilov went to Leningrad. I don't remember any of the others who went. I went to Leningrad with my group ("nine"). I can't recall the members of this group now. None of Stalin's assistants went with us to Leningrad. I don't remember which of Molotov's and Voroshilov's bodyguards and assistants went to Leningrad. I don't recall if Shtern (the military man) was among those who went to Leningrad. As I remember, IAgoda went to Leningrad, but was not in the same passenger car as Stalin, Molotov, and Voroshilov, and I can't recall how he travelled to Leningrad. I didn't see Ezhov or Kosarev during my trip to Leningrad. On the trip to Leningrad the guards travelled in a separate car. Pauker and Gul'ko were the two high-ranking *NKVD* operations commissars who went to Leningrad. None of Stalin's personal attendants went to Leningrad. After Stalin and the others arrived in Leningrad, they got into cars and went to Smolny or a house (I don't remember exactly). I don't remember the name of the Leningrad official who met us at the train station, because we immediately got into cars and drove off. I knew Medved', the head of the Leningrad *oblast' NKVD*, but I didn't see him at the train station. Stalin spent his off-time at a house on the islands and worked at Smolny. During Stalin's stay in Leningrad agents from the operations department of the *NKVD* provided security for him. I didn't know the Leningrad *NKVD* agents Matveev and Mikhal'chenko. As I recall, Medved' called on Stalin, Voroshilov, and Molotov at the house. When Stalin was at Smolny, I stayed in the waiting room of the office without leaving. I recall one occasion very well, when they brought Nikolaev in to Stalin, Molotov, and Voroshilov at the office. Nikolaev made a very bad impression: he was small, mean-looking, and so forth. Two agents were leading him by the arms, and he looked totally exhausted and said nothing. I don't remember the names of the agents who brought in Nikolaev. I can't say exactly how long Stalin, Molotov, and Voroshilov interrogated Nikolaev, but he stayed in the office quite a while. I didn't hear any loud talk, screaming, or noise from the office when they were interrogating Nikolaev. I don't recall if anyone besides Stalin, Molotov, and Voroshilov took part in or was present at Nikolaev's interrogation. I do recall that Pauker was with me in the waiting room when Stalin was interrogating Nikolaev. With respect to the death of Operations Commissar Borisov, I remember the following: Pauker walked into the waiting room and told me that they were taking Borisov in a truck to be interrogated by Stalin at Smolny, there was some ice on the road, the truck got into an accident, and Borisov was taken to the hospital unconscious, and Pauker was shaken up. I don't remember who told Stalin what happened to Borisov.

The relationship between Stalin and Kirov was a friendly one. Whenever Kirov came to Moscow, he would always stay with Stalin at his apartment in the Kremlin or at his dacha and would even go to Sochi for two or three days if Stalin was vacationing there.

[signed]

March 17, 1965   VLASIK

True Copy:

1 of 3

INTERROGATION
OF OPERATIONS COMMISSAR BORISOV
OF THE LENINGRAD *OBLAST' NKVD*

At 4:30 P.M. or thereabouts, Comrade Kirov got out of the vehicle alone and went into the *oblast'* committee building. I was walking about 15 paces behind him in the vestibule. I followed him at this distance up to the second floor. When I reached the first staircase, Kirov was already at the landing between the first and second floors, and I followed him up to the entrance to the third floor. After getting to the corridor, I followed him down the corridor at a distance of about 20 paces. I was about two steps away from turning into the left corridor when I heard a shot. As I was pulling my revolver out of my holster and cocking it, I heard a second shot. After running into the left corridor, I saw two individuals lying near the door to the waiting room of Comrade Chudov's office. They were lying about three-fourths of a meter apart. A Nagan pistol was lying on the floor off to the side. In the same corridor I saw the *oblast'* committee's electrician Platych. Some employees of the *oblast'* committee immediately rushed out the doors. I don't remember their names.

OPERATIONS COMMISSAR BORISOV

INTERROGATOR: MOLOChNIKOV

1 of 2 copies

December 7, 1965

This copy was found in Archives Case File No. 100807 for Nikolaev et al.
(Volume No. 25)

[handwritten:] There is also a copy in Volume No 15 notarized by A. Svetlova. This copy gives the date of the interrogation as December 1, 1934.

Copy of copy

TRANSCRIPT OF AN INTERROGATION

On December 2, 1934 I, L. G. Mironov, the head of the economic department of the Central Directorate of State Security of the *NKVD* of the USSR, interrogated the following individual:

1. Last name: Platych

2. First name and patronymic: Seliverst Alekseevich

3. Age and year of birth: January, 1895.

4. Place of birth: Latvia, Village of Maloe Rein [Little Rhine], parents peasants, Latvian, citizen of the USSR, acquired Soviet citizenship in 1922.

5. Place of residence: Leningrad, Krasnaia Sviaz' Street, 17/5, Apartment 114.

6. Occupation: electrician, Leningrad *Oblast'* Committee of *VKP(b)* since 1924.

7. Family: divorced, father and mother in Latvia, sister IUzefa in Latvia, sister Varvara Platych in Leningrad employed at the *Svetlana* Factory. Principal occupation electrician since 1913, elementary education, attended *TEKhMASS* (technical) classes in 1931–1932, currently taking general education courses offered by *TEKhMASS*.

8. Party affiliation: member of *VKP(b)* since 1925.

9. Information on political and social activity: In 1918 joined the Red Army Fourth Air Mobile Train as a volunteer. Served in the Red Army through 1922.

10. Information on convictions or arrests: in 1913 in Leningrad sentenced to two months in jail for insulting an officer.

11. Current military status: reserve officer

12. Never served in the White Army.

<u>Testimony on Essentials of Case:</u>

<u>Question:</u> Who told you to fix and repair the electric lights in the building of the *obkom* of the *VKP(b)* on December 1, 1934?

<u>Answer:</u> On December 1, 1934, an employee of the *oblast'* committee, Kutulov, came to me at about 4:20 P.M. and stated that a light had gone out in Room No. 447 where he, Kutulov, was working and asked me to fix the light in his office.

<u>Question:</u> What sort of procedure did you have for fixing lights at the building? Who was responsible for telling you to make repairs?

<u>Answer:</u> Usually I would get an order from Baskakov, the *obkom* facilities manager, or Pavlov, the *obkom*'s business manager. If these individuals were absent, I would make repairs without waiting for instructions from them, simply by getting a verbal or written request from one of the *obkom* employees telling me that his lights had gone out.

<u>Question:</u> So tell me what happened this time: did Kutulov come to you with an order from Baskakov or Pavlov in his hand or not?

<u>Answer:</u> Because neither Pavlov or Baskakov were around at the time, I received a verbal request from Kutulov and proceeded to make the repairs.

<u>Question:</u> So what steps did you take to fix the lights and in what order did you take them?

<u>Answer:</u> I got the key to the fusebox from the cabinet in my room where I keep my tools, went out into the corridor and headed to the electrical cabinet in my office on the third floor. After opening the fusebox, I used my test light to check the fuses and found that one phase out of the four wasn't working. After fiddling around with the box for about 8 or 10 minutes, I discovered that the problem was in the basement, and not on the third floor. At the time, the electrician on duty from the building superintendent's office (whose name I don't know) was fixing a light after checking the lights in the entire building, which I later found out from him.

<u>Question:</u> So what was the condition of the lights in the corridor where Kirov's office was located?

<u>Answer:</u> The lights were in good working order; none of them were out, because the problem with the phase didn't have any effect on the lights in that corridor.

<u>Question:</u> Did you hear any shots on the third floor, and if you did, where were you at the time?

<u>Answer:</u> I heard the shots, and at the time I was in front of Comrade Kirov and was on my way to close the glass door at the end of the corridor on orders from Vasil'ev, the storeroom manager.

<u>Question:</u> So where did you go and what did you do after you heard the shots?

<u>Answer:</u> After the first shot I turned around, and then the second shot rang out. Right away I saw Kirov lying on the floor and another man slumped against the wall and slowly falling to the floor. I rushed towards the other man, because I had already figured out that he was the gunman. After I got to him, I picked up a Nagan pistol off the floor, threw it aside, and hit the gunman twice in the face with my fist.

<u>Question:</u> Who else besides you was still in the corridor?

<u>Answer:</u> I was so agitated that, of all the people that showed up, I remember only two, the commandant of the guard, Comrade Mikhal'chenko, and Comrade Chudov. It seems to me that I was the first one to get to the murderer. By the time I threw the pistol aside and hit the murderer, there was already a crowd, but I can't say exactly how many people were there, because I was extremely upset at the time and wasn't thinking too clearly. The only person I remember in particular was Mikhal'chenko, because he was holding back everyone who wanted to hit the murderer. This transcript is a true record of my testimony and has been read aloud to me.

PLATYCh

<u>Question:</u> Was Borisov one of the people at the scene when you ran up to the murderer, threw his Nagan aside, and started to beat up the murderer?

<u>Answer:</u> I know Borisov well. Whether he was there at the time or not, I can't say, because, as I said before, I was very upset and can only remember two of the people who were there: Comrades Chudov and Mikhal'chenko.

PLATYCh

True Copy:

1 of 2 copies
December 7, 1965

This copy was found in Archives Case File No. 100807 for Nikolaev et al.
(Volume No. 25)

[handwritten:] There is also a copy in Volume No. 15 notarized by A. Svetlova. This copy gives the date of the interrogation as December 1, 1934.

To the Party Control Committee of the *TSK KPSS*
from Il'ia Aleksandrovich Aleksandrov,
b. 1903, member of the *KPSS* since January 1929,
party card no. 03937426, issued December 8, 1954

I was transferred to S. M. Kirov's personal security team sometime around October or November of 1934. Before that I worked in the *operad* [operations branch] in Gul'bis's division. This division was involved in exterior surveillance. Four other secret service agents were transferred along with me to S. M. Kirov's personal security team. To the best of my recollection, among these four agents were Smirnov, Trusov, and Kulanev. I can't remember their first names. Like me, all of them had worked in the exterior surveillance service before coming to the team. The very best agents were chosen for S. M. Kirov's personal security. The team was put together with *operad* agents from 11 other Directorate of the People's Commissariat of Internal Affairs [*UNKVD*] subdivisions in Leningrad *oblast'*. Earlier, S. M. Kirov's personal security team consisted of three or four men. It began to be enlarged in late 1933 or early 1934 and reached full strength by November 1934. Police agents were brought into S. M. Kirov's security team. Now I cannot say just how many men were on S. M. Kirov's security team. But I remember very well that in the driveway to S. M. Kirov's apartment building there was a round-the-clock sentry disguised as a doorman or porter who was one of the *operad* secret agents. Outside S. M. Kirov's family residence a police guard was posted. I can't recall right now whether the guard was posted round the clock or during the day or during the night. There was no permanent guard posted on the stairway of S. M. Kirov's apartment building. The security team accompanied S. M. Kirov on his trips around town. At S. M. Kirov's wish, he was accompanied on excursions by Bukovskii, who either wore an *NKVD* military uniform or sometimes dressed in civilian clothes.

Operations Commissar Borisov guarded S. M. Kirov at Smolny. This bodyguard met S. M. Kirov in the vestibule of Smolny, usually at the main portico, accompanied him to his work chamber, and then remained in his reception room. I do not know at what distance Borisov accompanied S. M. Kirov at Smolny.

S. M. Kirov's security at the office was also the responsibility of the Smolny commandant's agents.

Personally, I was part of S. M. Kirov's secret security team. Primarily I had to be on duty right outside Smolny. As a rule, there were two other *operad* secret agents on duty with me. We were assigned responsibility to: meet and guard S. M. Kirov upon his arrival at Smolny, accompany S. M. Kirov to the third floor of Smolny, and then ensure his security when departing from Smolny. The same type of post of *operad* secret agents was set up outside S. M. Kirov's residence. These agents were required to meet S. M. Kirov and ensure his security during his departure from the building. The post consisted of two secret service agents. Both our post and the secret agent post outside S. M. Kirov's apartment building came on duty early in the morning and usually went off duty late at night. To be specific, our post went off duty when S. M. Kirov departed from Smolny. If S. M. Kirov left Smolny on foot, our security team had to accompany him through the city and ensure his safety. In case S. M. Kirov left his apartment on foot, the other group of secret service agents on duty outside his building accompanied him and ensured his security during his movements around town. Right now I can't remember whether we, S. M. Kirov's personal security team, were assigned a special automobile to accompany him around town as he traveled in his own car from home to Smolny and, vice versa, from Smolny to home. Bukovskii usually rode in S. M. Kirov's car. But there were times when S. M. Kirov traveled around town alone with only a chauffeur and without Bukovskii in his car.

On December 1, 1934, along with other secret service agents (three of us all together), I was on duty outside Smolny. I can't recall who was on duty with me then. Toward evening (I don't remember what time it was) the Smolny commandant agent on duty (I forget who was on duty at the time) informed us that S. M. Kirov was arriving at Smolny. Before that S. M. Kirov had been at home, preparing for a speech to a party meeting that was supposed to take place that very evening at Tavricheskii Palace, and he had not come to Smolny either in the morning or in the afternoon. On this occasion, as on other routine days, the other group of secret service agents was on duty outside his apartment building (their names escape me now). A few minutes after the Smolny commandant agent's report, an automobile drove up to the main portico of Smolny, and S. M. Kirov emerged from it. Our entire group accompanied S. M. Kirov through the main portico into the vestibule where operations commissar Borisov met S. M. Kirov to the third floor of Smolny where the guard admitting persons into the *oblast'* party committee was located. We descended from the third floor, and Borisov followed S. M. Kirov down the large corridor to the right. A few minutes after we left Borisov, Smolny commandant agents informed us that S. M. Kirov had been murdered. Immediately all the entrances to and exits from Smolny were locked and the building itself was surrounded by *UNKVD* agents and soldiers. Personally, I did not hear the shots; I was not at the scene of the murder.

After S. M. Kirov's murder our group remained at Smolny several hours, I guess, in the commandant's office. I didn't take part in carrying out investigative and operational measures. Then at around midnight they sent us to the *UNKVD.* We stayed there all night in the operations division, and in the morning they sent us to provide security for a governmental commission that had arrived from "Moscow." Borisov had spent the entire night between December 1 and 2, 1934, with us in the *operad.* They kept us in one of the office rooms of the division. There were four of us there all together. Borisov came with us from Smolny to the *UNKVD* in an official vehicle; no one else accompanied us then. We, the secret service group, had weapons, and no one took them away from us. I don't remember whether Borisov had a weapon when he was with us at the *UNKVD.* The room where we spent the night, as far as I can recall, was not specially guarded. Borisov phoned home from this room and talked with his wife. I don't remember now what he said to her. The conversation was brief. It seems to me he said that S. M. Kirov had been murdered and that he would tell her all about it when he got home.

Borisov was in an agitated state and, like the rest of us, was distressed by what had happened. We barely spoke with him, and he cried the whole time. Borisov told us that S. M. Kirov was murdered next to Chudov's office in the small corridor of Smolny by some unknown person. He shot S. M. Kirov at point-blank range. Borisov did not tell us why he had been unable to prevent this attack on S. M. Kirov. Nor did Borisov tell us how far he had been walking behind S. M. Kirov. Nor did Borisov tell us how the murderer happened to be in the small corridor of Smolny. It could be that we didn't ask him this question because he was too distressed for us to talk with him and for him to explain anything. Borisov had never known the murderer. I recall that Borisov said the murderer wanted to commit suicide; he tried to shoot himself but missed.

I do not know why the terrorist murdered S. M. Kirov.

S. M. Kirov didn't like the security team, and so we were instructed to guard him surreptitiously, out of his sight.

During my work on S. M. Kirov's security team I never had occasion to arrest any suspicious persons. Some of my colleagues did arrest such persons. I heard (from whom I can't remember any more) that Nikolaev (who murdered S. M. Kirov) had been arrested earlier outside S. M. Kirov's residence. After Nikolaev's arrest he had been taken to police headquarters and from there to the *UNKVD* building. I no longer recall under what circumstances Nikolaev had been arrested—for what or by which security force agents. I never saw Nikolaev myself. After S. M. Kirov's murder there was talk about Nikolaev's arrest. I don't know when Nikolaev had been arrested.

On the morning of December 2, 1934, *operad* agent Agalii(?) came into the office room where we were being kept and told Borisov to get his things together at once because he had been summoned to Stalin for questioning. Borisov collected himself and left with Agalii (?). He (Borisov) was dressed in an overcoat and business suit. Within about 30 minutes Borisov was brought into the *UNKVD* clinic dead. I saw them carry him into the *UNKVD* building, and he was covered with a white sheet. Under exactly what circumstances Borisov died, I do not know; they didn't indicate where he had died, but there were rumors among the *UNKVD* agents (I no longer remember from whom I heard this) that the agents escorting Borisov threw him out of a moving truck onto a sidewalk and he was killed on impact. I do not know how reliable these rumors were. I didn't even see them putting him into a vehicle, and I really don't know whether he was being conveyed in a truck.

Borisov was an elderly man, physically weak, of a reticent nature, but modest. Clearly, a younger, more mobile agent than Borisov should have been assigned to protect S. M. Kirov. I do not know why Borisov in fact had been assigned to protect S. M. Kirov.

The chief of the *operad*, Gubin (?), and the head of the security force, Kotomin (?), treated their subordinates politely and built a proper, professional relationship with them. At meetings and conferences, they demanded that we (S. M. Kirov's personal security team) perform our task attentively and fulfill our responsibilities vigilantly and conscientiously. At the same time, they told us to stay out of S. M. Kirov's sight. Both they and we knew that S. M. Kirov did not view the security force favorably.

October 20, 1966, City of Leningrad   [signed] Aleksandrov

TSKhSD

DOCUMENT 36   *Materials from 1935 on the Kirov murder case*

Material regarding the question of the murder of S. M. Kirov

By order of the Central Committee Presidium, we investigated the questions raised in the letter from Comrade O. T. Shatunovskaia. We spoke with Comrades Kirchakov and Trunina, ex-party members who were mentioned by Shatunovskaia in her letter.

Dr. Kirchakov in essence verified that he told Shatunovskaia and Trunina about several puzzling circumstances related to the murder of S. M. Kirov, but he declared that he did not get this firsthand from Medved', as Comrade Shatunovskaia stated, but from Ol'skii (a former employee in the People's Commissariat of Internal Affairs [*NKVD*] who was transferred in 1931 to the national food system), with whom Medved' had discussed these circumstances.

In his statement Kirchakov writes, "A conversation started about the tragic death of Comrade Kirov and of the involvement of Medved', who suffered repression in connection with this case.

In this conversation Ol'skii decidedly stated the opinion that Medved' had suffered completely undeservedly, that Medved' was the closest and dearest friend of Comrade Kirov, and that Medved' was not guilty of the murder of Kirov.

Ol'skii also told me that Medved' was dismissed from the investigation of the Kirov murder case, that Agranov led the investigation, and that after Agranov there was someone else (I do not remember who it was).

During one interrogation, Ol'skii said that Comrade Stalin asked the murderer Nikolaev why he had killed Comrade Kirov. Nikolaev answered that he killed Comrade Kirov on the instructions of persons employed by the *Cheka* and at this he pointed to the men from the *Cheka* sitting in the room, but Medved' was not in this group."

In the statement by Comrade Trunina, who was a nurse in the hospital and who, with Comrade Shatunovskaia, had heard Kirchakov tell the above-mentioned story, this episode is related slightly differently: "I do not remember from whom Comrade Kirchakov heard all this, but he drew for us the following picture: After the death of Comrade Kirov, Comrade Stalin went to Leningrad and was the last person to question Nikolaev as to why he had killed Comrade Kirov. Nikolaev pointed to those employees of the *NKVD* who were standing there and said, 'They forced me to do it.' After these words, one of the *NKVD* men knocked Nikolaev to the floor with a blow to the head, and he was removed."

Kotolynov asked for the case of Nikolaev to be <u>investigated</u> in order to look into the obvious discrepancy of his testimony.

It seems this statement of Kotolynov made an impression on Ul'rikh, head of the Military Council. In a letter to the Party Control Committee (sic), Comrade Aristova-Litkene (actually the former wife of Ul'rikh), who was in Leningrad during the trial, says:

> When the judicial inquest came to a close and an adjournment for the passing of the sentence was announced, Comrade Ul'rikh, dissatisfied, it seemed, with the proceedings, phoned the direct line to the Kremlin asking permission for an investigation to clarify several facts that had been insufficiently illuminated but that promised to uncover deeper involvements and clues to this evil act. He received from Comrade Stalin a sharply terse answer: "What other investigations? No other investigations. Finish it."

[break in the text] . . . touched upon the far-flung counterrevolutionary organization of Zinoviev." Stalin corrected this to: "criminally skimmed over the <u>existence of the Zinoviev terrorist group.</u>" (Case of Medved', Zaporozhe Cossacks, and others kept in the Central Committee archives)

1. A few facts on the murder of S. M. Kirov and of the nature of the investigation of this case in 1934–35 and 1937–38.

The large quantity of factual evidence on the murder of S. M. Kirov makes it clear that this evil murder took several months for Nikolaev to plan.

What kind of person was the murderer L. Nikolaev?

Series of data indicate that without a doubt he was not a mentally normal person, an epileptic, unbelievably egotistic, who bore malice toward the party and the Soviet government (he was excluded from the party for refusing to accept work on the railroad and later was reinstated).

RTSKhIDNI, fond 629, op. 1, d. 150, ll. 10–11, 17, 29

DOCUMENT 37   *Report of March 4, 1935, assessing the Central Committee's confidential letter on the lessons derived from the Kirov murder*

Top Secret

Transport Department of the Central
Committee of the All-Union Communist
Party (of Bolsheviks) [*TSK VKP(b)*] to
Comrade Evgen'ev

On the Analytical Study of the Confidential
Letter of the *TSK VKP(b)*
about Lessons Learned from the Events
Surrounding the Heinous Murder of Comrade Kirov

The sealed letter of the *TSK VKP(b)* received January 20 by the rail line's Political Section was sent out on the same day to all party organizers.

Study of the letter of the *TSK VKP(b)* began with an instructional conference with the chiefs of political sections, with supervisors in the administration of the rail line's Political Section, and with the party organizers of the Moscow rail junction. The conference was conducted January 20 by the supervisor of the rail line's Political Section.

On January 22 study of the letter began at junction conferences of party organizers and the active party membership of branch political sections; these meetings were conducted by the chief of the rail line's Political Section and the deputy and members of the rail line's Party Collegium.

On January 25 study of the letter began in party committees with active party members and subsequently at closed party meetings.

For study of the letter at the closed party meetings, the rail line's Political Section appointed party workers as leaders in 46 party organizations.

The party organizations for transport received a great deal of help from territorial party organizations, especially in Moscow and in Tula and Gorkii as well; those organizations helped in the guidance of workers in the political sections and sent their workers to meetings of railway party organizations for study of the *TSK VKP(b)* letter.

In a vast majority of the party transport organizations, study of the *TSK* letter proceeded at the highest ideological-political level, showing the political strength and uncompromising nature of party organizations in the struggle for the overall party line, as well as their solidarity around the Stalin *TSK* and the party leader, Comrade Stalin.

The letter was heard with particular attention and exceptional interest at all the meetings.

The reading of the letter was accompanied by commentary and an emphasis on its exceptional clarity, precision, and Stalinist style.

In the majority of organizations the closed meetings were well prepared and distinguished by very large attendance and exceptional political activity.

At the Voitovich Plant, for example, of 280 persons who could have attended, 272 were present and 93 spoke. At the Krasnyi Put' Plant, 60 of 73 persons attended and 18 spoke. At the Moskva Paveletskaia Steam Engine Repair Shop, 81 of 96 persons attended and 15 spoke. In the 22nd Railway Region (Ranenburg), 19 of 24 Communists attended and 11 spoke. In the First Section, 98 to 100 percent took part in the party meetings.

Among Communists who were not present at the closed party meetings because of illness or assignment, supplementary meetings were held to study the letter.

Party organizers visited intermediate rail stations for study of the letter with individual Communists.

Stalin and Zhdanov as "honor guards" at Kirov's bier in the Tauride Palace, Leningrad, December 3–4, 1934. TSGAKFD. N V-149

Some party organizations conducted poor preparations, and therefore study of the letter proceeded at a low political level. For example, at Steam Engine Depot Moskva-1, study of the *TSK* letter at a meeting of the party committee and active membership missed the principal political meaning of the letter and debate was limited to minor production problems. The same thing occurred at the party meeting of the 18th Railway Region. At the Kashira depot, the double-dealing of former Trotskyites was not exposed to its full depth. Therefore, a second study of the letter was conducted in these organizations.

At this meeting it was also indicated that the work being conducted was only the beginning of accomplishing the basic tasks stemming from the *TSK VKP(b)* letter.

This especially concerns party organizations and individual Communists at small rural stations where study of the *TSK VKP(b)* letter was less vigorous, where existing scandals have still [not] been exposed, and where revolutionary vigilance, preparedness for struggle, and the ideological political work of Communists are not yet at the necessary level.

The meeting discussed in particular detail and provided concrete instruction on the question of improving propaganda work.

At present, study of the *TSK VKP(b)* letter has begun in *komsomol* organizations, in relation to which the political section discloses certain facts concerning party organizers who do not provide the required leadership for this study and sometimes do not even attend *komsomol* meetings for study of the letter. The divisional political sections and party organizers were notified of the impermissability of such occurrences and a proposal was made to the political section chiefs that they personally accompany the active members of *komsomol* organizations in the study of the *TSK VKP(b)* letter and single out proven Communists and responsible workers for study of the letter in all *komsomol* organizations to ensure an ideologically high political level for *komsomol* meetings in the study of the *TSK VKP(b)* letter.

Chief of the Rail Line Political Section

[signature indistinct]
(Kostanian)

RTSKhIDNI, fond 17, op. 120, d. 176, ll. 13, 14, 23? 33?

DOCUMENT 38 *Report to the Secretariat of the Party, November 19, 1935, concerning suicides that occurred after a review of party documents uncovered inconsistencies in personal records of party members*

ON SUICIDES

1. <u>Moscow</u>. On October 5, 1935, A. I. Sergeev, a member of the party since 1926, assistant head of the State Appropriations Committee of the USSR People's Commissariat for Finance, shot himself. A month earlier, he had undergone inspection of his party documents, at which time he gave an incorrect answer to *raion* committee secretary Comrade Andreasian's questions about his brothers' past. However, the investigation revealed that his two brothers had worked for the police before the revolution. For concealing this fact, the *raion* party committee expelled Sergeev from the party. After that, he shot himself.

(From the report of the Moscow City Committee
of the All-Union Communist Party (of Bolsheviks) [*VKP(b)*]
October 7, 1935

2. Arzamas, Gor'kii _krai_. On the night of September 2, second secretary of the _raion_ party committee Kirillov drove out of the city with Chufarova, a member of the _raion komsomol_ [_VLKSM_] committee. On the way, he shot and seriously wounded her, then shot and slightly wounded himself. Upon returning home, he attempted to cut his throat with a knife. Khaims has been sent to investigate the case on location.

(From _NKVD_ notes)

3. Sankovo _raion, Kalinin oblast'_. On September 21,1935, the secretary of the Sankovo _raion_ party committee, IA. P. Maksimchuk, who had been summoned to Kalinin by the _oblast'_ party committee secretary, Comrade Mikhailov, in connection with a review of his party documents, shot himself. His motives are unknown. A commission has been sent to Sankovo.

(From a report of September 22, 1935)

4. Moscow. On September 31, Grandberg, a party committee secretary in the People's Commissariat of State Farms, poisoned himself in his office. In the letter he left for the party committee, he explained that the reason for his suicide was the following discrepancy in his party documents (about which he informed the secretary of the Bauman _raion_ committee): his party card indicates membership since 1909, with a lapse between 1914 and 1918, but his file indicates membership began in 1918. There is also a note about party affiliation in the years 1909–14 in accordance with a 1929 decision by the commission on party purges.

(From the report of the Political Administration of the People's Commissariat of Agriculture, September 1)

5. Kharkov _oblast'_. On October 9, S. V. Grodnitskii, editor of the Savintsy _raion_ newspaper, committed suicide. He had been expelled from the party following inspection of his party documents. (Grodnitskii served in the Polish Army in 1919–20, and in 1923 crossed over from the Polish border.) In his suicide note, Grodnitskii writes, "I have never tried to conceal the fact that I am a Pole, that I came to the Soviet Union in 1923, and that I served in the Polish Army. So it was no accident that this was uncovered during the inspection of my party documents. In 1923 all this information on me was taken by the _NKVD_ after I had crossed the border."

(From the report of the Kharkov _Oblast'_
Committee, October 22)

Nov. 19, 1935

RTSKhIDNI, fond 17, op. 40, d. 787, ll. 141–142

TO THE SECRETARY OF THE
ALL-RUSSIAN COMMUNIST PARTY (BOLSHEVIK)

COMRADE STALIN

I am forwarding the report from the People's Commissariat of Internal Affairs (*NKVD*) of the Ukrainian Soviet Socialist Republic on the preliminary results of their investigations related to the inspection of party identification papers.

DEPUTY COMMISSAR OF
INTERNAL AFFAIRS OF THE
USSR   [signed] (Agranov)

November 24, 1935
No. 57673

TO THE DEPUTY COMMISSAR OF
INTERNAL AFFAIRS OF THE USSR

Comrade AGRANOV

REPORT

ON THE PRELIMINARY RESULTS OF INVESTIGATIONS RELATED
TO THE INSPECTION OF PARTY IDENTIFICATION PAPERS

As of November 20, agencies of the *NKVD* of Ukraine have arrested 1,890 individuals expelled from the party in the process of inspecting party identification papers.

The breakdown of arrests by regions is as follows:

Donets 534
Kharkov 314
Dnepropetrovsk 302
Kiev 277
Odessa 219
Chernigov 104
Vinnitsa 103
Moldavian Autonomous
Republic 37

Active counterrevolutionary elements accounted for 41.5% of the total number of individuals arrested in connection with the inspection of party identification papers.

Confirmation of this is provided by the data below on the social and political profiles and nature of the offenses committed by 1,803 persons under arrest.

Those arrested included:

```
spies . . . . . . . . . . . . . . . . . . . . . . . . . . . .  24
Trotskyites . . . . . . . . . . . . . . . . . . . . . . . 154
nationalists . . . . . . . . . . . . . . . . . . . . . . . 236
fascists and terrorists . . . . . . . . . . . . . . .  67
individuals concealing
a counterrevolutionary
past . . . . . . . . . . . . . . . . . . . . . . . . . . . . . 217
individuals suspected
of espionage . . . . . . . . . . . . . . . . . . . . . 304
individuals concealing
socially hostile
origins . . . . . . . . . . . . . . . . . . . . . . . . . . .306
criminal elements . . . . . . . . . . . . . . . . 495
```

The arrested persons included 184 Poles and 61 Galicians [Western Ukrainians]. Some of these individuals were suspected of *provocateur* activities during their membership in the Communist Party of Poland and the Communist Party of Western Ukraine and also espionage on behalf of Poland.

In a number of cases involving spy networks, we have definitely established that some Polish "political emigres" were sent over to the Soviet side by Polish intelligence agencies. These agencies assigned these individuals the mission of infiltrating the Communist Party in order to facilitate their espionage activity.

57 Germans were arrested. Predominantly, they were fascists who maintained ties to Germany, engaged in anti-Soviet agitation, and distributed fascist literature prior to their arrest. Some of the arrested Germans, who were members or candidates for membership in the Communist Party, remained foreign subjects and refused to accept Soviet citizenship.

Our undercover investigative work in connection with the inspection of party identification papers resulted in the exposure and liquidation of 62 active counterrevolutionary groups in Ukraine whose members had infiltrated the party, quite often with the cooperation and recommendations of the aforementioned counterrevolutionary elements.

The evidence produced by the investigation for most of the groups liquidated in connection with the inspection of party identification papers revealed that the members of these groups joined the Communist Party *in an organized manner.*

In terms of the nature of their day-to-day anti-Soviet activity, the liquidated groups may be classified as follows:

```
espionage and sabotage . . . . . . . . . . . . .  14
Trotskyite . . . . . . . . . . . . . . . . . . . . . . . .  14
nationalist . . . . . . . . . . . . . . . . . . . . . . . .12
fascist . . . . . . . . . . . . . . . . . . . . . . . . . . .  6
terrorist . . . . . . . . . . . . . . . . . . . . . . . . .  2
criminal activities . . . . . . . . . . . . . . . . .  14
```

In addition to our undercover investigative work on cases [break in the text]

In accordance with my instructions, several *oblast'* political directorates have conducted extensive inspections of general office procedures and the registration and storage of party identification papers and party archives at low-level party organizations, workplace party organizations, and at *raion* and municipal party committees.

These inspections have revealed a number of major deficiencies in general office procedures and the work of secret departments of certain party agencies that were corrected as a result of appropriate decisions by higher party authorities.

The evidence produced by the investigation has exposed the following basic ways in which class enemies infiltrate the Communist Party.

1. Joining the party on direct assignment from foreign intelligence agencies. This is often preceded by membership in fraternal Communist parties and flight to the Soviet Union in the guise of political refugees.

The spies planted by foreign intelligence agencies often take jobs as workers in industrial enterprises, in large industrial centers and large new projects, and they infiltrate the party in the first category.

2. The members of spy networks assist each other in infiltrating the party by making recommendations at party meetings.

3. In a number of cases the members of spy and counterrevolutionary networks have joined the party in response to directives from underground organizations.

4. By employing their basic tactical weapon of double agentry, Trotskyites and nationalists have sometimes been able to not only remain in the party but also occupy high offices in the party organization and thus allow persons associated with the Trotskyite-nationalist underground to remain in the party or join it.

5. The criminal element is involved in counterfeiting and laundering documents, which they quite often steal themselves. Publishing notices in the newspapers concerning the imaginary loss of party identification papers is the most common trick that criminals use to obtain party cards. Major deficiencies in the system for registering, storing, and keeping track of party identification papers and, in certain cases, sloppy housekeeping by party members have made it much easier for these characters to engage in their criminal activity.

6. Persons with active counterrevolutionary pasts have usually joined the party on the basis of recommendations provided by their former colleagues in the fight against Soviet power.

Our undercover investigations in connection with the inspection of party identification papers are ongoing.

PEOPLE'S COMMISSAR OF INTERNAL AFFAIRS
OF THE UKRAINIAN SOVIET SOCIALIST REPUBLIC   V. BALITSKII

November 23, 1935

City of Kiev   True Copy: [illegible signature]

RTSKhIDNI, fond 17, op. 120, d. 181, ll. 72–74, 99–100.

DOCUMENT 40   *Excerpt from a report on final results of the verification of party documents, January 15, 1937, listing reasons for expulsion from the party*

III. REASONS FOR EXPULSION FROM THE PARTY DURING A REVIEW OF PARTY DOCUMENTS

	In Absolute Numbers			In Percentages		
	Members of the *VKP(b)*	Candidate Members	All Communists	Members of the *VKP(b)*	Candidate Members	All Communists
Total expelled from the party	154,948	110,118	265,066	100.0	100.0	100.0
OF THIS NUMBER:						
Spies and those having connections with them	2,272	488	2,760	1.5	0.4	1.0
White Guards and *kulak*s	29,911	14,128	44,039	19.2	12.8	16.6
Trotskyites and Zinovievites	7,096	832	7,928	4.6	0.8	3.0
Rightists	394	95	489	0.3	0.1	0.2
Swindlers and petty criminals	12,968	5,554	18,522	8.4	5.0	7.0
Other class-aliens and enemy elements	27,515	13,822	41,337	17.7	12.6	15.6
Degenerates in morality and life style	25,353	15,618	40,971	16.4	14.2	15.5
In hiding	2,302	2,633	4,935	1.5	2.4	1.9
Refused	1,387	2,653	4,040	0.9	2.4	1.5
Expelled earlier but did not turn in documents and are still registered	1,532	705	2,237	1.0	0.6	0.8
Registered but automatically excluded from party	4,592	7,008	11,600	3.0	6.4	4.4
Did not pass the purge of 1929	2,207	306	2,513	1.4	0.3	0.9
Passive members	11,393	22,444	33,837	7.4	20.4	12.8
Criminals	1,752	914	2,666	1.1	0.8	1.0
Expelled for other reasons	24,274	22,918	47,192	15.6	20.8	17.8

RTSKhIDNI, fond 17, op. 7, d. 460, l. 5

Statistics on reasons for purges from the party, March 7, 1937

POLITICAL DEPARTMENT OF THE MAIN ADMINISTRATION OF THE BORDER AND INTERNAL GUARD [*GUPVO*], NKVD.

SECRET

Moscow

No. 505248   March 7, 1937

All-Union Communist Party (Bolshevik)

Central Committee [*VKP(b) TSK*]

Party Organs Management Department.

Party Statistics Sector .

Forwarded herewith are the final statistical reports as of January 15, 1937:

1) final totals for party documents verification;

2) totals for exchange of party documents;

3) results of review of appeals from members expelled during verification of party documents;

4) results of review of appeals from members expelled during exchange of party documents;

5) make-up of those expelled from the party in 1936 holding the new type of party documents

You are requested to return the statistical reports presented to you on February 20, 1937, under No. 502414.

ATTACHMENT: text

CHIEF OF THE POLITICAL DEPARTMENT, *GUPVO NKVD*

(Roshal')

Printed in triplicate   [signed] [illegible]

No. 1 - to addressee

Nos. 2–3 PO *GUPVO*

NS

REGISTER

RESULTS OF APPEAL REVIEWS OF DISMISSED PARTY MEMBERS DURING EXCHANGE OF PARTY DOCUMENTS AS OF JANUARY 15, 1937

Party Organizations of the Border and Internal Guard of the *NKVD* of the USSR

	Reasons appeals of dismissed party members were rejected by *okrug* political departments	Appeals submitted to polit. dept. of *GUPVO (TSPK)* by those expelled during exchange of party documents		Appeals reviewed by polit. dept. of *GUPVO (TSPK)* as of this date	
		VKP(b) members	*VKP(b)* candidates	*VKP(b)* members	*VKP(b)* candidates
1.	For passivity	1	2	1	2
2.	For concealing social background	10	3	10	3
3.	For moral turpitude/corruption	12	5	12	5
4.	For contacts with foreign/hostile elements	-	1	-	1
5.	For concealing service with the White forces	5	-	5	-
6.	For connections with counterrevolutionary (cr) Trotskyites, smuggling their contraband	4	1	4	1
7.	For concealing membership in cr Trotskyite movement	4	-	4	-
8.	For losing party documents	5	2	5	2
9.	For violating revolutionary law	1	-	1	-
10.	For failing to uphold party membership standards	11	3	11	3
11.	For violating party discipline	1	-	1	-
	TOTAL:	54	17	54	17

	Reasons appeals of dismissed party members were rejected by *okrug* political departments	Results of appeal review:						
		Expulsion decision by *okrug* polit. depts. reaffirmed		Readmitted to the party		Expulsion from party changed to reclassification		
						From *VKP(b)* member to cand.	To sympathizer	
		VKP(b) members	*VKP(b)* candidates	*VKP(b)* members	*VKP(b)* cand.		*VKP(b)* mem.	*VKP(b)* cand.
1.	Passivity	-	1	1	1	-	-	-
2.	Concealing social origin	5	3	4	-	1	-	-
3	Moral turpitude/corruption	8	5	3	-	1	-	-
4.	Contact with foreign/hostile elements	-	-	-	1	-	-	-
5.	Concealing service with White forces	5	-	-	-	-	-	-
6.	Contacts with cr Trotskyites & smuggling contraband	3	1	1	-	-	-	-
7.	Concealing membership in cr Trotskyite movement	4	-	-	-	-	-	-
8.	Losing party documents	1	1	4	1	-	-	-
9.	Violating revol. law	1	-	-	-	-	-	-
10.	Not upholding party membership standards	7	3	4	-	-	-	-
11.	Violating party discipline	-	-	-	-	1	-	-
	TOTAL:	34	14	17	3	3	-	-

RTSKhIDNI, fond 17, op. 7, d. 455, ll. 25–26.

Information, ca. January 1938, on the number of individuals expelled in 1937 from the Communist Party in Kuibyshev oblast'.

Information on the number of members of the All-Union Communist Party (Bolsheviks) [*VKP(b)*] expelled by *raion* and city committee of Kuibyshev *oblast'* in 1937

	Name of city committee [GK], raion committee [RK]	As of 1 Jan 1937			As of 1 Jan 1938		
		Total no. Communists in raion party org.	VKP(b) members	VKP(b) candidates	Total no. Communists in raion party org.	VKP(b) members	VKP(b) candidates
I	2	3	4	5	6	7	8
1.	Kuibyshevskii GK	10,100	7,586	2,244	9,341	7,204	2,137
2.	Ul'ianovskii	2,043	1,563	480	1,880	1,437	443
3.	Syzranskii	1,841	1,230	611	1,796	1,186	610
4.	Chapaevskii	1,411	1,034	377	1,326	964	362
5.	Alekseevskii RK	231	155	76	192	125	67
6.	B. Syzganskii	194	120	74	147	89	58
7.	Baituganovskii	200	114	86	171	89	82
8.	Baranovskii	147	90	57	114	61	53
9.	Baryshskii	769	476	293	697	429	268
10.	Bezenchukskii	317	190	127	262	161	101
11.	Bogatovskii	248	165	83	245	155	90
12.	Bogdashkinskii	276	179	97	243	147	96
13.	B. Glushitskii	339	232	107	299	204	95
14.	B. Chernigovskii	290	188	102	219	132	87
15.	Borskii	296	175	121	240	138	102
16.	Beshkaimskii	380	204	176	313	151	162
65.	Shigonskii	191	118	73	172	98	74
66.	Molotovskii	469	326	143	539	385	154
	TOTAL:	34,046	23,643	10,403	30,433	20,845	9,588

	Name of city committee [GK], raion committee [RK]	Expelled from VKP(b)						Automatically left party ranks
		Total no. Communists expelled in 1937	VKP(b) members	VKP(b) candidates	Expel. from VKP(b) in 1st half 1937	VKP(b) members	VKP(b) candidates	
1	2	9	10	11	12	13	14	15
1.	Kuibyshevskii *GK*	423	365	58	346	325	21	3
2.	Ul'ianovskii	153	121	32	104	85	19	9
3.	Syzranskii	121	85	36	91	65	26	9
4.	Chapaevskii	93	74	19	81	65	16	-
5.	Alekseevskii *RK*	36	29	7	33	28	5	2
6.	B. Syzganskii	64	42	22	63	42	21	2
7.	Baituganovskii	31	25	6	26	20	6	6
8.	Baranovskii	32	20	12	25	14	11	2
9.	Baryshskii	57	44	13	46	37	9	5
10.	Bezenchukskii	45	30	15	41	27	14	2
11.	Bogatovskii	37	31	6	32	26	6	2
12.	Bogdashkinskii	39	34	5	33	29	4	1
13.	B. Glushitskii	54	37	17	45	31	14	1
14.	B. Chernigovskii	66	54	12	65	53	12	1
15.	Borskii	48	37	11	40	30	10	3
16.	Beshkaimskii	88	68	20	75	60	15	-
65.	Shigonskii	32	24	8	28	23	5	1
66.	Molotovskii	28	25	3	23	21	2	-
	TOTAL:	3,541*	2,749	792	2,970	2,386	584	138

*The figure 3,541 does not include data on expelled *VKP(b)* members and candidates among those accepted into the party in categories 1 and 5, about which no decision was taken by the bureau of the *VKP(b) oblast'* committee.

HEAD OF THE REGISTRATION SECTOR
OF THE *VKP(b) oblast'* COMMITTEE [signed] Platonov
/GOLOLOBOV/

RTSKhIDNI, fond 17, op. 120, d. 329, ll. 1, 4

Minutes of the Moscow Oblast' Committee, June 29, 1938, confirming the deci-sion of the Kolomna State Committee to expel B. I. Katarskaia from the party

<u>MINUTES No. 5</u>
<u>MEETING OF THE BUREAU OF THE MOSCOW *OBLAST'* COMMITTEE OF THE ALL-UNION
COMMUNIST PARTY (BOLSHEVIK) [*MK VKP(b)*]</u>

<u>JUNE 29, 1938</u>

<u>PRESENT:</u>

Members and candidate members of the Bureau of the *MK VKP(b)*:	Comrades Gogolev, Dedikov, Maksimov, Tarasov, TSesarskii.
Secretaries of the *Raion* Committee [*RK*] *VKP(b)*:	Comrades Biriukov, Dymov, Ignatov, Kukharev, Milov, Sirotov
Deputy Manager for the Dept. of the *MK VKP(b)*:	Comrade Shchekin
Asst. Secretary of the *MK VKP(b)*:	Comrade Petrukhin

1.   <u>Decision of the Kolomna City Committee [*GK VKP(b)*] to expel B. I. Katarskaia from the party.</u> (Comrade Baev).

Katarskaia, Bronislava Iosifovna, born 1887, member of the *VKP(b)* since 1921, party card #0085151, social class - worker. At time of expulsion from party - housewife.

Katarskaia has been expelled from the party by the Kolomna *GK VKP(b)* for close relations with enemies of the people and for defending them.

Inquiry has established that Katarskaia arrived in 1919 from Latvia, together with her husband, now arrested by the organs of the People's Commissariat of Internal Affairs [*NKVD*]. She worked for one year before joining the party. She joined the *VKP(b)* with the help of her husband. Katarskaia has not worked anywhere since 1923. Arrested besides her husband were those living with her: her three sons, sister, and daughter-in-law. Katarskaia has expressed dissatisfaction with the organs of the *NKVD* and carries messages to her arrested relatives.

The decision of the Kolomna *GK VKP(b)* is confirmed. B. I. Katarskaia is to be expelled from membership in the *VKP(b)* for relations with relatives arrested by organs of the *NKVD*.

RTSKhIDNI, fond 17, op. 21, d. 3035, l. 7

Dissension within the Party

The Communist political leadership had always been riven with doctrinal and personal disputes, even before the 1917 revolution. Lenin first engineered a schism in the Russian Social Democratic Workers' Party in 1903. Among those who would later lead the party, Trotsky had once been a Menshevik, and Kamenev and Zinoviev had publicly condemned the Bolsheviks' planned seizure of power in October 1917. Nikolai Bukharin had been a radical Left Bolshevik in 1918, breaking with Lenin and calling for a renewed revolutionary war rather than peace with imperial Germany. During the Civil War disputes about high policy and tactics continued to rage within the party, and in early 1921, Lenin forced a showdown at the Tenth Congress of the Communist Party. Each faction came to the congress with its own official program. The assembled delegates heard them all out and then voted first of all to adopt the centrist platform of Lenin and next to invoke a future prohibition on all organized dissent within the party. The formation of factions, of organized opposition within the party, was henceforth to be punished by expulsion from the party.

This ban on factions did not end political disagreements within the ruling circles of the Communist Party. During the 1920s Trotsky had staked out his own position on economic and political policy, advocating rapid industrialization and world revolution as the only guarantee of the survival of the Russian Revolution. Stalin took the position that socialism could be built in one country, buttressing his claim with selected quotes from the works of Lenin, who had died in 1924. Kamenev and Zinoviev supported the internationalist position, but feared Trotsky as a potential dictator. Bukharin had shed his earlier leftism and now emerged as a defender of gradual economic development and of political pluralism. Stalin cleverly exploited all these divisions and rivalries, and when Trotsky, Kamenev, and Zinoviev came together at the party congress in 1927 in a last-ditch attempt to remove Stalin from the leadership, they were easily defeated. A commission chaired by Sergo Ordzhonikidze ruled that the oppositionists had violated the ban on party factions and ordered the expulsion and exile of seventy-five of them, including Trotsky, Zinoviev, and Kamenev.

With these left oppositionists discredited, Stalin now appropriated their program of rapid and forced industrialization, provoking opposition from his former allies, Bukharin, Aleksei Rykov, chairman of the Council of People's Commissars, and Mikhail Tomskii, the head of the trade unions. A growing attack emerged within the party on this "right deviation," culminating in the defeat and disgrace of the rightists late in 1929. Because they had not organized open opposition, Bukharin, Rykov, and Tomskii were not expelled from the party, but they and their followers were stripped of their posts and forced to apologize for their errors.

Zinoviev and Kamenev too had apologized and were readmitted to the party in 1928, but never again would any of these leaders be given responsible positions. Instead, they were hauled out of their political isolation to serve as scapegoats for the murder of Kirov. Zinoviev and Kamenev were arrested and tried in 1935, then tried again in 1936 on the grounds that they and Trotsky were engaged in a heinous conspiracy to assassinate *all* the members of the Soviet government. They were executed in August 1936 after their petitions for clemency, included here, were denied. The rightist leaders were next. Tomskii committed suicide in 1936 rather than face arrest. A new show trial in early 1937 implicated Bukharin and Rykov in the vast conspiracy. Their guilt was widely broadcast through the press and discussed at length in the extraordinary plenary meeting of the party Central Committee in February 1937, some of whose transcripts are included here. At the conclusion of this plenum, Rykov and Bukharin were arrested. They were tried a year later, found guilty, and executed in March 1938. Tentative attempts to rehabilitate Bukharin—to admit that the charges against him had been totally fabricated—came to nothing in the 1960s and 1970s. Not until Gorbachev had become the leader of the Soviet Union did the party officially exonerate Bukharin. The man whom Lenin had once labeled "the favorite of the party" was readmitted to that party in July 1988.

DOCUMENT 44   *Appeal from Kamenev and others to Ordzhonikidze, December 10, 1927, regarding resolutions on opposition in the Fifteenth Party Congress*

[Handwritten]

Comrade Ordzhonikidze

Dear Comrade, I am sending you for the commission our statement on the matter of the resolutions of the congress about the opposition. It would be desirable for this declaration also to be brought to the attention of the congress.

With Communist greetings,
[signed] L. Kamenev

December 10, 1927
The undersigned comrades and I can be reached at this address: Arbat 35, Apt. 59 - Zinoviev tel. 97-53
....

To the Commission Chairman, 15th Congress, Comrade Ordzhonikidze.

We request you report our following declaration to the commission and then to the congress:

The resolution of the congress on the report of the Central Committee declares that membership in the Trotskyite opposition and propagandizing its views are incompatible with remaining in the ranks of the Bolshevik party.

Thus, the 15th congress not only rejected our views, but also forbade their propagandizing. In defending our fundamental views, which we are convinced are correct, before the body of the congress, we simultaneously emphasized in our declarations to the congress that we find it necessary to submit to the decisions of the congress no matter how difficult they might be for us.

The whole situation raises the question of a second party. Under the conditions of a dictatorship of the proletariat, we fundamentally reject the path of a second party for ourselves.

With this in mind and submitting to the resolution of the congress, we, participants in the congress, declare: 1) that the opposition faction must cease and is ceasing its existence and 2) that the decision of the congress to prohibit propagandizing of its views is accepted and will be implemented by us all. We call on all of our confederates to come to the same conclusions from the decisions of the congress. Each one of us must take that place the party assigns him and implement its decisions in daily practical work with all of his energy, helping the party work toward the goals set forth by Lenin.

Comrades expelled from the party for opposition activities have already addressed the congress with a request to be reinstated in the party. We repeat and support their request, and, it goes without saying, we consider the release of those comrades arrested in connection with opposition activities absolutely necessary.

Dec. 10, 1927 [signed] L. Kamenev. G. Evdokimov I. Avdeev[?] [illegible]

RTSKhIDNI, fond 56, op. 2, d. 55, ll. 1,2

DOCUMENT 45   *Kamenev's plea to the Presidium of the Central Executive Committee to spare his life, August 24, 1936*

To the Presidium of the Central Executive Committee of the Union

Having deeply repented the terrible crimes that I committed against the Proletarian Revolution, I am begging you, if the Presidium finds no contradiction to the future interests of socialism—the interests of Lenin and Stalin, to spare me my life.

August 24, 1936   L. Kamenev

TSGAOR, fond 3316-sch, op. 2, d. 1842, l. 17

DOCUMENT 46   *Zinoviev's plea for mercy to the Central Executive Committee, August 24, 1936*

[Document handwritten in its entirety]

TO THE PRESIDIUM OF THE CENTRAL EXECUTIVE COMMITTEE
OF THE USSR

Statement

I have confessed all the details of the crimes I committed against the Party and Soviet power to the proletarian court. The Presidium of the Central Executive Committee is aware of them.

Please believe me when I say that I am no longer an enemy and that I ardently desire to give every last bit of my strength to the Socialist Motherland.

I hereby request the Presidium of the Central Executive Committee of the USSR to grant me a pardon.

[signed:] G. Zinoviev

August 24, 1936

4:30 A.M.

TSGAOR, fond 3316sch, op. 2, d. 1842, l. 18.

DOCUMENT 47 *Resolution of the Presidium of the Central Executive Committee, August 24, 1936, denying the petitions for pardon of Zinoviev, Kamenev, and others*

<u>RESOLUTION</u>
of the Presidium of the Central Executive Committee of the USSR

The petition for pardon of G. E. Zinoviev, L. B. Kamenev, I. N. Smirnov, and others, convicted by the Military Tribunal of the Supreme Court of USSR on August 24, 1936, in the case of the Trotskyite-Zinovievite Terrorist Center

Having considered the petition for pardon of Grigorii Evseevich ZINOVIEV, Lev Borisovich KAMENEV, Grigorii Eremeevich EVDOKIMOV, Ivan Petrovich BAKAEV, Sergei Vital'evich MRAChKOVSKII, Vagarshak Arutiunovich TER-VAGANIAN, Ivan Nikitich SMIRNOV, Efim Aleksandrovich DREITSER, Isaak Isaevich REINGOL'D, Richard Vitol'dovich PIKEL', Kruglianskii Il'ia, David Izrailevich FRITS-DAVID, Valentin Pavlovich OL'BERG, Konon Borisovich BERMAN-IURIN, Moisei Il'ich, Zmel' Aleksandr LUR'E, Natan Lazarevich LUR'E, convicted by the Military Tribunal of the Supreme Court of the USSR on August 24, 1936, in the case of Trotskyite-Zinovievite Terrorist Center to the highest degree of punishment- execution by shooting,

THE PRESIDIUM OF THE CENTRAL EXECUTIVE COMMITTEE OF THE USSR RESOLVES:

To DENY the petition for PARDON of:
ZINOVIEV Grigorii Evseevich
KAMENEV Lev Borisovich
EVDOKIMOV Grigorii Eremeevich
BAKAEV Ivan Petrovich
MRAChKOVSKII Sergei Vital'evich
TER-VAGANIAN Vagarshak Arutiunovich
SMIRNOV Ivan Nikitich
DREITSER Efim Aleksandrovich
REINGOL'D Isaak Isaevich
PIKEL' Richard Vitol'dovich
FRITS-DAVID Kruglianskii Il'ia, David Izrailevich
OL'BERG Valentin Pavlovich
BERMAN-IURIN, Konon Borisovich

LUR'E Moisei Il'ich, Zmel' Aleksandr
LUR'E Natan Lazarevich

Chairman of the Central Executive Committee of the USSR
(M. Kalinin)

For the Secretary of the Central Executive Committee of the USSR
(I. Unshlikht)

Moscow, Kremlin
August 24, 1936

TSGAOR, fond 3316-sch, op. 2, d. 1842, ll. 1,2

DOCUMENT 48   *Letter from Bukharin to the Politburo, February 20, 1937, denying the charges of treason and treachery made against him and declaring a hunger strike*

February 20, 1937   No. P3465

To the Politburo of the Central Committee
All-Union Communist Party (Bolsheviks)

Dear Comrades!

I have sent to the Plenum of the Central Committee a two-part "Deposition" of nearly 100 pages, responding to the cloud of slander contained in the testimony. I had to do this work in a very short time, and therefore it does not pretend to be complete. But it does repulse the stream of filth.

As a result of all this I am a nervous wreck. The death of Sergo [Ordzhonikidze], whom I loved as deeply as a member of my family, was the final blow. The position in which this slander has put me, when I can neither rejoice together with my Party comrades, together with the whole country (Pushkin Days), nor grieve and mourn over the body of Sergo, is an insufferable position and I cannot endure it any more.

I swear to you once again on the last breath of Il'ich [Lenin], who died in my arms, on my deep love for Sergo, and on all that I hold sacred that associating me with all these acts of terrorism, sabotage, Trotskyite pacts, etc., is unheard-of, base slander.

I cannot live like this anymore. I have written an answer to the slanderers. I am physically and emotionally not in a state to come to the Plenum: my legs fail me, I cannot bear the atmosphere that has been created, I am not in condition to speak, and I do not want to sob, to fall into hysterics or faint either when my own [friends] revile me on the basis of slander. My answer must be read, and I ask you to disseminate it. In this situation, when I, being whole-heartedly with all of you, am already viewed by many as a renegade and an enemy, all that is left to me is:

either to be rehabilitated or to leave the scene.

In this most extraordinary situation, from tomorrow I will go on a full hunger strike* until the charges of treason, sabotage, and terrorism against me are removed. I will not live with these accusations. So that there is not even the appearance of a dispute with you, comrades, I will not speak to anyone about this on the outside; therefore, I am not writing to the Plenum; therefore, I am not resorting to other measures. This hunger strike is aimed against the slanderers. It would be a good thing if they could be reinterrogated, with the understanding that they will be punished without mercy for slander. I know that here (I read the draft of the resolution on the report of Comrade Ezhov) the stick is bent in the other direction (in regard to me). I fought until the end, I did not evade anything, I endured outrageous insults, of my own accord I did not leave the room. I cannot go on; goodbye and farewell. I fervently wish you success. I mourn for Sergo. I cannot go on.

My final request: tell my wife of the decision of the Plenum on the first point. If I am condemned to follow the sorrowful path to the end, allow me to grow weak and die here. Do not drag me elsewhere and do not let them torment me.

Farewell.
Be victorious.

Yours, N. BUKhARIN.

P.S. I earnestly request that the members of the Plenum be acquainted with my detailed answer (insofar as it was physically possible to write an answer in such a short time.) From a <u>practical</u> point of view it is immeasurably better than rebuttals. I have an undeniable <u>right</u> to this. I ask you, comrades, to do this, especially as I invested so much of my final strength here.

---

*Already begun at midnight <u>Noted</u> at 10:00 A.M., February 21, 1937

RTSKhIDNI, fond 17, op. 2, d. 773, ll. 169, 170

DOCUMENT 49   *Excerpt from Bukharin's speech to the Central Committee Plenum of February 23, 1937, in response to charges made by Ezhov—with annotations in Bukharin's hand*

GRIGOR'EVA-KhATUNTSEV, Nikitina
[stenographer]

Tell me please, when a person makes a statement, does he transform his intrinsic self overnight? There are such cases and there are such people who say one thing today, tomorrow they are pressured, and they make a statement that says completely the opposite. Such a person does not feel bound by either the former or the latter: He is simply unprincipled.

GAMARNIK. This continued for 2 years after the statement.

BUKhARIN. Let me relate to you how I explained this matter. Comrade Mikoyan says the following: On the most <u>basic</u> question, he, Bukharin, has differences of opinion with the party. In essence, he stuck to his old positions. This is untrue. In no way have I stuck to my previous positions—not on industrialization, not on collectivization, not on village restructuring in general. But with regards to stimuli in agriculture, this question was not clear to me until the matter came round to the legislation on Soviet trade. I consider the entire problem, as a whole, was resolved after the introduction of laws on Soviet trade. Prior to this, this problem, very important but not all-embracing, was not clear to me. When this matter became pertinent to commodity exchange [break in the text]

KhATUNTSEV-VASIL'EVA, F-va
[stenographer]

I would like to make one more remark. Apparently Mikoyan has said: How, then, are you not responsible, as you say, for [illegible] this whole "school" sits? I do bear responsibility for this. But the question involves the <u>degree</u> of responsibility; it is a matter of the <u>quality</u> of this responsibility. During the process of confrontation, I told Kaganovich that I am responsible for the death of Tomskii because, in 1928–29, had I not headed up the group of rightists, it is possible that Tomskii's fate might also have been different. I bear responsibility for this fact. However, it is necessary to establish the <u>degree</u> and <u>nature</u> of this responsibility. Responsibility for what transpired with these youths over an indefinite number of years qualitatively and quantitatively differs from, let's say, the responsibility of a person who orders another person to do something and that person carries out the order. I am not shifting responsibility from myself; more than anyone else I accept the gravity of this responsibility. However, I would like to say that the measure of responsibility, the characterization of this responsibility, is absolutely specific in nature, and it should be expressed as I have expressed it here. [break in the text]

. . . two people? This is an obvious lie. How could Kulikov offer two versions in answer to this absolutely and exceptionally terrible question? How could Sokol'nikov advance two ideas at the same time?

(VOICE: Rozit, Slepkov, and others mention this).

BUKhARIN: In what regard about this? If one speaks "generally" in this way, nothing at all is said. It is the same as when a student is asked where Moscow is on the map, and he immediately covers the whole map with the palm of his hand.

Regarding the Riutin platform. It was presented by Ezhov as one of the top-priority issues requiring deliberation. This is very understandable from the point of view of constructing an indictment. The Riutin platform (if you could prove that I have any connection to it) would be a real treasure, because of its concern with the most crucial moments in the struggle with Soviet power, its concern with terror, and censorship, etc., etc. I studied the vast number of pages of [material?] especially from the angle of the Riutin platform. Nonetheless, I feel that it is necessary here to look closely at this matter which, after all, is in the testimony. Astrov testifies that the authors were Rykov [break in the text]

. . . Errio did not see. It is even there, they say, that I maintained contact with Skrypnik (for a right-wing deviation, I would have to be linked to the positions of Skrypnik). It has been established, they say, that I stand for a democratic republic and, at the same time, it is known that I spoke about it, let's say, at the constituent assembly, and a whole series of other things. I cannot answer all these questions separately, since it would require too much time, so I'll take only the fundamental ones.

I'd like to say a few words about terror. Comrades, the question of membership in the party seems to me simply to be naive: if a person takes the terrorist point of view against the leadership of the party, then the question as to whether he may be a party member is a naive question.

I have absolutely no relationship with terror, not by a single word or thought. When I hear these things, it seems to me that the conversation concerns other people. Perhaps I am sitting here and hearing about another person. I do not understand how I can be charged with such an accusation; to me this is absolutely incomprehensible, and I view this as "a sheep looking at new gates."

POZERN: These are not "new gates"—that's the problem.

BUKhARIN: To your way of thinking, perhaps they are not new gates, but then I'm not a sheep either. [break in the text]

ALTAEVA-PRIGORNAIA, Petrakova.

[stenographer]

STALIN: You should not and do not have the right to slander yourself. This is a most criminal thing.

MOLOTOV: That which you have stated concerning the hunger strike is simply an anti-Soviet thing.

VOICES FROM THE ROOM: A counterrevolutionary thing!

STALIN: You must come around to our position. Trotsky with his disciples, Zinoviev and Kamenev, at one time worked with Lenin, and now these people have negotiated an agreement with Hitler. After this, can we label such things as shocking? Absolutely not. After everything that has happened to these gentlemen, former comrades, who have negotiated an agreement with Hitler, a sellout of the USSR, there is nothing surprising in human affairs. Everything has to be proven and not replied to using exclamation points and question marks.

MOLOTOV: And anti-Soviet matters should not be engaged in.

MOLOTOV: Let us call a recess, comrades.

RTSKhIDNI, fond 17, op. 2, d. 578, ll. 7, 10, 22, 32, 53

DOCUMENT 50   *Transcription of Rykov's speech and consideration of the case of Rykov and Bukharin at the February 1937 Plenum of the TSK VKP(b)*

Prigornaia-Mokhova
Mikhailova E.

[Original typewritten version:]

He [Rykov] was the only one who was not guilty. He was doubtful about Bukharin; he probably had something to do with it, but he [Rykov] had nothing to do with it; Tomskii, there was no doubt about him. So why was there no doubt about Tomskii? Tomskii has taken a lot of yours with him in order to hide. Now you are saying that there is no doubt about Tomskii. We know that Tomskii was undoubtedly [involved], but you were standing right next to him. He didn't do it by himself. We have Schmidt's testimony. Now Rykov is saying that Schmidt never talked to me [him] about wrecking. Maybe he didn't say anything to you. Are you mad at him because he didn't say anything? But what Schmidt said to you, you would have said the same thing about it. But he probably told you a lot. He operated with you, was at the center and engaged in this work. There is no doubt. I think that this is unbelievable. They did work together and their work was counterrevolutionary. The party couldn't let the issue drag on. The issue could not be put off any longer. Rykov could stand on firm ground and not talk that way. And he knows that if he had some ground to stand on, he could talk. But it seems that he's lost his tongue and can't talk and put two words together. Why? Because it would be difficult to wiggle his way out of this issue. For some reason he believes that he might be able to sidestep the issue. (Laughter). But it won't happen. It's impossible for him to squirm out of this counterrevolutionary affair. He has to make a clean break and tell everything to the party.

VOICE: And Foma Smirnov acted the same way.

ShKIRIATOV: He did too. They're like identical twins. On this issue he was against the party. He has long worked against the party. He was a real *kulak* and leader of the *kulak*s. And he has long been opposed to the party even when he was a Central Committee Secretary. He was against the party the whole time. But what about Rykov? He was against Lenin, he was against Stalin, and he has been against our party the whole time. So why do we need him in the party, when he can't even stand on his own two feet in the party? Rykov doesn't know the road to the party, because he has another road. He doesn't know where to go when he hears counterrevolutionary conversations. His road is overgrown with brush, and he decided on another one. So why was he in the party? Why do we need a person like that in the party? Enough, we need to put an end to this and make a decision. We not only don't have any room for people like that in the *TSK*, we don't have any room for them, and if it proves necessary, we should conduct an investigation. Let them prove in the investigation that they weren't involved.

KOSIOR: Let them testify in court.

ShKIRIATOV: Why should we let them off so easy? What's the point. At a time when they're attacking the *TSK*, our party, when they're organizing conspiratorial cells to get rid of a particular member of the *TSK* or another, and all we're talking about is kicking them out of the party. No, we need an investigation.

KOSIOR: And a trial.

[Revised version (handwritten corrections over typed version):]

In his statement, Rykov wanted to represent the situation as follows. When he was asked about Bukharin and Tomskii he answered: Evidently Bukharin had worked against the party and, with respect to Tomskii, there is no doubt that Tomskii was involved in this counterrevolutionary activity. Why was Rykov so willing to assume and confess that Tomskii was undoubtedly guilty in this case? It's obvious to everyone that the easiest thing to do is blame someone who's no longer around for everything. We know that Tomskii undoubtedly took a lot of both your and his work against the party with him. And now it's much easier for you to dump all your guilt on Tomskii instead of splitting it evenly with him. We are well aware even without you that Tomskii undoubtedly took part in this "cr" [counterrevolutionary] activity, but there is no doubt that you were standing right next to Tomskii, he didn't do it alone, but with your very active involvement. Right here we have a document which implicates you, where it provides evidence of your counterrevolutionary activity. With respect to Schmidt's testimony that he had talked with Rykov about his counterrevolutionary activity, Rykov claims that Schmidt never talked to him about wrecking, about his wrecking activity. Why are you foaming at the mouth at him? Schmidt testified that he had a conversation with you about his counterrevolutionary activity, and you can't deny it. You can't deny his testimony that you and he read and discussed a counterrevolutionary platform together. Now there is no doubt that from all that has become clear at this Plenum, Bukharin and Rykov engaged in their subversive counterrevolutionary struggle against the party. This is the conclusion we should make. Rykov, if he was standing on firm ground, could talk coherently, and of course not talk the way he has been talking. But it seems that he's lost his tongue and can't talk and can't put two words together. Why? Because it would be difficult for him to wiggle his way out of this deep hole he's fallen into. I think he decided to play the fool and has some [illegible] the matter. (Laughter). But it won't happen. It's impossible for him to squirm out of this counterrevolutionary affair. He has to make a clean break and tell everything to the party.

VOICE: And Foma Smirnov acted the same way.

ShKIRIATOV: They're like identical twins. Smirnov is a real *kulak* and has long been against the party. He was against the party even when he was a Central Committee Secretary. When they were resettling the *kulak*s, Foma spoke out wholeheartedly in their defense. The party knows about Smirnov. But here Bukharin and Rykov are sitting before us. Both of them, Rykov and Bukharin, have always fought against Lenin, Comrade Stalin, and he has been working against our party the whole time. So why do we need him in the party, why do we need them in the party? Rykov doesn't know the road to the party, because he has another road. He doesn't know where to go and whom to inform when he hears counterrevolutionary conversations. His road to the *TSK* is overgrown with brush, and he found himself another one and has taken it, the road of counterrevolution. So why do we need him in the party? Enough, we need to put an end to this and make a decision. We not only don't have any room for people like that in the *TSK*, in the party either. They should be put on trial; they are state criminals; the only place for them is the defendants' bench.

KOSIOR: Let them testify in court.

ShKIRIATOV: Yes, they should be put on trial. Do you really believe, Bukharin and Rykov, that we should let you off so easy? Why? At a time when they were working so feverishly against our party, when they were organizing terrorist [cells] against the party, terrorist plots "to get" members of the Politburo "out of the way," we can't limit ourselves to kicking them out of the party. We just shouldn't allow this to happen. We need to apply the laws established by our socialist state against the enemy. We shouldn't just kick them out of the Central Committee and the party, we need to put them on trial.

[signed] *Shkiriatov.* March 5, 1937

RTSKhIDNI, fond 17, op. 2, d. 580, ll. 92–94.

DOCUMENT 51   *Minutes and draft resolution of the Central Committee's commission on the*
Bukharin and Rykov "affair," February 27, 1937, ordering their expulsion from the party and that
their case be referred to the NKVD

PROTOCOL No. 2

of the meeting of the Plenum of the Central Committee of the All-Union Communist Party (Bolshevik) [*TSK VKP(b)*] Commission on the Bukharin and Rykov Case.

February 27, 1937

PRESENT:

Comrade MIKOYAN - chairman.

Commission members: comrades Andreev, Stalin, Molotov, L. M. Kaganovich, Voroshilov, Kalinin, Ezhov, Shkiriatov, Krupskaia, Kosior, IAroslavskii, Zhdanov, Khrushchev, Ul'ianova, Manuil'skii, Litvinov, IAkir, Kabakov, Beria, Mirzoian, Eikhe, Bagirov, Ikramov, Vareikis, Budennyi, IA. IAkovlev, Chubar', Kosarev, Postyshev, Petrovskii, Nikolaeva, Shvernik, Ugarov, Antipov, Gamarnik.

H e a r d:

A draft resolution presented by the Subcommission on the Bukharin and Rykov Case.

R e s o l v e d:

1) To adopt the draft resolution on the Bukharin and Rykov case presented by the subcommission and submit it for approval by the Plenum of the *TSK VKP(b).*

(Passed unanimously)

2) To direct Comrade Stalin to report to the Plenum of the *TSK* on the work of the Plenum Commission.

CHAIRMAN OF THE COMMISSION

[signed] A. Mikoyan

(A. MIKOYAN)

DRAFT

RESOLUTION OF THE PLENUM OF THE *TSK VKP(b)* ON THE BUKhARIN AND RYKOV CASE.

1) Based on documents from the *NKVD* investigation, the confrontation of Comrade Bukharin with Radek, Piatakov, Sosnovskii, and Sokol'nikov in the presence of members of the Politburo, and the confrontation of Comrade Rykov with Sokol'nikov, as well as the thorough discussion of this matter at the Plenum, the Plenum of the *TSK VKP(b)* finds that, at a minimum, Comrades Bukharin and Rykov knew of the criminal, terrorist, espionage, and diversionary saboteur activity of the Trotskyite Center, and they not only did not fight it, but concealed its existence from the party by not reporting it to the *TSK VKP(b)* and thus abetted it.

2) Based on documents from the *NKVD* investigation, the confrontation of Comrade Bukharin with rightists Kulikov and Astrov in the presence of Politburo members of the *TSK VKP(b)* and the confrontation of Comrade Rykov with Kotov, Shmidt, Nestorov and Radin, as well as the thorough discussion of this matter at the Plenum of the *TSK*, the Plenum of the *TSK VKP(b)* finds that, at a minimum, Comrades Bukharin and Rykov knew about criminal terrorist groups being organized by their disciples and supporters—Slepkov, TSetlin, Astrov, Maretskii, Nestorov, Radin, Kulikov, Kotov, Uglanov, Zaitsev, Kuz'min, Sapozhnikov, and others—and they not only did not fight them, but encouraged them.

3) The Plenum of the *TSK VKP(b)* finds that Comrade Bukharin's letter to the *TSK VKP(b)*, in which he attempts to refute the testimony of the above-mentioned Trotskyites and right-wing terrorists, is, in its content, a slanderous document, which not only reveals Comrade Bukharin's total inability to refute the testimony against him by Trotskyites and right-wing terrorists, but which also, under the guise of a legal challenge to this testimony, makes slanderous accusations against the *NKVD* and permits attacks against the party that are unworthy of a Communist; therefore, Comrade Bukharin's letter cannot be viewed as other than a most untenable document undeserving of any trust.

Considering the testimony, and taking into account that even during Lenin's lifetime Bukharin led a struggle against the party and against Lenin himself both prior to the October Revolution (on the question of the dictatorship of the proletariat), as well as after the October Revolution (the Brest-Litovsk Peace, the party program, the nationalities question, the discussion on trade unions), that Comrade Rykov also conducted a struggle against the party and against Lenin himself both prior to the October Revolution and during the October revolt (he was against the October Revolution), as well as after the October coup (he called for a coalition with Mensheviks and Socialist Revolutionaries, and as a protest he resigned from the post of People's Commissar of Internal Affairs, for which Lenin branded him a strike breaker), which indicates without doubt that the political fall of Comrades Bukharin and Rykov is not accidental or unexpected. Considering all that, the Plenum of the *TSK VKP(b)* finds that Comrades Bukharin and Rykov deserve to be expelled immediately from the party and to be handed over to the Military Tribunal.

However, because Comrades Bukharin and Rykov, unlike the followers of Trotsky and Zinoviev, have not yet been subject to serious party penalties (they have not been expelled from the party), the Plenum of the *TSK VKP(b)* has resolved to restrict itself to the following:

1) to remove Comrades Bukharin and Rykov from the list of candidates for membership in the *TSK VKP(b)* and from the ranks of the *VKP(b)*;

2) to hand over the case of Bukharin and Rykov to the *NKVD*.

RTSKhIDNI, fond 17, op. 2, d. 577, ll. 25–27

DOCUMENT 52   *Plea for mercy to the Presidium of the Supreme Soviet of the USSR, March 13, 1938, from N. I. Bukharin*

TO THE PRESIDIUM OF THE SUPREME SOVIET OF THE USSR

from N. BUKhARIN
sentenced to be shot

A PLEA

I beg the Presidium of the Supreme Soviet of the USSR for mercy. I consider the verdict of the court to be just punishment for my most grave transgressions against the socialist motherland, its people, party, and government. There is not a single word of protest in my soul. I should be shot ten times for my crimes. The proletarian court passed its judgment, which I deserved for my criminal activity, and I am ready to bear my deserved punishment and die, cloaked in the just indignation, hatred, and contempt of the great and heroic people of the USSR, whom I have so basely betrayed.

If I allow myself to petition the highest government organ in our land, before which I appear on my knees, it is only because I believe that through a pardon I can be of value to my country; I do not say—and I am not able to say—that I can expiate my guilt; the crimes I committed are so monstrous, so enormous, that I cannot atone for the guilt—no matter what I may do for the rest of my life. But I assure the Presidium of the Supreme Soviet that my stay of more than a year in prison has forced me to do a great deal of thinking and to reconsider much from my criminal past, which I myself regard with indignation and contempt, and now none of that has remained in my mind. It is not from fear of the penalty I deserve, it is not from fear of death, on whose threshold I stand as before a just punishment, that I ask the Presidium of the Supreme Soviet for charity and mercy. If anything inimical to the party and the government remained in my heart, I would not be petitioning you for charity and mercy. I have been inwardly disarmed and have reeducated myself for the new socialist order. I have rethought all questions—starting with my theoretical errors which lay for me personally at the foundation of my initial deviations and subsequent, increasingly terrible transgressions. Step by step, I have reexamined my past life. The former BUKhARIN has already died; he no longer lives on this earth. If physical life were to be granted me, it would go for the benefit of the socialist motherland, under whatever conditions I would have to work: in a solitary prison cell, in a concentration camp, at the North Pole, in Kolyma, wherever you like, in any circumstances and under any conditions. My knowledge and capabilities, all my mental faculties, whose activity had previously been directed toward the criminal, have been preserved. Now these mental faculties have been retuned. I can work in the most diverse areas in any circumstances. In prison I wrote a series of works attesting to my complete reeducation. But I can work not only in the purely scholarly sphere. Thus I dare to call out to you, as the highest organ of government, for mercy, justifying this by my fitness for work and appealing to the cause of furthering the revolution. If I were no longer fit to serve, then this petition would not be occurring and I would only be awaiting the swiftest execution of the death sentence, for then nothing would justify my petition. Disarmed, but a useless enemy, unfit for work, I would be good for one thing only—my death might serve as a lesson for others. But because I am able-bodied, I presume to petition the Presidium for charity and mercy. Our mighty country, mighty party, and government have carried out a general purge. The counterrevolution has been crushed and neutralized. The motherland of socialism has set out on a heroic march into the arena of the greatest triumphant struggle in world history. Inside our country, a broad-based socialist democracy is emerging, founded on Stalin's constitution. A great creative and fruitful life is blossoming. Give me the chance, even behind prison bars, to participate in this life as much as I am able! Let me—I beg and implore you—contribute at least a tiny bit to this life! Let a new, second BUKhARIN grow. Let him even be [called] PETROV—this new man will be the complete antithesis of the one who has died. He has already been born. Give him the opportunity of any kind of work at all. I ask this of the presidium of the Supreme Soviet. The old in me has died forever and irreversibly. I am happy that the power of the proletariat has totally obliterated all that was criminal which saw me as its leader and whose leader I, in fact, was. I am absolutely sure: the years will pass, great historical frontiers will be crossed under STALIN'S leadership, and you will not lament the act of charity and mercy that I ask of you: I shall strive to prove to you, with every fiber of my being, that this gesture of proletarian generosity was justified.

Nikolai BUKhARIN.

Moscow, March 13, 1938
Internal *NKVD* prison

True copy:

Head, first department
Secretariat of the *NKVD* of the USSR
Senior Lt. for State Security
[signed] Kudriavtsev

Transcribed from handwritten copy, also provided.

TSGAOR, fond 7523 sch, op. 66, d. 58, ll. 1–5

DOCUMENT 53   *Plea for mercy from A. I. Rykov to the Presidium of the Supreme Soviet of the USSR, March 13, 1938*

To the Presidium of the Supreme Soviet

By order of the Military Tribunal of the Supreme Court on this 13th of March, I was condemned to death by shooting.

I ask for clemency.

[signed] A. I. Rykov

March 13, 1938
[stamp] True copy

To the Presidium of the Supreme Soviet of the USSR

On March 13 [of this year] the Military Tribunal of the Supreme Court condemned me to death by shooting. I ask for clemency.

My guilt before the party and my native land is great, but I have a passionate desire and, I think, enough strength to expiate it.

I ask you to believe that I am not a completely corrupt person. In my life there were many years of pure, honest work for the revolution. I can still prove that even after the crimes I have committed, it is possible to become an honest person and to die with honor.

I ask that you spare my life.

March 13, 1938

[signed] A. I. Rykov

[stamp] True copy

TSGAOR, fond 7523 sch, op. 66, d. 58, ll. 9–12

The Red Army Purge

All the while that attention was focused on the crimes of the Old Bolshevik leaders, the *NKVD* was preparing material for a purge of the army high command. Allegations of Trotskyite terrorist assassination plots were raised in 1936, and lower ranking officers began to fall victim to arrest and interrogation. At the end of the Central Committee plenum in February 1937 that had called for the arrest of Bukharin and Rykov, Stalin spoke about the harm "a few spies in the Red Army could do." Then on June 11, 1937, came the announcement that nine leading commanders of the Red Army had been arrested on charges of participation in a counterrevolutionary military fascist organization. The next day came the report that they had been tried and executed.

From the top the purge spread downward. Almost all of the heroes of the

Civil War and virtually the entire command structure disappeared into the prisons, the camps, or execution chambers: three of five marshals, three of four leading army commanders, all twelve second-tier army commanders, sixty of sixty-seven corps commanders, and the list goes on. Once again, the question remains "why?" The archives as yet offer only clues, no definitive answers. Documentary "evidence" proving conspiracies was allegedly destroyed by Stalin, and nothing ever emerged from the German archives. On the other hand, the danger that the military leadership was alarmed by Stalin's moves against Bukharin and other party leaders was very real, and Stalin may have moved swiftly in order to eliminate this source of opposition, actual or potential. It has been suggested that Stalin was already planning a rapprochement with Germany—the future Nazi-Soviet pact—and, fearing the army leaders would block this, he eliminated them to expand his room to maneuver. Despite the magnitude of the purge in the military, Stalin managed to retain the loyalty of the army. He had not destroyed the Soviet military, but had effectively neutralized any source of opposition to his policies.

DOCUMENT 54 *Order by Marshal Voroshilov, People's Commissar of Defense, to the Red Army, June 7, 1937, concerning another counterrevolutionary fascist organization uncovered within the military by the* NKVD

SECRET

Copy No. 1

Order

of The People's Commissar of Defense of the Soviet Union

No. 072

June 7, 1937

Moscow

Comrades of the Red Army, Commanders, Political Workers of the Worker-Peasant Red Army!

From the first until the fourth of June of the present year, with members of the government in attendance, there was convened a Military Council under the People's Commissar of Defense of the Soviet Union. In its sessions the Military Council heard and studied my report concerning the findings by the People's Commissar of Internal Affairs about the treasonous counterrevolutionary military fascist organization which, because it was an extremely clandestine conspiracy, existed for a long time and carried on espionage and other harmful, base, and subversive activities in the Red Army.

The Soviet Court has already more than once penalized deservedly the Trotskyite-Zinovievite gang of terrorists that was uncovered: saboteurs, spies, and murderers working their traitorous deals with money from Germany, Japan, and other spies under the command of that brutal fascist, the traitor and betrayer of the workers and peasants—Trotsky. The Supreme Court passed its sentence without mercy on the outlaws from the murderous band of Zinoviev, Kamenev, Trotsky, Piatakov, Smirnov, et al.

However, the list of counterrevolutionary conspirators, spies, and saboteurs is far from being exhausted by blaming earlier criminals. Many of them, under the guise of honest people, remain free and continue to perform their dark deeds of treason and betrayal.

To the number of these traitors and betrayers who still remain undiscovered should be added the participants in the counterrevolutionary band of spies and conspirators who have built themselves a nest in the Red Army. The top leaders of this military fascist-Trotskyite band consist of the people occupying the highest command positions in the Worker-Peasant Red Army.

As is clear from the evidence from the People's Commissariat of Internal Affairs, here belong: the former Deputy People's Commissars of Defense, Gamarnik and Tukhachevskii; the former military district commanders, IAkir and Uborevich; the former head of the Frunze Military Academy, Kork; the former deputy military district commanders, Primakov and Sangurskii; the former head of the Administration for Commanding Officers, Fel'd-man; the former military attache in England, Putna; the former chairman of the Central Council of the Society for the Promotion of Defense and Aero-Chemical Development, Eideman. The enemy was able by means of bribery, blackmail, provocation, and fraud to entangle in its criminal nets these morally-lapsed, putrescent people who forgot their duty and transformed themselves into outright agents of German-Japanese fascism.

The ultimate goal of this gang was to eliminate the Soviet system in our country at any cost and by any means possible, to destroy Soviet power in the country, to overthrow the workers and peasants' government, and to restore the yoke of the landowners and the factory owners.

The fascist plotters would go to any lengths to achieve their treasonous goals. They planned the murders of party and government leaders, they engaged in all sorts of malicious sabotage in the country's economy and system of defense, and they tried to undermine the might of the Red Army and pave the way for its defeat in the event of war. They reckoned that their treacherous acts and sabotage of the army's logistics and command of combat operations would result in the defeat of the Red Army and the overthrow of the Soviet government if war broke out.

These traitors were well aware that they would not be able to find support among the workers, peasants, and warriors of the Workers and Peasants' Red Army, so they operated by deception and by concealing themselves from the people and the Red Army soldiers, afraid to show their true faces. They sold state military secrets to the Soviet Union's enemies, engaged in sabotage and subversion in all areas of the country's defense system, attempted to sabotage the country's defense and civilian construction projects, tried to sabotage the manufacture and stockpiling of weapons and equipment, and endeavored to sabotage the combat training of military units; in short, committed sabotage wherever they could infiltrate.

These traitors and scoundrels, who hid themselves behind their high ranks as party members and commanders of the Workers and Peasants' Red Army, quietly did everything they could to undermine the defensive potential of our country and pave the way for the Red Army's defeat in any future war. They tried to sell our motherland to German and Japanese fascism. They awaited assistance from the German and Japanese fascists and were willing to give them Ukraine and Maritime Territory in the Far East in exchange for this assistance.

Now these enemies of the people have been caught red-handed. They have completely confessed their treason, sabotage, and espionage. We cannot be sure that these sworn enemies of the workers told everything they know about their deeds. And we can also not be certain that they have given up all their confederates and accomplices. But the principal organizers, leaders, and spies with direct links to the German and Japanese general staffs and their intelligence agencies have been exposed. They will get their just deserts from the hard hand of Soviet justice.

The Workers and Peasants' Red Army, the faithful and honorable backbone of Soviet power, is mercilessly lancing this festering abscess on its healthy body and is quickly removing it. Our enemies have miscalculated. The German and Japanese fascists will never see the Red Army beaten. The Red Army was and remains invincible. Trotsky, that agent of Japanese and German fascism, has once again learned that his faithful servants, the Gamarniks and the Tukhachevskiis, the IAkirs and the Uboreviches, and the other trash and lackeys of capitalism, will be wiped off the face of the earth, and their names will be damned and forgotten.

Comrades!

The Red Army was, is, and ever shall be the army of the victorious people, the army of socialist triumphs, and the army which is the flesh and blood of the people building a new socialist life. We will purge the Fascist spy Trotskyite rot from our ranks and will not let these despicable acts happen again. By cleansing our army of this rotten trash, we will make it even stronger and more invulnerable.

The Red Army must and will have its own true commanders who are honorable and dedicated to the cause of the workers and the peasants and the cause of their Motherland.

We must heighten our Bolshevik vigilance tenfold, elevate and radically improve our performance in all areas, step up our self-criticism, and thus hasten the total elimination of the handiwork of the enemies of the people.

Down with the Trotskyite fascist traitors! Death to spies and turncoats!

Down with the Japanese and German imperialist bosses of the Trotskyite turncoats and spies!

Long live our glorious Workers and Peasants' Red Army!

Long live our great party of LENIN and STALIN!

This order should be read at all companies, troops, batteries, squadrons, detachments, ships, depots, headquarters, directorates, and installations of the Workers and Peasants' Red Army!

PEOPLE'S COMMISSAR OF
DEFENSE OF THE SOVIET UNION
MARSHAL OF THE SOVIET UNION
[signed] (K. VOROShILOV)

TSGASA, fond 4, op. 11, d. 52, ll. 56–58

DOCUMENT 55 *Resolution of the Plenum of the Central Committee, March 3, 1937, on Ezhov's report of what was learned from the sabotage, subversion, and espionage committed by Japanese and German Trotskyite agents*

LESSONS OF WRECKING, SABOTAGE, SUBVERSION, AND ESPIONAGE BY JAPANESE-GERMAN TROTSKYITE AGENTS.

Decision of the Plenum of the Central Committee of the All-Union Communist Party (Bolsheviks) [*TSK VKP(b)*] on Comrade Ezhov's Report. March 3, 1937.

The Plenum of the *TSK VKP(b)* believes that all the facts established during the investigation of the anti-Soviet Trotskyite center and its local accomplices show that the People's Commissariat of Internal Affairs [*Narkomvnudel*] was at least four years late in unmasking these most vicious enemies of the people.

The Motherland's traitors—Trotskyites and other double-dealers, in union with German and Japanese counterintelligence—have managed with relative impunity to carry on wrecking, sabotage, espionage, and terrorist activities and to damage socialist progress in many branches of industry and in transportation. They were able to do this not only because of defects in the work of party and economic organizations, but also because of slipshod work by the Department of state security of the *Narkomvnudel.*

Despite numerous warnings by the *TSK VKP(b)* on redirecting all *Cheka* work toward a more organized and acute struggle against counterrevolution (March 8, 1933, instructions of the *TSK VKP(b)* and the Council of the People's Commissars of the USSR, secret letter of the *TSK VKP(b)* on lessons of events related to the vicious murder of Comrade Kirov, etc.), the *Narkomvnudel* has not carried out these party and government directives and has turned out to be unable to expose the anti-Soviet Trotskyite gang in time.

The major defects in the work of state security agencies that have decisively contributed to the delay in unmasking the Trotskyite anti-Soviet organization continue to be:

a) The *Narkomvnudel* has not established high work standards for its agents, a key in the struggle against counterrevolution. Agents have been recruited at random and without direction. As a rule attention has not been paid to those basic and decisive sectors where a network of agents should have been well established. The agent network has been particularly weak among the Trotskyites, Zinovievites, and rightists, even in the places of their highest concentration. There also were no agents in almost any of the anti-Soviet (including Trotskyite) organizations abroad. *Narkomvnudel* administrative officials as a rule never have dealt with agents personally. Poorly qualified regular functionaries have been meeting agents and picking up materials from them.

As a result of this poor supervision of agents, there turned out to be many traitors among them. During the investigation of the anti-Soviet Trotskyite center, 65 agent-traitors were discovered in Moscow alone; they systematically deceived organs of state security, tangled up all cases, actively facilitated the Trotskyites' ability to operate with impunity.

b) The absence of a qualified network of agents and the unskillful management of the agents already in place made poor investigative work inevitable. Without sufficient evidence from the agents, an investigation often depended on the criminal, his willingness to give comprehensive testimony, i.e., the entire investigation was built on the voluntary confession of the accused.

To a certain extent this also explains how the arrested Trotskyites have managed to conceal the darkest side of their anti-Soviet activity from investigators and, most importantly, to conceal the people organizationally connected with them.

c) In all aspects of its operation the *Narkomvnudel* has followed the wrong punitive policy, especially toward the Trotskyites and other enemies of the Soviet system.

Analysis of the arrests made during 1935–1936 shows that the brunt of state security organs' effort was directed not against organized counterrevolutionary formations, but primarily at isolated instances of anti-Soviet agitation, at all sorts of abuses of office, hooliganism, domestic crimes, etc. Of all those prosecuted in 1935–36, about 80% were petty crimes of all sorts that should have been handled by the police, not state security organs.

d) Even more intolerable is the *Narkomvnudel*'s prison policy for the most vile convicted enemies of the Soviet government, the Trotskyites, Zinovievites, rightists, Socialist Revolutionaries, and others.

As a rule, these enemies of the people have been sent to so-called political isolation facilities supervised by the *Narkomvnudel.* The political isolation facilities have been quite comfortable, resembling involuntary rest homes more than prisons.

Inmates in the isolated political prisons have had the opportunity to talk to each other, to discuss all political events in the country, to elaborate political plans of anti-Soviet activity for their organizations, and to establish contacts outside of prison. The prisoners have enjoyed access to literature, paper, and writing tools in unlimited quantity, and the right to receive unlimited numbers of letters and telegrams, to acquire their own equipment in their cells, and to receive along with prison food parcels from outside prison in any quantity or assortment.

e) A very serious flaw in the work of state security organs is the practice of selection, promotion, and training of *Cheka* personnel.

Narkomvnudel staff as a whole are unquestionably experienced, professional *Cheka*-men, selflessly devoted to the goals of our party. In spite of this, in practice, promotions and appointments of people have not been performance-based. In many cases people were promoted not by reason of their loyalty to the party, capabilities, or expertise, but for their servility and ability to flatter.

As a result, alien and criminal elements have infiltrated some units of state security organs. Several cases have been revealed where even foreign intelligence agents have managed to infiltrate state security organs (the Polish spies Sosnovski, Mazepus, the Polish-German spy Ilinich, et al.).

This very lack of professionalism in promoting people and also the lack of political training have created conditions that have enabled outright Trotskyite traitors to obtain supervisory positions in the *Cheka.*

Some of them have systematically informed members of the Trotskyite organization about *Narkomvnudel* materials on the anti-Soviet activities of the latter (Balaniuk, head of the Taganrog Department of the *Narkomvnudel;* Shapovalov, head of the Novocherkassk Department of the *Narkomvnudel;* Kozelskii, former head of the Secret Political Division [*SPO*] of the Ukrainian *Narkomvnudel,* et al.).

Moreover, it must be said that party political training of *Cheka* cadres has been very weak. People have been educated in narrow-minded departmental parochialism with no relation to the general work of the party. As a result, some of the *Cheka* personnel have separated themselves from party life and become immersed solely in departmental concerns.

That is how things stand in terms of the general flaws in the work of the *Narkomvnudel* of the USSR. [. . .]

The plenum of the *TSK VKP(b)* resolves:

1) To approve *TSK VKP(b)* measures to destroy the anti-Soviet, subversive, sabotaging, spying, and terrorist band of Trotskyites and other double-dealing scum.

To require the *Narkomvnudel* to finish the business of unmasking and destroying Trotskyites and other fascist agents and crush all manifestations of their anti-Soviet activity.

2) To approve *TSK VKP(b)* measures to improve the work of *Narkomvnudel* agencies, particularly measures to reorganize personnel of the *GUGB* [Main Administration of State Security] and augment it with new party cadres.

3) To approve *TSK VKP(b)* measures to improve state security organs by promoting to supervisory positions new *Cheka* personnel of proven loyalty to Bolshevism and firing rotten bureaucrats who have lost Bolshevik sharpness and vigilance in the struggle against the class enemy and who have shamed the glorious name of *Cheka*-men.

To approve in particular the arrest and trial of former head of the *SPO* of the *GUGB,* Molchanov—one of the major culprits in the shameful failure of state security organs in their struggle against Zinovievites and Trotskyites.

4) To continue and finish reorganizing *Narkomvnudel,* especially the *GUGB* staff, making it a real fighting agency capable of carrying out the missions charged to it by the party and the Soviet government to ensure state and public safety in our country.

5) Considering the vital economic and defence significance of railroad transportation and the necessity of protecting it from anti-Soviet subversion by enemies of the Soviet Union, to reorganize the Sixth Department of the *GUGB* of the *Narkomvnudel* (Department of Transportation and Communication), separating from it a special department of railroad transportation.

To assign to this department the mission of fighting all types of counterrevolution in the area of transportation, above all sabotage, subversion, and espionage by the enemies of the Soviet government.

To relieve the Transportation Department of the *GUGB* of the functions of maintaining public order in railroad transportation, guarding railroad stations, fighting theft of socialist property, vandalism, and child homelessness.

For maintaining public order and fighting crime in railroad transportation, to create a special railroad militia subordinated to the Main Directorate of the Worker-Peasant Militia of the *Narkomvnudel.*

The Transportation Department of the *GUGB* of the *Narkomvnudel* shall be organized linearly, subordinating the line-transport departments directly to the Transportation Department of the *GUGB* of the *Narkomvnudel.*

To organize as a part of the *GUGB* of the *Narkomvnudel* an Eleventh Department for water transportation, highways, and systems of the People's Commissariat of Communication.

7) The *Narkomvnudel* is to take strict measures to completely eliminate shameful cases where individual *Cheka* personnel, as a result of their own talkativeness, are themselves a source of secret information to enemies of the Soviet system.

8) To require all *oblast'* and *krai* party committees and the *TSK*'s of the republic Communist parties to give more attention to the work of *Narkomvnudel* organs, rendering them all possible assistance in their work, for which:

a) Systematically augment *Narkomvnudel* organs with the best, proven party cadres;

b) In every way possible, help the cause of political education and development of Bolshevik *Cheka* cadres;

c) Do not overburden state security organs and staff with assignments and instructions not directly related to the task of fighting counterrevolution.

9) Advise the *Narkomvnudel* on the basis of the present resolution of the Plenum of the *TSK VKP(b)* to draft a letter to all staff of state security organs of the *Narkomvnudel* on the lessons and missions of *Cheka* personnel deriving from this resolution.

The Plenum of the Central Committee of the *VKP(b)* expresses its absolute confidence that all *Cheka* personnel will absorb the lessons of past mistakes in exposing the anti-Soviet Zinovievite and Trotskyite conspiracy, will correct these mistakes as Bolsheviks should as soon as possible, and by their deeds will merit the exalted title of the leading armed detachment of the party of Lenin and Stalin.

RTSKhIDNI, fond 17, op. 2, d. 577, ll. 9, 90b, 10.

DOCUMENT 56 *Stalin's order of February 28, 1938, dismissing A. I. Egorov from the Red Army command and expelling him from the ranks of the Central Committee*

Proletarians of All Countries, Unite!   Top Secret

ALL-UNION COMMUNIST PARTY (OF BOLSHEVIKS) [*VKP(b)*]
CENTRAL COMMITTEE [*TSK*]

- -

No. P59/22   February 28, 1938

TO *TSK VKP(b)* FULL AND CANDIDATE MEMBERS

Comrade <u>Krupskaia</u>

Since, as was revealed in the confrontation of Comrade Egorov with the arrested conspirators Belov, Griaznov, Grin'ko, and Sed'iakin, Comrade Egorov has turned out to be politically more unreliable than could have been expected prior to the confrontation and considering that his wife, nee TSeshkovskaia, with whom he has lived in perfect amity, was found to be a longtime Polish spy, as she stated in her confession, the *TSK VKP(b)* and the Council of People's Commissars of the USSR have decided to relieve Comrade Egorov of his duties as

Commander of the Transcaucasian Military District and dismiss him from the army. Accordingly, the Politburo of the *TSK VKP(b)* has found it necessary to expel Comrade Egorov from the ranks of *TSK VKP(b)* candidate members.

The Politburo of the *TSK VKP(b)* is submitting this proposal to a vote by the *TSK VKP(b)* full and candidate members.

Secretary of the *TSK*

[On Krupskaia's copy of the memo, top left corner, is written:] I concur, N. Krupskaia. [On Poskrebyshev's copy is scrawled:] For expulsion from the ranks of *TSK VKP(b)* candidate members, Posk.

RTSKhIDNI, fond 17, op. 2, d. 640, ll. 116, 139.

DOCUMENT 57   *Resolution of a commission of the Central Committee, March 26, 1935, investigating the staff of the Central Executive Committee*

Top Secret

RESOLUTION
OF THE COMMISSION OF THE CENTRAL COMMITTEE OF THE ALL-UNION
COMMUNIST PARTY (BOLSHEVIKS)

On investigating the All-Union Central Executive Committee Staff

1. Varmashenko, G. I.	non-member	Secretary for minutes	Dismiss for concealing residence on "white" territory and lying about being in Red Army
2. Boitsov, E. P.	non-member	Adviser, former wartime adviser	Dismiss
3. Lazovskii, I. IU.	non-member	Adviser, former member of *Okrug* Court, hid aristocratic background	Dismiss for hiding his aristocratic background
4. Popova, T. N.	non-member	Techn. secretary	Dismiss
5. Serebrovskii, V. I.	non-member	Legal adviser, hid aristocratic background	Dismiss immediately for hiding his aristocratic background
6. Skalozubov, N. N.	non-member	Adviser, former member of *Okrug* Court	Dismiss

[Handwritten notations on document:] Comrade Ezhov, such a decision Comrade Belenok and I propose through the channels of the All-Union Central Executive Committee. In examining this proposal at the commission meeting, Diselev and Uspenskii can be called upon.
When do we convene the commission?
Tomorrow at 12.

RTSKhIDNI, fond 17, op. 120, d. 186, ll. 29, 30.

DOCUMENT 58   *Politburo announcement of* VKP(b) *Central Committee expulsions and arrests, signed by Stalin, December 1937*

Central Committee of the
All-Union Communist Party
(of Bolsheviks) [*TSK VKP(b)*]

Proletarians of All Countries, Unite!   TOP SECRET.

ALL-UNION COMMUNIST PARTY (of Bolsheviks)
CENTRAL COMMITTEE

No. P4128   December 4, 1937

TO MEMBERS AND CANDIDATE MEMBERS OF THE CENTRAL COMMITTEE OF THE *VKP(b)*
To Comrade Egorov

On the basis of incontrovertible evidence, the Politburo of the Central Committee of the *VKP(b)* has found it essential to expel from the membership of the Central Committee of the *VKP(b)* and to arrest as enemies of the people: Bauman, Bubnov, Bulin, V. Mezhlauk, Rukhimovich and Chernov, who proved to be German spies; V. Ivanov and IA. IAkovlev, who proved to be German spies and agents of the tsarist secret police; M. Mikhailov, linked in counterrevolutionary activities with IAkovlev; and Ryndin, linked in counterrevolutionary activities with Rykov, Sulimov. All of these individuals have admitted their guilt. The Politburo of the Central Committee requests approval for the expulsion of the above-named individuals from the Central Committee *VKP(b)* and their arrest.

SECRETARY OF THE CENTRAL COMMITTEE OF THE *VKP(b)*
[signed] J. Stalin

[signed] A. I. Egorov
December 8, 1937

[Handwritten note by Egorov on the left margin:]
All these reprobates and [illegible] are to be wiped off the face of the earth as the lowest possible scum and disgusting filth. [signed] A. I. Egorov, December 8, 1937

RTSkhIDNI, fond 17, op. 2, d. 640, ll. 116, 139.

Appeal through the Japanese press to the American people, January 4, 1939, by political refugee, General G. S. Liushkov, former head of the Far East Secret Police, to stop the despotism and crimes of Stalin

People's Commissar
of Defence of the USSR

Intelligence Department
Worker-Peasant Red Army
Section _____
January 4, 1939
No. 143009
Moscow, 19,
B. Znamenskii, No. 19
tel. 1-03-40, ext.

Top Secret
Copy No. 1

Of Particular Importance.
To People's Commissar of the USSR
Marshal of the Soviet Union
Comrade Voroshilov

Attached I submit a translation of a
communique from the "Domei" agency
Attachment: 3 Pages

Deputy Chief of the Intelligence Department
of the Worker-Peasant Red Army
Division Commander [signed] A. Orlov

Issued: 3 Copies

[Stamped]
No. 20
5 January 1939
People's Commissar of
Defence of the USSR

TOP SECRET

Tokyo

General Genrikh Samoilovich Liushkov, former head of the Far East Unified State Political Directorate [*OGPU*], who has now become a political emigrant in Japan, has issued the following declaration to the American people:

I wish to tell the democratic people of America of the truly great tragedy that has been taking place in the Soviet Union during the past several years and which, evidently, will not end soon. All the news that you are receiving about the Soviet Union comes from official sources. These sources announce that: Socialism has been constructed in the Soviet Union, that the Soviet Union has the most democratic constitution, that the Soviet people (as one) are now happily united around Stalin's leadership. If these declarations were correct, there would be no need to doubt the happiness of the Soviet people. However, if everything is as blissful as they officially declare, a question inevitably arises: Why has the Soviet government arrested 1,000,000 people during the last two or three years? In the Far East there are 5 concentration camps containing 500,000 persons. In the entire Soviet Union there are around 30 such camps with a population of 1,000,000 people. These numbers do not include those who have been shot and those permanently incarcerated.

If it is true that <u>IAgoda, Pauker, Tkalun (commander of the Kremlin garrison), Kork, Petrovskii (commander of the Moscow Proletarian Division), and Egorov participated in the terrorist plot against Stalin,</u> why did they fail to kill him at a time when they had full power?

The following data are available for the Far East:

From among the 8,000 persons under arrest, without any judicial process, 4,000 have already been shot and about 4,000 have been confined in concentration camps. From among those incarcerated in prisons, 5,000 have already been shot. In 1938 in the Far East, a total of about 10,000 persons were arrested, and of these 8,000 were shot and 2,000 are confined in concentration camps. From among those held in prisons 12,000 have already been shot. Additionally, 11,000 Chinese residents in the Far East have already been arrested. 8,000 Chinese were forced to move from the Far East to other locations. Also 180,000 Koreans were forced out of the Far East, and 2,600 of them were arrested.

About 1,000 Soviet citizens who formerly lived in Harbin and 6,000 who formerly lived in Poland were also arrested, together with several hundred Germans, Latvians, and other foreigners. About 2,500 Communist Party leaders, officers (commanders) of the Red Army, and personnel of the political department were shot in 1938. They are accused of originating or participating in intrigues and were condemned to death as a result of the "open" trials by military tribunal. Masses of people live in constant fear of sharing the same tragic fate. Such horrors are being perpetrated in the Far East, an area with a population of only 2 million. In this manner, Stalin is deceiving the peoples of his own and other lands. I do not have the space here to describe what is going on in other parts of the Soviet Union.

The material presented here is enough to draw your attention to how brutally Stalin is dealing with his opponents.

A bloody nightmare has engulfed millions of people in the Soviet Union. A full light must be cast upon the hypocrisy of Stalin, who cold-bloodedly condemns tens of thousands of people to death.

According to the laws of the Soviet Union, a wife is answerable for her husband. Does this law reflect Stalin's humaneness? Wives rarely lose their husbands, except to death. Yet in the Soviet Union, if husbands are arrested by the Soviet government, wives are also subject to arrest, shooting, incarceration in camps, or change of residence, even when they are totally innocent. Besides, all victims of the bloody putsch, by Stalin's order, are subjected to the confiscation of their property, and their children are placed in concentration camps for juveniles. The blood of tens of thousands of innocent people is being shed. Tears pour from unfortunate wives, mothers and orphans, who demand emancipation.

Americans! Are you deaf to the pathetic call of the unfortunate wives and children? No, I do believe in the humaneness of the American people. They will never fail to react to the shedding of blood and tears.

I call upon you to use all your public organizations, trade unions, and your press to stop the persecutions, despotism, and crimes of Stalin!

Send your protests to the Soviet Embassy!

Publicize your protests in the press!

Press your government to withdraw its support from the Stalin administration—a cabal of butchers and swindlers!

TSGASA, fond 33987, op. 3, d. 1233, ll. 2–5.

Beria's report to Stalin, May 8, 1944, on the number of cases examined by the
Special Commission

SPECIAL FOLDER
No. 1-1 page No. 115
Copy
<u>TOP SECRET</u>
Copy No. 2

Copying this document without
the permission of the Secretariat
of the People's Commissariat of
Internal Affairs [*NKVD*] of the USSR
is prohibited.

421/b

May 8, 1944

TO THE CENTRAL COMMITTEE
OF THE ALL-RUSSIAN COMMUNIST PARTY (BOLSHEVIK)

<u>Comrade STALIN</u>

I hereby report that on May 6, 1944, a Special Commission of the *NKVD* of the USSR examined the cases of 438 individuals and sentenced 3 individuals to be shot and 435 individuals to various terms of punishment.

PEOPLE'S COMMISSAR OF INTERNAL AFFAIRS
OF THE UNION OF SOVIET SOCIALIST REPUBLICS

(L. BERIA)

<u>2 copies typed</u>

1 copy to the recipient
2 copies to the Secretariat
of the *NKVD*
Typist: Zhurkina
Official: Comrade Ivanov

True Copy: [Ivanov]

TSGAOR.

The Doctors' Plot

In early 1953 central newspapers reported that a new conspiracy against the state had been foiled, this one an organization of doctors who had been engaged for years in cutting short the lives of leading officials, including Andrei Zhdanov, who had died in 1948 at the age of 52. The accusations carried strong anti-Semitic overtones. The doctors were allegedly agents of American and British foreign intelligence with connections to the international Jewish organization Joint, a charitable agency. The actor S. M. Mikhoels, who had been murdered in 1948, was one of the alleged intermediaries between the doctors and their foreign bosses. Many feared at the time that this signaled the start of a vicious new campaign targeted specifically against Jews.

The first evidence for the plot was said to come from a letter of denunciation from Dr. Lidiia Timashuk, a radiologist in the Kremlin hospital and an agent, historians have said, of the *MGB*. Her letter, included here, was written in 1948 at the time of Zhdanov's death. After the "unmasking" of the Plot in 1953, Timashuk was given the Order of Lenin, but when Stalin died three months later and the plotters were all exonerated, Timashuk's award was rescinded. Many people believed that Timashuk had played a leading role in preparing the accusations and were appalled that she continued to work as a radiologist in the Kremlin hospital even after the Twentieth Party Congress in 1956, at which Khrushchev revealed the extent of Stalin's crimes. According to the Soviet historian Roy Medvedev, when some old Bolsheviks learned she was still working, they refused to be x-rayed. Timashuk, however, maintained she was innocent and appealed to the Central Committee for justice in a letter written in 1966 and included here.

DOCUMENT 61   *Doctor Timashuk's report on the health of Zhdanov, August 30, 1948, with notes of Abakumov to Stalin*

Top Secret

TO: Comrade J. V. Stalin

I am forwarding the statement of Doctor M. F. TIMAShUK, the head of the Electrocardiography (EKG) Department at the Kremlin Hospital, concerning the health of Comrade _Zhdanov A. A._ .

As is evident from TIMAShUK's statement, she continues to insist on her conclusion that Comrade _Zhdanov_ suffered from a myocardial infarct in the area of the anterior wall of the left ventricle and the interventricular septum, even though EGOROV, the Director of the Kremlin Medical Department, and Academician VINOGRADOV have asked her to change the conclusion to eliminate any references to a myocardial infarct.

Attachments: The statement of Comrade TIMAShUK and the electrocardiogram of Comrade _Zhdanov_ .

[signed] V. ABAKUMOV

August 30, 1948

To the Chief of the Main Administration of Protection of the Ministry of State Security [*MGB*]
Comrade N. S. Vlasik

On August 28, 1948, I was summoned by the director of the LSUK, Professor Egorov P. I. to perform an EKG on Comrade A. A. Zhdanov.

On the same day, along with Prof. P. I. Egorov, Academician V. N. Vinogradov, and Professor V. Kh. Vasilenko, I flew from Moscow to the designated place, and at about 12 noon I performed an EKG on Andrei Aleksandrovich. Based on the data of that EKG, I diagnosed a "myocardial infarct in the area of the anterior wall of the left ventricle and the interventricular septum," of which I informed the consultation team on the spot.

Professor Egorov and Dr. Maiorov declared to me that this was an incorrect diagnosis and they did not agree with me—Andrei Aleksandrovich has no myocardial infarct, but there is a "functional disorder" because of sclerosis and hypertension. They suggested that I rewrite my conclusion with no reference to myocardial infarct and that I write "caution," just as Dr. Karpai had done on previous EKGs.

On August 29, 1948, after rising from his bed, Andrei Aleksandrovich suffered another serious heart attack, and once again I was summoned from Moscow, but, on the orders of Academician Vinogradov and Professor Egorov, no EKG was performed on August 29; but one was scheduled for August 30. Once again it was categorically suggested that I reformulate my conclusion, with no reference to myocardial infarct, of which I informed Comrade A. M. Belov.

I believe that the consultants and the attending physician Dr. Maiorov underestimate the absolutely serious condition of Andrei Aleksandrovich, permitting him to get out of bed, take a walk in the park; this physical stress exacerbated his heart condition, which was manifested on the August 28 EKG, which triggered another heart attack, which could have fatal consequences in the future.

Although, at the insistence of my chief, Prof. Egorov, I rewrote my conclusion, indicating no "myocardial infarct," I stand by my opinion, and I insist that the strictest bed rest regime be followed for Andrei Aleksandrovich.

Head of the Electrocardiography Department
of the Kremlin Hospital
Dr. Timashuk

August 29, 1948

APRF, fond 3, op. 58, d. 414, ll. 1–200b.

Ruling of the Presidium of the TSK KPSS *on the "doctor saboteurs," January 13, 1953, and excerpt from the newspaper* Pravda

Proletarians of All Countries, Unite!

The Communist Party of the Soviet Union. Central Committee [*TSK KPSS*]

No. BP7/83

......19....

Extract from Minute No. 7 of the Meeting of the Bureau of the Presidium of the Central Committee on January 9, 1953

83.   On the arrest of the group of doctor saboteurs

Decision: Approved draft of press release concerning the
          arrest of a group of doctor saboteurs and
          publication of this release along with an article
          in *Pravda* on the subject.

BUREAU OF THE PRESIDIUM
OF THE *TSK KPSS*

On the Subject of: January 9, 1953
Draft of press release
concerning the arrest of
a group of doctor saboteurs   Persons in attendance

Members of the Bureau of the
Presidium of the *TSK KPSS*

Comrades   Stalin J.V. (absent)
               ✓ Beria L. P.
               ✓ Bulganin N. A.
               ✓ Voroshilov K. E.
               ✓ Kaganovich L. M.
               ✓ Malenkov G. M.
               ✓ Pervukhin M. G.
               ✓ Saburov M. Z.
               ✓ Khrushchev N. S.

Secretaries of the *TSK KPSS*

Comrades   ✓ Aristov A. B.
               ✓ Brezhnev L. I.
               ✓ Ignatov N. G.
               ✓ Mikhailov N. A.
               ✓ Pegov N. M.
               ✓ Ponomarenko P. K.
               ✓ Suslov M. A.

✓Chairman of the Party Control Commission [*KPK*]
Comrade Shkiriatov M. F.

Comrades   ✓Ogol'tsov
                            ✓Golidze
                            ✓Shepilov

APRF, fond 3, op. 58, d. 420, ll. 67–69.

DOCUMENT 63   *Resolution of the Presidium of the Central Committee, April 3, 1953, adopting the report and recommendations of the Ministry of Internal Affairs on the "Doctors' Plot"*

Proletarians of All Countries, Unite!   SECRET
COMMUNIST PARTY OF THE SOVIET UNION. CENTRAL COMMITTEE [*TSK KPSS*]

No. PZ/1   Comrade L. P. Beria
April 3, 1953   To Members of the *TSK KPSS*
To the first secretaries of the *TSK*s of the union republic Communist parties and to the *krai* and *oblast'*
KPSS committees.
Extract from minutes No. 3 of the April 3, 1953, meeting of the
PRESIDIUM of the *TSK KPSS*
Report and recommendations of the Ministry of Internal Affairs of the USSR on the "affair of the physician-
saboteurs."
(To Comrades: Beria, Voroshilov, Bulganin, Pervukhin, Kaganovich, Saburov,
                 Mikoyan, Khrushchev, Molotov, Malenkov)

1. To adopt the proposal of the Ministry of Internal Affairs [*MVD*] of the USSR:

(a) on the complete rehabilitation and release from custody of physicians and members of their families arrested in connection with the so-called affair of the physician-saboteurs, numbering 37 persons;

(b) to institute criminal proceedings against the agents of the former Ministry of State Security [*MGB*] of the USSR who had deliberately fabricated this affair and distorted Soviet laws most grossly.

2. To approve the text of the attached communication for publication in the central press.

3. To suggest to the former minister of the *MGB*, Comrade S. D. Ignat'ev, that he submit to the Presidium of the *TSK KPSS* an explanation of the crudest distortions of Soviet laws and of the falsification of investigative materials permitted by the Ministry of State Security.

4. To make note of the communication by Comrade L. P. Beria that the Ministry of Internal Affairs of the USSR is taking steps to prevent further occurrences of such aberrations in the work of *MVD* agencies.

5. To annul the decree of the Presidium of the Supreme Soviet of the USSR of January 20, 1953, awarding the order of Lenin to Dr. L. F. Timashuk, as incorrect in light of the current state of affairs.

6. To submit for ratification by the Plenum of the *TSK KPSS* the following proposal of the Presidium of the *TSK KPSS*:

"In view of Comrade S. D. Ignat'ev's confession of having permitted serious errors in the operation of the former Ministry of State Security of the USSR, to consider it inadmissible for him to remain in the position of *TSK KPSS* secretary."

7. To send to all members of the *TSK KPSS*, to the first secretaries of the *TSK*s of the union republic Communist parties, and to the *krai* and *oblast'* committees of the *KPSS* the present resolution accompanied by

the letter of Comrade L. P. Beria and the resolution of the Special Investigating Commission of the *MVD* of the USSR.

PRESIDIUM OF THE *TSK KPSS*

Decree of the Presidium of the   Made public
Supreme Soviet of the USSR, no. 5, Apr. 3, 1953 Apr. 4, 1953

COMMUNICATION
OF THE MINISTRY OF INTERNAL AFFAIRS OF THE USSR

The *MVD* has conducted a comprehensive examination of all materials accumulated in the preliminary investigation and all other data relevant to the affair of the group of physicians accused of sabotage, espionage, and terroristic activities aimed at the leading personages of the Soviet state.

As a result of this examination it was determined that, without any legal justification, the former Ministry of State Security of the USSR had arrested Professor M. S. VOVSI, Professor V. N. VINOGRADOV, Professor M. B. KOGAN, Professor B. B. KOGAN, Professor P. I. EGOROV, Professor A. I. FELDMAN, Professor IA. G. ETINGER, Professor V. Kh. VASILENKO, Professor A. M. GRINShTEIN, Professor V. F. ZELENIN, Professor B. S. PREOBRAZhENSKII, Professor N. A. POPOVA, Professor V.V. ZAKUSOV, Professor N. A. ShEREShEVSKII, Doctor G. I. MAIOROV.

The examination has revealed that the accusations leveled against the listed persons are false and that the documentary data relied upon by the investigating agents are groundless. It also has been established that the depositions of the prisoners, admitting their guilt, had been obtained by the investigating agents of the former Ministry of State Security by methods of investigation inadmissible and strictly prohibited by Soviet law.

As a result of the decision of the Investigating Commission, specially appointed by the *MVD* of the USSR to conduct a review of this affair, prisoners M. S. VOVSI, V. N. VINOGRADOV, B. B. KOGAN, P. I. EGOROV, A. I. FELDMAN, V. Kh. VASILENKO, A. M. GRINShTEIN, V. F. ZELENIN, B. S. PREOBRAZhENSKII, N. A. POPOVA, V. V. ZAKUSOV, N. A. ShEREShEVSKII, G. I. MAIOROV, and others involved in this case are totally cleared of the accusations of sabotage, terrorism, and espioniage leveled at them and are released from detention in accordance with art. 4, paragraph 5 of the Criminal Code of RSFSR.

Persons guilty of the inappropriate conduct of the investigation have been arrested and are being criminally prosecuted.

APRF, fond 3, op. 58, d. 423, ll. 1–4

DOCUMENT 64   ***Letter from Dr. L. Timashuk to the Presidium of the Twenty-Third Communist Party Congress, March 31, 1966, asking to have her name cleared of any responsibility for the "Doctors' Plot"***

Copy

[stamp:] *TSK KPSS*
16644, Apr. 21, 1966
1st section
return to Gen. Dep.
of the *TSK KPSS*

To the Presidium of the XXIII Congress of the Communist Party of the Soviet Union [*KPSS*]

I am a doctor by profession, non-party-member, and 67 years old. After graduating from Moscow University No. 1, I joined the Kremlin Medical Department, where I was employed continuously for 38 years. In my last 16 years at the Kremlin I was head of the Functional Diagnosis Department of Hospital No. 1 of the Fourth Main

Directorate. I was forced to retire on May 28, 1964. For my long years of impeccable service I was awarded the "Badge of Honor," the Order of the Red Banner of Labor, and various medals. The Ministry of Public Health of the Soviet Union awarded me the "Outstanding Public Health Employee" badge. In 1962 I was assigned the classification of Category I functional diagnosis therapeutic specialist. The functional diagnosis department I headed was awarded the honorary title of "Communist Labor Brigade." I have published scientific treatises in medical journals and collections. During my career I trained a large number of young doctors and nurses. From 1953 to 1955 I was elected as a Workers' Deputy from the Lenin District of the City of Moscow to the Fourth Convocation [of Supreme Soviet?].

The matter that I bring to the court of highest appeal consists of the consequences of a medical dispute that arose between me and professors V. N. Vinogradov, V. Kh. Vasilenko, and P. I. Egorov, who were treating A. A. Zhdanov.

The reason for the dispute was a divergence of diagnosis, treatment, and regimen established by the professors for their patient A. A. Zhdanov.

Clinical evidence and methods of objective diagnosis (electrocardiogram, blood analysis, and other clinical data) indicated that the patient had suffered an <u>acute myocardial infarction</u> of the front-left ventricle and the transventricular partition. However, professors V. N. Vinogradov, V. Kh. Vasilenko, and P. I. Egorov insisted he had a <u>functional disorder of cardiovascular activity resulting from sclerosis and high blood pressure.</u> Such a divergence in diagnosis, and consequently in the treatment and prescribed regimen, was fraught with grave consequences for the patient. This caused me immediately to turn to the personal guard of A. A. Zhdanov, Major A. M. Belov, with the request to put me in touch with Moscow; I had no other recourse at this time in Valdai. I set forth my written opinion about the patient, according to the dictates of my medical conscience and my desire to help the patient. I gave this letter along with the electrocardiogram that I took in Valdai to Major Belov and asked him to send it as soon as possible to the Central Committee [TSK] of the KPSS.

A. A. Zhdanov died on Aug. 30, 1948. The results of the postmortem examination, performed in situ in Valdai by the pathologist A. F. Fedorov, confirmed the diagnosis of myocardial infarction that I had put forward while the patient was alive, but which the professors had rejected.

On September 6, 1948, Professor P. I. Egorov, the Chief of the Kremlin Medical Department, called a meeting. The persons summoned included Professor V. N. Vinogradov, V. Kh. Vasilenko, Doctor Maiorov, the anatomist Fedorov, and me (the stenographer was E. N. Rubchevskaia). At the meeting Professor Egorov opened the discussion of the discrepancies in the diagnoses, reminded me of my "complaint" in front of the professors in attendance, and did everything he could to discredit me as a physician by uttering unwarranted insults and calling me a "strange" and "dangerous" person. On September 7, 1948, I was summoned to the personnel department, where the personnel manager read aloud an order signed by the Chief of the Kremlin Medical Department transferring me from the hospital to a clinic office, ostensibly for the purpose of improving its performance.

On September 7, 1948, I wrote a letter to the TSK KPSS addressed to Secretary A. A. Kuznetsov in which I set forth my opinion of the diagnosis and treatment of A. A. Zhdanov (a copy of which I kept). I never received a reply to my letter of August 29, which I had sent to Moscow through Major Belov, or to my letter of September 7, 1948, to Kuznetsov at the TSK KPSS. The Secretariat staff answered my telephone calls to Kuznetsov by saying "We received your letter and you'll get a call very soon." After waiting four months for an answer or a call, on January 7, 1949, I wrote to the Central Committee again requesting an interview on the case of the late Zhdanov, but I never got an answer to this letter either, so I simply stopped writing.

Four and a half years later, I was suddenly summoned to the investigative department for sensitive cases of the Ministry of State Security [MGB]. I was interviewed on the case of the deceased Zhdanov, at first by Investigator Novikov and later by Investigator Eliseev, and I simply confirmed what I had written in my letter to Kuznetsov at the TSK.

A half year later, on Jan. 20, 1953, A. N. Poskrebyshev telephoned to invite me to the Kremlin to see G. M. Malenkov, who told me that a meeting of the Council of Ministers with Stalin present had just declared its gratitude to me for displaying, 4¹/₂ years ago, great courage when I entered into my lone fight with the distinguished professors who were treating Zhdanov, and for standing up for my medical opinion concerning the patient, and that I had been awarded the Order of Lenin. I was shaken because this was so unexpected, because I didn't think the doctors who treated Zhdanov could have been saboteurs. I told Malenkov that I didn't deserve such a high award because, as a doctor, I didn't do anything special, but rather what any Soviet doctor in my place would have done. The next day, Jan. 21, 1953, [several weeks before Stalin died] I was awarded the Order of Lenin, but on April 4, 1953, [several weeks after Stalin died] the Presidium of the Supreme Soviet abrogated the award as a mistake. When I turned in the order to the Supreme Soviet, A. F. Gorkin and N. M Pegov were present; they assured me that the government considered me an honorable Soviet doctor, and that the abrogation of the award did not reflect on my competence as a doctor or my position at work. I continued to work at the same Kremlin hospital in my former position, as head of the functional diagnostic department.

Three years later in 1956, in his secret letter to the *TSK KPSS*, N. S. Khrushchev mentioned my name in connection with the "doctors' affair."

On March 31, 1956, I wrote another letter to the *TSK* personally addressed to N. S. Khrushchev. In this letter I once again described my part in the examination of Zhdanov and the medical disagreements I had with Professors Vinogradov, Vasilenko, and Egorov and also mentioned that I had absolutely no connection to the other doctors and professors described as participants in the "doctors' plot" who never treated Zhdanov but who were victimized during the era of the personality cult.

As a result of my letter to Khrushchev, I was summoned to the *TSK* by V. V. Zolotukhin, who informed me that my letter had been read to the Presidium of the *TSK KPSS*, that it was not the right time to bring up my case, and that I should keep doing my job just like before and not worry about anything. And then he added: "If you have any problems, don't talk to anyone about them except for us at the *TSK*."

Thirteen years have passed, and my social position is still unclear. Some people are of the opinion that the "doctors' plot" had originated because I had defamed honest doctors and professors. These rumors continue to circulate and are always distressing to me.

In April 1964 the management of the Fourth Main Directorate, headed by Professor A. M. Markov, announced to me that I would no longer be able to remain in my position as head of the department of functional diagnostics because professors "who had suffered" were working in the fourth Directorate and circumstances for me were such that I would be forced to retire. <u>After retiring I lost my right to an apartment, and despite references and petitions I was refused the right to a personal pension, and so forth.</u>

After working at the Fourth Main Directorate for 38 years without a single black mark on my record, I have retired under a huge and undeserved black cloud. After all, I am not just a doctor who has devoted her entire life to serving the people and my beloved profession, I am also the mother of an officer in the Soviet Armed Forces, a fighter pilot who, while defending the Motherland on a combat mission, was burned and maimed in a burning aircraft and is now a Category I disabled veteran of the Great Patriotic War. He was awarded the Order of the Great Patriotic War. I have grandsons in the Pioneers and the *Komsomol*, and my husband is a doctor at the Central Military Hospital.

Only after suffering severe emotional stress for 13 years and many futile attempts to get justice, I have been forced to appeal to the Highest Body of the Communist Party, the Presidium of the 23rd Congress of the CPSU, to ask for justice for a person who has sacrificed her entire life and personal well-being to the sick. My position in society is quite tragic. After I was awarded the Order of Lenin in conjunction with the doctors' plot, the national newspapers published articles on the fabrication of the "doctors' plot" and the exoneration of the accused doctors which stated that I had been awarded the Order of Lenin by mistake but failed to publish any additional explanations which would have proven that I had absolutely nothing to do with the affair. These stories gave most people the impression that I had slandered these doctors, and in addition, their analysis of Khrushchev's secret letter in 1956 reinforced an opinion which was completely unfair.

I will not go on to describe the offensive and unfair reproach to which I am subjected when people make reference to me. Such a situation can no longer continue.

I petition the Presidium to introduce clarity and justice into this unprecedented "case."

Doctor L. Timashuk
March 31, 1966

My address: Moscow "19," Frunze Street 7, Apt. 1

True copy
[illegible signature]

APRF, fond 3, op. 58, d. 423, ll. 174–1790b

DOCUMENT 65   *Decree of the Supreme Soviet of the USSR, June 26, 1953, on the criminal anti-state activities of Beria*

DECREE
OF THE PRESIDIUM OF THE SUPREME SOVIET OF THE USSR

On the Criminal Anti-State Activities of L. P. Beria

In view of recent revelations of the anti-state activities committed by L. P. Beria aimed at undermining the Soviet state in the interests of foreign capitalists, the Presidium of the Supreme Soviet of the USSR in examining the reports submitted by the Council of Ministers of the USSR, resolves:

1. To deprive L. P. Beria of his position as Deputy of the Supreme Soviet.

2. To remove L. P. Beria from his post as First Deputy Chairman of the Council of Ministers of the USSR and from his post as Minister of Internal Affairs of the USSR.

3. To deprive L. P. Beria of all rights conferred on him as well as honors, medals, and other honorary awards bestowed on him.

4. To submit the case concerning these criminal activities committed by L. P. Beria to the Supreme Court of the USSR for review.

[SEAL]

Chairman of the Presidium of
the Supreme Soviet of the USSR - K.VOROShILOV

Secretary of the Presidium of the Supreme Soviet of the USSR (N. Pegov)

[signed] N. Pegov

Moscow, Kremlin
June 26, 1953

TSGAOR, fond 7523-sch, op. 85-s, d. 82, l. 5.

Directive to the Central Committee, December 26, 1962, revising procedures for informing families of causes of death of relatives while in police custody

Top Secret

Central Committee of the
Communist Party of the USSR

USSR
Committee on State Security [*KGB*]

December 26, 1962
no. 3265-S
City of Moscow

In 1955 the *KGB* issued through channels and with the concurrence of the Office of the Public Prosecutor of the USSR directive no. 10SS to local *KGB* organs. This directive defined the procedures to be used when considering the requests of citizens interested in determining the fate of persons shot upon the orders of nonjudicial organs (the former Collegia of the Unified State Political Directorate [*OGPU*]), three-person commissions of the *OGPU-NKVD-UNKVD*, and the Commission of the *NKVD* of the USSR and of the Public Prosecutor of the USSR). In accordance with these instructions, the state security organs were to notify the family members of those convicted that their relatives were sentenced to 10 years in the *ITL* [corrective labor camps] and died in their places of incarceration. And when settlement of property or other legal questions so required, the deaths of the executed persons were to be recorded at the registry office and certificates issued to the claimants indicating the dates of death within ten years of the day of arrest, with the causes of death to be invented.

The establishment of this procedure in 1955 was justified by the fact that during the period of mass repressions large numbers of people were convicted without grounds. Exposure of the actual fate of those subjected to this repression could negatively influence the status of their families. Moreover, it was also presumed that informing family members of those shot of the actual fate of their relatives might be exploited at that time by certain hostile elements to the detriment of the interests of the Soviet state.

The existing procedure of reporting fictitious information applies mainly to those Soviet citizens who were innocently victimized and were shot by decisions of nonjudicial organs during the period of mass repressions.

As a result of a review of criminal cases conducted from 1954 to 1961, almost half of those shot as the result of nonjudicial proceedings were rehabilitated. In most cases relatives of those executed were given untrue information about their death, which supposedly occurred in the places of incarceration.

After the investigation conducted by the Central Committee of the Communist Party exposing the lawlessness that existed during the period of the cult of personality surrounding Stalin, we believe it is essential to change the present procedure of examining citizens' applications with queries about the fate of their relatives.

Providing to citizens fictitious dates and circumstances of death of persons near to them places state security organs in a false situation, especially when the press prints the dates of death of individuals who once rendered great service to the party and state. Furthermore, registration of the death of those shot by decisions of nonjudicial organs and with fictitious periods of incarceration indicated in the documents places members of their families at a disadvantage compared with families of persons shot by a court verdict when determining the size of pensions.

The Soviet people have been informed of the massive violations of socialist law that occurred, and the motives behind the procedure established in 1955 for reporting to relatives about family members subjected to repression no longer exist.

In view of the above, we advise that in the future in response to queries from citizens about the fate of their relatives condemned to be shot in nonjudicial proceedings, the actual circumstances surrounding the death of these persons be communicated orally, and the date of their execution be entered in the registry bureau as the date of death, without stating the cause of death, as is done in the Military Collegium of the Supreme Court of the USSR and the military tribunals with regard to persons shot by court verdicts.

It is intended that this procedure will not be applied to persons previously given an answer under the guidelines established earlier and still in effect.

Notifying citizens of the actual circumstances concerning the death of the condemned persons will give the members of their families eligible for a pension (because of the loss of the breadwinner) grounds to submit a petition to the proper government agency for a pension on preferential terms, similar to those of relatives of people who died as a result of an industrial accident or who perished during official duty.

It should be pointed out that the number of applications concerning the fate of those convicted in a non-judicial procedure declines with each passing year (in 1954 there were 36,225, whereas for eight months of 1962 there were 8,018).

The procedure of reporting abroad the dates of death of those sentenced to be shot was established by the resolution of the Presidium of the Council of Ministers of the USSR on December 15, 1959, (min. no. 37), which determined on an individual basis that the date to be issued is not to be earlier than the date of the execution itself nor later than 10 years from the date of the actual arrest. In our opinion, there is no reason to change this procedure.

The proposal presented above has the concurrence of the Office of the Public Prosecutor of the USSR and the Supreme Court of the USSR.

Please examine.

Chairman of the
Committee of State Security

V. Semichastnyi

Source?

Gulag Origins and Operations

Aleksandr Solzhenitsyn made the acronym *Gulag* famous with the publication in 1974 of the first volume of his three-volume history of the Soviet prison camp system, *The Gulag Archipelago.* The term *Gulag* stood for *Glavnoe upravlenie lagerei*, the Main Directorate for Camps. It was established as a branch of the *OGPU* in 1930, but the system of forced labor and concentration camps had been created much earlier. The Soviet prison system emerged in the chaos of the Civil War amidst institutional rivalry between the People's Commissariat of Justice and the *Cheka*. The first concentration camps were created under *Cheka* supervision in July 1918. When Lenin wrote to his comrades in Penza in August 1918 (see Document 4), he stated that terror should be carried out among *kulaks*, priests, and white guards and that the suspicious ones should be placed in the concentration camp outside of town.

Forced labor camps developed separately, the result of attempts to rehabilitate petty criminals through labor. In 1919 the *Cheka* was given the responsibility of administering the camps in which such prisoners were placed, and it adopted the model previously developed for the concentration camps for political prisoners. As the regime's antireligious efforts intensified, confiscated monasteries were converted for use as camp buildings. One of the most notorious and tragic was the prison on the Solovetskii Islands in the far north. Once a center of religious monasticism, Solovki was first used as a prison to house Socialist Revolutionaries convicted as counterrevolutionaries in their 1922 show trial. Complaints about treatment of prisoners made their way back to the center, and in 1929 the writer Maksim Gorky made a well-publicized investigatory trip to Solovki, reporting that conditions there were humane and adequate. Gorky would also be pressed into service to laud the building of the White Sea Canal. The principle of "corrective labor" remained a central tenet of Soviet penology. Huge works projects, such as the White Sea Canal, a new trans-Siberian rail line between the Amur River and Lake Baikal, and later gold mines in Kolyma, were managed by the *NKVD* and staffed by prison labor. Indeed, one explanation for the magnitude of the purges of the 1930s was the *NKVD*'s insatiable demand for labor for its economic enterprises.

With the Nazi-Soviet Pact of 1939 the Red Army expanded Soviet power into the Baltic states and Poland, and prisoners of war taken in these actions were also used for labor purposes. Some prisoners, however, including Polish officers held in a camp near Katyn, were judged to be too dangerous to use for labor duties, and as is shown in Document 84, they were systematically executed in 1940.

The labor camp system continued in force after the war, swollen with hundreds of thousands of inmates whose wartime activities had brought them into disfavor. To conceal the magnitude of the system and to prevent the reinfection of society by these "hostile" elements, prisoners, once they had served their sentences, were forbidden to return to their homes and remained confined to exile in distant regions of the Soviet Union. Only after the death of Stalin, and with the relaxation of this prison regime during Khrushchev's "thaw," did hundreds of thousands of former prisoners finally return to their homes and families.

DOCUMENT 67   *Minutes of the June 25, 1919, meeting of the NKVD on organizing labor camps in Moscow, Petrograd, and the surrounding areas*

[Stamped in upper right corner:]
NKVD Central Division of Civil Affairs Records
(June 18, 1919)
incoming number 1079
copy

Protocol No. 49

Meeting of the Collegium of the Peoples' Commissariat of Internal Affairs [*NKVD*]

In attendance : Comrades Dzerzhinsky, Vladimirskii, Kanatchikov, Eiduk, Maksimovskii, Kedrov, Popov.
Chaired by: Comrade Vladimirskii
Minutes taken by: Comrade Siniavin

Proposal: 1. On the establishment of a children's center (camp for handicapped children) in the Savinkovskii Monastery in the city of Zvenigorod, Moscow *guberniia*.

Resolution: To inform the Moscow *Guberniia* Executive Committee that because of the agreement between the *NKVD*, the People's Commissariat of Health, and the People's Commissariat of Social Security in the city of Zvenigorod in Moscow *guberniia* a children's center for handicapped children is hereby organized with the consent of the Executive Committee of the city of Zvenigorod under the direction of the People's Commissariat of Social Security and the Department of Forced Labor of the *NKVD*.

Proposal: 2. On the granting of an advance which would be at the disposal of the assistant chief of the Department of Forced Labor, Comrade Popov, in order to equip the camps promptly and to cover other urgent expenses.

Resolution: a. To place at the disposal of the assistant chief of the Department of Forced Labor a one-time advance in the amount of 360,000 rubles for special expenses needed to equip the camps.

b. To grant him a permanent advance in the amount of 100,000 rubles for urgent operating expenses.

Proposal: 3. On the Central Collegium for Prisoners of War and Refugees [*TSentroplenbezh*] and its merging with *Moplenbezh* [Moscow Prisoners and Refugees].

Resolution: a. To instruct Comrade Shcherbakov to inspect accurately *Moplenbezh* and to present a detailed report with numerical data to the next meeting of the Collegium.

To invite Comrade Isaev from *Moplenbezh* and a representative of the Presidium of the Moscow Soviet to the next meeting of the Collegium.

b. To appoint Comrade Veinshtenker inspector general to permanently oversee the matter of supplies for the *TSentroplenbezh*.

Proposal: 4. On the occupation of the house at 3 Nastasinskii Street

Resolution: To instruct Comrade Kanatchikov immediately to occupy the building at 3 Nastaskinskii Street, for the establishment of a museum of the *NKVD* by order of the Housing-Land Department of the Moscow Soviet.

Proposal: 5. Report of Comrade Kedrov concerning the establishment of forced labor camps in Moscow, Petrograd and surrounding areas.

Resolution: a. To place citizens of countries which are at war with us in separate camps or specially designated quarters in order not to mix them with criminal elements.

b. To give forced labor camp prisoners who are foreign citizens paid work with the written consent of the prisoner.

Barracks in the concentration camp, at Ufa in the Urals 1919–20. TSGAKFD. N -2-3699, 2-3700

   c. To transfer within a five-day period all who have been sentenced to forced labor until the end of the Civil War from Butyrskaia Prison to the Novo-Andronievskii Camp.

   d. The Main Administration of forced labor camps must find and establish within a ten-day period a suitable area near Moscow to send prisoners from Petrograd who have been sentenced to forced labor.

   e. To direct the Moscow Emergency Committee to transfer the sealed property of the German Committee in Moscow to the *TSentroplenbezh* for supply to the forced labor camps (this duty to be fulfilled by Comrade Eiduk).

   f. To assign the Central Prisoner and Refugee Commission to supply the forced labor camps.

   g. To instruct Comrade Popov to present to the next meeting of the commission a detailed report about the activities of the Main Administration of forced labor camps, including a detailed financial accounting.

The original was signed by comrades: Chairman Vladimirskii, members Dzerzhinsky, Kanatchikov, Eiduk, Maksimovskii, Kedrov, Secretary Comrade Siniavin
True copy.
For the Secretary of the *NKVD* Collegium
                    [illegible signature]

TSGAOR, fond 393, op. 1, d. 19, ll. 144–144ob

RUSSIAN SOVIET FEDERATED SOCIALIST REPUBLIC
PEOPLE'S COMMISSARIAT OF INTERNAL AFFAIRS [*NKVD*]
DEPARTMENT OF FORCED LABOR

June 25, 1919

No. 359
MOSCOW
Malyi Znamenskii Lane, No. 3

URGENT

To the Deputy People's Commissar for Internal Affairs
Comrade VLADIMIRSKII

Now that the matter of the urgent organization of forced labor concentration camps has been resolved, the department entrusted to me is now faced with the very difficult problem of organizing regular supplies and transport for all the camps.

Currently, four camps have been organized and are in operation in Moscow, and in the near future we will open two more camps designed to accommodate the following numbers of individuals:

1) Novo-Peskovskii (Reception Center)	
capacity	450 people
current population	132 "
2) Pokrovskii (General Camp for Men)	
capacity	700 "
current population	457 "
3) Andron'evskii (Special Camp for Men)	
capacity	750 "
current population	192 "
4) Novo-Spasskii (Camp for Women)	
capacity	400 "
current population	178 "
Total of 4 camps with	
combined capacity of	2300 "
current combined population	959 "

In addition, the Kozhukhovskii No. 13 Reception Center with a capacity of 2,500 individuals has been placed at the temporary disposal of the department as a transit point to handle sudden influxes of large groups, and the *Detskii Gorodok* [Children's Village] Camp for Children with a capacity of 700 is being opened at Zvenigorod in Moscow *guberniia,* for a total of 6 camps with a combined capacity of 5,500 individuals.

The delivery of supplies and the performance of work details at the camps have been made extremely difficult by a shortage of transportation resources such as horses, carts, sledges, harness, and so forth. These items are urgently needed to set up the camps, especially because work details have been organized at the camps for gardening, the production of fuel from waste material, trash cleanup, delivery of materials from warehouses for the carpentry shops, metalworking shops, blacksmith shops, and sewing shops which are now being organized, the delivery of building materials for repairs, and so forth. Hence we need an emergency appropriation of funds to acquire the following items to provide transport for the camps:

for each camp	3 horses
" " "	2 summer drays
" " "	2 sledges
" " "	2 sets of harness
for the 6 camps as a whole	18 horses
" " "	12 summer drays
" " "	12 sledges
" " "	12 sets of harness

If we calculate the costs of all this on the basis of current local market prices, we arrive at the following figures:

1 horse	25,000–30,000 rubles
1 summer dray	7,000–8,000 rubles
1 set of harness	1,000–2,000 rubles
1 sledge	5,000–6,000 rubles

and thus the total amount required to provide transport for the camps may be expressed by the following figures:

horses	18 @ 30,000 rubles	540,000 rubles
summer drays	12 @ 8,000 rubles	96,000 rubles
harness	12 sets @ 2,000 rubles	24,000 rubles
sledges	12 @ 6,000 rubles	72,000 rubles
Total		732,000 rubles

If we consider that some of the horses and carts are already available and the carts are merely in need of repair or replacement, other carts will be built at the camps by the inmates or acquired from Soviet agencies free of charge, still others can be reconditioned for winter use using camp labor, and so forth, we might be able to cut these costs in half. In order to have sufficient funds for these purposes, the department must have up to 560,000 rubles at its disposal, which I ask you to appropriate as quickly as possible and place at my disposal. On my part, I will do everything I can to minimize transportation costs by procuring everything outside of Moscow in the provinces, where these items can obviously be procured at a lower cost.

Please be so kind as to notify me of your decision as soon as possible.

Head of the Department of Forced Labor [Illegible Signature]

TSGAOR, fond 393, op. 10, d. 1, ll. 240–241.

DOCUMENT 69   *Resolution of the Presidium of the Moscow Soviet, August 29, 1919, establishing a directorate of Moscow concentration camps*

Russian Federated Soviet Socialist Republic
Presidium of the Moscow Soviet of
   Workers' and Red Army Deputies
Moscow, Soviet Square, Building of the Moscow Soviet of
   Workers' Deputies, Sept. 1, 1919
No. 13252
Tel. 64-20, ext. 0-100

Excerpt from the resolutions of the Presidium of the Moscow Soviet of Workers' and Red Army
Deputies   August 29, 1919

To: People's Commissariat for Internal Affairs [*NKVD*]
To: Comrade Vladimirskii
For your information.

On establishing Concentration Camps located in the city of Moscow under the administration of the Moscow Soviet.

Decided:

I. To establish the Directorate of Moscow Concentration Camps under the Presidium of the Moscow Soviet of Workers' and Red Army Deputies.

II. To appoint Comrade VARDZIELI director of Moscow Concentration camps.

III. To instruct Comrade VARDZIELI without delay:

   1. to take over all Moscow concentration camps from the Department of Forced Labor of the *NKVD*

   2. to compile lists of all prisoners in Moscow concentration camps with the following data:
      a) last name, first name, patronymic;
      b) name of the agency whose decision sentenced the person to prison;
      c) crime committed by the person;
      d) date of the sentence;
      e) the term of imprisonment.

IV. To bring this resolution for ratification to the Executive Committee.

               Administrator,
               Member of the Presidium   [illegible]
               Secretary [illegible]

[Seal:] Russian Socialist Federated Soviet Republic [*sic*]. Moscow Soviet of Workers' and Red Army Deputies

TSGAOR, fond 393, op. 10, d. 1, l. 260.

Minutes of NKVD meeting, January 17, 1920, concerning the organization of forced labor camps

Protocol No. 1

Meeting of the Collegium of the People's Commissariat
of Internal Affairs

January 17, 1920

Present: Dzerzhinsky, Vladimirskii, Vasil'ev, Eiduk, Medved',
Zingvil' [?]
Chairman:Comrade M. Vladimirskii

No.	DISCUSSED	RESOLVED	Notes
1.	Information report of Comrade Vladimirskii on congresses of communal section managers and administrative section managers.	Convene a session of the Collegium by January 28 to discuss the situation of the administrative sections in the executive committees [ispolkoms].	
2.	Comrade Vladimirskii's motion to submit to the Council of People's Commissars a proposal to add to the Revolutionary Council of the Labor Army a representative of the People's Commissariat of Internal Affairs.	To delegate Comrade Vladimirskii to submit the following motion to the Council of People's Commissars: To add to the Revolutionary Council of the Labor Army an NKVD representative. Inform him of his rights, as stipulated in paragraphs 9 and 12 of the decree of the Council of Defense of January 15, to participate in decisions concerning transporting the labor force mobilized by means of compulsory conscription.	
3.	Report of Comrade Medved' on the work of forced labor.	a) Require the Central Collegium for Prisoners and Refugees [TSentroplenbezh] to establish, before Feb. 1, 1920, commissions under the Revolutionary Military Councils of the Army to register and transfer POWs to the rear /pursuant to the May 24, 1919, decree of the Soviet of People's Commissars/. The commissions will include a representative of the Dept. of Forced Labor. b) Create within the Dept. of Forced Labor a subsection for POWs to assign them to forced labor. c) Require the Dept. of Forced Labor to submit, within a week, a plan to organize, in several locations in the republic, special camps with especially strict regimes,	Done I/26/ 1920

		for prisoners with life sentences, and to organize forced labor in such camps.	
		Establish the first camp in Moscow. Notify the presidium of the Moscow Soviet for its approval.	
		All such camps will be under the jurisdiction of the Dept. of Forced Labor of the *NKVD*.	
4.	Report by Comrade Eiduk on the activity of the *TSentroplenbezh*.	a) The Central Collegium for Prisoners and Refugees is reorganized into Evacuation Dept. of the *NKVD*. b) The Statistical Department is reorganized into the Dept. of Statistics of the *NKVD*. All *NKVD* departments are to submit all statistical data to the Dept. of Statistics, except for data on special projects which are to remain in their departments. The head of the Dept. of Statistics should decide with the heads of *NKVD* departments what data should be submitted to the division. c) All transfers of workers required by the Dept. of Registration and Distribution of the Labor Force should be executed by the Dept. of Evacuation. d) Medical and eating facilities should remain under the control of the Dept. of Evacuation. The People's Com. of Health Care has jurisdiction to monitor health, sanitation, and distribution of medical resources. e) Comrade Eiduk is charged with presenting at the next Collegium meeting by January 26 a plan to organize the Dept. of Evac. and create local branches.	
5.	Motion by Comrade Vladimirskii to confirm the resolution concerning the periodic submission of statistical data by the heads of all departments.	a) By noon Monday, a weekly written report consisting exclusively of facts and figures about the Dept. activities of the previous week is to be presented to the Deputy People's Commissar. b) Heads of the branches and clerks are required to present to the Dept. heads the same kind of weekly reports. c) By the fifth of each month, a dept. monthly activity report is to be presented to the Deputy People's Commissar.	

Original copy signed: Chairman, M. Vladimirskii
Members: Dzerzhinsky, Vasil'ev, Eiduk
Approved by: Secretary of the Collegium: P. Margolis

TSGAOR, fond 393, op. 89, d. 61, ll. 2–3.

NKVD *circular, January 27, 1925, on measures for developing work in areas* *of labor camps*

RUSSIAN SOVIET FEDERATED SOCIALIST REPUBLIC [RSFSR]
PEOPLE'S COMMISSARIAT OF INTERNAL AFFAIRS [*NKVD*]
MAIN ADMINISTRATION
OF PLACES OF INCARCERATION OF THE REPUBLIC

January 21, 1925
No. .....

Moscow, Ilinka, 21
Switchboard Numbers: 21-91, 98-58, 2-29-24
2-61-29 and 2-04-20

Ref No. .....
dated .....

Original No. .....
In replies refer to No., date, and department
DEPARTMENT: ....

CIRCULAR No. 47

TO *KRAI*, GUBERNIIA, AND *OBLAST'*
INSPECTORATES OF PLACES OF INCARCERATION

On Steps to Develop Work Programs at Places of Incarceration

The Corrective Labor Code defines our basic mission as assigning inmates to productive employment for the purpose of imparting the benefits of corrective labor to them.

In order to develop inmate employment, inmates should be organized as self-supporting work units exempt from all national and local taxes and levies (see Articles 48 and 77 of the Corrective Labor Code).

In light of this acknowledgment of the importance of corrective labor for inmates, the aforementioned tax exemptions for the development of employment at places of incarceration, and the possibility of obtaining loans for the purpose of developing inmate employment, work programs must be organized without fail at all places of incarceration in the RSFSR to the extent permitted by local conditions, and in exceptional cases officials may organize work programs that do not require substantial investment of fixed or liquid capital and at the same time would be open to participation by most of the inmates.

According to our information, it is obvious that work programs for inmates have not been organized at a

The Vorkuto-Pecherskii forced labor camp, 1945, one of many camps run by the *NKVD*. TSGAOR, Fond 9414-s, op.6, d.24, 25

The Vorkuto-Pecherskii forced labor camp, 1945, one of many camps run by the *NKVD*. TSGAOR, Fond 9414-s, op.6, d.24, 25

large number of places of incarceration, thus depriving the inmates of the benefits of corrective labor, i.e., the places of incarceration are failing to accomplish their primary mission as defined by the Corrective Labor Code.

Deeming this situation to be improper and unacceptable, the Main Administration of Places of Incarceration believes that the organization of work programs is directly dependent on the energy and diligence of the *guberniia* Inspectorates of places of incarceration and recommends that you take additional steps immediately to organize work programs at all the places of incarceration entrusted to you without exception and describe the progress of your efforts in your quarterly reports, to include the following information:

1) the names of the places of incarceration where work programs have been organized, the types of work programs organized, the number of inmates employed therein, the source and amount of funds for these programs; and

2) the names of the places of incarceration where work programs cannot be organized and the reasons why they cannot be organized.

In the process we should provide the following clarifications:

1) If any place of incarceration has any unencumbered and unused operating funds, these funds should be put to use by extending them as repayable loans to those places of incarceration where work programs could be instituted but have been held up solely because of a lack of funds;

2) Inspectors of Places of Incarceration are responsible for organizing work programs, and the progress of work programs at places of incarceration shall constitute the yardstick for evaluating their performance and diligence.

CHIEF OF THE MAIN ADMINISTRATION
OF PLACES OF INCARCERATION   [signed] Shirvindt

HEAD OF THE DEPARTMENT OF WORK PROGRAMS
AND OPERATIONS   [signed] Burlachenko

TSGAOR, fond 393, op. 53, d. 42, ll. 93–94.

DOCUMENT 72   **NKVD *circular of January 1926 regarding staffing of the bureaus for forced labor***

RSFSR
People's Commissariat for Internal Affairs
Main Directorate of Penal Institutions
... Labor ... Dept.
Moscow, Il'inka, 21
Tel. switchboard 4-09-60

FOR CIRCULATION
Respond by ....
Moscow, January 1926 No. 3
Refer to the above No. when responding.

To Regional, District, and Provincial Inspectorates of Penal Institutions in the
RSFSR

Subject:
On determination of staffing
for the Bureaus ... Depts. of Forced
Labor ... keeping .... under guard

Having deemed it necessary, in accordance with articles 23 and 34 of the Correctional Labor Code [*ITK*], among other things, to determine staffing for the Bureaus for Forced Labor under the Inspectorates of Penal Institutions and their local branches, the *NKVD*, via the Main Directorate for Penal Institutions, proposes that no later than February 15, 1926, proposals concerning the aforementioned staffing be delivered to it for examination and approval; furthermore these should be supplemented with the following information for each separate bureau and its departments:

a) number of individuals currently serving sentences of forced labor, b) number of individuals who had served their sentences during the year, c) sums of the 25% deductions from wages, d) current salaries for the corresponding employees of the Bureau or Dept. of Forced Labor, e) positions which could be combined through substitutions.

It should be made clear that: 1) once exact staffing has been approved by the center, an increase in staff may be permitted only upon receipt of relevant authorization from the center, based on a petition justifying the request, and 2) for Inspectorates of Penal Institutions that have not submitted proposals for staffing, such determination will be made by the center.

People's Commissar for Internal Affairs A. Beloborodov

Head of the Main Directorate for Penal Institutions E. Shirvindt

TSGAOR, fond 393, op. 60, d. 26, l. 3.

The Vorkuto-Pecherskii forced labor camp, 1945, one of many camps run by the *NKVD*. TSGAOR, Fond 9414-s, op.6, d.24, 25

The Vorkuto-Pecherskii forced labor camp, 1945, one of many camps run by the *NKVD*. TSGAOR, Fond 9414-s, op.6, d.24, 25

Solovki Prison

Three monasteries, built on the remote Solovetskii Islands in the White Sea off the far north coast of Russia, had been used as a state prison between 1718 and 1903. They were again pressed into service as political prisons in 1923 to house the group of Socialist Revolutionaries convicted in a major Moscow show trial in 1922. In December 1923, to protest a tightening of the camp regime, the prisoners revolted, resulting in the killing of 6 of them. Again, in 1924, prisoners in the three monasteries coordinated a hunger strike to protest conditions, and they were rewarded with a transfer to an even stricter regime in the Verkhne-Ural'sk isolation prison. Solovki, as it was called, continued to serve as a special-purpose labor camp, specializing in logging; ordinary criminals, prostitutes, and juvenile delinquents were assigned there as well as political prisoners. The prison population grew from 3,000 in

1923 to around 50,000 in 1930. Conditions were notorious in Solovki; it was impossible to escape. An official newspaper published glowing reports about the benefits of corrective labor there, and Maksim Gorky made a special trip there soon after his return to the Soviet Union in 1929 in order to report on the re-education of former criminals. He was shown a model prison and returned to write glowingly of new Soviet methods for rehabilitating criminals. Solzhenitsyn describes Solovki as the mother of the *Gulag*. It was closed down and merged with another prison in 1939 on the eve of the Winter War with Finland.

DOCUMENT 73   ***Report by G. Zheleznov, Vinogradov, and F. Belinskii, December 14, 1926, on the intolerable conditions in the Solovki concentration camp***

To the Presidium of the Central Executive Committee of the All-Union Communist Party (Bolshevik)

We appeal to you, asking you to pay a minimum of attention to our request.

We are prisoners who are returning from the Solovetskii concentration camp because of our poor health. We went there full of energy and good health, and now we are returning as invalids, broken and crippled emotionally and physically. We are asking you to draw your attention to the arbitrary use of power and the violence that reign at the Solovetskii concentration camp in Kemi and in all sections of the concentration camp. It is difficult for a human being even to imagine such terror, tyranny, violence, and lawlessness. When we went there, we could not conceive of such a horror, and now we, crippled ourselves, together with several thousands who are still there, appeal to the ruling center of the Soviet state to curb the terror that reigns there. As though it weren't enough that the Unified State Political Directorate [OGPU], without oversight and due process, sends workers and peasants there who are by and large innocent (we are not talking about criminals who deserve to be punished), the former tsarist penal servitude system in comparison to Solovki had 99% more humanity, fairness, and legality. People (mostly proletariat) are sent to Solovki on no grounds whatsoever. During the years of devastation, poverty, hunger, and cold, they had the misfortune of falling into the whirlpool of the struggle for survival. They committed crimes, for which they have been punished by the law and society, and they have returned to the honest work from which they had (we repeat) temporarily strayed. So we feel that the nightmarish past with its hunger and torment is behind us. We have quietly and peacefully worked at state factories and plants, but despite that, most of the people incarcerated at Solovki were taken from their jobs, ripped from honest work and family. The families and children have been left to the mercy of fate, thereby greatly increasing the already large number of homeless waifs. This isn't fiction but facts that can always be verified. But that isn't enough, not when the law allows innocent people to be punished. Why can't people be allowed their meager existence without being doomed to torment and suffering? For example, people who have money come out all right because of that money, and the entire burden once again falls on the workers and peasants who unfortunately have no money but eke out a miserable existence in unbearable jobs—stripped almost bare, living on carrion, since rations given for the unbearable work are negligible. If I'm a shoemaker, then for 20–30 rubles, I can be a metalworker. There are hundreds and thousands of such examples. The beating and humiliation has reached such nightmarish levels, there aren't words to describe it. People die like flies, i.e., they die a slow and painful death. We repeat that all this torment and suffering is placed only on the shoulders of the penniless proletariat, i.e., on workers who, we repeat, were unfortunate to find themselves in the period of hunger and destruction accompanying the events of the October Revolution, and who committed crimes only to save themselves and their families from death by starvation. They have already borne the punishment for these crimes, and the vast majority of them subsequently chose the path of honest labor. Now because of their past, for whose crime they have already paid, they are fired from their jobs. Yet, the main thing is that the entire weight of this scandalous abuse of power, brute violence, and lawlessness that reign at Solovki and other sections of the *OGPU* concentration camp is placed on the shoulders of workers and peasants; others, such as counterrevolutionaries, profiteers and so on, have fat wallets and have set themselves up and live in clover in the Socialist State, while next to them, in the literal meaning of the word, the penniless workers and proletarians die from hunger, cold, and back-breaking 14–16-hour days under the tyranny and lawlessness of inmates who are the agents and collaborators of the State Political Directorate [*GPU*].

If you complain or write anything ("Heaven forbid"), they will frame you for an attempted escape or for something else, and they will shoot you like a dog. They line us up naked and barefoot at 22 degrees below zero and keep us outside for up to an hour. It is difficult to describe all the chaos and terror that is going on in Kemi, Solovki, and the other sections of the concentration camp. All annual inspections uncover a lot of abuses. But what they discover in comparison to what actually exists is only a part of the horror and abuse of power which the inspection accidently uncovers. (One example is the following fact—one of a thousand—which is registered in *GPU* and for which the guilty have been punished: THEY FORCED THE INMATES TO EAT THEIR OWN FE-CES. "Comrades," if we dare to use this phrase, verify that this is an actual fact about which, we repeat, *OGPU* has the official evidence, and you may judge for yourself the full extent of effrontery and humiliation in the super-vision by those who are furthering their careers. Everything that the commission manages to discover by accident is but one-hundredth of the real situation, because the commission is being shown everything just as the ILLUS-TRIOUS PRINCE POTEMKIN showed Catherine II living pictures during her journey through Taurida in the Crimea. And the commission visits once a year; the rest of the time, the prisoners are cut off from the entire world, naked, hungry, and moaning from the unbearable work 16 hours a day. They are controlled through abuse and various forms of humiliation, not daring to speak or complain. It is no exaggeration to say that this is the "Spanish inquisition." The law on labor and the eight-hour working day and time off for holidays are a fantasy. And if 50% come back from there, then in most cases (except for the people who have money, because they get along with their money) they are living corpses. But everywhere people say and write that Soviet authority does not punish but corrects. We are such living corpses, and we have decided to describe, to the best of our poor abili-ty, life in the Solovki concentration camps of the *OGPU*. And we cannot even apply the old saying, "THIS ISN'T LIFE, IT'S HARD LABOR," because people who have done time at hard labor say that this comparison doesn't fit. We are sure and we hope that in the All-Union Communist Party there are people, as we have been told, who are humane and sympathetic. It is possible that you might think that it is our imagination, but we swear to you all by everything that is sacred to us that this is only one small part of the nightmarish truth, because it makes no sense to make this up. We repeat, and will repeat 100 times, that yes, indeed there are some guilty people, but the major-ity suffer innocently, as is described above. The word law, according to the law of the *GPU* concentration camps, does not exist; what does exist is only the autocratic power of petty tyrants, i.e., collaborators, serving time, who have power over life and death. Everything described above is the truth and we, ourselves, who are close to the grave after 3 years in Solovki and Kemi and other sections, are asking you to improve the pathetic, tortured exis-tence of those who are there who languish under the yoke of the *OGPU*'s tyranny, violence, and complete lawless-ness. At the present time we are dispatching [this statement], in the same spirit, to the International Aid Society for Revolutionary Fighters [*MOPR*], to the Workers' and Peasants' Inspection [*RKI*], and (we are even ashamed to say) we want to describe to the fraternal workers of other countries, this unheard-of abuse of power and lawless-ness in Solovetskii concentration camps of the *OGPU* in the hope that justice will prevail.

To this we subscribe: G. Zheleznov, Vinogradov, F. Belinskii.

Dec. 14, 1926

True copy

RTSKhIDNI, fond 17, op. 85, d. 492, ll. 371, 371ob.

Prisoners taking a walk at the Solovki concentration camp, 1937. TSGAKFD, N 4-13347

List of arrested engineering specialists, August 26, 1931, to be assigned to work in Leningrad industries

R. S. F. S. R.
_____

Leningrad Regional
Executive Committee
Soviets of Workers, Peasants,
and Red Army Deputies
_____

**REGIONAL
ECONOMIC COUNCIL**
========
PRESIDIUM
_____

Leningrad, Postal Division 14
Canal Griboedova, 6

[Numerous telephone numbers given]

August 24, 193 1 No. 2585

Copy No. 1 _____

To respond, refer to this number

_T_O_P__S_E_C_R_E_T_

VSNKh SSSR _____

_____ Com. ORDZhONIKIDZE._____

_____

Subject No._____(N/Vx./No.____)

Subject:

The Presidium of the *LOSNKh* requests the assignment of the following arrested specialists to work in the indicated Leningrad industries

NAME OF ENTERPRISE	Nos. in Order	Last name and Initials	SPECIALITY
	1.	ShAKhT	Plumber
"Krasnyi	2.	ShIShKIN, V. M.	Mechanical engineer
Putilovets"	3.	SAKhARNOV, V. A.	Metallurgist
Plant	4.	ROBUSTOV, M. P.	Mechanical engineer
	5.	SAZONOV, V. P.	Mechanical engineer
	6.	MERZLIUTIN, B. G.	Electrician
	7.	NIKOLAEV, G. N.	Builder
	8.	MALYShEV, P. I.	Rolled metal worker
	9.	BER, M. M.	Rolled metal worker
	10.	VITTE, A. O.	Mechanical engineer
	11.	KATS-KAPLINSKII	Civil industrial engineer
	12.	BROIDES, M. A.	Technological engineer comrade director of the Dinamo plant
	13.	KORONOVSKII, P. N.	Automotive engineer
	14.	IVANOV, B. A.	Professor of automated machines
Stalin Metal	15.	SKVORTSOV, V. A.	Mechanical engineer
Plant	16.	KIRILLOV, I. I.	Technological engineer
	17.	ILARIONOV, I. E.	Cold metal engineer
	18.	NEUDAChIN, I. A.	Metal-working specialist
	19.	PYZh, O. A.	Cold metal-working specialist
	20.	KhRABROV, I. M.	Technological engineer
Lenin Plant	21.	GREINER, K. G.	Steam boiler designer
	22.	ZAKhAROV, B. A.	General machine technologist
	23.	PROKhOROV, V. Zh.	Technological engineer
	24.	PUKhAL'SKII, I. V.	" "
	25.	ShUL'TS, E. M.	Technician/mechanic

	26.	LANTSERE, N. K.	Architectural designer
	27.	BOBROVShchIKOV, S. A.	Turbine mechanic
Central	28.	BESIALOV, I. F.	Architect
Casting	29.	IVANOV, I. P.	Mechanical engineer
Machinery	30.	LOMACh', IU. IU.	Electrical engineer
Works	31.	SPIRIDONOV, A. G.	Technician/mechanic
	32.	FINIKOV, V. S.	Metallurgist
	33.	AGLITSKII, A. M.	Mechanical engineer
	34.	SPERANSKII, V. A.	Electrician
	35.	ShIShKO, L. P.	Civil engineer
	36.	AZNOBIShIN, V. N.	Draftsman
	37.	STAROSTIN, V. V.	Builder
	38.	GIUFEL', D. G.	Safety expert
Boiler-	39.	ABAKUMOV, I. T.	Metallurgist
Turbine	40.	ShTRETER, V. I.	Boilermaker
	41.	KIRPIChEV, M. V.	Boiler specialist
	42.	TATARChUK, V. A.	Technologist
Union	43.	BELONOZhKIN, A. I.	Technological engineer
Shipyard	44.	VAZILEVSKII, O. A.	Naval engineer/design engineer

ADDENDUM to page 3

Association of	—	EVANGULON, B. G.	Electrical engineer
Weak-Current	—	ZAKhAR'IN, N. L.	Electrical/mechanical engineer
Plants (Elec-			
trical Commun-	—	BOBROV, S. A.	Electrical engineer
ications	—	LEBEDEV, V. M.	Radio engineer
Works)			
	45.	GOINKIS, P. G.	Ship engineer
	46.	DUKEL'SKII, A. G. T.	Technological engineer/ specialist in art. systems
	47.	EFIMOV, M. I.	Naval engineer
	48.	ZVORYKIN, A. K.	Shipbuilding engineer
	49.	NERKO, A. A.	Naval engineer
	50.	KRIUGER, E. V.	Shipbuilding engineer
	51.	KOSTENKO, V. P.	Ship engineer
	52.	MALININ, B. M.	Ship engineer/technological engineer
	53.	SKORChELLETI, V. K.	Technological engineer/ ship mechanical engineer
	54.	SNEGIREV, D. K.	Naval shipbuilding engineer
	55.	SKOPIChENKO, G. V.	Mechanical engineer (mechanical section of the ship group)
	56.	PERTSEV, I. K.	Naval engineer (for boats)
	57.	POPOV, V. F.	Naval engineer
	58.	RUBROVSKII, K. I.	" "
	59.	KAZIN, L. Kh.	Ship engineer/technological engineer

Leningrad Construction	60.	STIZhA, IA. IA.	Sewerage specialist
	61.	KRUTIKOV, V. I.	Construction engineer
"Electric Power"	62.	KUZNETSOV, I. I.	Hoisting gear specialist
Plant	63.	KONDRAT'EV, A. A.	Military engineer
	64.	DUBROVIN, L. N.	Mechanical engineer
	65.	—KOV, P. N.	Technological engineer
	66.	LEVITSKII, M. N.	Electrician
	67.	SUKhORUKOV, M.	Internal combustion engines specialist
Karl Marx	68.	BRIADOV, G. I.	Mechanical engineer
Plant	69.	PEKVO, A. I.	Mechanic
	70.	AVILOV, B. Kh.	Mechanical engineer
"Red Chemist"	71.	NIKIFOROV, N. N.	Construction technician
plant	72.	AGRAChEV, I. Kh.	Technological engineer
4th State Constr. Combine	73.	PAVLOVSKII, V. A.	Civil engineer
Linen-Cotton	74.	OL', V. V.	Cotton spinning
Industry	75.	POLETAEV, N. A.	"
	76.	ROMANOV, P. S.	Textile production
	77.	GORBUNOV, V. A.	Cotton fabric production
	78.	KARABANOV, A. S.	Cotton spinning
Izhorsk Plant	79.	SAVEL'EV, S. I.	Technological engineer
	80.	IURINOV, I. K.	Steel-casting specialist
"Red Dawn"			
Plant	81.	BOBROV, S. A.	Electrical engineer
Spinning	82.	LAPShIN, P. S.	Color chemist
Combine	83.	ARAPOVSKII, K. P.	Cotton spinning
	84.	ZEBERG, V. G.	"
Sverdlov	85.	LEBEDEV, G. A.	Metallurgist
Plant	86.	DAMM, I. K.	Technologist
	87.	ZINOV'EV, P. I.	Machinery engineer
	88.	KRAUZ-, S. I.	Thermal technician
	89.	STEISKALLO, I. I.	Mechanical engineer
	90.	KREVER, G. L.	Economist
	91.	GAKIChKO, N. L.	Metallurgist
	92.	LAPShIN, B. F.	Heat treatment engineer
All-Union	93.	GUN, V. V.	Artillery engineer
Optical Instr.	94.	PEREPELKIN, IA. N.	Artillery equipment engineer
Ind. Assoc.			

CHAIRMAN OF THE LENINGRAD REGIONAL ECONOMIC COUNCIL

Head of the Cadres Sector

RTSKhIDNI, fond 85, op. 28, d. 30, ll. 2, 20b, 3, 4, 40b, 5.

A prison orchestra in an unidentified camp, 1927. TSGAKFD, N-3881

The White Sea-Baltic Canal

The White Sea-Baltic canal project begun in 1931 was one of the massive construction projects of the First Five-Year Plan and the first to be built exclusively with prison labor. The construction chief of the canal project was Naftali Frenkel', an entrepreneur and former prisoner who Solzhenitsyn alleges convinced Stalin to utilize *Gulag* labor for such projects. "The canal must be built in a short time and it must be built cheaply," ordered Stalin. It was begun in December 1931, using massive amounts of prisoner labor and the most primitive technology: wheelbarrows and sledges, wood and dirt instead of iron and concrete. The human toll was tremendous: Solzhenitsyn reports that one hundred thousand project workers died during its first winter. Although it was meant to be finished by the middle of 1932, construction took longer than planned. The canal was officially completed by May 1, 1933, and with great fanfare Stalin and his associates conducted a tour of the canal and its locks by pleasure steamer. Later that summer a team of one hundred twenty writers led by Maksim Gorky made an excursion through the canal in order to compile a volume on its heroic construction, part of the series Gorky directed on the history of plants and factories in the USSR. This book, with contributions by Gorky, Mikhail Zoshchenko, Aleksei Tolstoy, and other notable writers, extolled the rehabilitative benefits of the prison labor project; many of those who worked on the canal were rewarded subsequently with pardons. Yet immediately after the completion of the canal in 1933, plans were begun to expand it, to widen it, perhaps even to build another alongside it, for the canal was too shallow. In 1966 Solzhenitsyn was told by a lockkeeper, for example, that submarines had to be loaded on barges to be transported between the White Sea and the Baltic Sea via this canal.

DOCUMENT 75   *Resolution of the USSR Central Executive Committee, September 1, 1932, on privileges for convict-workers at the White Sea-Baltic Canal construction site*

18. Privileges for workers at the White Sea Canal construction site [*Belmorstroi*]

(Politburo, Aug. 16, 1932, order no. 112, para. 52)
(Comrades IAgoda, Postyshev).

To confirm the commission's draft resolution on privileges for workers at *Belmorstroi* (see attached).

[...]

Addendum to para. 18,
Politburo Minutes no. 114.

RESOLUTION OF THE USSR CENTRAL EXECUTIVE COMMITTEE
ON PRIVILEGES FOR WORKERS AT THE WHITE SEA CANAL CONSTRUCTION SITE
(Ratified by the Politburo of the *TSK VKP(b)*, Sept. 1, 1932)

Among the large-scale construction projects of the five-year plan—Magnitostroi, Dneprostroi, Berezniki and many others—is the White Sea-Baltic waterway, currently nearing completion. It connects the Baltic and White seas and has tremendous economic significance for the entire economy of the union, especially for the Autonomous Soviet Socialist Republic of Karelia and for the outer regions of the northern Soviet Union.

This is a vast construction, consisting of 19 locks, 13 dikes, 35 dams, and 40 kilometers of artificial canals. Begun in December 1931, it was basically finished in fewer than 400 days, creating a new waterway 227 kilometers long.

The year of construction on the White Sea-Baltic waterway demonstrated that the participants in the project, camp prisoners, showed themselves in significant numbers to be genuine and enthusiastic shock workers who overfulfilled the established output norms and actively conducted public, cultural, and educational work.

In connection with the successful completion of the basic work on the White Sea-Baltic waterway, this great new accomplishment of the Soviet regime, the USSR Central Executive Committee resolves:

1. To give the Unified State Political Directorate [OGPU] the right to free those prisoners who distinguished themselves on the construction project from serving the remainder of their sentences, and where needed, from serving supplementary sentences.

2. To instruct the OGPU to grant to all other prisoners (participants who worked conscientiously in the construction of the White Sea-Baltic waterway), in addition to existing ordinary privileges in the corrective labor camps, a reduction in the term of measures taken to ensure the defense of society.

3. To instruct the OGPU to present for review by the USSR Central Executive Committee the expunging of the convictions of those freed in accordance with paragraph 1 of this resolution.

RTSKhIDNI, fond 17, op. 3, d. 898, l. 4, 14.

DOCUMENT 76   *Decisions from the Politburo session, August 15, 1933, charging the* OGPU *with improving the White Sea-Baltic Canal and detailing plans for a hydroelectric power plant in Murmansk*

38/24. - On the White Sea-Baltic Canal.

1. In order to develop the White Sea-Baltic Canal and the surrounding areas, it is necessary to grant the White Sea-Baltic Combine exclusive rights to exploit the canal and adjacent natural resources.

2. The combine is charged with management of all existing installations at the canal and all new construction (ports, shipyards, etc.); to develop passenger and cargo shipping; to develop and exploit operations for saw-milling, timber chemistry, mining, stone quarrying, commercial fishing, agriculture, etc.

3. A commission, composed of Comrades Kuibyshev, Voroshilov, IAgoda, Firin, Frenkel', Kirov, Giulling (Karelia), Ivanov (Northern region), Lobov, IAnson, Mikoyan, and Mezhlauk, is instructed to draft within twenty days a statute on the combine that will specify its functions, organizational structure, and administrative staff.

4. The State Planning Committee [Gosplan] is instructed to review within 20 days the plan of the Unified State Political Directorate [OGPU] for wooden dikes, hydroelectric stations, and locks on the Svir' rapids; it should establish a construction timetable, a budget, and supplies for 1933, and report to the Central Committee of the All-Union Communist Party (Bolshevik).

5. The Canal Construction Section [Kanalstroi] of the OGPU is instructed to study within 20 days the following problems: a) the widening and deepening of the canal; b) the construction of the Kandalaksha-Murmansk Canal, and to report to the Central Committee of the All-Union Communist Party (Bolshevik).

39/25. - On Murmansk.

1. It has already been decided to construct a hydroelectric station on the Tuloma River in early 1934 using OGPU forces. The main energy department [Glavenergo] of the People's Commissariat of Heavy Industry [NKTP] is required immediately to begin exploratory and design work and to complete the project by April 1934.

2. The municipal power plant (coal) being built in Murmansk is restricted to 3,000 kilowatts of power, and the Murmansk Executive Committee of the Municipal Council of Labor Deputies [Gorispolkom] is ordered to adapt the station to burn wood.

3. It is necessary to electrify the railroad from Murmansk to Kandalaksha using the Niva River hydroelectric station. The People's Commissariat of Transportation [NKPS] and Gosplan should give its recommendation to the Central Committee within thirty days.

4. The People's Commissariat of Supply [NKSnab] must report to the Politburo within a month on the measures taken to organize the salting, smoking, and processing of fish, especially of herring, in the Murmansk basin.

5. The institute of the People's Commissariat of Agriculture [NKZem] that is located in Aleksandrovsk (State Institute of Oceanography [GOIN]) should be purged by the OGPU immediately, its administration transferred to the People's Commissariat of Supply [NKSnab], and be relocated to Murmansk.

RTSKhIDNI, fond 17, op. 3, d. 928, l. 10.

DOCUMENT 77   *Resolution of the USSR Council of People's Commissars on the organization of the White Sea-Baltic Canal enterprise, August 15, 1933*

<u>SUPPLEMENT</u>
to point 13, Politburo minutes No. 143

<u>ON ORGANIZING THE WHITE SEA-BALTIC COMBINE.</u>

<u>RESOLUTION OF THE COUNCIL OF PEOPLE'S COMMISSARS OF THE USSR.</u>

(Confirmed by the Politburo of the Central Committee of the All-Union Communist Party (Bolsheviks) on August 15, 1933)

1. Consider it essential for the purpose of developing the Stalin White Sea-Baltic Canal and the territory along it that the organization of the White Sea-Baltic Combine, abbreviated *BELBALT-KOMBINAT,* be given monopoly rights to exploit the canal and adjacent natural resources.

2. Confirm the proposal on the White Sea-Baltic Combine (see supplement).

Envision assignment of construction work to a special directorate within *BELBALT-KOMBINAT.*

3. Designate Comrade IA. D. Rapoport as chief of *BELBALT-KOMBINAT,* Comrade Verzhbitskii as deputy chief, representative of the People's Commissariat for Water Transportation, and chief engineer, Comrade Uspenskii as deputy chief and also chief of the White Sea-Baltic Camp [Belbaltlag].

Propose to People's Commissar of Forestry Comrade Lobov and People's Commissar for Water Transportation Comrade IAnson to select their representatives as deputy chiefs of *BELBALT-KOMBINAT* from the People's Commissariat for Forestry and the People's Commissariat for Water Transportation, coordinating their choice of candidates with Comrade IAgoda.

4. Propose to the Unified State Political Dictorate within two months to specify in conjunction with the government of Karelia and the Northern Territorial Executive Committee the regions involved in the White Sea-Baltic Canal.

5. Instruct the Unified State Political Directorate [OGPU] to accomplish the following in consultation with the appropriate agencies within two months' time:

a) determine sites for settlements in the region;

b) determine the forests and areas to be transferred to the combine and at the same time draw up a list of enterprises to be turned over to the combine in conjunction with the first transfer;

c) draw up a plan for the development of the region's mineral resources and a prospecting plan for locating new mineral deposits;

d) draw up a specific list of industrial plants whose construction could begin in the near future;

e) develop a surveying plan for the purpose of developing agriculture in the region;

f) determine the region's commercial fishing potential in terms of existing resources and aquaculture;

6. The funds required to cover the combine's operating expenses in 1933 will be provided from the funds appropriated for the *OGPU* for labor camps.

Require the *OGPU* to submit an estimate of the combine's operating expenses for 1933 to the Council of Labor and Defense [*STO*] (through the State Planning Committee [*Gosplan*]) within one month's time.

7. Require the *OGPU* to submit a plan for the construction of wharves and a program of tug and barge construction on a priority basis (within one month).

8. Instruct *Gosplan* to review the *OGPU*'s plans for a wooden dam, a hydroelectric power plant, and locks on the Svir' Rapids, determine construction completion dates, necessary appropriations, and materials for 1933, and submit its recommendations to the Council of People's Commissars for approval within 20 days.

9. Instruct Comrade Kuibyshev to monitor and resolve any routine matters which may arise in conjunction with the operation of the WHITE SEA-BALTIC COMBINE.

CHAIRMAN OF THE COUNCIL OF PEOPLE'S COMMISSARS OF THE USSR

BUSINESS MANAGER OF THE COUNCIL OF PEOPLE'S COMMISSARS OF THE USSR

True Copy: [signed] Khriankina

RTSKhIDNI, fond 17, op. 3, d. 928, ll. 48, 49.

DOCUMENT 78   *List of persons proposed to receive awards for work on the White Sea Canal construction site, May 1, 1933*

APPENDIX

LIST OF PERSONS NOMINATED
FOR AWARDS
FOR THE CONSTRUCTION
OF THE WHITE SEA-BALTIC CANAL
(Drafted by Comrade IAgoda
in Consultation with Comrade L. Kaganovich)

ORDER OF LENIN

1. IAGODA Genrikh Grigor'evich - Deputy Chairman of the Unified State Political Directorate [*OGPU*].

2. KOGAN Lazar' Iosifovich - Chief of the White Sea-Baltic Canal Construction Office, member of the All-Russian Communist Party (Bolshevik) [*VKP(b)*].

3. BERMAN Matvei Davydovich - Chief of the Main Directorate for Camps [*Gulag*] of the *OGPU*, member of the *VKP(b)*.

4. FIRIN Semen Grigor'evich. Chief of the White Sea-Baltic Camp and Deputy Chief of the *Gulag*, member of the *VKP(b)*.

5. RAPOPORT IAkov Davydovich - Deputy Chief of the White Sea-Baltic Canal Construction Office and Deputy Chief of the *Gulag*, and *OGPU*, member of the *VKP(b)*.

1. FRENKEL' Naftalii Aronovich. Assistant Chief of the White Sea-Baltic Canal Construction Office and project supervisor, no party affiliation.

Comments: He was convicted of embezzlement and crossing the border illegally (Articles 98 and 188 of the Criminal Code of 1925), but at the request of the *OGPU* he was pardoned by the Central Executive Committee of the USSR in 1932.

From the beginning to the completion of the White Sea-Baltic Canal project, he made sure the construction work was well-organized and of high quality and demonstrated considerable proficiency.

2. MOGILKO Nikolai Vasil'evich - Assistant Chief Engineer of the project, no party affiliation.

Comments: an outstanding engineer and one of the designers of the Canal.

3. ZhUK Sergei IAkovlevich - Deputy Chief Engineer of the project, no party affiliation.

Comments: One of the best and most conscientious engineers. His extraordinary knowledge and incredible capacity for work ensured that the construction was of high quality.

4. KOChEGAROV Arkadii Ivanovich - technician. Foreman at Lock 11, no party affiliation.

Comments: From the very beginning of the project to its completion, he demonstrated an extremely conscientious attitude towards his work and ensured that Lock 11 and its associated structures were built quickly and well.

5. GOSKIN Mikhail Fedorovich - Assistant Chief of White Sea-Baltic Canal Construction Office, member of the *VKP(b)*.

RTSKhIDNI, fond 17, op. 3, d. 926, l. 24.

DOCUMENT 79   *Minutes of a decision, July 5, 1933, to transfer construction of the Baikal-Amur Railway to the* OGPU

Directives Issued July 5, 1933

28/19. On the plan for major construction in 1933 in the Far East
(Politburo [*PB*] March 1, 1933, Minute No. 131, Item 120/85)

Decision: Special Folder

29/20. On construction of the Moscow headquarters of the All-Union Central Executive Committee

Approve the following directive of the Council of People's Commissars of the USSR:

1. Include the construction of a headquarters for the All-Union Central Executive Committee in the City of Moscow at 33 Miasnitskaia Street with construction costs of 1.5 million rubles in the itemized lists for 1933.

2. Instruct Comrade Grin'ko, the People's Commissar of Finance of the USSR, to consult with Comrade Kalinin on financing for the project.

30/21. On the delegation from the British Wholesale Purchasing Cooperative

Authorize a visit to the USSR by a delegation from the British Wholesale Purchasing Cooperative consisting of three board members (Robinson, McFadden, and Graham) and one specialist.

31/22. On the support committee for the construction of Baikal-Amur Railway
(*PB* October 10, 1932, Minute No. 118, Item 10)

In conjunction with the assignment of the construction of the Baikal-Amur Railway to the Unified State

Political Directorate [*OGPU*], grant Comrade Voroshilov's request to revoke the order of the Central Committee establishing a Government Support Committee for the Construction of the Baikal-Amur Railway.

32/33. <u>On Comrade Kuz'min P. V.</u>
(Organizational Bureau [*OB*] July 1, 1933, Minute 150, Item 49gs)

Relieve Comrade P. V. Kuz'min of his duties as a member of the collegium of the People's Commissariat of Justice of the Russian Soviet Federated Socialist Republic in conjunction with his reassignment to another position.

33/24. <u>On leave for Comrade Dogadov</u>
(*OB* July 1, 1933, Minute 149, Item 91gs)
Grant Comrade Dogadov leave of one and a half months.

RTSKhIDNI, fond 17, op. 3, d. 898, l. 4, 14.

DOCUMENT 80   ***On building the Baikal-Amur railroad, June 1, 1938***

<u>APPENDIX</u>
to Item 311
of Politburo Minutes no. 61

<u>ON THE CONSTRUCTION OF THE BAIKAL-AMUR RAILROAD [*BAM*]</u>

<u>Resolution of the Council of People's Commissars [*SNK*] of the USSR</u>
(Approved by the Politburo of the Central Committee of the All-Union Communist Party (Bolshevik) [*TSK VKP(b)*] on June 1, 1938)

For the purpose of clarifying and elaborating the Resolution of the *SNK* of the USSR of August 17, 1937 (No. 1402/317/*s*), concerning the construction of the Baikal-Amur Railroad, the Council of People's Commissars of the USSR has resolved to:

1. Approve the following timetable for construction of individual sections of the Baikal-Amur Railroad.

Name of section	Date line design and prelim. estimates turned over to construction organization	Date engineering designs and estimates turned over to construction organization	Construction start date	Date of opening to temporary traffic	Regular operation start date
Taishet-Padun	1/15/38 (done)	6/1/38	1938	5/1/40	11/1/41
Padun-Ust'-Kut	6/1/38	12/1/38	1939	5/1/41	11/1/42
Ust'-Kut-Delakor	1/1/40	4/1/40	1940	11/1/42	1/1/44
Delakor-Niukzha	9/1/41	4/1/42	1941	11/1/44	11/1/45
Niukzha-Tynda	9/1/39	4/1/40	1940	11/1/43	11/1/45
Tynda-Zeia	11/1/38	3/1/39	1938	11/1/41	11/1/42
Zeia-Ust'-Niman	9/1/40	3/1/40	1940	6/1/42	12/1/43
Ust'-Niman- Komsomol'sk	2/1–6/1/38	12/1/38	1938	11/1/41	11/1/42
Komsomol'sk Junction		8/1/39	1939		
Komsomol'sk-Sovetskaia Gavan'	1/1–10/1–38	4/1/40	1939	11/1/41	12/1/42
Izvestkovyi-Ust'-Niman	done	11/1/38	1938	5/1/40	1/1/41
Amur River Crossing	9/1/39	12/1/39	1939		6/1/42

2. Concentrate on building the following sections in 1938: the Izvestkovyi-Ust'-Niman (Urgal) Switching Track, Ust'-Niman (Urgal)-Komsomol'sk, and Taishet-Padun. Also in 1938 begin construction of the Tynda-Zeia section by appropriating 20 million rubles of additional funds from the Council of People's Commissars reserve fund over and above the 5 million rubles already appropriated.

3. Assign the People's Commissariat of Internal Affairs [*NKVD*] the task of providing the design specifications, engineering designs, and working blueprints, while leaving only the task of producing the basic technical specifications for the Baikal-Amur Line to the People's Commissariat of Transportation [*NKPS*].

Instruct the *NKPS* to transfer all its design offices and employees engaged in construction surveys and design work for the *BAM* to the *NKVD*.

4. Direct that the engineering designs for certain sections of the *BAM* are to be produced by the *NKVD* and, after review by the *NKPS*, to be submitted to the Economic Council of the Council of People's Commissars of the USSR for approval.

5. Instruct the *NKVD* and *NKPS* to establish firm deadlines for the review and approval of the engineering designs for the individual sections of the *BAM* and submit their proposed deadlines to the Economic Council by July 5, 1938.

6. Instruct the *NKPS* to submit the basic technical specifications for the *BAM* to the Economic Council by June 15, 1938.

7. Instruct the *NKPS* to submit its proposals for training personnel for putting the *BAM* into operation to the Economic Council by July 1, 1938.

8. Instruct the People's Commissariat of Finance to finance the construction, surveying, and design work for the entire length of the route in 1938 until the designs and detailed estimates are approved.

9. Exempt the Baikal-Amur Railroad construction project from payments by the stump for timber or for cutting areas and for any mineral royalties.

10. Approve the submitted special clothing and gear allowances for the construction surveyors.

11. Require the People's Commissariat of Agriculture of the USSR to supply 985 horses for use in the construction surveys to the *NKVD* prior to August 1, 1938.

12. Require the People's Commissariat of Procurement to supply the necessary quantities of fodder for horses and reindeer in a timely manner on the basis of requests submitted by the Main Directorate of Camps [*Gulag*] of the *NKVD*.

13. Require the People's Commissariats of Mechanical Engineering, Heavy Industry, Light Industry, and the Defense Industry to supply the *Gulag* of the *NKVD* with instruments, gear, and equipment for construction surveying and design of the Baikal-Amur Line in quantities to be approved by the *SNK* of the USSR.

14. Instruct the People's Commissariat of Agriculture of the USSR (Draft Animal Procurement) in consultation with the *NKVD* to procure 5000 horses and the People's Commissariat of State Farms to procure 1000 horses for the construction of the Baikal-Amur Line within the Buriat-Mongolian Republic, Irkutsk and Chita *oblast*'s, and Krasnoyarsk *krai* to be delivered no later than August 1, 1938.

15. Order the People's Commissariat of Mechanical Engineering to submit proposed deadlines for organization of production and production of the machinery and equipment needed for the construction of the Baikal-Amur Line in 1938 to the Economic Council of the *SNK* within one month's time. [break in the text]

33. Allocate materials for construction of the Baikal-Amur Line to be shipped in the third quarter from the third-quarter material allocations for the *Gulag* of the *NKVD*.

34. Require the people's commissariats designated as suppliers of equipment, spare parts, and track vehicles for the construction of the Baikal-Amur Line to ship these supplies from the approved allocations for 1938 in the third quarter.

35. Require the *NKPS* to establish a directorate for the construction of the Baikal-Amur Line and make it responsible for the quality of the construction work in accordance with the approved specifications, engineering designs, and detailed estimates.

The *NKPS* is responsible for drafting a charter for the directorate in consultation with the *NKVD* and submitting this charter to the Economic Council of the *SNK* of the USSR by July 1, 1938.

36. Require the People's Commissariat of Forestry and the People's Commissariat of Agriculture to:

a) reserve the necessary felled timber and land in a 25-kilometer strip on either side of the line and along the banks of log floating rivers leading to the route.

b) reserve felled timber in consultation with the *NKVD* of the USSR to supply wood processing plants for the construction project located outside the 25-kilometer zone.

37. Authorize the People's Commissar of Defense in consultation with the *NKVD* to issue conscription deferments of up to 5 years to engineers and technicians employed in the construction of the Baikal-Amur Line.

38. Reserve housing at their former places of residence for employees of the construction project and the planning and surveying expeditions of the *NKPS* for their entire term of employment on the project.

39. The People's Commissariat of Defense is instructed to call 400 reserve line and staff officers (including political officers) to active duty (in the *NKVD* troops) in the third quarter of 1938 to organize a para-military security force for the construction of the Baikal-Amur Railroad.

The following benefits will be established for the reserve officers and their families called to active duty:

a) payment of a one-time allowance at the job site amounting to twice the average monthly salary;

b) reservation of housing space for the reserve officers themselves and their families with the privilege of making a single payment for any resultant extra space (after the departure of the officer).

CHAIRMAN OF THE *SNK* OF THE USSR

BUSINESS MANAGER OF THE *SNK* OF THE USSR

True Copy: [signature illegible]

RTSKhIDNI, fond 17, op. 3, d. 999, ll. 88, 89, 93.

Memorandum from IAgoda to Stalin, January 17, 1935, on permanent exile of
released prisoners

UNION OF SOVIET SOCIALIST REPUBLICS
PEOPLE'S COMMISSARIAT OF INTERNAL AFFAIRS [NKVD]
January 17, 1935, No. 55137

Moscow, 2 Dzerzhinsky Square
Telephone: NKVD Switchboard
Brief Description of Contents: .....
[Handwritten:] 66/25.1.35. Correct. I. St.

TOP SECRET

Original No. .....dated.....193....71
(in replies refer to No, date, and [illegible])

TO THE SECRETARY OF THE CENTRAL COMMITTEE
OF THE ALL-RUSSIAN COMMUNIST PARTY (BOLSHEVIK) [TSK VKP(b)]

Comrade STALIN

The decree of the Central Executive Committee of the USSR, dated May 27, 1934, concerning the restoration of civil rights to forced labor deportees unconditionally requires persons who have had their civil rights restored to settle permanently in the areas to which they were deported.

Because no special clause was added to the law, however, forced labor deportees have been leaving the areas to which they were deported *en masse* as soon as their civil rights have been restored, which has frustrated our efforts to settle uninhabited areas.

The return of rehabilitated forced labor deportees to the areas from which they were deported would also be politically undesirable.

I believe it would be advisable for the Central Executive Committee of the USSR to issue an amendment to its decree of May 27, 1934, which should indicate that restoration of civil rights does not give forced labor deportees the right to leave the areas to which they were deported.

PEOPLE'S COMMISSARIAT OF INTERNAL AFFAIRS
UNION OF SOVIET SOCIALIST REPUBLICS

[signed] G. IAGODA

Source?

DOCUMENT 82 *Letter from Ordzhonikidze to Stalin, March 20, 1936, requesting that prisoners working at the Lake Balkhash construction site be left there until construction is completed*

USSR
People's Commissar
of Heavy Industry
March 20, 1936
Moscow
No. 70

Top Secret

To the Central Committee, All-Union Communist Party (Bolshevik)
To Comrade STALIN

This year work at the Lake Balkhash Basin Construction Trust [*Pribalkhashstroi—PBS*] is expanding with great energy. The plan allocated 140 million rubles to it, with the goal that in 1937 it will already yield copper.

The construction of *PBS*, as we know, is proceeding under very difficult conditions, and the problem of the *PBS* labor force is never easy to solve.

Last year, in agreement with the *NKVD*, prisoners were brought in to work on the *PBS* construction project. This year the *NKVD* is taking them away and transferring them to the Far East *krai*. Our negotiations with the *NKVD* have gone nowhere.

In view of the great importance of the *PBS* and its especially difficult working conditions, I request the *NKVD* be instructed to leave the prisoners at the *PBS* until construction is completed.

Comrade Mirzoian has also telegraphed Comrade IAgoda and us to leave the prisoners at the *PBS*.

[signed] S. Ordkhonikidze

[Upper right corner, handwritten words read:] "Not sent."

RTSKhIDNI, fond 85, op. 29, d. 357, l. 1.

The Katyn Forest Massacre

When the German army invaded Poland from the west in September 1939, the Red Army advanced into Poland from the east under the terms of secret protocols of the Soviet-German Non-Aggression Treaty. During this 1939 offensive some 15,000 Polish army officers were captured by the Red Army, and 11,000 of them disappeared without a trace. In April 1943 Nazi authorities announced that they had uncovered the remains of Polish officers in mass graves in the Katyn forest about ten miles west of Smolensk. The Soviet government immediately countered that the officers had been killed by the Nazis in 1941 and claimed to have discovered "proof" when the Red Army recaptured this territory in September 1943. This remained the official story until

1989. Over the years, rumors and bits of evidence came to light that implicated the *NKVD*: the evidence suggested that the officers had died in 1940, when Soviet troops controlled the area, not 1942, but the denials persisted. The Polish Communist government loyally backed the Soviet version until 1989, when the winds of *glasnost'* loosened the grip of Soviet power over its satellites. The Polish press began to write openly of the evidence incriminating the Soviets, and the government called for an official investigation by a joint Polish-Soviet commission. The Soviet government held to its story that the killings had been committed by Nazis in 1942, but in 1990 an article in a Moscow publication presented evidence from Soviet archives to implicate the highest Soviet officials in the massacre. In April 1990 Mikhail Gorbachev handed over the documents on the Katyn murders to Polish President Wojciech Jaruzelski, accepting Soviet responsibility for the tragedy and expressing official "profound regret." These documents were made public, however, only in October 1992, when Russian President Boris Yeltsin took the opportunity to denounce Gorbachev for concealing his knowledge of the truth of the Katyn massacre.

DOCUMENT 83   **NKVD *order, October 3, 1939, on disposition of prisoners of war in Soviet camps***

<u>Code 784</u>

<u>TO BE DECRYPTED AND HAND-DELIVERED IMMEDIATELY</u>

TO: L'VOV, TIMOShENKO, BORISOV, POZhIDAEV
       VOLKOVYSK, KOVALEV, SUSAIKOV, IVANOV

1) The following resolution of the Central Committee of the All-Russian Communist Party (Bolshevik) [*TSK VKP(b)*] dated October 2 concerning prisoners of war is reproduced below for your information and guidance:

Approve the following proposals of Comrades Beria and Mekhlis:

1. Prisoners of war of Ukrainian, Belorussian, and other nationalities whose homes are located in the Western Ukraine and Western Belorussia will be allowed to go home.

2. 25,000 prisoners of war will be kept to build the Novograd-Volynskii-Korets-L'vov Road until the end of December (completion of construction of this phase of the project).

3. Prisoners of war whose homes are located in the German part of Poland will be assigned to a separate category and will be detained in the camps until negotiations with the Germans begin and the issue of their repatriation is resolved.

4. A separate camp will be organized for officer prisoners of war. Officers with the rank of lieutenant

colonel to general and important government and military officials will be kept separate from the rest of the officers in a special camp.

5. Intelligence agents, counterintelligence agents, military policemen, prison guards, and policemen will be kept in a separate camp.

6. The Czech detainees (approximately 800 individuals) will be released after they have signed a pledge not to fight against the USSR.

7. The Economic Council will be instructed to provide the POW Affairs Administration with 20 mobile film projectors and 5 mobile print shops for the prisoners of war.

8. Officer prisoners of war will receive better rations than enlisted prisoners of war.

9. The Central Cooperative Organization [*TSentrosoiuz*] will be instructed to set up food and manufactured goods retail outlets at the camps.

10. All prisoners of war, including officers and enlisted men, will be required to surrender all valuables and any money over the limit established by the POW Affairs Administration to the administrations of the camps for safekeeping in exchange for a receipt.

11. Prisoners of war will be assigned to the following camps:

a) generals, lieutenant colonels, major military and government officials, and all other officers in the south (at Starobelsk);

b) intelligence agents, counterintelligence agents, military policemen, policemen, and prison guards to Ostashkovo Camp in Kalinin *oblast'*;

c) enlisted prisoners of war whose homes are located in the German part of Poland will be kept at the Kozel Camp, Smolensk *oblast'* and the Putivel Camp, Sumi *oblast'*.

Secretary of the *TSK* J. STALIN

2) We will have to use enlisted men taken prisoner by the Ukrainian Front to make sure that exactly 25,000 POWs are available to build the Novograd-Volynskii-Korets-L'vov road. Agents of the People's Commissariat of Internal Affairs [*NKVD*] will be employed to select POWs for the construction project.

3) All POWs whose homes are located in the German part of Poland will be temporarily confined to camps. We must explain to them that they will be repatriated in an orderly manner after our negotiations with the Germans on this issue.

[Handwritten:] Copy No. 18051

4) All other enlisted POWs, including Ukrainians, Belorussians, and other nationalities whose homes are located in our territory, should be immediately sent home. They should be given all possible assistance, including advice, in getting home. Major political indoctrination efforts should be initiated for these POWs to remind them that they will soon be citizens of the USSR. The soldiers should be informed of the forthcoming sessions of the two popular assemblies and the issues they will decide. The platform we are using in the election campaign should be explained to the soldiers. The indoctrinators should try to get the soldiers to become activists and advocates for our platform.

5) All officers, military policemen, counterintelligence agents, and other similar prisoners of war will without exception be confined in the camps. You must assist the *NKVD* agencies in settling this category of POWs in the appropriate camps.

6) The political departments of the Ukrainian and Belorussian Fronts will supply political officers fluent in Polish called up from the reserve to the *NKVD* to work with prisoners of war. Each front will supply 15 such officers. The political department of the Ukrainian Front will provide enough journalists for 3 Polish newspapers,

while the political department of the Belorussian Front will provide enough journalists for 2 Polish newspapers. Make sure that Red Army journalists who are fluent in Polish return to active duty no later than two months from now. The army urgently needs their services.

[signed] L. MEKhLIS

October 3, 1939

[illegible handwriting]   Received 3:00 October 3, 1939
                            Sent 7:00 October 3, 1939
                            No. 18051/52/53
                            Duty officer [illegible]

[Source: no source provided. The document has been repaginated (for archival registration) three different times.]

DOCUMENT 84   **NKVD order, March 5, 1940, to execute Polish, Ukrainian, and Belorussian prisoners of war**

[Handwritten cover sheet:]
    The documents in this file were received from Comrade K. U. Chernenko in sealed form.
    They were presented to Comrade IU. V. Andropov on April 15, 1981.
    They were received in this condition from Comrade Andropov after he had familiarized himself with these documents.

[signed] V. Galkin
April 15, 1981

[cover sheet:]

CERTIFICATE

    [I] Received from Comrade V. I. Boldin the documents in a sealed file along with the envelope of the unsealed package for No. 1, which [file] was submitted on the same day to sector VI in a new sealed package for No. 1.

[signed] V. Galkin
April 18, 1989

Point 13/144 Special File
<u>Top Secret</u>

USSR   March 5, 1940
People's Commissariat of
    Internal affairs [NKVD]
    <u>March 1940</u>   Central Committee, All-Union Communist   No. <u>794/5</u>
    Party (of Bolsheviks) [TSK VKP(b)]
Moscow
                            <u>To Comrade S T A L I N</u>

    NKVD USSR prisoner-of-war camps and prisons in western parts of Ukraine and Belorussia hold a large number of former Polish Army officers, former employees of Polish police and intelligence agencies, members of

Polish nationalist counterrevolutionary parties, participants in exposed counterrevolutionary insurgent organizations, deserters, i.a. They are all sworn enemies of Soviet authority, filled with hatred for the Soviet system.

The prisoner of war officers and policemen held in the camps are trying to continue c-r work and are conducting anti-Soviet agitation. Each of them is just waiting to be freed so that he can have the chance to actively engage in the struggle against Soviet authority.

NKVD organs in western Ukraine and Belorussia have exposed a number of counterrevolutionary insurgent organizations. In all of these counterrevolutionary organizations an active leadership role was played by former officers of the former Polish Army, former policemen, and gendarmes.

Many persons participating in counterrevolutionary spy and insurgent organizations also have been discovered among the arrested deserters and violators of the national border.

Excluding enlisted personnel and noncommissioned officers, the prisoner-of-war camps hold a total of 14,736 former officers, civil servants, landowners, policemen, gendarmes, prison guards, settlers, and intelligence agents—more than 97% are of Polish nationality. Among them are:

Generals, colonels, and lieutenant colonels	-	296
Majors and captains	-	2,080
Lieutenants, second lieutenants, and ensigns	-	6,049
Officers and junior commanders of the police, border guards, and gendarmerie	-	1,030
Rank and file policemen, gendarmes, prison guards, and intelligence officers	-	5,138
Civil servants, landowners, priests, and settlers	-	144

The prisons in the western parts of Ukraine and Belorussia hold a total of 18,632 internees (of which 10,685 are Poles), including:

Former officers	-	1,207
Former police intelligence agents and gendarmes	-	5,141
Spies and saboteurs	-	347
Former landowners, factory owners, civil servants	-	465
Members of various counterrevolutionary and insurgent organizations and various counterrevolutionary elements	-	5,345
Deserters	-	6,127

Because they all are inveterate, incorrigible enemies of Soviet authority, the *NKVD* USSR considers it essential to:

I. Order the *NKVD* USSR to give priority consideration (applying the supreme punishment of execution by shooting) to:

1) the cases of 14,700 persons held in prisoner-of-war camps, namely former Polish officers, civil servants, landowners, policemen, intelligence agents, gendarmes, settlers, and prison guards,

2) as well as the cases of 11,000 persons arrested and held in prisons in the western parts of Ukraine and Belorussia, namely members of various counterrevolutionary espionage and

sabotage organizations, former landowners, factory owners, former Polish officers, civil servants, and deserters.

II. Conduct the examination of cases without summoning the prisoners and without presenting the accusation, the investigation finding, or the conviction, as follows:

a) persons held in prisoner-of-war camps—according to information presented by the *NKVD* USSR Directorate of Prisoner of War Affairs,

b) arrested persons—according to information presented by the *NKVD* of the Ukrainian SSR and the *NKVD* of the Belorussian SSR.

III. Assign responsibility for examining these matters and executing the decision to the trio of Comrades MERKULOV, KABULOV [handwritten], and BAShTAKOV (Chief of the First Special Division of the *NKVD* USSR).

PEOPLE'S COMMISSAR OF INTERNAL AFFAIRS

OF THE USSR

[signed] L. Beria

[handwritten on first page]

Kalinin - for
Kaganovich - for

[handwritten:]

Excerpt.

Beria

point 13/144

March 5, 1940

To be returned within 24 hours
to Unit 2 of the Special Sector
of the *TSK* (Politburo of the *TSK*
Resolution of May 5, 1927,
protocol 100, point 5)

TOP SECRET
(special file)

All-Union Communist Party (of Bolsheviks). Central Committee

no. p. 13/144Comrade Beria
March 5, 1940

Extract from protocol no. 13, *TSK* Politburo session
of _____193__.

Resolution of March 5, 1940

144. *NKVD* USSR Matter.

I. Order the *NKVD* USSR to:

Give priority consideration (applying the supreme punishment, execution by shooting) to:

1) the cases of 14,700 persons held in prisoner-of-war camps, namely former Polish officers, civil servants, landowners, policemen, intelligence agents, gendarmes, settlers, and prison guards,

2) as well as the cases of 11,000 persons arrested and held in prisons in the western parts of Ukraine and Belorussia, consisting of members of various counterrevolutionary espionage and sabotage organizations, former landowners, factory owners, former Polish officers, civil servants, and deserters.

II. Conduct the examination of cases without summoning the prisoners and without presenting the accusation, the investigation finding, or the conviction as follows:

a) persons held in prisoner of war camps—according to information presented by the *NKVD* USSR Directorate of Prisoner-of-War Affairs,

b) arrested persons—according to information presented by the *NKVD* of the Ukrainian SSR and the *NKVD* of the Belorussian SSR.

III. Assign responsibility for examining these matters and executing the decision to the trio of Comrades Merkulov, Kabulov, and Bashtakov (Chief of the First Special Division of the *NKVD* USSR).

SECRETARY OF THE *TSK*

Source?

DOCUMENT 85   *USSR Supreme Soviet Presidium decree, February 21, 1948, ordering the exile to remote places of those especially dangerous state criminals who have completed their sentences*

No. 128/11

Not for publication

DECREE
OF THE PRESIDIUM OF THE SUPREME SOVIET OF THE USSR

On exiling to remote areas of the USSR especially dangerous state criminals upon the completion of their sentences.

1. The Ministry of Internal Affairs of the USSR is ordered to deport all inmates of special camps and prisons, namely, spies, saboteurs, terrorists, Trotskyites, right-wingers, Mensheviks, Socialist Revolutionaries, anarchists, nationalists, White emigrants, and members of other anti-Soviet organizations and groups, as well as persons dangerous by virtue of their anti-Soviet connections and inimical activity—upon the completion of their sentences—as directed by the Ministry of State Security of the USSR to the following exile areas under the supervision of organs of the Ministry of State Security [*MGB*]:

- the region of Kolyma in the Far North;
- the regions of Krasnoiarsk *krai* and Novosibirsk *oblast'* within 50 kilometers north of the Trans-Siberian Main Line;
- the Kazakh SSR, excluding the *oblast'*s of Alma-Ata, Gur'ev, South Kazakhstan, Aktiubinsk, East Kazakhstan, and Semipalatinsk.

2. The Ministry of State Security of the USSR is ordered to exile state criminals as listed in paragraph 1 who have served out their sentences in corrective-labor camps and prisons since the end of the Great Patriotic War.

The deportation of these persons is to be carried out in accordance with the decisions of a Special Conference of the *MGB* USSR.

Chairman of the Presidium of
the Supreme Soviet of the USSR, N. Shvernik

Secretary of the Presidium of
the Supreme Soviet of the USSR, A. Gorkin

Moscow, the Kremlin
February 21, 1948
Doc. No. 111/8

Chairman of the Council of Ministers of the USSR
[signed] J. Stalin

Manager of the Council of Ministers of the USSR
[signed] IA. Chadaev

TSGAOR, fond 7523, op. 36, d. 345, ll. 53, 54.

DOCUMENT 86   *Central Committee note, March 15, 1955, on the practice of exiling dangerous criminals upon completion of their prison sentences*

NOT FOR PUBLICATION

CENTRAL COMMITTEE
OF THE COMMUNIST PARTY OF THE SOVIET UNION [*TSK KPSS*]

The Administrative Department of the *TSK* of the *KPSS* possesses information indicating that many individuals convicted of counterrevolutionary crimes have not been released from punishment even after they have completed their sentences and instead have been sent directly from prisons and camps by orders of Ministry of Internal Affairs [*MVD*] agencies into indefinite exile.

There are more than 54,000 of these individuals. Exile on the basis of *MVD* orders instead of court sentences has continued until recently.

The practice of exiling individuals by this procedure is based on a Decree of the Presidium of the Supreme Soviet of the USSR dated February 28, 1948, "Concerning the Exiling of Especially Dangerous State Criminals Upon Completion of their Sentences to Remote Regions of the USSR." Despite the fact that our laws do not allow individuals to be punished twice for the same offense and do not provide for any punishment such as indefinite exile, this decree requires the *MVD* USSR to send all spies, saboteurs, and other especially dangerous criminals, as well as persons constituting a danger by virtue of their anti-Soviet associations and hostile activity, into exile for resettlement under the supervision of the state security agencies as directed by the Ministry of State Security [*MGB*] of the USSR.

The same decree established that persons convicted of these crimes but released from confinement prior to the issuance of this decree (after the Great Patriotic War) may be exiled on the basis of orders issued by a special board.

All individuals sent into exile on the basis of orders issued by the old Special Board are hereby released from exile. The decree of the Presidium of the Supreme Soviet of the USSR dated February 21, 1948, is no longer valid for this category of individuals and should not be enforced, but this decree is still valid for individuals exiled on the basis of orders issued by *MVD* agencies, even though extra-judicial punishment has been abolished.

We consider it necessary to examine this issue and instruct Comrades Rudenko, Kruglov, Serov, and Gorshenin to submit the necessary proposals to the *TSK KPSS.*

Head of the Administrative Department
of the *TSK KPSS*

[signed] (A. Dedov)

March 19, 1955
[See Document 85 for the text of the February 21, 1948, decree.]

TSKhSD, fond 5, op. 47, d. 68, l. 54.

Censorship

Censorship of publications and ideas had been firmly established under the tsarist regime. The ten months between the February and October revolutions in 1917 witnessed a brief flurry of freedom of the press, but with the coming of the Bolsheviks to power in October press censorship once again became a state priority. The Council of People's Commissars published its decree on the press on October 27, 1917, giving it the right to close down newspapers that agitated against the new government or that misrepresented facts in their attempt to discredit the government. This decree produced controversy within socialist ranks and prompted some Bolsheviks to break openly with Lenin's policies, but it remained in force.

An official agency responsible for control of the printed word was created in 1922, the Main Directorate for the Protection of State Secrets in the Press, more commonly known as *Glavlit.* It was charged with coordinating all forms of censorship, including review of domestic and imported printed works, manuscripts, photographs, and other matter intended for distribution. *Glavlit* also had the responsibility to draw up lists of banned works and to cooperate with the *GPU* to suppress the circulation of underground publications. A parallel agency was created in 1923 to monitor the content of plays, films, concerts, phonograph records, and other public performances.

The censoring function took a wide variety of forms. *Glavlit* after 1931 had the authority to impose pre- and post-publication censorship of all printed matter. Foreign publications were strictly controlled by customs and *Glavlit* review; censorship through translation constituted another important mechanism. Foreign radio broadcasts were regularly censored by electronic jamming until the 1980s. Editorial staffs learned to exercise the censor's function in anticipation of *Glavlit's* intervention; the discussion of Vasilii Grossman's manuscript, *Life and Fate,* in chapter 2 (Document 136) illustrates how this was done. Almost anyone who traded in the printed word learned to exercise self-censorship as well. Postal censorship of foreign and domestic mail was also regularly applied. In carrying out its functions *Glavlit* followed the prevailing party line, but its day-to-day activities were said to be governed by a book of rules known as the "Index" or the "Talmud." The *Glavlit* files included here offer a glimpse of the level of detail, and in some cases the logic (Document 92), of its removal of works and authors from libraries and the book trade.

DOCUMENT 87   *Letter from* Glavlit, *January 27, 1938, concerning incorrect removal of a book by Feuchtwanger*

Secret

Copy No

No. 135/s

Circular

January 27, 1938

TO ALL CHIEFS OF MAIN, *KRAI,* AND *OBLAST'* DIRECTORATES FOR
PROTECTING MILITARY AND STATE SECRETS IN THE PRESS [*GLAVLIT*]

Glavlit has been receiving information that attempts have been made in certain places to remove Feuchtwanger's book *Moscow 1937* from circulation. I would like to remind you that no one may take any literature out of circulation on his own without explicit instructions from *Glavlit* in Moscow. Feuchtwanger's book is not to be removed from circulation in any way.

Deputy Director of *Glavlit*   [signed]   (A. Samokhvalov)

[Illegible handwritten initials and notes of different officials]

TSGAOR, fond 9425 s, op. 1, d. 3.

DOCUMENT 88   *Order issued by* Glavlit, *January 21, 1943, banning a section of A. Tvardovskii's poem* Vasilii Terkin

SECRET

Copy #1

ORDER No. 3/52S
of the Representative of the USSR Council of People's Commissars
on Military Secrets in the Press and
the Chief of *Glavlit*

Moscow   January 21, 1943

Publication of the text of A. Tvardovskii's poem *Vasilii Terkin* (part 3) 'From the author', from the line

   "Friend and reader, do not be sad . . .

to

   They take cannons ass backwards to battle—
   That was not said by me"

is prohibited.

[signed] N. Sadchikov
Representative of the USSR Council of
   People's Commissars on Military Secrets
   in the Press and Chief of *Glavlit*

TSGAOR, fond 9425s, op. 1, d. 119, l. 3.

DOCUMENT 89   **Glavlit** *ban, June 10, 1947, on unpublished materials by or about Kalinin,* **IAroslavskii, Zemliachka, Gorky, Aleksey Tolstoy, and Bednyi**

CIRCULAR   Secret
No. 28/15766cc   copy no. 86
June 10, 1947
Moscow

TO ALL CENSORSHIP ORGANS

IT IS FORBIDDEN, without the special permission of the Directorate of Propaganda and Agitation of the Central Committee of the All-Union Communist Party (Bolshevik), to publish any previously unpublished materials by <u>M. I. Kalinin, E. IAroslavskii, R. Zemliachka, M. Gorky, Al. Tolstoy, D. Bednyi</u>, as well as any unpublished archival materials about them, either from their personal archives or from other sources.

Please notify the editors of newspapers, journals, and publishing houses of this decision.

Representative of the Council of Ministers of the USSR for the Protection of War and State Secrets in the Press

K. Omel'chenko

True copy

TSGAOR, fond 9425s, op. 1, d. 512, l. 129.

List published in 1948 by Party censorship organizations, of more than 1,000 names of persons whose works were banned in the period 1938–1948

Secret

LIST

of persons, all works of whom are designated for removal by the orders of the Representative of the Council of People's Commissars of the USSR and the Representative of the Council of Ministers of the USSR for preservation of military and state secrets in the press for the period 1938–1948.

_" A "_

ABRAMOV Arkadii Mikhailovich - 681 (party subjects)

AVERBAKh Leopol'd Leonidovich - 266 (literary criticism)

AVILOV Nikolai Pavlovich (Glebov-Avilov, N.) - 241 (trade union movement)

AVINOVITSKII IAkov Lazarevich - 266 (military-chemical)

AGIENKO Aleksandr Fedorovich - 683 (anti-religious)

AGOL Izrail' Iosifovich - 241 (philosophy)

AGURSKII (Samuil Khaimovich) - 372 (social-political literature)

ADAMIShVILI M. S. (Dzhavakhishvili, Mikhail Savvich) - 372 (fiction)

AZARKh Raisa Moiseevna - 73 (fiction)

AITAKOV Nadyrbai - 957 (party subjects)

AIKhENVAL'D Aleksandr IUl'evich - 241 (economics)

ALAZAN Vagram Martynovich - 266 (artistic subjects)

ALEKSANDROVICh Andrei Ivanovich - 372 (poetry)

ALKSNIS IAkov Ivanovich (Alksnis-Astrov) - 171 (military)

ALYPOV Stepan Akimovich - 683 (party topics)

AMAGLOBELI Sergo Ivanovich - 266 (playwright)

AMMOSOV Maksim Kirikovich, (Poliarnyi M.) - ts1506 (social and economic issues)

ANGAROV Aleksei Ivanovich - 646 (social and economic issues)

ANDREEV Sergei Dmitrievich - 683 (_komsomol_ topics)

ANIShEV Anatolii Isaevich - 647 (essayist on military topics)

ANTIPOV Nikolai Kirillovich - 681 (party topics, mathematics, communications, physical education, and tourism)

ANTONOV N. (Lukin Nikolai Mikhailovich) - 957 (historian)

ANTOShKIN Dmitrii Vasil'evich - 683 (labor movement)

ARZhAKOV Stepan Maksimovich - ts1506 (agricultural topics)

ARZhEKAEV Evgenii Andreevich - 681 (military topics)

ARNOL'DOV Aron Markovich - 681 (railroads)

ARONShTAM L. N. - 172 (party topics)

AROSEV Aleksandr IAkovlevich - 683 (artistic subjects)

ASNIK (Skrypnik Nikolai Alekseevich) - 671 (public education, the courts, the prosecutors)

ASTROV Vladimir Ivanovich - 683 (party topics)

AChKANOV Grigorii Pavlovich - 681 (trade union topics)

_" B "_

BABUShKIN Viktor Fedorovich - 163 (fiction)

BAZhANOV Vasilii Mikhailovich - 683 (coal industry)

BAZAREVSKII Aleksandr Khalilevich - 1085 (military topics)

BAKUNTS Aksel' - 266 (fiction)

BAKShI Mikhail Markovich - 1085 (military topics)

BALABANOVA Anzhelika - 82 (artistic, social, and political subjects)

BALITS'KII Vsevolod Apollonovich - 258 Ukrainian SSR (military topics)

BARAKhOV Isidor Nikiforovich - *ts*1506 (party topics)

BAUMAN Karl IAnovich - 171 (party topics)

BATAShEV Vladimir Nikitovich - 1085 (military topics)

BEIMBET (Mailin B.) - 372 (fiction)

BELITSKII Semen Markovich - 292 (military topics)

BELOI A. S. - 163 (military topics)

BELYKh Grigorii Georgievich - 266 (fiction)

BELIAVSKII Aleksei Grigorievich - 163 (military, energy, music, beekeeping)

BELIAKOV G. (Lelevich G., Labori Gileev, Kal'manson, Mogilevskii, L., Gavrilov N.) - 266 (fiction)

BERGAVINOV Sergei Adamovich - 978 (party topics)

BERLIN Vladimir Markovich - 683 (military topics, methodology)

BERLOGA Aleksandr Sergeevich - 1085 (military topics)

BERMAN IAkov Leont'evich - 241 (Soviet development and law)

BESSONOV Sergei Alekseevich - 266 (social and economic issues)

BIBIK Aleksei Pavlovich - 163 (fiction)

BLUMENTAL' Fridrikh Leopol'dovich - 683 (social and political issues)

BLIUKhER Vasilii Konstantinovich - 31 (military topics)

BOGAEVSKII Grigorii Vasil'evich - 163 (agriculture)

BOGUSLAVSKII Mikhail Solomonovich - 266 (Soviet development)

BOLDYREV Mikhail Fedorovich - 957 (public health)

BOLOTIN Zakhar Samuilovich - 646 (commerce and cooperatives)

BORISOV Nikolai Andreevich - 372 (artistic subjects)

BORN Georg - 266 (artistic subjects)

BOIAROV Aleksei Fedorovich - *ts*1506 (literature and art)

BRATKOVSKII IUrii Vatslavovich - 683 (international issues)

BRILIANT (Sokol'nikov Grigorii IAkovlevich) - 241 (foreign policy, finance)

BRONShTEIN (Semkovskii) Semen IUl'evich - 241 (philosophy)

BRONShTEIN (Trotsky Lev Davidovich, Takhotskii) - 292.

BUBNOV Andrei Sergeevich (A. Glotov, S. I. Glotov, S. Igotov) - 171 (party topics, public education in military affairs)

BUBIAKIN Nikolai Vasil'evich - *ts*1506 (topics of Soviet development)

BUISKII Anatolii Aleksandrovich - 292 (military topics)

BULAT Aleksandr Fedotovich - 256 (communications and transportation)

BULAKh Viktor Stepanovich - 683 (trade union and *komsomol* topics)

BUKhARIN Nikolai Ivanovich - 241 (social, political, economic, party, philosophical, and antireligious topics)

BUKhARTSEV Dmitrii Pavlovich - 241 (essayist, social and political issues)

"V"

VAGANIAN Vagarshak Arutiunovich - 241 (party and social and political issues)

VAINBERG Valentin IAkovlevich - 957 (education)

VANAG Nikolai Nikolaevich - 241 (history, social and economic issues)

VARAVVA Aleksei Petrovich - 482 (literary studies)

VARDIN (Illarion Vissarionovich Mgeladze, Visanov I.) - 266 (party topics)

VAREIKIS Iosif Mikhailovich - 171 (party topics)

VASILENKO Matvei Ivanovich - 292 (military topics)

VATSETIS Ioakim Ioakimovich - 1085 (military topics)

VEGER Evgenii Il'ich - 683 (party topics)

VEITSER Izrail' IAkovlevich - 688 (trade, politics)

VERKhOVSKOI Boris Klavdievich (Verkhovskii) - 292 (war fiction)

VERShKOV Petr Afanas'evich - 31 (*komsomol* topics)

VESELYI Artem (Kochkurov Nikolai Ivanovich) - 171 (artistic subjects)

VILENSKAIA Marfa Mitrofanovna - 681 (preschool education)

VILENSKII (Vilenskii-Sibiriakov V.) Vladimir Dmitrievich - 241 (essayist on Oriental subjects)

VINNIChENKO V. K. - 52 Ukrainian SSR (fiction)

VIRTANEN IAlmari Erikovich (IAlmari Vartanen) - 372 (fiction)

VIShNEVSKII Aleksandr Ivanovich - 683 (physical education and tourism)

VOGAU (Pilniak Boris Andreevich) - 171 (artistic subjects)

VOLOSEVICh Vladislav Ottonovich - 241 (party topics)

VOL'PE Abram Mironovich - 1085 (military topics)

VORONKOV Viktor Mikhailovich - 1085 (military topics)

VORONSKII Aleksandr Konstantinovich - 266 (artistic subjects)

VYGOTSKII Lev Semenovich - 957 (education)

"G"

GABYShEV Aleksandr Gavrilovich - *ts*1506 (Soviet development, party topics)

GAVRILOV N. (G. Lelevich, Labori Gileev, Kal'manson, Mogilevskii L., Beliakov G.) - 266 (fiction)

GAI (Gaia) Gaia Dmitrievich - 292 (military topics)

GAISTER Aaron Izrailevich - 683 (politics, collective farm development)

GAMARNIK IAn Borisovich - 513 (party, military topics)

GANETSKII IAkov Stanislavovich - 646 (bibliographer, essays, international issues)

GVOZDIKOV Karp Dmitrievich - 266 (military topics)

GEINTS Neiman - 390 (party topics)

GERASIMOV Mikhail Prokop'evich - 266 (fiction)

GERONIMUS Aleksandr Abramovich - 681 (military topics)

GIKALO Nikolai Fedorovich - 31 (party topics)

GILINSKII Abram Lazarevich - 957 (party topics)

GIL'BO Anri [GILBEAU, Henri] - 390

GIMMER (Sukhanov) Nikolai Nikolaevich - 671 (social, political, and agricultural issues)

GINDIN IAkov Isaakovich - 681 (labor issues)

GLEBOV-AVILOV N. (Avilov Nikolai Pavlovich) - 241 (labor movement)

GLOTOV A. (Bubnov Andrei Sergeevich, S. Igotov) - 171 (party topics, military, public education)

GLUDIN I. I. - 163 (military)

GOLENDO Matvei Semenovich - 683 (party topics)

GOLIKOV A. P. - 681 (military topics) (Not to be confused with Golikov (Gaidar), the writer of children's books,
    who also has written books for children on military themes)

GOLODED Nikolai Matveevich - 671 (Soviet development)

GOL'DMAN Boris Isaakovich (Gorev B. I.) - 647 (philosophy, history, biographical themes)

GOL'DMAN Emma - 82 (social and political subjects)

GOL'DShTEIN Isaak Iosifovich - 73 (social and economic issues)

GONIKMAN Solomon L'vovich - 681 (party topics)

GORBAChEV Georgii Efimovich - 266 (criticism)

GOREV B. I. (GOL'DMAN Boris Isaakovich) - 647 (philosophy, history, biographical themes)

GORNShTEIN Tat'iana Nikolaevna - 241 (philosophy - essays)

GOROKhOV F. A. - 822 (philosophy)

GRAVE Berta Borisovna - 681 (agrarian movement, history and theory of class struggle)

GRINShTEIN Grigorii Osipovich - 683 (railway transportation)

GRIN'KO Grigorii Fedorovich - 171 (finance)

GRIChMANOV Aleksei Petrovich - 957 (party topics)

GRIADINSKII Fedor Pavlovich - 957 (party topics)

" D "

DAVID Rudol'f Eduardovich - 163 (agricultural meteorology)
DAVID Frits (Fritz) - 646 (international issues)
DALIN Viktor Moiseevich - 681 (*komsomol* topics)
DANIShEVSKII Karl Khristianovich - 681 (forestry and wood products industry)
DAShINSKII S. (Nikonov Aleksandr Matveevich) - 644 (international issues)
DVOIChENKO Petr Abramovich - 486 (literary history)
DEMBO Vladimir Osipovich - 683 (international and trade union topics)
DERNOVA-IARMOLENKO Avgusta Aleksandrovna - 957 (education)
DZhAVAKhIShVILI Mikhail Savvich (Adamishvili M. S.) - 372 (fiction)
DIMENTMAN Anatolii Matveevich - 372 (*komsomol* topics)
DOGALOV Aleksandr Ivanovich - 683 (trade union topics)
DOMBAL' Tomash F. - 646 (international issues, social and economic issues)
DONSKOI Semen Nikolaevich - 1st *ts.*1506 (Russian-Yakut dictionary, trade and industrial topics)
DONSKOI Semen Nikolaevich - 2nd *ts.*1506 (topics of cultural development)
DROBNIS IAkov Naumovich - 646 (party topics)
DROZDOV Petr Stepanovich - 683 (historian and essayist)
DRIAZGOV Grigorii M. - 683 (*komsomol* topics)
DUBOVOI Ivan Naumovich (Dubovyi) - 957 (military)
DUBOVKO Viacheslav Nikolaevich - 1085 (military topics)
DUBROVSKII Sergei Mitrofanovich - 683 (agrarian history, social and economic issues)
DURNOVO Aleksandr Sergeevich - 957 (education)
DYBENKO Pavel Efimovich - 671 (naval topics)

" E "

EVDOKIMOV Grigorii Eremeevich - 646 (party topics)
EVSEEV Nikolai Fedorovich - 292 (military topics)
EGOROV Aleksandr Il'ich - 292 (military topics)
EZhOV Nikolai Ivanovich - 388 (party topics)
ELPAT'EVSKII Dmitrii Vladimirovich - 163 (agricultural topics)
ENUKIDZE Avel' Safronovich - 646 (party topics and Soviet development)
EFREMOV (Tomskii Mikhail Pavlovich) - 292 (party topics and trade union movement)

" Z "

ZAIDEL' Grigorii Solomonovich - 241 (international issues)
ZAITSEV Aleksandr N. - 681 (social and economic issues)
ZAITSEV Vladimir Alekseevich - 683 (*komsomol* topics)
ZAKONSKII Leonid Mikhailovich (Zakovs'kii L.) - 513 (intelligence)
ZALKIND Aron (Aaron Borisovich) - 957 (education)
ZALUTSKII Petr Antonovich - 671 (party topics)
ZARIN Petr Karlovich - 681 (antireligious topics)
ZATONSKII Vladimir Petrovich - 372 (social and political issues)
ZELENSKII Isaak Abramovich - 266 (party topics)
ZEL'TSER Vladimir Zel'manovich - 646 (historical and antireligious topics)
ZIMIN Nikolai Nikolaevich - 957 (party topics and transportation)
ZINOVIEV Grigorii Evseevich (Radomysl'skii G. E.) - 241 (party topics, international issues, social and political, social and economic issues)
ZORIN Boris Porfir'evich - 292 (military topics)
ZOF Viacheslav Ivanovich - 646 (navy)
ZUN Vladimir Aleksandrovich - 1085 (military topics)

" I "

IVANOV Vladimir Ivanovich - 266 (party topics)

IVONIN Nikolai Pavlovich - 1085 (military topics)

IGNAT S. B. - 683 (*komsomol* and Communist Party topics)

IGOTOV S. (Bubnov Andrei Sergeevich, Glotov A.) - 171 (party, military, public education)

IZRAILOVICh Abram Il'ich - 681 (coal industry)

IKRAMOV Akmal' - 266 (party topics)

IL'IN Fedor Fedorovich (Raskol'nikov R.) - 901 (social, political, artistic)

INGULOV Sergei Borisovich - 266 (party topics)

INSAROV Kh. (Rakovskii Khristian Georgievich, Stancheva E.) - 171 (social and political issues)

IOEL'SON Maksimilian Filippovich - 683 (international issues and economics)

ISAAK Don Levin [Isaac don Levine] - 82 (social and political issues)

ISAEV Uraz - 372 (party topics)

ISTMEN Maks [EASTMAN Max] - 82 (social and political issues)

ISTRATI Panait - 388 (artistic subjects)

IShchENKO A. G. - 681 (trade union topics)

" K "

KABAKOV Ivan Dmitrievich - 646 (party topics)

KAVALERIN (Rogovskii Aleksandr Antonovich) - 1085 (military topics)

KAKTYN' Artur Martynovich - 645 (social and economic issues)

KAKURIN Nikolai Evgen'evich - 683 (military topics)

KALMANOVICh Moisei Iosifovich - 681 (state farm topics and finance)

KAL'MANSON (Labori Gileev, Lelevich G., Mogilevskii L., Gavrilov N., Beliakov G.) - 266 (fiction)

KAMENEV L. (Rozenfel'd Lev Borisovich, Kamenev IU.) - 241 (party topics, international politics, social and political, social and economic issues, philosophy)

KAMENEV Sergei Sergeevich - 292 (military topics)

KAMINSKII Grigorii Naumovich - 646 (party topics, cooperatives, public health)

KAMKOV Boris Davydovich - 647 (party topics)

KANATChIKOV Semen Ivanovich - 266 (artistic and party topics)

KAPLINSKII Vladimir Viktorovich - 1085 (military)

KAREV Nikolai Afanas'evich - 241 (philosophical and artistic subjects)

KARELIN Vladimir Aleksandrovich - 647 (social and political issues)

KARPOV Ivan Karpovich - 372 (party topics)

KATAEV Ivan Ivanovich - 957 (artistic subjects)

KAShIRIN N. D. - 172.

KVIRING Emmanuil Ionovich - 171 (party and social and political issues)

KIVAL'ChICh (Serzh Viktor [Victor SERGE]) - 82 (social and political issues)

KIEVSKII Petr (Piatakov IUrii Leonidovich) - 241 (industrial economics)

KIN V. (Surovinin Viktor Pavlovich) - 266 (fiction)

KIRILENKO Ivan Ul'ianovich - 372 (artistic subjects)

KIRILLOV Vladimir Timofeevich - 292 (poetics)

KIRShON Vladimir Mikhailovich - 171 (artistic subjects)

KLIMENKO (Ivan Evdokimovich) - 681 (agricultural topics)

KNORIN Vil'gel'm Georgievich - 241 (party topics, international politics)

KOVTIUKh Epifan Iovich - 683 (military topics)

KOLBAS'EV Sergei Adamovich - 266 (artistic subjects)

KOL'TSOV Mikh. (Fridliand Mikhail Efimovich) - 31 (satirist and political and social commentator)

KONDRAT'EV Nikolai Dmitrievich - 683 (agricultural economics)

KONOVALOV Nikolai Alekseevich - 957 (education)

KORNILOV Boris Petrovich - 266 (fiction)

KOSAREV Aleksandr Vasil'evich - 31 (*komsomol* topics)
KOSIOR Stanislav Vikent'evich - 513 (party topics)
KOTOV Nikolai IAkovlevich - 1085 (military topics)
KOFANOV Pavel Evtikhaevich - 310 (fiction)
KOTSIUBA Gordii Maksimovich - 372 (fiction)
KOChKUROV Nikolai Ivanovich (Veselyi Artem) - 171 (fiction)
KRAVAL' Ivan Adamovich - 646 (social and economic issues)
KRESTINSKII Nikolai Nikolaevich - 266
KRIVOBOKOV (Nevskii Vladimir Ivanovich) - 292 (historical and biographical, history of Communist Party)
KRINITSKII Aleksandr Ivanovich - 681 (party topics)
KRYLENKO Nikolai Vasil'evich - 266 (government and law, tourism, chess)
KRYLOV Semen Nikolaevich - 681 (party and agricultural topics)
KSENOFONTOV Gavriil Vasil'evich - ts. 1506 (history)
KSENOFONTOV Filipp Alekseevich - 683 (party topics, agriculture)
KUZNETSOV Stepan Matveevich - 163 (finance)
KULIK Ivan IUlianovich - 372 (poetry and criticism)
KULISh Mikola Gur'evich - 284 Ukrainian SSR (artistic subjects)
KUN Bela - 646 (international topics)
KURAMYSOV Izmukhan Mukhashevich - 372 (agitation and propaganda among the masses)
KUTIAKOV Ivan Semenovich - 241 (military topics)
KUShNER Boris Akisimovich - 266 (fiction, essayist)

"L"

LAVLINSKOV Aleksei Ivanovich - 163 (agricultural topics)
LAVRENTIEV Lavrentii - 683 (party and collective farm topics)
LAVROV Mikhail Aleksandrovich - 683 (financial topics)
LAZAREVSKII Boris Aleksandrovich - 1088 (fiction)
LAKOBA Nestor A. - 681 (party and Soviet development)
LANTSUTSKII Stanislav [LANCUCKI Stanislaw] - 446 (fiction)
LAPINSKII Pavel Liudvigovich - 241 (international political issues)
LARIN V. F. - 957 (party topics)
LAUER Genrikh Bernardovich - 683 (ferrous metallurgy)
LEBED' Dmitrii Zakharovich - 681 (party, military, and Soviet development)
LEVIN (Isaac don Levine) - 82 (social and political issues)
LEVIN Miron Naumovich - 683 (economics and party topics)
LEVINA Revekka Saulova - 73 (social and political issues)
LEVIChEV Vasilii Nikolaevich - 681 (military topics)
LEZhAVA Andrei Matveevich - 646 (trade and social and economic issues)
LELEVICh G. (Kal'manson, Labori Gileev, Mogilevskii L., Gavrilov N., Beliakov G.) - 266 (fiction)
LEMUS Vladimir Ivanovich - 644 (economics and agriculture)
LENTSNER Naum Mikhailovich - 266 (international movement)
LEONIDOV Leonid Osipovich - 644 (party topics)
LIBERMAN Grigorii Borisovich - 266 (chemistry)
LIVShITS Vladimir Aronovich - 644 (trade union topics)
LIGNAU Aleksandr Georgievich - 1085 (military topics)
LILINA Zlata Ionovna - 644 (party topics and children's literature)
LITVINOV Ig. I. - 681 (social and economic issues)
LOBOV Semen Semenovich - 671 (timber industry)
LOMINADZE V. V. - 266 (*komsomol* topics and international movement)
LOMOV G. (Lomov A., Oppokov Georgii Ippolitovich) 646 (coal industry, petroleum industry, electrical power)

LUKAChEVSKII A. T. - 245 (antireligious topics)
LUKIN Nikolai Mikhailovich (Antonov N.) - 957 (history)
LUK'IANOV Dmitrii Dmitrievich - 646 (*komsomol* topics)
LUPPOL Ivan Kapitonovich - 1085 (philosophy)
LIUBIMOV Isidor Evstigneevich - 644 (local and light industry and cooperatives)
LIUBChENKO Arkadii Afanas'evich - 4 Ukrainian SSR (fiction)
LIUBChENKO Panas Petrovich - 671 (party topics and Soviet development)

" M "

MAD'IAR Liudvig Ignat'evich - 241 (essayist on Oriental topics)
MAILIN Meimbet (pseudonym Beimbet) - 372 (fiction)
MAKAROV Ivan Ivanovich - 266 (fiction)
MAKAR'EV Stepan Andreevich - 31 (ethnography)
MARETSKII Dmitrii M. - 241 (social and political issues)
MATORIN Nikolai Mikhailovich - 646 (antireligious topics and social and economic issues)
MGELADZE Illarion Vissarionovich (Bardin, Bisanov) - 266 (Communist Party topics)
MEZhENIKOV Sergei Aleksandrovich - 292 (military topics)
MEZhLAUK Valerii Ivanovich - 513 (economic topics)
MEISTER Georgii Karlovich - 163 (agricultural topics)
MELIKOV V. A. - 66/2398 (military history)
MEL'NIChANSKII Grigorii Natanovich - 241 (trade union topics)
MEN'ChUKOV Evgenii Aleksandrovich - 1085 (military topics)
METELEV Aleksandr Denisovich - 647 (agriculture)
MEShchERSKII Aleksandr Pavlovich - 644 (agriculture)
MIKITENKO Ivan Kondrat'evich - 372 (artistic subjects)
MIKULIN Vladimir Iosifovich - 1085 (military topics)
MILIUTIN Boris Trofimovich - 644 (social insurance)
MILIUTIN Vladimir Pavlovich - 241 (social and economic issues)
MIGULIN Ivan Georgievich - 644 (economics and the Communist International)
MIRZOIAN Levon Isaevich - 31 (party topics)
MIKhAILOV Vasilii Mikhailovich - 644 (trade union topics)
MILEVSKII L. (Lelevich G., Labori Gileev, Kal'manson, Gavrilov N., Beliakov G.) - 266 (fiction)
MOSKALEV Mikhail Abramovich - 50 (history of the Communist Party)
MURALOV Aleksandr Ivanovich - 646 (party and agricultural topics)
MURALOV Nikolai Ivanovich - 266 (agricultural topics)
MUSKIN Vasilii Antonovich - 644 (*komsomol* topics)
MUKhARDZhI Abani (Aboni) - 390 (international economics)

" N "

NEVSKII Vladimir Ivanovich (Krivobokov) - 292 (biographical history, Communist Party history, essayist)
NEIMAN Geints - 390 (party topics)
NEKRASOV Vsevolod Vladimirovich - 1085 (chemical warfare)
NIKITENKO Natalia Nikolaevna - 957 (education)
NIKONOV Aleksandr Matveevich (Dashinskii S.) - 644 (international issues)
NIKULIKhIN IAkov Petrovich - 671 (economics, agriculture, antireligious topics, textbooks)
NIN Andres - 671 (trade union topics)
NODEL' V. A. - 644 (party topics and Soviet trade)
NORKIN Boris Osipovich - 646 (social and economic issues)
NOSOV Ivan Petrovich - 644 (party topics)

OBOLENSKII (N. Osinskii) Valer'ian Valer'ianovich - 171 (essayist, satirist, agricultural topics, international situation)

OVALOV Lev Sergeevich - 599 (fiction)

OGLOBLIN Aleksandr Petrovich - 482 (history)

ODINTSOV Aleksandr Vasil'evich - 163 (collective farm and state farm development)

OIUNSKII (Sleptsov) Platon Alekseevich - ts.1506 (Soviet development issues and fiction)

OKOEMOV Nikolai Nikolaevich - ts.1506 (Soviet and party topics)

OL'KhOVYI Boris Semenovich - 644 (party topics)

ORAKhELAShVILI Mamiia Dmitrievich - 644 (party topics)

OREShIN Petr Vasil'evich - 171 (poetics)

ORLOV V. M. - 172

OSEPIAN G. A. - 172

OSINSKII Valer'ian Valer'ianovich (Obolenskii V. V.) - 171 (essayist, satirist, primarily on economics, agriculture, international politics, and Soviet development)

OSIPOVICh (Razumov Mikhail Iosifovich) - 671 (party and agricultural topics)

OTWAL'T Ernst - 390 (fiction)

PARIN Vas. Vas. - 69/2454 (medical topics)

PAS Madeleine (Madeleine Marx) - 82 (social and political topics)

PAShUKANIS Evgenii Bronislavovich - 241 (social and political topics, Soviet government and law)

PEVZNIAK Pavel Matveevich - ts. 1506 (party topics)

PEVNEV A. L. - 1085 (military topics)

PEGEL'MAN Gans (Hans) Gustavovich - 390 (economics)

PEPPER John - 671 (international affairs)

PEREL' Idel' Abramovich - 671 (cultural development)

PEROVSKAIA Ol'ga V. - 404 (children's topics)

PERChIK Lev Mendelevich - 241 (Communist Party, Soviet development, history and biography)

PETROV Petr Polikarpovich - 266 (artistic subjects)

PETROVSKII David Aleksandrovich - 266 (social, economic, international affairs and advanced technical education)

PIKINA Valentina Fedorovna - 372 (komsomol topics)

PIKKEL' Richard Vitol'dovich - 266 (political topics and criticism)

PIL'NIAK Boris Andreevich (Vogau) - 171 (artistic subjects)

PINKEVICh Al'bert Petrovich - 163 (education)

PIONTKOVSKII Sergei Andreevich - 266 (historian and essayist)

PIOTROVSKII Adrian Ivanovich - 266 (artistic subjects)

PISTRAK Moisei Mikhailovich - 241 (elementary education)

POZERN Boris Pavlovich - 978 (party topics)

POKUS IA. 163 - (military topics)

POLONSKII Vladimir Ivanovich - 645 (party, labor union topics)

POPOV Grigorii Andreevich - ts. 1506 (history)

POPOV Nikolai Nikolaevich - 671 (essayist, party history)

POSTYShEV Pavel Pavlovich - 342 (party topics)

POTAPOV Serafim Georgievich - ts. 1506 (history, social and economic topics)

PRAVDUKhIN Valerian Pavlovich - 266 (artistic subjects)

PRAMNEK Eduard Karlovich - 446 (party topics)

PREOBRAZhENSKII Evgenii Alekseevich - 292 (party topics and economic policy)

PRIGOZhIN Abram Grigorievich - 1085 (history, sociopolitical and socioeconomic topics)

PRIMAKOV V. M. - 645 (international affairs)

PUTNA Vitovt Kazimirovich - 292 (military topics)
PIATAKOV (Petr Kievskii) IUrii (Georgii) Leonidovich - 241 (industrial economics)
PIATNITSKII Osip (Iosif) Aronovich - 171 (social, political, party topics and trade union movement)

" R "

RABICh-ChERKASSKII M. - 671 (Communist Party history)
RADEK Karl Berngardovich (Sobel'son) - 241 (journalist, primarily international affairs)
RADOMYSL'SKII Grigorii Evseevich (Zinoviev G. E.) - 241 (international affairs, party, social and political topics)
RAZUMOV Mikhail Iosifovich (Osipovich) - 671 (party and agricultural topics)
RAKITIN Nikolai Vasil'evich No. 1085 (artistic subjects)
RAKOVSKII Khristian Georgievich (Insarov and Stancheva E.) - 171 (social and political topics)
RASKOL'NIKOV Fedor Fedorovich (Il'in) - 901 (social, political, and artistic topics)
RAFAIL Mikhail Abramovich - 645 (international workers' correspondent)
RAKhIMBAEV Abdula Rakhimovich - 647 (Soviet development)
RAKhIMBAEV M. A. - 172
REINGOL'D Isak Isakovich - 31 (financial topics, budget, and cotton)
REMMELE German - 647 (international affairs)
ROGOVSKII Aleksandr Antonovich (Kavalerin) No. 1085 (military topics)
ROZhDESTVENSKII M. - 163 (military topics)
ROZENGOL'TS Arkadii Pavlovich - 266 (foreign trade, social and political topics)
ROZENFEL'D Lev Borisovich (Kamenev L. B., Kamenev IU.) - 241
ROZIT David Petrovich - 671 (agricultural economics)
ROKOS Petr Nikolaevich - 671 (rail transportation)
RUBEN R. G. - 671 (party topics)
RUBIN Isaak Il'ich - 1085 (social and economic topics, political economy, philosophy)
RUDZUTAK IAn Ernestovich - 342 (party topics)
RUMIANTSEV Ivan Petrovich - 647 (party topics, agriculture)
RUT'KO Arsenii - 163 (artistic subjects)
RUKhIMOVICh Moisei L'vovich - 171 (party topics, economics)
RYKOV Aleksei Ivanovich - 266 (party topics)
RYKOV Pavel Sergeevich - 163 (archaeology)
RYNDIN Kuz'ma Vasil'evich - 645 (party topics)
RYSKULOV Turar Ryskulovich - 292 (party history, Soviet development)
RIULE (RUHLE) Otto - 82 (social and political topics)
RIUTIN Martem'ian Nikitich - 645 (party topics)
RIASTAS Otto - 390 (history)

" S "

SAVIN Viktor Alekseevich (Nebdins Viktor) - 446 (fiction)
SALTANOV Sergei Aleksandrovich - 646 (komsomol topics)
SAPRONOV Timofei V. - 646 (essayist, Soviet development)
SARKISOV S. A. (Sarkis) - 266 (social, political, and party topics)
SARYMULDAEV Kabuldek Sarymuldaevich - 372 (social and economic topics)
SAFAROV Georgii Ivanovich - 241 (party, social, and political topics)
SVEChNIKOV Mikhail Stepanovich - 1085 (military topics)
SEMKOVSKII Semen IUl'evich (Bronshtein) - 241 (philosophy)
SEREBROVSKII Aleksandr Pavlovich - 266 (gold and oil industry)
SEREBRIAKOVA Galina Osipovna - 671 (artistic subjects)
SERZh Viktor (Kibal'chich) - 82 (social and political topics)
SEF Semen E. - 671 (party topics)
SITKOVSKII Evgenii P. - 822 (philosophy)

SKRYPNIK Nikolai Alekseevich (Asnik) - 671 (public education, judicial system, prosecution)

SLEPKOV A. - 241 (party and agrarian topics, social policy)

SLEPTSOV (OIUNSKII) Platon Alekseevich - *ts.* 1506 (Soviet development, fiction)

SMILGA Ivar Tenisovich - 241 (economics, military topics)

SMIRNOV Anatolii Aleksandrovich - 957 (education)

SMIRNOV Aleksandr Petrovich - 645 (economics, agriculture, Soviet development)

SMIRNOV Mikhail Petrovich - 957 (Soviet trade)

SMIRNOV Sergei Aleksandrovich - 1085 (military topics)

SMUShKOV Vadim Vasil'evich - 446 (economic topics)

SOBEL'SON (Radek Karl Berngardovich) - 241 (journalist, primarily international affairs)

SOKOLOV I. G. - 446 (forestry industry)

SOKOL'NIKOV Grigorii IAkovlevich (Briliant) - 241 (international political and financial topics)

SOKOL'NIKOV Konstantin Alekseevich - *ts.* 1506 (poetry and drama)

SOLOGUB Nikolai Vladimirovich - 1085 (military topics)

SOSNOVSKII Lev Semenovich - 266 (artistic and party topics)

SPOKOINYI Leontii Feliksovich - 241 (philosophy)

STANChEVA E. (Rakovskii Khristian Georgievich, Insarov) - 171 (social and political topics)

STEN IAn N. - 266 (social and political topics)

STETSKII Aleksei Ivanovich - 342 (party topics)

STOLIAROV Aleksei Konstantinovich - 645 (philosophy, Communist Party development)

STROILOV Mikhail Stepanovich - 957 (mining)

STRUPPE Petr Ivanovich - 671 (agriculture, economics)

STUKOV Inokentii Nikolaevich - 647 (social and political topics)

SUVARIN Boris - 82 (social and political topics)

SULIMOV Daniil Egorovich - 266 (Soviet development)

SUROVININ Viktor Pavlovich (Kin V. P.) - 266 (fiction)

SUKhANOV (Gimmer) Nikolai Nikolaevich - 671 (social and political topics, agriculture)

SYRTSOV Sergei Ivanovich - 266 (party topics)

"T"

TAL' Boris Markovich - 513 (party press)

TAL'GEIMER (THALHEIMER) Avgust - 671 (social and political philosophy)

TANIN Mikhail Aleksandrovich - 266 (international politics)

TANIAEV Aleksandr Petrovich - 645 (party topics)

TATAEV Nikolai Andreevich - 671 (agricultural economics)

TVERIAK Aleksei Artem'evich - 266 (artistic subjects)

TEODOROVICh Ivan Adol'fovich - 645 (history of the revolutionary movement and agricultural topics)

TETERIN Mikhail Pavlovich - 372 (*komsomol* topics)

TOVEL' Aleksandr IUl'evich - 645 (international affairs)

TOMSINSKII Semen Grigor'evich - 241 (history, social and political topics)

TOMSKII Mikhail Pavlovich (Efremov) - 292 (party and trade union movement)

TRET'IAKOV Sergei Mikhailovich - 266 (artistic subjects)

TROEPOL'SKII A. - 163 (artistic subjects)

TROTSKY (Bronshtein, Lev Davydovich, Takhotskii) - 292

TUKhAChEVSKII Mikhail Nikolaevich - 292 (military topics)

"U"

UBOREVICh Ieronim Petrovich - 292 (military topics)

UGAROV Aleksandr Ivanovich - 31 (social and economic topics)

UGLANOV Nikolai Aleksandrovich - 647 (party topics)

UMANETS' IUrii (Khvil'ovii Mikola) - 288 Ukraine (fiction)

UNShLIKhT Iosif Stanislavovich - 645 (Defense Assistance Society and socialist development)
URANOV S. - 513 (intelligence)
URITSKII Semen Borisovich - 957 (party topics)
UKhANOV Konstantin Vasil'evich - 645 (Soviet development)

"F"

FAINBERG Evgenii L'vovich - 647 (*komsomol* topics)
FAL'KEVICh Isai - 372 (law and Soviet development)
FEL'DMAN Boris Mironovich - 646 (military topics)
FILOV Viktor - 163 (social and economic topics)
FIN IAkov Isaakovich - 645 (trade union movement)
FIShMAN IAkov Moiseevich - 266 (chemical warfare)
FLAKSERMAN IUrii Nikolaevich - 671 (engineering and electrification)
FRANKFURT Sergei Mironovich - 647 (party topics)
FRIDLIAND Grigorii (TSvi) Samoilovich - 671 (history)
FRIDLIAND Mikhail Efimovich (Kol'tsov Mikh.) - 31 (journalistic satire and pamphlets)
FRIDOLIN Sergei Petrovich - 671 (agricultural economics)
FROLOV I. V. - 163 (artistic subjects)

"Kh"

KhALATOV Artemii Bagrationovich - 647 (Soviet development, publishing)
KhALEPSKII Innokentii Andreevich - 645 (military topics)
KhARChENKO Ivan Ivanovich - 671 (*komsomol* topics, physical education, and sports)
KhATAEVICh Mendel' Markovich - 617 (collective and state farm development and party topics)
KhODZhAEV Faizulla - 266 (party and Soviet development)
KhOIUTANOV Georgii Prokop'evich - *ts.* 1506 (textbooks)
KhVIL'OVII Mikola (pseudonym of Umanets' IUrii) - No. 288 Ukraine (fiction)

"TS"

TSVI (Fridliand Grigorii Samoilovich) - 671 (history)
TSEITLIN Efim F. - 266 (international youth movement)
TSIFRINOVICh Vladimir Efimovich - 647 (party topics)
TSIFFER Richard Stanislavovich - 1085 (military topics)
TSYL'KO Fedor Andreevich - 647 (cooperative agriculture)
TSYTOVICh Nikolai Platonovich - 1085 (military topics)

"Ch"

ChAIKOVSKII Kas'ian Aleksandrovich - 1085 (military topics)
ChAPLIN Nikolai Pavlovich - 978 (*komsomol* topics)
ChAIANOV Aleksandr Vasil'evich - 645 (economics, agriculture)
ChEKIN A. (IArotskii Vasilii IAkovlevich) - 31 (trade union movement)
ChEMODANOV Vasilii Tarasovich - 31 (*komsomol* topics)
ChERNOV Mikhail Aleksandrovich - 171 (party topics, agriculture)
ChUBAR' Vlas IAkovlevich - 646 (party, social, and political topics)
ChUDOV M. S. - 172 (Soviet development)

"Sh"

ShADUNTS Suren Konstantinovich - 957 (party topics)
ShARANGOVICh Vasilii Fomich - 266 (party topics)
ShATSKII Lazar' - 266 (international youth movement)

ShVER Aleksandr Vladimirovich - 671 (agriculture)
ShEBOLDAEV Boris Petrovich - 671 (party and collective farm development)
ShEMShELEVICh Leonid Veniaminovich - 163 (fiction)
ShLEIFER I. O. - 647 (finance)
ShLIAPNIKOV Aleksandr Gavrilovich - 241 (history and Communist Party topics)
ShMELEV I. S. - 1088 (fiction)
ShMIDT Vasilii Vladimirovich - 647 (labor and wage topics)
ShOTMAN Aleksandr Vasil'evich - 647 (party topics)
ShTEINMAN Zelik IAkovlevich - 647 (fiction)
ShTETSA Konstantin - 482 (history)
ShUBERT Anna Mikhailovna - 957 (education)
ShUBRIKOV Vladimir Petrovich - 645 (party topics and agriculture)
ShUMS'KII Oleksandr IAkovlevich - 293 Ukraine (education)
ShUMIATSKII Boris Zakharovich - 446 (party topics)

" Shch "

ShchEGLOV Aleksei Vasil'evich - 163 (philosophy, Communist Party history)

" E "

EIDEMAN Robert Petrovich - 266 (military and artistic topics)
EISMONT Nikolai Boleslavovich - 647 (economic topics)
EIKhE Robert Indrikovich - 342 (party topics)
ELIAVA Shalva Zurabovich - 647 (economic topics)
EPShTEIN Moisei Solomonovich - 446 (education)
ESTREIKhER-EGOROV Rudol'f Anastas'evich - 1085 (military topics)

" IU "

IURINETS Volodimir Oleksiiovich - 300 Ukraine (literary studies)

" IA "

IAVORSKII Semen IAkovlevich - 241 (internationalist essayist)
IAVORS'KII Matvei Ivanovich - 293 Ukraine (history)
IAKIR Iona Emmanuilovich - 292 (military topics)
IAKOVLEV IAkov Arkadievich - 546 (party and agricultural topics)
IAKOVLEVA Varvara Nikolaevna - 647 (financial topics)
IAROTSKII Vasilii IAkovlevich (A. Chekin) - 31 (trade union movement)
IASENSKII Bruno - 171 (artistic subjects)

TSGAOR, fond 9425-sch, op. 1, d. 747, ll. 3–20.

DOCUMENT 91   **Glavlit *order, August 26, 1949, to remove from bookstores and libraries literature of certain authors published in the USSR***

97

Secret

ORDER

of the Representative of the Council of
Ministers of the USSR for Protection of
Military and State Secrets in the Press

26 August 1949   No. 22   Moscow

Outgoing No. 3351s

I ORDER:

1

Remove from the general public libraries and bookstores the following literature:

1. Simonov, K. *Slavic Friendship.* Military Publishing House of the Ministry of Defense of the USSR, 1945, 88 pp.

2. Simonov, K. *Yugoslav Notebook.* All editions.

3. Ternovoi, O. I. *International Significance of the Great October Socialist Revolution.* Stalingrad. *Oblast'* Publishing House, 1947, 31 pp., 10,000 copies.

4. Tikhonov, N. *Poems about Yugoslavia.* Moscow. Moscow Worker, 1947, 88 pp., 10,000 copies.

5. Usherenko, IA. *The Soviet Army—The Liberation Army.* Moscow. Military Publishing House, 1947, 55 pp.

6. Fish, Gennadii. *The Fires of Kamennyi Bor* [Stony Forest]. Petrozavodsk. State Publishing House of the Karelian-Finnish SSR, 1948, 211 pp., 45,000 copies.

7. Ehrenburg, I. *On the Roads of Europe.* Moscow. *Pravda,* 1946, 80 pp., 10,000 copies (The *Ogonek* Library, Nos. 12–13).

8. Ehrenburg, I. *The Roads of Europe.* Moscow. The Soviet Writer. 1946, 147 pp., 15,000 copies.

9. IAkovlev N. *The October Socialist Revolution and Its Place in the History of Our Country.* Moscow. State Publishing House of Political Literature, 1946, 62 pp., 50,000 copies.

2

Paragraphs 151–174 of the "Censor's Instructions" itemize the procedure and guidance for the removal.

Representative of the Council of Ministers of the USSR for Protection of Military and State Secrets in the Press

[signed]   K. Omel'chenko

[Illegible name and note]

To all censorship organs including
district censor
August 25
[Illegible signature]

TSGAOR, fond 9425-sch, op. 1, d. 732, l. 97.

UNION OF SOVIET SOCIALIST REPUBLICS

MAIN DIRECTORATE FOR THE PROTECTION
OF MILITARY AND STATE SECRETS IN THE PRESS [*Glavlit*]
OF THE COUNCIL OF MINISTERS OF THE USSR

DIRECTORATE FOR THE PROTECTION
OF MILITARY AND STATE SECRETS IN THE PRESS [*LENOBLGORLIT*]
OF THE LENINGRAD *OBLAST'* AND CITY EXECUTIVE COMMITTEES

February 15, 1964
No. 24s
Leningrad, D-88, Nevskii Prospect, No. 28
Telephone: A 4-94-72

TO:
The Deputy Chief
of the Main Directorate of the State Committee on the Press
of the Council of Ministers of the USSR
Comrade AVETISIAN S. P.

At the request of Comrade M. N. Kozitskii, we are forwarding the list of politically defective books.

ENCLOSURE: List (six pages of text).

Acting Deputy Chief of the *Lenoblgorlit*
(N. ISUPOV)

[signed]

[handwritten:]   Noted
For the file/books examined   April 20, 1964
by the commission

LIST OF POLITICALLY DEFECTIVE BOOKS

1. ALYPOV S. A. *How Our Government Works* (based on Comrade Rykov's speech to the Fourth All-Union Congress of Soviets of Workers', Peasants', and Red Army Soldiers' Deputies). Moscow-Leningrad, State Publishing House, 1927, 75 pp. 85,000 copies printed.

The entire book is based on Rykov's speech, and there is a portrait of Rykov on page 7.

2. ALYPOV S. A. *What the 15th Congress of the All-Union Communist Party (Bolshevik) Decided.* Moscow-Leningrad, State Publishing House, 1928, 96 pp. 35,000 copies.

Portraits of N. Bukharin and A. Rykov (pp. 22 and 29). The pages with the portraits cannot be easily removed.

3. ALYPOV S. A. *What the 15th Conference of the All-Union Communist Party (Bolshevik) Decided.* Moscow-Leningrad, State Publishing House, 1927, 48 pp.
(For peasants: on the decisions of the 15th Party Conference of the All-Union Communist Party (Bolshevik)). 35,000 copies.

The book discusses the speeches of N. Bukharin (pp. 8–15) and A. Rykov (pp. 15–30).

4. ALYPOV S. A. *Is Our State Proletarian? The Errors of the Opposition Concerning the Class Character of Our State.* Moscow-Leningrad, State Publishing House, 1927, 64 pp. (Library of the journal *Sputnik agitatora* [The Agitator's Companion], an organ of the Department of Agitation and Propaganda of the Central Committee of the All-Union Communist Party (Bolshevik) and the Moscow Committee of the All-Union Communist Party (Bolshevik). 10,000 copies.

Excerpts from speeches and quotations from and references to N. Bukharin (pp. 5, 18, 33–34, 50, 51–52, 54, 56–57).

5. *Op cit.* 2nd Edition. Moscow-Leningrad, State Publishing House, 1927, 64 pp.

The same political defects (pp. 5, 18, 33–34, 50, 51–52, 54, 56–57).

6. *Op cit.* Kazan', State Publishing House of the Tatar Soviet Socialist Republic, 1927, 83 pp. 3,000 copies (in Tatar).

Same political defects on same pages.

7. ANIShEV An. *Studies on the History of the Civil War, 1917–1920.* Leningrad, State Publishing House, 1925. 288 pp. (The Comrade Tolmachev Military Political Academy of the Workers' and Peasants' Red Army and Workers' and Peasants' Red Navy). 7,000 copies.

Numerous quotations and references to L. Trotsky (pp. 46, 131–32, 135, 157, 159–60, 228, 268), I. Smilga (p. 162), G. Sokol'nikov (pp. 8, 198), Kh. Rakovskii (pp. 167 and 269), A. Rykov (p. 175), and G. Safarov (p. 56).

8. VARAVVA A. (compiler). *Cooperation on the Stage. Cooperation in Music, on the Stage, in Literature, and Cooperative Chastushki [Ditties].* (A collection and reader compiled by Ol. Varavva). Kharkov, Knigospilka, 1927, 115 pp. 5,000 copies.

Article by P. Zagoruiko (pp. 81–86).

9. VOLOSEVICh V. *Bolshevism During the World War.* Leningrad, *Priboi,* 1929, 148 pp. 5,000 copies.

The author supports a number of points in his book with quotations of and references to G. Zinoviev (pp. 63, 69, 72, 77, 87–88, 90, 95, 98).

10. GONIKMAN S. *The History of the All-Union Communist Party (Bolshevik). For the Lay Reader (Up to and Including the 15th Party Conference).* Kharkov, *Proletarii,* 1927, 258 pp. 7,000 copies.

L. Trotsky, G. Zinoviev, A. Rykov, L. Kamenev, and N. Bukharin are included in two group photographs in the book (pp. 143 and 168). Overly mild criticism of the errors of Trotsky, Zinoviev, and Kamenev (pp. 46–47, 66–68, 103–5, 125, 144–45, 146, 160).

11. GONIKMAN S. *A Party Primer. A Textbook for Short Political Education Courses on the Program of the Central Committee of the Russian Communist Party.* Kharkov, *Proletarii,* 1926, 388 pp. (Textbooks for basic political education courses.) 30,000 copies.

L. Trotsky and L. Kamenev are included in two group photographs in the book (pp. 261 and 284), and there are also photographs of N. Bukharin, G. Zinoviev, and A. Rykov (p. 261). These individuals are also quoted, cited, and subjected to only mild criticism (pp. 75, 173, 191–92, 225, 226, etc.) There is a poem dedicated to A. Rykov on page 93.

12. GONIKMAN S. *The Path to Socialism. A Textbook for Short Political Education Courses on the Program of the Central Committee of the Russian Communist Party.* 2nd revised and supplemented edition. Edited by the Department of Agitation and Propaganda of the Central Committee of the Communist Party (Bolshevik) of Ukraine. Kharkov, *Proletarii,* 1926, 468 pp. (Textbooks for basic political education courses.) 20,000 copies.

L. Trotsky and L. Kamenev are included in two group photographs (pp. 307 and 334), while one photograph includes Zinoviev, Bukharin, and Rykov (p. 307). The author is overly mild in criticizing Trotsky's activity (pp. 285–87, 288–89, 330, 348, 356, 360, 366–68, etc.) A poem dedicated to Rykov is on page 100.

13. ZAITSEV A. *The Party's Important Decision on Peasant Farming. What the 14th Communist Party Conference Said.* Moscow-Leningrad, State Publishing House, 1925, 32 pp. 10,000 copies.

This book quotes Rykov's speeches at the conference extensively and flatteringly (pp. 13–14, 23, 27, 29–30).

14. *Op cit.* Chita, Publishing House of the Transbaikal Provincial Executive Committee of the Russian Communist Party (Bolshevik). 1925, 32 pp. 4,050 copies.

The same political defects on the same pages.

15. *Op cit.* Chita, Publishing House of the Transbaikal Province *PP* [acronym unclear]. 1925, 32 pp. 2,000 copies.

The same political defects on the same pages.

16. *Op cit.* Minsk, State Publishing House of Belarus. 1925, 34 pp. (Village Library No. 39). 5,000 copies (in Belorussian).

The same political defects.

17. *Op cit.* Kazan', State Publishing House of the Tatar Soviet Socialist Republic, 1926, 27 pp. 4,000 copies (in Tatar).

The same political defects.

18. ZAITSEV A. and ASTROV V. *Our Enemies on the Opposition.* Collection of articles by A. Zaitsev and V. Astrov. *Priboi,* 1926, 83 pp. 15,000 copies.

V. Astrov helped compile and contributed an article to the collection (pp. 72–83).

19. ZAKOVSKII L. *The Subversive Activities of Clergymen and Sectarians.* Leningrad, Leningrad *Oblast'* Publishing House, 1937, 16 pp. 100,000 copies.

Excerpt from book written by N. Ezhov (pp. 15–16).

20. ZAKOVSKII L. *Let's Wipe Out All the Spies, Saboteurs, and Wreckers!* Party Publishing House of the Central Committee of the All-Union Communist Party (Bolshevik). 1937, 47 pp. 1,000,000 copies.

The book praises and quotes N. Ezhov (pp. 46–47).

21. *Op cit.* Kiev. Party Publishing House of the Central Committee of the Communist Party (Bolshevik) of Ukraine. 1937, 37 pp. 100,000 copies. (in Ukrainian).

Same political defects (p. 37).

22. *Op cit.* Petrozavodsk, Karelian State Publishing House, 1938, 84 pp. 4100 copies. (in Karelian).

Same political defects (p. 83).

23. ZALUTSKII P. and Safarov G. *More on State Capitalism and Socialism.* Leningrad, *Priboi,* 1926, 36 pp. 10,000 copies.

G. Safarov coauthored one article and was the lone author of another article (pp. 11–36).

24. KONDRAT'EV N. D. *The World Grain Market and Our Grain Export Potential.* Moscow, Central Trade Union Council Publishing House, 1923, 52 pp. (Economist and Cooperative Manager's Library No. 1). 2,000 copies.

L. Trotsky quoted (pp. 10–11).

25. LELEVICh G. *V. IA. Briusov.* Moscow-Leningrad, State Publishing House, 1926, 258 pp. 3,000 copies.

The author uses material from an article by L. Kamenev to characterize Valerii Briusov's creative work and quotes Kamenev extensively on the subject (pp. 3–4, 7, 21, 49–50, 56, 59–60, 65, 66, 70, 72–73, 77, 84, 86, 89–90, 96, 126–28). The author also refers to Trotsky (p. 245).

26. LELEVICh G. *The October Revolution at Military Headquarters.* Gomel', *Gomel'skii rabochii* [The Gomel' Worker], 94 pp. + 83 pp. (Russian Communist Party (Bolshevik). 5,000 copies.

Trotsky is described as an active participant in the struggle for peace. The book reproduces a speech of his and a number of statements in full (pp. iii, 17, 38–43, 44, 45, 62). The book also quotes Kamenev (pp. 51, 53) and V. Chernov (pp. 64–66, 67, 68).

27. LELEVICh G. *At the Literary Battle Station.* (Articles and commentary.) Tver', *Oktiabr'* Party Publishing House, 1924, 170 pp. 3,000 copies.

The entire book is chock-full of quotes and statements from Trotsky and in some places contains very mild criticism of him (pp. iii, 6–7, 9–10, 11–12, 13, 16, 17, 18, 57, 80–81, 84, 87, 134, 154). The book also contains references to and quotes from Bukharin and Zinoviev (pp. 34, 118, 154).

28. LILINA Z. I. *The Great Teacher. A Lenin Reader.* Compiled by Z. I. Lilina. Leningrad, State Publishing House, 1924. 395 pp. 75,000 copies.

Articles by and references to Trotsky (pp. 101, 103, 326–28), Bukharin (224–26, 318–21), Kamenev (pp. 76, 83, 178–79), Zinoviev (pp. 74, 75, 78, 79, 84, 166–68, 208–12, 315–18), G. Safarov (pp. 344–45), Rykov (pp. 114, 321–23). Zinoviev in group photograph on page 117.

29. *Op cit.* 2nd edition. Leningrad, State Publishing House, 1924, 395 pp. 25,000 copies.

The same political defects on the same pages.

30. LILINA Z. I. *The Life of V. I. Lenin. A Short Biography for Komsomols and Pioneers.* Compiled by Z. Lilina. Moscow-Leningrad, State Publishing House, 1926, 112 pp. 4,000 copies.
Articles by, numerous references to, and photographs of Zinoviev (pp. 54, 69, 71, 72–73, 75, 82, 84, 85–90, 93, 94, 95, 97). Trotsky in group photograph on page 98.

31. LILINA Z. *The Red Calendar at the Vocational School.* Methodological articles, instructional material, and bibliography. Collection compiled by Z. I. Lilina. Leningrad, State Publishing House, 1924, 115 pp. 10,000 copies.

Article by Zinoviev (pp. 69–74), Zinoviev and Trotsky are quoted and referred to (pp. 43, 44, 45, 58, 65–66, 75, 77). Pages 101–15 contain a bibliography which refers to works by Trotsky, Bukharin, Zinoviev, Rakovskii, and others.

32. *Op cit.* 2nd edition, revised and supplemented. Leningrad, State Publishing House, 1925, 182 pp. 15,000 copies.

Same political defects (pp. 48, 85, 86, 87, 99, 106, 109–14, 117, 162–82).

33. PIKEL' R. *An Expert's Guide to Lenin Collections.* Moscow-Leningrad, *Moskovskii rabochii* [Moscow Worker], 1925, 72 pp. 5,000 copies.

Numerous quotes from Kamenev (pp. 6, 7, 10, 26, 33, 45) and Zinoviev (p. 11).

34. RAVICh-ChERKASSKII M. *History of the Communist Party (Bolshevik) of Ukraine.* Kharkov, State Publishing House of Ukraine, 1923, 248 pp. 10,000 copies.

The book is chock-full of references to, quotes from, and portraits of Piatakov (pp. 44, 51, 52, 53, 62, 63, 65, 72–73, 76, 78, 79, 81, and others), Trotsky (pp. 13, 20, 39, 131, 135, 166, 168, 176), Rakovskii (pp. 90, 107–108, 116, 132, 136, 161, and others), Kamenev (pp. 92–93, 95, 96, 167), and Zinoviev (p. 167).

35. *Op cit.* Kharkov, 1923, 180 pp. press run not indicated (in Ukrainian).

Same political defects (pp. 14, 20, 21, 31, 34, 35, 38, 41, 42, 43, 45, 47, 53, 60, 66, 69, 77, 78, 84, 85 etc.) and photographs (pp. 51, 153, 156).

36. RASKOL'NIKOV F. F. *Kronstadt and Petrograd in 1917.* Moscow-Leningrad, State Publishing House, 1925, 279 pp. (Party History Department of Central Committee of Russian Communist Party (Bolshevik) for Studying the History of the October Revolution and the Russian Communist Party (Bolshevik).) 7,000 copies.

Quotes, numerous references to, and sometimes praise of Zinoviev (pp. 53, 54, 57, 64, 65, 66, 101, 116, 117, 131, 175, and so on), Kamenev (pp. 111, 112, 115, 116, 117, 141, 142, 143, 145–46, 171, 203–4, 211–12, and so on), and Trotsky (pp. 77, 128, 129, 130, 131, 141, 142, 143, 167, 168, 170, 171, 175, 177, and so on).

37. ShLIAPNIKOV A. *On the Eve of 1917. Memoirs and Documents on the Workers' Movement and the Revolutionary Underground 1914–1917.* Moscow, 1920, 290 pp. Press run not indicated.

Description of the activity of Bukharin, Zinoviev, Kamenev, Trotsky, and Piatakov abroad on the eve of the revolution. (pp. 36, 37, 38, 51, 70–71, 73, 74, 77, 138, 188–89, 190, 193, 202–3).

38. ShLIAPNIKOV A. *The Eve of 1917. Memoirs and Documents on the Workers' Movement and the Revolutionary Underground 1914–1916.* Part 1. 2nd revised edition. Moscow-Petrograd, State Publishing House, 1923, 300 pp. (Party History Commission on the History of the October Revolution and the Russian Communist Party (Bolshevik). 5,000 copies.

Quotes from, references to, and flattering descriptions of the activity of Zinoviev, Bukharin, Kamenev, Trotsky, and Piatakov (pp. 41, 45, 60, 85, 88, 89, 92, 153, 203, 204–5, 208, 216, and so on).

39. ShLIAPNIKOV A. *1917.* Book 3. Moscow-Leningrad, State Publishing House, 1927, 380 pp. 3,000 copies.

Speeches, statements, and flattering references to Kamenev (pp. 107, 207, 209, 210, 217–20, 222, 227), Zinoviev (pp. 256, 261, 263), Sukhanov (pp. 174, 189), and Piatakov (pp. 201, 251).

40. ShLIAPNIKOV A. *1917.* Book 4. Moscow-Leningrad, *Sotsekgiz* [Social Sciences and Economics Publishing House], 1931, 445 pp. 5,000 copies.

Numerous references to, quotes from, and summaries of statements by Zinoviev (pp. 32, 155, 169, 185, 194, 196–97, 260, 261, 291–92, and so on), Trotsky (pp. 149, 150, 180, 181), Kamenev (pp. 171, 262, 321), and Rakovskii (pp. 157, 208, 281, 284, 290).

Acting DEPUTY DIRECTOR OF *LENOBLGORLIT*

(N. Isupov)   [signed]

Source: ?

Glavlit *complaint, November 15, 1967, on the unauthorized production of* Shatrov's play, **The Bolsheviks**

Secret

Copy No. 2

CENTRAL COMMITTEE
OF THE COMMUNIST PARTY OF THE SOVIET UNION [*TSK KPSS*]

The production *The Bolsheviks*, based on M. Shatrov's play *The Thirtieth of August*, premiered at the *Sovremennik* [Contemporary] Theater in Moscow on November 7, 8, and 12 of this year without registering with the Council of Ministers of the USSR Main Directorate for Protecting State Secrets in the Press [*Glavlit*]. This constituted a totally unacceptable and unprecedented violation of established procedures, which stipulate that all theatrical works by contemporary Soviet authors may only be staged after the scripts have been approved for production by *Glavlit*.

We did not approve the script of M. Shatrov's play *The Thirtieth of August* for production because it contained a number of major ideological and political defects.

This play was first submitted to *Glavlit* for inspection by the Ministry of Culture of the USSR in June of this year and was quickly recalled because of the negative evaluation it received from the Institute of Marxism-Leninism of the *TSK KPSS*. Despite this evaluation by the Institute of Marxism-Leninism, the Ministry of Culture resubmitted the play with only minor changes to *Glavlit* in September of this year.

An examination of the play revealed that it, for example, distorted a number of V. I. Lenin's ideas. In the script he is quoted as saying that we need to rethink all our theories from the very beginning. He himself wouldn't be able to do this, because "he is no longer capable of changing even his own ideas." The play obsessively emphasized Lenin's inconsistency in the tactics used to suppress the counterrevolutionary activity of the enemies of Soviet power. It even attempted to justify Zinoviev's failure to carry out Lenin's orders to send workers to the front to defend Petrograd.

We also doubted the historical accuracy and political soundness of including such figures as Steklov, Kollontai, and Krestinskii in the play. After all, these individuals were in opposition to Lenin both before and after the events depicted in the play, opposed party policy on fundamental issues, and joined different antiparty factions.

For example, we know that IU. Steklov was a Menshevik prior to the fall of 1917 and only joined the Bolshevik Party just before the October Revolution. In March 1917 he joined the Menshevik-Social Revolutionary "Contact Commission," which was organized for the purpose of establishing relations between the Provisional Government and the Soviets. Right up to July, 1917, Lenin mentioned Steklov in the same breath as TSereteli and Chkheidze on several occasions (see *Sobranie sochinenii* [Collected Works], Vol. 24, pp. 4, 13, 25, 29, 119, 201, et al.), calling him a "tail of the bourgeoisie" and a "sweet-talking strangler of the revolution," who is "pulling the revolution backwards."

In March 1918 Aleksandra Kollontai theatrically resigned from the Council of People's Commissars as a protest against Lenin's policy on the Treaty of Brest-Litovsk. In 1920 and 1921 she was an active member of the "workers' opposition," and her pamphlet entitled *The Workers' Opposition*, published right before the 10th Party Congress, became this group's ideological platform. Despite Lenin's resolution "On Party Unity" at the 10th Congress, which condemned the views of the "workers' opposition," Kollontai's pamphlet was distributed by oppositionists among the Comintern employees. Kollontai's antiparty activities were also severely criticized in the resolution of the 11th Party Congress (1922) "On Certain Members of the Former Workers' Opposition."

In 1918 N. Krestinskii joined the "left-wing Communists" in opposing Lenin on the Brest-Litovsk Treaty. He took a Trotskyite position during the "trade union" debates of 1920 and 1921. Subsequently he signed his name to the letter of the "eighty three."

We should mention that the author intentionally gave these and several other figures leading roles in the play and portrayed them as Leninists and the nucleus of the Bolshevik Party. This one-sided, subjective portrayal of their role distorts the historical truth and results in disinformation.

While writing a play on Lenin and the Bolsheviks and their actions in a very specific time frame, namely August 30, 1918, the author was very careless with the facts and created imaginary historical situations.

An example of this kind of invention in the play is his account of the discussion of "red terror" which supposedly occurred at the meeting of the Council of People's Commissars in the first few hours after the attempt on Lenin's life. The author's attempt to emphasize the question of the advisability of the "red terror" and its possible excesses and perversions in the future is also completely unjustified. The proposition that the terror could lead, as was the case under the Jacobin dictatorship, to the death of our revolution and turn against people devoted to the party and the country, is the central theme of the second act. All of these propositions are completely unrelated to the specific historical situation in August 1918 and are based on a large number of dubious political analogies.

The commissars' discussions of the danger of the dictatorship of a single class and possible disturbances of the proper balance between centralism and democracy and the associated establishment of a one-man dictatorship are also imaginary and hard to believe. "Yes, centralism and democracy are a hard nut to crack, and let's just hope we don't break our teeth on it," is Krestinskii's comment on the subject.

Those passages in the play which portray the helplessness of the Bolshevik commissars after the attempt on Lenin's life and their fear that without Lenin the party would be incapable of continuing his work successfully are also objectionable.

These and other complaints related to the ideological and political content of the play were detailed on October 25 and 29 in our letters to Comrade Tarasov, the director of the Theatrical Department of the Ministry of Culture of the USSR. On November 3 of this year, the Theatrical Department submitted a revised version of the play for inspection.

Our examination of the most recent version revealed that the author's scattered corrections and changes did not correct the basic deficiencies of Shatrov's *The Thirtieth of August.*

The revised version continues to focus on possible perversions of the "red terror" and the repetition of the errors of the Jacobin dictatorship in our country in the future, without Lenin. The revised version still portrays individuals who were in opposition to Lenin as Leninist Bolsheviks.

Glavlit did not consider it possible to approve the play for production in the form in which it was submitted and informed Comrade Vladykin, the deputy minister of culture, of this on November 5 of this year. Despite our complaints, on November 6, an official preview of the production of *The Bolsheviks* based on Shatrov's play, *The Thirtieth of August,* was held at the Contemporary Theater. After viewing the production the directors of the Ministry of Culture gave their approval for the staging of the play.

The fact that the advertising campaign for the production began far in advance of its premier draws attention to itself. Several press releases on the play contain inaccurate appraisals of its value as a work which reflects an important phase in the development of the Russian Revolution. For example, an item published in the November 13 issue of *Pravda* under the heading "Dedicated to the Revolution" (the theatrical chronicle) describes this production of the Contemporary Theater as the final play in a trilogy (*The Decembrists, The Narodnaia Volia,* and *The Bolsheviks*) conceived and produced by O. Efremov as a theatrical account of the three phases of the revolutionary liberation movement in Russia."

Please be so kind as to examine the issues discussed in the letter.

Chief of the USSR Council of Ministers
Main Directorate for Protecting
State Secrets in the Media

P. Romanov

November 15, 1967
No. 1081*s*

[illegible signatures and dates]

TSGAOR, fond 9425sch, op. 1, d. 1261, ll. 73–76.

DOCUMENT 94   *Instructions issued by Glavlit, April 11, 1969, forbidding publication of reviews and excerpts of Marshal Zhukov's memoirs*

Secret

copy no. 1

Council of Ministers of the USSR
Main Directorate for
Protection of State Secrets in the Press

April 11, 1969
no. 349
Moscow

To the chiefs of directorates for
protection of state secrets in the press

Until special instructions, publication of reviews of, references to, and excerpts from the book by the Marshal of the Soviet Union, G. K. Zhukov, *Memories and reflections*, Novosti Press Agency, Moscow, 1969, is forbidden.

Deputy Chief of the
Main Directorate

[signed] A. Okhotnikov

Basis: Instructions from the Office of Propaganda of the Central Committee of the Communist Party of the Soviet Union relayed by Comrade I. I. Chkhikvishvili, April 10, 1969.

TSGAOR, fond 9425-sch, op. 1, d. 1315, l. 49.

Aleksandr Solzhenitsyn

Aleksandr Solzhenitsyn emerged as one of the giants of the Soviet dissident movement in the early 1970s. He had first attracted attention as a writer with his novella, *One Day in the Life of Ivan Denisovich*, published in serialized form in 1962, and subsequently reprinted in Russian and several other languages of the Soviet Union. Its protagonist Ivan Denisovich was an ordinary political prisoner, a laborer in a post-war work camp, and this novel was the first published depiction of life in the *gulag.* Solzhenitsyn himself had been arrested during World War II for writing letters critical of Stalin while serving as a Red Army officer, and he spent eleven years in camps and in exile. Trained as a mathematician, he began to write fiction after his arrest, and he also began to collect materials and testimony for a study of the *gulag* system. During the 1960s he secretly composed his massive three-volume indictment of the Soviet repressive apparatus, *The Gulag Archipelago.* Two more of his novels, *The First Circle* and *Cancer Ward,* were published in the West to great acclaim.

When Solzhenitsyn was awarded the Nobel Prize for Literature in 1970, the Soviet government increased its attempts to discredit him and the dissident movement that had emerged during the regime of Brezhnev (see Document 140). In 1973 *KGB* authorities finally located and confiscated a hidden copy of the *gulag* manuscript. Solzhenitsyn then authorized its publication abroad. In quick retaliation, the *KGB* arrested him on February 14, 1974, and deported him the next day to West Germany. Solzhenitsyn eventually settled in the United States, from where he continued to attack the Soviet Union and the attempts by Western powers to reach any accommodation with it. The order banning his legally published books, issued February 14, 1974, must have already been prepared.

DOCUMENT 95   *Order from Glavlit, February 14, 1974, to remove the works of Solzhenitsyn from libraries and bookstores*

For official use

Copy no. 1

Order

of the Head of the Main Directorate

for the Preservation of State Secrets in the Press

under the Council of Ministers of the USSR

No. 10-den

Moscow   February 14, 1974

Content: Concerning the removal of the works of Aleksandr Solzhenitsyn from libraries and bookstores.

Remove from public libraries and bookstores the following separately published works of Aleksandr Solzhenitsyn, and also the journals in which the works were published:

One Day in the Life of Ivan Denisovich. Story. In journal *Novyi Mir*, 1962, No. 11.

Idem. Story. Moscow, Goslitizdat, 1963. 47 pp. (Roman-gazeta no. 1 [277].) 700,000 copies.

Idem. Story. Moscow, *Sovetskii pisatel'*, 1963. 144 pp. 100,000 copies.

Idem. Story. In two volumes. Moscow, Uchpedgiz, 1963. Vol. 1. 75 pp. 250 copies. For the blind.

Idem. Vol. 2. 80 pp. 250 copies. For the blind.

Idem. Story. Trans. by A. Pakalnis. Vilnius, Goslitizdat, 1963. 191 pp. 15,000 copies. In Lithuanian.

Idem. Story. Trans. from the Russian by L. Meri and E. Sarv. Tallin, Gazetno-zhurn. izd-vo, 1963. 114 pp. (Biblioteka "Looming," No. 11/12 [279/280].) 40,000 copies. In Estonian.

Two Stories. "An Incident at Krechetovka Station." "Matryona's House." In journal *Novyi Mir*, 1963, No. 1.

"For the Good of the Cause." Story. In journal *Novyi Mir*, 1963, No. 7.

Idem. Trans. from the Russian by O. Ingi. Tallin, Gazetno-zhurn. izd-vo, 1964. 108 pp. (Biblioteka "Looming," No. 38/39 [358/359].) 19,000 copies. In Estonian.

"Zakhar-the-Pouch." Story. In journal *Novyi Mir*, 1966, No. 1.

Also subject to removal are foreign editions (including journals and newspapers) that contain the works of this author.

[signed] P. Romanov

Basis: Directions of Central Committee of
       Jan. 28, 1974, according to No. 03879
       of Jan. 25, 1974 (Book and other
       publications).

TSGAOR, fond 9425, op. 2, d. 639, l. 7.

DOCUMENT 96   *Letter from the Ministry of Education, April 17, 1975, on the removal of works by Nekrasov from circulation*

COPY

FOR OFFICIAL USE ONLY

Copy No. 1

FROM:

THE DEPUTY
Minister of Education
of the USSR

April 14, 1975

No. 1-M dsp

Moscow, M-162
Shabolovka, 49.
Tel: 232-03-44

TO:

The Ministers of Education (Public Education) of the Union Republics

The Academy of Educational Sciences of the USSR

The Editors of the Newspaper *Uchitel'skaia Gazeta* [Teacher's Gazette]

The Teaching Methodology Council of the Ministry of Education of the USSR

SUBJECT: The Removal of V. P. Nekrasov's Works from Circulation

The Ministry of Education of the USSR requests that you give the necessary instructions to local educational authorities, schools, and adult education institutions that V. P. Nekrasov's works are not to be studied in all grades of general education secondary schools and should not be used in classes or extracurricular activities.

In light of the fact that this writer's name is mentioned in syllabi, textbooks, the elective curriculum, and instructional and teaching aids, these materials should be carefully scrutinized and revised and the appropriate instructions should be issued to publishing houses, public education agencies, and schools. In particular, references to Nekrasov's works should be deleted from the course on "The Literature of the Great Patriotic War and the Early Postwar Period" in the syllabus and from the textbook *Soviet Russian Literature* (A. Dement'eva et al., *Prosveshchenie* Publishing House, 1975, p. 252).

Any references to this author should also be deleted from syllabi, textbooks, the elective curriculum, and all instructional and teaching aids published in the various republics.

We also request that V. P. Nekrasov's works be removed from the libraries of elementary, eight-year, and secondary general education schools, teachers' schools and teachers' institutes, teachers' advanced training institutes, and other libraries of the public education system.

Signature:		M. KONDAKOV
True Copy:	[signed]	L. Nikol'skaia

April 14, 1976

[Illegible stamp]

TSGAOR, fond 9425sch, op. 1s, d. 1572, l. 13.

DOCUMENT 97   *Request to Glavlit from the Leningrad Directorate, October 12, 1977, to suppress the works of the writers N. A. Berdiaev and S. N. Bulgakov*

<u>Secret</u>

Copy No. 1

Council of Ministers
Main Directorate for Protection of
State Secrets in the Press

To the Chief of the
Main Directorate for Protection of
State Secrets in the Press
Council of Ministers of the USSR

Leningrad Directorate
191011. Leningrad, Nevskii Pr., 52/14
Tel. 214-71-30
10/12/77 No. 215s
On No. _____ of _____

To Comrade Romanov, P. K.

Concerning the works of the reactionary writers
N. A. Berdiaev and S. N. Bulgakov.

[handwritten]

to Comrade Siman'kov, V. IA.
to Comrade Vladimirov, V. V.
Illegible]
October 18

Upon investigation of bookstores, it was discovered that some of them were buying and selling books of the reactionary philosopher N. A. Berdiaev and the counterrevolutionary and reactionary economist and philosopher S. N. Bulgakov.

These names do not appear in the documents that govern antiquarian bookstore acquisition and sale of books. Nor do they appear in our documents.

The directorate requests an opinion as to whether the names of S. N. Bulgakov and N. A. Berdiaev should be included in the "List of persons whose works are excluded totally from circulation."

This question was discussed in the Leningrad City Committee of the *KPSS*, namely, by the Secretary of the Committee Comrade T. I. Zhdanov. We were told that propaganda agents have been addressing such questions to the city committee.

Head of the Directorate [signed] B. A. Markov

1870s

October 17, 1977

TSGAOR, fond 9425-sch, op. 1s, d. 1605, l. 19.

DOCUMENT 98   *Order of* Glavlit, *September 4, 1984, on the removal from libraries and bookstores of works by Aksenov, Voinovich, Liubimov, and others*

Secret copy № __1__

MAIN DIRECTORATE
FOR THE PROTECTION OF STATE SECRETS IN THE PRESS
USSR COUNCIL OF MINISTERS

ORDER

September 4, 1984   № __11s__

Moscow

┌On the removal of books from┐
public libraries and the book
trade

Remove from public libraries and the book trade all separately published works of the following persons:

Aksenov, Vasilii Pavlovich
Vladimov, Georgii Nikolaevich
Voinovich, Vladimir Nikolaevich
Zinoviev, Aleksandr Aleksandrovich
Kopelev, (IAkovenko, L., Kadashov, A.) Lev Zalmanovich

(Zinovievich)

Liubimov, IUrii Petrovich
Oganesian, Eduard Vagramovich
Orlova, (Kopeleva) Raisa Davydovna
Tarsis, Valerii IAkovlevich

Acting Chief of the Main Directorate   [signed] N.P. Zorin

Basis: agreement of the secretaries of the *TSK KPSS* of 8/22/84 № 21573. Communicated by telephone to Comrade Zorin, N.P. by Comrade Voronin A.P. 8/27/84

TSGAOR, fond 9425, op. 1, d. 1786, l. 13.

Proposal by Glavlit, January 23, 1989, recommending to the Central Committee that the works of twenty-eight emigre authors published earlier in the Soviet Union be reinstated in libraries and bookstores

Not for Publication   Secret

Central Committee of the Communist Party of the Soviet Union [*TSK KPSS*]

On the Subject of the USSR Main Directorate for Protection of State Secrets in the Press [*Glavlit SSSR*]

The Main Directorate for Protection of State Secrets in the Press under the Council of Ministers of the USSR (Comrade Boldyrev) reports that, in compliance with *TSK KPSS* resolution No. Art. 36/p.14 of January 13, 1987, an interagency commission of representatives from *Glavlit,* the Ministry of Culture of the USSR, and the State Committee on Publishing [*Goskomizdat*]) has completed its review of the "Comprehensive list of books subject to exclusion from libraries and the book trade" and, partially, of the list of authors all of whose works are to be banned. From March 1987 to October 1988, 7,930 editions have been returned to the general library collections; and 462 editions that are either of manifestly anti-Soviet character, slandering V. I. Lenin, the Communist Party, and the Soviet state and people, or are White Guard, Zionist, or nationalistic in nature, are to remain in special collections.

Simultaneously, *Glavlit* recommends a return to the general library collections of all works published in the Soviet Union of the following emigre writers: Aksenov, V. P.; Baumvol', R. L.; Belinkov, A. V. (dec.); Vladimov, G. N.; Vlestaru, B. M.; Voinovich, V. N.; Galich, A. A. (dec.); Gladilin, A. T.; Demin, M (Trifonov, G. E.); Zinoviev, A. A.; Kerler, I. B.; Kopelev, L. Z.; Kopytman, M. R.; Krotkov, IU. V.; Kuznetsov, A. V.; L'vov, A. L.; Liubimov, IU. P.; Maksimov, V. E.; Maltinskii, Kh. I.; Nekrasov, V. P. (dec.); Orlova, R. D.; Rudenko, N. D.; Siniavskii, A. D.; Solzhenitsyn, A. I.; Tabachnik, G. D.; Tarsis, V. IA. (dec.); Telesin, Z.A.; Etkind, E.G. A total of 28 authors.

Indicate your agreement
January 23, 1989
[signature illegible]

The proposal from *Glavlit SSSR* is in consonance with the position of the Writers' Union of the USSR (Comrade Karpov). The list of works of the writers named above and references to the supporting decisions are attached.

Glavlit SSSR is also requesting the interagency commission, as originally constituted, to carry out the task of transferring from the special collections to the general library collections the Russian-language works of some 600 authors who had emigrated between 1918 and 1988. Among them are well-known writers, such as I. Bunin, V. Nabokov, N. Gumilev, E. Zamiatin, and J. Brodsky, and philosophers and essayists, such as N. Berdiaev, V. Khodasevich, B. Zaitsev, et al. Works of these writers published abroad and occasionally received here were banned from circulation and placed in special collections simply as works of emigre authors, even though many of them are not anti-Soviet in nature. It is these works that we propose making available to the public in general libraries, subject to the criteria established in the directive of the Central Committee of the *KPSS.*

The ideological section of the *TSK KPSS* is supporting the proposal from *Glavlit SSSR.* The joint commission is advised to submit the results of its deliberations by January 1, 1990.

A consent is requested.

Head of the Ideological Section
of the *TSK KPSS*   [signed] A. Kapto

December 31, 1988

[Top of p. 1, handwritten notation:] Agreed.
[Nine illegible signatures]

FOR REFERENCE

Basis for Orders Issued by *Glavlit SSSR*
Withdrawing Books by the Following Authors
From the General Collections of Libraries

1. Aksenov V. P.

<u>Basis:</u> Approval of Secretaries of *TSK KPSS* (August 22, 1984) No. 21753. Relayed by telephone to Comrade Zorin N. P.

2. Baumvol' R. L.

<u>Basis:</u> Instructions from *TSK KPSS* to Comrade Okhotnikov A. P., relayed by Comrade Chkhikvishvili I. I. Section Head, Department of Propaganda of *TSK KPSS* (April 16, 1971)

3. Belinkov A. V.

<u>Basis:</u> Consultation with Secretary of *TSK KPSS* Comrade Demichev P. N. and Head of Department of Propaganda of *TSK KPSS* Comrade Stepakov V. I. June 12, 1969

4. Vladimov G. N.

See Item 1.

5. Vlestaru B. M.

<u>Basis:</u> Approval of Department of Propaganda of *TSK KPSS* relayed by Comrade Smirnov G. L. and Comrade Sevruk V. N. on July 20, 1976, and confirmed by Comrade Sevruk V. N. on July 30, 1976.

6. Voinovich V. N.

See Item 1.

7. Galich A. A.

<u>Basis:</u> Approval of Comrade Demichev P. N. on October 22, 1974, and Department of Propaganda of *TSK KPSS* (Comrade Smirnov G. L.)

8. Gladilin A. T.

See Item 5.

9. Demin M. (Trifonov G. E.)

See Item 3.

10. Zinov'ev A. A.

See Item 1.

11. Kerler I. B.

See Item 2.

12. Kopelev L. Z.

See Item 1.

13. Kopytman M. R.

See Item 5.

14. Krotkov IU. V.

See Item 3.

15. Kuznetsov A. V.

<u>Basis:</u> Approval of Department of Propaganda of *TSK KPSS* (Comrades Stepakov V. I. and Dmitriuk A. N.) on August 5, 1969

16. L'vov A. L.

<u>Basis:</u> Instructions of *TSK KPSS* relayed by Comrade Sevruk V. N. on October 2, 1979

17. Liubimov IU. P.

See Item 1.

18. Maksimov V. E.

See Item 7.

19. Mal'tinskii Kh. I.

See Item 5.

20. Nekrasov V. P.	See Item 5.
21. Orlova R. D.	See Item 1.
22. Rudenko N. D.	Basis: Instructions from Secretary of *TSK KPSS* Comrade Zimianin M. V. on October 4, 1978
23. Siniavskii A. D.	See Item 7.
24. Solzhenitsyn A. I.	Basis: Instructions from *TSK KPSS* on January 28, 1974, on basis of No. 03879 dated January 25, 1974, (books and other publications).
25. Tabachnik G. D.	See Item 7.
26. Tarsis V. IA.	See Item 1.
27. Telesin Z. A.	See Item 2.
28. Etkind, E. G.	See Item 7.

TSKhSD, fond 5, op. 35, d. 135, l. 22.

Anti-Nationality Policies

The relationship between socialism and nationalism was a complex one in the nineteenth century, when both doctrines attracted increasing popular support. Karl Marx had written "Workers have no fatherland," and some socialists interpreted this to mean that workers' class identity did and should transcend national identity: nationalist feeling and nationalist identity were a product of bourgeois culture, one that would disappear with the transition from capitalism to socialism. Other socialists, particularly those in the Austro-Hungarian empire, interpreted Marx differently. These Austrian socialists, led by Otto Bauer and Karl Renner, argued that the linguistic and cultural aspects of national identity were intrinsic to individuals and that they would not, and should not, disappear with a change in the economic structure of society. Only political nationalism was harmful, they argued; nation-states did indeed impede progress toward socialist internationalism, but national culture within the socialist state should be treated like religion: it was a matter of personal, individual preference.

Russian Marxists initially sided with the more orthodox point of view and rejected both cultural nationalism and any form of federalism; to recognize nationality would weaken the socialist state politically and ideologically. But the Austrian solution became increasingly attractive to certain groups among the Russian Marxists, particularly those in the Jewish Bund and from the Caucasus. In 1912 Lenin asked the young Joseph Stalin to write a pamphlet countering the Austrian position. This request was the beginning of Stalin's career as an expert on the nationality question. The nationality question continued to confound Lenin and the other socialists. As he sought to consolidate his own position in the center of the Bolshevik Party, Lenin gradually modified his views, and by the start of World War I, he had come around to supporting the right of nations to self-determination. For him, imperialism was now the main capitalist enemy, and movements of liberation, even along national lines, could help to weaken and defeat the imperialist powers, paving the way for a truly socialist revolution. Lenin's critics, such as Nikolai Bukharin, denounced this accommodation with nationalism, but in the end Lenin's pragmatic views, echoed by Stalin, shaped the nationality policy adopted by the young socialist state.

In the process of the Russian Civil War, theory gave way to reality and to improvisation. However much Lenin or his opponents believed in a centralized, nonfederal Russia, whether socialist or monarchist, as the center became weak, territories on the periphery fell away and established their own political identities. Russia itself was organized as a federation of national "autonomous republics," the Russian Soviet Federated Socialist Republic (RSFSR). Ukraine and Georgia became independent socialist republics; the Georgian Republic exchanged ambassadors with the RSFSR. The Baltic territories of Finland, Estonia, Latvia, and Lithuania declared their independence. On the Pacific coast, a Far East Republic also lived an independent existence for several years. Toward 1922 a series of bilateral treaties between the RSFSR and the independent republics of Ukraine, Belorussia, Georgia, Armenia, Azerbaijan, Bukhara, Khoresm, and the Far East began to cement these independent states into a federal union. Their needs were to be met by the People's Commissariat of Nationality Affairs, the *Narkomnats*, whose commissar was Joseph Stalin. But Stalin, even more than Lenin, was a centralizer, and his influence can be seen in the constitution of 1923 that created the Union of Soviet Socialist Republics. Nationality policy was officially expressed by the slogan, "nationalist in form, socialist in content," and the socialist content was enforced by the highly centralized Communist Party.

Stalin was a Georgian, and this was one reason that Lenin picked him to oversee nationality affairs. But like many members of national minorities in the Bolshevik Party, Stalin saw himself as an internationalist and communist first and always. Lenin had to rebuke Stalin for his high-handed treatment of Georgian communists in 1922, accusing him of "Great Russian chauvinism." Stalin's biographer Robert Tucker argues that Stalin became even more of a "national Bolshevik" as he consolidated his power, and his Great Russian chauvinism returned with a vengeance in the aftermath of the German invasion of the USSR.

Stalin and his followers evidently suspected all non-Russian citizens of disloyalty and took steps to remove the possibility of their collaboration with the Nazis or to punish entire ethnic populations for the collaboration of some of their members. The first to be dealt with were German residents in

Ukraine, who were forcibly resettled in Kazakhstan in September 1941. Nazi occupation of the Crimea and territories in the North Caucasus created the conditions for further repression of national minorities. Following the Soviet recapture of these territories, the regime launched a massive deportation of entire minority populations. In the North Caucasus region, the entire population of the Kalmyk Autonomous Republic was deported to Siberia and Central Asia in the span of four days in December 1943. The Chechen-Ingush Autonomous Republic was abolished and its inhabitants resettled in February 1944. The Kabardino-Balkar Autonomous Republic met the same fate in March 1944.

In May 1944 the State Defense Committee ordered <u>all</u> Tatars living in the Crimea to be deported to Uzbekistan, Kazakhstan, and Kirghizia. The resettlement was carried out secretly and swiftly as a military operation, and for years afterward it remained a state secret. Bulgarians, Greeks, and Armenians accused as collaborating peoples were also removed en masse from the Crimea and resettled elsewhere. The Crimean Autonomous Republic was downgraded to a simple region. After Stalin's death, restrictions on the rights and freedoms of these resettled peoples were gradually removed, and some of them agitated for a return to their homelands. In 1957 the Kabardino-Balkar and Chechen-Ingush areas regained their status as national autonomous republics, and Kalmykia and Karachai-Cherkessia were restored as autonomous regions. The Crimean Tatars and the exiled Germans, however, were ignored. Crimean Tatars began to organize and to agitate for a restoration of their rights and a return to their homeland, and their demands for recognition of their national identity constituted an important element of the dissident movement of the 1960s and 1970s. This unfinished business of Stalin's nationality policy remained for Gorbachev and his successors to resolve.

DOCUMENT 100   *Resolution of the State Defense Committee, September 22, 1941, on removal of Germans from certain areas of Ukraine*

Subject to return to the State Defense
    Committee Secretariat (Part II)

Top Secret

STATE DEFENSE COMMITTEE
Resolution No. GKO-702ss
September 22, 1941.   Moscow, the Kremlin.

Resettlement of Germans from Zaporozhskaia, Stalinskaia
and Voroshilovgradskaia *oblast*'s.

The State Defense Committee resolves:

1.   To resettle in the Kazakh SSR Germans from Zaporozhskaia *oblast'* (63,000 persons), from Stalinskaia *oblast'* (41,000 persons), and Voroshilovgradskaia *oblast'* (5,487 persons).

2.   To charge the People's Commissariat of Internal Affairs of the Soviet Union [*NKVD SSSR*] with managing the resettlement.

3.   To accomplish the resettlement by moving the people into existing *kolkhoz*es and *sovkhozes,* settling them in all existing buildings in the countryside, and increasing population density.

      To employ the resettled persons to build their own housing if none is available. To resettle townspeople in *raion* centers and other cities, excluding republic and *oblast'* centers.

4.   To allow the resettled persons to bring with them their personal property and a supply of provisions for the journey in the amount of 200 kilograms for each member of the family.

5.   Buildings, agricultural implements, livestock, and cereal/grain fodder belonging to the resettled persons will be handed over to the following commission representatives: the local executive committee, the People's Commissariat for Agriculture, the People's Commissariat for Meat and Dairy Production, and the People's Commissariat for State Purchases, and will be restored at the place of settlement in accordance with confirmed instructions from the Council of People's Commissars, the People's Commissariat for Agriculture, and the People's Commissariat for Meat and Dairy Production.

      Structures for *kolkhoz*es and *kolkhoz* farm personnel will be provided at the place of settlement by delivery of prefabricated houses.

      Those resettled persons not provided homes at the place of settlement will be given loans for construction and, if necessary, repair of housing from the Agricultural Bank in the sum of up to 2,000 rubles to be repaid in five years at 3% annual interest with amortization of the loan starting the second year after received.

6.   To charge the People's Commissariat for Transportation (Comrade Kaganovich) with transporting all resettled persons from Zaporozhskaia *oblast'* during the period Sept. 25–Oct. 2 of this year and from Stalinskaia and Voroshilovgradskaia *oblast'*s during the period Sept. 25– Oct. 10 of this year and organizing the supply of railroad passenger cars according to the schedule drawn up by the *NKVD SSSR.*

7.   To task the People's Commissariat of Foreign and Domestic Trade (Comrade Liubimov) with providing food to the resettled persons at locations as ordered by the *NKVD SSSR.*

8.   To task the USSR People's Commissariat for Health (Comrade Miterev) with providing medical service for the resettled persons in transit, for which medical personnel, medicines, and first-aid supplies will be allocated as ordered by the *NKVD SSSR.*

9.   To release from the reserve fund of the Council of People's Commissars and the *NKVD SSSR* the sum of 15 million rubles for resettlement expenses.

10.   To put the chairman of the Council of People's Commissars of the Kazakh SSR (Comrade Undasynov) and the

secretary of the Central Committee of the Communist Party (Bolshevik) [*TSK VKP(b)*] of Kazakhstan (Comrade Skvortsov) in charge of organizing the reception, settling, and household arrangements for the resettled persons.

11.   To allow the Council of People's Commissars of the Kazakh SSR to mobilize the necessary motor vehicles from local organizations and *kolkhoz*es to transport the resettled persons from the depot to the place of settlement.

CHAIRMAN OF THE STATE DEFENSE COMMITTEE J. Stalin

Excerpts sent to: Comrades Beria, Mikoyan, Chadaev; *TSK KP(b)* Kazakhstan - everything; *TSK KP(b)U*- 1, 2, 3, 4, 5, 6, 7, 8; Zaporozhskaia, Stalinskaia, and Voroshilovgradskaia *Oblast'* Committees - 1 (as required), 2, 3, 4, 5, 6 (as required), 7, 8; Benediktov, Subbotin, Lobanov, Smirnov - 1, 3, 5; Zverev - 1, 3, 5, 9; Kaganovich - 6, Liubimov - 7, Miterev - 8.

[Seal:] State Defense Committee, Protocol Dept., *GOKO.*

RTSKhIDNI, fond 644, op. 1, d. 10, ll. 62, 63.

DOCUMENT 101   *Telegram from the NKVD to officials in Alma-Ata, September 24, 1941, detailing actions taken to resettle Germans and Finns from the Leningrad region to Kazakhstan*

SECRET
NOTE FOR THE HIGH-FREQUENCY LINE

ALMA-ATA PEOPLE'S COMMISSARIAT OF INTERNAL AFFAIRS [*NKVD*] TO BABKIN

ORDERS SENT BY DEPUTY PEOPLE'S COMMISSAR OF THE KAZAKH SSR COMRADE BOGDANOV FOR RESETTLEMENT OF GERMANS AND FINNS FROM LENINGRAD *OBLAST'* TO THE *RAION*S OF SOUTHERN-KAZAKHSTAN *OBLAST'*. INDICATED TRANSFER OF 28,200 PERSONS. AMONG THIS NUMBER 20,000 PERSONS WERE TAKEN FROM ROSTOV *OBLAST'*. THEREFORE, IT IS NOT CLEAR WHAT PROMPTED YOUR QUESTIONS ABOUT TRANSFER OF PERSONS ABOVE THE SET NUMBER FOR SOUTHERN-KAZAKHSTAN *OBLAST'*. SEND A TELEGRAM.

KONRADOV

- -

Deputy Commander of the Department for
Special Resettlement of the *NKVD SSSR*
Captain of State Security

[signed] Konradov

186/22 September 24, 1941.

TSGAOR, fond 9479s, op. 1s, d. 86, l. 65.

Decree of the State Defense Committee, May 11, 1944, signed by Stalin, on deportation of Crimean Tatars to Uzbekistan

STATE DEFENSE COMMITTEE

State Defense Committee Decree No. 5859ss

May 11, 1944   Moscow, the Kremlin

On the Crimean Tatars

During the Patriotic War many Crimean Tatars betrayed the Motherland, deserted Red Army units that defended the Crimea, and sided with the enemy, joining volunteer army units formed by the Germans to fight against the Red Army. As members of German punitive detachments during the occupation of the Crimea by German fascist troops, the Crimean Tatars particularly were noted for their savage reprisals against Soviet partisans, and also helped the German invaders to organize the violent roundup of Soviet citizens for German enslavement and the mass extermination of the Soviet people.

The Crimean Tatars actively collaborated with the German occupation authorities, participating in the so-called Tatar national committees, organized by the German intelligence organs, and were often used by the Germans to infiltrate the rear of the Red Army with spies and saboteurs. With the support of the Crimean Tatars, the "Tatar national committees," in which the leading role was played by White Guard-Tatar emigrants, directed their activity at the persecution and oppression of the non-Tatar population of the Crimea and were engaged in preparatory efforts to separate the Crimea from the Soviet Union by force, with the help of the German armed forces.

Taking into account the facts cited above, the State Defense Committee decrees that:

1. All Tatars are to be banished from the territory of the Crimea and resettled permanently as special settlers in regions of the Uzbek SSR. The resettlement process will be assigned to the Soviet People's Commissariat of Internal Affairs [NKVD]. The Soviet NKVD (Comrade Beria) is to complete the resettlement by June 1, 1944.

2. The following procedure and conditions of resettlement are to be established:

a) The special settlers will be allowed to take with them personal items, clothing, household objects, dishes and utensils, and up to 500 kilograms of food per family.

Property, buildings, outbuildings, furniture, and farmstead lands left behind will be taken over by the local authorities; all beef and dairy cattle, as well as poultry, will be taken over by the People's Commissariat of the Meat and Dairy Industries, all agricultural production by the USSR People's Commissariat of Procurement, horses and other draft animals by the USSR People's Commissariat of Agriculture, and breeding cattle by the USSR People's Commissariat of State Farms.

Exchange receipts will be issued in every populated place and every farm for the receipt of livestock, grain, vegetables, and for other types of agricultural products.

By July 1 of this year, the NKVD SSSR, People's Commissariat of Agriculture, People's Commissariat of the Meat and Dairy Industries, People's Commissariat of State Farms, and People's Commissariat of Procurement are to submit to the USSR Council of People's Commissars a proposal on the procedure for repaying the special settlers, on the basis of exchange receipts, for livestock, poultry, and agricultural products received from them.

b) An on-site commission of the USSR Council of People's Commissars, consisting of Comrade T. Gritsenko (Deputy Chairman of the RSFSR Council of People's Commissars), commission chairman, and Comrade T. Krest'ianinov (collegium member of the USSR People's Commissariat of Agriculture), Comrade T. Nad'iarnykh (collegium member of the People's Commissariat of the Meat and Dairy Industries), Comrade Pustovalov (collegium member of the People's Commissariat of Procurement), Comrade Kabanov (Deputy USSR People's Commissar of State Grain and Animal Husbandry Farms), and Comrade T. Gusev (collegium member of the USSR People's Commissariat of Finance), will be dispatched to organize the receipt of property, livestock, grain, and agricultural products from the special settlers in areas from which they are being evicted.

To facilitate the receipt of livestock, grain, and agricultural production from the special settlers, the USSR People's Commissariat of Agriculture (Comrade Benediktov), USSR People's Commissariat of Procurement (Comrade Subbotin), USSR People's Commissariat of the Meat and Dairy Industries (Comrade Smirnov), and USSR People's Commissariat of State Farms (Comrade Lobanov) are to dispatch the required number of workers to the Crimea, in coordination with Comrade Gritsenko.

c) The People's Commissariat of Railroads (Comrade Kaganovich) is to organize the transport of the special settlers from the Crimea to the Uzbek SSR, using specially organized convoys, according to a schedule devised jointly with the *NKVD SSSR*. The number of convoys, loading stations, and destination points are to be determined by the *NKVD SSSR*.

Payment for the transport will be based on the rate at which prisoners are transported;

d) To each convoy of special settlers, the USSR People's Commissariat of Public Health (Comrade Miterev) is to assign, within a time frame to be coordinated with the *NKVD SSSR*, one physician and two nurses, as well as an appropriate supply of medicines, and to provide medical and first-aid care to special settlers in transit;

e) The USSR People's Commissariat of Trade (Comrade Liubimov) will provide all convoys carrying special settlers with hot food and boiling water on a daily basis.

To provide food for the special settlers in transit, the People's Commissariat of Trade is to allocate the quantity of food supplies indicated in Appendix No. 1.

3. By June 1 of this year, the Secretary of the Central Committee of the Communist Party (Bolshevik) of Uzbekistan, Comrade IUsupov, the Chairman of the Uzbek SSR Council of People's Commissars, Comrade Abdurakhmanov, and the Uzbek SSR People's Commissar of Internal Affairs, Comrade Kobulov, are to take the following steps in regard to the acceptance and settlement of the special settlers:

a) To accept and settle within the Uzbek SSR 140 to 160 thousand special settlers—Tatars, sent by the *NKVD SSSR* from the Crimean ASSR.

The settlement of the special settlers will occur in state farm communities, existing collective farms, farms affiliated with enterprises, and in factory communities, for employment in agriculture and industry;

b) To establish commissions in *oblast*'s where the special settlers are resettled, consisting of the chairman of the *oblast*' executive committee, secretary of the *oblast*' committee, and chief of the *NKVD* administration, charging them with the implementation of all measures connected with the acceptance and distribution of the newly arrived special settlers;

c) To organize *raion* troikas, consisting of the chairman of the *raion* executive committee, secretary of the *raion* committee, and chief of the *raion* branch of the *NKVD*, charging them with preparation for the distribution and organization of the acceptance of the newly arrived special settlers;

d) To arrange the automotive transport of the special settlers, mobilizing the vehicles of any enterprises or institutions for this purpose;

e) To grant plots of farm land to the newly arrived special settlers and to help them build homes by providing construction materials;

f) To organize special *NKVD* commandant's headquarters, to be maintained by the *NKVD SSSR*, in the *raion*s of settlement;

g) By May 20 of this year, the Uzbek SSR Central Committee and Council of People's Commissars are to submit to the *NKVD SSSR* (Comrade Beria) a plan for the settlement of the special settlers in the *oblast*'s and *raion*s, indicating the destination points of the trains.

4. Seven-year loans of up to 5,000 rubles per family, for the construction and setting up of homes, are to be extended by the Agricultural Bank (Comrade Kravtsov) to special settlers sent to the Uzbek SSR, in their places of settlement.

5. Every month during the June–August 1944 period, equal quantities of flour, groats, and vegetables will be allocated by the USSR People's Commissariat of Procurement (Comrade Subbotin) to the Uzbek SSR Council of People's Commissars for distribution to the special settlers, in accordance with Appendix No. 2.

Flour, groats, and vegetables are to be distributed free of charge to the special settlers during the June–August period, as repayment for the agricultural products and livestock received from them in the areas from which they were evicted.

6. To augment the automotive transport capacity of the *NKVD* troops garrisoned in the *raion*s of settlement in the Uzbek, Kazakh, and Kirgiz SSRs, the People's Commissariat of Defense (Comrade Khrulev) is to provide 100 recently repaired "Willys" motor vehicles and 250 trucks during the May–June 1944 period.

7. By May 20, 1944, the Main Administration for the Transport and Supply of Petroleum and Petroleum Products (Comrade Shirokov) is to allocate and supply 400 tons of gasoline to locations specified by the *NKVD SSSR*, and 200 tons of gasoline are to be placed at the disposal of the Uzbek SSR Council of People's Commissars.

To supply the gasoline for this purpose, all other consumers' gasoline allocations will be cut accordingly.

8. By May 15 of this year, the Main Supply Administration of the USSR Ministry of Forestry, USSR Council of People's Commissars (Comrade Lopukhov), is to deliver 75,000 2.75-meter boards for railroad cars to the People's Commissariat of Railroads, using any means at its disposal.

9. In May of this year the People's Commissariat of Finance (Comrade Zverev) is to transfer 30 million rubles from the reserve fund of the USSR Council of People's Commissars to the *NKVD SSSR*, for the implementation of special measures.

> J. Stalin
> Chairman, State Defense Committee

cc   :   Comrades Molotov, Beria, Malenkov, Mikoyan, Voznesenskii, Andreev, Kosygin, Gritsenko, IUsupov, Abdurakhmanov, Kobulov (Uzbek SSR *NKVD*), Chadaev—entire document; Shatalin, Gorkin, [illegible] Smirnov, Subbotin, Benediktov, Lobanov, Zverev,Kaganovich, Miterev, Liubimov, Kravtsov, Khrulev, Zhukov, Shirokov, Lopukhov—appropriate sections.

[Notation in upper left corner:] To be returned to the State Defense Committee Secretariat (Part II).
[Typed along left edge of first page:] Making copies or extracts of this decree is strictly prohibited.

RTSKhIDNI, fond 644, op. 1, d. 252, ll. 137–142.

Report from Beria to Stalin, May 19, 1944, on the progress of the resettlement of Crimean Tatars

May [illegible] 1944   SPECIAL FOLDER   Copy
No. 483/5   No. 1-1pp. 142   Top secret
                             Copy No. 2

STATE COMMITTEE FOR DEFENSE—

To Comrade J. V. S T A L I N

The People's Commissariat of Internal Affairs of the Soviet Union [*NKVD SSSR*] reports on the progress of the Crimean Tatar resettlement operation, as of May 19.

One hundred forty thousand persons have been brought to the railroad loading points, and 119,424 persons have been loaded onto special trains and sent to the places of resettlement.

The operation continues.

PEOPLE'S COMMISSAR OF INTERNAL AFFAIRS
    of the Union of SSR -

(L. BERIA)

Delivered 2 copies:
1st adr
2nd to *NKVD SSSR* Secretariat   A copy for the Special Folder was made
   [Executor] Comrade Mamulov   on May 21, 1944, by order of Comrade Zhukov.
   [Osn: t-ma] Comrades Kobulov, Serov from May 19, 1944.

Typed by Okunev
May 19, 1944.

                    True copy: [signed] Chernikov

TSGAOR.

State Defense Committee resolution, June 2, 1944, to evict from the Crimean Autonomous Republic 37,000 Bulgarians, Greeks, and Armenians, cited as German collaborators

Return to the Secretariat
of the SDC (Section II)

Top Secret

STATE DEFENSE COMMITTEE
Resolution of the SDC No. 5984ss of June 2, 1944.
The Kremlin, Moscow

The State Defense Committee resolves to:

1. Direct the People's Commissariat of Internal Affairs of the USSR [*NKVD SSSR*] (Comrade Beria) to evict from the Crimean Autonomous Soviet Socialist Republic [ASSR] 37,000 German collaborators from among the Bulgarian, Greek, and Armenian populations, in addition to the Crimean Tatars evicted under SDC Resolution No. 5859ss of May 11, 1944. The eviction will be carried out July 1–5 of this year.

2. Send the evicted Bulgarians, Greeks, and Armenians for resettlement in agriculture, on auxiliary holdings and at industrial establishments in the following *oblast*'s and republics:

Gur'ev *oblast'* of the Kazakh SSR	- 7,000 people
Sverdlovsk *oblast'*	- 10,000 "
Molotov *oblast'*	- 10,000 "
Kemerovo *oblast'*	- 6,000 "
Bashkir ASSR	- 4,000 "

3. Execute the eviction and resettlement in accordance with confirmed points 2 and 3 of Resolution No. 5859ss of the SDC.

Direct the People's Commissar of Agriculture (Comrade Andreev), the People's Commissar of the Meat and Dairy Industry (Comrade Smirnov), the People's Commissar of Procurement (Comrade Subbotin), and the People's Commissar of State Farms (Comrade Lobanov) to ensure that the evicted Crimean Greeks, Bulgarians, and Armenians receive livestock, grain, and collective farm products using exchange receipts.

4. Direct the People's Commissar of Transportation [*NKPS*] (Comrade Kaganovich) to organize the transfer of the special settlers from the Crimea by special convoys in accordance with the schedule worked out with the *NKVD SSSR*. The number of convoys, loading stations, and destination stations will be announced by the *NKPS* and the *NKVD SSSR*. The cost of transport will be set at the same rate as the transport of prisoners.

5. Direct the People's Commissar of Trade (Comrade Liubimov) to provide food for 37,000 people during the convoy of special settlers from the Crimea in accordance with the schedule set by the *NKPS* and the *NKVD SSSR*. The *Narkomtorg* will allocate foodstuffs for this purpose in accordance with Addendum No. 1.

6. Direct the People's Commissar of Public Health (Comrade Miterev) to supply the convoy for the special settlers from the Crimea, as ordered by the *NKVD* of the USSR, with medical personnel, medicines, and medical-sanitation services en route.

7. Direct the secretaries of the *oblast'* committees of the All-Union Communist Party (Bolsheviks) [*VKP(b)*] and the chairmen of the *oblast'* political executive committees: Gure'ev *oblast'* of the Kazakh SSR (Comrades Kruglov and Burbaev), Molotov *oblast'* (Comrades Gusarov and Kochergin), Kemerovo *oblast'* (Comrades Zadionchenko and Gogosov), Sverdlovsk *oblast'* (Comrades Andrianov and Nedosekin), the secretary of the *VKP(b)* regional committee and the chairmen of the Council of People's Commissars of the Bashkir ASSR (Comrades Ignat'ev and Vagapov) and people's commissariats whose collectives accept special resettlers to carry out measures

for receiving and settling the special resettlers, as provided for in point 3 of State Defense Committee resolution No. 5859ss.

8. Direct the People's Commissar of Procurement (Comrade Subbotin) to determine the methods to be used by the *oblast'* executive committees of Gur'ev, Sverdlovsk, Molotov, Kemerovo, and the Council of People's Commissars of the Bashkir ASSR in distributing provisions to the special resettlers during the first three months after resettlement (July–September) in equal monthly portions in accordance with Addendum No. 2. The distribution of foodstuffs to the special resettlers during July–September will be free of charge taking into account the collective farm foodstuffs and livestock received at the place of eviction.

9. Direct the Main Administration of Oil Supply (Comrade Shirokov) to allocate and ship 8 tons of gasoline by July 5, 1944, to each of the executive committees of Gur'ev, Sverdlovsk, Kemerovo, and Molotov *oblast'*s and the Council of People's Commissars of the Bashkir ASSR, and 250 tons of gasoline to the *NKVD* by June 28 to carry out its Crimean operations. This will be done by not delivering gasoline to all other users.

Chairman of the State Defense Committee [*GOKO*]
[Stamp of the *GOKO*]

J. STALIN

....

[Copies] sent to Comrades Mikoyan, Voznesenskii, Andreev, Kosygin, Gritsenko, Tiuliaev (Crimean *oblast'* committee of the *VKP(b)*), Nadaev; Shatalin [handwritten]. People's Commissariats, *oblast'* committees, *oblast'* political executive committees, the Central Committee and the Council of People's Commissars respectively.

RTSKhIDNI, fond 644, op. 1, d. 261, ll. 64–66.

DOCUMENT 105   *Telegram from Beria's deputy, June 27, 1944, confirming the execution of Beria's orders to begin deporting and resettling Crimean Tatars*

Top Secret
Received by High Frequency

From SIMFEROPOL'

MOSCOW, USSR PEOPLE'S COMMISSARIAT OF INTERNAL AFFAIRS [*NKVD*], to
Comrade BERIA.

In accordance with your instructions, the operation to move the special contingent from the Crimea began today, June 27, at daybreak.

As of 1600, 27,000 individuals have been moved from *raion*s to loading stations. Moreover, 1,500 foreign subjects were loaded into special trains.

There were no special incidents.

SEROV

Accepted by Sidorova
June 27, 1944, 1715.
[signed] Sidorova

4258
[Stamp in lower right corner:] Special Settlement Section of the *NKVD SSSR*

TSGAOR, fond 9479s, op. 1s, d. 179, l. 226.

DOCUMENT 106   *Report from Beria to Stalin, July 4, 1944, stating that resettlement of Tatars, Bulgarians, Greeks, Armenians, and others from the Crimea has been completed*

copy

top secret

copy No. 2

No. 693/b

STATE DEFENSE COMMITTEE

July 4, 1944

to Comrade J. V. S T A L I N

The USSR People's Commissariat of Internal Affairs [*NKVD SSSR*] reports that the resettlement of special settlers from the Crimea—Tatars, Bulgarians, Greeks, and Armenians—has been completed.

In total, 225,009 people have been resettled, including:

Tatars	183,155 persons
Bulgarians	12,422 "
Greeks	15,040 "
Armenians	9,621 "
Germans	1,119 "
and other foreigners	3,652 "

All the Tatars reached their places of settlement and have been resettled:

in the *oblast*'s of the Uzbek Soviet Socialist Republic (SSR)—151,604 persons

in the *oblast*'s of the Russian Soviet Federated Socialist Republic (RSFSR), in accordance with the decision of the State Defense Committee [*GOKO*] of May 21, 1944—31,551 persons

Bulgarians, Greeks, Armenians, and Germans, numbering 38,202 persons, are en route to the Bashkir Autonomous Soviet Socialist Republic [ASSR], the Mari ASSR, the Kemerovo, Molotov, Sverdlovsk, and Kirov *oblast*'s of the RSFSR and Gur'ev *oblast'* of the Kazakh SSR.

The 3,652 persons of other nationalities are destined for resettlement in Fergana *oblast'* of the Uzbek SSR.

All of the special settlers who have reached their destination have found satisfactory living conditions.

A significant number of the resettled, able-bodied Tatar special settlers have been engaged in agricultural work on collective and state farms, in logging, in industry, and in construction.

There were no incidents during the resettlement operation on site or during transit.

PEOPLE'S COMMISSAR OF INTERNAL AFFAIRS

of the Soviet Union

(L. Beria)

s-ta *NKVD*

Chernigov   One copy made for the special Crimea file.

July 3, 1944

True copy [signed] V. Popova

[Stamp at top of page:] No. 1-1 p. no. 198, SPECIAL FILE

TSGAOR

Report by M. Kuznetsov of the NKVD, September 26, 1944, on the number of Tatars, Bulgarians, Greeks, and Armenians deported from the Crimea and resettled

INFORMATION

on the number of resettled Crimean Tatars and Bulgarians, Greeks, and Armenians deported from the Crimea.

Name of republic, krai, oblast'	Crimean Tatars		Bulgarians, Greeks, Armenians		TOTAL	
	Families	Persons	Families	Persons	Families	Persons
Uzbek SSR	35,275	151,604	-	-	35,275	151,604
Mariiskaia ASSR	2,115	8,597	176	581	2,291	9,178
Bashkir ASSR	-	-	2,263	5,727	2,263	5,727
Gor'kovskaia "	1,450	5,122	-	-	1,450	5,122
Gur'evskaia "	-	-	1,096	4,289	1,096	4,289
Ivanovskaia "	696	3,200	-	-	696	3,200
Kemerovskaia "	-	-	2,594	6,791	2,594	6,791
Kirovskaia "	-	-	165	550	165	550
Molotovskaia "	2,342	10,002	2,951	10,023	5,293	20,025
Sverdlovskaia "	902	3,591	2,900	10,348	3,802	13,939
IAroslavskaia "	302	1,047	-	-	302	1,047
	43,082	183,163	12,145	33,309	55,227	221,472

HEAD OF THE DEPARTMENT OF SPECIAL SETTLEMENTS OF THE *NKVD SSSR*
Colonel of State Security
(M. KUZNETSOV)

TSGAOR

Report from the Uzbek NKVD on the incidence of hospitalization and death among Crimean deportees while in transit through Tashkent oblast' in 1944

INFORMATION

About specially resettled persons who were hospitalized and died in transit through Tashkent *oblast'*.

Name of *Raion*	Hospitalized on Debarking	Died Along the Way
Begovatskii	44	16
Khavastskii	none	1
Mirzachul'skii	14	18
Syr Dar'inskii	20	3
N. Chirchikskii	1	4
Ak. Kurganskii	-	1
Chirchikskii	37	9
Parkentskii	8	7
Pskentskii	5	-
Chinazskii	-	5
Tashsel'skii	12	1
IAngi-IUl'skii	27	3
Akhan Goranskii	-	6
TOTAL	168	74

CHIEF OF THE ADMINISTRATION OF THE PEOPLE'S COMMISSARIAT OF
        INTERNAL AFFAIRS OF THE UZBEK SOVIET SOCIALIST REPUBLIC,
        TASHKENT *OBLAST'* [*UNKVD UZB SSR T/O*]
LIEUTENANT COLONEL of STATE SECURITY   (MATVEEV)

Verified by assistant [head] of section to the commissioner of the   [illegible] *UNKVD*
for Tashkent *oblast'* [signature illegible].

        [signed] Romanov

TSGAOR [no cite]

DOCUMENT 109   *Resolution of the Central Committee Secretariat, June 13, 1991, concerning the rehabilitation of "repressed peoples," their rights, resettlement, and changes in their political boundaries*

Not for Publication

RESOLUTION

Of the Secretariat of the Central Committee of the Communist
Party of the Soviet Union [*TSK KPSS*]

On some problems related to the rehabilitation of repressed peoples

regarding this issue

1. To ratify the proposals introduced in the note from the Department of Nationalities Policy of the *TSK KPSS* (attached).

2. To send a note to the *TSK* of the Communist Party of the Russian Soviet Federated Socialist Republic [RSFSR] (Comrade I. K. Polozkov) for his consideration.

[signed] V. Mikhailov

Results of the vote:

For [signature illegible] May 29, 81 [sic]
Vl. Ivashko June 12, 1991

To be formulated along with corrections
(June 13, '91) of Comrade V. A. Ivashko

Supplement
to p. 7 g. note no. 30

TSK KPSS

Some Problems Related to the Rehabilitation
of Repressed Peoples

On April 26 of this year the Supreme Soviet of the RSFSR passed the law "On Rehabilitation of Repressed Peoples" and a resolution "On implementation of the RSFSR law on rehabilitation of repressed peoples." The law identifies repressed peoples, recognizes their right to national statehood and territorial integrity as it existed before forcible boundary changes were made, mandates the restoration of historical place names which were illegally changed after deportation, and provides compensation for losses caused by the state. Concomitantly, the law protects the rights and legal interests of citizens presently residing on the territories of the repressed peoples. In certain cases territorial rehabilitation may involve a transitional period. Decisions on the need for a period of transition and restoration of boundaries shall be determined by the Supreme Soviet of the RSFSR.

This law deserves ratification since it redresses a historical injustice.

At the same time, in our view, this law—and its implementation without a thorough impact analysis—may have serious consequences within the territory of the RSFSR and beyond.

Letters are being received from current residents of these areas who often were settled there against their will. Their concerns deal with potential boundary changes between the republics, *oblast*'s, *raion*s, and settlements.

Serious questions are also being raised about the fate of *raion*s in which demographic changes have occurred or which previously belonged to the states of the repressed nationalities.

The situation is particularly complicated in the relations between the North Ossetian ASSR and the Chechen-Ingush republic (and within the latter between the Chechen and the Ingush populations). In January 1957, in connection with the re-establishment of the Chechen-Ingush ASSR, the North Ossetian ASSR returned 4 of the 5 *raion*s in question to the former. However, Prigorodnyi *raion* remains in North Ossetia as do other small areas to which the Ingush have pretensions. At that time, by a decree of the Presidium of the Supreme Soviet of the RSFSR in 1957, the Karagalin, Shchelkov, and Naur *raion*s of Stavropol' *krai* were included in the territory of the Chechen-Ingush ASSR.

The proclamation of the Karachai republic on November 17, 1990, at a congress of peoples' deputies representing 6 *raion*s (formerly existing as the Karachai autonomous *oblast*' until 1943) met with ambiguous reception. The Zelenchuk and Urup *raion*s are populated largely by Cossacks who agitated for the transfer of areas settled by them to the Stavropol' or Krasnodar *krai*s. More than 40 thousand Karachais live in *raion*s populated by Cherkessians.

The Akkinians (an ethnic Chechen group) in Daghestan demand the re-establishment of the Aukhov *raion* (presently Novolak *raion*) and the restoration of Akkin geographical names used before their expulsion. They also demand return of their homes and farmsteads now occupied by Laks and Avars who were relocated there against their will.

A commission has been created in the Kalmyk republic to deal with the possible return of Narimanov and Liman *raion*s (presently in Astrakhan *oblast*') that were previously part of their republic, although today Kalmyks account for only 2 to 11 percent of the population there.

In accordance to a law passed by the Supreme Soviet of the RSFSR the Cossacks have been politically rehabilitated. This may entail territorial rehabilitation and re-establishment of Cossack *oblast*'s and regions. In November 1990 the Terek Cossacks and Nogais held a meeting calling for reversal of the *ukaz* of the Presidium of the Supreme Soviet of the RSFSR of January 9, 1957, No. 721/4, particularly as it pertains to partitioning of the Nogai Steppe among Daghestan, Checheno-Ingushetia and Stavropol' *krai*. Prior to 1957 the major part of the Nogai Steppe was included in Stavropol' *krai*; during tsarist times this constituted the Nogai *okrug*. The Terek Cossacks and the Nogais are demanding re-establishment of the territorial integrity of the Nogai Steppe and the creation of a corresponding republic in the RSFSR. This step will require review of boundaries of the existing national states within the RSFSR and the USSR as a whole.

If at present Prigorodnyi *raion* of the North Ossetian ASSR is a point of contention between Ossetians and Ingush we can assume, with certainty, that future demands will be raised for the restoration of territorial and administrative structures of the Terek Cossacks and the return of the Prigorodnyi and other *raion*s from which they were expelled in 1918.

The tragic events at the Troitsk stanitsa (currently populated by 5 thousand Cossacks and 1.5 thousand Ingush) in Sunzhensk *raion* in Checheno-Ingushetia have once again demonstrated that conflicts between Cossacks and the peoples of the North Caucasus may increase. This is due to an ever increasing perception among these people that the conquest of their lands during tsarist times was unjust.

The "Cossack problem" goes beyond the perimeters of the RSFSR and may impact on the Ukrainian, Kazakh, and Kirghiz SSRs (Ukraine includes part of the territory of the Don Cossacks, and Kazakhstan incorporates lands of the Ural, Siberian, and Semirechensk Cossacks). A movement is growing in the Ural and Gur'iev *oblast*'s of Kazakhstan for re-establishment of the Ural Cossacks and the transfer of their territory to Russia. In

November 1990 a founding congress of the Don Cossacks was held in Rostov. A sociopolitical union of the Don Cossacks was founded as an independent self-governing organization. A declaration was passed by the Great Council of the Union of the Don Cossack military *oblast'* on "Civil and Political Rehabilitation of the Cossacks," expressing their views on past anti-Cossack and antipeasant policies. In particular, demands are being made to rectify the consequences of territorial partitioning of the former Don Cossack military *oblast'* and recognition by the Supreme Soviet that these lands, lying in Russia and Ukraine, belong historically to the Don Cossacks and should be renamed the Don *oblast'*. They hold that these lands belong to the aboriginal Cossack and non-Cossack populations without ransom. There are plans to create a Cossack national guard, frontier, and other Cossack formations, and to accord the Cossack movement priority over other political organizations.

At a congress of the Buriat people a call was made for unification of the three autonomous Buriat entities (Buriat ASSR, Aginsk Buriat autonomous region in the Chita *oblast'*, and Ust'-Ordynsk Buriat autonomous region in Irkutsk *oblast'*.)

Adherence to the letter of the law would entail re-establishment of the Volga German autonomous republic. This proposal elicited a negative response in the Volgograd and, especially, Saratov *oblast'*s, that may hinder relocation of Soviet Germans to the Volga region and raises questions about recovery of their autonomy. At the May 7, 1991, meeting of the President of the USSR and representatives of Soviet Germans it was noted that re-establishment of German statehood in the Volga region must take into consideration the legitimate interests of all peoples living in that region. The problem has to be resolved in a rational manner within the framework of existing political and economic realities. This does not preclude the need for building national structures in places with a compact German population.

The public demands that implementation of this law be preceded by a detailed analysis of the means used to protect the rights of the people presently occupying the territories of repressed peoples.

Article 10 of the law is already the object of much discussion, since it advocates tripling the actual time spent in special settlements (places of exile) in considering entitlement to rehabilitation. Shouldn't this be applicable to others, for example, peasants exiled to Siberia during collectivization and those illegally repressed in 1937–1938 and at other times?

The difficulties inherent in the law on "Rehabilitation of Repressed Peoples" make it mandatory to involve communists, committees of the republics, *krai*s, *oblast'*s, cities, and *raion*s of the Communist Party of the RSFSR and first-line party organizations in its implementation. Consequently, the following measures appear to be necessary:

1. Recommendations to the *TSK* of the Communist Party of the RSFSR:
- Analyze the developing situation and together with the local party, Soviet organs, and scientific institutions identify all possible "hot" spots where territorial and other conflicts may arise. In accordance with Article 6, Communist deputies should make concrete proposals to the Supreme Soviet of the RSFSR regarding rehabilitation of a given repressed people and protection of citizens currently residing on these territories;

- Hold meetings in Rostov with secretaries of the committees of the republics, *krai*s, and *oblast'*s of the Communist Party of the RSFSR to exchange ideas and provide guidelines for party committees in resolving relationships among various nationalities and the activation of the Cossack movement;

- Provide the party committees with a special letter or guidelines with specific recommendations on implementing the law on "Rehabilitation of Repressed Peoples."

2. Educate the committees of the republics, *krai*s and *oblast'*s of the Communist Party of the RSFSR in the territories with repressed people not to display impatience and to avoid making hasty and intemperate decisions. To carry out these proposals people's deputies from all levels, senior citizens, veterans of war and labor, representatives of the creative intelligentsia, scholars, and clergymen could be drawn upon to create conciliation

commissions. Those articles of the law that provide for political solutions to territorial disputes should be emphasized first and foremost.

3. Recommend that the central and local press act in a reasonable and measured manner in reporting the implementation of the law, in advocating compliance and constructive dialogue, and in condemning extremism and arbitrariness.

Draft of the *TSK KPSS* declaration is appended.

Ratified by Comrade I. I. Antonovich, secretary, *TSK* of the Communist Party of the RSFSR.

Chief
Department of Nationalities Policy
TSK KPSS
[signed] V. Mikhailov

May 22, 1991

TSKhSD, fond 4, op. 42, d. 104.

Soviet Anti-Semitism

Official and popular anti-Semitism was widespread in tsarist Russia; hence it was no coincidence that many leaders of the Russian revolutionary movement and Communist Party were Jews. Special Jewish sections of the Communist Party existed until 1930 to aid in mobilizing Jews to join the party and support the regime. In 1927 the Soviet regime assigned the Birobidzhan territory in the Far East as a center of Jewish colonization, to become the Jewish autonomous republic. During World War II a leading Jewish actor, Solomon Mikhoels, was named to head the Jewish Anti-Fascist Committee, which appealed to Jews of the West and especially the United States to support the Soviet Union. The Soviet Union also supported the creation of the state of Israel in 1948, but policy toward Soviet Jews changed sharply with the visit to Moscow of Israel's first ambassador, Golda Meir. Her arrival met with an unexpectedly enthusiastic response by Soviet Jews. From that point on, Israel began to be denounced as a tool of Western imperialism. Soviet Jews were pronounced to have become assimilated and no longer in need of the protections of Soviet nationality policy. Jewish theaters, periodicals, and publishing houses were shut down, and Jewish writers and editors were purged. Mikhoels died mysteriously in 1948, allegedly in an automobile accident. Press reports denouncing "rootless cosmopolitans" and men of "uncertain allegiance" led to rumors that the entire Jewish population of the USSR would be deported to Birobidzhan, as the Crimean Tatars had been deported in 1944.

The revival of anti-Semitism became even more ominous with the declaration of the Doctor's Plot in 1953. Stalin's death removed much of the immediate danger, but latent and overt anti-Semitism continued to affect the lives of Soviet Jews for decades, reaching another peak in crude anti-Jewish propaganda and caricatures that followed Israel's lightning military victory in the 1967 Six Days' War. In subsequent decades, manifestations of anti-Semitism would remain a fixture of the Soviet and Russian political scene.

DOCUMENT 110   *Letter to M. A. Suslov from S. Mikhoels and I. Fefer, members of the Jewish Antifascist Committee in the USSR, June 21, 1946, providing information about the committee and its activities*

JEWISH ANTIFASCIST COMMITTEE IN THE USSR
Moscow, ulitsa Kropotkina, 10, Telephone: G-6-71-00, G-6-47-07
[letterhead also in Russian and Yiddish]

June 21, 1946

TO COMRADE M. A. SUSLOV, DIRECTOR OF THE SECTION FOR FOREIGN POLICY OF THE CENTRAL COMMITTEE OF THE ALL-UNION COMMUNIST PARTY (OF BOLSHEVIKS) [*TSK VKP(b)*]

Pursuant to the inquiry of Comrade Shumeiko, we are providing some information about the Jewish Antifascist Committee in the USSR and its activity.

The August 11, 1945, news release from the Soviet Information Bureau that was sent to you earlier gives a general idea of the work of the committee. We are also providing the information that Comrade Shumeiko requested about the organization and staff of the committee, its presidium, etc.

The Jewish Antifascist Committee in the USSR was formed soon after the first antifascist radio conference of representatives of the Jewish people held in Moscow in August 1941.

The committee consists of 70 members (a list of committee members is attached), and its presidium has 19 members (a list of presidium members is attached).

The working staff of the committee consists of:

1) Secretary of the Committee, whose duties (following the death of Comrade Shakhno Epshtein) are carried out by the writer I. Fefer, a member of the All-Union Communist Party (Bolsheviks) [*VKP(b)*] since 1919.

2) Deputy Secretary of the Committee, Comrade S. M. Shpigel'glias, *VKP(b)* member since 1919 and formerly a party worker.

3) Senior editors: N. IA. Levin, *VKP(b)* member since 1944 and veteran of World War II; L. A. Gol'dberg, not a party member, former director of the publishing house Der Emes; editor S. O. Berman, *VKP(b)* member since 1940, veteran of World War II; and three translators and several technical workers.

In the course of the last two years, representatives of a series of foreign Jewish antifascist organizations have visited the committee: the deputy chairman of the Jewish Antifascist Committee of Bulgaria, Mr. Zhak Vradzhali; one of the leaders of the Union of Jews of Czechoslovakia, Mr. Rozenberg; representatives of Jewish organizations of France, Poland, et al.

Recently Mr. Ben Zion Goldberg (Waife), the son-in-law of Sholem Aleichem, visited the Soviet Union. He is a prominent public figure in the United States, a member of the presidium of the Soviet-American Friendship Society (headed by Lamont), chairman of the Committee of Jewish Scientists, Writers, and Artists of the United States (Albert Einstein is president of the committee), vice-president of Ambidzhan, the All-American Society for Aid to Birobidzhan (president of Ambidzhan—Steffenson). Mr. Goldberg is also a major American journalist, a contributor to the newspapers *Toronto Star, Saint Louis Dispatch, New York Post,* and *Today,* and to the magazine *The New Republic.* Mr. Goldberg stayed in the Soviet Union from January 11 to June 8, excluding one month when he traveled to Finland, Sweden, and Denmark.

During his stay in the Soviet Union, Mr. Goldberg was received in Moscow by M. I. Kalinin and S. A. Lozovskii; he attended all meetings of the Supreme Soviet of the USSR; and he had a series of meetings with Soviet writers (including a banquet at the Union of Writers), with representatives of the Soviet Jewish community (at the Jewish Antifascist Committee in the USSR headquarters), with leaders of the State Jewish Theater, with the chief rabbi of the Moscow Jewish congregation, Shliffer, and with leaders of the Red Cross, among others.

Mr. Goldberg visited Riga, Tallin, Leningrad, Minsk, Vilnius, Kaunas, Kiev, Odessa, L'vov, Uzhgorod, Mukachevo, Brody, and Stalingrad. He was received by the leading workers and writers in the capitals of the union republics.

During his stay in the Soviet Union, Mr. Goldberg dispatched via the Soviet Information Bureau 33 articles to the American, Canadian, English, Palestinian, Polish, and Yiddish press. The articles were extremely friendly toward the Soviet Union.

Before his departure, Mr. Goldberg began to write a book in English entitled *England: The Opponent of Peace,* and a book in Yiddish entitled *Jewish Culture in the Soviet Union.*

Recently the committee has received a series of requests from prominent Jewish public figures from several countries seeking assistance in visiting the Soviet Union. Such requests were received from: N. Goldman, the chairman of the executive committee of the World Jewish Congress; Dr. Stephen Wise, chairman of the American Jewish Congress; Louis Levine, chairman of the Jewish Council for Soviet Aid under Russian War Relief; Mr. Raiskii, the editor-in-chief of the newspaper *Presse Nouvelle* in Paris; et al.

The Jewish Antifascist Committee in the USSR has sent during its entire existence one delegation, composed of Comrades Mikhoels and Fefer, to the United States, England, Canada, and Mexico. This delegation's trip report has been published in the book *The Jewish People against Fascism* (attached; see pp. 91–129).

[signed]

Chairman of the Jewish Antifascist Committee in the USSR: S. Mikhoels
Member of the Presidium of the Jewish Antifascist Committee in the USSR: I. Fefer

[Stamps at upper right:]
    Removed from the register; to the dossier of [blank] sector; date: Jan. 9, 1947.
    Secretariat *OMI,* Central Committee of the Communist Party
    No. 2074 July 1, 1946

[Handwritten at left margin, p. 1:]
    To the archive
    [illegible notations and signature]
    The book stays. [signed] G. Shumeiko
    25/1948

RTSKhIDNI, fond 17, op. 128, d. 76, ll. 3–5.

S. M. Mikhoels, director of the State Yiddish Theater and chairman of the Jewish Antifascist Committe, 1945.
TSGAKFD, N 4-25141

Memorandum from L. Baranov and V. Grigor'ian to Zhdanov, July 19, 1947, detailing shortcomings in the work of the Jewish Antifascist Committee in the USSR

TO THE SECRETARY OF THE CENTRAL COMMITTEE OF
THE ALL-UNION COMMUNIST PARTY (BOLSHEVIK) [*TSK VKP(b)*]

<u>COMRADE ZhDANOV, A. A.</u>

The Jewish Antifascist Committee, after an investigation of its operation by the Department of Foreign Policy of the *TSK VKP(b)*, is taking certain measures to improve its propaganda operations abroad. In addition to the articles on the life of the Jewish population in the USSR, the committee began sending materials abroad which illuminate the friendship of the peoples of the USSR.

However, the committee has not eliminated nationalistic errors in its propaganda and continues to present Soviet Jewish culture as cut off from the influence of the cultures of other peoples in the USSR, and it exaggerates the role of the Jewish population in various aspects of life in the USSR.

The committee does not make the necessary rebuttals to anti-Soviet campaigns that have been conducted by the imperialistic circles of England and the U.S.

The committee does not fight Jewish nationalism and Zionism in foreign countries. Neither in articles sent abroad, nor in their newspaper *Einikait* [Unity] are the highly active Jewish nationalists of various stripes and Zionists denounced; the nationalistic errors of Jewish democratic organizations and their activists are not criticized.

The committee has not exploited its ties with foreign Jewish scientists, social-political, and cultural figures to obtain useful scientific, engineering, or political information for the Soviet government.

In creating the Jewish Antifascist Committee it was not expected that this committee would have any function regarding the Jewish population in the USSR. However, the committee has without any prior permission developed its activities within the country, diverting itself from the issues of Jewish movements abroad. The committee conducts a broad correspondence with central and local Soviet party organs and obtains a significant number of letters from the Jewish population in the USSR, which contain complaints about the treatment of Jews by various Soviet organizations. Some of these complaints find support in the committee.

The publication of the newspaper *Einikait*, intended primarily for the Jewish population of the USSR, strengthens the improper functions of the committee within the country. The committee is not running the paper satisfactorily. The newspaper republishes official materials and TASS information and often fills its pages with a random assortment of articles, satires of little substance, and stories.

The newspaper is distributed primarily to Jews in the Baltic region, the western *oblast*'s of the Ukrainian SSR, Belorussian SSR, and Birobidzhan. Only 1,000 out of 10,000 copies of the paper are distributed abroad (primarily in the U.S., Argentina, Palestine, Poland, and Rumania).

The shortcomings of the operations of the Jewish Antifascist Committee and its paper *Einikait* are mainly due to the fact that the leadership of the committee and the editors lack politically trained party cadres and qualified internationalists. The positions of executive secretary of the committee and editor of *Einikait* have long been vacant. The poet, Fefer, a former member of the Bund, as secretary has in fact been in charge of both the committee and the newspaper and has been using his position for self-advertisement while gathering around him a group of poorly qualified journalists. The editorial responsibilities for publishing *Einikait* have been performed by Comrade Zhits, who has poor political training.

The presidium of the committee consists mostly of members who for all practical purposes do not take part in the work of the committee; the composition of the presidium includes qualified internationalists who study the problems of the Jewish movement abroad. During 1947 there was only a single meeting of the presidium, at which only 8 of 18 members were present. The last full meeting of the committee was in 1944.

In order fundamentally to improve the operation of the Jewish Antifascist Committee the Department of Internal Politics of the *TSK VKP(b)* and the Directorate of Propaganda and Agitation of the *TSK VKP(b)* believe that it is essential to accept the corresponding resolution of the *TSK VKP(b)*.

The draft of the *TSK VKP(b)* resolution is attached.

Deputy Department Head
of the *TSK VKP(b)*   (L. Baranov)

Deputy Head of the
Propaganda and Agitation Directorate
of the *TSK VKP(b)*   (V. Grigor'ian)

July 19, 1947

RTSKhIDNI, fond 17, op. 128, d. 1058, ll. 132–33.

DOCUMENT 112   *Report to Stalin, ca. February 8, 1949, with a proposal to dissolve the associations of Jewish writers in Moscow, Leningrad, and Kiev and to suppress Yiddish publications*

To Comrade J. V. STALIN

The general secretary of the USSR Union of Soviet Writers, Comrade Fadeev, raised the question of dissolving the associations of Jewish writers in Moscow, Kiev, and Minsk and also of closing the literary-artistic Yiddish-language miscellanies *Heymland* (Moscow) and *Der Shtern* (Kiev).

The Moscow Association of Jewish Writers has 45 writers, the one in Kiev has 26 writers, and the one in Minsk has six writers. The basic organizational principle of these associations—that of national homogeneity—seems to be mistaken. Other literary associations, created on the basis of such a principle, do not exist within the Union of Soviet Writers. Recently, the activity of these associations has acquired a nationalistic character. These associations have no prospects for increasing their cadre of writers. The works of the writers, the participants in these associations, do not have a wide readership.

The literary-artistic Yiddish-language miscellanies are a place for works of a nationalistic character.

The writer Stel'makh, in her story "Grandfather's Children," tells about the old Jewish intelligentsia, evacuated to the Urals from Ukraine. The writer gives significantly more attention to illustrating remnants of the past in the consciousness and behavior of the people described than to the sprouting of something new in their experiences and deeds. Traits of provincial narrow-mindedness stand out sharply in the story. The writer Der Nister, in his sketch "With the Immigrants to Birobidzhan," develops Zionist ideas; he talks about Birobidzhan: "Let the house of Israel be built anew"; and further: "How good that in the USSR there have already appeared small, daring Davids, who must even more actively be armed with the pride and worthiness of David, with love for his people . . . in order that no Goliaths frighten them anymore." At the basis of the stories printed in the publications *Heymland* and *Der Shtern* lies the mistaken idea that the task of Jewish literature consists of describing only Jews; these materials are mainly devoted to Jewish activists: Hero of Socialist Labor Baranbaum, engineer Dymshits, woman pilot Gel'man, the boxer Mekhanik, the director Rakhlin.

Nationalist tendencies also are manifested in poetic works printed in the publications *Heymland* and *Der Shtern*. In the verses of Markish, "The Caucasus," the joyful radiance of Caucasian nature is contrasted with the bitter experiences of the author: "At the foot of a mountain, in stony torpidness, I, brought there by my grief, had to sit in mourning for that which had been destroyed, obliterated in the suffering of millennia." In the verses of Gofshtein, "Golden Autumn," the author delights in the "dear square inscriptions at the railway station" (that is, signs in the Jewish language). In the poem of Vloshstein, "Letter to a Friend Abroad," the prophet Ezekial appears as the bearer of comfort for the Jewish population terrorized by the fascists and is the conveyer of a new life; the author writes, "I hear this voice and am comforted deep in my soul." The poet Velednitskii in the poem "By Mount Ararat," declares that this mountain is dear to him because it is mentioned in the Bible.

The publication of the miscellanies *Heymland* and *Der Shtern* is unprofitable.

The Central Committee of the Communist Party (of Bolsheviks) of Ukraine [*TSK KP(b)U*] (Comrade Khrushchev) agrees with the proposal to dissolve the Association of Jewish Writers in Kiev and to close the miscellany *Der Shtern*.

The Secretary of the Central Committee of the Communist Party (of Bolsheviks) of Belorussia [*TSK KP(b)B*], Comrade Gusarov, supports the proposal to dissolve the Association of Jewish Writers in Minsk.

It seems expedient to support the proposal of the USSR Union of Soviet Writers (Comrade Fadeev), of the *TSK KP(b)U* and the *TSK KP(b)B* to dissolve the associations of Jewish writers in Moscow, Kiev, and Minsk and also to close the publications *Heymland* and *Der Shtern*.

RTSKhIDNI, fond 17, op. 118, d. 305, ll. 21–22.

DOCUMENT 113   *Decision by the Central Committee, February 8, 1949, to disband organizations of Jewish writers and to suppress Yiddish publications*

Statute, no. 415, para. 5s, session XVIII.   <u>STRICTLY SECRET</u>

All-Union Communist Party (Bolshevik). [*VKP(b)*] CENTRAL COMMITTEE [*TSK*]

P 67/109   To Comrades   Malenkov, Shepilov, Fadeev,
February 1949   Khrushchev; the Organizational
                                          Bureau—everyone; Central Committee
                                          of the Communist Party (Bolshevik)
                                          of Belorussia - "a"

Excerpt from the minutes of meeting 67 of the Politburo of the *TSK VKP(b)*

Decision of February 8, 1949

109. <u>Concerning the dissolution of organizations of Jewish writers and the suppression of Yiddish-language literary miscellanies</u>

(Statute of February 2, 1949, order no. 415, para. 5-s)

To accept the proposal of the board of the Union of Soviet Writers of the USSR (Comrade Fadeev) to:

a) dissolve organizations of Jewish writers in Moscow, Kiev and Minsk;

b) suppress the Yiddish-language literary miscellanies *Heimland* (Moscow) and *Der Stern* (Kiev).

Secretary of the Central Committee
J. Stalin

[Stamp at bottom of document:] All-Union Communist Party (Bolshevik)

RTSKhIDNI, fond 17, op. 118, d. 305, l. 20.

chapter 2

INTELLECTUALS AND THE STATE

The term "intelligentsia" always possessed special meaning in Russian history. The intelligentsia were not merely intellectuals—individuals who earned their livings by mental and intellectual work. The term conveyed a sense of political engagement and, before the revolution, opposition to the principles and values of the autocratic regime. Most revolutionary leaders, from all political parties, came from the intelligentsia. But the position of intellectuals in the Marxist class-based analysis of the Bolsheviks was problematic. There was no place for intellectuals in this analysis; they were either products of their middle-class or aristocratic social origins, or else, as Marx wrote, they had renounced their loyalties to their class of origin and had come over wholeheartedly to the side of the vanguard class, the proletariat. There was no middle ground. Lenin, himself a product of the Russian intelligentsia, was especially hostile toward those who did not support his vision of the revolution, and in fact, the majority of Russian intellectuals either opposed the 1917 revolution or took a neutral position.

Yet the new state needed these intellectuals, as teachers, scientists, planners, managers, doctors, and engineers. Early state policy toward intellectuals thus vacillated between repression of those who would not support the regime, and incentives—such as food rations—for those who would serve it. At the same time the state pursued a policy to create its own intelligentsia from among class-loyal workers and peasants; the upward mobility of individuals from previously disenfranchised groups was an important hallmark of the Soviet revolution.

During the 1920s, despite Lenin's extreme revulsion toward intellectuals, the state permitted substantial cultural pluralism, whether measured in education, literature, music, or science. This toleration for intellectual diversity came to an end, however, in 1928, when the arrest of "bourgeois specialist" mining engineers in the town of Shakhty signaled a new assault on intellectual nonconformity. The class principle returned to public discussion about intellectuals, who were once again labeled as products of a hostile bourgeois class. During the next few years a fierce cultural revolution raged in Soviet society, with advocates of proletarian principles in all spheres of culture leading the attack on proponents of the older Russian intellectual traditions.

This battle came to an end toward 1931, symbolized by the return of Maksim Gorky from his self-imposed exile in Europe. Stalin called for a new accommodation with expertise and experts in the industrial sphere. In literature a new Union of Writers emerged from among the competing factions of the cultural revolution and, with Gorky's blessing, propounded the literary doctrine of "socialist realism." This doctrine would become the new cultural orthodoxy of the Soviet Union, and, although it represented a level of ideological conformity, it was more ecumenical than the modernist and avant-garde doctrines promoted by the radical factions in the cultural revolution. The new orthodoxy also called for a renewed concern with craftsmanship and quality. Thus began a rapprochement between intellectuals and the state in the Soviet Union. Although ideological conformity remained de rigueur, and many intellectuals would fall victim to the purges of the late 1930s, the place of the intelligentsia as a social stratum, now reinforced with a generation of those trained under the Soviet regime, was accorded equal status in 1937 with peasants and workers.

Henceforth, the intelligentsia enjoyed a privileged social and economic position, but its intellectual freedom remained tightly controlled. An attack on Leningrad writers led by the Central Committee's cultural chief Andrei Zhdanov signalled a renewed emphasis on party-sponsored orthodoxy in 1946. The heresy of "anticosmopolitanism" was discovered in literature, art, and science, and Soviet intellectuals found themselves cut off and isolated from developments in the West. Still the regime trained new generations of scholars and scientists, and after the death of Stalin, intellectuals were able to loosen the restraints of state control, to experiment with new artistic forms, and to establish contacts with non-Communist counterparts. When Leonid Brezhnev came to power in 1964, the new regime reintroduced strict state control on the intellectual freedom practiced under Khrushchev. Some intellectuals refused to submit, and their dissidence spread into many spheres of Soviet cultural and social life.

Early Attacks on the Intellectuals

Most Russian intellectuals greeted the October revolution with skepticism or hostility. The All-Russian Union of Teachers called a series of strikes against the regime in late 1917 and early 1918. A number of leading academics fled central Russia and lent their support to the White governments that formed on the periphery. Other scientists and scholars tried to work with the Bolshevik regime, proposing structures that would maximize their scholarly autonomy. In many cases the regime treated the cultural elite with favor.

The Civil War mentality and conditions of Red Terror dealt harsh revolutionary justice to intellectuals who joined opposition movements or who publicly criticized the Bolshevik regime. Many members of the liberal Constitutional Democratic Party (Kadets) among whom were numerous academics, scientists, and professionals, supported the White military movement of General Denikin. Faced with a mutiny at the Krasnaia Gorka fortress on the Gulf of Finland near Petrograd in June 1919, Bolshevik authorities blamed the Kadets and arrested many of them (Documents 114, 115). Repression took the form first of denying intellectuals the freedom to emigrate. But political opposition continued to percolate within the intelligentsia. A counterrevolutionary conspiracy led by intellectuals and officers was uncovered by the *Cheka* in July 1921; sixty-one participants, including the poet Nikolai Gumilev, were executed. Reaction toward intellectuals surfaced again during the 1922 trial of Socialist Revolutionaries charged with anti-Soviet activity. This peasant socialist party had attracted many members of the Russian intelligentsia before and after 1917; the trial provided the excuse for a further wave of deportations of intellectuals (Document 119) who belonged to this or to other moderate parties, such as the Mensheviks, Popular Socialists, and to the liberal Kadets. Among the victims in this round-up were the sociologist Pitirim Sorokin and the writer Evgenii Zamiatin.

Minutes of a Politburo meeting, September 11, 1919, discussing, among other matters, a review of the mass arrests of intellectuals belonging to the Constitutional Democratic Party

Minutes of the September 11, 1919, session of the Politburo of the Central Committee [*TSK*]

Present: Comrades Lenin, Stalin, Krestinskii, Kamenev, Stuchka, Mitskevich, Beloborodov, Stasova, Bukharin, Dzerzhinsky, Litvinov, Karklin, Beika, Rakhia, and Kalske.

Agenda:

1. The question of Finland's peace proposal.
2. Offer of peace to the Lithuanian government.
3. Offer of peace to the Latvian government.
4. Form of address of peace offers.
5. Timing of peace offers.
6. Address of Zinoviev to the government of the Estonian republic.
7. Issue of English actions in Murmansk.
8. Comrade Miliutin.
9. Comrade Larin.
10. Mass arrests of professors and scientists.
11. Halt in publication of the newspaper *Narod* [The People].
12. The question of the Bessarabian government.
13. The question of the Ukrainian government.
14. Report of the High Command on the situation at the front.
15. The People's Commissariat of State Control.

1.   On the question of proposing peace to the White government of Finland. Voting FOR: Lenin, Stalin, Kamenev, Krestinskii, the Lithuanian Mitskevich, the Finns Rakhiia, Kalske. Latvians abstaining: Stuchka, Karklin, Beika.

2.   Offer of peace to the Lithuanian white government (Taribe). FOR: members of the Politburo, Lithuanians: Mitskevich, and Finns Kalske, Rakhiia; three Latvians abstaining.

3.   Offer of peace to the Latvian government of Ulman. FOR: members of the Politburo; Comrade Mitskevich and Finns abstaining; three Latvians against.

4.   Form of address of peace offers. Negotiate with each government separately, with a concrete proposal; in addition, the People's Commissariat for Foreign Affairs [*Narkominodel*] should make a radio broadcast directed to the international proletariat explaining the completed agreement.

5.   Timing of peace offer. FOR: an immediate proposal, members of the Politburo; Latvians for a delay of the proposal to the Ulman government; others abstaining.

Comrade Beika, in the name of the Central Committee of Latvian Communists, requests that a decision on the question of negotiations with the Ulman government be transferred to a plenary session of the Central Committee, and to stay implementation of today's decision of the Politburo until that time. In view of the impossibility of convening a plenum immediately, the Politburo unanimously proposes to satisfy the Latvian comrades by summoning all members of the *TSK* present in Moscow. In case of disagreement, the question will be put before the session of the next plenum, but the decision of the Politburo will be implemented immediately. The Latvian comrades agree. Upon arrival of the members of the *TSK* listed above, the floor is given to Comrade Lenin to speak FOR peace negotiations and to Karklin to speak against, and the question comes to a vote. Voting For an immediate offer of peace to the Ulman government: Comrades Lenin, Stalin, Kamenev, Krestinskii, Bukharin, Dzerzhinsky, Beloborodov; voting against, Stuchka; abstaining, Comrades Mitskevich, Stasova. Kamenev is assigned to write a letter to the *TSK* of Latvia detailing the reasoning behind the decision of the *TSK*.

The following questions are decided within the Politburo.

6. The communication of Comrade Zinoviev to the government of the Estonian Republic.

In view of the decision of the *TSK* to enter into negotiations with the Estonian government, the *TSK* reminds Comrade Zinoviev of the inadmissibility of contacts between individual Soviets and foreign governments and requests him to refrain in advance from any public pronouncements that could give the governments of Finland, Estonia, Lithuania cause to break off peace negotiations.

Recommend to Comrade Podbel'skii to issue an order to all radio stations of the republic to make no radio broadcasts to foreign governments without the sanction of the *Narkominodel* or the Politburo.

7. The question of expulsion of communists from Murmansk by the English and executions of some of them.

Propose that the *Narkomindel* send a radio broadcast to protest the execution of prisoners and the aerial bombing of innocent civilians and declare that imprisoned English officers are to be sentenced to execution. The sentence will be carried out if the English engage in any further such actions.

8. Declaration from the Presidium of the Supreme Soviet for the National Economy [*VSNKh*] granting a two-week leave of absence to Comrade Miliutin and designating Comrade Lomov as acting Chairman of the *VSNKh* for this period.

9. Declaration from the *VSNKh* to confirm Comrade Larin as a member of the Presidium.

In view of the fact that Comrade Larin has full authority to apply his energies to economic construction in the positions he occupies as chairman of the Commission on Utilization and the *VSNKh* Economic Policy Committee, the *TSK* does not consider it necessary to include him in the Presidium.

10. Declaration of Kamenev, Lunacharskii, and Gorky on mass arrests of professors and scientists because of their former membership in the Constitutional Democratic [Kadet] Party. Recommend to Comrades Dzerzhinsky, Bukharin, and Kamenev to review jointly with them the cases of those arrested in the most recent mass arrests. Disagreements on the release of any arrested shall be referred to the Central Committee.

11. Declaration of Comrade Kamenev on the decision of the Vol'skii group to cease publication of the newspaper *Narod.* Transmit via Kamenev that the *TSK* sees no obstacle to publishing a weekly on poor paper and to commission Kamenev to supply the Vol'skii group for several issues if publication of a weekly is decided upon.

12. Question of the Bessarabian government.

Liquidate the Bessarabian government. If members of the government have committed any abuses, authorize Dzerzhinsky to treat them in the usual fashion.

13. Question of the Ukrainian government.

Liquidate the entire governmental apparatus, preserving the nominal existence of the government. Recall to Moscow all members of the government and all members of the *TSK* of the Communist Party of Ukraine who have not received military appointments or are conducting underground work behind lines to Moscow for use in all-Russian work.

14. Report of the High Command on the situation at the front.

The report is to be taken under consideration. Send Trotsky a telegram with a recommendation to detail Comrade Peters as a member of the Revolutionary Military Council to Silvachev's staff. Do not execute the decision to send Comrade Peters without the agreement of Comrade Trotsky.

15. On the People's Commissariat of State Control.

a) Confirm the previous decision of the Politburo on Lander.

b) Comrade Stalin is to remain People's Commissar of State Control, returning in $1\frac{1}{2}$ weeks to Moscow from the western front.

c) Comrade Avanesov is appointed his acting deputy and with this appointment is simultaneously freed of all other duties except as a member of the Presidium of the All-Russian Central Executive Committee [*VTSIK*] and chairman of the commission for transport repair. He is also freed from substantive work in the Presidium of the *VTSIK*.

RTSKhIDNI, fond 17, op. 3, d. 26, ll. 1–2.

DOCUMENT 115   *Letter from Lenin to Gorky, September 15, 1919, about the arrest of intellectuals belonging to the Constitutional Democratic Party*

                                                                          Secret

Sept. 15, 1919

Dear Aleksei Maksimovich!

I saw Tankov, and even before his visit and your letter, we had decided in the Central Committee [*TSK*] to appoint Kamenev and Bukharin to review and confirm the arrests of the bourgeois intellectuals of the quasi-Constitutional Democrat [Kadet] stripe and to free whom we can. For it is clear to us that here indeed mistakes were made.

It is also clear that, in general, the arrest of the Kadets (and quasi-Kadets) was the necessary and correct measure to take.

When I read your frank opinion on this subject, I recall a phrase you used during our conversations (in London, Capri, and elsewhere) that made a deep impression on me:

"We artists are irresponsible people."

Just so! What gives you cause to say these improbably angry words? This cause, that dozens (or even hundreds) of these Kadet and quasi-Kadet little gentlemen will spend several days in prison <u>in order to prevent conspiracies similar to the surrendering of the Krasnaia Gorka Fort,</u> conspiracies that threaten the lives of tens of thousands of workers and peasants!

What a tragedy, you're thinking! What an injustice! Intellectuals in prison for several days or even weeks just to prevent the massacre of tens of thousands of workers and peasants!

"Artists are irresponsible people."

It is erroneous to confuse the "intellectual energy" of the people with the "energy" of bourgeois intellectuals. Take Korolenko for example. Recently I read his *War, Motherland, and Mankind,* a pamphlet written in August 1917. Korolenko, you know, is the best of the "quasi-Kadets," almost a Menshevik. But what a vile, despicable, rotten defense of the imperialist war, dressed up with sugar-coated phrases! A pitiful petty bourgeois captivated by bourgeois prejudices! For such gentlemen, 10,000,000 men killed during an imperialist war is a matter deserving support (by <u>deeds,</u> while mouthing sugar-coated <u>phrases</u> "against" the war), but the death of hundreds of thousands in a <u>just</u> civil war against landlords and capitalists evokes only aahs, oohs, sighs, and hysterics.

No. It isn't a sin to jail such "men of talent" for short periods if that's what it takes to <u>prevent</u> plots (such as the one at Krasnaia Gorka) and the deaths of tens of thousands. We uncovered the conspiracies of the Kadets and quasi-Kadets. And we <u>know</u> that quasi-Kadet professors are giving assistance heart and soul to the conspirators. That is a fact.

The intellectual forces of the workers and peasants are growing and getting stronger in their fight to overthrow the bourgeoisie and their accomplices, the intellectuals, the lackeys of capital, who consider themselves the brains of the nation. In fact they are not its brains, but its shit.

We pay <u>above-average</u> salaries to those "intellectual forces" who want to bring learning to the people (rather than toadying to capital). That is a fact. We cherish them. That is a fact. Tens of thousands of officers are serving in the Red Army and are winning in spite of hundreds of traitors. That is a fact.

Regarding your frame of mind, I know how to "understand" it (once you asked whether I would understand you). Several times, on Capri and elsewhere, I told you, "You let yourself be surrounded by the worst elements of the bourgeois intelligentsia, and you give in to their whining. You hear and listen to the wail of hundreds of intellectuals about their "terrible" incarceration lasting several weeks, but you do not hear or listen to the voices of the masses, of millions—workers and peasants—who are threatened by Denikin, Kolchak, Lianozov, Rodzianko, the Krasnaia Gorka (and other <u>Kadet</u>) conspirators. I fully understand, fully, fully understand that this is how you can end your letter with the statement that these "Reds are just as much enemies of the people as the Whites" (fighters for the overthrow of capitalists and landlords are just as much enemies of the people as are the capitalists and the landlords), or even end up believing in a tin divinity or in "our father the tsar." I fully understand.

Really and truly you will perish* if you don't break away from this situation with the bourgeois intelligentsia. With all my heart I wish that you would break away as soon as possible.

Best regards
[signed] Yours, Lenin.

*But you're not writing! To waste yourself on the whining of decaying intellectuals and not to write—is that not ruin for an artist, is that not shame?

RTSKhIDNI, fond 2, op. 1, d. 11164, ll. 1–6

DOCUMENT 116 *Memorandum from Davydov of the* **Cheka** *to Molotov, June 28, 1921, recommending against foreign travel by Russian writers*

TOP SECRET EXTREMELY URGENT
Department <u>Foreign</u>

To the Central Committee of the Russian
Communist Party [*TSK RKP*], Workers' and
Peasants' Party, Comrade Molotov.
Copy to: the Kremlin, Comrade Trotsky
<u>No. 1596</u>

Copy to: the Council of People's
Commissars, Comrade Gorbunov
<u>No. 7461/admin.</u>

The Foreign Department of the Extraordinary Commission for Combating Counterrevolution, Speculation and Crime [*Cheka*] currently has applications for exit visas from a number of literary figures, in particular those of Vengerova, Blok, and Sologub.

In view of the fact that authors who have gone abroad are conducting a most active campaign against Soviet Russia and that some of them, such as BAL'MONT, KUPRIN, and BUNIN, do not stop at the vilest fabrications, the *Cheka* does not consider it possible to satisfy such petitions.

Unless the Central Committee has special reasons for considering a stay of one or another of these authors abroad to be more desirable than in Soviet Russia, the *Cheka*, for its part, sees no basis for permitting their departure in the near future.

In any case, we would consider it preferable that such questions be referred to the Organizational Bureau for resolution.

To illustrate the above, enclosed herewith is a copy of a letter from Comrade Vorovskii from Rome.

CHIEF of the FOREIGN DEPT. of the *Cheka*
[signed] L. Davydov

PERSONAL SECRETARY

[Letterhead on left:] Russian Socialist Federated Soviet Republic [as in original]
All-Russian Extraordinary Commission for Combating Counterrevolution, Speculation, and Crime, as authorized, of the Council of Peoples' Commissars
June 28, 19[21]
No. 5937/s
Moscow, Bol. Lubianka, 11
Tel. 2-02-09, 2-02-27, 5-79-23

[Handwritten comment on left:] Copies to all members of the organizational bureau for familiarization. On point (1) respond that Central Committee completely agrees on the matter of foreign travel of literary figures and others, in this case when the All-Russian *Cheka* deems it better to refer the matter to the organizational bureau.

RTSKhIDNI, fond 17, op. 84, d. 175, l. 48–490b

DOCUMENT 117 *Application submitted by the historian and scholar Florenskii, August 1, 1921, requesting an academic ration*

Pavel Aleksandrovich Florenskii, born 1882, graduated in 1900 from the Second Men's Gymnasium of the city of Tiflis Magna Cum Laude. In 1904 he graduated from the Department of Physics and Mathematics of Moscow University with a major in pure mathematics. He had been permitted to stay in the university for the purpose of increasing his knowledge in the fields of philosophy and history. He was accepted to the Moscow Religious Academy, from which he graduated in 1908 and where he remained as an instructor of history of philosophy. After 1912 he held a Master's degree and was an associate professor. In addition, he taught physics and mathematical sciences at the Sergiev-Posad Women's Gymnasium, and in recent years at the Sergiev-Posad Institute of Popular Education, where he has been teaching physics, mathematical sciences, and the history of material culture.

Since 1918 he has been a member and academic secretary of the Commission for the Protection of the Troitsko-Sergievskaia Monastery, and there he has compiled a description of encolpia in the monastery's sacristy, silverware, and an analytical description of the Monastery's best icons. These works are in the process of being published. In addition, he presented to the commission a series of reports of aesthetic and archeological content.
P. A. Florenskii's numerous works have been published in the journals *Novyi put'* [New Path], *Vesy* [Scales], *Voprosy religii* [Questions of Religion], etc., and especially in the Journal *Bogoslovskii Vestnik* [Theological Herald], published under the editorship of P. A-ch. His individually published large works include, among others *Chastushki of Kostroma guberniia, First steps of ancient philosophy, Reduction of numbers, Pillar and the establishment of Truth*, etc. Since 1921, P. A. has been working as a mathematician in the Department of Chemistry and Electricity in the Supreme Economic Council [*VSNKh*].

[illegible signature]

QUESTIONNAIRE

For persons receiving an academic ration

Name...................... Pavel Aleksandrovich Florenskii

Specialty................. Philosophy, mathematics

Place of employment........ Moscow Higher State Artistic and Technical Workshop

Kind of work................Lecturing on analysis of perspective

Scholarly experience....... 18 years of literary work, 13 years as a professor

List publications, if any.. See Curriculum Vitae

SIGNATURE OF PERSON GIVING INFORMATION [signed] P. Florenskii

[Handwritten note:] Comrade P. Florenskii approved by order No. 92–21 of August 1, 1921.

TSGALI, fond 681, op. 1, d. 2634, ll. 2–3.

DOCUMENT 118   *Letter from Lenin to Stalin, July 17, 1922, on deporting Mensheviks, Popular Socialists, and Constitutional Democrats*

Comrade Stalin!

On the matter of deporting Mensheviks, Popular Socialists [NS], Constitutional Democrats [Kadets], etc. from Russia, I would like to ask a few questions, since this operation, which was started before my leave, still has not been completed.

Has the decision been made to "eradicate" all the NSs? Peshekhonov, Miakotin, Gornfel'd, Petrishchev et al.?

As far as I'm concerned, deport them all. [They're] more harmful than any SR [Socialist Revolutionary]—because [they're] more clever.

Also A. N. Potresov, Izgoev and all the *Ekonomist* contributors (Ozerov and many, many others). The Mensheviks Rozanov (a physician, cunning), Vigdorchik, (Migulov or something like that), Liubov' Nikolaevna Radchenko and her young daughter (rumor has it they're the vilest enemies of Bolshevism), N. A. Rozhkov (he has to be deported, incorrigible), S. A. Frank (author of *Metodologiia*). The commission supervised by Mantsev, Messing et al. should present lists and several hundred such ladies and gentlemen must be deported without mercy. Let's purge Russia for a long while.

As for Lezhnev (former[ly associated with] *Den'*), let's think it over: shouldn't we deport him? He will always be the wiliest sort as far as I can judge based on his articles I have read.

Ozerov as well as all the *Ekonomist* contributors are the most ruthless enemies. All of them—out of Russia.

This must be done at once. By the end of the SRs' trial, no later. Arrest a few hundred and without a declaration of motives—get out, ladies and gentlemen!

Deport all authors of *Dom literatorov, Mysl'* from Piter [Petrograd]; ransack Kharkov, we do not know it, for us it is a "foreign country." We must purge quickly, no later than the end of the SRs' trial.

Pay attention to the writers in Piter (addresses, *Novaia Russkaia Kniga*, No. 4, 1922, p. 37) and to the list of private publishers (p. 29).

With communist greetings   Lenin

RTSKhIDNI, fond 2, op. 2, d. 1338, ll. 1, 1ob, 2–4.

DOCUMENT 119   *Memorandum from Lenin to Unschlicht, September 18, 1922, regarding a list of anti-Soviet intellectuals, with a response from IAgoda returning lists with notes and names of persons in Moscow and Petrograd*

[Handwritten note:] Sept. 17. Comrade Unshlikht! Please issue a directive: Return to me all enclosed papers with notes, who has been deported, who is in prison, who (and why) has been spared exile. [Make] Very short notes on this same paper.
Yours Lenin

....

RSFSR   September 18, 1922,   2345
    HEAD
  of the
Secret-Operations Directorate   To Comrade V. I. Lenin
of the State Political Directorate
[GPU]

No. 295

In accordance with your directive I am sending back to you the lists you had sent with corresponding notations on them and the names of persons (listed separately) who for one reason or another were left in Moscow and Piter [Petrograd].

With Communist greetings G. IAgoda

P.S. The first batch is leaving Moscow September 29 (Friday).

LIST OF ANTI-SOVIET INTELLIGENTSIA IN PETROGRAD

PERSON	STATUS
1. SOROKIN PITIRIM ALEKSANDROVICh	arrested; awaiting deportation
2. IZGOEV-LANDE A. S.	arrested; awaiting deportation; at liberty while settling affairs
3. ZUBAShEV E. L.	" " "
4. BRUTSKUS	" " "
5. KAGAN A. S.	" " "
6. LUTOKhIN	" " "
7. PUMPIANSKII	arrested; awaiting deportation; at liberty while settling affairs
8. FROMET	at large (whereabouts currently unknown)
9. ZAMIATIN E. I.	arrested; deportation postponed by [illegible] directive [illegible] dated August 31
10. PETRIShchEV A. B.	arrested; awaiting deportation
11. BULGAKOV S. N.	at large (whereabouts currently unknown)
12. VOLKOVYSSKII M.	arrested; awaiting deportation; at liberty while settling affairs
13. KhARITON BORIS	arrested; awaiting deportation; at liberty while settling affairs

14. ChAADAEV	at large (whereabouts currently unknown)
15. KARSAVIN	arrested; awaiting deportation; at liberty while settling affairs
16. LOSSKII	arrested; awaiting deportation; at liberty while settling affairs
17. GUTKIN A. IA.	arrested; awaiting deportation; at liberty while settling affairs
18. KANTSEL' EFIM SEMENOVICh	deportation suspended until [illegible] and justification for such [illegible] received from Comrade TSiperovich
19. ZBARSKII DAVID SOLOMONOVICh	at large (whereabouts currently unknown)
20. SADYKOVA IU. N.	arrested; awaiting deportation; at liberty while settling affairs
21. BRONShTEIN ISAI EVSEEVICh	arrested; awaiting deportation; at liberty while settling affairs
22. PAVLOV PAVEL PAVLOVICh	at large (whereabouts currently unknown)
23. KARGENS NIKOLAI KONSTANTINOVICh	at large (whereabouts currently unknown)
24. SOLOVEIChIK EMANUIL BORISOVICh	at large (whereabouts currently unknown)

LIST OF MEMBERS OF THE UNITED COUNCIL OF PROFESSORS OF THE CITY OF PETROGRAD

PERSON	STATUS
25. POLETIKA	at large (whereabouts currently unknown)
26. ODINTSOV BORIS NIKOLAEVICh	arrested; awaiting deportation; at liberty while settling affairs
27. LAPShIN IVAN IVANOVICh	arrested; awaiting deportation; at liberty while settling affairs
28. POL'NER SERGEI IVANOVICh	arrested; awaiting deportation; at liberty while settling affairs
29. ANTONOVSKAIA NADEZhDA GRIGOR'EVNA	at large (whereabouts currently unknown)
30. SELIVANOV DMITRII FEDOROVICh	arrested; awaiting deportation; at liberty while settling affairs
31. FRENKEL' GRIGORII IVANOVICh	at large (whereabouts currently unknown)
32. OSTROVSKII ANDREI	arrested; awaiting deportation; at liberty while settling affairs
33. BUTOV PAVEL IL'ICh	at large (whereabouts currently unknown)
34. VISLOUKh STANISLAV MIKhAILOVICh	arrested; awaiting deportation; at liberty while settling affairs
35. VETTSER GERMAN RUDOL'FOVICh	at large (whereabouts currently unknown)
36. KORSh	at large (whereabouts currently unknown)

37. NAROIKO	at large (whereabouts currently unknown)
38. ShTEIN VIKTOR MARITSOVICh	deportation rescinded by Commission chaired by Comrade Dzerzhinsky and allowed to remain in Petrograd . . . see [illegible]
39. SAVVICh	to be tried for participation in anti-Soviet organization abroad; not to be deported; to be kept in custody
40. BOGOLEPOV A. A.	at large (whereabouts currently unknown)
41. OSOKIN VLADIMIR MIKhAILOVICh	awaiting deportation; at liberty while settling affairs
42. BOL'ShAKOV ANDREI MIKhAILOVICh	at large (whereabouts currently unknown)
43. GUSAROV IGNATII EVDOKIMOVICh	[Passage below applies to individuals 43–46:]
44. ERMOLAEV NIKOLAI NIKOLAEVICh	By resolution of Commission chaired by Comrade Dzerzhinsky, to be prosecuted on charges of participation in anti-Soviet organization abroad. Not to be deported.
45. EREMEEV GRIGORII ALEKSEEVICh	To be bound over for trial and kept in custody [illegible]
46. TEL'TEVSKII ALEKSEI VASIL'EVICh	
47. EVDOKIMOV PETR IVANOVICh	arrested; to be deported; at liberty

<u>LIST OF PETROGRAD LITERARY FIGURES</u>

48. ROZhKOV	at large (whereabouts currently unknown)
49. GERETSKII VIKTOR IAKOVLEVICh	at large (whereabouts currently unknown)
50. KLEMENS	at large (whereabouts currently unknown)
51. KROKhMAL' VIKTOR NIKOLAEVICh	deportation rescinded by commission chaired by Comrade Dzerzhinsky on August 31 of this year on the basis of his personal letter to Comrade Dzerzhinsky of the 3rd. [illegible] He pledges his [illegible] of Soviet authority.

Original Signed by:

  L. KAMENEV
  D. KURSKII
  I. UNShLIKhT

True Copy: [illegible signature]

[Handwritten:] Comment: Pursuant to a decision of the Politburo of the Central Committee of the Russian Communist Party, a commission chaired by Comrade Dzerzhinsky examined applications to rescind the deportations of persons considered irreplaceable in their profession, for whom the appropriate institutions had submitted appeals to leave in place. [signed] Deputy Chairman of the *GPU* G. IAgoda.

LIST OF ACTIVE ANTI-SOVIET MEMBERS OF THE
INTELLIGENTSIA (PROFESSORS) IN MOSCOW

Professors at Moscow University No. 1

PERSON	STATUS
1. STRATONOV Vsevolod Viktorovich	awaiting deportation; at liberty
2. FOMIN Vasilii Emelianovich	deportation rescinded by decree of the commision, based on the appeal of Comrades IAkovlev and Bogdanov

Professors at the Moscow Higher Technical School

4. IASINSKII Vsevolod Ivanovich	awaiting deportation; at liberty
5. BRILLING Nikolai Romanovich	not deported; turned over to Counter-intelligence Department of *GPU* for prosecution on charges of counterrevolutionary activity
6. KUKOLEVSKII Ivan Ivanovich	deportation suspended until receipt of justification of appeal from Comrade Bogdanov
7. ZVORYKIN Vladimir Vasil'evich	awaiting deportation; at liberty

Professors at the Petrovskii-Razumovskii Agricultural Academy

8. ARTOBOLEVSKII Ivan Arsen'evich	to be tried by revolutionary tribunal for agitation against confiscation of church valuables
9. UShAKOV	awaiting deportation; at liberty

Professors at the Institute of Railroad Engineering

10. TIAPKIN Nikolai Dmitrievich	case turned over to counterintelligence department of *GPU* for prosecution on charges of counterrevolutionary activity; kept under guard

The Case of the Free Economic Society

11. UGRIMOV Aleksandr Ivanovich	awaiting deportation; at liberty

Professors at Miscellaneous Educational Institutions

12. OBNINNIKOV (Kazan')	not arrested; no information.
13. VELIKhOV Pavel [illegible]	case turned over to Counterintelligence Department of the *GPU* for prosecution on charges of counterrevolutionary activity
14. LOSKUTOV Nikolai Nikolaevich	at large (whereabouts currently unknown)
15. TROShIN (Kazan')	at large (whereabouts currently unknown)
16. NOVIKOV M. M.	awaiting deportation; at liberty
17. IL'IN N. A.	awaiting deportation; at liberty

List of Anti-Soviet Professors at the Archeological Institute

18. USPENSKII Aleksandr Ivanovich	Sentenced to 10 years confinement by revolutionary tribunal for agitation against confiscation of church valuables

19. TSVETKOV Nikolai Nikolaevich	awaiting deportation; at liberty
20. BORDYGIN Vasilii Mikhailovich	awaiting deportation; at liberty
21. KOROBKOV Nikolai Mikhailovich	released . . . . by order of commission. . . .after contracting tuberculosis

GENERAL LIST OF ACTIVE ANTI-SOVIET PERSONS INVOLVED IN THE CASE OF THE BEREG [shore] PUBLISHING HOUSE

22. TRUBETSKOI Sergei Evgenievich	awaiting deportation; at liberty
23. FEL'DShTEIN Mikhail Solomonovich	awaiting deportation; at liberty

LIST OF PERSONS CHARGED IN CASE NO. 813 (Group of Abrikosov)

PERSON	STATUS
24. ABRIKOSOV Vladimir Vladimirovich	awaiting deportation; at liberty
25. KUZ'MIN-KARABAEV Dmitrii Vladimirovich	awaiting deportation; at liberty
26. BAIKOV Aleksei L'vovich	awaiting deportation; at liberty
27. ARBUZOV Aleksei Dmitrievich	awaiting deportation; at liberty

LIST OF ANTI-SOVIET AGRONOMISTS AND COOPERATIVE MOVEMENT MEMBERS

28. RYNIKOV Aleksandr Aleksandrovich	at request of People's Commissariat of Agriculture deportation rescinded; under investigation
29. LIUBIMOV Nikolai Ivanovich	awaiting deportation; at liberty
30. MATVEEV Ivan Petrovich	awaiting deportation; at liberty
31. ROMODANOVSKII Nikolai Pavlovich	awaiting deportation; at liberty
33. KONDRAT'EV I.D.	charged with collaborating with the *SR*s; deportation suspended; keep under guard
34. KIL'ChEVSKII Vladimir Agafonovich	awaiting deportation; at liberty
35. BULATOV Aleksei Alekseevich (Novgorod)	awaiting deportation; at liberty
36. SIGIRSKII Aleksandr Ivanovich	awaiting deportation; at liberty
37. ShIShKIN Matvei Dmitrievich (Vologda)	awaiting deportation; at liberty
38. BAKAL (Left Socialist Revolutionary)	awaiting deportation; at liberty
39. MALOLETNIKOV Nikolai Vasil'evich	awaiting deportation; at liberty
40. KLEZITSKII (Tver')	at large (whereabouts currently unknown)

LIST OF PHYSICIANS

41. IZRAIL'SKII (Orel) — awaiting deportation to Kirghiz Territory for 2 years to work as doctor

42. FANIN (Vologda) — exiled to Vologda for 2 years to work as doctor

43. ROZANOV (Saratov) — awaiting deportation to Turkestan to work as doctor

LIST OF ANTI-SOVIET ENGINEERS (Moscow)

44. PAL'ChINSKII Petr IAkimovich — awaiting deportation; in custody

45. PARShIN Nikolai Evgrafovich — deportation postponed until matter reviewed with Comrades Steklov and Bogdanov; at liberty

46. IUShTIN Ivan Ivanovich — awaiting deportation; at liberty

47. VAISBERG — at large (whereabouts currently unknown)

48. KOZLOV Nikolai Pavlovich — at large (whereabouts currently unknown)

49. SAKhAROV Andrei Vasil'evich — released [illegible] *GPU*

LIST OF LITERARY FIGURES

50. FRANK Semen Liudvigovich — awaiting deportation; at liberty

51. ROZENBERG — awaiting deportation; at liberty

52. KIZEVETTER A. A. — awaiting deportation; at liberty

53. OZERETSKOVSKII Veniamin Sergeevich — awaiting deportation; at liberty

54. IUROVSKII Aleksandr Naumovich — deportation rescinded by resolution of Commission of Oct. 31, 1922, at request of Comrade Vladimir [illegible]

55. OGANOVSKII Nikolai Petrovich — at large (whereabouts currently unknown)

56. AIKhENVAL'D IUl'ii Isaevich — awaiting deportation; at liberty

57. BERDIAEV N. A. — awaiting deportation; at liberty

58. OZEROV Ivan Khristoforovich — deportation suspended until matter reviewed with Comrade Malbeshev

59. OSSORGIN Mikhail Andreevich — awaiting deportation; at liberty

60. MATUSEVICh Iosif Aleksandrovich — awaiting deportation; at liberty

61. EFIMOV (professor) — at large (whereabouts currently unknown)

July 31, 1922, KAMENEV, L. D. KURSKII, UNShLIKhT

SUPPLEMENTARY LIST OF ANTI-SOVIET INTELLIGENTSIA (Professors) (Moscow)

1. KRAVETS Terichan Pavlovich — case turned over to counterintelligence department of *GPU* for prosecution on charges of counterrevolutionary activity; in custody

2. IZGARYShEV Nikolai Alekseevich — deportation rescinded; formal investigation of his remaining in RSFSR underway

3.   KUDRIAVTSEV Vasilii Mikhailovich   awaiting deportation; at liberty

4.   MIAKOTIN Venedikt Aleksandrovich   awaiting deportation; at liberty

5.   PEShEKhONOV Aleksei Vasilievich   awaiting deportation; at liberty

6.   STEPPUN Fedor Avgustovich   at large (whereabouts currently unknown)

7.   ChERNOLUSSKII Vladimir Ivanovich   at large (whereabouts currently unknown)

8.   IZIUMOV Aleksandr Filaretovich   awaiting deportation; at liberty

     L. KAMENEV, D. KURSKII, UNShLIKhT

July 31, 1922

RTSKhIDNI, fond 2, op. 2, d. 1245, ll. 1,2,6,7,3–5.

DOCUMENT 120   *Decree of the Special Committee for the Organization of Artistic Tours and Art Exhibits, January 17, 1925, recommending against permission for S. Diaghilev to enter the USSR*

TO: The Administration of the State Actors' Theaters
ABOUT: Information

EXCERPT

from the Minutes of meeting no. 2 of the Special Committee for the Organization of Artistic Tours and Art Exhibitions under the Commission of Foreign Assistance.

from January 17, 1925

HEARD:	DECREED:
4. Inquiry of the People's Commissariat of Foreign Affairs on the desirability of the entrance into the USSR of S. P. Diaghilev, Director of the Russian Ballet in Monte Carlo, and P. Kay, an English citizen and dancer in his ballet.	4. Entrance into the USSR of S. Diaghilev and Kay considered undesirable.

True copy

TSGALI, fond 2310, op. 1, d. 3, l. 32.

The Industrial Party Affair and Related Attacks on Intellectuals

The Soviet "cultural revolution" is often dated from 1928, the first year of the five-year-plan in industry and the year of the trial of mining engineers from the town of Shakhty, the first in a series of show trials and arrests of the technical intelligentsia. According to documents produced by the *OGPU*, the Shakhty engineers had received letters from abroad, written in code, directing a foreign conspiracy to wreck Soviet coal mines. The case provided the pretext to raise again the banner of "class struggle," justifying police measures and repression against the foreign bourgeoisie and their internal "class agents" in the USSR. The Shakhty case was followed by the Industrial Party Affair, the most widely publicized show trial until the purge trials of the late 1930s. The trial was perhaps an invention to compensate for the ongoing mistakes of the industrialization effort; the charges were spectacular. The prosecution accused the so-called Industrial Party, led by Professor Ramzin, of conspiring to take over the government of the Soviet Union. The trial also served to discredit the quite real aspirations of the technical intelligentsia to exercise more technocratic control in Soviet society. Some of the testimony against the Industrial Party was provided by arrested members of the "Toiling Peasants' Party," including the noted agricultural economist Aleksandr Chaianov. They were implicated in a conspiracy to incite a *kulak* uprising against the regime.

Did Stalin believe in the validity of these conspiracies? His 1930 letter to the chief of the *OGPU* (Document 122) reveals two things: his minute involvement with the progress of the case and an obsession with foreign intervention. Proving these conspiracies would validate his message about foreign enemies and the need for rapid and forced industrialization, and it would also provide useful propaganda for foreign communists to use against their own "interventionist" governments.

Intellectuals also had supporters within the leadership. Industrial bosses tried to protect their engineers and obtained the release of many prisoners who had been obviously wrongly arrested. The well-known historian Evgenii Tarle was one such victim, indicted for his alleged role as future Minister of Foreign Affairs in the Industrial Party conspiracy and exiled to Alma-Ata. He was freed in 1933 upon the interventions of Anatolii Lunarcharskii, Lenin's Commissar of Education, and of leftist French intellectuals. Nikolai Bukharin, even after his political disgrace in 1929, continued to intercede successfully on behalf of intellectuals and scientists. In addition to Document 124, in which he appeals to Kirov to protect scientific researchers, Bukharin also helped the poet Osip Mandelshtam, according to the memoirs of Mandelshtam's widow, to survive the persecution of the *NKVD*.

Testimony of Professor Chaianov to the OGPU, **August–September 1930, on counterrevolutionary activities**

-86-

As reported to me, the Council of Engineering Organizations has been in contact with capitalist governmental circles in France and Poland and with conservative circles in England. I stopped attending meetings of the Council of Engineering Organizations in the autumn of 1928.

A. Chaianov
Interrogated by IA. Arganov

Additional Testimony of A. V. Chaianov

I, A. V. Chaianov, interrogated by Chief of the Secret Department of the Unified State Political Directorate [OGPU] IA. S. Agranov, have given the following testimony.

To supplement my cursory testimony at the end of a daytime interrogation on August 8, 1930, I hereby submit the following information and corrections.

1. In late 1926, I learned from conversations with Ramzin and Rabinovich about the political consolidation of engineering in various branches of industry, and I once was invited by Rabinovich to a meeting of one of the groups. The meeting took place after work hours, if my memory does not betray me, in one of the *Gosplan* RSFSR offices, under the guise of some sort of meeting. The political attitudes of the engineering sector were discussed. I do not recall the precise content of the discussion.

Since by that time the Central Committee of the Toiling Peasants' Party [TKP] had already been formed, I informed my comrades about this meeting and they felt it was extremely important to maintain this contact on behalf of the *TKP*, under no circumstances departing from the role of informer, and they instructed me to reveal the political physiognomy of this organization.

In early 1927, meeting Ramzin, I told him about my instructions to maintain informational contact with them on behalf of the *TKP* and I asked him to invite me to their most substantive meetings. After that, until the summer, which I did not spend in Moscow, I attended two meetings of the Engineering-Industrial Center. In the autumn I attended about the same number of meetings. I was abroad for about three months in the winter of 1927–28, and only upon the insistence of the Central Committee of the *TKP* did I resume attending meetings, preferring to receive information from individual members. However, because of the obvious incompatibility of the mind-set of the engineering organization with my convictions and the positions of the *TKP*, these meetings became more and more burdensome.

By the summer of 1928 I had already broken with my old ideas on agriculture. My job as liaison to the engineering and industrial center was becoming more and more oppressive, and I breathed a sigh of relief when five-man delegations were organized as liaisons to the engineering and industrial center in mid-1928. I was replaced as liaison from the *TKP* by Makarov and Kondrat'ev, because my comrades realized that it was psychologically impossible for me to continue as liaison because of my convictions in general and the changes they had undergone in particular. In addition to the new delegates, the new consolidated contact center included, as I have already testified, Makarov, Groman, and two representatives of the industrial center, whose names I can't recall exactly (Khrennikov? Bazarov? Charnovskii? or maybe someone else). Either Makarov or Kondrat'ev could tell you.

2. With respect to the engineering and industrial center itself, I can provide the following additional testimony:

a) Title - at our meetings we referred to the engineering and industrial center and its members colloquially as "the club" or "the council," while formally we referred to it as "The Council of Engineering Organizations." I am troubled when I remember our conversations concerning the need to give it a more politically militant title, but I don't remember what exactly this title was.

b) Membership - I never saw any lists or attendance sheets at the meeting, and I believe we didn't have any. Hence I can only guess what industries were represented there by my recollections of the speakers who spoke for a particular industry. I am absolutely certain that there were representatives of the transportation industry (Krasovskii), the textile industry (Fedotov), metallurgy, the defense industry, heat engineering (Ramzin), the mining industry, and the oil industry.

With respect to the individual members, I can't add anything to my original testimony.

c) The character of the organization, as I recall, gradually changed. In the beginning it was basically a contact bureau of diverse groups. With time, they increasingly took on political and even operational tendencies and forms. As for the final organizational form, I think our delegates to the unified center, Kondrat'ev and Makarov, can tell you much more than I. In any event, if it can be considered a political party, it was not one in the usual sense of the word. Political ideology was not its core; its concrete political goal was to be a fighting arm for the remnants of the bourgeoisie.

d) The executive organ was called the "executive bureau," because I was always hearing the expression "submit to the bureau," "assign to the bureau." I do not know its full make-up, because it was not selected in my presence, and in general, I think as an operational organ, in the final analysis, it was kept secret from the council as a whole, at least from the planning meetings that I attended. I believe its leader was Pal'chinskii, and that Khrennikov, Rabinovich, and Ramzin had dealings with it, because they made official announcements, accepted instructions from the bureau, and spoke with me as officials. It was through them that I came to a meeting for the first time, and no one but a member of the bureau naturally could have taken me there. The role of the others, besides taking part in the meetings, amounted to liaison with engineering groups. Various persons chaired. I can't remember exactly if Rabinovich or Ramzin chaired the meetings. Pal'chinskii sometimes chaired.

e) Minutes were not taken at the meetings. It could be they were compiled later in the bureau.

f) Meetings were conducted either in the "club" or in private apartments.

The term "club" referred to some sort of public place in Moscow in the evening. In addition to our meeting at the Supreme Economic Council, at the State Planning Committee [*Gosplan*], and in the office of some scientific and technical council near the Polytechnic Museum, there were all kinds of other phony agendas we used as covers. We discussed organizing a real miners' club with a legal charter, which was supposedly done. We had one meeting in some sort of club where Rabinovich took me after he dropped by my place, but this club belonged to some sort of agency. I remember attending meetings at apartments on Miasnitskaia (?) Street, where, as I remember, the same Rabinovich or Ramzin had taken me. My conversations with Ramzin took place at the cafeteria of the Central Commission for Improving the Living Conditions of Scientists [*TSEKUBU*].

The talks and discussions at the meetings I attended—and I specifically asked to be invited only to meetings where general basic principles were discussed, for the most part preferring to learn what the Engineering and Industrial Center's positions were in private conversations—covered different subjects at different times. [original ends at this point]

RTSKhIDNI, fond 17, op. 71, d. 30, ll. 470b, 48.

DOCUMENT 122 **Letter from Stalin to V. R. Menzhinskii of the OGPU, ca. 1930, regarding evidence in the political trial of two groups, the Industrial Party and the Trade-Industry Party [Torgprom]**

Comrade Menzhinskii!

I received the letter of October 2 and the materials. Ramzin's testimony is very interesting. In my opinion, the most interesting of his testimony is the problem of the intervention in general and, in particular, the problem of the <u>date</u> of the intervention. It turns out they had intended the intervention for 1930, but then postponed it to 1931 or even 1932. That's quite probable and important. It is even more important because this information came from a primary source, i.e., from the group of Riabushinskii, Gukaev, Denisov and Nobel', which represents the most powerful socio-economic group of all existing groups in the USSR and in emigration—the most powerful in terms of capital and in terms of its connections with the French and English governments. It might seem that the Toiling Peasants' Party [*TKP*] or the Industrial Party [*Prompartiia*] or the "party" of Miliukov represents the main force. But that's not quite right. The main force is the group of Riabushinskii-Denisov-Nobel', etc., i.e., *Torgprom*. The *TKP*, the *Prompartiia*, the "party" of Miliukov are at the beck and call of *Torgprom*. All the more interesting is the information about the <u>date</u> of the intervention coming from *Torgprom*. The intervention in general and the date of the intervention in particular, as you know, are issues of primary interest to us.

Here are my suggestions:

a) Make the question of the intervention and the date of the intervention one of the most important key points of new (future) testimony from the *TKP*, *Prompartiia* and especially, from Ramzin: 1) why they postponed the intervention in 1930; 2) Was it because Poland is not yet ready? 3) Maybe it is because Romania is not ready? 4) Maybe it is because the [illegible] had not yet closed ranks with Poland? 5) Why was the intervention postponed to 1931? 6) Why "might" they postpone it to 1932? 7) etc., etc.)

b) Bring to trial Larichev and the other members of the "Central Committee of the *Prompartiia*" and interrogate them severely about the same, having given them Ramzin's testimony to read.

c) Severely interrogate Groman, who, according to Ramzin's testimony, stated at the "United Center" that "the intervention was postponed to 1932."

d) Make Kondrat'ev, IUrovskii, Chaianov, etc., who are cleverly trying to deny "a tendency toward intervention" but support (indisputably!) the idea of intervention, run the gauntlet and severely interrogate them about the date of the intervention (Kondrat'ev, IUrovskii and Chaianov should have known this earlier, as Miliukov, to whom they were going for a "chat," also knew).

If Ramzin's testimony is <u>confirmed</u> and <u>clarified</u> by the testimony of the other defendants (Groman, Larichev, Kondrat'ev and company, etc.), it would be a noteworthy success for the *OGPU*—because the materials obtained by this method we will make available in one form or another to sections of the KP [Communist Party] and workers of all the other countries. We will carry out the widest campaign against the interventionists and thus paralyze and stop all attempts at intervention in the next 1–2 years, which is of utmost importance to us.

Understand?

Greetings! J. Stalin

RTSKhIDNI, fond 558, op. 1, d. 5276, ll. 1–5.

Stalin and Poskrebyshev, 1934. TSGAKFD

DOCUMENT 123 *Letter from Ol'ga Tarle to Lunacharskii, May 7, 1930, on the dire conditions of her husband's incarceration, and E. V. Tarle's letter to Lunacharskii of May 17, 1933, thanking him for his help*

Highly esteemed Anatolii Vasil'evich,

I am petitioning you on behalf of my husband Evgenii Viktorovich Tarle. He has been in the Pretrial Detention House since January 28 of this year. His chronic illness has now become acute. He writes that he is in agony from his [kidney] stones. For more than three months I have been struggling in vain to get permission to bring him food that is not standard prison fare, i.e., not exclusively meat, but also fruit, cheese, cottage cheese, fish, vegetables. He is on his fourth month of a meat diet, which he was absolutely prohibited from having by all the doctors who were treating him here and abroad. There can be no justification for damaging irreversibly a scholar's health and ability to work because of strict adherence to a prison diet. I ask you, Anatolii Vasil'evich, to help change the conditions of my husband's incarceration so that I might be permitted to deliver him the dietetic foods he needs for his health. I enclose the testimony of Dr. Gorash, who performed two operations on my husband.
Ol'ga Tarle.

May 7, 1930

Naberezhnaia 9-ogo IAnvaria, 30, 4

May 17, 1933   Phone G 3-85-34
                                                  Kropotkinsk. naber. 3 Dom Uchenykh

Dear and highly esteemed Anatolii Vasil'evich,

My Moscow telephone number is G 3-85-34. I provide it because I could not recall the number precisely when you asked me for it today. I would like to take this opportunity to thank you once again. Both Romain Rolland and S. Charlety, rector of the Sorbonne, asserted from the very beginning of this unfortunate misunderstanding, that you alone would help to eliminate it "to the full benefit of Soviet science." (Words of Charlety, a real friend of the USSR and author of a book about Saint-Simon.)

                                                  Sincerely yours,
                                                  Evg. Tarle

RTSKhIDNI, fond 142, op. 1, d. 647, ll. 31, 31ob, 34.

DOCUMENT 124 *Letter from Bukharin to S. M. Kirov, March 31, 1933, regarding the removal of directors of scientific institutes*

To Comrade Kirov

Dear Sergei Mironovich,

Having recovered from my chronic illness at your place in Leningrad and having returned to Moscow, I am taking the liberty to bother you with the following lines.
Serebrovskii has removed Ol'bert from *NISaliuminii* [Aluminum Scientific Research Institute]. He is telling everybody that he has your agreement in this matter. If this is true, he obviously has not informed you entirely correctly. The Leningraders (present on the commission) were all quite astonished by the obvious prejudice displayed by Serebrovskii's commission. In view of the series of failures in his department, he was looking for a whip-

ping boy and found "the real culprit" in Ol'bert. If I understand anything at all, I really must say that *NISaliuminii*, in terms of the concern shown for it, its construction, its relationship with the industry, and the pace of its scientific research, was one of the very best institutes. Even if it had some shortcomings, who doesn't have? I don't deny it. But to punish the institute for the faults of others isn't right in my opinion. Serebrovskii here obviously has his own reasons. He is a man that "aims from a distance," whose leadership skills, augmented by his knowledge of the situation, form the material basis on which [illegible] "the moral, political, and religious superstructure." In short, today I requested [we] wait for Sergo's arrival, and I beseech you, regardless of what your opinion is in this matter, to delay the final decision until my boss arrives.

On the whole, right now there is not only a slashing of money, but also:

1) continuous removal of people from the institutes ("above all from the institutes," as one of the directives on this subject proclaims);
2) breaking up, altering, splintering, when sometimes I am not even asked; I fear they now will tear up *Mekhanobr* [All-Union Scientific Research and Planning Institute for the Mechanical Processing of Minerals] (which has an excellent director, a Communist and engineer, very thoughtful, Comrade Norkin).
I therefore beg you, as the head of Leningrad, not to allow on the territory under your jurisdiction any unwarranted deviationism, extremism, or other "isms" that would cost us a pretty penny. (Regarding *NISaluminii* Sergo decided that its recently completed building will be handed over to the Main Administration of Geological Exploration, the staff will be reduced from 1,176 to 750 (together with four experimental plants).

      Greetings   Yours N. Bukharin   March 31, 1933

RTSKhIDNI, fond 80, op. 17, d. 64, ll. 19, 20.

Zhdanovshchina

The term *Zhdanovshchina*, translated loosely as the "bad days under Zhdanov," refers to the period after World War II when Soviet cultural policy shifted sharply away from its wartime relaxation back to strict control over content and ideology. The architect of this policy was Andrei Zhdanov, who had succeeded Kirov as Leningrad party boss in 1934, and who by 1945 had emerged as Stalin's chief lieutenant among the party secretaries. He was already active in cultural police work (Document 125) in 1938. The *Zhdanovshchina* proper, however, did not begin until August 1946 as the Cold War was settling in over Europe. The attack began with criticism of two Leningrad monthly literary journals, *Zvezda* [The Star] and *Leningrad*, but it focused in particular on two of the journals' frequent contributors, the satirist Mikhail Zoshchenko and the poet Anna Akhmatova. Zoshchenko had incurred the wrath of the party for stories such as "Adventures of a Monkey," in which a monkey escapes from a zoo during a wartime bombardment, encountering a series of adventures that poked fun at ration cards and other forms of everyday life. Zhdanov denounced Zoshchenko for not being interested "in the labor of Soviet people, in their heroism and high social and moral qualities." Akhmatova, who had gained fame as a poet in the rarified intellectual culture of prerevolutionary St. Petersburg, was attacked for her "amorously erotic themes mingled with sorrow, sadness, nostalgia, death, mysticism, and hopelessness. . . . A mixture of nun and harlot, that's what she is." Some scholars attribute this new assault on intellectuals to Stalin, with Zhdanov acting only as loyal henchman. Nonetheless, the Central Committee resolution reorganizing *Zvezda* and *Leningrad* (Document 126), sometimes attributed to Stalin, is written in Zhdanov's hand.

This initial attack was followed by a broad assault on all manifestations of nonconformity in intellectual life and was reinforced by an increasingly rigid xenophobia. Artists and writers were instructed to infuse their works with political purpose, to utilize their work to inculcate loyalty to the party and the state, and to expose the duplicity of the Western bourgeoisie. In music the world-famous composers Dmitrii Shostakovich and Sergei Prokofiev were criticized in a 1947 Central Committee resolution for "formalist perversions, anti-democratic tendencies which are alien to the Soviet people and their artistic tastes." The master film director, Sergei Eisenstein, incurred Zhdanov's wrath with his portrayal of Ivan the Terrible's secret police as "a gang of degenerates" rather than a "progressive army." Zhdanov dabbled in criticism of Soviet philosophy, and the scientific community also suffered from this new xenophobia, as the documents on the Kliueva-Roskin Affair demonstrate. These two Soviet cancer researchers, engaging in normal open dialogue with international colleagues, were suddenly taken to task for publishing preliminary results in a Western scientific journal and for permitting Americans to visit their research laboratories. The case was serious enough to be discussed at the level of the Politburo: it was one more sign of the dangerous influence of "Western bourgeois culture" and the need for the state to exercise more vigilance over the activities of its intelligentsia.

The *Zhdanovshchina* differed from the assaults on intellectuals in the 1930s in that its victims were not arrested or killed. But they were destroyed in other ways: Zoshchenko and Akhmatova were expelled from the Writers' Union and thus deprived of their right to publish. Zoshchenko died a broken man who never regained his earlier literary brilliance. Akhmatova lived in isolation, resuming her writing only in 1956. Eisenstein, who had won the Stalin Prize for his film *Alexander Nevsky* in 1941, did not recover from the attack on part two of his *Ivan the Terrible* and died in 1948 of heart failure at the age of 52.

A. A. Zhdanov, first secretary of the Leningrad Regional Communist Party Committee and secretary of the Central Committee addressing a meeting of the "October Contemporaries of the City of Lenin," 1935. RTSKhIDNI. Photograph collection.

DOCUMENT 125   *Politburo decision, August 5, 1938, based on Zhdanov's notes, concerning Marietta Shaginian's novel,* Bilet po istorii *(A Ticket through History)*

73. On the novel of Marietta Shaginian *A Ticket through History*, part 1, "The Ul'ianov Family."

Having familiarized itself with part 1 of Marietta Shaginian's novel *A Ticket through History* (subtitled "The Ul'ianov Family") and also with the circumstances of its publication, the Central Committee of the All-Union Communist Party (of Bolsheviks) [*TSK VKP(b)*] has established that the Shaginian book, which purports to be a biographically accurate novel about the life of the Ulianov family and also about the childhood and youth of Lenin, turns out to be a politically harmful and ideologically hostile work. The *TSK* also considers the publication of this work a gross political error on the part of Comrade Ermilov, the editor of *Krasnaia nov'*, and of Comrade Bol'shemennikov, the former director of the State Publishing House of Belles Lettres.

The *TSK* also censures the behavior of Comrade Krupskaia who, upon receiving the manuscript of the novel, not only did not prevent its publication but, on the contrary, encouraged Shaginian, gave the manuscript a favorable review, and supplied Shaginian with factual details of life in the Ulianov family, and thus bears full responsibility for this book.

The committee considers the behavior of Comrade Krupskaia all the more inadmissible and improper because she acted without the knowledge and consent of the committee, behind its back. She thus turned the party-wide task of compiling works about Lenin into a private, family matter and set herself up as the only authoritative source for comment on Lenin and his family in terms of their public and family life and their work. At no time and to no one has the committee given this right.

Accordingly, the committee issues the following resolutions:

(1) Relieve Comrade Ermilov as editor of *Krasnaia nov'*;

(2) Issue a reprimand to the former director of the State Publishing House of Belles Lettres, Comrade Bol'shemennikov;

(3) Point out to Comrade Krupskaia her errors;

(4) Prohibit publication of works about Lenin without the knowledge and consent of the Central Committee of the All-Union Communist Party (Bolshevik);

(5) Withdraw the Shaginian book from circulation;

(6) Recommend to the Board of the Union of Soviet Writers that it issue a reprimand to Shaginian.

[The original of this document is in the hand of Zhdanov.]

RTSKhIDNI, fond 17, op. 1, d. 873, ll. 1–4.

DOCUMENT 126   *Notes written by Zhdanov, ca. August 14, 1946, for a draft of a decree by the Central Committee concerning the journals* Zvezda *and* Leningrad

1. The editorial staff of the magazine *Zvezda* [Star] and the board of the Union of Soviet Writers are required to take measures to eliminate totally all the errors and deficiencies of this journal, as described in the present resolution. The political course of the magazine should be corrected and a high ideological and artistic standard should be secured. This can be achieved by eliminating publication of the contributions by Zoshchenko, Akhmatova and similar writers.

2. Considering the fact that at present conditions do not support publication of two literary-artistic journals in Leningrad, cease publication of the journal *Leningrad* and concentrate all literary talents available in the city in the magazine *Zvezda*.

3. For the purpose of bringing order to the functioning of the magazine's editorial office and significantly improving the contents of *Zvezda*, an editor in chief should be selected who will supervise the editorial staff. It should be stated that the editor in chief would be fully responsible for the ideological and political course of the journal, as well as for the quality of published material.

4. Confirm Comrade Egolin as editor in chief of the magazine *Zvezda*.

5. Instruct the Union of Soviet Writers to review and confirm the head editors of various departments of the journal, as well as the full editorial staff.

6. Cancel the decision of the City Committee [*GK*] of Leningrad, issued June 26, regarding the editorial staff of *Zvezda*, as politically incorrect. Reprimand the second *GK* secretary, Comrade Kapustin, for making such a decision.

7. Dismiss the secretary for propaganda from his job [illegible] and place him at the disposition of the Central Committee.

8. Place the *Oblast'* Committee [*OK*] of the city of Leningrad in charge of the party management of *Zvezda*. Make the *OK* and Comrade Popkov (?) personally responsible for undertaking all necessary steps to improve the journal's quality and strengthen ideological and political activity among the writers of Leningrad.

9. Reprimand Comrade Likharev for the poor management of the magazine *Leningrad*.

10. Require the board of directors of the Union of the Soviet Writers to take an active part in the improvement of *Zvezda* by extending regularly its expert help to the editors and by attracting a larger number of writers, even from outside Leningrad.

11. Taking into consideration the fact that the journal *Zvezda* appears with considerable delay, that its appearance and cover are not attractive, that there is no indication of the publication date of the next issue, the editors of the magazine *Zvezda* should be made fully responsible for its timely publication and attractive external appearance.

12. Place the Department of Propaganda of the Central Committee (Comrade Aleksandrov) in charge of verifying the implementation of this resolution of the Central Committee.

13. Request the editor in chief of *Zvezda* to submit in 2 months a complete progress report to the Organizational Bureau of the Central Committee.

[Draft of a decree by the Central Committee. No signature; no date.]

[The first 4 points of this resolution were published in *Pravda*, August 21, 1946. The resolution is in the hand of Zhdanov.]

RTSKhIDNI, fond 77, op. 1, d. 979, ll. 182, 183.

DOCUMENT 127 *Summary of an address by Zhdanov to the Writers' Conference, ca. August 16, 1946, on the journals* Zvezda *and* Leningrad, *including critical comments on the writers Zoshchenko and Akhmatova*

Summary of an address
delivered at the Writers' Conference

The Central Committee has made a decision on the journals *Zvezda* and *Leningrad*.

I have been assigned to clarify this decision in Leningrad.

Permit me to reveal the shortcomings of the journal *Zvezda*. Its most jarring error is allowing Zoshchenko space on its pages. His "Adventures of a Monkey" depicts people as loafers, freaks. He digs around in petty everyday life. There is not one positive type. The monkey plays the role of judge of the order of things. Preaches morals. "It is more secure to live in a cage." Who is Zoshchenko? His physiognomy. The Serapion brothers.

A vulgar man. His works are an emetic. In his person there emerges on the arena a lowly, limited, petty bourgeois, Philistine. His story "Before the Sunrise" is disgraceful. This renegade and degenerate is dictating literary tastes in Leningrad. He has a swarm of patrons. He is a foul, slimy scavenger.

Zoshchenko during the war. A man without morals, without conscience.

He does not like our ways.

He pines for others. Should we adapt our ways, our morals to Zoshchenko's? Let him himself adapt. If he doesn't want to, let him get out of Soviet literature.

The second to become "persona grata" [sic] is Akhmatova, a representative of poetry devoid of ideals, foreign to Soviet literature.

Gorky said that the decade 1907–1917 deserves the name the saddest, the most shameless decade in the history of the Russian intelligentsia.

Akhmatova is its representative.

RTSKhIDNI, fond 77, op. 1, d. 979, ll. 1,2.

DOCUMENT 128   *Order from the USSR Council of Ministers, August 27, 1946, to remove works by Zoshchenko and Akhmatova from bookstores and libraries*

Secret
copy No. 81

ORDER

Of the Representative of the Council of Ministers of the USSR for the protection of military and state secrets in the press.

Moscow   No. 42/1629s   August 27, 1946

§ 1.

Withdraw the following books from the book distribution network and public libraries:
Zoshchenko M. M. - *Stories.* Pub. by *Pravda*, Moscow, 1946, 46 pp., edition of 100,000 copies.

"   "   " - *Selected Works, 1923–1945. Goslitizdat*, Leningrad, 1946, 660 pp., edition of 30,000 copies.

"   "   " - *Essays, stories, novellas.* Published by *Lenizdat*, Leningrad, 1946, edition of 10,000 copies.

§ 2.

Suspend production and distribution of the following books:

Akhmatova A. A. - *Poems 1909–1945. Goslitizdat*, Leningrad, 1946, 340 pp., edition of 10,000 copies.

"   "   " - *Selected poems, 1910–1946.* Published by *Pravda*, Moscow, 1946. 48 pp., printing of 100,000 copies.

A. A. Zhdanov on vacation at the Black Sea resort of Sochi, January 1947. RTSKhIDNI. Photograph collection

Representative of the Council of Ministers of the USSR for the protection of military and state secrets in the press

1880
95 copies
zl

K. Omelchenko.

DOCUMENT 129   *Directive from the Leningrad Oblast' Committee, July 2, 1948, criticizing the editorial work of the journal* Zvezda

<u>Proletarians of All Countries, Unite!</u>

LENINGRAD *OBLAST'* COMMITTEE
OF THE ALL-RUSSIAN COMMUNIST PARTY (BOLSHEVIK) [*VKP(b)*]

No BO-334/1s <u>STRICTLY SECRET</u>
July 2, 1948

<u>DIRECTIVE</u>
of the Bureau of the Leningrad *Oblast'* Committee
of the *VKP(b)*
<u>June 4, 1948</u>

<u>ON THE WORK OF THE JOURNAL *ZVEZDA*</u>

Having heard and discussed the report of Comrade Druzin, the editor in chief of *Zvezda,* the bureau of the *oblast'* committee [*obkom*] of the *VKP(b)* noted that the directive of the Central Committee [*TSK*] of the *VKP(b)* of August 14, 1946, "On the Journals *Zvezda* and *Leningrad*" has led to radical changes in *Zvezda's* work, which have contributed to a remarkable improvement in its ideological and literary quality.

The journal has published ideologically and artistically important works by Soviet writers who have won Stalin Prizes, including the novels of E. Grin, *South Wind,* and V. Ketlinskaia, *Under Siege,* the plays of Konstantin Simonov, *The Russian Question,* and N. Virt, *Our Daily Bread,* and A. IAkobson's *Life in the Citadel* and *The War Without a Front.* The journal has published a number of works in translation by progressive foreign writers, including *Deep Are the Roots,* the politically penetrating play by the American playwrights Gow and D'Usseau and the posthumous memoirs of the Czech Communist J. Fucík, *Reporting with a Noose Around My Neck,* and others.

The journal's poetry department has made a useful contribution in introducing the readers to the work of poets from the fraternal republics, the Far East, the Urals, and so forth.

The journal has extensively advocated the ideas of party-mindedness in literature and has published a number of important critical articles opposing the lack of ideology and political apathy in literature.

At the same time, the *obkom* bureau noted that recently there has been a marked decline in the journal's quality with respect to its ideological and political content and the literary quality of its works.

In recent issues of *Zvezda* the prose department has been filled with mediocre works of little literary value which have not measured up to the growing demands of the readers and has left a mark of mediocrity on the entire journal. In the last six months the journal has failed to publish a single work which could be considered one of the best this year. The journal's publication of K. Vanin's ideologically and artistically immature *Father,* which provides an inaccurate portrait of the conduct of Soviet citizens in enemy-occupied territory, should be considered an error on the part of the editorial board.

Zvezda's presentation of such an important prose genre as literary essays on leading factories, the outstanding Stakhanovites of the postwar five-year plan, prominent people in the collectivized village, and major figures in Soviet science, culture, and the arts has also been poor. The journal has failed to use the essay as a flexible form for portraying the energetic postwar reconstruction of Leningrad, which is in the vanguard of the new Stalinist five-year plan.

Much of the poetry published in *Zvezda* is dreary in content and mediocre in form. These poems are still failing to reflect the creative postwar efforts of the Soviet people, especially the citizens of Leningrad. The journal has failed to publish any lyric poetry which would reflect the high moral character of the Soviet person, the breadth of his feelings and experiences, his attitudes towards people, towards his natural environment, and so forth.

The journal is also doing a poor job of publishing the most important works in translation by progressive foreign writers, first and foremost Slavic writers and poets.

The quality of the criticism department has especially deteriorated in recent issues and has lost its militant edge. The journal is no longer playing the role of a center of the fight against the formalist theories of a number of Leningrad literary critics and has not joined in the Soviet press criticism of the major shortcomings in Fadeev's novel *The Young Guard,* Simonov's story *The Smoke of the Fatherland,* and so forth. A number of critical articles and reviews have been objectivist and "evasive" in nature.

The journal's "art" department is practically defunct.

The primary reason behind *Zvezda*'s failure to keep up with the requirements of the party and the growing demands of its readers is major deficiencies in the work of the journal's editorial board.

The new editorial board, headed by Comrade Druzin, the editor in chief, has failed to follow the guidelines set forth by the historic *TSK VKP(b)* directive "On the Journals *Zvezda* and *Leningrad,*" has failed to implement this directive satisfactorily, and has not taken steps to correct the major deficiencies in its work. It has not eradicated any and all manifestations of cliques in the editorial board and among the Leningrad writers by faithfully implementing the *TSK VKP(b)* directive, nor promoted genuine collegiality and participation by all members of the editorial board, nor encouraged all Leningrad writers to take part in improving the journal. Instead Comrade Druzin, the editor in chief, and Comrade Prokof'ev, a member of the editorial board and the chairman of the Leningrad Branch of the Soviet Writers' Union, have allowed cliques, discord, and unprincipled backbiting to reemerge at *Zvezda* and in the Writers' Union and have even stooped so low as to betray the interests of the journal to narrow clique interests. All of this has had a negative impact on the journal and has naturally resulted in a decline in its ideological and literary quality.

Until recently the editorial board has not functioned in a properly organized manner and there has not been the proper coordination and collegiality in discussing the selection of material for publication.

Comrade Druzin, the editor in chief, has made no effort to unite prominent literary men and the city's literary community around the editorial board and has failed to demonstrate the proper fastidiousness and scruples in selecting material for publication.

The editorial board has not taken the necessary steps to recruit leading Soviet and Leningrad writers to work on the journal. Soviet citizens who could provide a wealth of interesting and enlightening accounts of what they have seen and experienced have also not been asked to take part in the journal. [break in the text]

4. The bureau of the *obkom* of the *VKP(b)* would like to emphasize in particular that *Zvezda* should be a vital concern for the entire Leningrad writers' organization and hereby orders the journal's editorial board and the Board of the Leningrad *Oblast'* Soviet Writers' Union to take effective steps to recruit leading Leningrad writers, poets, and critics to work on the journal and call on each of them to publish their latest and best works this year in the journal.

The bureau would like to make it clear to the writers of Leningrad that an ongoing improvement in the ideological and literary quality of *Zvezda* is a matter of literary honor for them and their duty to their country and their native city. They must justify the confidence expressed by the *TSK VKP(b)* that the Leningrad contingent of Soviet writers will once again occupy a worthy place in the ranks of Soviet literature by demonstrating greater concern for the journal *Zvezda*.

5. The bureau calls on the board of the Leningrad *Oblast'* Soviet Writers' Union to hold regular discussions of *Zvezda* at its board meetings, section meetings, and general assemblies of the members of the union involving reader participation, conduct critical reviews and discussions of the most important literary works published in the journal, and organize creative discussions of the important literary and artistic questions raised in the journal *Zvezda*.

The bureau deems it necessary to hold *Zvezda* readers' conferences at major industrial plants, libraries, houses of culture, intelligentsia clubs, and institutions of higher learning at least once every two months.

6. The bureau requests the board of the Union of Soviet Writers of the USSR (Comrade Fadeev) to exercise greater leadership over *Zvezda* and provide effective assistance to the journal's editorial board on a regular basis, and take the appropriate actions to recruit leading writers from Moscow and elsewhere in the country to work on the journal.

7. The bureau suggests that the editor in chief of *Zvezda* institute the necessary order in the proceedings of the editorial board, hire qualified staff members, and provide all the proper conditions for creative assistance to novice writers (to include consultation with editorial board members, prompt reviews of submitted manuscripts, and so forth). The editorial board should work towards the goal of making sure that every major work is reviewed by all the members of the editorial board, to include their written opinions, before it is accepted for publication in the journal.

8. The bureau requests the permission of the *TSK VKP(b)* to include leading writers and critics of Leningrad on the editorial board of *Zvezda* in order to improve the board and the journal.

9. In light of the fact that the Evgeniia Sokolova Printing Plant does not have the necessary capacity to print the journal's press runs quickly, the bureau hereby assigns the task of printing the journal to the Volodarskii Plant starting with the September 1948 issue. Comrade Anisimov, the director of the Leningrad Publishing House, and Comrade Fridliand, the director of the printing plant, are instructed to make sure that each issue of the journal is published on time. The bureau orders that each issue of the journal should be published no later than the 15th of its respective month.

Secretary of the *Obkom*
of the *VKP(b)*

[SEAL OF LENINGRAD *OBLAST'* COMMITTEE]

Copies to: *TSK VKP(b)*
               Department of Propaganda and Agitation
               Comrades Sintsov and Prokof'ev (Leningrad Branch of the
               Soviet Writers' Union)
               Comrade Druzin (*Zvezda*)
               Comrade Fadeev (Board of the Soviet Writers' Union)
               Comrades Smolovik and Dzerzhinsky
               (*Raion* Committee of the *VKP(b)*)

               Paragraph 9 to:
               Comrade Anisimov (Leningrad Publishing House)
               Comrade Fridliand (Volodarskii Printing Plant)

RTSKhIDNI, fond 17, op. 132, d. 78, ll. 5

DOCUMENT 130   *Report on the visit to the Institute of Epidemiology by U.S. Ambassador Smith, with comments by Zhdanov, August 3, 1946*

[Illegible Stamp]

[Largely illegible handwritten note from Zhdanov to Dekanozov]

TO THE SECRETARIES
OF THE CENTRAL
COMMITTEE OF THE
ALL-RUSSIAN
COMMUNIST PARTY
(BOLSHEVIK) [*TSK VKP(b)*]

Comrade A. A. ZhDANOV
Comrade A. A. KUZNETSOV
Comrade N. S. PATOLIChEV
Comrade G. M. POPOV

Report on The Circumstances Surrounding the Visit of
the American Ambassador to the Soviet Union,
Smith, To the Institute of Epidemiology,
Microbiology, and Infectious Diseases

On June 20 the American ambassador to the Soviet Union, Smith, visited the institute at which Professors Kliueva and Roskin are developing an anticancer vaccine.

Three days before his visit to the institute Smith visited Academician Abrikosov, who in Smith's presence called Professor Kliueva on the telephone and asked her to receive Smith and discuss her work with him. Professor Kliueva agreed to let Smith visit the institute. Then Smith visited the Minister of Public Health of the USSR, Comrade Miterev, and made the same request. Comrade Miterev gave his consent to the visit and called Professor Kliueva on the telephone to inform her that Smith was on his way.

Comrade Miterev first asked the Minister of Foreign Affairs, Comrade Zarubin, for his consent to Smith's visit. Comrade Zarubin gave his approval. Comrade Miterev also consulted with Comrade Lozovskii on the subject.

Smith's conversation with Professors Roskin and Kliueva took place in the office of the director of the institute, in the presence of Professor Timakov and Comrade Rabinovich, a representative of the Red Cross who speaks English. Smith never visited Professors Kliueva and Roskin's laboratory.

Both Smith and his interpreter were well informed of Professors Kliueva and Roskin's discoveries and research. From his questions and from his knowledgeable and correct use of highly specialized terminology, it was clear that Smith was well aware of the history and importance of the discovery.

Smith asked Professor Kliueva if she needed any help getting equipment. Smith made more sweeping and specific proposals "to join the efforts of American and Soviet scientists in the fight against cancer on behalf of mankind" to Comrade Miterev. As Smith envisioned it, Professors Kliueva and Roskin would provide the ideas and the concepts, whose value American and other scientists have already recognized, and America would provide equipment, microscopes, and so forth.

Comrade Ogol'tsov, the Deputy Minister of State Security of the USSR, believes that the interview between Smith and Professors Kliueva and Roskin was arranged in a proper manner.

Assistant Director of the
Personnel Department of the
TSK VKP(b)

[signed] (Andreev)

August 3, 1946

4-vshch

RTSKhIDNI, fond 77, op. 3, d. 147, ll. 1–2.

DOCUMENT 131   *Letter from Professors Kliueva and Roskin to Zhdanov, November 15, 1946,*
imploring him to improve conditions for their research on a cancer vaccine

SECRET

Moscow, November 15, 1946

Dear Andrei Aleksandrovich,

We have an important request to make of you—that you give your personal attention to the fate of our cancer research. Thanks to your help in May and June of this year, steps were taken permitting us to work normally. We were given sufficient staff and allotted laboratory facilities. So the impression was created that everything had been taken care of for the work of professors N. G. Kliueva and G. I. Roskin. But the matter of assistance was not carried through to the end. We received premises that do not give us the opportunity to set up a vivarium for laboratory animals or a hospital for our patients. More importantly, as before we are deprived of the <u>most necessary</u> instruments and reagents. We are working in <u>shameful</u> conditions of <u>scientific poverty.</u>

To the above must be added that the Americans, having found out about our research from the medical press, organized a special project on the same topic at the U.S.A. National Cancer Institute over a year ago, and well-known specialists were provided to head it.

For more than a year American researchers have systematically requested to come here and study our discoveries on the spot, especially after they obtained early corroborations in laboratory experiments. At the present time <u>three prominent</u> researchers who have been detailed by the U.S. government to work in our laboratory are awaiting visas.

U.S. Ambassador Smith, having visited the Academy of Medical Sciences vice president, the Minister of Health, and then us to discuss our work, proposed:
    a) to deliver by airplane all American technology necessary for our work,
    b) to work jointly on the "KR" problem together with American scientists.

On November 11 of this year, the deputy minister of the Union Ministry of Health told us that Viacheslav Mikhailovich Molotov gave instructions to send to Smith's U.S.A. address our book, *Cancer Biotherapy*, finished this fall and now at the publisher. Considering the interest in the U.S.A., the book will, of course, be published quickly. Work is going on there, and will certainly be expanded after concrete familiarization with our experiments. That they take up this work only enhances the authority of Soviet science, for our research really is a new and legitimate scientific endeavor.

But we, those very Soviet specialists now in the forefront, will <u>undoubtedly</u> be left <u>far behind</u> in the confusion, frequent trivialities, lack of minimal resources and technical equipment, wasting our efforts, knowledge, and experience not in the struggle with scientific problems, but with purely economic and bureaucratic difficulties.

We would not have troubled you with this, as we have not done in the many years of our previous work, if we were not now <u>fully convinced</u>:

    1) that a deep sense of our duty to the sick will not allow us to let this matter drift;
    2) that, deprived of instruments, instead of benefitting Soviet science we can only compromise it;
    3) that the request of minimal equipment (complete and modern) is fully justified.

With deepest respect,

    Associate Member
    USSR Academy of Medical Sciences
    [signed] Prof. Kliueva

Lomonosov Moscow State University
[signed] Prof. Roskin

[Handwritten notes, top left]
Com. Beria L. P.
Com. Mikoyan A. I.
Com. Voznesenskii N. A.

Request you familiarize yourselves with this. I think we need to discuss this issue.

November 19 Zhdanov

RTSKhIDNI, fond 77, op. 3, d. 148, ll. 7–8.

DOCUMENT 132   *Report from Zhdanov, May 7, 1947, on the case of the scientists Kliueva amd Roskin*

[Handwritten Note]

Comrade Stalin

I am forwarding my draft of a letter from the Party Committee of the Ministry of Public Health addressed to Minister Smirnov requesting that Professors Kliueva and Roskin be brought before a party honor court.

A. Zhdanov

May 7, 1947

TO THE MINISTER OF PUBLIC HEALTH OF THE USSR
Comrade E. I. SMIRNOV

The party organization of the Ministry of Public Health of the USSR possesses information which gives us reason to believe that two employees of the Ministry of Public Health, Professors Kliueva and Roskin, have committed a number of antistate and unpatriotic acts which have demeaned their honor and dignity as Soviet scientists and citizens.

As you are aware, Professors Kliueva and Roskin, who have been working on a cancer vaccine for more than 15 years, have achieved very remarkable initial results. They developed the *KR* preparation, whose preliminary trials involving treatment of several forms of cancer have given evidence indicating that they have made a discovery of the utmost scientific importance, which could spark a revolution in cancer treatment. Until now, science has been unable to provide a single effective medicine for treating cancer.

We also know that the antistate and unpatriotic actions of the former Minister of Public Health (Miterev) and the blatant crimes of the former Secretary of the Academy of Medical Sciences, Parin, who proved to be an American spy, resulted in the transfer of the *KR* preparation and its manufacturing process to the Americans in late 1946. This transfer threatened the Soviet lead in this field and caused considerable harm to our national interests.

So what exactly did the disreputable actions of Professors Kliueva and Roskin involve?

The actions of Kliueva and Roskin resulted in disclosure of the secrets of the *KR* preparation and its transfer to the Americans.

1. As early as 1945 and the first part of 1946, when the first successes in the use of *KR* to treat cancer pa-

tients were noted, Kliueva and Roskin, instead of maintaining the secrecy of their research, particularly if we consider the fact that their discovery was in an embryonic stage and had not undergone comprehensive clinical trials, began to publicize their research and disseminate information on it abroad for the sake of their own personal reputations. Thus foreign, primarily American, intelligence began to take a greater interest in Kliueva and Roskin's experiments and the work of their laboratory.

2. In their quest for personal popularity, Kliueva and Roskin proved to be completely defenseless at a later time, when they and their laboratory came under a genuine assault by American intelligence. In a very short time, starting in June 1946, Kliueva and Roskin were visited by the American ambassador to the USSR, Smith, the American academician Waxman, and the American professors Mead [?] and Leslie. All of them appeared at Kliueva and Roskin's laboratory with persistent requests for detailed information on Kliueva and Roskin's research and brazen offers of "assistance" in any amount. In exchange for this "assistance," which in essence was nothing less than bribery, the Americans asked Kliueva and Roskin to "cooperate" with American cancer researchers by giving them the *KR* preparation and its manufacturing formula with all subsequent modifications.

These meetings and interviews with the Americans culminated in Kliueva and Roskin's agreement to give Parin, the former Secretary of the Academy of Medical Sciences and an American spy, a manuscript entitled *Biotherapeutic Ways of Treating Cancer,* a description of the *KR* manufacturing process, and 10 vials of the preparation itself, before Parin's trip to America. Parin turned these items over to the Americans after he arrived in America.

The party organization considers this conduct on the part of Kliueva and Roskin disreputable, antistate, and unpatriotic. These individuals, who worked in a Soviet laboratory financed with Soviet funds for 15 years and received the attention and care of the Soviet government, were obligated to turn the fruits of their research over to the Soviet state and not to foreigners. Kliueva and Roskin released secrets of their own Soviet state. They willingly allowed the Americans to visit their laboratory. They let interviews take place which were harmful to the interests of the Soviet state. Finally, they committed the shameful act of giving Parin their manuscript, manufacturing process, and the preparation itself so he could turn it over to the Americans. This act, which demeaned the honor and dignity of a Soviet citizen, was also harmful to the interests of the Soviet state and Soviet science, because the transfer of the manufacturing formula for the *KR* preparation also meant that the Soviet Union would lose its lead in this field.

3. The Party Committee considers Kliueva and Roskin's attempt to deceive and hoodwink the government no less disreputable.

We know that as soon as a government investigation of the incident was initiated, Kliueva and Roskin apparently guessed that their conduct might be considered antistate, and in explaining their behavior they did everything they could to conceal the truth of the affair from the government, devalue the importance of the manuscript turned over to the Americans, and act as if the manuscript provided absolutely no key to the *KR* manufacturing process. In their account, because Parin did not turn the manufacturing process itself over to the Americans, the mere transfer of the manuscript was supposedly trivial. The Party Committee possesses information which indicates that the manuscript contained all the information needed to conduct the necessary experiments and thus revealed the secrets of the technology. Thus, Kliueva and Roskin's testimony was false and intended to deceive the Soviet government.

We should also mention that according to our information, Professors Kliueva and Roskin received gifts—bribes in the form of two parcels from the American spy Leslie—for their services to the Americans in revealing the secrets of the *KR* preparation.

In light of the above, the Party Committee of the Ministry of Public Health of the USSR believes that Professors Kliueva and Roskin have committed antistate, unpatriotic acts which are unworthy of Soviet citizens and have demeaned the honor and dignity of the Soviet state and the Soviet people.

Professors Kliueva and Roskin preferred to maintain relations with the Americans over going to the Soviet government and tried to conceal the transfer of their discovery to foreigners from the government in an attempt to deceive the government and cover up all the severe consequences of this undignified affair.

The transfer of the discovery to the Americans took place under the banner of a phony humanism, because any arguments that medical science should be guided by humane considerations are absolutely incapable of justifying the acts they committed. Everyone knows that the Americans have never and will never transfer their medical discoveries out of any sort of humanitarian motives . . . [illegible] Kliueva and Roskin must have been aware of this, but this didn't keep them from turning over the fruits of their long years of research, which was the property of the Soviet people and the Soviet state, to the Americans. ~~Thus Professors Kliueva and Roskin conducted themselves not as patriots and true Soviet citizens, but as persons bowing and scraping before foreigners.~~

The Party Committee of the Ministry of Public Health of the USSR believes that the actions of Professors Kliueva and Roskin fall within the jurisdiction of the Honor Court. On this basis, the Party Committee considers it necessary to bring Professors N. G. Kliueva and G. I. Roskin before the Honor Court of the Ministry of Public Health of the USSR.

Signatures of the secretary
and members of the Party Committee

RTSKhIDNI, fond 77, op. 3, d. 150, ll. 1, 8–11.

DOCUMENT 133 *Report by Zhdanov on the Kliueva/Roskin Affair, 1947*

TO THE FIRST SECRETARIES OF PARTY *OBLAST'* COMMITTEES,
KRAI COMMITTEES, CITY COMMITTEES,
AND *RAION* COMMITTEES,
THE CENTRAL COMMITTEES OF THE UNION REPUBLICS
THE MINISTRIES OF THE USSR,
THE DIRECTORS OF CENTRAL AGENCIES, AND
THE SECRETARIES OF THE PARTY ORGANIZATIONS
OF THE MINISTRIES OF THE USSR

The Central Committee [*TSK*] of the All-Union Communist Party (Bolshevik) [*VKP(b)*] has recently uncovered a number of facts which indicate that certain members of the Soviet intelligentsia have engaged in behavior unworthy of Soviet people by their fawning and servility to foreigners and the contemporary reactionary culture of the bourgeois West. One of the most shameful examples of this is the case of Professors Kliueva and Roskin, which was examined in June of this year by an Honor Court at the Ministry of Public Health of the USSR.

Because of the great political significance and instructive value of the Kliueva and Roskin case, the *TSK VKP(b)* has paid special attention to it and has closely followed its progress; from start to finish, it has considered it essential to report on the case to the party organizations.

The *TSK VKP(b)* is forwarding the following documents from the Honor Court at the Ministry of Public Health concerning the case of Kliueva and Roskin: the statement of the ministry's party organization, the stenographer's transcript of the proceedings, the speech of the procurator at the court, and the decision of the court. The *TSK VKP(b)* requests that you peruse these materials and the following letter signed by members of *oblast'* and *krai* party committees, members of the Central Committees of the Communist Parties of the union republics, and the party organizations of the ministries of the USSR, the central agencies, higher educational institutions, academies, and research institutes.

The materials of the Honor Court give a complete picture of this unprecedented case. Professors Kliueva and Roskin, with the acquiescence of Miterev, the former minister of public health, and with the active participation of an American spy, Parin, a former secretary at the Academy of Medical Sciences, turned over to the Americans an important discovery of Soviet science, a preparation for treating cancer, which Professors Kliueva and

Roskin had worked to develop for fifteen years in a Soviet laboratory at government expense. Driven mostly by personal fame and cheap popularity abroad, they were unable to withstand the flattery and promises of the American intelligence agents and turned over a major scientific breakthrough to the American capitalists to enhance their power and wealth. They ignored the basic interests of the Soviet state and the Soviet people. They betrayed their sacred duty to their homeland, which had attended to and nurtured them. With these antistate, unpatriotic deeds, Kliueva and Roskin jeopardized the leadership of Soviet science in this field and seriously harmed the national interests of the Soviet Union.

As it has been demonstrated, the vile deed of Professors Kliueva and Roskin is primarily the result of their servility toward decadent bourgeois culture, their fawning obsequiousness to foreigners. Only people who do not respect the dignity and worthiness of the Soviet scientist, who lack the feeling of Soviet patriotism, and who grovel before foreigners, people for whom the interests of bourgeois culture and science—inimical to us—took precedence over the welfare of their homeland and their own countrymen could embark on such an unworthy, despicable path.

The *TSK VKP(b)* has discovered that the case of Kliueva and Roskin is no isolated incident or coincidence and that there have been other incidents of unworthy behavior by certain Soviet citizens.

Last year, in resolutions concerning the journals *Zvezda* [The Star] and *Leningrad* and the repertoires of drama theaters, the *TSK VKP(b)* decisively condemned the bowing and scraping to the modern bourgeois culture of the West on the part of several of our writers and artistic workers. Despite the serious warnings of the *TSK VKP(b)*, however, Soviet scientists were found who were so infected with the vile sense of inferiority to foreigners that our most treasured patriotic sentiments and the welfare of the homeland and the Soviet people were of no consequence to them. This means that the evil and dangerous disease of worshipping foreign countries and bourgeois culture and science has spread to a certain segment of our intelligentsia.

So where are the roots of this disease? Why do the Soviet people, who have carried out a socialist revolution, opened a new age in the history of mankind, built socialism—the most advanced and ideal system for human life—and demonstrated the unparalleled depth of their patriotic feelings in the Great Patriotic War, still have some people in their midst who are capable of national self-abasement, losing their sense of dignity, and bowing and scraping to perform the lowest and most mercenary dirty work of the foreign capitalists? Where do certain Soviet citizens pick up these attitudes of fawning over and worshipping foreigners?

The roots of these kinds of unpatriotic attitudes and deeds by some Soviet citizens lie in the past, in tsarist Russia. For decades and decades the ruling reactionary classes of tsarist Russia, for their own egoistic class interests, drummed into the heads of the intelligentsia and the people all sorts of unpatriotic notions and feelings undermining their human dignity, feelings of permanent dependency on foreigners—grovelling before and worshipping them.

The exploiting classes of tsarist Russia, who were detached from the Russian people and hostile to them, tried to demean the great accomplishments of the Russian people, refused to believe in their creative potential, and would not allow Russia to pull itself out of backwardness by its own efforts. They licked the boots of foreigners. Hence, it is no coincidence that the Russian nobility in the 18th and 19th centuries had lost and betrayed their national traditions to such an extent that they essentially forgot their native language, spoke French almost exclusively, and slavishly copied French fashions. Subsequently the worship of French customs and French culture by Russia's ruling classes gave way to bowing down to the Germans.

The intelligentsia in tsarist Russia was brought up to feel unworthy, inferior to the outside world. Russian science and culture were not supported by the ruling classes because of this bootlicking of foreigners. The greatest discoveries of Russian scientists were handed over to foreigners or were stolen by the latter. Lomonosov's great discoveries in chemistry were attributed to Lavoisier; the invention of radio by the great Russian scientist Popov was credited to the Italian Marconi; and the same thing happened with IAblochkov's discovery, and with many others.

Both the policies and ideology of the Russian land owners and capitalists were aimed not at ensuring the political, economic, and cultural independence of Russia but at perpetuating the country's backwardness and making it a colony of West European imperialism.

Obviously the policy of the Russian ruling classes was quite advantageous for the foreign imperialists, because it made it easier for them to exploit the riches of Russia for their own selfish purposes and interests. They did everything they could to implant and encourage the ideology of foreigner worship in Russia.

The Great October Socialist Revolution cut off this path of economic, political, and spiritual enslavement of the country by foreign capital, which was destroying the peoples of Russia. The laborers of our country, casting off the dominance of the land owners and capitalists and installing their own Soviet rule, have achieved political independence from the capitalist world. Having built a strong socialist industrial base and a progressive collectivized agriculture, they have achieved economic independence from the bourgeois states. By carrying out a cultural revolution and creating its own Soviet intelligentsia, our people have shattered Russia's former spiritual dependence on the bourgeois West and have totally eliminated the foundations on which all sorts of servility and obsequiousness arise. But obsequiousness to foreign culture still exists among certain Soviet citizens as a loathsome relic of the past.

Such are the roots of the intolerable disease of obsequiousness to foreigners among certain Soviet citizens.

The *TSK VKP(b)* is paying heed to the fact that given the hostility of capitalist states toward the Soviet Union, unpatriotic and antistate deeds and displays of lackeyism and servility toward bourgeois culture pose a serious danger for the development of Soviet science and culture, for the entire endeavor of building socialism. We must keep in mind that international reactionary forces strive to support in every way and revive these very harmful relics of capitalism in the people's consciousness so as to weaken the Soviet state and demoralize ideologically and politically the most vulnerable Soviet citizens. And, as the Kliueva and Roskin case demonstrates, people infected with a slavish attitude of obsequiousness toward bourgeois culture become an easy target for foreign agents.

So what conclusions should our party organizations draw from the case of Kliueva and Roskin?

1. Grovelling and servility to Western bourgeois culture still exist to some extent. Therefore, party organizations have the very important task of educating all Soviet citizens, especially the intelligentsia, in the spirit of Soviet patriotism, devotion to the interests of the Soviet state, and in the spirit of intolerance for any worship of the depraved culture of the bourgeois West. They must constantly imbue Soviet citizens with a sense of national pride and their own worth and eradicate any and all traces of grovelling to the foreign world. Party organizations should constantly remind our people of Comrade Stalin's saying that even "the most humble Soviet citizen, who is free of the chains of capital, stands head and shoulders above any high-ranking foreign bureaucrat dragging the yoke of capitalist slavery on his shoulders."

2. By resolution of the *TSK VKP(b)* and the Council of Ministers of the USSR, Honor Courts have been set up in the ministries and central agencies of the USSR. The purpose of these courts is to promote the education of employees in state agencies in a spirit of Soviet patriotism, devotion to the welfare of the Soviet state, and a keen awareness of their civic and social duty. As early experience in their operation has shown, Honor Courts are a highly successful method of combatting the worship of bourgeois ideology and effective means of inculcating patriotism in our employees. Therefore, the party organizations of the ministries and central agencies of the USSR must skillfully use these courts in their political work.

3. The case of Kliueva and Roskin has revealed that certain echelons of our government and party apparatus have suffered an intolerable lapse in vigilance and have become complacent and lethargic. In the face of hostile capitalist encirclement, some of our people are acting not like statesmen but like unscrupulous, apolitical hustlers who have lost their Bolshevik edge. This is the only way to explain the fact that former minister of public health Miterev not only overlooked the shameful actions of Kliueva and Roskin but essentially arranged for their contact with Americans.

It is the task of the party organizations to heighten the vigilance of all our workers, to arm the Soviet people against the intrigues of foreign agents, to uncover the insidious techniques and methods of bourgeois secret services. Any of our people who have dealings with foreigners should act proud and independent, in a way befitting Soviet people, and not bow and scrape before them.

4. The case of Kliueva and Roskin has also revealed the deficiencies of party and political work at the ministries. This effort is not focused, is not aimed at inculcating in workers of state agencies a spirit of Soviet patriotism, and basically is limited to various sorts of campaigns. This major deficiency in the work of the party organizations of the ministries should be stamped out in the most decisive manner possible.

CENTRAL COMMITTEE OF THE VKP(b)

[The original typewritten document, translated here, was heavily edited in Zhdanov's hand, primarily stylistically. Because some of Zhdanov's emendations are illegible, this translation preserves the wording of the original typed draft.]

RTSKhIDNI, fond 77, op. 3, d. 153, ll. 1–7.

The Dissident Movement, 1954–91

The death of Stalin brought great hope for a reconciliation between the regime and Soviet intellectuals. Expressing the sentiment of many Soviet writers, Ilya Ehrenburg's novel *The Thaw* provided the label for the period of cultural accommodation under Khrushchev. Khrushchev's denunciation of Stalin's crimes at the Twentieth Party Congress in 1956 further signaled an expanding cultural freedom. A generation schooled in this climate of liberalism and relaxation looked forward to more openness and intellectual freedom. Anna Akhmatova began to write poetry again. Novelists and memoirists began to write about topics that once were forbidden, particularly about their experiences under Stalin.

But limits remained that were only determined through conflict with state authorities. The poet Boris Pasternak, who had escaped the purges, wrote a historical novel about revolutionary Russia. Too controversial for Soviet literary journals, the book was published only abroad. Vasilii Grossman's epic novel about the war, depicting Soviet villains as well as Soviet heroes, was likewise suppressed by cautious editors. The publication of Solzhenitsyn's novella, *One Day in the Life of Ivan Denisovich*, signaled a cultural breakthrough, but many other writers found their works, begun hopefully after the Twentieth Party Congress, were consigned "to the drawer," i.e., they were not publishable. Some of this literature circulated in typewritten copies, creating an underground library of "samizdat," from the term for "self-publishing." Others, such as Pasternak, published their works abroad. After Khrushchev was deposed in 1964, however, the cultural climate turned even frostier. Two writers, IUlii Daniel' and Andrei Siniavskii, were arrested in 1966 for having published satirical stories abroad under pseudonyms. Their crime was "spreading anti-Soviet propaganda." Even Stalin had not used this argument against intellectuals. Daniel' and Siniavskii were sentenced to terms in a labor camp, but their convictions spurred sixty-three members of the Moscow Union of Writers to protest the harm such persecution could do to Soviet culture (Document 137). Further arrests led to further protests, a phenomenon unknown under Stalin's terror. To coordinate this new dissenting activity, a samizdat journal began to publish in the spring of 1968, the *Chronicle of Current Events*, which took as its purpose the defense of the United Nations Declaration of Human Rights. The *Chronicle*, typed clandestinely in carbon copies, then distributed within the USSR and smuggled abroad, publicized grievances and abuses of authority; it spawned further groups concerned with the rights of religious groups, women, and national minorities. When Brezhnev signed the Final Act of the Conference on Security and Cooperation in Europe at Helsinki in 1975, new groups formed to monitor Soviet compliance with the human rights provisions of the agreement.

The state authorities fought back with censorship, refusal to give permission for public performances, arrests and show trials, deportations, involuntary incarceration in mental hospitals, and sometimes with naked force. By the mid-1970s the dissident movement came to reflect a number of sources of protest. Aleksandr Solzhenitsyn had become the spokesman for a nationalist, Orthodox Russophilia; he claimed that communism had been an alien force, imported from the West and inappropriate for the Russian soul. He was expelled from the USSR in 1974. Roy Medvedev, on the other hand, was a reform communist who believed that Stalin had perverted the originally positive Leninist ideals. His *Let History Judge*, published in the West in 1971, was the first Soviet analysis of the crimes of Stalin. Andrei Sakharov represented the large democratic humanist element of the dissident movement. Sakharov wielded such tremendous moral authority that the regime finally exiled him in 1980 to the city of Gorky, off-limits to foreign journalists. National groups such as the Crimean Tatars staged a series of demonstrations demanding the right to return to their homeland; Soviet Jews began to organize their own protests on behalf of the right to emigrate to Israel. Similar nationalist movements gathered momentum in Ukraine, the Baltic republics, and elsewhere.

By the early 1980s repression, deportation, and self-censorship had severely damaged the dissident movement, but as the response to Gorbachev's gradual relaxation of ideological conformity revealed, the intellectual currents of challenge and opposition had remained only barely below the surface of Soviet cultural life.

DOCUMENT 134   *Analysis by P. N. Pospelov, secretary of the Central Committee, June 19, 1954, of the errors in the political views of Mikhail Botvinnik, world chess champion from 1948–1957, expressed in his letter, "Is a Socialist Revolution Possible in the West without a Third World War?"*

Central Committee. Communist Party of the Soviet Union [*TSK KPSS*]

Not for publication.

Party member and world chess champion, Comrade M. Botvinnik, has sent me a letter along with his "notes" on the topic "Is a Socialist Revolution in the West possible without a Third World War?" Admitting that he is a "very weak political thinker" and, apparently, not sure of the correctness of his reasoning, M. Botvinnik essentially develops a liberal-pacifist, anti-Marxist conception of a "compromise" with the imperialists with the aim of avoiding a third world war. Without understanding the basic economic principles of contemporary capitalism—the striving of imperialists toward maximum profit and world domination—M. Botvinnik expresses a naive and ridiculous anti-Marxist idea: "Can't we put the monopolists in a situation where they would not find nuclear war necessary?" In order "not to scare" the bourgeoisie with a socialist revolution, Botvinnik proposes incorporating a pledge into the programs of Communist parties that in the event of a revolution, not only would the profit received by the capitalists from nationalized industries be preserved, it would even be increased thanks to reduced military expenditures.

M. Botvinnik's "notes" are of interest as the manifestation of bourgeois ideology of the Labor Party type and fear of capitalist encirclement.

I suppose we should call M. Botvinnik to the *TSK* Department of Propaganda and Agitation and explain to him the anti-Marxist flavor of his notes. If he insists on his un-Communist views, then, I think, he cannot remain a member of the party.

[signed] P. Pospelov
June 19, 1954

- -

To Comrade P. N. Pospelov

Dear Petr Nikolaevich!

Sometimes poor chess players turn to grand masters with their theoretical "findings." These findings, despite the most indulgent attitude toward them, as a rule, turn out to be useless.

Realizing that I am a very weak political thinker, and also counting on your indulgence, I ask you, Petr Nikolaevich, if you could find the time to familiarize yourself with the attached notes.

With heartfelt greetings   [signed] M. Botvinnik
May 29, 1954

M. M. Botvinnik
1st Meshchanskaia 52, apt. 15
Member *KPSS*, p/b #3334328

TSKhSD, fond 5, op. 30, d. 81, ll. 69–98.

Boris Pasternak

Boris Pasternak (1890–1960) was known as a brilliant, innovative lyrical poet in the years immediately before and after the 1917 revolutions, but he found himself under attack for his purported excessive individualism and his difficult style. He remained on the margins of official literary life, making his living translating Shakespeare and other works from English, German, French, and Georgian. He also had begun to write a novel of the revolution, *Doctor Zhivago*, which he attempted to publish in 1956, the year of Khrushchev's secret speech denouncing the crimes of Stalin. The literary journal *Novyi Mir*, however, refused to publish the work, claiming that its spirit was that of the nonacceptance of the socialist revolution. Pasternak submitted his novel to the Italian publisher Feltrinelli, and it appeared in Italian and other translations to great acclaim. Pasternak was awarded the Nobel Prize for Literature in 1958, but the response of the Soviet cultural establishment was a hue and cry against the "literary Judas, who betrayed his people for thirty pieces of silver, the Nobel Prize." He had circumvented Soviet censorship by publishing abroad, and this was not to be tolerated. Pasternak was forced to renounce the prize in 1959.

DOCUMENT 135   *Memorandum from D. Polikarpov, head of the Party's Cultural Department, to the Central Committee, April 16, 1959, recommending (with E. A. Furtseva's approval) that Pasternak's request for permission to accept money from Norwegian publishers for* Doctor Zhivago *be denied*

> Secret
> *TSK KPSS*
> Apr. 16, 1959
> To be returned to the
> General Dept., *TSK KPSS*

Not for publication

Central Committee of the Communist Party of the Soviet Union [*TSK KPSS*]

B. Pasternak turned to me for advice on what he should do in connection with the proposal of the Norwegian publishers to receive money for the book *Doctor Zhivago*.

Judging by the letter, Pasternak would like to receive this money, a portion of which he intends to give to the Literary Fund "for the needs of elderly writers."

I think that Pasternak should refuse receipt of money from the Norwegian bank.

I am asking for permission to express this point of view.

> [signed] D. Polikarpov
> April 16, 1959

Archive

Boris Pasternak refused to receive the money from the Norwegian publishers. See the copy of his letter to the Copyright Directorate (attached).

August 17, 1959

Secret
TSK KPSS
Apr. 16, 1959

Esteemed Dmitrii Alekseevich,

I was invited to the International Legal Board and informed that our embassy in Norway has offered to receive on my behalf an honorarium for the novel *Doctor Zhivago* deposited in a Norwegian bank.

As you know, until now I have received no money for publishing my novel abroad, and I have made no attempt to do so. Now that an offer to accept an honorarium has officially been made to me by a person in an official capacity, I suppose that in accepting such an offer I will not have done anything contrary to the interests of the state. You also know that my books are not being published at this time in the Soviet Union, and my contracts have actually been suspended, and therefore I cannot count on income in this country.

At the International Legal Board I was also told that I can receive money being held for me in a Swiss bank in English currency, and they requested my approval to receive it.

I would like to donate part of this money to the Literary Fund of the USSR for the needs of elderly writers.

If for some reason it is deemed inconvenient or contrary to state interests that I accept money from abroad and donate part of it to the Literary Fund, I earnestly request that you so inform me in order to prevent a mistaken move on my part that would have negative consequences.

[handwritten:] April 1, 1959

[signed] B. Pasternak

Please inform me of your permission or refusal at the following address: Moscow, Potapovskii pereulok, 9/11, apt. 18, c/o Ol'ga Vsevelodovna Ivinskaia

Not for publication.

[handwritten:]

To Comrade Polikarpov, D. A.

Comrade Furtseva, E. A., concurs with your proposal.

April 20, 1959 [signature illegible]

TO THE COPYRIGHT ADMINISTRATION

I relinquish the use of deposits made in my name for the publication of the novel *Doctor Zhivago* in Norwegian and Swiss banks, about which deposits I was informed in writing by the International Legal Board.

April 24, 1959

B. Pasternak

True copy: [signature illegible]

TSKhSD, fond 5, op. 36, d. 93, ll. 21–24.

DOCUMENT 136   *Memorandum from D. Polikarpov, head of the party's cultural department, to the Central Committee, December 9, 1960, about V. Grossman's manuscript,* Life and Fate

Not for Publication.

Central Committee of the Communist Party of the Soviet Union

The writer V. Grossman has submitted a manuscript of his work *Life and Fate* to the journal *Znamia*.

This work is a collection of malicious fabrications about our reality, filthy slander against the Soviet social and state structure.

In the interests of the matter, it is imperative for the editors of *Znamia* not only to refuse the manuscript but to have a serious political discussion with Grossman. It is also necessary for the following leaders of writers' organizations to participate in this conversation: Comrades Sobolev, Markov, Shchipachev. It is important for the writers themselves to make Grossman understand that any attempts to distribute the manuscript will meet an irreconcilable attitude on the part of the literary world and the severest denunciation.

I request your consent to recommend this to Comrades Kozhevnikov, Sobolev, Markov, Shchipachev.

Head of the Department of Culture
Central Committee of the
Communist Party of the Soviet Union   D. Polikarpov

December 9, 1960

[Handwritten note:]
Conversation with V. Grossman was held in the Writers' Union of the USSR; Comrades Markov, Shchipachev, Sartakov participated.

D. Polikarpov
March 18, 1961

To Comrade D. A. Polikarpov
Comrade M. A. Suslov has been informed.
No objections. December 9, 1960

On December 30, 1960, an interview was held at the Soviet Writers' Union with Vasilii Grossman, the writer, on the subject of his novel *Zhizn' i sud'ba* [Life and Fate]. In addition to me, the interviewers included S. P. Shinachev, the Chairman of the Board of the Moscow Branch of the Writers' Union, and S. V. Sartakov, the Secretary of the Board of the Writers' Union of the Russian Soviet Federated Socialist Republic.

We, who all evaluated Grossman's new work as hostile to our socialist system and antipatriotic in concept, expressed our opinions frankly, without pulling any punches. We especially emphasized the point that if the manuscript of the novel were to, by some misfortune, fall into the hands of Western reactionary circles, they would immediately attempt to use it in their campaign against our Homeland.

V. Grossman listened to our opinions attentively and with a surprising amount of restraint. His answer went something like this.

"I am fully aware of the seriousness of your assessment of my new novel. But I also remember the impassioned discussions of my previous novel *Za pravoe delo* [For a Just Cause]. At that time many people were inclined to call me a traitor, but experience has shown that my views were close to the truth. And after all, in the new novel I also wrote about what happened in real life."

During our discussion we informed Grossman that, despite a number of ideological weaknesses, the spirit of *For a Just Cause* was in harmony with the spirit of Soviet patriotism. In response, he said that it would be difficult for him to repudiate everything he had written right away, because he had worked on the novel for twelve years and had put a lot of work and his life into the book. But in light of the sincerity of our arguments and our great concern for the situation, he did say he would give it a lot of thought.

With respect to our fears that the manuscript might get to a foreign country, Grossman said that he pretty much keeps to himself and doesn't associate with anyone. "Of course, you won't be able to hide the fact that the editors of *Znamia* rejected the manuscript. The word will get out quickly, especially when you consider that the journal rejected the manuscript offhand, without offering any constructive criticism," Grossman added.

The day before the interview at the Writers' Union, Grossman went to a meeting at *Znamia* with V. M. Kozhevnikov, the editor in chief of the journal, and E. Galanov, a member of the editorial board. Grossman never showed up at the meeting of the editorial board where the manuscript would be discussed in his presence, complaining of illness. In his meeting with Kozhevnikov and Galanov, he took the same position that he did in his interview with us at the Writers' Union.

Our encounters with Grossman left us with the impression that his ideological and literary disaster has not shaken him in the least and has not yet made him eager to get out of the trouble which has befallen him.

Secretary of the Board
of the Soviet Writers' Union   [signed] G. Markov

January 2, 1961

Moscow

No. 1-s

COMMENTS

of the Members of the Editorial Board of the Journal *Znamia* on the Manuscript of Vasilii Grossman's Novel *Life and Fate*

To the Editor in Chief of *Znamia*

V. M. KOZhEVNIKOV

I have read Vasilii Grossman's novel *Life and Fate* as submitted to the editors of *Znamia* (over 1000 pages). In my opinion it cannot be published in its current form or revised, modified, or rewritten, because in this case we are not talking about partial errors or inaccurate statements or plot lines, but about the entire theme of the work, which is fallacious and pernicious and has permeated the plot, the heroes, and the very fabric of the novel.

The author considers the historical process to be some sort of contest between Good and Evil. Grossman interprets these concepts over his entire epic in the conflicts of his heroes and in the development of events and also (which takes up most of the novel) in long-winded social and political digressions. So where does he see Evil? In totalitarian social systems, which kill what is good in human beings, namely, what is human. So where is the power of Good? It lies in the arousal of simple "human" feelings and emotions, including love, pity, and the desire to do good for one's fellow man, and so forth.

But this antihistorical approach to actual current events results in the distortion of actual events and relationships between people and even to the distortion of history. It is amazing that the author, who fought in the Battle of Stalingrad and wrote patriotic articles about it during the Great Patriotic War, has now begun to draw parallels, on so-called humanitarian lines, between the sufferings of the defenders of Stalingrad and the Nazis. This would provoke heartfelt protest from any reader of the novel or, to put it bluntly, without any professional or editorial courtesy for the author, outrage (read, for example, the scene where the starving Nazi from the encircled Nazi garrison meets the Stalingrad women who went through the siege when they are both rummaging through the ruins of the city in search of food, and so forth). These kinds of "parallels" are drawn along many other lines, in particular with respect to the cruelty of both sides (read, for example, the scene where the Soviet snipers hold a "production meeting," the scene where the deserter is shot, and so forth). As a result of all these "parallels," our picture of the heroic battle of Stalingrad is distorted, despite the fact that it is sacred to all of us, and this "new look" at the events of our recent past personally elicited a feeling of profound disgust in me.

The author also presents a misleading picture of our country's domestic life. The author focuses all of his attention on the "dark sides" associated with the "cult of personality" (such as the scenes in the concentration camp, the arrests, interrogations, denunciations, and other scenes). Gradually, as the plot develops, the heroes emerge as persons who are overwhelmed by a feeling of fear. Fear controls all of their behavior, thoughts, and actions. The purpose of this plot development is to demonstrate how an inhuman system kills everything that is human in human beings. By the end of the novel, its main protagonists have turned into obedient and satisfied "cogs" of the system. The only thing I cannot understand is how we won the war, survived the postwar scares, and so forth. The author will not answer this question and would not even try to answer it, because then the entire framework of the novel would collapse.

So what sort of "positive ideal" does the novelist offer us? It is a worthless ideal: some sort of "humane," "kind," and essentially sweetly idyllic bourgeois democracy, without "bosses," without leaders, without any kind of party loyalty, and so forth. (Many of the digressions, episodes, and scenes are devoted to this subject.) In particular, this "bossless" democracy is embodied in "Building 6/1." It's a bitter pill to swallow when you think that our dear and sacred "Pavlov Building" in Stalingrad served as the prototype for this building. And evidently it never occurred to the author that this "ideal," to put it crudely, might have led us straight to the cremation ovens of Nazism, that very same "suffering" Nazism, which Grossman even believes is worthy of human sympathy. The author's ideological blindness and his denial or rejection of everything which has already been proven by history is amazing. In essence, Vasilii Grossman has taken positions which are ideologically hostile to Soviet ideology and has presented a tendentious and garbled picture of Soviet reality. The novel is incorrigible. In this case it can only be rejected, which is why I am adamantly opposed to the publication of the novel *Life and Fate.*

L. SKORINO

December 6, 1960

To the Editor in Chief of *Znamia*

V. M. KOZhEVNIKOV

With respect to the manuscript of Grossman's novel, I could ramble on or I could get to the point. I will get to the point.

One of the heroes of the novel says: "Our humanity and freedom are partisan and fanatical and have pitilessly sacrificed human beings in the name of an abstract humanity."

Grossman's entire novel is devoted to proving this slanderous proposition.

The author is aiming at a target which has long been a favorite of the advocates of bourgeois democracy and the slanderers of socialism.

The dyed-in-the-wool revisionist program of the Yugoslav Communist League is just a little less outspoken: "Socialism does not have the right to subordinate the personal happiness of human beings to any sort of higher goals." Of course this proposition completely ignores voluntary service to the people as the supreme happiness of the individual and the noblest expression of humanity.

The martyrs of the revolutionary struggle in all countries, from Karl Liebknecht and Rosa Luxemburg, to Julius Fucík, Musa Jalil, and the heroic General Karbyshev would turn over in their graves if they read this blasphemous sentence from Grossman's novel and the similar pernicious and vulgar proposition of the Yugoslav revisionists.

It may seem improbable, but it is true that the author, by alternating scenes from Hitler's Germany and the Soviet Union, draws divers parallels between the two, as if Nazism and the Soviet system were the same.

The author makes these comparisons in an epic calm tone of voice. He hovers "over the fray" and gives "everyone his due." And the Nazis are bad and the Nazi state is a totalitarian police state, but ours supposedly was not any better.

So it is completely unclear what the Soviet people were fighting for or defending in the Great Patriotic War.

And by the way, we are talking about a war in which millions of Soviet people died to save their nation from slavery, defend the freedom and independence of their homeland, and protect the individual liberties of Soviet people.

Where would all of us be, including Grossman, if our army, almost all of whose commanders and political officers he portrays as corrupt (Getmanov, Neudobnov) or stupid (Eremenko, Chuikov), or quasi-anarchists (Grekov and others), if our army and its commanders had not demonstrated martial skills, had not learned the art of war and, most importantly, had not been able to mold their soldiers, who included not 28, but tens of thousands of Panfilovs, into ideologically cohesive units?

I find it impossible even to understand why Grossman needed to demean the planning and conduct of the Stalingrad operation and try to spread the nonsense that it was not a brilliant or talented operation but an imitative effort, by comparing it to prehistoric people surrounding a pack of wolves. After all, he is very well aware that classical Cannae have been extremely rare in history and knows the axiom that every battle is unique, that one could compare Paulus's powerful army to a pack of wolves only in rhetorical terms, that Manstein's mighty forces were trying to break through to help Paulus (help from the outside, which was never encountered in the classical battles of antiquity), and that "a mechanized Cannae," such as the Stalingrad encirclement, was the first of its magnitude in the annals of the art of war.

But even though he knows all this, he still pooh-poohs the Stalingrad operation, which is studied by all the military academies in the world.

Nor did Grossman so assess the people of our army and the events of the war in his own publications appearing in the newspaper *Krasnaia Zvezda* [Red Star] during the war.

Grossman tells us nothing new when he talks about the wave of arrests. But he does reject the party's analysis of these events. The novel interprets the violations of legality which took place at the time as a phenomenon which is an organic part of the Soviet system.

One of Grossman's characters (who is far from repulsive) speaks at length on the need to disband the collective farms. The author writes at length on the excesses of collectivization but has absolutely nothing good to say about collectivization per se in the manuscript.

"In my opinion, it is the fault of the bureaucracy if a worker suffers in his own state," the officer Bova says about his own prewar ordeals. And the author notes that at this point the discussion was getting to the heart of the matter.

It seems that there is no aspect of our life in the novel which Grossman does not portray in the darkest colors, which are laid on so thick that it is impossible to see anything good through them.

I automatically began to compare the novel with Pasternak's *Doctor Zhivago*, which I also read and about which I signed a letter with other members of the editorial board of *Novyi Mir*. And if you will permit me to take this comparison to its logical conclusion, then *Doctor Zhivago* was simply a stinking little piece of trash which would have had the same harmful effect as Grossman's novel.

A. KRIVITSKII

REVIEW

of Vasilii Grossman's Novel *Life and Fate*

Vasilii Grossman's new novel, *Life and Fate*, left me with an oppressive, unpleasant feeling. What is the book about? Is it about the wartime exploits of our people? Is it about the historic victory of our forces at Stalingrad? Is it about the rear and the front? But if you read the novel, you might ask yourself what the purpose of all these great exploits and sacrifices was. Why did people like Grekov, Ershov, and Mostovskii suffer, fight, and die when, as the writer portrays it, they were surrounded by cruelty, corruption, and filth, if elementary human rights were trampled and violated, if human relations were dominated by cynicism and hypocrisy, and if even the most honest people were forced to dissemble, twist and turn, and play "an exhausting and difficult game" in order to avoid falling victim to denunciations and persecution. And after all, that is how Grossman depicts the Soviet front lines and the rear at the time of the Battle of Stalingrad.

The novel contains the following episode. Colonel Novikov, as he looks at some young tankers driving by and sees individuals who are quite different from one another, thinks that people have to fight for the right to be different and to think and live the way they see fit on the earth. "The eternal, only, and true meaning of the struggle for life lies in the human being, in his basic individuality, and in his right to this individuality." And Novikov's thought holds the key to much of the novel's symbolism. And this basic right to think and live as one sees fit is denied not only by the Nazi totalitarian regime but, as Grossman claims, by the Soviet system. The red thread of comparison between fascism and the Soviet system runs through the entire book. The spirit of the novel lies in its depiction of the misfortunes and sufferings of good Soviet people, whom the state punished and silenced and to whom it denied the right to "basic individuality." The reader is left with the impression that it was not the war or Nazism but the "Soviet system" and the Soviet political structure that was the cause of so much misfortune and human suffering, that the entire atmosphere around people was poisoned with suspicion, spying, and informing. And the author keeps returning to this idea with, as I would describe, a painful regularity. Getmanov denounces Novikov and puts Krymov in prison. In turn, Krymov "exposes" the now-deceased Grekov. Shtrum is tormented by the apparition of a certain Mad'iarov, with whom he was carelessly candid during the evacuation. In the prison cell, right in front of Krymov, are three district committee secretaries from Leningrad, each of whom exposed his predecessor.

All or practically all of the novel's heroes are victims of persecution, injustice, anti-Semitism, and official and bureaucratic arbitrariness. They are locked up in prisons, hounded from their jobs, and forced to endure cruelty, humiliation, and ridicule. Shtrum, Chepyzin, Zhenia Shaposhnikova did not escape participation in this. Their fates were much more bitter than the fates of Mostovskii or Sofia Osipovna Levington, who died at the hands of the Nazis, while these people were tormented and suffered as honest individuals who were devoted to the Soviet system.

I have not even mentioned many of the transitory figures in the novel, such as the worker who hanged himself at work after first putting the medals he won in the war on his chest, the Red Army man who was sentenced to be shot by a night firing squad, crawled out of his hastily dug grave, and ran back to the prison. There are many such episodes in the novel, and there is not enough space in this brief review to enumerate all of them. I merely cited the first episodes I could remember.

All the honest and talented people in the novel come to a bad end. But the cynical and hypocritical snitches and demagogues such as Getmanov and Neudobnov prosper. To put it bluntly, Soviet society "in cross section," which the writer claims to view from a sweeping perspective—all the way up to the Supreme Commander in Chief—does not look so appealing in Grossman's novel. That universal patriotic enthusiasm, which united not just a few people but the entire nation in the war with Nazism and which Grossman himself was able to portray so vividly in his articles from the Stalingrad front and his novels *Narod Bessmerten* [The People Are Immortal] and *Za pravoe delo* [For a Just Cause], almost never inspires the emotions and actions of the novel's protagonists in his new novel. If we are to believe Grossman, some people were motivated by personal advantage and cynicism, while others expended all of their spiritual energies in an unequal contest against mediocrities and phonies.

At several points throughout the novel, Grossman talks about the ascetic, abstract concept of humanity which prevails in our society. He returns to this theme in Novikov's thoughts that people must win the right to be different and when the heroes of the novel discuss Chekhov, who said that "people are first people and then bishops and bureaucrats." Grossman himself sees the embodiment of genuine democracy among the soldiers of Building 6/1 in Stalingrad, whose garrison withstood an enemy assault in a battle which raged for many days. Was this not because in this building, which was surrounded by Germans on all sides, people were left to themselves and cut off from others as if they were on an island? And in this building it became clear just exactly what each person was worth. "Here," Grossman writes, "was human brotherhood without officialdom." Here people are able to speak their minds about the collective farms and so forth. When Krymov, the commissar, came to Building 6/1, it even seemed to him that the "Leninist truth," which he, Krymov, had remembered on several occasions, was alive and well in these ruins.

But that was why "Grekov's building" was an eyesore for everyone else. People talked suspiciously about its defenders. "They're living like the Paris Commune over there." People start to build a "case" against Grekov. They sent Krymov to the building to restore "Bolshevik order." The sense of natural human equality which initially impressed Krymov soon aroused a sense of malice in him and the desire to suppress and stifle it. And ultimately he gets a bullet from Grekov because of it.

In the novel the commander and the commissar turn out to be irreconcilable enemies. They are hostile and profoundly alien to one another. Is Grekov fighting for Soviet power? We do not know. He is fighting for freedom. Dealing with the Germans is not the only thing he is thinking about. "The revolution," Grekov says, "was made so people wouldn't get bossed around." He is also one of the individuals who in the novel is denied the right to his "basic individuality."

I will not even go into how the author enumerates every minor little problem in such detail or the clashes of petty egos on which the author dwells in such length. Enough! Were the military and civilian milieus really as vulgar, petty, and trifling as the author describes them in the novel? Grossman is always looking for bad, weak, and ugly qualities, even in the characters and actions of his main protagonists, Shtrum and Novikov.

The artist has used his talent to seek out and to exaggerate all that is bad and insulting in the life of our society, in the temper of its people.

This is a perverted and anti-Soviet picture of Soviet life. An equal sign is essentially placed between the Soviet state and fascism.

The novel is unacceptable for publication.

B. Galanov

December 1960

To the Editor in Chief of *Znamia*

V. M. KOZhEVNIKOV

Vasilii Grossman's Novel *Life and Fate*

Grossman's novel *Life and Fate* primarily compels me to speak of the theme which the author used as the basis for his effort to portray the Battle of Stalingrad, and more broadly, Soviet reality in the war era. In the process he also writes a great deal about the prewar and postwar situation, massing incidents from different eras, in his words, on the axis of the main thrust. But what is important here is not the chronology but his rearrangement of different events and situations, namely, in the theme itself.

Let me enumerate its main points, which are glaringly obvious in the symbolic structure of the novel.

Grekov and Novikov, the characters who are the most appealing from the author's point of view, are fighting not for their Soviet motherland, but for the abstract ideal of freedom. Grekov tries to kill Commissar Krymov because he believes that Krymov is among the people opposed to freedom (Grekov is completely unaware of any of the complexities of Krymov's fate). The corps commander Novikov is "encircled" by Getmanov and Neudobnov, people who are only temporarily conceding this military specialist his command and are already gathering compromising materials on him.

Soviet commanders and commissars are generally depicted in sharp contrast to the rank and file soldiers. It is as if they were separated by an abyss. The commanders and commissars are supposedly cruel, intellectually limited, fight over personal glory and medals, get drunk, curse, and are not motivated by any lofty thoughts of the people, the motherland, or human beings but are merely concerned with their own selfish interests and brown-nosing their superiors. This frightening canvas of corruption is composed of a large number of large and small sketches. But these sketches are dispersed in such a way as to put this theme in the sharpest relief.

At the peak of the fighting officers sit in a bunker and play cards (which is repeated several times in different circumstances), at a meeting with Novikov a general discusses petty household details over the telephone with his wife (which is repeated almost exactly at Krymov's interrogation, when the investigator also discusses petty details with his spouse). The officers on the Steppe Front are all dying of boredom and give themselves over to petty jealousies and so forth.

We cannot deny a writer's right to create negative characters or to portray conflicting traits in the same characters. But after all, that is not the problem here. In this novel everything is portrayed as evidence of the inhumanity of the machinery of state, whose main engines prove to be people of the lowest possible character.

The author proceeds from a concept of the Soviet system as a totalitarian system which warps the human psyche and human nature. In addition to his portraits of the military men, this is especially evident in his sketches of the individuals with some sort of connection to Shtrum's case (Shinakov, Gurevich, Markov, Bad'in, and many others). And all of this comes from the author's own opinions as well as his images.

In his treatment of totalitarianism, the author uses his characters in a unique way. The good people are all victims. Instead of getting recognition for his heroism, the director Stalgress is severely punished. The posthumous award of the title of Hero of the Soviet Union to Grekov is withdrawn, and if he had lived he would have been punished. They are already trying to get Novikov. Krymov suffers torments in prison. Shtrum becomes the object of persecution. I will not begin to enumerate them all. The author sees everything through the prism of baseness, careerism, repression, treachery, and sly foxes and hawks pouncing on ants (this is on the last page of the novel, where this phrase is included as a kind of summary).

There was nothing sacred, progressive, or radiant about the people who triumphed at Stalingrad. Instead of Pavlov's heroic building, we get "Building 6/1," where the soldiers are supposedly fighting for freedom in general. Instead of an accurate account of the planning and then brilliant execution of the encirclement of the Germans at Stalingrad, we get the naive and moreover insulting theory that that is how hairy cavemen in the Stone Age used to surround packs of wolves. And instead of the people's self-sacrifice and truly legendary heroism which distinguished the Stalingrad era in particular, the reader gets hit with tales of brutality and treachery.

No matter what the author might say, to him everything is nothing but 1937, the tortures, the prisons, the concentration camps, and the mountains of corpses in collectivization. Everyone suspects everyone else of being an informant. All people are base. We must say that this concept of the human being as one who invariably carries within himself repulsive and base traits could just as easily apply to the people who were herded into ghettos and sent to death camps. Even though the author is apparently standing up for humanity, in reality his entire outlook on people is misanthropic.

The accusations of totalitarianism against the Soviet state are directly coupled with the assertion that Russia has always been hostile to freedom. And even in this case (in the scene of the so-called Kazan society of free thinkers, where scholars gather for evening discussions), Russian freedom without any restraints, from ancient times to our time, is interpreted as fanatical, partisan, and inhuman. The author cannot hide behind the words of his character Mad'iarov, because after all it is completely obvious that all of Mad'iarov's statements are in the spirit of the novel's theme.

By the way, this passage sheds a little light on what exactly Mad'iarov's and thus the author's ideal of humanity are, because they have the same points of view. In his discourse on Chekhov Mad'iarov proclaims that to Chekhov—everyone was the same—the factory owner, the drayman, and so forth, because they were all people. It is painful to hear such an outdated, ahistorical, and completely distorted picture as Mad'iarov's characterization of Chekhov.

I know the author will not agree with my criticism. And I was not counting on his agreement, because we stand at opposite poles. But I cannot help but mention that he has discarded all the principles of historicism. He completely discards them when he starts talking about such individuals as Bukharin, Trotsky, Rykov, Kamenev, and so forth. They also speak "as just people," with the author completely forgetting that they expressed definite political opinions.

He also discards the principles of historicism when in essence he returns to Chepyshin's "mixing bowl" theory from the novel *For a Just Cause*. After all, it would seem that it is quite clear: the author simply reworked the novel *For a Just Cause*, in particular Chapter 38, where in the new version (the book, not the journal version), Shtrum provides a persuasive critique of Chepyshin's mixing bowl theory (which he likens to the historical process), in which the dough and then the scum take turns rising to the top, i.e., in history the forces of good triumph, followed by the forces of evil. In the new novel this theory is for all intents and purposes resurrected (of course, without any reference to it by name). Moreover, now the author applies it not only to the Nazi state but to ours. And he applies it to our country to such a degree that now Stalin and everything associated with him are portrayed in such a way as to make the Nazis look like gentle little lambs. I certainly do not believe the author has lost any of his anger against Nazism, but this is not the point. He paints Nazi barbarism very vividly in his scenes of the destruction of the Jews. But he has shifted the focus of his gaze to our country, and the picture we get is extremely distorted. And it could not turn out any other way, because that is exactly where the entire theme of totalitarianism leads.

If the author should object that in his novel, in its passages concerning 1937 and other similar incidents, he relied on the examples of violations of socialist legality, it would still be impossible for him to justify his theme, which is extremely bizarre for a Soviet writer. It is true that violations of socialist legality did take place. We know of them from party documents. Stalin's errors and the damage they caused have been exposed. But could we really portray the Battle of Stalingrad and the life of the nation in this era solely through the prism of 1937? After all, the question does not require a long and involved answer. You could not get much of a novel if you completely ignored the exploits of the people who were fighting not for some sort of abstract freedom but for their socialist homeland, for communism, and for the triumph of the firmly intertwined ideals of patriotism and internationalism. And just think of how naive his opinions of the snipers' meeting at Stalingrad are. It was as if these snipers were primarily motivated by the sporting urge to kill people. But the snipers were not killing Germans per se, they were shooting Nazi occupiers. Once again we have to remind ourselves of these things, because in his study of human beings the author considers everything except for the specific historical manifestations of human emotions.

I hope that the author does not get the impression that his novel was too bold. Instead, it is simply wrong with respect to that just cause of the people which the author treated earlier. The novel is historically biased. It can only please our enemies. It is with a great deal of sadness that I write all this, but principles are principles.

V. Pankov

TSKhSD, fond 5, op. 36, d. (5845), ll. 70–88.

DOCUMENT 137   *Letter from members of the USSR Writers' Union to the Presidium of the Twenty-third Party Congress and the Russian and Supreme Soviets, March 23, 1966, appealing for release on bail of Siniavskii and Daniel', convicted for publishing their works abroad and for satirizing the Soviet Union*

To the Presidium of the 23rd Congress of the Communist Party of the Soviet Union

To the Presidium of the USSR Supreme Soviet

To the Presidium of the RSFSR Supreme Soviet

Dear comrades!

We, a group of Moscow writers, appeal to you to release to us on bail the recently convicted writers Andrei Siniavskii and IUlii Daniel'. We feel that this would be a wise and humane act.

Although we do not approve of the measures to which these writers resorted by publishing their works abroad, we cannot agree that in their actions there was any anti-Soviet intention, proof of which was necessary for such a severe punishment. This malicious intent was not proved during the course of the trial of A. Siniavskii and IU. Daniel'.

Meanwhile, the conviction of the writers for satirical writings sets an extraordinarily dangerous precedent capable of impeding the development of Soviet culture. Neither science nor art can exist without the possibility of expressing paradoxical ideas or creating hyperbolic images. The complex situation in which we live requires the expansion (not the constriction) of freedom of intellectual and artistic experimentation. From this point of view, the Siniavskii and Daniel' trial has already caused incomparably greater damage than all the errors of Siniavskii and Daniel'.

Siniavskii and Daniel' are talented people and should be offered the chance to correct their errors and their tactlessness. If free on bail, Siniavskii and Daniel' would more quickly realize the mistakes they made and through contact with the Soviet public would be able to create new works, the artistic and ideological value of which would make amends for the damage caused by their blunders.

For all these reasons, we ask you to release on bail Andrei Siniavskii and IUlii Daniel'. This is in the interests of our country. It is in the interests of peace. It is in the interest of the world communist movement.

[signed] Members of the USSR Writers' Union:

[63 signatures]

TSGAOR, fond 7523, op. 83, d. 150, l. 7

Aleksandr Tvardovskii

Aleksandr Tvardovskii (1910–71) is noted for two distinct and important careers in Soviet letters. He first earned fame and popularity as a poet, especially for his epic wartime poem *Vasilii Terkin*, which presented the war from the point of view of an ordinary foot soldier. A sequel appeared in 1963, *Terkin in the Other World*, which satirized Soviet bureaucracy and its administrative absurdities. Later his poetry became more bitter and sad; his meditations on the injustice of the Stalin system were too pessimistic for Soviet censorship, and he could not publish his last works. Tvardovskii is perhaps best known as a literary editor. In 1950 he became editor of *Novyi Mir* [New World], one of the USSR's leading literary journals. He was forced to resign in 1954 for prematurely publishing an essay calling for more truth and openness in Russian literature, but he returned to the editorship in 1958. In his twelve years as editor of *Novyi Mir* the journal gained fame as the leading venue for new writing and creative freedom. Solzhenitsyn's *One Day in the Life of Ivan Denisovich* first appeared in its pages in 1962, and many other young and promising writers published their stories and poetry in the journal. With the fall of Khrushchev in 1964, however, Tvardovskii found himself increasingly under attack, both for his own poetry and for the line taken by the journal. Tvardovskii was forced out of the editorship in 1970, and he died soon after.

Letter from noted Soviet writers, written in early February 1970, and documents concerning the campaign against the journal Novyi Mir *and its editor, Tvardovskii*

Not for publication.   [stamp:] *TSK KPSS*

                                                        04305
                                                        Feb. 9, 1970
                                                        Return to Gen. Dep. *TSK KPSS*

                    Dear and deeply respected Leonid Il'ich [Brezhnev]!

        Alarmed by a situation that has arisen within our country's literature, we consider it our duty to address you.

        Lately there has been a campaign against A. T. Tvardovskii and *Novyi mir,* the journal he manages, aimed at removing him from the editorship of the journal. Decisions about changing the editorial staff of the journal have already been made that are basically directed toward Tvardovskii's resignation.

        A. T. Tvardovskii can safely be awarded the title of national poet of Russia and people's poet of the Soviet Union. The significance of his work for our literature is immeasurable. We have no poet who equals him in talent or significance. The journal run by him sets the standard for high artistic merit, something that is extremely important for the communist education of the people. The journal follows the policies set by the 20th–23rd Party Congresses and analyzes complex questions of contemporary social development in scholarly depth. In its pages have appeared many of the most talented contemporary Soviet writers. The reputation it enjoys in our country, as well as among progressive intellectuals around the world, makes it a completely unique phenomenon. Not taking this fact into account would be a mistake with far-reaching implications.

        We are completely convinced, for the benefit of all Soviet culture, that it is necessary that *Novyi mir* continue its work not only under the leadership of A. T. Tvardovskii but also with the editorial staff that he considers best for the journal.

[signed]
A. Bek   A. Voznesenskii   Evg. Vorob'ev
V. Kaverin   Evg. Evtushenko   V. Tendriakov
B. Mozhaev   M. Aliger   IU. Nagibin
An. Rybakov   S. Antonov
IU. Trifonov   M. Isakovskii
Elizar Mal'tsev

                                                        [Stamp:] *TSK KPSS*
                                                        04306
                                                        April 9, 1970
                                                        Return to Gen. Dep. of
                                                        TSK KPSS

Dear Leonid Il'ich:

        I am writing to you in reference to matters which, for the first time in my more than fifteen years as an editor and my more than forty years as a literary man, are directly endangering my good name as a Soviet writer and Communist.

        Several days ago K. V. Voronkov, the Secretary of the Writers' Union, and A. A. Beliaev, an employee of the Cultural Department of the *TSK KPSS,* showed me the Western European publications which in November and December of last year published my poem *Po pravu pamiati* [By Right of Memory] under the provocative heading "Over Stalin's Ashes," with the blaring notice that the poem "was banned in the Soviet Union."

I believe there is no need to assure you that the poem traveled overseas by channels unknown to me, obviously against my will, but I can provide the following brief account of the affair.

This relatively short poem, on which, however, I had worked for more than five years, was in fact held up by the Main Office for the Protection of State and Military Secrets in the Press [Glavlit] in the proofs of the sixth (June) edition of Novyi Mir for 1969 without any recommendations for changes or deletions and without any explanations whatsoever.

At that point I asked K. A. Fedin, the First Secretary of the Writers' Union, to bring up the issue to the Secretariat and discuss the poem in the same way that the Secretariat had discussed the final chapters of my book Za dal'iu—dal' [Distance beyond Distance], which in its time had also been held up by the censors.

But the poem was never discussed and the matter remained open until I discovered that it had been published abroad.

Obviously, I could not help but be alarmed by the situation, and on January 19 I again asked K. A. Fedin to put the poem on the agenda immediately. But instead there was absolutely no mention of a discussion of the poem, and instead they asked me to issue a statement "expressing my response" to the publication of the poem, i.e., an appropriate response to all the various L'Expresses, Figaroes, and Posevs.

I was willing to make a very strong statement which would express all my disgust and dissatisfaction with the publication of a purloined and garbled work of mine in the foreign press, but I believed and continue to believe that the most effective response to this outrage would be to publish (after the appropriate discussion) my very own poem in the authentic version, which would have completely blunted the effect of these provocative attempts to discredit my poem.

On February 3, however, when the Secretariat of the Writers' Union heard Fedin's report on my letter and his conversation with me, their decision on the matter came as a complete surprise. They decided to appoint Comrade Bol'shov the first assistant editor in chief of Novyi Mir and appoint a commission, including the very same Comrade Bol'shov, to reorganize the journal's editorial board within three weeks' time.

I protested the decision (which had been made not only without any consultation with me, but in my absence) to the TSK KPSS and the Secretariat of the Writer's Union on the grounds that I had never seen Comrade Bol'shov's face before, was completely unfamiliar with him, and consider his appointment without my knowledge or consent to be an unprecedented encroachment on my authority as an editor in chief and an insult to me personally. But the very next day Comrade Voronkov, who had informed Fedin of my protest and my letter to Literaturnaia Gazeta [The Literary Gazette] concerning the foreign publication of my poem, notified me that five working members of the editorial board of Novyi Mir were gone and that new members had been appointed to replace them, once again without my knowledge and consent.

Thus, the issue of my poem resulted in organizational changes which for all intents and purposes forced me to resign and for all intents and purposes devastated the journal I edited. And this devastation of the editorial board of Novyi Mir was carried out precisely at the time when the journal was finally getting over its chronic delays in publication (primarily caused by censorship problems) and at a time when, in spite of a prolonged negative press campaign, our readers had demonstrated their trust and support for the journal by their subscriptions for 1970. (The circulation of the journal had grown by 26,000 new subscribers, including 10,000 in Moscow alone, while other "thick" journals had suffered substantial declines in readership.)

In the meantime the discussion of the poem was postponed indefinitely, and for all intents and purposes the subject has been declared "off-limits."

On several occasions people at the Writers' Union have compared me with Solzhenitsyn. But even though I considered and still do consider Solzhenitsyn's expulsion from the Writers' Union to be a major blunder which has done incredible harm to us both in and outside the country, I am not Solzhenitsyn, I am Tvardovskii.

The provocational character of the foreign publication of my poem is completely clear: our enemies are proceeding from the assumption that an atmosphere of neo-Stalinism is building in the Soviet Union and that the author of the poem, like Solzhenitsyn, is subjected to every form of ostracism and so ends up outside of Soviet literature.

Unfortunately, I have reason to believe that *Glavlit*'s holdup of my poem, with all the unfortunate consequences it had for me, can be attributed to the poem's unmistakable opposition to the Stalin personality cult and to the autobiographical nature of the poem. But it is obvious that the autobiographical nature of a particular work of literature and motives arising from a writer's personal experiences are not one and the same thing. As an artist I was formed by the years of the first five-year plans (*Strana Muraviia* [The Country of Muravia]) and the war years (*Vasilii Terkin*), and in purely personal terms I have no basis for considering myself abused by Stalin in any way. No matter how strange it may seem, Stalin showered me with decorations and medals when he was alive, while the Stalinists of today are hounding me. But, obviously, my poem looks at history not through the prism of my personal experiences, but rather in the spirit of the resolutions adopted by recent party congresses, which I welcomed from the bottom of my heart.

I am aware of the attempts to set Tvardovskii the poet in opposition to Tvardovskii the editor. But this sort of division is completely inappropriate. In the last twenty years all of my works, including lyric poems, articles, longer poems, including the poem *Za dal'iu—dal'*, which was awarded the Lenin Prize, have been published first in *Novyi Mir*. In other words, all my creativity has been inseparably linked with the journal to which I have given more than fifteen years of my life. To the best of my ability, I have tried to convey the same ideas in the journal that I have in my creative work, the ideas of the party, as expressed in the decisions of the 20th through 23rd Party Congresses and other documents, up to and including your speech to the most recent plenary session of the *TSK KPSS*.

It was the journal's social and political orientation that has defined its personality and has given it a good reputation both in our country and among our true friends abroad. The journal has become a magnet for the most talented and viable forces of our literature and has rallied dozens and hundreds of literary people, scholars, and political and social commentators and representatives of different generations and practically all the nationalities of the Soviet Union. Many works of literature which are now widely praised were first published in the pages of *Novyi Mir*, and it is no accident that our contributors have been awarded far more Lenin and State Prizes than the contributors to any other journal.

Hence, the current attempts to "tame" the journal will certainly have the most dire consequences, both literary and political. Our mass audience will inevitably perceive these attempts as a resurgence of Stalinism.

This appeal to you was dictated by necessity and could not be delayed. If you could find it in your heart to see me, I could discuss the poem, *Novyi Mir*, and the literary situation in general much more extensively and convincingly.

[signed] A. Tvardovskii

February 7, 1970

[stamp:] *TSK KPSS* 04383, 10 Febr 1970
Return to Gen. Dept. *TSK KPSS*

For the Information of the Secretaries of
the *TSK KPSS*
[illegible signatures]

As I have already reported, the Bureau of the Secretariat of the Writers' Union of the USSR has adopted a resolution to appoint Comrade D. G. Bol'shov first assistant editor in chief of the journal *Novyi Mir* and to improve the journal's editorial board.

On February 9 a meeting of the Bureau of the Secretariat of the Writers' Union of the USSR attended by Comrades K. Fedin, N. Tikhonov, L. Sobolev, S. Mikhailov, A. Chakovskii, V. Ozerov, S. Baruzdin, K. IAshen, and

K. Voronkov discussed proposals for partial changes in the membership of the journal's editorial board in the presence of the journal's editor in chief, A. Tvardovskii.

A commission consisting of Comrades Fedin, Markov, Voronkov, and Bol'shov recommended removing the deputy editor in chief A. Kondratovich and the department heads V. Lakshin, I. Vinogradov, and I. Sats from the editorial board and terminating their employment on the editorial staff.

They recommended adding Comrades V. Kosolapov, O. Smirnov, A. Rekemchuk, and A. Ovcharenko to the editorial board and at the same time appointed O. Smirnov to the position of deputy editor in chief.

The Bureau of the Secretariat of the Writers' Union of the USSR unanimously approved their recommendations.

A. Tvardovskii has stated that the candidates approved by the Secretariat were unacceptable to him and that because of this he is protesting the secretariat's actions to the *TSK KPSS*. He also stated that his continued service as editor in chief of the journal will be contingent on our response to this protest.

The Bureau of the Secretariat of the Writers' Union of the USSR has examined Tvardovskii's statement concerning the publication of his poem in foreign anti-Soviet publications and has decided to publish this statement in *Literaturnaia Gazeta*.

For your information.
Head of the Cultural
Department of the
TSK KPSS   [signed] V. Shauro

February 10, 1970

TSKhSD, fond 5, op. 62, d. 84, ll. 35–42.

DOCUMENT 139   *Report of the Central Committee section on science and educational institutions, March 1971, on an anti-Soviet group of young people in Saratov*

<u>TOP SECRET</u>
NOT FOR PUBLICATION

THE UNION OF SOVIET SOCIALIST REPUBLICS
COMMITTEE FOR STATE SECURITY [*KGB*]
OF THE COUNCIL OF MINISTERS OF THE USSR

April 28, 1970
No. 1159-*ts*
City of Moscow

CENTRAL COMMITTEE
OF THE COMMUNIST PARTY
OF THE SOVIET UNION [*TSK KPSS*]

[STAMP OF *TSK KPSS*]
April 29, 1970
RETURN TO THE
GENERAL DEPARTMENT
OF THE *TSK*

For your information, we are forwarding a copy of the report of Comrade VASKIN, the head of the *KGB* office for

Saratov *Oblast'*, on the steps which have been taken to suppress the hostile activity of an anti-Soviet youth group in the city of Saratov.

DEPUTY CHAIRMAN OF THE *KGB*
[signed]
TSVIGUN

Copy <u>Secret</u>

ok-4Copy No.

From January 5 through 16, 1970, the Saratov *Oblast'* Court heard a criminal case against a group of young people indicted for organized anti-Soviet activity, i.e., crimes falling under Articles 70 and 72 of the Criminal Code of the Russian Soviet Federated Socialist Republic.

This group formed in February 1967 and remained in existence until August 1969. Its members, who disagreed with the policies of the Communist Party and the Soviet government with respect to governance, economic development, and socialist democracy, set themselves the task of fighting the existing system in our country. They deemed it necessary to organize illegal circles and groups (to be followed by the consolidation of these groups into a party of a "new, authentically Marxist type") to train propagandists to work among the masses, and to use hostile propaganda to carry out a "new revolution" and overthrow Soviet power.

The group had a charter which spelled out its structure, its procedure for accepting new members (and the duties of the members), and the procedure for collecting monthly membership dues. The group considered the anti-Soviet tract *The Twilight of Capital* to be its platform. They prepared and copied anti-Soviet and politically harmful documents by various means and distributed them to their acquaintances. They also had connections to an anti-Soviet group in the city of Riazan'. The members of the group tried to cultivate and involve politically immature and "critical"-minded individuals in their criminal activity.

The members included:

> <u>SENIN Oleg Mikhailovich,</u> born 1947, Russian, *komsomol* member, married, correspondence student in his fourth year at the Saratov Law Institute, prior to his arrest employed as an investigator-trainee at a district prosecutor's office in the city of Riazan'.

He was the organizer of the anti-Soviet group in Saratov. He was able to influence and involve other individuals in the group's activity. He prepared and disseminated hostile literature and drafted the group's charter and secrecy rules. He has expressed terrorist intentions and attempted to send anti-Soviet material abroad through A. UChI-TEL', a student at Petrozavodsk University.

He comes from a white-collar family. His father is the director of a state farm in Riazan' *oblast'*, and his mother is a librarian. After graduating from middle school, he attended a construction technical school, then left the technical school and completed his secondary education at a regional correspondence school. He was a good student, was interested in philosophy, and took part in discussion clubs and debates. By nature he is power-hungry, aloof, an alcohol abuser, and has committed immoral acts. His wife is a student at the history faculty of Moscow State University and is a *komsomol* member.

> <u>KIRIKOV Valentin Ivanovich,</u> born 1942, Russian, Communist Party member, reserve officer in the Soviet Army, fourth-year student at the Saratov Law Institute.

Recruited into the group by SENIN, he worked on the charter, cultivated others, prepared and distributed anti-Soviet materials, and supported criminal ties with the Riazan' group.

KIRIKOV's father and mother were separated, and his mother, an accountant, raised him by herself. He graduated from the Saratov Artillery School. In the army he was considered a knowledgeable specialist but had an indifferent attitude towards the military. In October 1964 he applied to the political department for permission to quit the Communist Party. After his discharge from the army (due to back problems), his unit's political department recommended him for the law institute. In his first year he was appointed the party organizer of his group. He was a good student. By nature he is calm and sociable but reacts very painfully and sharply to any seeming injustice. His wife is a foreign language teacher at Vocational School No. 16.

> BOBROV Viktor Aleksandrovich, born 1946, Russian, *komsomol* member, single, fourth-year student at the Saratov Law Institute.

He was cultivated and recruited into the group by SENIN. He energetically supported SENIN in his efforts to mold a cohesive group, kept and distributed documents, and carried out anti-Soviet agitation by word of mouth.

He comes from a military family. His father is a Communist Party member, a reserve officer in the Soviet Army, and works as the head of the party office at a factory in the city of Krivoi Rog. His mother is a doctor. He graduated from night middle school. He has been employed as a writer at a district newspaper and an instructor for the City *Komsomol* Committee of Kimry. In his first year at the institute, he was elected secretary of the *komsomol* organization. He is a satisfactory student. By nature he is cunning, cowardly, and easily influenced by others.

> ROMANOV Aleksandr Ivanovich, born 1948, Russian, single, *komsomol* member, fourth-year student at the history faculty of Saratov State University.

He was recruited into the group by SENIN, was one of its active members, and was the co-author of several anti-Soviet tracts. He regularly copied anti-Soviet literature and acquired the necessary reproduction equipment, including typewriters and a camera. He tried to influence other people and organized a "second team."

He comes from a working-class family. His father was a driver and died in 1969 after being run over by a streetcar, while his mother is an ironing machine operator at a garment factory. He earned good grades at school and at the university. He was appointed a *komsomol* organizer in his first year. He was a class leader in the *komsomol* history group at the middle school he attended. By nature he is disorganized, scatter-brained, and easily influenced by others, and it is easy for others to put words into his mouth.

> KULIKOV Dmitrii Georgievich, born 1942, Russian, married, *komsomol* member, graduate of the physics faculty at the state university in 1966, prior to his arrest worked as a trainer at the *Sokol* children's athletic school.

He was cultivated and recruited into the group by SENIN and ROMANOV. He collected and kept the group's membership dues, kept and distributed anti-Soviet tracts, and became involved in the criminal activity of others, including working-class youths.

He comes from a white-collar family. In 1957 his father was expelled from the Communist Party for refusing to work in his field (in agriculture) and is now employed as a design engineer at the Saratov Radio Component Factory. His mother teaches English at Boarding School No. 3, is a member of the Communist Party, is of Jewish origin, and worked at the military school which KULIKOV attended until 1961. He earned good marks at the university but never went to work in his field, became a trainer, and enrolled in the correspondence department of the Moscow Physical Education Institute. People have described him as somewhat undisciplined and conceited. He is stubborn and has an opinion about everything.

In addition to these individuals, the following person was indicted on the basis of Article 70 of the Criminal Code of the Russian Soviet Federated Socialist Republic.

> FOKEEV Mikhail Georgievich, born 1947, *komsomol* member, single, night student in his fourth year at the biology faculty of the state university, prior to his arrest employed as a security guard at a garment factory.

Recruited by ROMANOV in 1967. He copied and kept anti-Soviet and *samizdat* literature. He intended to continue the group's hostile activity using the literature in his possession if ROMANOV was arrested.

He comes from a white-collar family. His father is a reserve officer in the Soviet Army and works as the manager of Construction Site No. 7. His mother is a salesperson at a bookstore. He had a poor upbringing because of family problems. By nature he is aloof, stubborn, and arrogant.

The arrests of the members of the group and their connections resulted in the seizure of a large quantity of anti-Soviet literature, including 20 handwritten manuscripts of 167 pages, 72 copies of typewritten manuscripts of 566 pages; 15 photocopies of 89 pages, and 100 rolls of microfilm with the text of anti-Soviet material and documents. Our agents also seized the equipment used to copy this material, including 4 typewriters, 4 cameras, and a microfilm viewer.

The confiscated literature (*The Twilight of Capital, Trumpets of Freedom, The Machinery of Lies, On the Subject of Stalinism, Marxism and Sorcerers, The Foreign Policy of Soviet Imperialism*) deny the socialist character of the October Revolution and distort the basic phases of the development of the Soviet state, claim that the USSR has a system of state capitalism, and provide guidelines for organizing illegal circles and groups in the country, conducting hostile propaganda campaigns, and organizing strikes, demonstrations, and uprisings. This literature slanders our social system, our education system, the activity of our government and party organs, crudely distorts our nationalities (ethnic) policy, and contains appeals for the overthrow of Soviet power.

This literature was used by the members of the group to recruit new members.

They distorted certain doctrines of the classics of Marxism-Leninism concerning the state and revolution, classes and class struggle, and the role of the masses and the individual in history, and tried to prove the bankruptcy of the Communist Party program and how the leaders of the party and government have supposedly deviated from Leninist principles for governing the country and the society.

They also used several literary works and articles of social and political commentary, including *A Day in the Life of Ivan Denisovich* by A. SOLZhENITSYN; *Not By Bread Alone,* by DUDINTSEV; *Memoirs of a Terrorist* by SAVINKOV (*Priboi* Publishing House, Kharkov, 1926); "From the Life of Fedor Kuzkin" by MOZhAEV (the July 1966 issue of *Novyi Mir*); *My Biography* by EVTUShENKO (manuscript); "Lenin on Trotsky and Trotskyism" and "The New Course" by L. TROTSKY (published in the journal *Universitet*, Nos. 1 and 2, 1925); "Tribes, Parties, and Bureaucracy," by M. FRENKEL (the November 1968 issue of the journal *Mirovaia ekonomika i mezhdunarodnye otnosheniia*); "Liberalism and Democracy" by LIFShITS (January 1968 issue of *Voprosy filosofii*); "A Nightstick for the Wiseguys" by A. GORBANOVSKII (January 1968 issue of *Nauka i zhizn'*); "Why I Don't Wear a Vest" by L. PLEShAKOV (June 28, 1967, issue of *Komsomol'skaia Pravda*); "The Dead Don't Feel Any Pain" by BYKOV (January 1966 issue of *Novyi mir*); "Janusz Korczak and Our Children" by A. ShAROV (October 1966 issue of *Novyi mir*); "The End" by TENDRIAKOV (March 1968 issue of *Moskva*); "*German Fascism* by A. GALKIN (*Nauka* Publishing House, 1967), and many others.

In the preliminary investigation and the trial, the defendants and the witnesses gave detailed testimony on the goals and tasks the group set for itself, on the group's operating methods, and on the conditions which gave them a distorted perception of Soviet reality.

SENIN testified,

> We believed that in its current phase of development the Soviet Union has state capitalism, not socialism. Therefore, we set ourselves the task of organizing circles and groups, recruiting new members, and fighting the system which currently exists in our country.
>
> The group used practically the same approach in recruiting all its new members. Initially they would work on the candidate's mind. They would tendentiously single out and exaggerate the problems in the country. They tried to make it seem as if the Soviet Union was totally unjust. They would exaggerate the dark side of the life of society and distort certain precepts of the classics of Marxism-Leninism.
>
> Then they would lead their target to the idea that the Soviet Union is under state capitalism,

not socialism, that the ruling class is the bureaucracy, which holds all political and economic power, that the working class in the Soviet Union is supposedly exploited by the bureaucratic class, and, therefore, that the existing system in the Soviet Union must be fought and a new revolution is necessary and inevitable to obliterate state capitalism and build a "truly socialist society."

Then they would recommend that the target read several journal articles such as "Radishchev and Robespierre," "20th-Century Bureaucracy," and "Russian Wheat," which were published in *Novyi mir* in 1966, and others. In their discussions they would emphasize the problems in our country and try to demonstrate the wickedness of the existing system and the need to fight it.

In October 1967 I was supposed to deliver a report on the Great October Socialist Revolution at the Department of the History of the *KPSS*. In the process of gathering material for the report, I met on several occasions with STEPANOV, the dean of the day department of the institute. To me STEPANOV seemed to be a bold thinker with a critical mind. He agreed with me that students should be bolder and more principled. Without making any blatant anti-Soviet statements to STEPANOV, I put forth the idea that the current government and party apparatus is partially infected with bureaucratism. STEPANOV agreed with me. I was impressed. I got the idea of recruiting STEPANOV for anti-Soviet activity. In trying to carry out my idea, in October 1967 I gave STEPANOV the manuscript of *The Twilight of Capital* to read in October 1967 and asked him for his opinion of the book. If STEPANOV approved of the book, I planned to begin his anti-Soviet indoctrination. At any rate, I believed that our discussion of *The Twilight of Capital* would remain a secret between us.

(From SENIN's testimony on August 25 and October 27, 1969)

I should mention that SENIN's belief proved to be wrong. After reading the manuscript, STEPANOV turned it over to the university administration.

Bobrov testified,

The primary mission of our group was to train propagandists for *The Twilight of Capital,* which I considered to be our group's platform. . . .

The members assumed that circles would form at other institutions of higher learning and in other cities and that the exchange of theoretical works such as *The Twilight of Capital* and opinions would make it possible to develop a general theoretical platform, which could then be used as the basis for organizing a new party by means of a charter convention attended by representatives of the circles. This party would express the true interests of the proletariat and would have its social base in the proletariat. And the proletariat, incited to revolution, would overthrow the ruling bureaucratic apparatus. We assessed the current period as a period of "economic stabilization," in which the proletariat was not yet prepared to fight the existing system. . . .

Our task in the "stabilization" period was to be active in the so-called Marxist circles, into which we were to recruit all critical-minded people. In order to develop our analysis of the current situation in the country and the tasks of fighting the ruling bureaucratic class, we had to study and write our own theoretical works and develop a common theoretical platform by means of collective discussions and exchanges between groups. . . .

I had tried to study the material offered by the social sciences department at the school. But the instructors' inability to answer many burning questions and their unwillingness to touch anything which required an explanation made me more willing to trust SENIN's judgments.

I gradually began to look at everything through the prism of Senin's views and began to look for answers to the questions that were troubling me in the direction where SENIN pointed.

(From BOBROV's testimony of August 30, 1969, and October 31, 1969)

KIRIKOV testified as follows at the investigation:

Our group considered the October Revolution to be a bourgeois-democratic rather than a socialist revolution. We believed that at present the Soviet Union is under state capitalism, not socialism, and that society is divided into the proletarian class and the bureaucratic class, and that in the future the proletariat might be able to carry out a so-called real socialist revolution. . . .

I was assigned the task of becoming a good photographer so that we could then make our own microfilms. I used my classes in forensic photography at the institute's criminology laboratory to learn how to photograph documents. I became such a good photographer that I was appointed the leader of the criminology group. Afterwards I microfilmed the anti-Soviet tracts *The Twilight of Capital* and *Psychology and Propaganda*. . . .

In trying to recruit critical-minded people for our group, we focused on the best students. . . .

At one class on the theory of the state and the law at the Institute of Law, I had a question on LENIN's work *State and Revolution.* In this treatise Lenin, on the basis of the history of the Paris Commune, concluded that the salaries of officials should not exceed the average wage of a skilled worker. I asked BORISOV, the instructor, why this principle doesn't apply here and why certain categories of white-collar workers get much higher pay than blue-collar workers. But I never got a complete answer from BORISOV. I realized that there was no point in asking the instructors these questions. I began to go to all kinds of sources to get an answer. For this purpose I obtained a pass for the scientific library. That's where I met SENIN, who targeted me as a "critical-minded individual." . . .

In the summer of 1968, NIKITIN, the head of the Department of History of the *KPSS* at our institute, asked me to start studying on an individualized program in my third year in order to stay with him at the department as a graduate student and defend a dissertation. In our conversation he told me that if I successfully defended my dissertation, I would earn a big salary and "make myself a career." This conversation was very distasteful to me.

(From KIRIKOV's testimony of August 28 and 29, October 2, 7, and 24, and November 1 and 8, 1969)

The witness KNIAZhENTSEV testified,

KULIKOV brought Evgenii EVTUShENKO's biography to one of our meetings. He called Evtushenko a revolutionary poet. He said we didn't have enough poets like him in Russia and that Evtushenko was one of the people fighting for truth and justice. . . .

At our next meeting, KULIKOV let me read a transcript of the speeches DANIEL' and SINIAVSKII made at their trials. Then he acquainted us (myself and FROLOV, a graduate student at Saratov State University) with SOLZhENITSYN's letter to the Writers' Congress. KULIKOV said that our country's censorship was too strict and that sometimes the works of writers which might be socially beneficial aren't published.

The next work KULIKOV introduced us to was *Marxism and Sorcerers.* I don't know who the author was, but I know the book was anti-Soviet. The author discussed the events in Czechoslovakia from a hostile point of view. He called the introduction of allied forces there an occupation and claimed that the intervention had retarded the democratic development of the Czechoslovak Socialist Republic. . . .

KULIKOV also introduced me to L. BORIN's work *The Twilight of Capital.* Its contents are pernicious, because the author's conclusions call for the violent overthrow of the existing system in our country.

From KULIKOV I learned that he had a stenographer's transcript of the proceedings of the 14th Congress of the All-Russian Communist Party (Bolshevik). I asked him to let me read it, and he did. After reading it I used the *Vega* electrograph at my job to print ZINOVIEV's report at the Congress's third session and KAMENEV's speech at the sixth session on a total of 40 sheets of regular paper.

(From KNIAZhENTSEV's testimony of November 19 and 24, 1969)

The witness MIKhAILOV testified,

> ROMANOV introduced me to the articles "Dialectical Materialism and the Effect of the Environment on an Object," *The Twilight of Capital*, "The Deroor" (or "Trumpets of Freedom"), "The Truth of Our Times," "Marxism and Reality," the afterword to *The Twilight of Capital*, and other works whose titles I can't recall.

> At my meetings with ROMANOV we systematically went over the problems in our country, including the shortcomings of our administrative and economic managers, whom we believed were responsible for a great deal of crime, mismanagement, and misappropriation. Then we proceeded to discuss the social and political system [break in the text]

ANIKIN S. P., born 1947, *komsomol* member, third-year correspondence student at the Saratov Teachers' Institute, employed as a lab technician at the Saratov State University satellite tracking station;

MIKhAILOV N. V., born 1948, *komsomol* member, fourth-year student at the History Faculty of Saratov State University;

ZELENSKAIA A. M., born 1949, *komsomol* member, third-year student at the History Faculty of Saratov State University;

KONSTANTINOV S. A., born 1948, *komsomol* member, fourth-year correspondence student at the History Faculty of Saratov State University, employed as a loading dock worker at the Saratov Office of the Russian Recreational and Sporting Goods Wholesale Agency [*Roskultorg*];

KNIAZhENTSEV V. IA., born 1946, *komsomol* member, secondary education, former senior technician at the state university computer center, currently employed at a retail services consortium;

FRONTAS'EVA M. V., born 1946, *komsomol* member, fifth-year student at the Physics Faculty of Saratov State University;

FROLOV V. B., born 1942, *komsomol* member, correspondence graduate student at Saratov State University, employed as an engineer at an electrical appliance factory;

RODIN A. N. born 1938, no party affiliation, secondary education, worker at the Saratov Stamping Plant;

BUNDUR V. F., born 1946, *komsomol* member, secondary education, metalworker at the Saratov Receiver and Amplifier Tube Factory;

SEMENOV A. V., born 1947, *komsomol* member, student at the Physical Education Faculty of the Turkmen State University.

The forenamed individuals gave candid testimony concerning the criminal activity of the group members that they were aware of and their participation in this activity and expressed remorse for their actions.

In light of the above and the change in circumstances caused by the arrest of the group members, the court ruled that IONOV, KLOPIChEV, and other persons were no longer socially dangerous by the time the investigation began. The interrogations of these individuals as witnesses in the preliminary investigation had served as an effective antidote. By agreement with the Procuracy and the courts on the basis of Article 50 of the Criminal Code of the Russian Soviet Federated Socialist Republic, findings were issued absolving these individuals of criminal liability.

On the basis of an analysis of the materials of the investigation, the court proceedings, and investigative notes, we concluded that bourgeois propaganda was the primary reason for the defendants' politically pernicious views and their involvement in anti-Soviet activity.

Their anti-Soviet views were also conditioned by poor political indoctrination, a lack of firm Communist convictions, their tendentious and critical attitude towards Soviet reality, their exposure to *samizdat* works and documents, errors and gaps in their education, deficiencies in social science instruction and political information, ideologically harmful works of literature and art, problems in the economy and with the availability of goods and services, and elements of formalism and bureaucratism in the work of certain officials.

In the court proceedings the evidence produced by the preliminary investigation was confirmed and the defendants confessed their guilt and provided detailed testimony on the crimes they had committed.

The court found the members of the group guilty.

On the basis of Part I Article 70 and Article 72 of the Criminal Code of the Russian Soviet Federated Socialist Republic, the following sentences were pronounced: SENIN was sentenced to 7 years of imprisonment and 2 years of exile; KIRIKOV was sentenced to 6 years of imprisonment and 2 years of exile; ROMANOV was sentenced to 6 years of imprisonment; KULIKOV was sentenced to 5 years of imprisonment; and BOBROV was sentenced to 4 years of imprisonment. FOKEEV was sentenced to a term of three years on the basis of Part I of Article 70 of the Criminal Code of the Russian Soviet Federated Socialist Republic.

Members of the higher education community, including the rectors, secretaries of the party and *komsomol* committees, department heads, social science instructors, and ideological and cultural employees, attended the proceedings at the invitation of the court.

No untoward displays were observed during or after the trial. The *oblast'* Procuracy played an active role in the proceedings. The *KGB* Office received the full-fledged cooperation of the party agencies.

At present we are analyzing the causes behind the emergence and activity of the group, are taking steps toward a more comprehensive study of negative processes among students and the intelligentsia, and are acting to expose and prevent anti-Soviet and politically unhealthy manifestations in a timely manner.

Original signed by the HEAD of the Saratov *Oblast' KGB* Office

[signed] VAS'KIN

February 5, 1970
No. 350/V City of Saratov

True Copy: HEAD OF THE *KGB* OFFICE

[signed] BOBKOV
April 16, 1970

TSK KPSS

On the Report of the Committee for State Security [*KGB*]
of the Council of Ministers of the USSR

The *KGB* (Comrade TSvigun) has informed us of the steps which have been taken to suppress the anti-Soviet activity of a youth group in the city of Saratov. In January of this year the Saratov *Oblast'* Court conducted criminal proceedings against this group and pronounced verdicts of guilty for its members.

In May of this year the Departments of Science and Educational Institutions and Departments of Party Organizational Work of the *TSK KPSS* and *Komsomol* Central Committee, based on material provided by the *KGB* concerning incidents of politically immature manifestations among young students at a number of educational institutions in the Russian Federation and the Ukrainian, Estonian, Lithuanian, and Armenian Soviet Socialist Republics, issued a report to the *TSK KPSS* concerning the steps which have been taken to improve ideological indoctrination for young people and improve monitoring of compliance with Central Committee directives concerning work with young people.

In drafting this report for the *TSK KPSS*, we also considered the incidents in Saratov *oblast'*.

At the present time the Saratov *Oblast'* Committee of the *KPSS* and party organizations at institutions of higher learning in Saratov are taking steps to prevent such manifestations in the future.

At this point we consider it possible to conclude our review of the report provided by the *KGB* on this problem.

Assistant Head of the Department
of Science and Educational Institutions
of the *TSK KPSS*

[signed] (S. Shcherbakov)

May 19, 1970

320*/4

Attachment to No. 14080

TSKhSD, fond 5, op. 62, d. 973, ll. 59–75.

DOCUMENT 140 *Information provided to the Central Committee's Department of Propaganda, October 23, 1970, about measures undertaken by the* Novosti *Press Agency regarding the award of the Nobel Prize to Solzhenitsyn*

<u>Secret</u>
no. 1
no. 785c
23 October 1970

Not for publication

Central Committee of the CPSU
Office of Propaganda

We are forwarding information concerning propaganda measures of *Novosti* Press Agency [*APN*] in connection with the award of the Nobel Prize to A. Solzhenitsyn.

Enclosure: The above-referenced pages

Chairman of the Board
Novosti Press Agency

[signed] I. Udal'tsov

October 23, 1970

<u>INFORMATION</u>

concerning propaganda measures of the *Novosti* Press Agency in connection with the award of the Nobel Prize to A. Solzhenitsyn

The *Novosti* Press Agency [*APN*] has taken measures to explain to the foreign public the Soviet point of view on the award of the Nobel Prize to A. Solzhenitsyn. The TASS release, "An unworthy game" (on the awarding the Nobel Prize to Solzhenitsyn), was transmitted by technical means to 45 recipients on the same day. The commentary, "Where is the Nobel Committee searching for literary talent and fame?" which exposes the treacherous character of Solzhenitsyn's behavior, was transmitted by technical means to 64 recipients on October 9. This material was featured in *Komsomol'skaia Pravda* on October 17.

The *APN* commentary about Solzhenitsyn has been published in Soviet embassy bulletins in Denmark, Sweden, Finland, Australia, Japan, Italy, Switzerland, England, Canada, France, the Congo (Brazzaville), Morocco, and Senegal. They were featured in the *APN* magazine *The Soviet Union Today* in Japan and in the newspaper *Soviet Weekly* in England. *APN* publications in other countries have also published these materials.

In the socialist countries the commentary, "Where is the Nobel Committee searching for literary talent and fame," was published in the newspaper *Zemledelsko zname* (Bulgaria), the newspaper *Magyar hirlap* (Hungary), the newspapers *Rude Pravo* and *Pravda* (Czechoslovakia).

In Yugoslavia the newspaper *Express Politika* published the *APN* commentary under the headlines "An act of provocation" and "An unworthy game." The publication notes: "In a straightforward manner the agency has begun to settle accounts individually with Solzhenitsyn, as a person and as a literary figure. In a commentary published by the agency it is said that Solzhenitsyn "in his self-isolation has created not a tragedy, but a business."

Accusations against the dismissed writer include that he is a person of pathological conceit and "easily succumbs to the flattery of those who are not choosy about the means when it comes to fighting the Soviet system." The commentary of *TANJUG* [Yugoslav News Agency] points to the possibility of a trip to Stockholm for Solzhenitsyn to receive the Nobel Prize. The newspaper *Politika* bears this phrase in the headlines of its publication.

Belgrade's *Politika* published the following report of its Moscow correspondent M. Marković: "The recent sharp criticism on the part of the secretary of the Board of Russian Writers Sergei Mikhailov and the *Literary Gazette* was joined today by *Komsomol'skaia Pravda*—a newspaper which in recent days has written more about Solzhenitsyn than others, probably due to the strong influence of his books on the younger generation. The organ of the Central Committee of the *komsomol* reprinted very sharp attacks published a few day ago by the Soviet agency *APN*, whose bulletins were primarily directed toward foreign editorial offices. . . . All of this, obviously, signifies an intensification of the campaign—writes the newspaper—which cannot but have an influence on the fulfillment of the writer's wish to go to Stockholm, and on his further creative fate as well."

According to a report from the *APN*'s representative in Bucharest, the editors of Romanian newspapers announced that materials received from *APN* about Solzhenitsyn would not be published because they "do not interfere in similar controversial questions." The same was officially announced to Soviet embassy employees by the Writers' Union of Romania.

The position of *APN* generated great interest in the Scandinavian press. The commentary, "Where is the Nobel committee searching for literary talent and fame?" was published in full in the prominent Norwegian newspaper *Aftenposten*, and in shorter form in the Dutch newspaper *Het parool*. In Sweden a version of the commentary was published in the prominent Göteborg newspapers *Göteborgs sjofarts och handelstidning* and *Göteborgsposten*. The full text was featured in the organ of the Swedish Communist party *Norjensflamman*, and a version in the newspaper *Soderhamnskuriren* and in the evening paper *Expressen*. In Finland the commentary was published in the newspaper *Helsingin sanomat*.

In Western Europe the *APN*'s material about Solzhenitsyn was published in a detailed version in the Paris *Le Monde*. In Switzerland the commentary was used by Swiss television in a program devoted to the award of the Nobel Prize to Solzhenitsyn as an exposition of *APN*'s opinion (with a subsequent critique). In England *APN*'s material was published in a summary in the newspapers *The Daily Telegraph* and *The Guardian*.

In Japan the commentary "Where is the Nobel Committee searching for literary talent and fame?" was published in full in the newspapers *Sovieto janaru* and *Nihon-no koe*. In Australia *APN*'s material was featured in excerpts by the newspapers *The Canberra Times* and *The Australian*. The full text was published in the newspaper *The Australian Socialist*.

Material about Solzhenitsyn attracted the attention of press organs of the Middle East, Near East, and Africa. In Morocco *APN*'s commentary was featured by the newspaper *Opinion*. In Algeria the most prominent newspaper in the country, *Al-Mujahid*, placed it under the headline "*APN*. The selection of Solzhenitsyn resembles a joke in poor taste." An account of the commentary was placed in the newspaper *Al-Shaċb*. In Lebanon

APN's material about Solzhenitsyn was published in the newspapers *Ar-Ranat* and *Al-Baykar*. In Mali the newspaper *Essor* printed excerpts from the commentary.

In connection with the fact that the central organs of the Communist Party of France *Humanité* and the Communist Party of Italy *Unita* came out practically justifying the decision of the Nobel committee to award the prize to Solzhenitsyn, defending their position by saying that Solzhenitsyn "suffers" as an opponent of the cult of personality, on October 15 the agency issued a rebuttal in the form of a commentary by the political observer V. Ardatovskii entitled "The prize—for what?" It is intended primarily for the press of the fraternal parties and not to enter into polemics with his French and Italian friends. It contains an analysis of their arguments and an exposition of the true face of Solzhenitsyn as an opponent of the socialist order. The data about the publication of this commentary has not yet been received.

The *Novosti* Press Agency continues to work for the further dissemination abroad of those materials which explain Soviet society's viewpoint concerning the award of the Nobel Prize to Solzhenitsyn.

Chief Secretariat

TSKhSD, fond 5, op. 62, d. 56, ll. 200–203.

DOCUMENT 141   *Sakharov's telegram to the Minister of Health, March 5, 1971, concerning the treatment of political prisoners Fainberg and Borisov, who were being held in a Leningrad psychiatric hospital, and reports on the matter by various officials*

MINISTRY OF HEALTH   <u>Secret</u>
OF THE USSR   Copy no. 1
<u>March 16, 1971</u>
No.704c
Moscow

CENTRAL COMMITTEE OF THE COMMUNIST PARTY OF THE SOVIET UNION

Not for publication

I am sending for your familiarization the text of a telegram from Academician Sakharov that was received in the Ministry of Health of the USSR.

<u>Enclosure</u>: The above-referenced text.

MINISTRY OF HEALTH
OF THE USSR

B. Petrovskii

MINISTRY OF COMMUNICATION OF THE USSR

TELEGRAM   MOSCOW 3502 71 15 1151

NOTIFICATION BY TELEGRAM
MOSCOW I-51 RAKhMANOV LANE 3
MINISTRY OF HEALTH OF THE USSR
TO THE MINISTER,
ACADEMICIAN B. V. PETROVSKII

DEEPLY ESTEEMED BORIS VASIL'EVICh:
FAINBERG AND BORISOV, POLITICAL PRISONERS IN THE LENINGRAD PSYCHIATRIC PRISON, HAVE
ANNOUNCED A HUNGER STRIKE <u>AGAINST COMPULSORY THERAPEUTIC TREATMENT WITH MED-
ICATIONS INJURIOUS TO MENTAL ACTIVITY.</u> I AM ENDORSING THEIR DEMANDS. I ASK YOU UR-
GENTLY TO INTERVENE TO PRESERVE THE HEALTH [AND] DIGNITY OF PRISONERS IN THE PSYCHI-
ATRIC PRISON. PROMOTE THE REMOVAL OF EVEN THE POSSIBILITY OF VIOLATIONS OF HUMAN
RIGHTS AND MEDICAL ETHICS IN THE RUNNING OF PSYCHIATRIC INSTITUTIONS AND THE CORREC-
TION OF VIOLATIONS PERMITTED THERE.
ACADEMICIAN SAKhAROV.

True copy: [signed] Krutova [?]

MINISTRY OF HEALTH OF THE USSR
March 25, 1971
No. 828 c
Moscow

TO THE HEAD OF THE DEPARTMENT OF SCIENCE AND
EDUCATIONAL INSTITUTIONS

CENTRAL COMMITTEE OF THE COMMUNIST PARTY OF THE SOVIET UNION

Comrade S. P. Trapeznikov

In connection with the telegram to me from Academician Sakharov, in which he requests the adoption
of measures against the alleged "compulsory therapeutic treatment with medications injurious to mental activity"
of "political prisoners" Fainberg and Borisov in the "Leningrad Psychiatric Prison," the chief specialist for neu-
ropsychiatry of the Ministry of Health of the USSR, Candidate of Medical Science Z. N. Serebriakova, and the
deputy director of the Scientific Department of the Institute for Psychiatry of the Academy of Medical Sciences of
the USSR, Prof. R. A. Nadzharov, were sent to Leningrad.

An investigation has established that the patients V. I. Fainberg and V. E. Borisov were sent for compulsory therapeutic treatment to the special psychiatric hospital of the Ministry of Internal Affairs of the USSR by
court order in compliance with existing legislation after they were found by forensic-psychiatric experts to be suffering from mental illness and mentally incompetent.

In the patient V. I. Fainberg are noted personality changes and persistent quasi-psychopathic disorders
(paranoid development of the social reforming type), carried over from a schizophrenic condition in his youth, for
which he has repeatedly been hospitalized in psychiatric clinics in Kharkov, Moscow, and Leningrad.

In the patient V. E. Borisov are also noted persistent, quasi-psychopathic personality changes (infantil-
ism, paranoia) against a background of residual, organic neurological symptoms. He has repeatedly undergone

compulsory therapeutic treatment in the special psychiatric hospital in Leningrad in connection with antisocial behavior.

An earlier transfer of the patient for treatment at a standard psychiatric hospital led to negative results.

The patient was returned to the special psychiatric hospital after an attempt to kidnap him by persons unknown who attacked the [hospital] personnel.

Both patients' protest reaction (refusal of food) was linked to the incorrect (in their opinion) prolongation of compulsory treatment and the circumstances of their being held at the indicated hospital.

Because of somatic contraindications, a course of active therapy with psychotropic medicines is not being conducted for patients V. I. Fainberg and V. E. Borisov.

Both patients are undergoing symptomatic treatment, which has no effect on the "intellect" (medicines having an effect on the intellect are unknown to medical science).

Taking into account the origin of the patients' situationally conditioned psychogenic reaction with refusal to eat and the limited possibilities for medical treatment, a change in the conditions of their custody in the given hospital was declared advisable, having in mind more active psychotherapeutic and readapting measures, but also the exclusion of undesirable influences from the outside that would lead to the reinforcement of their paranoid precepts.

Along with the investigation of said patients, the commission familiarized itself with the conditions of their being kept and treated at this hospital.

It was established that the existing internal regime of the special psychiatric hospitals of the Ministry of Internal Affairs of the USSR (on the basis of this hospital) does not meet current requirements for the rehabilitative treatment of mental patients at [regular] hospitals.

The members of the Commission expressed their views jointly with Professor G. V. Morozov, the director of the Serbskii Central Scientific Research Institute of Forensic Psychiatry, at a March 24 meeting conducted by the Directorate of Medical Service and the Main Directorate of Correctional-Labor Establishments of the Ministry of Internal Affairs of the USSR.

As a result of this discussion, a number of joint measures were identified to improve the medical treatment of mental patients in these hospitals.

MINISTER OF HEALTH OF THE USSR   [signed] B. PETROVSKII

CENTRAL COMMITTEE OF THE COMMUNIST PARTY OF THE SOVIET UNION

To No. 12065

In a telegram addressed to the Minister of Health of the USSR, Comrade Petrovskii, Academician Sakharov reports that "political prisoners Fainberg and Borisov of the Leningrad Psychiatric Prison have announced a hunger strike against compulsory treatment with medications injurious to mental activity" and asks that measures be taken to correct the violations permitted there.

The facts indicated in the telegram were investigated by the Ministry of Health of the USSR. It has been determined that the patients V. I. Fainberg and V. E. Borisov were sent for compulsory therapeutic treatment to the special psychiatric hospital of the Ministry of Internal Affairs of the USSR [MVD SSSR] in compliance with existing legislation after forensic-psychiatric experts declared them incompetent by reason of mental illness.

Patient Fainberg exhibits personality changes and persistent quasi-psychopathic disorders carried over from adolescent schizophrenia, for which he was repeatedly hospitalized in psychiatric clinics in Kharkov, Moscow, and Leningrad.

Patient Borisov exhibits persistent quasi-psychopathic personality changes against a background of residual organic neurological symptoms. He has repeatedly undergone compulsory treatment in a special psychiatric hospital because of anti-social behavior.

Both patients have had their symptoms treated in a way that has no effect on mental activity.

Considering that in both patients a situationally conditioned psychological reaction with refusal of food has arisen, specialists have advised more actively applying psychotherapeutic and readapting measures to them.

During the investigation, it was noticed that the internal regime of the special psychiatric hospitals of the *MVD SSSR* do not meet modern requirements for the rehabilitative treatment of the mentally ill in inpatient hospitals.

The *MVD SSSR* has now outlined a series of measures to improve medical service for the mentally ill in said hospitals.

Comrade Sakharov has been informed of the results.

Deputy Director of the Department
of Science and Educational
Institutions of the Central   [signed] V. Baltiiskii
Committee of the Communist
Party of the Soviet Union

June 10, 1971
320-A/7

TSKhSD, fond 5, op. 63, d. 136, l. 18.

DOCUMENT 142   *Note from Zamiatin, director of TASS, to Brezhnev, May 6, 1971, asking for a delay in upcoming political trials*

To Comrade L. I. Brezhnev

Esteemed Leonid Il'ich:

Presently under discussion is the question of the line our propaganda should take in regard to the trials planned for the first half of May in Leningrad (May 11), Riga, and Kishinev involving certain groups of persons charged with anti-Soviet and Zionist activities. The question arises of how to counter the negative propaganda that, undoubtedly, will make active use of these trials to develop a new anti-Soviet campaign of international proportions.

In this regard I would like to offer the following observations. At present, the proceedings of the Twenty-fourth Congress of the Communist Party of the Soviet Union are under lively discussion worldwide. The impact of the resolutions of the congress on the general international situation is enormous. In the international sphere at all levels—democratic, bourgeois—the foreign policy of the congress is characterized as one of peace. At the very moment when we are in such a favorable foreign policy position, it seems to me that we should not provide any grounds that imperialist propaganda could use to alter to its benefit the advantageous position of the Soviet Union in the world.

An additional point. The above-mentioned judicial proceedings coincide with the elections to the Supreme Soviets of the republics. It doesn't pay to provide Western propaganda a pretext to tarnish the impression created in the world by this broad demonstration of the unity between the party and the people. One can hardly doubt that in connection with these trials once more will be spread slanderous fabrications about the presence of "opposition groups" in various cities throughout the USSR, etc.

A third point. The actions by the government of the United States to put down peaceful demonstrations against the war in Vietnam outraged the world community enormously. In Washington alone, as is generally known, during the last few days more than ten thousand demonstrators were arrested. Our propaganda is energetically exploiting this now. However, the start of the trials in the Soviet Union will, in all likelihood, help the Americans to divert public attention away from their actions and once more to trumpet ballyhoo throughout the world about the so-called Jewish question in the USSR. And it's a dead certainty that this will again strike a responsive chord in certain liberal and even Communist circles in the West that are now actively protesting against the actions of the Nixon administration.

Leonid Il'ich! I do not know all the aspects of this affair, but it seems it would be possible (not to mention politically expedient) to delay the trials until a later, more reasonable date, well, let's say, until after the results of the elections to the Supreme Soviets—June 13.

[signed] L. Zamiatin

May 6, 1971

[Handwritten notation at top left of page 1:] To Comrade M. A. Suslov: please discuss this matter expeditiously with the comrades. L. Brezhnev

TSKhSD, fond 5, op. 63, d. 1, ll. 6–7.

DOCUMENT 143   *Letter from V. S. Vysotskii of the Moscow Taganka Theater to Central Committee Secretary Demichev, April 17, 1973, concerning permission to hold a concert and the Committee's denial of the request*

[Handwritten cover sheet:] To Comrade V. F. Shauro, per understanding. [signature illegible]
March 16, 1973. ....
                              [Handwritten:]   Vysotskii, V.

Central Committee of the Communist Party of the Soviet Union
[*TSK KPSS*]   No. 63382

Moscow Drama and Comedy Theater [Taganka] artist Comrade V. S. Vysotskii has addressed the Central Committee of the Communist Party of the Soviet Union in a letter in which he raises the issue of obtaining permission to perform his concerts and in which he voices disagreement with correspondence published in the newspaper *Sovetskaia kul'tura* on March 30, 1973, concerning his public appearances in Novokuznetsk.

According to the report of the RSFSR Ministry of Culture (Comrade E. V. Zaitsev) the tour of Comrade V. S. Vysotskii in the city of Novokuznetsk was conducted without the knowledge of *Roskontsert* [Russian Concert], which is responsible for the arranging and quality control of concerts. Comrade V. S. Vysotskii does not have the government permit required to have the right to give performances. Related to this, no schedule of fees has been set for his concerts.

Director of the Novokuznetsk Theater Comrade D. O. Barats and Director of the Kemerovo *Oblast'* Cultural Administration Comrade I. L. Kurochkin received harsh administrative penalties for violating regulations established by the USSR Ministry of Culture governing the arrangement and conduct of concert tours in the country.

In a conversation with B. V. Pokarzhevskii, chief of the Main Administration of Culture in the Moscow City Executive Committee, the author of the letter had received an explanation of the procedure for certifying performers and organizing their concert appearances.

The Kemerovo *Oblast'* Committee of the *KPSS* (Comrade Z. V. Kuz'min) confirmed the correctness of the criticism by the newspaper *Sovetskaia kul'tura* with regard to Comrade V. S. Vysotskii's concerts (the response of the Culture Department of the *KPSS* was printed in the newspaper *Sovetskaia kul'tura* on April 24, 1973).

Assistant Chief of the Culture Section
TSK KPSS [signed] Z. Tumanova (Z. Tumanova)
June 14, 1973

To Candidate Member of the Politburo, Secretary of the *TSK KPSS*
Comrade P. N. Demichev

From Artist of the Moscow Drama and Comedy Theater at Taganka
V. S. Vysotskii

ESTEEMED PETR NILOVICh!

Lately, I have become the object of the hostile attention of the press and the Ministry of Culture of the RSFSR.

For nine years I have been unable to receive official permission to perform my songs before a live audience. All my efforts to go through concert organizations and ministries of culture have been fruitless. That is why I am addressing you; at issue is the fate of my creative work, which is my own fate.

You probably know that in this country it is easier to find a tape recorder playing my songs than one that is not. For nine years I have asked for one thing only: to be allowed to perform live in front of an audience, to select songs at my concerts, to control my program.

Why have I been put in a position where my responsible civic creativity is construed as independence? I will answer for my art before the nation that sings and listens to my songs, even though they are not advertised on the radio or television or by concert promoters. But I see how the short-sighted caution of the cultural officials who must resolve these problems directly is undermining all my efforts to work creatively within the traditional performance framework. This has involuntarily provoked the explosion of pirated tapes of my music; moreover, my songs in the final analysis are life-affirming, and I am placed in the role of the sufferer, the persecuted poet. I realize that my art is somewhat unorthodox, but in all seriousness, I understand that I can be a useful tool for promoting ideas, not only those that are acceptable but also vitally necessary to our society. There are millions of spectators and listeners whom I can reach with my genre of song poetry, which almost no other artist performs.

That is why when I received the first official invitation in years to perform to audiences of Kuzbas workers, I happily accepted, and I can say that I gave the performance everything I had. The concerts went well. At the end of the show, the workers gave me a special medal cast in steel as an expression of their appreciation; the *oblast'* party and government functionaries thanked me for these performances, invited me to come again. I returned to Moscow a happy man, for I had hoped of late that my performance would finally enter official channels.

Instead, [I got] an undeserved spit in the face, an insulting commentary on a journalist's letter by A. V. Romanov in the newspaper *Sovetskaia kul'tura*, which could be a signal of a campaign against me, just as has happened before.

In the cosmonauts' village, in student dorms, in academic and almost any worker community in the Soviet Union, my songs are heard. Commanding such popularity, I want to place my talent in the service of spreading ideas about our society. It is strange that I am the only one concerned about this. This is not a simple problem, but can it really be solved by trying to shut me up or devising some way of publicly humiliating me?

I desire only one thing—to be the poet and the artist of the people, whom I love, of the people whose pain and happiness I seem to be able to express in tune with the ideas that shape our society.

And the fact that I am not like others is part of the problem that requires the attention and involvement of the leadership.

Your assistance will enable me to bring much greater benefit to our society.

V. Vysotskii

TSKhSD [no further cite]

DOCUMENT 144   *Memorandum from V. Shauro, director of the Department of Culture, to the Central Committee, June 20, 1975, regarding the publication in the West of Solzhenitsyn's* The Oak and the Calf *and proposing publication of a book to expose Solzhenitsyn as a slanderer—rejected by the Writers' Union*

<u>Secret</u>
TSK KPSS
June 20
23801

Not for Publication.

Central Committee of the Communist Party of the Soviet Union [*TSK KPSS*]
<u>Concerning A. Solzhenitsyn's Book</u>
<u>*The Oak and the Calf*</u>

In the spring of this year the bourgeois publisher YMCA-Press published in Russian a book by A. Solzhenitsyn, *The Oak and the Calf*. The book has the subtitle *Sketches of literary life* and is a slanderous version of the relationship of Solzhenitsyn with the USSR Union of Writers and Soviet society in the years 1961–1974.

In his new work Solzhenitsyn declares his long-standing hatred of the socialist social order, of Lenin and Leninism, of everything Soviet. Calling himself a "writer-member of the underground," he confesses that since his youth he nurtured plans to undermine the Soviet government. The book *The Oak and the Calf* represents the cynical confession of an ideological saboteur.

In the opinion of the USSR Union of Writers (Comrade Markov), in connection with the publication of *The Oak and the Calf* in the West it would be entirely appropriate to prepare and publish in foreign languages for distribution in foreign countries, as well as in Russian for the Soviet reader, a book consisting of reliable material about the activities of Solzhenitsyn hostile to socialism (articles from the Soviet press, verbatim reports of discussions in the secretariat of the USSR Union of Writers, critical speeches and statements of Soviet and foreign writers and artists about Solzhenitsyn, and so forth). Such a documentary publication would contribute to the further exposure of Solzhenitsyn as a slanderer and falsifier and would be a valuable illustration of the actual picture of the development of Soviet literature and attitude of society to the provocative activities of Solzhenitsyn.

Work on the book could be entrusted to the USSR Union of Writers and the *Novosti* Press Agency along with other interested departments. The *Novosti* Press Agency has experience in the preparation and dissemination of this type of publication (for example, the collections *The Press on Solzhenitsyn, Last Circle,* and others).

The cultural section of the *TSK KPSS* agrees with the opinion of the USSR Union of Writers.

We request your review.

Director of the Cultural
Section of the *TSK KPSS*
[signed] V. Shauro
June 20, 1975

[Handwritten note:] The Union of Writers (Markov) at the present time withdraws its suggestion.

TSKhSD, fond 5, op. 69, d. 625.

Report from KGB chief Andropov to the Central Committee, November 15, 1976, on the hostile activities of the "Group for Implementation of the Helsinki Accords in the USSR"

Not for Publication

	Secret
Committee for State	*TSK KPSS*
Security, Council	15.NOV76 52269
of Ministers of the USSR	To be returned to the
	General Dept.,

TSK KPSS

No. 2577
Moscow

Central Committee of the Communist Party of the Soviet Union [*TSK KPSS*]

On the hostile activities of the
so-called Group for Implementation
of the Helsinki Accords in the USSR

In recent years our adversary's special services and propaganda bureaus have attempted to give the impression that a so-called internal opposition exists in the USSR, rendering support to those who inspire antisocial activities and objectively promote the banding together of participants in a variety of anti-Soviet activities.

Accordingly, in 1969 antisocial elements headed by YAKIR and KRASIN founded an "initiative group" in order to form an organization made up of participants of the so-called movement for democratization.

In 1970, in order to energize the antisocial efforts of individuals with hostile attitudes, ChALIDZE established the so-called Committee for the Defense of Human Rights, which, in addition to himself, includes among its members Academician SAKhAROV and ShAFAREVICh, a corresponding member of the Academy of Sciences of the USSR.

In 1973 the so-called Russian Section of Amnesty International, headed by TURChIN and TVER-DOKhLEBOV, assumed organizational responsibilities for individuals with anti-Soviet attitudes.

Members of these organizations made contacts with selected anti-Soviet centers abroad and engaged in the collection and dissemination of defamatory materials to discredit the Soviet state and civic order.

As a result of measures taken by the Committee for State Security the "initiative group" and the "Committee for the Defense of Human Rights" have been completely compromised and have virtually ceased to exist. The activities of the "Russian Section" have been curtailed.

Nevertheless, despite the failure to create an "internal opposition" in the USSR, our adversary has not abandoned this idea.

On May 12 of this year, on the initiative of IURII F. ORLOV, born in 1924, unemployed, corresponding member of the Academy of Sciences of the Armenian SSR, the antisocial elements announced the formation of a "Group for Implementation of the Helsinki Accords in the USSR."

This "group" includes the following individuals: GINZBURG, A. I., who has on numerous occasions been charged with criminal actions, born 1936, Jew, without regular employment; GRIGORENKO, P. G., born 1907, Ukrainian, retiree; the professional criminal MARChENKO, A. T., born 1938, Russian, in exile in Irkutsk *oblast'*; the Jewish extremists: RUBIN, V. A., born 1913, Jew, emigrated to Israel; ShchARANSKY, A. D., born 1948, Jew, without regular employment; and SLEPAK, V. S., born 1927, Jew, without regular employment; participants in various hostile activities: SAKhAROV's wife BONNER, E. G., born 1922, Jew, retiree; BERNShTAM, M.

S., born 1949, Jew, emigrated to Israel; LANDA, M. N., born 1918, Jew, retiree, without regular employment; ALEKSEEVA, L. M., born 1927, Russian, without regular employment, and KORChAK, A. A., born 1922, Ukrainian, fellow at the Institute of Terrestrial Magnetism, Ionosphere and Radio Wave Transmission, Academy of Sciences of the USSR.

By the creation of this "group" the individuals just named have made it their provocative goal to put in doubt the Soviet Union's sincere efforts to implement the principles of the Final Act of the Conference on Cooperation and Security in Europe, and thereby to exert pressure on the Soviet government with respect to implementation of the Helsinki Accords, especially as concerns the "third basket."

Members of the "group" are collecting materials on the alleged noncompliance of Soviet authorities with the Final Act, especially on the "violation of the basic rights of Soviet citizens," "persecution of dissenters," etc.

The information collected on these topics is transmitted via various channels to governments that have signed the Final Act. It is the intention of the "group" to request that, in special cases, these countries form an international commission to investigate these matters. In addition, the "group" will rely on the pressure of Western public opinion on the Soviet government, and does not—in the words of ORLOV—"seek support among the people."

Antisocial elements are calling on the heads of states participating in the Helsinki Conference to create in their countries unofficial monitoring groups, which could subsequently be unified into an international committee.

During the period of its existence the "group" has attempted to gain official recognition in the U.S.A. For example, in his talk with RICHARD COMBS, first secretary for political affairs at the U.S. embassy in Moscow, in September of this year ORLOV insisted on official recognition of the "group" by the U.S. Department of State and on the use by Americans of information supplied by the "group" in dealing with other governments and heads of governments, including their use at the upcoming meeting in Belgrade.

The Committee for State Security is taking measures to compromise and put an end to the "group's" hostile activities.

Reported by way of information.

Chairman of the Committee on State Security

[signed] Andropov

Filed Nov. 29, 1976

TSKhSD, fond 5, op. 69, d. 2890.

Report from KGB chief Andropov to the Central Committee, December 6, 1976, regarding the "provocational" gathering of antisocial elements on Pushkin Square in Moscow and at the Pushkin monument in Leningrad the previous day, in silent protest about violations of the Soviet Constitution

SECRET

USSR
Committee on State Security [*KGB*]
USSR Council of Ministers

December 6, 1976
No. 2755-A
Moscow

To the CPSU Central Committee

On a provocational gathering of antisocial elements on Pushkin Square in Moscow and at the Pushkin monument in Leningrad

On December 5 of this year a group of antisocial elements gathered at Pushkin Square with the confrontational goal of expressing "silent protest" in connection with "violations" of the rights guaranteed to citizens by the USSR Constitution.

On the square at the Pushkin monument were the following: SAKhAROV, SEMENOVA and IANKELEVICh (the daughter and son-in-law of Bonner), the GRIGORENKOS, BUKOVSKAIA, ALEKSEEVA, SALOVA, ShATUNOVSKAIA, GASTEV, GENKIN, STARChIK, LANDA, Irina IAKIR, and others, in all about fifty people. At 6 P.M. some of them removed their hats and attempted to observe a so-called minute of silence.

The following foreign correspondents were present on the square at the time: REN, WILLIS, KRIMSKY, KENT, WALLACE (U.S.); KETLIN, EVANS, BLUETT (Great Britain); PREDE, JURGEN, ENGELBREChT, BRANDT (West Germany); and BOLENBACh (France), who photographed the participants in the demonstration.

Residents of Moscow and guests in the capital present on the square expressed their indignation at this demonstration by antisocial elements.

In Leningrad on the same day a group of ten hostile persons carried out a similar action at the monument to Pushkin on the Square of the Arts.

In both cases no incidents were recorded.

This is being provided for your information.

[signed] Andropov
Chair, Committee on State Security

TSKhSD, fond 5. op. 69, d. 2890.

NOT FOR PUBLICATION

Secret
February 2, 1979 03574
RETURN TO GENERAL DEPT
TSK KPSS

Central Committee, Communist Party of the Soviet Union
[*TSK KPSS*]

Concerning the Letter of a Group of Moscow Writers and the *Metropol'* Almanac

The writers V. Aksenov, B. Akhmadulina, A. Bitov, and others (a total of 6 persons) have complained to the *TSK KPSS* about what they allege to be the incorrect treatment of their literary almanac at the hands of the administration of the Moscow writers' organization.

In this connection we deem it necessary to relay the following information.

In mid-January of this year it became known that members of the USSR Writers' Union, A. Bitov and F. Iskander and the aspiring writers E. Popov and V. Erofeev who were recently accepted into the Union but have not yet received membership cards, produced an anthology entitled *Metropol'* and, bypassing standard procedures, intended to demand that the State Committee on Publishing [*Goskomizdat*] publish it immediately.

The massive anthology (about one-thousand typed pages) was preceded by a foreword, asserting that the editing/publishing practices now in place in the USSR are not acceptable to the authors, and that "the stifling inertia that exists in the journals and other publications is giving rise to an inflated, pervasive sense of responsibility for an "item" of literature that not only cannot be as it ought to be but even isn't what it was yesterday. This pervasive "responsibility" is creating a state of stagnant, silent fear, a striving to make a literary "item" conform to a rigid ranking. Literature that is not part of a set sometimes is doomed to many years of wandering and homelessness."

Some of the compositions included in the almanac pointedly focus on presenting negative aspects of our life. Some of them are ambiguous in their ideological and political leanings. Many of them are packed with erotic, at times explicitly pornographic scenes.

In all 23 writers were persuaded to contribute to *Metropol'*. Among them were 11 members of the USSR Writers' Union (in addition to those already mentioned: S. Lipkin, I. Lisnianskaia, A. Arkanov, B. Bakhtin), as well as nonmembers of the USSR Writers' Union: M. Rozovskii, E. Rein, F. Gorinshtein, P. Kozhevnikov, G. Sapgir, V. Vysotskii, IU. Karabichevskii, IU. Kublanovskii, V. Rakitin, V. Trostnikov, L. Batkin, and IU. Aleshkovskii. (IU. Aleshkovskii was expelled from the USSR Writers' Union because of his impending departure for Israel.)

To give his anthology greater prestige, V. Aksenov recruited two well-known Soviet writers to contribute. The anthology includes a few poems by A. Voznesenskii and a small prose work by B. Akhmadulina.

B. Messerer and D. Borovskii, who are members of the USSR Artists' Union, designed the almanac.

The almanac's organizers planned an evening at a Moscow cafe, with a large circle of artists from the capital in attendance, to celebrate the publication of the almanac; they also planned a press conference for foreign correspondents.

The Moscow writers' organization secretariat conducted individual interviews with A. Bitov, F. Iskander, E. Popov, and V. Erofeev (V. Aksenov declined). Attempts to make clear to the almanac's organizers the unseemly ideological character of their undertaking, the incompatibility of their actions with the standards of our literary life, were not crowned with success.

On January 22 the Secretariat of the Board of Directors and the Party Committee of the Moscow writers' organization met in joint session and reviewed the matter of the *Metropol'* anthology.

In their speeches, F. Kuznetsov, who is first secretary of the Directorate of the Moscow writers' organization, M. Baryshev, who is secretary of the Party Committee, and the well-known writers M. Alekseev, N. Gribachev, IU. Zhukov, A. Aleksin, IA. Kozlovskii, L. Ginzburg, IU. Drunina, and others, characterized the actions of the anthology compilers as a political provocation designed to ignite another anti-Soviet campaign in the West and an attempt to legalize "samizdat."

The organizers of *Metropol'* were advised to resolve the matter of publishing the works therein in accordance with Soviet copyright standards and the publishing practices existing in our country.

V. Aksenov, A. Bitov, F. Iskander, E. Popov, and V. Erofeev (all present at the session) naively attempted to portray their actions as "concern" for expanding the artistic richness of Soviet literature and offered assurances that they have no ties with foreign propaganda centers and do not intend to send the manuscript out of the country.

The next day they announced that they would not hold their "opening day" ceremony and press conference.

But on that very evening the radio station "Voice of America" reported that manuscripts of *Metropol'* were already outside the country and would soon be published in the U.S.A. and France.

The Secretariat of the Board of the Moscow writers' organization, with the agreement of the Moscow City Committee of the *KPSS* and the USSR Writers' Union, developed measures to neutralize this leak.

The large-circulation newspaper *Moskovskii literator* [Moscow Writer] is preparing to publish material on the joint session of the Secretariat and Party Committee of the Moscow writers' organization.

An issue of *Literaturnaia gazeta* also is being prepared which will present a basic critique of the anthology and show the unseemly role of its organizers.[1]

The Moscow writers' organization is planning an open party session with the agenda: "The Contemporary Ideological Struggle and the Mission of Moscow Writers."

The Moscow City Committee of the *KPSS* and the administration of the Moscow writers' organization continue their individual work with the anthology participants. Authors of works that do not contradict the ideological and aesthetic principles of Soviet art in terms of their spirit and tone will be advised to publish those works in appropriate Soviet publications.

Reported for your information.

Head of the Cultural Department
TSK KPSS [signed] V. Shauro

January 2, 1979

[handwritten:] <u>To the archives.</u> Relay comments of Comrade Kirilenko [?] A. G. to Comrade Shauro V. F. [illegible signature]

---

1. [This paragraph is bracketed for deletion. The handwritten annotation in the left margin reads] "Better without. Remove." [It is initialed] "Kru."

January 19, 1979

GENERAL SECRETARY OF THE *TSK KPSS*
CHAIRMAN OF THE PRESIDIUM OF THE SUPREME SOVIET OF THE USSR
Comrade L. I. BREZhNEV

copy: SECRETARY OF THE *TSK KPSS* Comrade M. V. ZIMIANIN

DEAR LEONID IL'ICh !

We, Moscow writers, earnestly request that you find the time to intercede in the conflict that has arisen in the Moscow writers' organization.

We have produced a new literary almanac that reflects the artistic aspirations of various generations of contemporary Soviet writers. The basic mission of our work is to expand the creative possibilities of contemporary Soviet literature, thereby enriching our culture and bolstering its prestige both inside and outside the country.

Unfortunately, the administration of the Moscow writers' organization greeted our initiative not only without enthusiasm but with inexplicable suspicion that has now degenerated to unfounded accusations and threats.

Without taking the trouble to read through the text of the manuscript thoroughly, the secretaries of the Moscow writers' organization have pronounced our almanac a dangerous undertaking and have inflated to hyperbolic proportions the importance of standard literary procedure.

We believe that this kind of treatment of writers is intolerable and sharply contradicts Leninist cultural policy.

With deep respect, on behalf of the almanac authors

Members of the USSR Writers' Union
[signed] V. Aksenov, Bella Akhmadulina, A. Bitov, Vik. Erofeev, Evg. Popov, F. A. Iskander

TSKhSD, fond 5, op. 76, d. 273.

Andrei Sakharov

Andrei Sakharov (1921–89) epitomized the educational and scientific accomplishments of the Soviet era. Trained as a nuclear physicist during World War II, he joined the research team that developed a Soviet hydrogen bomb in 1953, and he was elected that year to full membership in the Soviet Academy of Sciences, the youngest person to receive this honor. His science was infused with humanism, and like many other physicists of this era he was appalled at the implications of the weapon he had helped to develop. He wrote to Khrushchev in 1958 and 1961 about the dangers of nuclear weapons testing. During the 1960s he gradually became involved with the growing human rights movement; in 1968 he published his essay, *Reflections on Progress, Peaceful Coexistence, and Intellectual Freedom,* calling for an end to the Cold War and urging democratic reform. He continued to defend human rights and democratization, and he gained immense moral authority with his

quiet and consistent defense of the rights of conscience. His protection extended to Aleksandr Solzhenitsyn, although the two represented quite distinct political positions within the Soviet dissident movement; for his defense of Solzhenitsyn, both were subjected to rabid vilification in the Soviet
press in the early 1970s. Although Solzhenitsyn was arrested and deported,
Sakharov continued to enjoy a kind of immunity afforded by his status as a
scientific hero and full member of the Academy of Sciences. With his wife
Elena Bonner, Sakharov continued to support the emerging movement of
Helsinki Watch groups and to act as conduit between the dissident community and the Western press. In 1975 he was awarded the Nobel Peace Prize, but
he declined to accept the prize in person, fearing his citizenship would be revoked if he traveled abroad. Finally in 1980 the Soviet authorities could tolerate him no more, and Sakharov was exiled to the city of Gorky, a closed city
forbidden to foreigners. He languished there for six years until Gorbachev rescinded his sentence of exile. Sakharov immediately resumed his familiar role
of conscience of the people. When party officials conspired to block his nomination as a member of the Academy of Sciences slate for the Congress of People's Deputies in 1989, a grass-roots movement elected him anyway. He
served in the first elected congress as an eloquent supporter of nationality
rights and human rights; his death in late 1989 was mourned by world leaders
and by ordinary Russians who lamented, "We are all orphans now."

DOCUMENT 148   *Report from KGB chief Fedorchuk, August 31, 1982, on the squashing of
Sakharov's appeal to the May 1982 Pugwash Conference, one of many held since 1957 by scientists
and scholars on nuclear armaments and other world problems*

Top Secret

Committee of State Security
of the USSR [*KGB*]
August 31, 1982. No. 1789-F
Central Committee of the Communist Party of the Soviet Union [*TSK KPSS*]
31.AUG.82 23033

On the preparation of Sakharov's latest anti-Soviet "appeal"
to the West and its use by the Americans
for purposes hostile to the Soviet Union

In May 1982 Academician A. D. Sakharov prepared an "appeal" to the "Participants of the Pugwash
Conference," which contained sharp anti-Soviet evaluations of the internal and foreign policies of the CPSU and
Soviet government, accusing the USSR of "building up its army, navy, missile arsenal, and air force" and "interfering in the internal affairs of Afghanistan and Poland." Sakharov demagogically declares that the Soviet government remains a "closed society" and persecutes "fighters for human rights." He tries to compromise the broad antiwar movement in the West and its leaders. He accuses the participants of the Pugwash movement of "blindly
following" the policies of the USSR and incites scholars to meddle in the internal affairs of our country and come
to the defense of persons convicted for committing particularly dangerous state crimes.

Data in our possession indicate that this "appeal" was transmitted to the West by Sakharov's wife, Bonner.

The Americans tried to exploit this libel for purposes hostile to the USSR at the latest session of the Pugwash Conference in Warsaw as a counterbalance to the declaration of 97 Nobel Prize laureates reflecting the basic principles of the international movement of scientists for peace.

On August 28 Sakharov's "appeal" was distributed illegally among the delegates by the Americans, and the Canadian scientist Sommers planned to read it out and place it on the agenda for discussion by the conference delegates.

As a result of measures taken, the hostile plans of the adversary have been foiled.

Communicated for your information

Chairman of the Committee   [signed] V. Fedorchuk

TSKhSD, fond 5, op. 88, d. 1083.

DOCUMENT 149   *Materials from Central Committee discussions of Andrei Sakharov, 1980, 1982, 1988*

To the Central Committee [*TSK*] of the Communist Party of the Soviet Union [*KPSS*] (General Department, 1st Sector)

COMMUNIST PARTY OF THE SOVIET UNION, CENTRAL COMMITTEE

TOP SECRET

SPECIAL FOLDER

PERSONALLY

No. P.177/X

To Comrades Brezhnev, Andropov, Grishin, Gromyko, Kirilenko, Kosygin, Kunaev, Pel'she, Romanov, Suslov, Tikhonov, Ustinov, Chernenko, Shcherbitskii, Aliev, Gorbachev, Demichev, Kuznetsov, Masherov, Ponomarev, Rashidov, Solomentsev, Shevardnadze, Dolgikh, Zimianin, Kapitonov, Rusakov, Rudenko, Savinkin, Trapeznikov, Tiazhel'nikov, Georgadze, Smirtiukov - everything; Aleksandrov - point 1 (addendum, respectively), Alekseev - point 3.

Extract from minutes no. 177 from the January 3, 1980, session of the Politburo of the *TSK KPSS*

Issue for the *KGB* and Procuracy of the USSR.

1. Concur with the proposals of the *KGB* and Procuracy of the USSR presented in the memorandum of December 26, 1979, No. 2484-A (attached).

2. Approve the draft decrees of the Presidium of the Supreme Soviet of the USSR and the resolutions of the Council of Ministers of the USSR on the given matter (attached).

3. The editors of the newspaper *Izvestiia* to prepare and publish a communique on this matter; coordinate its text with the *KGB* (text attached).

Decree of the Presidium of the
Supreme Soviet of the USSR
pt. 2 No. 1390-x of February 8, 1980
    1389-x February 8, 1980

Resolution of the Council of Ministers
of the USSR, pt. 2, No. 22 of January 8, 1980   pt. 3 published Jan. 22, 1980 in *Izvestiia*

About Sakharov, D. A. [*sic!*]

To pt. 10, min. no. 177

<u>Top Secret</u>
<u>SPECIAL FOLDER</u>

TSK KPSS

<u>On Measures to Suppress the Harmful Activity of A. D. Sakharov</u>

Academician Sakharov, being a confirmed opponent of the socialist system, has been conducting a subversive effort against the Soviet state for more than ten years. Firmly holding to the positions of an opponent of socialism, he is urging aggressive circles in capitalist states to interfere in the internal affairs of socialist countries and toward military confrontation with the Soviet Union. He constantly is speaking out against official Soviet policy, which aims for the relaxation of international tension and peaceful coexistence. Moreover, Sakharov is undertaking measures to organize and unify anti-Soviet elements within the country and is inciting them to extremist actions.

Harming the national interests of the USSR, Sakharov is giving representatives of capitalist countries secrets relating to the most critical aspects of our national defense. Specifically, in 1974 during conversations with American, German, and Canadian journalists, he divulged the specifications of Soviet strategic missiles and launch sites and data on the number of warheads, and he named the ministries involved in their production. Experts have concluded that this information is classified Top Secret and constitutes a state secret. Delivery of such information to the enemy is covered by the law specifying guilt for treason.

Violating established regulations for working with foreigners, Sakharov maintains constant contacts with diplomatic representatives of capitalist countries in Moscow. In 1972–1979 he visited these representatives 80 times. He maintains closest contacts with the representatives of the U.S. embassy and with American correspondents, to whom he systematically expresses his negative reaction to the political measures implemented in our country; he informs them of inflammatory actions by antisocial elements. In turn, the diplomats and intelligence operatives working under diplomatic cover exploit contact with Sakharov to obtain political information and facts pertaining to his past work at an especially important facility.

Sakharov has established direct contact with antisocialist elements in Poland and Czechoslovakia; he has shown solidarity with Czechoslovak "chartists" and with members of the so-called Social Self-Defense Committee in Poland, and he is summoning them to organizationally unite to carry on antisocialist activity from unified, coordinated positions.

To undermine Soviet authority, Sakharov systematically renders assistance to foreign states in conducting hostile activity against the USSR. He actively participates in anti-Soviet agitation and propaganda. In 1968–1979 he authored and circulated abroad a number of anti-Soviet documents of a programmatic nature—more than 200 "declarations," "appeals," and "protests," in which he doggedly cautions the West against disarmament and asserts that the only acceptable form of interstate relations with the USSR can be the situation "when Vance has forces two or three times greater than the Soviet [forces]." In doing this he maliciously slanders, proclaiming the "totalitarian nature of our system," the "global challenge of socialism," the "concealed militarization of the Soviet economy," "communist expansionism," etc. In addition to contacts with embassy representatives, Sakharov had more than 600 meetings with other foreigners to discuss various aspects of organizing and conducting anti-Soviet activity. He held more than 150 so-called press conferences for Western correspondents. Based on his materials, Western radio stations prepared and transmitted about 1,200 anti-Soviet broadcasts.

The West generously compensates Sakharov's hostile activity, transferring tens of thousands of dollars to his account in foreign banks. They acknowledged his zeal by awarding him the Nobel Peace Prize and other monetary prizes.

In 1970 Sakharov established the so-called Human Rights Committee. Behind the facade of the "committee," Sakharov actively consolidated antisocial elements, established and maintained contacts with foreign subversive centers, and guided the execution of extremist and inflammatory anti-Soviet actions. Eleven persons were indicted and convicted for crimes conducted behind the facade of the "committee" and directly instigated by Sakharov. The "committee" gave rise to "groups aiding fulfillment of the Helsinki Accords in the USSR," "commissions to investigate the use of psychiatry for political purposes," and certain other antisocial groupings.

Party, Soviet, and public organizations, the procuracy, and security agencies repeatedly have warned Sakharov about the unacceptability of his hostile activity; prominent scholars have warned him; the deputy chairman of the Council of Ministers of the USSR has spoken with him on behalf of the Soviet government. Sakharov has been warned officially by the Procuracy of the USSR three times. He has ignored all these warnings.

Thus, Sakharov's activity is of the nature of a punishable crime. His actions completely fall within the description of crimes specified by point "a", art. 64 (treason), part I, art. 70 (anti-Soviet agitation and propaganda) of the Criminal Code of the RSFSR.

However, bringing Sakharov to trial may entail serious political costs. At least 2–3 months will be required to conduct a preliminary investigation of the matter and review it in court. During that time the West undoubtedly will organize loud anti-Soviet campaigns, which will be difficult to neutralize since criminal procedural law proscribes using criminal evidence for propaganda purposes before the court has concluded its examination of it.

Thus, administrative measures against Sakharov are called for, whereby his contacts with foreigners could be severed, and his inimical activity could be hampered seriously.

To suppress Sakharov's anti-Soviet activity, in our view, it is essential to implement the following measures:

- examine the possibility of depriving Sakharov of his exalted titles of Hero of Socialist Labor, recipient of the Lenin and State prizes of the USSR, and other state awards (drafts of a Decree from the Presidium of the Supreme Soviet of the USSR and a resolution from the Council of Ministers of the USSR are attached);

- adopt the Decree of the Presidium of the Supreme Soviet of the USSR, by which, as a preventive measure, he is administratively evicted from the city of Moscow to one of the areas of the country closed to foreign visitors (a draft Decree from the Presidium of the Supreme Soviet of the USSR is attached);

- the Academy of Sciences of the USSR should discuss at an expanded session of the Presidium (or at another representative gathering of scholars) the antisocial conduct of Academician Sakharov. The *KGB* should forward the necessary information to the Presidium of the Academy of Sciences of the USSR (information attached);

- publish in the press an appropriate communique on the measures taken with respect to Sakharov (attached).

Request your review.

IU. Andropov   R. Rudenko

December 26, 1979
No. 2484-A

Proletarians of All Countries, Unite!

COMMUNIST PARTY OF THE SOVIET UNION, CENTRAL COMMITTEE

TOP SECRET

No. P53/23

To Comrades Brezhnev, Tikhonov, Andropov, Gromyko,
Aleksandrov, Trapeznikov

Extract from Minutes No. 53 of the April 6, 1982, session of the Politburo of the Central Committee of the Communist Party of the Soviet Union

On Measures to Censure the Latest Inflammatory Statement by Academician Sakharov.

Instruct the Presidium of the Academy of Sciences of the USSR to introduce a motion in connection with the appearance of the latest so-called open letter from Academician Sakharov.

SECRETARY OF THE CENTRAL COMMITTEE

....

COMMUNIST PARTY OF THE SOVIET UNION, CENTRAL COMMITTEE

TOP SECRET

No. P138/XVII

To Comrades Gorbachev, Ryzhkov, Medvedev, Chebrikov,
Luk'ianov, Razumovskii, Kriuchkov, Menteshashvili.

Extract from minutes no. 138 of the October 20, 1988, session of the Politburo of the Central Committee of the Communist Party of the Soviet Union

On the Issue of Restoring A. D. Sakharov's Rights to Awards.

Changing the October 13, 1988, Central Committee of the Communist Party of the Soviet Union resolution on this matter, adopt the corresponding Decree of the Presidium of the Supreme Soviet of the USSR following further study. (Memorandum of Comrades V. M. Chebrikov and V. A. Medvedev is attached).

SECRETARY OF THE CENTRAL COMMITTEE

To point XVII, min. no. 138

CENTRAL COMMITTEE, COMMUNIST PARTY OF THE SOVIET UNION

In connection with the appearance of appeals and letters calling for the return to Academician A. D. Sakharov of state awards stripped from him by the Presidium of the Supreme Soviet of the USSR in January 1980, Comrade I. M. Makarov, the senior academic secretary of the Academy, had a conversation on the matter with academician A. D. Sakharov at the instruction of the Presidium of the Academy of Sciences of the USSR.

In the course of this conversation, Comrade A. D. Sakharov declared that he considers the return of the state awards to him inappropriate at this time, and, in his words, he feels uncomfortable taking this course when his wife, E. G. Bonner, and many other persons supporting his views have not yet been rehabilitated.

In this connection, without changing the basic decision on returning the state awards to A. D. Sakharov, we would advise adopting the relevant Decree of the Presidium of the Supreme Soviet of the USSR following further study of this matter.

V. Chebrikov   C. Medvedev

October 19, 1988

[Probably] APRF

chapter 3

THE COMMUNIST PARTY APPARATUS

The Communist Party was created at a small gathering of Russian Marxist revolutionaries in the Belorussian city of Minsk in 1898. It took its original name, the Russian Social-Democratic Workers' Party, from the similarly named German party, but unlike the Social Democrats in Germany the Russians were unable to function legally inside the tsarist empire. Led from abroad, with periodic congresses held in European capitals to determine policy, the party was destined to lead an underground, conspiratorial existence inside Russia. At a party congress in 1903, the group split into two factions, later named the "majority" (Bolshevik) and "minority" (Menshevik). The Bolsheviks' leader was Vladimir Lenin, who believed in a tightly controlled party of professional revolutionaries: only such a party could survive the repression of the tsarist police.

These repressive conditions changed in 1917 with the fall of the old regime. The Bolshevik Party and others grew rapidly in the months after the February Revolution; Lenin's conspiratorial model gave way to a much more democratic, mass party, where local units felt free to criticize the leadership and to reject its advice. Even when Lenin finally convinced his reluctant followers to seize power in the name of the Soviets in October 1917, party dissidents publicly opposed the plan. But the Bolshevik assumption of power quickly changed the form of the party. The necessities of ruling amidst great opposition and the conditions of civil war pushed the democratic side of the party to the background; gradually the electoral principle for selecting party leaders was abandoned. Other political parties were outlawed for opposing the regime. The Bolshevik Party renamed itself the Russian Communist Party (Bolshevik) in 1919 and soon established a monopoly over political life. Although the country was governed by a system of elected Soviets, to be active in political life one had to be either a Communist, a Communist sympathizer, or a member of no party. The party itself was extremely selective about who could become a member. Although activists were urged to join the party, their credentials were carefully checked before admission, and all members had to serve a probationary period before being granted full membership. Periodic purges and "verifications of documents" helped to weed out the opportunists and the free-loaders. Observing party discipline became a critical part of performance.

The Bolshevik party as envisioned by Lenin in 1903 was a highly centralized organization, coordinated by a newspaper and a central committee. In 1917 local party committees enjoyed considerable autonomy, but the Central Committee reasserted its authority during the Civil War years. Its powers were nominally subject to annual congresses of party members, which elected the Central Committee and adopted the party program, but the pattern set by Lenin in 1919–1921 prevailed: the Central Committee and the high party leadership set the agenda and determined policy. In practice, a smaller inner circle of the Central Committee, the Politburo, exercised great power over party and state policy; a separate Organizational Bureau (*Orgbiuro*) was designated to coordinate personnel assignments. Given the scarcity of reliable cadres and the crucial importance of the party's presence in various government and economic agencies, the assignment of personnel, a job given to Stalin beginning in 1919, vested the chairman of the *Orgbiuro* with great political power.

The Communist Party structure pervaded society. Each workplace and educational institution organized its Communists into a local cell; the cell in turn elected a bureau to run its affairs. The cells sent representatives to local committees, who were in turn subordinate to city and *oblast'* committees. Each administrative unit, whether soviet, trade union, or scientific council, had its party faction, through which policy decisions were transmitted from central party authorities. The function of the local members was to set a communist example and to follow orders from the center.

The Communist Party emerged from the Second World War in a state of disarray. Patriotic themes had triumphed over ideological ones in mobilizing wartime support. Political leaders, although all Communists, established their power bases in state agencies rather than in the party apparatus. Malenkov emerged as Stalin's second-in-command as chairman of the Council of Ministers; Lavrentii Beria accumulated great power as head of the police. The accession of Khrushchev and his 1956 denunciation of Stalin's crimes further contributed to a crisis in party identity. Khrushchev's political opponents capitalized on this crisis in 1964, when the Central Committee voted to dismiss him from his post as First Secretary of the party. His eventual successor, Leonid Brezhnev, owed his position to the party loyalists, and one of the hallmarks of his regime was to restore party membership to a position of power, status, and privilege. Party membership once again became the only path to public life and to professional mobility. Party members were rewarded for their loyalty with an increasing (and concealed) network of privilege: special access to scarce consumer goods, to vacation resorts and suburban villas, and to the best schools for their children.

The Communist Party remained the sole vehicle of public activism until the dissolution of the Soviet Union in 1991. When Gorbachev launched his policies of reform from within the party, enthusiasm for the party actually rose. Would-be reformers joined the party for the first time, believing that the party finally represented a meaningful agent for change. But party leaders who wished only to defend their privileges and preserve the old system continually blocked the reformers. The resignation from the party of Gorbachev's foreign minister, Eduard Shevardnadze, in July 1991 (Document 235), signaled the moral collapse of the party that had monopolized Soviet political life since 1918, and the ill-fated putsch attempt by hard-line opponents of reform in August 1991 led directly to disestablishment of the Communist Party as the country's privileged political vanguard.

From Party Leaders' Personal Files

True to its conspiratorial origins, the Communist Party preserved a cloak of secrecy throughout its existence. Party documents were routinely assigned "secret" classifications, and information about party leaders was officially circumscribed. These documents of party leaders from Stalin to Gorbachev give concrete form to the lives of many of the men who helped to shape Soviet history. Many of them need little introduction.

Joseph Stalin (Iosif Vissarionovich Djugashvili) (1879–1953) led the Soviet Union either alone or in a coalition from 1924 until 1953. When he died in 1953, the entire country mourned. His body was placed next to Lenin's in the mausoleum on Red Square, and his residences were sealed as shrines to his leadership. Only with Khrushchev's denunciation of Stalin's excesses at the Twentieth Party Congress in February 1956 did Stalin regain more normal human status, symbolized by the inventory of the contents of his Moscow apartments (Documents 162 and 163).

Nikita Sergeevich Khrushchev (1894–1971) came from a simple background and worked his way up through the party ranks as an organizer, as party leader of Ukraine and later Moscow, and as Stalin's assistant for agriculture. He served as First Secretary of the party and leader of the country from 1953 until 1964, when a coalition of conservatives forced him into retirement.

Leonid Il'ich Brezhnev (1906–82) rose in the party with the patronage of Stalin and Khrushchev, but in 1964 he helped engineer the conservative revolt that deposed Khrushchev. As Soviet leader from 1964 to his death in 1982, he surrounded himself with cronies from his early party days and presided over a gradual ossification of the Soviet economy and society. He emerged as an international statesman in the 1970s, as the USSR rose to the status of military and political superpower.

IUrii Vladimirovich Andropov (1914–84) gained political visibility with the assignment of "sovietizing" the portions of Karelia seized from Finland in the Winter War of 1939–40. As ambassador to Hungary, he oversaw the crushing by Soviet troops of the uprising there in 1956 and thereafter rose through the ranks of the *KGB,* becoming its chief in 1967. Andropov succeeded Brezhnev as Soviet leader in 1982, the first one to emerge from the ranks of the police. In his short tenure in office, he initiated some of the reforms that Gorbachev would later continue.

Konstantin Ustinovich Chernenko (1911–85) owed his party career to the protection of Brezhnev, who promoted him as his heir-apparent. A member of the Central Committee beginning in 1971 and Politburo beginning in 1978, Chernenko did not command much attention and was passed over in favor of Andropov when Brezhnev died. When Andropov succumbed to disease in 1984, however, Chernenko finally became Soviet leader; his regime was characterized mainly by his absence from public view, and he died in 1985.

Mikhail Sergeevich Gorbachev (1931–) was the first Soviet leader trained in the more liberal postwar era. He rose quickly to positions of power and responsibility and succeeded Chernenko as general secretary of the party in 1985, at the age of 54. Gorbachev launched a radical reform of the party and country under the slogans of "restructuring" *(perestroika),* "openness," *(glasnost'),* and "democratization" *(demokratizatsiia).* He was much criticized by intellectuals for not abandoning old habits rapidly enough, and by most of the rest of Soviet society for the continuing collapse of the economy. When the Soviet Union crumbled at the end of 1991, Gorbachev, as president of a nonexistent country, found himself in involuntary retirement.

Felix Edmundovich Dzerzhinsky (Polish Feliks Dzierżyński) (1877–1926), a Polish aristocrat turned revolutionary, became chairman of the *Cheka* in 1917. Later, his tireless energy was harnessed to economic administration, first in the Commissariat of Transportation and then as chairman of the Supreme Economic Council. A member of the Central Committee but never the Politburo, Dzerzhinsky remained known for his independence and his outstanding administrative abilities.

Sergei Mironovich Kirov (1886–1934) (real name Kostrikov) was born in a peasant family in northern Viatka province and rose to prominence in Bolshevik ranks during the Civil War in the North Caucasus. From 1921 to 1926 he was the party leader in Azerbaijan. A member of the Central Committee from 1923 and the Politburo from 1930, he replaced Zinoviev as head of the Leningrad party organization in 1926. Kirov, a popular figure in Leningrad and in the party, was murdered in December 1934.

Viacheslav Mikhailovich Molotov (real name Skriabin) (1890–1986) became an active Bolshevik party member in 1906, and thereafter worked as an underground revolutionary, serving several terms in prison and exile. He was appointed to the Politburo in 1925 and served Stalin loyally throughout the purges. He became People's Commissar of Foreign Affairs in 1939, negotiating the Non-Aggression Pact with Germany. In 1957, he joined an attempt as part of the "Anti-Party Group" to remove Khrushchev from power, and as punishment he was assigned to be ambassador to Mongolia. Molotov remained critical of Khrushchev's reform program, and after he accused the party's draft program of "revisionism" in 1962, he was expelled as a party member. His appeal for reinstatement in 1971 was denied.

Andrei IAnuar'evich Vyshinsky (1883–1954) left the Menshevik party for the Bolsheviks in 1921. He studied law at Moscow University and served as rector of Moscow University from 1925 to 1928. Earning his prosecutor's spurs in the Shakhty trial in 1928, he argued that confessions, however obtained, were the best guarantee of conviction, and he practiced this theory in his subsequent career in the Procurator General's office. In 1935 he was appointed Procurator General, and in this capacity he presented the government's case in the notorious show trials of the late 1930s.

Lavrentii Pavlovich Beria (1899–1953), the son of Georgian peasants, made his career in the Soviet secret police. Under the patronage of Stalin, he became first secretary of the Georgian Communist Party in 1931, and at the height of the great purges, he was named head of the *NKVD*. Thereafter, he served at the pinnacle of the Soviet government. When Stalin died, Beria allegedly plotted to take control of the government; he was arrested and executed by Stalin's successors.

Mikhail Andreevich Suslov (1902–1982) did not attract the world renown of some of the other Soviet leaders, but he served Stalin, Khrushchev, and Brezhnev as the guardian of party ideology. A member of the Central Committee from 1947, he supervised the party's efforts in culture, agitation and propaganda, science, schools, public organizations, the censorship apparatus, and the media. Suslov and his organization thus controlled the entire ideological life of the Soviet Union, and he was especially vigilant in the struggle with the dissident movement of the 1970s.

Semen Mikhailovich Budennyi (1883–1973), a hero of the Civil War, was founder of the Red Army cavalry. Having supported Stalin against Trotsky in the 1920s, he continued in various military posts through 1945, and he remained a favorite of Stalin. He did not distinguish himself militarily during World War II, although he was three times named "Hero of the Soviet Union," in 1958, 1963, and 1968.

Andrei Aleksandrovich Zhdanov (1896–1948), the son of a provincial school inspector, studied for the priesthood before the revolution but joined the Bolshevik Party in 1917. Zhdanov rose to prominence in 1934 when he replaced Kirov as head of the Leningrad party organization, and he was named in 1939 as one of five Central Committee secretaries. He led the postwar assault on cultural nonconformity, the campaign known as the *Zhdanovshchina*.

Anastas Ivanovich Mikoyan (1895–1978), the son of poor Armenian parents, Mikoyan, like Stalin and Zhdanov, passed through a theological seminary before joining the Bolsheviks. As commissar for trade from 1926 to 1939, and then minister of foreign trade, he loyally supported Stalin. He transferred his loyalty to Khrushchev after 1953, serving in a number of high-level posts, including special envoy to Cuba during the Cuban Missile Crisis of 1962. Mikoyan was forced out of office by Brezhnev in 1965, ostensibly because he had reached the retirement age of 70.

Klimentii Efremovich Voroshilov (1881–1969) joined the Bolshevik Party in 1903, while working in a locomotive plant in the Donbass region. After 1917 he worked in the early *Cheka*, and then became a Red Army commander. Ever a Stalin loyalist, he served as assistant to the Red Army chief Frunze until the premature death of Frunze in 1925, and then as head of the Commissariat for Military and Naval Affairs, even though he had had no formal military training. On bad terms with Khrushchev, Voroshilov returned to favor under Brezhnev.

Party membership cards and information cards for Party General Secretaries Stalin, Khrushchev, Brezhnev, Andropov, Chernenko, Gorbachev

[left half of card:]

ALL-UNION COMMUNIST PARTY
(OF BOLSHEVIKS)

Proletarians of All Countries, Unite!

PARTY MEMBERSHIP CARD
No. 0000002

Last Name_____Stalin_____

First Name_____Iosif Vissarionovich_____
Year of Birth_____1879_____

Date of Admission to Party__1898_____

Organization Issuing Card__Zamoskvoretskii *Raion* Committee, *VKP(b)*, Moscow_____

Personal Signature___[signed] I. V. Stalin_____

Place	[seal, outer to inner rings:]
Photo	All-Union Communist Party (of Bolsheviks)
Here	Moscow Organization
	Zamoskvoretskii, M. P. Secretary

[right half of card:]

PAYMENT OF MEMBERSHIP DUES--1927

Month	Monthly Salary	Dues	Secretary's Signature
January	225 rubles	6.75 rubles	[illegible]
February	"	"	"
		[. . .]	
October	"	6.75 rubles + 3.32 rubles	"
November	"	6.75 rubles + 3.38 rubles	"
December	"	6.75 rubles	"

REGISTRATION
CARD   No. 0 0 0 0 0 0 2
    for the Politburo

Upon Completion Must be Returned to the Central Committee of the All-Union Communist Party (of Bolsheviks)

To be Filled out Legibly in Ink in Russian Only

Last Name____Stalin_____

First Name and Patronymic___Iosif Vissarionovich____

Year of Birth____1879_____

Date of Admission to Party____1898_____

Name of organization issuing card___Red Guard *Raion* Committee, City of Moscow____

Personal Signature
[signed] I. Stalin

Raion Committee Secretary
[signed] Komarov

May 29, 1936

[seal, outer to inner rings:]

Red Guard *Raion* Committee 2600–F
Moscow
VKP(b)

[left half of card:]

Proletarians of All Countries, Unite!

COMMUNIST PARTY OF THE SOVIET UNION [*KPSS*]

PARTY MEMBERSHIP CARD

No. 00000004

Last Name_____Khrushchev_____

First Name and Patronymic____Nikita Sergeevich____

Year of Birth____1894_____

Date of Admission to Party___November 1918_____

Organization Issuing Card___Moscow Red Guard *Raion* Committee of the Communist Party of the Soviet Union___

____[signed] N. Khrushchev____

[seal, outer to inner rings:]
Red Guard *Raion* Committee, Moscow
Raion Committee Secretary

....

[right half of card:]

PAYMENT OF MEMBERSHIP DUES—1954

Month	Monthly Salary	Dues	Secretary's Signature
January	8000	240	[illegible]
February	"	"	"
March	"	"	"

[left half of card:]

PARTY MEMBERSHIP CARD

No. 00000002

Last Name____Brezhnev_____

First Name____Leonid_____

Patronymic____Il'ich_____

Year of Birth____1906_____

Date of Admission to Party___October 1931_____

Party Agency Issuing Card Party Committee for the Party Organization of the Central Committee Staff, *KPSS*_____

_____[signed] L. Brezhnev_____

Date issued_March 2, 1975____

....

[right half of card:]

PAYMENT OF MEMBERSHIP DUES—1973

Month	Monthly Salary	Dues	Secretary's Signature
January	--	--	--
February	--	--	--
March	800 r.	24 r.	[illegible]
April	"	"	"
May	"	"	"

[left side of card:]

PARTY MEMBERSHIP CARD

No. 00000017

Last Name_____Andropov_____

First Name_____IUrii_____

Patronymic_____Vladimirovich_____

Year of Birth____1914_____

Date of Admission to Party___February 1939____

Name of party agency issuing card___Party Committee of the *KGB* in the Council of Ministers of the USSR_____

[signed] Andropov

Party Committee Secretary
[signed] [illegible]

[seal, outer to inner rings:]
Party Committee of the *KGB*, City of Moscow
in the Council of Ministers of the USSR
Communist Party of the Soviet Union
Date issued____March 2, 1973_____

....

[right half of card:]

PAYMENT OF MEMBERSHIP DUES—1973

Month	Monthly Salary	Dues	Secretary's Signature
January	--	--	--
February	--	--	--
March	800	24	[illegible]
April	"	"	"
May	"	"	"
		[. . .]	

[left half of card:]

PARTY MEMBERSHIP CARD

No. 00000033

Last Name_____Chernenko_____

First Name_____Konstantin_____

Patronymic_____Ustinovich_____

Year of Birth____1911_____

Date of Admission to Party___February 1931_____

Name of Party Agency Issuing Card__Party Committee for the Party Organization of the Central Committee Staff, Communist Party of the Soviet Union_____

[signed] K. Chernenko

Party Committee Secretary

[signature illegible]

Date issued____March 7, 1973_____

....

[right half of card:]

PAYMENT OF MEMBERSHIP DUES—1973

Month	Monthly Salary	Dues	Secretary's Signature
January	--	--	--
February	--	--	--
March	550	16.50 [stamped: Moscow, Bauman *Raion* Committee]	
April	"	"	"
		[. . .]	
August	950	27.50	"
September	"	"	"
October	"	28.50	"
November	550	16.50	"
December	1100	33	"

REGISTRATION CARD for the Politburo, No. 0 1 1 4 0 0 0 1
To be filled out in Russian

Last Name_____Gorbachev_____

First Name_____Mikhail_____

Patronymic_____Sergeevich_____

_1931_   _worker_
Year of Birth   Social Position
Name of Party Agency Issuing Card

The Lenin *Raion* Committee of the Communist Party of the Soviet Union, City of Stavropol'
[signed] M. Gorbachev

Party Committee Secretary
[signature illegible]

Date issued   March 22, 1973

Date of Admission as a Candidate_June 1950_____

Name of Party Agency Confirming Acceptance
Red Guard *Raion* Committee of the All-Union Communist Party (of Bolsheviks), Stavropol' *Krai*_____

Name of Party Agency Confirming Acceptance as a Member
 Krasnopresnenskii *Raion* Committee of the All-Union Communist Party (of Bolsheviks), City of Moscow_____

JUSTIFICATION FOR ISSUING PARTY MEMBERSHIP CARD

1. In exchange for party membership card No._00152961_, 1954 form.

2. In exchange for card No._____accepted as a member, protocol of the *Raion* Committee, City Committee, Political Committee No.____of____[day]____[month]____19_____.

3. In exchange for party membership card No._____

Information on Elimination (to be filled out by the Central Committee of the Communist Party of the Soviet Union)

TSKhSD

Communist Party file on Felix Dzerzhinsky, July 21, 1926, noting his death

Russian Communist Party (of Bolsheviks) [*RKP(b)*]
Addendum to personnel registration record No. 4706

Dzerzhinsky Felix Edmundovich
     from the Moscow organization of the Russian Communist Party

Place and date of employment	Institution	Department	Position	Date of Termination
Moscow	*OGPU*[1]	Collegium	Chairman	
" "	*NKPS*[2]	Collegium	People's Commissar	Removed in '24
" " Febr 1924	*VSNKh SSSR*[3]	NA	Chairman	held these several positions simultaneously
" " Nov 1924	*Glavmetal*[4]	NA	Chairman	
" " Jan 1925	*TSRKP*[5]	*Orgbiuro*	Candidate	
" " Jan 1925	*TSRKP*	Politburo	Candidate	
" " May 1925	*TSRKP*	Third Conference	Member	
" " May 1925	*VTSIK*[6]	Twelfth Convocation	Member	
" " May 1925	*TSIK SSSR*[7]	Third Convocation	Member	

Died July 20, 1926 at 4:35
[Overwritten] See newspaper *Izvestiia* from July 21, 1926 N. 165 (2796)

RTSKhIDNI, fond 76, op. 4, d. 19, l. 4.

1. Unified State Political Administration
2. People's Commissariat of Transportation
3. Supreme Economic Council
4. Main Administration of the Metalworking Industry
5. Central Committee of the Russian Communist Party
6. All-Union Central Executive Committee of the USSR
7. Central Executive Committee of the USSR

Ordzhonikidze, Voroshilov, and other dignitaries on the occasion of Stalin's fiftieth birthday, December 1929. TSGAKFD

Sergei Kirov's party record, February 1934

<u>Proletarians of All Countries, Unite!</u>

Re: personnel matter No.10

Supplement to Personnel Registration Record

Last name __Kirov__ First name __Sergei__ Patronymic __Mironovich__

I. Data on work since registering (after personnel record filled out)

Post (show name of office, department, sector)	Name of Institution (show full name of the institution, organization, or enterprise)	Location of Institution (city, *raion*, and mandatory indication of *oblast'*, *krai*, or republic)	Date month, (year) --- Started work Left work	Basis of the entry --- About start of work About leaving work	Signature of person making entry --- About start of work About leaving work
Secretary	Central Committee of the Communist Party (Bolshevik) of Azerbaijan	Baku	August 1921 January 1926		
First Secretary	*Oblast'* Committee of the All-Union Communist Party (Bolshevik) *VKP(b)*	Leningrad	February 1926		Akimenko
First Secretary	City Committee of the *VKP(b)*	Leningrad	February 1932	Decision of the *TSK*, February 1932	Bromberg Akimenko
Secretary	Central Committee of the *VKP(b)*	Moscow	February 1934 February 1934	Congress decision	Bromberg Bromberg

II. Membership in Elective Organs

Name of Elective Organ	Location of Elective Organ	Elected capacity	Which Convocation	Date (month, year) of Election	Signature of Person Making Entry
TSK VKP(b)	Moscow	Candidate Member	10th and 11th		
TSK VKP(b)	Moscow	Member	12th–16th		Akimenko
Central Executive Committee of the USSR [*TSIK SSSR*]	Moscow	Member	3rd and 4th		

[Hand-written diagonally across the middle of the first table:] Comrade Kirov. Died at the hands of an enemy of the working class, December 1934 (newspaper December 2, 1934) [signed] uch.[?] Fedorova.

RTSKhIDNI, fond 80, op. 19, d. 1, ll. 100b.

DOCUMENT 153   *Central Committee resolution to expell Molotov from the party, July 26, 1962, and Molotov's party information form*

PARTY CONTROL COMMITTEE
Central Committee of the Communist Party of the Soviet Union

No. KPK-595/20s   TOP SECRET
TO: Supervisory Cadre Registration Sector, Central Committee of the Communist Party of the USSR [*KPSS*], Comrade IU. A. Polenov

August 2, 1962   D E C I S I O N

        of the COMMITTEE, Minutes No. 595, point 20s, July 26, 1962

20s. Appeal of MOLOTOV (SKRIABIN) Viacheslav Mikhailovich (has been a member of the *KPSS* since 1906, party card number 00000005).

        (Comrades Klimov, Molotov (Skriabin), Serdiuk, Andreeva, Pikina, Karavaev, Kompanets, Dzhurabaev, Markov, Fursov, Postovalov)

        Confirm the March 21, 1962, decision of the Moscow City Committee of the *KPSS* to expel V. M. Molotov (Skriabin) from the *KPSS* for abuses of authority, for infractions of socialist legality (as a result of which a large number of totally innocent persons perished), for antiparty activity and devious conduct at a session of the Party Control Committee of the Central Committee of the *KPSS*.

                First Deputy Chair, Party Control Committee
                    Central Committee of the *KPSS*   [signed] Z. Serdiuk

July 1, 1921

            Central Committee, Russian Communist Party (of Bolsheviks)

                        [stamp:] Party Card No. after
                        Exchange in 1954: 00000005

                P E R S O N A L   I N F O R M A T I O N   F O R M

*Guberniia*___Moscow___*Uezd*_____

City_____

Party organization (city, *raion*, *uezd*)_ Zamoskvoretskii *raion*,
___city of Moscow_____

1) Last name_____Molotov (Skriabin)_____

2) First name, patronymic__Viacheslav Mikhailovich___

3) Year of birth___1890_____

4) Nationality___Great Russian_____

5) Native language__Russian_____

6) Fluency in other languages: a) speaks b) writes___

---

7) Areas of RSFSR with which very familiar Viatskaia, Vologodskaia, Tatar Republic, Petrograd, Moscow, Nizhegorodskaia guberniia

8) Social position (former class, title, status, etc.) Office worker, former petty bourgeois

9) Primary occupation (source of income):

a) Before the war, 1914 journalism, teaching, party professional

b) During the war (until the October Revolution) occasional income from Zemgor [Municipal Land Administration] institutions, party professional

10) Profession journalist and party professional[8]

Household includes wife and niece.

SUPPLEMENT
To Personal Information Form for Cadre Registration

Last name MOLOTOV (SKRIABIN) First name Viacheslav   Patronymic Mikhailovich

1. Data on work (after completing personal information form)

POSITION	LOCATION	START DATE	END DATE
Secretary, Central Committee Ukrainian Communist Party	Kharkov	11-20	3-21
Secretary, Central Committee All-Union Communist Party	Moscow	3-21	12-30
Secretary Moscow *Oblast'* Committee, All-Union Communist Party	Moscow	11-28	4-29
People's Commissar of Foreign Affairs of USSR	Moscow	5-39	3-46
Chairman of the Collegium of the People's Commissariat of Foreign Affairs of USSR	Moscow	5-39	3-46
Member of the Bureau of the Council of People's Commissars of the USSR	Moscow	5-41	8-42
Deputy Chair of the Council of People's Commissars of the USSR	Moscow	5-41	8-42

TSKhSD

8. Stamps denoting various honors bestowed on Molotov indicate he was a deputy to the Supreme Soviet of the USSR, second, third, and fourth convocations; a deputy to the RSFSR Supreme Soviet; a four-time recipient of the Order of Lenin; a two-time recipient of the Order of Hero of Socialist Labor; and a member of the Central Committee of the Communist Party of the Soviet Union.

PROLETARIANS OF ALL COUNTRIES, UNITE!

PARTY CONTROL COMMITTEE
OF THE CENTRAL COMMITTEE
OF THE COMMUNIST PARTY OF THE SOVIET UNION
[*TSK KPSS*]

TOP SECRET

Not For Publication

MINUTE NO. 160
OF THE MEETING OF THE PARTY CONTROL COMMITTEE
OF THE *TSK KPSS*
of August 18, 1971
TO EXAMINE THE APPEAL TO THE 24TH
PARTY CONGRESS

Members in Attendance: Comrades   Pel'she, Grishin, Postovalov, Denisov,
                                                  Lazurenko, Osipov, Pikina, and Fursov.

1.   The Appeal of Molotov (Skriabin), Viacheslav Mikhailovich (member of the *KPSS* since 1906, Party Card No 00000005) to the Presidium of the 24th Party Congress Requesting Reinstatement of His Membership in the *KPSS*

(Report delivered by Comrade Mogilat. Comrade Molotov present.
Speakers: Comrades Molotov, Postovalov, Grishin, Fursov, Pikina, Lazurenko, Osipov, Denisov, Pel'she)

After reviewing the appeal of Comrade V. M. Molotov to the 24th Party Congress at the behest of the Political Bureau of the *TSK KPSS*, the Party Control Committee of the *TSK KPSS* does not deem it possible to reinstate his membership in the party because of his abuse of power and violations of socialist legality during the era of Stalin's personality cult, which resulted in mass repressions against honest Soviet citizens and because of his membership in the antiparty faction in 1957.

Chairman of the Party Control Committee
of the *TSK KPSS*   [signed] A. Pel'she

[Stamp:
Appeal to
24th Congress
of *KPSS*]

Top Secret

TO THE PARTY CONTROL COMMITTEE OF THE *TSK KPSS*

1. On the Appeal of V. M. Molotov to the Presidium of the 24th Congress of the Communist Party of the Soviet Union

V. M. Molotov submitted a statement to the Presidium of the 24th Congress of the *KPSS* which reads as follows:

Dear Comrades:

I am asking you to review my application for reinstatement of my membership in the Communist Party of the Soviet Union (I was a member from 1906 to 1962).

In my enclosed statement of August 14, 1962, to the *TSK KPSS*, I provided detailed explanations in connection with my request.

The *TSK KPSS* turned Molotov's statement over to the Party Control Committee of the *TSK KPSS* for review.

MOLOTOV (Skriabin) Viacheslav Mikhailovich, born 1890, former member of the *KPSS* since 1906, Party Card No. 00000005, Russian, incomplete higher education, and at the time the issue first arose, was serving as the Soviet representative to the International Atomic Energy Agency.

The issue of Molotov's continued membership in the party was raised under the following circumstances.

In their speeches, delegates to the 22nd Party Congress harshly condemned the factional activity of Molotov and other members of the antiparty faction which opposed the Leninist policy envisioned by the 20th Party Congress. Representatives of the Communist parties of Kazakhstan, Latvia, and Moldavia, the party organizations of Moscow, the Altai and Stavropol' *krai*s, Volgograd, Ivanovo, Irkutsk, Moscow, Novosibirsk, Rostov, Saratov, Sakhalin, Sverdlovsk, and Cheliabinsk *oblast'*s, the Bashkir Autonomous Soviet Socialist Republic, Tuva Autonomous *Oblast'*, the Soviet Army and Navy spoke for their delegations in saying that Molotov could not remain in the ranks of the Communist Party.

The 22nd Party Congress's resolution on the *TSK KPSS* report stated that:

In the name of the entire party, the 22nd Party Congress expresses its abhorrence and condemnation for subversive antiparty factional activity as incompatible with the Leninist principle of party unity. Anyone who engages in factional conflict and behind-the-scenes intrigues and machinations against the party's Leninist policies and its unity is acting in opposition to the interests of the entire nation and the interests of Communist development. In expressing the will of all Communists, the congress hereby affirms that the party will continue to adhere steadfastly to the Leninist law of preserving party unity and the purity of the party's ranks and will unflinchingly suppress any manifestations of cliquishness and factionalism.

In discussing the results of the 22nd Party Congress, the resolutions of party and *komsomol* organizations and workers of Moscow demanded that Molotov be expelled from the party and put on trial. The proposal to expel Molotov from the party was unanimously supported by Communists at meetings of the party organizations of the Business Office of the Council of Ministers of the USSR and the Soviet Delegation to the International Atomic Energy Agency, where Molotov's party records were kept.

In conjunction with this, the Bureau of Primary Party Organization No. 3 of the Business Office of the Council of Ministers of the USSR raised the issue of Molotov's party membership at a party meeting, expressing its judgment that Molotov could not remain in the ranks of the party. After discussing the issue, the party meeting adopted a resolution expelling Molotov from the party "as an active participant and chief ideologist of the antiparty faction which opposed the policies of the 20th Party Congress and party policy on key domestic and international issues and as a person who had committed gross violations (during the era of Stalin's personality cult) of revolutionary socialist legality, resulting in the deaths of large numbers of completely innocent persons, including many party members, statesmen, and military men who were devoted to our party and the Soviet state."

On February 10, 1962, the party committee of the Business Office of the Council of Ministers of the USSR approved the resolution adopted by the meeting of Primary Party Organization No. 3 expelling Molotov from the Communist Party with the comment that "Molotov has failed to provide a political assessment of his activity in the antiparty faction and his errors and his antiparty actions which caused grievous harm to the party and the Soviet state."

On February 14, 1962, the Bureau of the Sverdlov *Raion* Committee of the *KPSS* approved the decision of the party committee expelling Molotov from the party "for antiparty factional activity incompatible with the Leninist principle of party unity and for his active involvement in the mass repressions during the era of Stalin's personality cult against party, government, industrial, military, and *komsomol* personnel who were devoted to our party and the Soviet state."

On March 21, 1962, the Bureau of the Moscow City Committee of the *KPSS* adopted a resolution which "approved the decision of the bureau of the Sverdlov *Raion* Committee of the *KPSS* to expel V. M. Molotov (Skriabin) from the *KPSS* for his abuse of power and his violations of socialist legality which resulted in the death of a large number of completely innocent people and for his divisive antiparty factional activity."

The resolutions of the meeting of the primary party organization and party committee of the Business Office of the Council of Ministers of the USSR, the Bureau of the Sverdlov *Raion* Committee, and the Moscow City Committee of the *KPSS* expelling Molotov from the party were all adopted unanimously.

On July 26, 1962, the Party Control Commission of the *TSK KPSS*, after reviewing Molotov's appeal, affirmed the decision of the Moscow City Committee of the *KPSS* expelling him from the Communist Party for abuse of power and violations of socialist legality resulting in the deaths of a large number of completely innocent people and for his antiparty activity and insincerity at the meeting of the Party Control Commission of the *TSK KPSS*.

As is clear from the evidence at the disposal of the Party Control Commission, Molotov, as chairman of the Council of People's Commissars from 1930 to 1941, committed major abuses of power and the grossest possible violations of revolutionary legality.

As a high-ranking party and government official of long standing and the second highest man in the country after Stalin, Molotov contributed to the inflation of the Stalin cult and to the emergence of a situation of tyranny and lawlessness in the country. These were the years which witnessed the adoption of a number of extraordinary laws, the establishment of extrajudicial bodies vested with special powers, the institution of a system of mass repression based on so-called limits (or quotas) and national origins and family ties, and the emergence of the practice of certain officials deciding the guilt and punishment of citizens arrested on political charges before their cases had even gone to trial. All of this paved the way for unrestricted lawlessness and the massive destruction of honorable Soviet citizens.

Molotov is personally responsible for the politically incorrect and extremely harmful instructions issued at the February-March 1937 Plenary Session of the All-Union Communist Party (Bolshevik) and other public speeches. At the time he stated that the enemy had become clever, treacherous, and skillful and quite often concealed himself behind a party card, claimed that there were saboteurs in every sector of the economy and in all government agencies, and called for a sweeping campaign against saboteurs and ordered party members and others to look for saboteurs high and low. This marked the beginning of the extensive persecution of party, government, industrial, military, and other personnel.

Molotov committed a grievous violation of legality by his involvement in the destruction of party and government personnel on the basis of the so-called lists. Molotov took part in reviewing and approving 373 out of the 383 lists submitted to him by the People's Commissariat of Internal Affairs [NKVD], which judicial and extrajudicial bodies subsequently used as the basis for convicting 43,569 individuals on trumped-up charges, including 38,103 persons who were ultimately sentenced to death. Many of the executed victims were prominent party members and statesmen, the leaders of party, government, trade union, and *komsomol* agencies, major industrialists, military men, scientists, cultural figures, artists, and old party veterans. Lists approved with Molotov's participation were used as the basis for executing 29 out of 71 members of the *TSK KPSS* and 37 out of 68 candidate members in the *TSK KPSS*, i.e., about half the membership of the party's Central Committee, a large number of members of the Party Control Commission, Soviet Control Commission, and the Central Inspection Commission, and delegates to the 17th Party Congress.

Molotov's guilt was aggravated by the fact that many of the persons on the lists he approved were people he knew well as devoted party members from the revolutionary movement and long years of work together. Nevertheless, he approved their destruction. It has been proven beyond a doubt that Molotov personally approved the execution of E. I. Veger, a party member since 1918 and the wife of Shelekhas, the deputy chairman of the Council of People's Commissars of Ukraine. In August 1937 the *NKVD* had included Veger on a list of 92 persons to be sentenced to ten years of incarceration in corrective labor camps. In approving the list, Molotov wrote down "Supreme Measure of Punishment" [VMN: death penalty] next to Veger's name. Veger was shot on the basis of this notation, even though she never admitted her guilt in court and was later completely exonerated.

We also know of incidents where Molotov initiated the arrest of certain individuals and when he approved the arrest of honorable people on the basis of unsubstantiated accusations.

On June 24, 1937, a statement was issued in Stalin's name which indicated that G. I. Lomov-Oppokov, a party member since 1903 and a member of the bureau of the Soviet Control Commission of the Council of People's Commissars of the USSR, had supposedly maintained friendly relations with Rykov. Stalin sent this statement to Molotov with the notation: "Comrade Molotov. What should we do? J. Stalin." Molotov replied: "Arrest this scum Lomov immediately. V. Molotov." In turn, Stalin wrote: "Approved. St." Solely on the basis of these decisions, without any verification of the statement, Lomov-Oppokov was arrested, accused of membership in a "right-wing organization," and shot on September 2 of the same year. Lomov-Oppokov was completely rehabilitated in 1956.

In December 1937 Professor V. L. Levin, a top official of the People's Commissariat of Foreign Affairs [*NKID*], wrote a personal appeal to Molotov in which he asked him "to intervene" on behalf of his father, the well-known Doctor L. G. Levin, who had been arrested by *NKVD* agents. In the margins of the letter Molotov wrote: "Comrade Ezhov. Why is this Levin still at the *NKID* and not at the *NKVD*? V. Molotov." The very next day Levin was arrested and was subsequently executed on trumped-up charges. The case against him was finally dismissed for lack of elements of a crime.

Molotov, as a former head of government, is responsible for the absolutely inexcusable cruelties inflicted on the families of individuals arrested for "counterrevolutionary crimes," when both adult family members and children were subjected to unlawful persecution. He was directly involved in approving the executions of wives of "enemies of the people," even though the wives had committed no crimes whatsoever.

Our examination revealed that Molotov was well aware of the lawlessness that was going on but never did anything to stop it. Moreover, in a number of cases he resisted even the feeble attempts of certain top officials of the Procuracy and the courts to limit the tyranny.

We should emphasize that in the mass repressions of 1937 and 1938 alone 1,372,392 persons were arrested, and 681,692 of these individuals were shot. According to the incomplete information at our disposal, 116,885 party members were victims of the repressions of 1937 and 1938.

In reviewing the issue of Molotov's accountability to the party, he is also accused of active involvement in an antiparty faction which in 1957 opposed the new party policy adopted by the 20th Congress, resisted efforts aimed at ridding the country of the personality cult and its remnants, and attempted to seize control of the party for the purpose of changing its policies. This issue is discussed in detail in a resolution adopted by the June 1957 Plenary Session of the *TSK KPSS*, which was subsequently approved by the 21st and 22nd Party Congresses. We should mention that Molotov was not just an active member of the faction but was one of its masterminds, and that even after the resolution, as is evident from his subsequent letters to the *TSK KPSS*, he continued to oppose party policy on a number of fundamental issues, especially in the area of foreign policy, where he accused the party of revisionism.

In the face of all these accusations Molotov gave (and continues to give) inconsistent, contradictory, and at times, simply evasive explanations. While admitting, in a very general way, and with all kinds of qualifications, his personal responsibility for the violations of socialist legality and the repressions which occurred, he still considers them justified, because these actions, as he claims, were directed against Trotskyites, right-wing opportunists, and other enemies of the party and the Soviet state. Along with these incurable enemies of the party, Molotov wrote in his appeal to the *TSK KPSS* of August 14, 1962, "to our great misfortune, quite a few honorable party members and non-party-members also suffered." In an attempt to shift the blame for his own actions to the

Central Committee and party congresses, Molotov has stated that his attitudes at the time were no different from the attitudes of other members of the Politburo and that "the repressions occurred with the full knowledge and approval of all the members of the Politburo of the Central Committee." Molotov also claims that all the issues related to the responsibility of the leaders of that time were dealt with completely by the *TSK KPSS* resolution of June 30, 1956, "Concerning the Elimination of the Cult of the Personality and Its Harmful Consequences," and he considers the revival of these issues in 1962 with the accusations against individual members of the former leadership unwarranted.

Molotov's explanations of his involvement in the antiparty faction are also pro forma in nature. He admits that he "took part in a group within the Presidium of the Central Committee," but claims that this "group did not constitute a coherent faction," and that "it completely ceased to exist" after the July 1957 Plenary Session of the *TSK KPSS* condemned it as an antiparty faction.

In his appeal to the *TSK KPSS* for reinstatement in the party, Molotov has asked us to consider that he did not get into the party by accident, that he worked long and hard for the party for many years as part of the revolutionary underground, that he served several prison terms, was sent into exile, played an active role in the preparations for the October Revolution, and was directly involved in leading the armed uprising.

Molotov has held leadership positions in the party and the government from the early years of Soviet power. From 1921 to 1930 he was a secretary of the *TSK* of the party. In 1926 he was elected a member of the Politburo of the *TSK*. In December 1930 he was appointed Chairman of the Council of People's Commissars of the USSR, while from 1939 to 1955 (with a hiatus from 1949 to 1953) he served as Minister of Foreign Affairs of the USSR. From 1941 to 1955 Molotov was the Deputy Chairman of the State Defense Committee. In May 1941 after Stalin's appointment as Chairman of the Council of People's Commissars, Molotov was appointed Deputy Chairman of the same body. In 1953 Molotov was appointed First Deputy Chairman of the Council of Ministers of the USSR. In November 1956 he headed the Ministry of Government Oversight of the USSR. In August 1957 Molotov was appointed the Soviet Union's special envoy to the Mongolian People's Republic. From July 1959 to June 1962 he was the Soviet representative to the International Atomic Energy Agency.

Molotov is a Hero of Socialist Labor and the holder of four Orders of Lenin.

The matter of V. M. Molotov's appeal to the 24th Party Congress has been submitted to the Party Control Committee of the *TSK KPSS* for review.

A draft of the resolution is attached.

Executive Controller
of the Party Control
Committee of the *TSK KPSS*   [signed] S. Mogilat

3.3
Aug. 16, 1971
account no. 1292

TSKhSD, fond 6, op. 8, d. 167

DOCUMENT 155   *Personal information on Andrei Vyshinsky, including review of his case by a purge commission in 1933*

Extract from the minutes of a meeting of the commission to purge the All-Union Communist Party (of Bolsheviks) cell at the People's Commissariat of Justice [*NKIU*], August 3–September 10, 1933.

CONSIDERED:

15. Vyshinsky, Andrei IAnuar'evich. Born 1883. Member of the party since 1920. Party card No. 0051414. Education—higher. 1903–19, was a member of the Russian Social Democratic Workers' Party [*RSDRP*], Mensheviks. In 1905 took part in the Baku revolutionary workers' movement; was the strike committee secretary, joined the Menshevik faction. Influenced by the Armenian massacre of 1905, organized armed detachments of workers against the tsarist government. Was repeatedly arrested in 1906, 1907, 1908, and 1909, and right up to the revolution was a lawyer in Moscow. After 1917 was a member of the Menshevik committee of the Martov group, where he remained until 1919. In 1919 became a member of the All-Russian Communist Party (of Bolsheviks), where he fought determinedly against the Mensheviks, unmasking their treacherous role and his own errors. In the July days [1917], as chief of the *raion* militia in Moscow, assisted revolutionary activities of Bolshevik workers. Party assignment: Propagandist for the Moscow Committee, teaches at the University, conducts scholarly research. Published "History of Communism," in which he confessed his many errors and recognized his [earlier] book as a failure.
Comrades Kupriianov, Butkina, Markov, Burov testified at the hearings.
Testimonial—favorable.

Extract authentic: [signature illegible]

RESOLVED:

Consider verified.

Proletarians of All Countries, Unite!

Central Committee, All-Russian Communist Party (of Bolsheviks)

Party Card No._____

Personal Information Form No. 6055

*Guberniia*__Moscow__*Uezd*__Moscow_____
City____"_____
Party organization_(city, *raion, uezd*)__Moscow organization__

1) Last name__Vyshinsky_____

2) First name, patronymic__Andrei IAnuar'evich_____

3) Year of birth____1883_____

4) Nationality____Russian_____

5) Native language___Russian_____

6) Fluency in other Languages: a) speaks_____
b) writes_French, German, English_____

7) Areas of RSFSR with which very familiar_Caucasus_____

8) Social position (former class, title, status, etc.)_Former_

gentry official, attorney, son of an honored citizen _____

9) Basic occupation (source of income):⁹
a) before the war, 1914 ~~lawyer~~; bureaucrat; teaching _____
b) during the war (until the October Revolution)_ lawyer, _____
 bureaucrat _____

10) Married, three family members in household, including one dependent (child)

Personal characteristics: Responsible worker with a great deal of initiative, military service and experience. As a Communist, he was tough, a good manager. A very talented man.

SUPPLEMENT
to Personal Information Form For Cadre Registration

Last name _VYShINSKY_ First name_ Andrei_ Patronymic _IAnuar'evich_

1. Work record after personal information form was completed

POSITION name of institution, organization, enterprise, main directorate, ministry, or department	LOCATION city *raion*, *oblast'*, *krai*, republic	START DATE	END DATE	DECISION TO ——— APPOINT RELEASE
Commission representative in the Committee of Procurators in the International Military Tribunal		Sept. 45	Nov. 54	Central Committee 46/238 9/5/45
First Deputy Minister of Foreign Affairs of the USSR		Mar. 53	Nov. 54	USSR Council of Min. 3/7/53
Member of the collegium of the Ministry of Foreign Affairs of the USSR		Mar. 53	Nov. 54	USSR Council of Min. 11/10/53
Permanent representative of the USSR to the Security Council of the U.N.		Mar 53.	Nov. 54	USSR Council of Min. 3/7/53

TSKhSD

9. Stamps denoting various honors bestowed on Vyshinsky indicate he was a six-time recipient of the Order of Lenin; a member of the Academy of Sciences; A deputy of the Supreme Soviet of the USSR fourth convocation; a recipient of the Order of the Red Banner of Labor; a recipient of the medal "For Victorious Labor in the Great Patriotic War 1941–1945"; a recipient of the medal "For the Defense of Moscow"; a winner of the Stalin Prize; the holder of the degree of Doctor of Sciences; and a member of the Central Committe of the Communist Party of the Soviet Union.

Proletarians of All Countries, Unite!

ALL-UNION COMMUNIST PARTY (BOLSHEVIK) [*TSK VKP(b)*]

REGISTRATION FORM FOR DELEGATES
ATTENDING THE 17TH PARTY CONGRESS   No _306_

1. Last name _____Beria_____
First name and patronymic___Lavrentii Pavlovich____

2. Voting rights at congress
(full, advisory)_full_____

3. Delegate of which organization_Azerbaijan_____

4. Sex_m_ 5. Age_34_ 6. Nationality_Georgian___

7. Education:

a) Graduate of what school?_Baku Technical High School___

What year?_'20__

b) Currently attending what school___ Since when___

Specialty___technician_____

9. Social position__white-collar worker_____

For blue-collar workers, indicate:

a) Primary occupation as worker_____

b) Year in which individual last worked as
blue-collar worker_____

10. Primary occupation at present time:

a) Job title and name of office or organization:

Secretary of the Transcaucasian Krai Committee and the Central Committee of Georgia

b) Location of organization, office, or business:

_____Tiflis_____

Membership in elected party bodies:

a) Party committee_____

b) *Raion* committee, city ward committee_____

c) City committee____yes_____

d) *Oblast'* committee, *krai* committee__yes, yes____

e) Central Committees of National Communist Parties__yes_

f) *TSK VKP(b)* _____

g) Central Control Commission_____

13. Date of admission to All-Union
Communist Party (Bolshevik)___Feb. 1, 1917_____

14. Was individual ever member of other parties
(which parties and when)?____no____

15. Did individual take part in Civil War (Red Guards,
partisan detachments, Red Army), and if so,
when and for how long?____1918-~~19~~, Baku____
_____

16. To what sort of persecution was individual subjected for political activity before the war and during the Civil
War?_____

a) Prison term (how long)____6 months____

b) Hard labor (how long)_____—-_____

c) Exile (how long)_____—-_____

d) Police supervision (how long)____—-____

17. All-Union Party Congresses attended:

a) with full voting rights:_____

b) with advisory voting rights:____14th____

18. All-Union Party Conferences attended:

a) with full voting rights:____17th____

b) with advisory voting rights:_____

Signature of delegate____[signed] L. Beria____

Jan. 24, 1934

Signature of registrar____Kuznetsov____

RTSKhIDNI, fond 59, op. 1, d. 2, ll. 68, 68ob.

DOCUMENT 157 *Autobiography and personal information form for Mikhail Suslov*

AUTOBIOGRAPHY OF MIKhAIL ANDREEVICh SUSLOV

I was born in 1902 in the village of Shakhovskoe in the former Khvalynskii *uezd* of the Saratov *guberni-ia* (now the Pavlovskii *raion*, Kuibyshev *oblast'*). My father and mother were poor peasants; they ran a small peasant farm and didn't even have their own horse. For this reason, my father occasionally sought work as a carpenter (Baku, Archangel). Soon after the October Revolution, my father quit farm work in the village completely, but my mother, with my help, continued to farm for a time. Subsequently, my father worked as a laborer (storeroom keeper in a butter factory in the city of Vol'sk), as well as a leader in Soviet work. While a member of the Communist Party (Bolsheviks), he died in 1930. My father had been expelled from the party because of his drinking. My mother died in 1920.

In my immediate family I have a brother, Pavel, not a party member, who works as a bookkeeper in the Kuibyshev *oblast'* (I don't know exactly where since I haven't corresponded with him since 1929 or 1930). None of my relatives (in my immediate family) was in the White Army, was deprived of the right to vote, or went abroad.

Until 1920 I lived in the village of Shakhovskoe and helped my mother on the farm, and sometimes in winter I worked in the village Soviet and on the Committee of Poor Peasants as the assistant secretary (my father was the chairman of the committee).

In 1919 I began in earnest to be interested in Bolshevist political pamphlets and politics. At the beginning of 1920, I organized a *komsomol* branch in my village and was its secretary. I served the party at this time chiefly as a collector in the grain-appropriation system and as an organizer of aid to poor peasants at the expense of *kulaks.*

By the fall of 1920, on detail from the Khvalynskii *uezd* committee of the *komsomol*, I arrived in Moscow to study. I only settled down to study, however, at the beginning of 1921 at the Prechistenskii Workers' Faculty [*Rabfak*]. For a short time before this, I worked as a clerk in the People's Commissariat of Post and Telegraph. There in the party organization I joined the party as a candidate member, and in March 1921 I became a regular party member. [. . .]

In the fall of 1931, by decision of the Organizational Bureau of the Central Committee of the All-Union Communist Party (Bolsheviks) [*TSK VKP(b)*], I was sent to work at the USSR People's Commissariat of Workers' and Peasants' Inspection [*NKRKI SSSR*] of the Central Control Commission [*TSKK*] of the *VKP(b)*, where I worked as a senior inspector until the beginning of 1934. After the *TSKK* was abolished, I worked as a controller of the Commission of Soviet Control until August 1936. I took an active role in party work also in this period: in the culture and propaganda section of the party committee, the party organization, propagandist, for a large part of 1933 and 1934 I worked with the Urals party members, and after that in the Chernigov *Oblast'* Commission to purge the party, where I was the leader of the inspection unit.

In the fall of 1936 I was detailed by the *TSK VKP(b)* to the Economics Institute of the Red Professorate (for the 2nd year course). I studied here for one year, after which I was sent by the *TSK VKP(b)* to Rostov as the head of the Section for Leaders of Political Bodies [*ORPO*] of the *Oblast'* Committee [*Obkom*] of the *VKP(b)*.

For the entire period of my stay in the party, I have not been disciplined by the party in any way; I have never had any doubts about the general party line. . . .

PERSONAL INFORMATION FORM FOR PARTY REGISTRATION

Last name Suslov First name Mikhail Patronymic Andreevich
1. Gender male 2. Year/month of birth January 1902 3. Place of birth (use existing administrative divisions) Kuibyshev *oblast'*, Pavlovskii *raion*, village of Shakhovskoe 4. Nationality Russian 5. Social background: a) former social position (title) of parents poor peasants b) primary occupation of parents prior to October Revolution agriculture after October Revolution father—in soviet industrial and party work, died in 1930; mother—homemaker, died in 1920 6. Primary occupation up to entering party agriculture; from youth 7. Social position office worker 8. Party affiliation member *VKP(b)*
9. Which organization accepted you into membership in the *VKP(b)* City regional committee of Moscow 10. Party member since March 1921 Party membership card no. 1219627 11. Member of *komsomol* from February 1920 to 12. Other party memberships (which, where, how long) no other memberships 13. Were you formerly a member of the *VKP(b)* no 14. Did you participate in opposition activities (which groups, when) Did not 15. Trade union membership, from what year Workers in Government Agencies, from September 1920 16. Education higher General and special education: Prechistenskii Worker's Faculty, Moscow, Feb. 1921–July 1924, Graduated; Plekhanov Institute of National Economy, Moscow, 1924–1928, Graduated, specialty of economist Party and political education: Institute of Economics, Russian Association of Scientific Research Institutes of Social Sciences [*RANION*], Moscow, Fall 1929–Mar. 1931, did not graduate, completed 2nd year; Economics Institute of the Red Professorate, Moscow, Fall 1936–Oct. 1937, did not graduate, completed 3rd year.
17. Educational degree (title) do not have 18. Scholarly publications and inventions none 19. Have you traveled abroad no .

TSKhSD

DOCUMENT 158   *Appeal by the opera singer Mikhailova, March 12, 1949, that the location of her personal belongings be determined and that she be furnished documents identifying her as the wife of Marshal Budennyi, hero of the Civil War*

To the Chief of the Administrative Department of the *TSIKSA*

Former instructor of the Moscow State Conservatory.
Former artist of the Order of Lenin Bolshoi Theater opera singer
Ol'ga Stefanovna Budennaia Mikhailova.

Declaration

From 1927 to 1937 I lived at: Moscow, Granovskii Street, building 3, apartment 78 of *TSIKSA*

Please do not cease investigating the whereabouts of my property: clothing, gold, money, expensive furs, a piano, music, etc. The piano [was] at [my] Bakovko dacha on the Mozhaisk highway.

Since the management of Building 5 [sic] does not reply to my inquiries, I am turning to you.

I was registered [married] with S. M. Budennyi in 1927, and that fact was entered in the house records book on January 6, 1927.

Kindly send me a certificate of identification proving that I really am Budennaia Mikhailova, Ol'ga Stefanovna.

With respect to the subject of money received, please check my savings account books.

O. Budennaia Mikhailova

I now live in Eniseisk, Krasnoiarsk *krai*.

TSGAOR, fond 9542, op. 1, d. 136, l. 1.

DOCUMENT 159   *Autobiography of A. A. Zhdanov, written January 3, 1922*

Member of the Bureau of the Nizhnii Novgorod *Guberniia* Committee of the Russian Communist Party (Bolshevik) Andrei Zhdanov

Autobiography.

I was born on the 14th of February 1896 in the family of Master of Divinity, Inspector of Public Schools A. A. Zhdanov in the city of Mariupol' in Ekaterinoslav *guberniia*. My childhood was spent under the influence of the revolutionary ideas of my father (he did not belong to the party but maintained friendship with socialists and followers of Tolstoy), who provided the main impetus for the creation of my revolutionary world view. Because my father was drawn principally to the Social Democrats, the main direction of his educational work was Marxist. As soon as I began to live a conscious life, and for me it began in 1904–1905, I became a sympathizer with the Social Democrats and followed all the details of their work during 1906–1912, using the sources that I had (bourgeois press, pamphlets published during the first revolution of 1905–1906).

In 1910 I entered Tver' Technical School in its third class. I graduated in 1915. Due to the poverty in my family after the death of my father (1909), I worked as a tutor. I was always the best student in my school and graduated with top honors.

In 1912, when in the 5th class, together with my sisters (at present chauffeurs for the All-Russian Central Executive Committee) along with a number of comrades studying at the Tver' Technical School, the Commercial Institute and the Women's Gymnasium, I organized courses for Marxist work among the student youth. I participated in various groups in the circles of 1913, 1914, and 1915 maintaining a Social Democrat Bolshevik orientation. I maintained a subscription to *Pravda* under all its publication titles.

In 1915 I enrolled as a student at the Moscow Agricultural Institute. I worked in a group from my native region, forming an international wing with six friends from the Circle. In November 1915 I left this group and went to Tver' to begin intensive illegal work with the working masses. Through acquaintance with Iv. Mikh. Moskvin (at present, the head of the *Cheka* Organizational Section) who led the work in Tver', and also through acquaintance with Aleks. Iv. Kripitskii (secretary of the Omsk *Guberniia* Committee of the Russian Communist Party), I succeeded in obtaining a job with comrades doing party work in Tver'. In this way I worked from November 1915, at first as a propagandist, and later in March 1916 under appointment to the Tver' Committee of the Russian Social-Democratic Labor Party (Bolshevik), where I worked along with N. N. Patrikeev (code name Leonid, now the chairman of the Don *Guberniia* Executive Committee) and with Comrade Vil'ks [Wilkes?] (code name "Mexican," killed on the Western Front, who was, as I recall, the commissar of a division). I worked under the code name IUrii.

In July 1916 I was sent to military service. I served in the Tsaritsyn Student Battalion and the 3rd Tiflis Ensign School. I graduated as ensign in January 1917. In February 1917 I went to Shadrinsk, Perm' *guberniia*, to serve in the 139th Reserve Infantry Regiment. At the school, as well as in the regiment, I conducted propaganda among the cadets (at the school) and the soldiers of the 10th Company (in the regiment).

In 1917 I was a member of the Soviet of Soldiers' Deputies and a member of its executive committee (after February), then member of the Soviet of Workers' Deputies, deputy chairman of the Soviet of Workers' and Soldiers' Deputies, deputy chairman of the *Uezd* Soviet of Peasant Deputies, and member and chairman of the Committee of the Russian Social-Democratic Labor Party (Bolshevik) in Shadrinsk.

In 1918 I was *Uezd* commissar of agriculture in Shadrinsk, editor of the newspaper, and then inspector organizer of the Agitation Bureau of the Ural Peasant Committee in the city of Ekaterinburg. I headed the military-agitation courses in the *okrug* of the city of Perm'.

In 1919 I worked as the head of Cultural Education of the [illegible] *Guberniia* Military Committee, then headed the Agitation-Organization Section of the Tver' *Guberniia* Military Executive Committee, was editor of the *guberniia* newspaper, and taught political literacy at the Cavalry School. In October 1919 I was elected a member of the Tver' *Guberniia* Committee of the Russian Communist Party and a member of its Bureau in which capacity I remained until September 1922.

In 1920 I headed the Agitation Section of the *Guberniia* Committee, the cooperative department of the *Guberniia* Committee, and I conducted lectures. I was elected by the 8th Congress of Soviets to membership in the All-Russian Central Executive Committee, where I remained during two convocations (the 8th and 9th).

In 1921 I worked as the chairman of *Guberniia* planning and vice chairman of the Tver' *Guberniia* Executive Committee.

In 1922, from April to June, I worked as the chairman of the Tver' *Guberniia* Executive Committee.

In the month of June, by the resolution of the Central Committee of the Organization Bureau, I was appointed to the Nizhnii Novgorod *Guberniia* Committee, where I head the Agitation Section, being a member of the Bureau of the *Guberniia* Committee.

January 3, 1922.

A. Zhdanov

[Upper left corner:] Second copy for the Zhdanov file.

RTSKhIDNI, fond 77, op. 2, d. 62, ll. 27, 27ob, 28.

1939 Census blanks for the households of Mikoyan, Molotov, Stalin, and Vyshinsky

CENTRAL OFFICE OF ECONOMIC RECORDS
OF THE STATE PLANNING COMMITTEE [*Gosplan*] OF THE USSR

ALL-UNION POPULATION CENSUS OF 1939

Form approved by Council of Ministers of USSR July 26, 1938

Number of census bureau	Number of inspectorate	Number of counting office	Number of quarter	Number of consolidated report for housing development or household list

KEY TO TABLES

1. Relationship to head of family (wife, son, mother, sister, cousin, etc.)
2. Permanent or temporary resident?
3. Temporary residents: a) permanent residence b) time absent from place of permanent residence
4. Permanent residents who are temporarily absent, indicate "temporarily absent" and how long.
5. Sex (male, female)
6. Age in years, or for children less than one year old, in months.
7. Nationality (ethnic affiliation)
8. Native language
9. Married?
10. Citizenship (what country)?
11. Literacy: a) can read/write or only read in any language b) completely illiterate
12. Students: a) name of educ. inst., school, or courses; b) grade or year
13. Graduate of secondary or higher educational institution (write "secondary" or "higher")
14. Current occupation or other source of livelihood
15. Place of employment (name of business, collective farm, or office)
16. Social category: blue-collar, white-collar, collective farmer, cooperative craftsman, independent peasant, independent craftsman, independent professional, or clergyman or non-working element.

THE MIKOYAN HOUSEHOLD

CENSUS FORM No 1

Republic, *Krai, Oblast'* ___Russian Soviet Federated Socialist Republic (RSFSR)___
*Okrug*_____*Raion*_____
Name of urban settlement: _Moscow___   City ward (district): _Lenin____
Street, lane, square:_____   Building No:____
Apartment No: __

Address for rural areas:
Rural council:_____Name of community (village, *aul, kishlak*):_____
Street, lane:_____ House No: _____

	1. Mikoyan Anastas Ivanovich	2. Mikoyan Ashkhen Lazarevna	3. Mikoyan Stepan Anastasovich	4. Mikoyan Vladimir Anastasovich	5. Mikoyan Aleksei Anastasovich	6. Mikoyan Vano Anastasovich	7. Mikoyan Sergo Anastasovich
1	head of household	wife	son	son	son	son	son
2	permanent	permanent	permanent	permanent	permanent	permanent	permanent
3	N/A N/A	N/A N/A	N/A	N/A	N/A		
4	N/A	N/A	N/A	N/A	N/A	N/A	N/A
5	male	female	male	male	male	male	male
6	43 years	42 years	16 years	14 years	13 years	11 years	9 years
7	Armenian	Armenian	Armenian	Armenian	Armenian	Armenian	Armenian
8	Armenian	Armenian	Russian	Russian	Russian	Russian	Russian
9	yes	yes	no	no	no	no	no
10	Soviet Union	Soviet Union	Soviet Union	Soviet Union	Soviet Union	Soviet Union	Soviet Union
11	reads/writes	reads/writes	reads/writes	reads/writes	reads/writes	reads/writes	reads/writes
12	N/A	N/A	Spec. School no. 2, 9th gr	Mid. School no. 32, 7th gr	Mid. School no. 32, 6th gr	Mid. School no. 32, 4th gr	Mid. School no. 32, gr 2
13	secondary	secondary	secondary	secondary	N/A	N/A	N/A
14	People's Commissar	dependent of no. 1	dependent of no. 1	dependent of no. 1	dependent of no. 1	dependent of no. 1	dependent of no. 1
15	People's Commissariat of For. Trade of USSR	N/A	N/A	N/A	N/A	N/A	N/A
16	white-collar	white-collar	white-collar	white-collar	white-collar	white-collar	white-collar

THE MOLOTOV HOUSEHOLD

CENSUS FORM No. 2

Republic, *Krai, Oblast'* _RSFSR_____
*Okrug*____*Raion*_____
Name of urban settlement: _Moscow___   City ward (district): _Lenin_____
Street, lane, square: _Kremlin_____   Building No:____
Apartment No: __

Address for rural areas:
Rural council:_____Name of community (village, *aul, kishlak*):_____
Street, lane:_____ House No: _____

	1. Molotov Viacheslav Mikhailovich	2. Zhemchuzhina Galina Semenovna	3. Molotova Svetlana Viacheslavna	4. Zhemchuzhina Rita Aronovna
1	husband	wife	daughter	daughter
2	permanent	permanent	permanent	permanent
3	N/A	N/A	N/A	N/A
4	N/A	N/A	N/A	N/A
5	male	female	female	female
6	48 years	40 years	9 years	11 years
7	Russian	Jewish	Russian	Jewish
8	Russian	Russian	Russian	Russian
9	yes	yes	no	no
10	Soviet Union	Soviet Union	Soviet Union	Soviet Union
11	reads/writes	reads/writes	reads/writes	reads/writes
12	N/A	N/A	School no. 175, 3rd grade grade	School no. 175, 3rd
13	secondary	secondary	N/A	N/A
14	Chairman of Council of People's Commissars	Deputy People's Commissar of Food Processing Industry	dependent of no. 1 and 2	dependent of no. 1 and 2
15	Council of People's Commissars of the USSR	People's Commissariat of Food Processing Industry	N/A	N/A
16	white-collar	white-collar	N/A	N/A

THE STALIN HOUSEHOLD

CENSUS FORM No. *1*

Republic, *Krai, Oblast'* _RSFSR_____

*Okrug*____*Raion* _____

Name of urban settlement: _Moscow___   City ward (district): _Lenin_____

Street, lane, square:____   Building No.:____

Apartment No.: __

Address for rural areas:

Rural council:_____Name of community (village, *aul, kishlak*):_____

Street, lane:_____ House No.: _____

	1. Stalin Iosif Vissarionovich	2. Stalina Svetlana Iosifovna
1	head of household	daughter
2	permanent	permanent
3	N/A	N/A
4	N/A	N/A
5	male	female
6	59 years	12 years
7	Georgian	Georgian
8	Georgian	Russian
9	no	no
10	Soviet Union	Soviet Union
11	reads/writes	reads/writes
12	secondary	Full Middle School no. 175, 6th grade
13	secondary	no
14	Secretary of Central Committee of All-Union Communist Party (Bolshevik)	dependent of no. 1
15	Central Committee of All-Union Communist Party (Bolshevik)	N/A
16	professional revolutionary (white-collar)	white-collar

THE VYShINSKY HOUSEHOLD

CENSUS FORM No. 1–A

Republic, *Krai, Oblast'* _RSFSR_____
*Okrug*_____*Raion* _____
Name of urban settlement: _Moscow___   City ward (district): _Soviet____
Street, lane, square:_Gnezdikovskii Prospect_____   Building No.: _10___
Apartment No.: _828__

Address for rural areas:
Rural council:_____Name of community (village, *aul, kishlak*):_____
Street, lane:_____ House No.: ____

	1. Vyshinsky Andrei IAnuar'evich	2. Vyshinskaia Ka[illegible] Isidorovna	3. Vyshinskaia Zinaida Andreevna
1	head of household	wife	daughter
2	permanent	permanent	permanent
3	N/A	N/A	N/A
4	N/A	N/A	N/A
5	male	female	female
6	55 years	52 years	29 years
7	Russian	Russian	Russian
8	Russian	Russian	Russian
9	yes	yes	no
10	Soviet Union	Soviet Union	Soviet Union
11	reads/writes	reads/writes	reads/writes
12	N/A	N/A	N/A
13	higher	secondary	higher
14	procurator	dependent of no. 1	researcher
15	Procuracy of the USSR	N/A	All-Union Institute of Legal Sciences
16	white-collar	white-collar	white-collar

TSGAOR, fond 9430, op. 1s, d. 166, ll. 1–6

CENTRAL OFFICE OF ECONOMIC RECORDS
OF THE STATE PLANNING COMMITTEE [*Gosplan*] OF THE USSR
ALL-UNION POPULATION CENSUS OF 1939

Form approved by Council of Ministers of USSR July 26, 1938

Number of census bureau	Number of inspectorate	Number of counting office	Number of quarter	Number of consolidated report for housing development or household list

KEY TO TABLES

1. Relationship to head of family (wife, son, mother, sister, cousin, etc.)

2. Permanent or temporary resident?

3. Temporary residents: a) place of permanent residence; b) amount of time absent from place of permanent residence

4. For permanent residents who are temporarily absent, indicate "temporarily absent" and how long.

5. Sex (male, female)

6. Age in years, or for children less than one year old, in months.

7. Nationality (ethnic affiliation)

8. Native language

9. Married?

10. Citizenship (what country)?

11. Literacy: a) can read and write or can only read in any language; b) or completely illiterate

12. Students: a) name of educ. inst., school, courses; b) grade/year (courses less than one year, write "short-term")

13. Graduate of secondary or higher educational institution (write "secondary" or "higher")

14. Current occupation or other source of livelihood

15. Place of employment (name of business, collective farm, or office)

16. Social category: blue-collar, white-collar, collective farmer, cooperative craftsman, independent peasant, independent craftsman, independent professional, or clergyman or non-working element.

Republic, *Krai, Oblast'* *Russian Soviet Federated Socialist Republic* (RSFSR)
*Okrug*____   *Raion*_____
Address for urban areas:
Name of urban settlement: *Moscow*   City ward (district): *Krasnaia Presnia*

Street, lane, square: *Malaia Nikitskaia*   Building No.: 28
Apartment No.: 1
Address for rural areas:
Rural council:_____
Name of community (village, *aul, kishlak*):_____
Street, lane: _____   House No.:_

	1. Beria Nina Teimurazovna	2. Beria Marta Ivanovna	3. Beria Akesha Pavlovna	4. Beria Sergei Lavrentievich	5. Almeshtigler Ellia Emanuilovna
1	N/A	mother of husband	sister of husband	son	no relation
2	permanent	permanent	permanent	permanent	permanent
3	N/A	N/A	N/A	N/A	N/A
4	N/A	N/A	N/A	N/A	N/A
5	female	female	female	male	female
6	34 years old	66 years old	32 years old	14 years old	38 years old
7	Georgian	Georgian	Georgian	Georgian	German
8	Georgian	Georgian	Georgian	Georgian	German
9	yes	no	no	no	no
10	Soviet Union	Soviet Union	Soviet Union	Soviet Union	Soviet Union
11	reads/writes	reads/writes	reads/writes	reads/writes	reads/writes
12	N/A	N/A	N/A	Middle School 15; 8th grade	Moscow Inst. of Finance & Economics; 4th year
13	higher	N/A	N/A	no	secondary
14	researcher	white-collar dependent	white-collar dependent	white-collar dependent	education
15	Timiriazev Agr. Inst. of Moscow	N/A	N/A	N/A	Comrade Beria's office
16	white-collar	white-collar	white-collar	white-collar	white-collar

THE VOROShILOV HOUSEHOLD. CENSUS FORM No. 5

Republic, *Krai, Oblast'* _RSFSR_____Okrug____   Raion_____
Address for urban areas:
Name of urban settlement: _Moscow___ City ward (district): _Lenin___
Street, lane, square:_____ Building No.:__Apartment No.:__
Address for rural areas:
Rural council:_____Name of community (village, *aul, kishlak*):_____
Street, lane: _____   House No.:__

	1. Voroshilova Ekaterina Davydovna	2. Frunze Tatiana Mikhailovna	3. Frunze Timur Mikhailovich
1	N/A	adopted	adopted
2	permanent	permanent	permanent
3	N/A	N/A	N/A
4	N/A	N/A	N/A
5	female	female	male
6	61 years old	18 years old	15 years old
7	Jewish	Russian	Russian
8	Russian	Russian	Russian
9	yes	no	no
10	Soviet Union	Soviet Union	Soviet Union
11	reads/writes	reads/writes	reads/writes
12	N/A	Moscow State Univ., 1st year	Special School no., 9th grade
13	higher	secondary	secondary
14	Chairman, Communist Party History Dept.	pension	pension
15	Sverdlov Advanced Propaganda Training School, *TSK VKP(b)*	N/A	N/A
16	white-collar	white-collar	white-collar

TSGAOR, fond 9430, op. 1s, d. 166, ll. 1–2.

Beria, Stalin, and Stalin's daughter Svetlana at the dacha, 1930. TSGAKFD

Inventory of Stalin's personal effects, March 16, 1956, found in his Moscow apartment

<u>INVENTORY</u>
of STALIN'S Personal Effects Found in Bldg. 1, Apt. 1.

<u>Bed Room</u>

1. Iron case for binoculars	- 1 piece
2. Chest badges	- 3 pieces
3. All-Russian Central Executive Committee deputy's badge, no. 120	- 1 piece
4. Order of the Red Banner, old model no. 400	- 1 piece
5. Bronze decoration depicting a star and half moon (1922)	- 1 piece
6. Protective glasses	- 1 piece
7. Men's batiste underwear	- 4 pairs
8. Handkerchiefs	- 5 pieces
9. Men's field socks	- 7 pairs
10. Men's wool suit (jacket and trousers)	
11. Bedroom slippers (buckskin)	- 1 pair
12. Bedroom slippers (brown leather)	- 1 pair
13. Kidskin boots	- 1 pair
14. Key to interior lock (closet)	- 1 piece
15. Blank notebook	- 1 piece
16. Pencils	- 2 pieces
17. Smoking pipe	- 1 piece

<u>Study</u>

1. Blank notebook for a delegate to the 18th Congress of the All-Union Communist Party (of Bolsheviks), with a comb in it	
2. Photograph of Stalin's mother	
3. Ribbon racks [for military decorations]	- 2 pieces
4. Ballpoint pen in case	- 1 piece
5. Wooden cigarette box	- 1 piece
6. Ornamental inlaid box	- 1 piece

<u>Dining Room</u>

1. Smoking pipes	- 4 pieces
2. Cap (moth damaged)	- 1 piece
3. Horn goblets	- 2 pieces
4. Magnifying glass	- 1 piece

<u>Bathroom</u>

1. Hairbrush [handwritten annotation:] not turned in	- 1 piece

<u>Cool-Storage Room (in a trunk)</u>

1. White felt boots	- 1 pair
2. Men's galoshes	- 1 pair

3. Blue cloth muffler	- 1 piece
4. Dark gray wool jacket (civilian cut)	- 1 piece
5. Wool men's trousers, worn with boots	- 1 pair
6. Handkerchiefs	- 23 pieces
7. Cambric men's pants	- 17 pieces
8. Men's cambric undershirts	- 17 units
9. Deerskin slippers	- 1 pair
10. Canvas shoes	- 1 pair
11. Beige scarf	- 1 piece
12. Knitted wool sleeve	- 1 piece
13. Leather slippers	- 1 pair
14. Wool quilted blanket	- 1 piece

<u>In the Housekeeper's Room</u>

1. Men's wool suits	- 3 pieces
2. Wool trousers (separate)	- 3 pieces
3. Suspenders	- 1 pair

SUBMITTED BY COLONEL - [signed] P. TSvetkov (TSVETKOV).

ACCEPTED BY MAJOR Tech. Services - [signed] Kurkin (KURKIN).

<u>March 16, 1956.</u>

Personal belongings of J. V. Stalin found in Apt. no. 1, as per inventory no. 1 were all inventoried in my presence; no statement of value; I make no claim to a commission.

Submitted by Engineer-Major - [signed] Kurkin (KURKIN)

Accepted for custodial storage - captain - [signed] Viktorov

(VIKTOROV)

<u>July 29, 1959</u>

KGB archive.

DOCUMENT 163   ***Inventory of Stalin's personal effects, March 16, 1956, transferred from his Zubalovo dacha to his apartment in Moscow***

INVENTORY
of Stalin's Personal Effects
Transferred from Zubalovo Dacha to Bldg. 1, Apt. 1.

1. Crystal decanters mounted in metal	- 2 pieces
2. Green porcelain coffee service, consisting of teapot, cups, sugar bowl, saucer, creamer with tray (gilded tips broken off sugar bowl and pot)	
3. Porcelain vase with blue design	- 1 piece
4. Porcelain tea cups (two are cracked)	- 6 pieces
5. Porcelain saucers	- 10 pieces

6. Octagonal porcelain dessert plates with fruit design — 16 pieces

7. Porcelain dessert plates with fruit design — 9 pieces

8. White table setting — 1 set

9. Porcelain vase with Stalin's portrait — 1 piece

10. "Goose" porcelain figurine — 1 piece

11. "Hare" porcelain figurine — 1 piece

12. Pink tea cup with saucer — 1 piece

13. Colored down pillows — 4 pieces

14. Lilac porcelain vase — 1 piece

15. Drawn work linen napkins — 6 pieces

16. Embroidered silk pillowcases — 2 pieces

17. Embroidered table napkins — 2 pieces

18. Sewing machine, MPZ No. 441241 — 1 piece

19. "Chinese girls" figurines (on one figurine part of the fingers are broken off, on the other, part of the kimono) — 2 pieces

20. Metal drinking glass holders — 14 pieces

21. Small drinking glass — 7 pieces

22. A "fox" clock (fox's right ear broken off) — 1 piece

23. Crystal carafes with metal fixtures — 2 pieces

24. Tall crystal flower vase — 3 pieces

25. Six-piece coffee service (pot with broken spout) — 1 set

26. Blue glass candy dish on metal pedestal — 1 piece

27. Small porcelain "basket" vase — 1 piece

28. Oval dish with tower — 1 piece

29. Portable radio — 1 piece

30. Skiing boots with fitted socks — 1 pair

31. Ski boots — 1 pair

32. Hunting boots — 1 pair

33. Yellow embroidered table cloth (three-meters long) — 1 piece

34. Electric teapots — 2 pieces

35. Tall crystal flower vase with silver fixtures — 1 piece

36. 3–liter electric saucepans — 2 pieces

37. Wild strawberry pattern coffee service,
    consisting of :

cups	- 12 pieces
saucers	- 8 pieces
milk pitcher	- 1 piece
creamer	- 1 piece

38. Small rug with Stalin's portrait (torn)	- 1 piece
39. Gray suit (red pinstripe)	- 1 piece
40. House slippers	- 3 pairs
41. Underwear (undershirts)	- 5 pieces
42. Underwear (undershorts)	- 5 pieces
43. Silk socks	- 6 pairs
44. Handkerchiefs	- 12 pieces
45. Suspenders	- 2 pieces
46. White felt boots	- 1 pair
47. Porcelain pitcher inscribed, "Drink your fill but do not spill."	- 1 piece
48. 1946 geographic atlas for high school	- 1 piece
49. Ivory-handled letter opener	- 1 piece
50. Wood veneer portrait	- 1 piece
51. Woman's house slippers	- 1 pair
52. Worn slippers	- 2 pairs
53. Handkerchiefs	- 2 pieces
54. Gramophone	- 1 piece
55. Gramophone records (2 broken)	- 18 pieces
56. Record carrying case	- 1 piece
57. Device for measuring distance on a map	- 1 piece
58. Corded textile dressing gowns	- 8 pieces

SUBMITTED BY COLONEL - [signed] P. TSvetkov (TSVETKOV).

RECEIVED BY MAJOR of Tech. Services - [signed] Kurkin (KURKIN)

March 16, 1956.

Personal effects of J. V. Stalin, transferred from the Zubalovo dacha to Bldg. 1, Apt. 1, per inventory no. 4, were all inventoried in my presence; no statement of monetary value; I make no claims to a commission.

Submitted by Engineer-Major - [signed] Kurkin (KURKIN)

Received for custodial responsibility - Captain - [signed] Viktorov (VIKTOROV)

July 29, 1959

KGB archive.

Malenkov, Beria, Kaganovich, and Molotov walking to Red Square, May 1, 1953. TSGAKFD

Nomenclature Apparatus

As a monopoly political party, the Communists were concerned not only to suppress political opposition to their policies but also to take active measures to guarantee that the most important government posts would be held by reliable party cadres. As early as 1920 the Central Committee began to designate appointments to be made at that highest level of the party, and thus began the *nomenklatura* system. As the documents here suggest, in each government agency, whether the state planning committee, the state bank, the wine syndicate, or the *GPU*, a certain number of positions was reserved for the appointees of the Central Committee. Sometimes the interests of the party and the interests of the specific agency clashed, as illustrated in Document 165, in which the commissar for foreign affairs argues that certain high officials in his commissariat needed to select their own assistants, not have them sent by the party. The net effect of this system was to produce a network of officials who owed their appointments to their party patrons, not to their nominal bosses, and this helped to cement party control throughout the state bureaucracy.

Appointments made through the Central Committee and other party agencies were coordinated by the personnel assignments office, *Uchraspred*, which by 1922 was already responsible for over 10,000 appointments throughout the country. In 1924 *Uchraspred* merged with the *Orgbiuro* of the Central Committee and was named *Orgraspred*, under the leadership of Stalin's close associate L. M. Kaganovich. Through this agency every responsible appointment, whether in the party or in the state apparatus, was carefully checked and certified. The system remained in place throughout the history of the Soviet Union and reached its greatest refinement during the years of Brezhnev's rule, when the term *nomenklatura* came to signify the Soviet elite, the privileged ruling class.

DOCUMENT 164   *List of jobs at central institutions and their regional affiliates included in the special appointments (nomenclature) category*

[Note: ~~Stricken items~~ in original]

LIST OF CENTRAL AGENCIES AND THEIR LOCAL OFFICES
IN WHICH PERSONNEL APPOINTMENTS
AND REASSIGNMENTS
REQUIRE A RESOLUTION
OF THE CENTRAL COMMITTEE
OF THE RUSSIAN COMMUNIST PARTY (BOLSHEVIK) [*TSK RKP(b)*]

Item No	Title of position	Approximate number of authorized positions
I.	SUPREME ECONOMIC COUNCIL [*VSNKh*]	
1.	Chairman and members of the Presidium	10
2.	Department heads and members of the Collegium (or deputies) of major offices and departments of *VSNKh* such as Central Industrial Economic Administration, Mining Industry Administration, chairman and members of the Collegium of the Main Metallurgical Administration, director and deputy director of Electrical Industry Administration, director and deputy director of State Construction Administration, chairman, vice-chairman, and members of Collegium of Main Military Industry Administration, ~~Industrial Engineering Administration, Main Military Administration, director of Central Administration of Records and Statistics,~~ director of Commercial Finance Administration, and director and deputy director of the Central Supreme Survey Administration	26

Item No	Title of position	Approximate number of authorized positions
3.	Chairman and members of Syndicates' Board	17
4.	Chairman and members of boards of nationally important trusts	96
5.	Directors and managers of nationally important trusts	
6.	~~Oblast' representatives of syndicates~~	
7.	Directors of major enterprises	
8.	Chairman of and ~~members of oblast'~~ industrial bureaus	60
9.	All foreign representatives of VSNkh	
II.	STATE PLANNING COMMITTEE [*Gosplan*]	
1.	Presidium of *Gosplan*	12
2.	Members of *Gosplan*	11
III.	CENTRAL CONCESSIONS COMMISSION	
1.	Chairman and members of Central Concessions Commission	7
III. [sic]	INDUSTRIAL BANK	
1.	Chairmen and vice-chairmen of councils	32
2.	Chairman and Members of Board	6
3.	Managers of *krai* and *oblast'* offices of Industrial Bank	6
4.	~~All authorized representatives and agents, managers of foreign branches and offices of Industrial Bank~~	
IV.	PEOPLE'S COMMISSARIAT OF FINANCE	
1.	People's commissar, deputy people's commissar, and	8
2.	Heads of major departments of People's Commissariat of Finance, such as director of Administrative Office, director of Budget Office, director of Currency Office, director and deputy director of the Central Tax Inspectorate, director of Local Finance Office, director of Precious Metals Fund	8
3.	~~All foreign representatives and agents of People's Commissariat of Finance~~	
4.	Local offices: Authorized representatives of People's Commissar of Finance	14
5.	Heads of *guberniia* finance departments of major *guberniias*	~~30~~ 15
V.	STATE BANK	
1.	Chairman, vice-chairman, and members of the boards	10
2.	Directors of major departments, such as Foreign Department, Credit Department, Commercial Department, Agricultural Department, Grain Department, Audit Department	7

Item No	Title of position	Approximate number of permanent positions
3.	All authorized representatives, agents, and heads of foreign branches and departments of the State Bank	
4.	Local offices: heads of branch offices of State Bank	24
5.	Heads of branches of State Bank	104
VII.	CENTRAL NATIONAL INSURANCE ADMINISTRATION OF THE USSR [*Gosstrakh*]	
1.	Chairman and members of Board	5
VIII.	PEOPLE'S COMMISSARIAT OF FOODSTUFFS	
1.	People's commissar, deputy commissar, and members of Collegium	5
2.	Heads of major departments: including procurement, ~~distribution~~, meat and slaughterhouses, chairman and members of board of ~~State Dairy Administration,~~ head of Central Gut Supply	8
3.	Chairman and members of Board of *TSuprodkhoz* [acronym unclear]	3
4.	Chairman and members of Board of State Fisheries Industry Administration	3
5.	All authorized representatives, agents, and heads of foreign offices of the people's commissar of foodstuffs	
6.	Local agencies: authorized representatives: . . . . Heads of *oblast'* offices of Main Fish Administration . . . . *Guberniia* food commissars of major grain-producing *guberniia*s	5 7 20
7.	Head of Department of Flour Mills	1
8.	Head of Main Fish Administration	1
IX.	GRAIN ADMINISTRATION	
1.	Chairman, Deputy Chairman, and Members of Board	1
2.	Heads of major departments such as: fodder grains and inspection department	2
3.	All authorized representatives, agents, and heads of foreign offices of Grain Administration	
4.	Local agencies: heads of *oblast'* offices	7
X.	PEOPLE'S COMMISSARIAT OF AGRICULTURE	
1.	Commissar, deputy commissar, and members of Collegium	9
2.	Heads of major departments such as agriculture, veterinary services, land improvement and reclamation, the chairman of the Supreme Special Collegium for Land Affairs, head of the Central Forestry Administration	6

Item No	Title of position	Approximate number of permanent positions
3.	All authorized representatives, agents, and heads of foreign subsidiaries and offices of People's Commissariat of Agriculture	
XI.	STATE AGRICULTURAL SYNDICATE	
1.	Chairman and members of Board	
XII.	WINE SYNDICATE	
5.	Chairman and members of Board	
6.	Local agencies: Authorized representatives of people's commissar of Agriculture	5
7.	Heads of *guberniia* agricultural departments of major agricultural *guberniia*s	25
XIII.	PEOPLE'S COMMISSARIAT OF TRANSPORTATION [*NKPS*]	
1.	People's commissar, deputy commissar, and members of Collegium	8
2.	Heads of *major* central departments of *NKPS*	5
3.	Chairman and vice-chairman of Freight Commission	~~3~~
4.	~~Chairman and vice-chairman of Transportation Planning Commission~~	2
5.	Head of Transportation Districts River and Sea	12
6.	Authorized representatives and assistant representatives of *NKPS* (river and sea)	12
7.	Authorized representatives of people's commissar for railways	24
8.	Chairman ~~and vice-chairman~~ of railroad boards (river and seaways)	[illeg]
9.	Chairmen and members of boards of trusts	11
10.	Authorized representatives for ports	6
11.	All authorized representatives, agents, and heads of foreign subsidiaries and offices of *NKPS*	
XIV.	PEOPLE'S COMMISSARIAT OF POSTAL AND TELEGRAPH COMMUNICATIONS	
1.	Commissar, deputy commissar, and members of Collegium	6
2.	~~Heads of central boards~~	4
3.	Authorized representatives of people's commissar to republics	6
4.	Administrators of communications districts	22
5.	~~Manager of October Radio~~	1
6.	All authorized representatives, agents, and heads of foreign subsidiaries and offices of People's Commissariat of Postal and Telegraph Communications	

Item No	Title of position	Approximate number of permanent positions
XV.	PEOPLE'S COMMISSARIAT OF INTERNAL AFFAIRS	
1.	People's commissar, deputy commissar, and members of the Collegium	5
2.	Directors and heads of major directorates and departments, including Administrative and Organizational Bureau, Main Facilities Directorate, Main Administration of Places of Incarceration, Main Police Directorate	5
	~~Assistant Head of Police Administrative and Organizational Bureau~~	1
3.	~~Chairman of *oblast'* and *guberniia* executive committees~~	106
XVI.	STATE POLITICAL DIRECTORATE [*GPU*]	
1.	Chairman, vice-chairman, and members of Collegium	9
2.	Heads of major departments	3
3.	Head of Transportation Department of *GPU*	1
4.	Head of Special Department of *GPU*	1
5.	Head of Eastern Department of *GPU*	1
6.	Chief of Staff of *GPU* Troops	1
7.	~~Heads of District Transportation Departments of *GPU*~~	
8.	Local agencies: Chairmen of *GPU*s of union republics	3
9.	Authorized *oblast'* representatives	5
10.	Heads of *guberniia* and *oblast'* departments	25
XVII.	PEOPLE'S COMMISSARIAT OF JUSTICE	
1.	Commissar, deputy commissar, and members of Collegium	6
2.	~~Heads of major departments~~	5
3.	Assistant procurators of republics	4
4.	Procurators of People's Commissariat of Justice	8
5.	Procurators assigned to Supreme Court Collegium	8
6.	~~Assistant procurators~~	4
7.	*Guberniia* and *oblast'* procurators	105 [*153*]
XVIII.	SUPREME COURT	
1.	Chairman and vice-chairman of Supreme Court	2
2.	Chairmen and members of all the Collegia, including Military, Military Transportation, Civil, Civil Appeals, Criminal Appeals	32
3.	~~Local: Chairmen and members of local branches of Supreme Court~~	20

Item No	Title of position	Approximate number of permanent positions
4.	~~Chairmen of District Military Tribunals~~	20
5.	Chairmen of District and Corps Military Tribunals	52
6.	Military district procurators	12
XIX.	PEOPLE'S COMMISSARIAT OF WORKERS' AND PEASANTS INSPECTION	
1.	Commissar, deputy Commissar, and members of Collegium	11
2.	~~Heads of major inspectorates~~	8
3.	~~Head of Central Complaints Office~~	1
XX.	PEOPLE'S COMMISSARIAT OF FOREIGN AFFAIRS	
1.	Commissar, deputy commissar, and members of Collegium	6
2.	~~Department heads~~	4
3.	~~Subdepartment heads~~	17
4.	Foreign ambassadors	17
5.	Consuls	23
6.	First secretaries	17
7.	~~Second secretaries~~	4
8.	Ambassadorial advisers	4
9.	Special representatives	6
XXI.	PEOPLE'S COMMISSARIAT OF FOREIGN TRADE	
1.	Commissar, deputy commissar, and members of Collegium	5
2.	Heads of major departments such as ~~Economics Office, Transportation Office~~, Regulation Office, Export and Import Department, ~~Licensing Department, [illeg]~~, Customs Office, Customs, Tariffs, and Quotas, Contraband Control	12
3.	Foreign trade representatives and deputy trade representatives	16
4.	Secretaries	10
5.	Authorized representatives of People's Commissariat of Foreign Trade	
6.	Members of the boards of the State Export-Import Trade Office [*Gostorg*]	
XXII.	PEOPLE'S COMMISSARIAT OF LABOR	
1.	Commissar, deputy commissar, and members of Collegium	6
2.	~~Department heads~~	4
3.	Director of Central Social Insurance Administration	1
4.	Authorized *oblast'* and *raion* representatives of People's Commissariat of Labor	5

Item No	Title of position	Approximate number of permanent positions
XXIII.	**PEOPLE'S COMMISSARIAT OF HEALTH**	
1.	Commissar, deputy commissar, and members of Collegium	5
2.	~~Head of Department of Medical Care Facilities~~	1
3.	Head and assistant head of Central Medical Administration	2
4.	~~Head of Department of Medical Education~~	1
5.	Head of Health Resort Administration	1
6.	~~Head of Political Inspectorate~~	1
7.	~~Head of Department of Transportation~~	1
8.	~~Head of Department of Foreign Information~~	1
9.	~~Authorized *oblast'* representatives of People's Commissar of Health~~	5
10.	~~All authorized representatives, agents, and heads of foreign offices of People's Commissariat of Health~~	
XXIV.	**PEOPLE'S COMMISSARIAT OF SOCIAL INSURANCE**	
1.	Commissar, deputy commissar, and members of the Collegium	5
2.	~~Heads of central social insurance departments and agencies~~	1
3.	Chairman of Central Peasants' Committee of Mutual Aid Associations	1
4.	~~Authorized insurance agents for disabled war veterans and families of servicemen~~	1
5.	Chairman of Board of All-Russian Disabled Cooperative Association	1
XXV.	**PEOPLE'S COMMISSARIAT OF EDUCATION**	
1.	Commissar, deputy commissar, and members of Collegium	6
2.	Heads and assistant heads of major departments such as: Main Vocational Education Department, Main Children's Social Development and Political Indoctrination Department, Main Political Education Department, State Publishing Houses, Main Office for the Protection of Military and State Secrets in the Media [*Glavlit*], Central State Cinema Company, Main Administration of Research Institutes, Museums, and Art Research Institutes [*Glavnauka*], State Academic Council, etc.	25
3.	Head of Central Archives	1
4.	Head of the Russian Telegraph Agency	1
5.	Heads of Foreign and Domestic Information Departments and Commercial Telegraph Agency	3
6.	Editors of the major Moscow newspapers: *Pravda, Izvestiia, Rabochaia gazeta, Ekonomicheskaia zhizn', Bednota*	5
7.	Editors of periodicals: *Krasnaia nov', Molodaia gvardiia, Proletarskaia revoliutsiia, Pechat' i revoliutsiia, Pod znamenem Marksizma, Krasnaia letopis',* etc.	10

Item No	Title of position	Approximate number of permanent positions
8.	Institutions of higher education: Rectors of leading institutions of higher learning, such as the First and Second State Universities of Moscow, Petrograd University, Kazan University, the Petrovskii Agricultural Academy, the Higher Technical School, the Marx Institute of Economics, and so forth	10
9.	~~The deans of major workers' faculties, including the Pokrovskii Workers' Faculty at the First State University of Moscow, at the Marx Institute, the Petrovskii Agricultural Academy, and so forth~~	10
XXVI.	THE ALL-RUSSIAN CENTRAL EXECUTIVE COMMITTEE	
1.	Party members of the All-Russian Central Executive Committee and USSR Central Executive Committee	300
2.	Staff employees of the All-Russian Central Executive Committee and Central Executive Committee: business manager and head of Organizational Department	2
XXVII.	COUNCIL OF PEOPLE'S COMMISSARS [*Sovnarkom*]	
1.	Members of Small Council of People's Commissars	
2.	Staff: Business managers of *Sovnarkom*s of USSR and Russian Soviet Federated Socialist Republic (RSFSR), secretaries of Councils of People's Commissars of USSR and RSFSR, Supreme Arbitration Commission	8
XXVIII.	CENTRAL COUNCIL OF CONSUMERS' COOPERATIVES OF THE USSR	
1.	Board	15
2.	Auditing Commission	12
3.	Council	40
4.	~~Heads of major departments~~	12
5.	~~Heads of *oblast'* and *krai* offices of Central Council~~	18
6.	Members of Board of Transportation Section	10
7.	Members of Board of Central Workers' Section	2
	THE ALL-UNION CENTRAL COUNCIL OF TRADE UNIONS [*VTSSPS*]	
1.	Members and candidates for membership in All-Union Central Council of Trade Unions	114
2.	Members of Presidium of *VTSSPS*	115
3.	Chairmen of *oblast'* bureaus of *VTSSPS*	9
4.	Authorized representatives of *VTSSPS* at *oblast'* bureaus of *VTSSPS*	207
	TOTAL:	445

RTSKhIDNI, fond 17, op. 34, d. 106, ll. 151–156, 273, 276.

DOCUMENT 165   *Letter from Chicherin to Molotov, October 24, 1923, on classification of positions in the nomenclature system*

October 24, 1923

VERY URGENT   VERY SECRET

FOR A.M. DELIVERY

To: Comrade Molotov

Copy to Com. Kaganovich
Reference your No. 6530/s
Oct. 24

Esteemed Comrade,

Your letter was received very late in the evening, and only tomorrow will I have the opportunity to consider it in the Collegium. Besides, you require an answer tomorrow by 5 P.M. After considering your letter I shall write to you again. In the meantime, I note the following.

You have established a list of positions whose appointments are made solely by a decision of the Central Committee. This is confusing and imprecise. First of all, all transfers of party members are made by agreement with the Personnel Assignment Office [*Uchraspred*]. Regarding appointments by the Central Committee, these come from the Organizational Bureau [*Orgbiuro*] and the Political Bureau [Politburo].

Formerly, the Politburo appointed the people's commissars, deputy people's commissars, Collegium members, plenipotentiaries, and authorized representatives of the union republics. Recently, to these have been added counsellors, first secretaries—based on the fact that in the absence of a plenipotentiary they replace him. A common attribute of these positions is independent work of the most responsible nature. Consuls are appointed by the *Orgbiuro* since this position is not political, and even though these workers perform independent work, it is of a less responsible nature.

Therefore, the basis for appointments in the People's Commissariat of Foreign Affairs by the Central Committee, by both the Politburo and the *Orgbiuro*, is the independent and representational nature of the work.

In your list you have added the second secretaries of our plenipotentiaries, Section heads, and Subsection heads. All these positions are nonindependent since the work of these officials is conducted under the direct and constant supervision of the plenipotentiary in one case and the people's commissars, deputy commissars, or members of the Collegium in the other case. I therefore do not see the necessity of burdening the Central Committee with the appointment of these officials.

I even consider it absolutely undesirable for the Central Committee to appoint Section heads and Subsection heads. They are close and immediate coworkers of the people's commissar, deputy people's commissars, and Collegium members. They must work together with these officials and the success of their collaboration is of the first order. It is both impossible to burden a responsible worker with a personal secretary with whom he cannot work harmoniously or to burden the Collegium with Section and Subsection heads with whom collaboration will not be successful. Furthermore, for these workers most important are their technical qualifications, knowledge, and experience in one specific area. Finally, their appointment by the Central Committee can have a detrimental effect on the nature of their work. When Comrade Mikhailov in Tashkent, instead of fulfilling the directives of the People's Commissariat of Foreign Affairs, responded to these directives, as is his fashion, with polemics and all possible tricks, he incidentally sometimes alluded to having been appointed by the Central Committee. It is specifically the Section and Subsection heads who must absolutely carry out the directives from the people's commissar, deputy people's commissars, and members of the Collegium. If instead of this they engage in polemics with the Collegium members, alluding to having been appointed by the Central Committee, this will render the functioning of the Commissariat impossible.

Thus, I raise my personal objection to the appointment of Section and Subsection heads and second secretaries by the Central Committee.

Communist greetings,

/Chicherin/copies:

RTSKhIDNI, fond 17, op. 34, d. 106, ll. 283–284.

DOCUMENT 166   ***List of nomenclature positions in the NKVD, January 31, 1924***

Compiled January 31, 1924

NOMENKLATURA [LIST]
OF POSITIONS TO BE REGISTERED
AT THE PERSONNEL RECORDS AND ASSIGNMENT OFFICE [*Uchraspred*]
OF THE CENTRAL COMMITTEE [*TSK*]

FOR THE PEOPLE'S COMMISSARIAT OF INTERNAL AFFAIRS
RUSSIAN SOVIET FEDERATED SOCIALIST REPUBLIC [*NKVD RSFSR*]

Item	POSITION TITLES	Number of positions subject to registration (by *nomenklatura* list)			Comments
		I	II	III	
	People's Commissar	I	—	—	
	Deputy People's Commissar	I	—	—	
	Collegium Members	4			
	BUSINESS OFFICE	—	—	—	
	Business Manager				
	BUREAU OF STATISTICS				
	Head of Bureau (Chief Statistician of *NKVD*)	—	—		
	RECORDS SUBDEPARTMENT				
	Head of Records	—	—	I	
	CENTRAL ADMINISTRATIVE DIRECTORATE	—	—	I	
	Chief of Directorate (same individual is Chief of Police of the Republic)	I	—	—	
	DIRECTORATE SECRETARIAT				
	Secretary	—	—	3	

Item	POSITION TITLES	Number of positions subject to registration (by *nomenklatura* list)			Comments
		I	II	III	
	ADMINISTRATIVE DEPARTMENT				
	Chief of Department	—	I	—	
	Assistant Department Chief	—	—	I	
	SUBDEPARTMENT OF ADMINISTRATIVE OVERSIGHT				
	Head of Subdepartment	—	—	I	
	FOREIGN SUBDEPARTMENT				
	Head of Subdepartment	—	I	—	
	Assistant Head of Subdepartment	—	—	3	
	CIVIL REGISTRY SUBDEPARTMENT				
	Head of Subdepartment	—	I	—	
	DEPARTMENT OF POLICE				
	Chief of Department	I	—	—	
	Assistant Chief	—	I	—	
	DEPARTMENT OF CRIMINAL INVESTIGATION				
	Chief of Department	I	—	—	
	Assistant Chief	—	I	—	
	ADMINISTRATIVE ORGANIZATION SUBDEPARTMENT				
	Head of Subdepartment	—	—	I	
	PARTY ACTIVIST SUBDEPARTMENT				
	Head of Subdepartment	—	—	I	
	MAIN ADMINISTRATION OF PLACES OF INCARCERATION (has Central Administrative Headquarters subdepartment status)	I	—	—	
	Chief of Administration				
	Assistant Chief	—	I	—	
	RUSSIAN-UKRAINIAN JOINT COMMISSION ON REPATRIATION				
	Chairman	—	—	I	

RTSKhIDNI, fond 17, op. 34, d. 256, l. 54.

Stalin, Zinoviev, Bukharin, Kamenev, and Rykov leading a group of delegates at the Thirteenth Party Congress, Moscow, 1924.
TSGAKFD

APPENDIX No. 1
Item No. 1
Minute No. 122
Organizational Bureau
November 16, 1925

RESOLUTION OF THE ORGANIZATIONAL BUREAU OF THE
CENTRAL COMMITTEE
CONCERNING THE SELECTION AND APPOINTMENT
OF PERSONNEL
(Approved by the Organizational Bureau of the
Central Committee of the Russian Communist Party (Bolshevik) [*TSK RKP(b)*]
in its Meeting on November 16, 1925
Minute No. 122, Item 1)

While recognizing recent accomplishments in assigning party personnel to key government agencies and in organizing personnel records and assignments for personnel detailed to party assignments per se and appointed to administrative positions in government, economic, labor, and cooperative organizations, at this point the *TSK* deems it necessary to focus on direct selection of party personnel for key administrative positions in order to make the process as meticulous as possible, in fulfillment of which it resolves to:

1. Approve, in amendment of the Organizational Bureau Resolution of June 12, 1923, the lists of positions (*nomenklatura*) revised by the Organizational Assignments Office, while leaving the procedures for appointment to these positions established by the aforementioned resolution in effect, i.e., appointments to positions on *nomenklatura* No. 1 can only be made by resolution of the *TSK* regardless of whether the appointee is a member of the *RKP* or not a party member; and appointments to positions on *nomenklatura* No. 2 require consultation with the Organizational Assignments Office of the *TSK* (see *nomenklatura* [lists] No. 1 and 2, Annex 3).

2. In supplementation of *nomenklatura* No. 1, approve the list of elective positions (Supplement No. 1), having directed that special commissions assigned by the *TSK* to hold the appropriate congresses and meetings (see Annex No. 4) shall be responsible for approving nominees for these positions.

3. Require that selection and appointment to key staff positions in central agencies not included on *nomenklatura* Nos. 1 and 2 be based on a list drafted by each agency in consultation with the Organizational Assignments Committee (agency *nomenklatura* No. 3) or by the agencies on their own, with monthly notification of the Organizational Assignments Committee of any appointments which have been made.

4. Require the *Guberniia* Committees, *Krai* Committees, and Central Committees of the national Communist Parties to draft their own *nomenklatura* of positions in local agencies whose appointment would require the approval of or consultation with these party bodies, on the basis of the models provided by *TSK nomenklatura* (lists Nos. 1 and 2) and guidelines concerning consultation procedures for appointments of officials of local agencies.

5. Establish the following procedure for resolving any questions related to reassignments (from one party organization to another or one agency to another):

a) A resolution of the *TSK*, its Secretariat, its Organizational Bureau, or its Political Bureau adopted by the procedure established by the *TSK* Resolution of November 24, 1924, is required for the reassignment of personnel occupying the positions listed on *nomenklatura* No. 1 and top administrative personnel in *krai*, *oblast'*, and *guberniia* agencies based on the supplementary list of positions (Supplement No. 2) (see Annex 5) attached to *nomenklatura* No. 1.

b) Party members occupying positions on *nomenklatura* No. 2, top administrative personnel in other *guberniia* agencies, and top *uezd* officials and all other personnel coming from regional and local positions and placed at the disposal of the *TSK* may be given permanent or temporary assignments by the Organizational Assignments Office only with the approval of one of the secretaries of the *TSK*. The Organizational Assignments Office will submit weekly reports of personnel reassignments falling under the provisions of point b §5 of this resolution to the secretaries of the *TSK*.

c) Any matters related to the reassignment of other party members from one agency to another and temporary assignment from a central agency to a provincial agency and to the staffs of central agencies and any grievances on the part of certain party comrades pertinent to these reassignments shall be resolved in Moscow by the Moscow Committee and in other cases by the Organizational Assignments Office of the *TSK*.

6. Instruct the Organizational Assignments Office of the *TSK* to reduce the number of listed personnel while leaving individuals occupying positions on *nomenklatura* No. 2 on the permanent personnel registry of the *TSK*. The personnel records and assignments offices of central agencies shall be directly responsible for keeping the records of and reviewing other key agency personnel under the close supervision of the Organizational Assignments Office of the *TSK*.

7. In amendment to Item 9 of the regulations governing departmental personnel records, authorize departments to keep personnel records on key employees who are members of the *RKP* on the following basis:

a) Agencies shall limit themselves to keeping a single personnel information sheet for members of the *RKP* occupying positions on *nomenklatura* No. 1. Agencies should forward performance evaluations for these individuals to the *TSK* only at the request of the Organizational Assignments Office and should not be kept in agency personnel files.

b) Other key personnel at central agencies and the top officials of local agencies should be assigned agency personnel files consisting of personnel information sheets and indexed performance records and evaluations.

8. Order that central agencies shall obtain all references, recommendations, and evaluations for personnel of record only from the directors of their local offices and the inspection, instructor, and information departments of their agencies. Any requests by central agencies to local agencies for such materials may be forwarded only with the authorization of the Organizational Assignments Office of the *TSK*.

9. Instruct the Organizational Assignments Office of the *TSK* to draft regulations for personnel records and assignments on the basis of this resolution and submit them to the Secretariat of the *TSK* for approval.

TRUE COPY: OSIPOVA

RTSKhIDNI, fond 17, op. 68, d. 459, ll. 1–3.

DOCUMENT 168   *Two nomenclature lists for the Supreme Council of the Economy [VSNKh],*
November 1925

Schedule No. 3
For Item 1 Minute No. 123
of Proceedings of Meeting of
Organizational Bureau
on November 16, 1925

NOMENKLATURA   NOMENKLATURA
[List]   [List]
No. 1   No. 2

of positions at central agencies and local offices for which appointments and dismissals of employees require an order from the Central Committee of the All-Russian Communist Party (Bolshevik) [*TSK VKP(b)*]

of positions at central agencies and their local offices for which appointments and dismissals of employees require preliminary notification of the Central Committee of the All-Russian Communist Party (Bolshevik)

(Approved by the Organizational Bureau of the *TSK VKP(b)* at the September 25, 1925, session, transcript 111, no. 1; the October 19, 1925, session, transcript 115, no. 2; and the November 16, 1925 session, transcript 122, no. 1)

Titles of agencies and positions	A*	B**	Titles of agencies and positions	A*	B**
I.			I.		
Supreme Economic Council			Supreme Economic Council		
Presidium of Supreme Economic Council of USSR and Russian Soviet Federated Socialist Republic (RSFSR)	25		Department heads at Central Administration of State-Owned Industry of USSR: asset management, foreign trade, audit and control, finance and budget, Central Accounting Office	5	
Collegium of Central Administration of State-Owned Industry of USSR and chairman of Central Administration of State-Owned Industry of RSFSR	11		Department heads at Central Economic Administration of USSR: trade policy and pricing, financial policy, industrial organization, and foreign	4	
Chairman and vice-chairman of Central Economic Administration of USSR and director of Economic Administration of RSFSR	3		Directors of Central Administration of State-Owned Industry of USSR: a) bituminous coal industry b) assistant director of the forestry industry c) second assistant director of textile industry d) director of food processing industry	5	
Board of Central Administration of the Military Industry	7				
Chairman and deputy chairman of Scientific and Technical Department	2		Directors of administration of State-Owned Industry of RSFSR: a) construction industry b) chemical industry c) food processing industry d) fuel industry e) forestry industry	5	
Board of Central Administration of the Metallurgical Industry	7				
Director of the Central Publishing Administration	1				

*A - Number of persons **B - List (number and page)

NOMENKLATURA
[List] No. 1

NOMENKLATURA
[List] No. 2

Titles of agencies and positions	A*	B**	Titles of agencies and positions	A*	B**
I.			I.		
Director of the Industrial Economic Council	1				
Senior directors of the Central Administration of State-Owned Industry of USSR: a) for the mining industry b) for the textile industry c) for the forestry industry d) for the chemical industry e) for the food processing industry	5		Assistant director of Central Economic Administration of RSFSR	1	
			Chairman and assistant chairman of Industrial Planning Agency of USSR	2	
			Chairman of RSFSR Industrial Planning Agency	1	
			Head of Surveying Administration	1	
Chairmen of commissions: for inventions, concessions, military industry, Supreme Arbitration Commission, and chairman and deputy chairman of the Cotton Commission	10		Director of Administrative and Financial Office of USSR	1	
			Chairman of *Gosmetr* [acronym unclear]	1	
Boards of Central Trusts (of USSR and RSFSR)	114	1/1-3	Members of Board of Scientific and Technical Department	4	
Chairmen and vice-chairmen of syndicates	15	2/3	Chairman of Geological Commission	1	
Directors of major plants	73	3/3-6	Assistant director of Central Publishing Administration	1	
Foreign representatives of Supreme Economic Council, syndicates, central trusts, and stock companies	14	4/6	Boards of trusts and syndicates	182	6/6–9
			Directors of major plants	34	7/9–10
Chairmen of stock companies	9	5/6	Managers of local subsidiaries of syndicates and trusts	75	8/10-3
TOTAL	297		Representatives of trusts and syndicates abroad	28	9/13
			Members of boards of stock companies . . .	20	10/14
			Chairmen of Industrial Bureau, *krai* and *oblast'* economic councils and Central Economic Councils (Northwest, North Caucasus, Siberian, Ural, Ukrainian, Far East)	6	
			Chairmen of most important *guberniia* economic councils	8	11/14
			TOTAL	385	

*A - Number of persons **B - List (number and page)

NOMENKLATURA [List] No. 1			NOMENKLATURA [List] No. 2		
Titles of agencies and positions	A*	B**	Titles of agencies and positions	A*	B**
II.			II.		
STATE PLANNING COMMITTEE [Gosplan]			Gosplan		
Presidiums of Gosplan of USSR and RSFSR.	20		Members of Gosplan (not included on List 1)	8	
Heads of major departments of Gosplan of USSR (industry, agriculture, economic statistics, finance, internal) [section of this item missing]			Head of Market Analysis Department	1	
			TOTAL	9	
			Agents in territory of Soviet Union	24	52/37
			TOTAL	137	
XV					
PEOPLE'S COMMISSARIAT OF WORKERS' AND PEASANTS' INSPECTION					
Collegia of USSR and RSFSR	16				
TOTAL	16				
XVI			XVI		
PEOPLE'S COMMISSARIAT OF LABOR			PEOPLE'S COMMISSARIAT OF LABOR		
Collegia of USSR and RSFSR	8		Members of Council of Central Social Insurance Administrations of USSR and RSFSR	9	
Director and assistant directors of Central Social Insurance Administrations of the USSR and RSFSR	4		Department heads at People's Commissariat of Labor: Departments of Labor Organization and Labor Protection of USSR and RSFSR	4	
TOTAL	12		Oblast' representatives of people's commissar of labor and department heads	6	53/37
			TOTAL	19	

*A - Number of persons   **B - List (number and page)

[Pages 3–7 of original missing. Translation resumes at page 8.]

NOMENKLATURA [List] No. 1				*NOMENKLATURA* [List] No. 2		

Titles of agencies and positions	A*	B**		Titles of agencies and positions	A*	B**
XVII				**XVII**		
PEOPLE'S COMMISSARIAT OF INTERNAL AFFAIRS				PEOPLE'S COMMISSARIAT OF INTERNAL AFFAIRS		
Collegium	5			Deputy director of Administrative Headquarters	1	
Director of Central Administrative Headquarters (chief of police for republic) and director of Main City Services Administration	2			Head of Organizational Department	1	
				Head of Prison Administration	1	
TOTAL	7			Head of Central Investigative Office	1	
				TOTAL	4	
XVIII				**XVIII**		
STATE POLITICAL DIRECTORATE [*GPU*]				*GPU*		
Collegium.	7			Assistant directors of Offices of Secret Operations, Economics, and Administration and Organization	3	
Directors of Offices of Secret Operations, Economics, and Administration and Organization.	3					
Heads of Departments: Foreign, Special Department, Transportation Department, Special Counterintelligence, Eastern, and Chief Inspectorate of *GPU* Troops.	7			Heads of Departments of: Counterintelligence, Routine Political Surveillance, and Border Control	5	
Representatives of Unified State Political Directorate [*OGPU*] under Councils of People's Commissars of USSR, Republic, *Krai*, and *Oblast'* Executive Committees . .	9	54/38		Heads of *guberniia* offices of *GPU*	44	55/ 38-39
				TOTAL	52	
TOTAL	26					

*A - Number of persons   **B - List (number and page)

NOMENKLATURA
[List] No. 1

NOMENKLATURA
[List] No. 2

Titles of agencies and positions	A*	B**	Titles of agencies and positions	A*	B**
XIX			XIX		
PEOPLE'S COMMISSARIAT OF JUSTICE			PEOPLE'S COMMISSARIAT OF JUSTICE		
Collegium	4		Head of the Department of Procurators and Courts	1	
Procurator general and assistant	2				
Assistant procurators of the republics	4		Procurators assigned to People's . . . . Commissariat of Justice	27	
Procurators Assigned to Collegium of Supreme Court	4		Assistant procurators assigned to Collegium of Supreme Court	15	
Krai, oblast', and *guberniia* procurators	52	56/ 39-40			
TOTAL	66		TOTAL	43	
XX			XX		
SUPREME COURT			SUPREME COURT		
Presidium of Supreme Court of USSR and RSFSR.	12				
Collegium of Supreme Court of USSR, military, military transportation and RSFSR: criminal, civil, and appeals	37				
TOTAL	48 [sic]				

*A - Number of persons   **B - List (number and page)

RTSKhIDNI, fond 17, op. 68, d. 459, ll. 6–7, 13–14.

chapter 4

ECONOMIC DEVELOPMENT

The socialist state in Soviet Russia was born in the midst of years of devastating warfare. By 1921, after seven years of international and civil strife, the Soviet economy was in shambles. The 1921 harvest collected only 43 percent of the prewar average tonnage, and famine spread through many of the hardest hit regions. Industrial production had fallen to one-fifth of the prewar level. Planned industrial development had always been a key element of socialist policy, and ambitious plans were begun even during the Civil War to construct hydroelectric stations to provide new sources of efficient power. "Communism equals Soviet power plus electrification of the entire country," Lenin had written. In the meantime, however, government policies of forced requisition of grain to feed the cities had contributed to the decline in agricultural output, and so in 1921 the party congress adopted a new set of policies designed to liberalize trade between town and country. During the period of the New Economic Policy, small-scale private trade and manufacturing flourished, while the state controlled the "commanding heights" of the economy: large-scale industry, transport, finance, and trade. Using this leverage the regime attempted to implement measures that would raise productivity and the nation's overall standard of living.

The idea of central economic planning had always held great appeal as the most efficient mechanism to promote economic development, and throughout the 1920s Soviet economists, planners, and government officials debated methods and philosophies of the plan idea. By 1926, moreover, the economy under the New Economic Policy appeared to have reached its maximum level of recovery. A new approach was needed to go farther, and in 1927 the party approved the principle of all-union economic development coordinated by a series of five-year plans. The State Planning Committee (*Gosplan*) was charged with developing such a plan. Fierce debates ensued over the pace of development and the balance between economic sectors: how hard could agriculture be squeezed to generate a surplus to invest in construction and industry? Economists disagreed among themselves, and these issues also fueled high-level political debates about the direction of the revolution. Trotsky had favored rapid industrialization at the expense of the near-term standards of living of workers and peasants. Bukharin supported a more gradual approach, encouraging peasants to accumulate wealth before the country plunged into large-scale industrialization projects. Stalin first agreed with Bukharin until they had combined to defeat the Trotsky program. Then he appropriated that very program of rapid industrialization based on forced extraction of surplus from the countryside.

The first five-year plan as officially implemented in 1928 was ambitious enough in its own right, basing target figures on the most optimistic projections of industrial and agricultural growth, weather conditions, and international trade. Within this plan, agriculture was to be collectivized gradually and voluntarily. To work properly the balances projected by the plan had to be carefully observed, but from the very beginning the plan began to break down. Successes in some areas led to increased demands for investment of resources above and beyond the country's capacity; shortfalls in other areas led to revised plans and to the increasing imposition of coercive measures. The trial of the Shakhty mining engineers for their alleged treason was one response to the initial failures of the plan's implementation.

Even more serious was a serious shortfall in projected agricultural output, which led directly to the decision to implement full-scale collectivization during the winter of 1929–30. The results of this decision will be discussed below, but publicly the party claimed victory. The plan continued to be revised and distorted: the slogan "The Five-Year Plan in Four" illustrates the replacement of the principle of rational planning by appeals to proletarian and patriotic enthusiasm. Despite tremendous costs in agriculture, the plan was officially declared a success in 1933, a year ahead of schedule: gross industrial production had more than doubled, the labor force had doubled, and new industrial cities had sprung up in areas that had formerly been wildernesses. But accomplishments in other sectors had fallen far below plan, and these imbalances would plague the subsequent five-year plans, although substantial economic growth continued.

Stalin had argued for breakneck industrialization in 1931 on the grounds that the capitalist world would soon combine to attack the Communist

USSR. "We are fifty or a hundred years behind the advanced countries. We must make good this distance in ten years. Either we do so, or we shall go under." Historians still debate whether this extraordinarily costly policy of rapid industrial development did indeed make the difference in the USSR's victory over Germany, or whether the Soviet Union won the war despite the damage it had inflicted upon itself in the process of this industrialization.

Collectivization

Soviet economic development absolutely depended on improvement in agricultural productivity; many Soviet peasants continued to produce at subsistence levels into the 1920s, and such agrarian stagnation could not provide the surpluses necessary to raise investment funds abroad and to feed factory workers at home. One key to raising productivity was to improve cultural levels in the countryside by expanding literacy and promoting the study of new agrarian techniques. Another key was to invest in new agricultural technology: fertilizers and mechanization. A third key was to reduce the inefficient methods of traditional peasant farming, in which individual holdings consisted of widely scattered narrow strips of plowland. Model cooperatives were promoted during the 1920s to demonstrate how peasants could organize to purchase advanced machinery, and peasants were urged to combine their land in more efficient, collective operations. Still, by the end of 1927 only about 18,000 collective farms had been organized, combining roughly 300,000 peasant households out of a total of 25 million. Most of the early collectivists were relatively poor peasants; the richest stratum of the peasantry, the *kulak*s, preferred to remain in their individual holdings.

The *kulak* had long been perceived as the class enemy of socialism: as a landholder, the *kulak* was labeled a member of the bourgeoisie—the capitalist class—and was ipso facto an enemy of the proletariat. By the end of the 1920s the *kulak* was represented even more vividly as the source of opposition to agricultural reform, both political and economic. It was likely, then, that state policies to transform agriculture would be targeted at the *kulak* class.

The first five-year plan that began to operate in 1928 envisioned only limited collectivization, but it projected a substantial improvement in grain collections from private peasant farms. Grain procurements, however, fell below expectations in 1928, prompting the government to adopt "emergency" measures to extract grain forcibly from the countryside. These measures produced resistance; rather than relax their grain requirements, as Bukharin was arguing, state officials tried to rally the poorer peasants against the *kulak*s to break this resistance and to expropriate larger and larger amounts of grain. The leaders of the "*kulak* counterrevolution" were arrested or deported from their native regions. At the same time, substantial increases in the number of collective farms led Stalin to announce in November 1929 that the time for "The Great Turn" toward mass collectivization had come. And the key to mass collectivization was to destroy the resistance of the *kulak*s, by "eliminating the *kulak* as a class."

During the winter of 1929–30 thousands of zealous Communists flocked to the rural areas of the Soviet Union to assist in the formation of collective farms and in the dekulakization of agriculture. There was great resistance. Forced to contribute their livestock to the collectives, peasants instead slaughtered their cattle in order to convert them to cash. *kulak* heads of households and then entire families were arrested and deported to new labor sites: Documents 172 accounts for almost 1.7 million people relocated in this way. Others escaped to the cities or the construction sites to avoid this fate. Still others used the assault on *kulak*s to settle old scores, and the activists from the countryside could not easily distinguish a *kulak,* who was a class enemy and ineligible to join a collective farm, from a middle peasant, who was supposed to be won over to the collective.

By the spring of 1930 over half of all households had joined collective farms, but resistance, often led by women, was also fierce. In March, Stalin wrote a famous article, "Dizzy with Success," blaming local officials for overly zealous enforcement of the collectivization principle and calling a halt to the process. But the damage had been done. The most skillful farmers, the *kulak*s, had been driven out of agriculture. Horses and cows had been slaughtered, and there were not yet tractors to replace them in the fields. The harvest in 1932 was far below expectations, which led to renewed forcible grain collections, prohibitions on any free marketing of grain, and widespread conditions of famine by 1933. Despite some gradual recovery, rural standards of living remained extremely low, and some scholars argue that Soviet agriculture never recovered from the damage inflicted by the dekulakization and collectivization policies of 1929–30.

15-ГО ОКТЯБРЯ СОСТОИТСЯ ВСЕУКРАИНСКИЙ С'ЕЗД КОМИТЕТОВ НЕЗАМОЖНЫХ.

Незаможные! Готовтесь к вашему с'езду На нем вы докажете свою волю к победе над голодом, разрухой, генералами, помещиками и кулаками!

ВАШ С'ЕЗД СВЯЖЕТ УЗАМИ БРАТСТВА ПРОЛЕТАРСКИЙ ГОРОД И ТРУДОВОЕ СЕЛО!

Propaganda poster urging the poor peasants of Ukraine to attend a meeting about the battle against "hunger, economic ruin, generals, landlords, and *kulaks*." Reproduction of a woodcut. *October 15 the All-Ukrainian Congress of the Committees of the Unempowered will take place,* anonymous. Publisher: Vseukrainskoe izdatel'stvo, Nikolaev, 1920. Prints and Photographs Division, Library of Congress.

Party memorandum of May 1929 reporting on resistance in the countryside to grain requisitioning, food shortages, and the closing of religious institutions

To Comrade Moskvin

<u>Top Secret</u>

INFORMATION DEPARTMENT OF THE CENTRAL COMMITTEE
OF THE ALL-UNION COMMUNIST PARTY (OF BOLSHEVIKS) [TSK VKP(b)]

<u>POLITICAL REPORT No. 1</u>

<u>MASS UPRISINGS AMONG KULAKS IN THE COUNTRYSIDE</u>

Recently, in connection with the intensified offensive against the *kulak*s on two fronts—the grain requisition program and the restructuring of rural society—*kulak* anti-Soviet activities have increased significantly. More to the point, the *kulak*s no longer confine themselves to acts of individual sabotage but are beginning to adopt more sophisticated, openly counterrevolutionary tactics in the form of mass demonstrations, frequently connecting these demonstrations against the ongoing campaign to close churches, mosques, Islamic religious schools, and to remove veils, etc. As a result, this network of underground *kulak* groups, which has already made its presence felt in the Soviet election campaign, today has surfaced with impudent mass demonstrations with corresponding slogans and demands. These actions vary: in grain-procurement areas, they are against surrendering grain; in consuming areas, they focus on the difficulties of obtaining foodstuffs; in areas where campaigns are under way to close churches, they are in support of faith, religion, the old way of life; and almost everywhere, they are against collectivization, against new forms of land distribution, against the social restructuring of the countryside.

In Biisk *okrug* alone, when the public-pressure approach was being applied in the grain-requisition campaign, there were 43 mass actions, some with as many as 7,000 participants. Of these, 16 were very large and serious. (Report from the *okrug* committee, May 23)

A typical uprising took place in the village of Mikhailovskii on April 11 and 12, where "a mob under the control of confirmed counterrevolutionary elements ruled the village for two days. 150 armed men were required to bring the mob to heel." (Quoted from a letter dated April 15 from the representative of the grain procurement center)

The incident can be summarized as follows. The *kulak*s took advantage of a mistake committed by the authorities when the latter sealed the barns of 28 farms (farms belonging to 10 *kulak*s, 10 wealthy peasants, and 8 middle peasants). The *kulak*s managed to sway the most backward segment of the population, namely the women, and through them the men, with an openly counterrevolutionary platform and managed to disrupt the grain procurement drive. They beat up the chairman of the surplus confiscation commission, shut down auctions of *kulak* property, seized property which had already been sold at auction, and used the threat of mob violence to compel the authorities to release prisoners under arrest, unseal the barns, and provide guarantees of no reprisals for the uprising.

A meeting called by the *kulak*s (attended by 900 persons, including 700 women) adopted the following platform:

1. The return of all property, livestock, and buildings sold at auction along with confiscated grain.

2. Lifting of the boycott.

3. An inventory of all confiscated seed grain and edible grain and distribution of these supplies to the needy (?!)

4. Abolition of property auctions.

5. Election of a commission to investigate the activities of the surplus confiscation commission.

6. A halt to the grain procurement drive and cancellation of the most recent measures.

7. The return of all mills to the millers.

8. Equal shares for all cooperative members.

9. Restoration of voting rights to all voters.

10. Abolition of forced communization of the peasants. Disbandment of the existing communes.

In another village in the same Mikhailovskii *raion*, Verkhniaia Sliudianka, on April 12 an inventory of the property of peasants caught with surplus grain led a mob of 200 individuals (primarily women) under the leadership of the *kulak* Rubanovich to surround the village Soviet building, lock the 24 members of the village Soviet inside, and demand a halt to grain requisition. And if the Soviet refused, the mob threatened to burn down the building. The timely arrival of a police squad kept the mob from carrying out their threat. As soon as the police arrived, the mob began to disperse. While pursuing the *kulak* Rubanovich, one policeman's horse got stuck in the mud, and a *kulak* tried to kill the policeman with a knife, but was prevented from doing so by another policeman, who shot and wounded the *kulak* with his revolver. Ten persons were arrested in connection with the case. (Report of Biisk *okrug* committee)

In the village of Abash in Bashelak *raion* of Biisk *okrug*, a group of women (as many as a hundred) appeared at the village Soviet building shouting, yelling, and demanding a halt to grain procurement "because if we don't have any grain, we won't have anything to eat." They pulled the chairman of the village Soviet—a day laborer—out of the village Soviet building and tried to beat him up. At that point the representative of the Biisk *okrug* committee rode up. The mob attacked him and tried to pull him off of his cart. After a long talk with the representative, the mob calmed down and dispersed, and two of the women admitted that some local Cossack *kulak*s had incited them. (Report of the Siberian *Krai* Committee, April 12)

The Barnaul *Okrug* Committee reports that "in certain villages in Upper Irtysh *raion* mobs consisting primarily of women have staged demonstrations against the grain procurement drive." The Sungai village Soviet writes that "the measures adopted by the village Soviet to stop the demonstrations haven't worked. The mob continues to demonstrate in the village day and night and has organized rallies against the grain procurement drive. Drivers hauling grain to the cooperative have been turned around with the warning: 'If you haul off this grain, then you won't see any of your own grain.' The men have begun joining the mob of women. The demonstrators devised a plan to steal all the grain from the consumers' cooperative. The mob has freed individuals from custody, and any time the members of the village Soviet go outside they are threatened. The demonstrators have begun posting guards around seized property and putting their own locks on the buildings.

The following incident occurred in the same village. Communards from the Zuboskal Commune had received edible grain and seed grain from the Sungai Cooperative and had loaded it onto wagons, when a mob of 50 women appeared, seized the grain, put it back in a barn, and then locked the barn with their own lock. (Report from Barnaul *Okrug* Committee, April 26)

Siberia has been the scene of most of the mass uprisings and demonstrations organized by the *kulak*s in conjunction with the grain procurement drive. Nevertheless, isolated incidents have occurred in other regions.

In the Urals, in Uisk *raion* (Troitskoe), in the community of Kumliak, *kulak*s organized a public uprising (demonstration) against the grain requisitions on March 11. A mob began travelling around the farms and putting grain back in the barns which the *kulak*s had prepared to turn over to the collectors.

In Khoper *okrug* (Lower Volga), in the village of Bezymiannyi, a mob of 100 *kulak*s resisted attempts to seize the property of four individuals caught with surplus grain, and the police arrested three persons. (Report from the *krai* committee of April 20) [break in the text]

. . . the lack of systematic work with the active poor and middle peasants, the failure to study these activists and bring them closer to the party cells, and the lack of any communication between party members and nonmembers.

In a letter Comrade Vol, the authorized representative of the People's Commissariat of Trade, provides the following assessment of the condition of the party organizations in the Siberian countryside (based on his observations of four *okrugs*).

"The extraordinary inertia of our organizations, the political illiteracy of a large number of personnel, their reliance on "War Communism" tactics against the peasantry, and their lack of public respect have greatly obstructed and blunted the impact of most efforts." (He goes on to describe a large number of cases).

In his letter Comrade Khataevich arrives at the following conclusions:

"An investigation of the role of local party and Soviet organizations in all the aforementioned incidents which provoked mass uprisings has revealed that, in most cases, party and Soviet organizations were guilty of tactlessness, egregious blunders, and a lack of skill and proficiency in their preparations for vital efforts. This made the anti-Soviet activities of the *kulak*s and the clergy much easier. The latter were able to respond quickly, flexibly, and skillfully to the blundering, tactlessness, and ineptitude of our local party and Soviet organizations. The *kulak*s were particularly successful in taking advantage of incidents where local party and Soviet organizations closed churches and so forth by administrative fiat, without careful preparations at the lowest levels and without explaining, persuading, and gaining the support of most of the poor and middle peasants."*

2. <u>Women have been extremely active</u> in all the *kulak* uprisings, which is too alarming a situation not to draw attention to itself.

The extraordinary activity of women in the Soviet reelection campaigns (their participation in the reelection campaigns grew from 29.8% in 1927 to 46.9% in 1929; 19.1% of the members elected to village Soviets in 1929 were women, as opposed to 11.8% in 1927) can be described as a very <u>positive</u> development. And if women are now playing a no less <u>negative</u> role in all of the counterrevolutionary *kulak* uprisings, the only conclusion we can draw from this is that <u>local</u> party and Soviet organizations have rested on their laurels, have let the leadership of rural women slip out of their hands, have been unable to take advantage of their energy and guide it in the proper—<u>Soviet</u>—direction, and have conceded leadership and influence over these women to anti-Soviet *kulak* elements.

3. A new and noteworthy feature of the current phase of the class struggle in the village is the fact that in a number of places the *kulak*s have been able to expand by drawing the middle classes of the villages into their anti-Soviet uprisings. The <u>widespread support</u> for anti-Soviet uprisings in certain areas is a direct consequence of deficiencies in our work with the poor peasants and thus with the middle peasants, which should be blamed entirely on the party's disorganization in the countryside and the extreme shortage of rural party cells (there are only 23,000 rural party cells and probationary groups for the 75,000 village Soviets in the Soviet Union).

As the most recent reports indicate, the *kulak* counteroffensive is steadily growing in intensity and fierceness (as it must inevitably do in response to the sustained and systematic socialist offensive). This means that we must do everything we can to keep the *kulak* as isolated as possible in this merciless struggle.

4. This leads us to the <u>problem of strengthening our rural cadres</u>, which is now becoming more urgent than ever for the party. The *kulak*s' seizure of certain villages, the open mass uprisings against the party and Soviet power, the brazen and arrogant sabotage of our activities in a number of cases, and the excesses, perversions, and errors which have occurred and continue to occur may be attributed, for the most part, not to the unwillingness, but to the inability of rural cells to assume leadership of the villages in a fierce class struggle. And hence cities and industrial centers must play a much greater role than they have to this point in supplying and reassign-

---

*We cannot agree with Comrade Khataevich's statement of the issue. He says that almost all the cases of mass uprisings can be attributed to the tactlessness and excesses of local organizations. This is untrue. Obviously, excesses have pushed middle peasants into the arms of the *kulak*s. But a no less important problem (which has been confirmed by a number of incidents reported by Comrade Khataevich and others) is the fact that in many villages, the *kulak* has encountered no resistance from a cohesive bloc of poor peasants because of the lack or weakness of party cells, their unimportance, and so forth, and the fact that practically no efforts have been made to unite the poor and middle peasants against the *kulak*.

ing personnel capable of organizing the poor and middle peasants and, in many cases, reorganizing party cells from the bottom up.

Recently, some party committees have begun taking concrete action in this regard. For example, as early as December of last year, the Lower Volga *Krai* Committee resolved to "reinforce the *raion* and village party organizations with skilled personnel from the *krai* and *okrug* levels" and assigned 28 comrades each from the *krai* and *okrug* organizations to work in the countryside, and on February 14 decided to transfer an additional 315 party members from the *krai* and *okrug* organizations for field work in the cities and countryside and promote lower-ranking individuals to take their places.

The Kharkov *Okrug* Committee has mobilized 253 comrades, 178 of whom will be permanently reassigned and 75 of whom will receive temporary assignments (for five months). 151 individuals will be assigned to grass-roots electioneering efforts (conducted by cooperative shareholder meetings), while the others will be assigned to Soviet, agricultural, administrative, and party positions. In the near future the Kharkov *Okrug* Committee plans to transfer an additional 150 comrades and thus have one party employee assigned to each village Soviet (there are a total of 400 in the *okrug*).

There is no doubt that in this effort we will not only have to resort to mobilization, but we will also have to reduce our central and then *oblast'* and *okrug* staffs in order to send additional personnel to the countryside. This will be especially important for regions without any large industrial plants (such as the Central Black Earth Region, Siberia, Kazakhstan, and the Middle and Lower Volga).

5. On this basis the Information Department of the *TSK VKP(b)* deems it proper to <u>put the issue</u> of reinforcing rural party organizations on the agenda of the Organizational Bureau after first conducting a <u>careful study</u> of local experience by dispatching 3 to 4 senior instructors from the *TSK* to areas where this effort has already made substantial progress (such as the North Caucasus, Kharkov, and the Volga) so that a specially appointed commission can review the matter for one month to six weeks.

Head of the Information Department
of the *TSK VKP(b)*
(Bogomolov)   [signed] Bogomolov

<u>Copies distributed to:</u>

<u>Secretaries of the Central Committee:</u>
Comrade Kaganovich
Comrade Molotov
Comrade Stalin
and
Comrade Moskvin

RTSKhIDNI, fond 17, op. 85, d. 355, ll. 1, 10b, 4, 40b, 5.

Registration of volunteers to work on collective or state farms, 1929. TSGAKFD. N 256562

DOCUMENT 170 *Resolution of the Central Committee Politburo, January 5, 1930, on the pace of collectivization and the construction of collective farms*

[Handwritten:] Addendum no. 2 to point 13,
Politburo Minutes no. 112

RESOLUTION OF THE POLITBURO OF THE CENTRAL COMMITTEE [*TSK*] OF THE ALL-UNION COMMUNIST PARTY (OF BOLSHEVIKS) [*VKP(b)*] ON THE PACE OF COLLECTIVIZATION AND STATE AID MEASURES FOR KOLKHOZ CONSTRUCTION

[Handwritten:] Resolution of the *TSK VKP(b)* of January 5, 1930

1. In recent months the collective movement has taken a new step forward, encompassing not only separate groups of individual holdings but entire *raion*s, *okrug*s, and even *oblast*'s and *krai*s. The basis of the movement is collectivizing the means of production of poor and medium-sized peasant holdings.

All timetables for development of the collective movement projected by the plan have been surpassed. Already by the spring of 1930 the sown area of collectivized land exceeded 30 million hectares. Thus the current five-year collectivization plan, which was to encompass 22–24 million hectares by the end of the period, will be exceeded by a wide margin already this year.

Thus we have the material basis for replacing large-scale *kulak* agricultural production with large-scale production on the *kolkhoz*es, which is a powerful advance toward the creation of socialist agriculture, not to mention *sovkhoz*es, which are growing much more rapidly than the plan had envisioned.

This situation—of decisive importance for the entire Soviet economy—has provided the party the basis for moving from a policy in its practical work of restraining the exploitative tendencies of the *kulak*s to a policy of eliminating the *kulak*s as a class.

2. Based on all this, one can state with certitude that within five years, instead of collectivizing 20% of the cultivated area (as projected by the five-year plan), we will be able to collectivize the vast majority of peasant holdings. Collectivization of such important grain-producing regions as the Lower and Middle Volga and the North Caucasus may be accomplished by the fall of 1930 or by the spring of 1931 at the latest. Collectivization of the other grain-producing regions may be accomplished by the fall of 1931 or at least by spring of 1932. [break in the text]

4. Since the total transition from horse- to machine-drawn inventory cannot be achieved in a short period and requires a number of years, the *TSK VKP(b)* demands that tendencies to underestimate the role of horse-drawn inventory at this stage of the *kolkhoz* movement be firmly rejected; such tendencies lead to the waste and sale of horses. The *TSK VKP(b)* stresses the extraordinary importance under present conditions of transitional measures to establish horse-drawn-machine bases and mixed tractor-and-horse bases, which combine tractor and horse traction. [break in the text]

11. The *TSK VKP(b)* stresses the need for a decisive struggle with any attempt to restrain the development of the collective movement because of the shortage of tractors and sophisticated machinery. Furthermore, with all seriousness, the *TSK* warns the party organization against any kind of "decree issuing" from above the *kolkhoz* movement, which risks transforming true socialist competition in *kolkhoz* organizing into a kind of collectivization game.

[Crossed out:] POLITBURO COMMITTEE CHAIRMAN, IA. IAKOVLEV

True copy: [illegible]

RTSKhIDNI, fond 558, op. 1, d. 2900, ll. 1–5.

Session of a committee to select volunteers to work in the countryside, Moscow, 1930. TSGAKFD

Report from the commander of the Siberian Military District to Voroshilov, *chairman of the Revolutionary Military Soviet, April 30, 1930, regarding directives forbidding use of the military in operations against the* kulaks

N.K.V.M.D.	Series K 21
Revolutionary Military Council	Top secret
Siberian Military District	Copy 1
April 30, 1930	
No. 088/I	
Novosibirsk	

To the Chairman of the Revolutionary
Military Council of the USSR
Moscow

Re: No. 28/sh.

Based on your directives of February 2 and 5 of this year, on February 6 the Revolutionary Military Council [*RVS*] of the district issued orders to divisional commanders [*komdiv*] and military divisional commanders [*voenkomdiv*] categorically forbidding the use of military formations in the dekulakization operations.

In view of the fact that cases of isolated military involvement have come to light, in response to requests from local Soviet and party organs and from the *OGPU* for guard duty, convoying *kulaks*, and in the struggle against banditry (Achinsk—24 individuals conscripted for the struggle against banditry from the 118th infantry regiment, 40th infantry division; Tatarsk—4 individuals conscripted from the 35th infantry regiment to guard *kulaks*, 12th infantry division; in Barnaul—from the 63rd infantry regiment, 21st infantry division 2 men conscripted for convoying *kulaks*), the *RVS* of the district has on February 22 once again issued specific instructions to all garrison commanders ordering that such personnel immediately return to their units.

At the present time all commanders of military units (garrison by garrison) have reported compliance with the orders issued by the district *RVS*.

In fulfillment of your demands, delineated in directive No. 28/sh. of April 5, the district *RVS* has warned by its order of April 15, for the last time, commanders of military units and chiefs of garrisons about their responsibilities in adhering to the instructions given them.

Military Commander	Member *RVS*
Siberian Military District [signed] Mezis	

2 Copies: No. 1 - Chairman, *RVS* of the USSR
　　　　　No. 2 - Headquarter Files, Department 1

Chief, Department 1, Headquarters
　　[signed] Ignat'ev

TSGASA, fond 4, op. 1, d. 142, l. 21.

<u>Top Secret</u>

PROGRESS REPORT
ON THE EVICTION AND RELOCATION OF *KULAK* FAMILIES

<u>As of July 12, 1931</u>

I. RESETTLEMENT PLANS

The *kulak* family resettlement operation began on June 1. Our plans called for relocating a total of <u>185,281 families:</u>

A)	to Urals:	1) from the Ivanovo Industrial Region	5,000 families to *Magnitostroi*
		2) from the Belorussian SSR	5,000 families "
		3) from the Ukrainian SSR	30,000 families to *Uralles*
		4) from North Caucasus *krai*	15,000 families "
		TOTAL	55,000 families

B)	to Kazakhstan:	1) from Northern Volga *krai*	13,125 families
		2) from Lower Volga *krai*	14,000 families
		3) from Central Black Earth region	10,556 families
		TOTAL	37,681 families

C)	Within the same region:	1) in Ural region	12,000 families
		2) in Western Siberia *krai*	40,000 families
		3) in Eastern Siberia *krai*	12,000 families
		4) in Leningrad *oblast'*	4,000 families
		TOTAL	68,000 families

II. PROGRESS OF EVICTION AND RELOCATION

From June 1 through June 12 of this year we evicted and relocated 134,637 families, including 75,809 families relocated to other regions and 58,828 families relocated within the same region:

A)	to Urals:	1) from Ivanovo Industrial Region	3,655 families	18,020 persons to *Magnitostroi*
		2) from Belorussian SSR	4,645 families	20,501 persons to "
		3) from Ukrainian SSR	31,825 families	131,127 persons to *Uralles*
		4) from North Caucasus *krai*	15,400 families	71,658 persons to "
		TOTAL	55,525 families	241,306 persons

The eviction and relocation of *kulak*s from the Ivanovo Industrial Region, the Belorussian Soviet Socialist Republic, the Ukrainian Soviet Socialist Republic, and North Caucasus *krai* has been completed. Although all heads of households, i.e., able-bodied men, were completely evicted and relocated, a high dropout rate and high rate of family breakup meant that the numbers of families actually evicted and relocated from the Ivanovo Industrial Region and Belorussian SSR were short of the plan targets by the following amounts:

	a) from the Ivanovo Industrial Region	1,345 families
	b) from the Belorussian SSR	355 families
	TOTAL	1,700 families

On the other hand, the following numbers of families were evicted and relocated over and above the targets from the Ukrainian SSR and North Caucasus Territories:

a) from the Ukrainian SSR	1,825 families	
b) from North Caucasus *krai*	400 families of which 200 were sent to the *Uralryb*	
TOTAL	2,225 families	

B) <u>to Kazakhstan:</u>

1) from Northern Volga *krai*	9,603 families	41,046 persons incl 10,381 male heads of household
2) Central Black Earth Region	10,681 families	50,721 persons
3) Ivanovo Industrial Region	10,015 persons	
TOTAL	20,284 families	101,782 persons

Eviction and relocation from the Central Black Earth Region has been completed, and we exceeded our target by <u>125 families</u>.

We must still evict and relocate 3,522 families from Northern Volga *krai,* and the process will be completed by July 22.

The eviction and relocation of male heads of *kulak* households from Lower Volga *krai* has been completed. We plan to begin relocating the persons of the families whose heads have already been transported on July 15. The entire relocation process will be completed on August 8.

C) <u>within the same regions:</u> The eviction and relocation of heads of *kulak* households has been completed in the Ural region, Western Siberia *krai*, and Leningrad *oblast'*. The eviction and relocation of *kulak*s within Eastern Siberia *krai* began on June 15, is still in progress, and will be completed by July 30. All told, the following numbers of families and individuals were relocated within the same regions:

1)	Ural region	12,000 families	57,000 persons
2)	Western Siberia	39,788 families	170,784 persons
3)	Eastern Siberia	3,154 families	14,472 persons
4)	Leningrad *oblast'*	3,386 families	16,066 persons
	TOTAL	58,828 families	258,322 persons

III. PLANS FOR THE NEW RESETTLEMENT OPERATION

On July 16 we plan to begin a new operation of relocating *kulak*s from the following regions. The original plans called for relocating these individuals in KAZAKHSTAN, but the plans have been changed and they will be relocated in the URAL region and WESTERN SIBERIA *KRAI*:

1) from TATARIA	5,000 families	July 16 to August 5
2) from BASHKIRIA	6,000 families	July 18 to August 3
3) from MOSCOW *OBLAST'*	8,200 families	July 20 to August 10
4) from NIZhEGOROD *KRAI*	5,000 families	July 30 to August 7
5) from CENTRAL BLACK EARTH REGION	1,000 families	July 9 to August 11
TOTAL	15,200 families [sic]	

The evicted and relocated *kulak* families will be turned over to the following industrial organizations for employment:

Receiving industrial organization	Number of *kulak* families	region of origin of *kulak* families
1) *Senarstroi* [Senar Construction Trust]	1,000	additional evictees from Central Black Earth Region July 9– July 11
2) *Magnitostroi*	5,000	from Tataria July 16–Aug. 5
3) Anzhera-Sudzhi Mines	2,000	from Bashkiria July 18–Aug. 24
4) Prokop'ev Mines	3,000	from Bashkiria July 25–Aug. 3
5) Cheremkhov Mines	1,000	from Bashkiria July 30–Aug. 1
6) *Kuznetskstroi* [Kuznetsk Construction Trust]	5,000	from Moscow *oblast'* July 20–Aug. 1
7) Vysokogor Mining Directorate	500	from Moscow *oblast'* Aug. 2
8) Bakal Mining Directorate	1,200	from Moscow *oblast'* July 20–Aug. 1
9) Goroblagod Mining Directorate	1,000	from Moscow *oblast'* Aug. 7–Aug. 9
10) Zlatoust Mining Directorate	500	from Moscow *oblast'* Aug. 10
11) Sinar Mining Directorate	1,000	from Nizhegorod *krai* July 30–Aug. 1
12) Kalata, Ural Non-Ferrous Metallurgy Directorate	400	from Nizhegorod *krai* Aug. 2
13) Tagil Non-Ferrous Metallurgy Directorate	200	from Nizhegorod *krai* Aug. 3
14) Karabash Non-Ferrous Metallurgy Directorate	400	from Nizhegorod *krai* Aug. 4
15) Ural Platinum Trust	800	from Nizhegorod *krai* Aug. 5–Aug. 6
16) Kizel Mines	1,100	from Nizhegorod *krai* Aug. 2–Aug. 4
17) Cheliabinsk Mines	1,100	from Nizhegorod *krai* Aug. 5–Aug. 7
18) *Tagilstroi* [Tagil Construction Trust]	3,000	July 15–Aug. 15: 3,000 families previously destined for *Uralles*
19) Bukachach Mines, *Vostugol'* [Eastern Coal Trust]	500	July 15–July 25: *kulak*s previously destined for resettlement within Eastern Siberia *krai*
20) Minusinsk Mines, Eastern Coal Trust	500	July 15–July 20: *kulak*s previously destined for resettlement within Western Siberia *krai*

WHAT HAS BEEN ACCOMPLISHED SO FAR:

1) Central Black Earth Region: 3 trains containing 1,071 families (4,781 persons) sent to Senar Construction Trust July 9 to July 11.

2) Preparations have been completed in TATARIA, BASHKIRIA, MOSCOW *OBLAST'*, and NIZhEGOROD *KRAI* to evict and relocate the *kulak*s. A large number of able-bodied male heads of households to be evicted and resettled have already been removed.

3) Orders have been given to URAL REGION to transfer 3,000 *kulak* families previously destined for the *URALLES* to the *TAGILSTROI* [Tagil Construction Project] from July 15 to August 15.

4) Orders have been given to EASTERN SIBERIA *KRAI* to transfer 500 *kulak* families previously destined for resettlement within EASTERN SIBERIA *KRAI* to the BUKAChACh mines from July 15 to July 25.

5) Orders have been given to WESTERN SIBERIA *KRAI* to transfer 500 *kulak* families previously destined for resettlement within WESTERN SIBERIA *KRAI* to the MINUSINSK mines from July 15 to July 20.

ASSISTANT HEAD OF OPERATIONS DEPARTMENT
OF THE UNIFIED STATE POLITICAL
DIRECTORATE [*OGPU*]   [signed] (NIKOLAEV)

July 12, 1931

Moscow

TOP SECRET

REPORT ON THE NUMBER
OF RELOCATED *KULAK*S

Total families and persons relocated in 1930	113,013 families	551,330 persons
Total families and persons relocated in 1931	243,531 families	1,128,198 persons
Combined totals for 1930 and 1931	356,544 families	1,679,528 persons

of which:

a) relocated from one region to another	245,403 families	1,157,077 persons
b) resettled within the same region	111,141 families	522,451 persons
TOTAL	356,544 families	1,679,528 persons

3. The evicted *kulak*s were relocated in the following regions:

Region of relocation	Number of families	Number of individuals
1) Northern *krai*	58,800	288,560
2) Ural *oblast'*	123,547	571,355
3) Kazakhstan	50,268	241,331
4) Western Siberia *krai*	69,916	316,883
5) Eastern Siberia *krai*	28,572	138,191
6) Far Eastern *krai*	9,694	48,269
7) Yakutia (Aldan)	1,366	7,157
8) Leningrad *oblast'*	6,884	31,466
9) Nizhegorod *krai*	1,497	6,316
10) North Caucasus *krai*	3,000	15,000
11) Ukrainian Soviet Socialist Republic	3,000	15,000
TOTAL	356,544 families	1,679,528 persons

Addendum to point 20, Politburo minutes no. 94
of April 20, 1932

ON FORCED COLLECTIVIZATION OF LIVESTOCK

[Handwritten line:] Resolution of the Central Committee [*TSK*] of the All-Union Communist Party (Bolsheviks) [*VKP(b)*], Mar. 26, 1932

In many regions we can observe the collectivization of cattle and smaller livestock by forcible means. This practice is a flagrant violation of repeatedly issued directives by the party's Central Committee as well as of the provisions contained in the statute of the agricultural artel.

The Central Committee *VKP(b)* stresses that only enemies of the *kolkhoz*es would permit forced collectivization of livestock from individual *kolkhoz* members. The Central Committee emphasizes that forced requisition of *kolkhoz* members' cattle and smaller livestock is contrary to the party's political program. The goal of the party is that every member of the *kolkhoz* have a cow, some smaller livestock, and poultry. The further expansion and development of *kolkhoz*es should occur through breeding and raising younger animals and/or by purchasing cattle by the farmers.

The Central Committee of the *VKP(b)* proposes to all party, Soviet, and *kolkhoz* organizations:

1. Cease all attempts of forced collectivization of cattle and small livestock belonging to *kolkhoz* members and expel from the party those guilty of violating *TSK* directives;

2. Organize aid for the members of the *kolkhoz*es who have no cattle or small livestock to purchase and raise young animals for their own personal needs.

Signed: *TSK VKP(b)*

[A heavily edited and apparently discarded version of this page included these additional proposals:]

3. Recommend to *kolkhoz*es that have livestock departments and incubator stations to put into practice the sale of calves, chicks, and piglets to the *kolkhoz* members for [illegible]. Consider [illegible] from these livestock departments be sent this year up to ¼ of their [illegible] calves, piglets, and chicks;

4. During the planting of feed grains and the fodder and hay harvesting campaign, *kolkhozes* must plan for satisfying the feed needs not only of the *kolkhoz* livestock departments, but also of the livestock belonging to individual *kolkhoz* members;

5. The purpose of these measures is not only to improve the material situation of the *kolkhoz* members, but to increase the overall livestock inventory by expanding the total number of young animals held by *kolkhoz* members.

Toward these ends, the *kolkhoz* makes a contract with each *kolkhoz* member, whereby the *kolkhoz* assumes responsibility to supply the member with the necessary feed in terms of workdays, and the member assumes responsibility to raise the young livestock to an age determined by the *kolkhoz*.

[three signatures:] M. K——[illegible]
        A. Kaganovich
        IAkovlev

RTSKhIDNI, fond 17, op. 120, d. 52, ll. 16–20, 42–47, 59.

DOCUMENT 173   *Minutes of the March 23, 1932, meeting of a Politburo commission and the final version of a resolution on the forced collectivization of livestock*

Minutes of the meeting of the Politburo commission to edit the draft resolution on the forced collectivization of livestock

March 26, 1932

Chairman: M. I. Kalinin.
Attending: Comrades Kaganovich, IAkovlev, Tataev, Markevich.

Under consideration:
The draft resolution on the forced collectivization of livestock, as edited by Comrade IAkovlev.

Resolved:
To adopt the following version:

The practice of collectivizing cattle and small livestock belonging to individual collective farmers by means of actual coercion has been noted in several regions, in flagrant violation of the repeated directives of the Central Committee of the party and the regulation governing agricultural cooperative associations. The Central Committee of the All-Union Communist Party most strongly emphasizes that only enemies of collective farms could allow the forced collectivization of cattle and small livestock belonging to individual collective farmers.

The Central Committee would like to clarify that the practice of forced confiscation of cattle and small livestock from collective farmers has nothing to do with the policy [illegible] the aim of the party consists in seeing that each collective farmer has his own cattle, small livestock, and poultry. The further expansion and development of collective farms should progress only by means of allowing these collective farmers to rear young animals.

RTSKhIDNI, fond 3, op. 1, d. 3016, l. 1.

DOCUMENT 174   *Letter from Feigin to Ordzhonikidze, April 9, 1932, about conditions on the collective farms, and Dr. Kiselev's memorandum of March 25, 1932, about those conditions*

Dear Sergo,

I'm writing you from Novosibirsk. I have driven around several *kolkhoz*es and consider it necessary to inform you about a few items. I was in various *kolkhoz*es—not productive and relatively unproductive ones, but everywhere there was only one sight—that of a huge shortage of seed, famine, and extreme emaciation of livestock.

In the *kolkhoz*es which I observed I attempted to learn how much the livestock had diminished in comparison with the years 1927–28. It turns out that *kolkhoz* Ziuzia has 507 milch cows at present while there were 2000 in '28. *Kolkhoz* Ust'-Tandovskii collectively and individually has 203 head, earlier they had more than 600. *Kolkhoz* Kruglo-Ozernyi at present has 418 head of beef cattle and 50 held by individuals; in 1928 there were 1800 head. *Kolkhoz* Goldoba collectively and individually has 275 head; in 1929 there were 1000 plus head. This *kolkhoz* now has 350 sheep; in 1929 there were 1500. Approximately the same correlations were found also in the *kolkhoz*es Ol'gino and Novo-Spasski.

The *raion* which I visited (Barabinskii) is known for its butter export, but even in the other *raion*s of Western Siberia the decline of livestock farming during this period is not much smaller.

These are facts that I myself checked, and on this basis I think that the data in the general census recently carried out by *Gosplan* significantly embellish the real picture.

The situation of the *kolkhoz* livestock farms is a bad one, primarily because of lack of feed. Milk production has reached extremely low levels of 1, 2, or 3 liters per day instead of the 5–7 liters normal for this region in a high-yield year [crossed out: "as noted by *kolkhoz* members and individual farmers"]. The poor condition of the livestock cannot be blamed on poor care or poor labor organization since in most of the *kolkhoz*es I visited the situation in terms of care and labor organization, relatively speaking, is not bad (although it could be much better). But in any case it is immeasurably better than in the butter-producing *sovkhoz*es of the *raion* which I also visited.

And so, undoubtedly, if the collectivized livestock is sufficiently fed every year, we can increase greatly the yield of commodity production. But this still does not remedy the situation in that the *sovkhoz*es and *kolkhoz*es will not be able to meet the needs of the country for meat and butter in the next 2–3 years, and I think it is now necessary, when the socialistic sector of the villages has been strengthened, to speed up the growth of livestock farming in the private households of the *kolkhoz* members and individual farmers. The resolution of the Central Committee forbidding collectivization of the last cow is somewhat of a plus in this regard, but this is not the main issue. The main issue is the fact that almost all of the *kolkhoz* member's livestock is subject to expropriation and removed. This livestock consists of the last cows and last sheep. In addition, when this livestock is expropriated, the *kolkhoz* member and individual farmer slaughter the rest. As a result, in the villages where I have observed this situation, not more than 20–30% of the *kolkhoz* members have one cow each and a few sheep, but as a rule, the *kolkhoz* member and individual farmer not only do not raise livestock, but they try to get rid of or slaughter those they do own.

If this situation continues, in my opinion, next year the shortage of meat, hides, and fats will be greater than this year.

Regional officials firmly believe that the *sovkhoz*es and the commodity farms of the *kolkhoz*es will be able to supply the nation already this year with the necessary production and express the idea that private ownership of livestock by the *kolkhoz* members should cease.

I think we should undertake all measures to increase private ownership of livestock by the *kolkhoz* members or else there is no way out of the present periodic shortage of food products.

The second item concerns the sowing campaign. The situation is such that there is not enough seed in the *kolkhoz*es. There is no way that we will be able to fulfill the plan for grain production, and the shortfall in the *krai* will probably be 15–20 percent. Besides this, horses are quite emaciated (a significant number of them have already died) and, in addition, the people do not have provisions. And so the spring planting will occur in exceptionally tense circumstances, but I figure that with the right organization of seed distribution within the *krai* and among the *kolkhoz*es we can achieve such a level that the gross yield in 1932 will rise above not only the gross yield of last year, but even that of the bumper year of 1930.

How can we accomplish this? Here is the situation: all *kolkhoz*es have been given a plan for sowing. [crossed out: Some areas were given state subsidies in order to carry out this plan. As a result] some *kolkhoz*es have enough or nearly enough seed (including the state subsidy), but other *kolkhoz*es have barely any seed. Since the planting will be carried out according to plan, one group of *kolkhoz*es will sow all its fields, but another group with less seed will be faced with a large underfulfillment of the sowing plan. How does this relate to crop capacity? The point is that in these circumstances fields that may yield an extremely small harvest will be in the first group of *kolkhoz*es to be sown. Thus, if the plan is followed blindly (as it was last year), not only the fallow and autumn fields will be sown but even the salt-marshes, where absolutely nothing grows. Meanwhile, fallow and autumn fields in the second group of *kolkhoz*es that were prepared last year and are certain to be productive will remain unsown.

In order to prevent this situation it is necessary to change the existing plan, but no one wants to do this even though they understand perfectly well that it is imperative to review the plan. The situation that I observed in the *kolkhoz*es last year was that at least 30% of all the sown fields were sown by the *kolkhoz*es at too late a date, merely to carry out the sowing plan (this is one of the reasons for the crop failure); on the other hand, fields known to produce a less than decent harvest were sown, also merely to carry out the plan. This year the same story will be repeated if instructions on behalf of the Central Committee are not issued accordingly. In a time of acute seed deficiency a significant amount of seed will be wasted on worthless land, the sowing will occur at a time when the land is already drying out, that is, when it is too late to sow, but the fallow and autumn fields of the second group of *kolkhoz*es will remain underutilized. These conditions guarantee a meager harvest, and in some places complete crop failure, only because a plan was given based on a forecast of spring planting, using the most optimistic quantitative indicators, not considering that the fall harvest will result in extremely unfavorable qualitative results.

And so I come to my second conclusion—that the Central Committee give the order to all *krai* organizations (as soon as possible, there is little time left before the spring planting) depending on the conditions of each *raion* and *kolkhoz*, that the plan be changed in such a way as to produce the best qualitative results. For this it is imperative to conduct a review from the standpoint of 1) sowing all prepared fields (fallow and autumn fields) without exception; 2) redistribution of seed among the *kolkhoz*es in the time remaining before the planting date so that the planting be completed within 15 days, and under no circumstances more than 17 days; 3) and finally, that the improvement of fallow land be stipulated for 1933.

In fulfilling these conditions, given average or especially favorable climatic conditions, the gross yield, and consequently even the marketable output, of grain may yield not less but even more than in 1930, even if the sown area declines. In addition, I believe that in reality the sown area will not decline because last year and the year before all agricultural agencies and party organizations pushed madly for quantitative indicators. The planting season was extremely lengthy, they sowed worthless land and, as a rule, only lands that were suitable and were sown at the correct time were productive. If in following this course (to conceal the actual nature of things behind quantitative indicators) we immediately start and propose to review the plan from the standpoint of achieving the best qualitative indicators (taking into account the seed shortage), then we can reach the necessary results.

The third issue—the peasants' attitude.

Their attitude is utterly negative in light of the famine and the fact that they are losing their last cows through forced contracts. As a result the *kolkhoz* member has neither bread nor milk. I saw all this with my own eyes and am not exaggerating. People are starving; living on food substitutes they grow weaker, and naturally under such circumstances their mood is extremely hostile. I have not seen in a long time such an attitude as is now found in the villages due to famine and the confiscation of the last cows and sheep through contracting. I will inform you of the facts that substantiate this when we meet. Upon arriving in Moscow, I will try to see Stalin and inform him, or if he cannot spare the time I will write him a letter.

It seems that you told me in 1926–27 (in Morozovka), when the opposition was making quite furious attacks on the Central Committee that Stalin sees farther than the rest of you. This is undoubtedly so and was substantiated during the period from 1923 on and especially since the establishment of the five-year plan. But in order for him to see beyond everyone, one must, with absolute objectivity, relate to him those facts which are based on reality. I will attempt to do this upon my arrival in Moscow, and I will tell him what I have seen with my own eyes. Maybe I am drawing incorrect conclusions, but I acquainted myself thoroughly with the factual situation and it seems to me that it is utterly imperative that Stalin take up this matter. This sounds like those arguments the German Social Democrats made in Marx's lifetime, saying, "I know the factual situation, but let Papa Marx draw the conclusion." I have nothing new to say besides what I have already related, and I will just repeat what the German Social Democrats used to say: "Let Papa Stalin draw the conclusions, and I will describe the factual situation as it is."

Take care. Feigin

April 9, 1932

At the same time I am sending you the doctor's statement on the famine in peasant families and in turn I corroborate that I observed a similar situation.

Top Secret

TO THE HEAD OF THE WESTERN SIBERIA REGIONAL BOARD OF HEALTH Comrade TRAKMAN.

Copy to POKROV REGIONAL COMMITTEE OF THE ALL-UNION COMMUNIST PARTY (Bolsheviks), *RAION* EXECUTIVE COMMITTEE and RUSSIAN COMMUNIST LEAGUE

MEMORANDUM

On the instructions of the Regional Committee [*Raikom*] of the All-Union Communist Party (Bolsheviks), issued to Kiselev on March 24, 1932, on exposing illness due to hunger, several families of the Kartsovskii Village Soviet were observed and the following was found: as stated by Soviet chairman Comrade Sukhanov and Secretary of the Party Cell Comrade Medvedev, the Village Soviet received a series of written and oral statements from the *kolkhoz* members of this village that they and their families were suffering from starvation.

Statements were made by the following people: Mariia Gorokhova, Malan'ia Pautova, Irina Rogozina, Ustin'ia Logacheva, and others. The Soviet chairman, the secretary of the cell and other Communists substantiate the fact that the *kolkhoz* members use dead animals for food.

Together with the Soviet chairman and other citizens I visited the quarters of the above-mentioned *kolkhoz* members and also as per my wish I observed a series of homes besides the aforementioned in order to be convinced that the worst family cases were not chosen as examples.

From my observation of 20 homes in the first and second Karpov villages, I found only in one home, that of a Red Army veteran, a condition of relative nourishment, some flour and bread; the rest subsist on food substitutes. Almost in every home either children or mothers were ill, undoubtably due to starvation, since their faces and entire bodies were swollen.

An especially horrible picture comes from the following families:

1) In the family of Konstantin Sidel'nikov, who had gone to trade his wife's remaining shirts, skirts, and scarves for bread, the wife lay ill, having given birth 5 days earlier, and 4 very small children as pale as wax with swollen cheeks sat at the filthy table like marmots, and ate with spoons from a common cup. The cup contained a mixture of hot water and a white liquid of questionable taste and sour smell, poured from a bottle, which turned

out to be skim milk (the result of passing milk through a separator). Konstantin Sidel'nikov and his wife are excellent *kolkhoz* members—prime workers, experienced farmers.

2) IAkov Sidel'nikov has 2 children and elderly parents, both 70, living in one room, but they eat separately; that is, the elderly obtain their own food substitutes with their savings; the son, IAkov Sidel'nikov, with his own; they hide their food substitutes from each other outside (I have attached examples of these food substitutes to this memorandum). The elderly, in tears, ask: "Doctor, give us death!"

3) Filipp Borodin has earned 650 work-days, has a wife and 5 children ranging from one-and-a-half to nine years of age. The wife lies ill on the oven; 3 children sit on the oven. They are as pale as wax with swollen faces. The one-and-a-half year old sits pale by the window, swollen; the 9 year old lies ill on the earthen floor covered with rags; and Filipp Borodin himself sits on a bench and continuously smokes cigarettes made of repulsively pungent tobacco, cries like a babe, asks death for his children. In tears he asks Comrade Sukhanov: "Give us at least 1 kilo of potatoes, give us at least 1 liter of milk, after all, I worked all summer and even now I work unceasingly (now he takes care of the bulls and in the summer he tends the grazing cows).

According to the statement by Comrade Sukhanov and the brigadier of the "Red Partisan" *kolkhoz*, Borodin was not a complaining worker.

Borodin does not even have food substitutes for nourishment. Two days ago he and his family ate two dead piglets thrown out of the common farmyard. In the Borodin home there is unbelievable filth, dampness, and stench, mixed with the smell of tobacco. Borodin swears at the children: "The devils don't die; I wish I didn't have to look at you!" Having objectively investigated the condition of Borodin himself I ascertain that he (Borodin) is starting to slip into psychosis due to starvation, which can lead to his eating his own children.

My inspection of a number of families took place at the dinner hour, when they use those same food substitutes which they eat with hot water, but in several homes (2) on the table there were gnawed bones from a dead horse. According to the explanations of the *kolkhoz* members, they themselves prepare food in the following manner: they grind sunflower stems, flax and hemp seeds, chaff, dreg, colza, goosefoot, and dried potato peelings, and they bake flat cakes. Of the food substitutes listed above, the oily seeds are nutritious, which are healthy in combined foods since they contain vitamins. By themselves the vegetable oils do not contain vitamins and by not combining them with other food products of more equal nourishment and caloric value they are found to be toxic and will harm the body. Based on: *General Course on Hygiene* by Prof. G. V. Khotopin, pp. 301–4.

The homes are filthy; the area around the homes is polluted by human waste, by diarrhea caused by these substitutes. People walk around like shadows, silent, vacant; empty homes with boarded-up windows (about 500 householders have left their homes in Karpov village for destinations unknown); one rarely sees an animal on the street (apparently the last ones have been eaten).

In the entire village of 1,000 households, I found only 2 chickens and a rooster. Occasionally one meets an emaciated dog.

The impression is that Karpov village seems to be hit by anbiosis (hibernation, a freeze, falling asleep). The livestock is free to feed on thatched roofs of homes and barns.

In reporting the above-related to the Pokrov *Raion* Committee of the All-Union Communist Party (Bolsheviks), *Raion* Executive Committee, Russian Communist League, and to you, as the *raion* health inspector and doctor of the Pokrov region, I beg of you to undertake immediate measures to help the starving and to notify me of the practical measures taken.

March 25, 1932 *raion* health inspector, Doctor KISELEV

True copy:

RTSKhIDNI, fond 85, op. 27, d. 206, ll. 9–14, 8, 80b.

DOCUMENT 175   *Report by Akulov, Deputy Chief of the* OGPU, *September 15, 1932, on the illegal sale of grain at markets and directives to halt the trade*

ADDENDUM
to paragraph 17-limited Politburo minutes No. 116
October 15, 1932

Sverdlovsk Authorized Representative of the Unified State Political Directorate [*PP OGPU*] of the Urals, Comrade Rapoport,

Ufa *PP OGPU* of Bashkiriia, Comrade Pogrebinskii,

Kazan' *PP OGPU* of the Tatar ASSR, Comrade Matson,

Samara *PP OGPU* of Northern Volga *krai*, Comrade Bak,

Voronezh *PP OGPU* of the Central Chernozem *oblast'*, Comrade Dukel'skii,

Stalingrad *PP OGPU* of Lower Volga *krai*, Comrade Rud',

Rostov-Don *PP OGPU* of the Northern Kuban' *krai*, Comrade Piliar,

Alma-Ata *PP OGPU* of Kazakhstan, Comrade Karutskii,

Novosibirsk *PP OGPU* of Western Siberian *krai*, Comrade Alekseev,

Irkutsk *PP OGPU* of *VSK* [possibly: Eastern Siberian *krai*], Comrade Zirnis,

Kharkov State Political Directorate of the Ukrainian SSR, Comrade Redens.

According to available information, the sale of grain and flour from the new harvest is being carried out at bazaars and markets almost everywhere despite the government's decree prohibiting the sale of grain from the new harvest until January 15, 1933.

Moreover, local organs of the *OGPU* are not making sufficient efforts to combat this phenomenon and are allowing trade in grain and flour.

In connection with this and to propagate the circular letter No. 530 of the *OGPU* from August 15, concerning the decisive battle against unlawful trade in grain and flour,

I order that:

1. Measures be taken to provide full notification to the entire rural population about the government's decree prohibiting trade in grain before January 15, 1933, by making announcements at meetings, hanging posters at markets and other public places, placing announcements in regional newspapers, and so forth.

2. Every type of trade in grain and flour at markets and bazaars be stopped.

3. Flour and grain delivered to bazaars for sale be taken away in instances when the grain is delivered by the grower himself—either by a collective farmer or by an individual farmer—and be included in the accounts of the procurement plans of the collective farm or the self-employed farmer, and that receipts be issued to them by the collection center, as well as payment for the confiscated grain based on the procurement price. However, cordons are not to be erected at markets and bazaars, nor blockades and barriers on roads to markets.

4. Actual confiscation of grain and flour at markets be carried out by members of the militia and the State Association for the Procurement and Marketing of Grain [*Zagotzerno*].

5. In view of possible abuses in this sphere by the grain procurement staff, supervision and security operations be strengthened to intercept them immediately, bringing the guilty to account.

6. Special training for the militia and *Zagotzerno* be provided so that during the confiscation of grain and flour from farmers at bazaars agents of the militia and *Zagotzerno* do not use brute force and arbitrary actions to-

wards them. The latter must explain to the individual farmer and the collective farmer that grain is taken away in conformance with the law of the Soviet government prohibiting trade in grain before January 15, 1933.

7. Confiscation at bazaars of any other kind of agricultural products besides grain and flour be prohibited categorically.

8. Baked bread sold at bazaars not be taken away; however, sellers of large batches of baked bread be uncovered by secret agents and their flour suppliers be identified.

9. As for collective farmers delivering flour to bazaars for sale, that collective farm administrators be notified to bring civil proceedings against them after confiscation of their grain.

As regards collective farmers exposed for repeated or systematic sale of grain, that collective farm administrators be notified to hand them over for trial and impose fines or any other punitive measures that a trial by peers can mete out, right down to their expulsion from the collective farm as malicious violators of the laws of the Soviet regime.

10. Regarding individual farmers exposed for repeated sale of grain and flour, fines be imposed by administrative procedure.

11. Upon finding grain in the possession of middlemen and speculators, that the grain be confiscated and the guilty repressed in accordance with the decree of the government and the directives of the *OGPU*.

Responsibility for carrying out the measures for liquidating the trade in grain and flour be personally assigned to the *PP* and the chief of the Economics Section of the *PP OGPU*.

At the same time, I consider it necessary to emphasize the inadmissibility of extremes or distortions in carrying out this directive.

The major thrust must be directed toward the class enemy, the speculator and middleman who use collective farm trade for private gain and who disrupt the procurement of grain.

In connection with this, one must not waste energy on minor things: the confiscation of small amounts (10–15–20 pounds) of flour if this is not sold systematically, but, by a series of important operational measures correctly putting into practice the circular letter No. 530 of the chairman of the *OGPU*, it is necessary to achieve a real halt in the trade of grain and flour until the time set by the government.

Report the results to the Economic Administration of the *OGPU* once every ten days beginning this September 10, stating the measures taken, the amount of confiscated grain, the number of persons repressed and their social position.

Vice-Chairman of the *OGPU*—Akulov.

Verified : Khriapkina

177-to.

RTSKhIDNI, fond 17, op. 3, d. 900, ll. 43–45.

Propaganda poster issued during the drive to collectivize agriculture, exhorting peasants to go on the offensive against the *kulak*s because they were "an impediment to collectivization." Original in color. *We will annihilate the kulaks as a class,* by Kukryniksy. Publisher: Gosudarstvennoe izdatel'stvo, Moscow-Leningrad, 1930. Prints and Photographs Division, Library of Congress.

DOCUMENT 176 *Minutes of the Central Committee meetings, September 28–October 2, 1932, with a report by Kosior concerning the centralized procurement of goods*

(After the intermission)

CHAIRMAN: Comrade Kosior has the floor.

KOSIOR: Developing the organization of Soviet trade, progress, and production of consumer goods are unquestionably a basic link in better provisioning of workers in industrial centers. We cannot say that the supply situation is favorable. To the contrary, it seems to me the situation must be viewed as extremely unfavorable. We need to work with commitment, as congenially and energetically as possible, because we have the resources to solve these problems, and it all depends completely on how we work. This is especially important now, when centralized procurement plans for all types of products, for meat, butter, etc., have been lowered; when centralized supply as the basic source for all blue-collar and white-collar workers in all our industrial and urban centers clearly must be reevaluated and changed; when through centralized procurement we can ensure that only some of our most critical enterprises are provisioned adequately. The performance of our trade network, the development of *kolkhoz* trade, decentralized procurement—these are a big problem for us, because while the plan for centralized procurement of meat, butter, etc. has been reduced, we, the party, the cooperatives, the supply agencies still must bear responsibility for provisioning a colossal number of workers that we have placed in the second, third, and sometimes, even the first category. [. . .]

Of course, the work of Odessa, Kiev, and the Donbass cannot be compared. It would seem that the Donbass should have been more concerned than Odessa about local procurement since they have more opportunities and their problems are greater, a huge number of workers to supply. In reality, it has been the opposite. We are facing a difficult task: to force the worker cooperatives of large centers, which up to now have lived primarily on centralized provisioning, to turn to the market, to force them to organize local procurement, and not only to procure for themselves, but to affect the market with regard to lowering prices. I believe that the questions raised here in the resolution ought to force us to make the transition from the first, preliminary stage in the development of *kolkhoz* trade and production of consumer goods toward the second stage, toward more determined, systematic work, the kind of work that would ensure us genuine, major success.

RTSKhIDNI, fond 17, op. 2, d. 500, ll. 49–51.

DOCUMENT 177 *Letter from Stalin to Mikhail Sholokhov, May 3, 1933, on sabotage by the grain growers of the Veshenskii* raion

[Handwritten]

Dear Comrade Sholokhov:

As you already know, all of your letters have been received. The help for which you are asking has been approved. To investigate the matter, I am sending Mr. Shkiriatov to the Veshenskii *raion* to see you. I earnestly request you to render him assistance.
So that's that. But not all, Comrade Sholokhov.
The problem is that your letters create a somewhat one-sided impression. I would like to write you a few words about that.

I am thankful to you for your letters, as they reveal the open sores in party and Soviet work; they reveal how our officials, in their ardent desire to restrain the enemy, sometimes inadvertently beat up their friends and sink to the point of sadism.

But this does not mean, that I <u>completely agree</u> with you on everything. You see <u>one</u> side of the situation, and you do not see it too badly. But this is only <u>one</u> side of the matter. In order not to make political mistakes (your letters are not fiction, but outright politics), you must observe widely; you must be able to see things from both sides. The other side is that the esteemed grain growers of your region (and not only from your region) have conducted a "sit-down strike" (sabotage!) and were not against leaving workers and the Red Army without bread. The fact that this sabotage was peaceful and outwardly harmless (bloodless) does not change the fact that the esteemed grain growers actually carried on a "quiet" war against Soviet authority. A war of starvation, dear Comrade Sholokhov. Of course, this circumstance cannot to any degree justify those terrible acts that were allowed to happen, as you are convinced, by our officials. Those guilty of these terrible acts should be punished accordingly. But it is clear as day that these esteemed grain growers are not as innocent as they appear to be from a distance.

> Well, so long,
> shaking your hand
>
> Yours J. Stalin
>
> May 5, 1933

RTSKhIDNI, fond 558, op. 1, d. 3459, ll. 1–6.

DOCUMENT 178   *Letter written by A. E. Kirpichnikov, March 10, 1937, to Kalinin and Stalin about dismal conditions on the collective farms*

Moscow, the Kremlin, to the Chairman of the Central Executive Committee, Comrade Kalinin, March 10, 1937.

Comrade Kalinin and Comrade Stalin,

You are the wisest leaders of our government and politicians of Soviet power, but probably you are also deeply in error.

At present we accept [that] *kolkhoz*es and *kolkhoz* members are becoming prosperous. Living has become pleasant, joyful. As much as this is true, can it be cleared up whether this is in fact the case in the life of the *kolkhoz* village?

Dear leaders, you see very blindly, you also at various congresses and conferences of one sort or another hear from some people who are quite satisfied, i.e., the delegates, and our entire press are pulling the wool over your eyes concerning the *kolkhoz* village. Actually, *kolkhoz*es present a completely dismal picture.

Particularly if you compare [things] with the NEP years, i.e., with the life of the private farmer from 1925 to 1930, when with the appearance of all sorts of agricultural machines, agriculture noticeably grew and became wealthier.

To give [my] conclusion.

But I suggest verifying [this] in the *kolkhoz*es of at least our *oblast'* or *raion*. Whether I have faithfully described and expressed my opinion concerning the whole situation that can be observed in a present-day *kolkhoz* village. Especially from the *kolkhoz* members you can hear that now there's nothing not only to build with or even just to put a roof on your log hut, shed. All the rest is falling apart destroyed burned for firewood because there aren't enough horses (to haul firewood from the forest.) With each year it gets not better but worse. With each year less and less is achieved in the work-days.

> Eastern Siberian *oblast'*
> Cherenkovskii *raion*
>
> [signed]   A. E. Kirpichnikov.

RTSKhIDNI, fond 78, op. 1, d. 593, ll. 18, 190b.

Letter from a collective farm peasant to Mikhail Kalinin, May 18, 1937, on conditions on collective farms

Mikhail Ivanovich!

Not having any prospects, I, Vetluzhskii, decided to appeal to you as a leader of the proletariat and a man who knows agriculture. M. I.! I now find the *kolkhoz* the right path for the peasantry, as Comrade Lenin stated. This is the most correct path for the peasantry. I read a lot of books and newspapers nowadays. The newspapers write that construction is going on everywhere, that the *kolkhoz*es are also beginning construction. But if it is true, I mean about *kolkhoz* achievements, it is all on the surface, and if you look deeper inside the *kolkhoz*, you'll find the opposite. If you look among the *kolkhoznik*s, you'll see a completely different picture. This statement is supported by the flow of *kolkhoznik*s from the *kolkhoz*. And at present, only 50 percent of the former peasant population has stayed on the *kolkhoz*. This shows that people are reluctant to live on the *kolkhoz* and now are leaving the *kolkhoz* in very large numbers. The complicated machines that came to our fields to replace the people who left the *kolkhoz* need a work force to operate them. But how do you explain the flow of *kolkhoznik*s from the *kolkhoz*? I think that the *kolkhoz* and the *kolkhoznik* are wronged by the government. What I mean to say is that if you compare them with factory workers, the workers live a lot better than the *kolkhoznik*s. And, to prove this point, *kolkhoznik*s who left the *kolkhoz* two years ago and found jobs in factories and other enterprises write that their present life at the plants and factories is better than it was on the *kolkhoz*. There they know how much they make every day. They write that they can start in the thirteenth pay grade. And they can buy everything they need at the plant—fabrics and other goods. They can buy as much as they want. They write that they live a lot better life than on the *kolkhoz*.

And now I will take my *kolkhoz* as an example. Our *kolkhoz* is located far from the district center, and our Shurma *raion* pays Kirov *krai* a 2.5 centner grain levy in the first zone. The average in the second zone of the *raion* is 2.39 centners. But neighboring Kil'mez' *raion* pays 1.7 centners per hectare because of their sandy soil. But the soil in our *raion* is as sandy as in Kil'mez' *raion*, yet we pay 2.39 centners per hectare. So after we have paid all the levy, there isn't enough animal feed left, and we have to buy oats. In 1936 we spent 8,000 rubles on oats. So it turns out that the old saying has a new meaning, "Don't cry over the oats you sold for a ruble. I'll buy them back for ten."

M. Iv., I guess I could write more, but I have already written a lot. But I think that the policy in the countryside needs to be changed. Only then can we fulfill Stalin's slogan, "Make all *kolkhoz*es Bolshevik and the *kolkhoznik*s prosperous."

Please send your comments to this address: Kirov *oblast'*, Shurma *raion*, *kolkhoz* "Cheliuskinets," Vetluzhskii, Nikolai Petrovich.

May 18, 1937

Source: ?

Antireligious propaganda poster aimed at the peasants resisting collectivization and also suffering from the widespread famine that began in 1930. Original in color. *Enough trickery! We are the trappers of men's souls,* by P. P. Skapa. (Parody of Gospel reference to the Apostles being the fishers of men's souls.) Publisher: Bezbozhnik, 1930.

Famine in Ukraine

The central authorities continued to impose unrealistic demands on the agricultural population after the initial collectivization assault in 1929–30 and to blame *kulak*s and incompetent or allegedly subversive Communists for failures in delivering grain quotas. This situation peaked in 1932 when excessive grain targets combined with a poor harvest to reduce sharply the amount of grain available for delivery to the cities. Forced collections again provoked resistance, which prompted further repressive measures on the part of Soviet authorities: any theft of grain or agricultural produce was severely punished. Stalin himself ordered that Communists who showed mercy to the "saboteurs" be singled out for special punishment (Document 183).

Some historians link this famine with a parallel assault on Ukrainian nationalism and on overly independent Ukrainian Communists and, in fact, argue that the famine itself was a deliberate attempt by Stalin to starve the Ukrainian peasantry into subservience, to break the back of Ukrainian nationalism by wiping out the property-owning *kulak* class. They see the excessive quotas and the zeal with which they were collected as part of this policy of genocide, whose goal was to wipe out the Ukrainian nation.

There is no question that the harvest of 1932 was followed by a tragic famine in early 1933 and that Soviet authorities tried to cover up the very existence of the famine. When a representative of the Ukrainian Communist Party asked Stalin for special assistance for victims of the famine, Stalin reprimanded him, saying, "You've made up a fable about famine, thinking to frighten us, but it won't work." The writer Mikhail Sholokhov also appealed to Stalin to order the end to arbitrary methods of grain collection. Stalin's reply (Document 177) claimed the peasants themselves were to blame. For decades thereafter, the famine was a forbidden topic among Soviet historians and writers. It was not until 1987 that discussion of the famine began to appear in Soviet publications.

Recent evidence has indicated that part of the cause of the famine was an exceptionally low harvest in 1932, much lower than incorrect Soviet methods of calculation had suggested. The documents included here or published elsewhere do not yet support the claim that the famine was deliberately produced by confiscating the harvest, or that it was directed especially against the peasants of Ukraine. The poor harvest of 1932 and resultant famine were certainly due to the combined effects of the collectivization policy and coercive campaigns of grain procurement beginning in 1928, and thus were one of the consequences of the entire program of forced-draft economic development. In this sense, the famine was "man-made." As the central grain-growing area of the USSR, Ukraine suffered enormously, with some of the most seriously affected regions located in Ukraine, but the effects of the famine were observed and reported throughout the country.

DOCUMENT 180   *Ukrainian Communist Party Central Committee resolution, April 1, 1932, on the eviction of* kulaks *from the Poles'e region*

Proletarians of All Countries, Unite!

TOP SECRET

CENTRAL COMMITTEE OF THE UKRAINIAN COMMUNIST PARTY (BOLSHEVIK)
[*TSK KP(b)U*]

SPECIAL FILE.

No. PB-70/6
April 1, 1932

Central Committee of the All-Union Communist Party (Bolshevik)
[*TSK VKP(b)*] Official Directive to Comrade Kol'tsov

Extract from Protocol No. 70 of the Central Committee Politburo
session of March 29, 1932

On Poles'e.

1. It must be considered essential to purge the Poles'e region of *kulak* elements, as we have determined the number of families subject to deportation to be 5,000.

2. The deportees are to be utilized to develop quarries for stone, clay, etc., and for this purpose permanent *kulak* settlements are to be established on the left bank of the Dnepr River in regions where quarries are located.

3. It is ordered:

a) organizations which will utilize the labor of the special deportees are to provide fully the food supply, living quarters, and cultural-medical services to the special deportees. In particular, the People's Commissariat for Supply of Ukraine must exercise particular supervision in supplying food and manufactured goods to the special deportees.

b) Administrative Control of the special deportee settlements is to be undertaken by the State Political Directorate [*GPU*] of the Ukrainian SSR, which will conclude the appropriate agreements with managers.

4. The *GPU* of the Ukrainian SSR, together with the appropriate People's Commissars, is ordered to develop the policy and instructions which derive from the present resolution.

SECRETARY *TSK KP(b)U*
S. Kosior

Source: ?

DOCUMENT 181   *Resolution of the Politburo of the Central Committee of the Ukrainian Communist Party, November 27, 1932, concerning the harvest and measures to combat sabotage*

<u>Supplement to Politburo minutes No. 92</u>

<u>TO ALL *OBLAST'* COMMITTEES</u>

(Resolution of the Politburo of the Central Committee [*TSK*] of the Communist Party (of Bolsheviks) [*KP(b)*] of Ukraine, November 27, 1932)

The fifth five-day week in the four main *oblast'*s (Dnepropetrovsk, Odessa, Kharkov, Kiev) resulted in a decrease of 574 thousand poods. In the other *oblast'*s the level of grain procurement still has not ensured fulfillment of the procurement plan set for the period. Reductions in procurements have been allowed to happen in a number of key *raion*s and in these *oblast'*s.

Such a steep decline cannot be explained by any objective factors such as rain, etc. The *TSK* finds the primary cause to be poor organization of procurement in the *oblast'*s as well as in the *raion*s and villages.

After making a degree of progress during the fourth five-day week, these successes were not reinforced; instead, they rested on their laurels, assuming that an accelerated pace of grain procurement had been accomplished. The result of this complacency was a reduction in procurement for this five-day week, while a level that would have ensured fulfillment of the plan had not yet been achieved. The reduction in procurement during this period indicates that the measures called for in the *TSK*'s decree of November 18 have not yet been implemented. On the contrary, resistance and sabotage organized by *kulak* counterrevolutionary elements and their degenerate party member supporters have not yet been broken, and repressive measures against them have been insufficiently and indecisively applied.

In this connection the *TSK* orders:

1. Regarding *kolkhoz*es that have most persistently sabotaged procurement, allowing concealment and theft of grain while not significantly contributing to procurement, the *kulak* and anti-Soviet elements organizing sabotage must be exposed and isolated, speedily brought to trial, and the sentence of the court together with notice of its execution must be published in the local district press.

2. First to be held to judicial account must be the degenerate supporters of *kulak*s, party members in responsible positions in the *kolkhoz*es—accountants, storekeepers, and the like. Their arrest and trial must be publicized immediately. Communists who have abetted deception of the state and organized sabotage of procurement must be dealt with especially severely by the courts and the verdicts and notices of execution of sentences published in the district press.

3. *Oblast'* committees must take these matters directly in hand through the judicial system and the *GPU* to ensure that in the districts essential organizational steps are taken in accord with the party line to crush *kulak* sabotage of procurement, as well as to win support of the *kolkhoz* members and achieve fulfillment of the plan for grain procurement.

The *TSK* must be informed immediately of the most critical developments, particularly involving Communists.

4. From the case lists of recently arrested managers and accountants, *oblast'* committee secretaries, together with chiefs of *oblast'* sections of the *GPU*, must select the most serious cases, bring them to trial promptly with the severest of sentences, and forward them to Kharkov for confirmation. The *TSK* must be informed as to the execution of this point within five days.

5. In regard to Communists, especially key workers in villages and *raion*s expelled for consorting with a class enemy, a list must be compiled and sent via the *GPU* to Kharkov of those to be exiled as politically danger-

ous elements. In special cases, upon expulsion from the party, responsible Communists will immediately be arrested and brought to trial.

The *TSK* will send the *oblast'* and *raion* committees a separate directive regarding further measures.

SECRETARY OF THE *TSK KP(b)U* - S. KOSIOR

True copy

RTSKhIDNI, fond 17, op. 26, d. 55, ll. 21–22.

DOCUMENT 182   ***Resolution of the Ukrainian Council of People's Commissars and the Central Committee of the Ukrainian Communist Party, December 6, 1932, on blacklisting villages that maliciously sabotage grain collection***

Addendum to the minutes of Politburo [meeting] No. 93

RESOLUTION OF THE COUNCIL OF PEOPLE'S COMMISSARS [*SNK*] OF THE UKRAINIAN SOVIET SOCIALIST REPUBLIC AND OF THE CENTRAL COMMITTEE OF THE COMMUNIST PARTY (OF BOLSHEVIKS) OF UKRAINE ON BLACKLISTING VILLAGES THAT MALICIOUSLY SABOTAGE THE COLLECTION OF GRAIN

In view of the shameful collapse of grain collection in certain regions of Ukraine, the *SNK* and the *TSK* call upon the *oblast'* executive committees and the *oblast'* [party] committees as well as the *raion* executive committees and the *raion* [party] committees: to break up the sabotage of grain collection, which has been organized by *kulak* and counterrevolutionary elements; to liquidate the resistance of some of the rural Communists, who in fact have become the leaders of the sabotage; to eliminate the passivity and complacency toward the saboteurs, incompatible with being a party member; and to ensure, with maximum speed, full and absolute compliance with the plan for grain collection.

The *SNK* and the *TSK* resolve:

To place the following villages on the black list for flagrant disruption of the grain collection plan and for malicious sabotage, organized by *kulak* and counterrevolutionary elements:

1. Verbka village in Pavlograd *raion*, Dnepropetrovsk *oblast'*

2. Gavrilovka village in Mezhev *raion*, Dnepropetrovsk *oblast'*

3. Liuten'ki village in Gadiach *raion*, Kharkov *oblast'*

4. Kammennye Potoki village in Kremenchug *raion*, Kharkov *oblast'*

5. Sviatotroitskoe village in Troitsk *raion*, Odessa *oblast'*

6. Peski village in Bashtan *raion*, Odessa *oblast'*

The following measures should be undertaken with respect to these villages :

1. Immediate cessation of delivery of goods, complete suspension of cooperative and state trade in the villages, and removal of all available goods from cooperative and state stores.

2. Full prohibition of collective farm trade for both collective farms and collective farmers and for private farmers.

3. Cessation of any sort of credit and demand for early repayment of credit and other financial obligations.

4. Investigation and purge of all sorts of foreign and hostile elements from cooperative and state institutions, to be carried out by organs of the Workers' and Peasants' Inspectorate.

5. Investigation and purge of collective farms in these villages, with removal of counterrevolutionary elements and organizers of grain collection disruption.

The *SNK* and the *TSK* call upon all collective and private farmers who are honest and dedicated to Soviet rule to organize all their efforts for a merciless struggle against *kulak*s and their accomplices in order to: defeat in their villages the *kulak* sabotage of grain collection; fulfill honestly and conscientiously their grain collection obligations to the Soviet authorities; and strengthen collective farms.

> CHAIRMAN OF THE SOVNARKOM OF THE UKRAINIAN
> SOVIET SOCIALIST REPUBLIC - V. ChUBAR'

> SECRETARY OF THE *TSK KP(b)U* - S. KOSIOR

December 6, 1932.

> True copy

RTSKhIDNI, fond 17, op. 26, d. 55, ll. 71–72.

DOCUMENT 183 *Report of December 7, 1932—with a cover letter by Stalin—regarding sabotage of grain collection in the Ukrainian Orekhovskii raion of the Dnepropetrovsk oblast'*

<u>SECRET</u>

TO ALL MEMBERS AND CANDIDATE MEMBERS OF THE CENTRAL COMMITTEE AND CENTRAL CONTROL COMMISSION, TO ALL SECRETARIES OF *OBLAST'* COMMITTEES, *KRAI* COMMITTEES, NATIONAL DISTRICT CENTRAL COMMITTEES, TO ALL SECRETARIES OF *RAION* COMMITTEES AND TO ALL CHAIRMEN OF *RAION* EXECUTIVE COMMITTEES, TO ALL PARTY MEMBERS OF THE BOARD OF THE PEOPLE'S COMMISSARIAT OF AGRICULTURE OF THE USSR

Investigatory materials concerning the sabotage of grain collection in <u>Orekhov</u> *raion* of Ukraine, sent to the Central Committee of the All-Union Communist Party (Bolsheviks) by Comrade Redens, the chairman of the *GPU* of Ukraine, are being distributed for your information. Since these materials appear to be characteristic for a significant number of *raion*s of the Soviet Union, in my opinion, special note should be given to them. The materials show once again that the organizers of sabotage are, in the majority of cases, "Communists," i.e., people who carry party membership cards in their pockets, but who long ago degenerated and in fact broke away from the party. These are the very deceivers of the party and swindlers who cleverly carry out pro-*kulak* policies under the guise of their "agreement" with the general line of the party.

Here is what Lenin had to say about such swindlers and deceivers:

> Workers and peasants, laborers and exploited people! The land, the banks, the factories, the plants have become the property of the entire nation! Take responsibility <u>yourselves</u> to keep track and monitor the production and distribution of goods. This is the <u>only</u> road to the victory of socialism, the guarantee of its victory, the guarantee of victory over all forms of exploitation, over poverty and want! For Russia has enough grain, iron, lumber, wool, cotton, and linen for everyone, provided that labor and goods are properly distributed, that nationwide <u>business-like, practical</u> oversight of distribution is established, that <u>not only</u> in politics but in everyday economic life the enemies of the people are defeated: the wealthy, their spongers, then the swindlers, the parasites, and the hooligans.

No mercy for these enemies of the people, the enemies of socialism, the enemies of working people! War not on life, but to the death against the wealthy and their spongers, the bourgeois intelligentsia. War against the swindlers, the parasites, and the hooligans.

The wealthy and the swindlers—they are two sides of the same coin, the two main categories of <u>parasites</u> nurtured by capitalism, the main enemies of socialism. The entire population must place these enemies under special surveillance. We must deal with them without mercy for the slightest infraction of socialist rules and laws. Any weakness, any vacillation, any sentimentality in this regard would be the greatest crime against socialism.

(Lenin, vol. XXII, p. 164, "How to organize competition").

Since an enemy with a party membership card in his pocket should be punished more severely than an enemy without a card, people like Golovin (former secretary of <u>Orekhov</u> *raion* committee), Palamarchuk (former chairman of a *raion* executive committee), Lutsenko, Ordel'ian, Prigoda, and others ought to be arrested immediately and rewarded according to their merits, i.e., give them each from five to ten years of imprisonment.

> J. Stalin
> Secretary of the Central Committee,
> All-Union Communist Party (Bolsheviks)
> [*TSK VKP(b)*]

December 7, 1932
No. P4731

UKRAINIAN SOVIET SOCIALIST REPUBLIC
CHAIRMAN
OF THE STATE POLITICAL DIRECTORATE [*GPU*]

December 3, 1932
No. 1282/*SP*

City of Kharkov
Telephones: *GPU* Switchboard

TO THE SECRET DEPARTMENT
OF THE *TSK VKP(b)*

I am forwarding a copy of the materials of the investigation of the case of resistance to grain requisitions in Orekhov *raion*.

Prigoda, the former chairman of the *Raion* Collective Farm Union, has been arrested in connection with this case.

Redens

TO THE GENERAL SECRETARY OF THE *TSK*
OF THE COMMUNIST PARTY (BOLSHEVIK) OF UKRAINE [*KP(b)U*]
Comrade KOSIOR

In Orekhov *raion* of Dnepropetrovsk *oblast'* the *GPU* is conducting an investigation of resistance to grain requisitions by the boards of a number of collective farms.

This investigation has revealed that top *raion* officials, in the persons of the secretary of the *Raion* Party Committee Golovin, the chairman of the *Raion* Executive Committee Palamarchuk, the chairman of the *Raion* Collective Farm Union Prigoda, the manager of the *Raion* Land Office Lutsenko, the chairman of the Control

Commission Ordel'ian, and others, have issued instructions to rural party organizations and collective farms directing them not to fulfill the *raion* grain requisition quotas.

For reference purposes I am forwarding a copy of the transcripts of the testimony of the party member Masliuk, the chairman of the *Avangard* Commune, the party member Kostenko, the chairman of the *Svoboda* Commune, the party member Dikii, the manager of the Machine-Tractor Station [*MTS*], Moroz, the manager of the *raion* office of the Union of Collective Swine Farms, and Budiak, a planner and consultant at the *Raion* Executive Committee.

Although the top *raion* officials were dismissed by the Dnepropetrovsk Regional Committee of the *KP(b)U*, I deem it necessary, because of the facts which have come to light, to conduct an investigation for the purpose of holding the guilty parties accountable.

> Chairman of the *GPU*
> of the Ukrainian SSR
> S. Redens
>
> Copy

TRANSCRIPT OF AN INTERROGATION

On November 21, 1932, the following individual, interrogated as a witness, Citizen Masliuk, Gavriil Amvrosievich by name, born 1899, native of the village of Basan', Chubarevskii *raion,* from a family of poor peasants, citizen of the Ukrainian Soviet Socialist Republic, elementary education, Ukrainian, married, middle-rank political officer in the military, occupation farmer, chairman of the *Avangard* Collective Farm, Novo-Karlovskii Rural Soviet, Orekhov *raion,* no record of conviction or arrest, party member since 1925, party card No. 0787758, resident of the *Avangard* Commune, Novo-Karlovskii Rural Soviet, Orekhov *raion,* gave the following testimony:

" . . . The *raion* commission assigned the *Avangard* Commune a quota of 10,981 centners in mid-August of this year.

After we received the quota, we called a meeting of the party bureau which decided that, even though the commune's quota was high, we had to meet it.

Several days later the former secretary of the *Raion* Party Committee, Golovin, came to the commune with a copy of the bureau and commune's resolution, called a meeting of the bureau, and raised the issue of the grain requisition quota, after telling us: "You should admit your mistake in saying that the quota was unrealistic, you should accept the quota no matter how high it is, and then you should only meet it 30%. It's for us to say how unrealistic the quota is. Do you really believe that we at the *raion* don't know that the quota is unrealistic? But for the time being, you have to act as if you've accepted it."

At this point the bureau meeting was adjourned.

In my opinion, the secretary of the *Raion* Party Committee gave us these instructions in order to be able to tell the *Oblast'* Party Committee that everyone accepted the quota as it was and that everything is going well in the *raion*.

Some time afterwards Palamarchuk, the chairman of the *Raion* Executive Committee, also visited the commune. I asked him to reduce our quota, and in reply he gave me the following instructions:

" . . . Ship out as much seed grain as you can for the collective farms in Orekhov *raion,* and the amount will be deducted from your cereal quota, and then we'll reduce the commune's cereal quota by the same amount. In other words, the seed grain you ship will be counted twice, once by deducting the grain shipped as seed grain from your quota, and the second time by counting the same grain as cereal."

I refused to carry out these instructions because I thought they were wrong.

In late October this year I was with Kostenko, chairman of the *Svoboda* Commune, in the office of Prigoda, chairman of the *Raion* Collective Farm Union, and we were discussing grain requisitions. I said that the quota was high and that it would be hard to meet because we had already set stocks aside, and then Prigoda responded by saying the following to Kostenko and me:

"You've got to cover all your bases and set aside a stock of seed grain, an emergency stock, and all the other stocks, because if you don't, we'll put you on trial."

"But as far as the quota goes, you can wait, because Golovin, Palamarchuk, and Lutsenko (the former manager of the *Raion* Land Office) went to the *Oblast'* Executive Committee and asked them to reduce the quota, and they'll probably go along."

These instructions had the effect of making the communes and the cooperatives less enthusiastic about meeting their quotas.

The top *raion* officials were following this policy long before that time. They started with the spring planting and sent one commission after another through the *raion* to determine the yields and varieties to be planted for the purpose of reducing the quota. For some collective farms, such as the *Kolos* Cooperative, they wrote off 160 hectares worth of wheat as lost, even though in reality the cooperative harvested about 300 centners of grain from this land. As a result, the cooperative has met all its quotas in full and has lots of surplus that it doesn't need.

I was bothered by this and brought it up to Palamarchuk, chairman of the *Raion* Executive Committee and the representative of the *Raion* Party Committee, at a plenary session of the rural Soviet, but nothing was ever done about it. They even got the quota reduced, at a time when the *Kolos* cooperative could have easily met its original quota.

When the quota was reduced, I brought it to the attention of Kovalenko, the manager of the *raion* supply office, and asked him not to reduce the cooperative's quota and instead give the reduction to another cooperative which was truly incapable of meeting its quota, but nothing was ever done about it, and the *Kolos* Cooperative was given a 130-centner reduction.

Prigoda was in the army with the chairman of the *Kolos* cooperative. Obviously, this played a major role in determining the grain requisition quotas.

In corroboration of all the above, I could cite the fact that our commune, the *Avangard*, only met its quota by 60% when all of the officials mentioned above were in power, while after these *raion* party and government officials were dismissed, we met our quota 100% in two and a half days and harvested an extra 500 poods to boot.

I've given all the testimony I can. This transcript is a true record of my testimony, in witness thereof I affix my signature.

Masliuk

Interrogators: Kaluzhskii, Gaponov

Copy

TRANSCRIPT OF AN INTERROGATION

On November 22, the following individual, interrogated as a witness, Citizen Dikii, Luka Ilarionovich by name, 42 years of age, a native of the village of Chaikovshchina, Lubensk *uezd*, Poltava *guberniia*, Oritskaia *volost'*, from a family of poor peasants, property consisting of one house, a citizen of the Ukrainian Soviet Socialist Republic, with an elementary education, Ukrainian, married, exempt from military service, occupation agricultural machinery operator, currently employed as manager of the Machine-Tractor Station [*MTS*] in the town of Orekhov, no record of conviction, party member since 1928, member of the Soviet Retail Workers' Union, resident of the city of Orekhov, gave the following testimony:

"The following individuals, namely Burkivskii, the manager of the grain procurement office, Prigoda, the chairman of the *Raion* Collective Farm Union, Lutsenko, the manager of the *raion* land office, and Ordel'ian, the chairman of the Control Commission, traveled around the *raion* as members of a commission (I don't know who appointed it) to determine crop yields and wrote a report of their findings.

I happened to be in the village of Zherebets and, without knowing what was going on, was present at the rural Soviet office when Prigoda himself picked up samples from the fields (spikes of green wheat cut from the fields) and, sitting right there in the rural Soviet office, determined the yields from these samples.

Zhuravskii, an agronomist employed by the *Raion* Collective Farm Union, whom they had taken around the *raion* as the expert, did the least talking of anyone.

Prigoda determined that 100% of the winter wheat crop, the *ornautka* [?] wheat, the barley, and the oats were lost, even though the wheat was still completely green and hadn't even blossomed yet and it would have been absolutely impossible to determine the yield at that time.

A report was written, and two or three days later Prigoda issued a directive ordering that all the winter wheat crop certified as lost was to be mowed for hay.

Nevertheless, only a small part of the crop was mowed, and the rest remained, because most of the collective farmers refused to mow it for hay.

As soon as the *raion* received its annual grain requisition quota, Palamarchuk, the *Raion* Executive Committee chairman, showed up at the *Raion* Collective Farm Union building and huddled with Prigoda in his office. They asked me, a member of the board of the union, manager of an agricultural production department, and a party member, to leave the room.

After talking for two hours, Palamarchuk left and Prigoda called me in along with all the agronomists on the staff and told us:

"Boys, you've got to put together some figures on the yields and a cereal and fodder budget report, because we as the collective farm system have to stand up for the collective farms, and what kind of damn bosses would we be if we didn't stand up for the collective farms?"

Afterwards, Prigoda said the following to me when we were alone:

"Palamarchuk came and told me that it wouldn't be good for him as a member of the commission to talk about how unrealistic the quotas were and that we, as the collective farm system, would have to speak up on behalf of the collective farms and have some sort of cereal and animal feed budget report to back us up, which he's already worked out with Lutsenko, manager of the land office. He already knows about it."

Now we were supposed to put together a report on how much feed we needed for the cattle, the pigs, and the livestock operation which would overstate the number of head of livestock at the livestock departments indicated in the livestock breeding development plan for the *raion*.

The staff of the *Raion* Collective Farm Union spent three days working on the cereal grain and animal feed budget report.

RTSKhIDNI, fond 17, op. 85, d. 379, ll. 1, 10b, 2.

DOCUMENT 184   *Resolution of the Odessa* Obkom *of the Ukrainian Communist Party, December 31, 1932, confirming the expulsion of fifty Party members for sabotaging grain collection and confining them to a labor camp and exiling five hundred families for organizing the sabotage*

Top Secret

SPECIAL FILE

Communist Party (Bolshevik) of Ukraine. Odessa *Oblast'* Committee

No. B-22/25-[op].   Central Committee of the All-Union Communist
                                 Party (Bolshevik) [*TSK VKP(b)*], Central
                                 Committee of the Communist Party
                                 (Bolshevik) of Ukraine [*TSK KP(b)U*],
December 31, 1932   To Comrades Leplevskii, Konik, Kaptsan.

Excerpt from Minutes No. 22 of a December 29, 1932, meeting of the *Oblast'* Committee of the Communist Party (Bolshevik) of Ukraine [*Obkom KP(b)U*].

In accordance with its decision of December 27, the *Obkom* resolves:

1. To confirm the attached list of 50 party members expelled for sabotaging state grain purchases and plundering grain, and to publish the news of their exile to a concentration camp in the *oblast'* and regional press. (The list is attached).

The decision to expel them from the party is to be published in the name of the *Oblast'* Control Committee (*oblast' K.K.*).

The resolution to exile them and to imprison them in a concentration camp is to be published, with the above list, in the name of the *Oblast'* Executive Committee [*Oblispolkom*], along with the following justification:

"The *Oblispolkom* resolves:

For sabotaging grain collection and plundering state and *kolkhoz* grain, for the direct betrayal of the interests of the party and the working class, the former members of the Odessa *Oblast'* Party Organization listed below are hereby expelled from the *KP(b)U*, and they shall be imprisoned in concentration camps for various terms. . . ."

2. To publish simultaneously in the *oblast'* and *raion* press, in the name of the *Oblispolkom*, a confirmed resolution by the Council of People's Commissars of Ukraine [*SNK USSR*] to exile 500 families from Odessa *Oblast'* for organizing the sabotage and disruption of grain requisitions.

The City Party Committee and the *Raion* Party Committee [*Raiparkom*] are ordered to publish this decision in the *raion* press, along with a list of the heads of those families in that *raion* no later than January 1, 1933.

Comrade Kaptsan is charged with editing the layout of the resolution on this subject and distributing the galleys for final review by Comrades Maiorov, Liubchenko, and Leplevskii.

3. To propose that Comrade Kaptsan dedicate the lead article in *Chernomorskaia Kommuna* to the *Obkom* decision to imprison the 50 expelled party members in a concentration camp and to exile 500 families from Odessa *oblast'*; to publish the lists in separate issues of the newspaper in two lead articles.

Comrades Maiorov, Liubchenko, and Leplevskii are to be apprised of these lead articles.

4. To require the *oblast'* and *raion* press to place the resolution of the *Obkom* on exiling the "50" and the "500" on the front page of the newspaper.

5. To give the Head of the *oblast'* department of the Ukrainian News Agency [*RATAU*] responsibility for timely communication of these resolutions and the lead articles in *Chernomorskaia kommuna* to *raion* newspapers.

LIST

of members and candidate members of the Communist Party (Bolshevik) of Ukraine expelled for sabotaging state grain requisitions and slated for exile.

1. Grushchanskii, A. I.	Pervomaiskii *raion*
2. Dmitriuk, S. P.	Pervomaiskii *raion*
3. TSegel'nichenko, A. F.	Pervomaiskii *raion*
4. Dorosh, M. M.	Pervomaiskii *raion*
5. Kliment'ev, A. I.	Nikolaevskii *raion*
6. Dziurin, G. N.	Nikolaevskii *raion*
7. Rusulov, S. G.	N.-Mirgorodskii *raion*
8. Prisiazhniuk, E. A.	Frunzevskii *raion*
9. Mirza-Zmeul, P. I.	Frunzevskii *raion*
10. Valetarskii, M. A.	Frunzevskii *raion*
11. Shepel', P. K.	Frunzevskii *raion*
12. Krivda, G. I.	Frunzevskii *raion*
13. Popushoi, V. K.	Frunzevskii *raion*
14. Pokhilo, G. S.	Frunzevskii *raion*
15. Shepel', P. A.	Blagoevskii *raion*
16. Gafner, I. I.	Ochakovskii *raion*
17. Groshev, I. A.	Snegurevskii *raion*
18. Rudenko, N.	Khersonskii *raion*
19. Shevchenko, A. E.	Khersonskii *raion*
20. Kolesnichenko, I.	Liubashevskii *raion*
21. Lysenko, I. N.	Novo-Ukrain. *raion*
22. Belokon', I. K.	Novo-Ukrain. *raion*
23. Efremov, P. P.	N.-Bugskii *raion*
24. Prestinskii, N. T.	Arbuzinskii *raion*
25. Kolesnichenko, S. T.	Arbuzinskii *raion*
26. Garbuz, K. A.	Arbuzinskii *raion*
27. Isakov, K. A.	Arbuzinskii *raion*
28. Bondar, L. IA.	Arbuzinskii *raion*
29. Matros, E. I.	Gressulovskii *raion*
30. Shevchenko, F. R.	Khmelevskoi *raion*
31. Nedoroda, G. M.	Dobrovelichk. *raion*
32. Serdiuk, A. S.	Bashtanskii *raion*
33. Burlachenko, P. I.	N.-Odesskii *raion*
34. Ivanov, K. T.	Ol'shanskii *raion*
35. Ivanov, G. T.	Ol'shanskii *raion*
36. Samosenok, E. I.	Voznesenskii *raion*
37. Zasul'skii, L. D.	Voznesenskii *raion*
38. Merlianov, L. T.	Voznesenskii *raion*
39. Marchenko, A. P.	Vradievskii *raion*
40. Kalina, P. IA.	Znamenskii *raion*
41. Kolesnikov, A. F.	Znamenskii *raion*
42. IUrchenko, F. T.	Znamenskii *raion*
43. Braiko, I.	Znamenskii *raion*
44. Shestokryl, F. G.	Znamenskii *raion*
45. Polishchuk, N. M.	Zinov'evskii *raion*
46. Dobrovol'skii, I. M.	Zinov'evskii *raion*
47. Masan, M. N.	Zinov'evskii *raion*

48. Skirda, S. Z.   Zinov'evskii *raion*
49. Ozer'ian, I. S.   Odessa
50. [Khdelon?], G. [I].   Odessa

True copy

RTSKhIDNI, fond 17, op. 42, d. 51, ll. 237, 237ob.

DOCUMENT 185   *Excerpt from a speech by S. V. Kosior, general secretary of the Central Committee of the Ukrainian Communist Party, ca. January 12, 1933, concerning the Ukrainian rural economy*

IV

THE RESULTS OF "THE FIVE-YEAR PLAN IN FOUR YEARS"
IN AGRICULTURE

Now let us turn to the results of "the five-year plan in four years" in agriculture.

The five-year plan in agriculture means the five-year collectivization plan. So on what assumptions did the party proceed with carrying out collectivization?

The party proceeded on the assumption that strengthening the dictatorship of the proletariat and building a socialist society would require, in addition to industrialization, a transition from small-scale individual peasant farms to large collective farms equipped with tractors and modern agricultural machinery as the only firm foundation for Soviet power in the countryside.

The party also proceeded on the assumption that without collectivization, it would be impossible to lead our country onto the highway of constructing the economic foundations of socialism and free millions and millions of working peasants from destitution and ignorance.

Lenin said:

"Small farming will never solve the problem of poverty."

(Lenin, 3rd ed., Vol. XXIV, p. 540)

Lenin said that:

"If we continue to rely on small farms, even if they are operated by free citizens on free land, we will inevitably perish."

(Lenin, 3rd ed., Vol. XX, p. 417)

Lenin said:

"Only by means of common, cooperative, and communal labor will we be able to extricate ourselves from the impasse to which the imperialist war led us."

(Lenin, 3rd ed., Vol. XXIV, p. 537)

Lenin said:

"We must move towards common cultivation of large model farms; for otherwise it will be impossible for us to escape the ruin and the outright desperate situation which Russia finds herself in now."

(Lenin, 3rd ed., Vol. XX, p. 418).

On this basis, Lenin arrived at the following basic conclusion:

"Only if we succeed in providing genuine proof of the advantages of social, collective, communal, cooperative cultivation of the land to the peasants and only if we succeed in helping the peasantry by means of communal cooperative farming will the working class, which now holds political power in its hands, be able to provide genuine proof of its soundness to the peasantry and bring the millions and millions of peasants over to the side of the working class once and for all."

(Lenin, 3rd ed., Vol. XXIV, p. 579–580).

The party has based its agricultural collectivization program and its five-year plan for agriculture on these Leninist principles.

This meant that the goal of the five-year plan for agriculture was to consolidate scattered, small individual peasant farms, bereft of the opportunity to use tractors and modern agricultural machinery, into large collective farms equipped with all the latest implements of modern agriculture and establish model state farms or *sovkhoz*es on vacant land.

The goal of the five-year plan for agriculture was to transform the Soviet Union from a backward country of small peasant farms into a major agricultural power organized on the basis of collective labor and designed to produce the maximum possible amount of marketable surplus.

So what has the party accomplished in carrying out the five-year plan in four years in the field of agriculture? Has it succeeded in carrying out this program or has it failed?

Over the last three years the party has succeeded in organizing more than 200,000 collective farms and 5,000 state farms engaged in growing grain and raising livestock and, at the same time, in the last four years has increased the area of land under cultivation by 21 million hectares.

The party has succeeded to the extent that collective farms now include more than 60 percent of all peasant farms and 70 percent of all the land under cultivation by peasants, which means that the original five-year plan target was exceeded by a factor of three.

The party has succeeded to the extent that, instead of the 500 to 600 million poods of marketable surplus grain supplied at the time when individual farming predominated, the party can now procure up to 1,200 to 1,400 million poods of grain every year.

The party has succeeded to the extent that the *kulak*s as a class have been crushed, and, although the process is still incomplete, the working peasants have been liberated from the *kulak* yoke and exploitation, and Soviet power in the countryside is now undergirded by a firm economic foundation—the foundation of collective farming.

The party has succeeded to the extent that the Soviet Union has already been transformed from a country of small peasant farms into the country with the largest-scale agriculture in the world.

Such are the fruits of the "five-year plan in four years" in the area of agriculture.

Now judge for yourselves: after all of these accomplishments, what is the bourgeois press's babbling about the "collapse" of collectivization and the "failure" of the five-year plan in agriculture worth?

And what about agriculture in the capitalist countries which are now undergoing a brutal agricultural crisis?

Everyone is aware of the official statistics.

The area under cultivation in the major grain-producing countries has decreased 8 to 10 percent. The acreage planted in cotton in the United States has declined 15 percent, acreage planted in sugar beets has decreased 22 to 30 percent in Germany and Czechoslovakia, and flax acreage has declined 25 to 30 percent in Lithuania and Latvia.

According to the American Department of Agriculture, the gross agricultural output of the United States fell from 11 billion dollars in 1929 to 5 billion dollars in 1932, i.e., by more than 50 percent. The gross output of grain fell from 1.288 billion dollars in 1929 to 391 million dollars in 1932, i.e., by more than 68 percent. With respect to cotton there was also a decline from 1.389 billion dollars in 1929 to 397 million dollars in 1932, or more than 70 percent.

Don't all these figures prove the advantages of the Soviet system of agriculture over the capitalist system? Don't these facts show that collective farms are a more viable form of farming than individual and capitalist farms?

Some people say that collective farms and state farms are not completely profitable, that they swallow up resources, that there's no sense in establishing such farms, and that it would be better to break them up and only keep the most profitable operations. But only people who have no understanding of economics could talk like that. A few years ago, more than half of our textile mills were unprofitable. Some of our comrades were in favor of closing these plants. So what would have happened to us if we'd listened to them? We would have committed a heinous crime against our country and against the working class if we had ravaged our industry just as it was getting on its feet. But what did we do at the time? We waited a little more than a year, and then the entire textile industry became profitable. And what about our auto plant in Gorky? Wasn't it unprofitable at one time? So would you have ordered it shut down? Or what about our steel industry, which was also unprofitable at one time? Should we have shut it down, comrades? If we looked at profitability the way they wanted us to, we should have developed only a few of the most profitable industries, such as the confectionery industry, the flour industry, the perfume industry, the knitwear industry, the toy industry, and so on. Obviously, I'm not opposed to the development of these industries. They should be developed because the general public needs them. But, first of all, they could not be developed without the equipment and fuel supplied by heavy industry. Secondly it would be impossible to base our industrialization on them. And that's the cold hard fact of the matter, comrades.

We cannot look at profitability from a hustler's point of view, from the standpoint of this minute. Profitability must be viewed from the standpoint of the national economy over several years. Only this outlook could be termed truly Leninist and truly Marxist. And we must stick to this point of view not just for industry but to an even greater extent for collective and state farms. Just think about it: over the last three years we have established more than 200,000 collective farms and about 5,000 state farms; i.e., we have created completely new major enterprises which are just as important to agriculture as plants and factories are to industry. Just name a single country which has been able to create not 205,000 major enterprises but, let's say, 25,000 such enterprises, in just three years. You wouldn't be able to, because such a country has never existed. But we have managed to establish 205,000 new enterprises in agriculture. And, as it turns out, there are people in this world who demand that these enterprises start making a profit immediately, and if they don't, then they believe that they should be broken up and disbanded. Isn't it obvious that the laurels of Herostratos** wouldn't give these more than strange individuals any sleep?

In discussing the unprofitability of collective farms and state farms, I have absolutely no intention of saying that all of them are unprofitable. It's not that way at all! Everyone knows that even now there are a large number of highly profitable collective farms and state farms. We have thousands of collective farms and dozens of state farms which are earning a good profit even now. These farms are the pride of the party and Soviet power. Of course, collective farms and state farms aren't exactly alike everywhere you go. There are old farms, new farms, and very young farms. There are weak farms which have not completely gelled as economic entities. They are going through approximately the same phase in their organizational development as our plants and factories did in 1920 and 1921. We understand that the majority of them cannot yet be profitable. But there can be absolutely no doubt that in two or three years they will become profitable, just as our plants and factories did after 1921. Refusing them assistance and support on the grounds that not all of them are profitable at this very minute would mean committing a heinous crime against the working class and the peasantry. Only enemies of the people and counter-revolutionaries could suggest that collective and state farms are unnecessary.

In carrying out the five-year plan for agriculture, the party has carried out collectivization at a rapid

**Herostratos, a tailor in the ancient city of Ephesus, burned a sacred temple in order to win fame.

pace. Was the party right in doing so? Yes, the party was absolutely right, even though we did get carried away a bit. In carrying out the policy of liquidating the *kulak*s as a class and exterminating nests of *kulak*s, the party could not stop halfway but had to take everything to its logical conclusion. [break in the text]

So what sort of situation did we have in Ukraine by the end of the first five-year plan? I must say that, despite the difficulties and mistakes of last year in the area of grain procurement and despite the difficulties that exist now, it seems to me that there is absolutely no doubt that Ukrainian agriculture has grown and gotten much stronger than it was at the beginning of the five-year plan period or the first year. But despite the hesitation of the past year, and the hesitation among individual farmers was even greater, despite all this hesitation, we undoubtedly have very large areas under cultivation, much larger than was the case at the beginning of the period when we had individual farms.

We have greatly expanded and are maintaining our acreage planted in industrial crops. We have substantially increased and are firmly maintaining the winter wheat acreage which constitutes the foundation of grain production in Ukraine. And we have done so despite the very severe weather conditions of the last two years. Obviously, we as Bolsheviks cannot use this as an excuse, but in the past weather conditions have had a very dramatic and severe impact on individual farmers, and if, for example, we had faced this year's weather conditions with most of our farms in individual hands, we would have suffered innumerable disasters. We would not have been able to manage even half of what we did this year with respect to planting without collective farms accounting for 75% of Ukraine's farms. In Ukraine we have collective farms which are already strong, farms which are getting stronger, and farms which are developing, and this allowed us to maintain Ukrainian agriculture at a certain level despite last year's difficult conditions. With respect to the production of marketable surplus by Ukrainian agriculture, we have 50 to 100% more than we did at the beginning of comprehensive collectivization. This is what allowed us to increase grain procurement so substantially in past years, and all the mistakes of the past year, even the problems with the grain procurement drive of this year, cannot for one minute obscure the fact that the strength and performance of agriculture is now much greater and more solid than it was at the beginning of collectivization and the beginning of the five-year plan.

Obviously, we cannot deny that local officials, including us, have committed a great many practical errors, which have led a great many members of the opposition, including individuals who are secretly and openly in the opposition—right-wingers and left-wingers—to attempt to characterize them, either publicly or in private, as the results of an incorrect policy. This is a despicable deception which must be clearly exposed for what it is. If we have had difficulties on the grain procurement front, they can only be the result of shortcomings of our day-to-day leadership in the field, and nothing more. Every time we have reflected on our problems and looked at ourselves carefully and attentively to determine why things have gone wrong, we have been forced to admit time and time again that the party's policy is the correct one, that the Central Committee's instructions have been the right ones, and that the cause of our problems is our failure to absorb them completely and our misunderstanding of and inability to accomplish what the Central Committee has asked of us.

None of this in any way implies that we should retreat, as Zinoviev has suggested, but instead tells us that we should be bolder in attacking our own inability to lead, our own shortcomings, and the individuals who have taken advantage of these shortcomings, namely the *kulak*s, who have managed to slither in through certain cracks in our collective farms.

Of course, running the collective farms is a very difficult job. In Ukraine alone there are more than 25,000. And we must say that Comrade Stalin was absolutely right when he said that we've been afflicted by a kind of dizziness with success. In a large number of areas and a large number of collective farms, our inaction, inertia, and complacency have allowed the *kulak*s and other anti-Soviet elements to start showing themselves in the collective farms, while some collective farms have even fallen under the outright control of the *kulak*s.

All of this suggests that we should go on the offensive and work harder to improve the performance of our party organizations. This is the only conclusion that a real Bolshevik could draw on the basis of the shortcomings in his own work.

Obviously we might run into situations where certain employees simply aren't capable of handling their jobs and will have to be replaced. In cases where certain party organizations can't handle the job, the Central Committee will help. The party has made incredible strides in the area of collectivization. These accomplishments have made agriculture the area where we have managed to establish a firm socialist foundation that will allow us to develop agriculture even further and raise agricultural productivity to unheard-of heights. We haven't learned how to pull all the levers, but as we do, and the lessons of the past will teach us a great deal, we will be able to genuinely tap all the vast potential of our collective agriculture.

I have already discussed the effort to meet the grain procurement targets. While individual farms once produced 500 to 600 million poods of marketable surplus grain, now the collective farms are providing 1,200 to 1,400 million poods. But is Ukraine producing more or less grain than it did during the period of individual farming or at the beginning of collectivization? I must say that, without a doubt, Ukraine is producing more grain now than it ever did then. But if despite the greater volume of grain, we're having a hard time collecting it, it is the result of a number of other factors. And the most important factor is that in a large number of areas and regions, we have been asleep and allowed hostile elements to infiltrate the collective farms, allowed our party organizations to become clogged with filth, and have allowed counterrevolutionary nationalist elements to become active. These elements have taken advantage of the opportunities presented by our Ukrainian national republic, have infiltrated our agencies, machine and tractor stations, our collective farms, and so forth, and have even managed to plant their own cells in some places.

In order to eliminate this factor, we are now engaged in a fierce assault on these elements to reveal, expose, destroy, and neutralize them.

RTSKhIDNI, fond 17, op. 2, d. 514, v. 1, ll. 10, 11, 65.

DOCUMENT 186 *Decision of the Ukrainian Communist Party Central Committee, January 17, 1933, to request permission to deport* kulak *families from Kharkov* oblast'

Proletarians of All Countries, Unite!   TOP SECRET

COMMUNIST PARTY /BOLSHEVIK/ OF UKRAINE CENTRAL COMMITTEE [*TSK KP(b)U*]

Special file

No. PB-98/3

To the CENTRAL COMMITTEE of the ALL-UNION COMMUNIST PARTY/BOLSHEVIK/ Organizational Instructor Comrade Kol'tsov

January 17, 1933

Excerpt from minutes No. 98 of a meeting of the Central Committee Politburo from January 3, 1933

Concerning the Intensification of Repression in Kharkov *Oblast'*

1. Petition the Central Committee of the All-Union Communist Party to approve:

a) The deportation to the North of 400 families of malicious elements and *kulak*s from Kharkov *oblast'*.

b) The deportation to the North of 40 Communists expelled from the party.

SECRETARY OF THE *TSK KP(b)U*.- [signed] S. KOSIOR

Source: ?

DOCUMENT 187 **Supplement to minutes of the Ukrainian Party Kiev oblast' bureau, February 22, 1933, instructing that the famine be alleviated and that "all who have become completely disabled because of emaciation must be put back on their feet" by March 5**

<u>To be returned</u>   <u>Top Secret</u>

Note no. 82

Supplement to minutes no. 87
of the meeting of the Kiev
Oblast' Bureau of the
Communist Party (Bolsheviks)
of Ukraine

February 22, 1933

SPECIAL FOLDER

<u>On the elimination of food shortages in the collective farms, centers of acute malnutrition, and cases of famine.</u>

I. Approve the measures taken by the Secretariat and the party element of the *OIK* [*Oblast'* Executive Committee].

II. Require all *RPK*s [*Raion* Party Committees] to eliminate rapidly extreme exhaustion among collective and individual farmers resulting from severe malnutrition. By March 5 all cases of swelling must be eliminated and all who have become completely disabled because of emaciation must be put back on their feet.

For this purpose:

1. In 48 hours take all—both children and adults—who are swollen or unable to walk because of malnutrition to facilities specially designated and adapted for this purpose. Make food available to them for as long as it is necessary to rid them of their unhealthy condition. Under no circumstances are they to be allowed to stay at home in such a state.

2. In the villages affected, make the serving of hot breakfasts mandatory in schools, bringing in all the emaciated children of preschool age as well, and set up special food service stations for them.

3. Because of the many cases of acute malnutrition among collective farmers who have earned many labor-days—the result of abuses in the distribution of collective farm products or because of large family size—consider it necessary to use collective farm funds to help such families. The eligibility of these people is determined case by case by the administration of the collective farm.

4. Persons who were in conditions of severe malnutrition and have been made fit to work are to be offered jobs on the collective farms, state farms, and timber industries, providing them with appropriate advance pay.

5. Require the *Raion* Party Committees to make special funds available for the goals outlined.

6. Order the *Raion* Party Committees to submit a report to the *Oblast'* Committee on:

a) the number of villages that will receive such relief;

b) the number of people in need of relief;

c) the existence of resources—drawn from *raion* and the collective farms funds—that will be needed and could be allotted for this purpose from Feb. 25 through Apr. 1.

7. The *Oblast'* Committee categorically insists that all cases of extreme emaciation and swelling be eliminated by March 5.

8. As to the existing cases of squandering collective farm resources—especially in the form of continued public food service in the collective farms, and placing these resources in the hands of so-called permanent collective farm staff—the *Oblast'* Committee warns that expropriation of any collective farm resources not provided for by existing directives and not reported to the *Oblast'* Committee by the *Raion* Committee will be interpreted as actions directed against socialist property and will be punished most severely according to the law.

9. Require the *Raion* Party Committees to use the sale of grain, which was approved by the Kiev *oblast'*, to improve the food situation, developing spontaneous activities and initiatives of collective farms and collective farmers.

10. In view of the continued attempts by our enemies to use these facts against the creation of collective farms, the *Raion* Party Committees are to conduct systematic clarification work bringing to light the real causes of the existing famine (abuses in the collective farms, laziness, decline in labor discipline, etc.).

11. Organize special commissions in the *raions* for direct management of the relief efforts under the chairmanship of the chairman of the *Raion* Executive Committee, consisting of the director of the *Raion* Office of *GPU*, the Women's Organizations Committee, *Raion* Department of Health, a representative of the *Raion* Committee of the Communist Youth League, and the "Friends of Children" Society.

Secretary of the *Oblast'* Committee of the *KP(b)U*
[signed] DEMChENKO

37- 60-b-on.[illegible]

Copy 90 [Seal]

RTSKhIDNI, fond 17, op. 42, d. 82, ll. 82, 83.

DOCUMENT 188   *Plans by the Odessa Oblast' Party Committee, August 7, 1933, for distributing August bread rations according to occupation*

TOP SECRET

The Communist Party (Bolsheviks) of Ukraine. Odessa *Oblast'* Committee

No. S-29/67-op. *TSK VKP(b)* [Central Committee of the All-Union Communist Party (Bolsheviks)], *TSK KP(b)U* [Central Committee of the Communist Party (Bolsheviks) of Ukraine]; to Comrades Borisov, Klinovskii, Shul'kin, Klochko, Nizovskii; Pervomaiskii *Raion* Party Committee:

   August 7, 1933   SPECIAL FOLDER

Extract from Minutes No. 29 of the August 4, 1933, meeting of the SECRETARIAT of the *Oblast'* Committee of the *KP(b)U*.

On the plan to supply bread for the month of August.

1. Approve the plan introduced by the *Oblast'* Supplying Agency [*Oblsnab*] to supply bread throughout the *oblast'* in August.

2. Approve supply of the following quotas of bread for the month of August:

for the first list: to workers . . . . 800 grams

                          to white collar workers and dependents 400   "

for the second list: to workers 600   "

                          to white collar workers and dependents 300   "

to major enterprises:

        in Zinov'evsk — *The Red Star*

        in Kherson — *im. Petrovskogo*" and *Oboznyi*

                to workers . . . . 700 gr. per person.

for the third list: to workers . . . . 500 grams

                          to white collar workers 300   "

                          to dependents of blue and white collar workers . 200   "

3. Approve for the workers of Odessa and Nikolaev an issue of 50% of the bread quota in wheat flour and 50% in rye flour.

Suggest to the *oblast'* grain procurement agency to ensure timely issuing of the indicated assortment of flour.

4. Having thoroughly checked and eliminated all the "dead souls," advise the city and *oblast'* party committees of Odessa, Nikolaev, Kherson, Zinov'evsk, and Pervomaisk to abide strictly by the approved norms and quotas.

Advise *Oblsnab* to establish strict operational control of the actual consumption of bread in accordance with the approved norms, quotas, and plans.

SECRETARY of the *OBLAST'* COMMITTEE of the *KP(b)U*
/BRYChKIN/

Plan for the central supply of Odessa *oblast'* with bread in August 1933

NAME OF CITY	LIST	GROUP	QUOTA	DAILY BREAD NORM	
A) ODESSA	First	Workers	21,587	800	The leading enterprises from the 2nd list in Odessa: IAnv., Dzhut, Lenina, Starost., Krasina, Dzerzhinskii, Iodnyi, and the Electric Power Station will receive the same quotas as those on the 1st list.
		White-collar workers and dependents	24,830	400	
	First: ORS IAnv. z-da i Dzhutov	Workers	7,805	800	
		White-collar workers and dependents	7,068	400	
	Second	Workers	79,267	600	
		White-collar workers and dependents	80,814	300	
	Third	Workers	33,571	500	
		White-collar workers	11,899	300	
		Dependents	40,528	200	
B) NIKOLAEV	First	Workers	6,125	800	
		White-collar workers and dependents	7,840	400	
	Second	Workers	12,591	600	
		White-collar workers and dependents	11,002	300	
	Third	Workers	8,509	500	
		White-collar workers and dependents	588	300	

NAME OF CITY	LIST	GROUP	QUOTA	DAILY BREAD NORM	
C) ZINOV'EVSK	First	Workers	941	800	
		White-collar workers and dependents	1,521	400	
	Red Star	Workers	8,880	700	
		White-collar workers and dependents	12,685	300	
	Second	Workers	8,372	600	
		White-collar workers and dependents	11,320	300	

II. In order to supply the cities according to the above indicated contingents and quotas, approve the following plan of flour distribution for the month of August (in tons)

city Odessa	—	2,778.6 tons	
Nikolaev	—	1,125.6 "	(including 498.3 tons for Marti and 142.5 tons for "61" worker supply sections [ORS])
Zinov'evsk	—	487 "	
Kherson	—	494.8 "	
Pervomaisk	—	93.7 "	
Voznesensk	—	15 "	

For the craftsmen and the leading small manufacturing shops of the cities, employing [illegible] workers and having 3,000 dependents, appropriate 45.3 tons, in accordance with the agreement reached with the *oblast'* industrial council. In all, for the individual supply of the cities, 5,040 tons.

III. Plan for the distribution of flour for public food service:

a) Public food service for city enterprises — 386.2 tons

b) Public food service for *ORS* — 88 tons

　Including for *ORS* Marti and "61" — 63 tons
　ORS Dzhutova and IAnv. — 18 tons

RTSKhIDNI, fond 17, op. 42, d. 83, ll. 41–43.

Industrialization

Industrial development had been the raison d'être of the Communist system, and the first five-year plan named the expansion of industry as the key to national prosperity. The industrial front was deliberately touted as the symbol of the successes of Soviet planning: fifteen hundred big enterprises were built during the first five-year plan, including the Magnitogorsk metallurgical complex, the Ural machine factory, the Kharkov tractor plant, and automobile plants in Moscow and Nizhnii Novgorod. New industries were developed: in aviation, chemicals, machine tools, synthetic rubber, and more. To a world plunged into economic depression, the successes of Soviet planning looked very attractive.

It is now well known that these successes were not nearly as impressive as contemporary propaganda made them seem and that the genuine achievements in industry came at tremendous cost. The fulfillment of the entire plan had been contingent on the presence of three important factors: the absence of a major crop failure during any of the plan's five years, the expansion of world trade and availability of long-term credits for the purchase of machinery, and overall growth in quality of output. Instead, the collectivization drive devastated agriculture, the world depression drove down prices of raw materials and placed the price of machinery beyond the reach of Soviet industry, and the influx of untrained workers into the industrial labor force far above planned levels (the immediate result of the drive against the *kulak*s in the countryside) drove down productivity and quality of output in industry. The industrial labor force nearly doubled instead of increasing by just one-third as planned. Instead of the planned increase of real wages, standards of living plummeted; food rationing was the urban corollary to the famine in the countryside.

Official propaganda trumpeted only the successes of the industrialization drive. The five-year plan had been completed in four years and three months, boasted Stalin in January 1933, as millions of peasants were facing death by starvation. Output figures for coal extraction, the production of pig iron, building materials, agricultural machinery, and much else fell far below plan, but these shortfalls remained unreported. Just as harmful was the tremendous waste that accompanied industrial construction, noted in Document 190. Waste and inefficiency produced bottlenecks in construction and production that jeopardized the entire plan.

Propaganda poster urging peasants to get the harvest in and help the all-union drive for industrialization. The combine depicted in this idealized portrayal of modernized agriculture is American and is clearly marked "McCormick-Deering." Original in color. *The fight for the Bolshevik harvesting of the crop is the fight for socialism,* by Klutsis. Publisher: Izogiz, Moscow-Leningrad, 1931. Prints and Photographs Division, Library of Congress.

DOCUMENT 189   *Report from V. V. Kuibyshev, chairman of Gosplan, provided to the Associated Press through its general director, Kent Cooper, December 15, 1930, on the achievements of the Soviet economy after the second year of the first five-year plan*

Communication to "The Associated Press" in New York through Mr. Kent Cooper (General Director of the Agency).

The second year of the five-year plan has ended—the same five-year plan that excited the minds of the entire world and on whose account an embittered discussion has and continues to be conducted in the world press.

Who does not remember the statements uttered by the most prominent bourgeois economists and politicians, who claimed that projections of the five-year plan are "unreal," "utopian," and "fantastic"? Who does not remember the claims that the projections of the five-year plan are just another Bolshevik "bluff"? To this day there are cries about the failure of the five-year plan and the breakdown of the comprehensively thought-out plan of economic reconstruction.

The two years that the five-year plan has been in effect give enough data to test the validity of the plan's projections and to test the soundness of doubts and objections evoked by this plan in the minds of representatives of the school of bourgeois economics.

Especially significant have been the achievements of socialist industry, whose increase of output exceeded five-year plan projections by 5% (instead of the 20.2% increase called for by the plan, it has risen by 25%). In talking about this, it must be stressed that the growth of output in industries manufacturing capital equipment was around 40%, an increase exceeding the five-year plan's projection. In the most important branches of industry, the five-year projections were exceeded as follows: oil extraction for 1929–30 was projected at 14.6 million tons, but it was actually 17.1 million tons; the plan projected casting 4.7 million tons of cast iron, but 4.982 million tons were cast. [. . .]

Thus the ever-increasing pace of economic growth and the systematic increase in the relative size of the already dominant socialist sector of the economy ensure fulfillment of the slogan of millions of laborers, "the five-year plan in four years," and are steadily improving the material and cultural quality of life of the working class and peasantry.

Despite all predictions and prophecies by economists and politicians hostile to our country, and sabotage by bitter remnants of the old regime, the five-year plan is being fulfilled and will be realized quickly. This is the best testimony to the progressiveness of the Soviet system and Soviet methods of economic management.

However, we are not satisfied with the pace of growth, nor with the quality of our work. That is why we harshly criticize ourselves. But those who use this criticism to predict the failure of the five-year plan make fools of themselves, as the cited data indicate. It is a pity that the laughable predictions and cawing of economists hostile to the USSR are denying the business world profitable involvement in the giant economic construction under way in our country.

[signed] V. Kuibyshev

RTSKhIDNI, fond 79, op. 1, d. 539, ll. 1–6.

DOCUMENT 190   *Report of the Presidium of the Supreme Economic Council, January 1, 1931,*
on industrial statistics and plans for 1931, with a note from Ordzhonikidze and comments by Stalin

[Handwritten notation, upper left corner:] Soso*, this is the project about which I spoke yesterday. Request you read it and give me your instructions. Signed, Sergo December 2, 1931]

10. January 1, 1931   Draft
                                            RESOLUTION
of the Presidium of the All-Union Economic Council [*VSNKh*] of the USSR concerning the control figures for industry for the year 1931

The Council of People's Commissars of the USSR approved a national economic plan for 1931 (control figures).

The Soviet Union is entering the third, decisive year of the five-year plan.

The year 1931 should lead to the basic fulfillment of the grandiose plan of building socialism—the five-year plan.

The 1931 plan is based to a significant degree on those great achievements of the last two years, on the overfulfillment of the first two years of the current five-year plan.

During the first two years of the five-year plan, socialist state industry yielded production worth 30.5 billion rubles in comparison with 29.3 billion rubles set by the five-year plan.

Heavy industry yielded production of 13.8 billion rubles rather than the 12.5 billion rubles envisioned for these two years by the five-year plan.

The annual industrial output is twice the prewar annual industrial production.

In contrast to the capitalistic world, for which the year 1930 was an "unfortunate year" according to the leaders of this world themselves, unlike world capitalism, where production is sharply declining under the blows of an economic crisis, the Soviet state is entering the year 1931 with the perspective of an even sharper upturn of the curve of the Bolshevik economic growth rate.

In carrying out the words of the slogan "The five-year plan in four years" that was proclaimed by the working masses and confirmed by the 16th Party Conference, in contrast to the statements of the Trotskyites and Rightists, the country of proletarian dictatorship, led by the Communist Party and its Central Committee, in the third year will grow even more rapidly.

Since industry plays a leading role in the socialist transformation of the entire economy and the establishment of a foundation for the socialist economy of the USSR, the following enormous and crucial task falls to industry:
  - 25 billion rubles of gross output
  - 6.3 billion rubles of capital construction (together with regional electrostations)
  - 10% reduction in production costs
  - 28% increase in labor productivity
  - 6% wage increase

Our industrial output and industrial construction targets are designed to:

1. Concentrate investment in new construction in the most essential areas to ensure that the maximum possible number of new plants are put into operation in 1931 and thus lay the groundwork for even faster growth of output in 1932.

2. Supply 17 million tons of cast iron for the program in 1933.

3. Accelerate the development of heavy machinery manufacturing in order to ensure that mostly Soviet-

*Soso was Stalin's nickname. Sergo Ordzhonikidze was a fellow Georgian and one of Stalin's closest associates.

made equipment and machinery are used in the gigantic new integrated steel and iron works and the coal and oil industries.

4. Establish a machinery manufacturing infrastructure for modernization of the transportation system.

5. Develop agricultural machinery manufacture and the automotive and tractor industries in order to provide a solid industrial foundation for the burgeoning process of agricultural collectivization and develop the production of machinery for the cultivation of industrial crops.

6. Dramatically accelerate the growth of the chemical and nonferrous metals industries. To this point, the nonferrous metals industry has developed at an unacceptably slow pace and has thus retarded the development of a number of other industries, especially the electrical equipment industry.

7. Expand the economy's fuel and energy infrastructure.

The successful achievement of the 1931 plan targets should result in 17 billion rubles of Category A industrial output and 8 billion rubles in Category B output. By comparison with 1930, this would mean a 42% increase, 58% in Category A output and a 17.6% increase in Category B. In the process, machinery manufacturing output would rise 86%, while the same figures for electrical equipment, iron, and coal would be 72%, 52%, and 46%.

THE OUTPUT of essential products would be expressed in the following terms:

COAL - 82.5 million tons;
OIL - 25.5 million tons;
CAST IRON - 8 million tons;
STEEL - 8.8 million tons;
ROLLED METAL PRODUCTS - 6.7 million tons;
TRACTORS - 54,000 units (as opposed to the 53,000 units projected for the last year of the five-year

plan);

GENERAL MACHINERY PRODUCTS - 2,483 million rubles;
AGRICULTURAL MACHINERY - 760 million rubles;
ELECTRICAL PRODUCTS - 970 million rubles;
COTTON FABRICS - 2,785 million meters, or 13.4% more than in 1930;
FOOTWEAR - 84 million pairs, or 36% more than in 1930.

In the area of production, meeting the plan targets will require us to concentrate as much effort as possible on the following tasks:

1. Strict fuel economy and effecting major reductions in fuel consumption per unit of output by 15% in industry and by 9% at electrical power plants. Despite the rapid growth projected for the fuel industry in 1931, fuel producers and consumers will have to work hard to ensure that an adequate supply of fuel is available for the rapidly developing economy. Some consumers continue to squander fuel in a totally unacceptable manner (for example, by burning coking coal, high-grade coal, and so forth in boiler furnaces). All of our leading industrial managers, engineers, and technicians and the entire industrial community must be mobilized to use fuel thriftily and save it by whatever means possible.

2. Saving ferrous and nonferrous metals. All industrial and construction workers must enlist in the campaign to save metal in machining and to substitute wood and other materials for metal in industry and industrial and housing construction in order to ensure a fully adequate supply of metal for the manufacture of equipment and critical industrial construction projects where metal is absolutely indispensable. The efforts of all industrial workers and special brigades of shock workers and *komsomol* members must be focused on inventorying and keeping track of all available supplies of ferrous metal.

Determined implementation of these measures and efforts to save every possible kilogram of metal will guarantee the successful accomplishment of the incredible tasks which industry now faces, especially the machinery manufacturing industry, in terms of the amount of metal which must be produced in 1931.

We must also focus the attention and efforts of shock workers, worker inventors, managers, engineers, and technicians on saving nonferrous metals as much as possible, finding substitutes for them, and tapping the country's current resources of these metals. To this point we have not done enough in this area. The performance of research institutes in this respect has been especially inadequate.

We must economize on raw materials in all industrial sectors, mainly agricultural raw materials, which will still be in short supply in 1931 despite the growth in output by comparison with past years. We must be increasingly frugal in our use of imported raw materials and simultaneously do everything we can to produce the same raw materials in the Soviet Union and substitute other materials for imports.

4. Efficient utilization of existing equipment. We must fight tooth and nail with anyone who believes that industrial development in the future can rely exclusively on new construction and new equipment. We must remember that in many cases our existing equipment is as good as the equipment installed at British, French, and German plants but is being utilized much less efficiently. In order to build socialism with old equipment, we will have to squeeze everything out of it that we can. We must firmly oppose any lordly contempt for old equipment.

Within three months' time we must inventory and document all equipment, calculate its capacity and utilization, and determine which equipment is being badly used and underutilized or is standing totally idle. The examples of the Stalin Machinery Manufacturing Plant in Leningrad, whose inventory and documentation of its equipment revealed 500,000 machine-hours of unused capacity, and a number of other plants have shown how great this underutilization of equipment capacity still is and what a poor job we have done in inventorying the productive capacity of our industrial plants. In addition, the transfer of excess machines to other plants will relieve us of the burden of importing these machines and instead will allow us to import those machines which are truly in short supply.

In the area of major construction, we must use 5.5 billion rubles and the 850 million rubles appropriated for the construction of district electric power plants.

Of the 5.5 billion rubles, 500 million rubles will be used to begin new construction projects, while the remaining 5 billion will be used to develop and complete ongoing projects. This by itself provides a perfectly clear picture of the reasoning behind the plans for major construction in 1931.

We must avoid dissipating the funds earmarked for new construction projects. WE MUST CONCENTRATE THESE FUNDS ON VITAL SECTORS in order to complete and PUT INTO OPERATION AS MANY NEW PLANTS, SECTIONS, AND INSTALLATIONS as possible this year. We must not fritter away our efforts on every little construction project and every plant undergoing remodelling but must concentrate our efforts on essential projects so that individual production lines, sections, and aggregates can begin making products in 1931 or can facilitate the immediate expansion of output by the other sections of an existing plant. This kind of major construction plan for industry as a whole will dramatically expand the material resources at the country's disposal, will promote socialist accumulation, and will open up the possibility of even faster growth in output and construction.

In order to accomplish this key task of the construction plan we must:

1) make immediate preparations for the construction season so as to provide as much material and manpower as possible and the proper organization for key construction projects in each industry and at each individual plant;

2) complete all the designs, plans, and specifications for priority construction projects without fail and make this effort the battle mission of plant engineers and technicians and design and planning organization employees. In past years we have often encountered the totally unacceptable situation where new construction has begun without any designs, plans, or specifications.

We must ensure that cost estimates are completed within two months for priority construction projects and facilities to be completed in 1931. Until now a number of construction projects have not had completed and reviewed cost estimates. We must condemn any construction project which begins without an accurate cost estimate as a manifestation of mismanagement and a reckless attitude towards the resources of a proletarian country.

3. We must persistently eliminate any extravagances from construction projects by reviewing all cost estimates, first and foremost for the largest construction projects, in order to decisively eliminate overbuilding and needless expenditures of metal and concrete not dictated by any engineering requirements. In our new construction projects we must concentrate our resources on factory buildings, their equipment, and the construction of the necessary housing for the workers and factory schools.

The campaign to cut construction costs, eliminate extravagances, and give priority to factory and worker housing construction must become the mission of every manager, construction worker, engineer, and technician.

We must single out the issue of financial discipline in production and construction for special consideration. We need discipline in spending, which must be based on accurate estimates. We need regular and accurate reports. We need our managers to stick fast to their budgets for materials and money.

Until now, many builders have believed that their only responsibility is to turn over a completed construction project on time, while in fact they are directly accountable to the proletarian state for keeping accurate accounts of their expenditures, saving as much money as they can, completing their construction projects promptly and at low cost, and providing timely and accurate reports.

Many industrial managers have devoted far too little energy and attention to reducing the unit costs of production and improving product quality.

A 10% cut in the unit costs of production and a 12% reduction in construction costs are indispensable conditions for achieving the goals of the financial plan for industry.

In order to fulfill the plan for 1931, the sections of the *VSNKh* of the USSR shall take the following actions within the next few months:

1. The chief of the Construction Section, in cooperation with the appropriate manufacturing sectors, shall be responsible for monitoring the status and progress of designs, plans, and specifications. He shall submit a report to the Presidium of the Council on the status of designs, plans, and specifications for priority construction projects no later than February 1, 1931.

2. The chief of the Construction Section, with the assistance of the required number of engineers, shall review cost estimates to determine whether funds have been spent wisely and economically, starting with key projects. He shall submit a report to the Presidium every two months.

3. The chief of the Machinery Manufacture Section shall submit an equipment budget for major construction in 1931 no later than February 15. He shall review the plans of machinery manufacturing consortia to ensure that they will supply equipment on time to the construction projects scheduled to begin in 1931.

4. The chief of the Supply Section, in cooperation with the appropriate manufacturing sectors, shall examine the availability of materials and supplies for the coal industry and steel and iron industries with local spot checks in certain coal-producing districts and facilities over the next three months.

5. The chief of the Fuel and Power Sector, with the assistance of research institutes and fuel industry employees, shall conduct spot inspections of leading fuel consumers to determine whether they are complying with expenditure limits and fuel economy requirements. The first report shall be submitted on March 1.

6. Over the next four months, the Presidium shall hear reports from the chiefs of six major construction projects after members of the Presidium have first been dispatched to inspect the projects.

The colossal plan of production and construction in 1931 has imposed major responsibilities on all workers, shock workers, managers, engineers, and technicians.

The successful fulfillment of the 1931 plan will require us to meet specific quantity targets and work hard to meet the plan's quality targets (improving labor productivity and cutting unit costs) and improve product quality.

The fuel and metals sectors of the industrial front have been assigned an extremely critical mission. The success of the entire production plan depends on the aggressive efforts of the miners of the Donbass, the Urals, and the Kuzbass, the metalworkers of the Donbass and the Urals, the oil workers of Baku and Groznyi, and the employees of the peat industry. The tasks of these sectors have been made even more critical by the fact that they did not meet their special quarterly target, even though their output was higher than last year.

The fulfillment of all production targets, the fullest possible utilization of machinery, furnaces, and rolling mills, achievement of all quality goals, and raising the percentage of mechanized output to 80% of total output in the Donbass, 42% in the Eastern Coal Fields, and 53% in the Moscow Coal Fields, getting their heavy coal cutters to produce 2860 tons of coal per month in the Donbass, 2150 tons in the Urals, and 4000 tons in the Kuzbass, and improving the coefficient of utilization of blast furnace capacity to 1.25 in the South and 1.20 in the Urals (in terms of mineral fuel) are the primary battle missions of the fuel and metal sectors.

The performance of the <u>timber industry</u> must be dramatically improved, especially in light of its unsatisfactory performance with respect to the special quarterly plan. The success of the construction plan is highly dependent on the successful performance of the timber industry.

The working class achieved its major successes in the first two years of the five-year plan not by "inertia," but by fierce class struggle and surmounting difficulties. The 1931 plan will also not be achieved "spontaneously." We face major growing pains on the way to fulfilling this plan.

All managers should strive to encourage a new outburst of worker enthusiasm which will make the prospect of even more colossal achievements in 1931 inevitable and inspire more socialist competition, shock-worker ardor, and employee-sponsored production and financial plans. Without this we will not be able to solve our problems and fulfill the 1931 plan.

Faster rates of growth in socialist industry and the successful solution of our problems will require even more dramatic improvements in the quality of performance of all industrial sectors, hard and sustained efforts at all levels of management, and a fierce and determined effort to correct all our deficiencies in industrial performance.

The experience of the past year, especially the last quarter, has quite convincingly confirmed that the proper pace should be set at the very beginning of the year. The actions needed to establish and sustain this pace must be planned and taken in the first quarter, and the first quarter plan must be approved by the government at the same time as the yearly plan is approved. Successful fulfillment of the plan will require workers to concentrate on <u>a specific plan for every month and every day of work</u>, not just on the yearly plan in general. Unconditional fulfillment of the first quarter plan will lay the groundwork for further progress in the drive to fulfill the plan as a whole.

Socialist industry has extensive untapped potential for fulfilling the proposed plan.

A new upsurge in socialist competition and shock-worker enthusiasm should establish the foundations for even greater accomplishments in the new year of 1931.

Managers, shock workers, engineers, and technicians should be ready for the hard fight ahead to complete the foundations for the socialist economy of the USSR.

True Copy:

[handwritten annotation:]

1) Need to talk more forcefully about reducing production costs and not burdening enterprises with haphazard and unnecessary [illegible] of workers and office staff.

2) Need to say something about streamlined, timely implementation of inventions.

3) Need to add a point on one-man management and individual responsibility for efficient use of resources.

RTSKhIDNI, fond 558, op. 1, d. 2992, ll. 1–6.

Propaganda poster urging the Soviet nation to fulfill the Five-Year Plan in four years. Original in color. *5 in 4—for the general party line,* by Deni. Publisher: Ogiz-izogiz, Moscow-Leningrad, 1931. Prints and Photographs Division, Library of Congress.

Politburo meeting minutes, February 1, 1933, forbidding publication of five-year-plan results without approval of **Gosplan**

MINUTE No. 129
OF THE MEETING OF THE POLITICAL BUREAU [POLITBURO]
OF THE CENTRAL COMMITTEE
OF THE ALL-UNION COMMUNIST PARTY (BOLSHEVIK)
[*TSK VKP(b)*]
on FEBRUARY 1, 1933

PERSONS IN ATTENDANCE:

Members of the Politburo of the *TSK VKP(b)*:	Comrades Kalinin, Kuibyshev, Molotov, and Stalin
Candidates for Politburo Membership:	Comrade Mikoyan
Members of the *TSK VKP(b)*:	Comrades Bubnov, Zelenskii, Kviring, Knorin, Komarov, Krupskaia, Kubiak, Lebed', Lomov, Liubimov, Manuil'skii, Piatakov, Strievskii, Sulimov, Shvarts, Shvernik, IAkovlev.
Candidates for Membership in the *TSK VKP(b)*:	Comrades Bulat, Kalmanovich, Kiselev, Kosarev, Krinitskii, Mezhlauk, Nikolaeva, Osinskii, Perepechko, Polonskii, Popov, Serebrovskii, Sokol'nikov, Unshlikht, Chutskaev, Eliava, IAgoda
Members of Presidium of Central Control Commission [*TSKK*]:	Comrades Antipov, Belen'kii, Vermenichev, Enukidze, Nazaretian, Roizenman, Sol'ts, Ul'ianova, IAroslavskii

AGENDA

1. Item: The shortage of potassium chlorate for match factories
(Comrade Liubimov)

Decision: Instruct the Unified State Political Directorate [*OGPU*] to conduct an immediate investigation of the causes of the stoppages at the Berezniakov Factory, determine the guilty parties, and report their findings to the Politburo.

2. Item: The concentration of criminal elements in Magnitogorsk
(Telegram from Comrade Myshkov)
(Comrade Stalin)

Decision: Instruct the *OGPU* to assemble a special team of *OGPU* agents to purge Magnitogorsk of criminal and undesirable elements and inform the Politburo of the accomplishment of their mission. [break in the text]

15. Item: Deadlines for drafting the Second Five-Year Plan
(Politburo meeting of November 1, 1932, Minute No. 121, Item 13-f)
(Comrades Kuibyshev, Mezhlauk)

Decision: a) Instruct all people's commissariats and agencies to draft their own five-year plans for 1933–1937 and submit them to the USSR State Planning Committee [*Gosplan*] by March 10, 1933.

b) Require USSR *Gosplan* to submit a consolidated five-year plan for
1933–1937 to the Politburo for approval by April 10.

16. Item:	<u>Disclosure of classified information on the mining of gold and nonferrous metals</u> (Comrade Serebrovskii)
Decision:	a) Turn the case over to the *OGPU* for investigation b) Instruct the *OGPU* to arrest Shipek immediately c) Turn the matter of Simonov and Aleshin over to the *TSKK*
17. Item:	<u>The results of the first five-year plan</u> (Comrade Kuibyshev)
Decision:	1) Prior to the official publication by *Gosplan* of the results of the first five-year plan, forbid any agencies, republics, or regions from publishing any other reports, either consolidated or industrial and regional, and require that all other reports after the official publication of the results be published only with the permission of *Gosplan* 2) Require all agencies to forward all the material and reports on the results of the first five-year plan in their possession to *Gosplan* for its use in its own work and for the purpose of establishing a standard format for reports.
18. Item:	<u>The payment of accounts receivable and lottery winnings by agencies and organizations:</u> (Comrades Mekhlis and Popov)
Decision:	Turn over the matter for review to a commission consisting of Comrades Antipov, Mekhlis, Shvernik, Grin'ko, Zelenskii, and Piatakov. Commission coordinator: Comrade Antipov. Term of commission: ten days [break in the text]
121/103. Item:	<u>The case of the North Caucasus *Krai* Committee</u>
Decision:	Special file folder
122/104. Item:	<u>The permanent representative of the Transcaucasian Soviet Federated Socialist Republic to the Council of People's Commissars of the USSR</u> (Organizational Bureau, January 16, 1933, Minute No. 138, Item 32-*gs*)
Decision:	Grant the Transcaucasus *Krai* Committee its request to have Comrade A. Esaian appointed as the permanent representative to the Council of People's Commissars of the USSR and relieve Comrade G. S. Vashadze of these duties.
123/105. Item:	<u>Telegram from Comrade Shubrikov:</u>
Decision:	Accept the request of the Middle Volga *Krai* Committee to send Comrade Lazarev as the authorized representative of the People's Commissariat of Transportation Routes to Samara-Batraki Station instead of Kinel' Station.
124/106. Item:	<u>The authorized representative of the People's Commissariat of Transportation for Gorky *Krai*:</u>
Decision:	In amendment of Politburo Order No. 49-*opr.* of January 29, 1933, concerning Comrade Zashibaev, send Comrade T. Ostrovskii (deputy chairman of the Gorky *Krai* Executive Committee) to Arzamas as the authorized representative of the People's Commissariat of Transportation.

125/107. Item: Comrade Ikramov's leaving minutes of a Politburo meeting at the National Hotel:

Decision: Revoke Comrade Ikramov's authorization to receive minutes of *TSK* meetings for three months because of his unacceptable carelessness with *TSK* documents (he left minutes of a Politburo meeting behind in his room at the National Hotel when he left for Central Asia).

176*as/di* [Seal of *TSK*]

SECRETARY OF THE *TSK* [signed] J. Stalin

RTSKhIDNI, fond 17, op. 3, d. 914, ll. 1, 5, 28.

chapter 5

RELIGION

The Russian Orthodox Church was the established state church in the Russian Empire: the tsar served as "guardian of its dogmas," the state treasury subsidized its activities, and by law the Orthodox Church was the supreme religious institution of the country. Seventy percent of the inhabitants of the empire professed membership in the Church, which was a major economic and social presence as well. On the eve of the revolution it owned three million hectares of land, one-third of all primary schools in the empire, and sheltered ninety-five thousand religious persons in over one thousand monasteries and convents.

Other faiths were tolerated by the imperial government but none was given comparable privileges and status. Lutherans in Estonia and Latvia, Roman Catholics in Lithuania, Moslems in the Caucasus and Central Asia, and Jews were tolerated but not accorded special status. Numerous Protestant and Evangelical sects also competed for the allegiance of believers. Other religious denominations, including the Uniates in Ukraine, were subject to more severe persecution.

The Orthodox Church had faced challenges to its dominance even before the 1917 revolution: liberals called for a democratization of the church structure, others advocated a separation of church and state. The February Revolution of 1917 accelerated the movement for change: almost all political parties supported a formal separation of church and state, and the Provisional Government secularized the Church's parish schools in July of that year. Throughout the year, high-level church councils met to discuss an orderly transformation of the role played by the Orthodox Church in Russian public life. Divisions within the Church turned out to be acute: the conservative majority demanded that the Church retain its primacy among religious faiths in the new Russia. Orthodox teaching should be obligatory in all schools, ecclesiastical decisions should carry the force of law, the head of government must belong to the Orthodox faith. In October 1917 the conservative wing restored the office of Patriarch, liquidated by Peter the Great, as the head of the Orthodox Church. This led to a schism between the conservative majority and the liberal minority, who favored more democracy.

Bolshevik attitudes toward religion, as in other areas, were far from uniform. One view, shared by Lenin, saw religion as a product of economic exploitation; once the socialist transformation of society was complete, secularism would naturally replace religious faith. Many in the party recognized the strong appeal of spiritualism and the need to wean the population away from religion through persuasion and propaganda, not by coercion. The party's program of 1918 called for "systematic antireligious propaganda to free the masses from their prejudices, but without irritating the feelings of others." Other Bolsheviks, less patient with the survival of religious belief, were especially intolerant of the Orthodox Church's increasing leadership of the anti-Bolshevik movement. The new patriarch, Tikhon, pronounced anathema on the Bolsheviks in January 1918, as henchmen of Satan who would "burn in hellfire in the life hereafter and be cursed for generations." The conflict between supporters of gradual, culturalist measures to eradicate religion and supporters of vigorous intervention against all manifestations of religious life would characterize Soviet religious policy throughout its history.

The State and Religion

Initial Bolshevik policy toward religion relied on law as an instrument of revolutionary change, and it targeted the church as an institution rather than the personal beliefs of individuals. The January 1918 decree on religion laid down the new ground rules for the relationship between church and state: faith was a matter of individual conscience, neither to be punished nor rewarded. State subsidies were withdrawn from religious institutions, and church property was nationalized. Church leaders naturally saw these measures as an attempt to destroy religion, not just to place it on an equal footing with other civic organizations.

At the same time, the regime was quick to exploit the existing divisions within the Church and in organized religion. Some clergy had openly supported the White opposition to the Bolsheviks, appealing for support against the "Jewish-Masonic slavemasters." Patriarch Tikhon refrained from rallying open opposition to the Bolsheviks, calling on the faithful to resist by spiritual means. The more liberal leaders of the church believed an accommodation could be found with the Communists, and they entered into negotiations in 1919 with some of the party's leaders about an eventual accord.

The event that crystallized these divisions was the state order to confiscate Church valuables in order to aid the starving victims of the Volga area famine in 1922. Since 1921 the Church had organized collections for the relief of the starving, and Tikhon called on the parish churches to sacrifice for famine victims all articles of value, except those used in sacraments. The government at first supported this measure, but then on February 28, 1922, ordered <u>all</u> items of value to be confiscated. Church resistance to the order could be now labeled as callous indifference to the needs of the suffering. The party sent police and army activists to begin to remove the valuables; in the town of Shuia, in Kostroma province north of Moscow, this action provoked violent resistance. Lenin used this incident to provide an excuse to launch a new attack on "Black Hundreds'" resistance to Soviet rule, to be publicly headed by the ethnic Russian Kalinin (Document 195). Trotsky, as a Jew, was ordered to remain in the background. Over one thousand additional incidents of resistance were reported in the press. Church leaders who supported the resistance to the confiscation of church valuables, such as Metropolitan Veniamin of Petrograd, were tried and executed.

Church liberals now attacked the patriarch for not volunteering the Church's resources to aid the famine victims. Known collectively as the Renovationists, the liberals represented three major branches of the antipatriarch schism: the Living Church, the Union of Communities of Ancient Apostolic Churches, and the Union for Church Renovation. When Tikhon was placed under house arrest for resisting the Church valuables confiscation, the Renovationists assumed the leadership of the Church, called their own council, and made peace with the Communists. Lenin was hailed as a "great fighter for truth," and Tikhon was stripped of his titles and his monastic status. Priests loyal to Tikhon were steadily replaced with supporters of the Renovationists; by 1925 some two-thirds of all parishes had been formally won over to the Living Church.

Meanwhile, Tikhon, still under house arrest, decided to make his own peace with the Communists, and in June 1923 he confessed his errors and was released from house arrest. This permitted him to wage a struggle against the Renovationists for control of the Orthodox Church, the net effect of which was to weaken the authority of all organized Orthodoxy inside the Soviet Union.

Throughout the 1920s the regime continued its policy of propaganda and selective accommodation with various religious institutions. Disturbances of a religious nature were closely monitored. Alternatives to religion traditional to Russia, such as the Baptists and other evangelical groups, received government sanction as a further means to weaken the power of the Orthodox Church. The collectivization and anti-*kulak* campaign of 1929–30 brought this policy of toleration to a sudden end: exorbitant taxes were levied against priests and parishes, and failure to pay brought arrest and the closing of churches. Church bells were seized to be melted down and used in the industrialization effort. Priests and *kulak*s who voiced any resistance were tarred with the same brush as "counterrevolutionaries." By 1933, only one hundred open churches remained in Moscow out of nearly six hundred that had operated in the early 1920s. By 1939 something like two percent of the 1920 level of churches remained operating (fewer than one thousand), and some scholars estimate that as many as forty-two thousand Orthodox clergy had been executed between 1918 and the late 1930s.

The German invasion of the Soviet Union brought a sudden reversal in the regime's antireligious policy. The Orthodox Church vocally supported the Soviet war effort, and in 1943 the Patriarchate was revived. Some twenty thousand churches were permitted to re-open, and parish priests were recognized as responsible for the spiritual welfare of their parishioners and for the preservation of church properties. After the war the regime continued to promote secularization through education and propaganda, but it also tolerated local religious activity. Then in 1961 came another reversal: parish priests lost their jurisdiction over church properties, and a new wave of church closings ensued, allegedly at the request of local parishes that wished to assign their buildings to other, secular uses. The state also strengthened its control over non-Orthodox groups such as the Evangelical Christians and Baptists.

Religious resistance to these measures coalesced with the growing dissident movements in the 1960s, 1970s, and 1980s among intellectuals and nationalist groups, and the regime applied the same selective policies of partial accommodation, propaganda, and repression towards all of them. In the interests of détente with Western powers, the Soviet state attempted to advertise its religious toleration by sending delegations of loyal churchmen abroad. Meanwhile, signs of the persistence and revival of religious belief gained increasing visibility, especially in the Islamic republics of Central Asia and in the Baltic republics, where religion and national identity reinforced one another. When Gorbachev assumed the party leadership in 1985, he cautiously instituted a program of religious reform. For example, in 1988, he openly embraced the one-thousandth anniversary of the coming of Christianity to Russia, and he instituted the orderly return of churches to their congregations.

Decree of January 19, 1918, on freedom of conscience and on church and religious societies

Minutes No. 52
Point 2.

Confirmed at the meeting of the Collegium of the People's Commissariat of Justice, January 19, 1918.
Signed: M. Reisner.
True copy: Department worker, [illegible signature]

[Partly legible stamp in upper left:]
    Administration of Peasant Affairs
    Republic of Russia
    January 19, 1918
    Entry. No. 5354

DECREE
on freedom of conscience and of religious organizations.

1.   There is a separation of Church and State. [Original overstruck text:] Religion is a private matter for each citizen of the Russian Republic.

2.   Republics are forbidden to make any local laws or resolutions that restrict or limit freedom of conscience or to establish any advantages or privileges based on the religious affiliation of a citizen.

3.   A citizen can profess any religion or none. All legal restrictions on the profession or nonprofession of any particular faith are repealed. [Handwritten:] Addendum: All indications of religious affiliation or nonaffiliation on official documents are to be eliminated [overstruck:] forever.

4.   The activity of state or other public/legal civic institutions will not include any religious rituals or ceremonies.

5.   The free conduct of religious rituals will be permitted only insofar as they do not disturb the civic order and do not interfere with the rights of citizens and the [handwritten insertion] Soviet Republics. Local governments have the right in such cases to take any necessary measures to ensure public order and security.

6.   No one has the right, based on his religious views, to evade fulfillment of his civic duties. Exceptions to this rule or substitution of one civic duty for another will be permitted as decided by a people's court.

7.   Religious vows or oaths are abolished. If necessary, only a solemn promise will be given.

8.   Civil matters are conducted exclusively by the state, by the Departments of Records for Marriages and Births [overstruck:] and Deaths.

9.   Schools are to be separate from the church. The teaching of religious beliefs in all state and social organizations and also private educational institutions, in which general education takes place, is forbidden. Citizens may engage in religious teaching and learning on a private basis.

10.   All church and religious societies will be subject to general resolutions on private organizations and unions, and do not enjoy any special advantages or subsidies from the State or from any of its local autonomous and self-governing institutions.

11.   Compulsory collection of church donations or taxes for the use of church or religious organizations, which are equivalent to compulsory measures or penalties imposed by these organizations on their members, are not permitted.

12.   No church or religious organization may possess private property. They do not have the rights of legal persons.

13. All properties of churches and religious organizations in Russia are declared to be public property. The buildings and articles which are used specifically in the performance of religious services may be used free of charge by religious organizations, in accordance with special resolutions of the local or central government. [Original overstruck text:] The manner of accounting, storing, and disposing of buildings and articles used specifically for performing religious services is to be determined by resolutions of the local and central governments.

Chairman of the Council of People's Commissars
I. Ul'ianov (Lenin)

[signed] N. Podvoiskii   V. Algasov   V. Trutovskii   A.Shlikhter   N. Prosh'ian
Manager of government
   affairs Vlad. Bonch-Bruevich

V. Menzhinskii
A. Shliapnikov

Secretary of the Council of People's
   Commissars   N. Gorbunov

T. Petrovskii

Petrograd
20 Jan. 1918

RTSKhIDNI, fond 2, op. 1, d. 5212, ll. 1–3.

DOCUMENT 193   *Minutes of a Politburo meeting, March 11, 1922, discussing the removal of valuables from Moscow churches*

Proletarians of All Countries, Unite!   <u>Strictly Secret</u>

Russian Communist Party (Bolsheviks) CENTRAL COMMITTEE

No. P111/39

Excerpt from meeting no. 111 of the Politburo of the Central Committee [*TSK*] of the All-Union Communist Party (Bolsheviks) [*VKP(b)*] March 13, 1922

<u>By consultation with members of the Politburo on March 11, 1922.</u>

39. <u>The approval of a commission on removal of property of value from Moscow churches.</u>

    To approve the commission composed of Comrade Sapronov, chairman; members: Comrades Unshlikht (deputy), Medved', Samoilova-Zemliachka, and Galkin.

SECRETARY OF THE *TSK*

<u>Copy</u>

TO MEMBERS OF THE POLITBURO
TO COMRADES LENIN, MOLOTOV, KAMENEV, STALIN

    Work on the removal of property of value from Moscow churches has gone utterly awry due to the fact that, along with the commission that was established earlier, the Presidium of the All-Russian Central Executive Committee [*VTSIK*] has formed its own commission, with representatives from the Committee for Famine Relief [*Pomgol*] and the chairmen of the *Guberniia* Executive Committees and the *Guberniia* Finance Departments. Yesterday at a meeting of my commission, composed of Comrades Trotsky, Bazilevich, Galkin, Lebedev, Unshlikht, Samoilova-Zemliachka, Krasikov, Krasnoshchekov, and Sapronov we came to a unanimous conclusion on the need to form in Moscow a shock commission composed of: chairman — Comrade Sapronov; members: Comrade Unshlikht (deputy: Medved'), Samoilova-Zemliachka, and Galkin. This commission must simultaneously prepare in secret the political, organizational, and technical aspects of the affair. The actual removal should still begin in the month of March and finish in the shortest time. All that is required is that the Presidium of the *VTSIK*, the Presidium of the Moscow Soviet, and the Central Committee of the *Pomgol* should acknowledge this commission as the sole one in this affair and assist it in every manner. I repeat, this commission is completely secret, the formal removal in Moscow will come directly from the Central Committee of the *Pomgol*, where Comrade Sapronov will have his own office hours.

I request the fastest approval of this resolution, as necessary for all in order to avoid any possible further confusion.

L. Trotsky.

True copy: [illegible]

Source?

DOCUMENT 194   *Telegram from the Ivanovo-Voznesensk* Guberniia *Party Committee to the Central Committee, March 18, 1922, on the outbreak of violence in reaction to the confiscation of Church valuables in the town of Shuia*

Coded Telegram

From Ivanovo-Voznesensk
Received for decoding: March 18, 1922, at 11:30 A.M.
Entry no. 523/sh of the Encoding Section of the Central Committee of the Russian
Communist Party [*TSK RKP*]

Received by Balagurovskaia

MOSCOW *TSK RKP*

March 17, 1922. The *Guberniia* Committee [*Gubkom*] reports that in Shuia on March 15, in connection with the removal of property of value from the churches, police and a Red Army platoon were attacked by a mob influenced by priests, monarchists, and Socialist Revolutionaries. Some Red Army soldiers were disarmed by the demonstrators. The crowd was dispersed with machine guns and rifles by units of the Special Forces Units [*ChON*] and soldiers from the 146th regiment of the Red Army. As a result, 5 dead and 15 wounded were registered at the hospital. Among those killed was a soldier of the Relief Division of the Red Cavalry. At 11:30 A.M. on March 15, 2 factories rose up for this same reason. By evening order was restored in the city. On the morning of the 16th the factory workers returned to work as usual. The mood of the inhabitants and some of the factory workers is sullen but not volatile. The *Guberniia* Executive Committee has appointed a special commission to investigate the events. Details in letter [to follow]. No. 4

SECRETARY of the *GUBERNIIA* COMMITTEE KOROTKOV

Encoded SOKOLOV

Source?

Workmen removing bells from one of many churches destroyed in the 1920s. TSGAKFD. N 124804.

Copy

To Comrade Molotov   Strictly Secret
For members of the Politburo

Please make no copies for any reason. Each member of the Politburo (incl. Comrade Kalinin) should comment directly on the document. Lenin.

In regard to the occurrence at Shuia, which is already slated for discussion by the Politburo, it is necessary right now to make a firm decision about a general plan of action in the present course. Because I doubt that I will be able to attend the Politburo meeting on March 20 in person, I will set down my thoughts in writing.

The event at Shuia should be connected with the announcement that the Russian Telegraph Agency [ROSTA] recently sent to the newspapers but that was not for publication, namely, the announcement that the Black Hundreds in Petrograd [Piter] were preparing to defy the decree on the removal of valuable property from the churches. If this fact is compared with what the papers report about the attitude of the clergy to the decree on the removal of church valuables, in addition to what we know about the illegal proclamation of Patriarch Tikhon, then it becomes perfectly clear that the Black Hundreds' clergy, headed by its leader, with full deliberation is carrying out a plan at this very moment to destroy us decisively.

It is obvious that the most influential group of the Black Hundreds' clergy conceived this plan in secret meetings and that it was accepted with sufficient resolution. The events in Shuia are only one manifestation and actualization of this general plan.

I think that here our opponent is making a huge strategic error by attempting to draw us into a decisive struggle now when it is especially hopeless and especially disadvantageous to him. For us, on the other hand, precisely at the present moment we are presented with an exceptionally favorable, even unique, opportunity when we can 99 times out of 100 utterly defeat our enemy with complete success and guarantee for ourselves the position we require for decades. Now and only now, when people are being eaten in famine-stricken areas, and hundreds, if not thousands, of corpses lie on the roads, we can (and therefore must) pursue the removal of church valuables with the most frenzied and ruthless energy and not hesitate to put down the least opposition. Now and only now, the vast majority of peasants will either be on our side, or at least will not be in a position to support to any decisive degree this handful of Black Hundreds' clergy and reactionary urban petty bourgeoisie, who are willing and able to attempt to oppose this Soviet decree with a policy of force.

We must pursue the removal of church valuables by the most decisive and rapid fashion in order to secure for ourselves a fund of several hundred million gold rubles (do not forget the immense wealth of some monasteries and abbeys). Without this fund any government work in general, any economic build-up in particular, and any upholding of our positions at Genoa especially, are completely unthinkable. In order to get our hands on this fund of several hundred million gold rubles (and perhaps even several hundred billion), we must do whatever is necessary. But to do this successfully is possible only now. All considerations indicate that later on we will fail to do this, for no other time, besides that of desperate famine, will give us such a mood among the general mass of peasants that would ensure us the sympathy of this group or, at least, would ensure us the neutralization of this group in the sense that victory in the struggle for the removal of church valuables unquestionably and completely will be on our side.

One clever writer on statecraft correctly said that if it is necessary for the realization of a well-known political goal to perform a series of brutal actions, then it is necessary to do them in the most energetic manner and in the shortest time, because masses of people will not tolerate the protracted use of brutality. This observation in particular is further strengthened because harsh measures against a reactionary clergy will be politically impractical, possibly even extremely dangerous, as a result of the international situation in which we in Russia, in all probability, will find ourselves, or may find ourselves, after Genoa. Now victory over the reactionary clergy is assured for us completely. In addition, it will be more difficult for the major part of our foreign adversaries among the Russian emigres abroad, i.e., the Socialist Revolutionaries and the Miliukovites, to fight against us if we, precisely at this time, precisely in connection with the famine, suppress the reactionary clergy with utmost haste and ruthlessness.

Therefore, I come to the indisputable conclusion that we must precisely now smash the Black Hundreds' clergy most decisively and ruthlessly and put down all resistance with such brutality that they will not forget it for several decades.

The campaign itself for carrying out this plan I envision in the following manner:

Only Comrade Kalinin should appear officially in regard to any measures taken. Never and under no circumstance must Comrade Trotsky write anything for the press or in any other way appear before the public.

The telegram already issued in the name of the Politburo about the temporary suspension of confiscations must not be rescinded. It is useful for us because it gives our adversary the impression that we are vacillating, that he has succeeded in confusing us (our adversary, of course, will quickly find out about this secret telegram precisely because it is secret).

Send to Shuia one of the most energetic, clear-headed, and capable members of the All-Russian Central Executive Committee [VTSIK] or some other representative of the central government (one is better than several), giving him verbal instructions through one of the members of the Politburo. The instructions must come down to this, that in Shuia he must arrest more, if possible, but not less, than several dozen representatives of the local clergy, the local petty bourgeoisie, and the local bourgeoisie on suspicion of direct or indirect participation in the forcible resistance to the decree of the VTSIK on the removal of valuables from churches. Immediately upon completion of this task, he must return to Moscow and personally deliver a report to the full session of the Politburo or to two specially authorized members of the Politburo. On the basis of this report, the Politburo will give a detailed directive to the judicial authorities, also verbal, that the trial of the insurrectionists from Shuia, for opposing aid to the starving, should be carried out in utmost haste and should end not other than with the shooting of a very large number of the most influential and dangerous of the Black Hundreds in Shuia, and, if possible, not only in this city but even in Moscow and several other ecclesiastical centers.

I think that it is advisable for us not to touch Patriarch Tikhon himself, even though he undoubtedly headed this whole revolt of slaveholders. Concerning him, the State Political Administration [GPU] must be given a secret directive that precisely at this time all communications of this personage must be monitored and their contents disclosed in all possible accuracy and detail. Require Dzerzhinsky and Unshlikht personally to report to the Politburo about this weekly.

At the party congress arrange a secret meeting of all or almost all delegates to discuss this matter jointly with the chief workers of the GPU, the People's Commissariat of Justice [NKIU], and the Revolutionary Tribunal. At this meeting pass a secret resolution of the congress that the removal of valuables, especially from the very richest abbeys, monasteries, and churches, must be carried out with ruthless resolution, leaving nothing in doubt, and in the very shortest time. The greater the number of representatives of the reactionary clergy and the reactionary bourgeoisie that we succeed in shooting on this occasion, the better because this "audience" must precisely now be taught a lesson in such a way that they will not dare to think about any resistance whatsoever for several decades.

To supervise the quickest and most successful carrying out of these measures, there at the congress, i.e., at the secret meeting, appoint a special commission, with the required participation of Comrade Trotsky and Comrade Kalinin, without giving any publicity to this commission, with the purpose that the subordination to it of all operations would be provided for and carried out not in the name of the commission but as an all-Soviet and all-party procedure. Appoint those who are especially responsible from among the best workers to carry out these measures in the wealthiest abbeys, monasteries, and churches.

Lenin.

March 19, 1922.

I request that Comrade Molotov attempt to circulate this letter to the members of the Politburo by evening today (not making copies) and ask them to return it to the secretary immediately after reading it with a succinct note regarding whether each member of the Politburo agrees in principle or if the letter arouses any differences of opinion.

Lenin.

A note in the hand of Comrade Molotov:

"Agreed. However, I propose to extend the campaign not to all *guberniia*s and cities, but to those where indeed there are considerable possessions of value, accordingly concentrating the forces and attention of the party.

March 19. Molotov."

True copy: [illegible]

The original has been transferred to the Lenin Institute.

Source?

DOCUMENT 196   *Letter from Foreign Minister Chicherin to Stalin, April 10, 1923, arguing against a death sentence for Patriarch Tikhon because of likely negative international consequences*

April 10, 1923.

To Comrade S T A L I N, Secretary of the Central Committee, Russian Communist Party.

Dear Comrade,

The People's Commissariat of Foreign Affairs urges the Politburo to decide in advance against the death sentence for Tikhon. The facts have shown how much harm we have brought on ourselves by the execution of Butkevich. In America, Senator Bohr and his supporters have proposed to form a committee to work for reestablishing relations with Russia, but in view of the very unpleasant situation caused by Butkevich's execution, they have decided to hold off temporarily on this and not to form a committee. In the weeks ahead, Senator Bohr will not appear publicly in support of reestablishing relations with Russia. The proposed meeting of Bohr with Hughes never occurred. In England, as is well known, Morel deferred his speech to Parliament supporting our recognition. The large number of resolutions from workers' organizations received in the English Parliament, demanding intercession for TSepliak and Butkevich, has shown the extent to which this affair is being used by our enemies—particularly by moderate socialists and trade unionists—to make us even more unpopular. An English radio announcement about the French rejection of a Russian invitation for a follow-up on the Lausanne Conference, in view of the execution of Butkevich—demands cautious treatment but in any event shows the inclination of England to use widely this incident against us—not to mention how in the case of conflict with Poland our enemies now possess marvelous weapons to drum up fanaticism against us among the Polish peasantry. Everyone who knows even a little something about what's going on on the other side of the border posts can affirm that in everything our situation has gotten markedly worse as a result of this affair. And in the Butkevich affair we can allude to Polish espionage and a link with aggressive Polish chauvinism. In the Tikhon matter this will not be the case.

All the other countries see in his sentence nothing other than naked religious persecution. The Anglo-Saxon countries, totally hypocritical from top to bottom, are no less interested in Orthodoxy than they are in Catholicism; Anglicanism considers itself even closer to Orthodoxy. In a word, pronouncing the death sentence in the case of Tikhon would worsen to an even greater extent our international standing in all our relations. To pronounce the death sentence and then change it under the influence of other nations would be most disadvantageous for us and to a great extent would leave a bad impression. We propose therefore to reject in advance the death sentence for Tikhon.

With communist greetings,

ChIChERIN

TSGAOR, fond 5446, op. 55, d. 409, ll. 1–110.

DOCUMENT 197   *Minutes of the June 12, 1923, and September 18, 1923, meetings of the Central Committee's commission on the separation of Church and State, including the matter of Patriach Tikhon*

TOP SECRET
For Secret Storage

MINUTES no.24

Meeting of the Commission for Implementing
Separation of Church from State

Central Committee, Russian Communist Party [*TSK RKP*]
June 12, 1923

Attending: IAroslavskii, Menzhinskii, Popov, Tuchkov.

Agenda: 1. On Tikhon
          2. On Old Believers
          3. On Prokhanov
          4. On [the journal] *Bezbozhnik*
          5. On church holidays

          Old business: On Caucasian Molokans

Decisions:

I. On Tikhon.

1. The investigation of the Tikhon affair must be carried on with no time limit.

2. To inform Tikhon that, regarding his case, the length of his incarceration can be changed on condition that (a) he make a special statement that he repents the crimes he has committed against the Soviet government and the working and peasant masses and express loyalty to the Soviet government; (b) that he recognize as just his arraignment in court for those crimes; (c) that he openly and abruptly distance himself from all counterrevolutionary organizations, particularly from White Guard and monarchist organizations, whether secular or spiritual; (d) that he express a sharply negative attitude toward the [Sremski] Karlovci Conference and its participants; (e) that he announce his negative attitude toward the intrigues of the Catholic clergy and also of the Bishop of Canterbury and Patriarch Meletios of Constantinople; (f) that he express agreement with certain reforms in the religious sphere, e.g., the new calendar.

Patriarch Tikhon, 1917. TSGAKFD

3. If he agrees, to free him and transfer him to the Valaam Monastery, with no prohibition on his religious activities.

II. On the Old Believers: To permit the Old Believers, following the example of the Renovationists, to organize in Moscow a central administrative office, and to delegate Comrade Tuchkov to keep abreast of its activities.

III. On Prokhanov: To approve the proposal of the State Political Administration [*GPU*] for the disintegration of the sectarians. [revised text illegible]

IV. On the journal *Bezbozhnik:* To propose that each member of the Antireligious Commission write each month not less than two articles for *Bezbozhnik.*

V. On church holidays in the new calendar: The same number of church holidays should be established as last year.

VI. On the Molokans in the Caucasus: To delegate Comrade Tuchkov to negotiate on this matter personally with Comrade Mogilevskii, currently in Moscow.

The next meeting of the commission will be on Tuesday, June 19, 1923.

> [signed] IAroslavskii
> Chair of the Commission
>
> [signed] Tuchkov
> Secretary of the Commission

June 14, 1923.

TOP SECRET
KEEP SECRET

MINUTES No. 33
OF THE MEETING OF THE COMMISSION FOR
IMPLEMENTING THE SEPARATION OF CHURCH AND STATE
OF THE *TSK RKP*
ON AUGUST 5, 1923

PERSONS IN ATTENDANCE: Comrades IAROSLAVSKII, MENZhINSKII, AND TUChKOV

Agenda:

1. Putting Patriarch Tikhon on trial
2. The protest by the Main Office for Protecting State Secrets in the Press [*Glavlit*] concerning the confiscation of Tikhon's proclamation.
3. Inaccurate newspaper reports of Tikhon's rearrest
4. The nonparty *Ateist* [Atheist] Society
5. The incorrect line adopted by Petrograd newspapers concerning Tikhon's release.
6. Review of a draft of guidelines for the registration of communities of Orthodox believers.
7. Appeals and proclamations

ITEM	CONCLUSIONS AND DECISIONS
1. Putting Patriarch Tikhon on trial	1) Tikhon's release has caused absolute turmoil in the monarchist and White Guard ranks. 2) Tikhon's release has allowed us to expose the most prominent Black Hundreds' members, who have already begun to distance themselves from Tikhon as a result of his current attitude towards Soviet power. 3) The antagonism between Tikhon's followers and the

Renovationists has intensified, thus causing a great scandal in the church.

4) The antagonism between Tikhon's followers and the Renovationists aggravated by Tikhon's release has led to an official schism within the church.

5) The recent split between Tikhon's followers and the Renovationists is based on each side's accusations that the other has done more harm to Soviet power and that its side has done more to benefit Soviet power.

6) The conflict between these two currents is just beginning to unfold.

7) Putting Tikhon on trial right now would give him an aura of martyrdom, which could be totally removed by his subsequent collaboration with Soviet power.

8) We need to keep the threat of a trial hanging over Tikhon. Therefore, the commission deems it inappropriate to put him on trial right now.

2. The *Glavlit* protest concerning the confiscation of Tikhon's proclamation

2. a) Instruct the head of *Glavlit* to submit all materials of a religious nature (proclamations, missives, pamphlets, and so forth) to Comrade Tuchkov, a member of the commission, for preliminary review in Comrade Popov's absence.

b) The confiscation of Tikhon's proclamation was proper.

3. Inaccurate newspaper reports of Tikhon's rearrest

3. In light of the reports which have appeared in certain provincial newspapers (*Krasnyi Sever*, No. 18, Vologda) indicating that Tikhon has been rearrested, instruct Comrade Tuchkov to determine the source of these reports and take steps to correct the problem.

4. The nonparty *Ateist* Society

4. Instruct the founders of this society to submit their plans in accordance with the general procedure through the People's Commissariat of Internal Affairs.

5. The incorrect line adopted by Petrograd newspapers concerning Tikhon's release

5. Bring the incorrect line of supporting Tikhon and opposing the Renovationists adopted by the Petrograd newspapers and party publications to the attention of the head of the Agitation and Propaganda Department.

6. Review of a draft of guidelines for the registration of communities of Orthodox believers

6. Approve the guidelines and submit them forthwith to the Politburo after first consulting with the *NKVD* and People's Commissariat of Justice.

7. Appeals and proclamations

7. Instruct Comrade Tuchkov to distribute copies of appeals and proclamations to all members of the commission prior to publication.

Chairman of the Commission   [signed] IAroslavskii
Secretary of the Commission   [signed] Tuchkov

         True copy:

MINUTES No. 36

OF THE MEETING OF THE COMMISSION FOR
IMPLEMENTING THE SEPARATION OF CHURCH AND STATE
OF THE *TSK RKP*
September 18, 1923

PERSONS IN ATTENDANCE: Comrades IAroslavskii, Popov, Smidovich,
Krasikov, Menzhinskii, Tuchkov

Agenda:

1) The newspaper *Bezbozhnik*
2) Tikhon
3) The Russian Telegraph Agency [*ROSTA*]
4) Miletius's ecumenical patriarchate
5) Review of resolution of Kharkov *Guberniia* Committee concerning sectarians
6) Application of Baptists for permission to hold an all-Russian congress on October 30
7) Allowing priests in exile to conduct church services
8) Review of the Charter of the League of Active Atheists
9) Appeal of Archangel *Guberniia* Executive Committee to evict monks from the Solovki Monastery
10) Permitting German Baptists to hold an All-Russian congress in Odessa
11) Permitting the Baptists to publish a German-language magazine
12) Permitting Antonin to publish a leaflet
13) Comrade Krasikov's report on his conversation with the American senators
14) The congress of the evangelicals
15) Permitting evangelicals to obtain Bibles, Gospels, and hymnbooks from foreign countries on the basis of their application addressed to Comrade Smidovich

ITEM	CONCLUSIONS AND DECISIONS
1) The newspaper *Bezbozhnik*	1) In view of Comrade Galkin's illness, turn over the task of editing the newspaper to Comrade Popov and instruct him to hire appropriate comrades for the job. Instruct Comrade IAroslavskii to review the guidelines and the articles.
2) Tikhon (Comrade Tuchkov's report)	2) Take the report into consideration. Recommend that Tikhon and Company adopt a new style in church affairs, disband the parish councils, and allow priests to divorce and remarry, for which purpose they will be allowed to publish a journal.
3) The Russian Telegraph Agency	3) Emphasize to the Russian Telegraph Agency that no reports on church officials may be published without the preliminary approval of Comrade Popov.
4) Miletius's ecumenical patriarchate	4) Instruct Comrade Popov to hold discussions with Comrade Chicherin on the situation of Miletius and the Constantinople Synod and on this basis resolve the issue of returning the building in Moscow to representatives of the Synod.

5) Review of resolution of Kharkov *Guberniia* Committee concerning sectarians	5) Assign Comrade Popov the task of instructing the Kharkov *Guberniia* Committee to refrain from persecuting the sectarians by imposing oppressive taxes on them and also refrain from extending the terms of military conscript service of these individuals.
6) Application of Baptists for permission to hold a congress on October 30	6) Grant permission.
7) Allowing priests in exile to conduct church services	7) Allow the Synod and Patriarch Tikhon to decide the issue on a case-by-case basis.
8) Review of the Charter of the League of Active Atheists	8) Instruct Comrade Tuchkov to distribute copies of the charter to all members of the commission and raise the issue of approving the charter at the commission's next meeting.
9) Appeal of Archangel *Guberniia* Executive Committee to evict monks from the Solovki Monastery	9) Deem the eviction of the monks from Solovki feasible, but require that the monks be relocated within the Archangel *Guberniia*.
10) Permitting German Baptists to hold an All-Russian congress in Odessa	10) Authorize the congress on a contingency basis depending on the results of the All-Russian congress in Moscow
11) Permitting the Baptists to publish a German-language magazine	11) " "
12) Permitting Antonin to publish a leaflet	12) Instruct Comrades Popov and Tuchkov to review the leaflet and decide whether it may be published or not
13) Comrade Krasikov's report on his conversation with the American senators	13) Take the report into consideration. Instruct Comrade Menzhinskii to provide information to Comrade Krasikov on the number of church officials in exile
14) The congress of the evangelicals	14) Instruct Comrade Popov to insert several articles and the most important resolutions adopted by the congress in the press.
15) Permitting evangelicals to obtain Bibles, Gospels, and hymnbooks from foreign countries on the basis of their application addressed to Comrade Smidovich	15) Grant permission.

The Commission will hold its next meeting on Tuesday, September 25, 1923.

        September 19, 1923

        Chairman of the Commission
        [signed] IAroslavskii

Secretary of the Commission[signed] Tuchkov

True copy:

RTSKhIDNI, fond 89, op. 4, d. 118, ll. 4–6.

DOCUMENT 198   *Patriarch Tikhon's declaration of June 16, 1923, to the Russian Supreme Court*

Copy

To the Supreme Court of the RSFSR

From imprisoned Patriarch Tikhon (Vasilii Ivanovich Bellavin)

DECLARATION

Addressing with this declaration the RSFSR Supreme Court, I believe it the duty of my pastoral conscience to report the following:

Being educated in a monarchist society and being up to the very time of my arrest under the influence of anti-Soviet individuals, I actually was antagonistic toward the Soviet government, and this hostility from time to time has changed from a passive state to actions such as: a declaration on the occasion of signing the Treaty of Brest-Litovsk in 1918, anathematizing the government in the same year, and, finally, a proclamation against the Decree on confiscation of Church valuables in 1922. All my anti-Soviet actions, with a few inaccuracies, are described in the indictment issued by the Supreme Court. Recognizing the correctness of the court's decision to bring me to account for alleged violation of articles of the Criminal Code for anti-Soviet activity, I repent my offenses against the governmental system and ask the Supreme Court to change the circumstances of my punishment, i.e., to release me from prison.

With this I declare to the Supreme Court that I am not an enemy of the Soviet government any longer, and I definitively and utterly dissociate myself from external as well as internal Monarchist-White Guard counter-revolution.

Patriarch Vasilii Bellavin Tikhon

June 16, 1923.   [signed]

[handwritten: Received 6/20]
[signed] V. Sotskov

RTSKhIDNI, fond 78, op. 7, d. 172, l. 48.

DOCUMENT 199   *Communication by a delegation of the Holy Synod of the Orthodox Church, October 28, 1924, to A. I. Rykov concerning the counterrevolutionary activities of former Patriarch Tikhon*

USSR
Secretariat of the Chairman of the Council of People's Commissars
A. I. Rykov
October 28, 1924

SECRET

To Comrade Smidovich.

The Synod has phoned and asked Comrade Rykov to receive a delegation including Metropolitan Veniamin, Serafim, Archpriest P. Krasotin, and legal adviser A. I. Novikov.

The topic of discussion is presented in the attached statement.

Comrade Rykov requests your response to this statement.

The delegation insists on the soonest possible reception.

Please return the attached document with your response.

Manager of the Secretariat of the Chairman of the USSR Council of People's Commissars - NESTEROV.

True copy: [signed] M. Levitskaia

. . . .

In 1922 a remarkable event occurred in the Russian Orthodox Church. Ideological members of the Church, under the direction of canonically sanctioned bishops and priests, suspended communion with Patriarch TIKhON. The reason for this schism was TIKhON's anti-Soviet policy, which was equally harmful to civil tranquility and the welfare of the Church. TIKhON was forced to resign. The All-Russian Council of 1923 and the Council of Eastern Bishops in Constantinople on May 3, 1924, sanctioned TIKhON's removal. Henceforth, he is not the patriarch, but the defrocked layman VASILII BEL[L]AVIN.

TIKhON has not submitted to the decision of the Council of the Russian and Greek Church. Without official sanction he heads congregations that have remained loyal to him. From the Church's point of view he is a serious criminal, shattering Church tranquillity, and likewise [he is a criminal] from the state's point of view. TIKhON is particularly harmful, for Tikhonism is an ecclesiastic curse splitting the Church and a curse on the state because all the counterrevolutionary forces of the country from monarchists to Mensheviks are uniting around TIKhON.

The Holy Synod, safeguarding the Church and filled with sincere civil loyalty to Soviet authority, and having expressed true freedom of conscience with its decree on the separation of church and state, is conducting a tireless battle against Tikhonism, which is both a church and a state evil.

Tikhonism poses three obstacles for us: our non-Orthodoxy, our economic weakness, our loyalty to Soviet Rule. The first two factors we can neutralize, more or less. The Renovationists in the past months have established ties with other Eastern Orthodox churches, and a number of publications by Renovationist scholars have clarified the canonicity of the movement. This all has enormous significance in the eyes of true believers who were frightened by our perceived non-Orthodoxy, which we have now debunked quite authoritatively.

Tikhonism is hurting us economically. Their strength in this regard is enormous. The Tikhonites have restored their religious buildings, they are showering their bishops and priests with money. Meanwhile, the Renovationists are suffering extreme deprivation, literally a state of poverty (in the dioceses of Pskov, Ekaterinoslavka, Poltava, and a number of others), but they are not giving in on their positions. The Tikhonites have tried repeatedly to give bribes (to Metropolitan Aleksandr Vvedenskii and others), also tempting them with other material rewards. Little by little we are coping with this aspect of the problem, as have many of the diocese, without anybody's support whatever.

But Tikhonism is beating us on the political front, and here we are powerless because the Tikhonites operate using nonecclesiastical methods. They do not hide the connection between Tikhonism and monarchism. Not even to mention the fact that the majority of Tikhonite bishops and priests (starting with TIKhON himself) are former members of the Union of the Russian People and inveterate monarchists, and they remain so now. In Poltava, the archpriest Valabanov, in Irkutsk, the archpriest Vernomudrov, and many others in Metropolitan Aleksandr Vvedenskii's public debates and in ecclesiastical discussions have preached the superiority of tsarism over Soviet power. The people devour these speeches. The Tula archbishop (a Tikhonite) is disseminating to the people throughout the eparchy writings about TIKhON's connection with the ENTENTE. The hope is growing among the population that Soviet power will go away and that the "most holy" TIKhON will preserve Russia for new, better masters among whom the ecclesiastic class will live best. The political contagion is spreading. The effort is being carried to the working masses. In Baku (in Bibi-Eibit) and other oilfields the clergy is propagandizing the workers toward a blatantly pro-Tikhonist position. Tikhonist agitators are infiltrating Leningrad, Ivanovo-Voznesensk, Shuia, Egor'evsk, and other proletarian centers. Even in the Moscow region a large part of the devout workers are Tikhonites.

It is hard for us to combat the political propaganda of the Tikhonites [words missing in original document] our religious motives for fighting the counterrevolutionaries mean nothing. Here only state authority can fight the political contagion at its roots.

We are confident that once the leadership of the Tikhonite movement is eliminated the situation will gradually settle down. And it will be easier for the Synod to even out its work on a Russia-wide scale. The Synod, despite all its difficulties, has established normal ecclesiastical life in many dioceses: Tula, Vladimir, Kuban', Leningrad, Tashkent, Voronezh, all Siberia, Odessa, and others.

As long as the Tikhonist center exists, the work of the Synod cannot be as fruitful as the Synod would like—for the sake of both church and purely state interests.

For its part, the Holy Synod would propose that former patriarch TIKhON, as the culprit in this Church disunity and the instigator of civil troubles, should leave the city of Moscow and be accommodated in one of the country's remote monasteries. Throughout Church history (in both the Greek and Russian Church) deposed patriarchs have been treated in this way. Depriving TIKhON of the opportunity to direct a counterrevolution based on his cause would contribute [cropped] to the Church and would avert the possibility of a whole range of unimagined excesses of civil order against the regime of workers and peasants.

> Chairman of the Holy Synod
> Members of the Holy Synod
> Secretary of the Holy Synod

TSGAOR, fond 5446-s, op. 55, d. 647, ll. 13, 14, 16.

DOCUMENT 200   *Report of September 18, 1923, on the turmoil connected with the release of Patriarch Tikhon from house arrest and on the resolutions passed at the All-Russian Conference of Evangelical Christians held in Petrograd*

[Acronym on the stamp at head of title: *TS.K.K.R.P.* (Central Committee of the Peasant-Worker's Party)]

Extremely Urgent

Top Secret

Report

about the clergy and religious sects for the period from July 1 through September 15, 1923.

During the period under review, the increasing turmoil in the church in connection with the release of [Patriarch] Tikhon [from house arrest] was especially noteworthy.

The release, and especially Tikhon's confession, his order to pray for the Soviet regime, and his intention to adopt the new church calendar not only shocked the clergy but also was difficult for many more or less prominent Soviet public figures to understand. According to one version, Tikhon had lost his mind; according to another, he had sold out to the Bolsheviks; according to a third, all of this was a sham, and some believers even thought Tikhon had been replaced by a double. Most of all, they feared that Tikhon would join the Renovationist movement. This frightened the believers more than anything.

After Tikhon's first official proclamation the believers became convinced that Tikhon opposed the Renovationist movement, and their attitude toward him immediately changed for the better. His reconciliation with the Soviet regime made it possible for the believers to associate with him without fear.

Reactionary factions detested Tikhon's odd political ploys, and most of all they were disgusted by his connection to the State Political Directorate [*GPU*], about which they began to learn after his release. They began discussing how to stop the old man from doing something more disastrous.

Tikhon's release frightened the Renovationists because, initially, they interpreted this as a threat by the civil authorities to eliminate their movement . . . [illegible]. However, having become convinced that their position with the authorities was as strong as ever, and that Tikhon had by no means escaped judicial action, they began organizing their forces and developed a plan to fight the Tikhon faction. They began by reorganizing their forces and by attracting more prestigious bishops (older ones), so that they could present Tikhon with strong and serious opposition. With this goal in mind, they renamed the Supreme Church Administration [*VTSU*] with its former name, "Synod," and co-opted twelve old Tikhonovite bishops into its ranks. Thus, the schism between the followers of Tikhon and the Renovationists became increasingly severe. At present, these two hostile groups, each considering the other schismatics, have definitely and irreconcilably separated. This was acknowledged by the Tikhonovite Bishop Ilarion, who in his lectures has more than once stated that a schism has definitely taken place in the church. Previously, both he and Tikhon had considered the Renovationists to be insignificant. The priests of Moscow, seeing that the release of Tikhon did not diminish the significance of the Synod, began to pressure the Tikhonovite bishops to reconcile with the Synod. They gave as reasons that they were in a very difficult position because, from one side they were pressured and ordered by the Synod to implement its measures, and from the other the parishioners representing parish councils demanded on the contrary that they submit themselves to Tikhon and ignore the Synod. Consequently, Tikhonovite bishops held a secret meeting with the Renovationists and decided that Tikhon should be stripped of his leadership role, willingly abdicate as patriarch, and be sent to a monastery. But Tikhon would hear none of this.

Despite the fact that Tikhon's followers everywhere greatly outnumber the Renovationists, the latter are unwilling to relinquish their positions and desperately fight for control of the churches, secretly accusing one another of counterrevolution and openly reporting one another's anti-Soviet crimes to the authorities.

The hostility between these two groups has resulted in out-and-out fights in churches (Petrograd, Ivanovo-Voznesensk, Orel), eroding the authority of the church and providing favorable conditions for antireligious propaganda. At the present time, in order to strengthen their authority, the Synod proponents are seeking recognition from the Ecumenical Patriarch and are sending a delegation to Turkey for this reason.

For his part, Tikhon is trying very hard to rehabilitate himself in the eyes of the Soviet authorities in order to gain unfettered governance of the church.

THE SECTS

The All-Russian Congress of the Evangelical Christians held in Petrograd has ended. The congress was a great success and the work done regarding that sect produced excellent results. One of the most important questions dealt with the sects' attitudes toward the Soviet regime and military service; this question proved to be of such importance to the congress that it took six full days to resolve; after long discussions, the following resolution was adopted (204 voting for, 26 against, and 36 abstaining):

1) To act in good faith with the Soviet regime and in all possible ways to support it following Divine Scripture, not from fear but with a clear conscience.

2) It is inadmissible to agitate against military sevice and the paying of taxes, because this goes against Scripture, and therefore the congress condemns such actions.

3) The congress most strongly disapproves of all hostile forces fighting against the Soviet regime, of our capitalistic and monarchist emigres, and of anyone attempting to gain riches by exploiting the people.

4) Concerning charity and helping the poor, the congress concluded that help must be rendered not according to religious affiliation but to all others as well.

5) To acknowledge military service in Soviet Russia for the required time; the fulfillment of this duty is carried out by each Evangelical Christian according to his conscience but in accordance with the existing Soviet Republic laws on this question.

Other questions discussed at the Congress were of a purely internal religious nature.

Such resolutions, taken by the Evangelists, greatly disturbed the Baptists, who are not pleased with them for such provocative acts. However, since the teachings of the two are exactly the same, the Baptists have found themselves in a very disadvantageous position, from which they are now trying to extricate themselves.

Chief of the 6th branch of the Secret Section of the State Political Administration [SOGPU]: [signed] Tuchkov

September 18, 1923.

RTSKhIDNI, fond 89, op. 4, d. 118, ll. 4–6.

DOCUMENT 201   *Report from IAkov Peters, Director of the Eastern Division of the* GPU, *to IAroslavskii, September 22, 1923, on the Muslim clergy*

Top Secret
In your response refer to number, date
and Division.

Division <u>Eastern</u>

To the Chairman of the Commission on the Separation of Church and State <u>Comrade IAroslavskii</u>

On the work of the All-Russian Unified State Political Administration [VOGPU] with Muslim clergy and immediate plans in this area.

Until May of this year our local organs limited themselves to only passive cultivation of Muslim clergy, i.e., clarifying and elucidating the state of the clergy and its level of activity, using insignificant special-agent resources for this purpose. The impetus for active cultivation came from our circular no. 6, which identified basic schisms in the Muslim clergy and forced local organs to begin concerted preparatory work, the results of which already are being felt. The first phase of active cultivation concerns the All-Russian Congress of Muslim Clergy held in Ufa from June 10 to 20, for which we provided local organs with appropriate, very specific directives as well as a number of direct VOGPU measures.

The basic achievements of the congress were:

1) Strengthening sympathetic attitudes among the Muslim clergy toward Soviet rule.

2) Leaving leadership of the Muslim clergy in the hands of the previous (truly loyal) group in the Central Clerical Directorate [TSDU].

3) Adopting favorable resolutions on the issues of: a) attitudes toward Soviet power and its enemies (in part toward the Basmachi rebellion); b) attitudes toward Soviet schools; c) the place of women.

As for the issue of religious instruction to minors, it was not possible to obtain a ban on this, but the final resolution [illegible] opens the possibility of reaching an agreement not with the congress but with the TSDU, which is much more opportune.

Still during our pre-Congress effort, in some places at local congresses and meetings, we succeeded in guiding resolutions propitious to Soviet power and these somewhat prepared the ground for the above-mentioned resolutions at the All-Russian Congress. For example, 1) a resolution at the Chistopol' *Raion* Congress of Muslim clergy; 2) a resolution at a meeting of Muslim clergy and representatives of the parishes in Kazan' (all of this preceded the All-Russian Congress).

The second phase of our organs' work with Muslim clergy is under way in the immediate aftermath of the All-Russian Congress; those locales that have swung into action are using the experience and results of the congress. The Azerbaijan *Cheka* very successfully organized the publication of a special proclamation by the highest representatives of the Azerbaijan Muslim clergy calling for support of Soviet power, along with propaganda for the very principle of Soviet power and praise of Soviet policy in Transcaucasia.

In Simbirsk local Muslim clergy also published an appeal favorable to Soviet power, and, moreover, they organized a collection on behalf of the air force that yielded 120 rubles in gold (in Simbirsk, where there are few Muslims.)

In Tomsk an *okrug* meeting of Muslim clergy and laymen sent the Soviet government a telegram of greetings.

In a number of locales certain resolutions of the All-Russian Congress were published in the press with the goal of influencing the local Muslim population and clergy and at the same time preparing the ground to facilitate the effort (Crimea, North Caucasus).

Our immediate specific agenda is as follows.

The Central Clerical Directorate [*TSDU*] is undertaking publication of its own periodical, *Islam* (a monthly). Thus the *VOGPU* faces the important and complex task of injecting its maximum influence into this organ, to exploit it for essential influence on the international and national Muslim clergy. In particular, thanks to this organ, we will be able to disseminate all favorable materials more systematically and on a broader scale than before.

At this time we are observing that clerical organs are trying to establish contact with the new caliph by traveling to Turkey to greet him. The Crimean Clerical Directorate has already selected two representatives for the trip. Analogous information, thus far not completely clarified, has come to light in relation to Tashkent and Ufa. Our task is to monitor strictly (and if possible, to direct) these potential contacts, which could be very interesting to us. In particular, we have already taken such measures with regard to the Crimean delegation.

In the near future we should expect several local congresses of Muslim clergy. For example, soon there is to be a congress of Crimean clergy. Our mission will include guiding their successful completion, for which we are issuing appropriate assignments to local agents. As regards the expected Crimean congress, judging by preliminary data, we can say that the preparatory work done by the Crimean Political Administration is satisfactory and the congress apparently will be successful.

Our current tasks, described above, define the third, present phase of the effort.

The principal question on the basic direction of our active work with the Muslim clergy is still being resolved. Within the Muslim clergy, two opposing tendencies coexist, namely, factionalization and unification, neither of which has clearly manifested itself yet, so that the selection, or, more aptly, the resolution of the question is being delayed. We are taking further steps to elucidate this matter.

In our active work with Muslim clergy we have always taken into account that the positive results of this work (proclamations, sympathetic resolutions, etc.) could also be used abroad. But in a multifaceted and profound manner, the issue of using the Muslim clergy for influence abroad has arisen for us only relatively recently as a result of correspondence with the People's Commissariat of International Affairs [*NKID*]. These special orders of the *NKID* present us with the task of greatly accelerating and expanding our effort.

In conclusion we should say that at the moment special work with Muslim clergy is in the process of large-scale development and expansion.

HEAD OF THE EASTERN DIVISION OF THE *GPU*:
[Peters]   [signed] Peters

[Stamp at upper left corner of first page:] Russian Socialist Federated Soviet Republic. *NKVD* State Political Directorate. September 22, 1923. No. 81159.
Moscow, B. Lubianka, 2
Tel. [*GPU* switchboard]

RTSKhIDNI, fond 89, op. 4, d. 117, ll. 5–6.

SUMMARY REPORT ON THE RELIGIOUS MOVEMENT AMONG THE PEASANTRY

Drought Belt

PODOL'SK *Guberniia*. In Obodok *raion* the chairman of the *Raion* Executive Committee detained two villagers carrying a rejuvenated crucifix. 60 petitions have been submitted asking for permission to hold religious processions.

A religious procession was held in one village in Dzhusurin *raion*, while on the very same day other villages in the area held ceremonies which involved blessing water, which was then carried out to the fields by "sisters" and "brothers." 20 large and 60 small crosses were erected in the Iosofatov Valley in the month of June.

This movement is led by *kulak*s and priests. A certain Sulima Semen is leading the movement in Pepeleevka and Vzvedenka. (From party *guberniia* committee [*GK*] materials.)

The Catholic clergy is starting counterrevolutionary agitation in Proskurovo *okrug*. Many peasants attended the Festival of Saint Anthony in the village of Gorodka, and priests there agitated against the government's tax policy and Soviet power. In the village of Porokhna, Voitovets *raion*, a local priest delivered a counterrevolutionary speech at the farewell ceremony for the draftees born in 1902. In the village of Gibblovka a priest influenced crowds of peasants to dig up the corpses at the cemetery and pray for rain to them (based on information supplied by the State Political Directorate [*GPU*].

DON *Oblast'*. In Il'in *volost'*, Sal'sk *okrug*, rumors have been going around that Il'ia the Prophet appeared to some peasant children. The drought has resulted in a marked revival of religious sentiment (based on *GPU* information).

UL'IANOV *Guberniia.* The clergy organized a reception ceremony for the Zhadovo Icon which attracted a crowd of believers and local residents (*GPU*).

TAMBOV *Guberniia.* Kozlov *uezd*. Borisov *volost'*. At a meeting villagers discussed a holy well. Peasants spoke up for and against the well. As a result most of the villagers concluded that the appearance of the well was the work of priests and peasant ignorance (based on *GK* material).

"The drought has caused morale to decline among the workers at the tannery in the village of Razskazovo. As a result workers have begun to turn to religion and church services and to grumble about the Communists because of their denial of the existence of god [God]. The individual behind these problems is a certain Zheltov, a religious-minded worker who has close connections to a priest in a nearby village and has agitated in favor of religious processions, prayers, and fasts. In this case the old rural ways are holding sway over the workers" (from *GPU* material).

DONETS *Guberniia*. Village of Dmitrovka. Taganrog *okrug*. In early 1923 the *Raion* Executive Committee decided to close one of the churches in the village (the village had two churches). This decision was approved by the *Okrug* and *Guberniia* Executive Committees. The villagers petitioned Kharkov to have the church reopened in early May 1924. In Kharkov the parishioners' representative was given an official letter stating that "the closure of the church had not been approved by headquarters." Upon his return to the village, the parishioners' representative asked the *Raion* Executive Committee to reopen the church. Man'kovskii, the chairman of the committee, informed the representative that he would reopen the church only if he was authorized to do so by the *Okrug* Executive Committee. On June 5, 1924, Charikov, the manager of the *Raion* Rural Construction Trust, and some *komsomol* members began taking down the crosses and the bells at the church on the basis of a decree from the Dmitriev *Raion* Executive Committee. At this time a crowd of believers gathered near the church and told Charikov and his helpers not to touch anything, or they would kill them. Charikov and his helpers stopped taking down the bells. The crowd calmed down and dispersed. On June 8 a crowd of citizens gathered near the church again, walked up to the guard, and ordered him to hand over the keys. 3 policemen arrived and tried to disperse the crowd. Several individuals in the crowd attacked one of the policemen and tried to take his rifle away from him. Upon seeing this, the other two policemen began to fire into the air. The crowd flew into a rage and attacked them, and the policemen opened fire, killing two and wounding two. The crowd headed for the *Raion* Executive Committee and began demanding that the three policemen be turned over to them for a lynching. Man'kovskii refused. But then, at the instigation of one Citizen Zimin the crowd wanted to kill Man'kovskii, but by this time a company of pre-inductees arrived and dispersed the crowd. Several hours later a delegation of believers went to Man'kovskii and asked permission to open the second church (the one that was still active) for a meeting. Man'kovskii refused. A requiem was held for the dead and the wounded. Priests pronounced damnation on the persecutors of religion. After the service a group of up to 15 citizens chosen by the parishioners held a meeting with the priests in the rectory of the church, but what they discussed at the meeting is unknown.

TEREK *Oblast'* (The Mozdok Events of May 21–23, 1924). On May 21, on the Orthodox holiday of *pre-polovenie* [halfway between Easter and Pentecost], a day which draws crowds of believers to Mozdok every year, rumors began to spread at the shrine near the Terek River that the icons in the Uspenskii Cathedral had been miraculously rejuvenated. This attracted throngs of believers from Mozdok and the surrounding towns. On the basis of information supplied by Comrade Mezhentsev, the local *GPU* representative, the bureau of the *Raion* Party Committee issued Order No. 2 on the very same day instructing Baisagurov, the assistant prosecutor, the *GPU* representative, and the party fraction of the *Raion* Executive Committee to do everything in their power to identify the elements responsible for public agitation in connection with the rejuvenation of the icons in Uspenskii Cathedral. At Baisagurov's request nothing was done on May 21. On May 22 Baisagurov, accompanied by an art expert, a chemist, a representative of the believers, and the senior priest of the church (at a time when there were up to 200 people in the yard of the church and the inside of the church was packed), began to conduct an examination, which involved taking an icon off the wall of the church, taking it to the rectory, and replacing it, to the accompaniment of shouts and threats not only from the believers but from curiosity seekers who had come to see the "religious miracle," who outnumbered the believers. These curiosity seekers included Communist party members and members of their families. Early in the morning on May 23, on Baisagurov's orders, the icons were removed from the church, the church was sealed, and the priest Gaponenko was arrested. After learning of this, the believers became even more agitated than they were the day before and began discussing what they should do about it, all the while cursing the Communists and Soviet power for their actions and gathering around the church. They sent a delegation, consisting primarily of Ossetian women, to Baisagurov. The delegation was promised that the *Raion* Party Committee and *Raion* Executive Committee would review the matter within the next two hours. After waiting two hours the crowd dispatched another delegation, which now included some priests and the officer Gerasimov. The believers had prepared bread and salt to welcome the miraculous icons at the church in the hope that their request would be granted. Some members of the delegation were arrested, and the icons and the priest Gaponenko were not released. Then the angry crowd moved from the fence of the church towards the Procuracy and *Raion* Executive Committee building shouting, "We'll Free Them or Die Trying!" In order to keep the situation from getting out of hand, the chairman of the *Raion* Executive Committee and the secretary of the *Raion* Party Committee summoned a cavalry detachment and the entire police force, with a machine gun, and personally sat on a car with revolvers and pistols in their hands. By clicking the bolts at strategic moments, they succeeded in dispersing the crowd without firing a shot, but with some fisticuffs. Thus ended the affair of the "rejuvenated icons" (from the report of Petrov, a member of the Control Commission, and the Terek *Guberniia* Committee).

GOMEL' *Guberniia* (from the June report of the head of the *GPU* to the bureau of the *Guberniia* Committee). There was extensive missionary activity, and a "holy week" was held. Priests tried to call Red Army men bandits and insult the secretary of the Central Committee of the Russian Communist Party. Priests are also using their holy tricks, which we will have to deal with administratively. Two icons at the Chonsk Monastery were rejuvenated, an investigation is underway, and we will probably have to make some arrests. At the same time we have observed more activity in repairing old churches and building new ones. Attempts have been made to teach the law of god [God].

BRIANSK *Guberniia*. In Sevskii *uezd* in June, there were religious processions through the fields with prayers for a good harvest. A rejuvenated icon appeared at a well (10 *verst*s from the village of Zernovo on the Moscow-Kiev Railroad). The line of pilgrims stretched for several *verst*s, most of the pilgrims were "old wives," and many of the pilgrims carried canvas to the church services.

KHARKOV *Guberniia* (Sumi *uezd*) (report for June). There were two cases of rejuvenated icons at Belopol'e and IUnakovka. Commissions were appointed at Belopol'e, an expert called in, and in the presence of the citizens the expert proved that no rejuvenation took place and related the history of the last rejuvenation. The following day a priest from Sumi, Zelenskii by name, spoke at the church and rejected the rejuvenation, and then the whole affair died down. At IUnakovka "an icon was rejuvenated" before two mentally ill old men and an old woman. The believers did not fall for the rejuvenation, because they could see that somebody had cleaned the icon. Party comrades and a chemist were dispatched from Sumi. They performed a demonstration of chemical rejuvenation and spoke to a crowd of up to 160 people. The priest from IUnakovka also spoke to the crowd and explained that somebody had cleaned the icon and that the old men were mentally ill.

Recently the *okrug* has been visited by wandering priests who engage in counterrevolutionary agitation among the peasants. The *GPU* is taking steps to arrest and prosecute these priests.

IVANOVO-VOZNESENK *Guberniia*. The *kulak*s are employing an original type of religious agitation. They agree to give one or two sheep to a poor peasant if he agrees to pray to God and read the Gospel. They also tell him that if he doesn't meet their conditions they'll take the sheep back (from *GPU* report for July 12, 1924).

RIAZAN' *Guberniia*. The drought has led to a revival of religious belief. The peasants are organizing religious processions to the fields. A holy well with healing powers supposedly appeared at the village of Dubovoi in Ranenburg *uezd* (from *GPU* report for July 5, 1924).

KURSK *Guberniia*. In the village of Alekseevka in Shchigrovskii *uezd*, a Communist who tried to stop a religious procession was severely beaten. A well with "healing water" opened up in L'vov *uezd* (from *GPU* report for July 1, 1924).

NORTHERN DVINA *Guberniia*. A religious procession in the town of Velikii Ustiug on June 29 drew a throng of 8000 townspeople and peasants from the entire *guberniia* (from *GPU* report for July 1, 1924).

AMUR *Guberniia*. On May 17 we received a report indicating that a church in the village of Ivanovka had been robbed. After travelling to the scene of the crime, we discovered that members of the Ivanovka cell of the Russian Communist Youth League [*komsomol*] had taken part. As we were able to reconstruct them, the events leading up to the crime were as follows: the secretary of the cell had called a meeting of the activists at which they discussed closing down the church. Early in the morning on May 14 several armed men approached the deacon of the church and demanded the keys to the doors of the church. They opened the doors, removed all of the church's valuables, and then took them to a spot outside the village and buried them. The stolen valuables were found and taken to the city, where their value was appraised at 2,500 gold rubles. Eight persons were arrested and confessed to the robbery, citing their desire to get rid of the church once and for all as the motive for the crime. In ruling on the case, the Presidium of the *Guberniia* Committee decided that general procedures should be followed in the case of the Ivanovka church robbery and that, in accordance with basic party and *komsomol* policy in such matters, the case should be turned over to the Russian Communist Youth League and Procuracy.

July 2, 1924

[Signature of Author of Report]

Source: ?

Antireligious poster using images from folk theater and songs to lampoon the clergy and their alleged secret alliance with reactionary military leaders. Original in color. *Christmas puppet show: the fight against religion is the fight for socialism*, by A. Radakov. Publisher: Moskovskii rabochii (no place, no date indicated).

DOCUMENT 203   *Memorandum from the Information Division of the Central Committee to IAroslavskii, July 22, 1924, on issues connected with religious movements*

Secret
For Comrade IAroslavskii

REPORT FROM THE INFORMATION DEPARTMENT CONCERNING
RELIGIOUS MOVEMENTS

A certain resurgence in religious groups and greater activity by the clergy were noted during the last two months. Reports from provinces with poor harvests, as well as provinces partially affected by poor harvests (TSaritsyn, Stavropol', Tambov, etc.) indicate a connection between religious activity and poor harvests. This connection is further supported by those forms which the religious movement has adopted here (mass processions through the fields with crosses, sprinkling of the fields with holy water, setting up crosses, etc.). We do not have data on the political nature of this movement. Our antireligious propaganda is not in a position to combat this movement because it misses broad sections of the peasantry, does not know how to approach them, and most often has the character of pedantic arguments or Communist Youth League pranks.

In Podolia, where setting up crosses was widespread last year, the same thing is being repeated this year. Here, in the opinion of the *Guberniia* Committee [*Gubkom*], the movement has undergone a transition from a purely religious to a political movement of the *kulak*s. We have insufficient data to indicate that everything possible in the way of political agitation has been done here, but the *Gubkom* has already begun to apply purely administrative measures (exiling suspicious and hostile elements, judicial actions). As a positive aspect of this struggle with the religious movement and the "wearing of crosses," the *Gubkom* has raised the question of intensifying work with the [Ukrainian] Committee of Poor Peasants [*Komnezam*], of accelerating the resolution of land cases, etc. It seems to me, that one can achieve success in the struggle against religion in the Podolia region particularly through economic measures and the struggle against *kulak*s.

Sectarianism is active in a number of places. We have evidence from regions with crop failures about the widespread activity of followers of Hieromonk Iliodor [*iliodortsy*]; there is a communique from TSaritsyn and Saratov that sectarians are offering their help to organize famine relief. We have evidence about the sectarian movement from the Western regions. Here the principal hotbeds of sectarianism are the Latvian peasant colonies in the Smolensk and Novgorod *guberniia*s, from which sectarianism has spread to surrounding Russian villages. According to the communique of the Smolensk *Gubkom*, the leaders of the Russian sectarians are members of the impoverished urban petty bourgeoisie and bourgeoisie. Here, evidently, as with the Latvians, the Russian sectarian movement is political in nature and is an expression of the *kulak*/petty bourgeois opposition. In support, one can show that local sectarians agitate against reading newspapers, taking part in rallies and political meetings, etc.

All this goes to say that religious movements and the growth in clerical activism requires more serious scrutiny and that one must raise the question of political measures being applied to regions infected with sectarianism and mass religious movements.

Head of the Information Department of the
Central Committee [signature illegible]

RTSKhIDNI, fond 89, op. 4, d. 121, ll. 3, 30b.

DOCUMENT 204 *Minutes of the July 31, 1925, meeting of a special commission concerning removal of icons and frescoes from the walls and towers of the Kremlin*

to Comrade A. I. Rykov

P r o t o c o l no. 1

Meeting of the commission regarding the removal of frescoes, icons and other objects of religious worship from the walls and towers of the Kremlin.

July 31, 1925

Chairman Comrade A. S. Enukidze

In attendance: Comrades Prof. Grabar', Architect Sukov, Architect Mashkov, Ac[ademician] Shusev, All-Union Central Executive Committee [*VTSIK*] secretary Comrade A. S. Kiselev, P. G. Smidovich, Zhidelev [?], Sadovskii and Andreev.

D e c r e e d :

On the removal of some frescoes from walls and towers:

1. Having discussed the suggestion of Comrade Rykov, the chairman of the Council of People's Commissars of the USSR, having exchanged ideas with the representatives of art and architecture, and taking into consideration that the removal of the modern paintings, icons, etc. by no means diminishes the historical-artistic significance of the Kremlin but in many cases may improve its external appearance, the commission considers it necessary to remove from the towers and walls of the Kremlin all modern paintings that have no historical-artistic significance.

2. All frescoes and paintings of the fifteenth and sixteenth centuries will be preserved for their scholarly significance.

3. The Technical Department of *VTSIK* assisted by the representative of the Museum Department will be in charge of executing all work regarding the removal of icons, frescoes, and other religious cult objects.

The problem of restoring old paintings is to be discussed separately in the Presidium of *VTSIK*, and the Technical Department of *VTSIK* together with the representative of the Museum Department are to present a report and corresponding estimate for the restoration of the all historic-artistic paintings.

On removal of the pedestal in the gallery from the former statue of Alexander II:

1. The Commission considers it necessary to discuss separately in the Presidium of the *VTSIK* Smidovich's suggestion of placing a new monument to the overthrow of autocracy for the tenth anniversary of the establishment of Soviet power in the place where the statue of Alexander II once stood.

2. Regarding the middle portion of the monument [marquee] upon which stood the figure of Alexander II, it is necessary to remove what is above the base.

Assign the Technical Department of *VTSIK* the task of working out this problem in detail and presenting the Presidium with a cost estimate for removing the marquee.

All other parts of the monument are to remain until the question of replacement is finally resolved.

3. In order to reduce labor costs all measures must be taken to utilize the architectural drawings of the monument during the dismantlement of the marquee.

4. Suggest to the Technical Department of *VTSIK* that all materials removed be retained.

Commission Chairman A. Enukidze

Chairman of the Council of People's Commissars
A. I. Rykov
Moscow, Kremlin

July 24, [1925]

Avel' [Enukidze],

1. So how would you solve the problem of the old icons on the Kremlin gates?

It seems to me that if these paintings were genuine antiques and therefore of artistic and historical importance it would be improper to destroy them. The best solution would be to remove all of the latest additions, all the excess ritual accoutrements such as the icon mountings, the icon lamps, the icon cases, and so on, and thus make them look more like ordinary paintings, cover them with ordinary glass, and put up a plaque next to it saying that this old painting or fresco belongs to such and such an era, such and such a school, and was painted by such and such an artist.

I'm afraid that Comrade ZhIDELEV is demonstrating more revolutionary fervor than intelligence and tact in these matters. This entire incident will undoubtedly be discussed not only by the emigres but also by archaeologists, art historians, and scholars in Western Europe. It would not behoove us to give them any valid reason for accusing us of vandalism. Hence it would be good for us to allow any knowledgeable and reliable archeologist or art historian to take part in this project.

[signed] A. I. Rykov

TSGAOR, fond 5446-s, op. 55, d. 735, l. 4.

DOCUMENT 205   *Minutes of the meeting of the commission on closing churches, May 23, 1929, including guidelines to prevent negative results when closing churches*

TOP SECRET

Moscow, May 23, 1929

Minutes No. 1 of a meeting of the
COMMISSION ON THE CLOSING OF CHURCHES

PRESENT: Comrades KRASIKOV, TOLMAChEV, TUChKOV.

HEARD:
Information presented by Comrade TUChKOV on the closing of churches.

RESOLVED:
Many local party organizations are closing churches and other houses of worship without any kind of plan or without having properly prepared public opinion on the issue. They underestimate the number of believers (80%) and the level of residual religious superstition; they exaggerate the actual growth of antireligious sentiment among the peasantry; and they often rely excessively on antireligious and *komsomol* organizations in the campaign against religious organizations.

As a result of this attitude, the closing of houses of worship is taking place in an erratic, chaotic way, ignoring directives of the party and Soviets and sometimes with total disrespect for objects of worship (shooting at icons, throwing firecrackers into crowds of worshipers, etc.).

In many regions the Central Executive Committee resolution on the closing of churches and other places of worship is not being observed. Often the closing is decided upon by local authorities alone without approval of the higher Executive Committees and the Center. All this irregular activity provides fertile ground for rising agitation among *kulak*s, priests, and other elements who exploit these deeds for their anti-Soviet activity.

Frequently the authorities dealing with the problem of church closing ignore the actual situation in favor of a formal approach to the matter. Thus, if the majority present at a meeting vote for closing, that is considered adequate. But this ignores the fact that the absolute majority of the believing population is against the closing of churches.

Statements that only *kulak*s, NEP-men, and clergy are against the closing of churches are not only wrong but also harmful, because they generate friction in our relations with the believing masses, who come from the same social background as we do.

In the last 4–5 months (starting with the campaign for reelection to the Soviets), such attitudes toward a serious issue that directly concerns most peasants has contributed greatly to unrest and demonstrations in several regions. In some cases these disturbances have turned into violent riots and armed clashes.

To eliminate past miscalculations in the closing of houses of worship, the commission has concluded that it is urgent to issue some directives to the Union of the Godless and to explain the entire problem in the press. It is also necessary to instruct precisely the Unified State Political Administration, the People's Commissariat of Internal Affairs, and the People's Commissariat of Justice on the important matter of closing churches, mosques, synagogues, etc.

1. Instruct party organizations, the Soviets and all public institutions to adopt a more serious attitude toward the issue of church closings.

2. Persuade the organizations involved that only negative results come from substituting purely administrative measures for the ideological struggle against religious prejudice, the more so when laws and party directives are not observed.

3. Instruct all party organs that all churches and other places of worship already closed must be immediately put to practical use.

4. In view of the fact that the closing of churches often was done without regard for Soviet laws and party directives, this arbitrary behavior should be prohibited categorically. Certain cases of churches already closed should be reexamined, as well as of those still not being used for any practical purpose. All persons who by breaking the law and party instructions have generated popular unrest should be called to account.

5. It is also important to stress that local authorities should not tolerate hooliganism or any similar activity. Such incidents happened recently in several places during the celebration of so-called *paskha* [Russian Orthodox Easter].

Members of the Commission:
[3 signatures]

P. Krasikov
E. Tuchkov
Vl. Tolmachev

RTSKhIDNI, fond 89, op. 4, d. 125, ll. 4, 5

Ruins of Moscow's Cathedral of Christ the Redeemer (1837–83), built as a monument to the War of 1812 and destroyed in 1934.

TSGAKFD. N 116901

Memorandum from Khrushchev to Stalin, June 14, 1945, concerning the Ukrainian Greek Catholic Church

Central Committee of the All-Union Communist Party (Bolshevik)

> To Comrade Malenkov, G. M.

I am sending you copies of documents which I have sent to Comrade Stalin, J. V.

Please familiarize yourself with them.

> [signed] N. Khrushchev

> June 1[illegible], 1945

[Handwritten note covering most of the page:] Aleksandr [illegible] let us please discuss this matter. [signed] G. Malenkov June 14, 1945.

[Second handwritten note is illegible.]

Central Committee of the All-Union Communist Party (Bolshevik)

> To Comrade Stalin, J. V.

When I was in Moscow, I informed you about the work done so far to break up the Uniate Church and to persuade the Uniate clergy to join the Orthodox Church. As a result of that work, some members of the Uniate clergy have formed an "initiative group." This group has sent the Council of People's Commissars of the Ukrainian Soviet Socialist Republic the following documents:

1. A letter to the Council of People's Commissars on the status of the Greek Catholic Church in Western Ukraine.

2. A letter from the "Initiative Group" to all the clergy of the Greek Catholic Church. They will send out this letter to the clergy as soon as we approve the existence of the "initiative group."

When the above documents were presented to an *NKVD* agent, who identified himself as the person responsible for religious affairs in the Council of People's Commissars of the Ukrainian Soviet Socialist Republic, Danilenko, they asked that, if the steps they have taken receive approval, we do not publish their "Letter to the Council of People's Commissars" before they send the second letter to all the clergy in the dioceses. All the documents were drafted by the churchmen themselves, and our people took no part in the editing of these documents.

I am sending you the text of our response. I believe that we should accede to their request, allow them to send the letter to the clergy of the Greek Catholic Church, and then publish these documents in the newspapers in western *oblast*'s of Ukraine. We have recommended to the republic level newspapers that they introduce "special columns" for the population in western *oblast*'s of Ukraine, in which we also can publish these documents.

I await your instructions.

If you have any recommendations concerning the text of the Uniate documents, we will be able to insert these recommendations through our representative.

Concerning our response to the "Initiative Group," do you recommend that it be signed by me or should it be signed by the person in the Council of People's Commissars of the Ukrainian Soviet Socialist Republic responsible for matters concerning the Russian Orthodox Church?

> N. Khrushchev.

RTSKhIDNI, fond 17, op. 125, d. 313, ll. 28–30.

DOCUMENT 207   *Graph showing the number of Russian Orthodox churches active within the republics of the Soviet Union as of January 1, 1948, contained within an album presented by the Council for Russian Orthodox Church Affairs to M. A. Suslov*

Central Committee of the All-Union Communist Party (Bolsheviks) to Comrade M. A. Suslov:

The Council for Russian Orthodox Church Affairs in the Council of Ministers of the USSR provides you an album of diagrams with an explanatory note about the status of the Russian Orthodox Church in the USSR according to the council's data as of January 1, 1948.

Attachment.

[signed] Karpov

President of the Council for Russian Orthodox Affairs for the Council of Ministers of the USSR

Number of churches and houses of prayer: 14,329

Churches: 11,897
Houses of prayer: 2,432

Distribution of active churches among the Union republics as of January 1, 1948

Total	14,329
RSFSR	3,217
Ukrainian SSR	8,931
Belorussian SSR	1,051
Moldavian SSR	612
Estonian SSR	137
Latvian SSR	130
Lithuanian SSR	68
Georgian SSR	54
Kazakh SSR	52
Kirghiz SSR	31
Uzbek SSR	24
Karelo-Finnish SSR	9
Turkmen SSR	5
Tadjik SSR	4
Azerbaijan SSR	4

RTSKhIDNI, fond 17, op. 132, d. 7, ll. 1, 10, 11.

DOCUMENT 208   *Letter from Archpriest Khvedosiuk to Stalin, March 27, 1948, concerning persecution of the clergy*

Provost	<u>Copy</u>
Diocese of Rogachev	
Gomel' *oblast'*	To the Chairman of the
March 27, 1948	Council of Ministers,
No. 35	Generalissimo
Rogachev, Molotov Street, 23/7	Iosif Vissarionovich Stalin

The terrorist persecution of the Orthodox religion has begun in the city and *raion* of Rogachev. All individuals who are employed by the state and carry out religious ceremonies, particularly baptisms, are subjected to persecution—reprimands and the threat of being deprived of their jobs.

Not only those who baptize their children are persecuted, but also those who share apartments with priests or who have any contacts with them.

I respectfully ask Iosif Vissarionovich to explain: Do state employees, and also Communists, have the right to carry out religious ceremonies if they so desire, or should they be, without fail, atheists, or is this a matter of conscience?

I also ask Iosif Vissarionovich to explain whether the children of clergy, their wives, relatives, friends, and their acquaintances can occupy state positions, or do they lose this right as a result of such association? It is the understanding of the Rogachev authorities that [these individuals] are disenfranchised and that the priest should be completely isolated.

I beg Iosif Vissarionovich's pardon for the bother I have caused.

Archpriest Aleksandr Mikhailovich Khvedosiuk.

March 27, 1948

True copy: [signed] V. Spiridonov

RTSKhIDNI, fond 17, op. 125, d. 593, l. 99.

DOCUMENT 209 *Central Committee memorandum, July 24, 1953, on refitting facilities of inactive churches*

Council for Affairs   Secret
of the Russian Orthodox Church   Copy no. 2
under the Council of Ministers
of the USSR   Central Committee of the
July 24, 1953   Communist Party of the Soviet Union
No. 706/c   To Comrade N. S. Khrushchev

INFORMATION MEMORANDUM
on the refitting of the facilities of inactive churches.

The council reports that for the period from 1945 through 1953 the council reviewed 380 resolutions and applications from *oblast'* and *krai* executive committees of the councils of ministers of the republics (of these 318 were from the Russian Republic) to refit facilities of inactive churches as clubs, houses of culture, movie theaters, schools, and for industrial purposes.

Of the 380 resolutions and applications that were reviewed in sessions of the council, the council, in compliance with resolution no. 1643-486c of the Council of People's Commissars of the USSR [*SNK SSSR*] from Dec. 1, 1944, agreed to the refitting of 307 church facilities and in 73 cases denied the requests because refitting was considered inopportune. The council denied requests that involved the removal of crosses, cupolas, cult objects, etc. It also denied them when it was a matter of refitting church facilities as garages and workshops and when it was clear that the refitting of the church facility for other uses might produce an undesirable outburst among the believers and other protests.

For example, the council declared against the request of the Kalinin *Oblast'* Executive Committee dated December 17, 1952, and its repeated application through the Council of Ministers of the USSR dated February 4, 1953, for the transfer of the church building in the village of Strashevichi, Lukovnikovskii *raion*, to the machine tractor station [*MTS*] for refitting as a club, insofar as believers of said village over the course of many years have persistently applied to reopen this church, with one of these applications containing 1,149 signatures from believers. The structure has maintained the appearance of a church, and there is a graveyard around it, where the burying of the dead was discontinued in 1924.

On two occasions, the council has considered applications from the Ivanovo *Oblast'* Executive Committee and could not approve the conversion of the church building in Furmanovo into a garage and workshops, because a large group of believers had filed six applications to reopen the church after they discovered that the *Oblast'* Executive Committee had applied to convert the building.

The council also deemed an application to convert the Kazan Church building in Irkutsk into a movie theater inappropriate. This building is a very large, architecturally well-preserved, multidomed structure with a large number of crosses, and conversion of this church would lead to undesirable murmuring and protest among the believers. But the Irkutsk City Council has applied on three different occasions to convert this building into a movie theater.

In certain *oblast'*s there have been cases where the implementation of church conversion plans adopted by *oblast'* executive committees and approved by the council has been delayed. This has given certain church officials sufficient time to organize groups of believers to file applications and grievances for the purpose of halting conversion of the buildings.

For example, in August 1951, at the request of the Council of Ministers of the Chuvash Autonomous Soviet Socialist Republic, the Council for Orthodox Affairs authorized the conversion of a church building in the village of Chuvash-Timiashi, Ibresin *raion*, into a village club, but the conversion was never carried out and the building is now used as a grain storage facility. After learning of this decision, believers filed four applications in 1952 and 1953 for custody of the building for the purpose of holding religious services there.

In August 1950 the Kalinin *Oblast'* Executive Committee authorized the conversion of a church building in the village of Zakrup'e, Bezhets *raion*, into a club. The council approved the committee's decision. More than two years have gone by since then, but the church still has not been converted and is currently vacant.

Officials in certain republics and *oblast*'s have blundered in their preparations to convert church buildings by putting these issues up for debate at general assemblies or gatherings of the residents of a particular village.

These debates have inevitably set neighbor against neighbor and have had the extremely undesirable effect of dividing the residents into believers and nonbelievers.

For example, in early 1950 officials sponsored general assemblies of the residents of Toisi, Pervye Toisi, Kilei-Kasy, and Khoramaly, in Oktiabr'skii *raion* and the village of Kiser-Bosi in Churachinskii *raion* to discuss the conversion of an inactive church building in the village of Toisi into a school.

A general assembly of the collective farmers and blue- and white-collar workers in the village of Savostleika, Kulebak *raion*, Gorky *oblast'*, was convened to discuss the same issue in June, 1952, and was attended by more than 500 people.

In April of this year (1953) these assemblies were held at communities under the Kiper Rural Soviet, Morkin *raion*, Marii Autonomous Soviet Socialist Republic, at which the conversion of a church building in the village of Kiper into a seven-year school was discussed.

In individual places, even in this past year, there have been incidents where the *SNK SSSR* resolution of Dec. 1, 1944, has been violated when the refitting of church facilities has been done without the knowledge or assent of the council.

In Ivanovskaia *oblast'* during 1952–1953, by decisions of the executive committee, a church building in the village of Georgievskoe, Privolzhskii *raion*, was transferred to the balance sheet of the office of a linen factory with the right to refit it; in the village of Bogorodskoe, Ivanovskii *raion*, under the same circumstances a church building was handed over for a club; and in the village of Klement'evo, Lezhnevskii *raion*, one was transferred to the *Raion* Department of Health for refitting into therapeutic manufacturing workshops for a psychiatric colony.

In this regard the *raion* executive committees and *oblast'* executive committees of Riazanskaia and Tambovskaia *oblast*'s are especially notorious.

Following all such illegal actions, the council has undertaken measures through the councils of ministers of the republics and *oblast'* and *raion* executive committees to eliminate them.

Many years of practical work by the council have established that when the facilities of inactive churches stand [empty] or are even put to other use (for example, storehouses, depositories, etc.), but the issue of altering the exterior or interior of the church is not raised, great activity by groups of believers is not aroused; but, on the other hand, as soon as the question of refitting or demolishing the facilities of an inactive church is raised, activity immediately springs up, manifested mainly in applications for reopening the church. This does not apply to buildings whose exteriors have lost the appearance of a church or that happen to be in a state of ruin.

N.B.: The number of inactive churches throughout the USSR exceeds 19,000. Of these, more than 17,000 are in the Russian Republic because in Ukraine and Belorussia all church facilities were occupied by religious congregations during the temporary period of German occupation. Approximately 13,000 buildings have been taken over for storehouses, for cultural purposes, or even for industrial enterprises; around 3,000 buildings are in a semi-ruined condition; and more than 3,000 are vacant, with their cult fittings preserved and their keys in the possession of a church member, even though services are not conducted.

CHAIRMAN OF THE COMMISSION   [signed] Karpov

Sent to: Comrade G. M. Malenkov
          Comrade N. S. Khrushchev
          Comrade A. M. Puzanov

Source?

DOCUMENT 210   *Report from the Council for Russian Orthodox Church Affairs to the Central Committee, July 6, 1959, on mistakes made in closing monasteries*

Not for publication

Council for Affairs
of the Russian Orthodox Church
in the Council of Ministers of the Soviet Union
July 6, 1959. No. 339/s

Central Committee of the Communist Party of the Soviet Union [*TSK KPSS*]

Report on mistakes made in closing monasteries.

An October 16, 1958, resolution of the Council of Ministers of the Soviet Union proposed studying the possible reduction of the number of monasteries. In cooperation with local authorities, the council found it possible to consolidate 63 monasteries and hermitages into 29 in 1959–60. (In 1946 there had been 101 monasteries, of which 38 were eliminated painlessly.)

Patriarch Aleksii agreed to the reduction of 29 monasteries but expressed the wish that it be done over a period of two to three years.

Deputy Chairman of the Council of Ministers Comrade F. R. Kozlov in a council report of April 7, 1959, No. 155/s, on the issue of reducing the number of monasteries, proposed that the Council of Ministers of the Ukrainian, Moldavian, Belorussian, Latvian, and Lithuanian Socialist Republics resolve the issue in concordance with the union council.

The Council of Ministers of the Moldavian SSR in a decision dated June 5, 1959, No. 255-22/s, resolved to reduce the 14 existing monasteries to 8. Ignoring the preliminary agreement with the union council that the reduction was to be conducted systematically during 1959–60, the council set the dissolution timetable at three monasteries by July 1, 1959; two by August 1, 1959; and the last three by the first quarter of 1960. In actuality they accomplished this even more quickly.

On July 3, 1959, the council received a telephone call from Moldavia informing us that four monasteries, the Khirov and Varzareshti Convents and the Suruchan and TSyganeshti Monasteries had been closed and that some of the nuns and monks had been transferred to the remaining monasteries in Moldavia, while others had been put to work at collective and state farms. For example, at the Khirov Convent which had 165 nuns, 60 persons were taken into a collective farm, while from the Varzareshti Convent (100 nuns), 35 individuals also went to a collective farm.

At the same time, the undue haste in closing the Fifth Rechul Convent (where there were 225 nuns) and gross errors on the part of local party and government agencies, who failed to consider the significance of this convent and started to close the church, caused a major incident. They did not take the time to explain the closure of the monastery to the believers who attended the church or to the nuns, and the believers' request to leave the convent church open as a parish church was denied, even though in its letter the Council for Orthodox Affairs had explained that, when necessary, the churches of closed monasteries could be left open as parish churches for the general public.

The nuns from the convent, taking advantage of this bungling by the local authorities, informed their relatives and acquaintances in the nearby villages that the authorities were oppressing them, driving them out of the convent, and so forth, which led many residents of the villages around the convent to go there and organize a round-the-clock guard of 50 men armed with pitchforks, cudgels, and stones. Any time the local authorities and representatives of the public organizations came and tried to close the church, they would ring the bells, summon the people from the surrounding fields, and not let anyone near the church. These events began on June 23. In the first two or three days, the organizers succeeded in getting up to 200 to 250 collective farmers to come to the church, including certain individuals with shady pasts, by spreading rumors that all the nuns would be driven out of their homes and sent to the Far North.

Many of the nuns took the people into their homes for the night, fed them, and gave them wine.

After the situation was explained to them, most of the people went back to their villages, but on the following days until July 2, groups of 20 to 25 people remained at the convent church and began terrorizing the representatives of the authorities and public organizations. They administered a brutal beating to Budocherskii, an agronomist from the Frunze Collective Farm, and did bodily harm to several other individuals. One of the instigators of the beating, Davyd, a drunkard and a loafer, seriously wounded Police Lieutenant Dolgan' on July 1 with a pitchfork with the intent of murdering him, and Dolgan' shot this bandit to death in self-defense. Eleven organizers of the disorders and hooliganism were arrested, and an investigation is now underway.

On July 3 we received news from Moldavia that the Rechul Convent had been closed, that the church had been closed, and that the incident was over.

On July 3 I sent council member Comrade Sivenkov to Kishinev. He reported today that many serious mistakes were made. With the decree regarding the shutdown of monasteries through consolidation, municipal authorities proceeded to shut down all monasteries' churches, they seized all iconostases in the closed monasteries, they removed bells (the Rechul monastery), and they intend to remove all crosses from monastery churches. This, along with removing cult property, is the most sensitive issue for the believers and cannot be done without special permission from the council (resolution of the Council of People's Commissars of the USSR of Dec. 1, 1944, No. 1643-486).

The Council of Ministers of the Ukrainian SSR on June 17 of this year adopted the resolution to reduce the number of monasteries from 40 to 8 in 1959, but they had not set a timetable, as the council had proposed, for the consolidation of these monasteries. Municipal, *oblast'*, and *raion* authorities, inclined to hasten the reduction, are attempting without advance preparation and explanation to liquidate monasteries in 2 to 3 days. In the town of Kremenets in Ternopol' *oblast'* on June 21, a large group of residents of the town organized a protest demonstration against the closure of the Kremenets Convent, and the Council for Orthodox Affairs' representative for Ukraine, who had informed the council that the demonstration was a provocation organized by the Archbishop Palladii of L'vov and Ternopol', never bothered to inform us that the local authorities had shown up at the convent and had tried to close it within 24 hours. The Council of Ministers of the Ukrainian Soviet Socialist Republic ordered the closure of one large convent and two small convents in the Transcarpathian Region. The local authorities there did not try to close them, but instead had the Bishop Varlaam of Mukachevo and the Council for Orthodox Affairs' representative for the *oblast'* negotiate with the nuns of the Uspenskii Convent in the village of Chervenevo in Mukachevo *raion*. The nuns told them, "We'll die before we leave this convent. The Catholics ran us out in Hungary, and then the Uniates, and now they're trying to send us God knows where." The council has been getting signals that instead of resettling the nuns at other active convents, many of them, despite their wishes, have been told to go to all sorts of places, including nursing homes, back to their relatives, and so forth.

The patriarch and the patriarchate have been getting a lot of complaints. In a recent letter addressed to me dated June 24, 1959, the patriarch wrote from Odessa that:

"I must say that even here I can hear the crying from the convents. I have been getting letters or even visits from nuns complaining that they are being driven out into the world by force, with no consideration of their age or the local church conditions, which is not only making them restive but is also causing a commotion among the general public. The problem is that the local authorities are not following the principle laid down in Moscow, i.e., that nuns should not simply be driven out of the convents, but should be transferred to other cloisters. And according to a letter from Archbishop Nektarii in Kishinev, he has been told to remove all the priests who are monks from their parishes and thus leave more than 100 parishes without priests."

The council believes that in the process of liquidating monasteries there may be more difficulties and serious objections in other towns. It should be kept in mind that the majority of religious personnel (55%) are older than 55 and do not want to enter invalid homes. On the other hand, local officials are in a rush to shut down monasteries and hermitages, not through mergers and consolidation as suggested by the council, but by dispersing the religious personnel outright.

The council finds it essential to call upon the Central Committee or the Council of Ministers of the Soviet Union to warn party and local Soviet organs of the Ukrainian, Moldavian, Belorussian, Lithuanian, and Latvian Socialist Republics to be more cautious and gradual in their dealing with the reduction of monasteries and hermitages and to conduct this activity in accordance with the council's policy.

Signature: Karpov

cc:

TSK KPSS

Council of Ministers, USSR

TSKhSD, fond 5, op. 30, d. 89.

DOCUMENT 211   *Letter of protest from the Evangelical Baptists of Odessa to Soviet authorities, March 1962, asking for an end to repression, return of property, release of prisoners, and permission to hold a congress*

Copy

To: The Chairman for State Security of the USSR,

      The Chairman of the Presidium of the Supreme Soviet of the USSR,

      The Procurator General,

      The Chairman of the USSR Council of Ministers,

      First Secretary of the Central Committee of the Communist Party of the Soviet

            Union, Comrade N. S. Khrushchev,

      The All-Union Council of Evangelical Christian Baptists,

      The Director of the Ukrainian Committee for State Security [*UKGB*] for Odessa *oblast'*

From: the believers of the city of Odessa.

A PROTEST

The following is not the protest of one person but expresses the will and the hopes of all Christians of the Evangelical Baptist faith who are honest before God.

The degree of freedom of conscience is an expression of the degree of democracy in the social structure existing in a country. Soviet socialist democracy, which is the highest form of democracy, ensures a freedom of conscience that is unthinkable in any capitalist country.

The necessity of writing the following protest results from our being confronted with past and ongoing violations of the law of the Soviet government and the Constitution of the USSR, which forbid the restriction of freedom of conscience, persecution for religious convictions, offense of the sensibilities of believers, and, what is more, interference in the internal spiritual life of the church.

We are not without foundation in our demands, although for the sake of brevity we are forced to generalize certain facts which we can cite if necessary.

No protests were written at the time that, together with atheistic measures, administrative measures were taken, such as: slanderous attacks in the press and on the radio; all types of oppression in the workplace, including even dismissal on various pretexts and exclusion from higher and middle educational institutions; and oppression of children in school.

We remained silent even when believers were compelled to deny the Word of God and take on bonds of the human condition.

Although with deep sorrow, we remained silent even when the certification of the Peresyp' Community (Leninskii *raion*) was revoked and the facilities of the house of prayer, built with the hard-earned kopeks of our brothers and sisters, were used as a club for the "Poultry Combine."

One had to be surprised at the steadfastness and courage, the restraint and patience of the believers who conducted their worship services in rain, bitter cold, and blizzards outside the walls of their sealed building!

Similar protests also were not lodged when all petitions to the local authorities proved fruitless and the congregation was forced into semi-illegal status after reporting this to the authorities.

We were also silent when house-to-house searches were conducted to confiscate all spiritual and moral literature, not disdaining even personal correspondence and postcards, when such searches were not always sanctioned by the procurator, when during work-breaks, organs of the *KGB* interrogated people who were guilty only of confessing their faith in Jesus Christ.

As we have discovered, such methods of "atheistic work" are being practiced in other cities as well.

The best of our brothers in the city of Khmel'nitskii have been accused unjustly, and in the city of Kharkov they are under investigation. As we join in the demands for release of progressive fighters in other countries and of those struggling for national independence, we cannot remain indifferent when our brothers in faith are repressed before our own eyes, and are tried for various reasons, when once again the road to prison camps and exile is watered by the tears of children, wives, and parents because "As one member suffers, so shall all members suffer" (I Corinthians 12:26).

But it was not these measures that have forced us to turn to you, for we know that all those wishing to live devoutly in Jesus Christ will be persecuted.

In following in the steps of Christ, the Church has passed through Roman arenas and fires, through catacombs and quarry pits, through prisons and camps, nurturing the Evangelical burden with its innocent blood. Those persecutions were overt then.

But now, under the cover of Soviet legislation, a systematic and methodical war is being waged with the church from within, using for this purpose a caste of dictators calling itself the All-Union Council of Evangelical Christian Baptists [*VSEKhB*], with its field staff.

But the present *VSEKhB* does not speak for the interests of churches, does not represent them, and is not vested with their authority, for in thirty-five years there has been no congress, which is the only body having the right to elect and empower a *VSEKhB* and its executive organs; the representatives elected at the respective congresses in Moscow and Leningrad in 1926 have lost both their authority and any substance because of the many years intervening.

Pursuing its selfish interests, the *VSEKhB* imposes upon the churches secular decrees, in overt contradiction to Holy Writ, directed at the decomposition and destruction of the church through the church. Congregations wishing to lead a proper spiritual life based on the Word of God have been closed; brothers rising in defense of the truth have been repressed and condemned as parasites and under other pretexts, although they are conscientious and honest toilers for their country.

As a result of all that has been presented above, we request that you:

1. On the basis of the constitutional right of religious organizations to hold meetings, permit us to conduct an All-Union Congress of Evangelical Christian Baptists under the direction of an organizational group headed by brothers Kriuchkov and Prokof'ev along with representatives of all congregations and groups of believers in the designated faith.

2. Return the illegally seized house of prayer, and with it the certification of the Peresyp' Congregation.

3. Return all spiritual and moral literature that was seized: books, magazines, collections of hymn music, and Gospels.

4. Cease all intervention in the internal spiritual life of the Church.

5. Cease repression and interrogation of those guilty only of believing in Jesus Christ.

6. Rehabilitate unjustly accused brothers and sisters who everywhere have carried on spiritual work directed at the purification of the church and the improvement of its spiritual life, taking part in no political groupings.

We hope that our government will take a humanitarian attitude toward our requests, and for our part we will pray for you, for that is good and proper in the eyes of our God, who wishes that all people be saved and achieve knowledge of the truth (I Timothy 2:1–4).

March 1962

[65 signatures were attached to the original.]

TSGAOR, fond 6991, op. 4, d. 133, ll. 58–61.

DOCUMENT 212   *Decree of the USSR Supreme Soviet Presidium, September 30, 1965, removing residence restrictions in force since 1952 for members of religious sects*

To the Chairman of the Council on Religious Sects of the USSR Council of Ministers
     Not for publication

DECREE

OF THE PRESIDIUM OF THE
SUPREME SOVIET

On the removal of special residence restrictions on members of the sects "Jehovah's Witnesses," "True Orthodox Christians," "Innokentievists," "Reform Adventists," and members of their families.

The Presidium of the USSR Supreme Soviet resolves:
     1)   To remove special residence restrictions on members of the sects "Jehovah's Witnesses," "True Orthodox Christians," "Innokentievists," and "Reform Adventists," and members of their families and to release them from administrative supervision by organs for the protection of public order imposed in accordance with the Decree of the Presidium of the USSR Supreme Soviet of March 11, 1952, and by special order of the USSR Council of Ministers.

     2)   To establish that the removal of special residency restrictions from these stated persons does not entail the return of property confiscated at the time of exile.
     The return to prior place of residence of persons freed from special residency restrictions on the basis of the first article of the present Decree may be allowed only by approval of the Executive Committees of *oblast'*

(or *krai*) Soviets of Workers' Deputies, or by the Councils of Ministers of republics (lacking *oblast*'s) on whose territory they lived earlier.

Chairman of the Presidium
of the USSR Supreme Soviet A. Mikoyan

Secretary of the Presidium
of the USSR Supreme Soviet M. Georgadze

Moscow, the Kremlin.
September 30, 1965
No. 4020-VI.

Source?

DOCUMENT 213 ***Report by V. Kuroedov, chairman of the Council on Religious Affairs, to the Central Committee, June 18, 1976, on the positive results of a recent visit to the United States by a delegation of religious leaders: Russian Orthodox, Catholic, Baptist, Jewish, and others***

SECRET
Copy no.1

CENTRAL COMMITTEE, COMMUNIST PARTY OF THE SOVIET UNION

Report on Results of a Visit to the U.S. by a Delegation of
Religious Leaders

At the invitation of the American civic religious organization Appeal to Conscience, a delegation of representatives of various USSR religious organizations, totalling ten persons and headed by Russian Orthodox Church Metropolitan IUvenalii (V. K. Poiarkov, chair of the Section of External Church Relations of the Moscow Patriarchate) visited the U.S. from May 9 to May 19, 1976. Included in the delegation were religious leaders of the Russian Orthodox Church, the Jewish religion, the Catholic Church in Lithuania, the Lutheran Church of Latvia, the Armenian Church, and the All-Union Council of Evangelical Christian Baptists. This is the first time such an interreligious delegation has visited the United States.

The goal of the delegation was to expand the cooperation of religious leaders of both countries in the area of defending peace and to facilitate further reduction of tensions between the USSR and the U.S. Another goal was, via contacts with American citizens, to assist in the dispersal of misconceptions widely held in the U.S. about the situation of religion and the church in our country.

During the delegation's stay in the U.S., in addition to wide communication with religious leaders and believers, they visited schools and other institutions, met with American political and government leaders, were received at the U.S. State Department and at the United Nations, and visited the White House.

It is necessary to note that the delegation was everywhere met with good will, and much was mentioned about the importance of expanding contacts between religious leaders, which will undoubtedly assist in the deepening of mutual understanding between the Soviet and American peoples, and to the elimination of mistrust and prejudices that still remain from the Cold War period.

The president of the Appeal to Conscience organization, Rabbi Arthur Schneier, expressing the opinion of other U.S. religious leaders, noted several times in his presentations that "contacts between religious leaders are no less important than cooperation in the political, economic, scientific, and cultural areas. The most important thing is that in the process of contacts and cooperation we have reached mutual understanding and trust, notwithstanding the disputed nature of certain issues."

There was a press conference in New York for journalists of the leading American newspapers, at which members of the delegation answered many questions from journalists about the situation of churches in the USSR and about their struggle for world peace. At this press conference a decisive rebuff was given to certain attempts to question the existence of freedom of conscience in the USSR.

As he received the delegation, the Assistant Secretary of State [Arthur] Hartman noted, "I ascribe great significance to interreligious contacts, which assist the strengthening of relations between both countries, and we in the U.S. do not separate these ties from the context of economic and political contacts."

House of Representatives Speaker Albert, who received the delegation with other congressmen who reacted positively to their recent visit to Moscow, noted that "the arrival of the delegation of religious leaders from the USSR will cause the revival of contacts between believers in the USSR and the U.S., and the strengthening of ties between the peoples of these countries."

The mayor of the city of Washington, Mr. Washington; the assistant to the UN General Secretary, Buffem; Congressman Edward Koch; and former U.S. Ambassador to the USSR Harriman also gave positive evaluations of the visit.

According to information from the Soviet Embassy in Washington, the visit to the U.S. of the delegation of Soviet religious leaders "was a useful and positive event, particularly since the U.S. uses the area of religion for various sorts of anti-Soviet actions."

          [signed] V. Kuroedov
          Chairman, Council on Religious Affairs,
          USSR Council of Ministers.

June 18, 1976.

TSKhSD, fond 5, op. 69, d. 96.

DOCUMENT 214   *Results of a round-table discussion, December 16, 1988, on issues of freedom of conscience in the conditions of the democratization of Soviet society*

Not for Publication

[Handwritten Note]

To Comrades A. S. Kapto
                        E. Z. Razumetov

Hold a discussion with
the church leaders at
the Academy of Social Sciences -
[illegible]

[illegible signature]

No. 32238

STAMP OF
CENTRAL COMMITTEE OF
THE
COMMUNIST PARTY OF THE
SOVIET UNION [*TSK KPSS*]
December 16, 1988
CONTROL No. 32238

RETURN TO GENERAL
DEPARTMENT OF *TSK KPSS*

Not for Publication

TSK KPSS

Summary of a Round-Table Discussion of the
Problems of Freedom of Conscience
under the Conditions of the Democratization
of Soviet Society

On November 23, 1988, the Academy of Social Sciences [*AON*] of the *TSK KPSS* was the venue for a round-table discussion on "The Problems of Freedom of Conscience under the Conditions of the Democratization of Soviet Society." To us it seemed that this discussion would be important for the practical realization of the idea of a broad public dialogue, which would include representatives of religious organizations and which the general secretary of the *TSK KPSS*, M. S. Gorbachev, proposed in a meeting with the Patriarch and members of the Synod of the Russian Orthodox Church in April 1988.

The participants in the round table discussed the following topics: the status of religious organizations in Soviet society; the nature of the Soviet state; the duties and responsibilities of parents, schools, and churches in shaping the worldviews of children; and atheist and religious propaganda under conditions of a socialist pluralism of opinion.

The participants included representatives of the Council of Religious Affairs of the Council of Ministers of the USSR, the Soviet UNESCO Commission under the Ministry of Foreign Affairs of the USSR, the Public Commission for International Cooperation on Humanitarian Issues and Human Rights of the Soviet Committee for European Security and Cooperation, the Institute of the State and Law of the Soviet Academy of Sciences, journalists, and scholars from the *AON* of the *TSK KPSS*. The participants also included the Metropolitan IUvenalii of Krutitsa and Kolomna and Archbishop Kirill of Smolensk and Viazma of the Russian Orthodox Church; V. G. Kulikov, the editor of the journal *Bratskii vestnik* [The Bulletin of the Brethren] from the All-Union Council of Evangelical Christians and Baptists; M. P. Kulakov, the chairman of the Council of the Seventh Day Adventists in the RSFSR; and Father V. A. Aliulis, the chairman of the Liturgical Commission of the Roman Catholic Dioceses of Lithuania.

During the discussion participants noted the narrowness of the legal interpretations of the rights of citizens to perform religious rites. It was emphasized that in a number of cases the provisions of this law have been ignored, especially by certain officials at the local level. In this regard, certain participants were of the opinion that religious organizations should be given the status of public organizations of Soviet citizens with all the appurtenant rights to rectify the situation. The only restrictions imposed would be a ban on the church's involvement in politics and public education. The church leaders who spoke were of the opinion that all other areas of public life could be open to religious organizations.

The round table participants also stated that effective efforts to publicize the tangible achievements of *perestroika* and the advantages of socialism, to publicize the new political thinking, and to find allies among the democratic forces in foreign countries would to some extent prevent the ideological adversary from taking advantage of the belief that the Soviet state is atheistic in character.

In the process it was noted that, while it is "secular" in theory, the socialist state is essentially atheistic. The de facto inequality of believers and nonbelievers persists. In the opinion of the church leaders, this situation is rooted in the fact that for many years religion was considered a relic of the past and that religious beliefs were considered inappropriate for the builders of the new society.

The religious leaders also expressed their concern with different aspects of creating the necessary conditions for establishing a nation under the rule of law in Soviet society. And this would also require legislation governing different aspects of freedom of conscience and impartial enforcement of these laws for the benefit of society as a whole.

Most of the speakers agreed with the proposition that freedom of conscience implies freedom of opinion and the right to express spiritual attitudes and defend one's philosophy.

The representatives of the religious organizations were unanimously in favor of teaching religion to children, justifying their position by arguing that religion does not arise at the level of rational thought and thus that religious instruction would neither promote nor hinder the growth of religious belief. In their opinion young believers should know the basics of their creed, and they now meet their need for religious knowledge primarily with the assistance of foreign sources.

At the same time religious leaders demonstrated marked differences of opinion on one issue: while the hierarchs of the Russian Orthodox Church emphasized the need to keep religious instruction private, i.e., without any financial or organizational support from the government, the representative of the Catholic Church expressed his opposition to the separation of school and church.

In turn, the lay participants in the round-table discussion staunchly defended the principle of separation of school and church as the most viable democratic principle accepted in all the developed countries.

The participants also discussed the current status and future of atheist education in the schools and teaching the "Fundamentals of Scientific Atheism" at institutions of higher education and secondary schools. This is where our ideological adversaries see an attempt to impose a certain set of beliefs on the individual while ignoring the individual's own convictions. In the opinion of the representatives of academia, this issue might be resolved by adding to the curriculum a course on the history of world culture, which would contain essential information on the history of religion as well as atheism and Marxist religious studies (as a required course or an elective).

The participants were especially interested in the issue of freedom of atheist and religious propaganda. In a situation where atheist propaganda is given explicit preference, the church officials see expanding the opportunities for religious propaganda as the solution.

The legal scholars who took part in the round table <u>observed that formulating the issue as one of legal protection of the interests of believers would not be completely correct.</u> This would result in the artificial assignment of believers to a distinct social category. The solution lies in developing and expanding the rights and freedoms of all Soviet citizens. Efforts to strengthen guarantees of free expression of religious beliefs and the satisfaction of religious needs would take place within the framework of the development of a socialist pluralism of opinions.

During the discussion the participants expressed their desire to see a solution to the urgent problems of the ethnic political structure of the Soviet Union. Some were of the opinion that a <u>proposal to keep the establishment of basic laws governing freedom of conscience under the jurisdiction of the Soviet Union but make the union republics responsible for drafting specific legislation</u> should be submitted to a working group of the Supreme Soviet of the USSR for consideration.

The round table participants were wholeheartedly in favor of the idea of continuing the dialogue between Marxists and believers on the problems of the legal status of religious organizations and humanitarian issues.

For your information.

Rector of the Academy of
Social Sciences of the
TSK KPSS   [signed] <u>R. IAnovskii</u>

December 16, 1988
No. 1/0267

TSK KPSS

<u>On the Report of Comrade R. G. IAnovskii</u>

The rectorate of the Academy of Social Sciences of the *TSK KPSS* has informed us of a round-table discussion at the academy on the subject of "Problems of Freedom of Conscience under the Conditions of the Democratization of Soviet Society," whose participants included religious leaders as well as academics. The rectorate considered this meeting appropriate in light of the drafting of a law of the USSR on freedom of conscience and organized it for the purpose of discussing relevant topics.

However, the content, venue, and organization of the discussion were not carefully planned. The discussion did not include leading experts on the subject, and the choice of clergymen, whose statements could be considered banal, biased opinions, was also poor. A number of passages in the report submitted by Comrade IAnovskii give evidence of confusion in the positions of the organizers of the discussion and give us reason to believe they made unwarranted concessions to the representatives of the church.

This has been brought to the attention of the rectorate of the academy.

Deputy Director of the	Deputy Director of the Department of
Ideological Department of the	Party Development and Personnel
TSK KPSS	Management of the *TSK KPSS*
[signed] A. Degtiarev	[signed] IU. Ryzhov

January 20, 1989

No. 32238

02-25

Znd

TSKhSD

DOCUMENT 215   *Letter from scientific and cultural figures, February 12, 1990, via People's Deputy Averintsev, to Gorbachev concerning the return of the Kremlin cathedrals and churches and other churches and monasteries in Moscow to the Orthodox Church*

Not for publication

PEOPLE'S DEPUTY OF THE USSR 1989–1994

[stamped Feb. 20, 1990 03523]

February 12, 1990

To the Chairman of the Supreme Soviet of the USSR
Mikhail Sergeevich Gorbachev

Dear Mikhail Sergeevich:
I have familiarized myself with the letter to you from M. F. Antonov, V. V. Baidin, E. V. Selivanova, and A. I. TSvetaeva. Please consider the requests and proposals contained therein.

With respect,

[signed] S. S. Averintsev

(S. S. Averintsev, Corresponding
Member of the Academy of Sciences
of the USSR, Member of the Union
of Soviet Writers, Vice-President of the
Intergovernmental Commission of UNESCO
for the Ten-Year Program of Cultural Development)

Ref: No. 03523

OPEN LETTER

to the Chairman of the Supreme Soviet of the USSR
M. S. Gorbachev

Dear Mikhail Sergeevich:

Public opinion in our country is deeply satisfied with the transfer of inactive churches and monasteries to the Russian Orthodox Church, which has begun as part of the reform process. The world as a whole sees these long-awaited changes as a clear sign of democratization of our life and our respect for basic human rights, including freedom of religion.

At the same time, this nationally important process has unfortunately been given an undesirable twist, i.e., the Church is primarily getting semi-dilapidated churches in need of expensive and complicated restoration. This attitude on the part of the executive authorities has imposed a heavy financial burden on the communities of believers, most of whom are needy older people, and has greatly delayed the resumption of religious services. At the same time, the authorities have preferred to use the churches which have already been restored by the state (to no small extent by voluntary contributions from the Church, which is a corporate member of the All-Russian Society for the Preservation of Historical and Cultural Monuments [*VOOPIiK*] as museums, exhibition and concert halls, and for a variety of economic purposes. This biased attitude, which is the fruit of decades of efforts "to eliminate religious anachronisms once and for all," is out of touch with the realities of the times and should be completely overhauled. The very best buildings, created by the religious genius of the people themselves over the course of a millennium, should be returned to the sure and loving hands of religious citizens.

In hopes of receiving your understanding and support, we would ask you to consider two specific proposals:

1) for a long time now the Orthodox Christians of Moscow have been raising the issue of having the churches of the Moscow Kremlin transferred to church congregations. Fully aware of all the difficulties that granting this request would entail, we would ask you to turn over the Pokrovskii Cathedral (the Cathedral of St. Basil the Blessed) on Red Square by Easter of this year (April 15) to the believers of Moscow and all the Orthodox people of Russia and in foreign lands. This world-class architectural landmark could still retain the status of a national museum (but only with the interests of the Church taking absolute precedence), as is already the practice in a number of union republics and practically all foreign countries.

2) We also consider it the proper time to transfer to the Church all of the most religiously and historically valuable churches and monasteries in Moscow which would be practical venues for the resumption of religious services. This description is especially applicable to the Church of the Savior at the Spas-Andronikov Monastery, where the Venerable Andrei Rublev is buried, and All Saints' Church "at Kulishki", which is associated with the memory of the Battle of Kulikovo and the saintly Prince Dmitrii Donskoi.

It would be hard to exaggerate the social significance of these decisions. The transfer of the Holy Trinity Church "at Nikitniki" (the icons of the Georgian Madonna) and the Memorial Chapel to the Heroes of Plevna would serve to strengthen friendly relations between the Georgian, Bulgarian, and Russian peoples. The transfer of the largest monasteries in Moscow such as the Novodevichii, Donskoi, Novospasskii, and Vysoko-Petrovskii Monasteries and the Krutitskii Diocesan Monastery Church to the Russian Orthodox Church would promote the development of charitable activities in the capital, improve the social welfare of the neediest members of society, and multiply the altruistic services of monks and nuns. The monasteries would be natural sites for orphanages, hospices, and nursing homes for the most unfortunate members of society. The resumption of religious services in the next year or two at the Church of St. Tatiana in the old Moscow University building and the opening of a religious education center at the Andreev Monastery close to the new Moscow University building would promote the moral improvement of Muscovites, especially young people. The resumption of religious services at the old hospital chapels (the old Golitsyn and First City Hospitals, the Pilgrims' Home, and so forth) and prison chapels (Lefortovo Prison, the old Corps of Cadets building, and Butyrki Prison) would be just as beneficial.

Without a doubt, Moscow's noble example would greatly expedite the process of transferring all of the most valuable and suitable churches and monasteries in Russia to the Orthodox Church. A government decision to this effect would not only promote the further restoration and more efficient use of the country's historical and cultural monuments but would also foster a national spiritual rebirth.

We hope your attitude towards our proposals is a positive one.

Respectfully yours

[signed] Antonov, Mikhail Fedorovich, writer
113054, Moscow, Zatsepa Street, 22-73, Tel 235-37-82
[signed] Baidin, Valerii Viktorovich, historian
129281, Moscow, Yenisei Street, 34-280, Tel 470-34-05

[signed] Selivanova, Elizaveta Vladimirovna, doctor
107078, Moscow, Bolshoi Kozlovskii Lane, 3/2, Apt 16
Tel 921-07-96

TSvetaeva, Anastasia Ivanovna, literary critic
Moscow, Bol'shaia Spasskaia Street, 8-58, Tel. 280-84-71

February 12, 1990

COMMUNIST PARTY OF THE SOVIET UNION, Moscow City Committee

March 19, 1990

Central Committee of the Communist Party of the Soviet Union

On Turning Over to the Orthodox Church a Number of Historic Monuments in Moscow.

The authors of the letter raise the issue of returning to believers of the city the cathedrals of the Moscow Kremlin, the Pokrovskii Sobor [St. Basil's Cathedral], as well as a number of churches and monasteries located in the central part of Moscow.

Existing legislation provides for the transfer of individual churches either to the jurisdiction of the Moscow Patriarchate or to congregations of believers. At present no official appeals have been received from either the Patriarchate or congregations to return the cathedrals in the Moscow Kremlin or the Pokrovskii Sobor. We can also report that local government agencies have reacted attentively and with understanding to individual appeals by believers. Thus, for 1989 and the first months of the current year, eighteen Orthodox congregations have been registered or are in the process of registration. Practically all of these groups are given church buildings for their use.

An appeal by the Moscow Patriarchate to the Council on Religious Affairs of the USSR Council of Ministers for the return of the Donskoi Monastery is currently being considered. This case will be continued until the receipt of appropriate petitions to local government bodies and comments on them.

We also would consider inadvisable the transfer to any congregation of the Kremlin Cathedrals or the Pokrovskii Sobor, considering the important political and state significance of the Moscow Kremlin and Red Square, and also the unique status of these cathedrals as historical and architectural monuments and as the cultural inheritance of the entire population. At the same time their maintenance by the state as historical museums and monuments does not offend the sensibilities of believers. Furthermore, the provision of functioning churches in the central residential neighborhoods completely satisfies the needs of believers for religious buildings.

By agreement with Comrade A. B. Kazakov of the Ideological Section of the Central Committee of the *KPSS*, an answer to the authors of the letter will be given to the Central Committee of the *KPSS*.

Comrade S. E. Morgunov, consultant to the Ideological Section of the Moscow City Committee of the *KPSS*, worked on the response to the letter.

[signed] IU. Karabasov
Secretary, Moscow City Committee, *KPSS*

STAMP OF *TSK KPSS*

March 23, 1990
05993
Return to
General
Department
of *TSK KPSS*

CENTRAL COMMITTEE
OF THE COMMUNIST PARTY OF THE SOVIET UNION
[*TSK KPSS*]

Ref 03523 February 28, 1990

Subject: The Transfer of Historical and Cultural Monuments to the Orthodox Church

Per instructions, the Ministry of Culture of the USSR has reviewed the "open letter" from Comrades V. F. Antonov, V. V. Baidin, E. V. Selivanova, and A. I. TSvetaeva proposing the transfer of churches and monasteries to the Orthodox Church and hereby informs you of the following.

According to the Council of Religious Affairs, more than 950 churches and monasteries have been returned to the Orthodox Church. In Moscow alone, 11 churches were transferred in 1988 and 1989, including the fully restored Cathedral of the Virgin Birth at Simonov Monastery, the Church of the Miraculous Salvation in the Kuntsevo District, the Church of the Trinity in Voroshilov District, and others. We have also transferred such prominent monuments as the Valaam Island complex, the Iosif of Volokolamsk Monastery, and Optina Pustyn'. The planning, surveying, and restoration of all these monuments were financed by government agencies and the All-Russian Society for the Preservation of Historical and Cultural Monuments [VOOPIiK]. Thus, for the most part, the authors' claim that the churches which have been turned over to the Church were practically in ruins does not correspond to reality.

The Pokrovskii Cathedral (Church of St. Basil the Blessed) and the Trinity Church at Nikitniki are currently branches of the State Historical Museum. Because of their historical and cultural uniqueness, these monuments attract more than 650,000 tourists every year, and their closure as museums would detract from Moscow's drawing power as a cultural attraction and would also adversely affect the capital's cultural finances (revenues from the Pokrovskii Cathedral and the Church of the Trinity at Nikitniki amount to about 230,000 rubles per annum, with most of the revenues used for cultural development, while the entire contribution of the Russian Orthodox Church as a corporate member of the VOOPIiK amounted to 251,000 rubles in 1989). Moreover, the Pokrovskii Cathedral was never intended to accommodate large numbers of worshippers for daily services and is an unheated summer cathedral. At present, the physical condition of these two buildings requires careful examination by specialists, who must then develop recommendations concerning their use.

With respect to the Novodevichii, Vysoko-Petrovskii, and Donskoi Monasteries and the Krutitskii Diocesan Monastery Complex, they are currently housing the shows, exhibits, and collections of the State Historical and Literary Museums and the Shchusev Architectural Research Museum. The main building of the Historical Museum is undergoing repairs. Four million of its most valuable artifacts have been moved to the Novodevichii Monastery and Krutitskii Diocesan Monastery Complex because the Moscow City Soviet does not have any other storage space available, and the museum's loss of this storage space would cause irreparable damage to its collection.

The building of the State Literary Museum was torn down in 1968 in connection with the reconstruction of Dimitrov Street, and the museum was moved to the Naryshkin Chambers of the Vysoko-Petrovskii Monastery. The Ministry of Culture of the USSR has been applying to the Moscow Soviet Executive Committee for a new building since 1971, the plans have been drawn up, and a building lot has been set aside, but the building still has not been put on the schedule of construction projects for the city of Moscow. At the present time it would be impossible to house the State Literary Museum in any other place than the Naryshkin Chambers.

At the same time the Ministry of Culture supports the authors' proposal to convert the Andreev Monastery into a religious education center and resume religious services at the hospital chapels at the old Golitsyn and First City Hospitals and the Pilgrims' Home with the consent of their current tenants. The ministry also considers it possible, in exceptional cases, to hold services in the Pokrovskii Cathedral and at the Spasskii Cathedral of the Spas-Andronikov Monastery on major religious holidays with the consent of the directors of the museums on each specific occasion.

Concurrently, the Ministry of Culture of the USSR considers it necessary to spell out its position concerning the growing tendency to transfer religious buildings currently used as museums, exhibition halls, and libraries to religious organizations.

For a long time now, the ministry has been working to get local authorities to stop using church and monastery buildings as warehouses, vegetable and grain storage facilities, jails, and juvenile homes and place them at the disposal of cultural and educational institutions in order to preserve them better. As a result, more than half (and in the Russian SFSR about 70%) of all museums, museum exhibition halls, and exhibits are housed in religious buildings. Extremely interesting and internationally acclaimed museum exhibition halls have been established in old religious buildings in the cities of Vladimir, Suzdal', Novgorod, IAroslavl, Riazan', Samarkand, Bukhara, Khiva, and other cities. Depriving museums of this space, as has already occurred in Ivano-Frankovsk, Syktyvkar, Optina Pustyn', Valaam, and other places, at a time when it would be impossible to build replacements for them, would result in the collapse of the museum industry and the country's existing system of museums.

And after all, even now the Soviet Union only ranks 29th in the world in terms of the number of museums per 100,000 population.

Holding religious services in unique historical and cultural monuments, especially those which contain paintings, would be absolutely out of the question, because the gathering of large crowds of people during the services and the use of burning candles and incense would inevitably tarnish the paintings, while the changes and fluctuations of the temperature and humidity in the building would also have a devastating effect on the paintings.

The transfer of the entire complex of monuments in the Solovki Islands, which currently constitute the Solovki Architectural, Historical, and Nature Preserve, is worthy of special consideration. Solovki is not just the history of the Russian Orthodox Church, but a unique ensemble of historical, cultural, and natural landmarks which embrace every stage in the history of the Russian and Soviet states. It preserves the visible memory of tragic pages in our country's history, i.e., the Solovki Special Camps, which should be preserved and put on public display, not hidden in the rooms of monastic cells, in the same way that the world has preserved the terrible memory of Auschwitz, Buchenwald, and Mauthausen. Major restoration organizations, such as the *Soiuzrestavratsiia* [All-Union Restoration Organization] and *Rosrestavratsiia* [Russian Restoration Organization], have been employed to do the planning, surveying, and restoration work at Solovki and have completed 6.9 million rubles worth of research and restoration so far. At present almost 80% of the buildings in the central ensemble have been restored from a dilapidated and semi-dilapidated condition, and their original appearance, which was obscured by the most recent reconstruction, is being restored on the basis of painstaking research. The Solovki Architectural, Historical, and Nature Preserve is engaged in important research and collection work on all aspects of the history, culture, and natural environment of the Solovki Islands and the White Sea region. In considering the transfer of the Solovki Islands to the Russian Orthodox Church, we should first of all provide for the maintenance and development of this preserve as a state agency for safeguarding the monuments and natural environment of the Solovki Islands and as a research, cultural, and educational institution.

The Ministry of Culture of the USSR deems it necessary to implement a consistent national policy on returning religious buildings and property to religious organizations which would be designed to preserve and use religious landmarks of special historical, scholarly, and artistic value as museums.

Minister of Culture of the USSR   [signed] N. N. Gubenko

MOSCOW CITY SOVIET OF PEOPLE'S DEPUTIES
EXECUTIVE COMMITTEE

103032, Moscow, 13 Gorky Street   Telephone: ...   Telegraph: *Moskva-Mossovet*

May 7 No. 16 3/0-330

MAY 22, 1990

MEMORANDUM

SUBJECT: The Joint Letter Proposing the Transfer
                  of a Number of Monuments in the City of Moscow
                  to the Orthodox Church

The authors of the letter, Comrades Antonov, Baidin, Selivanova, and TSvetaeva, raised the issue of transferring the churches of the Moscow Kremlin, the Pokrovskii Cathedral, and a number of historical monuments located in the center of the city to the Orthodox Church.

The Executive Committee of the Moscow City Soviet has reviewed their joint entreaty on the subject and hereby informs you that current regulations allow the transfer of historical and cultural monuments to the church or a community of believers only after they have filed an official application with the authorities and the application has been reviewed by concerned parties.

For example, in 1988 and 1989 11 churches in Moscow were transferred to the Russian Orthodox Church.

At the same time the authorities received absolutely no requests for the transfer of the buildings mentioned in the letter from the Patriarchate or communities of believers.

In light of the political and state importance of these buildings and their status as nationally and globally important historical and cultural monuments, the Executive Committee of the Moscow City Soviet deems it inadvisable to transfer the cathedrals of the Moscow Kremlin and the Pokrovskii Cathedral to the Church.

For the Secretary of the
Moscow City Executive Committee   [signed] IU. A. Shilobreev

TSK KPSS

On the Suggestions of V. F. Antonov, V. V. Baidan, E. V.
Selivanova, and A. I. TSvetaeva

The authors of the letter raise the issue of transferring the cathedrals of the Moscow Kremlin, the Pokrovskii Cathedral, and a large number of monasteries and churches in the center of Moscow to the Russian Orthodox Church. Comrade S. S. Averintsev, a People's Deputy of the Soviet Union, has supported this proposal.

Per instructions, the matter has been reviewed by the Council of Ministers of the RSFSR, the Moscow City Committee of the *KPSS*, the executive committee of the Moscow City Soviet, and the Ministry of Culture of the USSR.

According to their information, religious buildings, especially those which have been used in a very inappropriate way, are being transferred to the Church throughout the country.

In recent years more than 950 churches and monasteries have been transferred to the Church, including 10 in Moscow. Currently, the Patriarchate's request to use the Donskoi Monastery, the All Saints Church at Kulishki, and the churches of the Ismailovo Monastery Farm and the Krutitskii Diocesan Monastery Church are in the process of review.

With respect to the cathedrals of the Moscow Kremlin and the Pokrovskii Cathedral at Red Square, the aforementioned agencies deem it inadvisable to transfer these buildings to communities of believers, in view of the political and national importance of the Moscow Kremlin and Red Square and the status of these cathedrals as nationally and globally important historical and cultural monuments. Moreover, holding church services in these cathedrals could disrupt the existing routine and security of the Kremlin and Red Square.

This opinion is shared by the Council of Ministers of the RSFSR, the Ministry of Culture of the USSR, the Moscow City Committee of the *KPSS*, the Executive Committee of the Moscow City Soviet, and the Commandant's Office (Security Force) of the Moscow Kremlin (Comrade G. D. Bashkin).

Many of the religious buildings which the authors recommended for transfer to the Church are unique architectural and cultural monuments and contain masterpieces of fresco and easel painting which require special care and handling and the proper conditions for scholarly study. Moreover, the Orthodox Church in Moscow does not have adequate capabilities for performing extensive restoration work with its own personnel and has not applied for the transfer of the churches and monasteries cited in the letter.

By law, religious buildings may only be transferred to registered religious organizations at their request. As soon as the authorities receive the required applications, these matters will be reviewed in accordance with the established procedure.

The Ideological Department of the *TSK KPSS* (Comrade Kazakov) has already forwarded a reply to the authors of the letter.

Assistant Head of the
Ideological Department
of the *TSK KPSS*

[signed] A. Kapto

April 25, 1990

TSKhSD, current archive.

Antireligious Activities

The socialist credo presumed that secularism would triumph over religion in the socialist utopia; socialists shared Marx's conviction that religion was the "opiate of the people," dulling their resistance to oppression and discouraging organized attempts to change the system. An important part of the revolutionary conversion of many Russian workers and intellectuals had included a rejection of religion, but most revolutionaries still recognized that atheism had to be acquired, not obtained by coercion. Despite the pressures on the church as an institution, antireligious efforts by the new socialist regime tended to prefer propaganda over agitation, gradualism over repression.

Communist Party members would lead the march to secularism through their own example: they were expected to renounce religion and to be the first to adopt the new socialist rituals of civil marriage and "Red christenings" or "Octobering" of their children. In the periodic purges of the party in the 1920s, religious observance was a significant cause for expulsion. The leading Communist proponent of cultural atheism was a second-generation revolutionary from Siberia, Emelian IAroslavskii (Minei Izrailovich Gubelman) (1878–1943), who founded the weekly newspaper *Bezbozhnik* (The Godless) in 1922. In 1925 the society created to support the newspaper evolved into an official Communist organization, the League of the Militant Godless, whose task was to coordinate the antireligious propaganda effort inside and outside the party.

IAroslavskii was always a staunch supporter of Stalin and of Stalinist orthodoxy; in antireligious matters his orthodoxy took the form of holding the line against far more radical antireligious militants, "priest-eaters," who delighted in offending believers with their audacious activities. In 1923, for example, antireligious activists from the Young Communist League (*komsomol*) organized an alternative carnivalesque Christmas, mocking and blaspheming organized religion and religious belief. IAroslavskii and others recognized that such offensive activities did more harm than good, and part of the purpose of the new League was to rein in the radicals. Instead, *Bezbozhnik* would use the written word, scientific debunking of so-called miracles, and public debates in order to convince believers of the folly of their ways. Secular feast-days were developed to overcome the pull of tradition: Trinity Sunday became Forest Day, the Feast of the Intercession became Harvest Day; International Workers' Day competed with Easter, and the secular New Year's celebration borrowed gift-exchange and the fir tree from Orthodox Christmas traditions.

The League of the Militant Godless existed only until the Second World War, but afterwards antireligious propaganda continued on a more "scientific" footing. Journals such as *Science and Religion* and *Science and Life* promoted materialism and science as the antidotes to religious superstition; scientific and historical studies of religion were also used in the increasingly urban society to demythologize belief. Museums of atheism (installed in former churches) and an Institute of Scientific Atheism also contributed to the effort to saturate Soviet education with official atheism.

DOCUMENT 216   *Letter from Gorky to Stalin, November 29, 1929, on the organization of an-*
tireligious propaganda

Letter from Gorky to Stalin

Dear Iosif Visarionovich:

Before my departure from Moscow, I did not have a chance to share some of my observations with you, which even if I had found the time to, I still would not have been able to relay to you in a clear and coherent way—I tend to speak poorly, I'll do better in writing.

The emigre and bourgeois press bases its perception of Soviet reality almost entirely on the negative information which is published by our own press for self-criticism with the aim of education and agitation. The products of the "individual journalists" of the bourgeois press are not as numerous and harmful as they are made out to be, in contrast to our own release of self-revealing facts and conclusions.

By strongly emphasizing facts of a negative nature, we open ourselves to our enemies, providing them an enormous amount of material, which they in turn very aptly use against us, compromising our party and our leadership in the eyes of Europe's proletariat, compromising the very principle of the dictatorship of the working class, because the proletariat of Europe and America feeds on the bourgeois newspapers for the most part. For this reason it cannot grasp our country's cultural-revolutionary progress, our successes and achievements in industrialization, the enthusiasm of our working masses, and of their influence on the impoverished peasantry.

It stands to reason, I do not think we can positively influence the attitude which the bourgeoisie has already formed towards the Union of Soviets, and I do know that European conditions are zealously raising the revolutionary consciousness of the European proletariat.

I also know that the one-sidedness of our treatment of reality—created by us—exerts an extremely unhealthy influence on our young people.

In their letters, and in their conversations with me, it seems that today's youth displays an extremely pessimistic mood. This mood is very natural. Direct knowledge of reality of our youth from the central areas, especially our provinces, is limited, insignificant. To acquaint themselves with what is going on they turn to the newspapers.[. . .]

It is furthermore imperative to put the propaganda of atheism on solid ground. You won't achieve much with the weapons of Marx and materialism, as we have seen. Materialism and religion are two different planes, and they don't coincide. If a fool speaks from the heavens and the sage from a factory they won't understand one another. The sage needs to hit the fool with his stick, with his weapon.

For this reason, there should be courses set up at the Communist Academy which would treat more than the history of religion, especially the history of the Christian church, i.e., the study of church history as politics.

We need to know the "fathers of the church," the apologists of Christianity, especially indispensable to the study of the history of Catholicism, the most powerful and intellectual church organization whose political significance is quite clear. We need to know the history of church schisms, heresies, the Inquisition, the "religious" wars, etc. Every quotation by a believer is easily countered with dozens of theological quotations which contradict it.

We cannot do without an edition of the "Bible," with critical commentaries from the Tübingen school, and books on criticism of biblical texts, which could bring a very useful "confusion into the minds" of believers.

There is a fine role to be played here by a popular book on the Taborites and the Hussite movements. It would be useful to introduce here *The History of the Peasant Wars in Germany,* the old book by Zimmerman. Carefully edited, it would be very useful for the minds.

It is necessary to produce a book on the church's struggle against science.

Our youth is very poorly informed on questions of this nature. The "tendency" toward a religious disposition is very noticeable—a natural result of developing individualism. At this time, as always, the young are in a hurry to find "the definitive answer." [. . .]

RTSKhIDNI, fond 89, op. 4, d. 121, ll. 3, 30b.

DOCUMENT 217   *Letter from IAroslavskii to Gorky, January 24, 1930, concerning antireligious propaganda*

To Comrade A. M. Gorky

Please forward a copy of
this letter to Comrade
Stalin

_____

Copy to Comrade Kalinin
Send to Gorky

Dear Aleksei Maksimovich,

Comrade Stalin showed me the letter from Nov. 29, 1929, that you wrote to him, and in which you touch upon the subject of the new antireligious campaign in the USSR. Because I was involved with it from the beginning, I am possibly better able than others to see its weak points. But they <u>are not</u> what you think them to be.

However, I would first like to discuss some of our accomplishments in this area. Currently the Union of Godless has <u>more than two million members</u>, close to half of which are nonparty workers and peasants. The union has more than doubled in size in one year. We have held 2 congresses of the union and have subsequently made great progress. There are now <u>tens</u> of godless villages; that is, villages where peasants <u>to a man</u> have rejected all priests, religious rituals, etc. In the enclosed eight-page summary (not a very complete one), which I received you will see what a large movement we are. Most important of all is that it is the workers and <u>the peasants</u> who are becoming atheists. Recently, <u>hundreds</u> of priests, mullahs, et al., have unfrocked themselves and rejected their professions. If we were to announce today that those who "renounced the cloth" were to receive voting privileges, Soviet certification, etc. and that they would no longer be considered parasites of the state, <u>thousands</u> of priests would abandon being priests.

You are correct in thinking that antireligious propaganda cannot be carried out solely according to doctrinaire Marxist teaching. Lenin was very clear in his opinion on this. I cite his view in the enclosed newspaper article from *Pravda* entitled "The Atheist Movement and the Progress of the Masses."

But in my view, your reasoning in regard to this idea is incorrect. Antireligious <u>propaganda</u> must always be based on <u>materialism</u>, on <u>Marxism</u>. Otherwise the proletarian party should not and cannot carry on its work. We cannot and should not argue from Divine Writ as did previous religious reformers or such peasant revolutionaries as Foma [illegible], et al. In the summary we are sending you of our published literature, you will find that we do hand out varied and diverse materials. I do agree with you that little of this Marxist antireligious literature is outstanding, but that only means that precisely this kind of literature must be created. It does not mean that we should argue from the notes of the Tübingen school and Divine Writ.

You are correct in saying that we need to prepare our antireligious specialists in a more serious manner. We are persistently striving towards this. (We have already achieved a few things. We already have more than 30 antireligious universities for workers.) But the press constantly attacks us (and me in particular) because I insist on the need to study the history of religion. Our *komsomol* members (who are under the influence of the ultra-left concerning this) do not think that this is necessary.

If you will recall, you mentioned during the Congress of the Godless that we should use good, artistic literature to appeal emotionally to religious people, especially to those who are shaky in their beliefs. I told you then that we would be very pleased if you would write something. Will you consider writing something?

Your other proposals will be discussed in the Union of Godless.

Wishing you good health and courage
With Communist greetings

E. IAroslavskii
Jan. 24, 1930

P.S. I am sending to you my pamphlet, the latest issue of *Pravda*
2 [ ] (No. 11 and 12), an antireligious manuscript from my
publication *Antireligion,* literature and various other
information.

RTSKhIDNI, fond 89, op. 4, d. 172, l. 1.

DOCUMENT 218 *Conversation between IAroslavskii and an American delegation headed by Sherwood Eddy, August 2, 1932, concerning antireligious propaganda*

Comrade IAroslavskii's conversation on August 2 with the American delegation under the leadership of Sherwood Eddy

Mr. Eddy states that all who have gathered here are believers and nonbelievers, but they all equally believe in science and evolution and denounce the previous religion of the old regime as Rasputin's belief and also a belief in primitive objects, such as relics, etc.; they consider that between themselves and Communists they can find a common language since they share a common ground.

Comrade IAroslavskii says that he will attempt to answer all questions put by the Americans.

Question 1: Why do we carry out antireligious propaganda in the USSR? We carried out antireligious propaganda when there was no USSR before 1917; we were always opponents of religion, atheists, as revolutionary Marxists and followers of Marx and Lenin. Our militant atheism is inseparably linked with our revolutionary worldview. It did not appear as an outgrowth that arose merely due to the conditions in the Soviet Union; this atheism is an integral part of our revolutionary worldview.

I could refer to articles by Lenin which he wrote during the first revolution, such as "Socialism and Religion," "On the Relationship of the Party's Work to Religion," and a series of others, and in his lengthy philosophical book [*Materialism and*] *Empirio-Criticism,* in which all religious and idealistic theories are subject to criticism, including the criticism of philosophers Bergson, James, and many others who lean towards religious worldviews.

Lenin and our entire party also battled with religion during the period between the two revolutions, when there were several comrades who wanted to reconcile communism with religion. We had groups called god-builders and god-seekers, and our party waged a very harsh battle with them. Lenin argued and we defended that communism and religion have nothing in common [break in the text]

Question no. 2: Which elements of religion do we denounce and are trying to overcome?

Comrade IAroslavskii: I will briefly answer the second question. Our program of antireligious propaganda consists of the masses not only breaking ties with churches but also overcoming elements of religious consciousness. We should help them free themselves of all traces of religious consciousness, help them cultivate a scientific, materi-

E. M. IAroslavskii and the American Young Pioneer Gary Eisman (center) and other participants at the First Young Atheists Meeting in Moscow, 1931. TSGAKFD. N 1-56486

alistic understanding of the world to free them of all elements of religiosity—this is the goal of our program. To separate not only church from state, but also the individual from the church.

This program is being fulfilled by propaganda, by organizing our Union of Militant Godless. It is carried out in literature, in public rallies, in our newspapers, magazines, books, brochures, theatres, movies, radio. The government does not forbid us to carry out this antireligious propaganda just as it does not forbid anyone to pray.

Our party program regarding religion shows that freeing the masses from religion is related to how succesfully we will implement planning of all facets of economic life in our country. This means, when we are able to organize our economy so that every worker, every peasant will know that the result of his work depends only on his collective or individual efforts and does not depend on any other powers, only then will the masses be free from religion. We place great importance concerning freedom from religion on the participation of the masses themselves in the building of socialism, so that they will rebuild their entire lives according to a conscious plan carried out by themselves [break in the text]

Question no. 3: How many churches are there in Russia?

Comrade IAroslavskii: This is a shortcoming in our society. We do not have exact statistics on all the churches located in Russia. These statistics, in all probability, are held by the Central Executive Committee [TSIK] of Soviets. In any case, the number of closed churches as a percentage of those open is still insignificant. I think that if among the population fewer than half are nonbelievers, then I doubt that more than 20% of the churches are closed. In the cities, of course, there are more closed churches, especially in large industrial cities such as Moscow, but nearly all the churches are open in the villages. At present maybe only 1 or 2% of the village churches are closed. Here in Moscow there are several dozen active churches; there are more than a hundred churches which are not being torn down, but are no longer active.

Unfortunately, I cannot give you a more accurate figure. During my conversation with American professors, the chairman of the Moscow Union of Godless listed 87 churches in Moscow where services are being held. In the entire country there are tens of thousands of churches open, active, if you also include synagogues, mosques, and buddhist temples. Last year we counted 46,000 active churches and sectarian houses of prayer.

Mr. Eddy: It is said that Moscow has forty times forty churches. If only 87 active churches remain then even more are closed.

Comrade IAroslavskii: Forty times forty is a fable. If you include all the chapels, the merchants' private chapels at home, all the churches connected with hospitals, schools, barracks, prisons, which were destroyed at the very beginning of the revolution when there were twice as many. Since the church was separated from the schools, parochial schools have ceased to exist now, in hospitals, prisons.

[Mr. Eddy]: When you say that God is in favor of war, prostitution, etc., you are talking about religion before the flood, but we believe in the religion of science; we have a more modern and more scientific outlook and for this reason it is silly to talk about such a God. Among those in attendance, there is not one who believes in such things, just as we do not believe in the nationalization of women. You must approach the real question even closer, you must study the real religion, as we study Communism. As we attempt to understand you, so must you attempt to understand us. We are all fighting against superstitions and against social injustice.

Comrade IAroslavskii: I will answer this briefly. If you did study us Communists just as intently as we study you, then maybe something would come of it. Unfortunately, you study us very little. In any case, you do very little to make our views, the views of the Communists to be indeed accessible to the general masses in other countries. The matter is not as simple as it seems to you, that there are a crude religion and prejudices against which we must fight, which you are fighting against, and there is a "refined" religion, as Mr. Eddy stated—a scientific religion which should not be fought, but instead should be studied. Between these two ideas, it seems there lies an unfathomable gulf, even though there are many scholars who consider themselves to be believers. It is also false that all scholars in the Soviet Union are atheists, we never maintained this, we also have scholars who are believers, attend church, we do not ask them about this. There are scholars who do not ascribe to the building of socialism. Religion, all religions, including a scientific one as you know it, is the ideology of a particular class. There is no ideology that embraces the interests of all classes. Each ideology envelops the interests of a particular class, serves its interests [original ends at this point]

RTSKhIDNI, fond 89, op. 4, d. 41, ll. 4, 6, 9, 16, 19.

DOCUMENT 219   *Report by Institute for Scientific Atheism, May 21, 1974, to the Central Committee on increasing effectiveness of atheistic education among youth*

CENTRAL COMMITTEE OF
THE COMMUNIST PARTY OF THE USSR
[*TSK KPSS*]

MARCH 25, 1974

CONTROL NO. 11883

RETURN TO THE GENERAL
DEPARTMENT OF THE *TSK KPSS*

Not For Publication

THE DEPARTMENT OF SCIENCE AND EDUCATIONAL INSTITUTIONS
OF THE *TSK KPSS*

DEPARTMENT OF PROPAGANDA OF THE *TSK KPSS*

The Rectorate of the Academy of Social Sciences of the *TSK KPSS* is forwarding for your perusal a report entitled "Improving the Effectiveness of Atheist Education for the Student Population," drafted by the Institute of Scientific Atheism of the Academy of Social Sciences of the *TSK KPSS.*

In our opinion it would be worthwhile to forward this report to the Central Committee of the *komsomol,* the ministries of Higher and Secondary Specialized Education, Public Education, and Culture, and several of the artists' unions and organizations cited in this report for discussion of the recommendations of the Institute of Scientific Atheism.

I hereby request your consent.

Rector of the Academy of
Social Sciences of the
TSK KPSS

[signed] M. Iovchuk

March 22, 1974
No. 41
4-ian

IMPROVING THE EFFECTIVENESS OF ATHEIST EDUCATION
FOR THE STUDENT POPULATION

Over the last two years the Institute of Scientific Atheism of the Academy of Social Sciences of the *TSK KPSS* has been studying the development of atheist convictions among the student population. This study involved sociological surveys of the students' attitudes toward atheism and religion at a number of higher educational institutions (in Moscow, Leningrad, Kaluga, Perm', Riazan', Groznyi, Grodno, Karaganda, Tallin, Chernovtsy, and other locales).

The absolute majority of Soviet students are free of any religious prejudices, which was confirmed by our sociological surveys. At the same time the absence of religion among most students cannot conceal the fact that at times one may encounter religious believers or individuals who have fallen under the influence of idealistic, quasi-religious beliefs. The percentage of students who to some degree or another accept the validity of idealistic views or religious beliefs and traditions among the total number of students is somewhat higher in the western regions of Ukraine and Belorussia, in the Central Asian republics, in the Baltic republics, and in the North Caucasus. There have been cases where certain students who were previously nonbelievers or indifferent to religion have begun to show an interest in religious beliefs and rituals. Their interest in religion is quite often associated with errant moral and philosophical "searchings" and at times with contrariness and the desire to stand out from the crowd. Misconceptions of religion as an effective regulator of moral behavior even now, under socialism, are common among certain students. Certain students believe that religion plays an important role in personal moral behavior by supposedly "humanizing us," "establishing a framework for moral behavior," "restraining us from immoral acts," and so forth. The persistence of these misconceptions has largely been facilitated by religious propaganda, which emphasizes that religion is the "only repository of morality." There have been cases where political nihilism, rejection of the Soviet way of life, nationalistic attitudes, and so forth are cloaked in the attraction to religion and heightened interest in religious antiquity.

Our attention is also drawn to the fact that large numbers of students have an indifferent attitude towards religion and a tolerant attitude towards different manifestations of religiosity. Indifference toward religion among certain students is associated with an indifference toward philosophical questions in general with a kind of "lack of spirituality," a lack of ideology, and with the mistaken belief that supposedly preparation for a career, and nothing else, is what's important for people today.

We cannot help but be alarmed by the tolerance of certain segments of the student population towards religious rituals and holidays. For example, in our surveys and questionnaires involving several groups of students in their first year at the University of Mordovia, 43% of these students stated that they could see themselves taking part in religious rituals and holidays. Quite a few young people, including students from secondary schools, and at times students from institutions of higher learning, gather near Orthodox and Catholic churches, Moslem mosques, and Jewish synagogues on religious holidays. Our interviews and surveys of students at a number of technical and liberal arts schools in Leningrad revealed that some students see religious rituals and holidays as folk customs that should be supported. Some students see religion as a vehicle of ethnic traditions and beliefs that connects the present to the past.

To some extent, these misconceptions and mistaken attitudes have been facilitated by misconceptions in evaluating the traditions and culture of the past, a tendency to idealize and revive the religious past, and attempts to identify religious art and other forms of religious culture of the past with folk culture and portray the "religious" as the "national." These mistaken views have been reflected in the work of certain writers (Soloukhin, Chendei, and several articles in the journal *Molodaia Gvardiia* [Young Guard] and have been subjected to well-deserved criticism in our media.

At times an excessive infatuation with the pageantry of different church rites and ceremonies, which have been portrayed "impartially" or even with a certain amount of admiration in certain movies, TV programs, and so forth, has played a negative role.

All of these problems and misconceptions have led to a situation where church rituals, religious symbols, and objects of religious worship such as icons, crucifixes, and so forth have remained or become even more fashionable among certain young people, including students. These fads, as sociological surveys have shown, provide evidence of the mental immaturity, philosophical and moral incoherence, and at times the low spiritual level of certain students.

The most common motive cited by the students who take part in religious rites is an interest in the aesthetic aspect of the church, which, in the minds of these students, is separate from the religious essence of the church and is merely a beautiful theatrical "pageant." For example, one third-year student at L'vov University made a statement that typifies the opinions of this part of the student body: "The church ceremonies, which are based on folk customs, are very interesting. There is no need to describe the church weddings and church festivals in the Carpathian villages, "the sepulcher" in the church," "Palm Sunday" in the Il'in Church, and so forth. All of them provide aesthetic enjoyment for the believer and nonbeliever alike. And therefore it is no surprise that scenes from religious rituals are the best scenes in many films."

The uncritical attitude towards religious art adopted by certain students, especially at the arts schools, has also led to the idealization of religion and the "rebirth" of religious beliefs and traditions. For example, our interviews and surveys of students at the Conservatory and Institute of Theater, Music, and Cinematography in Leningrad, the Gnesin Music Education Institute, and other institutions revealed that fascination with the masterpieces of their art, which in the past was associated with religion, has led some students to overestimate the importance of religion in the history of culture and social development and doubt the need for atheist education. This problem looks even more alarming when we consider that the students at art schools are our artistic intelligentsia of the future, who have been called on to develop and teach art from a scientific, materialistic, and socialist point of view.

We should mention that for some students a heightened interest in religious rituals and religious traditions, religious art, and so forth has gone beyond the realm of trendiness and has at times become an expression of antisocialist and nationalist attitudes.

At times, the party and *komsomol* organizations of higher educational institutions, propagandists, and educators have failed to give the proper attention to those students who may classify themselves as nonbelievers, have a hostile attitude towards religious views, and are averse to religious rituals but have not yet acquired the requisite scientific atheist knowledge and convictions. They quite often demonstrate a fundamental ignorance of topics related to religion, its history, and the current state of religious cults, the legal status of religious organizations in a socialist society, and ways of combatting religion. These kinds of students are most often encountered at technical schools. When they encounter religious and idealistic arguments in favor of religion, some students are helpless and incapable of resisting clerical and sectarian propaganda and at times fall prey to its noxious influence.

One may also encounter young male and female students whose minds have been polluted with all kinds of superstitions and prejudices, or so-called folk mysticism, even though they deny any belief in God, religious mythology, prayer, religious services, and so forth. For example, 15% of the students surveyed at several Leningrad higher educational institutions believe in omens. According to our surveys at the University of Mordovia, 22% of the first year students believe in omens and 23% believe in "fate." Obviously, superstitions cannot be lumped willy nilly with religiosity, but they can provide fertile soil for the growth of religiosity.

Thus, our analysis of the materials of the sociological surveys has confirmed that the primary source of the aforementioned problems is the fact that many students have not developed a profound and consistent scientific and materialist outlook or firm atheist convictions, which is largely due to the inadequacy of education in the schools and deficiencies in the educational process, especially in the organization of atheist education for young people.

In 1964, in accordance with the directive of the *TSK KPSS* "Concerning Efforts to Improve the Atheist Education of the Population," a required or elective course entitled "The Fundamentals of Scientific Atheism" was introduced at institutions of higher learning. Specialized departments of scientific atheism were organized at 20 institutions of higher learning. In 1973 a new textbook entitled *Scientific Atheism* was published.

However, the quality of instruction in "The Fundamentals of Scientific Atheism" has been characterized by major shortcomings. This course is not offered at many teachers' schools or even at some universities, even though it was established as a required course for this category of schools. The course is not offered at many technical schools, where it is considered an elective. Certain institutes have reduced the number of hours allocated to the course on scientific atheism, and under the pretext of including questions on scientific atheism in their philosophy exams, do not give any tests for the required course on scientific atheism. At a number of schools this course is taught by instructors who are poorly prepared theoretically and professionally. Despite the great demand for qualified teachers of scientific atheism, the system for training and retraining these instructors is still poorly organized. Given the prevailing "allocations" for retraining atheism instructors for higher educational institutions, the current advanced training institutes for social science instructors at higher educational institutions are only capable of giving refresher courses to these instructors once every 10 to 12 years instead of the required 4 or 5. And three-month on-the-job training periods, which are required for the graduates of a number of schools, have practically never been used for scientific atheism instructors.

The profile of the institute or the specific conditions under which the graduates will impart scientific atheist knowledge is not always taken into account in the atheist education of students. The lack of special scientific atheism teaching aids for art, medical, and agricultural schools has also had an adverse impact.

Different kinds of extracurricular activities such as the involvement of students in research on atheism, atheist discussion clubs and seminars, sociological surveys, atheistic propaganda for the general public, and so forth could play a major role in the atheistic education of students. Atheist clubs, which have been organized at several institutions of higher learning (the Leningrad and Daugavpils Teachers' Institutes, the Tallin Polytechnical Institute, and so forth), schools for organizers of alternative rituals, schools for young atheist lecturers, and so forth have become an effective tool for atheist education in a number of cities. These activities make it possible to train qualified atheist lecturers as well as improve the atheist knowledge of the students. For example, during the ten years of its existence, the young atheist lecturer school at Kazakhstan State University has trained more than 200 lecturers. The experience gained at a number of schools in extracurricular scientific atheism activities, however, has not been widely publicized and is still the exclusive property of certain institutes.

Individual counseling with religious students has not been adequately developed. There have been cases where believers have been expelled from schools under the pretext of academic failure. These incidents not only constitute an example of administrative arbitrariness and a violation of the laws guaranteeing freedom of conscience; they have also played into the hands of religious extremists and are extensively publicized and exaggerated by foreign anti-Communist propaganda.

In order to improve the effectiveness of atheist education for students, the Institute of Scientific Atheism considers it advisable to recommend that:

1. The Ministry of Higher and Secondary Specialized Education, the Ministry of Public Education, and the Ministry of Culture of the USSR: a) initiate the development of specialized programs of scientific atheism, in particular for universities, higher educational institutions and schools for teachers and artists; focus special attention on the methodology of atheistic education for preschoolers and elementary school students in the curricula for teachers' schools and institutes. The scientific atheism programs for art schools should include a study of topics related to the relationship between art and religion, the importance and role of religion in the history of art, the difference between the religious mind and the artistic creative mind, and the specific nature of religious ethical and religious aesthetic ideals. It would be desirable to reshuffle the hours allotted for the study of scientific atheism at higher educational institutions, especially teachers' institutes, to give more weight to the sections of the "Fundamentals of Scientific Atheism" course that describe the current state of religious affairs, the perniciousness of religious ideology, the danger of attempts to modernize religion under the conditions of a socialist society, and the predominantly negative role of religion and the church in the history of society and its culture, especially in the contemporary ideological struggle; b) initiate the production of specialized instructional aids for atheism that would develop, illustrate, and supplement the ideas of the textbook *Scientific Atheism (Politizdat)* approved by the Ministry of Higher and Specialized Secondary Education to fit the curricula of different higher educational institutions (universities, teachers' institutes, medical, art, technical, and agricultural institutes); c) in light of the growing interest in the philosophical aspects of atheism and the critique of religion on the part of students at technical schools, examine the issue of making the "Fundamentals of Scientific Atheism" a required course at technical schools; d) arrange for the production of graphic teaching aids for atheism, slides, and educational films on scientific atheism topics for use in the instruction process; e) commission the *Vysshaia shkola* [Higher Education] Publishing House to publish educational literature, instructors' manuals, and graphic teaching aids for atheism for the students and instructors at higher educational institutions; f) examine the issue of establishing permanent scientific atheism groups at advanced training institutes and sending more atheism instructors for refresher courses at these institutes; g) organize scientific atheism councils at higher educational institutions, primarily the largest ones, whose members would be drawn from the faculty and representatives of party and *komsomol* organizations; h) make more extensive use of such proven techniques of atheist education as student atheist clubs and young lecturers' schools and exhibits of atheist literature at student clubs, libraries, auditoriums, and dormitories; i) periodically hold scientific atheism lectures scheduled to coincide with important dates in the history of atheism and freethinking.

2. Request the Central Committee of the *komsomol* to consider the importance of getting *komsomol* or-

ganizations at higher educational institutions more involved in atheist education of the student body. To accomplish this it would be advisable to: a) hold special conferences on improving atheist education among students in the union republics and major educational centers; b) include scientific atheism (as a separate competition) in the national competitions for the best student research in the field of social sciences, the history of the *komsomol*, and the international youth movement; c) organize special teams to advocate scientific materialist and atheist ideas among the general public, especially among young people, within the framework of the National Agitation Campaign.

3. It would be advisable to request the Central Committee of the *komsomol*, the Philosophical Society of the Soviet Union, the National *Znanie* [Knowledge] Society, and the creative artists' unions to consider the question of publishing a special popular science journal for young people (including students) that would cover philosophical questions and atheist ideas in a bright and attractive format and would provide persuasive critiques of the contemporary forms of religious and idealistic philosophy. Journals of this kind already exist in Poland and a number of other socialist countries. The journal *Liudina i svit* [Man and the World], published in the Ukrainian Soviet Socialist Republic, has also gained some valuable experience in this area.

4. Request the Central Committee of the *komsomol* to instruct the editors of the newspaper *Komsomol'skaia Pravda, oblast'* and republic youth newspapers, and the youth departments of the national and republic radio and television networks on the need to provide greater coverage of scientific materialist and atheist education of young people, including students, while stepping up their criticism of the different misconceptions of religion and the church, the unhealthy fascination with church rituals, and indifference towards atheism and the critique of religion, and so forth.

5. Request the State Publishing Committee [*Goskomizdat*] of the Council of Ministers to instruct the *Mysl'* [Thought] and *Molodaia Gvardiia* [Young Guard] political publishing houses, as well as the *Znanie* [Knowledge] publishing house, to organize the production of a series of books and pamphlets designed for the young reader that would cover contemporary aspects of the fight against religion, the role of atheist philosophy in molding the new man, the conflicts between the Communist and religious conceptions of man, the questions of the meaning and purpose of life, and so forth; it would be desirable to create a special library on atheism entitled "Youth, Atheism, and Religion."

6. The journals *Nauka i religiia* [Science and Religion], *Nauka i zhizn'* [Science and Life], and others should publish more articles describing the experience of scientific materialist and atheist education of young people, including students, which would shed light on specific aspects of combatting religiosity and inculcating scientific materialist attitudes in young people, especially students.

7. Request the boards of the creative artists' unions and organizations (The Writers' Union, The Cinematographers' Union, the Artists' Union, the Journalists' Union, and so forth) to consider the need to portray the problems of atheist education of young people and efforts to combat attempts by religious organizations here and abroad to influence the young in artistic and documentary films and in other works of literature and art.

Director of the Institute
of Scientific Atheism
of the Academy of Social Sciences
of the *TSK KPSS*   [signed] A. Okulov

TSK KPSS

On the Report of the Institute of Scientific
Atheism of the Academy of Social Sciences
of the *TSK KPSS*

The Rectorate of the Academy of Social Sciences of the *TSK KPSS* has forwarded to the departments of propaganda, science, and higher educational institutes of the *TSK KPSS* a report by the Institute of Scientific Atheism concerning "Improving the Effectiveness of Atheist Education for the Student Population."

In light of the issues raised in the report, the Ministry of Higher and Secondary Specialized Education of the USSR and the Ministry of Public Education of the USSR are instructed to study the proposal to develop specialized programs for scientific atheism for universities, institutions of higher education, and schools for teachers and artists.

The State Publishing Committee of the USSR is hereby advised to include the publication of a cooperative series of pamphlets on "Youth, Atheism, and Religion" in drafting its next prospectus for literature on atheism; the new *Plakat* [Poster] publishing house is advised to include the publication of atheism posters in its prospectus.

At the same time we do not consider the publication of a special popular science journal for young people worthwhile, because the country already has more than 60 social, political, and literary journals for young people and children that cover philosophical questions, conduct atheist propaganda, and publish critiques of contemporary religious creeds.

The issues of encouraging newspapers, journals, and the youth departments of radio and television to become more active in advocating scientific materialist ideas and atheist education of young people will be resolved on the job as the occasion presents itself.

The Rectorate of the Academy of Social Sciences of the *TSK KPSS* has been informed.

Assistant Head of the
Department of Science
and Educational Institutions
of the *TSK KPSS*

[signed] N. Kuz'min

May 21, 1974

Attachment to No. 11883

Assistant Head of the
Department of
Propaganda of the *TSK KPSS*

[signed] V. Medvedev

TSKhSD, fond 5, op. 67, d. 170

chapter 6

CHERNOBYL

On Monday, April 28, 1986, Swedish monitoring stations reported heightened levels of atmospheric radiation and traced the source to Ukraine. Only that evening the Soviet television news included a brief report that an accident had taken place at the Chernobyl nuclear electricity-generating plant north of Kiev, that one of the reactors had been damaged, and that some casualties were receiving medical treatment. The next evening further details emerged: lives had been lost and "dangerous conditions" (rather than radiation) existed at the site. *Pravda* did not cover the story for another two weeks, and Gorbachev first acknowledged the accident on May 14, nearly three weeks after the explosion. The silence and cover-up of the Chernobyl accident constituted one of the most significant failures of Gorbachev's policy of *glasnost'*.

The documents included here speak to the extent of the cover-up, which began well before the explosion in the nuclear reactor on April 26, 1986. Construction flaws had already been reported at the nuclear plant as early as 1979. Even after the explosion, which released a radioactive cloud ten times more hazardous than the radiation released by the bomb dropped on Hiroshima, officials failed to acknowledge or did not appreciate the extensive dangers caused to the population. Faulty instruments were blamed for the high radiation readings, and even Andrei Sakharov, still in exile in Gorky, was fooled by the false assurances of the Soviet media. Ukrainian Communist Party officials refused to call for an evacuation, claiming that the "panic is worse than radiation," although some of them evacuated their own family members. Memoranda included here describe efforts to reassure foreign governments, including those of Soviet allies, that Soviet authorities had taken all necessary measures to contain the damage. Even a year after the event, the Central Committee expressed concern about managing international public relations: the trial of those responsible for the accident was to be conducted quietly, with minimal attendance by journalists (Document 22). Despite the increase in genetic abnormalities among livestock, radiation-contaminated meat continued to be shipped from the area for processing into sausage as late as 1990. A secret decree in effect from 1988 to 1991 ordered Soviet doctors not to cite radiation as a cause of death, even though 600,000 workers took part in the deadly clean-up job, and the deputy prime minister of Ukraine, Boris Shcherbina, who had participated in the cover-up, himself died of radiation poisoning.

DOCUMENT 220   *KGB memorandum from Andropov to the Central Committee, February 21, 1979, on construction flaws at the Chernobyl nuclear power plant*

40

Not for publication   Secret

                                                Feb. 21, 1979 05363
                                                Return to the General
                                                Section of the Central
                                                Committee of the *KPSS*

                                        Central Committee of the *KPSS*

USSR COMMITTEE OF STATE SECURITY [*KGB*]
February 21, 1979 No. 346-A
        Moscow
Construction Flaws at the Chernobyl Nuclear Power Plant [*AES*]

According to data in the possession of the *KGB* of the USSR, design deviations and violations of construction and assembly technology are occurring at various places in the construction of the second generating unit of the Chernobyl *AES*, and these could lead to mishaps and accidents.

The structural pillars of the generator room were erected with a deviation of up to 100 mm from the reference axes, and horizontal connections between the pillars are absent in places. Wall panels have been installed with a deviation of up to 150 mm from the axes. The placement of roof plates does not conform to the designer's specifications. Crane tracks and stopways have vertical drops of up to 100 mm and in places a slope of up to 8°.

Deputy head of the Construction Directorate, Comrade V. T. Gora, gave instructions for backfilling the foundation in many places where vertical waterproofing was damaged. Similar violations were permitted in other sections with the knowledge of Comrade V. T. Gora and the head of the construction group, Comrade IU. L. Matveev. Damage to the waterproofing can lead to ground water seepage into the station and radioactive contamination of the environment.

The leadership of the directorate is not devoting proper attention to the foundation, on which the quality of the construction largely depends. The cement plant operates erratically, and its output is of poor quality. Interruptions were permitted during the pouring of especially heavy concrete, causing gaps and layering in the foundation. Access roads to the Chernobyl *AES* are in urgent need of repair.

Construction of the third high-voltage transmission line is behind schedule, which could limit the capacity utilization of the second unit.

As a result of inadequate monitoring of the condition of safety equipment, in the first three quarters of 1978, 170 individuals suffered work-related injuries, with the loss of work time totalling 3,366 worker-days.

The *KGB* of Ukraine has informed the Ukrainian Communist Party [*KPU*] Central Committee of these violations. This is for your information.

Chairman of the Committee [*KGB*] [signed] IU. Andropov

42

Secret

Copy no. 1

USSR MINISTRY OF
POWER AND ELECTRIFICATION
[*MINENERGO* USSR]   Central Committee *KPSS*

Kitaiskii pr. 7
Moscow, K-74 103074
Minenergo USSR

Moscow K-11 A.T. 112604   MAR. 16, 79 07738
3-16-79 No. 1381-2c   Return to General Section of the Central Committee
No. ____ from _____

On checking the structural condition of the first unit of the Chernobyl *AES*.

At the instruction of the USSR Minister of Power and Electrification, a commission under the chairmanship of Deputy Minister Comrade F. V. Sapozhnikov was formed to check the quality of construction and assembly work on the first unit of the Chernobyl *AES*.

The commission visited the site on March 5–6, 1979, and examined the state of the buildings and structures of the first unit of the Chernobyl *AES* and the notes on the quality of construction and assembly work.

The Commission found that violations of construction technology and design deviations have been documented.

In each specific instance, engineering solutions were adopted (in the construction, in the operation, or by the designers) to eliminate deviations and make the structures conform to the specifications of the original design and normative documents.

Some of the measures have been realized; the rest of the work is being completed according to a rigid timetable set by the commission.

At the present time the power station is operating successfully, and there are no hindrances to its further operation.

Taking into account the specifics of nuclear power stations and attaching primary significance to the reliability and safety of their operations, the USSR Ministry of Power and Electrification has issued an order to enhance monitoring of the observance of technical standards and the quality of construction and assembly work at all *AES*s under construction.

A letter of similar content was sent to the Central Committee of the Communist Party of Ukraine.

Deputy Minister   [signed] P. P. Falaleev

CENTRAL COMMITTEE OF THE *KPSS*

<u>On Flaws in the Construction of the Chernobyl *AES*</u>

The chairman of the *KGB* of the USSR, Comrade IU. V. Andropov, reports about the low quality of construction work on various sections of the second unit of the Chernobyl *AES* of the USSR Ministry of Power and Electrification.

As instructed, Comrade Minister P. S. Neporozhnii has formed a special commission under the leadership of Deputy Minister Comrade Sapozhnikov to examine and analyze carefully the facts cited. The commission visited the site to conduct a thorough investigation of design deviations and to inspect the system of quality control of construction and assembly work.

It was found that in erecting individual pillars, wall panels, and crane track stopways, there indeed were instances of deviation from the reference axes and substandard construction practices. Most of these deviations were exposed by the design inspectorate of the *Gidroproekt* Institute and a technical site inspection, and they were documented.

The Chernobyl *AES* Construction Directorate along with the design organization and client have adopted coordinated engineering solutions ensuring design reliability and construction quality. Some of the deviations have been eliminated, and the rest of the measures are being carried out. A timetable under the control of the ministry leadership has been established to eliminate the noted deficiencies.

The specialists conclude that at present there are no obstacles to the subsequent operation of the Chernobyl *AES*, and the electric power station is operating reliably.

To raise the quality of construction and assembly work and strengthen control over fire and radiation safety, the ministry has published instructions stipulating strict verification of the quality of work at *AES* construction sites by ministry commissions, enhancing quality inspection laws, training engineers and technicians, strengthening fire-fighting procedures, and monitoring observation of safety regulations.

The head of the *Soiuzatomenergo* organization, Comrade Nevskii, the director of the Chernobyl *AES*, Comrade Briukhanov, and the head of the construction directorate, Comrade Kizima, were notified of their personal responsibility for eliminating the noted flaws and improving the quality of the work performed.

The Central Committee of the Communist Party of Ukraine has been informed of the measures taken by the ministry.

Head of the Section of Machine Building of the
Central Committee of the *KPSS*.   [signed]   (V. Frolov)

March 23, 1979

Nos. 05363,07738,
    60A/II.

TSKhSD, fond 5, op. 76.

DOCUMENT 221 *Urgent report on the Chernobyl accident from the first deputy minister of energy and electrification, April 26, 1986*

Not for Publication Secret

Copy No. __

First Deputy	Central Committee of the
Minister of	Communist Party of the Soviet Union
Energy and	
Electrification of the USSR	

103074, Moscow, K-74, Kitaiskii pr., 7,
Moscow, K-11, Ministry of Energy and Electrification
of the USSR, A.T. 112604
Telephone: 220-55-00

<u>April 26, 1986</u>   No. <u>1789-2c</u>

Regarding the accident in Unit No. 4 of the Chernobyl Nuclear Power Plant [*AES*]

URGENT REPORT

On April 26, 1986, at 1:21 A.M., in taking Chernobyl *AES* generating unit No. 4 off-load for planned repairs, after shutting down the reactor, an explosion took place in the upper part of the reactor compartment.

According to the report of the Chernobyl *AES* director, in the explosion the roof, part of the wall panels of the reactor compartment, several roof panels of the generator room, and the reactor compartment's auxiliary systems block collapsed, and also the roofing caught fire.

At 3:30 A.M the fire was extinguished.

Through the efforts of the *AES* personnel, measures are being taken to cool down the reactor core.

In the opinion of Main Administration 3 of the USSR Ministry of Health, implementation of special measures, including evacuation of the city's population, is not necessary.

Nine operations staff members and 25 paramilitary fire fighters were hospitalized.

Measures are being taken to remove the aftereffects and to investigate the incident.

A. N. Makukhin

TSKhSD. Current archive

Spectrometrists making tests at the Chernobyl nuclear power plant and environs, May 17, 1986. ITAR-TASS Photoagency

DOCUMENT 222 *Resolution of the Central Committee, April 29, 1986, on additional measures to be taken concerning the damage caused by the Chernobyl accident*

<u>Top Secret</u>

RESOLUTION OF THE CENTRAL COMMITTEE OF THE COMMUNIST PARTY OF THE SOVIET UNION
[*TSK KPSS*]

<u>On additional measures to eliminate the damage caused by the
accident at the Chernobyl Nuclear Power Plant [*AES*]</u>

1. Note for the record Comrade V. I. Dolgikh's report on progress of efforts to eliminate the damage caused by the accident at the Chernobyl *AES*.

2. Note that the situation in the vicinity of the Chernobyl *AES* remains complex and needs coordinated actions. To that end, create a task force in the Politburo of the *TSK KPSS*, consisting of N. I. Ryzhkov (head of the task force), E. K. Ligachev, V. I. Vorotnikov, V. M. Chebrikov, V. I. Dolgikh, S. L. Sokolov, and A. V. Vlasov.

3. Instruct the task force to concentrate above all on localizing the center of nuclear radiation, on stricter monitoring of soil and air conditions, and also on organizing medical and other assistance for the population in the Chernobyl *AES* area and in the radioactive fallout zone.

Establish that in fulfilling its functions the task force is empowered to give necessary instructions to the government commission (which has a changing staff), and also to all party, Soviet, and public agencies, ministries and departments, and scientific institutions.

4. Taking into account the discussions at the session of the Politburo of the *TSK* of the *KPSS*, consider it advisable to prepare information on the progress of efforts to eliminate the damage caused by the accident at the Chernobyl *AES*. This information should be prepared for the population of our country, for the leadership of fraternal parties of socialist states, and also for the heads of other European states, the U.S.A., and Canada (texts attached).

Assign responsibility for liaison and information release to foreign statesmen and organizations, in the event of inquiries, to the Chairman of the State Committee of the USSR on Utilization of Nuclear Energy, Comrade A. M. Petros'iants, assisted by a prominent scientist/specialist in nuclear energy.

Secretary of the *TSK*, Ukrainian Communist Party

TO Comrades:			
	Gorbachev	Sokolov	Slavskii
	Ryzhkov	Dobrynin	Burenkov
	Ligachev	Medvedev	Beliakov
	Vorotnikov	Yakovlev	IAstrebov
	Zaikov	Shcherbina	Smirtiukov
	Chebrikov	Aleksandrov	
	Shevardnadze	Vlasov	
	Dolgikh	Maiorts	P9/1

Adopted by the Politburo of the *TSK*, April 29, 1986
[signed] Sokolov

From the Council of Ministers of the USSR.

As already reported in the press, there has been an accident at the Chernobyl *AES*, located 130 kilometers north of Kiev. A government commission headed by the deputy chairman of the Council of Ministers of the USSR, Comrade B. E. Shcherbina, is working on location. The staff of the commission consists of the heads of ministries and departments, prominent scientists, and specialists.

Preliminary data indicate that the accident took place in one of the buildings of the fourth generating unit. The accident destroyed part of the reactor building's structure and released some radioactive materials. Three other generating units have been shut down, remain in operating condition, and have been placed in operational reserve. Two people were killed in the accident. We are taking emergency measures to eliminate the damage caused by the accident. At the present time the radioactivity situation at the power plant and immediate vicinity has been stabilized, and the victims are receiving necessary medical assistance. The residents of the *AES* community and three nearby settlements have been evacuated.

The radioactivity level at the Chernobyl *AES* and environs is being monitored continuously.

SOFIA, BUDAPEST, BERLIN, WARSAW, BUCHAREST, PRAGUE, HAVANA, BELGRADE—SOVIET AMBASSADOR.

Visit immediately Comrade Zhivkov (Kádár, Honecker, Jaruzelski, Ceauşescu, Husák, Castro, Žarković or his substitute) and, referring to this instruction, convey the following:

1. As already reported in the Soviet press, on April 26 there was an accident in one of the generating unit buildings of the Chernobyl nuclear power plant [*AES*], located 130 kilometers north of Kiev. The accident destroyed part of the reactor building's structure, damaged the reactor, and released some radioactive materials. The other three generating units have been shut down, [but] remain in working condition and have been placed in operational reserve.

2. Measurements taken continuously by the Soviet services indicated that radiation levels in the immediate vicinity necessitated partial evacuation of the population. As a result of measures taken, the radiation level has been stabilized. To eliminate the damage caused by the accident, additional measures are being taken.

3. According to data given by responsible Soviet organizations, radioactive contamination has been noted spreading in westerly, northerly, and southerly directions. The level of contamination somewhat exceeds acceptable norms but not to such a degree that it requires special measures to protect the population.

Explain that similar information will be conveyed to the leadership of the U.S.A. and a number of West European countries.

Add that we will give our friends additional information as needed.

Telegraph the execution [of these instructions]

WASHINGTON, LONDON, PARIS, ROME, BONN, HELSINKI, OSLO, STOCKHOLM, ATHENS, VIENNA, BERN, BRUSSELS, THE HAGUE, LUXEMBOURG, COPENHAGEN, MADRID, LISBON, DUBLIN, VALLETTA, NICOSIA, ANKARA, OTTAWA—SOVIET AMBASSADOR.

Referring to the instructions, immediately inform President Reagan about the following, (at other places inform highest possible level of leadership of the country of station) through the person you find most appropriate about the following:

1. As already reported in the Soviet press, on April 26 there was an accident in one of the generating unit buildings of the Chernobyl nuclear power plant [*AES*], located 130 kilometers north of Kiev. The accident destroyed part of the reactor building's structure, damaged the reactor, and released some radioactive materials. The other three generating units have been shut down, [but] remain in working condition and have been placed in operational reserve.

2. Measurements taken continuously by the Soviet services indicated that radiation levels in the immediate vicinity necessitated partial evacuation of the population. As a result of measures taken, the radiation level has been stabilized. To eliminate the damage caused by the accident, additional measures are being taken.

3. According to data given by Soviet responsible organizations, radioactive contamination has been noted spreading in westerly, northerly, and southerly directions. The level of contamination somewhat exceeds acceptable norms but not to such a degree that it requires special measures to protect the population.

(Only for Helsinki, Oslo, Stockholm, Copenhagen: Tell them that in case of new information of special interest to these countries, we will send additional reports.)
Telegraph the execution [of these instructions]

[Published in *Rodina*, No.1, 1992, pp. 83–87.]

TSKhSD, fond 3, op. 102, d. 67.

DOCUMENT 223   *Central Committee resolution of April 30, 1986, concerning progress in repairing damage caused by the Chernobyl accident*

Top Secret

A RESOLUTION OF THE CENTRAL COMMITTEE OF THE COMMUNIST PARTY OF THE SOVIET UNION

On the Progress of Operations to Remedy the Damage from the Accident at the Chernobyl Nuclear Power Plant

1. To confirm the text of the news release from the Council of Ministers of the USSR for the Soviet press, radio, and television (attached).

2. To confirm the texts of instructions to the Soviet ambassadors in socialist countries, other European countries, the U.S.A., and Canada (attached).

SECRETARY OF THE CENTRAL COMMITTEE

FROM THE COUNCIL OF MINISTERS OF THE USSR

Operations to remedy the aftereffects of the accident that occurred at the Chernobyl nuclear power plant continue. As a result of measures taken in the past 24 hours, the release of radioactive matter has decreased, and the levels of radiation around the power plant and nearby town have dropped.

Measurements, conducted by specialists using appropriate instruments, indicate that fission has stopped in the nuclear fuel and that the reactor is dead.

Extensive measures are being taken to decontaminate the local region. Special units equipped with the necessary, up-to-date technology and operative facilities have been called in.

Some agencies in the West are spreading rumors that supposedly thousands of people have died because of the nuclear power plant accident. As already reported, two people actually perished, a total of 197 were hospitalized; of these, 49 left the hospital after examination. The functioning of production facilities, collective farms, state farms, and establishments continues as usual.

TO THE SOVIET AMBASSADOR IN: SOFIA, BUDAPEST, BERLIN, WARSAW, BUCHAREST, PRAGUE, HAVANA, BELGRADE

Communicate immediately to Comrades Zhivkov (Kádár, Ceaușescu, Husák, Castro, Žarković, or their designates) the following additional information on the status of attempts to remedy the aftereffects of the accident at the Chernobyl nuclear power plant.

As a result of measures taken in the past 24 hours, the release of radioactive matter has decreased, and the level of radiation in the region near the incident has dropped.

Measurements are being conducted that indicate that fission has stopped in the nuclear fuel. The reactor is dead.

Extensive measures are being taken to decontaminate the local region. Special units have been called in to carry out these measures.

Through our ambassadors we reported to other countries that the Soviet Union has sufficient material, scientific, and technical resources to remedy the aftereffects of the accident and that at the present stage does not need assistance from other countries. No foreign nationals in the Soviet Union (particularly specialists or tourists) have made application to relevant Soviet organizations in connection with the Chernobyl nuclear power plant accident.

Confirm the execution of this order by telegraph.

TO THE SOVIET AMBASSADORS IN: WASHINGTON, LONDON, PARIS, ROME, BONN, HELSINKI, OSLO, STOCKHOLM, ATHENS, VIENNA, BERN, BRUSSELS, THE HAGUE, LUXEMBOURG, COPENHAGEN, MADRID, LISBON, DUBLIN, VALLETTA, ANKARA, OTTAWA.

After having referred to the message, transmit without delay to the leadership of the country of your residence, through whomever you consider most suitable, the following additional information regarding the status of efforts to remedy the aftereffects of the Chernobyl nuclear power plant accident.

As a result of measures taken during the past 24 hours, the release of radioactive matter has decreased, and the level of radiation in the region near the incident has dropped.

Measurements are being conducted that indicate that fission has stopped in the nuclear fuel. The reactor is dead.

Extensive measures are being taken to decontaminate affected areas.

The Soviet Union has sufficient material, scientific, and technical resources to remedy the aftereffects of the accident. At the present stage it does not need assistance from other countries. (If your country of residence offers its services, express your appreciation.)

No foreign nationals in the Soviet Union (particularly specialists or tourists) have made application to relevant Soviet organizations in connection with the Chernobyl nuclear power plant accident.

Confirm the execution of this order by telegraph.

[Published in *Rodina*, No. 1, 1992, pp. 83–87]

TSKhSD, fond 3, op. 102, d. 69.

Secret

Central Committee of the Communist Party of the Soviet Union

From the 4th to the 9th of May, I visited the Chernobyl nuclear power plant [*AES*] accident site. At this time, I feel obligated to share some of my observations with you:

1. The evacuation of Pripyat. Within one hour a radiation situation in the town was apparent. No provisional measures for an accident situation were in place. People just did not know what to do.

According to all rules and instructions, which have existed for 25 years already, local authorities should have made the decision to evacuate the population from the danger zone. By the time the government commission arrived, all of the people could have been evacuated from the zone even on foot. But not one person assumed this responsibility (by contrast, the Swedes evacuated people from the zone around their station first, and only then began to clarify that the release of radioactivity had not occurred at their plant).

2. Working in the danger zone (which included an area 800 meters from the reactor itself) were soldiers without any individual protective gear, particularly involved in the unloading of lead. In my conversations with them I found out that they did not even possess this kind of gear. The helicopter pilots found themselves in a similar predicament as well.

The officers corps, which included marshals and generals, showed off their bravery in vain, appearing near the reactor site in their regular uniforms. In such circumstances reason is called for, not a false sense of bravado.

3. The drivers involved in the evacuation of Pripyat, as well as in the construction of dikes on the river, were also working without any individual protection. The excuse that the dosage of radiation received "was within the yearly allotted amount" cannot be used here. These were mostly young people, and it follows that their future offspring will be affected.

Furthermore, "combat norms" for army subdivisions should have been in effect—an extreme measure used in military operations and in traversing a zone contaminated by nuclear weaponry. In my opinion this order was dictated at that time by the lack of individual protective gear, which only the special subdivisions possessed in the first stage of the accident.

4. The whole civil defense system was completely paralyzed. There were not even any operative geiger counters to be found.

5. The fire-fighting subdivisions did a marvelous job. They prevented the spread of the accident in its initial stages. But even the subdivisions located in Pripyat itself were not equipped with the proper gear to work in a highly radioactive zone.

6. The roof of the machine room was constructed from highly flammable materials. These same materials were used in a textile mill in Bukhara, which was totally destroyed by fire in the early 1970s. Even though certain employees were indicted because of the Bukhara incident, these same materials were employed in the *AES*.

7. The quality control standards for the Ministry of Energy are several times lower than for the Ministry of Medium Machine Building, in particular:

a) the number of service personnel is reduced;

b) commitments are regularly made to reduce planned maintenance times by 6–7 days, including repair of the fourth unit;

c) in the opinion of specialists the quality of equipment during the past 10 years has been reduced by half. The *AESs* receive much defective equipment from suppliers, and there are not enough monitoring and measuring devices or apparatus;

d) it requires 3–4 months for the Ministry of Energy to comply with even the most urgent request for repair because of the lengthy paperwork process involved. In contrast, the Ministry of Mechanical Engineering complies within a week at the longest.

e) the measure of protection surrounding the functioning units clearly is not adequate;

f) the attitude of the Ministry of Energy toward *AES*s in the last few years has become the same as that toward thermal and hydroelectric power plants, with no sharp distinction between nuclear and conventional facilities.

8. I was amazed <u>by the slow response time exhibited by the local authorities</u>. There were no clothes, shoes, or underwear to give the victims; they waited for orders from Moscow.

9. In Kiev <u>a state of panic</u> occurred for a variety of reasons, but first and foremost it was due to a total lack of information. Not even about what happened or about radiation conditions in the city itself. Propaganda from abroad was very influential, all the more so because not a single republic leader appeared on local radio or television stations to explain in simple terms that there was no need for panic and worry about dangers to the health of the children and to the general populace. Mr. Liashko was the first to finally appear on the television screen, but only after meeting with foreign journalists.

The information about Comrades Ligachev's and Ryzhkov's trip to the *AES* site had a positive influence. But the "silence" of the leaders of the republic in the following days, in my opinion, renewed the panic, especially <u>when it became known that the children and families of the leadership were being evacuated. There were thousands of people at the ticket windows of the Central Committee of the Ukrainian Communist Party</u>. Of course, the whole city was very well aware of this.

On May 5 the Ukrainian Minister of Health made an unsuccessful television appearance, which only generated more panic. Basically, the television was showing only dance programs along with other unrelated subjects, when they could have been giving out very basic information about radiation conditions in the city and conducting elementary discussions with scientists and specialists, of whom there were plenty in Kiev, and thereby lessening the tension, as was the case after the centralized newspapers stepped in. In general, the Central Committee of the Ukrainian Communist Party waited for instructions from Moscow, even though the initial panic could have been averted. By the way, we constantly heard the following phrase: "We did not receive those instructions from the center."

There were exceptions. The secretary of the Kiev *Oblast'* Committee Comrade Revenko was continually informing the secretaries of the *raion* party committees and through them the Communists about the actual state of affairs, since he visited Chernobyl on a regular basis. This bore fruit: in the *oblast'* there was not the kind of panic conditions that we noted in Kiev.

10. At this time, the mood of the people has changed abruptly. But the crux of the matter is that eliminating the consequences of the accident is just beginning. A new explosion has been averted, but severe radioactive contamination remains. The elimination of the damage will take from several weeks to many months. People will not be able to return to their homes for a long time. This needs to be explained clearly to them, as well as many other elementary aspects of life in the zone affected by radiation. Also such "trifles" as you should not gather mushrooms here this year, etc.

Most important of all, now it is vital that we categorically safeguard all of the people employed in this zone. If in the beginning there were exceptions because of the complicated situation, at this time there can be no justification for exposing people to radiation.

Now we must analyze carefully the lessons learned from this tragedy. This must be done in the name of all of the thousands of people who have so selflessly battled this misfortune. By rallying together the people have taken upon their shoulders all of the burden of this tragedy, without thinking of the consequences. There are many instances of true heroism. For example, a few people (in particular, Major L. Teliatnikov, Lieutenants V. Pravik and V. Kibenok, and others) localized the accident and saved the station. They knew that they were receiving fatal doses of radiation, but they did not abandon the unit until the fire was out. In my opinion they truly deserve the title of Heroes of the Soviet Union. They do not have long to live, so why wait until all the necessary paperwork will be formalized—this might take months!?

    I realize, that I do not have complete information about the events which took place, but I found it my duty to share with you what I saw.

B. Gubarev
Editor, *Pravda*
Science Division

TSKhSD, fond 3, op. 102, d. 86.

Chernobyl nuclear power plant eighty miles north of Kiev as it appeared in August 1986 following the catastrophic accident of April 26, 1986. ITAR-TASS Photoagency

"Sarcophagus" erected over reactor 4—where the accident originated—of the Chernobyl nuclear power plant, November 1986.

ITAR-TASS Photoagency

Central Committee memorandum, April 10, 1987, on controlling information about the investigation into the Chernobyl accident

CENTRAL COMMITTEE OF THE COMMUNIST PARTY OF THE SOVIET UNION

On the Criminal Court Investigation of the Accident at the Chernobyl Nuclear Power Plant

In accordance with the instructions relayed in a memorandum by the chairman of the Supreme Soviet of the USSR, Comrade Terebilov, concerning the procedures that need to be followed in conducting the criminal investigation, as well as organizational points connected with this case that need to be addressed, we find it imperative to report to you the following.

The anti-Soviet campaign abroad has intensified with the approach of the first anniversary of the Chernobyl accident. This is why this process should be started at a later date, say June–July 1987. Conducting the court hearing in the city of Kiev would not be advisable. It could be held in another Ukrainian city, for example, in the town of Chernobyl or the community of Zelenyi Mys in Kiev *oblast'*.

Since the Chernobyl accident has already been widely covered by the mass media, issuing detailed publications concerning these legal proceedings is not necessary. The press can publish short TASS reports about the beginning and the end results of these legal proceedings. [lined out: Nor is it necessary to have a large number of journalists present at the court hearings.] With the permission of the Government Commission, we suppose it might be possible to invite a TASS correspondent and foreign correspondents to two or three court sessions [lined out: to some of them].

Local state and party agencies, as well as the Ministry of Atomic Energy of the USSR and the Ministry of Medium Machine Building should be instructed to render the necessary assistance to the Supreme Court of the USSR in organizing these proceedings.

Request your concurrence.

[signed] N. Savinkin
[signed] IU. Skliarov
[signed] I. IAstrebov
[signed] V. Petrovskii
[signed] G. Ageev

April 10, 1987

Source?

chapter 7

PERESTROIKA AND *GLASNOST'*

The gerontocracy that ruled the Soviet Union from Brezhnev to Chernenko finally passed the torch to a younger generation when Mikhail Gorbachev became general secretary of the party in 1985. A contemporary joke conveyed the ennui felt for the old leaders: "What support does Gorbachev have in the Kremlin? None, he walks unaided." Gorbachev came to power determined to revitalize the decrepit Soviet bureaucracy and economy, to modernize relations with the international community, and to fulfill the consumerist promise of socialism. He labeled the old regime the "era of stagnation" and brought new slogans to promote his programs: "acceleration" of reform would be achieved through higher productivity and greater enthusiasm. *Perestroika* or restructuring of the economy would incorporate reforms developed by a new generation of Soviet economists. Greater independence for producers and managers would lead to more efficiency and more innovation. The state would withdraw from some enterprises, encouraging cooperatives to develop consumer services, such as restaurants and small manufacturing. Other state enterprises were encouraged to collaborate in joint ventures with foreign firms. Gorbachev called for a new honesty and openness, or *glasnost'*, in the work of government. Reform could not proceed cloaked in secrecy, ideas needed to be aired, and past and present mistakes also required public discussion. The policy of *glasnost'* spread to every corner of public life: historical figures were rehabilitated, banned literature reemerged from the library special collections, and a pluralist press began to flourish. "Democratization" also figured in Gorbachev's planned reforms: the stagnant Communist Party needed to be shaken up with new open elections. Also a more democratic workplace would be more receptive to innovation and reform. By 1989 elections to local and national Soviets were scheduled in order to reinvigorate political life, even though only one political party was permitted to operate. Internationally, Gorbachev touted his "new thinking": a scaling back of ideological warfare and a new willingness to enter into arms control and peace agreements. The Gorbachev government encouraged reform among its own allies, withdrew its troops from Afghanistan, and sought to cooperate more productively with the major Western powers.

Gorbachev became the darling of the West, but his reforms brought him less popularity domestically. Economic reform failed to produce dramatic improvements in the average standard of living, and the lifting of censorship and repression now brought old antagonisms out into the open. Chief among these were nationalist tensions: the intensity of independence movements in the Baltic republics and in the Caucasus apparently caught Gorbachev by surprise. Democratization and openness, initially meant to liberalize the party, led instead to a growing discrediting of that institution. Gorbachev's independent Moscow party boss, Boris Yeltsin, exercised his own form of democracy and so vehemently criticized the leadership that he was dismissed from his position. The national elections to a new Congress of People's Deputies in March 1989 were designed to revitalize the party; instead, voters threw out old party leaders in droves. The new pluralism weakened local authority, and an influx of foreign money contributed to an increase in urban crime and general sense of insecurity.

Liberals and democrats felt that Gorbachev was not moving fast enough to distance himself from the old regime. When interior ministry troops brutally suppressed a nationalist demonstration in the Georgian capital of Tbilisi in April 1989, many felt that this signaled a return to the old repressive policies. Conservatives openly called for a slowing down of reform and a return to the old Communist values. Symbolizing their anxiety was the accelerating breakup of the Soviet Union itself. Many of the fifteen Union republics demanded new relationships with the center, and some demanded complete independence. In Lithuania, as in Georgia, independence movements were countered with Soviet force. During the summer of 1991, as Gorbachev and his aides were negotiating a new Union treaty designed to accommodate these demands for autonomy, conservatives stepped up their attack on Gorbachev, on democracy, and on reform. Gorbachev's close ally, his foreign minister Eduard Shevardnadze, had warned of the danger of these "dark forces" and finally resigned from the Communist Party rather than be subjected to criticism by its conservatives. The crisis peaked in August 1991, on the day before the new treaty was to be signed. An emergency committee attempted to isolate Gorbachev and take over the government. Resistance to their putsch was led by Yeltsin, recently elected President of the Russian Federation, and other democrats. Gorbachev briefly returned to power, but the failed putsch had thoroughly discredited the Communist Party and the idea of the Soviet Union. The country formally dissolved at the end of 1991, to be replaced by an uneasy coalition of some of the former Union Republics, named the Commonwealth of Independent States. The Russian Federation, as the largest of the former Union republics, inherited most of the old Soviet institutions, wealth, and power.

Propaganda poster for the Twenty-Seventh Party Congress calling for the acceleration of *perestroika*. Original in color. *The policy is acceleration. Perestroika—to work actively, boldly, creatively, competently!*, by V. Sachkov. Publisher: Plakat, Moscow, 1987. Prints and Photographs Division, Library of Congress.

DOCUMENT 226   *Central Committee resolution, adopted April 10, 1989, concerning measures for normalizing the situation in Tbilisi*

<u>Top secret</u>

Do not publish.

RESOLUTION OF THE CENTRAL COMMITTEE OF THE *KPSS*

<u>Concerning measures for normalizing the situation in Tbilisi</u>

1. Approve the text of the address of Comrade M. S. Gorbachev, General Secretary of the Central Committee of the *KPSS* and president of the Presidium of the Supreme Soviet of the USSR, to the Communists and all working people of the Georgian SSR.

2. When implementing measures for normalizing the situation in Tbilisi, be guided by the considerations expressed at the meeting of the Politburo of the Central Committee.

POLITBURO of the CENTRAL COMMITTEE of the *KPSS*
April 10, 1989

Resolution No. 152

Agenda not for distribution

MEETING OF THE POLITBURO OF THE CENTRAL COMMITTEE OF THE *KPSS*

April 10, 1989

2:00 P.M.
Meeting Room of the Central Committee Secretariat

1. Concerning measures for normalizing the situation in Tbilisi.

2. Concerning periods for conducting elections for higher and local organs of power in the union and autonomous republics.

3. Concerning the Plenum of the Central Committee of the *KPSS* (April 25, 1989).

4. Concerning the idea of the report of the President of the Supreme Soviet of the USSR at the Congress of People's Deputies of the USSR.

5. Concerning a note by Comrade B. K. Pugo of April 7, 1989.

TSKhSD, fond 3, op. 102, d. 1137.

DOCUMENT 227   *Central Committee resolution, January 2, 1990, on socio-economic conditions in the USSR*

Top Secret

Not for publication.

RESOLUTION OF THE CENTRAL COMMITTEE OF THE COMMUNIST PARTY
OF THE SOVIET UNION [*TSK KPSS*]

On the Issue of the Socio-Economic Situation in the Country

1. The Secretariat of the *TSK KPSS*, together with the relevant departments of the *TSK*, is instructed to draw up a schedule of travel by senior officials of the *TSK KPSS* apparatus, the Council of Ministers of the USSR, and ministries and departments to study local socio-economic conditions and to provide practical assistance to local party and Soviet organs and to workers' collectives.

2. Comrades A. I. Luk'ianov, E. M. Primakov, and R. N. Nishanov are directed to introduce a resolution on the work of the Supreme Soviet of the USSR to implement the decisions of the Second Congress of People's Deputies of the USSR, taking into account the discussion at the meeting of the Politburo of the *TSK KPSS*.

SECRETARY OF THE *TSK*

To Comrades	Gorbachev	Stroev
	Ryzhkov	Usmanov
	Zaikov	Frolov
	Ligachev	Nishanov
	Masliukov	Beliakov
	Medvedev	Kapto
	Sliun'kov	Kruchina
	Yakovlev	Skiba
	Luk'ianov	Pavlov, A.
	Primakov	Falin
	Razumovskii	Mikhailov, V.
	Baklanov	Mozhin
P175/I	Girenko	Rubtsov
January 2, 1990	Manaenkov	Shkabardna
1-ri		

TSKhSD, fond 3, op. 102, d. 1287.

518   *Perestroika and Glasnost'*

Resolution of the Central Committee, February 7, 1990, on measures to in-tensify the fight against crime in Moscow

[Cover sheet:]
Valerii Ivanovich
This document
was prepared by
order of Mikhail Sergeevich
as urgent.
          [illegible]
          January 2, 1990

                    02292

On measures to intensify the struggle with crime and
to maintain public order in the city of Moscow.

          ISSUE PRESENTED BY Comrades Zaikov, Luk'ianov,
                    Prokof'ev, Saikin,
                    A. Pavlov
Not for publication

          VOTING:

Comrades	Gorbachev	— [✔] reported [illegible]
	Vorotnikov	— yes
	Zaikov	— yes
	Ivashko	— yes
	Kriuchkov	— yes
	Ligachev	— yes
	Masliukov	— yes
	Medvedev	— yes
	Ryzhkov	— yes
	Sliun'kov	— yes
	Shevardnadze	— yes
	Yakovlev	— yes

No. 178-16
February 2, 1990

          Verified by: [signed] Lobachev [?]
          Responsible for release: [signed] Doroshin
          [signature illegible]

Secret
[crossed out] Draft

RESOLUTION OF THE CENTRAL COMMITTEE OF THE COMMUNIST PARTY OF THE SOVIET UNION
[*TSK KPSS*]

On Measures to Intensify the Struggle with Crime and to Preserve
Public Order in the City of Moscow

Endorse the ideas outlined in the note (of February 1, 1990) of Comrades L. N. Zaikov, A. I. Luk'ianov, IU. A. Prokof'ev, V. T. Saikin, and A. S. Pavlov (attached).

[Typed, then crossed out: The draft of the decree of the USSR Council of Ministers on the present issue] [Overwritten with:] Resolution of practical issues is to be referred to the USSR Council of Ministers for consideration [Crossed out: (enclosed)]

SECRETARY OF THE CENTRAL COMMITTEE

P178/42
February 9, 1990

reported to Comrade V. V. [illegible]
February 9, 1990

02292

[illegible]

Re: point 42 of Minutes No. 178
Secret 74

TSK KPSS

On Measures to Intensify the Struggle with Crime and to Preserve
Public Order in the City of Moscow

Recently, the state of law and order in the city of Moscow has gotten noticeably worse. In public places there have been considerably more instances of dangerous crimes: murders, robberies, beatings, and malicious mischief. Crimes against persons, blatant types of extortion, theft of state and personal property, and vehicle theft have increased. Criminal actions are becoming more cruel and aggressive, and the use of weapons is becoming more prevalent, causing tension and feelings of personal insecurity among citizens. Crime in Moscow has reached menacing proportions; in 1989 the number of crimes rose by 40 percent, and serious crimes by nearly 76 percent. The trend continues at the beginning of this year.

The situation and public order are complicated by the many unsanctioned speeches of various informal citizen groups, during which anti-Soviet, antisocialist, and provocational acts aimed at destabilizing public order are allowed.

An additional negative factor in the condition of public order in the capital is an ever-growing migration from various regions by a large number of citizens, among whom are many convicts, jobless, prostitutes, drug addicts, and others with antisocial lifestyles. Many of them have committed blatant, illegal acts. In just the past year, the number of offenses in which they have taken part has nearly doubled.

In recent months, the migration of a large number of citizens from Azerbaijan and other republics of the Transcaucasus has increased sharply. These people are regularly holding rallies, demonstrations, and pickets of party, Soviet, and law enforcement institutions and the mass media, considerably complicating the work of their employees and arousing justifiable outrage among Muscovites. Among those who have arrived from the Transcaucasus, calls are issued for the formation of "self-defense groups" to repel possible attacks.

520 *Perestroika and Glasnost'*

Measures taken by Moscow city and *oblast'* party organs, Soviet and law enforcement organs, and public organizations are not sufficiently effective in such an extreme situation.

All of this arouses alarm among workers and residents of the capital region, who insistently demand decisive measures to impose proper order—in letters and appeals to the *TSK KPSS*, the Presidium of the USSR Supreme Soviet, the Moscow City Committee of the Communist Party of the Soviet Union [*MGK KPSS*], and the Moscow City Soviet Executive Committee [*Mosgorispolkom*].

Considering the wishes of the people and the fact that between February and June of 1990 Moscow will have a plenary session of the *TSK KPSS*, a session of the USSR Supreme Soviet, elections of the people's deputies to the Russian Soviet Federal Socialist Republic [RSFSR] and local Soviets, the 21st Congress of the All-Union Lenin Communist Youth League [*VLKSM*], and other social and political events, the *MGK KPSS* and the *Mosgorispolkom*, in conjunction with the Moscow Committee of the Communist Party of the Soviet Union [*MK KPSS*], the Ministry of Internal Affairs of the USSR [*MVD SSSR*], the USSR Committee for State Security [*KGB SSSR*], the procurators of the USSR, and other interested ministries and jurisdictions have developed a plan for additional measures to intensify the struggle with crime and to preserve public order in the city of Moscow. The plan details the organizational, ideological, legal, and material-technical measures to be directed toward strengthening law and order in the city and preventing and quickly curtailing extremist, terrorist and other anti-Soviet acts as well as incidents of mass hooliganism. The plan is intended for confirmation by the Executive Committee of the Moscow Soviet of People's Deputies.

At the same time, in order to resolve questions under the jurisdiction of the government of the USSR, the *MGK KPSS*, and *Mosgorispolkom*, a plan for a decree by the USSR Council of Ministers has been prepared, outlining measures to ensure proper order in the city of Moscow during the important social and political events between February and June 1990.

We must note that a large part of the measures outlined for strengthening the preservation of public order were applied earlier in Moscow during the Olympic Games in 1980, the 12th World Festival of Youth and Students in 1985, and the Good Will Games in 1986. Practice has shown that their application was justified and that they made a positive contribution to intensifying law and order in the city.

Considering the alarming situation that is developing relative to preservation of public order in the city of Moscow, it is considered advisable to respond positively to the measures that have been developed and to support them.

[In brackets, crossed out:] A draft of the decree of the Central Committee of the Communist Party of the Soviet Union is enclosed.

[signed] Zaikov	L. Zaikov
[signed] A. Luk'ianov	A. Luk'ianov
[signed] IU. Prokof'ev	IU. Prokof'ev
[signed] V. Saikin	V. Saikin
[signed] Pavlov	A. Pavlov

February 1, 1990

TSKhSD, fond 3, op. 102, d. 1313.

Propaganda poster condemning behavior that impedes *perestroika:* drunkenness, laziness, covetousness, bribery, speculation, embezzlement. Original in color. *This makes it difficult to live and work!,* anonymous. Publisher: Plakat, Moscow, 1988. Prints and Photographs Division, Library of Congress.

Resolution of the Central Committee, April 4, 1990, on temporary accommodation of E. Honecker and his wife in the military hospital of the Soviet Western Group of Forces

Secret. Copy No. I
Draft [crossed out]

RESOLUTION OF THE CENTRAL COMMITTEE OF THE COMMUNIST PARTY OF THE SOVIET UNION [*TSK KPSS*]

On the Temporary Accommodation of E. Honecker and His Wife in the Military Hospital of the Western Group of Forces

1. Concur with the considerations presented in the memorandum of the USSR Ministry of Foreign Affairs [*MID SSSR*] and the International Section of the *TSK KPSS* of April 4, 1990.

2. The USSR Ministry of Defense is to temporarily accommodate E. Honecker and his wife at the military hospital of the Western Group of Forces. They are to be provided with necessary medical treatment, as well as such accommodations whereby the legal organs of the German Democratic Republic would be able to continue their investigation into the E. Honecker affair, including summoning him to interrogations and to court.

3. *MID SSSR* is to inform H. Modrow on the decision made.

4. On April 5, 1990, publish in the Soviet press the text of the communique on the temporary accommodation of E. Honecker in the military hospital of the Western Group of Forces (attached).

SECRETARY OF THE *TSK*

P 184/34
April 4, 1990

k 332/OS

[signature illegible]

....

On point 34 of Minutes No. 184

Draft [crossed out]
Text of communique for the press

E. Honecker Accommodated for Treatment in
the Military Hospital of the Western Group of Forces

By request of the government of the GDR and the family of E. Honecker, who has undergone a serious operation, and in accordance with deeply humanitarian considerations, he [Honecker] has been accommodated for treatment in the military hospital of the Western Group of Forces. Since E. Honecker is under investigation, GDR legal organs will be able to visit him in the hospital, as well as to summon him [crossed out: "to interrogations and to court."] for the necessary juridical actions [handwritten].

Correction by [illegible] k 332/OS [signature illegible]

Not for publication

On the Temporary Accommodation of E. Honecker and His Wife
in the Military Hospital of the Western Group of Forces.

ISSUE PRESENTED BY Comrades Falin and Kovalev

VOTING:

Comrades   Gorbachev   - [illegible]
                   Vorotnikov   - leave of absence
                   Zaikov   - in Leningrad
                   Ivashko   -
                   Kriuchkov   - yes
                   Ligachev   - yes
                   Masliukov   - yes
                   Medvedev   - yes
                   Ryzhkov   - yes with a correction
                   Sliun'kov   - leave of absence
                   Shevardnadze   - in the U.S.A.
                   Yakovlev   - yes

No. 184-38
April 4, 1990

     Confirmed [signature illegible]

     Responsible for release [signature illegible]

     April 4, 1990

TSKhSD, fond 3, op. 102, d. 1345.

DOCUMENT 230   *Minutes of Politburo meeting, September 20, 1990, concerning current conditions in the USSR and problems facing the Communist Party in connection with conversion to a market economy*

Communist Party of the Soviet Union. CENTRAL COMMITTEE

Not for publication   <u>TOP SECRET</u>

MINUTES Of Meeting No. 2
of the Politburo of the Central Committee of the *KPSS*
September 20, 1990

Chairman: Comrade M. S. Gorbachev

Attending:

     Members of the Central Committee Politburo: Comrades M. M. Burokiavichius, S. I. Gurenko, A. S. Dzasokhov, V. A. Ivashko, I. A. Karimov, P. K. Luchinskii, A. M. Masaliev, K. M. Makhkamov, N. A. Nazarbaev, IU. A. Prokof'ev, A. P. Rubiks, G. B. Semenova, E. -A. A. [sic] Sillari, E. E. Sokolov, E. S. Stroev, O. S. Shenin

     Secretaries of the Central Committee: Comrades O. D. Baklanov, B. V. Gidaspov, V. A. Kuptsov, IU. A. Manaenkov, V. M. Falin
     Chairman of the Central Control Commission of the *KPSS*: Comrade B. K. Pugo

I. <u>On the state of the nation and the problems facing the *KPSS* in connection with the conversion to a market economy.</u>
(Comrades Gorbachev, Burokiavichius, Gurenko, Dzasokhov, Ivashko, Karimov, Luchinskii, Masaliev,

Makhkamov, Nazarbaev, Prokof'ev, Rubiks, Semenova, Sillari, Sokolov, Stroev, Shenin, Baklanov, Gidaspov, Kuptsov, Manaenkov, Falin, Ryzhkov, Aganbegian, Shatalin, Abalkin, Masliukov, Sitarian, Pavlov, Beliakov)

We adopt the position that was elaborated during the discussions of the Politburo of the Central Committee on the further activity to be taken by party organizations in connection with the conversion to a market economy, with the proviso that this matter is to be reviewed at the next Plenum of the Central Committee.

SECRETARY OF THE CENTRAL COMMITTEE OF THE COMMUNIST PARTY OF THE SOVIET UNION
[signed] M. GORBAChEV

TSKhSD.

DOCUMENT 231   *Resolution by the "Unity, for Leninism and Communist Ideals" society, October 28, 1990, expressing lack of confidence in the policies of Gorbachev as general secretary of the Central Committee*

To the *TSK KPSS*

RESOLUTION
of the 3rd All-Union Conference of the Society "Unity,
for Leninism and Communist Ideals"
October 28, 1990, Leningrad

ON THE LACK OF CONFIDENCE IN THE POLICIES OF THE GENERAL SECRETARY OF THE CENTRAL COMMITTEE OF THE COMMUNIST PARTY OF THE SOVIET UNION [*TSK KPSS*] M. S. GORBAChEV

Faced with catastrophic consequences for the people, the country, and the party due to M. S. Gorbachev's policy of so-called *perestroika*, and in view of the fact that this policy has absolutely revealed its bourgeois-restorationist character, and in consideration of the fact that we are on the brink of an even graver national catastrophe in connection with the planned implementation in the country of the "stabilization program" from the International Monetary Fund, which is disguised as a transitional program toward a market economy, the 3rd All-Union Conference of the "Unity, for Leninism and Communist Ideals" society <u>expresses its lack of confidence in the policies of M. S. Gorbachev as general secretary of the *TSK KPSS*</u>.

We feel that the only force in the country capable of changing the course of events in a constructive way, without leading to civil war, continues to be the party of Communists. We invite all honest, socialist and patriotic members of the *KPSS*, members of the Central Committee and the Central Control Commission of the *KPSS*, party organizations at all levels, and the Communist parties of all union republics to request the convening of a special congress of the *KPSS* to raise the question of:

1. The dismissal of M. S. Gorbachev and his more zealous associates who have been involved in the unleashing of a bourgeois counterrevolution in the Soviet Union from all elected party posts and their expulsion from the ranks of the Communist Party of the Soviet Union.

2. The recall of M. S. Gorbachev and said persons from positions as deputies, to which they were elected only because they were party functionaries.

3. The immediate withdrawal of the country from this general national crisis, not by way of a restoration of capitalism but of socialist renewal.

[4.] An investigation into the real reasons and processes that formed this crisis situation during 1985–1990, which is unprecedented in terms of severity and danger for the Soviet government, and calling the guilty to account before the party and the country.

The All-Union Society "UNITY" recommends that all members of the organization develop propaganda campaigns for this resolution at the local level, first, by means of conducting open party, trade-union and similar meetings to achieve the concurrence of *KPSS* party organizations.

Forward the proceedings from the open All-Union Party Conference to call M. S. Gorbachev to account before the party to the *TSK KPSS*, to newspapers, and to the political executive committee of "Unity."

The resolution was adopted unanimously.

Chairman of the political executive committee of the
All-Union Society "Unity—for Leninism and Communist Ideals"
[signed] N. ANDREEVA

TSKhSD.

DOCUMENT 232   *Central Committee report of January 11, 1991, on events in Lithuania*

Not for publication.
IU. [signature illegible]

CENTRAL COMMITTEE OF THE COMMUNIST PARTY OF THE SOVIET UNION

On the Events in Lithuania

According to a report from senior officials of the *TSK* of the *KPSS* (Comrades Kaziulin, Udovichenko) located in Lithuania, on January 11 of this year commandos took control of the publishing house and the *DOSAAF* [Voluntary Society for Assistance to the Army, Air Force, and Navy] building (where the country's security department is located) in the city of Vilnius. In the city of Kaunas they have taken over the officers' training building. On the whole this operation was carried out without violent clashes. At the same time, one must point out the lack of objectivity in reporting these events as heard on the radio program "Maiak." Specifically, there were reports of excesses committed by the military and alleged casualties and wounded.

A press conference was held at 5 P.M. local time, at the Central Committee of the Communist Party of Lithuania [*TSK KPL*], where the chief of the ideology department of the Central Committee, Comrade IU. IU. Ermolavichius, announced that the Committee of National Salvation of Lithuania had been established in the republic. That committee is assuming full power. It is located at the Plant for Radio-Measuring Devices (Comrade O. O. Burdenko, director). The Committee has made an appeal to the people of Lithuania and delivered an ultimatum to the Supreme Soviet of the Lithuanian SSR, in which it demands an immediate response to the appeal of the president of the USSR.

The Supreme Soviet of the Lithuanian SSR has rejected the ultimatum, declared the committee which was established to be "self-styled," with no legal basis to speak on behalf of the Lithuanian people.

Reported as information.

Chief of the Department
of State Policy of the
    TSK KPSS   [signed] V. Mikhailov
                                                       0116 OZN
                                           January 11, 1991 [stamped] Jan. 11, 1991

TSKhSD.

Minutes of the Politburo meeting, April 25, 1991, on the issue of Gorbachev's resignation as general secretary of the Communist Party

Communist Party of the Soviet Union.
Central Committee [*TSK KPSS*]

Not for publication

Top Secret

MINUTES of Meeting no. 8
of the Politburo of the Central Committee of the *KPSS*

April 25, 1991

Chairman: V. A. Ivashko

Attending:

       General Secretary of the *TSK KPSS* Comrade M. S. Gorbachev

       Members of the Politburo of the *TSK KPSS*: Comrades L. E. Annus, M. M. Burokiavichius, S. I. Gurenko, A. S. Dzasokhov, V. A. Ivashko, I. A. Karimov, P. K. Luchinskii, A. A. Malofeev, A. M. Masaliev, K. Makhkamov, A. N. Mutalibov, N. A. Nazarbaev, S. A. Niiazov, S. K. Pogosian, I. K. Polozkov, IU. A. Prokof'ev, A. P. Rubiks, G. V. Semenova, E. -A. A. Sillari, E. S. Stroev, I. T. Frolov, O. S. Shenin.

       Secretaries of the *TSK KPSS*: Comrades O. D. Baklanov, A. N. Girenko, V. A. Kuptsov, IU. A. Manaenkov, V. M. Falin

1. <u>On the issue raised by M. S. Gorbachev at the joint Plenum of the Central Committee and the Central Control Commission of the *KPSS* regarding his resignation from the position of General Secretary of the *TSK KPSS.*</u>

   (Comrades Gorbachev, Ivashko, Annus, Burokiavichius, Gurenko, Dzasokhov, Karimov, Luchinskii, Malofeev, Masaliev, Makhkamov, Mutalibov, Nazarbaev, Niiazov, Pogosian, Polozkov, Prokof'ev, Rubiks, Semenova, Stroev, Sillari, Frolov, Shenin)

Refer for consideration by the joint Plenum of the Central Committee and the Central Control Committee of the *KPSS* the following decision of the Politburo of the Central Committee: "In the higher interests of the country, the people, and the party, remove from consideration the proposal put forward by Mikhail Sergeevich Gorbachev to resign from the position of General Secretary of the Central Committee of the Communist Party of the Soviet Union."

       [signed] V. Ivashko

       Deputy General Secretary, *TSK KPSS*

TSKhSD.

DOCUMENT 234   *Central Committee resolution, May 23, 1991, concerning free economic zones in the USSR*

No. ST-27/12 dated May 25, 1991

Not for Publication

RESOLUTION
of the Central Committee of the
Communist Party of the Soviet Union [*TSK KPSS*]

On Approaches to the Establishment of Free Enterprise Zones
in the Territory of the Soviet Union

1. Approve the proposals on this issue contained in the report of the Department of Social and Economic Policy of the *TSK KPSS* (attached).

2. Forward the report to the Supreme Soviet of the USSR (Comrade A. I. Luk'ianov), the Cabinet of Ministers of the USSR (Comrade V. S. Pavlov), and the central committees of the Communist Parties of the Union Republics and the republic, *krai*, and *oblast'* party committees.

Results of voting: [signed] A. Vlasov
                          For V. Ivashko
                          May 15, 1991

For registration [handwritten] with emendations of Comrade Ivashko V.A.
                          May 23, 1991

Attachment
to Item 1*d*
Transcript
No. 27
TSK KPSS
June 17, 1991
No. 04797
RETURN TO
THE GENERAL
DEPARTMENT OF
THE *TSK KPSS*

TSK KPSS

On Approaches to the Establishment of
Free Enterprise Zones
in the Territory of the Soviet Union

Recently national governing bodies, including the *TSK KPSS*, have been receiving an increasingly large number of proposals from different regions of the country concerning the establishment of free enterprise zones [*ZSP*].

Broad segments of the public are engaged in a lively discussion of the subject. A number of republics, *oblast'*s, *krai*s, and *raion*s have gone beyond proposals and made specific decisions, referring to the well-known decree of the president of the USSR on "Foreign Investment in the USSR." In the process, they have largely emphasized their desire for special economic concessions and streamlined export procedures, primarily for raw materials.

Government and party bodies of the Karelian and Yakut Autonomous Republics, the Primorskii and Khabarovsk *krai*s, Amur, Kamchatka, Karaganda, Leningrad, Kaliningrad, Novgorod, and Odessa *oblast*'s, the cities of Sochi, Tartu, Zelenograd, and others have all come out with initiatives to establish *ZSP*s.

Another aspect of the process is that many of the election platforms of candidates for Soviets at different levels included planks calling for the establishment of such zones.

However, these planks did not contain any comprehensive preliminary evaluations of the feasibility or advisability of establishing specific zones.

We are also struck by the conflicting interpretations of *ZSP*s. The proposal drafts which we have received contain absolutely no assessments of the possible political, economic, and social impact of these zones. The proposals completely ignore the interests of the people who will have to live in the zones. No analysis has been made of the changes which may occur in the regions with respect to the movement of plants and factories, employment and political activity, or the population's standard of living. ~~In particular, this was one of the reasons why the public refused to approve enterprise zones in Novgorod and Leningrad.~~

The movement to establish enterprise zones has often been characterized by a lot of empty hoopla, incompetence, excessive dependence on the economy of the Soviet Union, union republics, and foreign investors, and intentions which are clearly in conflict with national goals and interests.

In short, the campaign to establish enterprise zones, which appeared on a wave of centrifugal processes in the country, is now becoming a problem of great political, social, and economic importance.

Our evaluation of existing plans indicates that their local sponsors have often interpreted the concept of a "zone" in different ways, do not have a basic understanding of this very specific economic concept, and have failed to consider the need for major initial investments, including appropriations from the central budget. For example, our estimates show that it would cost up to 8 billion rubles to make the necessary improvements for the Nakhodka zone, while the figures for Leningrad and Sakhalin are 7 and 2 billion rubles respectively.

The legal status of these zones has still not been defined. If we consider that *ZSP*s will require special customs, border, foreign trade, tax, labor, and environmental codes, the question of establishing these zones and regulating their activity should be placed under the exclusive jurisdiction of union and republican bodies. It will also require the establishment of basic guidelines for the process, the development of specific procedures for establishing these zones, operating procedures, oversight procedures, and methods for analyzing and evaluating the performance of these zones.

A study of the history of establishing free trade zones in a number of countries around the world has shown that they have a variety of functions, and that the purposes for which they were established and their success rates varied not only from region to region and country to country but even within the same country. For example, the economic zones of Brazil and China and the duty-free zones of India, the Middle Eastern countries, and many countries in Western Europe are totally inadequate.

For the developing countries, the primary purpose of establishing a *ZSP* is to promote exports by attracting foreign investment to export-oriented businesses while raising employment levels in the area of the zone and benefitting from advanced foreign technology and management expertise. These zones are usually established near ports and other international transportation hubs.

In the developed capitalist countries, the most common types of free-enterprise zones are "technopolises" and technology parks, which have largely been the product of national efforts and involve concentrating major scientific and engineering prowess in a single city for the purpose of providing a steady flow of scientific breakthroughs and engineering developments directly to manufacturing.

We should also emphasize that none of these countries has considered the establishment of free trade zones to be of primary importance in solving its economic and social problems, but rather they are viewed as an ancillary mechanism and a generally effective foreign trade tool. We should also realize that there have been outright failures in a number of countries due to strategic errors, siting errors, and errors in the choice of specific incentives and regulations.

Our country has no such strategy or concept for establishing free enterprise zones.

A careful study of foreign experience and an analysis of the proposals submitted by government organizations to establish free enterprise zones show that a number of major legal, financial, foreign trade, organizational, and other issues would have to be resolved before we could use this tool to attract foreign investment.

In the department's opinion, which is based on the proposals of scholars and experts who have studied the issue, any decisions to establish free trade zones in the Soviet Union should be based on the following initial premises:

1. An assessment of the country's overall economic and technological potential and the specific characteristics of this potential, its geographical location, its demographic situation, the development of its infrastructure, and its history of foreign trade and joint ventures with Western countries indicate that the following ventures might be considered acceptable for the Soviet Union in the current phase:

"technopolises" and technology parks which would concentrate Soviet and foreign science and engineering prowess for the purpose of developing new technologies on the basis of advanced concepts and major breakthroughs; small free trade zones at industrial centers with harbors and airports or international rail and highway hubs.

The acute shortage of investment opportunities in our country and the experience of foreign countries objectively leads us to the conclusion that the initiative could be implemented only in geographically small "zones." This would allow us to avoid large central appropriations for infrastructure development, housing, and social amenities. We must realize that solving these problems by diverting investment from other programs and regions would be practically impossible in the current environment.

2. We should also remember that zones in the USSR would require a favorable environment for joint, foreign, and domestic businesses, which would require the development of the necessary infrastructure and acceptable procedures for converting the ruble profits of foreign investors into hard currency.

3. The area chosen for a zone must have the necessary geographical advantages and should have an adequate infrastructure, manpower and material resources, local construction capabilities, and access to domestic and international transportation routes. In determining the configuration, specialization, and boundaries of these zones we must primarily be guided by considerations of economic and social expediency.

4. The general status of free economic zones should be defined by legislation, and the details of their status will require decisions by republic authorities on a case-by-case basis.

If we consider that the zones will remain the sovereign territory of the Soviet Union, all national and republic laws will apply in these zones with slight modifications to commercial and labor codes and border controls. Local, national, and economic authorities could take the initiative in establishing these zones. The interests of the republics (regions) in which the zones are located could be protected by giving their representatives a voice in governing the zones.

5. In economic terms a zone would be an autonomous entity with its own budget and bank. As an integral part of the Soviet economy, a zone might be subject to mandatory government purchase orders, allocation limits for supplies of materials and machinery, and national and regional tax and hard currency payments. Trade within the zone would primarily involve the use of Soviet rubles with controlled use of foreign currency. It would be inadvisable to create any kind of special currency for these zones.

6. Foreign investors and Soviet businesses would be granted concessions on an equal basis, with the exception of concessions established by law. They would be granted rent abatements, accelerated depreciation rights, the freedom to set their own prices for goods and services in the zone, and streamlined hiring and firing procedures. Foreign investors would have to receive guarantees and a reduction in the tax on repatriated profits, the opportunity to invest their profits in expanding their businesses, guarantees of supplies, access via the zone to the domestic market of the Soviet Union, and streamlined procedures for granting foreigners residence permits for the zone.

7. A zone could be the site of commercial ventures under different forms of ownership and organization. With respect to the foreign market, the zone would operate on the basis of hard-currency, self-financing principles and as an area open to any kind of foreign trade transaction. We must develop specific models for including Soviet, joint, and foreign ventures as organic parts of the economic structure of the zone and make sure the zone promotes regional development and trade with the rest of the USSR.

8. The economic subjects of the zone would have to draw their manpower from local manpower pools on the basis of high labor productivity. However, they could be allowed to recruit workers from outside the zone and from foreign countries on contracts.

In this case, free enterprise zones could contribute to training large numbers of workers and technicians in modern management and industrial engineering techniques.

9. Governmental authority in the zone should be exercised by a local Soviet of People's Deputies. The Soviet in turn would charter a development corporation, bank, and commodities exchange as its economic agencies, along with an Advisory Council consisting of representatives of Soviet and foreign business and experts.

These basic principles could be included in a concept for establishing free enterprise zones in the Soviet Union to be drafted by the appropriate departments of the Cabinet of Ministers of the USSR. We might submit the draft of the concept to foreign businessmen, scholars, and experts for review.

We also believe that the proposals in this report could be considered by Supreme Soviet committees and commissions in the process of a free enterprise zone law, which should define their legal status, the tax and customs privileges of the organizations and businesses in the zones, the terms for allowing foreign companies the use of land and natural resources, procedures for resolving disputes, and so forth. We need to speed up the process of drafting legislation for the establishment of free enterprise zones in the Soviet Union.

The Department of Social and Economic Policy of the *TSK KPSS*, while in general supporting the concept, considers it necessary to point out the inevitability of greater social tension in *ZSP*s. The difference between the incomes of those employed at plants and other facilities in the zone and those employed elsewhere will rise. The working conditions of employees will change dramatically, and many of them, who are unaccustomed to the stringent demands of the marketplace, may lose their jobs. We must always keep in mind that the emphasis on raw materials in several zones and the obvious desire of the developed capitalist countries to ship polluting industries out of their own countries and in particular relocate them in the USSR could result in deterioration of the environment and depletion of our natural resources, which we absolutely cannot permit to happen.

In light of these circumstances, local authorities and party committees must take a balanced approach to the issue of free enterprise zones and consider the possible economic, political, and social consequences. In the process it would be pointless to rely on the generosity of foreign investors. Instead, we must create a situation of mutual economic advantage and give full consideration to the interests of the USSR.

This report could be forwarded to party committees ~~of those regions whose leaders have proposed creating ZSPs,~~ and the Supreme Soviet and the Cabinet of Ministers for their guidance.

The draft of the resolution of the Secretariat of the *TSK KPSS* on the issue is attached.

Director of the
Department of Social and
Economic Policy of the
TSK KPSS   [signed] A. Vlasov   A. Vlasov
May 15, 1992

TSKhSD, fond 4, op. 42, d. 95.

DOCUMENT 235   *Resolution of the Presidium of the Central Control Commission of the Communist Party, July 23, 1991, concerning Eduard Shevardnadze's resignation from the party*

RESOLUTION
of the Presidium of the Central Control Commission
Communist Party of the Soviet Union [*KPSS*]

Minutes 9, point 15
of July 23, 1991.

Concerning the statement by E. A. Shevardnadze on resigning from the *KPSS*

KPSS Central Committee member E. A. Shevardnadze has announced his resignation from the party to the Central Control Commission of the *KPSS*. His local party organization, at the General Secretariat of the USSR Ministry of Foreign Affairs, examined this issue on July 18 and decided to consider Shevardnadze as having left the party by virtue of his own statement.

The Presidium of the Central Control Commission of the *KPSS* resolves:

To accept for the record the information of the Bureau of the Presidium of the *KPSS* Central Control Commission that E. A. Shevardnadze has left the ranks of the *KPSS* and thereby has severed all ties with the party. As a consequence, the issue of further investigation by the party on the matter of his statement is to be considered closed.

[signed] E. Makhov
Acting Chair, *KPSS* Central Control Commission

Addendum to point 15, minutes 9

To the Central Control
Commission, *KPSS*

004397

Upon receiving from the commission a summons related to the party decision to conduct an investigation into my public statements, I consider it necessary to state the following:

I am fundamentally convinced that my statements—on the necessity of forming in this country a party which would act parallel to the *KPSS*—give no legally or morally justified cause for such an action.

I am also convinced that there is not, nor should there be, a prohibition on the right of a party member to think or speak his own thoughts and opinions and to stand by them. This right has been returned to us by *perestroika* which, it has often been proclaimed, was begun by the party itself.

One would have expected that Comrades from the higher party structures—those who have announced their break with the practice of suppressing ideas and opinions that led the party to its current situation and that gave birth to repression, persecutions, and the deepest crisis of faith in the party—would be sympathetic to the motivation behind my statements.

Instead, as in the worst of the old days, a resolution is being adopted about an inquisitorial investigation, with unclear goals and unestablished procedures.

Under no circumstances will I be subject to investigation by such a tribunal, for by agreeing to do so, I would be attesting, against my will and convictions, to the validity and legitimacy of the return by the *KPSS* leadership to repressive methods of suppressing dissent.

Your resolution leaves no doubt that I have no other choice than to announce my unwillingness to identify myself with such practices.

By the present letter I am anouncing my resignation from the *KPSS*.

It was not easy for me to reach this decision, but I deem it necessary to take this step, all the while realizing clearly what will follow. Moreover, I am aware of the campaign being prepared to compromise me and others of like mind—in complete and direct accordance with the experience accumulated in the past and with procedures already perfected. The evidence on hand once again convinces me of the correctness of my decision. I retain the right to express publicly the motives behind my conduct.

[signed] E. Shevardnadze
July 3, 1991.

TSKhSD.

The August 1991 Putsch Attempt

In August 1991 Mikhail Gorbachev had finally succeeded in reaching agreement with leaders of most of the Union republics on a new treaty redefining the rights and obligations of the members of the Union of Soviet Socialist Republics. The new treaty would permit the eventual independence of any of the republics, something that Lithuania, Latvia, and Estonia had been especially eager to achieve and something that conservative party members and Russian nationalists opposed with great fervor. With Gorbachev vacationing with his family in the Crimea and the treaty due to be signed on August 20, conservative leaders in Gorbachev's government decided to act. Creating a State Committee for the State of Emergency, they declared a dictatorship in the USSR for the purpose of restoring order and reversing the reforms. Gorbachev would not go along with the scheme. On the morning of August 19, 1991, state media announced that Gorbachev was ill and incapacitated and the State Committee had assumed control of the country. Its leaders included Prime Minister Valentin Pavlov, the *KGB* chief Vladimir Kriuchkov, Minister of the Interior Boris Pugo, Defense Minister Dmitrii Yazov, Oleg Baklanov, chief of defense industries, Vice-President Gennadii Yanaev, Vasilii Starodubtsev, Union of Collective Farms chairman (an opponent of agrarian reform), and Aleksandr Tiziakov, president of the Association of State Enterprises.

The coup quickly fell apart. Boris Yeltsin personally led resistance in Moscow by rushing to the Russian Federation headquarters and organizing its defense. In Leningrad Mayor Anatolii Sobchak persuaded the local military chief not to carry out the orders of the coup leaders. Television, radio, and newspapers managed to evade the strict controls of the Emergency Committee, and within three days Gorbachev was back in Moscow and the coup leaders under arrest. Blame spread quickly to the Communist Party; the party tried to join the chorus of accusers of the coup leaders (Documents 236 and 237), but its conservatives and its policies were for the moment thoroughly discredited. On August 24 Gorbachev resigned as general secretary of the party and dissolved its Central Committee. In Moscow and other cities, jubilant crowds delighted in pulling down statues of Lenin and other symbols of Communist authority.

Communist Party Central Committee Secretariat resolution of August 22, 1991, condemning the attempted putsch and recommending disciplinary action

No. ST 38 / 8g of August 22 1991 .

Not for Publication.

RESOLUTION

Secretariat of the Central Committee [*TSK*]
of the Communist Party of the Soviet Union [*KPSS*]

Issue of the Secretariat of the *TSK KPSS*

The text of the coded telegram for No. 116/Ts dated August 19, 1991, was composed on the basis of disinformation communicated to members of the Secretariat of the *TSK KPSS* concerning the health of General Secretary of the *TSK KPSS*, President of the USSR M. S. Gorbachev and the circumstances for invoking the state of emergency.

The text did not reflect all the views expressed by the members of the Secretariat in discussing this matter and was passed on for urgent dispatch to local organizations.

In view of the above, consider the text of said telegram invalid.

Results of Vote:

[ten illegible signatures, dated August 22, 1991]

APPEND TO *TSK KPSS* SECRETARIAT RESOLUTION

No. St-38/8g of August 22, 1991

Decree sent to:

Comrades Gorbachev, Ivashko, Dzasokhov, Luchinskii, Semenova, Stroev, Shenin, Gidaspov, Girenko, Kalashnikov, Kuptsov, Manaenkov, Mel'nikov, Falin, Makhov
[illegible signature]

Not for return to the General Department, *TSK KPSS*

Executed: [illegible signature] August 22, 1991

No. St 38/8g, of August 22, 1991

Draft

RESOLUTION
OF THE SECRETARIAT OF THE *TSK KPSS*
August 22, 1991

The Secretariat of the *TSK KPSS* notes that a number of members of the *KPSS*, including members of the *TSK*, took part in ~~anticonstitutional~~ activities connected with the attempted coup d'etat. Their activities were kept secret from the party leadership, threatened the development of democratic processes, and inflicted enormous harm on the country and the *KPSS*. Unequivocally condemning the adventurists, the Secretariat of the *TSK KPSS* resolves:

1. To present to the Central Control Commission of the *KPSS* a proposal to immediately review the culpability before the party of *KPSS* members who took part in the ~~antistate~~ anticonstitutional activities, and to take the appropriate decisions.

2. To recommend that the *TSK* membership of persons guilty of these ~~anticonstitutional~~ actions be reviewed at the next *TSK KPSS* plenary session.

The Secretariat of the *TSK KPSS* regards it essential that the *TSK* plenary session develop measures to increase the responsibility and the role of the party in implementing democratic changes in the country.

Source?

DOCUMENT 237   ***Communist Party Control Commission resolution, August 23, 1991, denouncing the leaders of the putsch and expelling the survivors from the party***

<u>Proletarians of All Countries, Unite!</u>

RESOLUTION

OFFICE OF THE PRESIDIUM OF THE CENTRAL CONTROL COMMISSION OF THE COMMUNIST PARTY OF THE SOVIET UNION [*KPSS*]

Min. 16, item 2

August 23, 1991

<u>On the party responsibility of *KPSS* members who took part in the anticonstitutional State Emergency Committee [*GKChP*]</u>

1. To note that members of the anticonstitutional *GKChP*, Communist Party leaders O. D. Baklanov, V. A. Kriuchkov, V. S. Pavlov, B. K. Pugo, V. A. Starodubtsev, A. I. Tiziakov, D. T. Yazov, and G. I. Yanaev grossly violated the primary requirement of the Charter of the *KPSS*, whereby all organizations of the party and each Communist are required to act within the framework of the Constitution and Soviet laws. They forcibly removed M. S. Gorbachev from the leadership of the country and party, they flouted the decisions of the Twenty-Eighth Congress of the *KPSS*.

To expel *KPSS* members O. D. Baklanov, V. A. Kriuchkov, V. S. Pavlov, V. A. Starodubtsev, A. I. Tiziakov, D. T. Yazov, and G. I. Yanaev from the party for organizing the coup d'etat. To announce that B. K. Pugo has committed suicide.

2. To conduct a party investigation of the actions of individual members of the Politburo and Secretariat of the *TSK KPSS* during this period.

Acting Chairman
Central Control Commission of the *KPSS*   [signed] Makhov
                                    E. N. Makhov

[stamp:] Communist Party of the Soviet Union, Central Control Commission

Source:?

DOCUMENT 238   *Russian Federal Presidential decree, January 30, 1992, pardoning political prisoners arrested during the regime of Gorbachev*

DECREE
OF THE PRESIDENT OF THE RUSSIAN FEDERATION

On Amnesty for A. E. Dolzhikov, A. B. Konoval, and Others

Pardon:

1. DOLZhIKOV Aleksandr Eduardovich, born in 1959, convicted on April 27, 1984, by the Far Eastern Military District Military Tribunal, releasing him from the rest of his prison sentence

2. KONOVAL Aleksandr Borisovich, born in 1967, convicted on May 22, 1987, by the Military Tribunal of the Volga Military District, releasing him from the rest of his prison sentence

3. KUTSENKO Viktor Il'ich, born in 1955, convicted on January 18, 1991, by the Military Tribunal of the Moscow Military District, releasing him from the rest of his prison sentence

4. MAKAROV Viktor Borisovich, born in 1955, convicted on November 30, 1987, by the Military Tribunal of the Moscow Military District, releasing him from the rest of his prison sentence

5. PAVLOV IUrii Vasil'evich, born in 1935, convicted on April 19, 1985, by the Military Tribunal of the Leningrad Military District, releasing him from the rest of his prison sentence

6. POPOV Sergei Nikolaevich, born in 1954, convicted on May 6, 1988, by the Military Tribunal of the Moscow Military District, releasing him from the rest of his prison sentence

7. POTAShOV Vladimir Viktorovich, born in 1949, convicted on June 19, 1987, by the Military Tribunal of the Moscow Military District, releasing him from the rest of his prison sentence

8. FEDOTKIN Igor' Petrovich, born in 1967, convicted on May 22, 1987, by the Military Tribunal of the Volga Military District, releasing him from the rest of his prison sentence

9. ChERNOV Nikolai Dmitrievich, born in 1927, convicted on September 11, 1991, by the Military Tribunal of the Supreme Court of the USSR, releasing him from the rest of his prison sentence

10. IUZhIN Boris Nikolaevich, born in 1942, convicted on October 23, 1987, by the Military Tribunal of the Supreme Court of the USSR, releasing him from the rest of his prison sentence

President
of the Russian Federation   B. Yeltsin

Moscow, the Kremlin
January 30, 1992
No. 101

[round stamp:] Office of Administrative Affairs of the President of the RSFSR, General Department, No. 1.

[rectangular stamp:] Secretariat of the *KGB* of the USSR, SPECIAL FOLDER

Source?

PART II. THE SOVIET UNION AND THE UNITED STATES

chapter 8

ECONOMIC COOPERATION

The United States and Russia fought as allies during World War One, but economic ties between the two countries before the revolution were not as extensive as those between Russia and European countries such as France and Germany. French investors had provided much of the capital to finance Russian industrial expansion in the late nineteenth century, and German manufacturers had provided much of the equipment. The U.S. government expressed enthusiasm for Russia's first revolution in February 1917, but with the separate peace agreement between Germany and Soviet Russia signed at Brest-Litovsk in March 1918, relations between the two countries cooled rapidly. The U.S. government did not officially recognize the government of the Council of People's Commissars; informal diplomatic contacts were carried out by Colonel Raymond Robins, who had been sent to Russia as part of a Red Cross delegation, but these led to nothing. When leaders of the Allied governments met in Versailles in early 1919 to work out a peace agreement, neither German nor Russian representatives were invited. Diplomatically, Soviet Russia was isolated. Economically, the Allies declared a blockade in order to force the Soviets to make peace with their enemies and to live up to their prerevolutionary agreements.

U.S. diplomats and others made several attempts to reach across the gulf separating the former allies, even though the French, British, and U.S. governments were even then engaged in assisting the anti-Bolshevik armies in the Russian Civil War. British Prime Minister David Lloyd George and U.S. President Woodrow Wilson offered to organize a peace conference between the warring sides in the Civil War, but neither side accepted the offer. Next, Wilson sent a young diplomatic attache, William C. Bullitt, to Moscow to enter into conversations with Lenin and the Soviet leaders. Bullitt would later become the first U.S. ambassador to the Soviet Union in 1933, but his mission in 1919 failed to facilitate diplomatic relations. A third initiative, a humanitarian food relief program to be administered by the Norwegian Fridtjof Nansen also failed to gain the support of Allied leaders.

The end of the Civil War and consolidation of the Soviet government brought new opportunities and challenges for diplomatic and economic relations. U.S. firms had entered into economic agreements on White-held territory before 1920; now these were useless, and the Allied governments lifted their economic blockade of Soviet ports in early 1920. The Soviet government itself had become keenly interested in normalizing economic relations: it needed credits and trade in order to help build socialism. Lenin had expressed particular interest in American trade: "We shall need American industrial goods—locomotives, automobiles, etc., more than any other kinds of goods from other countries." The Soviets negotiated the Anglo-Russian Trade Agreement with Great Britain in 1921, but the United States policy continued to be one of nonrecognition. U.S. firms that wished to do business with the Soviets were told to trade at their own risk. On the other hand, in 1921, the American Relief Administration, under the direction of Herbert Hoover, was permitted to enter Soviet Russia and carry out food relief operations for victims of the terrible famine that had struck parts of the country that year.

The U.S. policy of nonrecognition of the Soviet government, however, continued in force. It was based on the principled understanding that the regime in Soviet Russia was "based upon the negation of every principle of honor and good faith, and every usage and convention, underlying the whole structure of international law." But despite the absence of regular diplomatic relations, trade between the United States and the Soviet Union developed during the 1920s, reaching a peak in 1930. The Soviets continued to work for diplomatic recognition, believing that this would facilitate trade, credits, and economic development. A small coterie of U.S. diplomats developed expertise on the Soviet Union and sought to influence their government's policy; their efforts were rewarded in 1933 when President Franklin D. Roosevelt and the Soviet Foreign Commissar Maxim Litvinov reached an agreement on diplomatic recognition. In the end formal diplomatic recognition did little to boost trade between the two countries, which did not return to its 1930, prerecognition level, until World War II.

Famine Relief

The idea of an international relief effort to aid the victims of the Russian Revolution and Civil War was first broached by Herbert Hoover in 1919. He suggested to President Woodrow Wilson that a neutral relief commission, similar to the one that had aided Belgium after the war, be organized under the direction of Fridtjof Nansen to convey food, medicine, and other relief supplies to Russia. This plan was rejected, but other agencies had already begun operations to bring humanitarian aid to Russia. The international Society of Friends, the Quakers, had conducted relief work in Russia between 1916 and 1918, and its American section re-entered Russia in 1920. The situation had deteriorated by the summer of 1921 due to a combination of the disruption of transport, the exhaustion of reserves, and a drought which was affecting the new harvest. On behalf of the Soviet government, Maksim Gorky released an appeal to the press: "I ask all honest European and American people for prompt aid to the Russian people. Give bread and medicine."

After intensive negotiations, agreements were reached between the Soviet commissar for foreign affairs, Litvinov, and a representative of the American Relief Administration, which was headed by Hoover. The first ARA party entered Moscow in August 1921 and began to organize the import and distribution of food and medical supplies to the areas most severely affected by the famine. The ARA was not alone in its relief work: numerous religious organizations in addition to the Quakers also sent food missions, including the American Jewish Joint Distribution Committee, the American Red Cross, Baptist Russian Relief, the Mennonite Central Committee (which fed 35,000 people in open kitchens), the National Catholic Welfare Council, the Federal Council of the Churches of Christ in America, and the National Lutheran Council. The Student Friendship Fund of the YMCA and the Volga Relief Society, a coalition of German-American groups, also sent assistance. The American Committee to Aid Scientists with Scientific Literature shipped 28,000 pounds of scientific literature to the Russian Academy of Sciences. Radical organizations also joined the effort to collect money and supplies for famine victims; chief among them were the Friends of Soviet Russia, the American Federated Russian Famine Relief Committee, and the Soviet Red Cross.

Despite the urgency of the suffering, it was often difficult to separate humanitarian goals from political ones. The ARA was subjected to intense political scrutiny in the United States, and many Soviet officials also looked upon the ARA with suspicion. The Communist Party Central Committee warned the ARA in 1921 against using its position to overthrow the Soviet government, and Trotsky echoed this theme in a speech to the Moscow Soviet in 1922, included here as Document 244. Others worried that ARA officials were using their activities to further their own commercial interests. But the official Soviet position was one of gratitude to the ARA as the only officially sponsored foreign agency in the effort, and the ARA continued to be active in Soviet Russia until 1923.

DOCUMENT 239   *Proposal by members of the British and American Society of Friends (Quakers), December 13, 1920, to set up a system for distributing food and clothing to children in Moscow*

[Original spelling and typographic errors preserved]

<u>FRIENDS INTERNATIONAL SERVICE.</u>

[stamped in left margin:]
Society of Friends, the Quakers
December 13, 1920
No.____ Moscow

To the Peoples	126. Hotel Savoy
Commissariat of Supplies	M O S C O W .
Moscow	

Dear Sirs,

The religious Society of Friends in England and America wishes in a spirit of love and universal brotherhood to do its best to help the people of Russia with gifts of food and clothing.

As our resources are small compared with the great population of Soviet Russia we consider it advisable in the first instance to limit what help we have to offer to the children of Moscow and particularly the sick and undernourished.

During the past six months we have distributed our supplies through many departments of various commissariats. This has resulted in the wastage of much time and transport. We therefore desire now to have all supplies donated by the Friends International Service stored in one warehouse under our supervision.

We therefore suggest the following plan for your consideration.:-

<u>WAREHOUSE AND TRANSPORT.</u>

1. That the Peoples Commissariat for Supplies (Narkomprod) through the Central Co-operative Association (CentroSous) provides a warehouse together with the necessary lighting and heating. Such warehouse to be used exclusively for the supplies donated by the Friends International Service or supplies entrusted to their care.

2. That the CentroSous supplies and maintains the necessary personel for the handeling and controling of all such supplies. (In our opinion this should include to begin with the full time service of a person capable of checking all stores in and out of the warehouse and of making the necessary arrangements for transport, and a clerk capable of typewriting in both English and Russian.)

3. We ask that the CentroSous provides the necessary transport. We hope however to import one or two motor vehicles and shall be glad to know whether you would provide the necessary garage, petrol and drivers.

<u>CONTROL OF SUPPLIES.</u>

1. We propose that all supplies and Bills of Lading should be handed over by our agent in Reval to the Representative of the R.S.F.S.R. Commissarriat for External Trade on his giving a receipt and agreeing to forward the supplies to "FRIENDS INTERNATIONAL SERVICE" c/o CENTROSOUS. MOSCOW.

2. We suggest that on arrival at Moscow all supplies should be checked by a representative of the Centrosous and ourselves and that a receipt signed by both should be sufficient. It being understood that the Workers and Peasants Inspection and the Extraordinary Commission may may send representatives if they so desire.

3. That in making the distribution to institutions we should do so in accordance with a scheme to be agreed upon by a representative of the Department of Childrens Health or such other Departments as may seem desirable, and ourselves.

4. Lists of all supplies received and distributed to be sent to the Centrosous and to the commissariats responsible for the institutions to which such supplies are sent.

5. All orders for goods to leave the warehouse to be signed by a representative of the Friends International Service and a representative of the Narkomprod.

6. All supplies to be distributed as gifts from the Friends International Service and without payment.

The above proposals form the basis on which we the undersigned feel that we can satisfactorily carry out the distribution of supplies donated by the Friends International Service. Such proposal to be subject to alteration by mutual agreement.

Yours sincerely.

	REPRESENTING THE
[signed] Anna J. Haines	FRIENDS INTERNATIONAL SERVICE.
Arthur Watts	

TSGANKh, fond 1943, op. 1, d. 1964, ll. 2, 20b, 7.

DOCUMENT 240   *Letter from Foreign Minister Chicherin to Kamenev, August 2, 1921, discussing Hoover's proposal for the release of American prisoners held in Soviet Russia at the time the American famine relief program was initiated*

August 3, 1921

To Comrade KAMENEV.

Respected comrade,

I am sending you Hoover's answer. He proposes our immediate freeing of American prisoners and their immediate delivery to the border. Director Brown will be in Riga on August 9, and if by that time the freeing of the Americans is a fait accompli, he will work out the details of the matter of hunger relief with your representatives. He requests a prompt answer as to whether this proposal is accepted.

It seems to me that once it is decided in principle to release the American prisoners, we lose nothing by releasing them immediately. Among them is Killi, sentenced by a tribunal. It must be emphasized that in the interests of hunger relief we are not following standard practice, releasing someone sentenced to a specific punishment, contrary to a court decision. Furthermore, it should be stressed that Killi is guilty of the most flagrant violation of trust, for we revealed everything to him, so to speak, and he used this in order to collect information for the American government.

With communist greetings,

[signature illegible]

RTSKhIDNI, fond 2, op. 2, d. 802, l. 1.

DOCUMENT 241   *Letter from Kamenev to the Politburo, October 18, 1921, with handwritten comments by Lenin, Trotsky, and Stalin, regarding the terms of the agreement to be signed with the American Relief Administration*

To all members of the Politburo.

I am enclosing the text of the Agreement with "Ara" [American Relief Administration] on organizing food shipments to Russia. Eiduk and I are completely in favor of signing the agreement. They are bringing in an additional quantity of food. We have the right to hold up (without appeal) any delivery if it exceeds 50 dollars for a private individual or 500 [dollars] for an organization (hospital, municipality). We are providing them FREE TRANSPORTATION FROM THE BORDER TO THE FOOD WAREHOUSES.

Litvinov opposes the last [point], considering it a privilege. His objection is not serious.

I request you take a vote and provide an answer by 2 P.M. Wednesday.

[signed] L. Kamenev

[Handwritten comments on the bottom of the document]

(If indeed the goal is trade, then we <u>should</u> do this [illegible] for they are giving us pure profit for the hungry and monitoring rights, and the right of refusal for three months. Therefore, we ought <u>not</u> take payment for shipment to the warehouses.) Designate, with Politburo confirmation, our monitor to <u>ARA</u> for this operation, [illegible] reliable ones on condition that all be monitored.

Agreed. October 19. Lenin.

[Handwritten comments, left margin]

Agreed. Trotsky

The issue is obviously trade and not charity. <u>I propose:</u>
1) Exempt the incoming food from customs and taxes, charge for transportation on a universal basis;
2) Provide warehouse facilities for a charge.

Agreed. October 19. J. Stalin

Agreed. October 19. [illegible]

RTSKhIDNI, fond. 2, op. 1, d. 21444, ll. 1, 10b.

Review of the American Relief Administration's activities from September 5 to November 26, 1921, detailing areas of operation and quantities of food, clothing, and medicine distributed

REVIEW
OF THE ACTIVITIES OF THE AMERICAN RELIEF ADMINISTRATION
from September 5 to November 26, 1921

During the three-month period since the signing of the Riga Agreement on August 20, the American Relief Administration [ARA] has played quite an intensive role in assisting starving Russian children.

On September 5—exactly two weeks after the signing of the agreement—the distribution of shipments of provisions around Moscow, and from there to regional bases, began. The network of these bases, initially not extensive, is constantly expanding as "ARA" develops its operation, bringing food shipments to the starving population. Thus, for example, in September shipments were sent to the following four points:

1) Moscow	3) Samara
2) Petrograd	4) Kazan'

In October the number of points increased to eight:

1) Moscow	5) Ufa
2) Petrograd	6) TSaritsyn
3) Samara	7) Saratov
4) Kazan'	8) Simbirsk

In November we see a further increase to twelve:

1) Moscow	7) Saratov
2) Petrograd	8) Simbirsk
3) Samara	9) Alatyr' (Simbirsk *guberniia*)
4) Kazan'	10) Orenburg
5) Ufa	11) Syzran' (Simbirsk *guberniia*)
6) TSaritsyn	12) Pokrovskoe (Saratov *guberniia*)

The development of a network of distribution points is closely related to the increase in food shipment arrivals. But there is no doubt that this is also the result of the search for points convenient for supplying newly emerging relief agencies. In the future, with the development of a network of primary relief agencies and the formation of new regions, the network of distribution points also will expand.

Moscow is the central depot for all the regions. With the exception of a relatively small number of shipments which arrive by sea at Petrograd to the ARA organizations stationed there, all the other shipments are distributed through Moscow. This offers major advantages, both in terms of ensuring that distribution is regular and orderly and providing the fullest possible accounting of all commodities arriving in Moscow and shipped from there to the various regions.

The tables below illustrate the delivery of goods to ARA in Moscow.

Table 1

Table 1 provides information on the arrival of shipments from the time the ARA began its operations through November 25. As we can see from the table, the September shipments consisted exclusively of foodstuffs, primarily flour, milk, rice, and beans. These foods combined accounted for more than 75% of the total September shipments. Medicines, manufactured goods, and clothing and canteen items (dishes and utensils) and vehicles (automobiles) began arriving in October. The November shipments primarily consisted of foodstuffs, mainly flour, which accounted for more than 50% of all the November shipments. More meat and fats arrived in November also. We still do not have the totals for November, but we can anticipate that they will be below October's levels. This may be due to the fact that large stockpiles have already been built up at the regional depots.

Table 1. Shipments to ARA in Moscow by months[1]

DESCRIPTION	Arrived							
	September		October		November 1–26		TOTAL	
	*Pood*s	Pounds	*Pood*s	Pounds	*Pood*s	Pounds	*Pood*s	Pounds
Flour	32,186	27	171,628	27	205,380	14	429,195	14
Rice	30,956	—	56,807	27	18,495	11	106,209	38
Beans	20,054	—	36,020	14	24,144	—	80,224	14
Rye	995	—	—	—	—	—	995	—
Wheat	6,780	—	—	—	—	—	7,680	—
Milk	50,887	14	34,480	16	50,630	30	186,024	10
Lard	10,537	—	22,427	23	26,724	02	39,688	25
Butter	—	—	2,805	—	1,804	—	4,700	—
Sugar	5,691	—	35,483	37	19,620	15	20,267	12
Cocoa	4,512	—	8,558	20	3,832	—	17,900	—
Medicines . . .	—	—	3,785	—	—	—	3,786	—
Manufactured goods	—	—	1,936	30	—	—	1,933	—
Woolen items	—	—	2,427	—	—	—	2,427	—
Miscellaneous items	3,277	—	17,817	35	31,478	—	34,372	35
TOTAL	190,177	01	540,735	29	386,190	08	1,026,920	37

In addition, there were 23 railcar loads of automobiles.

The amount of goods shipped to the ARA in Russia can be understood more clearly if we express the totals for the most important food commodities in terms of the number of food rations established by the ARA offices as supplementary nutritional allowances for children.

This approximate conversion of food by weight into rations has been carried out in the following table (Table 2).

1. Although some totals are erroneous, all figures are presented as in the original document. A *pood* is roughly equal to 36 pounds.

Table 2. Shipments Expressed in Terms of Children's Food Rations

Food	September	October	November 1–26	Total through November 26
Flour	8,558,000	28,147,000	23,841,240	70,346,240
Rice	14,801,000	27,186,000	8,840,000	33,827,000
Beans	16,444,000	29,541,000	19,798,000	65,783,000
Milk	28,182,000	38,488,000	22,074,000	84,745,000
Fats	30,164,000	48,289,000	51,183,700	110,616,700
Sugar	5,218,000	37,002,000	20,116,000	62,330,000
Cocoa	18,303,000	85,079,000	13,711,700	69,293,700

From Table 2 we can see that for individual food items the September shipments were equivalent to anywhere from 5.2 to 23 million rations, the October shipments were equivalent to 18 to 27 million rations, and the November shipments were equivalent to 5.8 to 51 million average daily children's rations.

Total shipments through November 26 were equivalent (for individual food items) to anywhere from 50.8 to 119.6 million daily rations. The variations in the amounts of food shipped (in terms of daily rations) may be attributed to the fact that the shippers did not maintain the exact proportions in which these items are included in the daily rations.

It is interesting that in terms of the number of rations, fats and milk rank one and two on the list of imported foods, followed by flour, cocoa, beans, sugar, and rice. In the first two months the pattern was somewhat different, especially with respect to flour, which was in last place on the list.

In order to get an idea of the significance of the ARA's food shipments from abroad, let us compare the quantities shipped to the ARA in Moscow with the quantities shipped to other organizations in Moscow.

As of November 1 the following shipments had arrived in Moscow:

a) food items

ARA	602,369 *poods*	or	88.3%
Central Famine Relief Committee	25,356 *poods*	or	3.9%
Quakers	6,244 *poods*	or	0.9%
International Children's Relief Alliance	47,392 *poods*	or	6.9%
TOTAL	682,204 *poods*		100%

b) all items

ARA	640,487 *poods*	or	86.8%
Central Famine Relief Committee	28,682 *poods*	or	2.9%
Quakers	9,341 *poods*	or	8.0% [sic]
International Children's Relief Alliance	59,385 *poods*	or	1.3% [sic]
TOTAL	738,045 *poods*		100%

All ARA shipments, with the exception of some shipments delivered to Petrograd by sea, have come to Moscow and were shipped from there to the famine regions.

Figures for the total shipments from Moscow to the famine regions are given in Table 3, which also indicates the amount of each item shipped to Moscow. The totals for shipments which arrived in Moscow are for the period up to November 26, while the totals for shipments from Moscow are for the period up to November 23. These figures were taken from reports from the Moscow Distribution Depot of the People's Commissariat of Food Supply [*Narkomprod*].

Table 3. <u>Shipments to Moscow and from Moscow</u>
<u>to ARA Regional Depots</u>

Food item	Received as of November 26		Shipped prior to November 23	
	*Pood*s	Pounds	*Pood*s	Pounds
Flour	429,195	14	409,440	18
Rice	106,309	33	102,667	08
Beans	80,224	14	59,117	34
Rye	995	—	—	—
Wheat	6,780	—	993	—
Milk	185,024	10	166,069	08
Lard	59,688	25	26,002	29
Meat	7,862	—	—	—
Butter	4,700	—	7,431	02
Sugar	60,207	12	54,544	15
Cocoa	17,900	29	12,528	13
Medicines	3,785	—	78,780	38
Manufactured goods	1,935	—	—	—
Miscellaneous clothing	4,319	20	396	31
Woolen items	2,427	—	74	—
Miscellaneous items	54,572	35	31,386	11
TOTAL	1,026,936	37	891,132	03

Table 4 illustrates the distribution of items by individual famine regions. The figures in this table were taken from the same source as the figures in Table 3 and cover the period through November 23. The table does not include any figures for the Moscow region, which will be given below in our summary of relief activity for that region.

Table 4 is given in an annex to this report.

According to the Riga Agreement, the American Relief Administration has the authority to choose food distribution stations and fix rations. But undoubtedly our authoritative recommendations based on our detailed knowledge of the famine have heavily influenced the ARA's determination of priorities in distributing food shipments. We have reviewed requests from local authorities for supplementary rations before forwarding them to the ARA, and the ARA has followed our guidance in its distribution activity and has eliminated any element of chance which might occur as a result of its unfamiliarity with the country and the magnitude of the famine, along with other conditions which must be understood in order for the organization to act effectively.

These rations are merely supplementary rations, not basic rations. This determines how the rations are distributed and the makeup of the rations. The food is distributed as a meal once a day, and the meal must be consumed at a canteen or equivalent facility. Except for rare exceptions, issuing meals for home consumption is prohibited. Taking leftovers outside the canteen is also prohibited to discourage speculation and also to ensure that the meal is used exclusively for its express purpose, i.e., that the entire meal is consumed only by the child and is not divided up among other members of the household.

The ration for children includes the following foods: 28 grams of cocoa, 112 grams of sugar, 262 grams of milk, 700 grams of flour, 140 grams of beans, 340 grams of rice, and 60 grams of fats, for a total of 5,446.2 calories per week or an average of 778 calories per day. The menu changes daily, and thus so do the rations, with the amount of calories varying from 707 to 896 per day. As we mentioned above, the aforementioned proportions of foods in the children's rations are reflected in the total amounts of different foodstuffs included in the shipments to food distribution stations. In most cases the trains carrying ARA shipments are made up so that all of the required foods are present in the established proportions. This has streamlined the process of getting foods to primary food distribution agencies.

We have already mentioned that in September there were four depots to which ARA food was shipped, namely Moscow, Petrograd, Samara, and Kazan'. Three of these depots distributed meals in September, namely Kazan', Petrograd, and Moscow, with Kazan' distributing the most meals (300,000) and Petrograd distributing less (45,000), and Moscow distributing only 554 meals. The Kazan' depot fed an average of 10,000 children per day in September, while the same figures for Petrograd and Moscow were 1,500 and 16 respectively.

It was not until October 2 that two canteens were opened in Samara. Obviously, no food was provided there in September, and the first shipment of food did not leave Moscow for Samara until September 21.

ARA activity rose substantially in October. The pace of development of food relief is illustrated by the following figures.

ARA organizations operated:

314 food distribution stations in the first half of October;

more than 1481 food distribution stations in the second half of October.

The progress of the effort at the end of October is evident from the following table:

REGION	Number of food distribution stations	Number of children fed	Number of meals issued during month	Average number of persons fed per day
Kazan' guberniia	1,230	135,000	2,090,000	103,000
Samara gub.	120	36,281	486,000	15,533
Saratov gub.	2	1,530	4,000	133
Simbirsk gub.	16	4,075	14,000	400
TSaritsyn gub.	no information	2,045	no information	no information
	112	25,000	903,000	30,100
Petrograd	1	2,000	36,510	1,220
City of Moscow				
TOTAL, ≥	1,481	216,001	≥ 4,513,610	150,452

As we can see from this table, the number of persons fed in October was as high as 150,458 [*sic*], while the number of persons fed on average per day varied from day to day over the month, with the highest number of persons fed on a single day equal to 216,001.

The following plans were made for November.

Guberniia	Number of children to be fed	9-week food supply for following numbers of children
Kazan'	200,000 children	150,000
Samara	200,000 children	150,000
Saratov	150,000 children	75,000
Simbirsk	150,000 children	75,000
TSaritsyn	100,000 children	75,000
City of Petrograd	35,000 children	50,000 for five months
City of Moscow	30,000 children	15,000 for two weeks
Bashkir Republic	50,000 children	no information
Kirghiz Republic	50,000 children	no information
TOTAL	965,000 children	590,000

We have not yet received complete information on the implementation of this plan. The information at our disposal is fragmentary and applies to different periods of time. The table below contains this incomplete information for each individual region and gives the dates for the information.

REGIONS	Number of food distribution stations	Number of children fed	COMMENTS
1. Samara guberniia	438	85,451	as of November 15
2. Saratov gub.	—	30,000	as of November 15
3. Simbirsk gub.	—	33,411	as of November 18
4. TSaritsyn gub.	—	4,187	as of November 18
5. Astrakhan gub.	—	10,000	as of November 20
6. Tatar Republic (Kazan' raion)	—	170,000	as of November 15
7. Bashkir Republic	—	no information	no information
8. Kirghiz Republic	6	2,959	as of November 18
9. Volga German communities	—	12,000	no accurate information
10. City of Petrograd	112	35,000	as of November 15
11. City of Moscow	24	9,529	as of November 25
TOTAL		392,547	

As we can see from the table, the information contained therein only describes ARA activity in the first half of November. The only exception is the Moscow office, whose activity is described through November 25. We should mention that, given the condition of our postal and telegraph systems, any accurate description of ARA activity would be unimaginable. ARA representatives were ordered to submit very detailed weekly reports by telegraph. However, they have sometimes encountered insurmountable obstacles in trying to meet this requirement, because even if it is possible to compile more or less accurate information in a guberniia capital, it is often completely impossible to obtain this information in backwater district towns, let alone the villages. Most of the reports contain the brief statement "no information" for individual districts.

This circumstance makes it possible to assume that the total number of persons fed given in the table above (392,547) is much lower than the actual number. We have tabulated information on all the regions. Below we provide tables for Samara and Simbirsk guberniias, the Kirghiz Republic, and the Moscow Office of the ARA.

Summary of ARA activity in the Samara region
as of November 15, 1921

1. The operation of food distribution stations

AREA	Number of ARA canteens	Number of children fed	Number of children's facilities receiving food supplies	Number of children fed in these facilities
City of Samara	6	4,100	22	5,000
Samara *uezd*	307	63,192	63	3,200
Melekessy *uezd*	3	650	—	—
Stavropol' *uezd*	9	3,100	—	—
Pugachev *uezd*	2	1,000	—	—
Balakovskii *uezd*	16	4,300	10	1,000
Total	343	76,242	95	9,200

As of November 15 the ARA had fed 35,451 children.

2. The Supplies Received by the Samara Depot
and Its Distribution Activity from September 27
to November 15

Food item	Received	Distributed	Left
		In *poods*	
Flour	52,486	43,246	9,240
Sugar	7,805	5,431	2,384
Milk	32,096	21,052	11,044
Lard	6,853	4,515	1,773
Beans	17,387	10,681	6,706
Cocoa	2,842	1,241	1,601
Rice	14,945	8,339	6,615
Salt (received from *guberniia* food commissar)	747	398	349
TOTAL FOOD	134,596	94,883	38,713

In addition, the depot received one carload of medicine, which was distributed among seven *guberniias*, hospitals, and one children's pharmacy, and three carloads of clothing, which was to be distributed to orphanages.

Summary of ARA activity in the Simbirsk region
as of November 18, 1921

1. The operation of food distribution stations

AREA	Number of ARA canteens	Number of children fed there	Number of hospitals and sanatoria	Number of children fed there	Number of children's facilities receiving food supplies	Number of children at facilities	Total number of children fed
City of Simbirsk	5	4,265	2	391	—	2,500	7,206
Simbirsk *uezd*	—	—	—	—	—	—	24,015
City of Sangilai	—	1,669	—	117	—	404	2,190
Total	—	5,934	—	447			33,411

Note: There is no information from the *uezd*s.

2. The Supplies at the Simbirsk Depot
and Its Distribution Activity from November 11
to November 18

Food item	Distributed	Undistributed
Flour	88,525 metric tons	345,934 metric tons
Sugar	14,006 metric tons	46,569 metric tons
Milk	1,611 crates	10,359 crates
Fats	7,573 metric tons	36,433 metric tons
Beans	16,457 metric tons	81,464 metric tons
Cocoa	3,540 metric tons	22,151 metric tons
Rice	31,297 metric tons	171,404 metric tons

3. A total of 21,242 rations were issued
at canteens in the city of Simbirsk from
November 11 to November 18

ARA Activity in the Kirghiz Republic as of November 18, 1921

According to the liaison of the RSFSR at the ARA, the ARA received from Moscow its first shipment for the Kirghiz Republic on November 12 at Orenburg. The shipment consisted of flour, oats, beans, sugar, rice, condensed milk, cocoa, and vegetable fats.

The local Russian American Children's Relief Committee [*RAKPD*] organization began providing medical examinations for children. The scheduled completion date for these examinations was November 19.

By November 19 there were already 6 ARA canteens in operation in Orenburg. These canteens fed a total of 2,959 children. By November 22 the organization planned to be feeding up to 20,000 children.

There is an urgent need for medicines and medical care.

Information on the Activity of the Moscow Organization as of November 26

Type of facility	Number of facilities	Number of children fed
1. Canteens	19	8,572
2. Correctional facilities for morally defective children.	1	50
3. Red Army restricted distribution centers	1	115
4. Pokrovskii distribution center	1	620
5. Institutions for the children of emigres	1	66
6. Reception and transshipment station No. 20	1	116
TOTAL	24	9,539

The movement of food to and from the warehouse as of November 27, 1921

Item	Food	INCOMING	OUTGOING	LEFT OVER
1.	Cocoa	944.13	606.76	337.37
2.	Sugar	3,784.96	2,312.29	1,471.67
3.	Milk	324 crates, 46 cans	235 crates, 26 cans	39 crates, 20 cans
4.	"	97 crates	—	97 crates
5.	Flour	23,588.62	16,334.26	8,214.36
6.	Beans	4,676.49	2,644.76	2,031.73
7.	Rice	8,097.02	1,906.17	3,191.83
8.	Lard	2,118.52	1,264.03	854.79
9.	Potatoes	1,000	229.28	770.72

Information on the distribution of warm clothing to children

Item No	Item	RECEIVED	DISTRIBUTED
1.	Caps	2,971	1,681
2.	Children's stockings	11,310	5,119
3.	Armlets	2,554	230
4.	Woolen scarves	57	57
5.	Long dresses	1,726	347
6.	Bloomers	1,046	—
7.	Boys' shirts	89	—
8.	Boys' knickers	157	37
9.	Suits for boys and girls	1050	—
10.	Scarves	168	168
11.	Undershirts	32	32
12.	Gloves	27	27
13.	Shawls	237	237
14.	Boxes of old children's toys	1	75 items

We have very little information on ARA activity in providing medical care. This can be attributed to the fact that this kind of relief is not as specific as the ARA's food relief activities and that the demand for medical care is extremely diverse. The illnesses which have developed in the famine regions can largely be attributed to malnutrition, which means that the primary form of medical care should be improving the diets of the patients. We do have information on ARA activity in this area. In TSaritsyn the ARA has supplied supplementary rations to 13 facilities of the *Guberniia* Public Health Department with 1,080 patients and will do the same in other areas, and the ARA plans to supply supplementary rations to as many as 30,000 patients. In addition, the ARA is also supplying medicines to patients. Moscow has received a wide variety of medicines for a total of 3,785 *poods*. These medicines have been distributed to different regions, which is why medicines are included in the report for Samara *guberniia*.

Finally, the ARA is also providing relief by distributing items of clothing to the general public. The ARA depot in Moscow has received 1,925 *poods* of manufactured goods, 4,319 *poods* and 20 pounds of miscellaneous clothing items, and 2,427 *poods* of woolen items. In addition, some of these items, like the medicines, were included in the "miscellaneous items" category.

The ARA has also taken steps to have suits made and distributed to the starving population. Some of these items have already reached the famine regions and have been distributed, which we can see from the reports for Samara *guberniia* and Moscow. Currently we cannot provide an accurate accounting of ARA's activity in this area due to a lack of information, but we can say that the organization has become more active and focused in this area also.

Moscow

November 29, 1921

TSGANKh, fond 478, op. 3, d. 1366, l. 9–22.

DOCUMENT 243   *Transcription of a telephone message from Eiduk to Politburo members, December 29, 1921, notifying them of the passage of American legislation donating milk and grain to victims of famine in the Volga region*

Telephone message No. 4328

From the Plenipotentiary Representative of the Government of the RSFSR to all foreign famine-relief organizations, Comrade Eiduk.

To Comrades: Lenin, Kamenev, Molotov, Chicherin, TSuriupa, Lobachev, Dzerzhinsky, Lezhava, Menzhinskii, Kalinin, and Rakovskii.

The board of directors of ARA [American Relief Administration], Colonel Lomergan, has just relayed to me a telegram from HOOVER with the information that Harding's proposal in the U.S. Congress to donate 20 million bushels of grain and milk [1 bushel=72 pounds] for the famine victims of the Volga region has been ratified. Furthermore, HOOVER urged ARA in the telegram to harness all its energies to see to it that the wish of the American people to aid the starving of the Volga be successfully completed. The telegram ends with a wish for complete success. Tomorrow I will forward the English text of the telegram with a copy of the cover letter.

At the same time, I have informed the editors of *Pravda*, *Izvestiia*, and *ROSTA* [Russian Telegraph Agency] to publish his communication. Colonel Lomergan has asked me to call a meeting of the responsible representatives of the People's Commissariat for Transportation, the People's Commissariat for Foodstuffs, the People's Commissariat for Foreign Trade, officials of ARA, and the representatives of the RSFSR government to ARA to discuss transportation of the designated cargo. I have assigned Comrade Pines to conduct discussions with the various commissariats regarding the meeting. Signed: Plenipotentiary Representative of the RSFSR Government to all foreign famine-relief organizations, Comrade Eiduk.

Transmitted by Petrova

Accepted by Sheirent [?]   (time) 2245 Dec. 29, 1921

Telephone No. 66-50

RTSKhIDNI, fond 17, op. 84, d. 224, ll. 74, 74ob.

DOCUMENT 244   *From a stenographer's transcript of a speech delivered by Comrade TROT-SKY on March 12, 1922, at the Bolshoi Theater to a plenary session of the Moscow Soviet.*

OUR FRIENDS, OUR ENEMIES, AND THE FAMINE

Every starving Volga peasant would say that we need the army, even though he knows that the army, by its very existence, is diverting precious resources and food. The famine is a major disaster, which has meant the death of hundreds of thousands and even millions of human beings, but if we let the enemy tighten the noose around the neck of the Russian people, this would mean the death of the entire nation or slavery, which would be worse than death. The starving Volga peasant knows this, which is why he supports the Red Army as long as we have enemies. And we do have enemies. We can see this from the famine itself. Haven't they tried to use and aren't they still trying to use the famine as the starting point for an attack against us? Feverish debates are raging all over Europe over the efforts to alleviate the famine. And what about all the haggling over whether to send relief or not? And what about the British government's decision? Doesn't this prove how large segments of the bourgeoisie, especially the ruling cliques, view the famine not as a terrible disaster and calamity, but as a political event and a godsend for their diplomats and their financial aristocracy? We have been getting help—and not just from the working class—but from the bourgeoisie and that American quasi-governmental official agency known as the ARA [American Relief Administration]. This help is growing day by day, and at this point it is obviously playing a gigantic role in our lives. We can't help but mention it. I recently received a report on the amounts of aid we are receiving from our representative to the ARA and other relief organizations (at the same time the U.S. Senate voted 20 million dollars to aid the starving people of Russia). Once the ships arrive and the effort is fully underway, the ARA alone will feed 5 million starving adults. If we compare this figure with the aid provided by European organizations, we can see that the ARA is doing ten times more than all of the others put together.

We know about the heroic efforts of Nansen, that altruistic friend of Russia's toiling and starving masses; and we know how his heroic efforts are being stymied by the callousness and organized resistance of the governments of Europe.

Along with Nansen's organization, we have the Quakers, "The Society of Friends," who are feeding many thousands of children and adults, and the Swedish Red Cross, the Czechoslovak Red Cross, and so forth. These organizations have brought their own people here, who are engaged in difficult work. Of the 117 employees of the ARA, 15 have caught typhus. Two employees of Nansen's organization, Farer and Para, have died of typhus. Miss Peterson and Violet Kilara [?] of the Quakers, the Swedish nurse Karina Lindson, and Doctor Hertenberg of the German Red Cross also died of typhus.

When you think of these sacrifices, you want to remind yourself that there are still people in these bloody, heroic, but harsh and terrible times who are motivated exclusively by feelings of humanity and inner nobility regardless of their class affiliation.

I read the obituary of Violet Kilara, the Anglo-Saxon woman. She was probably no different from the others who died in service to humanity: her obituary said that she, a young, weak, and fragile creature, came to Buzuluk to live in very harsh, backward, and barbaric conditions. She died doing her duty and was buried there. Here tonight we have counted six such graves (there might be, or most likely will be, more). These sacrifices were a kind of harbinger of the new relationships between people in the future, relationships which will be based on solidarity and moral sympathy and unstained by avarice.

As soon as, and we are very certain of this, the Russian people become a little wealthier, they will build a large memorial to these fallen ardent champions of a brighter, better, more humane moral order.

We are fighting in the name of this moral order. If we did not believe that in the future people would treat each other like brothers and sisters, it would be absolutely pointless for us to fight, build barricades, and wage war.

Obviously, altruistic feelings don't always go hand in hand with philanthropy, but we won't insist on it. We will merely state the simple truth that the Great Republic Across the Ocean has shown ten times more generosity than all of Europe and has sent us large quantities of food, which are unfortunately insufficient, but are substantial nonetheless, in order to feed and save peasant men, women, and children from starvation.

We will remember this forever, just as the working masses of Russia have already remembered this for eternity!

But for the sake of honesty, we should admit that we have mixed emotions. They are clouded. I have asked myself more than once how we can explain why Nansen's name is covered with an aura of glory in our country, while we are merely grateful to the ARA. There is no doubt that the feelings this organization could arouse in the hearts of the working mass have not yet been aroused. And this can be attributed to the fact that we still do not know what the Great Republic Across the Ocean wants from us.

We often hear and read the names of the individuals who are the leaders of the ARA. And these names are associated with statements that are extremely hostile to us. We have been getting information from the newspapers and all sorts of other sources indicating that "Wrangel has received a new subsidy from influential circles," and some sources have attempted to prove connections between these circles and the individuals who have joined the ARA.

We would like to believe that this isn't so. Moreover, we are positive that it isn't. But we would very much like to see full and absolute honesty on the part of the ruling circles of the American Republic in this regard. The day when the men in Washington and New York firmly and clearly state that the United States believes that it has had enough of Wilson's experience with Kolchak, that the United States will not try to find a replacement for Kolchak, and that the United States will not provide any support, be it direct or indirect, financial or moral, to any new candidates for the role of executioner of the Russian workers and peasants, will be a great day of celebration for Soviet Russia. And then we will be able to see the role of the ARA—its great and benevolent role—in its true light. And then the attitudes of the working masses to this organization will not only be one of gratitude, but one of ardent and passionate feeling.

One might say that in making this assessment of the situation, I am equating the government's opinion with the attitudes of the people. Yes I am, and I am doing so intentionally. And as long as the people in Washington, New York, and the other world capitals don't realize this, they will not understand anything about us.

Our greatest achievement is the fact that the revolution has aroused and developed the revolutionary statist instincts of the Russian people. The Russian people are no longer the abject pawns of the "destiny of the state"; they are taking their political cues from the situation and are drawing conclusions. And the ambiguity which exists in our attitudes towards the ARA arises from the situation because the entire situation is telling us to be careful.

TSGASA, fond 33987, op. 1, d. 505, ll. 42

M. I. Kalinin (second from right) and S. M. Budennyi with other Soviet officials and several unidentified American senators, Moscow, 1923. TSGAKFD

DOCUMENT 245   *Note of thanks by Kalinin, March 20, 1923, acknowledging the $1500 raised by the New York newspaper* Russkii Golos [Russian Voice] *for famine victims in the USSR*

Mikhail K A L I N I N,
Chairman of the All-Russian Central Executive Committee [*VTSIK*]
and the Committee for Famine Relief, Moscow

/One thousand five hundred dollars/

[handwritten section:]

One thousand five hundred thousand [sic] dollars received

Chairman of the *VTSIK* M. Kalinin

As chairman of the Central Committee for Famine Relief, I bring on behalf of Russia's famine victims the deepest gratitude for the aid sent in the name of the newspaper *Russkii golos* collected by Russian workers.

I will make this enormous assistance known to the starving workers and peasants.

With salutations   M. Kalinin

May 20, 1923   Moscow, the Kremlin

RTSKhIDNI, fond 78, op. 9, d. 16, ll. 1, 10b.

American Capital Investments

Even before the introduction of the New Economic Policy in 1921, Soviet leaders recognized that economic recovery would require assistance through foreign trade and foreign credits. Investors abroad also recognized that the new Soviet state could provide a valuable market for their products. To this end the British government negotiated the Anglo-Soviet Trade Agreement in 1921, and the Soviet-German Treaty of Rapallo in 1922 paved the way for an expansion of trade between those two countries. The United States declined to pursue similar negotiations, although it quietly abandoned the trade embargo in 1920. In the ensuing years there was little coordination between the State Department, which discouraged diplomatic relations, and the Commerce Department, which urged the expansion of trade with Soviet Russia. This impasse led to a default policy of "trade at your own risk," and individual entrepreneurs soon entered the Soviet market.

As early as 1919 a "Soviet Bureau" in New York, organized by Ludwig Martens, arranged trade deals between U.S. firms and the Soviet government. Over nine hundred firms approached Martens with inquiries about contracts, including Chicago meat-packing firms, the Ford Motor Company, the Packard Motor Company, numerous machine-manufacturing firms, and producers of agricultural implements. Although Martens was deported in 1921 for radical activities, the Soviet Bureau continued to organize trade deals, and it was joined by several other intermediary agencies.

One of the most flamboyant of the early U.S. investors in Soviet Russia, whose contacts with the Soviet government lasted his long lifetime, was Armand Hammer. Hammer first traveled to Soviet Russia in 1921 as a recently graduated medical doctor in order to help with famine relief. His father, Julius Hammer, was a physician and entrepreneur who was also an active member of the Socialist Labor Party; he had helped to finance the office of the Soviet Bureau in New York headed by a family friend, Ludwig Martens. During his trip to Russia, Hammer visited some industrial sites in the Urals, accompanied by Martens, who after his deportation from the U.S. had become chief of the Soviet Metallurgical Trust. Through Martens, Hammer met Lenin in August 1921, who offered him the concession to develop the mining of asbestos. This led to Hammer's extensive involvement in Soviet trade: he quickly became the local representative of a number of foreign firms doing business with the Soviets, including Ford, and in 1925 he opened a huge pencil plant, which supplied "Hammer" pencils throughout the Soviet Union. When Nikita Khrushchev first met Hammer in 1961, he recalled learning to write with a Hammer pencil.

Other firms actively sought Soviet trade in the 1920s despite the official policy of nonrecognition of the Soviet Union by the U.S. government. By 1925, for example, the Soviet Union was purchasing 10 percent of the Ford Motor Company's tractor production. Toward the end of the 1920s Soviet trade representatives began to recruit not just American capital, but also labor and technology. A variety of agencies operated throughout the U.S. to recruit specialized engineers and workers for employment on Soviet projects; the Soviet Auto and Tractor Trust opened a special office in Detroit to assist in this recruitment. In 1927 the Supreme Economic Council [*VSNKh*] appointed the American engineer, Hugh Cooper, as its chief consultant for the construction of the Dnepr River hydroelectric dam. Ford was hired to design a new automobile plant in the city of Gorky in 1928, and the Cleveland-based Austin Company carried out the actual construction.

DOCUMENT 246   ***Appeal for Russian emigres living in the U.S. to aid Russia, May 10, 1919***

Translation   July 8, 1920

STATEMENT OF L. K. MARTENS,
THE REPRESENTATIVE OF THE
RUSSIAN SOCIALIST FEDERATED SOVIET REPUBLIC
IN THE UNITED STATES

I welcome the State Department's press release announcing the removal of restrictions in connection with the restoration of trade relations between Soviet Russia and the United States.

I should mention, however, that today's press release is hardly adequate to resolve the issue of restoring trade relations between Russia and the United States. It contains absolutely no mention of whether and how Russia will be allowed to pay American companies for the goods it purchases. Quite some time ago we stated our readiness and willingness to open a line of credit in Estonia for American manufacturers. But the government agency in charge of the banks (Federal Reserve Board) has issued letters warning American banks against accepting any drafts on Estonian banks. As a result, our payments for American goods by drafts have been frozen. We cannot establish credit by depositing Russian gold in American banks as long as the danger exists that these deposits will be seized or subjected to other restrictions. The government's announcement in today's newspapers provides absolutely no guarantee that we will be able to open lines of credit. According to the press release, no plans have been made to restore postal services or free transfers of funds. It is quite obvious that trade relations could not be restored without these conditions, which are absolutely essential for restoring international trade. Trade is based on an intricate system for transferring funds with the appropriate guarantees and security from both parties to a transaction, and thriving trade would be absolutely impossible without postal and telegraph services, the freedom to transfer funds, and international relations. Although its announcement apparently removed all the obstructions, in reality the State Department is continuing its policy of restrictions.

Even though diplomatic recognition of the Soviet government with all the associated formalities could be postponed indefinitely, de facto restoration of trade relations will require a minimum level of political relations. The British and Canadian governments have recognized this fact in their trade negotiations with Russia. Krasin left London for Moscow with the express purpose of handling the political aspects of the negotiations, which are essential for restoring trade. The Canadian government has sanctioned the opening of a Soviet government trade mission in Canada and has given its official blessing to trade agreements concluded between Canadian companies and the Russian government.

Of course today's press release aroused a great deal of interest in business circles, and we have been inundated with questions from American businessmen, who would like to know what role they could play in restoring trade relations with Soviet Russia. We can only tell them to talk to the American government if they want an explanation of U.S. policy. We will do everything we can to meet any practical proposal halfway. All we are asking for is the right to buy goods in the American market, ship them to Russia, and pay for them. If the American government's announcement means that we will be able to do this, then we are simply overjoyed. But the spirit of this press release, with all of its qualifications and ambiguities, will compel us to await further developments before making any statements about its tangible results.

TSGANKh, fond 413, op. 3, d. 515, ll. 4–6.

DOCUMENT 247 **Agreement between the Russian Republic and American Allied Drug and Chemical Corporation, November 2, 1921, on asbestos mining in the Urals**

Copy of Copy

CONCESSION AGREEMENT

FOR THE MINING OF ASBESTOS DEPOSITS IN THE URALS
BY THE AMERICAN ALLIED DRUG AND CHEMICAL CORPORATION

The government of the Russian Socialist Federated Soviet Republic, hereafter referred to as "the Government," hereby grants a concession for the mining of asbestos to the American Allied Drug and Chemical Corporation in the person of the individuals Armand Hammer and Boris Mishell, acting on behalf of the corporation, hereafter referred to as "the Concessioner" on the following terms.

§1.

The Government hereby grants the Concessioner the asbestos mines of the Alapaevsk *raion*, formerly the property of the Alapaevsk Mine District, located in Ekaterinburg *guberniia*, Alapaevsk *uezd*, 25 *verst*s from Alapaevsk Station on the Northeast Ural Railroad and 5 *verst*s from the Alapaevsk-Susunna Mine Spur, with all of the buildings at the mines, their equipment, machinery, and other property enumerated in a special inventory drafted by the procedure described in §3, with the exception of the materials and asbestos at the mine.

On this basis the Concessioner shall be assigned the tract of land occupied by the aforementioned mines. The exact contours of the tract shall be determined and a survey of its boundaries shall be conducted by the commission described in §3.

The tract shall be assigned to the Concessioner for his use of the surface and for subsequent prospecting and mining of asbestos on the basis of the Law Governing Mineral Leases.

§2.

The asbestos mines shall be transferred to the Concessioner for the purpose of producing at least 80,000 *pood*s [approximately 1440 tons] of unprocessed graded (separated from gangue) asbestos in the first year of operation.
[Original ends at this point.]

TSGANKh, fond 413, op. 5, d. 1249a, ll. 256–265.

DOCUMENT 248 *Proposals made by American commercial firms during the years 1921–1922 to export goods to Russia*

[English-language original]

[Typed in Russian:] 10. Proposals of American companies on exporting goods to Russia (on company stationery). Originals. (4 documents). 1921–1922

Technical service	**VOLGA**	New York
Engineering	*Engineering & Trading Co., Inc.*	
	EXPORT– IMPORT	Chicago
Mining	63 Park Row, New York, U.S.A.	
		Toronto
Trade Departments		
Agricultural Imple-		Montreal
ments		Harbin
Hardware & Building		London
Materials		Paris
Trucks & Automo-		Prague
biles		Constantinople
Electrical Machinery		Gothenburg
and Equipment		Danzig
Mining Machinery		Reval
and Equipment		Riga
Coal		Helsingfors
Anthracite		Vladivostok
Chemicals		
Medicaments		
Foodstuffs		
Raw Materials		

Feb. 1, 1922

People's Commissariat for Foreign Trade
Moscow, Russia

RE: SAMPLES OF CIGARETTES, REF
APPLICATION FOR IMPORT LICENSE FOR
50,000,000 AMERICAN CIGARETTES

Gentlemen:

With reference to our letter of January 28th, we are sending you herewith samples of cigarettes, as per enclosed specification.

Very truly yours,

VOLGA ENGINEERING & TRADING CO., INC.

per [signed] Omeltchenko

EIO:MC
Enc.

Saint Louis Machine Tool Co.

CABLE ADDRESS: 932 LOUGHBOROUGH AVE.   Manufacturers

MACHINTOOL   GRINDING MACHINES
        SAINT LOUIS   **Saint Louis, U.S.A.**   POLISHING MACHINES
WESTERN UNION CODE,   Dec. 5, 1921   TAPPING MACHINES
FIVE LETTER EDITION   TAPPING CHUCKS

Russian Export & Import Co.
Moscow, Russia

Gentlemen:

We have noticed an item in the current issue of the trade papers in reference to your organization and take pleasure in sending you a copy of our catalog, under separate cover. We beg to inquire whether the product there shown would be of interest to you.

If you should desire it, we would be glad to quote you our extreme export discounts and put your name on our permanent mailing list.

Very respectfully yours,

SAINT LOUIS MACHINE TOOL CO.

JTM:CER

1 catalog

CHICAGO CURLED HAIR CO.

Manufacturers of
Sterilized
Curled Hair

Chicago, U.S.A.

29 December 1921

[Russian stamp:]   Department of Foreign Trade, Peoples'
Commissariat of Trade

Russian American Chamber of Commerce
Moscow, Russia

Gentlemen:

We take the liberty of advising you that we are manufacturers of CURLED HAIR which we are interested in exporting. This article is used for Upholstering by

Automobile manufacturers,
" Body "
Furniture manufacturers
Mattress   "
Upholsters,
       ETC.

We would be pleased to have you place our name before anyone interested in these articles, or if convenient, would appreciating your sending us a list of all possible users in your territory.

Anything you can do for us along this line, will be more than greatly appreciated.

Yours very truly,

CHICAGO CURLED HAIR CO.

By J.P. Donohue

JOH. M. BRAUN - RIGA
Wood and Metal Processing Plant

Riga February 23, 1921
Koengol'mskaia 12.

I have the honor to offer for sale American winnowing machines:

No. 00 - 20 units at the price of 3900. — rubles per unit
No. 0 - 18   "   "   "   "   " 3450. — "   "   "
No. 1 - 85   "   "   "   "   " 3000. — "   "   "
No. 2 - 27   "   "   "   "   " 2850. — "   "   "
No. 3 - 31   "   "   "   "   " 2700. — "   "   "
No. 4 - 2   "   "   "   "   " 2600. — "   "   "

It is understood that the price includes delivery to the railroad station in Riga, in Latvian currency, however, payment must be made in cash at the time of shipment of the winnowing machines.

Respectfully,

Joh. M. Braun
    Riga

TSGANKh, fond 413, op. 3, d. 1001a, ll. 10, 21, 22, 87.

Translation
E. K.

Engel and Gevenor
Engineering Company, New York

May 5, 1922

Mr. Lev Trotsky
Minister of War
Moscow

Dear Sir,

I would like to offer you my services as a transportation engineer.

We have a large company in the United States which builds streetcar and railroad tracks and has already completed a number of major projects of this type.

I believe that you have a large number of projects in this field and that you could offer extensive opportunities to an individual who has specialized in this business his entire life.

I could furnish you references of my work, if you had a vacancy in government service, or I could sign a contract with you to perform a specific job of this type.

We would be very grateful for a reply.

Your faithful servant

Gevenor
Consulting Engineer

TSGASA, fond 33987, op. 1, d. 528, l. 4–5, 7.

[English-language original; typographical errors preserved]

STAR IRON WORKS
G. W. Porter. Prop.
DIAMOND DRILLS & DIAMOND DRILL TOOLS
GENERAL MACHINISTS
PUNXSUTAWNEY, PA.,

PHONES
SUMMERVILLE
BELL 5-R

June 8, 1922

Mr. Leon Trotzky,
Moscow, Russia

Dear sir,
I enclose you a letter giving some of the fundimental principals that made our Government one of the leading nations of the world. If any of the suggestions will help you in the upbuilding of your nation I will be delighted, as I am an ardent republican and very much interested in the success of Russia.

Your. Respect.
G. W. Porter

Punxsutawney Penn. April 6th 1922

Mr. Leon Trotzky.
Moscow, Russia.

Dear sir,
This is a good adage.   Give ear to all advise.   Then do as you please.
We Americans understand that you have a difficult problem to solve, a few suggestions from a retired business man may not come amiss.
I am a retired manufacturer and have been a student of political economy all my life.
Altho not a socialist — I believe to a certain extent in government ownership. The people in this country are very much interested in Russia and hope in the near future to see her one of the leading Republics of the world. You have wonderful resources. Something similar to our own, and if your country is properly organized, in time it should become as free and as prosperous as our own United States. It seems to me the first thing the leaders of a nation should do when changing a form of government is to carefully study the lives of the patriotic men who laid the foundation of a successful republic and you will not find in all history a more noble class of men than the founders of this republic. Washington the greatest patriot that the world ever produced a man of honesty, temperance, will, and gratitude. Jefferson the great commoner — equal to any peer who ever lived. The one who wrote the Declaration of Indipendence, a document together with our constitution well worth careful study. Franklin our philosopher. Adams. Lincoln. Roosevelt — all these a beacon light to all true Americans. Our nation is divided into states each to a certain extent having souvereign power one state may work out a certain problem and after due time if it is all right other states adopt it — such as our 18 and 19 amendment and other reforms.

To a certain extent I believe in government ownership. The government should by all means own the banks, never allow the money houses to get hold of the purse string of the nation. The post office, telephones, telegraphs, and railroads and it may be best to own the coal mines. These are the life currents of a nation. In time this government will own a part if not all of these utilities as they are utilized by all the people.
When it comes to mills, factories, farming and other utilities we find private ownership has proven to be the best, as it brings out individual competition, invites foreign capital and will bring some of the best brain of Europe and America into a country.

With foreigners doing business in your country it will bring foreign trade. We found this to be true in the early development of our own country. A large number of people of this country believe Russia has a right to adopt her own form of government. But a government to be successful must carry out some of the leading factors of our declaration of independence. All men are created equal as far as life, liberty and the persuit of happiness is concerned. They must be allowed to worship the deity according to the dictates of their concience providing it is done righteously.

A republic cannot last unless it has compulsory education, and one universal language. Peeples should be compelled to study one universal language other languages allowed. The nation must provide for the safety of life, guarantee protection of private property. The sancty of contract and right of free labor, fulfill national obligations and take care of individual and association's investments. The above recited statements in part is what has made our republic one of the world's leading nations.

Your Respect.

G. W. Porter

Punxsutawney, Pa.

TSGASA, fond 33987, op. 1, d. 528, ll. 54–61.

DOCUMENT 251   *Minutes of the meeting of the Scientific-Technical Council on Agricultural Industry, October 9, 1923, regarding the activities of the Russian Agricultural Bureau in America*

MINUTES NO. 12, OF THE MEETING OF THE SCIENTIFIC-TECHNICAL COUNCIL ON AGRICULTURAL INDUSTRY, October 9, 1923.

IN ATTENDANCE: D. D. Artsybashev, A. F. Bukhgol'tz, F. A. Aver'ianov, L. L. Nemirovskii, E. E. Keri, A. A. IArilov, N. Sergeev, A. Pimenov, N. F. Charnovskii, V. Talanov, A. N. Reformatskii, I. D. Shimanovich

Chairman - D. D. Artsybashev

Secretary - N. V. Vinogradov

HEARD:

After brief introductory remarks by D.D. Artsybashev, a report by A. F. Bukhgol'tz "On the Russian Agricultural Bureau in America, its goals and the necessity of supporting it."

The bureau, organized according to the idea of Professor N. I. Vavilov, in the first period of its existence was engaged exclusively in the introduction of seeds.

Similar organizations have existed for a long time in America and have been very active.

The existence of a Russian bureau in America was important because of similarities of American and Russian climatic zones.

The bureau transported to Russia up to 3,000 various types of plants, among which certain ones that had especially favorable results should be noted: corn (up to 700 samples), tomatoes (up to 600 samples), sunflowers (up to 600 samples), and potatoes.

Later the bureau expanded its activities in response to Russian needs. It began to serve as a link between Russian and American experimental and scientific institutions.

The bureau began to supply the latest American agricultural literature, to disseminate the latest scientific achievements in the field.

Recently the bureau has been studying methods of combatting plant pests; bureau Director D. N. Borodin is especially interested in the possibility of using airplanes for this purpose.

In America the bureau is already becoming quite well known and is becoming even more so as American firms show an increasing interest in Russia. Russian experimental and scientific institutions have become accustomed to consulting the bureau.

Due to a complete lack of funds the bureau is currently experiencing a crisis that has become so serious that they are preparing to sell their typewriters.

In answering questions of those in attendance, A. F. Bukhgol'tz reports that the bureau has full technical possibilities to develop its work to the extent desired.

In cases where there are particular requests from various institutions concerning different aspects of agricultural activity, such as advice on special matters, information about American experience, the supplying of special literature, agricultural machinery, and so forth, the bureau is capable of fulfilling these requests if adequate funding is provided.

Professor V. V. Talanov asserts that the activity of agricultural agencies in general has had enormous importance and that among them the Russian Agricultural Bureau in America is especially important. A number of examples can be cited where new crops have completely altered the agricultural make-up of a region, greatly increasing productivity. New types of corn and fodder crops are examples. Last year the People's Commissariat of Agriculture [NKZ] was able to effect a mass distribution of American seed grains thanks to the help of the bureau and its director D. N. Borodin. The introduction of these seeds will undoubtedly increase the harvests.

The Russian bureau in America is no less significant when it comes to the Supreme Economic Council [VSNKh]. In America special crops are highly developed as is processing of agricultural products. The significance of agricultural industry in such an agricultural country as Russia should be enormous and a promising future lies ahead for it. In this respect it is essential that there be an informational link and that appropriate machinery be delivered. VSNKh and the NKZ must allocate funds for the work of this bureau.

N. Sergeev, recognizing the importance of the bureau's existence, insists that this support must be rendered by state institutions.

D. D. Artsybashev suggests that the merits of the bureau are enormous and the bureau's assistance to experimental institutions and Institutes is so great that there can be no doubt about its continued existence and development.

The VSNKh and NKZ should be equally interested in this issue. The activity and work of the bureau needs to be widely publicized.

The latest information from America and an organization of links with America is necessary to all workers in various agricultural fields.

D. D., addressing A. F. Bukhgol'tz and thanking him for his interesting report, asks him to maintain close ties in the future with the Scientific Technical Stations [NTS] of the agricultural industry.

RESOLVED: Acknowledging the highly useful activity of the Russian Agricultural Bureau in America, which ensures the supply of high quality seeds for Russian agriculture and forestry and provides the Russian scientific community with new achievements in American agricultural thought, the Council of Agricultural Industry of the Scientific-Technical Section [NTO] of VSNKh resolved:

a. To submit considerations via the Council of the NTO regarding the need for all possible support for the bureau with the intent that a corresponding resolution be issued by the Council of People's Commissars [SNK].

b. To request from the NKZ, via the collegium, support for the bureau as an institution equally important to the NKZ and the VSNKh, which currently uses the bureau in America and will use it to an even greater extent in the future.

c. To apply with the same request to Gosplan, having selected for this purpose, with the consent of the collegium, an appropriate delegation for talks with Chairman Comrade Krzhizhanovskii.

d. To ask N. F. Charnovskii and V. V. Talanov to compose a special appeal to the Presidium of the *VSNKh* in which they outline why material support for the bureau from the Presidium is essential.

e. To connect the bureau with the projected Bureau of Introduction, whose activity will be fruitless without the existence of the Russian Bureau in America.

f. To ask the Main Exhibition Committee to pay the expenses for using the works of the bureau at the exhibition.

g. To inform cooperative organizations such as *TSentrosoiuz*, *Sel'skosoiuz*, and others about the full activities of the bureau.

Chairman [signed] Artsybashev   Secretary [signed] Vinogradov

TSGANKh, fond 480, op. 7, d. 43, l. 1547.

DOCUMENT 252   *Report by the People's Commissariat for Agriculture, November 20, 1925, regarding the possibility of sending fifty tractor mechanics to be trained at a Ford plant in the United States*

Secret

Material for question no. 3 of the secret agenda

Report on the possibility of training 50 Soviet tractor mechanics at the FORD plant
in the U.S.A.

Background:

In the summer of 1924 the question of training tractor mechanics for the USSR (initially in Canada) was suggested to the Official Agent of the USSR in Canada, Comrade IAZYKOV, by Professor ZhIVOTOVSKII of the Lomonosov Electromechanical Institute and formerly the deputy chairman of the Union of Match Manufacturers. The idea was to organize courses in Montreal for training tractor and automobile operators and mechanics from the Soviet Union. The courses would cost $1,575; salaries of the instructors an additional $250 per month; and rent another $50 monthly. The proposal was unacceptable to us because of its cost. It was also rejected by the People's Commissariat for Agriculture, which believed that the First Tractor School in Moscow would be able to train an adequate number of tractor operators and mechanics under our own supervision. Therefore, Professor ZhIVO-TOVSKII's proposal was declined, and we so informed Comrade IAZYKOV.

Later Professor ZhIVOTOVSKII submitted a different plan to comrade IAZYKOV. A representative of the Ford plant had suggested accepting at their plant 50 persons for a six-month course, whereby the plant would pay each of them six dollars per day for their labor. After consulting with the RSFSR People's Commissariat for Agriculture, we set the following conditions whereby we could accept this proposal:

1. All 50 candidates would be detailed to America upon approval by the *Guberniia* agriculture departments from among citizens permanently living within the boundaries of the USSR and already having sound experience in the use of tractors in farming.

2. On Ford's side, these citizens must be provided conditions at the plants to ensure successful practical training of tractor mechanics so that on completion of training, they will have been qualified for a rank no lower than tractor instructor-mechanic.

3. Ford must agree to cover all expenses of the trainees during their stay in the United States, as well as their travel expenses from the USSR to America and back.

[Document is undated and unsigned and appears incomplete.]

TSGANKh, fond 478, op. 1, d. 1911, ll. 3–5.

Henry Ford (center) with Soviet specialists V. I. Mezhlauk (left), deputy chairman of the *VSNKh,* and S. G. Bron of the American-Soviet Trading Company. TSGANKh. Fond 5240, op. 9, d. 485, 1. 147

Speech given by Colonel Cooper of the United States to the American section of the All-Union Western Chamber of Commerce, September 14, 1928, on his impressions of the USSR during four visits lasting a total of eight months

A Meeting of the American Section of the All-Union Western Chamber of Commerce
September 14, 1928

The meeting was opened by Comrade Aralov.
Agenda: A speech by Col. Cooper on his impressions from a trip around the USSR and about the electrification of the USSR.

(This is a translation of the speech, which Col. Cooper delivered in English.)

For a number of reasons I did not prepare a special speech for this occasion. First, I have not finished my studies of the Russian language, and so I will have to speak to you through an interpreter.

I have had occasion to speak to audiences in many countries through interpreters, and my experience has been that I do not know precisely whether the audience has understood what I was presenting. Interpreters take great liberties with the text and interject their views without making them consistent with what the speaker was saying. (Laughter)

I remember how I once spent a great deal of time preparing a speech and thinking that I had made a rather decent presentation. But when I saw what was written about it in the newspapers the next day, I discovered that even the title was incorrectly rendered, and I was positively amazed to read that my speech had produced a profound impression on the audience.

After that incident, I concluded that I cannot achieve my objective speaking to an audience through an interpreter. Moreover, even now I am not completely confident that the interpreter is translating my words correctly. (Laughter) I see among the listeners a few persons who I know speak good English, and I am counting on their help just in case.

In the course of two years I have visited the USSR four times; in toto these four visits lasted eight months. I find that for my part the time I have spent in Russia has been extremely interesting, and I now leave Russia with the serious intention of advancing the time when I will return here again.

During these four visits to the USSR I traveled from six to seven thousand kilometers, the entire distance from the Black Sea to Leningrad. I was also in a number of other places, and I have accumulated a mass of impressions that I would like to share with you.

In general I notice great improvements at the present time as compared to 1926/27. It is extraordinarily pleasant to me, an American, to certify this improvement. I figure that this improvement will increase even further with the passage of time. When I compare the conditions in your country with those of other countries in which I have happened to travel, I come away with an impression that is exceptionally favorable toward you.

When I was in America (after my visits to the USSR), I gave many lectures about Soviet Russia. I was astonished by the enormous interest in the USSR throughout America. I have to say that in America there is more incorrect information about Russia than about any other topic whatsoever.

I delivered my speeches with the aim and in the hope of rectifying the incorrect impression that has been created about Soviet Russia in other countries. I have to say that in Russia there is much incorrect information about America as well. I figure that one of the important factors hindering the establishment of normal relations between these two countries is that ignorance, the ignorance of one country about the other.

The speeches that I gave in America were presented to a wide spectrum of audiences. What distinguished my speeches was the fact that I never managed to finish them. I see that many of you sitting here are surprised, and now I will explain what I mean.

In America you very rarely hear of an engineer giving a speech, but when in our age an engineer does make a speech, the public gathers to hear him, because there is the popular belief that if an American engineer is speaking, he is telling the truth. I did not use very refined style to express the truth, but the audience understood it was the truth. [break in the text]

I am genuinely interested in engineering in Soviet Russia, and I believe in the future of the country. I can see myself getting involved in several other hydroelectric construction projects in Soviet Russia. I believe it would be extremely important for your country to introduce electricity whenever it is economically feasible. If it were possible to single out any one force which was responsible for the incredible development of American industry, this force could only be electricity. By using electricity American workers are now capable of producing eight to ten times more than they used to. In today's America anything that can be done with electricity is being done with electricity. I would hope that the same factor which contributed so much to the development of the United States will contribute just as much to the development of your country.

The next thing I would like to mention are the opportunities I see for Americans in your country. As I see it, the Soviet Union is the best country for Americans as pioneers. As far as I know, Russia has more natural resources than any other country in the world. I have found that my audiences have been so knowledgeable that there is no need to try to prove to them that the development of national natural resources constitutes a basic precondition for general development. No matter how hard you work in a desert, you'll never be able to build yourself a house. The development of the immense natural resources which the Soviet Union possesses should lead to the development of a level of prosperity that cannot be achieved in countries without such natural riches.

Because Americans are coming here with nothing more in mind than to help Russia, they should work here without any selfish motives. I am well aware that the Soviet Union will develop its own natural resources with the efforts of its own citizens and for their benefit, and I would hate to see the day when these incredible natural riches were exploited for selfish purposes.

In this day and time Americans are coming to Russia as technical consultants for the purpose of working here as engineers and teaching your engineers to develop the natural wealth of your country on their own.

As I see it, the Soviet Union's greatest need right now is for practical engineers. No one can ever learn how to play the violin by just reading music. One has to start at the beginning and go step by step through the process in order to get a complete education. In the near future I would like to see the very best American engineers come here and give Russian engineers the practical skills and knowledge which American engineers have and Russian engineers need. The only danger I see is that you won't always get the best people.

All of you should realize that there are a large number of worthless people in America, and the mere fact that a person is an American doesn't mean he's a good man. Americans have their good sides, but they also have their bad sides, and there are good people and bad people there, just as there are in every country. I consider it my obligation to make sure that only the best American people come here to do the work I mentioned. Genuine unity and friendship between Americans and Russians can only come when the United States recognizes the Soviet Union. And recognition of the USSR by the United States will come much sooner than you or I might imagine.

One of the most important benefits of recognizing the Soviet Union as soon as possible would be the elimination of one country's ignorance and lack of knowledge of the other. I am a member of a group involved in promoting recognition of the Soviet Union. Our work would be made much easier by having Russians visit America, as one group did recently. For all the time that I have worked to bring the USSR and America closer together, I have never seen a single Soviet citizen whom I would not consider someone his country could be proud of.

The cause of recognition would be considerably advanced if as many Russians as possible came to America.

I would like to tell you a funny story which actually happened, although I don't know if there are many people here who are tall enough to fit the story.

About four or five months ago your engineer Veselonov came to America. Professor Graftio, who is in the audience, can confirm that what I'm telling you actually happened. Engineer Veselonov is about 6'6", and I introduced him to the representatives of a large number of organizations, and when I took him to a bank in New York whose chairman of the board is extremely pessimistic, I asked the chairman to take a look at Engineer Veselonov. The Chairman of the Board of the Bank looked him up and down and when I said that there were 114,000,000 guys like that in Russia, the chairman exclaimed: "My God! We should recognize them immediately."

I don't know if I have anything more to say, but I get the feeling that my interpreter is running out of steam. If you have any questions, please ask them, and I will be very happy to answer them.

QUESTIONS FROM THE AUDIENCE TO COLONEL COOPER

1. You said that after your speeches the questions lasted for up to two and a half hours. What sort of questions were they, and what were the people of the United States most interested in?

Answer: They asked me if it was safe to travel in Russia and if I had to sleep outside. They also asked me if I had taken my wife with me, and when I told them I had, they said I obviously wanted to get rid of her. However anyone who knows Colonel Cooper well knows that this couldn't be true. Most of the questions revealed lack of understanding and ignorance about the Soviet Union. [original ends at this point]

TSGANKh, fond 160, op. 1, d. 174, ll. 1–15.

DOCUMENT 254   *Letter from Armand Hammer to the People's Commissariat for Foreign and Internal Trade, October 16, 1928, detailing problems with his office supply export business*

American Industrial Concession
A. HAMMER
Manufacture of pencils, pens, and other office supplies
Office in Moscow: Sofiika, no. 6/3
Telephone numbers: 2-60-66, 2-60-73, 4-02-92, 3-27-55, 1-14-49
Head office: 165 Broadway, New York

No. 6968   Moscow, October 16, 1928

To: Comrade I. O. Schleifer, member of the Collegium of
People's Commissariat for Foreign
and Internal Trade [*Narkomtorg*]

Since our company's future export business is in real danger and may have to cease altogether, I earnestly request to meet with you today or tomorrow, if only for a few minutes.

As you probably know, we have expanded our export business. At present our company has exported over 80,000 gross of pencils, and the results in the international market fully justify all our hopes regarding demand for our products and their price. In order to develop further our export business we have opened offices in London and China, hired a staff of traveling salesmen, established consignment warehouses and advertised our products widely. Our company and its goods have received excellent press abroad, convincing us of guaranteed success for further export activity. Please find attached a translation of an article recently published in one of the most influential trade publications in England.

Up to now we have invested 600,000 rubles in our export business (including the cost of exported goods), which should eventually be converted into foreign currency.

We have never pressed on the matter of financing from *Narkomtorg* because we were assured that this question would be solved in the near future and is being reviewed by the Committee on Foreign Concessions. However, this question remains unsolved.

Even the matter of exempting our company from duties on raw material imported to manufacture export goods has been resolved only temporarily, until November 1, 1928, by special decree of the deputy commissar of the People's Commissariat of Finance, Comrade M. I. Frumkin, so that we might reach in the meantime an agreement with *Narkomtorg* on financing our export business (enclosed are copies of memoranda from *Gosnalog* [State Tax Bureau]).

At this moment we must submit the following specific request: we need to obtain a guarantee from Soviet banks abroad to safeguard our export goods. We have already received the approval from the Special Foreign Currency Conference and from the deputy head of the *Narkomtorg* Financial Department, Comrade Shpindel, to obtain a guarantee of 10,000 British pounds from GARKREBO. As we have not yet received it, we are asking you to instruct GARKREBO by cable to issue the guarantee without further delay. As a matter of fact we must make several urgent payments abroad; the nonpayment of these bills could ruin our export business.

We also wrote on October 11, 1928, to *Narkomtorg* (see attached copy) asking to instruct ARKOS Bank in London to extend our 10,000 British pound guarantee, which expires on October 22, 1928. The requirement that we cover this loan with the possible guarantee from GARKREBO cannot solve our financial situation abroad, because in this case we would not have any funds at our disposal to cover our current foreign debts.

If ARKOS Bank does not receive your cable instructions, they might protest our bill for failure to receive timely payment of our promised financing in accordance with our export agreement with *Narkomtorg*.

Considering all the above we are asking you again to send the cables and to arrange an appointment, so that I can explain to you verbally the results already achieved by my company and set out a course for more normal operations in the future, in which *Narkomtorg* and the government are no less interested than I myself.

AMERICAN INDUSTRIAL
CONCESSION
A. HAMMER

[signed in Cyrillic] A. IU. Gammer

TSGANKh, fond 5240, op. 19, d.231, ll. 94–95.

DOCUMENT 255   *Report by Armand Hammer, October 19, 1928, detailing measures taken in order to carry out successfully his company's export business*

Item no. 2699   Moscow, Oct. 19, 1928
[signed] A. Hammer

REPORT

by Dr. A. J. Hammer

In order to carry out successfully our export activities, we have taken the following measures:

<u>England</u>

On June 4 we leased a 3-story building in the center of London, in a district where businesses dealing with office supplies are located. The street-level floor has been transformed into a retail and semiwholesale salesroom. The huge windows facing the street are very effective and useful as display showcases. The rest of the building consists of a warehouse where up to 200,000 gross of pencils may be stored, an area for sorting pencils, an area for sharpening pencils, an area for attaching pencils to advertisement cards, a packaging area, and a dispatching area and office. Also there are premises for receiving outside buyers on visits to London, where samples of our products and our advertising displays are presented in a very elegant and artistic manner. A large electric sign displaying a Hammer pencil hangs across the building's facade and can be seen from a great distance.

We have a staff of traveling salesmen who visit all regions of England, Ireland, and Scotland. In addition we have subagents at various locations.

The office supplies trade in England functions as follows: there exists a small number of large wholesalers who trade in thousands of products and have in their employ a large number of traveling salesmen and agents. These firms publish their own catalogs and price lists and operate as middlemen between the manufacturers and the small wholesalers and retailers. Of the latter there exist about 25,000 all told. At the beginning of our activities we encountered serious opposition from the large wholesalers, who categorically refused to handle our goods or to include our products in their catalogs or price lists. Apparently the position they took was based on the fact that it was easier for them to continue handling already well-known brands.

In view of the situation, we decided to make an effort to distribute our goods directly to the small wholesalers and retailers via the direct-sale methods. Although that course of action was somewhat risky and entailed considerable outlay of funds up front, the results achieved prove that our plan of action was correct in concept and thus fulfilled all of our expectations.

The figures given below show the gradual increase in the numbers of clients from the beginning of our operations in London up to Dec. 29th (the date of the last London inventory):
As of Aug. 18, 1928, we had 268 clients (small wholesalers and retailers)
As of Sept. 15, 1928, we had 507 clients
As of Sept. 29, 1928, we had 622 clients [. . .]

Judging by the preliminary statistics regarding our trade with England, it seems evident that even these fine results can make a great leap forward as soon as our export agreement with the People's Commissariat for Trade [*Narkomtorg*] becomes effective, along with the stipulated financial assistance to aid our export operations. Delays in the conclusion of that agreement have caused great losses in our export activities. For example, we have been forced to turn down many large special orders because we were not certain that *Narkomtorg* would be forthcoming with financial assistance to cover possible losses. And even now, as we compete with other firms for an annual order of pencils by the government of Egypt (a very large order), we remain uncertain of success because we are unable to include in our calculations the compensation that we are supposed to receive from *Narkomtorg*, and therefore we cannot lower our bid sufficiently to compete with the other firms. [. . .]

[UNITED STATES]

In the United States of America the import of pencils does not pay (except for those of premium quality) due to the high, protective tariff. At the same time the American market is one of the most interesting both with regard to prices and sales. According to official statistics, pencils valued at $25 million are used annually in the domestic market. Since there are businesses in the U.S. that import German leads to use in wooden pencils (the import tariff for the leads is very small), it occurred to us to establish our own wood processing unit in New York in the near future and then to supply that unit with our own ready-to-use USSR leads. In this way we can be part of the American market and thereby earn a fairly sizable amount of hard currency from the sale of semi-finished products manufactured in the USSR.

Summarizing the above, we can state that the accomplishments of the first few months of export activities, into which we entered with no expectation of an agreement with *Narkomtorg*, completely fulfilled our initial expectations on the possibility of success for our export products and the penetration of foreign markets. Our continued success depends exclusively on our ability to reduce prices and also on our ability to invest further in advertising and organizational needs, which in turn depends on:
1) concluding the agreement with *Narkomtorg*, whereby it undertakes to cover our losses at a rate of 20% of our costs; and

2) the immediate regulation of the matter of our financial needs inside the country, as well as providing guarantees with Soviet banks abroad to cover our needs. We are attaching a copy of our Oct. 2, 1928 (no. 6778) letter to *Narkomtorg SSSR* which includes a full plan regarding said financial assistance, which must be put into effect immediately.

TSGANKh, fond 5240, op. 19, d. 231, ll. 102–103.

DOCUMENT 256   ***Resolution of the Council of People's Commissars, February 18, 1930, regarding the purchase of Armand Hammer's office supplies concession and receipts due the Soviet government***

-2-

7. In compliance with paragraph 6 of this resolution, direct the People's Commissariat on Finances of the USSR to provide the Moscow Chemical Trust [*Moskhimtrest*] with an accounting of receipts due to the government from A. J. Hammer's pencil concession based on expenditures and excess profits, with the payments to be prorated on the basis of the annual balance sheets of the enterprise on October 1, 1929, 1930, and 1931.

CHAIRMAN, COUNCIL OF PEOPLE'S COMMISSARS OF THE USSR

ADMINISTRATIVE DEPARTMENT
COUNCIL OF PEOPLE'S COMMISSARS
OF THE USSR

SECRETARY, COUNCIL OF
PEOPLE'S COMMISSARS
OF THE USSR

Moscow, Kremlin
"........ 1930"

TSGASA, fond 4, op. 1, d. 1186, ll. 111–149.

DOCUMENT 257 *Letter from the Austin Company, July 11, 1931, offering to participate in the construction of the Soviet aviation industry*

[English-language original]

NEW YORK	PHILADELPHIA	DETROIT	CINCINNATI	SAN FRANCISCO	
PORTLAND					
CHICAGO	PITTSBURGH	ST. LOUIS	DALLAS	LOS ANGELES	SEATTLE
		PHOENIX	VANCOUVER, B.C.		

THE AUSTIN COMPANY
ARCHITECTS, ENGINEERS AND BUILDERS
16112 EUCLID AVENUE, CLEVELAND
[logo: The Austin Method
founded 1878]

Foreign Office
Nijni Novgorod
U.S.S.R
July 11, 1931

CIVIL AIR CRAFT INDUSTRY
Nikolskaya, 6
Moscow

Attn. M. Silin

Subject:- Austin Company technical
assistance for the civil
air craft industry in the USSR

Gentlemen:-

We acknowledge receipt of your letter from July 3rd No. 2207 with reference to having our Company do some work for you in civil air craft industry of USSR.

We expect to be in Moscow in the nearest future, and we will cable to you about our arrival there or we will get in touch with you on our next arrival to Moscow, to fully discuss the above matter with you.

We are very thankful for your prompt answer and we anticipate our pleasure in seeing you and discussing the question about our technical assistance with you in Moscow.

Yours very truly,   THE AUSTIN COMPANY

[signed] H. F. Miter

Vice President Foreign Work

TSGANKh, fond 9527, op. 1, d. 273, ll. 88–89.

DOCUMENT 258   ***Report of S. A. Levanevskii on his flight from Los Angeles to Moscow, September 1936***

[handwritten:] Main Arctic Seaways Administration in the Council of People's Commissars of the USSR. Operations Division.

THE *SOKOL* [FALCON] BINDERY

Literature:

City:

Office or Business:

Subject:

from: August 5, 1936

to: September 13, 1936

Comments:

THE REPORT OF
HERO OF THE SOVIET UNION
S. A. LEVANEVSKII
ON HIS FLIGHT FROM LOS ANGELES TO MOSCOW
AUGUST–SEPTEMBER 1936

Archives of the Central Arctic Seaways Administration
1936

Department: Polar Aviation
Division: Operations
Inventory No.: No. 337d 34ev

[Trademark of *SOKOL* Bindery]

___Report___   1 page

On the flight from Los Angeles to Moscow, August 5–September 13

Preparations:

Flight testing of the airplane, engine, and equipment was done using standard landing gear and then pontoons. The following tests were carried out: 1) structural strength; 2) landing gear strength (landings on two-meter ocean waves); 3) performance of the engine and engine systems; 4) fuel consumption per hour and per kilometer of flight; 5) checking the radio-compass regulator.

A few flights were made in the area of Los Angeles airport and airports on the routes Los Angeles—Phoenix, Los Angeles—San Diego.

Fuel consumption amounted to 34.284 gal./h. at an altitude of 2,500 m, an average speed of 247 kph, and a carburetor pressure of 25, maintaining the fuel mixture quality according to "mixture specs" at 28.

At the same altitude and an average speed of 247 kph, fuel consumption per kilometer of flight amounted to 0.158 gal. or 0.537 kg.

Tests of the radio compass initially did not yield favorable results (inaccurate regulation); after eliminating the inaccuracies, the radio compass accurately read out to a working radio station antenna. In testing the engine there were instances of oil temperature rising to 120 degrees and oil being thrown out of the crankcase through the [illegible] shaft, in which case the temperature of the cylinder heads 1 and 6 remained normal. This happened because the propeller nosecap was deflecting (blanketing) the air flow from the crankcase, and so the crank case was not being cooled, which in California conditions resulted in the oil's overheating. As soon as the "nosecap" was removed, this phenomenon was no longer observed.

TSGANKh, fond 9527, op. 2, d. 1144, ll. 1–26.

Fraternal Economic Assistance

The February 1917 revolution in Russia drew back the exiles of the Russian revolutionary movement, including numbers of radicals who had found refuge in the United States both before and during the war. Leon Trotsky had been working on a Marxist newspaper in New York when the revolution overthrew the autocracy; he returned to Russia in May. On the same boat was an anarchist organizer, Maksim Raevskii, who had been editing the weekly journal of the syndicalist Union of Russian Workers of the United States and Canada. His collaborator Vladimir (Bill) Shatov, who had worked at a number of manual jobs in the U.S., sailed to Russia via the Pacific, arriving in Petrograd in May. Mikhail Borodin left the progressive school that he ran in Chicago to participate in the revolution. Other exiles returned less voluntarily: the anarchists Emma Goldman and Alexander Berkman joined 247 other Russian-born leftists who had been deported on the *U.S. Buford* by the U.S. government in 1919.

Most of these returnees found positions in Soviet government and in the party. But the regime also appealed to Russian-born workers to return to their homeland and help to build socialism. One conduit for their recruitment was the Society for Technical Assistance to Russia, organized by Ludwig Martens in 1919, who was already running the Soviet Bureau at 110 W. 40th Street in New York. Martens was an engineer, the son of German-speaking Russians, who had come to the U.S. on a trade mission in 1916. The society soon established branches in other cities and encouraged Russian immigrants with technical skills and political sympathy to return, preferably bringing their tools and machinery. Martens claimed that by 1921 the society had recruited tractor-equipped teams for thirty model farms in Russia. In 1922 the U.S. Amalgamated Clothing Workers organized a joint enterprise, the Russian-American Industrial Corporation, which set up nine clothing and textile factories in Soviet Russia. The joint venture provided machinery and technical advice: skilled craftsmen from several U.S. cities made the journey to Russia to offer technical advice and training for the local workers. Later in the decade many more Americans, both skilled workers and engineers, lent their services to the construction of the Soviet economy.

BERDIANSK
May 12, 1919   Copy

RESOLUTION
ADOPTED AT A GENERAL MEETING OF THE MEMBERS
OF THE FIRST LABORING COMMUNE OF RUSSIAN-AMERICAN MACHINISTS

After hearing the report of Comrade ShAMRAEVSKII, the representative of the Department of Industrial Organization of the Supreme Economic Council, on the situation of toolmaking in Russia and on the decision of Soviet agencies to begin bringing order and organization to toolmaking on a nationwide scale immediately, the General Meeting of the members of the FIRST LABORING COMMUNE OF RUSSIAN-AMERICAN MACHINISTS ADOPTED THE FOLLOWING RESOLUTION:

In a desire to cooperate with the efforts of Soviet power and its economic development program and in the belief that the organization of toolmaking is a matter of the utmost importance and that the participation of the Labor Commune would have a quite beneficial and powerful impact on the organization of general-purpose tool production, thanks to our many years of American experience, the General Meeting has RESOLVED to play a very active role in the organization of this industry, having taken the initiative in organizing a tool factory and having no objections to the nationalization of our property and the plant under the condition that several terms of our agreement are met:

1. The organization will retain the principle of the equality of all members of the commune in matters of wages, which are to be determined on the basis of the productivity of the plant, and in resolving internal matters.

2. The commune will reserve the right to accept new members and expel old members in accordance with the existing charter of the General Meeting.

3. The election and dismissal of members of the Board and Technical Commission are subject to the internal rules of the organization.

4. The commune is to remain independent and is not to be absorbed into any other factory or organization.

The chairman of the MEETING:

Secretary:

TSGANKh, fond 3429, op. 2, d. 877, ll. 69–690b.

Council of Labor and Defense minutes discussing turning over a Russian automobile plant to returning American workers, February 28, 1921

EXTRACT FROM MINUTE No. 193
OF THE MEETING OF THE COUNCIL OF LABOR AND DEFENSE
on February 28, 1921

Agenda Item:	Decision:
7. A report on the transfer of the *AMO* [Moscow Automotive Company] Plant to returning American Communist immigrants (Miliutin, Gladun)	7a. Instruct the Presidium of the Supreme Economic Council [*VSNKh*] to conclude an agreement with the American workers turning over the Russian Renault Plant in Petrograd to them (if this proves impractical, turn over the technically more suitable *AMO* plant in Moscow to them). b. Instruct the Presidium of the *VSNKh*, People's Commissariat of Agriculture, the People's Commissariat of Transportation, the People's Commissariat of Labor, and the All-Union Central Council of Trade Unions to nominate candidates for membership in a commission with the following assignments: 1) monitor the proper implementation of the agreement indicated in point "a" of this decision; 2) take steps to ensure that similar plants are used to train workers and young people in Russia and to offer similar agreements to new groups of foreign workers. The candidates should be high-ranking officials. Deadline—as soon as possible. c) Instruct Comrade Karakhan to nominate additional candidates to the commission in consultation with Comrade Martens. d) The commission should work with the People's Commissariat of Labor (Comrade Martens) to gather information on the admission of worker immigrants from foreign countries (in what numbers and under what conditions).

EXTRACT ACCURATE:

Personal Secretary
of the Business Office
of the Council of
People's Commissars   [illegible signature]

RTSKhIDNI, fond 5, op. 1, d. 146, ll. 30

CHARTER
OF THE RUSSIAN-AMERICAN CENTRAL BOARD
OF COMBINED INDUSTRIAL ENTERPRISES

The Council of Labor and Defense hereby resolves that:

In order to improve the industrial base of the Russian Soviet Federated Socialist Republic (RSFSR) and satisfy the desire of American workers to play an active role in the economic development of the Russian Soviet Republic, the charter below establishes a Russian-American Central Board of Combined Industrial Enterprises [*RATSPRAV*], consisting of representatives to be appointed by the Supreme Economic Council [*VSNKh*] of the RSFSR and the American workers' association known as the American-Russian Trade and Industrial Association [*ARTPRA*].

Section I.

1. The Central Board shall organize enterprises and associations of enterprises in different industrial sectors designated by the *VSNKh* and shall manage them as self-sustaining entities.

2. The Central Board shall be granted the authority to organize enterprises and engage in commercial transactions outside the RSFSR in accordance with a special procedure to be established by the Council of Labor and Defense.

3. The Central Board shall consist of representatives appointed by the *VSNKh* and *ARTPRA*, with each party having the same number of votes regardless of the number of representatives. The chairman of the board shall be appointed as a supernumerary member over and above the total number of board members by agreement between the *VSNKh* and *ARTPRA*.

COMMENT: In the event that the chairman alone constitutes the deciding vote on a particular matter, each party shall have the right to turn the matter over for final resolution to the *VSNKh* and *ARTPRA*, before which time the decision will not be valid.

Section II.

4. The board shall be responsible for:

a) general administrative and technical supervision of all its enterprises and associations.

b) setting production targets and monitoring their fulfillment.

c) general supervision of all transactions involving the procurement of raw materials and fuel, food, machinery, accessory materials, and equipment for its factories.

d) the sale and marketing of products.

e) all plant expansion and improvement projects.

5. The board shall be responsible for the safety and security of property, the fulfillment of production targets, and successful management of the business and shall submit reports on its activity to the *VSNKh* and *ARTPRA* by a procedure, in a format, and within a time frame to be determined by a special agreement between the *VSNKh* and *ARTPRA*.

Section III.

6. The assets of the Central Board shall consist of chattels and real estate contributed by the *VSNKh* and *ARTPRA* to an association of enterprises, with the *VSNKh* turning over factory buildings, machinery, equipment, supplies of raw materials and fuels, vehicles, accessory materials, and ancillary operations to the Central Board,

and the *ARTPRA* turning over the necessary monetary assets, machinery tools, machine accessories, semi-finished products, and food to the Central Board. The Central Board shall take an inventory of all the property it receives and appraise its value in gold-backed currency based on international market prices.

7. All of the property invested by *ARTPRA*, as well as its capitalized revenues in equivalent shares minus depreciation shall be returned to *ARTPRA* at its monetary value in the event of liquidation of the *RATSPRAV* or in other cases provided for by an agreement.

Section IV.

8. The Central Board is obligated to abide by all current laws and decrees on the territory of the RSFSR. The activity of the Central Board and its forms, procedures, and time frame shall be governed by a special agreement between the *VSNKh* and *ARTPRA* subject to approval by the Council of Labor and Defense.

The relationships between the Central Board and the Boards of the Associations and Factory Managements shall be governed by special guidelines to be drafted by the Central Board.

CHAIRMAN OF THE COUNCIL
OF LABOR AND DEFENSE   V. Ul'ianov (Lenin)

SECRETARY OF THE COUNCIL
OF LABOR AND DEFENSE   L. Fotieva

Moscow, The Kremlin

May 12, 1921

AGREEMENT BETWEEN THE *VSNKh*
OF THE RSFSR
AND THE AMERICAN-RUSSIAN
TRADE AND INDUSTRIAL WORKERS' ASSOCIATION
[*ARTPRA*]

Not for disclosure. NP October 10.

In order to improve the industrial base of the RSFSR and satisfy the desire of American workers to play an active role in the economic development of the Russian Soviet Republic, the Presidium of the Supreme Economic Council of the RSFSR in the person of ...., the party of the first part, and the American workers' association the "American-Russian Trade and Industrial Workers' Association," in the person of ...., the party of the second part, hereafter referred to as *VSNKh* and *ARTPRA* respectively, have concluded this agreement concerning the following:

1. The *VSNKh* and *ARTPRA* shall organize a Russian-American Central Board in Russia to manage combined enterprises.

2. The *VSNKh* shall turn over all the necessary equipment and supplies of raw materials, fuel, and food necessary to operate plants, factories, and workshops in different industries to the control of the Central Board, while *ARTPRA* shall turn over monetary assets, industrial equipment, inventory, raw materials, and food to the control of the Central Board.

3. The *VSNKh* shall initially turn over a group of garment industry factories with more than 7,000 employees located in Moscow and Petrograd along with all buildings, machinery, equipment, ancillary operations, and supplies of raw materials and fuel at these factories at the time of the transfer, while *ARTPRA* is obligated to finance the Central Board with funds acquired by issuing stock to be sold to American workers' organizations, the members of these organizations, and then private individuals.

COMMENT 1:   All of the property transferred to the Central Board shall be inventoried and its value shall be appraised in gold-backed currency based on international market prices.

COMMENT 2:   The Central Board's receipt of the aforementioned plants from the *VSNKh* should not cause production to stop at these plants.

4. *ARTPRA* is obligated to do everything in its power to ensure that elements hostile to the organization will not be able to form a majority of stockholders in the organization. For this purpose *ARTPRA* shall impose restrictions allowable by law of the United States.

5. At the same time that the *VSNKh* transfers the aforementioned property to the Central Board, *ARTPRA* is obligated to transfer the sum of 1 million dollars in monetary form or a suitable equivalent to the board.

6. All the capital invested by *ARTPRA* in the territory of the RSFSR shall be guaranteed by the *VSNKh* of the RSFSR.

7. From the profits it earns from the operation of the enterprises, the Central Board shall issue dividends to the *VSNKh* and *ARTPRA* in an amount not to exceed 7% of the latter organizations' respective shares of invested capital. All remaining profits shall go towards expanding operations.

8. The Central Board in Russia shall consist of members appointed by the *VSNKh* and *ARTPRA* for a term of .... and shall operate on the basis of a Central Board Charter subject to approval by the Council of Labor and Defense of the RSFSR.

9. In the event that the Central Board finds it impossible to resolve any disputes which may arise, the matters under dispute shall be turned over to the *VSNKh* and *ARTPRA* for review.

10. The Central Board shall be granted preferences in receiving orders and also allocations of raw materials, fuel, and transportation from economic agencies of the RSFSR and shall be obligated to fill government requisition orders on a priority basis.

11. Each of the contracting parties shall have the right to demand liquidation of the Central Board if 1) one of the contracting parties violates the basic provisions of this agreement; 2) one of the contracting parties acts in a way harmful to the other; or 3) if any unresolved disputes should arise concerning the basic provisions of this agreement.

12. In the event of liquidation of the Central Board, a liquidation commission consisting of representatives of the *VSNKh* and *ARTPRA* shall be appointed to manage the liquidation.

13. In the event of liquidation, all property of the Central Board located on the territory of the RSFSR shall become the property of the *VSNKh*, while any investment and capitalized revenues belonging to *ARTPRA* shall be returned to it minus any depreciation at its monetary value. All sums due to *ARTPRA* shall be paid to *ARTPRA* by the *VSNKh* within the time periods determined by the liquidation commission.

Chairman of the Council
of Labor and Defense   V. Ul'ianov (Lenin)

Secretary of the Council
of Labor and Defense   L. Fotieva

Moscow, The Kremlin, October 12, 1921   True Copy: [initials]

DRAFT OF A RESOLUTION
OF THE COUNCIL OF LABOR AND DEFENSE
CONCERNING THE ESTABLISHMENT OF
THE RUSSIAN-AMERICAN
TRADE AND INDUSTRIAL ASSOCIATION

Top Secret
Do not Publish
And do not disseminate

In a meeting on "........." September, the Council of Labor and Defense RESOLVED:

I. In light of the desire of American workers to play an active role in rebuilding the economic might of the RSFSR, to acknowledge the desirability of the establishment of a Russian-American Trade and Industrial Association [*RATPRA*], in accordance with the proposal of Comrade GILMAN, the president of the American Union of Men's Tailors, through the agency of the organization headed by Comrade GILMAN, on the basis of the following principles:

> 1) *RATPRA*'s primary mission is to combine the efforts of organizations, institutions, and individuals sympathetic to the RSFSR for the purpose of assisting the Soviet government and rebuilding the country's industrial base.
>
> 2) *RATPRA* shall enter into an agreement with the Soviet government concerning the assignment of a number of enterprises in different industrial sectors whose revitalization is a matter of particular concern for the RSFSR.
>
> 3) *RATPRA* shall assist these enterprises in the following ways:
>
> > a) by providing financial backing;
> > b) by supplying equipment, raw materials, food, and other basic and ancillary materials;
> > c) by supplying essential administrative, technical, and training personnel;
> > d) by improving and developing industrial technology.
>
> 4) In order to carry out the missions outlined in §1 a and b, *RATPRA* shall issue shares of stock, which shall primarily be sold to workers' organizations, the members of these organizations, and then to private individuals and only with *RATPRA*'s approval of the sale.
>
> > COMMENT: The American Union of Men's Tailors, on whose
> > initiative *RATPRA* was created, guarantees the
> > distribution of shares in the sum of at least
> > one million dollars.
>
> 5) The industrial enterprises assigned to *RATPRA* shall remain the property of the state, which shall also become the owner of any acquired equipment, plant, and so forth with the proviso that all capital invested by *RATPRA* in the territory of the RSFSR shall be guaranteed by the Soviet government.
>
> 6) A Central Board shall be established to manage the enterprises and associations of enterprises assigned to *RATPRA*. The members of this Board shall include representatives of *RATPRA* and the Soviet government with equal status for the representatives of both parties. *RATPRA*'s initial nominees for Board membership shall be appointed to the Board with the approval of the Soviet government.
>
> 7) Dividends amounting to no more than 7% of the capital invested by *RATPRA* and no more than 7% of the appraised value of the chattels and real estate contributed by the Soviet government to the Central Board shall be paid respectively to *RATPRA* and the Soviet government from the profits earned from the operation of the enterprises. The balance of the profits shall be used to expand and develop the enterprises.

8) The Central Board shall be granted preferences with respect to government purchase orders and privileges with respect to government allocations of raw materials, fuel, transportation, manpower, food, and so forth for its enterprises.

9) The Central Board shall be granted the general authority to engage in commercial transactions in the domestic and foreign markets to facilitate the development of its enterprises and if necessary, open foreign offices through *RATPRA*.

10) In accordance with §3, the Soviet government shall initially assign several garment factories with all their equipment, plant, chattels, and real estate and as many as 7,000 employees to the Central Board.

II. Within one week's time, the Presidium of the *VSNKh* shall draft a model charter for the enterprises assigned on the basis of the aforementioned principles and a model agreement between the RSFSR and *RATPRA* and submit it to the Council of Labor and Defense for approval.

V. Kuibyshev

VKh. 8654

18-?-2?

To Sklianskii

R E S O L U T I O N

Rejecting the commission's draft (Comrade Bogdanov and other members of the *VSNKh* Presidium), which also failed to receive the complete approval of the American group, the Council of Labor and Defense suggests that agreement could be reached if the initiating group would:

1) change the composition of the basic group and management by augmenting to 6–8 representatives of the American labor movement or other workers' organizations;

2) reduce [illegible] expenditures to 300,000 dollars.

3) reduce and focus our expenditures in case the agreement is broken. For its part, the Council of Labor and Defense agrees to honor the desire of the American group that their organization be put into direct contact with the Council of Labor and Defense and its local offices, i.e., *oblast'* and *guberniia* [illegible].

CHAIRMAN OF THE COUNCIL OF LABOR AND DEFENSE	V. Ul'ianov /Lenin/
SECRETARY OF THE COUNCIL OF LABOR AND DEFENSE	L. Fotieva

Moscow - The Kremlin

Oct. 17, 1921

[seal of the Council of Labor and Defense] [signed] A. Paderina

TSGASA, fond 4, op. 3, d. 653, ll. 109.

Appeal from Society for Technical Assistance to Russia for American workers to return to help build socialism, October 24, 1921

Now, comrades, it's up to you. Over there in the homeland, the dawn of freedom, equality, and brotherhood has arrived, and great opportunities have opened up for building a new life, in which there will be neither slaves nor masters. And who can see the changes which have taken place better than you who have experienced all the horrors of the despotic regime and the autocracy? We would like to believe that you comrades would consider it your duty to hurry home to help our long-suffering brothers who have won their freedom.

Soviet Russia needs you. Our liberated motherland is calling you, dear exiles, back to its spacious and open fields, which you must turn not only into fertile fields, but into Oases of Communism and Brotherhood. Get ready, comrades, because now it's your turn.

As a start, it would be best to send representatives to Russia to choose a place to settle. According to our information, the North Caucasus is a good place. It would be desirable if you could inform us of your decision as quickly as possible.

For more information, please write the Central Bureau of the Society for Technical Assistance to Soviet Russia, and we will answer your letter as soon as we possibly can.

We are eagerly awaiting your letters

With Comradely Greetings

Feodor P. Vil'ga
Secretary of the Central Bureau

[seal of the Society for Technical Assistance to Soviet Russia]

COPY   The Central Bureau of the Society for Technical Assistance
              to Soviet Russia
              110 West 40th Street, Room 303, New York

                                                                    October 24, 1921

Dear Comrades:

The persecution of the tsarist government forced you to leave your homeland and seek food, happiness, and freedom in a strange and faraway land.

Comrades! Your brothers, the workers and peasants of Russia, have overthrown the despicable tsarist system and have established a People's Soviet Government, which is encouraging and supporting any activity based on fraternal and Communist principles. The people's government has decided to give large tracts of land to farmers, sectarians, and associations of landsmen wanting to come back home, will assist them in any way possible, and will guarantee their complete freedom.

Because Russia is a country in which 85% of the population is employed in agriculture, Soviet Russia is obviously most in need of experienced farmers. Your many years of experience in a country with a highly developed agriculture would undoubtedly be of invaluable assistance to Soviet Russia. Any model farms you might build with modern machinery and the most advanced agricultural methods would serve as a splendid example for your backward fellow tillers of the soil, who under the tsarist system never had the opportunity to learn or use decent farm implements or the latest advances in agriculture.

We assume that you know about the Society for Technical Assistance to Soviet Russia of the United States and Canada. The purpose of our society is to assist Soviet Russia in rebuilding its economy, which was ruined by the imperialist war, the counterrevolution, and civil strife. The Society for Technical Assistance to Soviet

Russia of the United States and Canada is recognized by the Soviet government and is authorized to organize and send groups to Soviet Russia, which you can see for yourselves by reading the following telegram from Comrade Lenin:

After receiving the report from your congress and its telegram of greetings to Soviet Russia, I would like to express our sincere gratitude on behalf of the Council of People's Commissars. I myself would like to add that we are desperately in need of technical assistance from the United States and Canada. If you could send teams without insisting on a particular location, factory, and so forth, we would guarantee you a two-year supply of food, clothing, and other items. We need to deal with Russia's immediate problems, such as food shortages and so forth. People coming to Russia should be ready for this. You should read the directive from the Department of Industrial Emigration of the Supreme People's Agricultural Council,[1] which we are forwarding.

Chairman of the Council of People's Commissars. V. Ulianov-Lenin. Chicherin.

RTSKhIDNI, fond 5, op. 1, d. 249, ll. 41

DOCUMENT 263   *Correspondence with American workers in Russia to assist in agriculture, 1922*

No. 2485

Comrade KAMENEV:

I am forwarding documents pertinent to the American expedition.

June [illegible], 1922   [signed] L. Trotsky

[Stamp of the Office
of the Revolutionary
Military Council
No. 487
June 20, 1922]

TO COMRADE TROTSKY

Dear Lev Davydovich:

A group of Americans has arrived with 20 tractors and other machinery. Their purpose is to cultivate a large tract of land and then leave the machinery to the People's Commissariat of Agriculture.
For three weeks already the group has been moping around and asking for an audience with you (the "Communist organizer"). Please contact them if you will be able to see them (Lux Hotel, Room 151, Harrow).

[signed] R. Menzhinskii

1. Ed: an error in the text; it should be the Supreme Economic Council (VSNKh).

[English original; spelling and typographical errors preserved]

Hotel Lux Room 151

Moskow,

June 19th, 1922.

Comrade Trotsky:

The purpose of the American Agricultural Relief Unit is summarized in the attached paper.

Our Russian success will be of tremendous value in propaganda work among the Agrarian masses in America.

Our particular difficulties are to locate three freight cars lost in transit between Riga and Moscow. Also to obviate further delays in getting to a location and to work.

Your assistance is most urgently requested.

[signed] H. Harrow
Director of Unit and Agrarian Organizer
C.P. of A.

[signed] James Cook
Delegate to Commintern   C.P. of A.

[English original; spelling and typographical errors preserved]

SUMMARY OF FREINDS OF SOVIET RUSSIA AGRICULTURAL RELIFE UNIT.

1.   <u>Working Conditions</u>

The Unit was organised by the "Friends of Soviet Russia", an American Organisation which is a member, being the American Section, of the Arbeiter Hilfe Auslands Kommitte. The Unit should have definite contracts arranged for fuel, land, and the feeding of the extra men supplied by the Narkomsem. It should have autonomy in its direction and not be subject to the whims of red tape of local authorities. It comes partly to demonstrate American methods and machinery and should have the utmost freedom to accomplish its purpose.

The men with the unit give their time and labour without question or compensation. Several, who had some money, contributed part of their expences. All they ask is an opportunity to get to work. To hurry the Unit thru is imperative. Everyday's delay means 125 desiatinas of wheat lost. The Comrades in America are awaiting telegraphic instructions and are prepared to send thousands of bushels of seed for the Unit to plant just as soon as the locality is settled upon.

2.   <u>Object of Unit.</u>

First, to act as a Relief Unit producing food in the famine area as a concrete demonstration that the workers of America are supporting their Russian Comrades.

Second, to be the basis for further relief appeals in America thru pictures and publicity supplied from the actual working of the Unit.

Third, its results to be used as a vehicle for propaganda among the agrarian masses in America.

Fourth, to serve as the Russian experts think best, in an agitational capacity among the peasantry in Russia.

3.   <u>Local.</u>

We should have ten thousand desiatinas of level land in a climate which permits of seeding winter grains as late as September 20 with sufficient average rain fall to produce a crop. The soil conditions are a limiting factor in tractor farming. The Unit should average 125 desiatinas per day with fairly light soil in ploughing, and double that average for all other operations such as seeding, harrowing, and etc.

4. <u>Equipment.</u>
     The equipment consist of a complete outfit of grain planting farming machinery which may briefly be outlined as follows;

20 15–27 horsepower tractors pulling 60 plows
One Fordson tractor
10 foot double disc harrows
10 smoothing harrows
soil packers
14 eleven foot disc seed drill planters
5 fuel tank wagons, 7,00 gallons
Tents and beds, food and medical supplies for the eleven American workers
Complete machine shop, including large lathe, acetyline welding outfit, drills and forge so that with this and spare parts any repairs can be made at the farm.
Electric lighting outfit with two thousand feet of service wire and 40 lights.
12,000 feet of educational films, motion picture projector and camera with 4,000 feet of raw film
This total comprises 18 cars of freight.

5. <u>Personnall.</u>
    1. Director, agricultural college graduate and practical farmer
    2. Doctor, Russian American,
    3. Tractor expert from the Case Tractor Company
    4. Wife of director in charge of Commissary.
    5. Expert machinist
    6. Six experienced tractor farmers, most of them from North Dakota and members of the Non-Partisan League (An American Radical Agrarian Organisation)

6. <u>Future Plans of Friends of Soviet Russia</u>
    If this effort proves satisfactory it is the purpose of the Friends of Soviet Russia to send other agricultural Units, particularly an harvesting Unit eqipped with the most modern reapers, stackers, and thrashing machines directly to harvest the same grain planted by the first Unit.

Transcript of Telephone Message No. 160

Comrade ZIMMER, Lux Hotel, Room 21

    Please inform Comrade Klara Zetkin that I have received her letter concerning the American delegation. I have already spoken with Comrade Kamenev on the subject and have asked Comrade Eiduk to take all the necessary steps. I hope that the matter will be settled soon.

June 22, 1922   Trotsky

Forwarded

Received

Dear Comrade Trotsky:

    From a discussion with the leader of the American delegation, it would not seem absolutely necessary for you to take up too much of your time getting involved in talks; <u>admittedly, a discussion with the comrade would be valuable</u> with respect to its propagandistic effect in America.

What the Americans bring and what they need, you can see from the attached exhibit. It all depends upon whether strong pressure can be placed upon the authorities under question so that the work can be moved forward as quickly as possible. Every lost day means the loss of 135 *desiatina*s of cultivated land. <u>The first thing is to put pressure on the *Narkomzem*</u>. <u>It would also be important</u> to make sure that the three missing railcars identified in the attachment <u>be recovered in Moscow</u> as quickly as possible, and, furthermore, that the required 35 men and necessary gasoline and machine oil be dispatched as quickly as possible.ˣ⁾

The expedition is supposed to be sent off to Perm' without anything being readied there and without any assurance that anything can really be done there.

This matter deserves support not only in and of itself but also because of its political significance. Soviet Russia has a great interest in a viable organization, based on its experiences, being able to counter the anti-Bolshevik movement in the United States.

I would urgently request that you personally devote every effort to this matter so that failure can be avoided.

I request that you contact me by phone (Lux, Room 21).

Warm regards,

[signed] Clara Zetkin

[handwritten:]
x) The comrades hope that the Army Administration can make tents available to you temporarily for the 35 men. Would it really be possible?

No. 2492

<u>TO L. B. KAMENEV</u>

Lev Borisovich:

Comrade Eiduk believes that the Americans themselves were to blame by contacting me instead of him. But obviously it is also the fault of poor organization on our end if our guests don't know who to contact.

With comradely greetings   [signed] Trotsky

June 23, 1922

Ref. No. 4937

Moscow, June 21, 1922

[translated from German]

Dear Comrade Trotsky

I have yet to receive any report from the agricultural group of Workers' Aid under General Schaffner. I would therefore assume that everything is in order. The troop was supposed to have been dispatched from Petrograd to Cheliabinsk and then sent out to lands around Pinaevo. I have not as yet received the letter with the promised information regarding deliveries of cattle and other items with long-term credits from Switzerland.

However, there is a new, more important matter about which I had you called this morning. A delegation of the "Friends of Soviet Russia" arrived here from America with 21 tractors, a repair facility, 9 drivers, as well as 4 or 5 thousand dollars in cash to set themselves up, which they hope to have completed by autumn and then return and send back an even larger shipment. No one is looking after these people and their things, although everything was supposed to have been readied for them here. In the next couple of days they will be dispatched to Perm' without anything being readied for them there. The leader of the delegation, General Ware, has firmly stressed that he first, and as soon as possible, speak with you. He requests that you receive him and my son, who can serve as interpreter and intermediary. This matter is very important, dear Comrade Trotsky, also for the sake of the future.

With warm regards,

[signed] Clara Zetkin

[Translated from German]

Moscow, June 22, 1922

To: Comrade Eiduk   Moscow

In response to your inquiry dated the 22nd of this month, and with respect to the material related to the matter of the American tractors with the International Workers' Aid, we inform you of the following:

The Committee of Workers' Aid was notified from New York via Berlin on May 15 regarding the departure of the tractor ship to Libau (Liepaja), with the observation that these tractors belong to the group working in Russia in the Tambov government. This telegram did not contain the name of the steamship and the harbor of destination. We immediately notified all government representatives in the Baltic harbors of such a steamship and have requested arrival reports, even though the Tambov group does not belong to our organization and has no relationship to us.

In a second telegram dated May 27 directly from New York, we received the news that this tractor group is to be considered a part of International Workers' Aid and that we see to all the preparations for taking care of the personnel, the procurement of land, etc. Based on this telegram we notified the Russian government representatives in the Baltic harbors and saw to getting a further travel passport for one of our representatives. By that time the steamship had already arrived in Libau and through our efforts had the local railway administration immediately make the necessary railcars and platforms available to send the tractors on farther.

From Libau we received a telegram that the tractors would be shipped out by the most expeditious means possible. In the meantime, we conducted negotiations with the People's Commissariat of Agriculture [Narkomzem] regarding making land available. It was decided after evaluating the conditions to send the tractors to Perm' and to do so in such a way that the tractor group within the framework of our organization in connection with the Ural-Prom-Bureau [Urals Industrial Office] would assist in improving the conditions of the Urals workers. The propaganda evaluation was established in connection with the Central Committee of the Party and several comrades were sent to the Urals in order to immediately make preparations. Likewise, an order went out from the Narkomzem to the Agricultural Trust in Perm' to make all preparations for the tractor facility, in particular, to accumulate the necessary materials for the arrival of the tractors.

The 8 individuals accompanying the tractor group declared to not engage in any negotiations until Comrade Ware, the leader of the tractor group, had arrived. Comrade Ware, who lost three railcars from his shipment while en route, is waiting in Sebesh with his entire shipment until these railcars arrive. We telegraphed Ware to come immediately and committed the local responsible railway officials to continue the search for the three railcars.

Upon Comrade Ware's arrival, we ran into the difficulty that the tractors loaded onto Latvian railcars had to be reloaded. The railcars had to be shipped to the Nikolai Station. We made every effort to directly order all responsible parties to hasten the shipment of tractors. A number of responsible workers from our organization have been working solely on speeding up the further shipment of the American tractors since their arrival.

Comrade Ware lost several days trying to deal with the Narkomzem until he came to the same results as we did. Likewise, Comrade Ware had to deal with various officials who were not responsible for this matter, such as Comrade Mileshanskii, chairman of the Transport Workers' Union, and who gave him information in an improper manner and upset the issue of shipping the tractors by making false promises. It turned out that Comrades Delgas and Zifirov, who were responsible for the shipment, did not know anything about the negotiation. Only today did Comrade Mileshanskii declare that he could do nothing regarding this matter.

It should be further stressed that all responsible parties among the transport authorities are searching for the lost railcars. Furthermore, the 15 railcars that had been readied on the 21st for shipment are being held up through the intervention of Comrade Ware, who still wants to wait for the arrival of the three railcars. This has resulted in a total disruption of transportation. Furthermore, Comrade Ware has delayed his trip to Perm' by two days, for which tickets were prepared yesterday. Comrade Ware is expected in Perm' by the Plenipotentiary of the Tractor Facility of the *Narkomzem,* General Sharnotskii, who had been notified by telegraph communication and we have received telegraph notification that all preparations had been undertaken so that Comrade Ware could examine the land that had been made available for the Tractor Group. Comrade Ware has been officially notified a number of times that these decisions are not a matter of the Central Office here, but rather of the local representatives of the *Prombureaus* [Industrial Bureaus] and the representatives of the Agricultural Trust.

The correspondence of Comrade Zetkin dated June 21 regarding the American Tractor Group is based on false information. The Collegium of International Workers' Aid will take down one statement by a single responsible worker who has been involved in that matter of the American tractors, and this statement together with the telegram will be transmitted to you as quickly as possible to resolve this matter.

International Workers' Aid
Chairman [signature illegible]
Member of Collegium [Schäfer]

[Russian Stamp:]
Office (Bureau of the International Workers'
Committee [illegible] of the Communist
International - COMINTERN)

No. 400

TO COMRADE EIDUK

Please give me answers to these extremely important questions as soon as possible. Who is directly responsible for receiving the American group? Who is on the job right now? What sort of preparations have been made in Perm'?

June 21, 1922   [No signature or name]

TELEGRAM   Time Sent   [illegible]

TO: MOSCOW REVOLUTIONARY MILITARY COUNCIL TROTSKY

[?] FROM PERM' 8507/648 2/7 18 20

TO REVOLUTIONARY MILITARY COUNCIL TROTSKY
COPY TO MOSCOW INTERNATIONAL WORKERS' FAMINE RELIEF ORGANIZATION
LUX HOTEL JURG

THIS IS TO INFORM YOU THAT THE FIRST AMERICAN WORKERS' TRACTOR STATION WITH TWO TRACTORS HAS BEEN ORGANIZED UNDER THE URALS OFFICE OF THE INTERNATIONAL WORKERS' FAMINE RELIEF ORGANIZATION PERIOD WE NEED TWENTY OFFICER-TYPE TENTS COMMA THE DE-

TACHMENT IS OUTDOORS WITH NO SHELTER PERIOD PLEASE SEND THESE TENTS TO PERM' PERIOD ORGANIZER OF THE TRACTOR DETACHMENT URAL OFFICE OF THE INTERNATIONAL WORKERS' FAMINE RELIEF ORGANIZATION BAUM NO. 55——

Moscow, June 22, 1922

[translated from German]

Moscow, June 28, 1922

My Dear Comrade Trotsky:

I request your assistance in the following matter. International Workers' Aid has come to me to ask your assistance if at all possible. International Workers' Aid has received an urgent telegram from the Tractor Group in Perm', of which you are already aware, to supply them on a loan basis some 20 "military officer style" [in Russian] tents from the Military Administration. These people are forced to work far from any populated place on the steppe. I sincerely ask of you to do whatever possible to look into this matter, which really warrants support. The address of International Workers' Aid is Bol'shaia Tverskaia IAmskaia 3, Telephone number 5 62 15.

With sincere Communist greetings

Yours truly,

Clara Zetkin

[handwritten:] I cannot determine the size of the needed tents. Perhaps the above information will suffice.

TSGASA, fond 33987, op. 2, d. 156, ll. 151–167, 194–195.

chapter 9

COMMUNIST PARTY OF THE U.S.A.

The history of the Comunist Party of the United States, while closely entwined with that of the Russian Communist Party and the Communist International, is also embedded in that of the American left. The CP U.S.A. emerged from a vibrant but fragmented socialist landscape in the aftermath of World War I, the Russian Revolution, and widespread labor activism and social unrest that had spread throughout the industrialized world by 1919. This situation had led to an explosion in the growth of the American Socialist Party, but also contributed to acute differences about revolutionary forecasts and strategies. The U.S. Communist movement was no less riven by doctrinal disputes, and its founding congress in September 1919 produced two parties, the Communist Party of America, which attracted many immigrants and pursued a more radical policy, and the Communist Labor Party of America, dominated by native-born American radicals such as John Reed. The movement continued to suffer factional splits among its adherents and was subject to harsh antiradical repression from the government. Its relations with the Russian Communist Party were similarly tortured. In 1920 the U.S. Communists achieved momentary unity and joined the Communist International as a constituent party. The Comintern provided financial aid to its affiliated parties, and also sought to manage the disputes that threatened to damage the ability of the U.S. Communists to build a mass movement. The U.S. section of the Comintern archive, some of whose documents are included here, thus contains a wealth of material on the relations between these two organizations.

Although the Comintern's consistent goal was unity within the U.S. Communist movement, and many of the movement's leaders were grateful for the Comintern's assistance, disputes over strategy and tactics continued to divide the Americans. With urging from Moscow, unity and legality were again momentarily achieved in 1923 with the formation of the broad-based Workers' Party of America. The relationship between this party of the left and American trade unions, however, remained strained. The Comintern leaders urged their American comrades to pursue strategies to bring rank-and-file trade unionists into the party. This was the goal as well of William Z. Foster, who had joined the Communist Party via his leadership of the Trade Union Educational League [TUEL], which provided a radical opposition to the more conservative leadership of the American Federation of Labor.

Conflicts in the U.S. party were played out against the backdrop of divisions inside the Soviet Union. By 1929 the Soviet party had expelled Trotsky as a schismatic and had launched a new assault against the "right deviation" in the party, epitomized by Nikolai Bukharin, head of the Comintern. In the United States the CP U.S.A.'s tumultuous 1929 congress tried to use Bukharin's disgrace to oust his former supporter, Jay Lovestone, from the party's leadership and to install Foster as general secretary. After the attempt failed, supporters of both factions were summoned to Moscow in April, where they presented their cases to the Russian party's Central Committee (Document 269). According to Lovestone's ally Benjamin Gitlow, Gitlow was unable to present this statement to the committee plenum because it publicly would have linked Stalin too closely with the Comintern's anti-Bukharin campaign in the United States.

This trip to Moscow brought the fall of Lovestone and the ascendancy of a leadership more loyal to the Comintern. Although divisions continued to plague the CP U.S.A., the party enjoyed its greatest success in the years 1935 to 1945 under the leadership of Earl Browder, a Comintern loyalist. Browder's native roots and trade union background made him an attractive leader during the period when the Comintern's policy supported popular fronts, alliances with other leftist and democratic parties against the rise of fascism. The party proclaimed itself as the heir to the diverse American radical tradition; its Sunday newspaper reached a circulation of 100,000 by 1938. Gradually, the U.S. party pulled away from Moscow, formally severing its membership in the Comintern in 1939. (The Comintern was officially dissolved in 1943, in the midst of the war with Germany.) This evolution reached a crisis at the CP U.S.A.'s 1944 Central Committee plenum, when the party, led by Browder, changed its name to the Communist Political Association in order to fit better into the mainstream of American politics. But a strong current in the party, represented by Foster, defended an alternative imperialist critique of the U.S. and called for a harder line against capital. In 1944 the moderate position carried the day with the apparent endorsement of Moscow, but a year later the French Communist Jacques Duclos published a scathing attack on this revisionist position, and this gave new life to the hard-liners in the U.S.

party. In June 1945 Foster replaced Browder as chairman of the party. The renewed anti-imperialist line of the CP U.S.A. brought new government repression, heightened because of the increasing international tensions between the U.S. and the USSR. Foster and ten of the party's leaders were arrested for sedition in 1947. Their eventual sentencing in 1951 coincided with the intensive hunt for Communist enemies by the U.S. House of Representatives Committee on Un-American Activities and by other government bodies.

The CP U.S.A. faced its most severe crisis, along with Communist parties elsewhere, with Khrushchev's 1956 revelations about the crimes of Stalin. Khrushchev's secret speech coincided with the party's own internal reevaluation of its political role. The Soviet Communists refused to countenance a more polycentric U.S. organization, and Foster retained the leadership of an officially orthodox CP U.S.A. The U.S. party, however, soon began to disintegrate and lost its position as a political force on the American left.

DOCUMENT 264   *Report on money transferred to representatives of foreign Communist parties, September 1919 to June 1920*

According to Krumina's archive of receipts released by her

Date yr/mo/day	Released to	Document no.	Denomination	Amount
1919/9/1	Hungar. Com.Party, Rudnianok for Dige	1/7	value[1]	250,000
1919/12/6	Hungar. Com.Party, D. Zerlei	2	" "	207,000
1919/12/15	Hungar. Com.Party, Brasler Kalush	3	" "	194,000
1920/?/24	The Czech lands, Iv. Sinekom for Genglerz and Mush	4	" "	288,000
1919/11/19	The Czech lands, Name illegible	5	" "	215,000
1919/5/30	Germany, Reich for Thomas	1/2	" "	350,000
	" "	" "	DM	100,000
	" "	" "	Swed. Kron.	3,000
	" "	" "	Finn. Marks	4,500
	" "	" "	Russian Rubles	6,500

1. The Russian word appears to be *tsennost'*, which translates as "value" or "object of value." In the present context, the latter might be the more appropriate meaning. Presumably, the amount indicated is the ruble equivalent value.

Date yr/mo/day	Released to	Document no.	Denomination	Amount
1919/9/9	Germany, Proletariat for Thomas	1/8a	ostensibly, value	639,000
1919/9/28	Germany, Rudolf Rothegel for Thomas	6	value	639,000
1919/2/20	Germany, Rozovskii for Reich for Thomas	4	" "	275,000
1919/5/30	Italy, Liubarskii, Carlo " " " " " "	1/2 " " " " " "	D.M. Finn. Marks Swed. Kron. Russ. Rubles	15,200 331,800 13,000 300,000
1919/9/21	Italy, via Berzin for whom not clear	8	value	487,000
1919/7/16	America, Kotliarov	1/4	" "	209,000
1919/9/30	America, Khavkin	1/9	" "	500,000
1920/1/31	America, Anderson	9	" "	1,011,000
1920/1/22	America, John Reed	10	" "	1,008,000
1919/7/5	England, Levin	1/3	" "	500,000
1919/7/15	England, Levin via Kantorovich, for whom not clear	11	" "	1,039,000
1919/9/29	[illegible] for England, to Krasin	12	" "	7,040,000
1919/7/30	Balkan countries	1/5	" "	1,000,000
1919/12/29	Yugoslavia, Beloshevich	13	" "	300,000
1919/12/26	Amer. Com. Party Shaw [?] Mikhail	14	" "	503,000
1919/8/13	Country not known Sgurskii	1/6	" "	298,000
1919/9/1	Country not known Inoderev via Balabanova	1/8	Kron?	83,300
1919/10/28	Country not known Leo, last name unclear	15	value	2,020,000
1920/5/5	Country not known, to whom not known	16	" "	5,239,000
1919/9/19	Reuters " " " " " "	17 " " " " " "	Swed. Kr. DM value Pounds	10,000 5,000 4,050,000 50,~~000~~
1919/12/?	Swedish Office, A. Uoffe	18	Pounds Dollars Swed. Kr. Marks	4,000 4,000 52,000 25,000

Date yr/mo/day	Released to	Document no.	Denomination	Amount
1919/12/?	Poland	19	ostensibly, value	10,000,000
1919/12/27	Loriot Kost group	20	value	28,000
1919/6/18	Thomas	21	value	1,000,000
	" "	" "	roman.	150,000
	" "	" "	DM	1,600,000
	" "	" "	" "	35,600

RTSKhIDNI, fond 495, op. 82, d. 1, ll. 10, 100b.

A group of English and American delegates at the Second Congress of the Comintern. RTSKhIDNI

Secret
to Comrade Piatnitskii

N K V D
Business Manager
B. I. Kantorovich

October 16, 1922

E. Shelepina is the wife of Arthur Ransome. The two of them left together then, according to the instructions given to me by Comrades Chicherin and Karakhan. I took these valuables at the appropriate time from Comrade Ganetskii at the People's Bank and handed them over to A. Ransome's wife, to which the list attests.

B. Kantorovich

[The above note is a later attachment to the following documents.]

No. 1512	4 diamonds	12.20 carats	150,000 rubles
No. 1510	9 diamonds	13.20 carats	158,000 rubles
No. 1443	3 diamonds	5.70 carats	69,000 rubles
No. 1510	2 diamonds	4.45 carats	45,000 rubles
No. 1510	9 diamonds	13.20 carats	152,000 rubles
No. 1443	8 diamonds	10.50 carats	115,000 rubles
No. 923	3 strands of pearls (206 pearls)		350,000 rubles
		total	1,039,000 rubles

I received seven packets of diamonds and pearls totalling thirty-five diamonds and two hundred six pearls with a total value of one million thirty-nine thousand rubles for the People's Commissariat of Foreign Affairs.

B. Kantorovich

October 24, 1919

[Handwritten:] to receive money from Kantorovich

INVENTORY

Valuables received by me for England:

No. 1512	4 diamonds weighing 12.20 carats worth 150,000 r.		
1443	8 diamonds	10.50	115,000 r.
1510	2 diamonds	4.45	45,000 r.
1510	9 diamonds	13.20	158,000 r.
1510	9 diamonds	13.20	152,000 r.
1443	3 diamonds	5.70	69,000 r.
923	3 pearl strands (206 pearls)		350,000 r.
in all			1,039,000 r.

one million thirty-nine thousand rubles
All valuables were received in full by E. Shelepina
Moscow, October 25, 1919

No. in order	Quantity	Carats	Amount
No. 256	9 diamonds	39.40	360,000
No. 267	2 diamonds	14.35	145,000
			505,000

for England

July 5, 1919, handed over to Comrade Levin hidden in a suitcase (with a false bottom)

No. 278	2 diamonds	8.90	81,000
No. 366	2 diamonds	10.75	120,000
			201,000

for Holland

July 5, 1919, handed over to Comrade TSebrikov hidden in a suitcase (with a false bottom)

No. 302	2 diamonds	12.17	94,000
No. 305	4 diamonds	5.48	22,000
No. 367	1 diamond	4.	41,000
No. 384	2 diamonds	11.	143,000
			300,000

for France

July 5, 1919, handed over to Comrade Zabrezhnev hidden in a suitcase (with a false bottom)

Hereby acknowledged by the Executive Committee of the Communist International to have received:

> 300,500 (three hundred thousand five hundred) rubles in valuables,

according to the enclosed inventory;

> 65,000 (sixty-five thousand) Rubles
> 100,000 (one hundred thousand) German Marks
> 3,000 (three thousand) Swedish Krone
> 7,500 (seven thousand five hundred) Finnish Marks

James Reich

Moscow, May 30, 1919

R 65,000

VALUABLES RELEASED TO THE EXECUTIVE COMMITTEE OF THE COMMUNIST INTERNATIONAL

No. 167	Sapphire brooch		6,000 r.
No. 172	Platinum bracelet with diamond		2,000 r.
No. 173	4 strands of pearls		3,000 r.
No. 175	67 diamonds	13 carats	17,000 r.
No. 176	2 fine diamonds	10.85	108,000 r.
No. 181	Diamond ring with dark pearl		2,000 r.
No. 186	Pearl pin		2,000 r.
No. 189	Diamond ring		3,000 r.
No. 193	Diamond ring		3,000 r.
No. 195	18 diamonds	6.90	10,000 r.
No. 198	Brooch with 3 large diamonds and pave diamonds		55,000 r.
No. 202	8 diamonds	13.25	47,000 r.
No. 205	Diamond brooch with sapphire		5,500 r.
No. 212	4 diamonds	10.35	37,000 r.
		total sum	300,500 r.

James Reich

Moscow, May 30, 1919

VALUABLES RELEASED TO THE THIRD INTERNATIONAL

No. 214	Pendant		5,000 rubles
No. 216	12 diamonds	8.50 carats	21,500 r.
No. 218	Diamond pendant		3,500 r.
No. 219	Pearl stud		4,000 r.
No. 220	Diamond stud with sapphire		2,500 r.
No. 223	Diamond ring with ruby		2,000 r.
No. 224	Horseshoe charm with diam. and sapphire		4,500 r.
No. 225	Platinum bracelet with diamond		4,500 r.
No. 228	1 diamond	2.30 carats	7,500 r.
No. 229	27 diamonds	13.30	32,000 r.
No. 230	1 diamond	4.05	16,000 r.
No. 231	1 diamond	3.30	19,000 r.
No. 232	14 diamonds	8.50	17,000 r.
No. 233	11 diamonds	16.40	56,000 r.
No. 235	2 pearl earrings		14,000 r.
No. 236	Charm with 2 pearl mount with diam.		12,000 r.
No. 238	Circular diamond brooch set in platinum		12,000 r.
No. 240	Diamond brooch		13,000 r.
No. 291	5 diamonds	5.08 carats	22,500 r.
No. 320	Diamond ring		21,000 r.
No. 351	2 diamonds	2.55	10,500 r.
Total amount			300,000 r.

Moscow, May 28, 1919 Received by [illegible]

Source?

DOCUMENT 266   *Letter from I. Amter to Zinoviev, April 6, 1924, describing the political conditions faced by the American Workers' Party*[2]

April 6, 1924

Dear Comrade Zinoviev,

Concerning the persecution of the "Workers' Party," I can relate the following.

The district and local bureaus were searched and party and printed documents were seized. In several places the party prohibits the convening of a meeting because the American Legionnaires oppose it. In the trade unions the Communists are subjected to persecution and are kicked out because they are members of the Trade Union Educational League [TUEL]. It is believed that the league is working toward a split in the union movement. In the fall of 1923 an attempt was made on Foster's life. The Section for International Workers' Aid is being subjected to attacks. In several places films depicting Soviet Russia have been forbidden.

2. Russian text mistranslates a few passages of the German original, e.g., in the final paragraph the Russian version reads "economic repression" instead of "economic depression."

A group of American delegates to the Fourth Congress of the Comintern, 1922. RTSKhIDNI

In general, one can say there has been no particularly strong persecution. The bourgeoisie and the government vigilantly follow the activities of the "Workers' Party." But, because the party learned after the raid of 1922 (during the Congress of the Communist Party of America) to ally itself closely with the organized proletariat, it is not so easy for the government to persecute it. (I mention this because Comrade Nogin expressed to me, and, it seems, to you as well his surprise that the government no longer persecutes communists and that the bourgeois press is no longer harassing them. The bourgeois newspapers have written a great deal about and against communists, but, as a consequence, have seen that this serves as the best advertising possible for communists, and thus have also fallen silent.)

After the presidential election, with economic depression looming on the horizon, persecution of Communists will probably begin.

With Communist greetings,
I. Amter

RTSKhIDNI, fond 515, op. 1, d. 273, ll. 19–20.

DOCUMENT 267   *Excerpt from Zinoviev's speech, February 27, 1926, given at the 6th Comintern Executive Committee Plenum on the status of the American workers' movement, the role of the American Communist Party in trade unions, and factional politics therein*

[Fragments]

AMERICAN COMMISSION, February 27, 1926

ZINOVIEV:

I will try to illuminate for you in general outline the resolution we are proposing on the American question. The draft has not taken its final form, but I will present it in general terms and hope that the American commission will find it acceptable. Much has been said on the question of the American labor movement, and the genuine difficulties of the American position, which in recent times are truly significant, have been greatly emphasized. If the English working class for a number of years was under the thumb of the labor aristocracy because of the unique position England occupied in the world, then it can be assumed that the American bourgeoisie, which currently is reaping excess profits significantly larger than those of the English bourgeoisie in its time, will succeed for some time in seducing the working class and strongly influencing the proletariat. But it goes without saying that the situation now differs from the situation before the war, especially before the Russian revolution. The arsenal of the American bourgeoisie is very extensive, however, and the counterattack has increased significantly. Thus, there are reasons to assume, that [break in the document]

We feel that the American party up to now has given too little attention to trade union work. We still have accomplished very little in the trade unions. The issue of trade union work must hold the central place in the party's field of vision. The international movement favoring recognition of the Soviet Union, the campaign to send workers' delegations, etc., all gain poignancy in America as well, being closely linked with the trade union issue. In this connection I consider it essential to explain thoroughly the internal party issue. I suppose that no radical changes are needed and that it is not necessary to search for a new line. One has to accept the line that had been planned at the last party congress and recognize the Central Committee it elected. In no circumstances should there be new tests of strength that could rekindle animosity between the two factions. The party will not survive it, and the differences are not so great as to make it necessary. Thus, one should not create a situation when, inevitably, a new factional struggle will flare up. By no means does this mean that the current position is perfectly clear. No, we think that the majority has a responsibility vis-à-vis the minority. In all of our parties we observe that the minority, having become the majority, frequently tries to imitate the mistakes of the deposed majority. We will ask them not to make this mistake and in no circumstances wage a destructive struggle against Comrade Foster's faction. We feel that it is necessary to have a systematic division of labor between the two groups. What division? Based on our knowledge of the history of the American party, we propose the following divisions of labor: Comrade Foster and like-minded colleagues ought to conduct trade union work. It goes without saying, in the Communist Party it is inconceivable to divide up the work in such a way that some are involved only with political issues, others exclusively with trade union issues; there is a close connection between the two. The Central Committee has to keep an eye on all the work, supervise it completely, direct all the work, etc. But some division of labor is still essential and possible. Thus, Comrade Foster should be occupied primarily with trade union work. Why? Because Comrade Foster and like-minded colleagues have roots in the trade union area. They have more contact with trade union comrades, and it is necessary for them to conduct the work, of course, under the direction of, with the assistance of, and according to the instructions of the Central Committee. In order to carry out such an ambitious division of labor, of course, it is necessary to have good [break in the document]

. . . attract more nonparty workers who do not presently side with us; and so at this moment it is necessary to change the program and the composition of the League, and not rename it at all. Maybe it will be necessary to rename it, but only at such time as new questions crop up. Then, perhaps, it will be necessary to find a new name for it: the Committee for Unity, the Left Wing, or something else.

We also feel that the Politburo of the American party ought to be strengthened by admitting some comrades from Foster's group. As far as I know, the Politburo is intended to have five full and two candidate members.

We favor getting another comrade from Foster's group. These are more or less our suggestions on the American question. As I already indicated, it would be wrong to think that we are attempting to find a new line. The starting point for the work has to be the decision of the last congress of the party and the Central Committee. The point of all this is that the majority be able to give the minority a genuine chance to work and not attempt again to put the blame on Comrade Foster for all mistakes on the trade union issue.

RTSKhIDNI, fond 495, op. 164, d. 384, ll. 1, 7, 8, 11.

DOCUMENT 268   *Letter from Arnold Petersen, national secretary of the Socialist Radical Party of America, to Stalin, August 19, 1926, requesting the minutes of the July 22 session of the Central Committee—with a note by Bukharin refusing the request*

Secretariat of the National Executive Committee
Arnold Petersen, National Secretary
 of the Socialist Radical Party of America
45-51 Roz. Street
New York Aug. 19, 1926

To Citizen Joseph Stalin
Secretary of the Communist Party of the USSR

Moscow, the Kremlin, USSR.
Esteemed Comrade!

In the interests of my party I would like to ask you to be so kind as to send me a copy of the minutes of the July 22 Session of your Central Committee, as well as those papers which were presented at this session of the Central Committee. If these documents contain materials not intended for publication, this should be indicated or communicated.

You of course understand that we are following with the liveliest interest the development of Soviet Russia. Since we constitute the oldest and solely Marxist party in our country, we always structure our decisions on Marxism and on reliable facts, and this results in our great desire to supply ourselves first and foremost with information on the question which is of the greatest interest for the Russian Revolution and for the revolutionary movement of the proletariat of the entire world.

With fraternal greetings -
I remain sincerely yours Arnold Petersen,
National Secretary.

[Stamp at top center:] Affair No. 257; Box No. 35.
[Handwritten notation:] Since the SRP is not part of the Comintern, [certain] materials (*TSK* [Central Committee] steno transcripts) cannot be sent to them. Other materials (published speeches, etc.) can be. [signed] Bukh
[Stamp in greeting:] Secret Section of the *TSK VKP(b)* [Central Committee of the All-Union Communist Party (Bolshevik)]; Sept. 24
[Stamp at bottom right:] Secret Archive of the *TSK VKP(b)*. Inventory No...; Convocation; F-GR.

RTSKhIDNI, fond 17, op. 85, d. 39, l. 1.

William Z. Foster at the Sixth Congress of the Comintern, 1928. RTSKhIDNI

Declaration by Benjamin Gitlow to the Plenum of the Central Committee, April 22, 1929, on the genesis of the American Communist Party resolution against Bukharin

STATEMENT OF COMRADE GITLOW TO THE PLENUM
OF THE ALL-UNION COMMUNIST PARTY (Bolshevik)
(April 22, 1929)

[illegible] 12
secret, urgent

Comrades! Inasmuch as a resolution of the VI Congress of our American Communist Party concerning Comrade Bukharin's situation has become the subject of debate at this session of the Plenum of the Central Committee of our fraternal party of the Soviet Union and inasmuch as Comrade [Philip] Dengel has issued a statement on that subject which needs further elucidation, I consider it necessary to give the following information about the facts in this matter.

1) The Central Committee of our party has more than once made clear and, in precise language, formulated into resolutions the fact that our Central Committee unreservedly follows the line of the Central Committee of the All-Union Communist Party (Bolshevik) [*VKP(b)*]. Our Central Committee has fully acknowledged the necessity of expanding the socialist base of the Soviet economy as fast as possible as the only means of quickly fortifying the strength of our proletarian revolution for its struggle against capitalist enemies, both at home and abroad. The most recent expressions of our Central Committee's view of this matter can be found in our Politburo's resolution dated November 14, 1928; in a declaration in the December 3 issue of our organ, the *Daily Worker*; in a Politburo resolution of February 7, 1929; and in the resolution of our VI Party Congress concerning decisions of the Moscow Party Conference.

2) Despite these repeated unanimous declarations by the Central Committee, the opposition in our party has mounted a campaign throughout the whole party—a campaign led by the chief All-American Bureau of the League of Trade Union Propaganda—whereby they accused our Central Committee of supporting Comrade Bukharin in his fight against the policies of the Central Committee of the *VKP(b)*. Our opposition asserted itself as the only "true supporters of Stalin" in America.

3) At our congress Comrade Browder, speaking for the opposition, brought forward that same accusation and announced that they (the opposition) "will not let this congress off with just a declaration on this political question, but will force it to submit to an open vote the question of Comrade Bukharin's condemnation, calling him by name." We could not fail to understand the meaning of this announcement, for we knew that representatives of the ECCI [Executive Committee of the Communist International] served in fact as an integral part of the opposition faction, directing its strategy at the congress.

4) The same day that Comrade Browder made his statement, leaders of the Central Committee held an all-night meeting with representatives of the ECCI. At that meeting Comrade Dengel told us openly that the ECCI considered us adherents of Bukharin and that that fact influenced the ECCI in its assessment of the American question. We were informed that our repeated political declarations refuting that view were insufficient to absolve us from this suspicion. We were told that our statements should be much more concrete and that specific names should not be included.

5) At the same time the opposition at our congress prepared a statement, publication of which was later demanded by the ECCI representatives. In that statement, for the first time in our party, the names of Stalin and Bukharin were specifically mentioned in a document concerning disputes in the *VKP(b)*. The relevant passage said:

Loyalty with regard to the Comintern demands at the present time rejection of the openly opportunistic viewpoint of right-wing elements in the German CP and in the *VKP(b)* represented by [Otto] Brandler, Frumkin, etc., and also the most energetic struggle against the conciliationist viewpoint (Ewert, Ember-

Dro, etc.), which are based on the interpretation given by Bukharin to the decisions of the VI Congress and on his article "Notes of an Economist" and on his speech at the Moscow conference dedicated to Lenin's memory, also titled "Lenin's Political Testament." Loyalty with regard to the Comintern demands unconditional support of the line of the ruling party of the Comintern, the *VKP(b)* and of its Central Committee, led by Comrade Stalin.

6) Comrade [William W.] Weinstone, who worked under the direct supervision of Comrade Dengel and has never taken a single step without Dengel's approval, presented the statement, which further said:

The congress supports the Central Committee of the *VKP(b)*, under the leadership of Comrade Stalin. Further, inasmuch as Comrade Bukharin has been estranged for the last few months from the Comintern leadership—in view of his position, in view of his vacillating stance in the struggle with right wing and conciliationist groups in the Comintern, insomuch as Comrade Bukharin's position hinders the development of the ruthless struggle against right wing and conciliationist groups, we therefore propose that the Comintern make a final decision on Comrade Bukharin's leadership of the Comintern.

7) Given this situation, leaders of the Central Committee finally recommended that the Presidium of the congress present the congress with a resolution on the question of Comrade Bukharin's future work in the Comintern. Comrades Dengel and Pollitt were both present at that session of the Presidium and at that session of the congress at which the resolution was unanimously adopted; they absolutely did not protest it nor raise any question in conjunction with that resolution. Likewise, neither of the two Comintern representatives made any remarks nor posed any questions when the statements of Comrade Weinstone and the opposition were presented to the congress.

I offer these facts for the information of your Plenum.

With Communist greetings,

Benjamin Gitlow

translated by
[illegible] Reinshten and
[illegible] Mikhailov

RTSKhIDNI, fond 495, op. 72, d. 63, ll. 271–73.

DOCUMENT 270　　*Letter from S. A. Lozovskii, May 10, 1929, on the Trade Union Educational*
League Convention

[English original]
RW/H.4.1929　　　　　　　　　　　　　　　[handwritten:] Comrade Williams SECRET
　　　　　　　　　　　　　　　　　　　　　　no. 132/21/2.
　　　　　　　　　　　　　　　　　　　　　　May 10, 1929

AMERICAN COMMISSION Comintern
DELEGATION OF COMMUNIST PARTY OF AMERICA

ON TRADE UNION EDUCATIONAL LEAGUE [TUEL] CONVENTION
[stamped:] May 10, 1929

Dear Comrades,

　　At the Red International of Labor Unions (RILU [*Profintern*]) Executive Bureau Meeting of May 8, Comrade Foster made a report on the forthcoming Convention of the Trade Union Educational league to be opened June 1. From the report and other materials in the RILU, it was clear that preparations for the Convention were very weak. But judging from the appeal, this Convention has to solve many important problems, and insofar as several independent unions are embraced, this Convention must create a militant centre of the revolutionary TU movement. Preparations for the Convention are extremely slack which may mean that this Convention will be turned simply into a meeting where a few score speeches will be made and nothing more. Confronted as it is with such important problems, this Convention should be carefully prepared. The whole Party should get down to work, and articles dealing with the Convention should be a prominent feature now in all the publications of the Party and the Trade Unions, while all the local Party organisations and the TUEL Groups should now be mobilised, this being the only way to realise effectively the tasks contemplated. The absence of a whole group of responsible Party leaders from the U.S.A. and the internal condition of the Party may well have an unfavourable effect on the coming Convention. At best the Convention will be attended in the main by Communists, who will start another fractional struggle, and in this way this gathering will be disrupted. Hence, the Executive Bureau is of the opinion that it would be expedient to postpone the Convention for a few months, make careful preparations and take care to mobilise all the forces of the Party and the TUEL.

　　The RILU Executive Bureau did not decide on the date for the Convention. But it is plain that to open this Convention on June 1 would be altogether unfeasible. The American comrades themselves must decide on when the Convention should be opened. At all events it would be inexpedient to call the Convention before next September.

　　　　　　　　　　　　　　　　　　With comradely greetings,
　　　　　　　　　　　　　　　　　　[signed in Roman alphabet] A. Lozovsky

RTSKhIDNI, fond 495, op. 72, d. 56, ll. 8–9.

Interview of E. M. IAroslavskii with an American delegation of professors at the Central Council of the League of Militant Atheists, July 13, 1932

<u>INTERVIEW WITH A DELEGATION OF AMERICAN PROFESSORS
AT THE CENTRAL COUNCIL OF THE UNION OF MILITANT ATHEISTS
ON JULY 13, 1932</u>

1. What were the party's primary objectives and tasks in 1931?

<u>Comrade IAroslavskii.</u> These objectives and tasks were spelled out in published resolutions. Essentially, the goal was to complete the five-year plan in 1931 and 1932. This was our main objective.

2. With respect to the Central Control Commission, could you give us some specific examples of what exactly it is you do?

<u>Comrade IAroslavskii.</u> Our Central Control Commission is a party agency, the supreme inspection agency in the party, and is at the same time a people's commissariat, the People's Commissariat of Workers' and Peasants' Inspection. These two party and government agencies are combined into a single agency with a single chairman. The Central Control Commission monitors the implementation of party and government decisions. If these decisions are not being implemented, the Central Control Commission has the authority not only to demand that they be implemented immediately or that the obstacles interfering with their implementation be removed, but also has the power to punish the individuals responsible, fire them from their jobs, or impose party sanctions, including reprimands and severe reprimands, and may even initiate proceedings to have them expelled from the party. This applies to organizations and individuals with respect to their implementation of party and government decisions. If individual party members violate these orders or the party platform or party discipline, the Control Commission may call these individuals in for a friendly chat to correct their errors or, if it deems necessary, impose party sanctions, dismiss them from their jobs, give them some sort of reprimand, or even expel them from the party.

The Central Control Commission studies the procedures in effect in our economy or different government agencies. If experience shows that some sort of reorganization is required, the Central Control Commission will resolve the matter in cooperation with the Central Committee of the Party and the supreme governing bodies. [break in the text]

7. In America there is the widespread opinion that [the Soviet Union] is an absolute dictatorship.

<u>Comrade IAroslavskii.</u> Of course, any talk of Comrade Stalin's dictatorship is utter nonsense. Comrade Stalin is not a dictator but the extremely beloved leader of our party, who enjoys unlimited trust and extraordinary prestige because he has carried out the correct line of the party for more than 30 years, never wavered at the most critical moments, and always walked side by side with Lenin. No one in our party ever considered, considers him, or could ever consider him a dictator because Comrade Stalin's proposals are discussed by the supreme bodies of our party, including the Central Committee, the Political Bureau, the Presidium of the Central Executive Committee, and the congresses, which may disagree with Comrade Stalin. If they do agree with him, it is because his policy is the correct one. In this respect, Lenin was also "justifiably" or, more probably, without any justification, called a dictator in his day, even though his authority was based on boundless trust and respect, not subordination. In Comrade Stalin's writings you can find a number of articles and letters in which he argues with his comrades who disagree with him and <u>tries to persuade</u> them. Of course, if the rumors you're talking about were true, he wouldn't even try to persuade or argue with his comrades.

8. We personally don't doubt that Comrade Stalin is a great man and a great leader, but have there not been cases, despite all his prestige, where the proposals he has submitted to the Central Committee have failed to win a majority of votes? After all, Lenin was sometimes in the minority.

<u>Comrade IAroslavskii.</u> I don't remember any instances where Comrade Stalin has submitted incorrect proposals. With respect to your comments that Lenin was sometimes in the minority, during the Brest peace negotiations

many people disagreed with Lenin. I myself was opposed to the Brest Treaty, which I have always deeply regretted, because I was wrong and Lenin was right. Even then Comrade Stalin supported Lenin's policy.

9. We believe that the Russian Communist Party influences the Communist movement throughout the world and is currently directing the policies of the Communist parties in the Western countries. For example, the Russian Communist Party supported Foster in America, who at a convention of the American Communist Party received only two votes, with the rest going to Rutner (?). This is a policy of imposing one's own influence in the West. Don't you think that the Western Communist parties should be given some independence in their affairs?

Comrade IAroslavskii. I have never heard and I categorically deny that the Russian Communist Party ever nominated anyone for president in America. Every Communist party is an independent actor, but all the parties belong to the Comintern, which has the authority to intervene wherever a dispute may arise. We have equal status in the Comintern with all the other parties. We would be happy if we could move the executive committee of the Comintern to Berlin, Paris, or New York, but unfortunately this would obviously be impossible at the present time. But, anyway, the Comintern Executive Committee is located in Moscow only in a geographical sense. Our party has its central newspaper, *Pravda*, which is not particularly noted for its reticence, and if we really dictated, as you say, our policies to the other Communist parties, we would do so in our own central newspaper. But you can be sure that we don't even give any advice to other Communist parties, because we believe that the Western Communist parties are mature enough to solve their own problems. If they learn from us, then I believe it's only because we have something to teach non-Communists as well as Communists.

10. We consider your assistance to the American Communist Party to be quite proper, but could you tell us if you actually do provide financial assistance to the American Communist Party?

Comrade IAroslavskii. As far as I know, we don't provide any financial support to the American Communist Party or other parties. The Comintern gets its funds from its publishing operations, from its membership dues, and from other sources and disposes of these funds as it sees fit. I know that at one time we provided assistance through our trade unions to the striking miners in Great Britain. But when we make contributions, we make them public by putting a notice in our newspaper that we are sending such and such an amount of money. We don't provide any secret assistance. After all, we all know what kind of harm we could do to a foreign Communist party if we actually provided such assistance, because we know that the bourgeoisie would take advantage of this situation to the detriment of the Communist Party.

(The Americans express their doubts.)

Comrade IAroslavskii. I personally don't know of any cases where we have ever sent money secretly.

11. Don't you think that revolutions could break out in other countries without necessarily requiring a new world war?

Comrade IAroslavskii. I, for example, am convinced that what is going on in Belgium right now cannot be called anything but a revolutionary movement. And there's no other war going on there right now except a class war. Class wars and class revolutions may break out, regardless of whether a conventional war is going on or not, such as the Spanish Revolution, for example. The possibility of such revolutions also exists in other countries. Another example is the Chilean Revolution, which has nothing to do with a war but has a lot to do with the crisis which is now underway. A world war would accelerate the pace of revolutions and would aggravate the conflicts within each country.

12. So what kind of success has your antireligious campaign had among the peasants?

Comrade IAroslavskii. We are not conducting an antireligious campaign right now. A campaign implies that we have set ourselves some sort of <u>temporary</u> goal and are using special means to achieve it. We are <u>systematically</u>, day in and day out, spreading antireligious propaganda and are organizing the masses who want to spread this antireligious propaganda themselves. Right now the council has five and a half million members, but this doesn't mean that there are only five and a half million atheists here. I could cite several very rough figures to give you an idea of the number of atheists here. More than 40% of the trade union members are atheists [original ends at this point]

RTSKhIDNI, fond 89, op. 39, d. 4, ll. 14, 17, 18, 19.

Letter to Stalin from Frank Jefferies, Socialist Party of New Jersey, March 11, 1934

[English original; spelling and punctuation errors preserved]

SOCIALIST PARTY OF NEW JERSEY
SOUTH JERSEY DISTRICT
814 Broadway Camden, N.J. U.S.A.

EXECUTIVE COMMITTEE   March 11, 1934

Josef Stalin
Sec't'y., Central Committee.
U.S.S.R.

Dear Sir and Comrade:-

Realizing that the time has arrived when all working class groups must, of a necessity, unite on common ground to fight off the reaction of a dead capitalist system, and having had numerous requests for a united front with the Communist Party in this section, we are at a loss to know what course to follow due to the fact that there are at present, four separate Communist groups here in America, all of them having weak reformist programs.

Therefore, we are asking at this time if any of the American Communist groups are affiliated with the Moscow Communist Internationale. Your answer will be held in strictest confidence. We have endeavored to secure the above information thru other sources, but have failed, due to the fact that Communist Party members in this section seem to know little or nothing in reference to the Moscow Internationale.

Your answer will also be the means of shaping the course that we shall take in the future. Hoping for a speedy reply to this letter, I am

Yours for the Socialist Revolution

[signed] Frank Jefferies

952 North 34th Street
Camden, New Jersey, U.S.A.

Executive Committee Organizer
in South New Jersey District.

[Handwritten note across the top:] comrade Kuusinen. I am sending for your information the letter we received. Could you write a few words about this to Edwards?
April 11, 1934 [signature illegible]

RTSKhIDNI, fond 515, op. 1, d. 3730, l. 1.

Letter from Sidney Bloomfield to Dimitrov, August 12, 1938, discussing changes in the policies of the U.S. Communist party [CP U.S.A.]

[English original; spelling and punctuation errors preserved]
"8"
5882/1
rc copy
16.8.38

August 12, 1938

Dear Comrade Dimitroff:

A short while ago I was called in by Comrade Panamarov [Ponomarev], who told me to inform the comrades back home about the attitude here to the slogan of the CP U.S.A. "Communism Is Twentieth Century Americanism."

I told Comrade Panamarov that I would write to the comrades and convey to them the information, which I did. I also told him that while I surmised the reason for this attitude, I would however, like to have a little more clarification which could come from a discussion of the matter and I would particularly like to hear your views.

I informed Comrade Panamarov that this is one of our popular slogans which has influenced large masses. It serves as the main theme under which the Party claims and carries forward the revolutionary and democratic traditions of America. This slogan can be found in all our literature and agitation since the 9th Party Convention of June 1936. This slogan has fired the imagination and revolutionary idealism of the movement and the wider masses supporting it. On the basis of this slogan or the ideas implied by it the whole movement was spurred on to Americanize itself in the spirit of the 7th World Congress of the Communist International.

For these reasons I asked for more information in order to be more clear. However, I think that the reason for the position taken here against this slogan is that it is unscientific. Communism is the classless society in which the exploitation of man by man has been abolished; in which the state has withered away; in which the economic and other material conditions of life are on such a high level that the relations between man are on a high idealistic plane based upon the contribution of the individual to society according to his ability and from which the individual receives according to his needs; that Communism, which is the highest development of Socialism (which can be realized in one country) is universal. Now, since Americanism has not yet shown any sign of any society higher than capitalism, and since even in its development (in one country) the most it possibly could develop to, would be Socialism, therefore to call it "Communism" (regardless of which century) would be incorrect from a Marxian standpoint.

I have had no adequate explanation for the position here on the slogan. Therefore I can only conclude that what I have here stated as the possible reason for objection is correct. Perhaps the comrades in the U.S.A. will also think as I do in search of an explanation. A further explanation would clear up matters.

However, I would like to call to your attention the following important literature which may throw light on the slogan insofar as one can thereby see the reasons for its use by the Party:

1)   *The Democratic Front for Jobs, Security, Democracy and Peace.* Page 86, Chapter VI entitled "The American Tradition and Socialism."

This is the pamphlet containing Comrade Browder's report to the 10th Convention of the Party in May 1938.

2)   "The Revolutionary Background of the United States Constitution," by Earl Browder in *The Communist* for September 1937, or in *The People's Front*, the book by Browder, on Page 249.

Comradely yours,

Sidney Bloomfield

Referent, CP U.S.A.,

Secretariat, Marty

RTSKhIDNI, fond 495, op. 74, d. 466, ll. 32

DOCUMENT 274 *Notification and marketing plans submitted to the Comintern, March 13, 1939, for the publication of the American edition of the* History of the All-Union Communist Party (Bolshevik)

MASS DISTRIBUTION IN THE UNITED STATES PLANNED FOR *HISTORY OF THE ALL-UNION COMMUNIST PARTY (BOLSHEVIK)* [VKP(b)]

The Central Committee of the Communist Party of the U.S.A. [CC CP U.S.A.] has announced an American edition of *History of the VKP(b)* [All-Union Communist Party (Bolshevik)] in 100,000 copies, to be issued March 15, 1939.

The delayed release of *History* evidently stems from a desire to withhold the book pending establishment of an organization for its immediate mass distribution. In this regard measures are being taken to ensure that all 100,000 copies of the book <u>will in fact have been sold</u> in advance. It is expected that another large printing will be issued immediately. Within its own ranks as well as those of the workers' movement the party has developed a broad campaign so that party members, and through them their friends, will purchase the book, aimed at ensuring an advance sellout of the first 100,000 copies.

The initial printing will be issued in plain cardboard binding and sold through Communist organizations (at 40 cents per copy). Shortly thereafter another printing, in a cloth binding, will be released for sale in all bookstores at 1 dollar per copy.

The first printing of 100,000 copies will be distributed among all 35 district and state party organizations.

To secure prepublication sale of 100,000 copies, the Literary Section of the CC has issued "advance subscription coupon cards" consisting of 8 coupons at 10 cents each. With each weekly payment of 10 cents duly noted on the card, after 8 weeks a party member will have paid for 2 copies: one for himself, the other for a friend. The coupon is sized to fit the party card wallet.

In the effort to explain to the masses the significance of the *History*, and tied to the book's distribution, announcement has been made of a nationwide essay contest on the topic "The Significance of the *History of the VKP(b)* for American Workers." The winning composition will be published in the journal *Communist*, and its author will be invited to attend a regular Plenum of the CC.

All district organizations are urged to convene at least one meeting at which one of the party leaders will report on the book.

The Section for Party Education at the CC CP U.S.A. is preparing for publication explanatory materials for those studying *History of the VKP(b)*.

The Communist press will publish a series of articles by leading comrades on specific topics dealt with in the book.

The party will make good use of *History* in connection with its 20th anniversary and in the drive to raise the political and theoretical level of the mass membership.

[signed] Pat [Touhey]?

[Stamps above header:]   3 entry no. 77 3/13/1939
                           8 entry no. 79 3/13/1939

[Inscriptions by different hands, following stamps:]
                           U.S.A., Archives

RTSKhIDNI, fond 495, op. 14, d. 126, ll. 8, 11.

DOCUMENT 275   *Telegram, located in the Comintern archive, from the American Communist Party, January 10, 1944, outlining the changes to be made in name, organization, and activities*

TELEGRAPHIC COMMUNIQUE OF SUPRESS [sic] FROM NEW YORK

Decision of the Plenum of the
Communist Party of the U.S.A.

New York, January 10, 1944—Yesterday the Communist Party issued a press release declaring that for the past three days a plenum of the Central Committee of the party was held in New York, the work of which ended yesterday. The plenum dealt with a single issue, namely the report of Comrade Earl Browder, who presented an analysis of the international and domestic situations, discussed the upcoming elections, and proposed far-reaching plans and measures regarding party politics and the organizational structure of the party. Comrade Browder proposed that the party congress scheduled for May change the name of the Communist Party. His proposal calls for dropping the word "party" from the name, suggesting that after the May congress the Communist organization be renamed the Communist Association for Political Education to reflect its true character. Furthermore, Browder suggested that this proposal be widely discussed in a forum open to the American people at large before the May congress. This proposal was approved by all of the 28 members of the Central Committee present at the plenum. The Central Committee accepted the text of the proposal, which is cited below, and instructed Comrade Browder to present the plenum's decision and rationale on which it is based at a mass rally in Madison Square Garden in New York this evening.

Text of the Central Committee's Declaration:

The favorable course of military activities and the conclusion of international agreements by participants of the coalition of Allied nations have created a completely new situation in the world and in our country. The present circumstances will ensure victory in the war and open new perspectives for a long period of world peace and for regular postwar restructuring. Complete defeat of the Fascist Axis and destruction of the regimes of Hitler and the Quislings, and their replacement by democracies in Europe, will fundamentally alter for the better perspectives for the future, while annihilation of the imperialistic regime in Japan will give greater impetus to national liberation forces and democracy among the peoples of Asia. The agreements reached in Moscow, Teheran, and Cairo have presented us with a program for avoiding the dangers of civil wars and wars among countries for generations to come. The world is faced with the prospects of prolonged global peace never before seen in history, as well as with the onset of economic interdependence, cooperation and development, and the implementation of social reforms.

In our country cooperation among the members of the Allied nations in the period of postwar reconstruction will create a basis for restructuring our industry after its wartime expansion for the benefit of the working class, farmers and capital. For the working class this program creates a prospect of full job security and orderly social progress based on collective agreements, and the promise of reforms and full participation in the political sphere as guaranteed by our constitution. The agreements reached in Moscow and Teheran will make it possible for our government to engage in political cooperation as regards world prices for farm products and with respect to their sales, and thereby create prospects for improving American agriculture. [break in the text]

The Communist Party emphasizes national unity as a key factor in ensuring a rapid and victorious conclusion to the war in Europe and Asia, continued high-level wartime productivity, and reinforcement of peace and cooperation among nations, which became possible as a result of the agreements. The Central Committee will convene a Communist Party Congress on May 1. The site for the congress will be selected by the Political Committee before February 1. Prior to the congress the Central Committee will make a number of proposals, one of which will be to discontinue designation of the Communist organization as a party; the name should more accurately reflect its broad unifying role in the nation as an organization that does not possess any party-like aspirations. An appropriate name might well be "American Communist Political Association."

RTSKhIDNI, fond 495, op. 14, d. 1460 (or 146a), ll. 78, 780b, 790b.

THE COMMUNIST PARTY OF
THE UNITED STATES OF AMERICA

During the war the Communist Party of the United States experienced a major political crisis. The American Communists, who at that time were led by Browder, adopted a Marxist revisionist policy, renounced the class struggle, and disbanded their party.

Browder, the theoretician of American revisionism, and his supporters believed that a trend towards peaceful coexistence and cooperation had developed between socialism and capitalism during the war. Therefore, the task of Communists would be to facilitate the further convergence of socialism and capitalism by promoting "national unity" and establishing a political coalition which would include everyone "from the working people to the capitalists."

On the basis of this concept, Browder asked the National Committee to disband the Communist Party and establish a nonparty association. Browder's proposal served to betray the Communist Party and the working class of the United States, because the disbandment of the Communist Party meant the ideological and organizational disarmament of the working class and the elimination of its militant vanguard.

Browder's platform of liquidation was opposed by Foster, the chairman of the National Committee. Browder's proposal, however, was supported by the majority of the members of the National Committee and a number of regional organizations.

As a result, the so-called Communist Political Association (CPA) was established at the May 1944 congress to replace the disbanded Communist Party. The congress also decided to disband party organizations at factories and trade unions. The association's "cultural and educational" activities were turned over to regional clubs.

The anti-Marxist stance of Browder and his supporters was subjected to scathing criticism by leading European Communist parties, including the Italian, French, and others. The most comprehensive critique of the idea of class peace and "national unity" in a capitalist country was provided by the Secretary of the Central Committee of the French Communist Party, Comrade Jacques Duclos, in an article published in the April 1945 issue of the journal *Cahiers du communisme*.

This article was reprinted by the New York *Daily Worker* and evoked lively debate in the CPA. Most Communists spoke out in favor of restoring the Communist Party of the U.S.A.

An emergency party congress convened in July 1945 by decision of most of the organizations acknowledged the validity of Duclos' critique and took steps to rectify the errors committed by the American Communists. The Communist Party was resurrected. The congress adopted a new charter for the CP U.S.A.

The charter's introduction emphasized that "the Communist Party of the U.S.A. is a political party of the American working class based on the principles of scientific socialism and Marxism-Leninism."

The congress reinstated the Leninist formula for membership in the party. The charter reads: "Anyone who accepts the goals, principles, and platform of the party, who is a member of one of its organizations and attends its meetings, who acts in the interests of the party, who reads the party newspapers and literature, and who regularly pays his membership dues shall be considered a member of the party."

In defining the rights and duties of party members, the congress required each member of the party to belong to a trade union, to fight for the interests of the workers, and to help strengthen mass progressive organizations.

In its new charter the congress emphasized the need to combine the party's current missions of defending the rights of the working class and expanding the democratic rights of the American people with the task of preparing the working class to carry out its historical mission of "building socialism on the basis of the freely expressed choice of the majority of the American people."

Thus, the congress totally rejected Browder's opportunistic strategy and laid the groundwork for the advancement of the Communist Party of the United States.

The Communist Party's return to Marxist principles aggravated the discord within the party. The opportunistic faction led by Browder sabotaged the congress' decisions and hindered the reform of party organizations. [break in the text]

The party's weak link is its low-level organizations, which are inadequately led, poorly organized, and, in most cases, politically inactive.

The growth in the dissatisfaction of the working class with its deteriorating economic situation and the establishment of a number of large progressive organizations with a broad democratic platform are laying the groundwork for a more active Communist Party, despite the intense pressure applied by the reactionaries.

Addendum No. 2

THE GOALS OF THE COMMUNIST PARTY
OF THE UNITED STATES FOR 1947

A plenary session of the Central Committee of the CP U.S.A. was held on December 5, 1946. The plenary session formulated the goals which the party would work for in 1947.

1. Substantial wage hikes for all workers. The passage of a law raising the minimum wage to 75 cents per hour. The introduction of the 30-hour workweek with no cut in pay. The establishment of a guaranteed annual income.

2. A reduction in taxes for all categories of low-income persons and a tax hike for high-income persons.

3. The adoption of a five-year plan for housing construction, which would include the construction of at least 3 million new housing units per year.

4. An increase in unemployment benefits for unemployed war veterans and payment of these benefits over the entire period of unemployment.

5. The introduction of social security allowances to compensate for inflation. The extension of social security benefits to the many categories of workers currently not covered by them.

6. An increase in government subsidies for agriculture to guarantee stable prices for agricultural commodities and thus provide relief for working farmers.

7. Enforcement of the labor laws passed during the term of President Roosevelt and the repeal of antilabor laws.

8. The passage of a law prohibiting discrimination against certain ethnic groups, a ban on lynching, and effective action against the Ku Klux Klan and other fascist organizations.

9. The establishment of public ownership of the railroads, mining industry, power plants, utilities, communications companies, and food processing plants.

10. Criminal prosecution of major monopolists and speculators, especially the owners of steel, defense, chemical, and other plants who profited from the war. The prosecution of all American companies who joined with German, Japanese, and Spanish firms in cartel agreements.

11. The adoption of a program of universal and immediate disarmament. A reduction in U.S. military and naval spending to at least 1939 levels. A ban on the production, stockpiling, and use of nuclear weapons. Opposition to the militarization of young people, educational institutions, science, and industry. The nationalization of all defense plants and all military patents, as well as the generation and use of nuclear power.

12. A break in diplomatic and economic relations with Fascist Spain. Rejection of American imperialist intervention in China. The withdrawal of all American forces from China. The cancellation of credit and aid to

the Kuomintang government. Full and unrestricted independence for Puerto Rico. The withdrawal of American forces from the Philippines. Opposition to "inter-American" defense plans. The abolition of the Anglo-American staff committee and repudiation of the Anglo-American defense treaty.

13. Unconditional compliance with the Teheran, Moscow, and Berlin agreements. Greater solidarity among the Big Three, and most importantly, greater friendship and cooperation between the U.S.A. and the USSR.

14. The organization of joint demonstrations by the AFL, CIO, and railroad workers' unions in defense of the vital interests, trade union rights, and democratic freedoms of the people. The unionization of nonunion workers. An improvement in relations with the World Federation of Trade Unions. The creation of a powerful antimonopoly and antifascist democratic front.

Addendum No. 5

THE POLITICAL ACTION PROGRAM OF THE
CONGRESS OF INDUSTRIAL ORGANIZATIONS (CIO) FOR 1948

The Executive Committee of the CIO has reviewed the political action program for 1948.

The program emphasizes that next year's election campaign should be based on the people's current fight against laws that, if adopted, would paralyze the labor unions.

The Executive Committee adopted the following resolution concerning political activity:

The working class and masses of people are living through a time of crisis.

The basic democratic rights, standard of living, and well-being of the broad masses of the American people are facing a major threat.

The majority of the U.S. Congress have mindlessly taken the path of reaction. Ignoring the wishes of their constituents, these individuals are carrying out the orders of the monopoly owners, who are demanding ever greater power, privileges, and profits for themselves at the expense of the public welfare.

This majority is working to destroy the remnants of the price stabilization program by abolishing rent controls. The majority is launching an attack on the minimum wage and set workday length and is attempting to emasculate the law on fair working conditions. They are insisting on a tax system which will "bleed the poor white." They want to paralyze all of the social legislation passed over the last 14 years by cutting off the necessary appropriations.

In the knowledge that labor unions are the staunchest defenders of economic stability and the civil liberties of all the people, this reactionary majority has launched a concentrated assault on the democratic rights of the workers to join unions, conclude collective bargaining agreements, and strike.

Largely ignored by public opinion, the legislatures of certain states have already implemented these reactionary policies. Six states have already passed laws restricting the rights of the workers, and other states are threatening to follow their example.

Disregarding the national interest, popularly elected representatives have chosen to listen to the voices of the privileged few. They have put the interests of the public and the welfare of the country in grave danger. They are threatening to repeat the history of the 1920s, when the country was led to the brink of disaster under Hoover after a period of normalcy under Harding.

This disaster can be prevented only by the political mobilization and determined resistance of the people, primarily the working class.

RTSKhIDNI, fond 575, papka mat. po SShA, ll. 31, 32, 49, 65, 66, 73.

Top Secret
October 28, 1948

Copy 2

To Comrade Baranov

<u>On Actions to Be Taken in Connection with the Trial</u>
<u>of the Leaders of the Communist Party of the United States</u>

Upon my arrival in Paris on October 12, I had a conversation with Comrades Jacques Duclos and Etienne Fajon [?], the French delegates to the Information Bureau, and informed them of the actions which must be taken in connection with the trial of the leaders of the Communist Party of the U.S.A.. That same evening the editors of *L'Humanité* called the editors of the *Daily Worker* in London and the editors of *Drapeau Rouge* in Brussels to notify them that *L'Humanité* was launching an extensive media campaign.

On October 13, 14, 15, 16 and the following week, *L'Humanité* ran a special series on the trial, most of which were written by Marcel Cachin, the director of the newspaper, and Pierre Courtade, the head of the newspaper's foreign policy department.

The *Daily Worker* also published a special article on October 13.

On October 13 I had a talk with Comrade Maurice Thorez on the subject. We decided that Comrade Jacques Duclos would personally assume the overall direction of the campaign.

On the same day I gave the necessary instructions to a French comrade, who immediately left for London. Comrade Duclos made contact with a representative of the Argentinean Communist Party, whom Comrade Duclos instructed to notify all the Latin American parties. He also received several Communist delegates from the Dutch trade unions who were attending the congress of the French Confederation of Labor as invited guests for a talk on the subject.

The Political Bureau of the French Communist Party met on the morning of the 14th. They heard a report from Comrade Duclos and devoted a special section in the published transcript of the proceedings to the trial. Comrades Thorez and Duclos and I had breakfast that day with Comrade Horner, a Communist leader and Secretary of the British Federation of Miners, and we emphasized the importance of the actions which must be taken.

On October 15 we held a closed meeting of Communist activists who were directly concerned with the trial, including journalists, lawyers, foreign policy experts, and so forth, chaired by Comrade Duclos with the secretary of the Paris party organization, R. Guilleau [?], in attendance. The following decisions were made:

1) A special party commission to organize the entire campaign was appointed. This commission, headed by Jacques Duclos, was placed under the direct supervision of the secretary of the Foreign Policy Commission of the party Central Committee, M. Manien [?]. The special commission's members included three journalists, one lawyer, and one instructor, who were appointed as capable and experienced activists.

2) The meeting decided to begin careful preparations for a protest rally on October 20. They decided that special public invitations to participate and speak at the rally would be extended to the following Americans in Paris: Madame Eleanor Roosevelt, John Foster Dulles, Warren Austin, and Charles Bohlen.

3) The meeting made plans to get interviews with a number of non-Communist figures in order to convince them to sign a letter of protest and join in forming a broad Action Committee. This letter would be extensively advertised. Affiliates of the Paris Committee would be organized in the provinces.

4) The meeting also made plans to publish a number of articles on the history of major trials against freedom of thought in friendly newspapers in order to highlight the reactionary and barbarous nature of this trial.

5) The meeting decided that Comrade Duclos, who is highly respected by American journalists of all political persuasions, would call a press conference immediately after the rally.

6) The party's federations were advised of the need to support and encourage the adoption of protest resolutions everywhere and appeals to the newspapers and American Embassy in Paris.

7) The meeting decided that a special issue of the weekly *Action* would be devoted to the trial and would go on sale on October 19. The initial press run would be 25,000 copies.

8) The necessary instructions were given to the Communist leaders of the International Association of Jurists to send a delegation to the United States.

9) The organizers ultimately envisioned a broad-based, highly publicized counter-trial in Paris which would indict the persecutors of the American Communist Party and the rampaging reactionary enemies of freedom. Steps were taken to recruit the best-known French jurists for this purpose, such as the former General Prosecutor Mornet.

The special party commission appointed on October 15 held its first working meeting the following day and met almost every day afterwards.

INDICTMENT AGAINST THE
AMERICAN COMMUNIST PARTY

Below follows the text of the indictments presented by the Federal Superior Court for the Southern District of New York against 12 leaders of the Communist Party.

The first indictment was presented against all 12 leaders as a group. The second indictment was presented against each leader as an individual.

The reader can read and reread the indictments as many times as he likes, but he won't find the slightest accusation or even insinuation that any of the individuals mentioned in the indictment or the Communist Party as a whole actually committed or encouraged any acts of violence against the government.

Superior Court Indictments:

1. That since April 1, 1945, or about that time, and until the time of writing of this indictment, in the Southern District of New York and other places, the accused, namely William Foster, Eugene Dennis, John B. Williamson, Jack Stachel, Robert G. Thompson, Benjamin J. Davis (Jr.), Henry Winston, John Gates, Irving Potash, Gilbert Green, Carl Winter, and Gus Hall intentionally, unlawfully, and consciously entered into—with various other persons unknown to the Superior Court—a conspiracy for the purpose of organizing an association, group, and assembly of persons, under the guise of the Communist Party of the United States, for the purpose of advocating and defending the idea of the violent overthrow and destruction of the government of the United States, which is prohibited by Article 2 of the Law of June 28, 1940 (Article 10, Paragraph 18 of the United States Code), which in common parlance is known as the Smith Act.

2. In the first part of this conspiracy the accused planned to convene, on June 2, 1945, or thereabouts, in the Southern District of New York a meeting of the National Council of the Communist Political Association for the purpose of adopting a resolution aimed at disbanding the Communist Political Association and organizing under the guise of the Communist Party of the United States an association, group, and assembly of persons dedicated to Marxist-Leninist principles and calling for the violent overthrow and destruction of the United States government.

3. Subsequently, in the following part of this conspiracy, the accused planned to convene on June 18, 1945, or thereabouts in the Southern District of New York a meeting of the National Committee of the Communist Political Association, at which the aforesaid resolution would be adopted and elaborated.

All of the above constitutes a violation of Articles 3 and 5 of the Law of June 28, 1940 (Articles 11 and 13, Paragraph 18 of the United States Code), which in common parlance is known as the Smith Act.

<u>Individual Indictments</u>

Below follows the text of the individual indictment presented against John Gates, the editor of the *Daily Worker*. Similar indictments were presented against each of the other 11 Communist leaders.

<u>Superior Court Indictments:</u>

1. That since July 26, 1945, or thereabouts, until the time of writing of this indictment, the Communist Party has been an association, group, and assembly of persons which has advocated and defended the violent overthrow and destruction of the government of the United States.

2. That since July 26, 1945, or thereabouts, until the time of writing of this indictment in the Southern District of New York, the accused, John Gates, was a member of the Communist Party of the United States, even though he was aware during the aforementioned period that the aforesaid Communist Party of the United States was and continues to be an association, group, and assembly of persons who advocate and defend the idea of the violent overthrow and destruction of the government of the United States.

The above constitutes a violation of Articles 10 and 13, Paragraph 18, of the U.S. Code.

RTSKhIDNI, fond 575, op. 5, d. 20, ll. 87–88, 501, 503.

DOCUMENT 278   *Resolution of the Secretariat of the Central Committee, July 31, 1954, organizing support for the Communist Party of the U.S.A. campaign for the liberation of political prisoners and congratulating the incarcerated Eugene Dennis on his fiftieth birthday*

No. [illegible]   <u>TOP SECRET</u>

Not for publication   <u>FOR VOTING</u>

R E S O L U T I O N

OF THE SECRETARIAT OF THE CENTRAL COMMITTEE

of the Communist Party of the Soviet Union

(Protocol No. Point from year 195___)

<u>A Matter of the National Committee of the Communist Party of the U.S.A.</u>

1. In connection with the appeal by the National Committee of the Communist Party of the U.S.A. for support in the campaign being conducted by the Communist Party of the U.S.A. for the liberation of political prisoners, representatives of Soviet public organizations in the World Federation of Trade Unions, the International Democratic Federation of Women, the Worldwide Federation of Democratic Youth, the International Association of Democratic Jurists, the International Organization of Journalists, and the International Federation of Fighters for Resistance to [Fascism] and Victims and Prisoners of Fascism are charged with raising the question, in these organizations, of increasing the struggle to liberate victims of Fascist persecution in the U.S.A. To entrust to the editors of the newspapers *Pravda, Komsomol'skaia Pravda, Literaturnaia Gazeta* to publish the appropriate materials on this question.

2. Send to the General Secretary of the Communist Party of the U.S.A., Eugene Dennis, a telegram of greeting (attached) from the Central Committee of the Communist Party of the Soviet Union on the occasion of his 50th birthday.

3. [illegible]

TO THE NATIONAL COMMITTEE OF THE COMMUNIST PARTY OF THE U.S.A.

The Central Committee of the Communist Party of the Soviet Union sends a fraternal greeting to Comrade Eugene Dennis, General Secretary of the Communist Party of the U.S.A., languishing in prison, in conjunction with his 50th birthday.

The fortitude and steadfastness manifested by Comrade Dennis in his struggle for the vital interests of the American working class, for peace, and for the democratic rights of the popular masses evoke sincere sympathy and respect among all proponents of peace and progress.

THE CENTRAL COMMITTEE OF THE COMMUNIST
PARTY OF THE SOVIET UNION

TSKhSD, fond 4, op. 9, d. 126, ll. 200–202.

DOCUMENT 279 *Transcription of a talk with the secretary of the National Committee of the Communist Party of the U.S.A., Williamson, August 20, 1956*

29524

NOT FOR PUBLICATION

TO THE CENTRAL COMMITTEE
OF THE COMMUNIST PARTY OF THE SOVIET UNION [*TSK KPSS*]

Comrade Williamson, the Secretary of the National Committee of the Communist Party of the United States, who has come to the Soviet Union for a vacation and medical care, expressed the views of our American comrades on the situation of the U.S. Communist Party in interviews with employees of the *TSK KPSS* Department of Relations with Foreign Communist Parties. I am forwarding the transcript of an interview with Comrade Williamson on the subject.

Head of the Department of Relations
with Foreign Communist Parties
of the *TSK KPSS*   [signed] B. Ponomarev

August 20, 1956

No. 25-S-1779

TRANSCRIPT OF AN INTERVIEW
With Comrade Williamson,
The Secretary of the National Committee
of the Communist Party of the United States

Comrade Williamson, the Secretary of the National Committee of the Communist Party of the United States (CP U.S.A.), who has come to the Soviet Union for a vacation and medical care, informed us that the situation in the U.S. Communist Party is bad and getting worse. Comrade Williamson said that in a recent letter to him, Dennis described the current situation in the party as tense and even more critical than in 1945, i.e., at the time of the Browder faction's short-lived triumph. [According to Williamson:]

For all intents and purposes, the party is divided into two factions. On one side there is the faction led by Foster, Dennis, Davis, and Winter. This group understands the issues correctly, but has been slow to respond to events as they unfold and has failed to take an energetic and resolute stance. The second faction, which has been acting in a provocative manner, is led by Gates, the editor of the *Daily Worker* newspaper. It consists of such prominent employees of the *Daily Worker* as Alan Max and Joseph Clark and the writer Howard Fast. All the evidence indicates that Steve Nelson supports this faction. By the way, it would be worth mentioning that Nelson was born in Yugoslavia. For many years he supported the correct policies. As we know, Nelson was the leader of one of the internationalist brigades in Spain. After the break between the *KPSS* and the Communist League of Yugoslavia, Nelson led the U.S. Communist Party's campaign against Tito. This factor may have played some role in Nelson's current stance. With respect to Max Weiss, he is obviously wavering and has refused to take a stand, although he is leaning to the right-wingers.

Gates's faction is panic-stricken. The recent troubling events have shaken the faction. The situation has been made even more complicated by the support for this faction from the party's New York organization, which contains a large number of Jews. As we know, New York is not an industrial center. The middle and petty bourgeoisie account for much of the population, a large percentage of which are Jews. But the New York organization plays a unique role in our party, because it accounts for 40% of our membership. In light of all this, Comrade Dennis, as he indicated in his letter, was forced to make certain concessions to the right-wingers on some issues, which was dictated by his desire to avoid an irreversible split in the party.

In the spring of 1956 the *Daily Worker* newspaper, whose editor is John Gates, initiated a so-called discussion of topics related to the 20th Congress of the *KPSS*. Gates steered the discussion in the wrong direction from the very beginning. The newspaper almost never mentions the successes of the Soviet Union. It has viewed all the issues solely through the prism of the personality cult. The newspaper has published a large number of anti-Soviet articles. The *Daily Worker* printed and distributed a version of Khrushchev's speech on the personality cult originally published by the U.S. State Department, which provided even more encouragement to the party's enemies in their efforts to split the party. We should also point out that the Connecticut state party organization published an open letter to Comrade Mao Tse Tung demanding the release of Americans arrested in China.

Gates placed the so-called Jewish question in the Soviet Union at the center of the "discussion." He launched a scathing attack on George Allen, who had analyzed the issue from the correct point of view. It is typical that a major article I submitted to the *Daily Worker* which was critical of the current policies of the editors was never published under the pretext that I was out of the United States at the time.

The situation has been made even more difficult by the fact that, in the face of fierce attacks of the American bourgeois propaganda machine against the Soviet Union and the *KPSS*, the Soviet press has failed to respond in any way to the assaults on the Soviet Union on the Jewish question.

The tone which has characterized the newspaper's "discussion" is completely incompatible with the attitude a Communist newspaper should have towards the Soviet Union and its Communist Party as a fraternal party. After the news of Bagirov's execution, Max Weiss wrote a new article for the *Daily Worker* which poured even more oil on the fire. Weiss also published an article which praised American bourgeois democracy and totally rejected the doctrine of the dictatorship of the proletariat and the class struggle. The paper has also launched systematic attacks on the principle of democratic centralism in the *KPSS* and other Communist parties.

The right-wing faction has not limited itself to attacks on the Soviet Union. It has begun a sweeping revision of what the U.S. Communist Party has accomplished over the last decade. It has declared that the U.S. Communist Party accomplished absolutely nothing over the last decade. In my opinion it was no coincidence that they raised the issue at this particular juncture. The fact that the newspaper spends all its time looking back instead of ahead is also noteworthy. We also cannot ignore the fact that the paper has published materials which have resurrected the old idea of "American exceptionalism" in a new form. The paper has also attacked the works of Comrade Foster. In their attacks on our party, the right-wingers have attributed the difficult situation in the party not to the circumstances which have emerged in the United States in recent years but to our party's supposedly servile devotion to the *KPSS* and Soviet Union over the years.

After the *TSK KPSS* resolution of June 30, the situation in the party began to improve somewhat. Nevertheless I consider the CP U.S.A. National Committee's resolution on the *KPSS* resolution a step backward. The National Committee's resolution emphasizes that the CP U.S.A. is "an independent Marxist party." But independent of whom, we might ask?

Comrade Dennis's letters have also informed me that the party's New York organization is having the most difficulty, and that the farther away you get from New York the better the party's situation is. Comrade Foster's health has steadily deteriorated. Comrade Dennis, who is suffering from heart disease, is also in poor health. The doctors have insisted that Comrade Dennis take a two-month vacation.

It seems to me that despite the extremely critical situation in the party, it could be changed for the better. I believe that the majority on the National Committee, which supports the correct policies, will be able to keep control. In this case it will be extremely important to maintain the unity that exists between Foster and Dennis. We should remember that they have had disagreements in the past. I know that Foster gave a certain amount of support to Thompson and Davis, who once advocated sectarian policies. But Dennis also has his shortcomings. He is incapable of getting the entire collective involved and only works with a certain group of comrades. But I am convinced that at present the party doesn't have anyone who is Dennis's equal and who could take his place.

So what are the root causes of the current predicament the CP U.S.A. now finds itself in? I would like to focus on two issues which I believe deserve special consideration.

First of all, the State Department's publication of Comrade Khrushchev's secret speech shocked the party. The situation became even more difficult when the Polish Yiddish newspaper, *Folks-Shtime* [The People's Voice], published its well-known article on the persecution of Jews in the Soviet Union.

I would like to emphasize that the Jewish question is especially important for our party. There are 2,000,000 Jews in New York alone. Jews have always played a major role in the progressive movement in our country, including a prominent role in the Communist Party. Before the war, a process of Jewish assimilation was underway. The Nazi atrocities against the Jewish population temporarily halted this process and became a factor which strengthened Jewish solidarity. Jews have begun to react more painfully than before to everything pertinent to the situation of Jews in other countries, including the Soviet Union. Over the entire history of the Soviet Union, Soviet Jewish policy, especially after Comrade Stalin's statement that anti-Semitism was banned in the Soviet Union, led American Jews to develop a profound respect for the Soviet Union. Now the situation has changed dramatically. I believe that the bourgeois press has stepped up its agitation over the Jewish question in the Soviet Union for the express purpose of distracting attention from the plight of the Negroes in America.

We, the leaders of the American Communist Party, believe that the Soviet Union cannot remain indifferent to the attacks against it on the Jewish question. Our Soviet comrades should provide a clarification. There is an urgent need for the publication of some sort of statement from the Soviet leadership on the matter. I personally believe that they had the opportunity to do so in drafting the *TSK KPSS* resolution of June 30. I also believe that the Soviet comrades made a mistake when they deleted the passages on the Soviet Jewish question from Dennis's article in *Pravda*. This merely gave American reactionary circles a new pretext for attacks on the Soviet Union. I should also mention that Comrade Furtseva's interview with Petran, the correspondent of the newspaper *The National Guardian*, was unsatisfactory and is being used by American reactionaries to intensify their anti-Soviet campaign.

In my opinion the second most important reason for the situation in the American Communist Party is that the party's leadership, in the person of Comrades Foster and Dennis, has taken a wait-and-see position and has not launched an active and decisive campaign against the right-wing faction led by Gates.

With respect to Comrade Potash and myself, I was in complete agreement with the *TSK KPSS* resolution of June 30. It answered many previously unanswered questions. I personally believe that if

Comrade Khrushchev's speech on the personality cult had been delivered in the same way that this resolution was written, we could have avoided a lot of problems.

Digressing somewhat from the main topic, I would like to say that I am profoundly convinced that in the current political environment, it would be very important for the Communist parties of the world to establish some sort of body or forum where they could exchange views on important policy matters.

What do I believe should be done to help our party in its current difficult situation?

1) In light of the importance of the Jewish question in the United States, we desperately need the Soviet comrades to issue some sort of policy statement on the issue. We are in desperate need of some kind of speech, interview, or lead editorial which would say, for example, that a number of Jewish figures did suffer in the Soviet Union in past years, but that this could in no way be construed as anti-Semitism, because Russians, Ukrainians, Georgians, and others suffered even more. The statement should then go on to say that the *TSK KPSS* is now taking steps to rectify the situation. Our Soviet comrades should realize that without this kind of statement it will be very difficult for us to operate and that the situation of the CP U.S.A. could hardly change for the better.

2) I understand very well that the *KPSS* has no need to intervene directly in our party's current affairs. But at the same time the *KPSS* cannot remain indifferent. I believe it would be very useful for the *TSK KPSS* to send personal letters to Comrades Foster and Dennis to offer them moral support in their efforts to preserve the party.

3) We need to find some kind of forum for Comrade Mao Tse Tung or Comrade Togliatti to give their assessment of the situation in the CP U.S.A. which would express their confidence that the party will be able to extricate itself from its current predicament in the right way under the leadership of Comrades Foster and Dennis. I believe that these speeches should place special emphasis on the issue of proletarian internationalism, on the proper standards for relationships between fraternal parties, and the proper limits for criticism of fraternal parties, in order to make the point that the Gates faction has exceeded these limits in its criticism of the *KPSS*. They should also emphasize how Marxists should interpret the concept of democratic centralism in the party.

4) It would also be advisable to send articles on the *Daily Worker*'s position to the newspapers *L'Humanité* and *Unità*. In particular, it would be worthwhile for these articles to describe the good examples set by the international Communist press in discussing the issues related to the 20th Congress of the *KPSS*.

5) It would be useful if the leading newspapers and journals of the *KPSS* published any kind of material in support of Comrades Foster and Dennis.

6) It would be appropriate to ask Comrades Thorez, Pollitt, Prestes, and other prominent figures in the world Communist movement to write letters to Comrades Foster and Dennis.

7) If all these efforts fail to improve the situation in the CP U.S.A., I believe we should ask Comrade Duclos to write a major article which would frankly discuss the situation in the CP U.S.A.. Comrade Duclos is the best man for the job, because his article against Browder earned him great popularity in our party.

8) With respect to Howard Fast, I believe we shouldn't consider him a defector to the enemy camp at this point. It would be useful if our Soviet comrades were to provide moral support for Fast in some way or another and avoid alienating him. For example, it would be worthwhile to continue publishing his works in the Soviet Union. I believe it would also be good if Sholokhov or another prominent Soviet writer were to write Fast a friendly letter and try to influence him. It would also be quite helpful if some prominent French writers would write these kinds of letters to Fast.

Transcript of interview by: [signed] V. Korionov

TSKhSD, fond 5, op. 28, d. 438.

chapter 10

WARTIME POLICIES AND WARTIME ALLIANCE

World War II brought the United States and the Soviet Union together as allies for the first time. Even before Germany's declaration of war against the United States after the Japanese attack at Pearl Harbor forced America to enter the war against Hitler as well as Japan, the U.S. government had contributed material aid to the Soviet defense effort through the Lend-Lease Act. But the alliance between the United States, Great Britain, and the Soviet Union was not a foregone outcome of the diplomatic maneuvering that preceded Hitler's war in Europe.

The Soviet government had used a war scare as early as 1927 to help justify rapid mobilization of its industry and population. In that year the alleged enemy was Great Britain; Hitler was still an insignificant politician in Weimar Germany. Again, in 1931, Stalin stressed the danger of war and the need for Soviet industrialization to prepare for the nation's defense: "One feature of the history of old Russia was the continual beatings she suffered for falling behind, for her backwardness. . . . All beat her—for her backwardness: for military backwardness, for industrial backwardness, for agricultural backwardness. She was beaten because to do so was profitable and could be done with impunity. . . . That is why we must no longer lag behind. We are fifty or a hundred years behind the advanced countries. We must make good this distance in ten years. Either we do it, or they crush us."[1] When Hitler came to

1. Joseph Stalin, *Leninism* (Moscow, 1940), pp. 365–6, as quoted in John Barber and Mark Harrison, *The Soviet Home Front, 1941–1945* (London, 1991), pp. 3–4.

power in 1933 with his explicit anti-Communist program, Germany and fascism assumed the role as the most dangerous enemy, and the USSR sought to join the European collective security network in order to ward off German aggression. The Soviet armaments industry also began to develop new weapons, including bacteriological ones, as indicated in Document 280.

Excluded from the 1938 Munich accord that appeased Hitler's demands for expansion into Czechoslovakia, the Soviet Union continued to try to form an alliance with France and Great Britain against Germany, but diplomatic talks faltered in the summer of 1939. Nonetheless, the world was stunned when on August 23, 1939, Germany and the USSR announced that they had signed a mutual nonaggression pact, pledging neutrality in the case of war with a third party. The public features of the pact left Hitler free to invade Poland without fear of Soviet retaliation, and he did so on September 1, 1939, plunging Europe into the Second World War. The secret supplementary protocols, included here as Document 281, carved Eastern Europe into spheres of influence between Germany and the Soviet Union. Shortly after the Germans invaded Poland, the Red Army advanced first into eastern Poland, then attacked Finland and won territorial gains, and in 1940 annexed the three Baltic republics of Estonia, Latvia, and Lithuania.

Mysteries remain about the intentions of the Soviet Union and its preparedness for war. Did Stalin seek the Nazi-Soviet Pact to buy time to strengthen his defenses, or was expansion into Eastern Europe his primary goal? Was Stalin preparing a preemptive offensive strike against Germany? Did Stalin suffer a nervous collapse when he heard the news of the German invasion on June 22, 1941, as certain memoirists alleged in the 1960s? Some argue that if Stalin had known that war was inevitable, he would not have eliminated the cream of the general staff in the military purge of 1937. The psychological atmosphere created by the agreement between Germany and the Soviet Union and the call for peace with fascism disarmed foreign communists, particularly in France, and rendered that country much more vulnerable to the coming Nazi invasion.

Grave doubts remain about Soviet military preparations in the spring and early summer of 1941. It is well documented that Stalin received numerous warnings about an imminent German invasion, but there were serious deficiencies in Soviet defenses. Old interior defense lines had actually been dismantled after the signing of the Nazi-Soviet Pact, and new installations were not scheduled for completion until 1942. There is some evidence, including that of troop movements, that Stalin may have been planning an offensive strike against Germany in the summer of 1941. New discussions and historical accounts in Gorbachev's USSR have given much more weight to the role of the common soldiers and popular patriotism in the eventual victory over the Nazis, diminishing Stalin's canonic role as the hero of the war. These new documents offer tantalizing glimpses into greater treasures still to be found, but writing the history of the USSR's Great Patriotic War will require much more sifting of memoirs and masses of archival documents.

The United States' role in the alliance has been documented from the American side, but these documents from Soviet archives provide fuller detail than ever before. Joseph Davies, the U.S. ambassador to the Soviet Union during the purge trials, included much of his letter to Stalin (Document 284) in his 1941 memoir, *Mission to Moscow*, but he omitted the initial fawning praise of Stalin. The extent of United States support, through Lend-Lease and other programs, was never fully admitted by the Soviet leadership. Some of the correspondence included here between Roosevelt, Truman, and Stalin had been published previously in the U.S., but it is significant that these documents were preserved in the highly sensitive Archive of the President of the Russian Federation.

DOCUMENT 280   ***Memorandum to Stalin on the use of bacteria in future warfare, March 27, 1934***

> March 27, 1934
> <u>Top Secret</u>
> <u>For personal signature</u>
> <u>on packet only</u>

> To Comrade Stalin

I am sending you a draft of the principles, staff, and estimates for the chemical-bacteriological effort which were worked out by the commission of Comrades Fishman, Gai, Velikanov, and Demikhovskii per our instructions.

The suggested organization, which (with your assistance) we shall attempt to staff with suitable people, should satisfy the preconditions to undertake this effort.

I request your approval of the attached proposals.

Please return the eight-page attachment to me, since this is the only copy.

> K. Voroshilov

To the People's Commissar of Military and Naval Affairs and Chairman of the Military Council of the USSR, Comrade K. E. Voroshilov

> from Senior Scientists of Section 9
> Scientific Research Chemical Institute,
> Chemical Warfare Directorate,
> Workers' and Peasants' Red Army,
> Comrades Nikolai Nikolaevich Ginsburg and
> Abram Moiseevich IUrkovskii

> Memorandum

The question of using bacteria in future warfare has received considerable attention among imperialist countries over the years. A large number of the scientists and military specialists listed below are involved in theoretical and practical research on this topic. The information that finds its way into the press and the echelons on which the topic is being discussed demonstrate beyond a doubt that this issue has long since passed from the discussion stage as a hypothetical matter and is now at a stage where the technical means and tactical conditions for its application are being developed.

Now the problem of bacteriological warfare has begun to be examined for the first time in the USSR at the initiative of the head of the Chemical Warfare Directorate, Comrade IA. M. Fishman. From 1926 to 1928 in a special laboratory created for this purpose, the first satisfactory results were achieved, making it possible to continue research on special offensive and defensive topics. From 1928, with the arrival of Comrade Velikanov as director of the laboratory, a man who underestimated the possibility of simultaneous and balanced research on both defensive and offensive topics, until mid-1930 the laboratory almost completely switched over to research on bacteriological defense. This development caused substantive disagreements and conflict between Comrade Velikanov and some of his colleagues in the Military Medical Directorate of the Workers' and Peasants' Red Army. After mid-1930 it switched over to research on offense and mechanical defense. In three years of work it has achieved concrete results that make it possible at this time to state with confidence that not only has a fundamental resolution of the feasibility of bacteriological warfare been accomplished in principle, but also a concrete prototype of a bacteriological weapon has been developed.

In the intervening period the efforts of the section have proven: 1) that a number of already-studied bacteria—anthrax, tularemia (causing plaguelike illness)—have weapon applications and that there is no reason in principle not to transfer this conclusion [break in the text]

. . . in the course of conducting the work, required an unnecessary expenditure of effort and energy, injected a great deal of tension into their work, and hindered the observance of critical safety technology requirements, and as a result of the latter, a number of specific illnesses (anthrax, tularemia, and "Maltese fever") infected employees of the section.

But the view that prevailed in our country, the USSR, toward the research conducted by Section 9 was manifested not only in difficult living conditions. Constant uncertainty regarding the prospects of developing [cropped term], constantly changing research directions and paces, the failure of plans, and many other similar phenomena were common occurrences in the life of Section 9. As an illustration we might point out just two canceled expeditions (1931, 1933) to a remote location for practical field testing of the section's laboratory innovations; in preparation for the expeditions much energy and effort were expended, a waste that painfully affected the section staff members.

The underestimation of the entire problem also was manifested in personnel policy. The often-raised question of the need to enlist communist professors (Suknev, Elin, and others) to research this problem did not find the requisite support from the leadership of Section 9 for reasons that cannot be considered honorable. Meanwhile, the scientific staff of the section (by and large young) in the course of their work had to cope with a whole range of problems that required specialized knowledge and vast experience, which, given the complete isolation of the scientific staff of the section from the outside world, created additional difficulties and greatly retarded solution of the problems assigned to the section.

The preceding discussion far from covers the large number of organizational and other deficiencies that slowed the necessary development of the effort undertaken by Section 9. The entire work of Section 9 was permeated by these troubles, which affected the work of the section in the most adverse way. The majority of these troubles were not insurmountable, but the complete lack of initiative and character of the former director of Section 9 Comrade Demikhovskii, his inability to supervise, his lack of authority within the section, and his inability to demonstrate to the command the necessity and importance of large-scale development of the project entrusted to him led to the mothballing of the department as a result of recent events, and all of its staff have been released.

Working in this area from the very beginning of its research in the USSR, and understanding the extraordinary importance and the urgency of this problem for our defense, we consider it our civic duty to protest most categorically the lack of appreciation we in the USSR have had with regard to this topic. The suspension of this effort at a time when it is being actively researched abroad is simply intolerable.

In bringing all the above to your attention, we ask you to get this effort back on track immediately and resolutely and assign it the priority and resources that it deserves.

We believe that it is necessary to:

1) Reactivate this project as quickly as possible.

2) Give it the fullest opportunity to grow and develop normally within the Chemical Warfare Directorate system, having made the appropriate decisions on personnel, resources, facilities, etc.

3) Replace the front-line management of the section, i.e., Demikhovskii, who could not cope with his assigned task, who was not able to provide authoritative leadership for the project, who discredited himself and led the project to its suspension.

We are certain that your personal involvement will inspire the staff of former Section 9, which always approached its work with exceptional love, enthusiasm, and selflessness in completing the most weighty mission entrusted to it by the Party and the Government—to give our Red Army prototypes of a new state-of-the-art weapon.

Senior Scientist: Dr. Nik. Nik. Ginsburg

Senior Scientist: Dr. A. M. IUrkovskii

Moscow

March 28, 1934

Source?

Molotov-Ribbentrop Pact

Along with the public sections of the pact negotiated between the two foreign ministers, Molotov and Ribbentrop, a series of secret protocols was negotiated that divided the countries between the USSR and Germany into spheres of influence. Initially, the treaty granted the Soviet Union freedom of action in Finland, Estonia, Latvia, and eastern Poland in the north, and Bessarabia in southeastern Europe. After the fall of Poland in September, an additional codicil gave the USSR control over Lithuania in exchange for specified payments in gold and commodities. Acting on these understandings, the USSR moved into "its" half of Poland shortly after the German invasion from the west, declared war on Finland in the autumn of 1939, annexed Estonia, Latvia, and Lithuania in the summer of 1940, and extended Soviet power in areas of Ukraine and Belorussia that had formerly belonged to Poland. Various justifications for these moves have been offered by Soviet leaders and historians. Khrushchev, for example, claimed that control of the Baltic republics prevented their being used as a beachhead for a capitalist assault after the end of World War Two.

Existence of the secret supplementary protocols was widely assumed and was confirmed with publication of German war documents. But the Soviet Union always denied the existence of any secret treaties, for to acknowledge them would have discredited the official claim that the annexation of the Baltic republics represented a popular liberation. When the Estonian press announced the details of the Molotov-Ribbentrop Pact in August 1988, Soviet authorities still stubbornly denied that they existed. The dissident historian Roy Medvedev speculated that Stalin had destroyed the protocols; Soviet officials claimed that efforts to find the original protocols in Soviet archives had proved fruitless, and questioned the authenticity of the documents cited in the West. But in 1992, after the collapse of the Soviet Union, the protocols published here were released from the special archive of the Central Committee, confirming what the rest of the world had known all along.

DOCUMENT 281   *Secret Texts of the Molotov-Ribbentrop Nonaggression Pact*

1. Original texts of Soviet-German secret
    <u>agreements concluded in the 1939–1941 period</u>

1) Secret supplementary protocol on the border of the spheres of interest of Germany and the USSR. Signed by V. M. Molotov and Ribbentrop on August 23, 1939. [handwritten annotation:] *Copy to Comrade Stalin

2) Clarification of the secret supplementary protocol of August 23, 1939. Signed by V. M. Molotov and Schulenburg on August 28, 1939.

3) Confidential protocol concerning the possibility of resettling the population residing within the spheres of interest of the governments of the USSR and Germany. Signed by V. M. Molotov and Ribbentrop on September 28, 1939.

4) Secret supplementary protocol on changing the Soviet-German agreement of August 23 with regard to the spheres of interest of Germany and the USSR. Signed by V. M. Molotov and Ribbentrop on September 28, 1939.

5) Secret supplementary protocol on preventing Polish agitation on the territory of the other treaty signatory. Signed by V. M. Molotov and Ribbentrop on September 28, 1939.

6) Protocol on Germany's renunciation of claims to the part of the territory of Lithuania indicated in the secret supplementary protocol of September 28, 1939. Signed by V. M. Molotov and Schulenburg on January 10, 1941.

7) September 28, 1939, declaration of the Soviet and German governments on mutual consultation.
    (In Russian and German)

8) Exchange of letters between V. M. Molotov and Ribbentrop on September 28, 1939, concerning economic relations between the USSR and Germany.
    (In Russian and German, along with drafts)

9) Two maps of Polish territory with the signatures of J. V. Stalin and Ribbentrop.

<u>Ministry of Foreign Affairs of the USSR</u>
1. Secret supplementary protocol on the border of the spheres of interest of Germany and the USSR. Signed by V. M. Molotov and Ribbentrop
<u>   August 23, 1939   </u>

<u>SECRET SUPPLEMENTARY PROTOCOL.</u>

In signing the nonaggression pact between Germany and the Union of Soviet Socialist Republics, the undersigned plenipotentiaries of the two sides discussed in strict confidentiality the issue of delimiting the spheres of mutual interest in Eastern Europe. This discussion led to the following result:

1. In the event of territorial-political reorganization of the districts making up the Baltic states (Finland, Estonia, Latvia, Lithuania), the northern border of Lithuania is simultaneously the border of the spheres of interest of Germany and the USSR. The interests of Lithuania with respect to the Vilnius district are recognized by both sides.

2. In the event of territorial-political reorganization of the districts making up the Polish Republic, the border of the spheres of interest of Germany and the USSR will run approximately along the Pisa, Narew, Vistula, and San rivers.

The question of whether it is in the [signatories'] mutual interest to preserve the independent Polish State and what the borders of that state will be can be ascertained conclusively only in the course of future political development.

In any event, both governments will resolve this matter through friendly mutual agreement.

3. Concerning southeastern Europe, the Soviet side emphasizes the interest of the USSR in Bessarabia. The German side declares its complete political disinterest in these areas.

4. This protocol will be held in strict secrecy by both sides.

Moscow, August 23, 1939

[handwritten:]
With the authorization of
the Government of the USSR
[signed] V. Molotov

For the Government of Germany
[signed] Ribbentrop

Ministry of Foreign Affairs of the USSR

2. Clarification of the secret supplementary protocol of August 23, 1939. Signed by V. M. Molotov and Schulenburg on August 28, 1939

CLARIFICATION OF THE "SECRET SUPPLEMENTARY PROTOCOL" OF AUGUST 23, 1939.

In order to clarify the first paragraph of point 2 of the "Secret Supplementary Protocol" of August 23, 1939, this is to explain that said paragraph is to be read in the following final version, namely:

"2. In the event of the territorial-political reorganization of the districts making up the Polish State, the border of the spheres of interest of Germany and the USSR will run approximately along the Pisa, Narew, Vistula, and San rivers."

Moscow, August 28, 1939.

WITH THE AUTHORIZATION OF
THE GOVERNMENT OF THE USSR

[signed] V. Molotov.

FOR THE GOVERNMENT OF
GERMANY

[signed] F. W. Graf v. d. Schulenburg

SECRET PROTOCOL.

SECRET PROTOCOL

The Chairman of the Council of People's Commissars of the USSR V. M. Molotov, with the authorization of the Government of the USSR on one side, and German Ambassador Count von der Schulenburg, with the authorization of the Government of Germany on the other side, have concurred on the following:

1. The government of Germany renounces its claims to the part of the territory of Lithuania indicated in the Secret Supplementary Protocol of September 28, 1939, and shown on the map that is attached to this Protocol;

2. The Government of the USSR agrees to compensate the Government of Germany for the territory indicated in point 1 of the present Protocol with a payment to Germany in the amount of 7,500,000 gold dollars, the equivalent of 31,500,000 German marks.

Payment of the sum of 31.5 million German marks will be made as follows: one-eighth, i.e., 3,937,500 German marks, in deliveries of nonferrous metals over a three-month period beginning from the day of signing of the present Protocol, and the remaining seven-eighths, i.e., 27,562,500 German marks, in gold through deductions from German payments of gold that the German side has to make before February 11, 1941, based on an exchange of letters between the People's Commissar of Foreign Trade of the USSR A. I. Mikoyan and the Chairman of the German Economic Delegation Mr. Schnurre that took place in conjunction with the signing of the "Agreement of January 10, 1941, on Mutual Deliveries of Commodities for the Second Treaty Period according to the Economic Agreement of February 11, 1940, between the USSR and Germany."

3. The present Protocol has been prepared in two Russian and two German originals and comes into force immediately upon signing.

Moscow, January 10, 1941

With the authorization of   For the Government of Germany
the Government of the USSR

[signed] V. Molotov   [signed] Schulenburg

Ministry of Foreign Affairs of the USSR

> 3. Confidential protocol concerning the possibility of resettling the population residing within the spheres of interest of the governments of the USSR and Germany. Signed by V. M. Molotov and Ribbentrop on September 28, 1939.

CONFIDENTIAL PROTOCOL.

The Government of the USSR will not impede German citizens or other persons of German ancestry residing within its spheres of interest should they desire to move to Germany or to German spheres of interest. It agrees that this resettlement will be conducted by persons authorized by the German Government in accordance with responsible local authorities and that in the process the property rights of the resettled persons will not be infringed.

The German Government assumes the same obligation with respect to persons of Ukrainian or Belorussian ancestry residing within its spheres of interest.

Moscow, September 28, 1939

With the authorization of
the Government of the USSR

For the German
Government

[signed] V. Molotov

[signed] J. Ribbentrop

Ministry of Foreign Affairs of the USSR

4. Secret supplementary protocol on changing the Soviet-German agreement of August 23 concerning the spheres of interest of Germany and the USSR. Signed by V. M. Molotov and Ribbentrop on September 28, 1939.

SECRET SUPPLEMENTARY PROTOCOL.

The undersigned plenipotentiaries state the concurrence of the German Government and the Government of the USSR in the following:

Point 1 of the secret supplementary protocol signed on August 23, 1939, is changed so that the territory of the Lithuanian state is included in the sphere of interest of the USSR because, on the other side, Lublin voivodeship and parts of Warsaw voivodeship are included in the sphere of interest of Germany (see map accompanying the Treaty on Friendship and the Border between the USSR and Germany, signed today). As soon as the Government of the USSR takes special measures on Lithuanian territory to protect its interests, the present German-Lithuanian border, with the objective of making it a natural and simple border, will be adjusted so that the Lithuanian territory that lies southwest of the line shown on the map goes to Germany.

It is further stated that economic agreements between Germany and Lithuania now in force must not be broken by the aforementioned measures by the Soviet Union.

[handwritten:]

With the Authorization of
the Government of the USSR
[signed] V. Molotov

For the Government of
the German Reich
[signed] J. Ribbentrop

September 28, 1939

5. Secret supplementary protocol on preventing Polish agitation on the territory of the other treaty signatory. Signed by V. M. Molotov and Ribbentrop <u>on September 28, 1939.</u>

SECRET SUPPLEMENTARY PROTOCOL

The undersigned plenipotentiaries, in concluding the Soviet-German treaty on the border and friendship, have stated their concurrence in the following:

Neither side will permit on their territories any sort of Polish agitation affecting the territory of the other country. They [will] abort such agitation on their own territories and will inform each other as to effective measures to accomplish this.

With the authorization of the Government of the USSR	For the Government of Germany
[signed] V. Molotov	[signed] J. Ribbentrop

Moscow, September 28, 1939.

Archive of the Central Committee

DOCUMENT 282   ***Troop strength orders for the Red Army, May 9, 1940***

<u>TOP SECRET</u>
<u>EXTREMELY URGENT</u>
Copy No. 3

PEOPLE'S COMMISSAR
OF DEFENSE OF THE USSR

May 9, 1940

TO THE POLITBURO OF THE CENTRAL COMMITTEE
ALL-RUSSIAN COMMUNIST PARTY (BOLSHEVIK) [*TSK VKP(b)*]

<u>Comrade STALIN J. V.</u>

TO THE COUNCIL OF PEOPLE'S COMMISSARS
OF THE USSR

<u>Comrade MOLOTOV V. M.</u>

[Stamp of Soviet Army
Central National Archives]

The operational organization and strength of the Red Army for all service arms were reviewed and approved by the Defense Committee on December 1, 1939 (Order No. 433 of the Commissar of Defense). However the military operations underway against the White Finns made it impossible to implement the government's decisions. The war with the White Finns resulted in the organization of new artillery, air, and other service arms and an increase in the strength of the Red Army.

After the end of the war, we reviewed and on April 4, 1940, approved the organization and strength of the infantry and efforts to reinforce the troops assigned to the Transcaucasus, North Caucasus, Odessa, and Kiev Military districts, but did not review the organization and strength of other service arms. At present, a commission of the Central Military Council is in the process of submitting a number of valuable proposals for the organization of certain service arms based on the experience of the Finnish War. I, however, without waiting for the commission to complete its work, consider it necessary to review and approve the current organization of the Red Army, while making the necessary changes and additions to the organization of each service arm which are clearly needed right now, and adjust the numerical strength of the Red Army so as to eliminate the unneeded personnel who have been called up from the reserves. Subsequently, after the commission has completed its work, we can make the appropriate changes in the organizational structures of the individual service arms as needed within the authorized manpower limits.

For this purpose I would like to submit the following proposals for your consideration:

INFANTRY

The organization and strength of the infantry should be left as approved on April 4, 1940, with the following recent additions:

1. The strength of the infantry divisions in the First and Second Red Banner of Labor Armies should be increased by 550 men each, which would give us 15 12,550-man infantry divisions.

2. We should organize a Karelian-Finnish division with a strength of 9,000 men over and above the 160 authorized divisions but within the manpower limits established for the infantry of the Leningrad Military District. To accomplish this we should convert one 12,000-man division in the Leningrad Military District into a 6,000-man division and one 12,000-man division into a 9,000-man division.

Thus, the total number of infantry divisions in the Red Army would be equal to 161, with the following breakdown by numerical strength:

a) 14,000-man infantry divisions	3
b) 12,550-man infantry divisions	15
c) 12,000-man infantry divisions	80
d) 12,000-man mechanized infantry divisions	3
e) 12,000-man mechanized divisions	4
f) 9,000-man infantry divisions (the Sakhalin and Karelian-Finnish Divisions and one division in the Leningrad Military District)	3
g) 9,000-man mountain infantry divisions	10
h) 6,000-man infantry divisions	43
Total	161

The total numerical strength of the infantry, including corps headquarters, corps units, and supernumerary infantry units, would be equal to:

52 infantry corps headquarters with corps units but no corps artillery at peacetime strength	57,400 men
3 14,000-man infantry divisions	42,000 men

15 12,550-man infantry divisions	188,250 men
80 12,000-man infantry divisions	960,000 men
3 12,000-man mechanized infantry divisions	36,000 men
4 12,000-man mechanized divisions	48,000 men
3 9,000-man infantry divisions	27,000 men
10 mountain infantry divisions	90,000 men
43 6,000-man infantry divisions	258,000 men
3 6,098-man separate infantry brigades in the Far East	18,294 men
6 1,520-man airborne brigades	9,420 men
3 600-man motorcycle battalions	1,800 men
Total	1,736,164 men

This infantry strength does not include the separate infantry brigade dispatched to Hankow, because this brigade will be transferred to the navy.

CORPS AND HIGH COMMAND RESERVE ARTILLERY

Corps artillery has the same strength as authorized on December 1, 1939. Corps artillery has an authorized peacetime strength of 62 artillery regiments, but currently there are 61, because one regiment has been transferred to the High Command Reserve artillery.

My proposal calls for leaving corps artillery at 61 regiments and in wartime expanding them into 75 artillery regiments as soon as ordnance becomes available, which would give us a wartime strength of 29 corps consisting of two artillery regiments each and 35 corps consisting of one artillery regiment each. At present only some of the artillery regiments are at peacetime strength. My proposal calls for putting all the corps units at peacetime strength, with the exception of four artillery regiments which will be transferred to the Transcaucasus Military District.

During the war with the White Finns, the High Command Reserve artillery was augmented with 6 conventional artillery regiments, 5 152-mm howitzer regiments, 3 203-mm howitzer regiments, two separate BR-5 280-mm howitzer battalions, and two separate BR-2 conventional artillery battalions.

At present the High Command Reserve artillery consists of the following units:

Conventional artillery regiments	7
Howitzer regiments	17
Heavy conventional artillery regiments	1
Heavy howitzer regiments	20 [handwritten:] 35
Separate 152, 280, and 205-mm howitzer battalions	10
Separate BR-2 batteries	2

My proposal calls for keeping all of the current artillery regiments and bringing them to peacetime strength, with the exception of three 152-mm howitzer and two 203-mm howitzer regiments and a heavy battalion to be transferred to the Transcaucasus Military District.

Due to manpower problems, the artillery of the Transcaucasus Military District and the corps artillery of this district must be left at wartime strength for the time being, which will require additional manpower of 10,5000 men.

The total peacetime strength of the corps artillery and High Command Reserve artillery would be 153,000 men.

Keeping the Transcaucasus Military District artillery at wartime strength and the associated addition of 10,500 men would be accomplished by drawing from the reserve manpower pool.

CAVALRY

With respect to the cavalry, the partial reductions in force planned in December 1939 were never implemented because of the war with the White Finns. Instead of the planned conversion into a cavalry brigade, the 25th Cavalry Division was reorganized into a wartime mechanized cavalry division. The 72nd Cavalry Division of the Kiev Special Military District, which was to be reorganized into a mountain cavalry division, was left unchanged. During this time the 24th Cavalry Division was brought up to wartime strength and transferred to the Transcaucasus Military District.

Based on the earlier decision, my proposal calls for converting the 25th Cavalry Division of the Leningrad Military District into a separate cavalry brigade while leaving the other units with the same organization at peacetime strength as follows:

Cavalry corps headquarters with corps units	5	total of	2,030 men
6,560-man cavalry divisions	13	total of	85,280 men
6,821-man cavalry divisions in the Far East and Transbaikal Military Districts	4	total of	27,284 men
Mountain cavalry divisions	5	total of	14,750 men
3,543-man cavalry divisions	2	total of	7,086 men
Reserve cavalry regiments	6	total of	4,320 men
Separate cavalry brigades	2	total of	6,448 men
Maintenance detachments		total of	170 men
Total			147,428 men

In this case my proposal calls for returning the two cavalry regiments and artillery battalion of the cavalry division belonging to the Transbaikal Military District and currently stationed in the Mongolian People's Republic to their divisions, which had already been provided for by Order No. 433 of the Commissar of Defense.

ARMOR (TANKS)

During the war with the White Finns, our armor strength grew, with three separate tank regiments expanded into three separate tank brigades, along with a new BT (high-speed) tank brigade and two T-26 tank brigades. In addition, a tank regiment is now being converted into a tank brigade, and a new T-26 brigade is being organized in the Transcaucasus Military District.

At present the tank brigades which fought in the war against the White Finns are still at wartime strength, and our armor forces still include a separate machine gun infantry brigade which was previously part of an armor corps and fought in the war with Finland.

My proposal calls for reducing the tank brigades which are now at wartime strength to peacetime strength, with the exception of the three tank brigades which are currently stationed in Estonia, Latvia, and Lithuania and the two tank brigades in the Transcaucasus Military District, leaving the latter at wartime strength. The armor training battalion in the Transbaikal Military District which trained armor cadre from the Mongolian

People's Republic and the 15th Machine Gun Infantry Brigade should be disbanded. The 34th BT (High-Speed) Tank Brigade, which is underequipped, should be reorganized and assigned to a mechanized division.

In this case our tank and armor forces would be as follows:

T-35-*KV* tank brigades	1
T-28 tank brigades	3
BT (high-speed) tank brigades	16
T-26 tank brigades	18/38
Mechanized armor brigades	3
Separate tank regiments	6
The tank training regiment of the Military Mechanization and Motorization Academy	1
The mechanized armor training battalion	1
The total strength of tank and armored forces would be equal to	96,785 men

AIR FORCE

The strength of the air force was authorized at 230,000 men by Order No. 433 of the Commissar of Defense in 1939. Order No. 97 of February 26 of this year added 31,210 men to this total for the purpose of organizing new air regiments, while Order No. 139 of March 11 of this year authorized an additional 30,711 men for training pilots and maintenance personnel.

Thus the total authorized strength of the air force is   291,210 men

At present the actual strength of the air force is 293,271 men, including 103,646 men in military schools.

My proposal calls for leaving the air force at the strength authorized by the Government (291,210 men).

THE FORCES ASSIGNED TO FORTIFIED AREAS

The number of troops assigned to fortified areas was set at 48,000 men by Order No. 433 of last year. Keeping the forces assigned to the Dniester fortified areas at wartime strength has meant that fortified area troops continue to be overstrength and currently number 105,500 men.

In light of the impossibility of reducing the forces in the Dniester fortified areas to peacetime manpower levels and the need to organize units for the new fortified areas in the Transcaucasus and Kiev Military Districts, we must, for the time being, authorize a strength of 75,000 men for the forces assigned to the fortified areas.

CHEMICAL FLAMETHROWER UNITS

At present our chemical flamethrower units include 3 flamethrower tank brigades, two separate flamethrower battalions, and 1 experimental flamethrower battalion. My proposal calls for disbanding the separate flamethrower battalions and giving the flamethrower tank brigades a total authorized strength of 6,700 men.

MORTAR UNITS

Until now mortar units have been classified as chemical units. During the Finnish War these units were extensively used as High Command Reserve mortar units. My proposal calls for beefing up the mortar units and organizing two new separate High Command Reserve mortar battalions this year. Subsequently, as ordnance becomes available, the number of mortar units will become even larger.

This year the Red Army should have a total of 8 separate High Command Reserve mortar battalions with a total strength of 2,900 men.

AIR DEFENSE FORCES

The total authorized strength of the air defense forces in December of last year was set at 75,000 men.

The war with Finland and the need to reinforce the Transcaucasus, Odessa, and Kiev Military Districts made it necessary to strengthen the air defense forces. The following units were organized for this purpose: an air defense artillery regiment in Baku, five air defense artillery battalions in Moscow, and twenty medium-caliber air defense artillery battalions and seven small-caliber air defense artillery battalions to reinforce the Transcaucasus, Odessa, and Kiev Military Districts.

The air defense forces now include:

Anti-aircraft artillery regiments	23
High Command Reserve anti-aircraft artillery regiments	1
Separate anti-aircraft artillery battalions	51
Air defense regiments	12
Separate air defense battalions	45
Anti-aircraft machine gun regiments	4
Separate anti-aircraft machine gun battalions	2
Obstruction balloon regiments	3
Separate obstruction balloon battalions	5
Air observation, warning, and communications regiments	6
Separate air observation, warning, and communications battalions	20
Separate air observation, warning and communications companies	9
Searchlight regiments	4
Separate searchlight battalions	11
Moscow Air Defense regiments	3
Moscow Air Defense battalions	4
Air defense signal battalions	4

Plans call for bringing all units to peacetime strength, with the exception of the Transcaucasus and Odessa Military Districts, which will be left at wartime strength. In this case the total numerical strength of the air defense forces would amount to 93,000 men.

SIGNAL CORPS

The total authorized strength of the signal corps was set at 21,000 men last December. The war with the White Finns resulted in major increases in signal corps strength. We will have to maintain a large signal establishment due to the need for communications and training in the Transcaucasus and Odessa Military Districts. My proposal calls for the following signal corps establishment:

Signal regiments	13
Signal battalions	28
Line signal battalions	3
Cable and pole climber companies	7
Telegraph construction companies	14
Telegraph operation companies	4
Military postal transports	5
Military postal facilities	2
Radio battalions	4
Special (*OSNAZ*) radio battalions	14

All of the above signal units will be manned at peacetime levels, with the exception of units in the Transcaucasus, Odessa, and part of the Kiev Military Districts, where establishments will be maintained at wartime levels.

The total numerical strength of the signal corps, including district signal establishments, will amount to 45,250 men.

ENGINEERS

The authorized strength of the engineers was set at 25,000 men. The war with the White Finns revealed the inadequate size of our engineer corps and the obsolescence of our engineering technology. Such engineering technologies as camouflage and demolitions proved to be deficient. Currently engineer units have a cumulative strength of 34,600 men. My proposal calls for a strength of 20,400 men and a comprehensive review of the entire organizational structure of the engineer corps on the basis of the experience of the war with Finland.

RAILROAD TROOPS

The authorized strength of the railroad troops was set at 13,912 men. During the war with Finland their manpower level rose to 45,398 men.

In light of the need to build and improve the railroads, I consider it necessary to leave the strength of the railroad troops at 20,000 men.

MOTOR TRANSPORT UNITS

The government authorized 12 motor transport regiments and 17 motor transport battalions. In order to supply active forces, the motor transport units were beefed up and reached a cumulative strength of 121,437 men.

My proposal calls for the following motor transport units:

Automobile regiments	12
Automobile battalions	45
Tractor battalions	1
Separate automobile companies	5
Automobile training regiments	1
Automobile training battalions	4

The increase in the number of battalions was due to the need to provide more vehicles available for the Transcaucasus and Odessa Military Districts and retain vehicles to meet the needs of the northern units of the Leningrad Military District.

The total numerical strength of MT units in the proposed organization will amount to 44,000 men.

ROADBUILDING UNITS

The authorized peacetime strength of these units was 5,710 men. They primarily included units supporting forces in the Mongolian People's Republic. Currently the roadbuilding units have a strength of 69,216 men. Because of training and road maintenance requirements, my proposal calls for retaining the following units for the Transcaucasus, Odessa, and Leningrad Military districts:

Reduced-strength road maintenance regiments	6
Military roadbuilding battalions	7
Mechanized military roadbuilding battalions	4
Military bridging battalions	2

The total strength of the roadbuilding units would be 19,000 men.

MILITARY SCHOOLS

The total authorized strength of military schools and military academies for 1940 was set at 170,300 men. Recruitment of an additional 30,000 men over and above this figure was authorized due to a shortage of command personnel.

The major shortage of command personnel which occurred after the expansion of units for the front compelled us to strengthen our system of military schools. For this purpose we organized 27 new infantry schools, bringing the cumulative strength of the military schools to 288,220 men. We had to organize an additional four mortar schools to meet the Red Army's growing needs for certain specialized command personnel.

Because of this, we must temporarily, until sufficient numbers of command personnel are trained, authorize a strength of 290,000 men for the military schools, with 20,000 making up for the shortage of command personnel.

RESERVE UNITS

My proposal calls for the following numbers of reserve units:

Reserve infantry brigade headquarters	5
Reserve infantry regiments	27
Reserve artillery regiments	3
Reserve tank regiments	1
Reserve anti-aircraft artillery regiments	2

The combined numerical strength of these reserve units would be 26,000 men.

ARMORED TRAINS

A cumulative peacetime strength of 3,271 men was authorized for armored trains. My proposal calls for leaving this figure unchanged at 3,271 men.

TOPOGRAPHICAL UNITS

My proposal calls for leaving the strength of these units unchanged at 3,530 men.

LOCAL INFANTRY UNITS

My proposal also calls for leaving the authorized strength of these units unchanged at 42,810 men.

CENTRAL, DISTRICT, AND LOGISTICAL SERVICES

My proposal calls for maintaining the following services at their current strengths:

Central and district headquarters and draft boards	40,584 men
Medical units	6,392 men
Veterinary services	1,254 men
Food supply	4,625 men
Uniform and equipment supply	2,038 men
Political education	3,469 men
Artillery depots, firing ranges, and workshops	14,147 men
Motor transport depots and workshops	6,965 men
Map depots	261 men
Fuel depots	1,463 men
Military transportation agencies, food service facilities, and general labor units	5,000 men
Total	86,193 men

THE TOTAL STRENGTH OF THE RED ARMY

The total numerical strength of the Red Army after the aforementioned proposals are implemented would be equal to 3,212,666 men.

Considering that 30,000 trainees will be enrolled at military schools to offset the shortage of command personnel without any rise in total strength, I hereby request an authorized strength of:

	3,182,666 men
Reserve	17,334 men
Total	3,200,000 men

As of May 1 the total number of men in the Red Army, not counting demobilized reservists, was equal to

3,886,329 men

Thus, at present the Red Army has the following number of men in excess of the proposed authorized strength

686,329 men

In order to bring the Army to its authorized manpower levels, I hereby request authorization to put the following categories of personnel on reserve status in the month of May:

a) the personnel of units and services to be reduced to peacetime strength and the units organized during the war in the Leningrad, Kiev Special, Baku Special, Kaliningrad Special, Odessa, Kharkov, Moscow, Orel, Volga, Ural, Siberian, and North Caucasus Military Districts, with the exception of units to be transferred to the Transcaucasus Military District:

173,461 men

b) all rank-and-file personnel called up from the reserves and awaiting discharge from military hospitals and convalescent battalions:

70,000 men

c) the temporary personnel of reserve units called up from the reserves:

140,000 men

d) the excess assigned personnel of infantry divisions to be reduced to peacetime strength:

	302,865 men
Total	686,329 men

Subsequently we plan to discharge unneeded temporary personnel and replace them with Category II conscripts born in the years 1912–1919 after we have determined the age distribution by units, about which I will issue a supplemental report.

I ask you to confirm the proposed actions and numerical strength of the Red Army.

People's Commissar of Defense of the USSR
Marshal of the Soviet Union

K. Voroshilov

IDU MID

Report on the evacuation of individuals from the Baltic Region and Moldavia, June 19, 1941

To Comrade Nasedkin
Top Secret

[illegible handwriting]

TABLE NO. 4

ON THE MOVEMENT OF SPECIAL TRAINS
FROM THE BALTIC REGION AND THE
MOLDAVIAN SOVIET SOCIALIST REPUBLIC

As of June 19, 1941

Point of departure	Number of people	Destination	Way points
Kishinev Railroad	432	Omsk Railroad Shartandy Station	June 18 0740 hours Alekseevka Station South East Railroad
" "	827	Orenburg Railroad Aktiubinsk Station	June 17 [illegible] Kupansk Station Northern Don Railroad
" "	863	Tashkent Railroad V. Alekseev Station	June 18 0740 hours Alekseevka Station South East Railroad
" "	934 [?]	Karaganda Railroad Akmolinsk Station	June 19 0010 hours Chuguevo Station
" "	1185	Orenburg Railroad Shurup [?] Station	June 15 [illegible] Chuguevo Station
" "	775	Omsk Railroad Omsk Station	June 17 [illegible] Chuguevo Station Southern Railroad
" "	928	Tashkent Railroad Kyzyl-Tuva Station	June 17 0010 hours Chuguevo Station Southern Railroad
" "	997	Omsk Railroad Omsk Station	June 19 0600 hours Chuguevo Station Southern Railroad
" "	1021	Orenburg Railroad Sea of Aral Station	June 18 0400 hours Poltava Station Southern Railroad
" "	1342	Orenburg Railroad Martuk Station	June 18 0010 hours Valunin Station Northern Don Railroad

TABLE NO. 4 (CONTINUED)

Point of departure	Number of people	Destination	Way points
" "	1094	Tashkent Railroad Kyzyl-Tuva Station	June 18 0101 hours Chuguevo Station Southern Railroad
" "	1120	Omsk Railroad Omsk Station	June 18 1158 hours Osnova [?] Station Southern Railroad
" "	816	Tomsk Railroad Novosibirsk Pier Station	June 18 0415 hours Valunin Station Northern Don Railroad
" "	784	Tomsk Railroad Novosibirsk Pier Station	June 16 2250 hours Kupansk Station Northern Don Railroad
" "	680	Tomsk Railroad Novosibirsk Pier Station	June 27 22[?] hours Chuguevo Station Southern Railroad

Source?

DOCUMENT 284   *Letter from former U.S. Ambassador Joseph Davies to Stalin, September 10, 1938*

[English-language original]

Brussels, Belgium,
September 10th, 1938.

PERSONAL

My dear Mr. Stalin:

Upon my arrival in Belgium sometime ago I was delighted to receive from Minister Rubinin your autographed photograph. I shall always value it. It will occupy a prominent place in my photographic gallery of the Great of the Earth.

May I say, also, that I was deeply gratified at the opportunity of meeting you personally before I left Moscow. It has been my privilege to meet the most (and to know quite well some) of the great men of my time. I was, therefore, very glad to meet, and measurably to feel that I now know, the leader of the Great Russian people; and to find in him a greatness of spirit that is absorbed in the cause that he is serving, and one who has the courage to dare and to do what he considers to be for the benefit of the common man.

There is another reason that I found satisfaction in our talk. It is this: it has served to clear up certain possible misunderstandings that existed. It has, I am sure, resulted in better understanding between the governing forces of our two great countries and in better relations between them. As Premier Molotov said to me in parting (and very wisely): whatever may come of the specific matters we discussed, good will have resulted through this better mutual understanding. I am much gratified that during my tenure as Ambassador to the U.S.S.R., and in no small measure due to the abilities and frankness of your great Foreign Minister, Mr. Litvinov, the relations between the Soviet Union and the United States were never on a better basis of mutual understanding.

Through Mr. Rozov, who was always very helpful, I transmitted to you a message concerning the debt question which we discussed. Doubtless you have received it before this and have been advised as to the situation as I found it. It is to be regretted that the exigencies of the moment in my country made it advisable temporarily to defer further discussion just at this time.

I am free to say, however, that the President and Secretary Hull were most favorably impressed with the spirit which you and the government of the Soviet Union manifested in a desire to complete in spirit the Roosevelt-Litvinov agreement. The President hopes quite definitely that some arrangement can be worked out later that will be within the practical possibilities that confront both governments.

I shall keep in touch with the matter and will always be ready to aid in bringing the principals together in a mutually advantageous agreement when it should be considered desirable. In the meantime, the record of these proposals, together with the discussions in my government concerning them, are being kept strictly confidential.

It was a matter of much gratification to me that the battleship matter had been satisfactorily worked out.

If Ambassador Troyanovsky is still in Moscow please give him and Mrs. Troyanovsky the kindest remembrances of Mrs. Davies and myself.

Thanking you again for the photograph, and with assurances of my great respect and esteem, I am

Yours sincerely,

[signed] Joseph E. Davies

The Honorable
  Joseph Stalin,
    The Kremlin,
      Moscow, U.S.S.R.

APRF, fond 45, op. 1, d. 375, ll. 14–18.

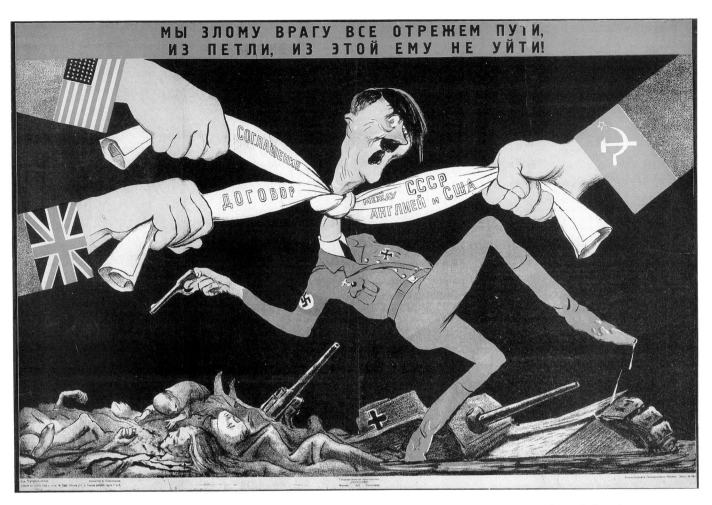

Propaganda poster depicting Hitler caught in a noose being pulled by each of the Allies. Original in color. *We will cut off all roads to the evil enemy, he will not escape from this noose!*, by Kukryniksy. Publisher: Iskusstvo, Moscow-Leningrad, 1942. Prints and Photographs Division, Library of Congress.

DOCUMENT 285   *Report by Vyshinsky to Molotov, August 1941, concerning trade and economic cooperation between the Soviet Union and the United States*

To Comrade V. M. Molotov

I present for your confirmation:

1. The draft resolution of the USSR Council of People's Commissars [*SNK SSSR*] on extending the trade agreement currently in effect between the USSR and the U.S.A. to August 6, 1942.

2. The text of notes which will be exchanged this August 4 in Washington between Umanskii and Welles.

The *SNK SSSR* resolution and notes which will be exchanged this August 4 in Washington are subject for publication.

In addition to this note on extending the agreement, two other notes will be exchanged:

a) on the U.S.A. rendering economic cooperation to us (with subsequent publication);

b) on the inapplicability for us of discretionary conditions concerning our gold and silver (without publication).

The texts of the last two notes are not yet in our possession.

[handwritten:] I am also enclosing a draft response to Comrade Umanskii.

Sent

[signed] A. Vyshinsky

[illegible]

"   "   August 1941

IDU MID

DOCUMENT 286   *Dinner hosted by Stalin in honor of Joseph Davies, President Roosevelt's personal representative, at 7:00 pm May 23, 1943*

MENU

May 23, 1943

Cold Appetizers

Soft and pressed caviar, rastegais
White salmon, pink salmon, herring with garnish, smoked *shamaia*
Jellied sturgeon
Cold suckling pig with horseradish, English roast beef with garnish
Cold ham with *lanspig,* wild game and *shefru* in aspic, braised duck
Galantine
"Olivier" and "Spring" salads
Fresh cucumbers, garden radishes
Assorted cheeses, butter, and toast

Hot Appetizers

Champignons au gratin
Medallion of wild game poivrade

<u>Main Course</u>

Soupe de poularde à la reine, pirogi pies
Consommé, borsht
White salmon in white wine
Roast veal with potatoes
Roast turkey and chicken with lettuce
Cauliflower, asparagus
Strawberry parfait, ice cream [illegible]
Coffee
Assorted cheeses
fruits, petits-fours, almonds
liqueurs

[Editor's note: Attending the dinner were the U.S. Ambassador to the USSR, William H. Standley, the British Ambassador to the USSR, Sir Archibald Clark Kerr, and their assistants; V. M. Molotov, K. E. Voroshilov, L. P. Beria, A. I. Mikoyan, G. M. Malenkov, A. Vyshinsky, M. M. Litvinov, and others.]

AVP RF, fond 6, op. 5, p. 9, d. 337, ll. 57, 60, 61

DOCUMENT 287 **Letter to Stalin from Donald M. Nelson, November 12, 1943**

[English original]

WAR PRODUCTION BOARD
WASHINGTON, D.C.

OFFICE OF
Donald M. Nelson
    Chairman

November 12, 1943

My dear Marshal Stalin:

As I review the events of my recent trip, I feel that I must add to the brief wire, which I sent you before leaving Russia, by expressing my great pleasure at having met and talked with you in Moscow and the profound impression which the magnificent spirit and determination of your people made upon me.

The opportunity to see many of your factories at first hand, and to talk with Soviet industrial and military leaders was an honor which I deeply appreciate. I shall never forget the kindness and hospitality shown us, wherever we went.

My visit to Russia has left me with the warmest respect for your country's industrial and military achievements and has strengthened my conviction that our joint war effort is moving swiftly toward complete and final victory. Moreover, my observations of the way in which your production has been carried on under the stress of wartime conditions leave no doubt in my mind that your country is assured of an impressive industrial future.

Sincerely,

[signed] Donald M. Nelson

Marshal Joseph Stalin
Moscow
Russia

APRF, fond 45, op. 1, d. 374, ll. 60–61.

DOCUMENT 288   *Report from Mikoyan to Stalin and Molotov, May 21, 1944, on Lend-Lease shipments from the United States during the period October 1, 1941, to May 1, 1944*

Copy No._____

To Comrade STALIN J.V.
To Comrade MOLOTOV V.M.

I am sending you information <u>on deliveries to the Soviet Union of arms, industrial equipment, materials, and food by the United States of America</u> under the Law on the Transfer of Loans or Leases (under Lend-Lease); this information is intended for publication in the press.

It is obvious from this information that during the period of October 1, 1941, to May 1, 1944, the U.S.A., under Lend-Lease, sent the Soviet Union arms, equipment, materials, and food totalling <u>$5,357,300,000</u> and weighing 8,514,000 long tons, not including the weight of 92 delivered ships or the weight of 3333 airplanes, which arrived by air.

The shipment figures for worth and weight <u>do not include</u>:

cargo from American steamers unloaded in England in 1942 and 1943, and transferred by the English and Americans, amounting to	115,000 tons	
cargo shipped from the U.S.A. in English deliveries	239,000 tons	
Canadian cargo shipped via ports in the U.S.A.	18,000 tons	
cargo we purchased in the U.S.A. for cash before the Lend-Lease Law	372,000 tons	
worth	$105.3 million	
Red Cross cargo and gifts from various public organizations	25,500 tons	
worth	$36.4 million	

<u>Of the total amount of cargo shipped by the U.S.A. under Lend-Lease as of May 1, 1944</u>:

		% of What Was Shipped	Worth	% of What Was Shipped
Arrived in the USSR	7,410,600 t	87.0	$4.6116 billion	86.1
In Iran	166,700 t	2.0	$155.7 million	2.9
En route	517,400 t	6.1	$288.8 million	5.4
Sunken	419,000 t	4.9	$297.5 million	5.5
Losses of airplanes in flight	28 units	—	$3.7 million	0.1

In addition to the above data on cargo losses, 17,000 t of Canadian and English cargo sent to us under Lend-Lease and shipped from ports in the U.S.A. was sunk.

The losses at sea of Lend-Lease cargo are shown by year:

1942	311,500 tons	14.2% of cargo shipped
1943	56,100 tons	1.2% " " "
1944 (Jan.–Apr.)	51,400 tons	3.2% " " "

I am also enclosing more detailed information, which is not for publication; this information includes data on shipments of the most important types of arms, equipment, materials, and food, all delivered under Lend-Lease.

[signed] A. Mikoyan

Sent to: Comrade Beria
Comrade Malenkov
Comrade Voroshilov
Comrade Voznesenskii

4-1/51 May 21, 1944

AVP RF.

DOCUMENT 289   ***Draft of a telegram for Stalin's signature, February 27, 1945, expressing gratitude to President Roosevelt for his greetings on the twenty-seventh anniversary of the Red Army***

N386/February 26, 1945
To: Comrade Stalin
From: V. Molotov
For confirmation
February 25   Draft

TELEGRAM

To Mr. FRANKLIN D. ROOSEVELT,
PRESIDENT OF THE UNITED STATES OF AMERICA.

Washington, the White House

Requesting you, Mr. President, accept my gratitude for your cordial greeting on the 27th Anniversary of the Red Army.

I am sure that further strengthening of the cooperation between our countries, reflected in the decisions of the Crimean Conference, will bring about in the near future the utter defeat of our common enemy and the establishment of a lasting peace based on the principle of cooperation among all freedom-loving peoples.

To: Comrade Molotov, V. M.
For confirmation
[illegible signature]
February 24

APRF, fond 45, op. 1, d. 370, l. 32.

(Seated) Churchill, Roosevelt, and Stalin and (standing left to right) Eden (behind Churchill), Stettinius, Molotov, and Harriman at the Yalta Conference in Crimea, June 16, 1945. TSGAKFD. N A-6695.

DOCUMENT 290 *Telegram from Stalin to Truman, June 16, 1945, on the preparation of a Soviet-Chinese accord*

People's Commissariat
for Foreign Affairs
Department 10

Ref. No. 9299
Rec'd 2:00 June 16 1945
Sent 4:30 June 16 1945
Spec. No. 1729

TOP SECRET
Copying
Prohibited

CODED TELEGRAM

- -

Destination: Washington
To whom: Soviet Ambassador   Copy 1

- -

URGENT SPECIAL
PRIORITY

In the message of June 15 to Comrade Stalin, Truman reported the June 15 departure of Sun-Tzi Ven from the U.S.A. for Moscow via Chungking. Sun should arrive in Moscow at the end of June to discuss preparation of a Soviet-Chinese Accord. Truman also reported that Hurly, the American ambassador to Chungking, was instructed to support Soviet proposals in this connection.

Give Truman the following messsage from Comrade Stalin:

"PERSONAL AND TOP SECRET FROM PREMIER J. V. STALIN
TO MR. PRESIDENT H. TRUMAN

Received your message concerning preparation of a Soviet-Chinese Accord and your instructions to Mr. Hurly. Thank you for the measures you have taken.

June 15, 1945."

Confirm execution by telegraph.

MOLOTOV

copies to:
1. Comrade STALIN
2. Comrade MOLOTOV
3. DEPARTMENT 10   For information to comrades: Vyshinsky,
                                                  Dekanozov.
                         True copy: [illegible initials]

APRF, fond 45, op. 1, d. 370, ll. 33, 34.

Telegram from Stalin to Harry Hopkins, via Molotov and the Soviet ambassador to the United States, April 15, 1945, expressing condolences on the death of President Roosevelt

NKVD	Dispatch No. 5460	Form No. 17	
Department 10	Received 5:15	Apr. 16, 1945	TOP SECRET
	Forwarded 8:25	Apr. 16, 1945	copying prohibited
		No. 1077	

ENCODED TELEGRAM

DESTINATION: Washington   TO WHOM: Soviet Ambassador

URGENT

On April 14 a telegram from Hopkins to Comrade Stalin was received via Harriman. Hopkins wrote that he heard on the radio the text of a telegram sent by Comrade Stalin expressing condolences on Roosevelt's death and that in his opinion Russia had lost a great friend in Roosevelt.

Send Hopkins the following telegram response from Comrade Stalin:

"Mr. HOPKINS.

I received your message of April 14 concerning President Roosevelt. I heartily agree with you in your estimation of the role and significance of Roosevelt for the Soviet Union. I am personally deeply saddened by the loss of a tested friend, a man of great spirit.

J. Stalin

April 15, 1945."

Telegraph execution.

MOLOTOV

True copy: [illegible initials]

Copies:
1. Comrade Stalin
2. Comrade Molotov For the information of: Comrades Vyshinsky,
3. Department 10 Dekanozov, TSarapkin

APRF, fond 45, op. 1, d. 375, l. 10.

Generals Tedder of the RAF (second from left), Zhukov of the Soviet Union (third), Spaatz of the United States (fourth), and Keitel of Germany (far right) at the ratification in East Berlin, May 8, 1945, of the surrender signed by Germany on the previous day at Rheims. TSGAKFD. NG-115

ТАК БУДЕТ
С ФАШИСТСКИМ ЗВЕРЕМ!

Propaganda poster done shortly after the fall of Berlin depicting the "Fascist beast" defeated by the Allied Forces of Great Britain, the United States, and the Soviet Union. Original in color. *Thus it will be to the Fascist beasts!*, by A. Kokorkin. Publisher: Iskusstvo, Moscow-Leningrad, 1945. Prints and Photograph Division, Library of Congress.

chapter 11

PRISONERS OF WAR

<hr />

One of the important signs of the rapprochement between Gorbachev's USSR and the United States was a willingness for Soviet officials to assist in resolving cases of U.S. soldiers missing in action during World War II, the Korean War, the Cold War, and the Vietnam War. Boris Yeltsin took this policy of cooperation a major step farther in June 1992 when he wrote a letter to the U.S. Senate Select Committee on POW-MIA Affairs, acknowledging that 716 American soldiers had been unlawfully detained during World War II. All of these men were evidently freed after the war, along with some 23,000 other U.S. soldiers who had been liberated by the Red Army from German prisoner-of-war camps. These and other allied soldiers were interned in transit camps, as the formerly secret documents here show. Some soldiers died before they could be repatriated: Document 302, for example, lists the names of 20 prisoners who died in April 1945, including 1 American.

Prisoners of war were not the only U.S. citizens detained in Soviet prisons. Numbers of U.S. citizens had emigrated to the USSR during the 1920s and 1930s; some of them ran afoul of Soviet law or were victims of the arbitrariness of Stalin's terror, and they joined the millions of Soviet citizens in the Gulag and exile systems. One example is Alexander Dolgun, a young U.S. Embassy employee who had accompanied his family to the USSR in the 1930s. He was arrested in 1948 and sentenced to twenty-five years in prison. Although he was released in 1956, he was able to leave the Soviet Union only in 1971, after strenuous efforts by his relatives abroad. Shortly after the close of the Russian archives exhibit at the Library of Congress, in August 1992, a Moscow newspaper published a new list of 39 Americans imprisoned after World War II and possibly still alive. Subsequent research by the U.S. press revealed that some of these individuals had returned to the U.S. long before this, and continuing research in Russian archives found no evidence of U.S. citizens still detained against their will in Russia or the republics of the former Soviet Union.

DOCUMENT 292   *Regulation on Prisoners of War, 1941*

<u>SECRET</u>

ORDER
OF THE PEOPLE'S COMMISSARIAT OF
INTERNAL AFFAIRS [*NKVD*]
For 1941

CONTENTS:

No. 0342   Announcement of the resolution of the Council of People's Commissars
of the USSR concerning "Approval of Prisoner-of-War Regulations."

No. 0342   July 21, 1941, City of Moscow

Resolution No. 1798-800s of the Council of People's Commissars of the USSR of July 1, 1941, concerning "Approval of Prisoner-of-War Regulations" is hereby brought to your attention.

Attachment: Resolution No. 1798-800s of July 1, 1941, "Approval of Prisoner-of-War Regulations."

Deputy People's Commissar of Internal Affairs of the USSR

Commissar of State Security Third-Grade

ChERNYShOV

RESOLUTION No. 1798-800s
of the Council of People's Commissars of the USSR
July 1, 1941, Moscow, Kremlin

SUBJECT: APPROVAL OF REGULATIONS ON PRISONERS OF WAR

The Council of People's Commissars of the USSR hereby resolves to:

1. Approve the attached Regulations on Prisoners of War

2. Revoke the current Regulations on Prisoners of War approved by Resolution No. 46 of the Central Executive Committee and Council of People's Commissars of the Soviet Union on March 19, 1931.

Chairman of the Council of People's Commissars of the USSR

J. STALIN

Business Manager of the Council of People's Commissars of the USSR

IA. ChADAEV

SECRET
Annex to Resolution No. 1798-800s
of the Council of People's
Commissars of July 1, 1941

REGULATIONS ON PRISONERS OF WAR

I. General Provisions

1. The following persons shall be considered prisoners of war:

a) persons belonging to the armed services of countries in a state of war with the Soviet Union and captured in the course of military operations and citizens of these countries interned on the territory of the USSR;

b) persons belonging to armed detachments which are not part of the enemy's armed forces if they are openly bearing arms;

c) civilians accompanying the enemy's army and navy with the appropriate authorization such as correspondents, suppliers, and other persons captured in the course of military operations.

2. The following shall be prohibited:

a) humiliation or cruel treatment of prisoners of war;

b) the use of violence and threats against prisoners of war for the purpose of extracting information from them on the situation of their country, be it military or other information;

c) confiscation of uniforms, undergarments, footwear, and other personal items and personal papers and insignia in the personal possession of prisoners of war;

Valuables and money may be taken from prisoners of war for safekeeping in exchange for official receipts by persons authorized to do so.

3. Any instructions and rules issued by the *NKVD* of the USSR pursuant to these Regulations must be posted in places where they can be read by all prisoners of war. These instructions and rules and any orders and directives pertaining to prisoners of war must be published in the Russian language and languages understood by the prisoners of war.

II. The Evacuation of Prisoners of War

4. Prisoners of war must be sent to prisoner-of-war camps immediately after they are captured.

5. Prisoners of war must be registered after capture on the basis of instructions provided by the command of the unit or formation.

In the registration procedure, each prisoner of war shall be required to give his true last name, first name, patronymic, age, place of origin, and serial number.

This information should be forwarded at the same time as the prisoners of war to their intermediate and final destinations.

6. Wounded or ill prisoners of war in need of medical attention or hospitalization must be sent immediately by unit commanders to the nearest hospitals.

The hospital administration shall be responsible for transferring these prisoners of war to prisoner-of-war camps after they have convalesced.

7. The maintenance of prisoners of war (food, sanitation, medical care, and so forth) shall be the responsibility of:

a) the army command (before the prisoners of war arrive at the reception stations of prisoner-of-war camps);

b) agencies of the *NKVD* of the USSR (thereafter).

III. The Conditions of Internment of Prisoners of War and Their Legal Status

8. Camp reception stations for prisoners of war should be organized in the army rear area as directed by the army command, while camps should be organized outside the area of military operations as directed by the *NKVD* of the USSR in consultation with the People's Commissariat of Defense.

9. Prisoners of war must be provided living quarters, undergarments, clothing, footwear, food, and other basic necessities and money allowances according to standards set by the Directorate of Prisoner-of-War and Internee Affairs [*GUPVI*] of the *NKVD* of the USSR.

The list of items and food to be supplied to prisoners of war and the allowances for these items must be posted in a conspicuous place in barracks, hospitals, and other places where prisoners of war are interned.

Any food and other assistance received by prisoners of war from third parties shall not result in a reduction of their allowances issued by the government.

10. Prisoner-of-war officers and other persons with equivalent status must be interned separately from other prisoners of war and be supplied with living quarters, clothing, undergarments, footwear, food, and other basic necessities and a money allowance at the prescribed allowances.

11. Prisoners of war may wear their uniform and insignia. Prisoners of war may not carry or keep weapons.

12. Prisoners of war must be given access to medical care on an equal footing with Red Army personnel.

Enemy prisoner-of-war medical personnel may be used to provide medical services at prisoner-of-war camps in addition to the camps' regular medical staffs.

13. Prisoners of war shall have the right to:

a) send a message home concerning their captivity at the first opportunity;

b) purchase food, clothing, undergarments, footwear, and other personal items and basic necessities at their own expense;

c) receive packages from their homeland and neutral countries containing food, clothing, and other basic necessities free of duty, free of license, and free of excise tax;

d) receive money orders from their homeland and neutral countries.

14. In order to maintain internal order and communications with prisoners of war, the camp administration shall

appoint certain prisoners of war as liaisons or leaders of rooms, groups, barracks, and so forth (depending on how the prisoners are housed), who shall serve as intermediaries between the prisoners of war and the camp administration on all matters.

15. Postal correspondence (letters and postcards, money orders, and letters with a declared value) sent and received by prisoners of war must be <u>forwarded free of charge</u> by a procedure determined by the *GUPVI* of the *NKVD* of the USSR.

16. Foreign currency sent to prisoners of war shall be exchanged for Soviet currency at the prevailing rate.

Prisoners of war will be authorized to keep money in their possession within the limits established by the *GUPVI* of the *NKVD* of the USSR. Any money over this limit shall be turned over to the camp administration and deposited in state laborers' savings banks. Money over and above the prescribed limits may be disbursed with the permission of the camp administration.

17. Prisoners of war may draw up wills and testaments. The death certificates of prisoners of war and their gravesites must be duly registered.

18. Any money and papers of deceased prisoners of war to be sent to their heirs shall be turned over to the Central Information Bureau of the Executive Committee of the Union of Red Cross and Red Crescent Societies.

Any food parcels addressed to deceased prisoners of war should be turned over to the prisoner-of-war liaisons or leaders to be divided among the prisoners of war.

19. Prisoners of war are required to obey the camp administration and all the rules indicated in these Regulations and any camp rules issued by the *GUPVI* of the *NKVD*.

IV. The Employment of Prisoners of War

20. Enlisted and noncommissioned-officer prisoners of war may be employed for work in and outside the camp in Soviet industry and agriculture on the basis of special regulations to be drafted by the *GUPVI* of the *NKVD*.

Officers and persons of equivalent status may be employed for work only with their consent.

21. The regulations governing labor protection and working hours which are applicable to Soviet citizens in a particular area working in the same types of occupations are also applicable to prisoners of war.

22. Prisoners of war employed in different sectors of the economy are to be compensated for their work in amounts to be determined by the Directorate of Prisoner of War and Internee Affairs of the *NKVD*.

Maintenance expenses (for living quarters, utilities, and food, if common dining facilities are provided) may be deducted from the wages of prisoners of war.

23. Housing and utilities are to be provided to prisoners of war at the expense of the businesses and organizations that employ them.

24. Prisoners of war shall become ineligible to receive all the rations authorized them at the expense of the government as soon as they are employed.

25. The use of prisoner-of-war labor is prohibited:

a) for work in areas of combat operations;

b) for the performance of personal services for administrative personnel or personal services for other prisoners of war (valet services).

V. The Criminal and Disciplinary Liability of Prisoners of War

26. Cases of crimes committed by prisoners of war come under the jurisdiction of Military Tribunals on the basis of the laws of the Soviet Union and Union Republics.

Any failure of a prisoner of war to carry out the orders of his superiors or any resistance or insult offered to these persons in their performance of their official duties shall be considered equivalent to the corresponding court martial offense.

27. Prisoners of war shall be liable to disciplinary punishments for any minor offenses not entailing criminal liability in a judicial proceeding.

The forms which these punishments may take, the procedures for imposing and appealing them, and the procedure for serving these punishments shall be determined by rules issued by the *GUPVI* of the *NKVD* in conformity with the Disciplinary Code of the Red Army.

28. Prisoners of war under investigation or sentenced to any kind of punishment by a court or disciplinary punishment may not be subjected to any additional restrictions for the same offenses over and above the restrictions related to their status as persons under investigation or convicts or to their serving disciplinary punishments or judicial punishments already imposed.

29. The appropriate court must inform the Executive Committee of the Union of Red Cross and Red Crescent Societies of any guilty verdict no later than 20 days after pronouncement of sentence. A copy of the sentence should be enclosed with the message.

The Executive Committee of the Union of Red Cross and Red Crescent Societies must be notified of any death sentence pronounced against a prisoner of war immediately after it is pronounced, and the sentence may be carried out no sooner than one month after the sentence has been pronounced.

VI. Communications and Assistance for Prisoners of War

30. The exchange of rosters of prisoners of war and communications on prisoner-of-war matters with foreign and international Red Cross societies or information bureaus is the responsibility of the Executive Committee of the Union of Red Cross and Red Crescent Societies.

A Central Prisoner-of-War Information Bureau shall be established for this purpose under the Executive Committee of the Union of Red Cross and Red Crescent Societies and shall operate on the basis of a special charter to be approved by the aforementioned committee in consultation with the *NKVD* of the USSR and the People's Commissariat of Foreign Affairs.

31. Representatives of foreign and international Red Cross and other organizations may be allowed to enter the territory of the Soviet Union to render assistance to prisoners of war only with special authorization of the People's Commissariat of Foreign Affairs.

TSGA

DOCUMENT 293   *Order from the USSR People's Commissar of Internal Affairs, October 18, 1944, regarding changes in the standards of food supplies for prisoners of war*

Top secret

ORDER
of the People's Commissar of Internal Affairs of the USSR
for 1944

CONTENTS:
No. 001282 Regarding the change in the standard for food to be supplied to prisoners of war.

October 18, 1944   Moscow

In compliance with the resolution by the State Defense Committee from Oct. 14, 1944 for No. 6725/ss—regarding the regulation of the use of labor and the increase of labor productivity among prisoners of war,

I ORDER:

1. That these announced standards for food to be supplied to prisoners of war be implemented.

2. Directors of *NKVD* camps for prisoners of war:
a) provide for the study of the present order by the regular personnel of the camp;
b) impement the new standards for feeding prisoners of war;
c) set a daily check for the correct application of the standards for provisioning prisoners of war and provide for the carrying out of the prescribed standard of rations for prisoners of war.

3. That the directors of initial processing centers, collection points, and camps are personally responsible for providing food to prisoners of war according to the standards set for them.

4. That *NKVD* division chiefs, in dealing with prisoners of war attached to commanders at the rear of fronts, be obliged:
a) to supply the prescribed provisions for prisoners of war at initial processing points, collection points, and camps at the front;
b) to provide a daily hot meal for prisoners of war, not allowing their physical condition to deteriorate;
c) to disallow the movement of prisoners of war to camps in the rear without providing supplies for the journey and reserves for the detraining as well as mess articles needed for the preparation of hot meals en route.

5. Those guilty of misuse, stealing, and expending provisions intended for prisoners not according to their designated purpose will be held strictly accountable.

6. The director of the *GUPVI* of the *NKVD* of the USSR, Major-General Comrade Petrov, is directed to ensure:
a) timely delivery of the prescribed provisions for prisoners or war to the commanders of assembled units before departure and at mess stops en route;
b) daily hot meals, a water supply, and a sanitary and healthful regimen for the prisoners of war en route to prevent the deterioration of their physical condition.

7. The director of the Directorate of Military Supplies of the *NKVD* of the USSR, Major-General of the Commissariat Service Comrade Vurgaft, is directed to ensure an uninterrupted supply of provisions in accordance with the announced standards to *NKVD* prisoner-of-war camps.

8. The director of the *GUPVI* of the *NKVD* of the USSR and the director of the Directorate of Military Supplies of the *NKVD* of the USSR are directed to present to me by Oct. 25, 1944, for confirmation a new table reporting the listed number of camp personnel and prisoners of war and the corresponding provisions supplied according to the announced standards.

9. Addendum No. 1 of the *NKVD* of the USSR order No. 00683 of Apr. 9, 1943 is canceled.

Deputy People's Commissar of Internal Affairs of USSR,
        commissar of state security of the second rank
                KRUGLOV

for cooked food for prisoners of war in camps and at *NKVD* initial processing centers
(per person per day in grams)

No. in sequence	Listing of products	Quantity
1	Rye bread (96% ground flour)	600
2	Wheat flour, second class	10
3	Various groats	70
4	Macaroni-vermicelli	10
5	Meat	30
6	Fish	50
7	Fatback or combined fats	10
8	Vegetable oil	10
9	Tomato puree	10
10	Sugar	17
11	Tea substitute	2
12	Salt	10
13	Bay leaf	0.1
14	Pepper	0.1
15	Vinegar	0.7
16	Potatoes	400
17	Sauerkraut and cabbage	100
18	Carrots	30
19	Beets	50
20	Onions	10
21	Root vegetables, greens, cucumbers	10
22	Household soap (per month)	300

Footnote 1. All prisoners of war held at initial processing centers, collection points, and *NKVD* camps are to be provisioned according to the set norms, except for:

a) officers,

b) the sick,

c) the weak,

d) those performing strenuous labor,

e) those held in guardhouses, excluded from work.

2. Bread for prisoners of war performing strenuous labor is distributed thusly:
for those performing up to 50% of POW production norm, 650 grams;
for those performing 50–80% of POW production norm, 700 grams;
for those performing 80–100% of POW production norm, 750 grams;
for those performing over 100% of POW production norm, 800 grams.

3. The bread ration for prisoners of war performing other tasks is set at 600 grams.

4. For prisoners of war performing light duty, unrated camp service tasks, not fulfilling work norms, for those who do not work due to lack of jobs at the front, preparing for departure, the ration of bread is set at 600 grams.

5. Brigadiers and foremen (released POWs) who lead brigades that perform at a level higher than the designated output norms receive 100 grams of bread extra.

6. During transportation prisoners of war will receive provisions according to their physical condition:
the healthy—basic norm;
the weak—norm for the weak;
the sick—the hospital norm.

In the event that it becomes impossible to set up mess en route, food (dry rations) will be issued, substituting products listed in the norms with provisions more suitable for meals en route.

7. The norm of nourishment for the weak will be increased by 25%. The increase of nourishment will be achieved by either adding more dishes or by preparing the food separately according to increased norms.

8. For prisoners of war performing strenuous labor the provision norm, except for bread, increases by 25%. Bread is distributed according to output norms as in point 2.

9. For those prisoners of war fulfilling or overfulfilling their production quota 100% or more (in both strenuous and light jobs), in addition to their ration limit they will receive provisions calculated per person per day (24 hours):
various groats—50 grams
meat—25 grams
fish—25 grams
fats—10 grams

10. Those prisoners of war in quarantine before being released for work are accorded the norm for the weak.

11. Nourishment for those in guardhouses and those not permitted to work is distributed per the following norm:
bread—400 grams
85% wheat flour—7 grams
groats—55 grams
fish—55 grams
vegetable oil—7 grams
potatoes—200 grams
vegetables—150 grams
salt—7 grams
sugar—7 grams

12. The monthly allotment of 300 grams of soap is distributed thusly:
a) 100 grams for personal hygiene;
b) 100 grams for bathing;
c) 100 grams for laundry.

13. In calculating the output norms for distribution to physically disabled prisoners of war and invalids, adjustment coefficients of 25–50% of the groups able to work are used, and for those 100% disabled, a lowered norm will be calculated by a medical-labor commission. Invalids who are fully released from work will be given 600 grams of bread per day.

14. Prisoner-of-war meals on days off and days without work will be supplied according to the previous work day.

15. Prisoners of war on sick leave (but having worked previously) are to be fed according to their norm before their illness. Bread will be supplied according to the average output for the 5 days preceding the illness but in no case less than 600 grams per day.

16. The bread norm for prisoner-of-war cadets is set at 700 grams per day.

17. Those prisoners who surrendered voluntarily will receive an extra 100 grams of bread (total 700 grams) at receiving and collection points and in camps at the front, those in labor camps will receive according to their output norms.

18. In the absence of fresh vegetables, one dose of vitamin C per person will be distributed.

Director of Military Supplies
NKVD of the USSR
Major-Gen. of the Commissariat Service
VURGAFT

Director of POW and Internee Affairs
NKVD of the USSR
Major-Gen. PETROV

TSGOA

DOCUMENT 294 *Letter from the chief of the NKVD directorate for prisoners of war, February 15, 1945, on different categories of prisoners*

SECRET
Copy No. .....

TO OFFICERS IN CHARGE OF PRISONER-OF-WAR DEPARTMENTS
REAR SERVICES COMMANDS OF THE FRONTS

COPIES TO: FRONT REAR SERVICES COMMANDERS

The authorized representative of the Council of People's Commissars [SNK] of the USSR for repatriation affairs has issued a directive to the officers in charge of repatriation under the war councils of the fronts concerning the procedures for handling foreign citizens liberated from enemy captivity by the Red Army.

On the basis of the aforementioned directive, the Main Directorate of Prisoner of War and Internee Affairs [GUPVI] of the NKVD of the USSR would like to provide the following clarifications:

1) Military and civilian personnel of allied countries held in German captivity and liberated by Red Army units must be processed by the front system of repatriation departments, who will handle this category of individuals in accordance with their directives.

2) Allied countries include Great Britain and its dominions, the United States, Poland, France, Yugoslavia, Czechoslovakia, Norway, Belgium, and Holland. Consequently, enlisted personnel, officers, and civilians who are subjects of these countries and have been liberated from German captivity constitute the clientele of the front repatriation departments.

3) Any subjects of these allied countries who served in the German or Hungarian Army, fought against Red Army units and were taken prisoner while bearing arms or who surrendered voluntarily are prisoners of war and should be processed by the front system of NKVD POW departments and should subsequently be sent to NKVD rear area camps on the basis of instructions from the GUPVI of the NKVD.

4) If any of the citizens listed in point 2 of this directive should arrive at the reception and collection points or front camps, these individuals should be transferred immediately to the appropriate repatriation department for their nationality.

While they are at reception points, collection points, or front camps, the aforementioned citizens should be kept separate from the prisoners of war until they are transferred to the repatriation departments.

5) The officers in charge of reception points, collection points, and front camps must explain to these citizens that they are only being held temporarily and that they will be transferred to the agencies responsible for repatriating allied citizens.

6) The officers in charge of the prisoner-of-war departments are INSTRUCTED TO:

a) Transfer all allied military personnel and civilians held in German captivity and subsequently liberated by the Red Army and received at reception points, collection points, and front camps to the collection points of the repatriation departments after preliminary coordination with the officers in charge of these departments;

b) In view of the fact that instructions have been issued to keep Italians liberated by the Red Army from German captivity separate from the military personnel and civilians of the Allied countries who fought in the war against Nazi Germany from the very beginning of the war, transfer Italians to repatriation departments separately;

c) In consultation with the officers in charge of the repatriation departments, devise an appropriate plan for coordinating the transfer of the aforementioned category of individuals from NKVD reception points to repatriation department collection points, to include individuals who are now being held and individuals who may arrive in the future.

Any of the repatriated citizens described in this order and Italians arriving at reception and collection points should not be counted or mentioned in prisoner-of-war reports.

Officers should submit a report on transfers of repatriated individuals and information on the number of repatriated individuals transferred once every ten days by courier under separate cover using the standard format for a personnel status report.

Please confirm receipt of this directive.

Deputy Commander of *GUPVI*
NKVD of the USSR
Lieutenant General (PETROV)

February 15, 1945

No. 28/11

TSGA

DOCUMENT 295   ***Circular letter on prisoners of war liberated by Red Army troops, December 2, 1944***

CENTRAL PRISONERS-OF-WAR
AND INTERNEES DIRECTORATE

Dec 29 [?]
   1/22992

<u>TOP SECRET</u>

TO:

THE ASSISTANT REPRESENTATIVE OF THE COUNCIL OF PEOPLE'S COMMISSARS OF THE SOVIET UNION FOR REPATRIATION AFFAIRS LIEUTENANT GENERAL Comrade GOLUBEV

No. [Illegible]

DEPUTY PEOPLE'S COMMISSAR FOR FOREIGN AFFAIRS
Comrade DEKANOZOV

CHIEF OF THE *GLAVUPRAFORM* OF THE RED ARMY
COLONEL GENERAL Comrade SMORODINOV

ASSISTANT CHIEF OF THE GENERAL STAFF OF THE RED ARMY FOR [illegible]
MAJOR GENERAL Comrade SLAVIN

The People's Commissariat of Internal Affairs of the USSR [*NKVD*] has reception, transit, and collection stations at the fronts exclusively for enlisted and officer prisoners of war of the enemy armed forces. Keeping enemy and Allied prisoners of war together at these facilities would be absolutely out of the question.

There is no practical need to organize a special system of camps for Allied prisoners of war under the *NKVD*, not to mention the fact that confining Allied military personnel liberated from enemy captivity at *NKVD* camps would not exactly be in the spirit of good Allied relations.

The *NKVD* of the USSR believes that Allied prisoners of war should remain at the enemy camps where they were held after the camps have been liberated by Red Army units prior to repatriation to their home countries. All that would have to be done is change the security procedures, rations, and living conditions.

The direction and organization of this effort should be the exclusive responsibility of the front commands, which have all the material resources they need to feed and provide medical care, clothing, maintenance, and transportation for the Allied prisoners of war.

The effort would require a small central staff either under the General Staff of the Red Army or under the Repatriation Directorate. This staff would be responsible for keeping personnel records of Allied prisoners of war liberated from captivity, coordinating through the *NKVD* the practical aspects of turning these individuals over to the Allied authorities, and issuing instructions to the front command concerning direct transfers of these individuals from the camps to designated border stations to be followed by repatriation.

Any matters related to special services for this contingent should be coordinated with the Main Directorate of Counterintelligence [*SMERSh*] of the People's Commissariat of Defense of the USSR.

DEPUTY PEOPLE'S COMMISSAR OF INTERNAL AFFAIRS OF THE USSR
COMMISSAR OF SECURITY, SECOND GRADE

(KRUGLOV)

7 COPIES
Copies 1, 2, 3, and 4
to addressees
Copies 5 and 6 to
Secretariat of the *NKVD*
Copy 7 to Secretariat
of the Central Prisoners-of-War
and Internees Directorate

TSGA

DOCUMENT 296   *Instructions from the USSR Commission on Repatriation, directed to commandants of assembly points, March 27, 1945, for the repatriation of prisoners of war and citizens of Allied States liberated by the Red Army*

March 27, 1945

INSTRUCTIONS

FOR COMMANDANTS OF ASSEMBLY POINTS (COMMANDANT'S OFFICES) FOR THE REPATRIATION OF PRISONERS OF WAR AND CITIZENS OF ALLIED STATES LIBERATED BY THE RED ARMY

I. Summary

1. Assembly points (commandant's offices) for the repatriation of prisoners of war and interned citizens of Allied states who have been liberated are being created on active fronts and in districts in the rear, each with a capacity of up to 3,000 persons.

2. At the head of each assembly point (commandant's office) is a commandant with an office per order No. 03/502, who is guided in his activity by the present Instructions.
The commandant of the assembly point (commandant's office) is directly subordinate to the chief officer of the de-

partment of repatriation attached to the Military Council of the front. In the districts in the rear, the commandant is subordinate to the commander of the rear-line district.

3. The commandant of an assembly point (commandant's office) for the repatriation of prisoners of war and citizens of Allied states liberated by the Red Army bears full responsibility for assembling, registering, and accommodating all persons at the assembly point, maintaining internal order, and providing economic and medical services.

4. When establishing internal order, the commandant of an assembly point (commandant's office) is guided by the following:
a) all personnel at the assembly point (commandant's office) are separated according to nationality (Americans, Englishmen, Frenchmen, Poles, Czechoslovaks, Yugoslavs, Norwegians, Belgians, and Dutchmen). Italians are separated from the other liberated prisoners of war and citizens of other nationalities of Allied states, and separate camps or assembly points are created for them. Servicemen are brought together into military subunits (squad, platoon, company, battalion), with responsible commanders appointed from among the commissioned and non-commissioned officers of the given nationality. [. . .]

TSGOA

DOCUMENT 297   *Report on the organization of transit camps for Allied prisoners liberated by the Red Army, March 22, 1945*

TO THE DEPUTY CHIEF OF
REAR SERVICES OF THE RED ARMY
COLONEL GENERAL Comrade
VINOGRADOV

REPORT
On the Organization of Transit Camps and
a Transit Station in the City of Odessa
As of March 22, 1945

I. QUARTERING

Four sanatoria, four schools, and one apartment building, to wit, a total of nine buildings with a total floor space of 11,300 square meters, have been provided by the City Executive Committee for transit camps. These buildings could accommodate 8,500 persons, including 800 officers. All the rooms have been prepared and provided with all the necessary furniture. Water lines and electrical lines have been run to all the buildings, and mess halls have been prepared, but we do not have enough sinks and outdoor field toilets.

Officers will be housed in separate four-man rooms with beds, while bunks are being built for the enlisted men, and, as of March 22, 1945, double-decker bunks for 500 men had been completed. Temporary cast iron stoves have been installed in the quarters.

The facilities of the old Infantry School with a total floor space of 15,061 square meters have been prepared for the transit station. Water and electricity have been restored at the post, and mess halls have been prepared, along with sinks and field toilets. The men are being provided straw bedding on the floor.

Conditions at the transit camps and the transit station are satisfactory, but a large number of minor improvements are needed.

II. ARRIVAL AND DEPARTURE OF CONTINGENTS

As of March 22, a total of 11,711 Allied prisoners of war had arrived, including:

British 2,163 men
Americans 2,486 men
French 7,062 men

The following numbers of prisoners of war departed on three ships from March 7 through March 15:

British	1,837 men
Americans	1,709 men
French	2,839 men
Total departures	6,385 men

Left in camp:

British	326 men
Americans	777 men
French	4,223 men

89 men arrived on March 22 at 1900 hours, including:

British	6 men
Americans	8 men
French	75 men

435 men were expected to arrive on March 23, including:

Americans	20 men
British	415 men

Two transports were expected to arrive on March 22–23:

1. The ship *Sarkasha* with 1,641 men
2. The ship *Duchess of Richmond* with 3,702 men.

7,740 men arrived at the Red Army former POW transit station, and all of them had departed by March 22.

III. MEDICAL CARE AND SANITATION

The medical department of the Odessa Military District has set aside 300 beds at Hospital No. 1266 to receive Allied prisoners of war and 200 beds at Hospital No. 1777 for the special contingents and 50 beds at the isolation hospital for patients suffering from infectious diseases.

Medical units have been organized at the transit camps and the collection and transit station to provide medical care and sanitation.

Adequate resources (Bath-Laundry-Disinfection Train No. 72, Cleansing and Disinfection Company No. 100, and the Garrison Baths) have been provided for sanitation. (We are keeping Bath-Laundry Train No. 433 in reserve if needed.)

We have enough medicine and soap.

No cases of infectious diseases were observed while the contingents were at the transit camps and at the collection and transit station.

The medical and sanitation resources we received were quite adequate for the collection and transit station and the transit camps.

IV. CLOTHING AND PERSONAL ITEMS

<u>We have all the bedding we need</u>. The enlisted men have been issued straw mattresses, while the officers have been issued a full set of bedding.

As for the arriving Allied prisoners of war, almost all of the British and Americans were well dressed, and we have only had to issue missing items of clothing to a few. Most of the French were poorly dressed, and as of March 22 we had issued up to 2,500 sets of clothing.

We have to resolve the problem of towels. The district only has coarse calico towels, which we don't like to issue to this group because they often throw them away. The district cannot issue waffle-weave towels because we don't have them. <u>The district needs regular shipments of items of clothing in order to provide them to all incoming personnel.</u>

V. FOOD

From the rations we issue and the additional food they get from their military missions, all of the Allied prisoners of war are getting three hot meals per day, with the officers served with table settings in the mess hall and the enlisted men served from kettles in their bays. The district has food, but we aren't getting enough groats. We have almost no vegetables, and we don't have all the spices we need. We haven't received any complaints about the food from the prisoners of war or the missions. All we've heard are compliments.

VI. RETAIL SERVICES

The canteens are open, but they aren't open everywhere and can't meet everyone's needs because of the scarcity of goods and the low quality of the goods that are available. <u>The barbershops are open, but not all of them. We need help from the Central Military Canteen Directorate and the People's Commissariat of Retail Trade.</u>

CONCLUSIONS:

1. The operation of the camps can be considered quite satisfactory, which has been noted more than once in the national newspapers, but it took a lot of work to get them working properly, because the district only began carrying out Directives 1/240645 and 1/240646 after I got here.

<u>I should mention that the district's Military Council and the entire staff of the deputy commander for Rear Services has spent the last 15 to 20 days getting the camps ready.</u>

2. <u>April was a good time for putting the camps in municipal buildings, at any rate the schools, because putting the men in tents would have forced us to supply camp tents for 5,000 to 6,000 men to the district and about 300 cubic meters of materials.</u>

3. <u>Orders should be given to maintain a permanent stock of items of clothing and personal issue sufficient for 10,000 persons, including women and children, in order to avoid running out of these items. It would be desirable to issue the prisoners of war waffle-weave towels, duffel bags, and shoeshine kits.</u>

4. <u>We need to resolve the problem of augmenting the rations of generals and officers.</u>

5. <u>We need to resolve the problem of financing the prisoner-of-war camps.</u>

6. Four groups consisting of 50 men each, including one group from the Rear Services Command and three separate groups from the Repatriation Office, were sent from Moscow to supervise and assist the district. <u>All of these groups operated independently and without any coordination whatsoever, and at times they did not help at all and just stood around carping, which is why</u> we need a single coordinator for these efforts.

The district does need supervision from the Rear Services Command, because it has several missions in addition to its primary mission, including maintaining the camps, and considers the camps an extra burden. That is why much of the work was done only after I insisted on it.

MAJOR GENERAL [signed] KARABAEV

March 25, 1945

THE NUMBER OF LIBERATED, COUNTED, AND REPATRIATED ALLIED AND FOREIGN PRISONERS OF WAR AND CIVILIAN INTERNEES AS OF MARCH 1, 1946

Row No	Nationality	Total liberated	Of which		
			Repatriated	Repatriated across front lines	Currently in the Soviet Union and at Red Army facilities in other countries
1	2	3	4	5	6
1.	Americans	22,487	22,479	19,013	8
2.	British	22,468	22,465	20,006	3
3.	French	311,254	310,030	277,062	1,224
4.	Italians	166,531	166,263	159,869	268
5.	Poles	173,826	173,749	——	77
6.	Yugoslavs	127,646	127,182	71	264
7.	Belgians	35,043	34,846	30,457	197
8.	Czechoslovaks	44,573	43,312	——	1,261
9.	Dutch	35,668	35,032	33,773	636
10.	Norwegians	1,156	1,151	1,062	5
11.	Luxemburgers	2,373	2,295	2,164	78
12.	Danes	1,017	968	963	49
13.	Swedes	36	30	15	6
14.	Romanians	29,029	28,907	41	122
15.	Hungarians	23,113	22,823	——	290
16.	Greeks	7,940	7,929	36	11
17.	Bulgarians	2,009	1,998	1	11
18.	Swiss	847	822	820	25
19.	Spaniards	212	149	91	63
20.	Albanians	9	9	6	——
21.	Turks	50	26	——	24
22.	Austrians	11,801	11,766	65	35
23.	Finns	100	95	——	5
24.	Palestinians	13	13	——	——
25.	Chinese	3	——	——	3
26.	Brazilians	19	17	17	2
27.	Argentineans	3	3	3	——
28.	Panamanians	22	22	22	——
29.	Serbs	25	25	——	——
30.	Scots	4	4	4	——
31.	Egyptians	6	6	6	——
32.	Polish Gypsies	170	170	——	——
33.	Indians	1	1	1	——
34.	Iranians	1	1	1	——
	TOTAL:	1,021,455	1,016,588	544,569	4,867

Source?

DOCUMENT 298   *Lists covering the period from March 23 to May 3, 1945, of American citizens liberated from German POW camps and sent home*

Not Classified

OFFICE OF THE REPRESENTATIVE
OF THE COUNCIL OF MINISTERS OF THE SOVIET UNION
FOR REPATRIATION

Department of Repatriation of Foreign Citizens

1945

No. 27, v. 2

Including statements and personal records of foreign citizens repatriated from the USSR via the port of Odessa.

From: March 23, 1945
To: May 3, 1945
198 leaves

Head of the office

LIST of
Allied POWs of AMERICAN CITIZENSHIP dispatched from
Odessa Transit Camp No. 138
... May 1945

Sergeant Clifton Mains's detachment

Name	Military Rank	Date of Birth	Nationality	Remarks
Mains, Clifton	Sergeant	1922	American	
Hill, Eugene	Private	1917	"	
Dole, Wilfrid	"	1919	"	
Consecci, John	Sergeant Major	1918	"	
Kazmarik, John	Corporal	1924	"	
Allen, Frank	Sergeant	1922	"	
Dussey, Albert	"	1922	"	

Total   7 people
Including: Officers   —
               Sergeants   5
               Privates   2

COMMANDANT of Transit Camp No. 138
Colonel of the Guard [signed] Stoev

Head of the Directorate of Border Security [UPO]
Captain [a/c] [signed] Veipan

TSGOA

DOCUMENT 299   *Letter from Major General Kobulov to an NKVD commander, July 17, 1945,*
with suggestions about treatment of British and American POWs prior to repatriation

Top Secret

Main Directorate of Prisoner-of-War and Internee Affairs [*GUPVI*]
July 17, 1945

To the head of Dept. of Prisoner-of-War and Internee Affairs [*OPVI*] of the Directorate of the People's Commissariat of Internal Affairs [*UNKVD*] of Tambov *oblast'*

Major—

Comrade Livshits
Tambov

The *GUPVI NKVD* has issued a decree to commanders of the *OPVI* to send all British and American prisoners of war, whose number will not exceed 70–75 men, to Radinskii Camp No. 188.

Since British and American POWs will have to be transferred in the near future to repatriation agencies to return them to their countries,

I ORDER:

1. That all British and American POWs, those who are already in *NKVD* Camp No. 188 as well as those who will come later, be billeted separately from the other POWs, that they be dressed in the best captured uniforms and shoes, and that they no longer be sent to work.

2. That detailed questionnaires on each British and American POW be compiled, describing at length why they consider themselves citizens of America or England and what facts support their declarations.

Said questionnaires are to be given to *GUPVI NKVD* of the USSR before July 28 of this year.

Said questionnaires are to be compiled for American and British POWs immediately upon their arrival at Camp No. 188 and are to be sent without delay to the *GUPVI NKVD* of the USSR.

Deputy chief of *GUPVI NKVD* of the USSR
Major General
(A. Kobulov)

True copy: A. Makeechev

TSGOA

Registration card of the American Robert Lovein (Levin), liberated from German captivity by the Red Army and returned home on the British ship Circassia, *March 25, 1945*

REGISTRATION CARD

For Allied prisoners of war liberated by the Red Army

1. LAST NAME Lovein_____

2. FIRST NAME Robert___3. PATRONYMIC_____

4. YEAR OF BIRTH 1920_____5. PLACE OF BIRTH_____

_____USA_____New York_____

6. NATIONALITY_____American_____

7. CITIZENSHIP_____USA_____

8. RANK _____Private_____

(Military rank)

9. HELD AT_____Germany____in the city of Schubin [Szubin]

in which country, in which camp

10. WHEN AND FROM WHERE ARRIVED IN THE CAMP_____

___March 1, 1945____Poland_____city of Regshen [ILLEGIBLE]___

11. NAME OF THE CAMP_____Odessa Transit Camp 139_____

12. REGISTRATION NUMBER_____3695_____

13. CONDITION OF HEALTH_____Healthy_____

I CONFIRM THE CORRECTNESS OF THE INFORMATION
WRITTEN ABOUT ME Robert Levin

(Signature)

SIGNATURE OF THE INDIVIDUAL FILLING OUT THE
CARD_____Second Lt. Klimov_____

(Signature)

14. SENT "_____"_____194_____

_____

Indicate correct address, sent to which transit camp, etc.

_____

15. WHEN AND WHERE SENT FROM THE TRANSIT CAMP_____March 25, 1945_____

English steamship *Circassia*_____

TSGOA

SECRET

AFFIDAVIT

January 16, 1946

City of Kiev,
Pushcha-Voditsa

I, the senior assistant head of the Department of Prisoner-of-War and Internee Affairs [*OPVI*] of the Ukrainian *NKVD* for Kiev District, Senior Lieutenant Comrade FUNDRIAKA, in the presence of the assistant chief of security for Special Hospital No. 1035, Senior Lieutenant Comrade Kuptsov, on this day inspected Special Hospital No. 1035 for the purpose of determining whether the hospital's records of deceased POWs and their graves are in order.

1. The hospital keeps a grave registration book into which a copy of a diagram of the cemetery has been sewn to keep records of deceased prisoners of war. Entries in the book include the last name, first name, and patronymic of the deceased prisoner of war, his date of birth, nationality, military rank, date of death, date of burial, and number of the grave and section.

2. A tract of land has been set aside 200 to 300 meters from the hospital as a cemetery for deceased prisoners of war. This tract is cordoned off with three strands of barbed wire. The cemetery is divided into sections. Each section is divided into graves, and each grave is marked. The exhumation of a deceased prisoner of war in October 1945 proved that it is possible to disinter and examine deceased prisoners of war at Special Hospital No. 1035.

CONCLUSION

Special Hospital No. 1035 is keeping proper records of deceased prisoners of war in compliance with Directive No. 28/2/23-1944 of the Main Prisoner of War and Internee Affairs Directorate [*GUPVI*] of the *NKVD*.

In witness thereof I have written and signed this affidavit.

1. Senior Assistant to
the Head of the Prisoners-of-war
and Internees Department of the
Ukrainian *NKVD*, Kiev District

    Senior Lieutenant: [signed]   FUNDRIAKA

2. Assistant Chief of Security
for Special Hospital No. 1035

    Senior Lieutenant: [signed]   KUPTSOV

[Seal of Special Evacuation Hospital No. 1035, Dnepropetrovsk]

TSGA

Copy of a page from the register of Pushcha-Voditsa Cemetery, listing prisoners of war and internees from Special Military Hospital No. 1035 buried there

Copy

LIST   Secret

Deceased Prisoners of war and internees from Special Military Hospital 1035 buried at the cemetery in Pushcha-Voditsa, according to the cemetery register.

Last Name First Name Patronymic of Deceased[1]	Nationality	Year Born	Military Rank	Date of Death	Burial Date	Grave No./ Square
1. Dam Genrikh Matias	French	1920	Private 1st Class	4/20/45	4/25/45	1/I
2. Rakovskii Robert-Karl Adol'f	German	1904	Private 1st Class	4/25/45	4/25/45	2/I
3. Gibler Gererd Karl	German	1922	Senior Private 1st Class	4/22/45	4/25/45	3/I
4. Fen'vegin Ferents Androsh	Hungarian	1902	Soldier	4/23/45	4/25/45	4/I
5. Tykve Gergard Paul'	German	1924	Private 1st Class	4/21/45	4/25/45	5/I
6. Tuderlan Vasilii Ion	Romanian	1920	Soldier	4/25/45	4/25/45	6/I
7. Katuko Laslo Laslo	Hungarian	1920	Soldier	4/24/45	4/25/45	7/I
8. Egert Gobert Frants	German	1914	Private 1st Class	4/23/45	4/25/45	8/I
9. Leps Rol'f Karl	German	1924	Private 1st Class	4/25/45	4/25/45	9/I
10. Gol'kamp Genrikh	German	1926	Soldier	4/24/45	4/25/45	10/I
11. Ketter Vil'gel'm Gustav	German	1905	Soldier	4/27/45	4/27/45	11/I
12. Dotsin Il'ia Pavlov	Moldavian	1905	Soldier	4/21/45	4/21/45	12/I
13. Chernyi Arkadii Il'ia	Romanian	1898	Soldier	4/26/45	4/27/45	13/I
14. Lessinger Erikh Mikhael'	German	1913	Senior Private 1st Class	4/22/45	4/27/45	14/I
15. German Karl Avgust	German	1914	Senior Private 1st Class	4/?/45	4/27/45	15/I
16. Shlag German German	American	1923	Private 1st Class	4/26/45	4/27/45	16/I
17. Shoer Gel'mut Adol'f	German	1923	Soldier	4/26/45	4/27/45	17/I
18. Fuksh IAnush Ferents	Hungarian	1922	Soldier	4/27/45	4/27/45	18/I
19. Petriuk Ivan Dmitrievich	Ukrainian	1921	Soldier	4/24/45	4/27/45	19/I
20. Rikhter Gerebert Rikhard	German	1921	Soldier	4/23/45	4/27/45	20/I

TSGOA

1. Transliterated from the Russian Cyrillic alphabet.

Proletarians of All Countries, Unite!

STRICTLY SECRET

COMMUNIST PARTY OF THE SOVIET UNION
CENTRAL COMMITTEE [*TSK KPSS*]

No. P101/U   To: Comrades Molotov (Ministry of Foreign Affairs [*MID*]), Kruglov, and Korobov

December 31, 1954

Extract from Transcript No. 101 of the Meeting of the Presidium of the *TSK* on December 30, 1954

(Return within seven days to the Chancellery of the Presidium of the *TSK KPSS*)

On the Transfer of Three American Citizens to the American Authorities

   1. Authorize the Ministry of Internal Affairs of the USSR (Comrade Kruglov) to:

   a) transfer the American citizens Marchuk and Noble, who i.ave served prison terms in the Soviet Union, to the American authorities in Berlin;

   b) transfer the American citizen Berdin to the American authorities in Berlin 2 to 3 weeks after the transfer of Marchuk and Noble;

   2. Approve the suggestion of the *MID* of the USSR that the message to the American embassy concerning the release of the American citizens Marchuk and Noble raise the issue of the repatriation of eleven children of Soviet citizens currently under detention by the American authorities.

SECRETARY OF THE *TSK*

7610
December 31, 1954
RETURN TO
Secret
[illegible]
"Special File"
[illible] Dept.
TSK KPSS

TSK KPSS

   In a memorandum dated October 23, 1954, and a note dated December 29, 1954, Bohlen, the U.S. ambassador, has requested us to expedite the release of three American citizens, Marchuk, Berdin, and Noble, currently in confinement in the Soviet Union.

   These individuals were arrested by Soviet security organs on the territory of the German Democratic Republic and were sentenced to long terms of confinement.

   Marchuk was detained by the Soviet military police in Potsdam in February 1949 and in July 1950 was sentenced to 25 years at a corrective labor camp for taking part as an interpreter in the interrogations of several Soviet citizens who had betrayed their country; at this time Marchuk was in the service of the American intelligence agencies.

   Berdin was detained in February 1949 by the German People's Police [*Volkspolizei*] and in April 1952 was sentenced by Soviet agencies to 25 years at a corrective labor camp for crossing into the Soviet occupation zone in Germany. Prior to crossing into the Soviet zone Berdin had been a member of an American police squadron in West Germany.

Noble was detained by Soviet agencies in July 1945, was interned at the special camp at Buchenwald, and in June 1950 was sentenced to 15 years at a corrective labor camp because a camera factory in Germany owned by his family had manufactured certain parts for military vehicles during the war in addition to cameras and because after Germany's surrender Noble's apartment was used for a certain period of time to conceal his relative who had previously engaged in espionage on behalf of Nazi Germany.

In light of the fact that Marchuk, Berdin, and Noble were sentenced to long terms of incarceration without sufficient cause, the *TSK KPSS* on May 8, 1954, decided to reduce their terms of incarceration to time served and release them from confinement to be followed by deportation from the Soviet Union.

However, in connection with the delay in the American response to our inquiries with respect to Rastvorov of the *MID*, the *TSK KPSS* issued instructions [break in the text]
[handwritten:] Send to members of the Presidium of the *TSK KPSS*

Top Secret
Draft

RESOLUTION
OF THE PRESIDIUM OF THE *TSK KPSS*

Concerning the Case of RASTVOROV

Approve the proposal of the *MID* of the USSR (Comrade Zorin) and the Committee for State Security [*KGB*] of the Council of Ministers of the USSR (Comrade SEROV) to summon the Ambassador of the United States in Moscow to the *MID* of the USSR to clarify the status of the case involving the Soviet diplomat RASTVOROV detained by the American authorities.

Instruct the *MID* of the USSR (Comrade ZORIN) to explain to the U.S. ambassador in this interview that a positive attitude on the part of the U.S. government to the Soviet government's request concerning RASTVOROV, as contained in the Soviet note of February 15, 1954, would expedite the process of providing the American Embassy in Moscow with the information it desires on the American citizens MARChUK, BERDIN, and NOBLE.

Refrain from transferring these citizens to U.S. representatives until the U.S. government clarifies its position concerning the release of RASTVOROV to Soviet authorities.

Source ?

Draft note to the U.S. Embassy from the Ministry of Foreign Affairs, August 9, 1956, denying that any American servicemen are detained in the USSR

Top Secret

Communist Party of the Soviet Union. Central Committee
No. P31/XXXVII

To Comrade Shepilov (Ministry of Foreign Affairs [*MID*])

Excerpt from minutes No. 31 of the Presidium of the Central Committee from August 9, 1956

Draft note in answer to the United States Embassy on the question of American servicemen allegedly detained in the Soviet Union.

The *MID* draft note responding to the United States Embassy on the question of American servicemen alleged to be detained in the Soviet Union (appended) is approved.

The text of the *MID* response is to be published in the press.

Secretary of the Central Committee

To item XXXVII, minutes No. 31

Secret

The Ministry of Foreign Affairs of the Union of Soviet Socialist Republics sends its respects to the Embassy of the United States of America, and, in regard to the embassy's note No. 42 from July 16 of this year, we have the honor to inform you of the following.

A careful investigation, carried out by responsible Soviet agencies in connection with the request of the government of the U.S.A., as presented in the referenced note from the embassy, has confirmed that there are no American citizens who are U.S. Air Force or Naval Aviation personnel on the territory of the Soviet Union.

The results of the investigation leave no doubt that the conjecture expressed in the note from the embassy about the detention of American servicemen in the Soviet Union has no factual basis and is erroneous.

In connection with the above, the Soviet government considers it necessary to note that the U.S. government evidently has been misinformed by persons who, with their disinformation, are attempting to hinder the development of normal relations between the Soviet Union and the United States.

Secret. Copy No. 1

CENTRAL COMMITTEE, COMMUNIST PARTY OF THE SOVIET UNION

The U.S. Embassy has sent to the Ministry of Foreign Affairs [*MID*] of the Soviet Union a note from July 16, in which, in reference to reports received from persons from various countries who have recently been released from imprisonment by the Soviet Union, it is stated that the U.S. government is in possession of reports about the detention of several U.S. Air Force or Naval Aviation personnel.

In the note it states that although the U.S. government is not able to identify these persons by name, it requests that the Soviet government inform it in detail about all American servicemen who have been detained in the Soviet Union at any time, beginning with Jan. 1, 1949, about whom the U.S. government has not yet been informed.

The U.S. government desires, it states in conclusion, that the Soviet government conduct the most careful investigation possible of this matter and as soon as possible inform the American Embassy about the results of this investigation.

An investigation carried out by the Committee of State Security [*KGB*] has determined that there are no American citizens who are U.S. Air Force or Naval Aviation personnel on the territory of the Soviet Union.

The *MID* of the USSR deems it advisable to send the U.S. Embassy a note in reply, in which it will be pointed out that, as the careful investigation of the matter touched upon in their note has shown, there are no American citizens of the designated categories on Soviet territory and that, consequently, the reports referenced in the note of the U.S. Embassy are mistaken.

The draft of the resolution is appended.

Request your review.

[signature illegible]

Source?

chapter 12

COLD WAR

Relations between the Soviet Union and the United States after the Second World War followed an uneasy course between cooperation and outright hostility and on several occasions led to armed confrontation. The documents in the next two sections illuminate some of the crises of the Cold War, the period of hostility between the two postwar superpowers that never exploded into open warfare. Commentators generally agree that the Cold War began during 1947, as attempts to cooperate on a postwar world settlement foundered on the shoals of mutual suspicions and recriminations. In March of that year, President Harry Truman issued his "Truman Doctrine," an appeal for a global commitment to protect the world from Communist expansion. The Marshall Plan of massive economic aid to rebuild Europe was the cornerstone of this doctrine, and it was the Soviet Union's rejection of Marshall aid for itself and for the Eastern European countries under Communist rule that confirmed the division of Europe by the "iron curtain" that Winston Churchill had described a year earlier. But there is less agreement on the causes and responsibilities for the onset of the Cold War, for there were many conflicting political currents inside each of the belligerent countries. Both the Soviet and the U.S. governments were divided between hard-liners and conciliators. Did the American hard-liners' fears of Soviet aggressive intentions correspond to reality? Or were Soviet moves after 1947 more a defensive response to perceived American hostility? The availability of these and additional documents from the newly opened Russian archives should provide historians with substantial new sources of evidence to reconsider the causes and conduct of the Cold War.

The Cold War was waged globally: in Europe, Germany remained the flash point of tensions until the collapse of the Communist regime in the German Democratic Republic in 1989 and the unification with West Germany the following year. In Asia, conflicts in Korea and Vietnam played out against the backdrop of superpower rivalry. The third world of newly independent nations in Africa, Asia, and Latin America also served as a major and continuing theater of Cold War operations.

Conflicts between the U.S. and USSR already had emerged in the course of wartime negotiations about the fate of postwar Europe. Poland, which had been divided between Germany and the USSR since 1939, was one point of contention: rival governments emerged under the respective protection of the Western allies in London and the USSR in Lublin. The big power conference in Yalta produced a compromise between President Roosevelt and Joseph Stalin, but the Red Army's occupation of Poland facilitated the manipulation of democratic elections and the eventual emergence of a Polish government loyal to Moscow.

Germany constituted an even greater center of conflict. The four allied powers, France, Great Britain, the USSR, and the U.S.A, had agreed to partition Germany into zones of occupation to be administered by an international Allied Control Council. To counter Soviet fears of a remilitarized Germany, U.S. Secretary of State James F. Byrnes had suggested an addendum to the postwar Potsdam agreements on Germany, proposing the unification of Germany with a guarantee of its demilitarization. This proposal was discussed by Kremlin officials between February and May 1946 (Document 307) and was ultimately rejected. By 1948 the three Western powers had decided that they must strengthen their zones in order to counter what they perceived as Soviet aggression in eastern Germany. In June 1948 the allies introduced a currency reform in their zones. The Soviets responded by blockading the western sectors of Berlin, which was located 110 miles inside the Soviet zone. The allies countered with an airlift of supplies to their sectors of Berlin that lasted nearly a year, until the Russians lifted their blockade in May 1949. That fall the division of Germany was sealed with the creation of the Federal Republic of Germany in the west and the German Democratic Republic in the east.

Events in Europe were overshadowed in 1950 by the invasion of South Korea by the Communist government in the north, which led to a military response headed by the United States under the flag of the United Nations. The bloody Korean War lasted until 1953, when an armistice perpetuated the division of the peninsula.

This and other episodes of Cold War hostilities remain relatively undocumented in the materials released for this collection, with the exception of the

Cuban Missile Crisis, which is presented in the following section. In particular, no documents were produced to shed light on the decisions behind Soviet interactions with the Eastern European satellites. Soviet military intervention to crush a general strike in East Germany in 1953, the armed suppression of the Hungarian revolt in 1956, and the invasion of Czechoslovakia in 1968 that put an end to the Prague Spring (the Czechoslovak Communist Party's attempt to refashion "socialism with a human face")—all these episodes reaffirmed Western fears and suspicions of Soviet aggression and militarism.

Throughout the years from 1950 until Gorbachev's assumption of power, Soviet and U.S. foreign policy assumed a fundamental hostility between the two powers, as both nations competed for the allegiance of developing and unaligned nations and sought to keep the other from gaining strategic or diplomatic superiority. Berlin returned to center stage in 1958, the "barometer," in Khrushchev's words, of the world's political atmosphere. In November 1958, Khrushchev attempted to force a resolution to the problem of a divided and remilitarized Germany by demanding an end to the Western occupation of West Berlin and the establishment of Berlin as a "free city" under the control of the German Democratic Republic. Issued in the form of an ultimatum, Khrushchev's demand provoked a flurry of diplomatic activity and summit meetings that failed to resolve the Germany question but that considerably raised world tensions and threatened to lead to war in Europe. The Berlin crisis escalated in August 1961, when the Soviets constructed the Berlin Wall in order to shut off the flow of emigration from East to West Germany and renewed their demands to resolve the German question more generally. This crisis led to a confrontation of Soviet and U.S. tanks at the borders of their Berlin sectors in October 1961 before Khrushchev relented and proclaimed his willingness to negotiate the status of Berlin and Germany.

The Soviet Union's position as unquestioned leader of the Communist world was damaged in the early 1960s, when the People's Republic of China denounced the USSR for abandoning its revolutionary élan. This rivalry in turn shaped the Soviet response to the war in Vietnam, which began as a conflict between the partitioned countries of North and South Vietnam and eventually involved more than 500,000 U.S. troops in the attempt to support the anti-Communist government of South Vietnam. The Soviet Union did not intervene militarily in the struggle but sent aid to the North Vietnamese government and worked for a settlement that would protect its ally. At the same time, these documents of Soviet foreign policy indicate the extensive propaganda machinery employed to turn this conflict and other episodes to the advantage of the Soviet Union in its bid to counter what it described as U.S. imperialism.

Propaganda poster calling for revolution in the Third World. Original in color. *For the power of the Soviets*, by Gershanin and Mikhailov. Publisher: Khudozhestvennoe Izdatel'skoe Aktsionnoe Obshchestvo, Moscow, ca. 1930.

DOCUMENT 305   *President Roosevelt's letter to Stalin, February 6, 1945, written while both were at Yalta, on an acceptable compromise regarding the composition of the postwar Polish government*

[English original]

THE WHITE HOUSE
WASHINGTON

February 6, 1945

My dear Marshal Stalin:

I have been giving a great deal of thought to our meeting this afternoon, and I want to tell you in all frankness what is on my mind.

In so far as the Polish Government is concerned, I am greatly disturbed that the three great powers do not have a meeting of minds about the political setup in Poland. It seems to me that it puts all of us in a bad light throughout the world to have you recognizing one government while we and the British are recognizing another in London. I am sure this state of affairs should not continue and that if it does it can only lead our people to think there is a breach between us, which is not the case. I am determined that there shall be no breach between ourselves and the Soviet Union. Surely there is a way to reconcile our differences.

Marshal V. I. [*sic*] Stalin,
Koreis, The Crimea

I was very much impressed with some of the things you said today, particularly your determination that your rear must be safeguarded as your army moves into Berlin. You cannot, and we must not, tolerate any temporary government which will give your armed forces any trouble of this sort. I want you to know that I am fully mindful of this.

You must believe me when I tell you that our people at home look with a critical eye on what they consider a disagreement between us at this vital stage of the war. They, in effect, say that if we cannot get a meeting of minds now when our armies are converging on the common enemy, how can we get an understanding on even more vital things in the future.

I have had to make it clear to you that we cannot recognize the Lublin Government as now composed, and the world would regard it as a lamentable outcome of our work here if we parted with an open and obvious divergence between us on this issue.

You said today that you would be prepared to support any suggestions for the solution of this problem which offered a fair chance of success, and you also mentioned the possibility of bringing some members of the Lublin government here.

Realizing that we all have the same anxiety in getting this matter settled, I would like to develop your proposal a little and suggest that we invite here to Yalta at once Mr. Beirut [Bierut] and Mr. Osubka [Osóbka] Morawski from the Lublin government and also two or three from the following list of Poles, which according to our information would be desirable as representatives of the other elements of the Polish people in the development of a new temporary government which all three of us could recognize and support: Bishop Sapieha of Cracow, Vincente [Wincenty] Witos, Mr. Zurlowski [Żulawski], Professor Buyak [Bujak], and Professor Kutzeba [Kutrzeba]. If, as a result of the presence of these Polish leaders here, we could jointly agree with them on a provisional government in Poland which should no doubt include some Polish leaders from abroad such as Mr. Mikolajczyk, Mr. Grabski, and Mr. Romer, the United States Government, and I feel sure the British Government as well, would then be prepared to examine with you conditions in which they would dissociate themselves from the London government and transfer their recognition to the new provisional government.

I hope I do not have to assure you that the United States will never lend its support in any way to any provisional government in Poland that would be inimical to your interests.

It goes without saying that any interim government which could be formed as a result of our conference with the Poles here would be pledged to the holding of free elections in Poland at the earliest possible date. I know this is completely consistent with your desire to see a new free and democratic Poland emerge from the welter of this war.

Most sincerely yours,

Franklin Roosevelt

APRF, fond 45, op. 1, d. 370, ll. 6–12.

DOCUMENT 306   *Report from Marshal Zhukov to Stalin, July 30, 1945, about the first meeting of the international coalition set up to control Berlin*

TO SUPREME COMMANDER-IN-CHIEF GENERALISSIMO OF THE SOVIET UNION

COMRADE STALIN

On July 30 at 1300 hours Berlin time, in the headquarters of General EISENHOWER in Berlin, the first meeting of the Control Council took place.

Present at the meeting were:

General EISENHOWER, Field Marshal MONTGOMERY, and General KOENIG, along with their political advisers and deputies.

The meeting dealt with the question of the organization and structure of the Control Council and some particular issues raised by Field Marshal MONTGOMERY, General EISENHOWER, KOENIG, and myself.

On the question of the organization and structure of the Control Council, General EISENHOWER proposed that the Allies' conclusions on this issue be turned over to the Deputy Commanders-in-Chief for finalization so that the matter can be closed and a decision reached at the next meeting of the Control Council.

The Control Council agreed to General EISENHOWER'S proposal and entrusted this work to Generals SOKOLOVSKII, CLAY (American), ROBERTS (English), and KELTZ (French).

General EISENHOWER further proposed that a meeting of the Control Council be convened the tenth, twentieth and thirtieth of every month and at any time proposed by the Commanders-in-Chief.

The chairman of these sessions is to be elected for a term of one month.

The Control Council approved these proposals.

Field Marshal MONTGOMERY proposed that chairmen be elected in the alphabetical order of the countries:
- For the month of August: General EISENHOWER;
- For the month of September: Field Marshal MONTGOMERY;
- For the month of October: General KOENIG;
- For the month of November: Marshal ZhUKOV.

This proposal also was approved by the Control Council.

Field Marshal MONTGOMERY then introduced a proposal to designate to the French the following two districts of Greater Berlin: Wedding and Reinickendorf

Since designation of these districts came at the expense of the English sector of Greater Berlin, the proposal met no objection from the Control Council.

Field Marshal MONTGOMERY proposed that a decision be taken on assigning one airport to each of the Allies in Berlin.

Since this proposal was not known to us earlier, I asked Field Marshal MONTGOMERY to present his position in writing.

Field Marshal MONTGOMERY requested that until a decision on this matter is reached the English maintain the right to use Kladow airport.

I did not object, and the Control Council accepted my proposal.

General KOENIG asked the representatives of the Control Council to help the French organize the French sector of Berlin as quickly as possible.

The Control Council promised this help.

At the conclusion of the meeting, I directed the attention of the Control Council to the Allies' poor performance of their responsibilities to deliver oil and foodstuffs to Berlin.

General EISENHOWER and Field Marshal MONTGOMERY suggested that this matter be turned over to their deputies for resolution and that all requisite measures be taken to ensure fulfillment of their responsibilities.

The meeting of the Control Council concluded at 1500, July 30, 1945.

MARSHAL OF THE SOVIET UNION

G. Zhukov

APRF, fond 3, op. 64, d. 703, ll. 3–5.

DOCUMENT 307   *Comments to Stalin from Zhukov and Litvinov, May 24, 1946, on the American Secretary of State Byrnes's proposals for the disarming and demilitarization of Germany and Japan*

Proletarians of All Countries, Unite!   STRICTLY SECRET
All-Union Communist Party (Bolsheviks) [*VKP(b)*]

CENTRAL COMMITTEE [*TSK*]
No. P32   May 22, 1946

TO MEMBERS AND CANDIDATES OF THE POLITBURO OF *TSK VKP(b)*,
MEMBERS OF THE COLLEGIUM OF THE USSR MINISTRY OF FOREIGN AFFAIRS
AND MEMBERS OF THE HIGHER MILITARY SOVIET.
Comrade_____

Forwarded to you for your familiarization are two proposals of U.S. Secretary of State Byrnes: 1) Draft treaty on the disarmament and demilitarization of Germany and 2) Draft treaty for the disarmament and demilitarization of Japan.

Request that you report to *TSK VKP(b)* within 5–6 days your comments on these proposals.
Secretary *TSK VKP(b)* J. Stalin

<u>The Byrnes draft treaty was distributed to the following Comrades:</u>

1. Andreev - reply received
2. Beria
3. Voroshilov - reply received
4. Zhdanov
5. Kaganovich -reply received
6. Kalinin - reply received
7. Malenkov
8. Mikoyan - documents returned [illegible]
9. Molotov
10. Stalin
11. Khrushchev - documents returned
12. Bulganin
13. Voznesenskii - reply rec'd
14. Kosygin
15. Shvernik - reply rec'd
16. Vyshinsky - reply rec'd
17. Dekanozov   "   "
18. Litvinov   "   "
19. Lozovskii   "   "
20. Gerashchenko
21. Golunskii - not sent
22. Maiskii - reply received
23. Novikov - reply received
24. Pavlov
25. Silin
26. TSarapkin - not sent
27. Antonov - not sent
28. Budennyi - reply received
29. Vasilevskii
30. Vershinin - reply received
31. Voronov - reply received
32. Govorov - reply received
33. Zhukov - reply received
34. Konev - documents returned
35. Kuznetsov - documents returned
36. Rokossovskii - reply received
37. Sokolovskii
38. Khrulev

To *TSK VKP(b)*

To Comrade S T A L I N

Reporting my comments on the draft treaty of U.S. Secretary of State Byrnes on the disarmament and demilitarization of Germany.

It is my opinion that the true purpose of the draft treaty is:
-the desire to end the occupation of Germany and to remove the armed forces of the Soviet Union from Germany as soon as possible. This is necessary to the Americans and British in order to raise the question of the withdrawal of our forces from Poland, and in the future also from the Balkan states;
-the desire to disrupt the export of equipment and manufactured goods as reparations from Germany to the Soviet Union;
-the desire to preserve military potential in Germany as the necessary base for fulfilling their aggressive objectives in the future;
-the desire to inhibit the growth of political activity of the masses and the growth of Communist party influence in Europe.

Everything that BYRNES proposes in the draft treaty for the disarmament and demilitarization of Germany is already contained in the German surrender and was announced in the proclamation of Germany's defeat.

In the introductory section of the draft treaty, BYRNES states that the disarmament and demilitarization of Germany have already been accomplished for the most part and that all that remains to be done is ensure that Germany stays completely disarmed and demilitarized.

This assertion does not correspond to reality and is false. The actual state of affairs with respect to Germany's disarmament is quite different, especially in the British and American occupation zones.

Consequently, instead of drafting and adopting a new treaty, what we should do now is ensure that the existing treaties are scrupulously enforced.

Byrnes's proposal to institute quadrilateral inspection and organize a control commission is unworthy of consideration, because even a Control Council based on the occupying powers has not managed to achieve any tangible results, except in the Soviet occupation zone, and a commission would be even less capable of completing the task of German disarmament.

A control commission to foil any attempts to revive German militarism and Germany's ability to wage war could be accepted only when the occupation authorities complete the task of disarmament and demilitarization.

I suggest:
1. Abstain from accepting the treaty.
2. Accept a coordinated document obliging the Control Council in Germany to issue a declaration on the defeat of Germany and the decision of the Potsdam Conference and to recognize that raising the issue of ending the occupation is premature.

In view of my weak knowledge of the situation in Japan, I can make no comments on the draft [treaty] for disarming Japan.

May 24, 1946   MARSHAL OF THE SOVIET UNION [signed] G. ZhUKOV

Copy No. 1
May 25, 1946

[handwritten: From Litvinov]

TO GENERAL SECRETARY OF THE *TSK VKP(b)*
Comrade J. V. STALIN

Comments on the American "Draft Treaties"

The substance of these documents is far less than what the Americans advertised. They wrote and talked about some kind of allied treaties, allied guarantees, and so forth. We might have imagined that they were talking about a quadrilateral treaty of mutual assistance in the event of renewed German aggression. But in fact, it is hardly possible to speak of any sort of treaty or agreement whatsoever.

These documents are merely drafts of provisions for German and Japanese disarmament which should be included in the peace treaties. We might ask why the Americans had to draft a separate agreement for one section of a peace treaty whose basic provisions had already been outlined at the Potsdam Conference and had provoked no disagreement whatsoever. Obviously Byrnes's gesture is designed solely for ulterior political propaganda motives, namely, creating the illusion of guaranteeing complete security vis-à-vis Germany and Japan. Once our security is assured, ostensibly, our various actions and demands that have given rise to disagreements between us and the western powers will lose their rationale. One might even assume—and this poses the greatest danger of all—that signing the proposed "treaties" will serve as a prelude to the demand for an early end to the occupation of Germany.

It is true that Article IV mentions a subsequent agreement which would stipulate "the size and kinds of armed forces that each country should provide for the purpose of enforcing the treaties." The draft, however, provides absolutely no indication of whether these forces should be stationed in German territory at all or for how long. Article III, which states that "Germany's acceptance of Articles I and II will constitute a necessary condition for the termination of the allied occupation," is particularly suspicious. This could be interpreted as providing for termination of the occupation after Germany's acceptance of Articles I and II even before Germany has signed a peace treaty.

In my opinion, our response to Byrnes's proposal should be to point out the nature of the proposed drafts as soon as possible, i.e., we should publicly explain that Byrnes's proposal merely covers one section of the future peace treaties and does not constitute the basis for any special agreement by which the United States would assume any obligations over and above the obligations which it would be forced to assume pursuant to the peace treaties. In the process we might express our doubts concerning the timeliness and benefits of such a special agreement on issues which have never been in dispute before. But if for some reason the Americans insist on a special agreement, we would not have any fundamental objections as long as they do not try to split up the peace treaties and as long as they work towards an agreement for the disarmament of Germany and Japan. As a basic precondition, however, we would have to insist on an agreement which would maintain some kind of occupation of Germany, at least until Germany signs a full-fledged peace treaty, and for a long time afterward.

Certain clauses of the drafts elicited the following comments:

Article A-I-a of the Potsdam Resolutions on disarmament are somewhat more complete than Article I-A in Byrnes's draft. Moreover, Article I of Byrnes's draft says absolutely nothing about a ban on the production and importation of toxic agents or the construction of fortifications. For some mysterious reason, Point D-2 of Article I of the draft treaty with Germany prohibiting "fissionable materials" was omitted from the draft of the treaty with Japan.

By the way, the very same clause of the draft treaty with Germany permits fissionable materials under conditions approved by the treaty powers. Experience has shown that any provisions involving approval and consent should always stipulate unanimity.

The same comment applies to Point [illegible] of Article I, which talks of the possibility of exceptions to disarmament under conditions to be determined by the treaty powers.

Article IV discusses violations of the disarmament provisions which would call for action deemed suitable "by a majority of the members of the commission" and stipulates that in general action could only be taken "by general agreement." The principle of making decisions by a majority of votes contained in this clause is especially dangerous. In my opinion we must stipulate that in the event of a disagreement, any treaty power may act alone, at its own risk and responsibility and with its own resources, to prevent violations of the disarmament provisions.

It is interesting that the very same Article IV of the draft treaty with Germany requires that reports of inspection results be submitted to the Security Council of the United Nations. Whether by accident or intention, the Security Council is never mentioned in the same article of the draft treaty with Japan.

The effective term of the agreement should run 50 years instead of 25 years, with the provision that after 25 years the treaty powers should consult with one another every five years on the possibility of amending the treaty or terminating it altogether.

[signed] M. LITVINOV

Two copies made
copy 1 to Stalin
copy 2 to file

APRF, fond 3, op. 64, d. 704, ll. 3–5, 14, 63–70.

DOCUMENT 308   *Note from Abakumov, Minister of State Security, to Stalin, May 21, 1947, detailing an American request to Soviet occupation forces to accept 1,950 German POWs accused of committing war crimes in Soviet-controlled zones in Germany and in the USSR*

[an. 4]   Top Secret
                                              Copy No. 1

USSR
Ministry of State Security

USSR Council of Ministers

May 21, 1947
No. 2774/a
City of Moscow

To: Comrade J. V. S T A L I N

Recently the American occupation forces in Germany have appealed several times to the Soviet military administration proposing [that the administration] accept Germans arrested by them: members of the SD [*Sicherheitsdienst*—Security Service], gestapo, SS [*Schutzstaffeln*—Special Military Forces], and other war criminals numbering 1,950 persons, guilty of crimes committed on USSR territory or in the Soviet occupation zone in Germany.

The USSR Ministry of State Security considers it advisable to have representatives of the Soviet military administration in Germany accept from the American occupation forces the 1,950 war criminals arrested by them, accommodate them in one of the camps of the USSR Ministry of Internal Affairs in the Soviet occupation zone, and with the forces of workers from the plenipotentiary organ of the USSR Ministry of State Security in Germany conduct an investigation of the crimes committed by them.

I request your instructions.

Sent to: [signed] ABAKUMOV
Comrade Stalin
Comrade Molotov

APRF, fond 3, op. 64, d. 705, l. 79.

DOCUMENT 309   *Note from Gromyko to Stalin, September 30, 1949, on the forming of a separate government in Western Germany*

Politburo Minutes No. 71 [?], pt. 2229 [?]

To Comrade STALIN J. V.

On September 20, 1949, a separate government was formed (in Bonn) for the western zones of Germany. In connection with this new step by the governments of the U.S.A., Great Britain, and France, designed to deepen the division of Germany, we ought to react to these divisive actions by sending the appropriate notes to the governments of the three powers.

Sending notes to the governments of the U.S.A., Great Britain, and France is called for not only because of the need to react to the new step by the three powers to divide Germany, resulting in the establishment of a separate government in Bonn, but also by the impending formation of the Government of the German Democratic

Republic in Berlin. These notes are part of a general plan of measures to be carried out in connection with the planned formation of a government in Berlin.

The Ministry of Foreign Affairs of the USSR also advises that the Soviet ambassadors to Poland, Czechoslovakia, Hungary, Romania, and Bulgaria and the envoy to Albania be instructed to visit the foreign ministries and inform them of the impending delivery of the aforementioned notes from the Soviet government. Furthermore, we should express our desire that the governments of Czechoslovakia and Poland, in light of the formation of the puppet government for the western zones of Germany, also send notes to the governments of the U.S.A., Great Britain, and France, and that the Romanian, Bulgarian, Albanian, and Hungarian ministries of foreign affairs issue appropriate statements on this matter. Being informed well in advance of the impending delivery of the notes to the three powers, the governments of these countries will be able to prepare themselves better to support the Soviet Union and its position on the German question.

A draft note to the governments of the U.S.A., Great Britain, and France and a draft resolution are attached.

Please review.

[signed] A. Gromyko

September 30, 1949

APRF, fond 3, op. 64, d. 707, ll. 56–57.

DOCUMENT 310 *Gromyko's entry of October 1, 1949, in his daily record, detailing his individual meetings with American Ambassador Kirk, British Ambassador Kelly, and French Chargé d'Affaires Frankfort*

Secret, copy 1

From the diary of
A. A. Gromyko October 4, 1949
No. 175/ag

RECEPTION

OF U.S. AMBASSADOR KIRK, BRITISH AMBASSADOR KELLY,
AND FRENCH CHARGÉ D'AFFAIRES FRANKFORT

October 1, 1949

Today I invited U.S. Ambassador Kirk, British Ambassador Kelly, and French Chargé d'affaires Frankfort, who visited me separately between 1900 and 2000.

I told each of them that I have been instructed by the Soviet government to present a note on the question of creating a separate government for West Germany.

Kirk, Kelly, and Frankfort said they would make the text of the note known to their governments immediately.

Frankfort, accepting the text of the note, asked me if the note was analogous to those notes handed today to the British and American ambassadors in Moscow.

I said that the text of the note to the French government was analogous to the texts of the notes to the English and the American governments.

Kirk, who recently returned from a trip to Stalingrad, shared in conversation his impressions from the excursion, saying that he was very much satisfied with the trip. Kirk also reported that he plans to leave Moscow within the next few days and visit France and a few other countries in Western Europe.

DEPUTY MINISTER OF FOREIGN AFFAIRS
OF THE USSR

[signed] A. Gromyko

APRF, fond 3, op. 64, d. 707, l. 58.

DOCUMENT 311   *Note from Gromyko to Stalin, October 9, 1949, on the U.S., British, and French response concerning the German issue*

To Comrade J. V. Stalin

The Ministry of Foreign Affairs [*MID*] of the USSR has received responses from the American, English, and French governments to the communiqué of October 1, 1949 from the Soviet government on the matter of the formation of a separate government in Bonn. In these responses the above-mentioned governments dispute the fact that the puppet "government" of West Germany created by them represents a direct violation by these governments of the decisions of the Potsdam Conference.

MID would advise replying to the English and French governments through communiqués in which the position of the Soviet government, stated in its communiqué of October 1 on the German question, is reaffirmed.

As for the American reply, *MID* proposes to return to the American embassy its communiqué with the attached text of the statement by Acting Secretary of State Webb, distributed to representatives of the press in Washington on October 6 of this year. This statement by Webb contains a series of coarse and slanderous attacks on the Soviet Union.

The draft resolution and draft communiqués to the governments of the U.S.A., Great Britain, and France are attached.

I request your review.

October 19, 1949   [signed] A. Gromyko

APRF, fond 3, op. 64, d. 707, l. 1.

Propaganda poster depicting the Soviet Union's former allies as partners in the "Anti-Comintern Pact." (Left to right) Benelux, de Gaulle, Bevin, Churchill, United States. Original in color. *An old song in a new key*, by B. Efimov and N. Dolgorukov. Publisher: Iskusstvo, Moscow-Leningrad, 1949. Prints and Photographs Division, Library of Congress.

DOCUMENT 312   *Resolution of the Central Committee, September 16, 1950, to revise a diplomatic note on the question of general elections in Germany and Gromyko's note to Stalin on this matter*

Proletarians of All Countries, Unite!   STRICTLY SECRET

All-Union Communist Party (Bolsheviks) [*VKP(b)*]. CENTRAL COMMITTEE.
Minutes 77/393
September 16, 1950   To Comrades Malenkov, Gromyko.

Excerpt from minutes No. 77 of a *VKP(b)* Politburo session

Decision of September 16, 1950

393. Draft of a note from the Soviet government to the governments of the U.S.A., England, and France concerning Germany-wide elections.

1. Observe that the USSR Ministry of Foreign Affairs is late in presenting to the Politburo the draft note from the Soviet government to the governments of the U.S.A., England, and France on the issue of Germany-wide elections.

2. Consider unacceptable the draft note presented by the USSR Ministry of Foreign Affairs and instruct Comrade Gromyko to revise it within 5 days based on the discussion that has occurred.

Central Committee of the *VKP(b)* Politburo

[handwritten:] From the notes of Com. Gromyko of October 9, 1950.

To Comrade J. V. STALIN

On behalf of their governments, the English, U.S., and French Supreme Commanders in the western zones of Germany have sent letters to Comrade Chuikov proposing to start negotiations on preparing a draft electoral law and holding Germany-wide elections to the National Constituent Assembly of Germany.

They propose taking as the basis for the talks the declaration by the foreign ministers of England, the U.S.A., and France concerning the unification of Germany and also the resolution of the "Bonn government" on holding Germany-wide elections. These documents contain conditions that are clearly not acceptable to us. In particular they envisage that the electoral law be prepared by representatives of the four occupying powers, and not by representatives of the German people, and they contain a demand that reparations from current production be stopped, that Soviet joint-stock companies in Germany be liquidated, et al.

Considering the upcoming October 15 elections in the German Democratic Republic, the USSR Ministry of Foreign Affairs advises giving an answer to these letters on behalf of the Soviet government to the governments of the U.S.A., England, and France after October 15.

The draft answer prepared by the Ministry of Foreign Affairs evaluates the proposals by the representatives of the three powers and contains our counterproposals concerning Germany-wide elections; our positions are consistent with the decisions of the Potsdam Conference.

The draft resolution of the *VKP(b)* Central Committee is attached. I request your review.

A. Gromyko

September 14, 1950
    112-gi. copy No.1

APRF, fond 3, op. 64, d. 707, ll. 120–21.

DOCUMENT 313   *Communication from Gromyko to Stalin, September 22, 1950, concerning a draft reply to the United States, England, and France on the matter of the national police of the German Democratic Republic*

All-Union Communist Party (Bolsheviks) [*VKP(b)*]. CENTRAL COMMITTEE [*TSK*].
P.78/32   To Comrades Malenkov, Gromyko

September 25, 1950. Excerpt from Minutes No. 78, session of the Politburo of the Central Committee of the *VKP(b)*

Decision of September 25, 1950

32. Draft communiqué from the Soviet government to the governments of the U.S.A., England, and France on the matter of the national police of the German Democratic Republic.

To instruct Comrade Gromyko to present within 3 days, based on an exchange of opinions, an explanatory note and amended reply from the USSR government to the governments of the U.S.A., England, and France concerning the national police of the German Democratic Republic.

Politburo *TSK VKP(b)*
To Comrade J .V. STALIN

The governments of the U.S.A., England, and France have sent to the Ministry of Foreign Affairs [*MID*] of the USSR communiqués of similar content asserting that the national police of the German Democratic Republic do not perform normal police functions but have the character of an army. In connection with this the communiqués charge the Soviet government with violating the decisions of the Potsdam Conference and other quadrilateral international agreements on the demilitarization of Germany.

The *MID* advises sending the governments of the U.S.A., England, and France replies deflecting these assertions as groundless, pointing out that the national police of the GDR was created for the protection of the democratic processes established in the GDR in accordance with the decisions of the Potsdam Conference on the democratization of Germany.

Facts about the creation of an army in the guise of armed police by the governments of the U.S.A., England, and France in West Germany appear in this communiqué.

The *TSK VKP(b)* has already examined the matter of sending replies to the governments of the three powers. It was decided to return to this question later.

Considering the meetings of the western powers now taking place on the question of rearming West Germany and the launching of a broad campaign in the west European press for the creation of German armed forces, the *MID* requests again your review of the Soviet government's response.

The draft resolution is attached.

I request your review.

September 22, 1950   [signed] A. Gromyko
No.147-GI

Copies sent to Comrades: Molotov,
                            Malenkov,
                            Beria,
                            Mikoyan,
                            Kaganovich,
                            Bulganin,
                            Khrushchev.

APRF, fond 3, op. 64, d. 707, ll. 143–45.

Central Committee resolution, June 28, 1963, on the U.S. request for assistance in securing the release of U.S. pilots stranded in North Korea

COMMUNIST PARTY OF THE SOVIET UNION, CENTRAL COMMITTEE

Top Secret

No. P104/24

To Comrades Suslov, Andropov, Gromyko

Excerpt from minutes No. 104 of the June 28, 1963, meeting of the Presidium of the Central Committee of the Communist Party of the Soviet Union

About the appeal of the U.S. government requesting assistance in the return of members of the crew of an American military helicopter that landed in the territory of the People's Democratic Republic of Korea [KNDR] on May 17, 1963.

1. Inform the government of KNDR about the appeal of the U.S. government to the Soviet government requesting assistance in the return of two members of the crew of a U.S. Armed Forces helicopter that landed in North Korean territory May 17, 1963 (a draft of the directive to the Soviet ambassador in Pyongyang is appended).

2. Do not reply to the request of the U.S. government. If the Americans raise this question again, inform them that their request has been brought to the attention of the North Korean government.

Secretary of the Central Committee

Secret. Copy No. 2

CENTRAL COMMITTEE, COMMUNIST PARTY OF THE SOVIET UNION

The U.S. government has addressed an appeal through the American Embassy in Moscow to the Soviet government with a request to render "good offices" and assist in the return of two members of the crew of a U.S. Armed Forces helicopter that made a "forced landing" in North Korean territory.

According to available information, this helicopter was brought down by the North Korean military after it had violated the demarcation line and appeared over North Korean territory.

During an oral report from the American Embassy on this matter, it was noted that attempts by American representatives to gain the return of the helicopter and its crew through the Military Commission for Armistice in Korea had been unsuccessful, although the American side had counted on a positive resolution of the matter, all the more because on May 27, 1963, the "United Nations Command of Forces in Korea" had turned over to North Korean authorities several North Korean fishermen who had been detained earlier.

We do not know either the details of the incident with the American helicopter or the disposition of our Korean comrades in regard to this incident.

The Ministry of Foreign Affairs of the USSR deems it advisable to inform our Korean comrades about said request from the U.S. government, emphasizing when doing this that the Soviet side, of course, has made no promises to the Americans.

It is deemed advisable to make no reply to the request from the U.S. government. If the Americans raise this matter again, it would be possible to inform them that their request has been brought to the attention of the North Korean government.

A draft of the resolution is appended.

Please review it.

June 25, 1963   A. Gromyko

No. 1957/GS

True copy

Source?

SPECIAL FOLDER/ Top Secret
Politburo Minutes No. 73, Point 47

USSR
KGB, Council of Ministers of the USSR

February 24, 1968

No. 438-A
Central Committee [*TSK*] of the Communist Party of the Soviet Union [*KPSS*]

Information in our possession indicates that the Japanese committee "Peace to Vietnam" (*Beheiren*) continues to provide active assistance to American military deserters in their illegal departure from Japan to seek political asylum in third countries.

In early November 1967 *Beheiren* organized the transportation of four American sailors deserting the aircraft carrier *Intrepid* to the Soviet Union. In February of this year the same committee illegally sent an American serviceman of Korean ancestry to Hong Kong [handwritten], from where he was to travel on to the Korean People's Democratic Republic [handwritten].

Beheiren made extensive and effective use of these incidents in a propaganda campaign to expose American aggression in Vietnam as well as to strengthen anti-war sentiment among U.S. servicemen and to entice them to refuse to participate in the war in Vietnam.

At the present time, the Japanese committee "Peace to Vietnam" is preparing to transport illegally from Japan three American servicemen who abandoned their units: Corporal I. L. Knets [handwritten] and privates E. S. Arnett and F. E. Collicot [handwritten], proposing to send them to Europe through the Soviet Union.

The *Beheiren* leaders are planning to accomplish the transportation of this group of Americans from Japan to the territory of the Soviet Union using the committee's own resources.

At one of the meetings with our representative, the secretary of the "Peace to Vietnam" committee, YOSHIKAWA, appealed for financial support, specifically to accomplish this undertaking, in the amount of 200,000 yen (500 transferrable rubles). At the same time, YOSHIKAWA reported that in late February of this year, the chairman of the Japanese committee "Peace to Vietnam," ODA, will travel through Cambodia to the Soviet Union and several European countries to establish closer contacts with European pacifist organizations that are taking up the cause of Vietnam.

In view of the above, the *KGB* recommends the following course of action:

1. Exploiting the *KGB*'s secret contact with the leaders of the Japanese committee "Peace to Vietnam," assist the committee to continue its activities including material support when needed to expand its propaganda activity and to accomplish illegal transportation of American military deserters from Japan to third countries.

2. The *KGB* should inform the secretary of the committee "Peace to Vietnam" YOSHIKAWA, that the Soviet Union cannot at this time permit the illegal transportation of Americans to the territory of the USSR using Soviet means of conveyance. At the same time, let it be known that if the committee finds other means to transport Americans to USSR territory (e.g., from the island of Hokkaido onboard Japanese fishing boats), the Soviet side will not prevent this.

3. Instruct the Soviet Committee of Solidarity with the Nations of Asia and Africa, in the name of the Vietnam Support Committee, to receive the American military deserters arriving from Japan, to work with them in a plan that is beneficial to the Soviet Union, and to provide for their departure to countries offering them political asylum (agreed to by Comrade ZASOKhOVOI).

Instruct the Vietnam Support Committee to establish close contacts with the Japanese committee "Peace to Vietnam," exploiting for this end the proposed visit to the USSR by the committee's secretary ODA.

For its part, the *KGB* is prepared through unofficial means at its disposal to assist in maintaining contact with the leadership of the Japanese committee "Peace to Vietnam" as well as in influencing it to the advantage of the Soviet Union.

A draft resolution is attached.

Request your review.

CHAIRMAN OF THE *KGB*

[signed] Andropov ANDROPOV

Source?

DOCUMENT 316 *Report to the Central Committee by A. Yakovlev, assistant chief of the Department of Propaganda, January 21, 1971, on additional measures for the anti-imperialist propaganda campaign*

Secret

CENTRAL COMMITTEE. COMMUNIST PARTY OF THE SOVIET UNION [*TSK KPSS*]
Additional Measures To Expose Imperialist Policies

With the goal of intensifying the struggle to expose the policies of imperialism it seems advisable to plan propaganda campaigns in advance centered around events that most clearly characterize the essence of these policies. Such an approach, in our opinion, will make our anti-imperialistic propaganda more concrete and convincing.

We intend to make use of concrete facts to expose capitalist reality, political and ideological sabotage of imperialism, the totalitarian character of the bourgeois state, and the strengthening of reactionary thought in the bourgeois apparatus and in capitalist society as a whole.

The realization of such measures will permit us to coordinate the Soviet press, radio, and television in such a way that the public's attention will be directed to the concrete manifestations of the antipopular nature of imperialism.

Such propaganda campaigns will help the press agency Novosti and politically oriented radio programs transmitted abroad to force our ideological enemy onto disadvantageous paths in the ideological struggle.

A calendar of this type of events, mainly pertaining to the U.S.A., is attached. Similar plans pertaining to other imperialist states could be developed in due course.

We request your review.

Assistant Chief of the Propaganda Department (A. Yakovlev)
TSK KPSS
January 21, 1971

[Upper left corner:] Without right of publication.
[Upper right corner:] Stamp of the *TSK KPSS*.

Attachment 170 <u>Calendar of Certain Events</u>

January 1, 1863 - In the U.S.A. the act to free Black slaves went into effect. Provides a rationale to point out the severity of the ethnic problem in the United States of America.

January 5, 1957 - President Eisenhower in a message to Congress set forth an expansionist U.S. policy for the Near East and Middle East that became known as the "Eisenhower-Dulles Doctrine."

January 5, 1970 - In the U.S.A. progressive trade union activist Yablonsky was killed.

January 17, 1966 - In Spain, in the Palomares region, an American bomber plane with 4 nuclear bombs on board crashed.

- 140 years ago in the U.S.A., the so-called Lynch law went into effect.

February 2, 1848 - End of the Mexican-American War, which resulted in the U.S.A. seizing from Mexico Texas, New Mexico, and Upper California and part of Arizona

February 1951 - In the U.S.A. seven falsely accused Blacks executed

February 7, 1965 - Beginning of systematic bombing of the Democratic Republic of Vietnam by the U.S.A.

February 9, 1950 - Beginning of the "McCarthy Era"

March 1, 1961 - Decade of the "Peace Corps U.S.A.," an organization engaging in subversive activity in Africa and Asia

March 5, 1946 - Churchill's speech at Fulton—the beginning of the "Cold War" against socialist countries

March 12, 1947 - Acceptance in the U.S.A. of Truman's aggressive foreign policy doctrine

March 16, 1965 - Bloody reprisals against participants in the Black freedom march in Selma

March 23, 1947 - Truman's order to verify the loyalty of all government employees

April 1914 - Shooting of participants in Colorado strike

April 4, 1949 - Creation of NATO

April 4, 1969 - The leader of the movement for the civil rights of American Negroes, Martin Luther King, is assassinated in the U.S.A..

April 14, 1865 - President Abraham Lincoln is assassinated.

April 15–19, 1961 - Attempted armed invasion of Cuba by the U.S.A.

April 1861 - Beginning of the Civil War in the U.S.A.

April 25, 1898 - Beginning of the Spanish-American War. The first war of imperialism for the redivision of the world, resulting in U.S.A. seizure of the Phillipines, Guam, Puerto Rico, and Cuba.

April 27, 1965 - U.S.A. intervention in the Dominican Republic

April 30, 1970 - Invasion of American forces into Cambodia

May 1, 1886 - Chicago strike in U.S.A.

May 4, 1970 - Shooting deaths of students at Kent State University in the U.S.A.

May 11, 1894 - Beginning of the Pullman strike

May 24, 1918 - Beginning of U.S.A. intervention in the Soviet North

May 26, 1938 - Creation in the U.S.A. of the Un-American Activities Committee

June 5, 1947 - U.S.A. adopts expansionist "Marshall Plan"

June 5, 1968 - Robert Kennedy assassinated

June 23, 1947 - U.S.A. adopts antilabor Taft-Hartley Act

June 1950 - Beginning of U.S.A. intervention in Korea

June 25, 1968 - Destruction of the American poor people's "Resurrection City" in Washington

June 28, 1932 - "Bloody Thursday"—shooting of war veterans—participants in a march on Washington

June 1963 - Murder of Medgar Evers, famous Negro activist in U.S.A.

July 16, 1877 - Beginning of a railroad strike—the first national strike in the U.S.A. to spread to all main railroads in the country

July 20, 1948 - Trial of 11 U.S.A. Communist Party leaders begins

July 1960 - Belgian government with U.S.A. support begins direct armed intervention in the Republic of the Congo

August 4, 1964 - Provocations by U.S.A. armed forces against Democratic Republic of Vietnam in the Gulf of Tonkin

August 4, 1953 - U.S.A. intervention in Guatemala

August 6, 1945 - Atomic bomb dropped on Hiroshima and Nagasaki

August 1918 - U.S.A. intervention in the Soviet Far East

August 23, 1927 - Execution of Sacco and Vanzetti

August 24, 1954 - U.S.A. adopts law "to monitor Communist activity"

August 27, 1968 - Political reprisals against participants in mass antiwar demonstration in Chicago

September 23, 1950 - U.S.A. adopts the McCarran-Wood "law on internal security"

September–October 1919 - National strike in the U.S.A. in which 2 million people take part

October 31, 1956 - Triple aggression of England, France, and Israel against Egypt

November 19, 1915 - Poet Joe Hill shot in the U.S.A.

November 22, 1963 - Assassination of John Kennedy

November 22, 1970 - Portuguese colonizers commit act of armed aggression against the Republic of Guinea

December 1931 - Two "hunger marches" on Washington by U.S.A. poor

TSKhSD, fond 4, op. 29, d. 1110.

DOCUMENT 317 **Report to the Central Committee by Defense Minister Ustinov, June 22, 1978, on reactions of military personnel to the Pravda editorial, "On the Current Policy of the U.S. government."**

Central Committee of the Communist Party of the Soviet Union
Responses of army and navy personnel to the editorial
"On the current policy of the U.S. government."

In connection with the editorial "On the current policy of the U.S. government," published in *Pravda* and other newspapers, wide-ranging and multifaceted popular/political work has been conducted among all branches of the Armed Forces, in all military districts, in groups of forces, and in the fleet. Political organs have held conferences in which the specific assignments of propaganda and interpretation of this important document were defined for commanders, political workers, and party organizations, along with instruction of staff and non-staff propagandists.

Everywhere there have been organized sessions to listen to radio programs and watch television broadcasts based on these materials. The leadership of the branches of service, military districts, army groups, fleets, strategic formations, and combined units are taking an active part in propaganda and explanation. Staff meetings, readings of the editorial, political information meetings, discussion groups have been held in subunits and units, on ships, in military institutions and schools. The contents of the editorial were quickly transmitted to ships at sea, to subunits and units on alert duty, to remote garrisons.

The members of the army and navy unanimously support and agree with the principled and consistent activity of the Communist Party and the Soviet government regarding the implementation of foreign policy goals set by the 25th congress of the Communist Party of the Soviet Union, and they emphasize the notable role of Comrade Leonid Il'ich Brezhnev in the work of strengthening peace, security, and cooperation among peoples.

Thus, flight commander, pilot first class Captain I. N. Dergachev (Borisoglebsk Higher Military Aviation Pilots' School) announced: "I read the piece with careful attention. I wholeheartedly agree with and support the principled evaluation of U.S. policy, which is directed at aggravating relations with the Soviet Union, returning to the times of the Cold War. Neither the arms race nor the crude attacks on the USSR will scare the Soviet people and the soldiers of the Armed Forces."

Major V. S. Bondarevskii (commander of a bridge battalion working on the construction of the Baikal-Amur Main Line) emphasized: "Railroad troops fervently and unanimously agree with each line of the editorial and conclusively condemn the adventuristic path of the Carter administration, which is riddled with the danger of starting a new war."[. . .]

In discussions of the editorial army and navy personnel showed profound understanding of the need to combine the indefatigable fight for peace with constant attention to reinforcing the defense capabilities of our country and with further increasing the vigilance and combat readiness of the Armed Forces.[. . .]

The words of the soldiers are backed by patriotic deeds. Information coming to us from the ranks shows that in recent combat training drills, personnel are striving to fulfill socialist obligations and are persistently mastering military technology and weapons.

In connection with the publishing of the editorial in the newspaper *Pravda*, the work of the army and navy is being directed at further rallying personnel around the Communist Party of the Soviet Union and its Leninist Central Committee, the successful completion of military and political training assignments in the summer session, the further strengthening of discipline, organization and order, and the enhancing of vigilance and combat readiness of combined formations, units, and ships.

Reported for your information.

[signed] D. Ustinov

[signed] A. Epishev

June 22, 1978

TSKhSD, fond 5, op. 75, d. 33, ll. 16–19.

DOCUMENT 318   *Report to the Central Committee by Yakovlev and Zamiatin, September 25, 1985, concerning erroneous quotes attributed to Lenin by President Reagan in his speeches*

Not for Publication

Secret
TSK KPSS, 2nd Sector
September 25, 1985 25374
Return to General Department
of the *TSK KPSS*

Central Committee of the Communist Party of the Soviet Union

On the Hostile Speeches of the President of the U.S.A.

Recently, the president of the U.S.A., in his official speeches, has more frequently resorted to falsified quotes, attributing them to V. I. Lenin.

Reagan has done this in the past, but now this is becoming standard practice. During one of his recent statements (September 18, 1985), Reagan attributed to Lenin plans to seize Eastern Europe, China, Latin America, and the United States.

The Soviet press often has rebuffed strongly the slanderous attacks of R. Reagan, but nevertheless this line [of speech] by the head of the White House continues.

The propaganda and external political propaganda departments of the Central Committee of the Communist Party advise instructing the Ministry of Foreign Affairs [*MID*] of the USSR, via the Soviet Embassy in Washington, to categorically protest to the U.S. Department of State the falsifying of the works of the founder of the Communist Party of the Soviet Union and the Soviet state, V. I. Lenin, emphasizing that this practice is not acceptable, insults the Soviet people, and causes justifiable indignation among the Soviet people. We demand the American administration end such antagonistic attacks against the Soviet Union and the gross falsification of Lenin's works.

The text of the protest to the State Department is to be published in the Soviet Press.

Draft instructions to Soviet embassy in the U.S.A. enclosed.
We request concurrence.

Chief of the Propaganda Department of the *TSK KPSS*	Chief of the Department of Foreign Political Propaganda of the *TSK KPSS*
[signed] A. Yakovlev	[signed] L. Zamiatin
25 September 1985	Communicate concurrence
19-03-134	1 October 1985 [signature illegible]

Enclosure

WASHINGTON.   SOVIET AMBASSADOR

In his recent appearances, the head of the White House has frequently falsified quotes that he attributed to V. I. Lenin. For example, during Reagan's interview with ABC on September 18, 1985, the president of the U.S.A. acknowledged that he "often quoted Lenin's statements," which allegedly speak of seizing Eastern Europe, organizing East Asian hordes, taking over Latin America and the United States. Grossly distorting the history and politics of the Soviet State, the American president attempted and continues to cast a shadow on the external and internal politics of the Soviet state. As is known, there are no such statements by V. I. Lenin.

This is not the first time that such allegations have been made. Such a practice is unacceptable in relations between countries. It creates justifiable indignation in the Soviet Union, as an insult to the Soviet people, a premeditated distortion of the history of the Soviet state.

The Soviet Union demands the American side end such practices which are incompatible with normal relations between countries.

[signature illegible]   25374

TSKhSD, fond 4, op. 29, d. 245.

Resolution of the Central Committee, July 31, 1986, regarding measures to strengthen Soviet opposition to the American policy of "neoglobalism"

Not for publication

RESOLUTION OF THE CENTRAL COMMITTEE OF
THE COMMUNIST PARTY OF THE SOVIET UNION [*TSK KPSS*]

On Measures to Strengthen our Opposition to
the American Policy of "Neoglobalism"

1. To concur with the observations on this matter that are set forth in the memorandum by Comrades Eduard A. Shevardnadze, Viktor M. Chebrikov, Sergei L. Sokolov, Anatoly F. Dobrynin, Vadim A. Medvedev, and Alexander N. Yakovlev (attached).

2. To commission the Ministry of Foreign Affairs of the USSR, the Ministry of Defense of the USSR, the Committee for State Security of the USSR, International Department, and the Department of the *TSK KPSS* for Communication with Communist and Workers' Parties of Socialist Countries, and the Propaganda Department of the Central Committee to enlist the institutes of the Academy of Sciences of the USSR to develop and present in three months time a proposal of systematic measures to be taken to strengthen our opposition to the policy of "neoglobalism" presently pursued by the United States of America.

3. To authorize the departments and sections of the *TSK KPSS* indicated in par. 2 to implement practical measures relative to the observations set forth in the memorandum.

Secretary, Central Committee

CENTRAL COMMITTEE OF
THE COMMUNIST PARTY OF THE SOVIET UNION

On Measures to Strengthen Our Opposition to
the American Policy of "Neoglobalism"

Analysis of the practical manifestations of the Reagan policy of "neoglobalism" and statements concerning it by the president himself allow us to characterize it, in essence, as follows.

Reagan's policy of "neoglobalism" reflects the attempt of right-wing groups, which have come to power in the United States, to restore the United States to the position of power in foreign affairs that it held immediately after the war. In the final analysis, it is directed at establishing the United States as the preeminent world power.

Although the target of the policy of "neoglobalism" at present is the "third world," especially countries with progressive regimes, its ultimate target is the Soviet Union and socialism in general.

Realizing the impossibility of attaining these goals under the present balance of power in the world, the Reagan administration has made it its mission, after having first altered the balance of power, not only to halt the further spread and consolidation of socialism in the world but also to exhaust the Soviet Union and its allies, to throw off course the socioeconomic development of socialism both through an acceleration of the arms race and by involving us in conflicts in different regions of the world.

This policy is organically linked with the effort to attain military superiority over the USSR, which the U.S.A. would like to exploit in order to restrict our ability to deny them a free hand in the international arena.

The main concrete manifestations of the policy of "neoglobalism" at this stage appear to be the following:

— to declare that practically all regions of the nonsocialist world are of vital interest to the United States and to attempt to involve its military-political allies in defending these interests, while reserving the right to act independent of or even in spite of these allies.

— to expand overt military support (including delivery of new highly efficient weapons systems) to counterrevolutionary forces fighting the governments of their countries (Afghanistan, Nicaragua, Angola, Kampuchea).

— direct use of American military force on one pretext or another (guaranteeing security of American citizens, "retribution" for territorial infringements, and so on) whenever the United States judges that it can act with impunity (Grenada, Lebanon, and Libya).

— to increase significantly the economic pressure on developing countries, especially those with a progressive political orientation (e.g., the position of the U.S.A. and its allies at the special session of the UN General Assembly on the critical situation in Africa, measures taken by the American administration to limit and destabilize the foreign economic relations of Libya, Angola, Ethiopia, and others).

— to scorn openly the decisions of international organizations, especially the UN, and often the positions of their own allies; this is associated with the rise of the chauvinistic atmosphere within the U.S.A. and the resurgence of neoconservative, reactionary forces.

Along with the growing use of force in the spirit of the doctrine of "neoglobalism," the American administration is engaged in political maneuvering to maintain control over countries in social upheaval. It is achieving this by replacing bankrupt dictatorial regimes with governments that have a democratic facade (e.g., El Salvador, Haiti, the Philippines).

At the same time that regional conflicts are ignited, the importance of regulating them on American terms is stressed. But without their preliminary resolution, there can be no relaxation of international tensions and no substantive progress in arms control and disarmament and in establishing a fruitful American-Soviet dialog.

Of course the main thing that will spell the downfall of the policy of "neoglobalism" will be successfully fulfilling plans for the social and economic development of our country and other socialist states, maintaining their military strength at the necessary level, continuing a dynamic, thoughtful foreign-policy course, including increased ties with the developing nations of Asia, Africa, and Latin America, as our resources allow.

In this connection it is essential to develop special long-term measures to strengthen our resistance to the policy of "neoglobalism" in its concrete manifestations in various regions. This set of well-reasoned measures ought to be incorporated into our conception of a comprehensive system of international security.

Prior to the complete [development of long-term measures], which require a set time to develop, it is important now to map out the chief direction to take to oppose this policy of "neoglobalism" and as far as possible to implement some concrete measures:

1. In view of the fact that the severest policies of "neoglobalism" are aimed against the entire socialist commonwealth, it is expedient to discuss questions concerning the strengthening of countermeasures to this policy when the secretaries of the central committees of fraternal parties hold their next scheduled meeting to discuss international questions.

2. Measures toward building a coalition to oppose U.S. "neoglobalism" among developing nations would be of great significance, particularly within the nonaligned movement, e.g., at the upcoming eighth conference of the heads of state and government of nonaligned countries in Harare, at the UN, and in other major international forums.

3. Since there are indications that the Chinese government is uneasy in regard to the dangerous consequences of Reagan's policy of "neoglobalism," it may be possible to initiate a dialogue with the Chinese about this problem, starting, let's say, with scientists.

4. In the interest of opposing the policy of "neoglobalism," we ought also to exploit our work with those political circles in the West (including those in the United States itself) that are anxious not only about the danger of a sharp deterioration in the international situation as a result of the Reagan administration's adventurist actions in "flash points" around the world but also about the possibility of being drawn into conflicts as a result of Washington's attempt to turn its policy of "neoglobalism" into a general NATO policy.

5. This plan would be usefully conducted in a coordinated effort with other fraternal communist and workers' parties and also with democratic-revolutionary parties as well as with social democratic parties.

6. The Soviet mass media must be very systematic and cogently sound in its statements in order to expose the sources, concrete manifestations, and dangerous consequences of the American policy of "neoglobalism." Our foreign policy propaganda must make effective use in this regard of the results of the scientific analysis of the basic aspects of this policy.

7. In addition to carrying out the courses of action enumerated above coupled with using official channels, there is also the possibility of using the Committee for State Security [*KGB*] to implement some countermeasures to the policy of "neoglobalism."

[crossed out] Draft resolution of the *TSK KPSS* attached.

[signed] E. Shevardnadze V. Chebrikov A. Dobrynin V. Medvedev A. Yakovlev
S. Sokolov

July 31, 1986

TSKhSD, fond 3, op. 104, d. 32.

chapter 13

THE CUBAN MISSILE CRISIS

The turn towards socialism on the part of Fidel Castro's revolutionary Cuban government in 1959 created great anxiety in a United States government already deeply involved in the tense confrontation over Berlin. A U.S.-supported invasion by Cuban exiles failed miserably at the Bay of Pigs in 1961, but the Cuban government and its Soviet ally remained fearful that socialist Cuba would remain vulnerable to the threat of a United States invasion. To protect the Castro regime the Soviet leadership decided upon a secret installation of nuclear missiles in Cuba. In the most recent and complete version of Nikita S. Khrushchev's memoirs, the former leader alleges that Soviet intention was never to use the missiles to threaten the U.S. itself but merely to protect Cuba from further threats of invasion.

The "Cuban Missile Crisis" began when aerial reconnaissance flights by U.S. intelligence on October 14, 1962, revealed the construction of missile-launching sites. Anxious planning meetings in Washington led to President Kennedy's announcement on October 22 of the existence of the missiles, and the United States' determination to force their removal. The U.S. declared a naval quarantine of Cuba; any Soviet ship approaching the island would be stopped and searched. The world lived in fear of imminent catastrophe over the next six days, while Kennedy, Khrushchev, and their intermediaries negotiated a resolution to the crisis. On October 28 Khrushchev agreed to the removal of the missiles, in exchange for the removal of aging missiles in Turkey and Italy targeted on the Soviet Union and a pledge by Kennedy not to invade Cuba.

The Khrushchev-Kennedy correspondence, some of which is included here, was released to the public only in January 1992, but revelations concerning the crisis had begun to circulate during Gorbachev's era of "new thinking" on foreign policy. In January 1989, a Moscow conference brought together some of the diplomatic participants in the crisis. Khrushchev's son revealed there that Castro had been much more hotheaded than the Soviets in his suggested response to the U.S. ultimatum. The latest volume of Khrushchev's memoirs confirms that Castro wanted to launch a preemptive nuclear strike against the U.S. once the missiles were discovered and that Castro had ordered Soviet antiaircraft personnel to shoot down a U-2 reconnaissance plane against Soviet wishes. "We felt obliged to send Mikoyan to Cuba," recalled Khrushchev, in order to convince Castro that the Soviets had only his welfare at heart. Mikoyan had "the special ability to repeat the general line over and over again without giving an inch and without losing his temper." Documents 327 and 328 present Mikoyan's report on this meeting and reveal the tension and lack of trust between the two countries.

Continuing scholarly discussion and access to these once-secret documents will illuminate further the causes and dimensions of the crisis. A 1992 conference in Havana suggested that nuclear warheads had already been installed on the missiles, contrary to Soviet claims and historians' beliefs. Later in 1992 the CIA organized a symposium to discuss this "defining Cold War moment." Further revelations have suggested that Khrushchev never succeeded in extracting an ironclad pledge from Kennedy not to invade Cuba. And there is still no definitive answer to the question of who was to blame for the crisis. Khrushchev insisted that by aiming Soviet missiles at U.S. targets only 90 miles away, he was merely compensating for the fact that the U.S. missiles had longed ringed Soviet borders. U.S. participants believed that the missile ploy was part of Khrushchev's risky strategy to force the U.S. to make concessions on other contentious issues in the relations between the East and the West, a position echoed by the Communist People's Republic of China at the time. Who won this showdown in the Caribbean? The Soviets agreed to withdraw their nuclear missiles and their IL-28 bombers and appeared to back down. But Khrushchev still claimed victory: the Soviet goal was to preserve socialist Cuba, while the U.S. wanted to destroy it. Indeed, the socialist sytem in Cuba would remain in place, despite severe economic deterioration, for decades after the missile crisis.

Nikita Khrushchev (right), Cuban revolutionary leader Che Guevara (left center), and Politburo member A. I. Mikoyan (left) during a reception at the Cuban Embassy in Moscow, 1960. TSGAKFD. N 160512

DOCUMENT 320 *Excerpt from minutes of the Presidium of the Central Committee, April 18, 1961, concerning measures taken in connection with the American aggression against Cuba*

Proletarians of All Countries, Unite!　　　　　Top secret

COMMUNIST PARTY OF THE SOVIET UNION. CENTRAL COMMITTEE [*TSK KPSS*]

No. P324/1

To Comrades Khrushchev, Kozlov, Kosygin, Gromyko, Stepanov

Extract from minutes No. 324 of the April 18, 1961, meeting of the Presidium of the *TSK KPSS*
On measures taken in connection with the aggression against the Cuban Republic.

　　　1. Confirm, with amendments, the declaration of the Soviet government in relation to an armed invasion of Cuba (attachment 1).
　　　Instruct the Ministry of Foreign Affairs of the USSR to deliver to the ambassador of the U.S.A. the text of the declaration of the Soviet government and also to transmit the text of the declaration with a covering letter to all accredited embassies in Moscow. To countries without representation in Moscow the text of the declaration shall be sent through the Representative of the USSR at the United Nations Organization [UNO]. The declaration of the Soviet government shall be broadcast on the radio and published in the press.
　　　2. Confirm the message of the chairman of the Council of Ministers of the USSR, Comrade N. S. Khrushchev, to President of the U.S.A. Kennedy (attachment 2). The message shall be handed to the ambassador of the U.S.A. in Moscow. The text of the message shall be broadcast on the radio 2 hours after the promulgation of the declaration of the Soviet government.
　　　3. Confirm the instructions to the ambassadors of the USSR in neutral countries (attachment 3).
　　　4. Confirm the instructions to the representative of the USSR to the UN (attachment 4).
　　　5. Instruct the Ministry of Foreign Affairs of the USSR to inform the governments of the socialist countries through the ambassadors of these countries in Moscow of the steps undertaken by the Soviet government in connection with the aggression against Cuba by transmitting to them the texts of the declaration of the Soviet government and of the message of N. S. Khrushchev to President Kennedy.
　　　6. Instruct the Ministry of Foreign Affairs of the USSR to inform F. Castro, Dorticos, and Cuban friends, through the Soviet ambassador in Havana, of the measures undertaken by the Soviet government in support of Cuba.

Secretary of the *TSK*

11-iav ks

APRF, fond 3, op. 66, d. 310, ll. 12–13.

Weapons captured during the aborted Bay of Pigs invasion, Cuba, 1961. TSGAKFD. N 166267.

DOCUMENT 321   *Coded cable from Soviet Ambassador Menshikov, April 23, 1961, concerning his talks in Washington, D.C., with Supreme Court Justice Douglas on relations with Cuba*

TOP SECRET

Copying prohibited

Copy No. 30

A CODED TELEGRAM

Copy No. 1	Original	Copy No. 22	Kosygin
2	Gromyko	23	Kuusinen
3	Kuznetsov	24	Mikoyan
4	Malik	25	Mukhitdinov
5	Orlov	26	Podgorny
6	Pushkin	27	Polianskii
7	Semenov	28	Suslov
8	Sobolev	29	Furtseva
9	Firiubin	30	Khrushchev
10	Dobrynin	31	Khrushchev
11	Podtserob	32	Shvernik
12	Tugarinov	33	Voronov
13	Kharlamov	34	Grishin
14	TSarapkin	35	Kalnberzin
15	Copy	36	Kirilenko
16	Section 10	37	Korotchenko
17	File	38	Mazurov
18	Aristov	39	Mzhavanadze
19	Brezhnev	40	Pervukhin
20	Ignatov	41	Pospelov
21	Kozlov		

From Washington No. 18561   rec. 8:40   4/24/1961

Special No. 717

Had a discussion with U.S.A. Supreme Court member Douglas; the following remarks merit attention:

1. As regards the latest action of the Kennedy government with respect to Cuba, Douglas emphasized that Kennedy had embarked on this adventure after being egged on by Allen Dulles, generally regarded a sinister person; it was Allen Dulles, said Douglas, who pulled a fast one on Eisenhower with the U-2 flight and now nudged Kennedy into this risky step with Cuba.

Douglas noted that the preponderant public opinion in the U.S.A., despite their attitude toward Castro, has been opposed to Kennedy's Cuban adventure. In support of his statement he related that more than two-thirds of the 180 newspaper editors polled at the annual editors' conference at which Kennedy spoke on Cuba on April 20 expressed disapproval of his action in one form or another.

2. Douglas stated that he had received State Department approval for his planned trip this summer to the People's Republic of China, if the government of the latter presents him with the opportunity. To his question on how and where to obtain a Chinese visa, Douglas was told that this can be done in any capital with a Chinese embassy representation.

3. In connection with his remark that he intends also to visit the People's Republic of Mongolia, en

route from the USSR to the People's Republic of China, if he receives a Chinese visa, Douglas stated that he has no knowledge of Rusk's opinion concerning the recognition of the Mongolian People's Republic by the U.S.A., but all others in the State Department—"from Bowles down"—hold a positive position in this regard.

4/23/1961   M. MEN'ShIKOV

24 cop.
Dopech.(?) 25.IV.21-30
Issued by Lagoiskii   True copy: Illegible

APRF, fond 3, op. 66, d. 310, ll. 36–37.

DOCUMENT 322   *Coded telegram from Soviet Ambassador Dobrynin in Washington, D.C., to the Central Committee, October 9, 1962, reporting on a meeting between Bol'shakov (vice-chairman of the USSR State Committee for Cultural Relations with Foreign Countries) and Robert Kennedy*

Top secret
Copying prohibited
Copy No. 12

CODED TELEGRAM

Copy No.		Copy No.	
1	Original	18	Mzhavanadze
2	Brezhnev	19	Shcherbitsky
3	Voronov	20	Gromyko
4	Kirilenko	21	Malinovskii
5	Kozlov	22	Kuznetsov
6	Kosygin	23	Lapin
7	Kuusinen	24	Orlov
8	Mikoyan	25	Pushkin
9	Podgorny	26	Sobolev
10	Polianskii	27	Firiubin
11	Suslov	28	Il'ichev
12	Khrushchev	29	Podtserob
13	Khrushchev	30	Smirnovskii
14	Shvernik	31	TSarapkin
15	Grishin	32	Copy
16	Rashidov	33	Section 10
17	Mazurov	34	File

From Washington	No. 46178	rec. 3:15	10/9/1962

46177
Special No. 1647-1648

EXPEDITE

Upon returning to Washington from vacation Bol'shakov met with R. Kennedy.

Bol'shakov said that he had been received by N. S. Khrushchev, who, upon hearing the President's message, instructed Bol'shakov to convey to the president an oral message.

R. Kennedy remarked that, apparently, the president will receive him for this purpose within the next few days.

Then, in a very pessimistic tone of voice, as if emphasizing his regret, R. Kennedy noted that, to the disappointment of the president, as well as his own, there has been in the last two months an obvious deterioration of Soviet-American relations, which, on the whole, greatly reduces the possibility of reaching any kind of agreement between our countries. Saying this, continued R. Kennedy, I have in mind, first of all, the political atmosphere in our country. At times it seems to us that Moscow does not always interpret correctly our political conditions and, as a result, takes steps that lead to the needless and serious exacerbation of our relations.

Speaking frankly, the president was angered by the latest moves of the Soviet Union in Cuba, and we interpreted it all as moves against us. Accordingly, in our election politics we find it necessary to devote considerable attention to the question of Cuba.

Bol'shakov answered that he had just returned from Moscow and is confident Moscow appraises the state of mind in the United States quite realistically. The crux is not in some moves of the Soviet Union but, mainly, in the actions of the United States government, which, as is known, are well detailed in the last message of N. S. Khrushchev to Kennedy. Transparent in all these actions is the tendency to talk with us from "positions of strength," which the U.S. does not hold, as the president himself had admitted in Vienna. In order to solve problems rationally, emphasized N. S. Khrushchev, it is necessary to be realistic in the appraisal of the balance of forces, to respect the sovereign rights of other countries, and not to meddle in their internal affairs.

R. Kennedy, who was in—for him—an unusually somber mood, listened to Bol'shakov in silence. Then, after a pause, he said that the President is now working on the answer to N. S. Khrushchev's message, which he had relayed from Ambassador Dobrynin. R. Kennedy also added that, as he sees it, an agreement on West Berlin will not be reached as long as the USSR entertains a notion to throw the American forces out of Berlin. We cannot accept this.

As regards the ban on nuclear testing—he continued—we shall not accept a five-year moratorium on underground nuclear testing.

R. Kennedy avoided elucidating whether this means that the U.S.A. is, in general, against moratoria on underground nuclear testing.

Concluding the conversation, R. Kennedy, in passing, expressed interest in whether N. S. Khrushchev is planning a visit to the U.S. Bol'shakov answered that, as far as he knows, N. S. Khrushchev has no plans to attend the General Assembly of the UN before the congressional elections. However, if it becomes necessary for N. S. Khrushchev to address the General Assembly, he will come to New York after the elections. R. Kennedy refrained from any remarks on this information.

October 8, 1962   A. Dobrynin

34 copies vk [?]
printed 10/9 10:30
issuer: Shiriaev   True copy: [Illegible signature]

APRF, fond 3, op. 66, d. 318, ll. 1–3.

DOCUMENT 323 *Resolution of the Central Committee, October 23, 1962, approving Khrushchev's letter to Kennedy in response to the American declaration of a naval blockade of arms shipments to Cuba*

Proletarians of All Countries, Unite!   Top secret

Communist Party of the Soviet Union. Central Committee [*TSK KPSS*]

No. P60/1

Extract from minutes No. 60 of the October 23, 1962, meeting of the Presidium of the *TSK*.

On measures related to U.S. President J. Kennedy's declaration of October 22, 1962.

1. Approve the draft Declaration of the Soviet government (attachment 1). Publish the declaration on October 23 of this year.

2. Approve the text of the letter of Comrade N. S. Khrushchev to the president of the U.S.A., J. Kennedy (attachment 2). Transmit the text of the letter, together with the Declaration of the Soviet government, to J. Kennedy through the ambassador of the U.S.A. in Moscow.

Secretary of the *TSK*.

2-ak.

[Printed vertically in left margin:] To be returned within 7 days to the *TSK KPSS* (General Dept., Sector 1)

Attachment 2
To para. 1 of minutes No. 60
Moscow, October 23, 1962

Mr. President:

I have just received your letter and have familiarized myself with the text of your statement of October 22 on Cuba.

I must say frankly that the measures proposed in your statement represent a serious threat to the peace and security of nations. The United States is blatantly embarking on the path of gross violation of the Charter of the United Nations Organization, the path of violation of the international standards of freedom of navigation on the open seas, the path of aggressive actions against both Cuba and the Soviet Union.

The Declaration of the Government of the United States of America cannot be interpreted as other than an undisguised intervention in the internal affairs of the Cuban Republic, the Soviet Union, and other nations. The Charter of the United Nations Organization and international standards of behavior do not bestow on any nation the right to set up in international waters inspection points for ships sailing toward the shores of the Cuban Republic.

Obviously, we cannot acquiesce in the right of the United States to institute control over the armaments that the Republic of Cuba needs to enhance its defense capability.

We assert that the armaments now located in Cuba, regardless of their type, are intended exclusively for defensive purposes, to protect the Cuban Republic from attack by an aggressor.

I hope that the government of the United States will display prudence and will reject the actions you have taken which may lead to catastrophic consequences for the peace of the entire world.

To His Excellency
John KENNEDY
President of the United States
of America

[bottom of first page of original]

The point of view of the Soviet government with regard to your declaration of October 22 is set forth in the Declaration of the Soviet government, which is being forwarded to you through your ambassador in Moscow.

APRF, fond 3, op. 66, d. 318, ll. 133, 141–142.

DOCUMENT 324   *Letter from Khrushchev to President Kennedy, October 24, 1962, about the blockade of Cuba*

Dear Mr. President,

I have received your letter of October 23; I have familiarized myself with it and am responding to you.

Imagine, Mr. President, what if we were to present to you such an ultimatum as you have presented to us by your actions. How would you react to it? I think you would be outraged at such a move on our part. And this we would understand.

Having presented these conditions to us, Mr. President, you have thrown down the gauntlet. Who asked you to do this? By what right have you done this? Our ties with the Republic of Cuba, as well as our relations with other nations, regardless of their political system, concern only the two countries between which these relations exist. And, if it were a matter of quarantine as mentioned in your letter, then, as is customary in international practice, it can be established only by states agreeing between themselves, and not by some third party. Quarantines exist, for example, on agricultural goods and products. However, in this case we are not talking about quarantines, but rather about much more serious matters, and you yourself understand this.

His Excellency
Mr. John F. Kennedy
President of the United States of America
Washington

[bottom of first page of original]

You, Mr. President, are not declaring a quarantine, but rather issuing an ultimatum, and you are threatening that if we do not obey your orders, you will then use force. Think about what you are saying! And you want to persuade me to agree to this! What does it mean to agree to these demands? It would mean for us to conduct our relations with other countries not by reason, but by yielding to tyranny. You are not appealing to reason; you want to intimidate us.

No, Mr. President, I cannot agree to this, and I think that deep inside you will admit that I am right. I am convinced that if you were in my place you would do the same.

The reference to the resolution of the Organization of American States can in no way strengthen the demands presently set forth by the United States. This organization has no authority or grounds whatsoever to pass resolutions like those of which you speak in your letter. Therefore, we do not recognize these resolutions. International law exists, generally accepted standards of conduct exist. We firmly adhere to the principles of international law and strictly observe the standards regulating navigation on the open sea, in international waters. We observe these standards and enjoy the rights recognized by all nations.

You want to force us to renounce the rights enjoyed by every sovereign state; you are attempting to legislate questions of international law; you are violating the generally accepted standards of this law. All this is due not only to hatred for the Cuban people and their government but also for reasons having to do with the election campaign in the U.S.A.. What morals, what laws can justify such an approach by the American government to international affairs? Such morals and laws are not to be found, because the actions of the U.S.A. in relation to Cuba are outright piracy. This, if you will, is the <u>madness of a degenerating imperialism</u>. Unfortunately, people of all nations, and not least the American people themselves, could suffer heavily from madness such as this, since with the appearance of modern types of weapons, the U.S.A. has completely lost its former inaccessibility.

Therefore, Mr. President, if you weigh the present situation with a cool head without giving way to passion, you will understand that the Soviet Union cannot but decline the despotic demands of the U.S.A.. When you lay conditions such as these before us, try to put yourself in our situation and consider how the U.S.A. would react to such conditions. I have no doubt that if anyone attempted to dictate similar conditions to you—the U.S.A.—you would reject such an attempt. And we likewise say—no.

The Soviet government considers the violation of the freedom of navigation in international waters and air space to constitute an act of aggression propelling humankind into the abyss of a world nuclear-missile war. Therefore, the Soviet government cannot instruct captains of Soviet ships bound for Cuba to observe orders of American naval forces blockading this island. Our instructions to Soviet sailors are to observe strictly the generally accepted standards of navigation in international waters and not retreat one step from them. And, if the American side violates these rights, it must be aware of the responsibility it will bear for this act. To be sure, we will not remain mere observers of pirate actions by American ships in the open sea. We will then be forced on our part to take those measures we deem necessary and sufficient to defend our rights. To this end we have all that is necessary.

Respectfully,   [signed] N. Khrushchev

                                            N. KhRUShchEV

Moscow
October 24, 1962

AVP RF.

[English original]

THE WHITE HOUSE
Washington

October 25, 1962

Dear Mr. Chairman:

I have received your letter of October 24, and I regret very much that you still do not appear to understand what it is that has moved us in this matter.

The sequence of events is clear. In August there were reports of important shipments of military equipment and technicians from the Soviet Union to Cuba. In early September I indicated very plainly that the United States would regard any shipment of offensive weapons as presenting the gravest issues. After that time, this Government received the most explicit assurances from your Government and its representatives, both publicly and privately, that no offensive weapons were being sent to Cuba. If you will review the statement issued by Tass in September, you will see how clearly this assurance was given.

In reliance on these solemn assurances I urged restraint upon those in this country who were urging action in this matter at that time. And then I learned beyond doubt what you have not denied—namely, that all these public assurances were false and that your military people had set out recently to establish a set of missile bases in Cuba. I ask you to recognize clearly, Mr. Chairman, that it was not I who issued the first challenge in this case, and that in the light of this record these activities in Cuba required the responses I have announced.

I repeat my regret that these events should cause a deterioration in our relations. I hope that your Government will take the necessary action to permit a restoration of the earlier situation.

Sincerely yours,

John F. Kennedy

N. S. Khrushchev
Chairman of the Council of Ministers of the
   Union of Soviet Socialist Republics
Moscow, USSR

AVP RF

DOCUMENT 326 *Instructions from the Politburo to the Soviet mission to the United Nations, November 9, 1962, to protest American attempts to inspect Soviet ships returning dismantled missiles from Cuba to the USSR*

24

<u>Proletarians of All Countries, Unite!</u>

<u>Communist Party of the Soviet Union</u>. <u>CENTRAL COMMITTEE</u> [*TSK KPSS*]

<u>Top secret</u>

No. P65/47

To Comrades Khrushchev, Gromyko

Extract from Minutes No. 65 of the November 9, 1962, meeting of the Presidium of the *TSK KPSS*.

Concerning instructions issued to Comrade Kuznetsov relative to the Americans' impeding of movement of Soviet vessels returning from Cuba.

Affirm the draft of the instructions to Comrade Kuznetsov (attached).

Secretary of the *TSK*

9-ae.

ks

[Printed vertically, left margin:] To be returned within 7 days to the *TSK KPSS* (General Dept., Sector 1)

25

Re: Item 47 of Minutes No. 65

NEW YORK

<u>Secret</u>

SOVIET MISSION to Comrade KUZNETSOV

Copy: to Comrade A. I. Mikoyan in Havana

Immediately get in touch with McCloy and Stevenson and declare the following:

We have received information from three Soviet vessels—*Aleksandrovsk*, located on November 9 at 1400 Moscow time in the area 25°20' North and 60°41' West; *Divnogorsk*, located on November 9 at 1400 Moscow time in the area 25°26' North and 60°19' West; and *Volgoles*, located on November 9 at 1400 Moscow time in the area 32°14' North and 77°37' West—that American destroyers have demanded that each vessel stop and open its hold and at the same time have threatened to use force if these arbitrary and illegal demands are not complied with. These demands are in gross contradiction with the agreement arrived at between the American and Soviet sides that the vessels transporting the dismantled rockets may only be photographed from the air and observed visually from the American vessels. *Divnogorsk* and *Volgoles* are the vessels carrying the rockets, and they were visually observed by the American side. But the motorship *Aleksandrovsk* was not at all on the list of Soviet vessels submitted by us to the American side that were to be subjected to visual observation.

The Soviet government expects that the pertinent vessels of the U.S. Navy will immediately receive instructions not to obstruct the passage of the above-named vessels proceeding from Cuba to the Soviet Union.

Also, in your conversation emphasize that obstructions to the movement of the Soviet vessels furthermore are occurring outside the quarantine zone delineated by the government of the U.S.A.

APRF, fond 3, op. 65, d. 909, ll. 24–25.

DOCUMENT 327   *Transcript of talks between Mikoyan and Castro, November 12, 1962, in which Mikoyan attempted to persuade Castro of the tactical necessity of acceding to the American demand to remove all Iliushin-28 bombers from Cuba*

To the Central Committee Department and the International Department of the Central Committee of the Communist Party of the Soviet Union [*TSK KPSS*]

<u>Copy</u>   <u>Top Secret</u>

TRANSCRIPT OF CONVERSATION BETWEEN A. I. Mikoyan AND FIDEL CASTRO
[Typewritten footnote:] Transcript not reviewed by A. I. Mikoyan

<u>November 12, 1962</u>

Ambassador A. I. Alekseev
present at conversation

FIDEL CASTRO informed us that he had had very little rest and had spent the last few days on a trip to experimental farms in the provinces. He also informed us that one farm had discovered an interesting new variety of beans, or more precisely four different species of beans, which he was greatly interested in. Castro told Mikoyan that these beans, which grow like grapes, are perennials. The peasants who grow these beans say the plants stay alive for four or five years. He took some of the beans home with him, Castro went on, and saw for himself that they were easy to cook and tasted good.

<u>Mikoyan</u> noted that this was the first time he had heard of perennial beans.

<u>CASTRO</u> said that he too had never heard of perennial beans before. But the peasants convinced him of this. He added that one peasant household had gotten 25 pounds of beans from just a few bushes of beans, which grow like grapes in bunches. The peasants' families who grow this variety of beans are practically self-sufficient in food.

"So what did our country produce before?" Castro went on. "For all intents and purposes, just sugar and tobacco. In my opinion, the use of these beans could help us solve our food problem. I should mention that this variety of beans even withstood an eight-month drought, when most of the crops in our country were lost."

<u>A. I. Mikoyan.</u> Comrade Fidel, I would like to discuss with you an important problem. We are interested in the earliest possible resolution of the existing conflict to the advantage of Cuba. Our country has fulfilled its obligations, but the Americans are continuing with their quarantine. They fear complications, look for snags, and try to find reasons to avoid keeping promises Kennedy made to N. S. Khrushchev. They promise that if the Soviet Union removes its offensive weapons, the U.S. will not attack Cuba and will restrain its allies. Then the situation in the Caribbean should normalize. Kennedy is being criticized in the U.S. for promising not to attack Cuba. This is happening because those in the U.S. who favor a war have become more strident. A number of American public figures advocate resolving the situation by force. They are unhappy that the problem is being resolved in a peaceful manner. In our view, Kennedy wants to strangle Cuba with an economic blockade. Such attempts have been made against our own country in the past. You must have read about the economic blockade instituted against the young Soviet republic by the imperialists and what hopes they placed on starving out Russia. By creating economic difficulties the Americans hope that Cuba will collapse from within. Kennedy openly stated that he will create conditions that will weaken Cuba economically. Then, the thinking goes, the Soviet Union lacks the resources to help her and the Cuban government will collapse.

The U.S. military circles disagree with Kennedy and insist on resolving the Caribbean crisis by force.

As long as there is no military tension or military blockade, a break in trade relations with the Western countries would not interfere with Cuba's development. The Soviet Union will provide comprehensive assistance to revolutionary Cuba so that Cuba can become a genuine model and shining example for all of Latin America. This is completely realistic. We believe in this deeply, and we would be able to ensure the requisite conditions for it.

Kennedy and a number of other American politicians believe that the Soviet Union has failed to meet all of its obligations. We believe that the agreement applied to missiles only. The Americans believe that it also applied to the Il-28 bombers. Kennedy discussed the bombers in his message on October 22. He also mentioned the bombers in his proclamation.

They believe that we have not fully met our obligations because of the Il-28 bombers. Taking a formal, legalistic stance, they have stated that we have failed to meet our obligations, and because of this, consider it their prerogative to repudiate their obligations of lifting the quarantine and providing guarantees. We have refused to remove the Il-28 bombers from Cuba and may continue to do so. We do not believe a war will start because of them. Of course, no one who knows the nature of these madmen can guarantee that they will not resort to armed conflict. However, if we do not formally meet Kennedy's demand to remove the bombers from Cuba, the United States will continue the blockade, extend the quarantine for an indefinite period of time, repudiate its obligations to refrain from attacking Cuba, and prolong the crisis in the Caribbean for the purpose of launching an attack on Cuba at some other time. That is one possible scenario.

There is also another possible scenario. We could agree to withdraw the Il-28 bombers from Cuba along with their crews and equipment, if the Americans provide full guarantees and promises not to attack Cuba, completely end the quarantine, and put an end to the crisis in the Caribbean. Of course, one might ask what the price of the American guarantees would be. Obviously they can't be trusted all the way. Imperialism and socialism are irreconcilable enemies.

However, we cannot completely mistrust any promises given by representatives of the bourgeois countries. There are certain international procedures, legal standards, laws, and international public opinion. All of these factors force the imperialists to keep their word. But if the objective conditions should change, they may forget their word and drastically alter their position.

We need to be extremely wary. Nevertheless, we cannot categorically deny the possibility of an agreement, because this denial would constitute evidence of our failure to recognize the coexistence of two opposing social systems. After all, our party's program, adopted by the 22nd Congress of the Communist Party of the Soviet Union, the declaration of the Conference of Representatives of Communist and Workers' Parties in 1957, and the Statement of the 81 Fraternal Parties at a Conference in 1960 clearly spell out the fact that peaceful competition between the two systems, not war, will decide the issue in favor of socialism. In other words, all of these very important documents were discussing the co-existence of the two systems and the preservation, as the lawyers say, of a modus vivendi.

We believe that the passage of UN resolutions containing passages in support of Cuba would constitute an important diplomatic factor. These documents would restrain the imperialists, tie their hands, and prevent them from unleashing aggression.

Despite this, we must rely on our own strengths and consider the balance of power in the world. In this respect the forces of socialism and capitalism are about equal. We are incapable of destroying imperialism. They are incapable of destroying socialism. Consequently there is only one path open to us, and that is the path of peaceful coexistence. We can see for ourselves how the socialist countries are growing rapidly and gaining strength. The prosocialist forces in the capitalist countries are also getting stronger. Liberation movements are developing in the colonial countries. The number of neutral countries is growing. So you might ask if a war is possible. Yes, war is possible, but it is not a fatal inevitability. It would be possible to prevent a war. Could the United Nations prevent a world war? This is highly unlikely. But the United Nations is one of the instruments of peace. It is true that the League of Nations existed at one time. The growing conflicts between socialism and capitalism caused the league to fall apart. The United Nations could also disintegrate. However, at the present time we can and must use the United Nations, because of the large number of neutral countries represented there. It is true that the representatives of neutral countries have often let us down at inopportune times, but within the UN the balance of power is changing in our favor.

We must struggle for peaceful coexistence and must use the representatives of the neutral countries in this struggle.

At this time it seems to me that we must free ourselves from the power of all, even the most noble, emotions, put aside all of our normally very important psychological concerns, and make a sober and rational decision which will be the best decision for Cuba.

We must assess the positive and negative aspects of the two options I mentioned earlier. We must soberly assess the value of the Il-28 bombers and realize what we might lose if we agreed to remove these weapons from Cuba.

Of course, we would obviously suffer a loss in morale. After all, this would amount to a new concession. It would cause you pain and depression. But these planes are of practically no real military value to Cuba.

CASTRO. So what is the point of all the discussion? You should get to the point and say exactly what the Soviet government wants.

Mikoyan. We delivered 42 Il-28 bombers. Only 2 of them have been assembled, and the others are still in their containers. The Il-28 was a good bomber, but now it is very obsolete. Our defense industry has discontinued production of the bomber.

ALEKSEEV. Our own air force does not have it any more.

Mikoyan. We think that the Il-28, although it has a long range, is of no significance for Cuba, because it only has a ceiling of 12,000 meters. Any type of air defense artillery can shoot it down. These aircraft could only be used near the coast of Cuba. And the Americans themselves realize that the plane is obsolete. Cuba has MiG-21s. The MiG-21 is an advanced aircraft whose performance is far superior to the obsolete Il-28 bomber. We should mention that the MiG-21 can carry bombs and missiles, bomb and strafe infantry, strike ground and air targets, and knock out ships. The MiG-21 is also capable of aerial combat. Cuba has 40 of these aircraft. And they will stay here regardless. Kennedy knows these planes are in Cuba. But he has not said a word about them. From a military standpoint the Il-28 is insignificant. In the near future we plan to deliver more MiG-21s to Cuba, as it is a highly advanced aircraft which can engage in aerial combat and hit ground and sea targets.

If we decide to remove the Il-28 bombers from Cuba, then we will deprive the Americans of the formal complaint which they are trying to take advantage of. And even though the Americans admit that the bombers do not pose any threat to them, they are still saying that the Il-28s pose a terrible threat to the governments of the Latin American countries, because these countries don't have good air defense systems. If we decide to remove these bombers with their crews and equipment and thus fulfill our promise to remove all weapons the Americans classify as offensive weapons from Cuba, we will force the Americans to fulfill their obligations and normalize the situation in the Caribbean.

As the saying goes, eating whets the appetite. And of course, we must put an end to these ravenous appetites. But it would be difficult to argue about the Il-28. After all, it is a bomber, albeit only in formal terms.

With respect to any other military assets, we will firmly and categorically reject any American demands. If we were to remove the bombers from Cuba, we would thus assure ourselves of UN support. In this case it would be easier to adopt the U Thant plan and normalize the situation. I have a few more arguments in favor of this decision, but I will not give them for the time being and shall instead say that I am speaking with you, Comrade Castro, in the name of the Central Committee of the Communist Party of the Soviet Union. As Marxist-Leninists we should decide the issue in a way which will save Cuba from the blockade and force the U.S. to meet its obligations.

We cannot provide adequate escorts for our ships proceeding to Cuba because the U.S. has superiority in the region. A continuation of the blockade could sap your strength and help the imperialists in carrying out their plans. If the Il-28 bombers are removed from Cuba, then this would only be a fleeting episode in the train of events. But in this case the interests of peace would triumph. The peace of Cuba would no longer be in jeopardy.

We implore you, Comrade Fidel, to understand us correctly. I am not asking for an answer right away. Think about it and talk it over. You might decide to meet with your comrades. This matter is worthy of the most careful study.

We trust you completely. You obviously realize that we are not pursuing any other goals except for defending the Cuban Revolution and the entire revolutionary movement from the imperialist predators.

We are not pursuing any commercial or national interests on Cuba. We are motivated exclusively by internationalist goals.

We understand you completely. We admire the great spirit of the Cuban people. As you are aware, in our country's early years, we were faced with a very difficult situation. The imperialists wanted to destroy us with a blockade. We understand quite well the great political significance of your motto *"Patria o muerte"* ("The Fatherland or Death"). During the civil war and the foreign intervention we were inspired by exactly the same motto. We recall how our patriots, who were much like the Cuban patriots, sang "We shall die as one man for Soviet power" as they went to the front to defend Soviet power. Our people demonstrated great endurance. We encountered incredible difficulties, but we overcame them and grew much stronger. V. I. Lenin, the leader of our country at the time, knew how to maneuver. He believed that maneuvering and flexibility were necessary to preserve the gains of the revolution. All of our considerable experience in the fight for the triumph and preservation of the revolution has given us a clue as to what the correct decision with respect to withdrawing the bombers should be. We are speaking with you and sharing our views as brothers and comrades and are telling you all of this with a clean heart. We assure you that the Soviet people, all of us, will be with you and will always walk shoulder to shoulder with you in our common struggle. You know that we sent our people to Cuba in order to be with you at all times in the difficult moments of the struggle. We ordered General Pavlov to defend Cuba with you. Our only interest in this regard is to defend Cuba and preserve the Cuban Revolution. Some people believe that you can fight the imperialists by cursing at them. However, no matter how strong the curses are, the imperialists never blush. At one time our country had the Comintern radio station. It constantly cursed the imperialists in broadcasts in different languages. However, this station could never provide any practical assistance to our friends abroad. We have given Cuba military, economic, and diplomatic assistance. We have sent military advisers here. We are doing all of this to preserve Cuba as a revolutionary beacon on the American continent. We are with you, Comrade Fidel, as brothers and friends. It is true that even brothers can have disagreements. But you should be fully aware of the sincerity of our intentions.

CASTRO. It seems to me that you are talking about the torpedo bombers at the San Julian base.

Mikoyan. The Il-28 bombers can in fact carry torpedoes.

I would like to emphasize once again that Cuba also has MiG-21s. As soon as the Cuban personnel are trained, we will turn them over to you. These planes can engage in aerial combat, can be used to attack ground targets, can be used to attack enemy landing parties, and can also perform dive bomber missions. As far as the Il-28s go, we would have scrapped them completely if the Berlin crisis hadn't flared up and Kennedy had not called 150,000 reservists to active duty. We are not saying that the MiG-21 has the same offensive capabilities as the Il-28. The United States knows that the Il-28 is an obsolete aircraft and that U.S. air defense artillery could easily shoot it down. However, we must take Latin American opinion into account. In documents you are aware of Kennedy also cited the bombers as offensive weapons in addition to the missiles.

CASTRO. (without waiting for Mikoyan to conclude his arguments, posed the following question) Could they not raise the issue of inspections of Cuban territory at a later date?

Mikoyan (continuing). Kennedy says that if the bombers are not removed from Cuba, then there will not be any guarantees that the United States will not attack Cuba. Even though the Americans are not afraid of them, the Il-28 is still classified as a bomber. In its day it was a good warplane. However the Il-28 is completely useless for defensive purposes, and Cuba is not planning on attacking the United States. The MiG-21 fighter, as we have already mentioned, is a very powerful fighting machine, although its range is somewhat less than the Il-28's. These fighters can be used for aerial combat missions and against ground targets and enemy ships.

These aircraft are so new that even we do not have enough of them. They are fully capable of defending Cuba. The MiG-21s could stay in Cuba, along with all the other military assets.

With respect to the possibility that the United States might raise the issue of inspecting Cuban territory and monitoring the withdrawal of the Il-28 bombers, I would like to state the following. We could agree to the same type of monitoring which was used for the ships removing the missiles from Cuba. Of course, the Americans would like to inspect Cuban territory, but we respect the Cuban position and will never allow unilateral inspections on Cuban territory. We could agree to visual monitoring at sea of the withdrawal of the bombers.

We have accurate information. Kennedy is maneuvering. If he is able to get his demands met, then he will be forced to keep his promises, i.e., provide guarantees that the United States and its allies will not attack Cuba and lift the blockade. If Kennedy's demand is not met, then the United States will maintain the blockade and continue to maintain it while accusing us of failing to keep our promises. And in this case the UN would not support us.

In our expert opinion, the presence of such advanced fighters as the MiG-21 makes the Il-28 bombers irrelevant for the defense of Cuba. We believe that we could meet Kennedy's demand if the Americans lifted the blockade and gave substantial guarantees that they will not attack Cuba. If we leave the bombers in Cuba, then we would thus give the Americans sufficient grounds to repudiate their promise of guarantees and maintain the blockade. This would be bad for both of us. Think about it long and hard, Comrade Fidel. Think calmly and then make your decision. If we stubbornly refuse to remove the Il-28s from Cuba, then the negotiations will hit a blank wall. This would allow the U.S. to maintain the blockade and make Cuba's economic situation worse. In this case Cuba's example would no longer inspire other peoples. Consequently you would suffer a moral defeat. You must get the U.S. to guarantee that it will not attack Cuba, with the support of the Soviet Union and the other socialist countries. Then Cuba's economy would be able to develop rapidly, which would be very important for Latin America and the entire world. Predators are predators, but you often have to maneuver in order to achieve a great goal. We, Comrade Fidel, will always act in the interests of revolutionary Cuba. This statement reflects the resolve of the entire Central Committee of the Communist Party of the Soviet Union. We believe that this solution is best for Cuba. Cuba's defensive capabilities are quite considerable. And Cuba is in the right. And reaching an agreement in the United Nations would foil any attempts to strangle Cuba by military force.

F. CASTRO. What will be the position of the Soviet Union if, despite removal of the bombers, the U.S. insists on an inspection and, using the excuse that Cuba does not agree to an inspection, continues with the blockade?

A. I. Mikoyan. We will only remove the bombers if the U.S. adheres to its commitments. We will keep the bombers in Cuba until the Americans agree to lift the blockade. The question of inspection was exhaustively discussed during my talk with McCloy in New York. We will be steadfast in defending your position. We feel that the procedure used to monitor removal of the airplanes from Cuba can be the same as that employed in removing the missiles. This can be conducted at sea in order not to compromise Cuba's interests. This is in accordance with the wishes of the revolutionary government and there is no question of inspecting Cuban territory.

F. CASTRO. I want to assert, Comrade Mikoyan, that we will never consent to an inspection. Please transmit to the Soviet government the fact that our decision is final and irrevocable.

A. I. Mikoyan. I have already informed the Soviet government that the Cuban government will never allow its territory to be inspected. This is no longer an issue. By allowing a visual inspection of our vessels we have fulfilled all of our obligations. We will not yield, no matter how insistent the American side may become. We are in full agreement on this. We respect your sovereignty. I will transmit your views to my government.

F. CASTRO. I will meet with the other members of our government to discuss this, although I personally see no need to hurry.

A. I. Mikoyan. I would like to add that removal of the missiles deprived you only of offensive weapons. The missiles were a means of holding the enemy at bay. However, Cuba has no intention of attacking the U.S. Consequently, you don't need the Il-28 bombers. They, as you know, have no such deterrent value. All of the other military hardware is state-of-the-art defensive weapons.

Obviously, if the U.S. were to attack you in force all of these powerful weapons would not be enough to protect you. But if the governments of the Latin American countries decided to attack Cuba without direct U.S. involvement, they would be badly defeated. The firepower of Cuba is very great. I think that no other socialist country, excluding the Soviet Union, has such powerful modern weapons as you have.

F. CASTRO. Right now I want to meet with my comrades. I will remember all of your arguments. I am in the process of reaching a decision.

Mikoyan. I am prepared to meet with you or with all the leaders of the United Revolutionary Organizations of Cuba together at any time to provide additional clarification if necessary.

I could cite other arguments if the arguments I have cited today were unpersuasive.

Please say hello to your comrades for me.

CASTRO. Thank you. Tell me, Comrade Mikoyan, are you going to the University of Havana today where you were invited this evening?

Mikoyan. Should I?

CASTRO. Of course you should. It would be very enjoyable and worthwhile. Are you going to Turiguano tomorrow?

Mikoyan. Maybe it would be better if I did not go to Turiguano and instead used the time for more discussions.

CASTRO. No. I think the trip would be very interesting. I would definitely advise you to go. We could schedule a discussion for tomorrow evening after you get back from your trip, or on Wednesday.

Mikoyan. OK. Goodbye, Comrade Fidel.

CASTRO. Thank you. Until we meet again, Comrade Mikoyan.

Transcript recorded by   [signed] V. Tikhmenev

AM-4470s

APRF, fond 3, op. 65, d. 909, ll. 120–133.

DOCUMENT 328   *Mikoyan's telegram to Khrushchev and the Politburo, November 12, 1962, characterizing his meeting with Castro in Havana and the Cuban leader's reaction to Soviet proposals to remove Iliushin-28 bombers from Cuba*

170

To Comrade N. S. Khrushchev

COMMITTEE OF STATE SECURITY [*KGB*]
COUNCIL OF MINISTERS OF THE USSR

Copying categori-
cally prohibited

RETURN TO.....
sector, General
department, *TSK KPSS*
No. 3397... 11/13/62

Top Secret
(when completed)

INCOMING CODED TELEGRAM No. 32918

Copy No. 1 to Comrade Khrushchev
copy No. 2 to Comrade Khrushchev

Copy No. 3 to Comrade Kozlov
Copy No. 4 to Department 8

From Havana   Received 1220   November 13, 1962   For decisions and remarks

Central Committee, Communist Party of the Soviet Union

I met Fidel Castro and carried out the instructions (your No. 1013, concerning everything connected with the Il-28), discussing nearly all the arguments summarized in Comrade Khrushchev's letter to me.

In the middle of our talk he was nervous and almost blew up, stating that he is not interested in arguments but wants to know directly what the Soviet government wants. Without losing my composure, I presented to him our proposal and for two hours supported it with our arguments. Fidel said very little.

I shall describe his reactions in full in the next telegram.

Toward the end of the discussion he calmed down, said that he understood our arguments, and has formed an opinion (he didn't say what), which he will discuss with his comrades, and then he will meet us again.

To comprehend Fidel's mood, these facts are typical: he asked whether I would go to the university, where I was invited this evening, I asked if it was necessary. He replied that it would be good and useful. Then he switched to tomorrow's excursion out of town, and I ventured an opinion that our time might be more usefully spent in discussions. However, he insisted on the excursion and said that we would be able to talk tomorrow evening after the trip, or on Wednesday.

We parted in a friendly mood, having said our good-byes in a fraternal fashion.

No. 864
Nov. 12, 1962

A. Mikoyan
printed: 1250, November 13 Issue: 4 copies

[Note in left margin:]
To be returned to Sector 8 of the Main Directorate of the *KGB*, Council of Ministers of the USSR, within 10 days of receipt.

APRF, fond 3, op. 65, d. 909, ll. 170–171.

Premier Fidel Castro of Cuba with Politburo member A. I. Mikoyan (right), 1960. TSGAKFD. N 164632.

DOCUMENT 329 *Excerpt from the minutes of the November 18, 1962, session of the Presidium of the Central Committee, confirming Mikoyan's instructions to the Russian military in Cuba not to fire on American planes, as the Cubans were doing*

Proletarians of All Countries, Unite!
Communist Party of the Soviet Union, CENTRAL COMMITTEE

Top Secret

No. P67/16

To Comrades Khrushchev, Gromyko

Excerpt of minutes No. 67 of the November 18, 1962, session of the Presidium of the Central Committee of the Communist Party of the Soviet Union.

On instructions to Comrade A. I. Mikoyan with regard to the Cubans' decision about firing on American airplanes.

Confirm draft instructions to Comrade A. I. Mikoyan, (attached)

Secretary of the Central Committee

[Left margin:] Return within 7 days to the Central Committee of the Communist Party of the Soviet Union (General department, first sector).

Re: Point 16, Minutes No. 67

Secret   PRIORITY

HAVANA
Soviet Ambassador for Comrade A. I. Mikoyan

1841. I am relaying instructions from above.

If our Cuban friends approach you with regard to the decision about firing on American airplanes, you are to tell them:

Since the decision to fire on American airplanes was not coordinated with us, we consider it impossible to take part in it. Therefore, our forces have been instructed not to open fire on American airplanes.

APRF, fond 3, op. 65, d. 911, ll. 116–117.

chapter 14

PEACEFUL COEXISTENCE AND DÉTENTE

The Cold War was facilitated by the prevailing Soviet view of the world
that had first been propounded by Stalin in the 1920s: the world was divided
into two hostile camps, and military confrontation between the two was inevitable. World War II had demonstrated the reality of Soviet fears of capitalist encirclement, and Soviet postwar policies could be interpreted as the
country acting in the continuing belief of the two-camp thesis. Nikita
Khrushchev shared this assumption of polarization as he rose to power within
the Soviet leadership in the early 1950s, but he added a new wrinkle to Soviet
foreign policy assumptions, the idea of "peaceful coexistence." By the 1950s
war between the superpowers meant nuclear conflict and mutual annihilation. So ways had to be found to manage tensions and to coexist. Class struggle would continue, but Khrushchev now believed it could take peaceful
forms. Until the ultimate and inevitable victory of socialism over capitalism,
a belief which Khrushchev never relinquished, the two sides should seek
ways to manage tensions, to limit armaments, and to understand each other
better.

Khrushchev's domestic thaw was thus accompanied by increasing openness and overtures toward the West on a scale unseen since the days of the
wartime alliance. The USSR acquiesced to a mutual withdrawal of forces
from occupied Austria in 1955, followed by a major gathering of heads of state
in Geneva. This meeting produced no concrete results, but the "spirit of
Geneva" signaled a new readiness by the Soviet Union to engage diplomati-

cally as an equal. At the same time, the Soviet foreign ministry began to up-grade its own information-gathering capabilities, evidenced by the briefings prepared in 1958 on President Eisenhower and Secretary of State John Foster Dulles (Documents 334 and 335). A sophisticated new generation of Soviet diplomats cultivated contacts across a broad spectrum of the U.S. policy es-tablishment, including those with Supreme Court Justice William O. Douglas (Document 337). Cultural exchange agreements led to increased travel by young Americans to the USSR and more openness and exchanges of ideas.

Khrushchev himself became the first Soviet leader to travel to the West, including a highly publicized visit to the United States in 1959. He continued his pattern of high-level summitry with a meeting in Vienna with the new U.S. president, John F. Kennedy, in 1961, during which Khrushchev demon-strated an aggressive and belligerent defense of Soviet interests in Europe and with regard to nuclear testing. Khrushchev recalled his disappointment with U.S. intransigence in his memoirs: "The difference in our class positions had prevented us from coming to an agreement—despite all possible efforts on my part." But Document 336 suggests that his behavior played well in the Krem-lin.

With the rise of the Chinese People's Republic in the 1960s as a rival to So-viet leadership in the socialist world, and the increasing unwillingness of de-veloping countries to be aligned with either the socialist or capitalist camp, Stalin's old two-camp theory seemed less valid than ever. Western European Communists began to develop their own version of socialism, labeled Euro-communism, further damaging the ideological hegemony of the Soviet Union. Old problems of security and mutual relations remained, such as the fate of Germany and the issue of nuclear arms, but new leaders sought new ways to manage these tensions. In August 1970 the Soviet Union and the Fed-eral Republic of Germany signed a landmark treaty, confirming the division of Germany and the permanence of the borders that had been drawn at the end of World War II. This treaty included a clause confirming that "détente," or a relaxation of tensions, was to be an object of Soviet-German policies. In the following years the search for détente extended to the other European powers and to the United States. The Final Act of the Conference on Security and Cooperation in Europe was signed in Helsinki in 1975, and the U.S. and the USSR engaged in a series of high-level negotiations to limit the expansion of their nuclear arsenals, culminating in the Strategic Arms Limitations Treaty (SALT) agreements. Economic and scientific cooperative efforts in-creased, illustrated by the 1986 agreement on cooperation in space (Docu-ment 338). These agreements must have generated some degree of debate and discord, but the documents released here shed little light on the inner work-ings of the Soviet foreign policy process.

DOCUMENT 330   *Biographical material on Wendell Wilkie, former Republican presidential candidate and then personal representative of the president, sent by S. Lozovskii, September 3, 1942, to Stalin and Molotov*

SECRET

item No. 2

September 3, 1942

TO CHAIRMAN OF THE STATE COMMITTEE OF DEFENSE
Comrade J. V. Stalin

TO PEOPLE'S COMMISSAR OF FOREIGN AFFAIRS
Comrade V. M. Molotov

I am sending you a detailed description of Wendell Wilkie. I direct your attention to the demagogic announcement by Wilkie on August 23, reported by the newspapers before his U.S. departure. Wilkie deliberately demonstrates his antifascism because of his German background and fears that he will be accused of insufficient American patriotism. All of his pro-Soviet declarations carry a clear campaign character, since he hopes to ride a wave of sympathy towards the Soviet Union to the presidential elections in 1944.

ATTACHMENT: the above-mentioned on 9 pages.

DEPUTY PEOPLE'S COMMISSAR
OF FOREIGN AFFAIRS

S. Lozovskii

[Overwritten, top of document:]
The information is fairly good (a rarity for the People's Commissariat
of Foreign Affairs!) Must distribute to those to whom we send cipherings.
        V. Molotov   Sept. 23

[handwritten:] Send to Comrades:
        Mikoyan
        Voroshilov
        Beria
        Kaganovich   Losovskii
        Vyshinskii   Zarubin
        Dekanozov [?]

SECRET
Copy No. 2

September 2, 1942

No. 485/SShA [U.S.A.]

WENDELL WILKIE

Wilkie was born February 18, 1892, in Elwood, Indiana, a typical small Midwestern town. His grandmother and grandfather were immigrants from Germany. During his election campaign Wilkie stated that his mother's and father's parents had left Germany to "breathe the free air of America." Wilkie's father was a lawyer and at one time was director of schools. Wilkie's mother was a school teacher.

After finishing school in Elwood, Wilkie attended the university in Bloomington, Indiana. During his summer vacation, Wilkie, like other students, worked different jobs in different parts of the country. He worked at a steel mill, harvested wheat in the state of Dakota [sic], and worked as a cook.

In his speeches in the 1940 election campaign, Wilkie tried to portray himself as a poor boy who worked his way up to where he is now. "Like you, I have walked the thorny path," Wilkie said to his supporters in the state of Iowa at one of his many campaign rallies.

But, as *The New Republic* reported in a special supplement devoted to Wilkie, "Wilkie's actual path was about as thorny as Roosevelt's. Wilkie was raised by parents who gave an education to all their children and helped them get their start in life."

In his first few years after college, Wilkie demonstrated an interest in teaching. In 1913 he became a high school teacher in Coffeyville, Kansas, where he taught history, public speaking, and basketball. But he soon grew disenchanted with teaching and left after a year for Puerto Rico, where he worked as a lab technician at a sugar mill. Finally, after realizing that his father's profession was much better, Wilkie returned to his native Indiana and, after earning a law degree, went to work at his father's law office in Elwood.

Wilkie served in the American Army during the First Imperialist War as a member of the expeditionary forces in Europe. After he returned from Europe as a captain, Wilkie went to work as a lawyer for the Firestone Tire Company of Akron, Ohio. After several months with the company, Wilkie got the opportunity to become an associate partner in a law firm in the same city.

Over the next few years at the firm, Wilkie became a prominent figure in Akron. He was greatly assisted in this process by the speeches he delivered, as a talented public speaker and lawyer, on cases involving the defense of democratic rights. Playing the Democracy Game and a desire to portray himself as a man of the people and as a liberal devoted to the American freedoms inscribed in the Constitution and ready to defend them have characterized Wilkie and his later political career. One example: Although he is a ferocious enemy of the American Communist Party, as a lawyer Wilkie never hesitated to plead the case of Schneider, the Secretary of the California Communist Party, before the Supreme Court of the United States after the California courts had issued a deportation order against Schneider as an "undesirable alien."

Wilkie's talents and energies attracted the attention of the directors of several major utilities companies. In 1926 a director of the Penn-Ohio and Commonwealth Power Company said, "Don't let this young man go."

Wilkie began to enter the national arena in 1927 and 1928, and in 1929 he was invited to New York, where as a member of the board of a major electrical company Commonwealth and Southern Corporation, affiliated with the Morgan Banking House, he founded the legal office of Wheelock and Wilkie. In 1933, when the need arose to name a director for this company, Commonwealth and Southern Corporation, the choice fell on Wilkie. Wilkie remained in the post of chairman of this company from 1933 to 1940, when he left the position in order to prepare for the presidential campaign.

As chairman of the board of directors of the Commonwealth and Southern Corporation, Wilkie earned a salary of at least $75,000 a year. If we consider that he simultaneously served as the director of several smaller companies belonging to the Commonwealth and Southern Corporation (including Consumers Power Co., Central Illinois Light Co., Trustee Edison Electric Institute, Ohio Edison Company, Southern Indiana Gas and Electric Company), then we can quite confidently say that Wilkie earned a salary of $100,000 to $125,000 per year.

Wilkie's life story does not resemble that of Edison or Ford—he never employed wage earners. Wilkie had a reputation as a public speaker and a liberal, whom the directors of Akron's public utility companies employed to defend their interests.

During his election campaign Wilkie almost never referred to his attitudes towards labor organizations, with the exception of a few comments in his speeches. However, as the director of the largest electrical company, Wilkie revealed what his views on this matter are. Commonwealth and Southern Corporation, a company with a capital of more than one billion dollars, conducted a campaign against labor organizations. This fact made it very difficult for Wilkie's supporters to wage an election campaign in his favor.

According to the "Civil Liberties Committee," which at the time was headed by Robert La Follette, seven of the ten subsidiaries of the Commonwealth and Southern Corporation used the services of "notorious spies known as persecutors of labor unions." From 1934 to 1936, one of Wilkie's companies, the Georgia Power Company, spent $31,000 on spies, who also worked at the same time for the Alabama Power Company. Another of Wilkie's companies, Central Illinois Light, purchased bombs, tear gas guns, and grenades from a defense company. Three of Wilkie's companies, namely Consumers Power of Michigan, Ohio Edison Power, and Pennsylvania Edison Power, used the services of the spy agency known as the Corporation Auxiliary Company. La Follette's committee was unable to determine the amount of money Wilkie had spent to defeat the labor unions, which obviously means that the picture is incomplete.

Wilkie's companies did battle with workers belonging to unions affiliated with the Congress of Industrial Organizations. They used every means at their disposal, up to and including terrorism. Wilkie waged a fierce battle against the state-owned electric company established on Roosevelt's initiative as part of his "New Deal" program. Roosevelt's purpose in establishing this company was to limit Wilkie's monopoly.

According to *The New Republic*, the magazine of the American liberal intelligentsia, which provided extensive coverage of Wilkie during the presidential campaign of 1940, Wilkie is an ardent advocate of big business and opposed to any government intervention in the affairs of entrepreneurs. Wilkie primarily believes that public supervision, which is ostensibly exercised on behalf of consumers, workers, and farmers, is in reality not in the best interests of the people and can be attributed to the power hunger of politicians. What we have to fear, Wilkie says, is not big business, but the power-hungry government. Wilkie blames the Great Depression and the hardship it caused more on government intervention in business than on the activities of industrialists and financiers. Wilkie believes that the essence of freedom lies in free enterprise and that striving for profit is the foundation of civilization. In Wilkie's opinion, "the nation and business are inseparable" and that "defending the freedom of the people against the omnipresent oversight of government is the liberalism of today."

In opposing Roosevelt's candidacy for a third term, the *New York Times* wrote that "Wilkie enjoys the trust of business circles and is an industrialist himself." Wilkie's candidacy was supported by the biggest and most influential financiers and industrial magnates such as DuPont, Rockefeller, Vanderbilt, Whitney, Thomas Lamont (one of Morgan's main partners), Davis, the attorney for one of Morgan's companies, Stingley, the president of one of the Morgan companies, Mooney, a vice-president of General Motors (who was awarded a Nazi Iron Cross), and many others.

Despite Wilkie's close connections to every corner of Wall Street, this has not kept him from demagogically playing the role of a defender of democratic rights. For example, in a speech to the Republican Convention, Wilkie said that "the democratic forces are facing a very decisive test, and we as Republicans and Americans must support the principles of the United States, which is a major bulwark of democracy in the world. I intend to run a determined campaign in order to unite America and its farmers, workers, and all classes of people behind the cause of freedom."

Wilkie's position towards aid to Great Britain can be best summarized by the following quote: "We must continue to help Great Britain, which is our first line of defense and our only remaining friend. We must render aid to Great Britain within the bounds of reason and efficiency as determined by impartial experts" (from a speech on September 21, 1940, in San Francisco).

In one of his campaign speeches Wilkie defined the reasons why Americans should help Great Britain in the following way: "We must realize that the loss of the British fleet would greatly weaken our defenses. If the British fleet were lost or captured, Germany could dominate the Atlantic and, if so, it would gain control over most of the ships and shipyards of Europe. This would be a real disaster for us. We would be open to attack from the Atlantic. Our defenses would be weakened if we were unable to build a navy and air force strong enough to defend both oceans. Our foreign trade would also be seriously impaired. This trade is absolutely essential for our prosperity, but if we had to trade with a Europe dominated by Germany's current trade policy, we might also have to adopt certain totalitarian methods. Each and every one of us who loves democracy must reckon with this prospect" (from a speech delivered August 17, 1940, in Indiana).

Now for a brief digression on the conflict which flared up between the Republicans and Democrats in the 1940 campaign in order to provide the reader with a better understanding of Wilkie and his supporters' positions on U.S. domestic and foreign policy.

In their platform adopted at the Republican Convention in Philadelphia, the Republicans assured their constituents that they were against involving the country in a European war. They were in favor of supporting Britain "within the bounds of international law" and "without detriment to the national defense." Like the Democrats, the Republicans demanded enforcement of the Monroe Doctrine. Sharply criticizing the Democrats for doing too little to arm the country, the Republicans came out in favor of a higher defense budget.

Thus, the Republicans and Democrats had no fundamental disagreements on foreign policy. The situation was somewhat more complex with respect to domestic policy. The Republicans were forced to disguise carefully all of their reactionary ideas, because they obviously realized that large segments of the voters had voted for Roosevelt in the past as a man who stood up for their interests.

In their campaign platform, the Republicans made no specific promises to the voters in the area of domestic policy. Although they refrained from any direct attacks on Roosevelt, the Republicans and Wilkie, their presidential candidate, accused the president of dictatorial inclinations, promised to preserve democracy and "make America strong," asking for substantial sacrifices in return.

In his campaign speeches, Wilkie alluded to a possible tax increase due to the war, a cut in wages, and military conscription. In order to win workers' votes, Wilkie demagogically declared that he was for collective bargaining, unemployment compensation, the minimum wage and a standard work day, and better conditions for farmers.

During the 1940 presidential campaign, there was no unity in the ranks of the Republican Party. The party had already divided into two camps. On one side was a strong faction which rallied around Wilkie and his interventionist policy, basically tended to support Roosevelt's policy of unlimited assistance to the countries fighting aggression, and had broken with isolationism. On the other side was a second faction, which was no less powerful and was led by such stalwarts of isolationism as Herbert Hoover, Senators Taft, Vandenberg, Nye, Brooks, and Barton, and Representatives Fish, Tinkham, and others. This faction (the Hoover-Taft faction) accused Roosevelt of inaction in the area of war preparations (while the members of the faction in Congress always voted against appropriations for military needs and defensive fortifications), was sharply critical of any aid to Great Britain and the other countries fighting Nazi aggression and called for mediation between Great Britain and Germany and for appeasement of the aggressor nations.

From the entire period between the elections and the attack on Pearl Harbor, Wilkie and his supporters (Senators Austin, Lodge, Danaher) attempted to convince the Hooverites of the perniciousness of the policy of isolationism, which would lead the party to ruin. In turn, the Hooverites accused Wilkie of betraying the Republicans and said that he could just as easily call himself a Democrat as a Republican.

In the summer of 1941 the discord between the two factions was so great that there was serious talk in the American press of the possibility of a split in the Republican Party and the organization of a new Republican Party under Wilkie's leadership. This was especially evident after all the reactionaries of the right wing of the Republican Party (Hoover, Landon, Taft, Brooks, Dewey, Fish, Tinkham, and so forth) rallied around the Lindbergh-Wood fascist America First Committee and launched a despicable profascist campaign against Roosevelt and his foreign policy.

This treasonous activity on the part of the Hooverites in cahoots with such outright fascists as Lindbergh, Wood, the radio priest Father Coughlin, the black shirt Pelley, and others did not cease even after the Nazi hordes invaded the Soviet Union. Perhaps it would be more accurate to say that the America First Committee's activity became especially frenzied after Nazi Germany's attack on the Soviet Union.

With powerful newspapers behind them (the *Chicago Tribune*, the *New York Daily News*, the Scripps-Howard papers), the right-wing reactionaries of the Republican Party with the support of reactionary Democrats such as Senators Reynolds, Clark, Wheeler, and others endeavored to sow discord between the USSR and the United States, get the Germans and the British to stop fighting, appease Japan at the expense of China and the USSR, and so on and so forth. They even revived the old bogeyman of the red menace which would imperil Europe and the entire world if Bolshevik Russia was victorious.

The discord between the Wilkie faction and the Hoover-Taft supporters has not died down yet. It reemerged at a meeting of the National Committee of the Republican Party on April 20, 1942, when the party was adopting a policy resolution. Wilkie proposed one resolution, while Taft, the senator from Ohio, proposed another.

Wilkie's draft resolution on the issue called for unconditional continuation of the war, regardless of the cost, "until the United States and the Allies win a total victory over Germany, Italy, Japan, and their auxiliaries." Wilkie declared, "We cannot agree to peace terms with the aforementioned powers except for peace as a result of victory, and we shall unconditionally reject any offers, no matter how appealing they may be, until total victory is won."

Wilkie also advocated that the United States "should do everything it can both now and in the future that may prove helpful in meeting its international obligations in the modern world."

In their draft resolution, Wilkie's opponents in the Republican Party from the Hoover-Taft faction promised the president unconditional support in waging war to total victory, but the resolution was not opposed to considering any enemy peace offers and also did not come out in favor of the United States assuming international obligations.

The fierce debate which raged over the two draft resolutions culminated in the adoption of Wilkie's resolution in somewhat modified form. The entire American press described the Republican National Committee's resolution as a total defeat for the isolationist elements and a victory for Wilkie, who had demanded that the party decisively reject a policy of appeasement or compromise.

In an interview with American reporters, Wilkie himself stated that the adoption of the resolution constituted evidence of the Republican Party's rejection of isolationism and that in its resolution the party's National Committee had "spoken out against any policy of appeasement and had expressed the intention of the American people to continue the war mercilessly, unconditionally, and all the way to total victory over any enemy."

Wilkie's attitude towards the Soviet Union is typified by his article published in *Fortune* magazine during the Soviet-Finnish conflict. "We wholeheartedly sympathize with the Finns in their struggle against the Soviet Union. If Finland succeeds in repulsing the Soviet Union, then the general peace and economic order will be more secure, but if the Soviet Union defeats Finland, then the general peace and economic order will be gravely imperiled. We are eager to help Finland as much as we can without taking part in the war."

After June 22, 1941, Wilkie came out wholeheartedly in favor of assisting us in the war against Nazi Germany. In a telegram of greetings to a New York rally on July 22, 1942, in support of opening a second front, Wilkie wrote, "I had hoped to be with you this evening, but because I could not, I want you all to know that in my opinion, you're doing great work." And he went on to say: "You are telling the Russian people that we Americans are enthralled by their courage, resolve, and heroism and would hope that their sacrifices are not in vain. You are telling the intrepid defenders of that great country that we Americans intend to back up our talk with action."

And finally, we should cite Wilkie's statement to the *TASS* correspondent in New York in connection with his forthcoming visit to the Soviet Union. Wilkie stated that "this visit will lead to greater mutual understanding between the Soviet and American peoples. Russia and the United States should work together not only in the present, but in the future. By making this trip, I hope to get the opportunity to explain the Russian point of view to the United States and to communicate the American point of view to Russia. I am anxiously awaiting my meeting with Mister Stalin and intend to learn as much as possible about Russia. I have wanted to do this for a long time, and I am very grateful to the government for allowing me to make this trip."

In Wilkie's opinion, the Red Army's heroic resistance is one of the most remarkable events in history. Wilkie enthusiastically spoke of the "fighting spirit of the Russian people, who are waging the war under splendid leadership."

Wilkie continues to enjoy great prestige and influence in the Republican Party. But he still must contend with opposition from rivals who aspire to leadership of the Republican Party. In particular, Wilkie is opposed by certain elements who objected to Wilkie's support of Roosevelt's foreign policy before the events at Pearl Harbor. These disagreements within the Republican Party were especially evident at the convention of the New York Republican Party which took place several years ago (for the purpose of nominating a candidate for governor of the state and to formulate the party's platform). Currently, the party's organization in the state is under the control of the former Chief Prosecutor for the City of New York, Dewey, who was an unsuccessful presidential candidate in 1940.

A meeting of the executive committee of the Republican Party of New York drastically altered a resolution proposed by Wilkie's supporters which called on the Republican Convention to approve a resolution expressing the convention's hope for the success of Wilkie's mission to the Soviet Union and the Near East and praising Wilkie's leadership. However, the final resolution approved by the Committee expressed the convention's hope for the success of Wilkie's mission but did not contain any praise of his leadership of the party. Afterwards the *New York Times* wrote that "the original draft aroused fierce debate because Wilkie was coming out against Dewey, and in addition, Wilkie was out of favor with the party organization of New York because of his support for Roosevelt's foreign policy" (*TASS*, August 26, 1942).

Wilkie's attitude towards the current war against the Axis powers is typified by his latest radio speech on August 21, 1942, which was broadcast to the entire country. In this speech Wilkie said: "If we are intent on destroying our enemies, we should be prepared to fight and die for our cause. Too many of us believe that this war is just a war of guns, airplanes, and industry and that we can win the war simply by producing more than the Axis powers. But the only way we can lose the war is if our production of guns, airplanes, and tanks is not backed up by our firm and unshakable dedication to our cause" (*Izvestiia*, August 22, 1942).

HEAD OF THE DEPARTMENT OF THE AMERICAS

(Zarubin)

September 8, 1942
7 copies made

SINFORM New York (241840)

<u>Washington</u>. Wendell Wilkie, who will soon be heading to Moscow and other allied countries, published an appeal to the Russian people on August 23:

A long time has passed since I first planned to visit the various countries which President Roosevelt recently spoke about. I am anxiously awaiting the opportunity to visit the USSR and exchange views with the people of this country, which could be called the largest country occupied by Germany, on issues which the Russian people and I consider common and pertinent to the destruction of German, Japanese, and Italian militarism.

My personal meeting with Joseph Stalin, the leader of Russia in its memorable defense against the Nazi hordes, will be an experience which I shall treasure forever. The valor and wisdom of this great leader has aroused as much admiration in the Allied countries as it has struck terror and fear among Adolf Hitler's satellites. I would like to talk to the people of this great country, with the men, the women, the young, and the old—in short, all those who have given and continue to give all of their energy, talent, and life to this harsh struggle against the Nazi hordes. I would like to tell these heroic people how much Americans appreciate the incredible work they are doing.

I would hope that the visits I am planning to make to other countries will be just as memorable.

Despite my status as a private citizen, the fact that I represented one of the major political parties of the United States in the most recent presidential election has given me the passionate desire to tell the Russian people and the entire world that the unity of the United States and its war effort is indestructible and that the entire American people have wholeheartedly dedicated themselves to the total war which we are waging. All of us are walking hand in hand with our allies to total victory without flinching.

True Copy

AVP RF

DOCUMENT 331   *Letter from American writer Robert Major to Gosplan Director Voznesenskii, April 15, 1946, on lessening Cold War hostilities*

[English original]

Special Speech Instructor	President
For	Major School of Acting
Los Angeles City High Schools	Special Lecturer
International Toastmasters Club	for
Beverly Hills Drama Workshop	Southern California Women's Clubs
Motion Picture Players Guild	Los Angeles Business Men's Clubs
Hollywood Screen Scribes	College Student Organizations
Adventurers' Club	Motion Picture Actors' Club
College Forum	

Robert W. Major

Dramatic Coach - Playwright - Director - Lecturer

Mabel V. Morey, Executive Secretary

Hollywood, California

April 15, 1946

Mr. M. A. Voznesensky
Head of State Planning Dept.
MOSCOW, Russia

My dear sir:

For many months I have intended writing a letter to Premier Stalin or Foreign Minister Molotov on a very serious matter. I did not know which one I should address. Then, several days ago I read the enclosed Associated Press Article in the *Los Angeles Times*. I read it carefully and decided you were the appropriate Official for me to address.

Mr. Voznesensky, my object in writing this letter is profoundly serious. I am sorry I cannot write it in Russian so you could get my meaning expressed in my own words. Since the end of the War, there has been a growing restlessness throughout the world. That restlessness in America is deliberately stirred up by financial interests who would welcome another war, if it served their own greed and selfishness. As you know, my Country is made up of many races, religions and nationalities. These groups are often very antagonistic. We have religious freedom, but not religious harmony. We have peace, but not tolerance. We are united in war only.

There is one church in this country with millions of members which is bitterly opposed to Russia. This church, (which I shall not identify for fear this letter may fall into other hands,) supported the Franco Regime in the Spanish Revolution. This church has its roots in a country that fought with the Axis and is antagonistic to American principles. Also, there are millions of Americans violently opposed to Russia because they are wealthy and they oppose any system that prevents wealth falling into the hands of a few to the detriment of the working people.

Then, there is a third group whose membership is less numerous, who oppose Russia because of ignorance. They believe all of the anti-Russian propaganda that they hear over the radio and read in the newspapers.

But, balancing these three groups there are about 40 or 50 million Americans composed largely of the working classes, teachers, writers and intellectuals, who fervently favor Russia and many of them openly support Communism without belonging to the Communist Party.

Anti-Russian propaganda in the United States originates among the wealthy families. It is financed by big corporations, newspapers and manufacturers. The working people have no way of knowing the truth because all they see in the capitalistic press and all they hear over the radios is anti-Russian propaganda.

I belong to the Democratic Party, the party which elected President Roosevelt four times. But, I generally vote for the most honest candidate, regardless of his party. However, I hate capitalism. All my life I have hated it. Because, in my opinion, it is the source of more evil than good. It causes wars, class distinction, strikes, revolutions, crime, civil war, broken homes, wrecked youth, hopelessness, despair, famine, and most every scourge known to mankind for ages past.

For years I have read and studied Russian History, particularly since the Karensky [sic] Revolution. I have studied the lives of Lenin, Stalin, Molotov and your other great leaders. I have also followed your diplomatic course before, during and since the War. And, I am definitely convinced that the present Russian Government is sincerely and ardently devoted to the cause of the common man. I have noticed that territory conquered by Russian Troops is given back to the people who work on it instead of to the wealthy landowners who for centuries have exploited peasants throughout the world.

If the people of the United States really understood the motives of the Russian Government and the ideals of the Russian people, there would not be friction between our Counties, and the Iranian case would never have been brought into the United Nations Security Council. But so long as the big corporations broadcast over the radio anti-Russian propaganda and the newspapers print anti-Russian propaganda, the American people will continue to misunderstand the objectives of the Russian people and the Soviet government. Of course, if this misunderstanding grows acute enough there is always the possibility of another terrible war.

I love my Country very deeply and I admire Russia more than any other Country in the world. I believe with all my heart that Russia and the United States should and can work together, if the American people could learn to know the truth about the Russian Government and the Russian people.

That brings me to the object of this letter. As you will notice in the pamphlet that I am attaching, I am an author, director, teacher and former actor. I am a professional speaker and an expert in radio and motion picture entertainment. I was formerly connected with Warner Brothers Pictures Corporation, as chief dramatic coach. At present I am a supervisor for speech, drama and radio for the Los Angeles School System. But, I am so agitated over the growing friction between the United States and Russia that I will gladly give up all my other positions to devote my entire time to writing, directing and broadcasting a series of radio programs dealing with Russian life, Russian ideals, Russian romances, Russian traditions and Russian family life. I am a gifted speaker as I have been professor of Public Speaking in both American High Schools and Universities. These radio stories and programs can be written in Russia, translated, and sent to me, or ideas and subject matter can be sent to me and I will write the stories and submit them to the Russian Consul for approval. The programs could consist of a continued story about the romance of an American soldier with a Russian girl, or the comradeship of American and Russian soldiers who met in Germany. There could be a new chapter of the story each week. The story could be made lifelike and so interesting that it would be looked forward to each week by millions of Americans. Continued stories are very popular in America. It would be my suggestion not to make it obviously propaganda, but to tell the truth so forcefully that all prejudice for Russia would be changed to admiration.

I am so enthusiastic about such a program that I would be willing to make a trip to Moscow to discuss with the proper Russian officials all the details of such a broadcast. Being an American and well-known in radio circles, I could lease in my own name or in the name of the Russian Consul or in some other name, time on one of the National Broadcasting Systems and give one or more programs each week.

Such a program devoted to eliminating friction between our great Countries and showing the mass of American people what a wonderful, generous people the Russians are, would, I believe, do inestimable good for our two nations, and pave the way for harmony, brotherhood, and permanent peace!

I am 38 years old, a graduate of an American University, in Washington, D.C., and the University of Poitiers, France. I hold both A.B. and M.A. degrees. I am well-known in motion picture and radio circles and have a very high standing in both.

Naturally, if you launched such an important and extensive program, you would want to know more about me. I can give you, if you desire them, the names of United States Senators and Representatives in the American Congress who are close friends of mine. Also, the Governors of two American States. In addition to these, any number of prominent educators and school officials in Los Angeles.

This undertaking is so deep in my heart that I would be willing to devote the rest of my life in promoting it until the United States and Russia were linked in such close brotherly union that it would be impossible for them to ever go to war. When that is a fact, I can die happy!

I will deeply appreciate your kindness in replying to my letter and telling me if you are interested in my comprehensive suggestion. I would love to come to Russia and discuss this vast undertaking, and also visit the villages and cities to gather material for a series of thrilling and romantic stories.

Awaiting with eager interest your reply,

> Very respectfully yours,
>
> [signed] ROBERT W. MAJOR
> 1221 Malcolm
> West Los Angeles 24, California
> [handwritten:] United States of America
> P.S. Next page, please.

TSGANKh, fond 4372, op. 46, d. 50, ll. 82–96.

DOCUMENT 332   *Draft letter from Bulganin to Eisenhower, September 16, 1955, on the results of the Geneva Conference*

> U.S.A.-04/5
> DECLASSIFIED
> April 7, 1992
> SECRET
> Copy No. 1

> To Comrade V. M. MOLOTOV
>
> Here is the draft of Comrade N. A. BULGANIN's message to Eisenhower.
>
> [Illegible Signature]
>
> September 16, 1955
>
> No. 655/VK

> Draft

Moscow, Kremlin

Esteemed Mr. President:

During our memorable meetings in Geneva, we both acknowledged that maintaining person-to-person contacts and frank exchanges of opinions on topics of interest to both our countries would be very important for achieving better mutual understanding. At this time I believe it would be useful for both sides to exchange their opinions on different aspects of disarmament which are of interest to the Soviet government, and, I am certain, the U.S. government.

I think that you would agree with me that positive results in arms reduction and a ban on nuclear weapons could be extremely important for reducing international tension and for preserving and strengthening peace.

Disarmament is not a new subject. Both before and after the Second World War, these topics were constantly on the minds of our governments. Unfortunately, we have yet to achieve any positive results in reducing armaments and in lightening the heavy burden on the shoulders of our peoples inflicted on them by the incessant growth in military spending.

The Soviet government believes that we cannot reconcile ourselves to this unsatisfactory situation and that we must keep trying to find ways which would make it possible to move this very important endeavor from its current standstill.

At the Geneva Conference of the Heads of the Four Powers, which included a discussion of disarmament, you made a proposal which provided evidence of your desire to find a way to resolve this difficult problem and thus contribute to our common efforts to improve the international situation.

During our unofficial meetings in Geneva, I and my colleagues already had the opportunity to express our initial reactions to your proposal. You are also probably aware of my statement of August 5 indicating that the Soviet government has studied your proposal attentively and thoughtfully, motivated by the desire to bring our positions closer together and reach the necessary agreement.

Now that we have had the opportunity to study your proposal of July 21 as subsequently submitted by the U.S. government to the Subcommittee on Disarmament, I would consider it useful to discuss several topics related to disarmament in this letter. I believe that this would be in accord with your wishes.

As you know, your proposal includes the following steps:

a) a mutual exchange of military information on armaments and armed forces;

b) allowing each country the opportunity to take aerial photographs of the territory of the other country.

You have claimed that these steps would provide a guarantee against a surprise attack and would facilitate the establishment of an effective inspection system.

I will permit myself to candidly express my views on these subjects.

1. I cannot help but point out that, first of all, your proposal contains absolutely no mention of the need to resolve the main issue; namely, the issue of reducing armaments and armed forces and banning nuclear weapons. And unless this problem is resolved, it will be impossible to limit the arms race, lighten the heavy burden which our peoples are bearing as a result of it, or eliminate the threat of a military attack by one country against another involving the use of nuclear weapons.

The implementation of aerial reconnaissance and mutual exchanges of military information by themselves, without any agreement on the fundamental issues of disarmament (reducing armaments and armed forces and banning atomic weapons), would obviously be absolutely useless for limiting the arms race or the stockpiling of military equipment at certain places, including such weapons of destruction as atomic and hydrogen bombs. Even if we were to implement aerial reconnaissance and exchange military information, the threat of a nuclear surprise attack would not be diminished in the least.

Under these conditions, the need to exchange military information could hardly be justified by the requirements of disarmament control. In addition, it is unclear what kinds of armaments should be included in this information. Should the information include both information on conventional weapons and information on atomic weapons, which are the most dangerous and destructive kinds of weapons?

2. As we already pointed out in our talks at Geneva, your proposal could be interpreted to mean that aerial reconnaissance would be limited to the territories of the Soviet Union and the United States. With respect to the territory of U.S. allies in Europe, Asia, and other parts of the world where there are large numbers of American bases, one might conclude from your proposal that it does not provide for aerial reconnaissance of these territories. Thus, areas where major U.S. forces are stationed, including U.S. ground, naval, and air bases in Great Britain, West Germany, Italy, France, Spain, North Africa, Turkey, Greece, the Near and Middle East, Japan, Taiwan, the Philippines, and so forth, would be exempt from this aerial reconnaissance. This means that the Soviet Union would be put at a disadvantage vis-à-vis the United States.

3. I would like to discuss one more topic. We have focused our attention on the statement you made, Mr. President, after the Geneva Conference, in which you said that certain zones, which would be declared restricted zones, should be off-limits to aerial photography. In our opinion one could hide just about anything one wanted to in a territory as vast as the Soviet Union or the United States. Restricted zones would merely make this task even easier. Under these conditions, massing large concentrations of armaments and troops without any inspection would not pose any particular difficulty. This means that aerial reconnaissance would be rendered ineffective as an inspection procedure.

4. The considerations cited above make it possible to conclude that the implementation of your proposal to exchange military information and conduct aerial photographic surveys without any agreement on the issues of reducing armaments and the armed forces and banning atomic weapons would be incapable of eliminating the danger associated with the arms race. At the same time, these measures could create a sense of false security among the peoples of our nations and slacken their efforts to preserve and strengthen peace.

5. I am candidly expressing the views of the Soviet government concerning your proposals. At the same time I would like to emphasize several very important issues which we believe deserve careful consideration in examining the problem of disarmament.

First of all, we must reckon with the fact that inspection cannot be considered apart from steps to reduce international tension, to strengthen trust between nations, and to implement programs to reduce armaments and ban atomic weapons. We must remain cognizant of the very important fact that the necessary level of trust has not been established between the two most important countries in the world and that the Soviet Union, which is encircled by large numbers of military bases, must take the necessary precautions for its own security.

An examination of the issue of the forms of monitoring and inspection and their use without any agreement on what specifically should be monitored (arms reductions, bans on atomic weapons) would make such monitoring (inspections) pointless and without any basis in reality.

The Soviet government is in favor of the establishment of effective international monitoring, not as an end in itself, but as a means of monitoring the countries' compliance with their obligations to reduce their armaments and armed forces and ban atomic and hydrogen weapons.

It would be desirable, and in our opinion, quite feasible at this early stage for us to reach an agreement on those disarmament issues, including monitoring issues, on which the positions of our respective sides have gotten closer. In this regard I would like to focus your attention, Mr. President, on such topics as, for example, the issue of the levels of the armed forces of the five great powers, the schedule for instituting a ban on nuclear weapons, and the subject of establishing monitoring posts at strategic and key transportation points in each country. Implementation of the proposal to establish monitoring posts at this time would allow us to prevent the buildup of dangerous concentrations of armaments and armed forces at key points and thus prevent a surprise atomic attack, which, as I understand, is a subject of concern for the United States government as well as ours.

Reaching an agreement on these issues would undoubtedly strengthen the trust between our countries, which would create favorable conditions for the implementation of a more comprehensive disarmament and inspection program.

Dear Mr. President, in sending you this letter, I was motivated by the sincere desire to use a candid exchange of views on the subject of disarmament to achieve better mutual understanding and thus make it easier for us to arrive at mutually agreeable solutions to this very important problem.

Sincerely yours,

N. Bulganin

To His Excellency
Dwight Eisenhower
The President of the
United States of America

Washington

IDU MID

DOCUMENT 333   *Central Committee correspondence on Americans missing in Afghanistan,*
July 1956

CODED TELEGRAM

No. 1. [illegible]	No. 11. Suslov	No. 21. Fedorenko
No. 2. Bulganin	No. 12. Khrushchev	No. 22. Zamchevskii
No. 3. Voroshilov	No. 13. Khrushchev	No. 23. Il'ichev
No. 4. Kaganovich	No. 14. Shepilov	No. 24. Kozyrev
No. 5. Kirichenko	No. 15. Dudorov	No. 25. Kostylev
No. 6. Malenkov	No. 16. Gromyko	No. 26. TSarapkin
No. 7. Mikoyan	No. 17. Kuznetsov	No. 27. Copy
No. 8. Molotov	No. 18. Zakharov	No. 28. 10th Department
No. 9. Pervukhin	No. 19. Patolichev	No. 29. File
No. 10. Saburov	No. 20. Semenov	No. 30.

_____KABUL   29779/29780   0800 HOURS

July 26, 1956   Copy No. 12

Special Nos. 468 and 469

Several days ago in a conversation with me at a reception, Meyer, an adviser at the American Embassy in Kabul, expressed his opinion on the construction of the Helmand irrigation works in connection with the arrival of American experts to inspect the project. He observed that this project was begun in 1946 without any decent planning, which is why a lot of money has been spent on it. It has yet to produce any economic benefits, and there is no end in sight to the project. The experts have been assigned the task of developing proposals for the use of the irrigation system and determining the prospects for completion of the project.

The American repeated what he had told me earlier—that the United States had no intention of drawing Afghanistan into the Baghdad Pact but was merely interested in developing economic cooperation. He then stated that the Americans were interested in establishing better relationships with the other countries involved in Afghanistan.

We have observed that in their bulletin the Americans have begun to publish less information directed against us.

Meyer then asked me, after first saying that he was doing so unofficially, if I could obtain some information from our border guards on whether an American citizen, Peter Wynant [?] (about 32 years of age) and a Swedish citizen (female), Gunnell Gutmison had crossed the border. These individuals had come from India to Kabul and in late May had taken an Afghan bus to Baghlan and Mazar-i-Sharif. No information has been received on them since that time.

Without making any promises, I told him that I would look into the matter if I could.

We would consider it possible, if you deemed it advisable, to give the Americans an answer to their question after making an inquiry with the border guards.

July 25, 1956   DEGTIAR'

29 copies
Printed July 26, 2310 hours
Released by Plotnikov

True copy: [signed]

CODED TELEGRAM

No. 1. [illegible]   No. 11. Suslov   No. 21. Fedorenko
No. 2. Bulganin   No. 12. Khrushchev   No. 22. Zamchevskii
No. 3. Voroshilov   No. 13. Khrushchev   No. 23. Il'ichev
No. 4. Kaganovich   No. 14. Shepilov   No. 24. Kozyrev
No. 5. Kirichenko   No. 15. Dudorov   No. 25. Kostylev
No. 6. Malenkov   No. 16. Gromyko   No. 26. TSarapkin
No. 7. Mikoyan   No. 17. Kuznetsov   No. 27. Copy
No. 8. Molotov   No. 18. Zakharov   No. 28. 10th Department
No. 9. Pervukhin   No. 19. Patolichev   No. 29. File
No. 10. Saburov   No. 20. Semenov   No. 30.

KABUL   0044   1815 HOURS   July 27, 1956   Copy No.

Special No. 477

Ref Nos 468-469.

Meyer also informed that several days ago the Second Secretary of the American Embassy accompanied by representatives of the Afghan government traveled to the northern provinces in search of Wynant and Gutmison but was unable to find any trace of the missing persons. They did establish that on May 27 these individuals were in the village of . . . ibergan in Mazar-i-Sharif Province, but since that time there has been no news of them.

Meyer asked me for information on whether Wynant and Gutmison are in the Soviet Union, so that he could inform their relatives. In the process he allowed that they might have crossed the border for political reasons.

The American also stated that if we could not provide any information unofficially, the U.S. Embassy could contact Washington and the American government could send an official inquiry to the Soviet Union on the matter.

Meyer emphasized that in view of the improving relations between our countries and our embassies in Kabul, it would be desirable if the request were granted.

Please inform me of what my reply to Meyer should be.

July 27, 1956   DEGTIAR'

REF: No. 468-469 (Original No. 29778) dated July 25, 1956. Comrade Degtiar' indicated that at a reception, Meyer, an adviser at the U.S. Embassy in Kabul, asked for information on whether an American citizen Peter Wynant and a Swedish citizen (female) Gunnell Gutmison had crossed the border.

29 copies
printed July 28, 1900 hours
Released by Nikitin

True copy: [signed]

To be returned within 7 days to Section 1 of the General Department
of the Central Committee of the Communist Party of the Soviet Union

COMMUNIST PARTY OF THE SOVIET UNION
CENTRAL COMMITTEE [*TSK KPSS*]

No. PRO/XXXII[?]

To Comrade Shepilov (Ministry of Foreign Affairs)

Extract from Minute No. 30 of the Meeting of the Presidium of the
Central Committee on August 3, 1956

SUBJECT: The telegrams from Comrade Degtiar' in Kabul of July 25, 1956
                  (No. 468-469) and July 27, 1956 (No. 477)

Instruct the Ministry of Foreign Affairs of the USSR to inform Comrade Degtiar', the Soviet Ambassador in Kabul, that the persons indicated in his telegrams did not cross the Soviet border.

SECRETARY OF THE *TSK*

4-ak

Source?

DOCUMENT 334   ***Biographical data on Eisenhower prepared in the Soviet Ministry of Foreign Affairs, December 18, 1956***

Dwight David EISENHOWER

President of the United States of America from January 1953 to the present.

He was born October 14, 1890, in Denison, Texas, into the family of a farmer who immigrated from Switzerland. He graduated from the following military schools: the military school at West Point [USMA] (1915); tank school [armor school] (1921); the General Staff Academy [Command and Staff College] (?) (1926); the Army War College (1928); and the Industrial War College, which trains specialists in industrial mobilization for military purposes (1933).

From 1929 to 1933, at the same time that he was attending the Army Industrial War College, Eisenhower held the office of the Assistant Secretary of War. From 1933 to 1935 Eisenhower was on the staff of General MacArthur, the Chief of the General Staff of the United States. In 1935, when MacArthur was appointed head of the American military mission to the Philippines, Eisenhower went with him. In 1936 he was promoted to lieutenant colonel.

In 1939 Eisenhower returned to the United States and received a number of command assignments in the American Army. In 1941 he was promoted to brigadier general and served as Chief of the War Plans Department of the General Staff (February 1942), Assistant Chief of Staff for Operations (April 1942), Supreme Commander-in-Chief of the Allied Forces in North Africa (November 1942), Supreme Commander-in-Chief of the Allied Expeditionary Forces in Europe (December 1943), commander of the American occupation forces in Germany (1945), and Chief of Staff of the United States Army.

In April 1946 Eisenhower received the permanent rank of General of the Army, which had been given to him temporarily in December 1944.

For a number of years American propaganda has been making efforts to glorify Eisenhower as an outstanding general and major political figure.

The progressive and liberal press in the United States has pointed out that in his career Eisenhower has followed the principles of the most conservative elements of the American ruling circles. Examples of this include Eisenhower's cooperation with the Yugoslav quisling Mihajlović, and his act of sending a telegram of greetings praising his activity when the Mihajlović deal with the Nazi and Italian occupiers was already common knowledge. In his appeal to the French population on the occasion of the Anglo-American invasion of Sicily, Eisenhower called on the French people to avoid any "premature" uprisings against the Nazi occupiers. Eisenhower's conservative leanings were also reflected in his policy towards Italy, where during the invasion he sought the support of the remnants of the fascist regime, monarchists, and reactionaries.

In February 1948 Eisenhower resigned from his position as Chief of the General Staff and went on reserve status. In summer 1948 he became President of Columbia University in New York. As the December 4–18, 1951, issue of *Look* magazine reported, Eisenhower was not particularly successful in this job.

During the 1948 election campaign, movements were underway in the Republican and Democratic parties to nominate Eisenhower as a candidate for President of the United States. At that time the general's party affiliation was still unknown. However, the clamor in the press died down almost as quickly as it started when Eisenhower refused to accept the nomination of either party in the forthcoming elections.

On December 19, 1950, President Truman appointed Eisenhower Supreme Commander of the Armed Forces of the North Atlantic bloc [NATO]. Eisenhower's efforts in this assignment were focused on establishing the NATO armed forces.

In mid-1951 both ruling parties in the United States again asked Eisenhower to announce his candidacy in the 1952 presidential elections. Eisenhower agreed to run on the Republican ticket. On May 30, 1952, he officially turned over the office of Supreme Commander-in-Chief of the NATO Armed Forces to General Ridgeway, his replacement.

In the election campaign, Eisenhower received the support of representatives of the major financial and industrial monopolies, including the Rockefeller, Morgan, Du Pont, and Mellon monopolies, which own a substantial portion of the military industry of the United States and reap huge profits from the arms race. These are the groups that are most interested in intensifying the aggressive and expansionist tendencies of U.S. foreign policy and in capturing new sources of raw materials and markets.

Most of the American press, including such influential newspapers as the *New York Times*, the *New York Herald Tribune*, the *Chicago Sun Times*, and others, and *Time, Life, Fortune, Look, Collier's*, and other magazines, supported Eisenhower.

After Eisenhower was elected president on November 4, 1952, he organized his administration in direct consultation with such individuals as Nelson Rockefeller, Winthrop Aldrich, the chairman of the board of Rockefeller's Chase National Bank, George Whitney, chairman of the board of John P. Morgan and Company, Henry Ford II, Bernard Baruch, Lawrence Lee, who at the time was president of the U.S. Chamber of Commerce, Ernest Weir, chairman of the board of the National Steel Corporation, Thomas Watson, chairman of the board of the International Business Machines Corporation, Paul Hoffman, General Clay, and others. As a result, Eisenhower's administration came to include direct representatives of the largest U.S. financial and industrial monopolies and politicians in the service of these monopolies who had played a major role in Eisenhower's election campaign. This statement is equally applicable to Eisenhower's other appointments.

Eisenhower himself is a stockholder in such major American companies as the Standard Oil Company of New Jersey and the Aluminum Company of America. He also owns stock in the Charm More Company, which manufactures hair cream, and the Howard Johnson company, which owns restaurants.

Eisenhower's term in office has been marked by further suppression of the remnants of democratic freedoms in America, more stockpiling of armaments, and greater militarization of the economies of the United States and its dependencies under the motto of establishing a "position of strength" and an orientation towards "a pro-longed period of international tension," and the establishment of a large number of military alliances and bases against the Soviet Union and the people's democracies.

Despite the fact that Eisenhower took part in the Geneva Conference of the Heads of Government of the USSR, United States, Great Britain, and France, which resulted in a certain relaxation of international tension, he did so only under great pressure from public opinion in the United States and other countries, and, moreover, al-most immediately after the Geneva Conference, Eisenhower, Dulles, and other members of the U.S. government did everything they could to bury "the spirit of Geneva."

The United States has invariably rejected all Soviet proposals aimed at normalizing relations between the USSR and U.S. and reducing the tension in international relations.

In his work as president, Eisenhower has shown a tendency to delegate the responsibilities of running the country and turn over a large number of tasks to his subordinates. For example, in the field of foreign policy Eisenhower has relied on Dulles and Lodge, the U.S. Ambassador to the UN, and has almost always followed their recommendations.

Eisenhower's immediate circle, including his unofficial "advisers" (McCloy, president of Rockefeller's Chase National Bank, General Clay, director of the Lyman Corporation, and so forth) have played a very impor-tant role in formulating U.S. policy.

With respect to Eisenhower's personal characteristics, people who have had close contact with him say that intellectually he is quite limited: he rarely reads the newspapers, rarely goes to the theater or the movies, and his reading largely consists of mysteries and Westerns.

For the American monopolies Eisenhower is a very useful figure, who has faithfully carried out all the wishes of the largest monopoly cartels of the United States, as his six years in office have shown.

This explains why the American monopolies supported him and why he was unanimously nominated by the Republican Convention in August 1956 as the party's candidate for a new four-year term as president, de-spite the fact that he was suffering from a severe heart ailment and was for all intents and purposes a semi-invalid.

This support, coupled with Eisenhower's broad but undeserved popularity among vast segments of the American public as a man working for peace and as the man who led the United States out of the Korean War, as-sured him victory over Stevenson, the Democratic candidate, in the elections on November 6, 1956. An important factor which contributed to Eisenhower's victory in the presidential elections was the relative stability of the U.S. economy and the comparatively high levels of industrial employment.

After the 1956 elections, noticeable changes took place in Eisenhower's government: Secretary of De-fense Wilson, the Secretary of the Treasury Humphrey, cabinet member Stassen, and Secretary of Commerce Weeks all resigned. Political circles in the United States saw the departure of Wilson, Humphrey, and Stassen as a major victory for Secretary of State Dulles and his supporters, including the Northeastern monopolies, the mili-tary, highly influential congressmen, and so forth. In addition, Eisenhower's major illness in late 1957 caused his role and influence in affairs of state to decline somewhat. Dulles, one of the main advocates of the Cold War and the arms race, which has recently put the world on the "brink of war" once again, has come to play an even greater role in determining U.S. foreign policy, and Nixon, who has been called the most likely Republican candi-date for president, has become more important.

The growing criticism of Dulles's policies in the United States and abroad compelled Eisenhower to make statements praising Dulles and stating that he fully supports him on foreign policy issues. At the same time, Eisenhower has tried to speak more calmly than Dulles in his public statements and pass himself off as a "peacemaker."

The Soviet Union's lead over the United States in a number of fields of science and technology, the set-backs in U.S. foreign policy, and the economic crisis which began in the fall of 1957 have led to new attacks in the United States not only against the Republican administration but Eisenhower himself. Dissatisfaction with the policies of the Eisenhower administration was expressed in the congressional elections of November 1958, in which the Republican Party suffered a major defeat, despite the fact that Eisenhower became actively involved in the last phase of the election campaign in hopes that his prestige would make possible an improvement in the position of the Republican Party. The congressional elections of 1958 demonstrated that the Republican Party is losing its influence in the country as a whole. We should also mention the decline in Eisenhower's prestige in the country, although he remains a very popular figure in the United States.

Eisenhower's presidential term expires in January 1961. By American law Eisenhower cannot be elected to a third term as president.

Written by the Second Secretary
[signed] V. Lomovtsev

[signed] A. Soldatov
December 18, 1958

IDU MID

DOCUMENT 335 *Biographical data on John Foster Dulles, prepared by the Soviet Ministry of Foreign Affairs, December 19, 1958*

John Foster DULLES

(Secretary of State since 1953)

Dulles was born in 1888 in Washington, D.C., into the family of a teacher at a theological seminary. Dulles's maternal grandfather, John Watson Dulles, was Secretary of State of the United States in 1892–93.

In 1908 Dulles graduated from Princeton University with a Bachelor of Arts degree. In 1908–1909 he attended lectures in international law at the Sorbonne University in France. In 1911, back in America, he was awarded a bachelor's degree in law, and in 1939 he earned a doctor of law degree.

In 1907, at the age of 19, Dulles took part in the Hague Conference as a secretary for the American delegation.

Before America's entry into World War I, Dulles was sent by President Wilson to Panama to organize the defense of the Panama Canal. During the war Dulles served on the General Staff with the rank of major.

In 1919 Dulles was a member of the American delegation to the Versailles Peace Conference and later worked for the Allied Reparations Commission and was one of the inspirations behind the "Dawes Plan," which enabled the rebirth of German heavy industry.

In 1933 Dulles was a legal adviser involved in implementing a financial stabilization plan for Poland.

In 1938 Dulles was a special envoy sent by President Roosevelt to the Far East "to study the political and economic situation."

In 1941, when the National Council of the Christian Church [National Council of Churches] established a "commission to assist international organizations in studying the foundations for a just and lasting peace," Dulles was appointed chairman of the commission.

In June 1944 Dulles became the vice-president of the New York Bar Association and chairman of this organization's international law committee.

In 1945 Dulles took part in the San Francisco Conference as an adviser to the American delegation. He was an adviser to the U.S. Secretary of State in the proceedings of the Council of Ministers of Foreign Affairs in 1945 in London, in 1946 in New York, and in 1947 in Moscow.

Dulles was a member of the American delegations at the first and fifth sessions of the UN General Assembly.

On April 6, 1950, Dulles was appointed a foreign policy adviser to the State Department.

In January 1951 Truman designated Dulles as his special representative with ambassadorial rank for the peace treaty negotiations with Japan.

In March 1952 Dulles resigned as special adviser to the State Department for foreign policy matters in connection with the election campaign.

Dulles's name became well known in the United States in 1944 when he became the chief adviser to the governor of New York, Dewey, the Republican presidential candidate, and drafted Dewey's foreign policy platform.

In 1948 Dulles served once again as Dewey's chief foreign policy adviser and, according to press reports, might have become Secretary of State if Dewey had won the election.

Dulles played an active role in the 1952 election campaign as a supporter of Eisenhower, the Republican candidate. He wrote the Republican Party's foreign policy platform.

As soon as the Republican administration came to power, Dulles was appointed Secretary of State of the United States (in January 1953).

Dulles is a major capitalist who represents the interests of the Rockefeller group.

Starting in 1911, Dulles worked as an attorney for the law firm Sullivan and Cromwell and later became a co-owner and head of the firm. According to American press reports, as of 1952, the partners in this firm included the directors and chief legal advisers to 57 American companies encompassing almost all sectors of industry and insurance and banking as well.

Dulles's name is closely linked to the American monopolies, which after the German defeat in 1918 used the Schröder Bank as an intermediary for financing German cartels, especially the *Vereinigte Stahlwerke* [Consolidated German Steelworks], which was to become one of Hitler's primary sources of support.

The historical handbook *The Falsifiers of History* states that:

> A prime example of the close intermingling of American and German capital as well as British capital was the notorious Schröder Bank, in which a leading role was played by the German steel cartel the *Vereinigte Stahlwerke*, organized by Stinnes, Thyssen, and other Ruhr industrial magnates with major offices in New York and London. Allen Dulles, the director of the London, Cologne, and Hamburg Schröders and in New York, the company "I. G. Schröder Banking Corporation," played a leading role in the affairs of this bank. The prominent law firm Sullivan and Cromwell, headed by John Foster Dulles, played a leading role at the New York office of this bank. [Original footnote:] *Falsifikatory istorii* [Falsifiers of History]. *Gospolitizdat* [State Political Publishing House], 1952, p. 11.

"Dulles not only represented the interests of such Nazi cartels as the 'German Steel Trust' all the way up to 1939, he also operated with government funds obtained from Hitler," wrote *Time* magazine in its July 10, 1939, issue.

Dulles was a member of the executive board of the International Nickel Company and was the de facto head of this global nickel conglomerate. During the Russo-Finnish war, this company took a pro-Finnish position.

Dulles was Franco's lawyer when the latter filed a lawsuit against the New York Federal Reserve Bank in 1939 seeking the transfer of gold which had belonged to the Spanish republican government.

The law firm of Sullivan and Cromwell was a member of the profascist "America First" organization established by the renowned American fascist Charles Lindbergh. Dulles and his wife personally contributed large sums of money to this organization.

Dulles is one of the main architects and the prime conductor of the American policy of achieving global supremacy, the policy of "position of strength," the policy of resurrecting German and Japanese militarism, and all of the major postwar foreign policy expansionist programs and efforts of the American government, including the "Truman Doctrine," the "Marshall Plan," the North Atlantic Alliance, and so forth. He was the author of the separate peace treaty with Japan and a large number of military treaties in the Far East, including the SEATO military and political alliance, and was also the architect and primary organizer of the American aggression against Korea and the People's Republic of China. Dulles does not recognize the Yalta, Potsdam, and other agreements concerning postwar peace arrangements, and he initiated the campaign to revise the UN Charter.

Dulles is an ideologue and a warmonger. In his book *War, Peace, and Change,* which came out in 1938, Dulles wrote that "war is an age-old and necessary tool for resolving international disputes which cannot be resolved by conventional peaceful means to make the necessary changes in international relations."

In advocating a new war, Dulles has attempted to justify the use of nuclear and other weapons of mass destruction. On October 26, 1952, in an interview with the *St. Louis Post Dispatch,* Dulles made the following statement:

> I believe that from a moral standpoint, it makes absolutely no difference whether death is caused by a nuclear weapon or any other weapon. I saw Tokyo, Hiroshima, and Nagasaki. And if I had to choose between them, I would rather die in the city where the atomic bombs were dropped instead of the city where the incendiary bombs were dropped. The atom bomb causes a much easier death. In Tokyo far more people died an agonizing death from burns than suffered in Hiroshima and Nagasaki.

The January 16, 1957, issue of *Life* magazine contained an article by Dulles in which he openly admitted that his policy was constantly placing the world on the brink of war. "Risks have to be taken for peace just as they do for war. Some people say that we have been led to the brink of war. The ability to stay on the brink of war . . . is a necessary skill. . . . If you try to avoid it, if you're afraid to go to the brink, then you'll die."

Eisenhower's most recent major illness in late 1957 has made Dulles even more important in the U.S. government. He now plays the decisive role in formulating American foreign policy.

Dulles has proven to be a very active and effective Secretary of State, making frequent public statements (at press conferences, on radio and television, at various meetings, conferences, and so forth) on foreign policy issues; and despite his age, he makes frequent trips to other countries to meet with statesmen and participate in various conferences and meetings. He has shown consistency and perseverance in pursuing his goals. The operation of the State Department staff has become much more centralized under him than it was under his predecessors.

Written by the Third Secretary of the
OSA   [signed] IU. Sokolikov
                  [signed] A. Soldatov
                            December 19, 1958

IDU MID

DOCUMENT 336 *Khrushchev's report to the Presidium of the Central Committee, June 17, 1961, on his discussions with President Kennedy in Vienna on June 3–4, 1961*

Proletarians of All Countries, Unite!   Top secret

COMMUNIST PARTY OF THE SOVIET UNION. CENTRAL COMMITTEE [*TSK KPSS*]
No. P334/1
To Comrades:

> Aristov, Brezhnev, Ignatov, Kozlov, Kosygin, Kuusinen, Mikoyan, Mukhitdinov, Podgorny, Polianskii, Suslov, Furtseva, Khrushchev, Shvernik, Voronov, Grishin, Kalnberzin, Kirilenko, Korotchenko, Mazurov, Mzhavanadze, Pervukhin, Pospelov;
> members and candidates for membership in the *TSK KPSS*, members of the *TSRK* [Central Auditing Commission] of the *KPSS*, Secretariat of the *TSK KPSS*, *TSK*s of the communist parties of the union re-publics, *krai*, *oblast'*, municipal and *raion* committees of the party—all of the communiqué below;
> to Comrades Satiukov, Goriunov, Adzhubei, Kaftanov—paragraphs 1, 2, 4, 5.

Extract from minutes No. 334 of the June 17, 1961, meeting of the Presidium of the *TSK KPSS*.

Report of Comrade N. S. Khrushchev on his meeting and discussions with President of the U.S.A. J. Kennedy in Vienna.

1. The Central Committee *KPSS* totally approves the extensive and fruitful work of Comrade N. S. Khrushchev at the time of his meeting and discussions with President of the U.S.A. J. Kennedy in Vienna on June 3–4, 1961.

In the course of the discussions Comrade N. S. Khrushchev thoroughly and argumentatively laid out the position of the Central Committee *KPSS* and the Soviet government on the subjects of disarmament and cessation of nuclear weapons testing, of the German peace treaty, of a peaceful settlement in Laos, of the problem of peace-ful coexistence, and of other important international problems.

In these discussions Comrade N. S. Khrushchev displayed his extensive mastery of the subjects and his aggressive spirit.

The *TSK KPSS* totally approves and supports the firm position adopted by Comrade N. S. Khrushchev relative to the normalization of the situation in West Berlin on the basis of concluding a German peace treaty.

The Central Committee *KPSS* considers that the meeting and discussions of Comrade N. S. Khrushchev with J. Kennedy were useful. They open up possibilities of further contacts between the governments of the two countries for the consideration and solution of important international problems. The discussions provided an op-portunity to present the position of the Soviet government directly to the President of the U.S.A. and at the same time to ascertain better the position of the present government of the U.S.A. on topics under the discussion. The meeting revealed that no illusions should be entertained concerning the position of the present president of the U.S.A. and of the American government in the coordinated resolution of international disputes and serious im-provement of Soviet-American relations in the near future.

2. The *TSK KPSS* considers it essential that the transcripts of the conversations of Comrade N. S. Khrushchev with President of the U.S.A. J. Kennedy be made available to the members and candidates for mem-bership in the *TSK KPSS*, members of the Central Auditing Commission, members of the Bureau of the *TSK*s of the communist parties of the union republics and of the *oblast'*, *krai*, municipal, and *raion* party committees, re-sponsible workers within the *TSK KPSS* and the central government administration, editors of the central newspa-pers and magazines, responsible workers in republics, *krai*s, and *oblast'*s, and also secretaries of major party orga-nizations as determined by the municipal and regional committees of the party.

3. The *TSK* considers it expedient:

(a) to transmit the total transcript of the discussions of Comrade N. S. Khrushchev with the President of the U.S.A. J. Kennedy to the first secretaries of the *TSK*s of the communist and workers' parties of the socialist countries, and also to Fidel Castro;

(b) to instruct the USSR ambassadors in France and Italy to acquaint Comrades M. Thorez and P. Togliatti with the transcripts of the discussions of Comrade N. S. Khrushchev;

(c) to instruct the Ministry of Foreign Affairs of the USSR to inform confidentially (orally) of the contents of the discussions of Comrade N. S. Khrushchev the heads of countries or governments of Afghanistan, Burma, Brazil, Ghana, Guinea, India, Iraq, Cambodia, Morocco, Mali, Mexico, Nepal, UAR, Somalia, Finland, Ceylon, Ethiopia, and also Yugoslavia.

4. The *TSK* instructs the *TSK*s of the communist parties of the union republics and the *krai*, *oblast'*, municipal, and *raion* committees of the party to organize sessions explaining the political significance of the meeting and discussions of Comrade N. S. Khrushchev with J. Kennedy, based on the speech of Comrade N. S. Khrushchev broadcast via radio and television on June 15, 1961.

5. Require the editorial staffs of *Pravda*, *Izvestiia*, and other central newspapers and magazines and the radio and television organizations to propagandize systematically the Leninist foreign policy of the Soviet Union, with particular emphasis on clarification of the proposals of the Soviet government relative to total general disarmament, the German question, and other questions expounded by Comrade N. S. Khrushchev in his discussions with J. Kennedy and in his radio and television speech on June 15, 1961.

Secretary of the TSK

34-am
bb

Mass distribution
P 1030

APRF, fond 3, op. 66, d. 312, ll. 36–37.

DOCUMENT 337   *Report to Central Committee on proposed trip by Justice Douglas from Moscow to Vladivostok, May 14, 1962*

Not for Publication

Article 22/29s

May 12, 1962

| 22 | 29s | May 8 | 62 |

On the Trip of United States Supreme Court Member Douglas to the Soviet Union

The attached text of the telegram to the Soviet Ambassador to the United States is hereby approved.

SECRETARY OF THE CENTRAL COMMITTEE

Copies to: Comrades Gromyko, Ponomarev, Mironov, Semichastnyi

WASHINGTON

SOVIET EMBASSY

520. Instruct an Embassy employee who knows Douglas to explain to him tactfully that the Soviet Union has designated routes for foreign tourists, in particular for foreign tourists traveling through Siberia, which, for a wide variety of circumstances, including the lack of amenities (the unavailability of Intourist services), may not be deviated from in any way.

Douglas should be informed that he may travel through Siberia if he agrees to abide by the Intourist rules and routes. According to these rules, travel on the Moscow-Vladivostok Railroad is open to foreigners from Moscow to Irkutsk, and foreigners may only stop in Irkutsk. Tourists may travel by plane to Khabarovsk from Irkutsk. However, due to the construction underway at Irkutsk Airport in the summer of 1962, he would be able to fly to Khabarovsk only from Moscow.

Douglas should also be informed that if he wants to take photographs, he will have to abide by current Soviet rules for photography by foreigners.

The employee should exercise due caution when talking to Douglas in order to ensure that he understands our explanations correctly.

Please confirm compliance with these instructions by telegram.

SECRET COPY
[Illegible]

CENTRAL COMMITTEE OF
THE COMMUNIST PARTY OF THE SOVIET UNION [*TSK KPSS*]

William Douglas, a member of the Supreme Court of the United States, has informed the Ministry of Foreign Affairs of the Soviet Union that he is interested in the possibility of arranging a trip by train from Moscow to Vladivostok this summer with stops of several days at different major cities along the way. In his letter he explained that the purpose of his trip, which the American *National Geographic Magazine* had suggested, would be to produce an illustrated article on the life and activities of Soviet people living in Siberia. He also indicated that the magazine was not interested in the railroad itself but in the communities, schools, churches, factories, farms, and so forth along the way. The assumption is that Douglas would be accompanied by his wife and a photographer from the magazine. We cannot rule out the possibility that Douglas might also be accompanied by employees of the U.S. Embassy in Moscow.

The nature of Douglas's letter indicates that American intelligence agencies probably intend to take advantage of Douglas's trip.

The Ministry of Foreign Affairs and the Committee for State Security [*KGB*] of the Council of Ministers of the USSR deem it advisable to send a reply to Douglas through the Soviet Embassy in the United States which would tactfully explain to him that the Soviet Union has designated routes for travel by foreign tourists, in particular trips through Siberia, which, for a wide variety of circumstances, including a lack of amenities (the unavailability of Intourist services), cannot be deviated from in any way. Douglas should be told that he could, of course, travel through Siberia in accordance with Intourist routes and rules, which prohibit foreigners from visiting certain restricted zones and cities. Douglas should also be informed that any photographer accompanying him would have to abide by the rules established in the Soviet Union for photography by foreigners.

(Draft resolution attached).

Please review.

[signed] V. Semichastnyi   [signed] V. Kuznetsov

SECRET COPY

RESOLUTION OF THE *TSK KPSS*

On Instructions to the Soviet Embassy in the United States
Concerning William Douglas's Request

Approve the draft of the instructions to the Soviet Embassy in the United States concerning the request of William Douglas, a member of the Supreme Court of the United States, concerning his journey on the Moscow-to-Vladivostok route (attached).

Attachment to 1201/Gs

15328

TSKhSD, fond 4, op. 18, d. 123

DOCUMENT 338   *Resolution of the Central Committee, August 20, 1986, on cooperation with the United States in the peaceful exploration of space*

On cooperation with the U.S.A. in the peaceful exploration of space.

Not for publication

The matter was presented to Comrades Shevardnadze, Sokolov, Stroev, Fedoseev, Baklanov, and Luzhin

[How they] voted:

Gorbachev	- [illegible] (reviewed with Luk'ianov)
Aliev	- on leave
Vorotnikov	- for
Gromyko	- on leave
Zaikov	- for
Kunaev	- for
Ligachev	- for
Ryzhkov	- for
Solomentsev	- on leave
Chebrikov	- for
Shevardnadze	- for
Shcherbitskii	- for

<u>Register Officially</u>

Original
No. 24-21
August 16, 1986   Verified

To Comrade N. M. Luzhin

Request you prepare a draft resolution.

L. Zaikov
August 1, 1986
K No. 22854

Secret

<u>On collaboration with the U.S.A. in the peaceful exploration of space</u>

As instructed by the Central Committee of the Communist Party of the Soviet Union [*TSK KPSS*] on January 9, 1986, the Academy of Sciences of the USSR, the Ministry of Foreign Affairs of the USSR, the Ministry of General Machine Building, the Ministry of Defense, and the Council of Ministers State Commission on Military-Industrial Issues have considered the question of establishing large-scale collaboration with the U.S.A. in the peaceful exploration of space and advise implementing the following measures.

To propose to the Americans to renew collaboration in space in areas such as space physics, space meteorology, space biology and medicine, and improvement of satellite search/rescue systems, and in other areas of mutual interest.

In the area of manned flight, proposals might be considered for mutual installation of scientific and technological equipment for research in extra-atmospheric astronomy, biology, medicine, and technology in Soviet space vehicles, special-purpose modules and orbital stations, as well as in manned U.S. space vehicles.

In the exploration of Mars, such collaboration could involve exchange of information and coordination of upcoming programs to study the planet, e.g., the "Phobos" and "Mars" projects in the USSR and "Mars Orbiter" in the U.S. The European Space Agency, France, Japan, and other countries could also be included in such projects.

A prospective project for the second half of the nineties might be to develop a joint project to bring to Earth specimens of Martian soil using robotic stations and other Soviet and American space technology.

These coordinated and joint investigations of Mars could be considered a preparatory step toward a possible manned flight to Mars in the future. To propose joint development of such a project at this time, however, is premature considering its extraordinary complexity, labor intensivity, and high cost.

It also seems advisable to support the U.S. Senate recommendation declaring 1992 the International Year of Space. In this framework it would be possible to carry on a program on the international and national levels since 1992 is the seventy-fifth anniversary of the October Revolution and the five-hundredth anniversary of the discovery of America.

We are presenting a draft resolution on this matter to the *TSK KPSS*.

We request a review.

Addendum: mp. 4/0215, for I l., secret.

[signed] E. Shevardnadze
[signed] S. Sokolov
[signed] IU. Masliukov
[signed] A. Aleksandrov
[signed] O. Baklanov

TSKhSD, fond 3, op. 104, d. 29.

chapter 15

AFGHANISTAN

The mountainous country of Afghanistan, located between the USSR on the north, Iran on the west, and Pakistan on the south, had constituted a strategic goal in the 19th-century "great game" of colonial powers seeking hegemony or balance in their international relations in South Asia. In the 1970s, Afghanistan figured in Soviet planning as one of a number of non-aligned states whose future leaders could be trained in Soviet universities and whose governments should be treated with respect and delicacy. But at the time, Afghanistan, like its neighbor Iran, was a troubled and divided country. In April 1978, the government of Mohammed Daud was overthrown in a bloody coup by the Marxist leader of the People's Democratic Party of Afghanistan (*NDPA*), Noor Mohammed Taraki. Taraki drew his country closer to the USSR, signing a treaty of friendship in December 1978, but his policies of radical social, educational, and economic reform soon led to a growing revolt among rural Afghan tribesmen and others. Taraki also faced rivals within his own movement, and in September 1979, he was overthrown by his former ally, Hafizullah Amin.

Meanwhile, opposition to the regime had spread so widely that by December, only a few cities remained under the control of Amin's shrinking army. The Soviet leadership discussed the Afghan crisis at least as early as June 1979, before Amin's coup, and considered then the idea of sending select troops disguised as civilians to prop up the Marxist regime (Document 339). In December 1979, the Soviets airlifted troops into Kabul, perhaps at the request of President Amin (Document 340), but Amin himself was overthrown in a coup in late December that elevated Babrak Karmal to the Afghan presidency. Like his predecessors, Karmal was a member of the People's Democratic Party of Afghanistan and loyal to his Soviet patrons.

World reaction to the Soviet Union's first use of troops beyond its bloc was swift and negative. The United States denounced the move and declared a boycott of the Olympic games scheduled to take place in Moscow in 1980. The second round of negotiations on the Strategic Arms Limitation Treaty and other pending agreements collapsed. European Communists and leaders of developing countries also condemned the invasion, and a United Nations Security Council resolution opposing the invasion failed only because the USSR exercised its right to veto the measure.

World opinion remained divided as to the Soviet motives for intervention. The most sinister interpretation argued that the move into Afghanistan was the beginning of a Soviet march toward warm-water ports in the Indian Ocean, part of a determined strategy to establish hegemony in the increasingly unstable Middle East. Others argued that the Soviet move was defensive, that support for the Marxist regime in the first place and then the use of Soviet troops to prop it up were necessary to prevent the emergence of another anti-Communist Islamic republic on Soviet borders. This view also held that the fear of the spread of Islamic militancy into nearby Soviet Central Asia was a major concern.

By 1981 the Soviet Union had sent 110,000 troops into Afghanistan, fighting alongside a shrinking Afghan government army and facing well-armed rebel soldiers quite comfortable fighting a guerrilla war in the mountainous terrain. Resistance to the foreigners spread, the Afghan government remained weak, and Soviet casualties mounted, with no visible light at the end of the tunnel.

Domestic repercussions were eventually felt inside Soviet society. Letters to newspapers began to complain that official reporting ignored the mounting Soviet casualties and the failure of the Soviet troops to establish effective control. Allegations that senior officials had used their influence to keep their sons from serving on the front lines also damaged public support for the occupation. Drug addiction and alcoholism emerged as major problems among returning Afghan veterans. Rumors of thousands of Soviet casualties were confirmed in 1989, when Soviet officials admitted that 14,000 Soviet soldiers had lost their lives in Afghanistan, 11,000 of them in combat. Consequently, one element of Mikhail Gorbachev's new thinking on foreign policy was to find a way to extricate the USSR from its Afghan quagmire. Talks were initiated with foreign governments to design a peace agreement that would preserve the neutrality of Afghanistan and permit phased Soviet troop withdrawals. Plans to prepare the Soviet public for this agreement are reflected in Document 343. Finally, on February 15, 1989, the last of the Soviet troops in Afghanistan returned home.

DOCUMENT 339   *Politburo memorandum on the deteriorating situation in Afghanistan, June 29, 1979, with provisional authorization to send Soviet troops*

Return within 3 days to
the Central Committee [*TSK*] of the
Communist Party of the Soviet Union [*KPSS*]
(General Department, 1st sector)

Communist Party of the Soviet Union. CENTRAL COMMITTEE

TOP SECRET
Special Folder

No. P156/IX

To Comrades Brezhnev, Kosygin, Andropov, Gromyko, Kirilenko, Suslov, Ustinov, Ponomarev, Zamiatin, Smirtiukov - everything;
to Comrades Pegov, G. Pavlov - item 3.

Excerpt from minutes no. 156 of the June 29, 1979, session of the
Politburo of the *TSK KPSS* from June 29, 1979

On the situation in the Democratic Republic of Afghanistan and potential measures to improve it.

1. Concur with the suggestions proposed in the June 28, 1979, memorandum from the Ministry of Foreign Affairs of the USSR, the *KGB*, the Ministry of Defense, and the International Department of the *TSK KPSS* (attached).

2. Ratify the draft instructions to the Soviet ambassador in Kabul with the text of the address from the Politburo of the *TSK KPSS* to the Politburo of the *TSK* of the People's Democratic Party of Afghanistan (attached).

3. Endorse the idea of Comrade B. N. Ponomarev's travelling to Kabul to discuss with the leaders of the Democratic Republic of Afghanistan the questions posed in the address.

TSK Secretary [signed] L. Brezhnev

To item IX, Min. No. 156

Top Secret

SPECIAL FOLDER

TSK KPSS

The situation in the Democratic Republic of Afghanistan (*DRA*) is becoming more complicated. The actions of rebel tribes are growing more widespread and organized. The reactionary clergy is stepping up its anti-government and anti-Soviet agitation, promoting the idea of creating in the *DRA* an "independent Islamic republic" following the Iranian model.

The difficulties confronting the formation of the *DRA* are largely of an objective nature. They are associated with economic backwardness, the small size of the working class, and the weakness of the People's Democratic Party of Afghanistan (*NDPA*). These difficulties also are exacerbated, however, by subjective factors: in the party and state there is absent a collegial leadership, all power is in reality concentrated in the hands of N. M. Taraki and Kh. Amin, who often allow mistakes and infractions of the law; there is no Popular Front in the country; local organs of revolutionary authority have not yet been set up. Our advisers' recommendations on these matters have not been practically implemented by the Afghan leadership.

The primary support for the Afghan government in its struggle with counterrevolution continues to be the army. Lately, security forces, border troops, and emerging self-defense detachments have been taking a more active part in this struggle. However, the attraction of a broad spectrum of social strata to this struggle against reaction has been inadequate, and as a result, the measures undertaken by the *DRA* to stabilize the situation are not turning out to be very effective. In these conditions, the counterrevolution is concentrating most of its efforts on demoralizing the Afghan army. A variety of techniques are being used for this: religious fanaticism, bribery, and threats. They are using methods to work on officers individually and tempt them toward treason. Such activities by the reaction are becoming widespread and might have dangerous consequences for the revolution.

In connection with all this, the Ministry of Foreign Affairs of the USSR, the *KGB*, and Ministry of Defense, and the International Department of the *TSK KPSS* recommend the following course of action:

1. On behalf of the Politburo of the *TSK KPSS*, send to the Politburo of the *TSK NDPA* a letter, which in a comradely fashion frankly expresses the concern and unease of the Soviet leadership regarding the real danger of losing the gains of the April Revolution and spells out recommendations to step up the struggle with counterrevolution and consolidate popular rule. Note certain mistakes in the management of the party and state and recommend measures to correct them, paying particular attention to collegiality in the work of the *TSK NDPA* and the government of the *DRA*. Advise the political leadership of the *DRA* to create an effective system of local organs of popular rule in the form of revolutionary (people's) committees, and significantly improve the ideological and political/educational effort among the population and ranks of the armed forces.

2. Adopt measures to strengthen the office of the party adviser and expand the scope of his activities and approve sending party advisers to provincial and municipal government agencies.

3. To assist the chief military adviser, send an experienced general and group of officers to Afghanistan to work directly with the troops (in divisions and regiments). The primary mission of this group will be to help the commanders of the formations and units to organize combat operations against the insurgents, improve the command and control of units and sub-units. Additionally, detail to the *DRA* Soviet military advisers down to the battalion level, including the brigade protecting the government, and tank brigades (40–50 men, including 20 political advisers), as well as military counterintelligence advisers to all *DRA* regiments.

4. To protect and defend airplanes of the Soviet air squadron at the "Bagram" airport, send to the *DRA*—with the concurrence of the Afghan side—a paratrooper battalion in the uniform (fatigues) of aircraft-technician personnel. To protect the Soviet embassy, send to Kabul a special *KGB* detachment (125–150 men) disguised as embassy service personnel. In early August of this year, after preparations are completed, send to the *DRA* ("Bagram" airport) a special detachment of the *GRU* of the General Staff to be used in case the situation sharply deteriorates to protect and defend particularly important government facilities.

5. Using the channels of the *KGB* and the *GRU* of the General Staff, bring to the attention of the Indian leadership the useful information about plans to incorporate Indian Kashmir along with Afghanistan in a "world Islamic republic" in order to provoke the Indian government to take active steps to resist the anti-Afghan activities of Pakistan.

6. Using Soviet mass media resources, intensify propaganda against attempts to interfere in the internal affairs of Afghanistan by Pakistan, Iran, China, and the U.S.A., using the slogan "Hands off Afghanistan." Facilitate the publication of similar material in the press of the Third World.

Request your review.

A. Gromyko   IU. Andropov   D. Ustinov   B. Ponomarev

June 28, 1979
No. 0552/gs

[Probably] APRF

Return within 3 days to
Central Committee
Communist Party of the Soviet Union
(General Dept., sector 1)

<u>Communist Party of the Soviet Union. Central Committee</u>

Top Secret
Special File

No. P176/82

To Comrades Brezhnev, Andropov, Gromyko, Suslov, Ustinov

Excerpt from min. 176, December 6, 1979, meeting of the Politburo of the Central Committee, Communist Party of the Soviet Union

<u>On sending a special detachment to Afghanistan</u>

Concur with the proposals in this matter as set forth in the December 4, 1979, memorandum from the *KGB* of the USSR and the Ministry of Defense, no. 312/2/0073 (appended).

SECRETARY OF THE CENTRAL COMMITTEE

To item 82, minutes no. 176

Top Secret
Special File

CENTRAL COMMITTEE OF THE COMMUNIST PARTY OF THE SOVIET UNION

Recently Chairman of the Revolutionary Council, General Secretary of the Central Committee of the People's Democratic Party of Afghanistan, and Prime Minister of the Democratic Republic of Afghanistan [*DRA*] H. Amin has urgently pressed the issue about the necessity of sending a Soviet motorized infantry battalion to Kabul to protect his residence.

Considering the current situation and the request of H. Amin, we deem it advisable to send to Afghanistan a specially trained Main Intelligence Directorate [*GRU*] detachment from the General Staff of 500 men wearing uniforms that do not reveal they belong to the armed forces of the Soviet Union. The possibility of sending this detachment to the *DRA* was provided for by Politburo decision no. P156/IX of June 29, 1979.

Since the issues involved in sending the detachment to Kabul have been coordinated with the Afghan side, we consider it possible to transport the detachment by military transport planes in the first ten days of December of this year. Comrade D. F. USTINOV has agreed.

Request your review.

IU. Andropov   N. Ogarkov

December 4, 1979
No. 312/2/0073

10 copies

[Probably] APRF

DOCUMENT 341　　*Central Committee decree on hostile propaganda concerning events in Afghanistan, February 7, 1980*

No. 04014

NOT FOR PUBLICATION

FOR THE INFORMATION OF THE SECRETARIES OF
THE CENTRAL COMMITTEE OF THE COMMUNIST PARTY
OF THE SOVIET UNION [*TSK KPSS*]

[Mostly illegible signatures and initials of various individuals]

SECRET

TSK KPSS

February 7, 1980

RETURN TO THE
GENERAL DEPARTMENT
OF THE *TSK KPSS*

Not for Publication

TSK KPSS

Report on Aspects of Hostile Propaganda
In Connection with the Events in Afghanistan

In connection with the events in Afghanistan, U.S. propaganda agencies have launched an extensive anti-Soviet campaign in the spirit of the "Cold War" for the purpose of inflicting the maximum possible political damage on the Soviet Union.

The dissemination of disinformation, falsehoods, and other fabrications via various Western information channels for the purpose of discrediting Soviet policies and putting the Soviet Union on the defensive has greatly intensified. The propaganda now underway is also designed to facilitate Carter's implementation of his long-term militaristic programs aimed at altering the balance of power.

Western propaganda is diversified in its content and focus for different countries and regions, but it does have general features which constitute the core of the hostile propaganda directed against us. This core includes the assertions that:

- Soviet troops have invaded Afghanistan and are engaged in a military intervention (the propaganda cites information indicating that the Soviet forces entered Afghanistan before the formation of a new government was announced);

- The Soviet Union has violated the principles of international law (the use of force to solve domestic problems and the rejection of our claim that there was external aggression);

- The Soviet Union intends to seize oil-producing regions, including the countries of the Persian Gulf and the Arabian Sea (the propaganda asserts that Soviet troops are now taking up positions to launch a direct "assault" on Iran and Pakistan and that the United States has been compelled to act as the "defender" of both its "national security" and the interests of other countries);

- Soviet military personnel are taking part in military and punitive operations in Afghanistan; anti-Soviet sentiment among the local population is growing; and Soviet units have suffered heavy losses of personnel and equipment.

In its broadcasts <u>to the Soviet Union</u>, American propaganda has attempted to prove that the Soviet Union miscalculated the consequences of its actions in Afghanistan. American propaganda has cynically emphasized that the United States' rejection of trade and other relations with the Soviet Union have made the Communist Party's programs to raise the standard of living of our country impossible or difficult. The purpose of this hostile propaganda is to arouse dissatisfaction among certain unstable segments of the population, create an atmosphere of hysteria and alarm, and provoke antisocial demonstrations.

In its propaganda aimed <u>at the socialist countries</u>, the United States has tried to take the fullest possible advantage of the events in Afghanistan to show that the steps taken by the Carter administration were directed against the Soviet Union, but not against the socialist countries. For a number of countries, such as the Polish People's Republic and Hungarian People's Republic, American propaganda has emphasized the expansion of economic aid and the development of relations with the United States. With respect to the German Democratic Republic, the United States prefers to influence its population through West German propaganda.

The Americans are praising Romania's and Yugoslavia's "independent policies" and are taking advantage of Tito's illness to spread invidious claims that the Soviet Union is supposedly preparing to send its troops into Yugoslavia. The Western mass media continue to publicize this conjecture, despite the denials of the Yugoslavs.

The Carter administration is focusing particular attention on public opinion in <u>Western Europe</u>. Their propaganda claims that the "Soviet invasion" of Afghanistan is directly responsible for the growing difficulties experienced by the NATO countries in obtaining energy and other resources. In light of the diversity of the responses by the Western European countries to the sanctions announced by the U.S. president against the Soviet Union, the American propaganda services have essentially implied that their demonstration of "Atlantic solidarity" by the Western European countries is totally dependent on their loyalty to the change in U.S. policy towards the Soviet Union, including the boycott of the Olympic Games in Moscow.

The propaganda clamor is also being used in an attempt to justify NATO's decision to deploy American medium-range missiles in a number of Western European countries.

In its propaganda aimed at the <u>developing countries</u>, the United States wants to show that the political and economic relations between the Soviet Union and these countries might serve as a pretext for interference in their internal affairs. American propaganda has claimed that treaties and agreements of cooperation signed by the Soviet Union and developing countries, especially the Arab countries, might be used for an armed invasion. American propaganda has placed special emphasis on the proposition that "Communists have been and continue to be the enemies of any religion, including Islam."

The propaganda campaign against the Soviet Union, as is evident from the statements of officials of the American administration, is designed for the long term. Evidence of this is provided by the fact that official U.S. government propaganda agencies (Office of International Communications and "Voice of America") are reorganizing their operations to provide more radio broadcasts to the Soviet Union. They plan to schedule more programming in Russian and the Central Asian and Transcaucasian languages. The "Voice of America" is quickly organizing broadcasts to Soviet military units in Afghanistan for the purpose of undermining their morale.

The Soviet mass media have responded to this situation in their counterpropaganda efforts and are energetically exposing the aggressive policies of the United States.

For your information.

Head of the Department of
Foreign Policy Propaganda
of the *TSK KPSS*

[signed] L. Zamiatin

February 7, 1980

Original No. 7D-24

4-na

[illegible signature]

TSKhSD, fond 5, op. 77, d. 926.

DOCUMENT 342   *Politburo memorandum of April 1, 1982, confirming continued support to the Afghanistan government of President Karmal*

To be returned within 3 days
to the *TSK KPSS* (General Department, Section 1)

COMMUNIST PARTY OF THE SOVIET UNION, CENTRAL COMMITTEE [*TSK KPSS*]

TOP SECRET
SPECIAL FILE

No. 1152/IV

To Comrades Brezhnev, Tikhonov, Andropov, Gromyko, Ustinov, Ponomarev, Kapitonov, Arkhipov, Baibakov, Martynov, Patolichev, Skachkov, Shchelokov, Zamiatin, Smirtiukov.

Extract from Protocol No. 52 of the *TSK KPSS* Politburo session of April 1, 1982

On measures to stabilize the situation in Afghanistan.

1. Approve the work of the *TSK KPSS* Politburo Commission on Afghanistan and the considerations it has submitted on this question (attached).

2. Instruct the Soviet ambassador in Kabul, together with the representative of the Ministry of Defense, the leader of the group of party advisers, and the representative of the USSR Committee on State Security [*KGB*] to inform B. Karmal of those considerations that concern the Afghan side and to provide assistance in the development of measures for 1982 based on this plan for the stabilization of the situation in the country.

3. Require those ministries and agencies listed in the attached materials to fulfill the designated measures in accordance with established procedures.

4. Instruct the *TSK KPSS* Politburo Commission on Afghanistan to examine the question relative to the coordination of recommendations to the Afghan leadership, taking into account the exchange of views having occurred at the session of the *TSK* Politburo.

TSK SECRETARY

13-ke
nsh

[Probably] APRF

No. ST-78/148ge Dated February 13, 1988   N68   TOP SECRET

Not for publication.

RESOLUTION

OF THE SECRETARIAT OF THE CENTRAL COMMITTEE OF THE COMMUNIST PARTY OF THE SOVIET UNION [*TSK KPSS*]

On propaganda support of the political settlement concerning Afghanistan

To confirm the orientation of mass media on this question (attached).

Voting result:

For: [10 illegible signatures]

Registered
February 13, 1988

0530	Excerpt to Comrades: Vorotnikov,
	Chebrikov, Shevardnadze,

	Yazov, Dobrynin, Medvedev,
February 2, 1988	Razumovskii, Skliarov

Distributed: Feb. 15, 1988

_____
(see continuation)

Secret   Appendix
to p.148gs, pr. No. 78

On propaganda support for a political settlement concerning Afghanistan
(orientation for mass media)

Soviet mass media propaganda on the question of Afghanistan within the country and abroad shall be guided by the following positions and theses.

Resolutely advance the idea that a political settlement in Afghanistan that excludes a military solution of the problem and a policy of national reconciliation are concrete paths to a peaceful solution of the Afghan problem, based on new political thinking, and are an example of realistic possibilities in the task of resolving the most complex regional situations and conflicts.

The mutually beneficial influence and interrelationships of a policy of national reconciliation and its practical realization with improvement in the general situation in international relations must be shown. Toward this goal, our propaganda ought to promote the thesis that efforts toward national agreement and reconciliation in Afghanistan are not only in the interests of the entire Afghan people and their future, but also in the interest of strengthening world peace. The Soviet Union accordingly is guided by such an approach.

Now Western propaganda is even more actively promoting the thesis of "responsibility for Soviet military actions," and "the military and political defeat of the Soviets in Afghanistan." We must also keep in mind the fears expressed in one form or another in certain circles among friends and national liberation organizations, which wonder if the Soviet Union, by removing its troops from Afghanistan, is retreating from principled internationalist positions or is showing "excessive pliancy."

To counterbalance this, it should be explained that Soviet troops are leaving Afghanistan with the consent of the Afghan government, having completely fulfilled their international duty, that the USSR will withdraw its troops in light of reliable preconditions for a future settlement in the country in the interest of the broad masses of the Afghan people, the establishment of peace, and an end to bloodshed on Afghan land. It should be recalled that, arriving in Afghanistan, Soviet troops defended the freedom and independence of this country and foiled the attempts of imperialism to tie it to its path of development by military means. It was our military assistance that enabled the creation of objective conditions for the realization of a policy of national reconciliation, the discovery of a path to a peaceful settlement.

It is necessary to constantly underline that the Soviet Union is interested in an independent, sovereign, neutral, nonaligned Afghanistan. The Soviet Union does not and has never had any expansionist interests in this country, and, moreover, its plans have never included an attempt to secure an outlet to warm waters through Afghanistan, as the Western press has attempted to portray. The USSR is making no attempt to ensure a pro-Soviet regime, but it will not accede, as M. S. Gorbachev has stated, to a pro-American regime. It is interested in a political settlement that would guarantee the security of our southern borders and the preservation of neighborly relations with Afghanistan, which have historical roots and a long tradition.

In illuminating the policy of national reconciliation in Afghanistan it is necessary to show objectively its successes and difficulties, not to embellish the state of affairs, and not to simplify the complexity of the path of the Afghan people towards this goal, which requires sincere, committed movement by diverse political forces and currents towards each other.

It is necessary to expose those groups among the enemies of the Afghan government that refuse political dialogue and to show that in so doing they are placing their narrow group and personal interests above those of the entire Afghan nation.

In propaganda directed toward the U.S.A. and its allies, the idea should be promoted that the USSR considers the faithful execution of obligations undertaken by the U.S.A. and its ally Pakistan for the settlement of the Afghan problem as an indispensable condition, which will not only permit the cessation of violent conflict but would also prevent the danger of recidivism, a development in the process of the political resolution of the situation that would be fraught with negative consequences for the world community. It is also necessary to actively expose those circles in the U.S.A. who are trying in every possible way to hamper the achievement of an Afghan settlement and continue to count on a military solution.

It is necessary to increase the attention given in our domestic and foreign press to nonmilitary aspects of Soviet-Afghan cooperation, especially in terms of direct contacts. We should continue to publish materials on Soviet soldiers in Afghanistan who have fittingly fulfilled their international obligation by showing more clearly the heroism of their exploits, worthy of their fathers; to show in the press the fate of soldier-internationalists after their return to the Motherland, while not avoiding objective exposure of the social and psychological problems they have encountered.

It would be appropriate to make propaganda use of the anniversary of the signing of the February 1921 Treaty of Friendship between the Soviet state and Afghanistan to promote our policy on the Afghan problem.

Given that we completely subscribe to the policy of national reconciliation and are actively supporting the proposal of President Najibullah for the creation of a coalition government with the participation of all political groupings who are prepared for it, we also need to shift to a new terminology in our propaganda. It is hardly appropriate to speak of reconciliation with "counterrevolution," of participation in a government coalition with "bandits" or "dushmans" (which in translation means "enemies"). These terms may be used: "opposition," "opposition forces," "Islamic parties"; expressions such as "armed opposition," or "military forces of the opposition" may be used in reference to their armed forces.

TSKhSD

AES (atomnaia elektrostantsiia)—nuclear power plant

AON (Akademiia Obshchestvennykh Nauk pri TSK KPSS)—Academy of
Social Sciences attached to the Central Committee of the Communist Party

APN (Agentstvo Pechati Novosti)—*Novosti* News Agency

ARA—American Relief Administration

ASSR—Autonomous Soviet Socialist Republic

Belmorstroi (Belomorskoe Stroitel'stvo)—White Sea Canal construction
project

*Cheka (Chrezvychainaia Komissiia po Bor'be s Kontrrevoliutsiei,
Sabotazhem, i Spekuliatsiei)* — Extraordinary Commission for
Combatting Counterrevolution, Sabotage, and Speculation [cf. *VChK*]

dekulakization—dispossessing *kulak*s of their property and status during 1929–30

desiatina—land measure equivalent to 2.7 acres

Dobrokhim—Voluntary Association to Assist the Development of the Chemical
Industry

DRA—Democratic Republic of Afghanistan

ECCI [see *IKKI*]

GDR—German Democratic Republic

GKO [see *GOKO*]

Glavenergo (Glavnoe Energeticheskoe Upravlenie)—Main Power Supply
Administration

*Glavlit (Glavnoe Upravlenie po Okhrane Gosudarstvennykh Tain v Pechati pri Sovete
Ministrov SSSR)*—Main Office for the Protection of Military and State Secrets in
the Press [censorship agency]

Glavmetall (Glavnoe Upravlenie Metallicheskoi Promyshlennosti)—Main Administration of the Metallurgical Industry

GOKO (Gosudarstvennyi Komitet Oborony)—State Defense Committee

gorkom (gorodskoi komitet)—city [party] committee

gorparkom [see *gorkom*]

Goskomizdat (Gosudarstvennyi Komitet Izdatel'stva)—State Committee on Publishing

Gosplan (Gosudarstvennyi Planovyi Komitet)—State Planning Commission

Gostorg (Gosudarstvennaia Importno-Eksportnaia Torgovaia Kontora)—State Import-Export Trade Office

GPU (Gosudarstvennoe Politicheskoe Upravlenie)—State Political Directorate [cf. *OGPU, VOGPU*]

Great Patriotic War—Soviet term for World War II

GRU (Glavnoe Razvedyvatel'noe Upravlenie)—Main Intelligence Directorate [military]

guberniia—province

gubkom (gubernskii komitet)—*guberniia* [party] committee

GUGB (Glavnoe Upravlenie Gosudarstvennoi Bezopasnosti NKVD)—Main Directorate for State Security under the People's Commissariat of Internal Affairs

GULAG (Glavnoe Upravlenie Lagerei)—Main Directorate for Camps

GUMZ (Glavnoe Upravlenie Mestami Zakliucheniia)—Main Administration of Places of Incarceration

GUPVI (Glavnoe Upravlenie po Delam o Voennoplennykh i Internirovannykh)—Main Directorate of Prisoner of War and Internee Affairs (sometimes known as *GUVPI* or *GUVI*)

GUPVO (Glavnoe Upravlenie Pogranichnoi i Vnutrennei Okhrany)—Main Administration of the Border and Internal Guard

IKKI (Ispolnitel'nyi Komitet Kommunisticheskogo Internatsionala)—Executive Committee of the Communist International [ECCI in English-language documents]

Il'ich—Vladimir Il'ich Lenin

ITL (ispravitel'nyi-trudovoi lager')—corrective labor camp

Kadet (Constitutional Democrat)—liberal political party in 1917 in opposition to Bolsheviks

KGB SSSR (Komitet Gosudarstvennoi Bezopasnosti)—Committee on State Security of the USSR

KNDR (Koreiskaia Narodnaia Demokraticheskaia Respublika)—Korean People's Democratic Republic

KNR (Kitaiskaia Narodnaia Respublika)—Chinese People's Republic

KNS (Komitet Nezamozhnikh Selian)—Committee of Poor Peasants [in Ukraine]

kolkhoz (kollektivnoe khoziaistvo)—collective farm

kom (komitet)—committee

Komnezam [see *KNS*]

komsomol [see *VLKSM*]

KPA (Kommunisticheskaia Politicheskaia Assotsiatsiia)—Communist Political Association

KPK (Komissiia Partiinogo Kontrolia)—Party Control Commission

KPSS (Kommunisticheskaia Partiia Sovetskogo Soiuza)—Communist Party of the Soviet Union *krai*—a large territorial and administrative subdivision

kulak—a successful independent farmer of the period before collectivization of Soviet agriculture

lavra—a large men's monastery directly subordinate to a synod

Lenoblgorlit (Leningradskoe Oblastnoe Upravlenie po Okhrane Gosudarstvennykh Tain v Pechati)—Leningrad *Oblast'* Office for the Protection of Military and State Secrets in the Press

LOSNKh (Leningradskii Oblastnoi Sovet Narodnogo Khoziaistva)—Leningrad *Oblast'* Economic Council

Magnitostroi (Magnitogorskoe Stroitel'stvo)—Magnitogorsk Construction Trust

MGB (Ministerstvo Gosudarstvennoi Bezopasnosti)—Ministry of State Security

MGK KPSS (Moskovskii Gorodskoi Komitet KPSS)—Moscow City Committee of the Communist Party

MID (Ministerstvo Inostrannykh Del)—Ministry of Foreign Affairs

Miliukovites—left wing of the Kadet party, followers of Pavel Miliukov

MK VKP (Moskovskii Komitet Vsesoiuznoi Kommunisticheskoi Partii)—Moscow Committee of the All-Union Communist Party

MNR (Mongol'skaia Narodnaia Respublika)—Mongolian People's Republic

MTS (mashino-traktornaia stantsiia)—machine-tractor station

MVD SSSR (Ministerstvo Vnutrennikh Del SSSR)—Ministry of Internal Affairs of the USSR

Narkomindel (Narodnyi Komissariat Inostrannykh Del)—People's Commissariat of Foreign Affairs

Narkomprod (Narodnyi Komissariat Prodovol'stviia)—People's Commissariat of Food Supply

Narkomzag (Narodnyi Komissariat Zagotovok)—People's Commissariat of Procurement

NDPA (Narodnaia Demokraticheskaia Partiia Afganistana)—People's Democratic Party of Afghanistan

Nepman—businessman engaging in economic activities for private gain [term of opprobrium]

NKID [see *Narkomindel*]

NKIU (Narodnyi Komissariat IUstitsii)—People's Commissariat of Justice

NKPS (Narodnyi Komissariat Putei Soobshcheniia)—People's Commissariat of Transportation

NKTP (Narodnyi Komissariat Tiazheloi Promyshlennosti)—People's Commissariat of Heavy Industry

NKVD (Narodnyi Komissariat Vnutrennikh Del)—People's Commissariat of Internal Affairs

NKZ (Narodnyi Komissariat Zemledeliia)—People's Commissariat of Agriculture

NTO (Nauchno-Tekhnicheskii Otdel)—Scientific and Technical Section

OB [see *Orgbiuro*]

obkom (oblastnoi komitet)—oblast' [party] committee

oblast'—a territorial and administrative subdivision directly subordinate to a union republic

oblispolkom (oblastnoi ispolnitel'nyi komitet)—oblast' executive committee [of soviets]

OblKK (oblastnaia kontrol'naia komissiia)—oblast' control commission

oblsnab (oblastnoe snabzhenie)—oblast' supply agency

OGPU (Ob"edinennoe Gosudarstvennoe Politicheskoe Upravlenie)—Unified State
   Political Directorate [cf. *GPU, VOGPU*]

OIK (oblastnoi ispolnitel'nyi komitet)—*oblast'* executive committee [of soviets]

okrug—a territorial and administrative subdivision of a *krai* or *oblast'*

OPVI (Otdel po Delam o Voennoplennykh i Internirovannykh)—Department of
   Prisoner-of-War and Internee Affairs

Orgbiuro—(Organizatsionnoe biuro) Organizational Bureau [of the Communist Party]

*Osoaviakhim (Obshchestvo Sodeistviia Oborone i Aviatsionno-khimicheskomu
   Stroitel'stvu SSSR)*—Society for Assistance to the Defense and Aero-Chemical Development of the USSR

PB [see Politburo]

PBS [see *Pribalkhashstroi*]

"Piter"—nickname for St. Petersburg, Petrograd

Poles'e (Ukr. Polissia; Pol. Polesie)—forested basins of the Pripiat', Pina, Dnieper, and
   Desna rivers in Belorussia and Ukraine

Politburo—Political Bureau [of the Communist Party]

Politsvodka (Politicheskaia Svodka)—political report

Polpred (Polnomochnyi Predstavitel')—authorized representative

PP OGPU (Polnomochnyi Predstavitel' OGPU)—authorized OGPU representative

Pribalkhashstroi—Lake Balkhash Basin Construction Project

Procuracy—the most powerful institution in the Soviet system of justice, a hierarchi-
   cal organization representing all public prosecutors from the procurator general (appointed by the Supreme Soviet) all the way down to the city level (see procurator)

procurator—a member of the Procuracy whose responsibilities can include conducting
   investigations, supervising investigations carried out by the *MVD* and the *KGB*,
   prosecuting criminal and civil offenders, referring judicial decisions to higher
   courts for review, supervising prisons, administering parole and release of prisoners,
   and overseeing the legality of operations of all government bodies.

Rabkrin [see *RKI*]

raion—a low-level territorial and administrative subdivision

raiispolkom (raionnyi ispolnitel'nyi komitet)—*raion* executive committee [of soviets]

raiparkom (raionnyi partiinyi komitet)—*raion* party committee

RAKPD (Russko-Amerikanskii Komitet Pomoshchi Detiam)—Russian-American
   Children's Relief Committee

RILU—Red International of Labor Unions [*Profintern*]

RKI (Raboche-Krest'ianskaia Inspektsiia)—Workers' and Peasants' Inspectorate

RKK (Rastsenochno-Konfliktnaia Komissiia)—Rates and Conflict Commission

RKP(b) (Rossiiskaia Kommunisticheskaia Partiia [bol'shevikov])—Russian
   Communist Party (of Bolsheviks)

*Roskontsert (Gosudarstvennoe kontsertno-gastrol'noe ob"edinenie Ministerstva kul'-
   tury RSFSR)*—State Concerts and Touring Agency of the Ministry of Culture,
   RSFSR

ROSTA (Rossiiskoe Telegrafnoe Agentstvo)—Russian Telegraph Agency

RPK (raionnyi partiinyi komitet)—*raion* party committee

RSDRP (Rossiiskaia Sotsial-Demokraticheskaia Rabochaia Partiia)—Russian Social
   Democratic Workers' Party, predecessor of the Bolshevik (Communist) Party and
   the Menshevik Party

RSFSR—Russian Soviet Federated Socialist Republic. (In documents from the early years of the Revolution, the sequence Russian Socialist Federated Soviet Republic is often encountered.)

RVS (Revoliutsionnyi Voennyi Sovet)—Revolutionary Military Council

Sel'skosoiuz (Vserossiiskii soiuz sel'skokhoziaistvennoi kooperatsii)—All-Russian Union of Agricultural Cooperatives

Sergo—Sergo Ordzhonikidze

SMERSh (Glavnoe Upravlenie Kontrrazvedki)—Main Directorate of Counterintelligence; from *smert' shpionam* [death to spies]

SNK [see *Sovnarkom*]

sovkhoz (sovetskoe khoziaistvo)—state farm

Sovnarkom (Sovet Narodnykh Komissarov)—Council of People's Commissars

SR (Sotsialist-Revoliutsioner)—Socialist Revolutionary, member of agrarian radical party during the revolution

SSD (Sovet Soldatskikh Deputatov)—Soviet of Soldiers' Deputies

SSSR (Soiuz Sovetskikh Sotsialisticheskikh Respublik)—Union of Soviet Socialist Republics

TKP (Trudovaia Krest'ianskaia Partiia)—Toiling Peasants' Party

TSDU (TSentral'noe Dukhovnoe Upravlenie)—Central Clerical Directorate

TSekubu (TSentral'naia Komissiia dlia Uluchsheniia Byta Uchenykh)—Central Commission for Improving the Living Conditions of Scientists

TSentrosoiuz (TSentral'nyi Soiuz Potrebitel'skikh Obshchestv SSSR)—Central Union of Consumers' Cooperatives, USSR

TSentroplenbezh (TSentral'nyi Komitet po Delam Plennykh i Bezhentsev)—Central Committee for Prisoners of War and Refugees

TSK KP(b) Azerbaidzhana (TSentral'nyi Komitet Kommunisticheskoi Partii [bol'shevikov] Azerbaidzhana)—Central Committee of the Azerbaijan Communist Party (of Bolsheviks)

TSKK (TSentral'naia Kontrol'naia Komissiia)—Central Control Commission

TUEL—Trade Union Educational League [U.S.]

Uchraspred (Uchetno-Raspredelitel'nyi Otdel)—Personnel Assignment Office

uezd—administrative unit smaller than a *guberniia*, larger than a *volost'*

UKP (Ukrainskaia Kommunisticheskaia Partiia)—Ukrainian Communist Party

UNO—United Nations Organization

Uralles—Ural Timber Trust

Uralryb—Ural Fisheries Trust

USD (Ukrainskie Sotsial-Demokraty)—Ukrainian Social Democrats

USR (Ukrainskie Sotsial-Revoliutsionery)—Ukrainian Social Revolutionaries

USSR (Ukrainskaia Sovetskaia Sotsialisticheskaia Respublika)—Ukrainian Soviet Socialist Republic

VCHK [Cheka] *(Vserossiiskaia Chrezvychainaia Komissiia po Bor'be s Kontrrevoliutsiei, Sabotazhem, i Spekuliatsiei)*—All-Union Extraordinary Commission for Combatting Counterrevolution, Sabotage, and Speculation

verst—approximately one kilometer

VKP(b) (Vsesoiuznaia Kommunisticheskaia Partiia [bol'shevikov])—All-Union Communist Party (of Bolsheviks)

VLKSM [komsomol] *(Vsesoiuznyi Leninskii Kommunisticheskii Soiuz Molodezhi)*—All-Union Lenin Young Communist League

VMN (vysshaia mera nakazaniia)—the supreme measure of punishment, the death penalty

VOGPU (Vserossiiskoe Ob"edinennoe Gosudarstvennoe Politicheskoe Upravlenie)— All Russian Unified State Political Administration [cf. *OGPU, GPU*]

volost'—a small rural administrative unit, a subdivision of an *uezd*

VOOPIiK (Vserossiiskoe Obshchestvo Okhrany Pamiatnikov Istorii i Kul'tury)— All-Russian Society for the Preservation of Historical and Cultural Monuments

VSEKhB (Vsesoiuznyi Sovet Evangel'skikh Khrestian'skikh Baptistov)—All-Union Council of Evangelical Christian Baptists

VSNKh (Vysshii Sovet Narodnogo Khoziaistva)—Supreme Economic Council

VTSIK (Vsesoiuznyi/Vserossiiskii TSentral'nyi Ispolnitel'nyi Komitet Sovetov)— All-Union/All-Russian Central Executive Committee of Soviets

VTSU (Vysshee TSerkovnoe Upravlenie)—Supreme Church Administration

Zagotzerno (Vsesoiuznaia kontora po zagotovkam i sbytu zerna)—All-Union Office for Procurement and Marketing of Grain

Zemgor (Vserossiiskii zemnoi i gorodskoi soiuz)—All-Russian Union of Cities and Rural Councils

BIOGRAPHICAL NOTES

Akhmatova, Anna Andreevna (1888–1966), pseudonym of Anna Andreevna Gorenko, Russian poet, was born in Odessa and studied in Kiev before moving to St. Petersburg. With her first husband, Nikolai Gumilev, she started the neoclassicist Acmeist movement. In the 1930s her husband Nikolai Punin and son (by Gumilev) were arrested and imprisoned, an experience she memorialized in the poem "Requiem." In the 1940s her writing was banned, but she was rehabilitated in the 1950s.

Andropov, IUrii Vladimirovich (1914–84) gained political visibility with the assignment of "Sovietizing" the portions of Karelia seized from Finland in the Winter War of 1939–40. As ambassador to Hungary he oversaw the crushing of the uprising there by Soviet troops in 1956 and thereafter rose through the ranks of the KGB, becoming its chief in 1967. Andropov succeeded Brezhnev as Soviet leader in 1982, the first leader to emerge from the ranks of the police. In his short tenure in office he began to initiate some of the reforms that Gorbachev would later continue.

Beria, Lavrentii Pavlovich (1899–1953) was the son of Georgian peasants who made his career in the Soviet secret police. Under the patronage of Stalin, he became first secretary of the Georgian Communist Party in 1931, and at the height of the Great Purges he was named head of the *NKVD*. Thereafter, he served at the pinnacle of the Soviet government. When Stalin died, Beria allegedly plotted to take control of the government; he was arrested and executed by Stalin's successors.

Botvinnik, Mikhail Moiseevich (1911–95), a chess prodigy, at age fourteen, after having played chess for only a year, defeated the world champion Raul Capablanca in an exhibition. A graduate of the Leningrad Polytechnic Institute in 1932, member of the Communist Party from 1940, he earned a doctorate in 1951 and worked as a research associate in electrical energy. Known for an eclectic style of play, he won the world chess championship in 1948 and, except for short periods, held the world title until 1963, when he retired from active competition.

Brezhnev, Leonid Il'ich (1906–82) rose in the party with the patronage of Stalin and Khrushchev, but in 1964 he helped engineer the conservative revolt that deposed Khrushchev. As Soviet leader from 1964 to his death in 1982, he surrounded himself with cronies from his early party days and presided over a gradual ossification of the Soviet economy and society. He emerged as an international statesman in the 1970s, as the USSR rose to the status of military and political superpower.

Browder, Earl (1891–1973), born into a poor farming family in Kansas, became active in the Socialist Party and then the Workers' Educational League as well as the local trade union organization by 1914. He became an early adherent of the Communist movement in the United States and served as U.S. representative to the Trade Union International (*Profintern*) from 1926. He emerged as a leader of the U.S. party in 1930 and was elected its general secretary in 1934. An advocate of a continued policy of cooperation between capitalism and communism toward the end of World War II, he fell from favor and was expelled from the Communist Party in 1946.

Budennyi, Semen Mikhailovich (1883–1973) was a hero of the Civil War and founder of the Red Army cavalry. Having supported Stalin against Trotsky in the 1920s, he continued in various military posts through 1945, and he remained a favorite of Stalin. He did not distinguish himself militarily during World War II, although he was three times named "Hero of the Soviet Union," in 1958, 1963, and 1968.

Bukharin, Nikolai Ivanovich (1888–1938), member of the Bolshevik Party after 1906, was a noted theorist and economist. In 1917 and during the Civil War he was known as a Left Communist, and could often be found in disagreement with Lenin, but during the 1920s his position became more moderate and he favored balanced economic growth and concessions to the peasantry. He attempted to organize an opposition to Stalin in 1928 and was dismissed from his major posts, although he remained on the Central Committee. He helped to draft the Soviet Constitution of 1936 but was arrested in 1937, along with Rykov and Tomskii, and was executed in 1938.

Bulganin, Nikolai Aleksandrovich (1895–1975) spent his early career in the *Cheka* in Central Asia and the Russian Federation, working his way up through party positions to the post of chairman of the Moscow City Soviet in 1931. Under the protection of Khrushchev, he was named chairman of the Russian Federation Council of People's Commissars in 1937 and member of the party Central Committee in 1939. During the war he was named a marshal of the Soviet Union and joined the Politburo in 1948. Loyal to Khrushchev, he replaced Malenkov as prime minister in 1955 but confessed in 1957 to complicity with the "Anti-Party Group" of Molotov, Malenkov, and Kaganovich that opposed Khrushchev. He retired on his pension.

Byrnes, James Francis (1879–1972), United States Senator from South Carolina and later state governor, served one year as Supreme Court Justice in 1941 before resigning to direct the Office of Economic Stabilization in 1942 and then the Office of War Mobilization in 1943. He was U.S. secretary of state from 1945 to 1947.

Chaianov, Aleksandr Vasil'evich (1888–1939), an agricultural economist, joined the Agricultural Institute of Petrovskoe Razumovskoe near Moscow in 1913 and later served as the director of its successor, the Institute of Agricultural Economy, until 1930. His original and enduring contribution to economics is his *Theory of the Peasant Economy*, published in 1925, but he wrote numerous other studies as well as plays and novels. His theories came under attack for being un-Marxist, and in 1930 he was arrested as a member of the allegedly counterrevolutionary Toiling Peasants' Party and forced to give evidence against other academics and engineers. He spent the rest of his life in labor camps.

Chernenko, Konstantin Ustinovich (1911–85) owed his party career to the protection of Brezhnev, who promoted Chernenko as his heir-apparent. A member of the Central Committee after 1971 and Politburo after 1978, he did not command much attention and was passed over in favor of Andropov when Brezhnev died. When Andropov succumbed to disease in 1984, however, Chernenko finally became Soviet leader; his regime was characterized mainly by his absence from public view, and he died a year later.

Chicherin, Georgii Vasil'evich (1872–1936) was born into a family of liberal nobility, and after service as a tsarist civil servant he emigrated to Western Europe in 1904, became a convert to Marxism, and eventually joined the Menshevik organization abroad. He became commissar for foreign affairs in 1918 and served as the USSR's leading diplomatic representative until 1927. In general, his foreign policy was isolationist and anti-Western; he stayed outside of the internal party struggles among Stalin, Trotsky, and the other oppositionists in the 1920s. He retired from public life in 1930 because of poor health.

Davies, Joseph E. (1876–1958), a native of Wisconsin, earned a law degree at the University of Wisconsin and was active in the Democratic Party in Wisconsin and nationally. He assisted Woodrow Wilson at the Versailles Conference in 1919. As an attorney, he represented a number of foreign countries in international legal matters, served as U.S. ambassador to the Soviet Union from 1936 to 1938, and later was Ambassador to Belgium. During the Second World War he served Presidents Roosevelt and Truman as special envoy.

Dennis, Eugene (Francis Eugene Waldron) (1905–61), born in Seattle, worked at a number of trades after leaving college because of his family's financial troubles. He joined the International Workers of the World and participated in its general strike in Seattle in 1919 and joined the Communist Party of the U.S.A. in 1926. He studied at the Lenin Institute in the USSR in the 1930s and continued as a Communist Party organizer in the United States. He was appointed the U.S. party's general secretary in 1945, when it abandoned its conciliationist policies, and served a prison sentence from 1951 to 1955 for advocating the violent overthrow of the U.S. He criticized the party after the 1956 invasion of Hungary but served as its national chairman from 1959 until his death.

Diaghilev, Sergei Pavlovich (1872–1929) earned a law degree in Russia but devoted his adult life to the arts, becoming editor of the *World of Art* journal in 1898 and, as impresario, arranging exhibitions and demonstrations of Russian art and music. His permanent company, based in Monte Carlo, was the Ballet Russe de Diaghilev, founded in 1911. Among the artists who performed or contributed music or stage sets for his ballets were Nijinsky, Balanchine, Picasso, Goncharova, and Stravinsky.

Douglas, William O. (1898–1980), U.S. jurist, native of Minnesota, educated at Whitman College and Columbia University, taught law at Yale University and served during the New Deal as chairman of the Securities and Exchange Commission. He was named to the Supreme Court in 1939 and was known as a strong supporter of civil rights and liberties and of freedom of speech and the press. In later life, he traveled widely and wrote autobiographical works and many books about his travels.

Dzerzhinsky [Dzierzynski], Felix Edmundovich (1877–1926), was a Polish aristocrat turned revolutionary, who became chairman of the *Cheka* in 1917. Later, his tireless energy was harnessed to economic administration, first in the Commissariat of Transportation and then as chairman of the Supreme Economic Council. A member of the Central Committee but never the Politburo, Dzerzhinsky remained known for his independence and his outstanding administrative abilities.

Egorov, Aleksandr Il'ich (1883–1939), born to a peasant family, rose to regimental commander in the Imperial Army and distinguished himself in the Red Army during the Civil War. Later he was associated with the secret military collaboration with Germany, served as marshal of the Soviet Union, became head of the Red Army General Staff in 1931, and rose to deputy defense commissar in 1937–38. He fell victim to the purge of military officials and died in 1939.

Enukidze, Avel' Safronovich (1877–1937), a native of Georgia, joined a seminationalist, semi-Marxist student revolutionary group while in school in Tiflis, and then became involved, along with Stalin, with the Social Democratic movement in Baku beginning in 1899. He participated in the 1917 revolution as a soldier in Petrograd and served thereafter in the Executive Committee of Soviets. He came under attack in 1935 for his allegedly erroneous views about the Baku workers' movement, was expelled from the party, and was executed after a secret trial in 1937.

Ezhov, Nikolai Ivanovich (1895–1939), a minor Soviet official, was elected to the Central Committee for the first time at the Seventeenth Party Congress in 1934 and replaced IAgoda as commissar for internal affairs (*NKVD*) in 1936. Ezhov was dismissed from the *NKVD* in December 1938 and was blamed by Stalin for the worst excesses of the purges. He was arrested and disappeared in 1939.

Florenskii, Pavel Aleksandrovich (1882–1943), a theologian, philosopher, and mathematics graduate of Moscow University, became an Orthodox priest in 1911. During the 1920s and 1930s, he taught in a technical institute and remained actively involved in science and technology until his arrest in 1933. He died in a labor camp.

Foster, William Zebulon (1881–1961), son of Irish immigrants, worked in a variety of occupations and became involved first with the Socialist Party in 1901 and then the Industrial Workers of the World; he helped to organize packing house and steel workers between 1917 and 1919 and founded the Trade Union Educational League in 1920, serving as its national secretary. He joined the Communist Party of the U.S.A. in 1921 after attending the congress of the Communist International in Moscow. A prolific writer and pamphleteer, he ran for president on the Communist ticket in 1924, 1928, and 1932 and served as the party's national chairman from 1932 until 1957. He was known as a firm supporter of the Stalin leadership and reemerged as a leader of the U.S. party in 1945, when the moderate position of Earl Browder was rejected.

Gorbachev, Mikhail Sergeevich (1931–) was the first Soviet leader trained in the more liberal postwar era. He rose quickly to positions of power and responsibility and succeeded Chernenko as general secretary of the Communist Party in 1985 at the age of fifty-four. Gorbachev launched a radical reform of the party and country. He was criticized by intellectuals for not abandoning old habits rapidly enough and by most of the rest of Soviet society for the continuing collapse of the economy. When the Soviet Union crumbled at the end of 1991, Gorbachev, as president of a nonexistent country, found himself in involuntary retirement.

Gorky, Maksim (Aleksei Maksimovich Peshkov) (1868–1936), was the son of a lower-middle-class family, who in his autobiographical writings described his early nomadic life as a peddler, dock hand, tramp, and writer. His prerevolutionary works carried a determined socialist and revolutionary message. He was a friend of Lenin in the days of prerevolutionary exile, during which Gorky sponsored a radical intellectual colony in Capri. He never joined the Bolshevik Party and tried to use his influence with Lenin to protect intellectuals after the revolution. Gorky returned to the USSR from an extended stay abroad in 1929 and was pressed into service glorifying the achievements of socialism and the first five-year plan. Known as the sponsor of the doctrine of socialist realism as it evolved in the early 1930s, Gorky nevertheless continued to try to protect intellectuals and dissident party leaders such as Bukharin until his own death in 1936.

Gromyko, Andrei Andreevich (1909–89), born near Minsk, the son of peasants, studied agriculture and economics and entered the Soviet diplomatic service. In 1939 he joined the staff of the Soviet Embassy to the United States, and was named ambassador to the United States in 1943, in which capacity he attended the Allied conferences at Teheran, Yalta, and Potsdam. Later he served as USSR delegate to the United Nations Security Council and as ambassador to the United Kingdom; he was named foreign minister in 1957 and held this post until 1985, demonstrating a keen ability to adapt his profile to the shifts in leadership and the shifts in policies from Cold War to détente.

Grossman, Vasilii Semenovich (Iosif Solomonovich) (1905–64), a novelist, was born in Ukraine, earned a degree in the physics and mathematics faculty at Moscow State University, and worked as a chemical engineer. His first stories in the mid-1930s treated themes of industrialization, the Civil War, and the revolutionary movement. He served as a war correspondent in World War II. Grossman's epic novel about the war years, *Life and Fate*, was deemed unacceptable by Soviet censors and was published in the West only after his death.

Hammer, Armand (1899–1990), trained as a physician, served with the U.S. Army Medical Corps at the end of World War I, and in 1921 traveled to Soviet Russia to aid in the famine relief effort. His activities led to trade deals with the Soviet government, and he continued trading connections with the USSR in one form or another for much of his life. In 1957 Hammer bought a small oil company, Occidental Petroleum, and developed it into a giant corporation. An avid art collector, he purchased many masterpieces from the Soviet government, some of which he later returned as gifts.

Honecker, Erich (1912–1994), son of a miner, joined the German Communist Party in 1929, and was imprisoned for opposition to the Nazis from 1935 to 1945. He became first secretary of the Socialist Unity Party of the German Democratic Republic in 1971 and served as head of state from 1976 until shortly before the demise of the GDR. Suffering from cancer, Honecker was arrested in 1990 for treason, corruption, and abuse of power. He sought refuge in the USSR and was subsequently allowed to join his family in Chile, where he died in 1994.

Hopkins, Harry Lloyd (1890–1946), an Iowa native, was educated at Grinnell College and made a career in government administration during the New Deal. Hopkins headed projects in the Works Progress Administration from 1935 to 1938, served as secretary of commerce from 1938 to 1940, and supervised the lend-lease program. In his capacity as President Franklin D. Roosevelt's special assistant and closest aide, he carried out several diplomatic missions during World War II.

IAgoda, Genrikh Grigor'evich (1891–1938) joined the Bolshevik Party in 1907 and worked as a statistician in the medical insurance office of the Putilov factory before the revolution. On active duty in the tsarist army during the revolution, he held various military posts from 1917 to 1919 and worked in the Commissariat of Foreign Trade from 1919 to 1922. In 1920 he joined the *Cheka*, and became deputy chairman of the *GPU* in 1924. As commissar for internal affairs from 1934 to 1936, he supervised the investigation of the Kirov murder and the first stage of the purges. He was arrested in 1936 and tried as a member of the Anti-Soviet Bloc of Rights and Trotskyites in 1937.

IAroslavskii, Emel'ian Mikhailovich (Minei Izrailevich Gubel'man) (1878–1943), born in Chita to a family of political exiles, joined the Russian Social Democratic Party in 1898, was an active participant in the 1917 October Revolution in Yakutia and in Moscow, and sided with the Left Communists in 1918. His chief responsibilities after the revolution were historical and antireligious: he was chairman of the Society of Former Political Prisoners, chairman of the Society of Old Bolsheviks, and contributor of historical articles to many journals. As head of the League of Militant Godless, he directed the antireligious campaigns in the USSR.

Kaganovich, Lazar' Moiseevich (1893–1991) was born in Ukraine to a poor Jewish family, joined the Bolshevik Party in 1911, and served as secretary of the Ukrainian Communist Party after the revolution. He became a loyal supporter of Stalin, joined the Central Committee in 1924, and played an important role in the collectivization campaign, in the building of the Moscow metro system, and in the Great

Purges of 1936–38. In 1957 he joined the opposition to Khrushchev, labeled the "Anti-Party Group," with Malenkov and Molotov and disappeared from public life, living out his days as a Moscow pensioner.

Kalinin, Mikhail Ivanovich (1875–1946), the son of poor peasants, came to symbolize the alliance between peasants and workers in the Soviet Union. He joined the Social Democratic Party as a young factory worker in 1898, served several terms of arrest and exile, and was an active participant in the October Revolution in Petrograd. He was elected to the Central Committee of the Communist Party in 1919 and became president of the Central Executive Committee of Soviets, the titular head of the government of the USSR. In this capacity he loyally supported the policies of Stalin and represented the public face of the Soviet regime.

Kamenev, Lev Borisovich (Rosenfeld) (1883–1936) was born in Moscow, the son of veterans of the revolutionary student movement of the 1870s, and became a Social Democrat and revolutionary activist in 1902. He loyally supported Lenin until 1917, when, along with Zinoviev, he opposed Lenin's call for a seizure of power. He served with Zinoviev and Stalin as the three-man leadership team during Lenin's illness and after his death in 1924, but he joined with Zinoviev in opposition to Stalin in 1926 and was expelled from the Central Committee in 1927, his political career over. Along with Zinoviev he was accused of organizing the murder of Kirov and was tried in 1936 in the first big show trial of the Great Purges. He was executed in 1936.

Khrushchev, Nikita Sergeevich (1894–1971) came from a simple background and worked his way up through the party ranks as an organizer, as party leader of Ukraine and later of the Moscow organization, and as Stalin's assistant for agriculture. After Stalin's death in 1953, Khrushchev played a prominent role in the removal of Beria and won a power struggle with Molotov and Malenkov. Among the milestones of his career as first secretary of the party and leader of the country were the cultivation of virgin lands in Kazakhstan, the policy of "peaceful coexistence" with the capitalist West, de-Stalinization, relaxation of state censorship, the irreconcilable rift with the People's Republic of China, and the Cuban missile crisis. In 1964 a coalition of conservatives forced Khrushchev into retirement.

Kirov, Sergei Mironovich (Kostrikov)(1886–1934) was born in a peasant family in northern Viatka province and rose to prominence in Bolshevik ranks during the Civil War in the North Caucasus. From 1921 to 1927 he was the party leader in Azerbaijan. A member of the Central Committee from 1923 and the Politburo from 1930, he replaced Zinoviev as head of the Leningrad party organization in 1926. He was a popular figure in Leningrad and in the party until his murder in December 1934.

Kosior, Stanislav Vikent'evich (1889–1939), the son of a Polish worker living in Ukraine, joined the Bolshevik Party in 1907. After the 1917 revolution, he directed revolutionary activities in Ukraine, becoming a member of the Central Committee of the Ukrainian Communist Party in 1922. He had sided with Stalin in 1920 in a split within the Ukrainian Communist Party and from then on became a loyal member of Stalin's party machine. He was also a leading figure in the Ukrainian Communist Party, becoming first secretary of its Central Committee in 1928 and playing an active role in the collectivization drive and the struggle against nationalism. His star began to fall in 1938, when he was recalled to Moscow. He was arrested in February 1939 on the charge of being a Polish agent and shot without a trial.

Kosygin, Aleksei Nikolaevich (1904–80), Communist Party and government leader, held a variety of industrial posts and served as a member of the Central Committee from 1939 to 1960 and the Politburo from 1946 to 1952. In 1964 he succeeded Khrushchev as chairman of the Council of Ministers (prime minister). His attempts at modest reforms were blocked during the regime of Leonid Brezhnev, and he gradually lost influence and visibility.

Krupskaia, Nadezhda Konstantinovna (1869–1939), daughter of impoverished gentry, became involved in revolutionary circles as a student and through her devotion to workers' education met fellow Marxist Vladimir Il'ich Ul'ianov (Lenin). Sentenced to exile, they married in 1899, and she served throughout his life as his secretary and collaborator. She and Stalin clashed during the last months of Lenin's life, and she joined the opposition to Stalin led by Zinoviev and Kamenev in 1925–26. With the defeat of that opposition, she capitulated to Stalin and was relegated to the symbolic position of Lenin's widow. She continued to be involved in educational policy, in which she had been active during the 1920s, until her death.

Kuibyshev, Valerian Vladimirovich (1885–1935), born the son of an army officer in Omsk, Siberia, became involved in Bolshevik activism as a student in the Military Medical Academy in 1905. He participated in the October Revolution in Samara and worked to consolidate Soviet power in Central Asia. Kuibyshev became a full member of the Central Committee in 1922, attaching himself to Stalin's political machine. He chaired the Party Central Control Commission until 1926 and in that year succeeded Dzerzhinsky as chairman of the Supreme Economic Council, where he favored the policy of rapid industrialization. Kuibyshev supported Stalin against the "right deviation" of Bukharin and Rykov in 1929 but may have joined the moderate Communist opposition to Stalin in 1932, along with Kirov. He died suddenly of a heart attack in 1935; the city of Samara was renamed in his honor.

Latsis, Martyn Ivanovich (IAn Fridrikhovich Sudrabs) (1888–1938), son of a Latvian farm laborer, attended the Shaniavskii People's University in Moscow and became a schoolteacher. He joined the Bolshevik Party in 1905, participated in the October Revolution in Petrograd, became a member of the Collegium of the Commissariat of Internal Affairs, and from 1918 a member of the *Cheka* Collegium. After 1921 Latsis held a number of economic and party positions; from 1932 he was director of the Plekhanov Economic Institute. He was arrested in 1937.

Lenin, Vladimir Il'ich (Ul'ianov) (1870–1924), son of a tsarist official, was a university law graduate who became dedicated to Marxism and revolution during the 1890s. He engineered the split in the Russian Social Democratic Party in 1903 that led to the creation of the Bolshevik Party and served as the party's leader from abroad until the February Revolution of 1917. Having urged the party to seize power in the name of the Soviets in October 1917, he served as chairman of the Council of People's Commissars from 1917 until his death in 1924. Lenin's views changed throughout his life, and he was often challenged by dissenters from the right and left within his party, but his voluminous writings became the canon of Communist Party orthodoxy after his death.

Ligachev, Egor Kuz'mich (1920–), an engineer by training, joined the Communist Party in 1944 and made his career as the party chief of the science city in Siberia, Akademgorodok. Promoted by Khrushchev in 1961, he fell from favor along with his patron in 1964 but returned to a position of influence under Andropov, becoming secretary for ideology in 1984. He was promoted to the Politburo in 1985, but as a cautious "centrist" he was perceived as a serious rival to Gorbachev. Ligachev suffered a major setback in September 1988, when he was removed as secretary for ideology. His association with the economically disastrous antialcohol campaign of the late 1980s badly damaged Ligachev's political career, and on July 13, 1990, he was dropped from the Central Committee and its politburo after only 15 percent of the delegates at the Twenty-eighth Party Congress voted for him.

Litvinov, Maksim Maksimovich (Meer Genokh Moiseevich Wallakh) (1876–1951) became attracted to Marxism while a student and joined the Bolshevik Party in 1903. He was a close collaborator of Lenin while in exile before the revolution. After the revolution Litvinov demonstrated diplomatic skills as head of Soviet delegations at numerous conferences, and in 1930 he became head of the People's Commissariat for Foreign Affairs. The outward symbol of the USSR's policy of seeking allies in the struggle against fascism, he also conducted the talks in Washington that led to the establishment of diplomatic relations between the U.S. and the USSR. He was replaced as commissar for foreign affairs in early 1939, and although he was utilized diplomatically, for example as ambassador to the U.S. from 1941 to 1943, he never returned to Stalin's favor.

Lozovskii, Solomon Abramovich (Dridzo) (1878–1952), was born into a poor Jewish family, worked his way through secondary school, and became active in Social Democratic circles in 1901. Although Lozovskii claimed to be a Bolshevik, he belonged to the "conciliationist" group in opposition to Lenin. In 1917 he was actively involved with trade union organization, joined the protest of Kamenev and Zinoviev against the Bolshevik seizure of power, and was expelled from the Bolshevik Party in 1918. He returned to party membership in 1920 and served until 1937 as general secretary of the Red International of Trade Unions (*Profintern*). He supported Stalin throughout the purges but fell victim to the attack on the Jewish Anti-Fascist Committee in 1949. He died in a camp in 1952.

Lunacharskii, Anatolii Vasil'evich (1875–1933), the son of a tsarist official, received a university education in Switzerland, where he became attracted to Marxism. Lunacharskii gravitated toward the Bolshevik position in 1904 while living abroad, returning to Russia (by sealed train through Germany) only after the February revolution in 1917. Known as a brilliant intellectual but also anticonformist by nature, he was named the first commissar for education in the new revolutionary government after the October Revolution. He continued in this post until 1929 but refrained from participating in the party's internal political struggles. He died in 1933 on his way to Spain, where he was to become the USSR ambassador.

Malenkov, Georgii Maksimil'ianovich (1902–88) joined the Communist Party in 1920 and began his party career in the Organizational Bureau. By the early 1930s he directed the Organizational Bureau for the powerful Moscow party organization. Malenkov operated in the wings of the party until he became a member of the Central Committee in 1939. He served as a member of the State Defense Committee during the war, and by 1949 he ranked as one of Stalin's leading lieutenants. An ally of Beria after the death of Stalin in 1953, Malenkov at first held high office but gradually lost favor, and in 1957 he joined the opposition to Khrushchev, labeled the "Anti-Party Group," with Kaganovich and Molotov. This move failed, and Malenkov was dismissed from most of his party posts, retiring in 1968.

Menzhinskii, Viacheslav Rudol'fovich (1874–1934), a graduate of the law faculty of St. Petersburg University, joined the Bolshevik Party in 1902. After the October Revolution he worked in the Commissariat of Finance and the Commissariat for Internal Affairs. In 1920 he was made a representative of the special section of the *Cheka* and served as the chairman of the *OGPU* from 1926 to 1934. Menzhinskii was named to the party Central Committee in 1927. His ashes were buried in the Kremlin wall.

Mikhoels, Solomon Mikhailovich (Vovsi) (1890–1948), born in Dvinsk, joined the Jewish Theater Studio in Petrograd in 1919, and later founded the State Jewish Theater, where he served as actor and director, performing many classical plays in Yiddish. During World War II he actively supported the Soviet cause as a member of the Jewish Anti-Fascist Committee, touring the United States and raising money for the Soviet defense effort. Mikhoels was killed in Minsk by the secret police during the repression against Jewish culture in 1948; his death was officially reported as an accident.

Mikoyan, Anastas Ivanovich (1895–1978), the son of poor Armenian parents, passed through a theological seminary, like Stalin and Zhdanov, before joining the Bolsheviks. As commissar for trade from 1926 to 1939 and then minister of foreign trade, he loyally supported Stalin. Mikoyan transferred his loyalty to Khrushchev after 1953, serving in a number of high-level posts, including special envoy to Cuba during the Cuban Missile Crisis of 1962. He was forced out of office by Brezhnev in 1965, ostensibly because he had reached the retirement age of seventy.

Molotov, Viacheslav Mikhailovich (Skriabin) (1890–1986) became an active Bolshevik Party member in 1906 and thereafter worked as an underground revolutionary, serving several terms of prison and exile. He was appointed to the Politburo in 1925 and served Stalin loyally throughout the purges. Molotov became people's commissar of foreign affairs in 1939, negotiating the Nonaggression Pact with Germany. In 1957 he joined an attempt as part of the "Anti-Party Group" to remove Khrushchev from power, and as punishment he was assigned to be ambassador to Mongolia. Molotov remained critical of Khrushchev's reform program, and after he accused the party's draft program of "revisionism" in 1962, he was expelled from the party. His appeal for reinstatement in 1971 was denied, but he was restored to party membership in 1984.

Ordzhonikidze, Grigorii (Sergo) Konstantinovich (1886–1937) was born into the family of a minor nobleman in Georgia. He joined the Bolshevik Party in 1903 while in medical school, and during his years in the Bolshevik underground he became a close friend of Lenin and Stalin. During the Civil War Ordzhonikidze was instrumental in establishing Soviet power in the North Caucasus, and he became a leader of the effort to unite the Transcaucasian republics of Georgia, Azerbaijan, and Armenia into a single republic. This activity led to a rebuke from Lenin, but Ordzhonikidze used his association with Stalin to continue to rise within the party. He was named to the Politburo in 1930, appointed commissar of heavy industry in 1932, and played an important role in the drive for industrialization. After quarreling with Stalin about the fate of his deputy, Piatakov, who had been arrested in 1936, Ordzhonikidze died suddenly, perhaps by suicide, in March 1937.

Piatakov, Grigorii Leonidovich (1890–1937), the son of a refinery director in Ukraine, became active in Bolshevik circles while an economics student at St. Petersburg University from 1910 to 1912. In 1917 he was active in the revolution in Kiev, and after he was brought to Petrograd in early 1918 to head the State Bank, he joined the Left Communists who opposed the Brest-Litovsk peace. During the 1920s Piatakov supported Trotsky's positions against Stalin and was expelled from the party with Trotsky and others in 1927. With the start of the five-year plan, he was granted readmission to the party and helped to implement the industrialization plan. These efforts earned him membership in the Central Committee in 1934, but he was arrested and tried in 1936 as a member of the Trotskyite anti-Soviet center and executed in 1937.

Polikarpov, Dmitrii Alekseevich (1905–65), a member of the Communist Party from 1924, served in a variety of *komsomol*, military, and party posts. Educated through correspondence courses, he worked during World War II as deputy chief of the Propaganda and Agitation Administration of the Central Committee and twice, in 1944–46 and in 1954–55, served as secretary of the Board of the Union of Writers. From 1955 to 1962 Polikarpov headed the Department of Culture of the party Central Committee, serving as Khrushchev's point man on cultural matters.

Poskrebyshev, Aleksandr Nikolaevich (1891–1966?) was a relatively obscure figure who directed Stalin's private secretariat from the 1930s to 1953. The son of working-class parents, he joined the Bolshevik Party in 1917 and worked his way up through the party within the Central Committee apparatus. From 1924 to 1928 Poskrebyshev was the assistant to the secretary of the Central Committee, Stalin. Later, working behind the scenes, he may have been directly involved in selecting targets for the purges of the 1930s. He continued his private and influential role during World War II but perhaps lost favor with Stalin after the war. Poskrebyshev's wife was said to have been arrested, and he himself was often made the target of Stalin's malicious jokes. His fate after Stalin's death is unknown, but he was rumored to have survived until 1966.

Potresov, Aleksandr Nikolaevich (Starover) (1869–1934), an early convert to Marxism in the 1890s, joined the Menshevik faction in 1903 and was a strong supporter of its defensist position during World War I. An opponent of the October Revolution, Potresov was arrested in 1919. He emigrated from Russia in 1925 and from abroad engaged in writing, publication, and criticism of the Soviet regime.

Radek, Karl Bernhardovich (Sobelsohn) (1885–1939) grew up in a Galician Jewish family in Austrian Poland and became a Marxist in 1902 while in school. During the war he was associated with Russian and German Marxist antiwar activists. After the 1917 Revolution Radek helped to organize the German Communist Party and then became active in Moscow in the Communist International. The peak of Radek's career came in 1919, when he became secretary of the Communist International and member of the Russian Communist Party Central Committee. Thereafter, he became active in some of the oppositions to Stalin. In 1927, as director of the Sun Yat-Sen University in Moscow, Radek opposed Stalin's China policies, and he was expelled from the party and exiled to Siberia. After confessing his errors, he returned to Moscow, where he helped Bukharin write the 1936 Soviet constitution and called for the death sentence for Zinoviev and Kamenev during their 1936 show trial. Radek himself was arrested as a Trotskyite and sentenced to ten years' imprisonment in 1937. He probably died in a special *isolator* prison.

Rykov, Aleksei Ivanovich (1881–1938), of peasant background, was first elected to the Bolshevik Central Committee in 1905. He succeeded Lenin as the chairman of the Council of People's Commissars (*Sovnarkom*) in 1924 and supported moderate, "right-wing" policies in the late 1920s until he was forced to resign from the *Politburo* and as chairman of the *Sovnarkom* in 1930. Rykov was arrested with Bukharin in 1937 and convicted and executed in 1938.

Shaginian, Marietta Sergeevna (1888–1982), born in Moscow, the daughter of a physician father and aristocratic mother, earned degrees in philosophy and philology. She began to write poetry and fiction in 1909, adhering for a time to the symbolists Gippius and Merezhkovskii. After the revolution, Shaginian explored many genres of writing, including journalism and crime fiction. Under the pen name "Jim Dollar" she wrote a series called *Mess Mend* (1923–25). In her entire career Shaginian wrote seventy-nine books. Her historical documentary novels on Lenin provoked criticism in the 1930s but were awarded the Lenin Prize in 1972.

Shatrov, Mikhail Filippovich (Marshak) (1932–), playwright, whose uncle Aleksei Rykov and his own father perished in the purges, graduated in 1956 from the Moscow Mining Institute. He began to write plays in 1955, many on historical and revolutionary themes. Shatrov's historical plays about Lenin and the October Revolution, *The Peace of Brest* (1987) and *Onward, Onward, Onward!* (1988), raised provocative questions about the conflict between revolutionary ideals and contemporary realities, and his historical reevaluations placed him well in advance of Soviet historians, some of whom attacked the harsh treatment of Stalin in his works.

Shevardnadze, Eduard Amvrosevich (1928–), son of a Georgian teacher, became chief of the Georgian Communist Party in 1972 and gained a reputation for agricultural innovation and strict opposition to corruption. A supporter of Gorbachev, he became a full member of the Politburo and foreign minister in 1985, acting as the main spokesman for the "new Soviet thinking" in foreign policy. After publicly warning of the possibility of an antireform coup, Shevardnadze resigned from the Communist Party before the August coup in 1991 and returned to Georgia, where he was elected president in October 1992.

Shkiriatov, Matvei Fedorovich (1883–1954), a tailor by trade, joined the Bolshevik Party in 1906 and participated in the 1917 revolution as a member of the Soviet of Soldiers' Deputies in Moscow. He held many posts in trade union and party organizations after the revolution. From 1933 to 1936 Shkiriatov was a member of the Central Commission for the Purge of the Party, and in 1939 he was elected a member of the Central Committee. During the 1930s he cooperated actively with the Commissariat of Internal Affairs in purging party and government organizations.

Sholokhov, Mikhail Aleksandrovich (1905–84), Soviet writer, served in the Red Army from 1920 to 1922 and worked also as teacher, clerk, playwright, actor, and journalist. Sholokhov's early works looked at relations among Don Cossack families in the years just after the Revolution. His book *And Quiet Flows the Don* recapitulated these themes and received wide acclaim, although Sholokhov's authorship has sometimes been questioned. A second major book, *Virgin Soil Upturned*, dealt with the collectivization of agriculture in the USSR. He received the Nobel Prize for Literature in 1965.

Siniavskii, Andrei Donatovich (Abram Tertz) (1925–), literary critic and writer who used the pseudonym Abram Tertz, wrote a number of works on socialist realism and satiric fiction, which were smuggled abroad and published in the West. In 1965 he was arrested and imprisoned for this activity. Released in 1971, Siniavskii was allowed to emigrate to France in 1973, where he taught at the Sorbonne.

Sokol'nikov, Grigorii IAkovlevich (Brilliant) (1888–1939), son of a physician, joined the Bolshevik Party in 1905 and earned a doctorate in Paris in economics before the 1917 revolution. In 1920 he organized the Bolshevik uprising in Bukhara. Sokol'nikov supported Trotsky in 1921 on trade union policy and while serving as commissar for finance was associated with the group favoring moderate industrialization. Always a conciliator, Sokol'nikov joined Zinoviev's opposition to Stalin and later supported Bukharin and the right faction in 1929. Removed from the Central Committee in 1930, he held a series of minor posts until his arrest in 1936. He was sentenced to ten years' imprisonment and died in prison.

Sosnovskii, Lev Semenovich (1886–1937), was drawn into the revolutionary movement in 1905 in the Urals, where he returned as an activist in the 1917 revolution. During and after the Civil War he supported the opposition positions of Trotsky and criticized the bureaucratization of the party. As editor of the peasant newspaper *Bednota*, Sosnovskii also criticized government policy toward the *kulak*s. He was expelled from the party as a Trotsky supporter in 1927 and deported to Siberia in 1928. Sosnovskii finally capitulated and petitioned for reinstatement into the Communist Party in 1934 but was expelled and rearrested in 1936.

Stalin, Joseph (Iosif Vissarionovich Dzhugashvili) (1879–1953), the son of a Georgian shoemaker, joined the Social Democratic movement in 1898 and worked in the revolutionary underground in Tiflis and Baku before the 1917 revolution. Stalin served as commissar of nationalities from 1917 to 1923, and he led the Soviet Union either in a coalition or alone from 1924 until 1953. When Stalin died in March 1953, the entire country mourned. His body was placed next to Lenin's in the mausoleum on Red Square but was removed in 1961 as part of Khrushchev's continuing campaign to diminish the mystique of Stalin.

Suslov, Mikhail Andreevich (1902–82) did not attract the world renown of some of the other Soviet leaders, but he served Stalin, Khrushchev, and Brezhnev as the guardian of party ideology. A member of the Central Committee from 1947, he supervised the party's efforts in culture, agitation and propaganda, science, schools, public organizations, the censorship apparatus, and the media. Suslov and his organization thus controlled the entire ideological life of the Soviet Union, and he was especially vigilant in the struggle against the dissident movement of the 1970s.

Tarle, Evgenii Viktorovich (1875–1955) was a noted Russian diplomatic and military historian. Not initially a Marxist or supporter of the Soviet regime, Tarle was swept up in a purge of academic historians in 1929–31 and was exiled for several years to Alma-Ata in Kazakhstan. After his return from exile in 1933, his writings more consciously adhered to acceptable models of Marxist historiography. Tarle's works in Russian include *Napoleon's Invasion of Russia in 1812*, *The Crimean War*, and *The Northern War and the Swedish Invasion of Russia*. His work on Napoleon's invasion fell under renewed attack in the early 1950s.

Tikhon (Vasilii Ivanovich Bellavin) (1865–1925), Metropolitan of Moscow and Patriarch of All Russia from 1917, led the Orthodox Church opposition to Bolshevik rule until his arrest in 1922. He attempted to make his peace with the regime, and after his release from incarceration Tikhon worked to combat the rival Renovationist Church until his death in 1925.

Tomskii, Mikhail Petrovich (1880–1936) was a printer by trade who began his revolutionary career in 1905. He became active in Bolshevik trade union circles in 1917 and continued his career as leader of the Soviet trade union movement, serving as chairman of the Central Council of Trade Unions from 1919 to 1929. Tomskii joined the moderate opposition to Stalin's industrialization policies in 1928, along with Rykov and Bukharin, and together with them fell from favor in 1929. With the acceleration of the purges after the murder of Kirov, Tomskii committed suicide in 1936.

Trotsky, Lev Davidovich (Bronshtein) (1879–1940), born in Kherson province to the family of a prosperous Jewish farmer, began his revolutionary activities while in school. Initially a Menshevik but always fiercely independent, Trotsky came to support the Bolshevik Party during the summer of 1917, helped to orchestrate the October 1917 seizure of power, and later became the architect of the Red Army victory over the opposition forces in the Civil War. A theorist and writer, Trotsky was a poor politician and was repeatedly outmaneuvered by Stalin in the struggle for power after Lenin's death. For leading active opposition to Stalin and his policies, he was expelled from the Central Committee in 1927 and exiled to Alma-Ata in Kazakhstan and later to Turkey. From his places of exile in the 1930s, Trotsky led a public outcry against the show trials of Stalin, in which he figured as the chief villain. He was assassinated in 1940 in Mexico by an agent of the *NKVD*.

Voroshilov, Klimentii Efremovich (1881–1969) joined the Bolshevik Party in 1903 while working in a locomotive plant in the Donbass. After 1917 he worked in the early *Cheka* and then became a Red Army commander. Ever a Stalin loyalist, Voroshilov served as assistant to the Red Army chief Frunze until the premature death of Frunze in 1925 and then as head of the Commissariat for Military and Naval Affairs, even though he had had no formal military training. After Stalin's death Voroshilov participated in the various oppositions to Khrushchev, but he returned to favor under Brezhnev.

Vyshinsky, Andrei IAnuar'evich (1883–1954) left the Menshevik Party for the Bolsheviks in 1921. He studied law at Moscow University and served as rector there from 1925 to 1928. Earning his prosecutor's spurs in the trial of the Shakhty mining engineers in 1928, Vyshinsky argued that confessions, however obtained, were the best guarantee of conviction, and he practiced this theory in his subsequent career in the Procurator-General's office. In 1935 he was appointed Prosecutor-General, and in this capacity he presented the government's case in the notorious show trials of the late 1930s.

Vysotskii, Vladimir Semenovich (1938–80), poet, actor, and ballad singer, rose to fame as a member of the experimental troupe of the Taganka Theater in Moscow. Recordings of his gravel-voiced guitar-poems circulated widely, but underground, during the years of Brezhnev's rule. Vysotskii was idolized by millions, and his death from heart failure in 1980 provoked a huge demonstration of mourners in Moscow.

Zetkin, Clara (neé Eissner) (1857–1933) was a major figure in the German Social Democratic movement, where she specialized in the organization of women workers. In 1919 she helped found the German Communist Party. Zetkin was a strong supporter of the Russian Revolution and lived many years in the Soviet Union.

Zhdanov, Andrei Aleksandrovich (1896–1948), the son of a provincial school inspector, studied for the priesthood before the revolution, but joined the Bolshevik Party in 1917. Zhdanov rose to prominence in 1934 when he replaced Kirov as head of the Leningrad party organization, and he was named in 1939 as one of five Central Committee secretaries. He led the postwar assault on cultural nonconformity, the campaign known as the *Zhdanovshchina*.

Zhukov, Georgii Konstantinovich (1896–1974), son of a peasant family, served as an ensign in the tsarist army during World War I and joined the Red Army in 1918. A specialist in tank warfare, Zhukov commanded Soviet tanks in Mongolia in 1939, and became army chief of staff in 1941. He commanded the armies that "liberated" Warsaw and captured Berlin in 1944–45, and he accepted the German surrender on May 8, 1945. After the war Zhukov was commander in chief of the Soviet zone of occupation in Germany. He became minister of defense in 1955 and supported Khrushchev against Malenkov, Molotov, and Kaganovich of the "Anti-Party Group" in 1957. He was dismissed soon thereafter for "Bonapartism" in his leadership of the armed forces. His memoirs, first published serially, were heavily censored because of their criticism of Stalin's role in World War II.

Zinoviev, Grigorii Evseevich (Apfelbaum) (1883–1936), born in Kherson province, the son of a dairy farm owner, joined the Bolshevik Party in 1903 and supported Lenin and his policies up until 1917. He was notorious in October 1917, along with Kamenev, for having opposed the violent seizure of power, but he later returned to firm support of Lenin's positions. Zinoviev became president of the Executive Committee of the Communist International in 1919, and he ruled Leningrad as its strong-armed party boss until his opposition to Stalin forced him out of those offices in 1926. In 1927 Zinoviev joined forces with Trotsky to renew his opposition to Stalin and was subsequently expelled from the Central Committee. He was the first of the Old Bolsheviks to be placed on trial after the murder of Kirov and was executed in 1936.

Zoshchenko, Mikhail Mikhailovich (1894–1958) was a Russian writer of satiric short stories, including *Adventures of a Monkey* and the autobiographical novel *Before Sunrise*. He belonged in the 1920s to the experimental Serapion Brothers group. Zoshchenko's stories provided wry and telling commentaries on everyday Soviet life. He came under attack in 1946 for the anti-Soviet character of his writing. His work, however, began to appear again in the early 1950s, and his skits were performed in Moscow by the popular comic Arkadii Raikin.

INDEX

Numbers in boldface type refer to illustrations.

Bazarevskii, Aleksandr Khalilevich, 173
Bazhanov, Vasilii Mikhailovich, 173
Bazilevich, G. D., 68, 438
Bednota (For the Poor) (newspaper), 42
Bednyi, D., 172
Begovatskii *raion,* 213
Beimbet, 174
Bek, A., 278
Bekker, I. M., 67
Belen'kii, 430
Belen'kii, A. IA., **18**
Belen'kii, Z. M., 68
Beliaev, A. A., 278
Beliakov, G., 174, 525
Beliankin, Efim Mikhailovich, 20–21
Belinkov, A. V., 198, 199
Belinskii, F., on Solovki concentration camp, 146–47
Beliavskii, Aleksei Grigorievich, 174
Beloborodov, A., 144
Beloi, A. S., 174
Belokon', I. K., 411
Belonozhkin, A. I., 150
Belov, A. M., 117, 124
Beltskii, Semen Markovich, 174
Belykh, Grigorii Georgievich, 174
Benediktov, 204
Ber, M. M., 149
Berdiaev, N. A., 196–97, 198, 238
Berevo-Luka *volost',* election campaigns, 49
Berezin, N. S., 67
Bergavinov, Sergei Alekseevich, 174
Beria, Lavrentii Pavlovich, 26–27, 108, 122; anti-state activities of, 130; arrest of, 58; Census family records, 344; Central Committee member, 65; communist party delegate questionnaire, 333–34; Crimean Tatar resettlement program, 205–8, 210, 210–11; on disposition of prisoners of war, 163–67; on doctors' plot, 125, 126–27; German resettlement program, 204; and Kliueva and Roskin affair, 258; profile of, 313; at Red Square, **351;** with Stalin at the dacha, **ii, 346**
Berkman, Alexander, 578
Berlin (Germany), Control Council, 687–88
Berlin, Vladimir Markovich, 174
Berloga, Aleksandr Sergeevich, 174
Berman, IAkov Leont'evich, 174
Berman, Matvei Davydovich, White Sea Canal project award, 155
Berman, S. O., 218
Berman-IUrin, Konon Borisovich, 102
Bernshtam, M. S., 298
Beshkaimskii, 96, 97
Besialov, I. F., 150

Bessonov, Sergei Alekseevich, 174
Bezenchukskii, 96, 97
Bezhetskii *uezd,* anarchists in, 29
Bibik, Aleksei Pavlovich, 174
Biisk *okrug:* election campaigns, 48; grain collections, 376–77
Bilet po istorii (A Ticket through History) (Shaginian), 249
biological warfare, 627–29
Birobidzhan territory, 217
Biseneks, G. IA., 70, 72–73
Biseneks, V. IA., 73
Bitov, A., 301–3
Black Hundreds' clergy, 435, 441–42
Blagonravov, G. I., 66
Bliukher, Vasilii Konstantinovich, 66, 174
Bloomfield, Sidney, 612
Bluett, 300
Blumental', Fridrikh Leopol'dovich, 174
Bobkov, 288
Bobrov, S. A., 150, 151
Bobrov, Viktor Aleksandrovich, 283, 285–86, 288
Bobrovshchikov, S. A., 150
Bogaevskii, Grigorii Vasil'evich, 174
Bogat, A. P., 68
Bogatovskii, 96, 97
Bogdanov, I. A., 32, 68
Bogdanov *volost',* election campaigns, 48
Bogdashkinskii, 96, 97
Bogen, 75
Bogolepov, A. A., 6, 235
Bogomolov, 379
Bogushevskii, V. S., 67
Boguslavskii, Mikhail Solomonovich, 174
Boiarov, Aleksei Fedorovich, 174
Boitsov, E. P., 118
Bokii, G. I., **18**
Boldin, V. I., 165
Boldyrev, Mikhail Fedorovich, 174
Bolenbach, 300
Bolotin, Zakhar Samuilovich, 174
Bol'shakov, Andrei Mikhailovich, 235, 714–15
Bol'shemennikov, 249
Bolshevik Party. *See under its later name* Communist Party
The Bolsheviks (Shatrov), 191–93
Bolshevism during the World War (Volosevich), 187
Bol'shov, D. G., 280, 281
Bonch-Bruevich, 6
Bondar, L.IA., 411
Bonner, Elena G., 298, 304, 308
Bordygin, Vasilii Mikhailovich, 237
Borin, L., 286
Borisov, 163

Borisov, M. V.: interrogation of, 79; and Kirov murder, 70, 76, 77, 80–83
Borisov, Nikolai Andreevich, 174
Borisov, V. E., 291–94
Born, Georg, 174
Borodin, D. N., 567
Borodin, Mikhail, 578
Borovskii, D., 301
Borskii, 96, 97
Botvinnik, Mikhail, 265
Braiko, I., 411
Brandt, 300
Bratkovskii, IUrii Vatslavovich, 174
Braun, Joh. M., 563
Brezhnev, Leonid Il'ich: Afghanistan situation, 759, 764; doctor saboteurs and, 125; intellectual freedom under, 225, 278; Khrushchev-Kennedy meeting, 751; Moscow writers' literary almanac, 303; party membership card, 317; political trials, 294–95; profile of, 312; Sakharov and, 308
Briadov, G. I., 151
Briansk *guberniia:* election campaigns, 49; political situation report, 32; religious movement, 458
Brikke, S. K., 67
Briliant, 174
Brilling, Nikolai Romanovich, 236
Brodsky, J., 198
Broides, M. A., 149
Broido, G. I., 66
Bron, S. G., **569**
Bronshtein, 174
Bronshtein, Isai Evseevich, 234
Bronshtein, Semen IUl'evich, 174
Browder, Earl, 595–96, 606, 614–16
Brutskus, 233
Bubiakin, Nikolai Vasil'evich, 174
Bubnov, Andrei Sergeevich, 65, 119, 174, 430
Bubyrev, 52
Budennyi, Semen Mikhailovich, 66, 108; with American senators, **557;** profile of, 313–14
Buiskii, Anatolii Aleksandrovich, 174
Bukatyi, V. L., 68
Bukeevskaia *guberniia,* bandit report, 34
Bukhanov, A. A., 68
Bukharin, K. I., Party Control Commission member, 67
Bukharin, Nikolai Ivanovich: at 13th Party Congress, **363;** ban on books by or about, 174, 186–87; Central Committee meeting minutes, 604; Central Committee member, 66; as Comintern leader, 595, 606–7; denial of charges, 103–6; economic policy, 99; expulsion from party, 57,

103–11; intercession for intellectuals and scientists, 240, 245–46; on more liberal policies, 4, 18–19; plea for mercy, 109–10; show trial (1938), 58, 100

Bukhartsev, Dmitrii Pavlovich, 174
Bukhgol'tz, A. F., 566, 567
Bukovskaia, 300
Bukovskii, 81–82
Bulakh, Viktor Stepanovich, 174
Bulat, Aleksandr Fedotovich, 174, 430
Bulatov, Aleksei Alekseevich, 237
Bulatov, D. A., 67
Bulgakov, S. N., 196–97, 233
Bulganin, N. A., 66, 125, 126, 740–42
Bulgarians, deportations, 209, 211–12
Bulin, A. S., 66, 119
Bullitt, William C., 540
Bundur, V. F., 287
Bunin, I., 198
Burbaev, 209
Bureau of Statistics, 361
Burlachenko, P. I., 143, 411
Burokiavichius, M. M., 524
Business Office, 361
Butkevich, 64, 443
Butov, Pavel Il'ich, 234
Bykin, IA. B., 66
Byrnes, James F., 683, 688–91

C

Cachin, Marcel, 618
Cancer Biotherapy (Molotov), 257
cancer research, 247, 256–63
Cancer Ward (Solzhenitsyn), 194
Castro, Fidel, 708, 721–27, **728**
Cathedral of Christ the Redeemer, ruins of, **464**
Cathedral of the Virgin Birth, 483
censorship: of the post, 170–71; of the press, 17; of public performances, 264; of publications, 170–98; of radio broadcasts, 170
Census records, 338–45
Central Administrative Directorate, 361
Central Collegium for Prisoners of War and Refugees *(Tsentroplenbezh)*, 134–35
Central Concessions Commission, 353
Central Council of Consumers' Cooperatives of the USSR, 359
Central Executive Committee: expulsions and arrests, 119; investigation of, 118; special appointments, 359
Central National Insurance Administration of the USSR *(Gosstrakh)*, 354
Chaadaev, 234
Chadaev, IA., 169, 204, 659
Chaianov, Aleksandr Vasil'evich, 183, 240, 241–42, 243

Chaikovskii, Kas'ian Aleksandrovich, 183
Chakovskii, A., 280
Chalidze, 298
Chapaevskii, 96, 97
Chaplin, Nikolai Pavlovich, 183
Charlety, S., 245
Charnovskii, N. F., 566, 568
Chebrikov, Viktor M., 57, 308, 505, 705, 765
Chechen-Inqush Autonomous Soviet Socialist Republic, 202, 215
Cheka (secret police): administration of labor camp system, 132–33; arrests and investigations, 11; counterrevolutionary conspiracy, 226; creation of, 5; dissolution of, 5; foreign travel of Russian writers, opposition to, 230–31; information summaries on political groups, 29–30, 32–35; Lenin assassination attempt, response to, 12–14; members of, **8;** purpose of commission, 7
Chekin, A., 183
Chemenko, K. U., 165
Chemodanov, Vasilii Tarasovich, 183
Cherepovets *guberniia,* election campaigns, 48
Chernenko, Konstantin Ustinovich: party membership card, 319; profile of, 312
Cherniak, Dr., 74, 75
Chernikov, 208
Chernov, Nikolai Dmitrievich, 536
Chernobyl nuclear plant accident, 499–510, **511, 512,** 513
Chernolusskii, Valdimir Ivanovich, 239
Chernov, Mikhail Aleksandrovich, 66, 119, 183
Chernov, Nikolai Dmitrievich, 536
Chernyi, Arkadii Il'ia, 677
Chernyshov, 658
Chicago Curled Hair Co., 562–63
Chicherin, 360–361, 443–44, 543, 554
Chinazskii *raion,* 213
Chirchikskii *raion,* 213
Chronicle of Current Events, 264
Chubar', Vlas IAkovlevich, 66, 108, 183
Chubin, IA. A., 67
Chudov, M. S., **63,** 66, 73, 80–81, 183
Chufarova, suicide attempt, 88
Chugurin, I. D., **8**
Church of the Miraculous Salvation, 483
church properties: closing of monasteries, 470–72; closing of, 435–36, 462–63; removal of valuables, 13, 17, 435, 438–39, **440,** 441–43; removing icons and frescoes from

Kremlin, 461–62; restoration of, 468–69; return to Orthodox Church, 480–86; ruins of, **464**
Church of the Trinity, 483
Churchill, Winston, **652,** 682
Chutskaev, 430
Chuvyrin, M. E., 66
Civil Registry Subdepartment, 362
Clark, Joseph, 621
Clay, 687
clergy: Muslim, 454–55; Orthodox, execution of, 436; Orthodox, persecution of, 467
clothing industry, 578
Cold War, 682–707
collectivization, 373–99, 435; conditions on farms, 390–92, 398–99; construction of farms, 381; famine on farms, 392–93; of livestock, 388–89; volunteer workers, **380.** *See also kulaks*
Collicot, F. E., 699
Combs, Richard, 299
Comintern: Bukharin leadership of, 595, 606–7; Communist Party history distribution plans, 613; dissolution of, 595; Second Congress, delegates at, **598;** Fourth Congress (1922), delegates at, **602;** history of, 595–96; Sixth Congress, Foster as delegate, **605;** Sixth Congress, Zinoviev speech, 603–4
Committee for the Defense of Human Rights, 298
Committee of Poor Peasants (KNS), 48–49
Committee on State Security (KGB), 5; criticism of Soviet government report, 56–57
Commonwealth of Independent States, 516
Communist International. *See* Comintern
Communist Party: Central Committee membership, 65–66; creation of, 5, 309–10; dissension within, 99–111; history of, proposed, 613; nomenclature apparatus, 351–70; Party Control Commission members, 67; Soviet Control Commission members, 68. *See also* party purges
Communist Party of the U.S.A., 594–624; campaign to liberate political prisoners, 620–21; changes in policies of, 612; court indictment against, 619–20; history of, 594–96; leadership of, 618–19; money transfers to foreign parties, 596–98; plans and goals of, 614–17; Williamson interview, 621–24

concentration camps. *See* labor camp system

Congress of Industrial Organizations (CIO), political action program, 617

Consecci, John, 673

Constitutional Democratic Party (Kadets): deportations of, 232; mass arrests of, 226, 227–29

Cook, James, 588

Cooper, Col., 570–72

Cooper, Hugh, 559

Cooper, Kent, 423

Cooperation on the Stage. Cooperation in Music . . . (Varavva), 187

Cossacks, political rehabilitation of, 215–16

Council of Engineering Organizations, 241–42

Council of Labor and Defense, 580

Council of People's Commissars *(Sovnarkom)*: on creation of *Cheka*, 5, 6–7; execution of the Romanovs, 10; nomenclature list, 359; prisoner-of-war regulations, 659–62

crime, in Moscow, 519–21

Crimea, Tatar deportation from, 202, 205–13

Crimean Autonomous Soviet Socialist Republic (ASSR), 202, 209–10

Criminal Investigation, Department of, 362

Cuban missile crisis, 684, 708–29

cultural revolution (Soviet), 225, 240, 433–34

Czechoslovakia, Soviet invasion, 684

D

Dalin, Viktor Moiseevich, 176

Dam, Genrikh Matias, 677

Damm, I. K., 150, 151

Daniel', IUlii, 264, 276–77

Danishevskii, Karl Khristianovich, 33, 176

Dashinskii, S., 176

Daud, Mohammed, 757

David, Frits, 176

David, Rudol'f Eduardovich, 176

Davidson, R. E., 67

Davies, Joseph, 627, 645–46, 648–49

Davis, Benjamin J. Jr., 619, 621

Davydov, L., 230–31

death of prisoners, informing families of, 131–32

Dedov, A., 170

Degtiarev, A., 479

Deich, M. A., 68

Dekanozov, 667

Delizhan *raion*, political situation report, 31

Dembo, Vladimir Osipovich, 176

Demchenko, N. N., 66, 418

Demichev, P. N., 296

Demin, M., 198, 199

Dengel, 606

Deniken, 58

Denisov, 243

Dennis, Eugene, 619, 620–21, 623

Department. *See under name of department*

Der Shtern (Yiddish miscellany), 222–23

Deribas, G. D., 66

Dernova-IArmolenko, Avgusta Aleksandovna, 176

détente, 730–56

Detskii Gorodok (camp for children), 136

Diaghilev, S., 239

Dikii, Luka Ilarionovich, 408–9

Dilizhan *raion*, farm workers, 54

Dimentman, Anatolii Matveevich, 176

diplomatic relations: with Germany, 625–26; with U.S., 539, 558; U.S. ambassador to Soviet Union, 540

Directorate Secretariat, 361

disarmament, 731, 740–42

dissident movement (1954–91), 263–308. *See also* Solzhenitsyn, Aleksandr

Dmitriuk, S. P., 411

Dobrotvorskii, Prof., 74, 75

Dobrovol'skii, I. M., 411

Dobrynin, Anatoly F., 705, 714–15, 765

Doctor Zhivago (Pasternak), 266–68, 272

Doctors' Plot, 123–30

Dogadov, 68, 158

Dogadov, A. I., 68

Dogalov, Aleksandr Ivanovich, 176

Dole, Wilfrid, 673

Doletskii, 33

Dolgikh, V.I., 505

Dolgun, Alexander, 657–58

Dolzhikov, Aleksandr Eduardovich, 536

Dombal', Tomash F., 176

Don *oblast'*, religious movement, 456

Donets *guberniia*, religious movement, 456

Donetsk, 30

Donohue, J. P., 563

Donskoi, Semen Nikolaevich, 176

Dorosh, M. M., 411

Doroshin, 519

Dotsin, Il'ia Pavlov, 677

Douglas, William Orville, 713–14, 731, 752–54

Dreitser, Efim Aleksandrovich, 102

Driazgov, Grigorii M., 176

Drobnis, IAkov Naumovich, 176

Drozdov, Petr Stepanovich, 176

Druian, 64

Drunina, IU., 302

Druzin, 253–55

Dubovko, Viacheslav Nikolaevich, 176

Dubovoi, Ivan Naumovich, 176

Dubrovin, L. N., 151

Dubrovskii, Sergei Mitrofanovich, 176

Duclos, Jacques, 595–96, 618–19

Dukel'skii, A. G. T., 150

Dulles, Allen, 713

Dulles, John Foster, 731; biographical data, 748–50

Dureiko, N. N., 76

Durnovo, Aleksandr Sergeevich, 176

Dussey, Albert, 673

Dvinskii, B. A., 67, 74

Dvoichenko, Petr Abramovich, 176

Dybenko, Pavel Efinmovich, 6, 176

Dzasokhov, A. S., 524

Dzerzhinsky, Felix Edmundovich: censorship of *Zvezda*, 255; *Cheka* director, **8, 18**; communist party file on, 321; on creation of *Cheka*, 5, 6–7; on information summaries, 19, 28; labor camps in Moscow, 134–35, 139–40; on liberal attitudes, 18–19; profile of, 312; U.S. food relief programs, 554; warrant for Ernest Kal'nin, 9

Dzhanalidze, Prof., 74–75

Dzhavakhishvili, Mikhail Savvich, 175

Dziurin, G. N., 411

E

economic aid, U.S. famine relief programs, 540–57

economic conditions, 518. *See also* famine

economic cooperation, 533–93; Russian-European countries, 539; U.S.-Soviet, 648

economic development, 371–432; five-year plan, 372; free enterprise zones, 528–31; market economy conversion, 524–25; U.S. capital investments, 558–77. *See also* collectivization

Eddy, Sherwood, 490–92

Eden, Anthony, **652**

Efimov, M. I., 150, 238

Efremov, P. P., 176, 411

Efremovich, Vasilii, 13

Egert, Gobert Frants, 677

Egorov, Aleksandr Il'ich, 176; Central Committee member, 66; on expulsion of enemies of the people, 119; expulsion from Red Army, 117–18, 120

Egorov, IA. G., 68

Egorov, P. I.: arrest and release of, 127;

on health of Zhdanov, 123–24; medical dispute, 128–29

Egorovich, IAkov, 13

Ehrenburg, Ilya, 185, 263

Eideman, Robert Petrovich, 113, 184

Eiduk: forced labor camps, 134–35, 139–40; U.S. agricultural workers in Russia, 590–92; U.S. food relief programs, 544, 554–55

Eikhe, Robert Indrikovich, 66, 108, 182

Einstein, Albert, 219

Eisenhower, Dwight, 687–88, 731, 740–42; biographical data, 745–47

Eisenstein, Sergei, 247

Eisman, Gary, with atheist youth, **491**

Eismont, Nikolai Boleslavovich, 184

Ekaterinburg, 29–30

election campaigns, in USSR, 48–50

Eliava, Sh. Z., 66

Eliseev, 128

Elizarov, 6

Elpat'evskii, Dmitrii Vladimirovich, 176

Engel and Gevenor Engineering Co., 564

Engelbrecht, 300

engineering specialists, in forced labor camps, 149–51

England: The Opponent of Peace (Goldberg), 219

Enukidze, Avel' Safronovich, 65, 176, 430, 461–62

Epishev, A., 703

Epshtein, Moisei Solomonovich, 184

Eremeev, Grigorii Alekseevich, 235

Eremin, I. G., 66

Ermilov, 249

Ermloaev, Nikolai Nikolaevich, 235

Erofeev, Vik., 301–3

Esaian, A., 431

Esiak, 64

Esin, Anatolii Aleksevich, 20–21

Essen, 6

Estonia: bandit report, 33; Lutherans in, 433; Soviet invasion of, 629

Estreikher-Egorov, Rudol'f Anastas'evich, 184

Etinger, IA. G., 127

Etkind, E. G., 198, 200

Evangelical Baptists, 472–74

Evangulon, B. G., 150

Evans, 300

Evdokimov, Grigorii Eremeevich, 65, 101, 102, 176

Evdokimov, Petr Ivanovich, 235

Evgen'ev, 85

Evseev, Nikolai Fedorovich, 7, 176

Evtushenko, Evg., 278

exiles, in U.S., 578

An Expert's Guide to Lenin Collections (Pikel'), 189

Extraordinary Commission for Combatting Counterrevolution and Sabotage. *See Cheka* (secret police)

Ezhov, Nikolai Ivanovich, 65, 67, 78, 104, 108, 118, 176; report on Japanese and German Trotskyite agents, 114–17

F

Fadeev, 222–23, 255

Fainberg, Evgenii L'vovich, 183

Fainberg, V. I., 291–94

Fajon, Etienne, 618

Falaleev, P. P., Chernobyl nuclear plant construction flaws, 501

Falin, V. M., 523–25

Fal'kevich, Isai, 183

famine: U.S. food relief program, 540–57; in Ukraine, 401–20. *See also* American Relief Administration

Fanin, 238

Fast, Howard, 621, 624

Father (Vanin), 254

Federal Council of the Churches of Christ in America, 541

Federal Republic of Germany (West Germany), 683, 692–93

Fedin, K. A., 279–81

Fedorchuk, V., 304–5

Fedorov, A. F., 128

Fedorovich, 64

Fedotkin, Igor' Petrovich, 536

Fedotov, 242

Fefer, I., 218, 221

Feigin, V. G., 68, 390–92

Feirman, 75

Fel'dman, 113

Fel'dman, A. I., 127

Fel'dman, Boris Mironovich, 183

Fel'dshtein, Mikhail Solomonovich, 237

Fel'tstag, Dr., 74

Fen'vegin, Ferents Androsh, 677

Feuchtwanger, 171

Filatov, N. A., 66

Filippovich, Semen, 13

Filov, Viktor, 183

Fin, IAkov Isaakovich, 183

Final Act of Conference on Security and Cooperation in Europe (Helsinki), 264, 298–99, 731

Finikov, V. S., 150

Finns, resettlement programs, 204

The Fires of Kamennyi Bor (Stony Forest) (Fish), 185

Firin, Semen Grigor'evich, White Sea Canal project award, 156

The First Circle (Solzhenitsyn), 194

Fish, Gennadii, 185

Fishman, IAkov Moiseevich, 183

five-year plan, 372, 412–16, 421, 423;

propaganda poster, **429**; results of, 430–32

Flakserman, IUrii Nikolaevich, 183

Florenskii, Pavel Aleksandrovich, 231–32

Fokeev, Mikhail Georgievich, 283–84, 288

Fomin, F. T., 71

Fomin, V. V., **8**

Fomin, Vasilii Emelianovich, 236

For a Just Cause (Grossman), 269, 275

forced labor camps. *See* labor camp system

Ford, Henry, 558–59, **569**

Foreign Subdepartment, 362

Foster, William Z., 595–96, **605**, 619, 621–23

Fotieva, L., 15, 582–83, 585

Frank, Semen Liudvigovich, 232, 238

Frankfurt, Sergei Mironovich, 183

Free Economic Society, 236

free enterprise zones, 528–31

Frenkel', A. A., 67

Frenkel', Grigorii Ivanovich, 234

Frenkel', Naftali Aronovich, White Sea Canal project, 152, 157

Fridliand, 255

Fridliand, Grigorii Samoilovich, 183

Fridliand, Mikhail Efimovich, 183

Fridman, 75

Fridolin, Sergei Petrovich, 183

Friends of Soviet Russia, 541

Frits-David, Kruglianskii Il'ia, David Izrailevich, 102

Frolov, I. V., 183

Frolov, V., Chernobyl nuclear plant construction flaws, 502

Frolov, V. B., 287

Fromet, 233

Frontas'eva, M. V., 287

Frumkin, M. I., 573

Fuksh, IAnush Ferents, 677

Fundriaka, 674

Furtseva, 751

G

Gabyshev, Aleksandr Gavrilovich, 175

Gafner, I. I., 411

Gai, Gaia Dmitrievich, 174

Gaister, Aaron Izrailevich, 68, 175

Gakichko, N. L., 150, 151

Galanov, B., 274

Galanov, E., 269

Galich, A. A., 198, 199

Galkin, V., 165, 438, 439

Gal'perina, Dr., 74, 75

Gamarnik, Ian Borisovich, 65, 104, 108, 113, 175

Ganetskii, IAkov Stanislavovich, 175

gangs, in USSR, 36

Gannin, V. P., 73
Garbuz, K. A., 411
Gastev, 300
Gates, John, 619, 621–22, 624
Gavrilov, N., 175
Gei, K. V., 68
Geints, Neiman, 175
Gemmervert, M. I., 68
Geneva Conference (1955), 740–42
Genkin, E. B., 67, 300
Georgadze, M., 475
Georgia, Tbilisi independence movement, 515, 517
Gerasimov, Mikhail Prokop'evich, 6, 175
Geretskii, Viktor IAkovlevich, 235
German Democratic Republic (East Germany), 683–84; national police of, 697
German, Karl Avgust, 677
German question, 683, 692–94
Germans: deportations, 209; resettlement programs, 201–4
Germany: demilitarization of, 688–91; elections, 696
Geronimus, Aleksandr Abramovich, 175
Gertsenberg, 73, 74
Gesse, 75
Gevenor, 564
Gibler, Gererd Karl, 677
Gidaspov, B. V., 524, 525
Gikalo, Nikolai Fedorovich, 66, 175
Gil'bo, Anri, 175
Gilinskii, Abram Lazarevich, 175
Gilman, 584
Gimmer, Nikolai Nikolaevich, 175
Gindin, IAkov Isaakovich, 68, 175
Ginsburg, Nikolai Nikolaevich, 627–28
Ginzburg, A. I., 298
Ginzburg, L., 302
Gitlow, Benjamin, 595, 606–7
Giuffel', D. G., 150
Gladilin, A. T., 198, 199
Gladshtein, IU. M., 68
glasnost', 28, 56, 163, 514–38
Glavlit. See Main Directorate for the Protection of State Secrets in the Press
Glebov, 6–7
Glebov-Avilov, N., 175
Glotov, A., 175
Gludin, I. I., 175
Glukhov *okrug*, election campaigns, 49
Gogosov, 209
Goinkis, P. G., 150
Goldberg, Ben Zion, 219
Gol'dich, L. E., 68
Gol'dman, Boris Isaakovich, 175
Goldman, Emma, 175, 578

Goldman, N., 219
Gol'dshtein, Isaak Iosifovich, 175
Golendo, Matvei Semenovich, 175
Golidze, 126
Golikov, A. P., 175
Gol'kamp, Genrikh, 677
Goloded, Nikolai Matveevich, 66, 175
Golubev, 667
Golubovich, 29
Gomel' *guberniia*, religious movement, 457
Gomfel'd, 232
Gonikman, Solomon L'vovich, 175, 187–88
Gorash, Dr., 245
Gorbachev, Georgii Efimovich, 175
Gorbachev, Mikhail Sergeevich, 28; Afghanistan policy, 758; Chernobyl accident cover-up, 499–513; commission on Kirov murder, 69; conceals Katyn massacre, 163; confidence in, lacking, 525–26; coup attempt, 515–16, 533–35; exoneration of Bukharin, 100; party membership card, 320; *perestroika and glasnost'*, 514–38; profile of, 312; reform policies, 311; religious reform, 436, 480–486; resignation as general secretary, 527; Sakharov censure and, 308
Gorbunov, V. A., 37, 64, 151
Gorchaev, 64
Gorev, B. I., 175
Gorinshtein, F., 301
Gorkin, A. F., 129
Gor'kovskaia ASSR, 212
Gorky, Aleksei Maksimovich: on antireligious propaganda for youth, 488–90; ban of materials by and about, 172; declaration on mass arrests of intellectuals, 228, 229–30; exile in Europe, 225; humanitarian aid to Russia, 541; investigation of labor camps, 133, 146; on Russian intelligentsia, 251; on White Sea-Baltic Canal project, 153
Gornshtein, Tat'iana Nikolaevna, 175
Gornunov, N., 438
Gorokhov, F. A., 175
Gorshenin, 170
Goskin, Mikhail Fedorovich, White Sea Canal project award, 157
Gosplan. See State Planning Committee
Gosstrakh. See Central National Insurance Administration of the USSR
GPU. *See* State Political Directorate
Grabar', 461
Grain Administration, 354
grain collections, 371, 376–79, 397–98; growers' strike, 397–98; illegal sales, 394–95; sabotage of, 403–12

Grandberg, suicide, 88
Granovskii, M. L., 67
Grave, Berta Borisovna, 175
Great Purges (1930s): arrests and investigations during, 5; explanation of, 3–4; victims of, 57. *See also* party purges
The Great Teacher: A Lenin Reader (Lilina), 189
Greek Catholic Church. *See* Ukrainian Greek Catholic Church
Greeks, deportations, 209, 211–12
Green, Gilbert, 619
Greiner, K. G., 149
Griadinskii, F. N., 66
Griadinskii, Fedor Pavlovich, 175
Griaznov, 117
Gribachev, N., 302
Grichmanov, Aleksei Petrovich, 175
Grigorenko, P. G., 298, 300
Grigor'eva-Khatuntsev, Nikitina, 104
Grigor'ian, V., 221–22
Grigoruk, 52
Grin, E., 253
Grin'ko, Grigorii Fedorovich, 66, 117, 175
Grinshtein, A. M., 127
Grinshtein, Grigorii Fedorovich, 175
Grishin, 64, 751
Grishin *uezd*, 30
Grodnitskii, S. V., suicide, 88
Groman, 241, 243
Gromyko, A., 308, 692–94, 696–98, 711, 759, 764
Groshev, I. A., 53, 411
Grossman, Vasilii, 67, 170, 263, 268–75
Group for Implementation of the Helsinki Accords, 298–99
GRU. *See* Main Intelligence Directorate
Grushchanskii, A. I., 411
Gubarev, B., Chernobyl nuclear plant accident report, 509–11
Gubenko, N. N., 484
Gubin, 83
Guevara, Che, at Cuban Embassy (Moscow), **710**
Gukaev, 243
Gulag, origins and operations of, 132–69
The Gulag Archipelago (Solzhenitsyn), 132, 194
Gul'ko, 78
Gullinger, deportation from Moscow, 17
Gumilev, Nikolai, 198, 226
Gun, V. V., 150, 151
GUPVI. See Prisoner-of-War and Internee Affairs
Gurenko, S.I., 524
Gurev *oblast'*, resettlement programs, 209–11

Gurevich, 64
Gur'evskaia ASSR, 212
Gusarov, Ignatii Evdokimovich, 209, 235
Gusev, A. N., 59, 68
Gusev, T., 206
Gutkin, A. IA., 234
Gutmison, Gunnell, 743–44
Gvozdikov, Karp Dmitrievich, 175

H

Haines, Anna J., 543
Hall, Gus, 619
Hammer, Armand, 558, 560, 572–75
Harriman, William Averell, **652**
Harrow, H., 588
Helsinki Accords. *See* Final Act of Conference on Security and Cooperation in Europe (Helsinki)
Heymland (Yiddish miscellany), 222–23
Hill, Eugene, 673
The History of the All-Union Communist Party (Bolshevik), 187
History of the Communist Party (Bolshevik) of Ukraine (Ravich-Cherkasskii), 190
Hitler, Adolf, 105, 625–26
Honecker, E., 523–24
Hoover, Herbert: famine relief program, 540; prisoners of war, 543
Hopkins, Harry, 654
How Our Government Works (Alypov), 186
humanitarian aid. *See* economic aid
Hungary, revolt (1956), 684

I

IAsenskii, Bruno, 184
IAgoda, 430; and Kirov murder conspiracy, 70, 77, 78; political situation report, 45–50
IAgoda, Gengrikh Grigor'evich, 66, 120; lists of anti-Soviet intellectuals, 233–39; on permanent exile of prisoners, 161; White Sea Canal project award, 154, 155
IAkir, Iona Emmanuilovich, 66, 108, 113, 184
IAkir, Irina, 300
IAkobson, 64
IAkobson, A., 253
IAkovlev, 430
IAkovlev, A. I., 67
IAkovlev, IAkov Arkandievich, 66, 108, 119, 184, 381, 389
IAkovlev, N., 185
IAkovleva, Varvara Nikolaevna, 184
IAngi-Iul'skii *raion*, 213
IAnkelevich, 300

IAnovskii, R. G., 479
IAnson, 155
IArilov, A. A., 566
IAroslavskaia, 30
IAroslavskaia ASSR, 212
IAroslavskii, 430
IAroslavskii, Emelian, 67, 108, 172; antireligious propaganda for youth, 487–92; Central Council of the League of Militant Atheists, 609–10; Muslim clergy, 454–55; religious movements, 460; separation of church and state, 446–47, 448–49; with young atheists, **491**
IArotskii, Vasilii IAkovlevich, 184
IAshen, K., 280
IAsinskii, Vsevolod Ivanovich, 236
IAstrebov, 64
IAstrebov, I., 513
IAvors'kii, Matvei Ivanovich, 184
Iavorskii, Semen IAkovlevich, 184
Ignat, S. B., 177
Ignat'ev, S. D., 126, 209
Ignatov, N. G., 125, 751
Igotov, S., 177
Ikramov, 432
Ikramov, Akmal', 65, 108, 177
Ilarionov, I. E., 149
Il'ia, Kruglianskii, 102
Il'ich, Moisei, 102
Il'in, 64
Il'in, Fedor Fedorovich, 177
Il'in, N. A., 236
Il'in, N. I., 68
Ilinich, 116
Industrial Bank, 353
Industrial Party *(Prompartiia)* affair, 240, 243
industrialization, 421–32. *See also* five-year plan
Infosvodka (Information summaries), 28
Ingulov, Sergei Borisovich, 177
Insarov, Kh., 177
Institute of Epidemiology, Kliueva and Roskin affair, 256–63
Institute of Railroad Engineering, 236
Institute for Scientific Atheism, 493–98
intellecutals, and the state, 224–42
intelligence reports, and public opinion, 28–57
International Significance of the Great October Socialist Revolution (Temovoi), 185
International Society of Friends (Quakers). *See* Society of Friends
Ioel'son, Maksimilian Filippovich, 177
Iovchuk, M., 493
Is Our State Proletarian? . . . (Alypov), 187

Isaak, Don Levin, 177
Isaev, Uraz D., 66, 134, 177
Isakov, K. A., 411
Isakovskii, M., 278
Isanchurin, 64
Ishchenko, A. G., 177
Isihim *raion*, political situation report, 31
Iskander, F. A., 301–3
Istmen, Maks, 177
Istrati, Panait, 177
Isupov, N., 186, 190
IUdenich, 59
IUrchenko, F. T., 411
IUrevich, E. I., 67
IUrinets, Volodimir, Oleksiiovich, 184
IUrinov, I. K., 151
IUrkin, T. A., 66
IUrkovskii, Abram Moiseevich, 627–28
IUrovskii, 243
IUrovskii, Nikolai Petrovich, 238
IUshkin, Trotsky supporter, 37
IUshtin, Ivan Ivanovich, 238
IUskin, I. G., and Kirov murder, 71
IUzhin, Boris Nikolaevich, 536
IUzovka *uezd*, 30
Ivan the Terrible (Eisenstein), 247
Ivano-Voznesensk *guberniia*, political situation reports, 29, 32
Ivanov, 64, 163
Ivanov, A., and Kirov murder case, 73
Ivanov, A. A., 68
Ivanov, B. A., 149
Ivanov, G. T., 411
Ivanov, I. P., 150
Ivanov, K. T., 411
Ivanov, N. G., 68
Ivanov, Vladimir Ivanovich, 65, 119, 177
Ivanovich, Aleksandr, 13
Ivanovich, Ivan, 13
Ivanovich, Nikolai, 13
Ivanovich, Sergei, 13
Ivanovich, Valerii, 519
Ivanovo-Voznesensk *guberniia*, confiscation of church valuables, 439
Ivanovo-Voznesensk *guberniia*, religious movement, 458
Ivanovo-Voznesensk Guberniia Party, 439
Ivanovskaia ASSR, 212
Ivashko, V. A., 214, 524, 527, 528
Ivonin, Nikolai Pavolvich, 177
Izgaryshev, Nikolai Alekseevich, 238
Izgoev, 232
Izgoev-Lande, A. S., 233
Izhevsk *raion*, 30
Izrailovich, Abram Il'ich, 177
Izrail'skii, 238
Izumov, Aleksandr Filaretovich, 239

Kucherov, 50
Kuchmenko, 58
Kudriavtsev, Vasilii Mikhailovich, 64, 110, 239
Kuibyshev, 6
Kuibyshev, N. V., 67
Kuibyshev *oblast'*, persons expelled from, 96–97
Kuibyshev, V. V., 65, 68, 423, 430
Kuibyshevskii, 96, 97
Kukolevskii, Ivan Ivanovich, 236
Kulagin, 64
kulaks, 11, 49, 60, 240, 373–74, 376–79; and collectivization, **396;** eviction and resettlement, 384–88, 402, 416; use of military against, 383
Kulanev, 81
Kulik, Ivan IUlianovich, 178
Kulikov, Dmitrii Georgievich, 105, 108, 283, 286, 288
Kulish, Mikola Gur'evich, 178
Kul'kov, M. M., 66
Kun, Bela, 178
Kuptsov, V. A., 524, 525, 674
Kuramysov, Izmukhan Mukhashevich, 178
Kurgaev, Mikhail, 14
Kuritsyn, V. I., 66
Kurochkin, I. L., 295
Kuroedov, V., 475–76
Kursk *guberniia*: political situation report, 33; religious movement, 458
Kurskii, D., 235, 239
Kushner, Boris Akisimovich, 178
Kutiakov, Ivan Semenovich, 178
Kutsenko, Viktor Il'ich, 536
Kutulov, 80
Kuusinen, 751
Kuz'min, A. I.: Bukharin and Rykov case, 108; Kirov murder investigation, 73, 77
Kuz'min, Karabaev, Dmitrii Vladimirovich, 237
Kuz'min, N., 497–98
Kuz'min, P. V., 158
Kuznetsk *okrug*, election campaigns, 48
Kuznetsov, A., 64; and Kirov murder case, 73
Kuznetsov, A. A.: Kliueva and Roskin affair, 256; Timashuk letter on doctors' plot, 128
Kuznetsov, A. V., 198, 199
Kuznetsov, F., 302
Kuznetsov, I. I., 151
Kuznetsov, M., resettlement programs, 212
Kuznetsov, Stepan Matveevich, 178
Kuznetsov, V., 754
Kviring, Emmanuil Ionovich, 177, 430

L
labor camp system, 132–69; camp conditions, 146–47; construction projects, 152–62; creation of, 3; development of work areas, 141–43; directorate of Moscow camps, 138; engineering specialists assigned to, 149–51; staffing of, 143–44; supplies and transport for, 136–37. *See also under names of individual forced labor concentration camps*
Lagoiskii, 714
Laida, 58, 59
Lake Balkhash Basin construction project, 162
Lakoba, Nestor A., 178
Lakshin, V., 281
Landa, M. N., 299, 300
Lantsere, N. K., 150
Lantsutskii, Stanislav, 178
Lapidus, 64
Lapinskii, Pavel Liudvigovich, 178
Lapkin, S., 301
Lapshin, B. F., 150, 151
Lapshin, Ivan Ivanovich, 234
Lapshin, P. S., 150, 151
Larichev, 243
Larin, V. F., 178
Latsis, Martyn IAnovich, on excesses in Ukrainian *Cheka*, 5, 15–16
Latvia: Lutherans in, 433; Soviet invasion of, 629
Lauer, Genrikh Bernardovich, 178
Lavinskov, Aleksei Ivanovich, 178
Lavrent'ev, L. I., 65
Lavrov, Mikhail Aleksandrovich, 178
Lazarevskii, Boris Aleksandrovich, 178
Laziukov, P. P., 76
Lazov, Viacheslav, 14
Lazovskii, I. IU., 118
League of the Militant Godless, 487, 609
Lebed', Dmitrii Zakharovich, 65, 178, 430
Lebedev, 438
Lebedev, G. A., 150, 151
Lebedev, V. M., 150
Lelevich, G., 178, 189
Lemus, Vladimir Ivanovich, 178
Lena, A. K., 66
Lend-Lease Act, 625, 627, 650–51
Lenin, Vladimir Il'ich: on anti-Soviet intellectuals, 229–30, 232–39; assassination attempt, 11, 12–14; at 10th party congress, 99; ban on works about, 249; as Bolshevik leader, 309; church valuables, removal of, 438–39, 441–43; on class militance, 4; on creation of *Cheka*, 6; death of, 103; misquoted by Reagan, 703–4;

on nationality question, 200–201; Romanovs' execution and, 10; U.S. food relief program, 544, 554; U.S.-Soviet trade relations, 581–85
Leningrad (literary journal), 246–47, 249–50, 253, 261
Leningrad *oblast'*: criticizing *Zvezda*, 253–55; German and Finn resettlement, 204
Lentsner, Naum Mikhailovich, 178
Leonidov, Leonid Osipovich, 178
Leps, Rol'f Karl, 677
Leslie (Amerian spy), 259
Lessinger, Erikh Mikhael', 677
Let History Judge (Medvedev), 264
Let's Wipe Out All the Spies . . . (Zakovskii), 188
Levanevskii, S. A., 577
Levichev, Vasilii Nikolaevich, 178
Levin, 178
Levin, A. A., 67
Levin, Miron Naumovich, 178
Levin, N. IA., 218
Levin, Robert, 675
Levin, V. S., 71
Levina, Revekka Saulova, 178
Levine, Louis, 219
Levitin, 64
Levitskaia, M., 451
Levitskii, M. N., 151
Lezhava, 554
Lezhava, Andrei Matveevich, 178
Lezhnev, 232
Liberman, Grigorii Borisovich, 178
Life in the Citadel (IAkobson), 253
Life and Fate (Grossman), 170, 268–75
The Life of V. I. Lenin (Lilina), 189
Ligachev, E. K., 505
Lignau, Aleksandr Georgievich, 178
Lilina, Zlata Ionovna, 178, 189
Lisnianskaia, I., 301
Lithuania: independence movement, 515, 526; Roman Catholics in, 433; Soviet invasion of, 629
Litvinov, Ig. I., 178
Litvinov, M. M., 65, 108, 541, 544, 646, 688, 690–91
Liubchenko, Arkadii Afanas'evich, 179
Liubchenko, Panas Petrovich, 66, 179
Liubimov: Crimean Tatar resettlement program, 206; five-year plan results, 430; German resettlement program, 204; resettlement programs, 209
Liubimov, Isidor Evstigneevich, 65, 179
Liubimov, IUrii Petrovich, 197–99
Liubimov, Nikolai Ivanovich, 237
Liushkov, G. S., 120
Livshits, Vladimir Aronovich, 178
Lloyd George, David, 539
Lobachev, 519, 554

Lobanov, 76, 204, 209
Lobov, 155
Lobov, P. M., 71
Lobov, S. S., 65
Lobov, Semen Semenovich, 178
Lomach', IU. IU., 150
Lominadze, V. V., 178
Lomov, G., 178
Lomov, G. I., 68, 430
Lopukhov, Crimean Tatar resettlement
    program, 207
Loskutov, Nikolai Nikolaevich, 236
Losskii, 233
Lovein, Robert, 675
Lozovskii, S. A., 66, 219, 256, 608, 732
Luchinskii, P. K., 524
Lugansk *uezd*, 30
Lukachevskii, A. T., 179
Luk'ianov, 308
Luk'ianov, A. I., 518–21
Luk'ianov, Dmitrii Dmitrievich, 179
Lukin, Nikolai Mikhailovich, 179
Lunarcharskii, Anatolii Vasil'evich, 228,
    240, 245
Luppol, Ivan Kapitonovich, 179
Lur'e, Moisei Il'ich, Smel' Aleksandr,
    102–3
Lur'e, Natan Lazarevich, 102–3
Lutokhin, 233
Lutsenko, 409
L'vov, 163
L'vov, A. L., 198, 199
Lychev, I. A., 67
Lysenko, I. N., 411

M
machinists, Russian-American coopera-
    tion, 579
Mad'iar, Liudvig Ignat'evich, 179
Mailin, Meimbet, 179
Main Administration of Places of Incar-
    ceration, 362
Main Directorate for the Protection of
    State Secrets in the Press (*Glavlit*),
    170–98
Main Intelligence Directorate (*GRU*),
    761
Mains, Clifton, 673
Maiorov, G. I., 124, 127, 128
Major, Robert W., 738–40
Makar'ev, Stepan Andreevich, 179
Makarov, 241–42
Makarov, I. G., 66
Makarov, I. M., 308
Makarov, Ivan Ivanovich, 179
Makarov, Viktor Borisovich, 536
Makhkamov, K. M., 524, 525
Makhov, E. N., 532, 535
Maksimchuk, IA. P., suicide, 88
Maksimov, V. E., 198, 199

Maksimovskii, 134–35
Makukhin, A. N., Chernobyl nuclear
    plant accident, 503
Malapura, 52
Malenkov, 223
Malenkov, G. M., 125, 126, 128–29, 310;
    at Red Square, **351**; church renova-
    tions, 469
Malinin, B. M., 150
Maloletnikov, Nikolai Vasil'evich, 237
Maltinskii, Kh. I., 198, 199
Mal'tsev, Elizar, 278
Mal'tsev, K. A., 68
Malyshev, P. I., 149
Mamushin, 75
Manaenkov, IU. A., 524, 525
Mandelshtam, Osip, 240
Mandel'shtam, S. O., 71
Manfred, S. A., 68
Manien, M., 618
Mantsev, 232
Manuil'skii, D. Z., 65, 108, 430
Mao Tse Tung, 624
Marchenko, A. P., 411
Marchenko, A. T., 298
Marchik, 64
Maretskii, 108
Maretskii, Dmitrii M., 179
Margolis, P., 140
Margulis, 64
Mariiskaia ASSR, 212
Mariupol' *uezd*, 30
Markevich, 389
Markin, 52
Markitan, 64
Markov, A. M., 129
Markov, B. A., 197
Markov, G., 268–69, 281
Marshall Plan, 682
Martens, Ludwig K., 558, 559–60, 578
Martynov, 764
Marx, Karl, 200
Masaliev, A. M., 524
Masan, M. N., 411
Mashkov, 461
Masliuk, Gavriil Amvrosievich, 407–8
Masliukov, IU., 525, 756
Matkovskii, 52
Matorin, Nikolai Mikhailovich, 179
Matros, E.I., 411
Matusevich, Iosif Aleksandrovich, 238
Matveev, Ivan Petrovich, 78, 213, 237
Max, Alan, 621
Maximalists, 30
Mazepus, 116
Mazurov, 751
McCloy, 720
Medved', 77, 78, 83, 139, 439
Medvedev, 765
Medvedev, C., 308

Medvedev, Roy, 58, 123, 264, 630
Medvedev, V., atheist education, 497–98
Medvedev, Vadim A., 705
Meerzon, Zh. I., 67
Meir, Golda, 217
Meister, Georgii Karlovich, 179
Mekhlis, L. Z.: Central Committee
    member, 66; on disposition of pris-
    oners of war, 163–65; five-year plan
    results, 431
Melamed, G., 68
Melikov, V. A., 179
Mel'nichanskii, Grigorii Natanovich,
    179
Memories and Reflections (Zhukov),
    193
Men'chukov, Evgenii Aleksandrovich,
    179
Mennonite Central Committee, 541
Mensheviks: *Cheka* information sum-
    maries of, 30; deportation of, 226,
    232; Lenin assassination attempt
    and, 13
Menshikov, 713–14
Menteshashvili, 308
Menzhinskii, V. R., 5, 6–7, **18**, 243, 438;
    American workers in Russia, 587;
    Dzerzhinsky letter on more liberal
    attitudes, 19; separation of church
    and state, 446, 448; U.S. food relief
    programs, 554
Merkulov, 167
Merlianov, L. T., 411
Merzliutin, B. G., 149
Meshcherskii, Aleksandr Pavlovich, 179
Messerer, B., 301
Messing, 232
metalworkers, strikes, 46–47, 50
Metelev, Aleksandr Denisovich, 179
Metropol' almanac, 301–3
Meyer, 743
Mezhenikov, Sergei Aleksandrovich,
    179
Mezhlauk, Valerii Ivanovich, 65, 119,
    179, 430, **569**
Mezis, 383
Mezlauk, I. I., 68
MGB. See Ministry for State Security
Mgeladze, Illarion Vissarionovich, 179
Miakotin, 232
Miakotin, Venedikt Aleksandrovich,
    239
Miasnikov, N. P., 71
Migulin, Ivan Georgievich, 179
Mikhailov, 58, 360–61, 607
Mikhailov, M. E., 66, 119
Mikhailov, N. A., 125
Mikhailov, N. V., 287
Mikhailov, Sergei, 280, 290
Mikhailov, V., 214, 217, 526

Rozit, David Petrovich, 181
Rozov, 646
Rozovskii, M., 301
Rubchevskaia, E. N., 128
Ruben, R. G., 181
Rubenov, R. G., 67
Rubikis, A. P., 524, 525
Rubin, Isaak Il'ich, 181
Rubin, V. A., 298
Rubinshtein, M. I., 67
Rubrovskii, K. I., 150
Rudenko, N. D., 198, 200, 411
Rudenko, R., 170, 307
Rudzutak, Ian Ernestovich, 65, 181
Rukhimovich, Moisei L'vovich, 65, 119, 181
Rumiantsev, Ivan Petrovich, 65, 181
Rumiantsev, V. V., 71
Rusanov, 14
Russian Agricultural Bureau, 566–68
Russian Communist Party (Bolshevik). *See* Communist Party
Russian Orthodox Church, 433–36; closing of monasteries, 470–72; number in Soviet Union, 466; return of churches and monasteries in Moscow to, 480–86
The Russian Question (Simonov), 253
Russian Social Democratic Workers' Party, 99
Russian-Ukrainian Joint Commission of Repatriation, 362
Russkii Golos (Russian Voice), 557
Rusulov, S. G., 411
Rut'ko, Arsenii, 181
Rybakov, An., 278
Rykov, Aleksei Ivanovich, 181; at 13th Party Congress, **363**; banned books about, 186–87; Central Committee member, 66; church property renovations, 461–62; expulsion from party, 4, 106–11, 119; opposition to Stalin, 99; Patriarch Tikhon's counterrevolutionary activities, 450–51; plea for mercy, 111; show trial (1938), 58, 100
Rykov, Pavel Sergeevich, 181
Ryndin, Kuz'ma Vasil'evich, 65, 119, 181
Rynikov, Aleksei Dmitrievich, 237
Ryskin, 64
Ryskulov, Turar Ryskulovich, 181
Ryzhkov, 525
Ryzhkov, IU., 308, 479
Ryzhkov, N. I., 505

S
Saburov, M. Z., 125, 126
Sadchikov, N., 172
Sadovskii, 461

Sadykova, IU. N., 234
Safarov, Georgii Ivanovich, 181, 187, 188
Saikin, V. T., 519–21
St. Basil's Cathedral, 482, 483
St. Petersburg. *See* Petrograd
Saint Louis Machine Tool Co., 562
Sakharnov, V. A., 149
Sakharov, 298, 300
Sakharov, Andrei D., 264, 291–92, 303–8
Sakharov, Andrei Vasil'evich, 238
Sakharova, P. F., 67
Sakh'ianova, M. M., 67
Salova, 300
SALT. *See* Strategic Arms Limitations Treaty
Saltanov, Sergei Aleksandrovich, 67, 181
Samara, Revolutionary Committee, 6–7
Samara *guberniia*, election campaigns, 48–49
Samoilova-Zemliachka, 438, 439
Samokhvalov, A., 171
Samosenok, E. I., 411
Sangurskii, 113
Sankovo *raion*, 88
Sapgir, G., 301
Sapozhnikov, F. V., 108, 501
Sapronov, Timofei V., 181, 438, 439
Sarkisov, S. A., 66, 181
Sartakov, S. V., 269
Sarymuldaev, Kabuldek Sarymuldaevich, 181
Sats, I., 281
Savel'ev, S. I., 151
Savin, Viktor Alekseevich, 181
Savinkin, N., 513
Savvich, 235
Sazonov, V. P., 149
Sazykin, 14
Shchipachev, 268
Shcherbakov, 134
schools, separation of church and, 434
Schulenburg, F. W. Graf v. d., 631, 632
Scientific-Technical Council on Agricultral Industry, 566–68
secret police, origins and operations, 4–27
Sedel'nikov, A. I., 66
Sed'iakin, 117
Sef, Semen F., 181
Selivanov, Dmitrii Fedorovich, 234
Selivanova, Elizaveta Vladimirovna, 481–86
Semashko, 32
Semenov, A. V., 287

Semenov, B. A., 66
Semenova, 300
Semenova, G. B., 524, 525
Semichastnyi, V., 132, 754
Semin, 64
Semkovskii, Semen IUl'evich, 181
Senin, Oleg Mikhailovich, 282, 284–85, 288
Serdiuk, A. S., 411
Serebriakova, Galina Osipovna, 181
Serebriakova, Z. N., 292
Serebrovskii, 245–46, 430, 431
Serebrovskii, Aleksandr Pavlovich, 66, 181
Serebrovskii, V. I., 118
Sergeev, A. I., suicide, 87
Sergeev, N., 566, 567
Sergeevich, Mikhail, 519
Sergo, 7
Serov, 170
Serzh, Viktor, 181
Shablievskii, G. V., 68
Shaburov, Aleksei, 38–42
Shaburova, M. A., 67
Shadunts, Suren Konstantinovich, 67, 183
Shafarevich, 298
Shaginian, Marietta, 249
Shakhgil'dian, 64
Shakht, 149
Shakhty case, 240
Shamraevskii, 579
Shapovalov, 53
Sharangovich, V. F., 67
Sharangovich, Vasilii Fomich, 183
Shatalin, 525
Shatov, Vladimir "Bill," 578
Shatrov, M., 191–93
Shatskii, Lazar', 183
Shatskii, N. N., 71
Shatunovskaia, O. T., 83–84, 300
Shauro, V. F., 281, 297, 302
Shcharansky, A. D., 298
Shcheglov, Aleksei Vasil'evich, 184
Shchelokov, 764
Shcherbakov, S., 289
Sheboldaev, Boris Petrovich, 66, 184
Sheirent, 555
Shelepina, E., 599
Shemshelevich, Leonid Veniaminovich, 184
Shenin, O. S., 524, 525
Shepel', P. A., 411
Shepel', P. K., 411
Shepilov, 126, 223
Shereshevskii, N. A., 127
Shestakov, V. I., 64, 67
Shestokryl, F. G., 411
Shevardnadze, Eduard A., 311, 705; Afghanistan situation, 765; resigna-

tion from party, 532–33; space exploration, 756
Shevchenko, A. E., 411
Shevchenko, F. R., 411
Shibaev, I., 14
Shigonskii, 96, 97
Shilkhin, 64
Shimanovich, I. D., 566
Shinachev, S. P., 269
Shipigel'glias, S. M., 218
Shir-Mukhamedov, 64
Shirokov, Crimean Tatar resettlement program, 207, 210
Shirvindt, E., 143, 144
Shishkin, Matvei Dmitrievich, 237
Shishkin, V. M., 149
Shishko, L. P., 150
Shkiriatov, M. F., 67, 106–7, 108, 126
Shlag, German German, 677
Shleifer, I. O., 184
Shliapnikov, Aleksandr Gavrilovich, 6, 184, 190, 438
Shlikhter, A., 438
Shmelev, I. S., 184
Shmidt, Vasilii Vladimirovich, 108, 184
Shoer, Gel'mut Adol'f, 677
Shokhin, A. P., 67
Sholokhov, Mikhail, 397–98, 401, 624
Shostakovich, Dmitrii, 247
Shotman, Aleksandr Vasil'evich, 6–7, 184
show trials: (1922), of Socialist Revolutionaries, 145; (1928), Shakhty case, 240; (1936) of Zinoviev and Kamenev, 57, 100; (1937), of Bukharin and Rykov, 100; (1938), of Bukharin and Rykov, 100
Shtein, Viktor Maritsovich, 235
Shteingardt, A. M., 66
Shteinman, Zelik IAkovlevich, 184
Shtetsa, Konstantin, 184
Shtreter, V. I., 150
Shubert, Anna Mikhailovna, 184
Shubrikov, Vladimir Petrovich, 66, 184
Shuia (town), confiscation of church valuables, 439, 441–43
Shul'ts, E. M., 149
Shumeiko, G., 218, 219
Shumiatskii, Boris Zakharovich, 184
Shums'kii, Oleksander IAkovlevich, 184
Shusev, 461
Shustin, A. IA., 67
Shvarts, S., 66, 430
Shver, Aleksandr Vladimirovich, 184
Shvernik, N. M., 66, 73, 108, 430, 751
Siberia: bandit report, 34; election campaigns, 48–49. See also Tobol'sk raion
Sidorova, 210

Sigirskii, Aleksandr Ivanovich, 237
Sikirskii, 53
Silin, M., 576
Sillari, E.-A. A., 524, 525
Siman'kov, V. IA., 196
Simferopol', 210
Simon (prior of moastery), 13
Simonov, Konstantin, 185, 253
Siniavin, 134–35
Siniavskii, Andrei D., 198, 200, 264, 276–77
Sintsov, 255
Sitarian, 525
Sitkovskii, Evgenii P., 181
Skachkov, 764
Skalozubov, N. N., 118
Skirda, S. Z., 412
Skliarov, IU., 513, 765
Skopichenko, G. V., 150
Skorchelleti, V. K., 150
Skorino, L., 269–70
Skrypnik, Nikolai Alekseevich, 182
Skvorstsov, V. A., 149
Slavic Friendship (Simonov), 185
Slavin, 64, 667
Slepak, V. S., 298
Slepkov, A., 108, 182
Sleptsov, Platon Alekseevich, 182
Slopovronskii, 53
Smidovich, P. G., 448, 450, 461
Smilga, Ivar Tenisovich, 182, 187
Smiriukov, 759
Smirnov, 64, 204; Crimean Tatar resettlement program, 206; resettlement programs, 209
Smirnov, A. V., and Kirov murder, 76, 81
Smirnov, Aleksandr Petrovich, 182
Smirnov, Anatolii Aleksandrovich, 182
Smirnov, E. I., Kliueva and Roskin affair, 258–60
Smirnov, Ivan Nikitich, 102
Smirnov, Mikhail Petrovich, 182
Smirnov, O., 281
Smirnov, Sergei Aleksandrovich, 182
Smirtiukov, 764
Smith (U.S. Ambassador), 256
Smolensk guberniia: election campaigns, 48; political situation report, 33
Smolovik, 255
Smorodin, P. I., 66
Smorodinov, 667
Smushkov, Vadim Vasil'evich, 182
Smykova, 20–21
Snegirev, D. K., 150
Sobchak, Anatolii, 533
Sobel'son, 182
Sobolev, L., 268, 280
Socialist Party of New Jersey, 611

Socialist Radical Party of America, 604
Socialist Revolutionaries (SRs): anti-Soviet activities, 226; at Solovki prison, 145; Cheka information summaries of, 29–30; hiring of, 6; Lenin assassination attempt and, 13; tsarist regime and, 11
Society of Friends (Quakers), 541, 542–43, 555
Society for Technical Assistance to Russia, 578, 586–87
Sokolikov, IU., 750
Sokol'nikov, 430
Sokol'nikov, Grigorii IAkovlevich, 66, 105, 108, 181, 187
Sokol'nikov, Konstantin Alekseevich, 182
Sokolov, 439
Sokolov, E. E., 524, 525
Sokolov, G. V., 71
Sokolov, I. G., 182
Sokolov, Sergei L., 505, 705, 756
Sokolovskii, 687
Soldatov, A., 748, 750
Sologub, Nikolai Vladimirovich, 182
Soloveichik, Emanuil Borisovich, 234
Solovki (forced labor camp), 145–47, **148**
Sol'ts, 430
Solzhenitsyn, Aleksandr, 198, 200; ban on works by, 194–95; expulsion from Writers' Union, 279; and the Gulag, 132, 146; Nobel Prize for literature recipient, 194, 289–91; publication in Russia, 263, 277; Sakharov defense of, 304; on White Sea-Baltic Canal project, 152–53; and Writers' Union, 297
Soms, K. P., 68
Sorokin, M. L., 67
Sorokin, Pitirim Aleksandrovich, 226, 233
Sositskii, L. I., 71
Sosnovski, 116
Sosnovskii, Lev Semenovich, 108, 182
South Wind (Grin), 253
The Soviet Army—The Liberation Army (Usherenko), 185
Soviet-Chinese Accord, 653
Soviet-German Treaty of Rapallo (1922), 558
Soviet Jews: anti-Semitism, 123, 217–24, 623; demonstrations, 264; dissolution of Jewish writers associations, 222–23; persecution of, 622–23; toleration of, 433
Soviet Red Cross, 541
Soviet Russian Literature (Nekrasov), 196
Soviet Writers' Union. See Writers' Union of the USSR

Sovnarkom. See Council of People's
    Commissars
space exploration, 755–56
Spaetz, Carl, **655**
Speranskii, V. A., 150
Spiridonov, A. G., 150
Spiridonov, V., 467
Spokoinyi, Leontii Feliksovich, 182
srikes, of textile workers, 47–48
Stachel, Jack, 619
Stakun, 64
Stalin, Joseph V.: antireligious propagan-
    da, 488–89; at 13th Party Congress,
    363; at Yalta Conference, **652;** with
    Beria and Stalin's daughter, **346;**
    Bukharin and Rykov affair, 105, 108;
    Census family records, 341; Central
    Committee member election, 65;
    church valuables, removal of, 438–
    39; on creation of *Cheka,* 6–7; death
    of, 58; despotism and crimes of,
    120–21; on exiling dangerous crimi-
    nals, 168–69; fiftieth birthday cele-
    bration, **322;** German invasion, 626;
    German question, 692–94; German
    war criminals, 692; grain collection
    sabotage, 405–6; Industrial Party tri-
    al, 243; industrialization projects,
    372–73, 424–28, 430–32; at Kirov's
    bier, **86;** Kirov murder and, 69, 73,
    83–84; Kirov, relations with, 77, 78;
    Lend-Lease shipments, 650–51; let-
    ter on, grain growers, 397–98; letters
    to Crimean Tatar resettlement pro-
    gram, 208; from peasants, 37–38,
    42–43; on Lake Balkhash construc-
    tion, 162; Nelson on trip to Russia,
    649; on penalty reductions for rein-
    stated party members, 54–55; on
    permanent exile of prisoners, 161;
    on prisoners of war, 165–67; meet-
    ing with W. Wilkie, 737; on nation-
    ality question, 200–201; on *NKVD*
    arrest procedures, 22–26; party
    membership cards, 315–16; personal
    effects inventory, 347–50; with
    Poskrebyshev, **244;** profile of, 311;
    resettlement programs, 203–4, 209–
    11; Roosevelt condolences, 654; So-
    viet Jews and, 222–23; Soviet–Chi-
    nese Accord, 653; trip to Leningrad
    (1934), 77–78; U.S. ambassador
    Davies and, 645–46, 648–49; U.S.
    food relief program, 544; Uniate
    church and, 465; Yalta Conference,
    686
Stalinskaia *oblast',* German resettle-
    ment, 203–4
Stancheva, E., 182
Stapnenko, A., 29

Star Iron Works, 565
Starchik, 300
Starodubtsev, Vasilii, 533
Starostin, V. V., 150
Starukhin, 64
State Agricultural Syndicate, 355
State Bank, 353–54
State Defense Committee: Crimean Au-
    tonomous Republic deportations,
    209–10; German resettlement pro-
    gram, 203–4
State Planning Committee *(Gosplan),*
    353, 368; five-year plan, 372
State Political Directorate *(GPU),* 5,
    356, 369; Bukharin opposition to,
    18–19
Stavskii, V. P., 67
Steiskallo, I. I., 150, 151
Steklov, IU., 191
Sten, IAn N., 182
Stepanov, 711
Stepanovich, Mikhail, 13, 67
Steppun, Fedor Avgustovich, 239
Stetskii, A. I., 65
Stetskii, Aleksei Konstantinovich, 181
Stettinius, Edward Reilly, **652**
Stevenson, 720
Stizha, IA. IA., 151
Stoev, E. S., 524
Storilov, Mikhail Stepanovich, 182
Strategic Arms Limitations Treaty
    (SALT), 731
Stratonov, Vsevolod Viktorovich, 235
Strel'tsov, G. M., 68
Strievskii, K. K., 66, 430
strikes: by type of worker, 50; of gov-
    ernment agency employees, 6; of
    metalworkers, 46–47, 50; of textile
    workers, 47–48, 50
Stroev, E. S., 524, 525
Struppe, Petr Ivanovich, 66, 181
Stuchka, 6
Student Friendship Fund of the YMCA,
    541
*Studies on the History of the Civil War,
    1917–1920* (Anishev), 187
Stukov, Inokentii Nikolaevich, 182
Subbotin: Crimean Tatar resettlement
    program, 207; German resettlement
    program, 204; resettlement pro-
    grams, 209–10
Subdepartment of Administrative Over-
    sight, 362
*The Subversive Activities of Clergymen
    and Sectarians* (Zakovskii), 188
Sud'in, S. K., 68
suicides, of party members, 87–88
Sukhanov, Nikolai Nikolaevich, 182
Sukhorukov, M., 151
Sukov, 461

Sulimov, Daniil Egorovich, 65, 119, 182,
    430
Sulkovskii, F. V., 68
Supreme Court: nomenclature lists,
    356–57, 370; October Revolution
    dockyard, 20–21; Patriarch Tikhon's
    declaration, 450
Supreme Economic Council *(VSNKh):*
    industrial statistics, 424–28; nomen-
    clature lists, 352–53, 366–67; and
    Russian Agricultural Bureau, 567;
    special appointments, 352–53
Surovinin, Viktor Pavlovich, 182
Susaikov, 163
Suslov, Mikhail Andreevich, 125, 218,
    268, 295; Afghanistan situation,
    759; American pilots downed in
    North Korea, 698; autobiography
    and personal information form,
    334–35; Khrushchev-Kennedy meet-
    ing, 751; profile of, 313; Russian Or-
    thodox churches, 466
Suvarin, Boris, 182
Suzdal' *uezd,* 30
Svechnikov, Mikhail Stepanovich, 181
Sverdlov, 6
Sverdlovsk *oblast',* resettlement pro-
    grams, 209–10
Sverdlovskaia ASSR, 212
Swedish Red Cross, 555
Syr Dar'inskii *raion,* 213
Syrtsov, Sergei Ivanovich, 182
Syzranskii, 96, 97

T
Tabachnik, G. D., 198, 200
Tal', Boris Markovich, 182
Talanov, V. V., 566, 568
Tal'geimer, Avgust, 182
Tambov *guberniia:* political situation
    report, 31; religious movement, 456
Taniaev, Aleksandr Petrovich, 182
Tanin, Mikhail Aleksandrovich, 182
Taraki, Noor Mohammed, 757, 759
Tarasov, 64
Tarle, Evgenii Viktorovich, imprison-
    ment of, 240, 245
Tarle, Ol'ga, 245
Tarsis, Valerii IAkovlevich, 197, 198,
    200
Tashkent *oblast',* 213
Tashsel'skii *raion,* 213
Tataev, Nikolai Andreevich, 182, 389
Tatarchuk, V. A., 150
Tatars, Crimean: demonstrations, 264;
    resettlement programs, 202, 205–13
Tedder, Gen., **655**
Telesin, Z. A., 198, 200
Tel'tevskii, Aleksei Vasil'evich, 235
Temkin, M. M., 67

Temovoi, O. I., 185

Tendriakov, V., 278

Teodorovich, Ivan Adol'fovich, 182

Ter-Vaganian, Vagarshak Arutiunovich,
102

Terek *oblast'*, religious movement,
457

Terekhov, R. IA., 68

Terkin in the Other World (Tvardovskii), 277

Teterin, Mikhail Pavlovich, 182

textile workers, strikes, 47–48, 50

The Thaw (Ehrenburg), 263

The Thirtieth of August (Shatrov),
191–93

Thompson, Robert G., 619

Thorez, Maurice, 618, 624

Tiapkin, Nikolai Dmitrievich, 236

A Ticket through History (Shaginian),
249

Tikhomirov, 14

Tikhon, Patriarch Vasilii Bellavin,
434–35, 441, 444, **445**, 446–454;
death sentence for, 443–44

Tikhonov, N., 185, 280, 308, 764

Timakov, 256

Timashuk, Lidiia, on health of Zhdanov, 123–24, 126, 127–30

Timoshenko, 163

Tiziakov, Aleksandr, 533

Tkachenko, 53

Tkalun, 120

Tobol'sk *raion*, political situation report, 31

Toiling Peasants' Party *(TKP)*, 243

Tolmachev, Vl., 462–63

Tolmazov, A. I., 71

Tolmosova, A. N., 54

Tolstoy, Aleksei, 153, 172

Tomsk *guberniia*, 29

Tomskii, Mikhail Pavlovich, 66,
99–100, 104, 106, 182

Tomskii, Semen Grigor'evich, 182

Tovel', Aleksandr IUl'evich, 182

Tovstukha, I. P., 66

trade embargo, U.S. with Russia, 558

trade relations: Soviet-British, 558; Soviet-German, 558; Soviet-U.S.,
559–60, 648; Soviet-U.S. firms,
558–59; U.S. "trade at your own
risk" policy, 558

Trade Union Educational League
(TUEL), 595, 601, 608

transportation workers: political attitudes and morale of, 51–53; strikes,
50

Trapeznikov, 308

Tret'iakov, Sergei Mikhailovich, 182

Trifonov, IU., 278

Trifonov, V., 7

Trilisser, M. A., 68

Trinity Church at Nikitniki, 483

Troepol'skii, A., 182

Trofimovich, Andrei, 13

Troshin, 236

Trostnikov, V., 301

Trotsky, Leon: assassination (1940), 57;
ban on books by and about, 182,
187–90; on capitalist intervention,
541; *Cheka* member, 6; church valuables, removal of, 438–39; expulsion
from party, 57, 99, 595; factory
workers support for, 36–37; famine
relief programs, 555–56; industrialization policy, 372; on Romanov execution, 10; U.S. agricultural workers in Russia, 587–93; U.S. exile,
578; U.S. road-building firm, 564

Trotskyite-Zinovievite Terrorist Center,
57, 69, 102, 108, 111, 112

Troyanovsky, 646

Trubetskoi, Sergei Evgenievich, 237

Truman, Harry, 653, 682

Truman Doctrine, 682

Trunina, 83–84

Trusov, N. M., 76, 81

Trutovskii, V., 438

TSarev, P. S., 68

TSaritsyn. *See* Volgograd

TSatskin, Dr., 74, 75

TSegel'nichenko, A. F., 411

TSeitlin, Efim F., 183

TSentroplenbezh. See Central Collegium for Prisoners of War and
Refugees

TSepliak, 443

TSetlin, 108

TSiffer, Richard Stanislavovich, 183

TSifrinovich, Vladimir Efimovich, 183

TSikhon, A. M., 68

TSinarev, Nikolai Andreevich, 20–21

TSuriupa, 554

TSvetaeva, Anastasia Ivanovna, 481–86

TSvetkov, 14

TSvetkov, Nikolai Nikolaevich, 237

TSvetkov, P., 348, 350

TSvetkovskii, 53

TSvi, 183

TSvigun, 282, 288

TSyl'ko, Fedor Andreevich, 183

TSytovich, Nikolai Platonovich, 183

Tuchkov, E., 446–47, 448–49, 462–63

Tucker, Robert, 201

Tuderlan, Vasilii Ion, 677

TUEL. *See* Trade Union Educational
League

Tukhachevskii, M. N., 66, 113

Tukhachevskii, Mikhail Nikolaevich,
182

Turchin, 298

Tvardovskii, A., banning of poetry of,
172

Tvardovskii, Aleksandr, 277, 278–81

Tver' *guberniia*: election campaigns, 48;
political groups, 29

Tverdokhlebov, 298

Tveriak, Aleksei Artem'evich, 182

The Twilight of the Capital (Borin), 286

Tykve, Gergard Paul, 677

U

Uborevich, Ieronim Petrovich, 66, 113,
182

Uchraspred. See Personnel Assignment
Office

Udovichenko, 526

Ugarov, Aleksandr Ivanovich, 66, 108,
182

Uglanov, Nikolai Aleksandrovich, 108,
182

Ugrimov, Aleksandr Ivanovich, 236

Uisk *raion, kulak* uprising, 377

Ukhanov, Konstantin Vasil'evich, 66,
183

UKP. See Ukrainian Communist Party

Ukraine: Chernobyl nuclear plant accident, 499–513; election campaigns,
48–50; famine in, 401–420; German
resettlement program, 201–2, 203–4;
political groups, 29–30; political situation report, 31; Uniates in, 433

Ukrainian Communist Party *(UKP)*,
29–30; and Chernobyl nuclear plant
accident, 499–500, 505; famine in,
401, 417–18; grain collection sabotage, 403–12; *kulak* deportations,
402, 416

Ukrainian Greek Catholic Church, 433,
465

Ukrainian Social Democrats *(USD)*, 29

Ukrainian Socialist Revolutionaries
(USR), 29

Ul'ianov family, 249

Ul'ianov *guberniia*, religious movement, 456

Ul'ianov, I., 438

Ul'ianov, Vladimir Il'ich. *See* Lenin,
Vladimir Il'ich

Ul'ianova, 108, 430

Ul'ianova, M. I., 68

Ul'ianovskii, 96, 97

Ul'rikh, 84

Umanets', IUrii, 182

Under Seige (Ketlinskaia), 253

Uniates. *See* Ukrainian Greek Catholic
Church

Unified State Political Directorate, and
Baikal-Amur Railway construction
project, 157–58

Unified State Political Directorate

(OGPU), 5; political situation in USSR, 45–50

Union of Militant Atheists, 609–10

Union of Writers. See Writers' Union of the USSR

United Press, tendentious reports from, 17

Unshlikht, Iosif Stanislavovich, 183, 235, 239; Central Committee member, 66; confiscation of church valuables, 438–39; five-year plan, 430; lists of anti-Soviet intellectuals, 233–39; purging party membership, 58, 59, 103

Ural *guberniia*, political situation report, 34

Uralov, S. G., **8**, 68

Urals: asbestos mining, 560; election campaigns, 48–49; *kulak* uprising, 377; public opinion, 37; Ufa concentration camp barracks, **135**

Uranov, S., 183

Uritskii, Semen Borisovich, 183; *Cheka* member, 6; murder of, 12

Urunichi *raion*, bandit report, 34

Ushakov, K., 73, 235

Usherenko, IA., 185

Uspenskii, Aleksandr Ivanovich, 155, 236

Ustinov, D., 702–3, 759–61, 764

Uzbek SSR, 212

Uzbekistan, Crimean Tatars resettlement, 202, 205–8

V

V. IA. Briusov (Lelevich), 189

Vabib, Dr., 74

Vaganian, Vagarshak Arutiunovich, 174

Vagapov, 209

Vaichurin, 64

Vainberg, Valentin IAkovlevich, 174

Vainov, 64

Vaisberg, 238

Vakhlamov, 64

Valetarskii, M. A., 411

Vanag, Nikolai Nikolaevich, 174

Vanin, K., 254

Varavva, Aleksei Petrovich, 174, 187

Vardin, 174

Vardzieli, 138

Vareikis, Iosif Mikhailovich, 65, 108, 174

Varmashenko, G. I., 118

Vashadze, G. S., 431

Vasilenko, Matvei Ivanovich, 174

Vasilenko, V. Kh., 124, 127, 128–29

Vasil'ev, S. V., 67, 139–40

Vasil'evich, Konstantin, 13

Vasil'evich, Nikolai, 13

Vasil'evskii, 7

Vasilii Terkin (Tvardovskii), 172, 277

Vas'kin, 281, 288

Vatsek, 64

Vatsetis, Ioakim Ioakimovich, 174

Vazilevskii, O. A., 150

Veger, Evgenii Il'ich, 66, 174

Veinbaum, E. I., 68

Veinberg, G. D., 66

Veinshtenker, 134

Veipan, 673

Veitser, Izrail' IAkovlevich, 174

Velen'kii, 64

Velikhov, Pavel I., 38, 236

Vengerova, R. S., 68

Verkhne-Ural'sk (forced labor camp), 145

Verkhovskoi, Boris Klavdievich, 174

Verkhovykh, 64

Vermenichev, 430

Vershkov, Petr Afanas'evich, 175

Verzhbitskii, 155

Veselyi, Artem, 175

Veshenskii *raion*, grain growers' strike, 397–98

Vetluzhskii, Nikolai Petrovich, 399

Vettser, German Rudol'fovich, 234

Viatka *guberniia*, 30

Viatkin, 64

Vietnam War, 684, 699–700

Vigdorchik, 232

Viksnin, 64

Vilenskaia, Marfa Mitrofanovna, 175

Vilenskii, Vladimir Dmitrievich, 175

Vil'ga, Feodor, 586

Vinnichenko, V. K., 29, 175

Vinogradov, 669; on Solovki concentration camp, 146–47

Vinogradov, I., 281

Vinogradov, N. V., on Russian Agricultural Bureau, 566–68

Vinogradov, V. N.: cleared of accusations, 127; on health of Zhdanov, 123–24; medical dispute, 128–29

Virt, N., 253

Virtanen, IAlmari Erikovich, 175

Vishnevskii, Aleksandr Ivanovich, 175

Visloukh, Stanislav Mikhailovich, 234

Vitte, A. O., 149

Vladimir, 29–30

Vladimir *guberniia*, political situation report, 32

Vladimirov, V. V., 196

Vladimirskii, 33, 134–35, 136, 138, 139–40

Vladimov, Georgii Nikolaevich, 197–99

Vlasik, Nikolai Sidorovich: Kirov murder investigation, 77, 78; Zhdanov treatment, 124

Vlasov, A. V., 505, 528–31

Vlestaru, B. M., 198, 199

Vogau, 175

Vogin, 74

Voinovich, Vladimir Nikolaevich, 197, 198, 199

Volga Engineering & Trading Co., Inc., 561

Volga German Oblast', 30

Volga Relief Society, 541

Volgograd *guberniia*, 29

Volkov, V. L., 20–21, 67

Volkovysk, 163

Volkovysskii, M., 233

Volobuev, K. M., **8**

Vologda *guberniia*: election campaigns, 48; political situation reports, 29, 33

Volosevich, Vladislav Ottonovich, 175, 187

Vol'pe, Abram Mironovich, 175

Volsit, 64

Vorkuto-Pecherskii (forced labor camp), **141, 142, 144, 145**

Vorob'ev, Evg., 278

Voronezh: dissatisfaction of Lenin plant worker, 51; Social Revolutionaries in, 30

Voronezh *guberniia*, election campaigns, 48

Voronin, A. P., 197

Voronkov, K. V., 278, 281

Voronkov, Viktor Mikhailovich, 175

Voronov, 751

Voronskii, Aleksandr Konstantinovich, 175

Voroshilov, Klimentii Efremovich, 65, 73, 108, 125, 126; biological warfare, 627; Census family records, 345; on counterrevolutionary fascists, 112–14; *kulak* uprisings, 383; profile of, 314; Red Army troop strength, 643; at Stalin's fiftieth birthday, **322;** trip to Leningrad, 77–78

Voroshilovgradskaia *oblast'*, German resettlement, 203–4

Vorotnikov, V. I., 505, 765

Vovsi, M. S., 127

Voznesenskii, A., 301

Voznesenskii, M. A., 738

Voznesenskii, N. A., 68, 258, 278

Vradzhali, Zhak, 218

VSNKh. See Supreme Economic Council

VTSSPS. See. All-Union Central Council of Trade Unions

Vygotskii, Lev Semenovich, 175

Vyshinsky, Andrei IAnuar'evich, 26, 74; Census family records, 342; personal information on, 331–32; profile of, 313; U.S.-Soviet relations, 648

Vysotskii, V. S., 295–97, 301